A DICTIONARY
of EARLY
CHRISTIAN
BELIEFS

A DICTIONARY
of EARLY
CHRISTIAN
BELIEFS

A Reference Guide to More Than 700 Topics
Discussed by the Early Church Fathers

DAVID W. BERCOT, EDITOR

HENDRICKSON PUBLISHERS

© 1998 David Bercot

Hendrickson Publishers, Inc.
P.O. Box 3473
Peabody, Massachusetts 01961–3473
All rights reserved
Printed in the United States of America

ISBN 1–56563–870–0

Sixth printing—January 2006

Library of Congress Cataloging-in-Publication Data

A dictionary of early Christian beliefs / compiled and edited by David
Bercot.
    ISBN 1–56563–357–1
    1. Fathers of the Church—Dictionaries.   2. Theology—Dictionaries.
    3. Fathers of the Church—Quotations.   4. Theology—Quotations,
    maxims, etc.
    I. Bercot, David W.
    BR66.5.D53 1998
    270.1—dc21   98-8259
                                                                              CIP

Table of Contents

How to use this Dictionary

A Dictionary of Early Christian Beliefs allows the user to quickly ascertain what the early Christians[1] believed on over 700 different theological, moral, and historical topics, and it functions as an index to the writings of the ante-Nicene writers, specifically as collected in the ten-volume work, the *Ante-Nicene Fathers*.[2]

Why are the beliefs of these early Christian authors important? Because early Christian testimony holds that many, such as Clement of Rome and Polycarp, personally knew the apostles of Jesus. They were approved by the apostles and appointed by the apostles to positions of church leadership. Modern students of church history must largely depend on these and other early Christian writers for information on topics of major import, such as who wrote the New Testament documents and how the Christian canon of Scripture came into being. Furthermore, these early Christians' interpretation of the Scriptures is among the most valuable commentary on Scripture anywhere. To be sure, none of these writers claimed divine inspiration; nor did they equate their own writings with Scripture. They did, however, claim that they were faithfully passing along the faith that the apostles had delivered to the church.

THE ESSENCE OF EARLY CHRISTIANITY

Users of this dictionary should first grasp the ethos of early Christianity. That ethos can be summarized in two basic principles: (1) the earliest Christians focused on living in the light of the Christian message and explaining that message to nonbelievers rather than on sharpening their theological prowess; and (2) early Christian doctrine is less elaborate and less defined than later formulations.

To say that the early Christians focused on living the gospel rather than on theological hair-splitting does not mean that individuals taught whatever they wanted. There were recognized boundaries that prevented such a laissez-faire attitude. Nonetheless, to the early Christians, the heart of their faith consisted of an obedient love relationship with Christ, not the ability to articulate dogma. None of the testimony of the writers in this volume arose from some professional theologians; rather, like the apostle Paul, many lived in the trenches, on the cutting edge of Christian life, and in fact, a substantial number of these early Christian writers died as martyrs.

The early church concentrated chiefly on the nature of Christian living because the essential core of Christian belief (i.e., the "rule of faith") can be expressed quite briefly. The church believed that the Christian faith is a fairly simple one. Cyprian wrote,

---

[1]When I use the term "early Christians" or "early church," I am referring to the pre-Nicene Christians and the pre-Nicene Church.

[2]*The Ante-Nicene Fathers* (ed. Alexander Roberts and James Donaldson; 1885–1887; repr. 10 vols. Peabody, Mass.: Hendrickson, 1994).

> When the Word of God, our Lord Jesus Christ, came unto all, he gathered alike the learned and unlearned. He published the teachings of salvation to each sex and every age. He made a concise summary of His teachings, so that the memory of the scholars might not be burdened with the heavenly learning. Instead, we could quickly learn what was necessary to a simple faith. (ANF 5.455).

Echoing those sentiments, Lactantius remarked,

> The secrets of the Most High God, who created all things, cannot be attained by our own ability and perceptions. Otherwise, there would be no difference between God and man, if human thought could reach to the counsels and arrangements of that eternal majesty. (ANF 7.9)

Irenaeus criticized the heretics for going beyond the simple teachings of the faith, saying, "They form opinions on what is beyond the limits of understanding. For this cause also the apostle says, 'Be not wise beyond what it is fitting to be wise, but be wise prudently'" (ANF 1.548).

WORKING THROUGH A SAMPLE TOPIC

Suppose a reader wants to know what the early Christians believed about the fall of man. Under the entry "Fall of Man," a number of early Christian texts are cited. Note, though, that selected Scriptures precede the early Christian quotations. The intent is not to include every biblical passage concerning the fall of man. Rather, these are some of the key texts used by the early church.

Following the Scripture passages are quotations from early Christians, listed in approximately chronological order:

> The human race . . . from Adam had fallen under the power of death and the guile of the serpent. Each one had committed personal transgression. *Justin Martyr (c. 160, E), 1.243.*

The citation identifies the source as *Justin Martyr*. His name is followed by *(c. 160, E)*. The parenthetical information indicates that Justin wrote around the year A.D. 160; the *E* verifies that he was an *Eastern* writer.[3] This affords brief information about the writer, but more information is required to place his statement in a proper perspective. A section entitled "Who's Who in the Early Church" following this introductory chapter furnishes the added information.

> **Justin Martyr** (JƏS-tən MÄRT-ər) *c. 100–165.* Philosopher who converted to Christianity and became a tireless evangelist and apologist. Justin wrote more concerning Christianity than any other person prior to his time. He is classified herein as eastern, since he was a native of Samaria and his thought patterns were eastern. However, he spent the last years of his life in Rome, where he was executed as a martyr (c. 165). See JUSTIN MARTYR herein.

The closing statement, "See JUSTIN MARTYR herein," indicates that the main section contains an entry under "Justin Martyr." That entry contains quotations from other early Christians concerning Justin Martyr.

---

[3] The stated dates of writing are not intended to be precise. For persons whose writings span a period of only a few years, I have usually attributed all of that person's writing to one median date. For example, all of Cyprian's works are dated herein as c. 250; however, the writings of authors who wrote over an extended period of time (such as Origen) are assigned an approximate date for each work.

For a fuller understanding of Justin Martyr's remarks concerning the topic "the fall of man," the quotation can be consulted in its full context in the *Ante-Nicene Fathers*. (In fact, one of the primary purposes of this dictionary is to serve as an index to the *Ante-Nicene Fathers*.) The citation ends with the reference, *1.243*, which refers to volume one, page 243 in the *Ante-Nicene Fathers*.[4] In *Ante-Nicene Fathers* 1.243, the source of the quotation is identified as Justin's *Dialogue with Trypho, a Jew*. The preface to *Dialogue with Trypho, a Jew* explains that it is an apologetic work written to the Jews. This procedure can be followed with each citation within a given entry.

A careful reader will discover that the *Dictionary's* translation does not exactly match that in the *Ante-Nicene Fathers*. That is because I rendered the citations into contemporary English. I endeavored, however, not to alter the meaning. My basic procedures in making these adaptations were as follows: (1) I have replaced archaic and academic words with contemporary, common words. (2) I have broken down long sentences into two or more smaller sentences. In doing so, I sometimes reused certain nouns and verbs to make complete sentences. (3) When appropriate, I have rearranged sentence structures to follow a contemporary English pattern. (4) Where the antecedent of a pronoun lies outside the passage being quoted, I have supplied it. For example, in the course of discussing the heretical teachings of Marcion, a writer may begin a sentence: "He also teaches. . . ." In such an instance, I would render the quotation, "Marcion also teaches. . . ." (5) Some early Christian writers used the editorial "we" when speaking about themselves. When it is clear that the writer is speaking only for himself, I have rendered his plural pronouns in the singular.

These steps should render these passages from the early Christians more accessible for the modern reader. No attempt, however, was made to retranslate the pre-Nicene writings from the available Latin and Greek texts.

Even though I collected several quotations, these are obviously only representative, not comprehensive. At the end of the last quotation is a further directive: *See also 2.102, 103*. This indicates that additional relevant material appears in volume 2, pages 102 and 103. The full text has not been given since they are similar in nature and are from one of the same authors as those already cited. For a more thorough study, look up those texts as well. A final instruction occurs at the end of the article.

"SEE ALSO ADAM; ATONEMENT; DEATH; EVE; EVIL, PROBLEM OF; FLESH; FREEWILL AND PREDESTINATION; MAN, DOCTRINE OF; SALVATION; TREE OF KNOWLEDGE."

These additional subjects are related concepts that should be examined in any full treatment of the topic, "fall of man." Thus to better grasp the early church's view of the fall of man, understanding early Christian teachings about death, the atonement, salvation, and the nature of man becomes critical.

I offer one caveat: Please remember that what the early Christian writers do *not* say can often be just as important as what they *do* say. In some cases, the early Christian writers knew nothing at all about some of the doctrines that certain Christians today regard as fundamental tenets of the faith. So do not be alarmed if a cross-reference does not lead to a fuller discussion. That should not happen very often, but when it does, it is not a mistake;

---

[4]Note that the Hendrickson Publishers' edition reorders the sequence of the volumes to make the index volume, volume 10 (not 9 as in past editions), the last volume. Volume 10 now includes an expanded index (Annotated Index of Authors and Works) and two appendixes (A. Patristic Exegetical Works and B. The Liturgical Year).

rather, in this manner I attempted to index what the early Christians did *not* say. For example, at the end of the list of quotations under Mary, you will find a cross-reference to "Woman Clothed with the Sun and Moon." However, when you check the various quotations under "Woman Clothed with the Sun and Moon," you will find that all of the writers understood this woman in Revelation to be the church, not Mary. In short, I have indexed what the early Christian writers did *not* say.

ACQUIRING A FOUNDATIONAL UNDERSTANDING

To accurately grasp what the early Christians said about a given topic it becomes important to have a basic understanding of three concepts: (1) Marcion and the Gnostics, (2) the early Christian concept of the Logos, and (3) the Scriptures of the early church.

Marcion and the Gnostics

Many early Christian writings were polemical works directed against the heretic Marcion or against various Gnostics.[5] Both Marcion and the Gnostics taught that the earth and everything in it (including people) were created by a God they called the Demiurge. They regarded the Demiurge not as the God of the New Testament; rather, the Demiurge was thought to be more of a demigod, with certain imperfect traits. Gnostics sometimes portrayed him as an unmerciful, unloving, and vengeful God. On occasion they referred to him as the "just God" of the Old Testament in contrast with the "good God" of the New Testament.

Marcion and the Gnostics also taught an exaggerated view of the fall of man. They believed that all physical creation—including the physical body—was inherently flawed and incapable of salvation. Accordingly, they denied the resurrection of the body, as well as the efficacy of baptism and communion. Many taught that the Son of God did not really become man and that he did not really die on the cross. In their teaching, the Son only *appeared* to do so. These Gnostics (including a group called Docetists, from the Greek word *dokeō,* "seem, appear") are the persons whom John spoke of as the "antichrists," for they denied that Jesus had come in the flesh (2 John 7).

Logos

It would be quite difficult to understand most of the early Christian writings without some appreciation of the meanings and significance of the Greek word *logos,* particularly as a title of Christ. Since our English translations usually translate *logos* as "Word" when this title is applied to the Son, English-speaking Christians usually fail to appreciate the term *logos* and its significance. The Moffatt version of the New Testament, however, often leaves *logos* untranslated when it is used as a title for the Son. For example, it renders John 1:1: "The Logos existed in the very beginning, the Logos was with God, the Logos was divine." It translates Revelation 19:13 as follows: "He is clad in a robe dipped in blood (his name is called THE LOGOS OF GOD.)"

---

[5] Treatment of the "Gnostics" as a defined and understood group is problematic. Modern scholars use the expression "Gnosticism" to describe a wide variety of groups and beliefs among those groups. The "origins" and nature of "Gnosticism" remains a point of scholarly debate.

Moffatt left the term *logos* untranslated because in Greek that term means far more than simply "word." Its range of meaning could include "reason," "rational principle," and even "mind." Early Christians use the term *logos* extensively when speaking about the Son of God. When John refers to the Son as being the Logos of God, the early Christians understood him to mean that the Son is the eternal Rational Principle of the Father, the Father's Counselor before all ages.[6]

The Early Christian Scriptures

To comprehend and appreciate what the early Christians have to say, a thorough knowledge and grasp of Scripture are indispensable. That is because the early Christians grounded all of their fundamental beliefs on Scripture. Nonetheless, a first reading of early Christian quotations from Scripture can be perplexing. Not infrequently, their citations do not read the same as do our modern Bibles. There are several reasons for this. First, when quoting from the Old Testament, the early Christians nearly always quoted from the Septuagint (i.e., the Greek Old Testament, including the Apocrypha)—as did the apostles. [See SEPTUAGINT herein.] In contrast, modern Old Testament translations are usually based on the Masoretic Text. Secondly, we must remember that the early Christians had no concordances, topical Bibles, study aids, computer Bibles, or even handy personal Bibles. As a result, the early Christians often had to quote Scriptures from memory, which meant they sometimes misquoted a verse or two. Furthermore, particularly in the case of the Latin writers, citations seem to have come from a version or text that differed slightly from later versions or editions.

THE *ANTE-NICENE FATHERS* AS A SOURCE FOR EARLY CHRISTIAN WRITINGS

Of course, the *Ante-Nicene Fathers* are not the only available translations of the pre-Nicene writings. Still, I chose the present edition of the *Ante-Nicene Fathers* as the basis for this work for several reasons. First, the translations in the *Ante-Nicene Fathers* are usually more literal than more recent translations. Secondly, other sets of translations contain only a small portion of the pre-Nicene writings. Finally, as a practical matter, the *Ante-Nicene Fathers* is the only set of the pre-Nicene writings affordable to the average person.

Theological Bias

I have made every effort to make this volume as theologically neutral as I can. I have indexed and cross-referenced most topics under terms familiar to both Catholics and Protestants. Although the *Dictionary* does not purport to be exhaustive, I have attempted to include every significant quotation under each of the indexed topics. No essential quotation has been purposefully omitted.

Scope of this Work

The *Dictionary* does not include all of the works contained in the *Ante-Nicene Fathers* because a number of those works are either spurious, post-Nicene, or Gnostic in origin.

---

[6]For examples of how the early Christians understood the word *logos*, see CHRIST, DIVINITY OF; LOGOS; and WORD OF GOD (CHRIST) in this digest.

This volume covers only recognized pre-Nicene works whose authors are considered orthodox by the pre-Nicene church. Therefore, I have excluded the following works:

- The spurious letters of Ignatius (vol. 1).

- The Martyrdom of Ignatius, which is post-Nicene (vol. 1).

- The apocryphal and Gnostic Gospels (vol. 8).

- The pseudo-Clementine literature (vol. 8).

- The false papal decretals (vol. 8).

- The post-Nicene works incorrectly attributed to Hippolytus, such as *Against Beron and Helix* (vol. 5).

- The post-Nicene works incorrectly attributed to Gregory Thaumaturgus (vol. 6).

- The quotations from the ninth-century bishop, Photius (vol. 6).

- The various liturgies, all of which are in a post-Nicene form (vol. 7).

- The various Syriac works, except for a few scattered references (vol. 8). Although these works are worth reading, nearly all of them are from the fourth or fifth centuries.

After considerable deliberation, I have included the *Apostolic Constitutions* (vol. 7) in this index, even though strong arguments exist to exclude this work. By way of objection, these *Constitutions* were not compiled until nearly the end of the fourth century—a half century or more after Nicea. Furthermore, the documents betray a spurious facade, pretending to have been written directly by the apostles themselves. The editor of the *Apostolic Constitutions* even makes the ludicrous attempt to include the *Constitutions* in the New Testament canon (ANF 7.505). Despite these objectionable elements, the bulk of the *Constitutions* is pre-Nicene in origin, and is thus included. I did exclude material in the *Constitutions* that is almost certainly post-Nicene in nature (or else I have included such passages in this digest with the caveat "post-Nicene"[7]).

Three Mistakes to Avoid

Perhaps the most common mistake would be to employ this resource as a database for proof-texts. It would be tempting to sift through it, noting quotations that bolster our personal beliefs and discarding those that do not fit. Such an approach, however, inevitably misuses the early Christian writings. By selectively choosing quotations, we make it appear that the early Christians believed exactly as we do (which is sometimes not the case). In short, instead of *learning* from those close to the apostles in time and spirit, we simply *use* them for our own designs.

Another common mistake is to read the early Christian writers as though these writers were making dogmatic theological pronouncements every time they spoke. Generally, the pre-Nicene Christian writers were not attempting to define precise points of dogma for the rest of the church. Most of their theological discussions come up in the context of

---

[7] Since chapters 1 through 32 of Book 7 of the *Constitutions* simply reiterate the Didache, I have not indexed those chapters. All of that material is included under the citations for the Didache.

either (1) explaining to outsiders what Christians believed or (2) contrasting the tenets of particular heretics with what the general body of Christians believed. They were not normally trying to convince other "orthodox" Christians what to believe.

We also must be careful not to read technical or post-Nicene meanings into theological terms used by the pre-Nicene Christians. Very rarely did "orthodoxy" (itself a fifth-century term) in the early church turn on the issue of using *this* word instead of *that* word. The early Christians understood orthodoxy in terms of general concepts, not meticulous theological definitions. As Clement of Alexandria put it, "Those who are particular about words, and devote their time to them, miss the point of the whole picture" (ANF 2.347). Although theology was important to the early church, it took a back seat to *living* the Christian life.

Who's Who in
the *Ante-Nicene Fathers*

Alexander of Alexandria (AL-ig-ZAN-dər) *d. 328.* Bishop of the church at Alexandria, Egypt, at the outbreak of the Arian controversy. He strongly opposed the heresy of Arius.

Apollonarius (ə-PÄL-ə-NAR-ē-əs) *2d century.* Bishop of Hierapolis and Christian apologist. He also wrote a short work against the Montanists.

Archelaus (ÄR-kə-LĀ-əs) *3d century.* A Christian bishop who publicly debated Manes, the founder of Manichaeism. A purported record of this debate is chronicled in the *Disputation of Archelaus and Manes.*

Aristides (AR-ə-STĪD-ēz) *early 2d century.* A converted Greek philosopher of Athens who wrote one of the earliest Christian apologies.

Aristo of Pella (AR-ə-STŌ) *2d century.* Early Christian apologist about whom little is known. Only brief excerpts remain of his apology.

Arius (AR-ē-əs) *c. 250–336.* Presbyter in the church at Alexandria who disputed with his bishop over the nature of Christ. Arius taught that Jesus was of a different nature than the Father and that Jesus was created out of nothing. His views were condemned at the Council of Nicea. See ARIUS herein.

Arnobius (är-NŌ-bē-əs) *d. c. 330.* Noted pagan teacher of rhetoric at Sicca, North Africa, who converted to Christianity. According to Jerome, the local bishop demanded proof of Arnobius's sincerity before admitting him into the church. That was because Arnobius had previously been an outspoken opponent of Christianity. So Arnobius wrote a lengthy apologetic work entitled *Against the Pagan*, which is included in the *Ante-Nicene Fathers*. Although orthodox in intent, this work reflects the fact that its author did not have a thorough grasp of the totality of Christian doctrine.

Athenagoras (ATH-ə-NAG-ə-rəs) *2d century.* Christian apologist who had been a Greek philosopher before his conversion. His apology was presented to Emperors Marcus Aurelius and Commodus about A.D. 177.

Bardesanes (BÄRD-i-SĀ-NĒZ) *c. 154–222.* A Syriac convert to Christianity who later lapsed into heresy, espousing many Gnostic tenets. The work, *The Book of the Laws of Divers Countries*, may have actually been written by his student, Philip. However, it is credited to

Bardesanes in the *Ante-Nicene Fathers* (under the name "Bardesan"). This work has been included in this dictionary only sparingly and only where it contains historical information or else theological teachings that are wholly consistent with pre-Nicene orthodoxy.

Barnabas, Epistle of (BÄR-nə-bəs) *c. 70–100.* An anonymous work widely circulated among the early Christians. Many early Christians believed this work to have been written by Barnabas, the well-known companion of the apostle Paul. Some writers, such as Clement of Alexandria, even considered it to be Scripture. It is included in the early manuscript, Codex Sinaiticus, which contains much of the modern New Testament. Most modern scholars doubt it was actually written by the historic Barnabas. See BARNABAS, EPISTLE OF herein.

Caius (KĀ-(y)əs) *early 3d century.* Presbyter in the church at Rome who wrote several works against major heresies of his day. Also known as Gaius.

Celsus (SEL-səs) *2d century.* Pagan Roman philosopher who wrote a blistering attack on Christianity (c. 178). Over a half century later, his attack was brilliantly answered by Origen. In the quotations found herein under Origen, I have noted where the speaker is Celsus rather than Origen. In such instances, it should be understood that the view being presented is that of a pagan critic.

Clement of Rome (KLEM-ənt) *1st century.* Bishop of the church at Rome; he may well have been a companion of both Peter and Paul (Phil. 4:3). On behalf of the church in Rome, he wrote a letter to the Corinthian church (c. 95) in aid to the church leaders who had been ousted by a minority faction. The work designated as *Second Clement* was at one time erroneously attributed to Clement of Rome. However, it is actually an early sermon or homily, the authorship of which is unknown. See CLEMENT OF ROME herein.

Clement of Alexandria (KLEM-ənt) *c. 150–215.* Learned Christian teacher at Alexandria, Egypt, who was in charge of the catechetical school there. Origen was one of his pupils. In his largest extant work, *Miscellanies*, Clement attempted unsuccessfuly to wrest the term "gnostic" (one who knows) away from the heretics and give it a Christian meaning. To avoid confusion, I have rendered his Christian "gnostic" as "spiritual man" herein. A few of the quotations herein from Clement have been translated from the Latin passages appearing in the *Ante-Nicene Fathers*. See CLEMENT OF ALEXANDRIA herein.

Cyprian (SIP-rē-ən) *d. 258.* Bishop of the church in Carthage, North Africa, during a period of fierce persecution. He often had to work underground. However, he was eventually captured and executed by the Romans. An extensive collection of letters written by and to Cyprian still remains, along with various treatises written by him. These works give tremendous insight into the structure of the church in the middle of the third century. See CYPRIAN herein.

Dionysius of Alexandria (DĪ-ə-NIS(H)-ē-əs) *d. c. 264.* Pupil of Origen, later head of the catechetical school in Alexandria, and eventually bishop of Alexandria (from 247). He wrote against Sabellianism, and he opposed Paul of Samosata.

Dionysius of Corinth (DĪ-ə-NIS(H)-ē-əs) *2d century.* Bishop of Corinth, some of whose letters are extant.

Dionysius of Rome (DĪ-ə-NIS(H)-ē-əs) *d. 268.* Bishop of Rome who entered into a controversy with Dionysius, bishop of Alexandria, concerning the divine nature of Christ.

Edict of Milan (mi-LÄN) *313.* Decree issued jointly by Constantine and Licinius, rulers of the Western and Eastern portions of the Roman Empire, giving legal recognition to Christianity for the first time.

Eusebius (yü-SĒ-bē-əs) *270–340.* Bishop of the church in Caesarea during the time of Constantine's reign. His *Ecclesiastical History* is a principal source for the history of the church from the first century down through the time of Emperor Constantine.

Firmilian (fər-MIL-yən) *c. 200–268.* Bishop of Caesarea in Cappadocia. He was a friend of Origen, and he sided with Cyprian against Stephen, bishop of Rome, in the controversy concerning baptism by heretics.

Hegesippus (HEJ-ə-SIP-əs) *c. 110–180.* Early church historian. Only fragments of his works are still extant, preserved in Eusebius's *Ecclesiastical History.* Hegesippus drew up one of the earliest lists of the succession of bishops in the church in Rome.

Hermas (HER-məs) *1st or 2d century.* Author of an allegorical work entitled *The Shepherd,* which was widely read and held in great esteem by many early Christian churches. Origen believed the author to be the same person referred to by Paul in Romans 16:14. The Muratorian Fragment asserts that he was the brother of Pius, second century bishop of Rome. See HERMAS, SHEPHERD OF herein.

Hippolytus (hip-ÄL-ət-əs) *c. 170–236.* A leading presbyter in the church in Rome near the beginning of the third century. He attacked the theology and discipline of two Roman bishops, Zephyrinus and Callistus, and apparently led a schism in the Roman church for awhile. His principal work was the *Refutation of All Heresies.* Among other works, he also wrote commentaries on Daniel and the Song of Songs. He died as a martyr.

Ignatius (ig-NĀ-sh(ē-)əs) *c. 35–107.* Bishop of the church at Antioch and a personal disciple of one or more apostles. He was executed in Rome c. 107. On his way to Rome as a prisoner, Ignatius wrote letters to several churches; these letters give considerable insight into the structure and beliefs of the churches in Asia Minor at the close of the apostolic age. See IGNATIUS herein.

Irenaeus (Ī-rē-NĒ-əs) *c. 130–200.* Bishop of the church at Lyons (in modern-day France). When he was a boy, Irenaeus had heard Polycarp teach. From this, it is generally supposed that Irenaeus was a native of Smyrna. In 190, Irenaeus wrote to Victor, bishop of Rome, pleading tolerance for the Christians of Asia Minor who celebrated Easter on a different day than did Rome. He is classified herein as both Eastern and Western, since he was from an Eastern background but ministered in the West.

Julius Africanus (JÜL-yəs AF-ri-KĀ-nəs) *c. 160–240.* Roman military officer, friend of kings and emperors, and convert to Christianity. Only a few letters from his writings remain.

Justin Martyr (JƏS-tən MÄRT-ər) *c. 100–165.* Philosopher who converted to Christianity and became a tireless evangelist and apologist. Justin wrote more concerning Christianity than any other person prior to his time. He is classified herein as Eastern, since he was a native of Samaria and his thought patterns were Eastern. However, he spent the last years of his life in Rome, where he was executed as a martyr (c. 165). See JUSTIN MARTYR herein.

Lactantius (lak-TAN-sh(ē-)əs) *c. 250–325.* Prominent Roman teacher of rhetoric who later converted to Christianity. In his old age, he was summoned by Emperor Constantine to Gaul (France) to tutor Constantine's son, Crispus.

Manes (MĀ-nēz) *c. 216–276.* Also known as Mani and Manichaeus. He founded a religious sect in Persia that incorporated many gnostic elements, particularly dualism. It spread throughout the East as a distinct religion, but it emerged in the West primarily as a Christian heresy. See MANES, MANICHAEANS herein.

Marcion (MÄR-s(h)ē-ən) *d. c. 160.* Heretical second-century teacher who eventually founded his own church. His teachings incorporated many gnostic elements, including the belief that the God of the Old Testament was a different God than the Father of Jesus. Marcion accepted only the Gospel of Luke and the writings of Paul for his New Testament canon, and he was forced to alter even these to fit his teachings. See MARCION herein.

Mark Minucius Felix (mə-N(Y)Ü-sh(ē-)əs FĒ-liks) *2d or 3d century.* Roman lawyer who converted to Christianity. He wrote one of the finest apologies of early Christianity in the form of a dialogue between a Christian and a pagan. When reading quotations attributed to Mark Minucius Felix, the reader should take note whether the speaker is the pagan antagonist or the Christian apologist.

Melito (MEL-ə-tō) *d. c. 190.* Bishop of Sardis in Asia and a prolific writer. Unfortunately, only fragments of his works remain.

Methodius (mi-THŌ-dē-əs) *d. c. 311.* Apparently bishop of Lycia, the author of several theological and moral works.

Montanus (MÄN-tə-nəs, män-TĀ-nəs) *2d century.* Founder of a spiritual movement that began in Phrygia in the latter part of the second century. After the death of Montanus, the movement was led by two self-proclaimed prophetesses, Priscilla and Maximilla. The Montanists referred to their movement as the New Prophecy. The church, however, usually called them "Phrygians," "Cataphrygians," or "Montanists." The Montanists referred to the catholic Christians as the "psychics," or "unspiritual." See MONTANISTS herein.

Novatian (nə-VĀ-shən) *d. 257.* Roman presbyter and author of several theological works in Latin. He later led a schism when Cornelius was ordained as bishop of Rome (c. 251).

The Novatianists held to the same theological doctrines as the church, but were stricter in matters of discipline. The Novatianists lingered through the fifth century. The quotations herein that are credited to Novatian, but marked with an asterisk, are works that the *Ante-Nicene Fathers* attribute to Cyprian but which most scholars now attribute to Novatian. See NOVATIAN, NOVATIANISTS herein.

Origen (ÄR-ə-jən) *c. 185–255*. A pupil of Clement of Alexandria who took over the famous catechetical school in Alexandria after the departure of Clement. He has been called the "father of Christian theology." Origen was also the most prolific writer of the pre-Nicene church, dictating around two thousand works. He wrote not only doctrinal and apologetic works, but also commentaries on most of the books of the Bible. Many of his teachings reflect brilliant spiritual insights. On the other hand, some of his teachings exhibit strained or unsound theological speculation.

Origen traveled widely and defended the church against heretics. During Origen's travels through Palestine on church interests (c. 233), he was ordained as a presbyter by the bishop of Caesarea. This led to a great controversy with his bishop in Alexandria and to Origen's dismissal from the church in Alexandria. Origen spent the remainder of his life at Caesarea in Palestine as a presbyter, where he publicly preached and taught. He eventually died as a confessor, having endured excruciating tortures for Christ during the Decian persecution. Many of Origen's works exist only in the Latin translations made by the fourth-century monk, Rufinus. At one time, it was generally thought that Rufinus's translations were seriously tainted and that he tried to make Origen appear more orthodox than he really was. Modern scholarship, however, has tended to vindicate Rufinus's translations as being much more theologically honest and sound than was once thought. See ORIGEN herein.

Papias (PÅ-pē-əs) *c. 60–130*. Bishop of Hierapolis in Asia Minor and a disciple of John and a friend of Polycarp. His testimony concerning the Gospels of Matthew and Mark has been invaluable to the church. See PAPIAS herein.

Polycarp (PÄL-ē-KÄRP) *c. 69–156*. Faithful bishop of the church at Smyrna, friend of Ignatius, and a disciple of the apostle John. He was arrested in his very old age and was burned to death (c. 156). See POLYCARP herein.

Polycrates (pə-LIK-rə-TĒZ) *2d century.* Bishop of Ephesus who opposed Victor, bishop of Rome, when the latter attempted to coerce all Christians to conform to Rome's date for celebrating Easter.

Tatian (TÅ-shən) *2d century.* A disciple of Justin Martyr and Christian apologist. His most famous work is the *Diatessaron*, a harmony of the Gospels. It was originally written in Greek, but Tatian translated it himself into Syriac. Sadly, after the death of Justin, Tatian deviated into heresy, becoming a leader of the Encratite sect. All of the quotations herein are from Tatian's orthodox period. See TATIAN herein.

Tertullian (tər-TƏL-yən) *c. 160–230*. Fiery Christian writer in Carthage, North Africa. He may have been an ordained presbyter. He wrote numerous apologies, works against heretics, and exhortations to other Christians—nearly all of which are in Latin. Near the beginning of the third century, he came under the influence of the Montanist sect. Around 211, he seems to have left the church to join a Montanist congregation, although this is not certain. Since the Montanist sect differed from the church primarily on matters of discipline, not theological doctrines, Tertullian's writings during his Montanist phase have been included herein. When the view he expresses appears to be unique to the Montanists, this is noted. See TERTULLIAN herein.

Theonas (thē-ÄN-əs) *d. 300.* Bishop of Alexandria who succeeded Dionysius.

Theophilus (thē-ÄF-ə-ləs) *2d century.* Bishop of Antioch and Christian apologist. He was the first person to use the word "Triad" in speaking of the Father, Son, and Holy Spirit.

Trypho (TRĪ-fō) A Jewish literary character (and possibly an historical person) in Justin Martyr's *Dialogue with Trypho the Jew.* In quotations from this work herein, I have noted the quotations where Trypho is the speaker. Such quotations reflect Jewish beliefs and attitudes, not those of the Christians.

Victorinus (VIK-tə-RĪ-nəs) *d. c. 304.* Bishop of Poetovio in Syria and a martyr. He wrote commentaries on a number of the books of the Bible; however, only his commentary on Revelation has survived.

ABANDONMENT OF INFANTS

SEE ABORTION, INFANTICIDE.

ABEL

And the Lord respected Abel and his offering. Gen. 4:4.

By faith Abel offered to God a more excellent sacrifice than Cain. Heb. 11:4.

On you may come all the righteous blood shed on the earth, from the blood of righteous Abel to the blood of Zechariah. Matt. 23:35.

We show that both earthly oblations and spiritual sacrifices were foreshadowed.... Cain foreshadowed those of the elder son, that is, of Israel. And the opposite sacrifices are demonstrated to be those of the younger son, Abel. He represents our [Christian] people. *Tertullian (c. 197, W), 3.156.*

Beloved brethren, let us imitate righteous Abel, who initiated martyrdoms. For he was the first to be slain for righteousness' sake. *Cyprian (c. 250, W), 5.348.*

In the sacrifices that Abel and Cain first offered, God looked not at their gifts, but at their hearts. Abel was acceptable in his *gift* because he was acceptable in his *heart*. Abel was peaceable and righteous; he sacrificed in innocence to God. He thereby taught others that when they, too, bring their gift to the altar, they should come with the fear of God and with a simple heart. *Cyprian (c. 250, W), 5.454; see also 2.105.*

ABGAR, KING

Abgar was the customary name given to various kings of Edessa. The passages below apparently refer to two different Abgars. The first one refers to Abgar the Black, c. A.D. 13–50.

King Abgar was renowned for his valor among the nations that were east of the Euphrates. However, his body was wasting away with a grievous disease, one for which there was no cure among men. But when Abgar heard and was informed of the name of Jesus and about the mighty works that He did, . . . he sent a letter of request [to Jesus] through one of his slaves. Abgar begged Him to come and heal him of his disease. However, our Savior did not comply with his request at the time that he asked. Still, He sent Abgar a letter in reply. *Eusebius (c. 315, E), 8.651.*

This Abgar was called Avak-air (great man) because of his gentleness, wisdom, and size. Not being able to pronounce well, the Greeks and the Syrians called him Abgar. In the second year of his reign, all the districts of Armenia became vassals to the Romans. *Moses of Chorene (date uncertain, E), 8.702; extended discussion: 8.651–8.653.*

SEE ALSO ARMENIA; EDESSA; SEVENTY, THE (DISCIPLES).

ABLUTION

Ablution refers to ceremonial washing before prayer or other religious observance.

It is said that we should go to the sacrifices and prayers washed, clean, and bright. It is said that this external adornment and purification are practiced as a symbol. *Clement of Alexandria (c. 195, E), 2.435.*

[DESCRIBING A LOVE FEAST:] After washing the hands and the bringing in of lights, each person is asked to stand forth and sing a hymn to God, as best he can. This can be either a hymn from the Holy Scriptures or one of his own composing. *Tertullian (c. 197, W), 3.47.*

What reason is there to go to prayer with hands indeed washed, but the spirit foul? It is *spiritual* purities that are necessary for our hands, so that they can be "lifted up pure" from falsehood, and from murder. . . . These are the true purities. The true ones are not those which most persons are superstitiously careful about—such as using water at every prayer, even when they are coming from a bath of the whole body. When I was carefully making a thorough investigation of this practice, . . . I ascertained that it was a commemorative act, relating to the surrender of the Lord [when Pilate washed his hands]. However, we *pray* to the Lord; we do not *surrender* him. *Tertullian (c. 198, W), 3.685.*

In this manner, the Essenes perform ablutions in cold water. And after being cleansed in this manner, they retire together into one room. *Hippolytus (c. 225, W), 5.134.*

SEE ALSO PRAYER (II. PRAYER POSTURES AND CUSTOMS).

ABOMINATION OF DESOLATION
SEE DANIEL, BOOK OF.

ABORTION, INFANTICIDE
The term "exposing infants" refers to the practice of abandoning infant children along roadsides, leaving them either to die of exposure or to be taken by someone, usually to be raised as a slave or a prostitute.

If men fight and hurt a woman with child, so that she gives birth prematurely . . . [and] if any lasting harm follows, then you shall give life for life, eye for eye, tooth for tooth, hand for hand, foot for foot. Exod. 21:22, 23.

You shall not kill the child by obtaining an abortion. Nor, again, shall you destroy him after he is born. *Barnabas (c. 70–130, E), 1.148.*

You shall not murder a child by abortion nor kill one who has been born. *Didache (c. 80–140, E), 1.377.*

They bear children, but they do not destroy their offspring. *Letter to Diognetus (c. 125–200), 1.27.*

We say that those women who use drugs to bring on abortion commit murder. And we also say they will have to give an account to God for the abortion. So on what basis could we commit murder? For it does not belong to the same person to regard the very fetus in the womb as a created being (and therefore an object of God's care)—yet, when he has passed into life, to kill him. We also teach that it is wrong to expose an infant. For those who expose them are guilty of child murder. *Athenagoras (c. 175, E), 2.147.*

Fathers, forgetting about their children who have been exposed, often unknowingly have intercourse with a son that has debauched himself and with daughters who are prostitutes. *Clement of Alexandria (c. 195, E), 2.276.*

Although keeping parrots and curlews, the [pagans] do not adopt the orphan child. Rather, they expose children who are born at home. Yet, they take up the young of birds. So they prefer irrational creatures to rational ones! *Clement of Alexandria (c. 195, E), 2.279.*

What cause is there for the exposure of a child? The man who did not desire to beget children had no right to marry at all. He certainly does not have the right to become the murderer of his children, because of licentious indulgence. *Clement of Alexandria (c. 195, E), 2.368.*

In our case, murder is once for all forbidden. Therefore, we may not destroy even the fetus in the womb, while as yet the human being derives blood from other parts of the body for its sustenance. To hinder a birth is merely a speedier way to kill a human. It does not matter whether you take away a life that has been born, or destroy one that is not yet born. *Tertullian (c. 197, W), 3.25.*

First of all, you [pagans] expose your children, so that they may be taken up by any compassionate passer-by, to whom they are quite unknown! *Tertullian (c. 197, W), 3.26.*

Although you are forbidden by the laws to kill newborn infants, it so happens that no laws are evaded with more impunity or greater safety. And this is done with the deliberate knowledge of the public. *Tertullian (c. 197, W), 3.123.*

Among surgeons' tools there is a certain instrument that is formed with a nicely-adjusted flexible frame for first of all opening the uterus and then keeping it open. It also has a circular blade, by means of which the limbs within the womb are dissected with careful, but unflinching care. Its last appendage is a blunted or covered hook, by which the entire fetus is extracted by a violent delivery. There is also a copper needle or spike, by which the actual death is brought about in this treacherous robbery of life. From its infanticide function, they give it the name, "killer of the infant"—which infant, of course, had once been alive. *Tertullian (c. 210, W), 3.206.*

Indeed, the Law of Moses punishes with appropriate penalties the person who causes abortion. For there already exists the beginning stages of a human being. And even at this stage, [the fetus] is already acknowledged with having the condition of life and death, since he is already susceptible to both. *Tertullian (c. 210, W), 3.218.*

Are you to dissolve the conception by aid of drugs? I believe it is no more lawful to hurt a child in process of birth, than to hurt one who is already born. *Tertullian (c. 212, W), 4.57.*

I behold a certain ceremony and circumstance of adultery. On the one hand, idolatry precedes it and leads the way. On the other hand, murder follows in company. . . . Witness the midwives, too! How many adulterous conceptions are slaughtered! *Tertullian (c. 212, W), 4.78.*

There are some women who, by drinking medical preparations, extinguish the source of the future man in their very bowels. So they commit murder before they bring forth. And these things assuredly come down from the teaching of your gods. *Mark Minucius Felix (c. 200, W), 4.192.*

Women who were reputed believers began to resort to drugs for producing sterility. They also girded themselves around, so as to expel what was being conceived. For they did not wish to have a child by either a slave or by any common fellow—out of concern for their family and their excessive wealth. See what a great impiety the lawless one has advanced! He teaches adultery and murder at the same time! *Hippolytus (c. 225, W), 5.131.*

The womb of his wife was hit by a blow of his heel. And, in the miscarriage that soon followed, the offspring was brought forth, the fruit of a father's murder. *Cyprian (c. 250, W), 5.326.*

I cannot find language to even speak of the infants who were burned to the same Saturn! *Lactantius (c. 304–313, W), 7.35.*

[SPEAKING OF PAGANS:] They either strangle the sons born from themselves, or if they are too "pious," they expose them. *Lactantius (c. 304–313, W), 7.144, 145.*

Let no one imagine that to strangle newborn children is allowable. For this is the greatest impiety! God breathes into their souls for *life*, not for *death*. Men . . . deprive souls that are still innocent and simple, of the light that they themselves have not given. . . . Or can those persons be considered innocent who expose their own offspring as prey for dogs? As far as their participation is concerned, they have killed them in a more cruel manner than if they had strangled them! . . . Therefore, if any-one is unable to bring up children because of poverty, it is better to abstain from marriage than to mar the work of God with wicked hands. *Lactantius (c. 304–313, W), 7.187.*

You shall not slay your child by causing abor-tion, nor kill the baby that is born. For "every-thing that is shaped and has received a soul from God, if it is slain, shall be avenged, as being unjustly destroyed" [Ezek. 21:23, LXX]. *Apostolic Constitutions (compiled c. 390, E), 7.466.*

SEE ALSO CONCEPTION; PROCREATION.

ABRAHAM

Now it came to pass after these things that God tested Abraham, and said to him . . . , "Take now your son, your only son Isaac, whom you love, and go to the land of Moriah, and offer him there as a burnt offering." Gen. 22:1, 2.

I say to you that God is able to raise up children to Abraham from these stones. Matt. 3:9.

If you are Christ's, then you are Abraham's seed, and heirs according to the promise. Gal. 3:29.

Now we, brethren, as Isaac was, are children of promise. Gal. 4:28.

This man was not only the prophet of faith, but also the father of those who from among the Gentiles believe in Jesus Christ. That is because his faith and ours are one and the same. *Irenaeus (c. 180, E/W), 1.492.*

The promise of God that He gave to Abra-ham remains steadfast. . . . For his seed is the church, which receives the adoption of God through the Lord, as John the Baptist said: "For God is able from the stones to raise up children to Abraham." Thus also the apostle says in the Epistle to the Galatians: "But you, brethren, as Isaac was, are the children of the promise." *Ire-naeus (c. 180, E/W), 1.561.*

God had commanded even Abraham to make a sacrifice of his son. He did not do this to *tempt* [Abraham], but to *prove* his faith. *Tertullian (c. 198, W), 3.684.*

SEE ALSO ISRAEL OF GOD.

ABRAHAM'S BOSOM

SEE DEAD, INTERMEDIATE STATE OF; PARADISE.

ABSOLUTION

In the early church, absolution was the formal act of a bishop or presbyter in pronouncing forgiveness of sin to a repentant Christian.

Whatever you bind on earth will be bound in heaven, and whatever you loose on earth will be loosed in heaven. Matt. 18:15.

If you forgive the sins of any, they are forgiven them; if you retain the sins of any, they are retained. John 20:23.

Some, not able to find this peace [i.e., ecclesiastical forgiveness] in the church, have been seeking it from the imprisoned martyrs. *Tertullian (c. 197, W), 3.693.*

Is it better to be damned in secret than absolved in public? *Tertullian (c. 203, W), 3.664.*

The next four quotations from Tertullian reflect the Montanist view that the church cannot extend forgiveness for serious postbaptismal sins, such as adultery.

I am not speaking of the type of repentance after believing that receives pardon from the bishop for lighter sins. For greater and irremissible ones, [pardon comes] from God alone. *Tertullian (c. 212, W), 4.95.*

Apostolic sir, therefore, demonstrate to me even now prophetic evidence, so that I may recognize your divine virtue and so that you can vindicate to yourself the power of remitting such sins! If, however, you have only had the function of *discipline* allotted you, . . . who are you, how great are you, to grant indulgence? *Tertullian (c. 212, W), 4.99.*

You say, "But the church has the power of forgiving sins." This I acknowledge and adjudge. . . . But now I ask you, "From what source do *you* usurp this right of the church"? Is it because the Lord has said to Peter, "Upon this rock I will build My church" and "to you I have given the keys of the heavenly kingdom"? Or "Whatever you shall have bound or loosed in earth shall be bound or loosed in the heavens"? From these [Scriptures], do you presume that the power of binding and loosing has derived to you—that is, to every church of Peter? If so, what sort of man are you, subverting and wholly changing the manifest intention of the Lord, conferring this [authority] on Peter personally? *Tertullian (c. 212, W), 4.99.*

You go so far as to lavish this power [of forgiveness of sins] on martyrs as well! No sooner has anyone . . . put on the chains, . . . than adulterers beset him and fornicators gain access to him. Prayers immediately echo around him. Instantly, there are pools of tears. *Tertullian (c. 212, W), 4.100.*

The impostor [i.e., Callistus, bishop of Rome], having ventured on such opinions, established a school in antagonism to the church. And he adopted the foregoing system of instruction: He first invented the device of conniving with men in regard to their indulgence in pleasures, saying that everyone has their sins forgiven by him. For if anyone who commits any transgression, if he is called a Christian (even though he normally attended the congregation of someone else), they say the sin is not counted against him—provided he hurries off to the school of Callistus. And many persons are gratified with his regulation. . . . Now, some of those persons had been by us forcibly ejected from the church in accord with our judicial sentence. However, they simply went over to him and helped to crowd his school. *Hippolytus (c. 225, W), 5.131.*

In smaller sins, sinners may do penance for a set time and come to public confession according to the rules of discipline. They then receive the right of communion through the imposition of the hand of the bishop and clergy. *Cyprian (c. 250, W), 5.290.*

Let no one say, "He who accepts martyrdom is baptized in his own blood. Therefore, he does not need peace [i.e., absolution for serious sins] from the bishop. For he is about to have the peace of his own glory. He is about to receive a greater reward from the mercy of the Lord." First of all, no one can be fitted for martyrdom if he is not armed for the contest by the church. *Cyprian (c. 250, W), 5.337.*

They do violence to His body and blood [i.e., the Eucharist]—before their sin is expiated, before confession of their crime has been made! They do this before their consciences have been purged by sacrifice and by the hand of the priest! *Cyprian (c. 250, W), 5.441.*

I entreat you, beloved brethren, that each one should confess his own sins while he is still in this world—while his confession can still be received and while the satisfaction and remission made by the priests are still pleasing to the Lord. *Cyprian (c. 250, W), 5.445.*

Falling sick, he [a lapsed believer] continued three successive days dumb and senseless. Recovering a little on the fourth day, he called his grandchild to him and said, . . . "Hurry, I entreat you, and absolve me quickly. Summon one of the presbyters to me." . . . The boy ran for the presbyter. But it was night and the presbyter was sick and was, as a result, unable to come. However, I had issued an injunction that persons at the point of death, if they requested it, . . . should be absolved in order that they might depart this life in cheerful hope. So the presbyter gave the boy a small portion of the Eucharist, telling him to steep it in water and drop it into the old man's mouth. *Dionysius of Alexandria (c. 262, E), 6.101.*

O bishop, just as you receive a pagan after you have instructed and baptized him, likewise let everyone join in prayers for this [penitent] man and restore him to his former place among the flock, through the imposition of hands. For he has been purified by repentance. And the imposition of hands shall be similar to baptism for him. For, by the laying on of hands, the Holy Spirit was given to believers. *Apostolic Constitutions (compiled c. 390, E), 7.415.*

SEE ALSO BINDING AND LOOSING; CONFESSION OF SINS; DISCIPLINE, CHURCH; REPENTANCE.

ACOLYTE

In the early church, an acolyte was a man who assisted the bishop, presbyters, or deacons in administering the Eucharist and in other duties.

I have sent another share to the same person by Naricus the acolyte. *Cyprian (c. 250, W), 5.314.*

I have read your letter, dearest brother, which you sent by Saturus our brother, the acolyte. *Cyprian (c. 250, W), 5.338, 339.*

The letter that you sent to us by . . . Lucian, Maximus, and Amantius, the acolytes. *Lucius to Cyprian (c. 250, W), 5.405.*

SEE ALSO MINOR ORDERS.

ACTS OF THE APOSTLES

SEE CANON, NEW TESTAMENT.

ADAM

As in Adam all die, even so in Christ all shall be made alive. 1 Cor. 15:22.

Adam was formed first, then Eve. And Adam was not deceived, but the woman being deceived, fell into transgression. 1 Tim. 2:13, 14.

Because he was still an infant in age, Adam was not yet able to receive knowledge worthily. For even nowadays, too, when a child is born, he is not at once able to eat bread. Rather, he is first nourished with milk. . . . It would have been the same with Adam. The reason God commanded him not to eat of knowledge was not because God begrudged him, as some suppose. Rather, He wished to test Adam, to see whether he would obey His commandment. At the same time, He wished man, infant as he was, to remain simple and sincere for a while longer. *Theophilus (c. 180, E), 2.104*

The Lord came to the lost sheep. He made a recapitulation of a very comprehensive dispensation, and He sought after His own handiwork. Therefore, it was necessary for Him to save that very man who had been created after His image and likeness—that is, Adam. . . . Man had been created by God to live. However, he was injured by the serpent who had corrupted him. Now, if after losing life, man would never again return to life (but would be utterly abandoned to death), then God would have been conquered. The wickedness of the serpent would have prevailed over the will of God. *Irenaeus (c. 180, E/W), 1.455.*

Inasmuch as man is saved, it is fitting that he who was created as the original man should be saved, too. . . . It was for this reason that, immediately after Adam had transgressed (as the Scripture relates), God pronounced no curse against Adam personally, but only against the ground. *Irenaeus (c. 180, E/W), 1.456.*

Adam showed his repentance by his conduct. He did this by means of the girdle of fig-leaves by which he covered himself. For there were many other leaves that would have been less irritating to his body. However, he adopted a garment fitting for his disobedience. For he was awed by the fear of God. . . . Adam had been conquered, and all life was taken away from him. Therefore, when the enemy was conquered in its turn, Adam received new life. So the last enemy, death, is destroyed. For it had taken possession of man at the first. . . . Therefore, everyone who disallows Adam's salvation, speaks falsely. *Irenaeus (c. 180, E/W), 1.457.*

It was possible for God to have made man perfect from the beginning. However, man could not receive such perfection, being as yet an infant. *Irenaeus (c. 180, E/W), 1.521.*

Disobedience to God brings death. For that reason, Adam and Eve came under the penalty of death. From that very moment, they were handed over to it. Therefore, they did die in the same day that they ate, for they became death's debtors. Furthermore, it was one day of the creation. . . . And there are some, again, who relegate the death of Adam to the thousandth year. For since "a day of the Lord is as a thousand years, " he did not go beyond the thousand years, but died within that period, thereby fulfilling the sentence of his sin. *Irenaeus (c. 180, E/W), 1.551.*

Before the Law, Adam spoke prophetically concerning the woman and the naming of the creatures. *Clement of Alexandria (c. 195, E), 2.331.*

Adam readily chose what was wrong, following his wife. So he neglected what is true and good. On which account he exchanged his immortal life for a mortal life—but not forever. *Clement of Alexandria (c. 195, E), 2.369.*

Adam was perfect as far as his formation. . . . So the cause [of his sin] lay in his *choosing*—his choosing what was forbidden. God was not the cause. *Clement of Alexandria (c. 195, E), 2.437.*

The question propounded to us by the heretics is: Was Adam created perfect or imperfect? If imperfect, how could the work of a perfect God . . . be imperfect? And if Adam was created perfect, how did he transgress the commandment? They shall hear from us in reply that he was not perfect [or complete] at his creation. Rather, he was adapted to the reception of virtue. . . . For God created man for immortality and made him an image of His own nature. *Clement of Alexandria (c. 195, E), 2.502.*

I cannot easily be silent about that thing concerning which also the very head and fountain of the human race, and of human offense, is not silent. I mean Adam, who was restored by penitential discipline [Gr. *exomologēsis*] to his own Paradise. *Tertullian (c. 203, W), 3.666.*

God did not actually curse Adam and Eve, because they were candidates for restoration. That is because they had been relieved by confession. *Tertullian (c. 207, W), 3.317.*

Since Adam was a figure of Christ, Adam's sleep foreshadowed the death of Christ (who was to sleep a mortal slumber). Similarly, the church, the true mother of the living, was pictured by the wound inflicted on His side. *Tertullian (c. 210, W), 3.222.*

Adam gave the various names to the animals before he picked the fruit of the tree. So, before he ate, he prophesied. *Tertullian (c. 210, W), 3.592.*

Jesus delivered from the lowest Hades the first man of earth, when that man was lost and bound by the chains of death. *Hippolytus (c. 205, W), 5.170.*

We could not have received such a benefit . . . had He not taken up man, the first man of all—the man more precious than all others, purer than all others and capable of receiving Him. But after that man, we, too, will be able to receive Him. *Origen (c. 228, E), 9.384.*

God, having made man, . . . placed him in Paradise—that is, in a most fruitful and pleasant garden. He planted the garden in the regions of the east with every kind of wood and tree. This was so that man could be nourished by their various fruits. Being free from all labors, man could devote himself entirely to the service of God his Father. Then He gave to man fixed commands, by the observance of which he might continue immortal. Or, if he transgressed them, he would be punished with death. *Lactantius (c. 304–313, W), 7.62.*

SEE ALSO CREATION; EVE; FALL OF MAN; TREE OF KNOWLEDGE; TREE OF LIFE.

ADOPTION OF CHILDREN

[CONCERNING A CHRISTIAN WOMAN ABOUT TO BE MARTYRED:] She gave birth to a little girl, which a certain sister brought up as her daughter. *Passion of Perpetua and Felicitas (c. 205, W), 3.704.*

Although keeping parrots and curlews, the [pagans] do not adopt the orphan child. Rather, they expose children who are born at home. Yet, they take up the young of birds. *Clement of Alexandria (c. 195, E), 2.279.*

When any Christian becomes an orphan, . . . it is good for one of the brethren who is without a child to take the young man and value him in the place of a son. *Apostolic Constitutions (compiled c. 390, E), 7.433.*

SEE ALSO ORPHANS AND WIDOWS; PROCREATION.

ADVENT

SEE BIRTH OF JESUS; CALENDAR, CHRISTIAN.

ADVENTS OF CHRIST

SEE JESUS CHRIST (II. TWO ADVENTS OF CHRIST).

AESCULAPIUS

Aesculapius was the Roman god of medicine and healing.

They bring forward Aesculapius as another god. They say that he is a physician and that he prepares drugs and plasters in order to maintain his livelihood. In other words, this god is in need! Eventually, he was struck with lightning by Dios, . . . and he died. If, then, Aesculapius was a god, how can he possibly give help to others? After all, when he was struck with lightning, he was unable to help himself. *Aristides (c. 125, E), 9.271.*

Although Aesculapius was a great physician, he was struck by a thunderbolt and ascended to heaven. *Justin Martyr (c. 160, E), 1.170.*

When the devil brings forth Aesculapius as the raiser of the dead and healer of all diseases, may I not say that in this matter also he has imitated the prophecies about Christ? *Justin Martyr (c. 160, E), 1.233.*

What action worthy of divine honors did Aesculapius perform—other than his healing of Hippolytus? Furthermore, his birth was not without disgrace to Apollo. His death was certainly more famous, for he earned the distinction of being struck with lightning by a god. *Lactantius (c. 304–313, W), 7.19.*

Even after his punishment and his death by lightning, have you not named Aesculapius the discoverer of medicines and as the guardian and protector of health, strength, and safety? *Arnobius (c. 305, E), 6.424.*

Aesculapius presides over the duties and arts of medicine. So why cannot more persons with various kinds of diseases and sickness be restored to health and soundness of body? *Arnobius (c. 305, E), 6.470.*

SEE ALSO GODS, PAGAN.

AFTERLIFE

SEE DEAD, INTERMEDIATE STATE OF; ETERNAL PUNISHMENTS AND REWARDS.

AGAPE

SEE LOVE; LOVE FEAST.

AGE OF ACCOUNTABILITY

In pursuance of that aspect of the association of body and soul that we now have to consider, we maintain that the puberty of the soul coincides with that of the body. Generally speaking, they both attain together this full growth at about the fourteenth year of life. The soul attains it by the suggestion of the senses, and the body attains it by the growth of the bodily members. I do not mention [the age of fourteen] because reflection begins at that age (as Asclepiades supposes). Nor do I choose it because the civil laws date the commencement of the real business of life from this age. Rather, I choose it because this was the appointed order from the very first. For after their obtaining knowledge of good and evil, Adam and Eve felt that they must cover their nakedness. Likewise, we profess to have the same discernment of good and evil from the time that we experience the same sensation of shame. Now, beginning with the aforementioned age, sex is suffused and clothed with a special sensibility. This eye gives way to lust and communicates its pleasure to another. It understands the natural relations between male and female, and it wears the fig-leaf apron to cover the shame that it still excites. *Tertullian (c. 210, W), 3.218, 219.*

SEE ALSO CHILDREN, INFANTS; FALL OF MAN; MAN, DOCTRINE OF.

ALCOHOLIC BEVERAGES

SEE WINE.

ALEXANDER THE GREAT

Having defeated Darius during this period, Alexander of Macedon began to reign. Therefore, the times of the Macedonian kings can be computed as follows: Alexander, eighteen years. *Clement of Alexandria (c. 195, E), 2.329.*

"Look! Another beast like a leopard." In mentioning a leopard, he refers to the kingdom of the Greeks, over whom Alexander of Macedon was king. . . . "The beast also had four heads." When the kingdom of Alexander was exalted, grew, and acquired a name over the whole world, his kingdom was divided into four principalities. For, when near his end, Alexander divided his kingdom among his four colleagues of the same nationality: Seleucus, Demetrius, Ptolemy, and Philip. *Hippolytus (c. 205, W), 5.189.*

In the reign of Alexander of Macedon, the [Jews] received no injury from him. This was even though they refused to take up arms against Darius because of certain covenants and oaths. They say that on that occasion, the Jewish high priest, clothed in his sacred robe, received homage from Alexander. For Alexander declared that in his sleep he had beheld an individual clothed in such a robe. And [in his dream] the man announced to him that he was to be the conqueror of all of Asia. *Origen (c. 248, E), 4.565.*

Did *we* produce and stir into action the cause by which one youth, starting from Macedonia, subjected the kingdoms and peoples of the East to captivity and to bondage? *Arnobius (c. 305, E), 6.415.*

ALEXANDRIA

Alexandria in Egypt became the second most important city in the Roman Empire.

It would be easier for someone . . . to cross from east to west than to travel from one point in Alexandria to another. For the most central pathway in this city is more vast and more impassable than even that extensive and untrodden desert that it took Israel two generations to cross. Our smooth and waveless harbors have become an image of that [Red Sea]. . . . The river, too, that flows by the city, has sometimes appeared drier than the waterless desert. . . . At other times, it has overflowed all the country around it. *Dionysius of Alexandria (c. 262, E), 6.109.*

ALLEGORY

SEE HERMENEUTICS; ORIGEN; TYPE, TYPOLOGY.

ALMS, ALMSGIVING

I. Exhortations and counsel on almsgiving

II. Rewards for almsgiving

III. Making friends with unrighteous mammon

I. Exhortations and counsel on almsgiving

Give to him who asks you, and from him who wants to borrow from you do not turn away. Matt. 5:42.

Take heed that you do not do your charitable deeds before men, to be seen by them. Otherwise you have no reward from your Father in heaven. Matt. 6:1.

This is pure and undefiled religion in the sight of our God and Father, to visit orphans and widows in their distress. Jas. 1:27 [NAS].

If a brother or sister is naked and destitute of daily food, and one of you says to them, "Depart in peace, be warmed and filled," but you do not give them the things which are needed for the body, what does it profit? Thus also faith by itself, if it does not have works, is dead. Jas. 2:15, 16.

But whoever has this world's goods, and sees his brother in need, and shuts up his heart from him, how does the love of God abide in him? 1 John 3:17, 18; see also Matt. 25:34–40.

Do not be ready to stretch forth your hands to receive, while you draw them back when it comes to giving. . . . You shall not hesitate to give, nor murmur when you give. "Give to everyone who asks you." *Barnabas (c. 70–130, E), 1.148.*

If one having need receives alms, he is without guilt. However, if someone receives alms who does not have a need, he will pay the penalty. . . . He will be examined concerning the things that he has done and he shall not escape from there until he pays back the last coin. Now, concerning this, it has been said, "Let your alms sweat in your hands, until you know to whom you should give them." *Didache (c. 80–140, E), 7.377.*

Do not be one who stretches forth his hands to receive but draws them back when it comes to giving. If you have anything, through your hands you shall give ransom for your sins. You shall not hesitate to give, nor murmur when you give. *Didache (c. 80–140, E), 7.378.*

Give to all the needy in simplicity, not hesitating as to whom you are to give or not to give. Give to all, for God wishes His gifts to be shared among all. *Hermas (c. 150, W), 2.20.*

Therefore, instead of lands, buy afflicted souls, according as each one is able. And visit widows and orphans. *Hermas (c. 150, W), 2.31.*

The wealthy among us help the needy.... Those who are prosperous, and willing, give what each thinks fit. And what is collected is deposited with the president, who gives aid to the orphans and widows. *Justin Martyr (c. 160, E), 1.185, 186.*

They should take care of elderly people.... "He that pities the poor lends to the Lord." Also, "Inasmuch as you have done it unto the least of these My brethren, you have done it to Me." *Clement of Alexandria (c. 195, E), 2.279.*

It is right to supply need, but it is not well to support laziness. *Clement of Alexandria (c. 195, E), 2.301.*

It is said, "I want mercy, not sacrifice" [Hos. 6:6]. By the merciful, he means—not only those who do acts of mercy—but those who *desire* to do them, yet are unable. Nevertheless, they do whatever they can. For sometimes we truly desire to provide mercy to someone by a gift of money or by personal attention. Sometimes we truly want to assist someone in need, help someone who is sick, or stand by someone who is in any emergency. However, sometimes we are unable to carry out our desire—because of poverty, disease, or old age. *Clement of Alexandria (c. 195, E), 2.416.*

Alms are to be given, but to the deserving, using judgment. That way, we may obtain a reward from the Most High. But woe to those who have enough, but who receive [alms] under false pretenses. Woe to those who are able to help themselves, yet want to take from others. For he who takes ... out of laziness shall be condemned. *Clement of Alexandria (c. 195, E), 2.578.*

"Give to everyone who asks you." For truly such is God's delight in giving. And this saying is above all divinity—not to wait to be asked, but to inquire yourself as to who deserves to receive kindness.... O divine merchandise! One purchases immortality for money. And, by giving the perishing things of the world, one receives in exchange for these an eternal mansion in the heavens.... Do not try to judge who is worthy or who is unworthy. For it is possible that you may be mistaken in your opinion. As in the uncertainty of ignorance, it is better to do good to the undeserving for the sake of the deserving—than by guarding against those who are less good to fail to provide for the good. By being sparing and trying to test who deserve to receive or not, you may neglect some of those who are loved by God. *Clement of Alexandria (c. 195, E), 2.600.*

Though we have our treasure chest, it is not made up of purchase money, as of a religion that has its price. Rather, on the monthly day, if he likes, each puts in a small donation—but only if it is his pleasure and only if he is able. For there is no compulsion; all is voluntary. These gifts are ... to support and bury poor people, to supply the needs of boys and girls destitute of means and parents, and of old persons now confined to the house. These gifts also help those who have suffered shipwreck. And if there happens to be any of us in the mines, or banished to the islands, or shut up in the prisons—for no reason other than their faithfulness to the cause of God's church—they become the nurslings of their confession. *Tertullian (c. 197, W), 3.46.*

Our compassion spends more in the streets than yours does in the temples! *Tertullian (c. 197, W), 3.49.*

The brother oppressed with want, nearly languishing away, cries out with distended belly to the splendidly fed. What do you say of the Lord's Day? If he has not placed himself before, call forth a poor man from the crowd, whom you may take to your dinner. *Commodianus (c. 240, W), 4.215.*

If your brother should be weak (I speak of the poor man), do not visit such a one empty-handed when he lies ill. Do good under God. Pay your obedience by your money.... Similarly, if your poor sister lies upon a sick bed, let your matrons begin to carry food to her. God himself cries out, "Break bread to the needy." There is no need to visit with merely words, but with aid. It is wicked for your brother to be sick because of lack of food. Do not satisfy him with words! He needs meat and drink! *Commodianus (c. 240, W), 4.217.*

If we give alms to men with the thought of appearing charitable before men, and if we desire to be honored because of our generosity, we receive only the reward from men. In fact, universally, everything that is done by someone who is conscious that he will be glorified by men has no reward from Him who beholds in secret. For He renders the reward in secret to those who are pure. *Origen (c. 245, E), 9.444.*

Let the poor be taken care of as much and as well as possible. I speak especially of those who have stood with unmovable faith and have not forsaken Christ's flock. *Cyprian (c. 250, W), 5.283.*

When one has pity on the poor, he lends to God. And he who gives to the least, gives to God. These are spiritual sacrifices to God, an odor of a sweet smell. *Cyprian (c. 250, W), 5.456.*

You are wealthy and rich. Do you think that you can celebrate the Lord's Supper, not at all considering the offering? Can you come to the Lord's Supper without a sacrifice and yet take part of the sacrifice that the poor man has offered? Consider in the Gospel the widow who remembered the heavenly teachings, doing good despite the difficulties and limitations of poverty. For she cast into the treasury two small coins, which were all that she had. *Cyprian (c. 250, W), 5.480.*

By almsgiving to the poor, we are lending to God. When it is given to the least, it is given to Christ. Therefore, there are no grounds for anyone preferring earthly things to heavenly—nor for considering human things before divine. *Cyprian (c. 250, W), 5.480.*

See how much he sins in the church—he who prefers himself and his children to Christ! Such a person preserves his wealth and does not share his abundant estate to relieve the poverty of the needy. *Cyprian (c. 250, W), 5.481.*

How much more could He stimulate the works of our righteousness and mercy than by saying that whatever is given to the needy and poor is given to Himself? *Cyprian (c. 250, W), 5.483.*

Let us consider, beloved brethren, what the congregation of believers did in the time of the apostles. Back then, at the beginning, the mind flourished with greater virtues. The faith of believers burned with a warmth of faith that was still new. Back then they sold houses and farms and gladly and generously presented the proceeds to the apostles, to be distributed to the poor. *Cyprian (c. 250, W), 5.483.*

On this same subject, in Solomon in Proverbs, it says: "He who has pity on the poor lends unto the Lord." . . . Also, in the same place: "Sins are purged away by almsgiving and faith." [Prov. 16.6]. . . . Of this same thing in Hosea: "I desire mercy rather than sacrifice." . . . Of this same thing also in the Gospel according to Matthew: . . . "Blessed are the merciful, for they shall obtain mercy." Also, in the same place: "Lay up for yourselves treasures in heaven." . . . Even a small work is of advantage, for it says in the same place: "And whoever shall give to one of the least of these to drink a cup of cold water in the name of a disciple, truly I say unto you, his reward shall not perish." That alms are to be denied to none, it also says in the same place: "Give to everyone who asks you." *Cyprian (c. 250, W), 5.531, 532.*

Of this same matter, in the Epistle of John, it says: "Whoever has this world's sustenance and sees his brother in need and shuts up his bowels from him, how does the love of God dwell in him?" *Cyprian (c. 250, W), 5.532.*

What shall I say of [a certain pagan] who changed his possessions into money and then threw it into the sea? . . . If you have so great a contempt for money, use it in acts of kindness and humanity! Give it to the poor. In this manner, that which you are about to throw away may be of aid to many others, so that they may not die because of famine, thirst, or nakedness. *Lactantius (c. 304–313, W), 7.93.*

If anyone were surrounded by fire, crushed by the downfall of a building, plunged in the sea, or carried away by a river, would they not think it is the duty of a man to assist him? . . . So what reason is there to think that aid is to be withheld when a man suffers from hunger, thirst, or cold? . . . Yet, the pagans make a distinction between these things. That is because they measure all things by present usefulness—not by the truth itself. For they hope that those whom they rescue from peril will return a favor to them. However, because they cannot hope for this in the case of the needy, they think that whatever they give to men of this type is "thrown away." . . . However, we must not bestow our funds on suitable persons [i.e., ones who will repay us], but as much as possible on *unsuitable* objects. For when you do it without the hope of any return, you will truly do it for the sake of justice, piety, and humanity. *Lactantius (c. 304–313, W), 7.174, 175.*

Why do you discriminate between persons? Why do you look at bodily forms? . . . Be generous to the blind, the feeble, the lame, and the destitute. For they will die unless you bestow your gifts upon them. They may be useless to men, but they are serviceable to God. For He preserves life in them and endows them with breath. *Lactantius (c. 304–313, W), 7.175.*

This is the chief and truest advantage of riches: not to use wealth for the particular pleasure of an individual, but for the welfare of many. It is not for one's own immediate enjoyment, but for justice—which alone does not perish. *Lactantius (c. 304–313, W), 7.176.*

The ransoming of captives is a great and noble exercise of justice. . . . Yet, he who does it to a stranger and an unknown person, he truly is worthy of praise. For he was led to do it by kindness alone. . . . Nor is it less of a great work of justice to protect and defend orphans and widows who are destitute and stand in need of assistance. Accordingly, the divine law prescribes this to all. *Lactantius (c. 304–313, W), 7.177.*

No Christian should be prevented from undergoing death on behalf of justice and faith [i.e., martyrdom], because he is concerned for his dependents. Rather, he should meet death promptly and boldly, for he knows that he leaves his beloved ones to the care of God and that they will never lack protection. . . . To undertake the care and support of the sick, who need someone to assist them, is the part of great kindness and love. . . . The last and greatest office of godliness is the burying of strangers and the poor. *Lactantius (c. 304–313, W), 7.177.*

Someone may say: "If I do all these things, I will have no possessions. What if a large number of people are in want, suffer cold, have been taken captive, or should die? If anyone acts this way, he will deprive himself of his property in a single day! Shall I throw away the estate acquired by my own labor or by that of my ancestors? Must then I myself live by the pity of others?" . . . [LACTANTIUS'S ANSWER:] Why do you fear to turn a frail and perishable asset into one that is everlasting? Why do you

fear to entrust your treasures to God as their preserver? For in that case you will not need to fear thief and robber—nor rust, nor tyrant. He who is rich towards God can never be poor. If you esteem justice so highly, lay aside the burdens that oppress you and follow justice. Free yourself from bondage and chains, so that you can run to God without any hindrance. *Lactantius (c. 304–313, W), 7.177, 178.*

God admonishes us that the doer of justice should not be boastful. Otherwise, he will appear to have given charitably, not so much from a desire of obeying the divine commands, but from the desire to please men. In which case, he will already have the reward of glory that he has aimed at. Therefore, he will not receive the reward that is heavenly and divine. *Lactantius (c. 304–313, W), 7.183.*

If anyone is in need because of gluttony, drunkenness, or idleness, he does not deserve any assistance. *Apostolic Constitutions (compiled c. 390, E), 7.397.*

What if some persons are neither widows nor widowers, but stand in need of assistance—either because of poverty, disease, or the responsibility of a great number of children? It is your duty to oversee all people and to take care of them all. *Apostolic Constitutions (compiled c. 390, E), 7.427.*

He that . . . receives in hypocrisy or through idleness—instead of working and assisting others—shall be deserving of punishment before God. For he has snatched away the morsel of the needy. *Apostolic Constitutions (compiled c. 390, E), 7.433.*

From the righteous labor of the faithful, maintain and clothe those who are in need. And such sums of money as are collected from them in the aforesaid manner, designate these to be used for the redemption of the saints, the deliverance of slaves, captives, and prisoners. They should also be used for those who have been abused or have been condemned by tyrants to single combat and death on account of the name of Christ. *Apostolic Constitutions (compiled c. 390, E), 7.435; extended discussion: 5.476–5.484, 5.530–5.533.*

II. Rewards for almsgiving

He who has pity on the poor lends to the Lord, and He will pay back what he has given. Prov. 19:17.

It is better to give alms than to store up gold; for almsgiving saves one from death and expiates every sin. Tob. 12:8, 9.

Sell what you have and give alms; provide yourselves money bags which do not grow old, a treasure in the heavens that does not fail, where no thief approaches nor moth destroys. Luke 12:33.

When you do a charitable deed, do not let your left hand know what your right hand is doing, that your charitable deed may be in secret; and your Father who sees in secret will Himself reward you openly. Matt. 6:3, 4.

Your prayers and your alms have come up for a memorial before God. Acts 10:4.

Charity shall cover the multitude of sins. 1 Pet. 4:8 [KJV].

When you can do good, do not hesitate. For "alms delivers from death" [Tob. 4:10]. *Polycarp (c. 135, E), 1.35.*

Therefore, almsgiving is a good thing, as is repentance from sin. Fasting is better than prayer. But almsgiving is better than both. "For love covers a multitude of sins." *Second Clement (c. 150), 7.522.*

As Solomon says, "He that has pity upon the poor lends unto the Lord." For God, who stands in need of nothing, takes our good works to Himself for this purpose: that He may grant us a reward from His own good things. For our Lord says: "Come, you blessed of My Father, receive the kingdom prepared for you. For I was hungry and you gave Me something to eat." *Irenaeus (c. 180, E/W), 1.486.*

Sins are purged by alms and acts of faith. *Clement of Alexandria (c. 195, E), 2.363.*

It is written, "Alms do deliver from death." Assuredly, this is *not* from that [original] death that the blood of Christ has extinguished and from which the saving grace of baptism and of our Redeemer has delivered us. Rather, it is from the death that creeps in afterwards through sins. *Cyprian (c. 250, W), 5.332.*

Be earnest in righteous works, by which sins may be purged. Frequently apply yourself to almsgiving, by which souls are freed from death.... Let good works be done without delay. *Cyprian (c. 250, W), 5.447.*

Those who pray should not come to God with fruitless or empty prayers.... Therefore,

Holy Scripture instructs us, saying, "Prayer is good with fasting and almsgiving" [Tob. 20:8]. He will give us in the Day of Judgment a reward for our labors and alms. Moreover, even in this life, He is a merciful Hearer of one who comes to Him in prayer associated with good works. For example, Cornelius, the centurion, when he prayed, had a claim to be heard. For he was in the habit of doing many deeds of charity towards the people and of constantly praying to God. An angel appeared . . . to this man . . . saying, "Cornelius, your prayers and your alms have gone up in remembrance before God." *Cyprian (c. 250, W), 5.456.*

The infirmity and weakness of human frailty would have no resource, unless the divine mercy, coming once more in aid, should open some way of securing salvation by pointing out works of justice and mercy. Therefore, by almsgiving we may wash away whatever foulness we subsequently contract [after baptism]. The Holy Spirit speaks in the sacred Scriptures and says, "By almsgiving and faith, sins are purged" [Prov. 16:6].... Moreover, He says again, "As water extinguishes fire, so almsgiving quenches sin" [Sir. 3:30]. *Cyprian (c. 250, W), 5.476.*

In the bath of saving water, the fire of Gehenna is extinguished. Likewise, by almsgiving and works of righteousness, the flame of sins is subdued.... The Lord teaches this also in the Gospel.... "Give alms, and behold all things are clean unto you." *Cyprian (c. 250, W), 5.476.*

Showing how he can be clean and purged, He added that alms must be given.... He seeks to save those whom at a great cost He has redeemed. Therefore, He teaches that those who, after the grace of baptism have become foul, may once more be cleansed. *Cyprian (c. 250, W), 5.476.*

He shows that our prayers and fastings are of less avail if they are not aided by almsgiving.... Life is redeemed from dangers by almsgiving. Souls are delivered from death by almsgiving. *Cyprian (c. 250, W), 5.477.*

Make Christ a partner with you in your earthly possessions, that He also may make you a fellow-heir with Him in His heavenly kingdom. *Cyprian (c. 250, W), 5.479.*

The matter comes to this: whatever a man has bestowed upon another person with no thought of receiving an advantage from him—

he really bestows upon himself. For such a man will receive a reward from God. God has also admonished us that if at any time we prepare a feast, we should invite to the entertainment those who cannot invite us in return. *Lactantius (c. 304–313, W), 7.176.*

However, just because offenses are removed by almsgiving, do not think that a license is given you to sin.... For if you consciously sin, relying on your almsgiving [for pardon], your sins are not done away with.... To this should be added that no one can be without defect as long as he is burdened with a covering of flesh.... So, if the condition of mortality does not allow a man to be pure from every stain, the faults of the flesh should therefore be done away with by continual almsgiving. *Lactantius (c. 304–313, W), 7.178, 179.*

"By acts of righteousness and faith, iniquities are purged." ... Give the necessities of life to the needy. *Apostolic Constitutions (compiled c. 390, E), 7.413.*

If you have acquired anything through the work of your hands, then give—so that you may labor for the redemption of your sins. For "by alms and acts of faith, sins are purged away." You should not begrudge giving to the poor. And when you have given, you should not complain. For you know who will repay you your reward. *Apostolic Constitutions (compiled c. 390, E), 7.435.*

III. Making friends with unrighteous mammon

I say to you, make friends for yourselves by unrighteous mammon, that when you fail, they may receive you into everlasting habitations. Luke 16:9.

The rich man refreshes the poor and assists him in his necessities. He believes that what he does to the poor man will be able to find its reward with God. For the poor man is rich in intercession and confession, and his intercession has great power with God. *Hermas (c. 150, W), 2.32.*

There follow us a small (and in some cases, a large) amount of property that we have acquired from the mammon of unrighteousness. For from what source do we derive the houses in which we dwell, the garments in which we are clothed ... unless it is from those things which, when we were Gentiles, we acquired by avarice or received from our unbelieving parents? This is not to mention that even now we acquire such things when we are in the faith. For who is there that sells and does not wish to make a profit from him who buys? ... Or who is there that carries on a trade and does not do so that he may obtain a livelihood thereby? *Irenaeus (c. 180, E/W), 1.502, 503.*

Whatever we acquired from unrighteousness when we were unbelievers, we are proved righteous when we have become believers, by applying it to the Lord's advantage. *Irenaeus (c. 180, E/W), 1.504.*

Contrary to what is the case with the rest of men, gather for yourself an unarmed, unwarlike, bloodless, peaceful, and a stainless army— an army of godly old men, orphans dear to God, widows armed with meekness, and men adorned with love. Obtain with your money such guards for your body and soul.... All these warriors and guards are trustworthy. Not one of them is idle; none are useless. Some of them can obtain your pardon from God. Others can comfort you when sick. And still others can weep and groan in sympathy for you to the Lord. *Clement of Alexandria (c. 195, E), 2.601.*

If you have no interpreter with you, you may learn again from Himself what He would have understood by mammon.... "I say to you, 'Make to yourselves friends with the mammon of unrighteousness.'" That is to say, with money, even as the steward had done. Now, we are all aware that money is the instigator of unrighteousness, and is the lord of the whole world. *Tertullian (c. 207, W), 3.403.*

SEE ALSO ORPHANS AND WIDOWS; SALVATION (III. ROLE OF OBEDIENCE IN SALVATION); TITHES, TITHING.

ALPHA AND OMEGA
SEE JESUS CHRIST (III. TITLES OF JESUS).

ALPHABET
SEE WRITING, ORIGIN OF.

ALTAR
If you bring your gift to the altar, and there remember that your brother has something against you, leave your gift there before the altar, and go your way. First be reconciled to your brother, and then come and offer your gift. Matt. 5:23.

When he opened the fifth seal, I saw under the altar the souls of those who had been slain for the word of God. Rev. 6:9.

Let no man deceive himself. If anyone is not within the altar, he is deprived of the bread of God. *Ignatius (c. 105, E), 1.51.*

He that is within the altar is pure. However, he that is outside of it is not pure. I mean, he who does anything apart from the bishop, the presbyters, and the deacons, such a man is not pure in his conscience. *Ignatius (c. 105, E), 1.69.*

Therefore, take heed to have only one Eucharist. For there is one flesh of our Lord Jesus Christ and . . . one altar. *Ignatius (c. 105, E), 1.81.*

It is, therefore, also His will that we, too, should offer a gift at the altar, frequently and without intermission. The altar, then, is in heaven. For our prayers and oblations are directed towards that place. *Irenaeus (c. 180, E/W), 1.486.*

The altar, then, that is with us here, the terrestrial one, is the congregation of those who devote themselves to prayers. They have, as it were, one common voice and one mind. *Clement of Alexandria (c. 195, E), 2.531.*

Will they not believe us when we say that the righteous soul is the truly sacred altar, and that the incense arising from it is holy prayer? *Clement of Alexandria (c. 195, E), 2.531.*

Does, then, the Eucharist cancel a service devoted to God—or does it bind it more to God? Will not your station be more solemn if you have stood at God's altar? *Tertullian (c. 198, W), 3.687.*

Do you think that we conceal what we worship just because we do not have temples and altars? *Mark Minucius Felix (c. 200, W), 4.193.*

He relates that he saw under the altar of God—that is, under the earth—the souls of those who were slain. For both heaven and earth are called God's altar. This was shown in the Law, commanding that two altars be made, symbolizing the realities. . . . By the testimony that our Lord bears to it, we perceive that the golden altar is therefore called heaven. For he says, "When you bring your gift to the altar and there remember that your brother has something against you, leave your gift there before the altar." Assuredly, our gifts are the prayers that we offer, and certainly our prayers ascend to heaven. *Victorinus (c. 280, W), 7.351.*

No one worships [at] the holy altar except the one who confesses this faith. *Victorinus (c. 280, W), 7.354.*

SEE ALSO EUCHARIST; INCENSE; REVELATION, BOOK OF.

AMEN

If you bless with the spirit, how will he who occupies the place of the uninformed say "Amen" at your giving of thanks? 1 Cor. 14:16.

When he had said the "Amen, "and thereby finished his prayer, those who were appointed for the purpose lit the fire. *Martyrdom of Polycarp (c. 135, E), 1.42.*

When he has concluded the prayers and thanksgivings, all the people who are present give their assent by saying "Amen." This word *amen* means "so be it" in the Hebrew language. *Justin Martyr (c. 160, E), 1.185.*

The president in like manner offers prayers and thanksgivings according to his ability. And the people assent, saying "Amen." *Justin Martyr (c. 160, E), 1.186.*

Out of the mouth from which you said "Amen" over the holy thing, you now shout in a gladiator's favor! *Tertullian (c. 197, W), 3.90.*

SEE ALSO PRAYER (II. PRAYER POSTURES AND CUSTOMS).

ANDREW

The fourth Gospel is that of John, one of the disciples. When his fellow-disciples and bishops entreated him, he said, "Fast now with me for the space of three days, and let us relate to each other whatever may be revealed to each of us." On the same night, it was revealed to Andrew, one of the apostles, that John should narrate all things in his own name—as they called them to mind. *Muratorian Fragment (c. 200, W), 5.603.*

SEE ALSO APOSTLES, TWELVE; JOHN.

ANGEL, ANGELS

I. Nature and position of the angels

II. Guardian angels

III. Fallen angels

I. Nature and position of the angels

Who makes His angels spirits, His ministers a flame of fire. Ps. 104:4.

You made [man] a little lower than the angels. Heb. 2:7.

Whereas angels, who are greater in power and might, do not bring a reviling accusation against them before the Lord. 2 Pet. 2:11.

To the angel of the church of Ephesus write . . . Rev. 2:1.

Let us consider the whole multitude of His angels—how they stand always ready to minister to His will. For the Scripture says, "Ten thousand times ten thousand stood around Him, and thousands of thousands ministered to Him" [Isa. 50:10]. *Clement of Rome (c. 96, W), 1.14.*

Although I am in chains [for Christ], that does not mean that I am able to understand heavenly things. I do not comprehend the places of the angels and their gathering all things visible and invisible under their respective princes. *Ignatius (c. 105, E), 1.68.*

"This," he replied, "is the angel of punishment. He belongs to the just angels and is appointed to punish. He accordingly takes those who wander away from God, and who have walked in the desires and deceits of this world, and he chastises them." *Hermas (c. 150, W), 2.37.*

We recognize also a multitude of angels and ministers, whom God, the Maker and Framer of the world, distributed and appointed to their various posts by His Logos. *Athenagoras (c. 175, E), 2.134.*

The other angels were created by Him, and entrusted with the control of matter and the forms of matter. . . . Just as with men, they have freedom of choice as to both virtue and vice. . . . Some men are diligent in the matters entrusted to them by you, and others are faithless. It is the same among the angels. They are free agents, being created that way by God, as you will observe. Some of them have continued in those things for which God had made them. They have remained over the things to which He had ordained them. But some outraged both the constitution of their nature and the oversight entrusted to them. . . . These angels fell into impure love of virgins and were subjugated by the flesh. . . . Those who are called giants were begotten from these lovers of virgins. *Athenagoras (c. 175, E), 2.142.*

Blessed are those who watch for Him. For they make themselves like the angels, whom we call "watchers." *Clement of Alexandria (c. 195, E), 2.258.*

By an ancient and divine order, the angels are distributed among the nations. *Clement of Alexandria (c. 195, E), 2.524.*

At the highest extremity of the visible world are the blessed band of angels. *Clement of Alexandria (c. 195, E), 2.525.*

The spiritual man prays in the company of the angels, . . . and he is never out of their holy keeping. Although he prays alone, he has the choir of the holy ones standing with him. *Clement of Alexandria (c. 195, E), 2.545.*

God works through archangels and kindred angels, who are called spirits of Christ. *Clement of Alexandria (c. 195, E), 2.571.*

Plato also admits the existence of angels. *Tertullian (c. 197, W), 3.36.*

Every spirit possesses wings. This is a common property of both angels and demons. So they are everywhere in a single moment. The whole world is as one place to them. It is easy for them to know everything that is done over the whole extent of the world, and to report it. *Tertullian (c. 197, W), 3.36.*

The angels, likewise, all pray. *Tertullian (c. 198, W), 3.691.*

You have sometimes read and believed that the Creator's angels have been changed into human form, and have carried about so real of a body that Abraham even washed their feet and Lot was rescued from the Sodomites by their hands. An angel, moreover, wrestled with a man so strenuously with his body, that the latter desired to be let loose. *Tertullian (c. 210, W), 3.523.*

Even if [the human body] had been the work of angels, as Menander and Marcus want to think, . . . the body would still be an object of respect, having the support and protection of even a secondary deity. For we know the angels rank next to God. *Tertullian (c. 210, W), 3.548.*

The angels are likewise possessed of personal freedom. For we can be sure that if the angels had not possessed personal freedom, they would not have consorted with the daughters of men, thereby sinning and falling from their places. In like manner, also, the other angels, who did the will of their Lord, were raised to a higher rank because of their self-control. *Bardesanes (c. 222, E), 8.725.*

This also is a part of the teaching of the church that there are certain angels of God and certain good forces, which are His ministers for accomplishing the salvation of men. However, it is not clearly stated when the angels were created, of what nature they are, or how they exist. *Origen (c. 225, E), 4.241.*

Moreover, other nations are called a part of the angels. This is because "when the Most High divided the nations and dispersed the sons of Adam, He fixed the boundaries of the nations according to the number of the angels of God" [Deut. 32:8, LXX]. *Origen (c. 225, E), 4.241.*

We should not suppose that it is the result of accident that a particular responsibility is assigned to a particular angel. For example, to Raphael, has been assigned the work of curing and healing. To Gabriel, there is assigned the conduct of wars. To Michael, there is the duty of attending to the prayers and supplications of mortals. For we are not to imagine that they obtained these positions otherwise than by their own merits and by the zeal and excellent qualities that they individually displayed before this world was formed. As a result, afterwards, in the order of archangels, this or that position was assigned to each one. At the same time, others deserved to be enrolled in the order of angels and to act under this or that archangel. *Origen (c. 225, E), 4.264, 265.*

In the Holy Scriptures, we find that there are princes over individual nations. For example, in Daniel we read that there was a prince of the kingdom of Persia and another prince of the kingdom of Greece. By the nature of the passage, these princes are clearly shown *not* to be human beings. Rather, they are certain [spiritual] powers. Also, in the prophecies of Ezekiel, the prince of Tyre is unmistakably shown to be a type of spiritual power. *Origen (c. 225, E), 4.335.*

It is enough to know that the holy angels of God are favorably disposed to us and that they do all things on our behalf. So our disposition of mind towards God should imitate the example of these holy angels, as far as it is within the power of human nature to do so. *Origen (c. 225, E), 4.544, 545.*

Those angels who were made spirits by God—those who are a flame of fire and ministers of the Father of all—cannot have been

excluded from also being evangelists. For that reason, an angel stood over the shepherds and made a bright light to shine around them. *Origen (c. 228, E), 9.304.*

We are already taught by the parable of the tares and the subject parable [of the dragnet] that the angels are to be entrusted with the power to distinguish and separate the evil from the righteous. *Origen (c. 245, E), 9.420.*

From this it does not follow, as some suppose, that men who are saved in Christ are superior even to the holy angels. . . . Although I say this, I am not ignorant that the men who will be saved in Christ surpass *some* angels (namely, those who have not been entrusted with this office), but not *all* of them. For we read, "which things angels desire to look into." However, it is not said "all angels" so desire. Again, we know this, that "we shall judge angels." But again, it is not said that we judge "all angels." *Origen (c. 245, E), 9.421.*

The passage might be taken from *The Shepherd*, concerning some who are put in subjection to Michael as soon as they believe. However, falling away from him because of love of pleasure, they are put in subjection to the angel of luxury, then to the angel of punishment. *Origen (c. 245, E), 9.509.*

When one is able to philosophize about the mystery of names, he will find much to say concerning the titles of the angels of God. One of them is called Michael, another Gabriel, and another Raphael. All of these names are appropriate to the duties that they administer in the world. *Origen (c. 248, E), 4.406.*

The divine and holy angels of God are of a different nature and a different resolution than all the demons on earth. *Origen (c. 248, E), 4.479.*

We know that in this way the angels are superior to men. So that when men are made perfect, they become like the angels. *Origen (c. 248, E), 4.509.*

Having thus learned to call these beings "messengers" [i.e., angels] from their duties, we find that because they are divine, they are sometimes called "god" in the sacred Scriptures. But this is not said in the sense that we are commanded to honor and worship them in place of God—even though they minister to us and bear His blessings to us. For every prayer, supplication, intercession, and thanksgiving is to be sent up to the Supreme God through the High Priest— the living Word and God, who is above all the angels. *Origen (c. 248, E), 4.544.*

He does no less than to set His own angels over His devout servants, so that none of the hostile angels—nor even he who is called "the prince of this world"—can do anything against those who have given themselves to God. *Origen (c. 248, E), 4.653.*

In the Apocalypse, the angel resists John, who wishes to worship him, and says, "See that you do not do this. For I am your fellow-servant and your brother. Worship Jesus the Lord." *Cyprian (c. 250, W), 5.491.*

He created angels and archangels before he created man, placing spiritual beings before earthly ones. *Victorinus (c. 280, W), 7.341.*

God, in His foresight, sent angels for the protection and improvement of the human race— lest the devil . . . should either corrupt or destroy men through his snares. *Lactantius (c. 304–313, W), 7.64.*

The angels neither allow nor wish themselves to be called gods, since they are immortal. For their one and only duty is to submit to the will of God and not to do anything at all except at His command. *Lactantius (c. 304–313, W), 7.65; see also 2.575; extended discussion: 4.264–4.266.*

II. Guardian angels.

The angel of the Lord encamps all around those who fear him, and delivers them. Ps. 34:7.

Take heed that you do not despise one of these little ones, for I say to you that in heaven their angels always see the face of My Father who is in heaven. Matt. 18:10.

They said to her, "You are beside yourself!" Yet, she kept insisting that it was so. So they said, "It is his angel." Acts 12:15.

There are two angels with a man—one of righteousness, and the other of iniquity. . . . The angel of righteousness is gentle and modest, meek and peaceful. When he ascends into your heart, he speaks to you of righteousness, purity, chastity, contentment, and every other righteous deed and glorious virtue. When all of these things come into your heart, know that the angel of righteousness is with you. *Hermas (c. 150, W), 2.24.*

The Scripture says, "The angels of the little ones, and of the least, see God." So he does not shrink from writing about the oversight . . . exercised by the guardian angels. *Clement of Alexandria (c. 195, E), 2.466.*

Regiments of angels are distributed over the nations and cities. And perhaps some are assigned to individuals. *Clement of Alexandria (c. 195, E), 2.517.*

To one angel, the church of the Ephesians was entrusted. To another, that of Smyrna. One angel was to be Peter's; another, Paul's. And so on down to each of the little ones that are in the church. For such and such angels as even daily behold the face of God must be assigned to each one of them. And there must also be some angels who encamp around those who fear God. *Origen (c. 225, E), 4.265.*

Every believer—although the humblest in the church—is said to be attended by an angel, who the Savior declares always beholds the face of God the Father. Now, this angel has the purpose of being his guardian. So if that person is rendered unworthy by his lack of obedience, the angel of God is said to be taken from him. And then that part of him—the part belonging to his human nature—is torn away from the divine part. And it is assigned a place along with the unbelievers. For it has not faithfully observed the admonitions of the angel assigned to it by God. *Origen (c. 225, E), 4.296.*

The book of *The Shepherd* declares the same, saying that each individual is attended by two angels. Whenever good thoughts arise in our hearts, they are suggested by the good angel. But when those of a contrary kind arise, they are the instigation of the evil angel. *Origen (c. 225, E), 4.332.*

Perhaps it was the angel to whom he had been assigned—if we are to say that every human soul is placed in subjection to some angel. *Origen (c. 245, E), 9.478.*

"The angel of the Lord" is said "to encamp around those who fear him and to save them." . . . So long as we are imperfect, and need someone to assist us so that we may be delivered from evils—we stand in need of an angel. Of such an angel, Jacob said, "The angel who delivered me from all the evils." *Origen (c. 245, E), 9.490.*

One might inquire as to when those who are called "their angels" assume guardianship of the little ones pointed out by Christ. . . . It may be said that there is no holy angel present with those who are still in wickedness. Rather, during the period of unbelief, they are under the angels of Satan. However, after our regeneration, He who has redeemed us with His own blood assigns us to a holy angel. *Origen (c. 245, E), 9.491.*

It is possible that the angel to whom any soul has been entrusted at birth may be wicked at the first, but afterwards may at some time believe in proportion as the man believes. In fact, that angel may make such an improvement that he may become one of the angels who always beholds the face of the Father in heaven. *Origen (c. 245, E), 9.491.*

They thought that it was quite impossible that Peter truly stood before the gate. So they said, "It is his angel." For the objector will say that, as they had learned once for all that each of the believers had some definite angel, they knew that Peter also had one. But he who adheres to what I have previously said, will say that the word of Rhoda was not necessarily a dogma. *Origen (c. 245, E), 9.491.*

His "angel," who "always beholds the face of his Father in heaven," offers up his prayers through the one High Priest to the God of all. He also joins his own prayers with those of the man who is committed to his keeping. *Origen (c. 248, E), 4.653.*

We entrust ourselves to the Supreme God through Jesus Christ, who has given us such instruction. We ask of Him all help and for the guardianship of holy and good angels, to defend us from the earth-spirits intent on lust. *Origen (c. 248, E), 4.662.*

I mean that holy angel of God who fed me from my youth. *Gregory Thaumaturgus (c. 255, E), 6.24.*

We have learned from the inspired writings that all who are born—even if it is through adultery—are committed to guardian angels. *Methodius (c. 290, E), 6.316; see also 9.509.*

III. Fallen angels.

Now it came to pass, when men began to multiply on the face of the earth, and daughters were born to them, that the sons of God saw the daughters of men, *that they were beautiful; and they took wives for themselves of all whom they chose.* Gen. 6:1, 2.

God did not spare the angels who sinned, but cast them down to hell and delivered them into chains of darkness, to be reserved for judgment; and did not spare the ancient world, but saved Noah. 2 Pet. 2:4, 5.

The angels who did not keep their proper domain, but left their own habitation, he has reserved in everlasting chains under darkness for the judgment of the great day. Jude 6.

The angels transgressed this appointment and were captivated by love of women. And they begat children, who are those who are called demons. *Justin Martyr (c. 160, E), 1.190.*

Angels sinned and revolted from God. *Justin Martyr (c. 160, E), 1.238.*

When the angels had transgressed, they fell to the earth for judgment. *Irenaeus (c. 180, E/W), 1.481.*

In the days of Noah, He justly brought on the Deluge for the purpose of extinguishing that most infamous race of men then existent, who could not bring forth fruit to God. For the angels who sinned had commingled with them. *Irenaeus (c. 180, E/W), 1.516.*

The Lord has said that there are certain angels of the devil, for whom eternal fire is prepared. *Irenaeus (c. 180, E/W), 1.524.*

An example of this are the angels who renounced the beauty of God for a beauty that fades, and so fell from heaven to earth. *Clement of Alexandria (c. 195, E), 2.274.*

The angels who had obtained the superior rank, having sunk into pleasures, told the women the secrets that had come to their knowledge. In contrast, the rest of the angels concealed them, or rather, reserved them for the coming of the Lord. *Clement of Alexandria (c. 195, E), 2.446.*

He knows that some of the angels were hurled to the earth, because of lack of diligence. They had not yet quite reached that state of oneness [with God]. *Clement of Alexandria (c. 195, E), 2.536.*

He says, "But the angels who kept not their own pre-eminence . . . He has reserved these to the judgment of the great day, in chains, under darkness." He means the place near the earth, that is, the dark air. Now, by chains, he means the loss of the honor in which they had stood and the lust of feeble things. *Clement of Alexandria (c. 195, E), 2.573.*

By our sacred books, we are instructed how from certain angels, who fell of their own free will, there sprang an even more wicked demon brood. *Tertullian (c. 197, W), 3.36.*

Those angels who invented them [jewelry, etc.] are assigned under condemnation to the penalty of death. They are the same angels who rushed from heaven on the daughters of men. . . . If it is true, they laid bare the operations of metallurgy, divulged the natural properties of herbs, promulgated the powers of enchantments, and traced out every curiosity, even to the interpretation of the stars. They conferred appropriately—and as it were, peculiarly—upon women that instrumental means of womanly ostentation: the radiances of jewels, . . . the dyes of orchil with which wools are dyed, and that black powder itself with which the eyelids and eyelashes are made prominent. *Tertullian (c. 198, W), 4.14, 15.*

These are the angels whom we are destined to judge. These are the angels whom we renounce in baptism. *Tertullian (c. 198, W), 4.15.*

I lay down this one proposition: that those angels—the deserters from God, the lovers of women—were likewise the discoverers of this curious art [of astrology]. And on that account, they were also condemned by God. . . . For we know the mutual alliance of magic and astrology. *Tertullian (c. 200, W), 3.65.*

If it is on account of the angels—those whom we read of as having fallen from God and from heaven because of lusting after females—we can presume that such angels yearned after bodies that were already defiled and were relics of human lust. *Tertullian (c. 207, W), 4.32.*

Although there is also assigned to angels perdition in "the fire prepared for the devil and his angels," yet a restoration is never promised to them. No directive about the salvation of angels did Christ ever receive from the Father. *Tertullian (c. 210, W), 3.533.*

Do you fear *man*, O Christian? You who ought to be feared by the angels, since you are to judge angels? You who ought to be feared by evil spirits, since you have received power also over evil spirits? *Tertullian (c. 212, W), 4.122.*

Apostate and refugee powers that have departed from God—because of the very wickedness of their mind and will, or from envy . . . invented these errors and delusions of false doctrine in order to prevent any progress. *Origen (c. 225, E), 4.336.*

Such was the beauty of women that it turned the angels aside. As a result, being contaminated, they could not return to heaven. Being rebels from God, they uttered words against Him. Then the Highest uttered His judgment against them. And from their seed, giants are said to have been born. By them, arts were made known in the earth. They taught the dyeing of wool and everything that is done. When they died, men erected images to them. *Commodianus (c. 240, W), 4.203.*

When men multiplied on the earth, the angels of heaven came together with the daughters of men. In some copies, I found "the sons of God." What the Spirit means, in my opinion, is that the descendants of Seth are called the sons of God, because of the righteous men and patriarchs who have sprung from him (even down to the Savior himself). However, the descendants of Cain are named the seed of men, as having nothing divine in them, because of the wickedness of their race. . . . However, if it is thought that these refer to angels, we must take them to be those who deal with magic and sorcery, who taught the women the motions of the stars and the knowledge of things celestial. By the power of those angels, they conceived the giants as their children, by whom wickedness reached its peak on the earth. Finally, God decreed that the whole race of the living should perish in their impiety by the deluge. *Julius Africanus (c. 245, E), 6.131.*

All of these things [i.e., the making of jewelry] the sinning and apostate angels put forth by their arts, when, lowered to the contagions of earth, they forsook their heavenly vigor. They also taught women to paint the eyes with blackness drawn around them in a circle and to stain the cheeks with a deceitful red. *Cyprian (c. 250, W), 5.434.*

God, in His foresight, sent angels for the protection and improvement of the human race—lest the devil . . . should either corrupt or destroy men through his subtlety. Since He had given these angels a free will, He admonished them above all things not to defile themselves with contamination from the earth and thus lose the dignity of their heavenly nature. . . . However, while the angels lived among men, that most deceitful ruler of the earth, by his very association, gradually enticed them to vices and polluted them through sexual relations with women. Thereafter, not being admitted into heaven because of the sins into which they had plunged themselves, they fell to the earth. *Lactantius (c. 304–313, W), 7.64.*

Although they are the destroyers of men, they wish to appear as men's guardians—so that they themselves will be worshipped and so that God will not be worshipped. *Lactantius (c. 304–313, W), 7.64.*

They strive to turn men away from the worship and knowledge of the true Majesty, so men will not be able to obtain immortality. That is because these angels lost [immortality] because of their wickedness. *Lactantius (c. 304–313, W), 7.66.*

Certain of the angels, refusing to submit themselves to the commandment of God, resisted His will. And one of them indeed fell like a flash of lightning upon the earth, while others, harassed by the dragon, sought pleasure in sexual relations with the daughters of men, and thus brought on themselves the deserved recompense of the punishment of eternal fire. *Disputation of Archelaus and Manes (c. 320, E), 6.205.*

SEE ALSO ANGEL OF THE LORD; DEMONS, DEMON POSSESSION; MICHAEL; SATAN; TOWER OF BABEL (II. ANGELIC DIVISION OF THE NATIONS).

ANGEL OF THE LORD

Then the Angel of the Lord said to her, "I will multiply your descendants exceedingly, so that they shall not be counted for multitude." . . . Then she called the name of the Lord who spoke to her, You-Are-the-God-Who-Sees; for she said, "Have I also here seen Him who sees me?" Gen. 16:10, 13.

Then Jacob was left alone; and a Man wrestled with him until the breaking of day. . . . And Jacob called the name of the place Peniel: "For I have seen God face to face, and my life is preserved." Gen. 32:24, 30.

And the Angel of the Lord appeared to him in a flame of fire from the midst of a bush. . . . So when the Lord saw that he turned aside to look, God called to

him from the midst of the bush and said, "Moses, Moses!" Exod. 3:2, 4; see also Exod. 23:23; Judg. 2:1.

Now the Word of God is His Son, as we have before said. And He is called Angel and Apostle. . . . For thus it is written in them, "And the Angel of God spoke to Moses, in a flame of fire out of the bush, and said, 'I am that I am, the God of Abraham, the God of Isaac, the God of Jacob.'" *Justin Martyr (c. 160, E), 1.184.*

"And the Lord spoke to Moses, 'Say to this people, Behold, I send My angel before your face, to keep you in the way. . . . Give heed to Him, and obey Him . . . for My name is in Him.'" . . . The name of the One who said to Moses, "for my name is in Him," was Jesus. *Justin Martyr (c. 160, E), 1.236.*

That Christ would act in this manner when He became man was foretold by the mystery of Jacob's wrestling with Him. *Justin Martyr (c. 160, E), 1.262.*

Christ Himself even testified back then that this name was His own, when He talked with Moses. For who was it who talked with Moses, but the Spirit of the Creator, who is Christ? *Tertullian (c. 207, W), 3.335.*

The Lord Himself at that very time appeared to Abraham among the angels. He had not yet been born; yet, he was undoubtedly in the flesh. *Tertullian (c. 210, W), 3.527.*

To me, He became a man. To the angels, He became an angel. . . . In several passages, angels speak in such a way as to suggest this, such as: "the Angel of the Lord appeared in a flame of fire. And He said, 'I am the God of Abraham, Isaac, and Jacob.'" *Origen (c. 228, E), 9.315.*

This was the work of one who was not simply an angel, but the "Angel of Great Counsel" (as the prophecy regarding Him said). For He announced to men the great counsel of the God and Father of all things regarding them. *Origen (c. 248, E), 4.566, 567.*

The Angel met with Hagar, Sarah's handmaid. . . . Now, was it the Father who was seen by Hagar, or not? The Angel is declared to be God. But far be it from us to call God the Father an Angel [i.e., Messenger]. Otherwise He would be subordinate to another whose angel He would be. . . . So we ought to understand it to have been God the Son. Since He is of God, He is rightly called God. For He is the

Son of God. However, because He is subjected to the Father, and because He is the Announcer of the Father's will, He is declared to be the Angel of Great Counsel. *Novatian (c. 235, W), 5.628.*

Moreover, Moses added the instance of God being seen by Abraham at the oak of Mamre.... Now, if they [i.e., the Monarchians] will have it that the Father was seen at that time and was received with hospitality in the company of two angels, the heretics have believed the Father to be visible.... Unless because, in order that His proper invisibility may be restored to the Father and the proper inferiority be remitted to the angel, it was only God the Son (who is also God) who was seen by Abraham. *Novatian (c. 235, W), 5.628.*

In another place also, we read in like manner that God was described as an Angel.... He says that the Angel of God had said to him in a dream, "Jacob, Jacob.... I have seen all that Laban has done to you. I am God, who appeared to you in the place of God." ... He who promises those things is manifested to be both God and Angel. So reasonably there must be a distinction between Him who is called God only, and Him who is declared to be not God simply, but Angel also.... Moreover, if this is Christ—which it is—the person is in terrible risk who says that Christ is only either man or angel, withholding from Him the power of the Divine name. *Novatian (c. 235, W), 5.630.*

Therefore, let no one who does not shrink from speaking of Christ as an Angel, shrink either from declaring Him also to be God. *Novatian (c. 235, W), 5.631.*

Christ is at once both Angel and God. In Genesis, to Abraham: "And the Angel of the Lord called him from heaven and said unto him, 'Abraham, Abraham.'" ... Also in Exodus: "But God went before them by day indeed in a pillar of cloud." ... Yet, in the same place: "And the Angel of God moved forward, who went before the army of the children of Israel." Also in the same place: "Lo! I send my Angel before your face.... For my Name is in Him." *Cyprian (c. 250, W), 5.517.*

He calls Him an Angel, that is, a Messenger of the Father. For He is called the Messenger of Great Counsel.... The great voice is to tell the words of the Omnipotent God of heaven to men. *Victorinus (c. 280, W), 7.353.*

His beloved Son, God the Word, the Angel of His great counsel. *Apostolic Constitutions (compiled c. 390, E), 7.408; see also 1.223–1.228.*

SEE ALSO CHRIST, DIVINITY OF; THEOPHANIES.

ANGER OF GOD

The anger of the Lord was kindled against Moses. Exod. 4:14.

Let all bitterness, wrath, anger, clamor, and evil speaking be put away from you. Eph. 4:31.

He possesses neither wrath nor indignation. For there is nothing that can stand against Him. *Aristides (c. 125, E), 9.264.*

When we read of the anger of God either in the Old Testament or in the New, we do not take such expressions literally. *Origen (c. 225, E), 4.278.*

Indeed, we speak of the wrath of God. However, we do not maintain that it indicates any passion on His part. Rather, it is something that is assumed in order to discipline by stern means those sinners who have committed many and grievous sins. For that which is called God's wrath and His anger is actually a means of discipline. *Origen (c. 248, E), 4.529.*

When we read of His anger and consider certain descriptions of His indignation, ... we are not to understand them to be attributed to Him in the same sense in which they are to humans. For although all these things can corrupt man, they cannot at all corrupt the Divine power.... All those angers or hatreds of God, or whatever there is of this kind, are displayed for our healing. ... They arose out of wisdom, not from vice. *Novatian (c. 235, W), 5.615.*

It is the fear of God alone that guards the mutual society of men. By this, life itself is sustained, protected, and governed. However, such fear is taken away if man is persuaded that God is without anger. For not only the common advantage, but also reason and truth itself, persuade us that He is moved and is indignant when unjust actions are done. *Lactantius (c. 304–313, W), 7.269.*

There is a just and also an unjust anger.... The unjust anger ... is to be restrained in man—lest he should rush into some very great evil through rage. This type of anger cannot exist in God, for He cannot be injured....

There is also just anger. This anger is necessary in man for the correction of wickedness. Plainly, then, it is also necessary in God, who sets an example for man. Just as we should restrain those who are subject to our power, so also God should restrain the offenses of everyone. *Lactantius (c. 304–313, W), 7.274.*

The patience of God is very great and most useful. Nevertheless, although patient, He punishes the guilty and does not allow them to proceed further—once He sees that they are incorrigible. *Lactantius (c. 304–313, W), 7.277.*

We should understand that since God is eternal, His anger also remains to eternity. On the other hand, since He is endowed with the greatest excellence, He controls His anger. He is not ruled by it; rather, He regulates it according to His will. What I am saying is not contrary to what I had previously said. For if His anger were completely inextinguishable, there would be no place after a sin for satisfaction or reconciliation. Yet, He Himself commands men to be reconciled before the setting of the sun. In other words, the divine anger remains always against those who sin *always*. . . . He who ceases to sin renders the anger of God extinguishable. *Lactantius (c. 304–313, W), 7.277; extended discussion: 4.529, 7.259–7.280.*

See also God, Attributes of.

ANIMALS
The animals are called wild beasts because they are hunted, not as if they had been made evil or venomous from the first. For nothing was made evil by God. But all things were made good—in fact, very good. But the sin in which man was entangled brought evil upon them. For when man transgressed, the animals also transgressed with him. For example, if the master of the house himself acts rightly, the domestics also of necessity conduct themselves properly. However, if the master sins, the servants also sin with him. In like manner, it came to pass, that in the case of man's sin—he being master—all who were subject to him sinned with him. When, therefore, man again shall have made his way back to his natural condition, and no longer does evil, those creatures also shall be restored to their original gentleness. *Theophilus (c. 180, E), 2.101.*

ANOINTING
See Baptism, Holy Spirit; Oil, Anointing With.

ANTHROPOLOGY, THEOLOGICAL
See Fall of Man; Man, Doctrine of.

ANTHROPOMORPHISMS
In theology, an anthropomorphism is the attributing of a human body and human characteristics to God.

And they heard the sound of the Lord God walking in the garden. Gen. 3:8.

I watched till thrones were put in place, and the Ancient of Days was seated; His garment was white as snow, and the hair of His head was like pure wool. Dan. 7:9.

Therefore being exalted to the right hand of God, . . . He poured out this which you now see and hear. Acts 2:33.

God has no form, nor any bodily members. *Aristides (c. 125, E), 9.264.*

We do not consider that God has such a form as some say, for they try to imitate it [in images] to His honor. *Justin Martyr (c. 160, E), 1.165.*

Form, motion, standing, throne, place, right hand or left—these are not at all to be conceived as belonging to the Father of the universe, although it is so written. But what each of these means will be shown in its proper place. The First Cause is not, then, in space; rather, He is above space, time, name, and conception. *Clement of Alexandria (c. 195, E), 2.461.*

There are certain expressions that occur in the Old Testament, such as when God is said to be angry or to repent, or when other human affections or passions are ascribed to Him. Because of these, our opponents think that they are furnished with grounds for refuting us. For we maintain that God is altogether impassible and is to be regarded as wholly free from all affections of this kind. *Origen (c. 225, E), 4.277.*

Those who do not understand these expressions (and similar ones) in the sacred Scriptures imagine that we attribute to God . . . a form like that of a man. According to their conceptions, it follows that we must think the body of God is furnished with wings. *Origen (c. 248, E), 4.513.*

The Scripture makes use of such expressions [i.e., anthropomorphisms] as an aid to men. *Origen (c. 248, E), 4.529.*

If you understand the words, "work with His own hands" literally, then neither are they applicable to the second God [i.e., the Son], nor to any other being partaking of divinity. . . . Truly, indeed, God can have no voice—if we are speaking of a voice that is a concussion of the air. *Origen (c. 248, E), 4.601.*

The Scriptures plainly speak of God as of a Being without a body. Hence it is said, "No man has seen God at anytime." *Origen (c. 248, E), 4.621.*

The heavenly Scripture often speaks of the Divine appearance as if it were a human form. For example, it says, "The eyes of the Lord are upon the righteous" [Ps. 34:15]. Or, "the Lord God smelled the smell of a good aroma" [Gen. 8:21]. . . . For the prophet then was still speaking about God in parables, according to the stage of man's faith. He was not speaking as God really was, but as people were able to receive Him. *Novatian (c. 235, W), 5.615, 616.*

Let no one charge us with Jewish fables and those of the sect of the Sadducees—as though we, too, attribute material forms to the Deity. For supposedly this is taught in their writings. *Arnobius (c. 305, E), 6.467.*

We are far from attributing bodily shape to the Deity. *Arnobius (c. 305, E), 6.469; see also 3.316–3.317.*

ANTICHRIST

He shall speak pompous words against the Most High, shall persecute the saints of the Most High, and shall intend to change times and law. Then the saints shall be given into his hands for a time and times and half a time. Dan. 7:25.

That day will not come unless the falling away comes first, and the man of sin is revealed, the son of perdition, who opposes and exalts himself above all that is called God or that is worshiped, so that he sits as God in the temple of God, showing himself that he is God. 2 Thess. 2:3, 4.

Little children, it is the last hour; and as you have heard that the Antichrist is coming, even now many antichrists have come. 1 John 2:18.

They worshiped the beast, saying, "Who is like the beast? Who is able to make war with him?" And he was given a mouth speaking great things and blasphemies, and he was given authority to continue for forty-two months. Then he opened his mouth in blasphemy against God, to blaspheme His name, His tabernacle, and those who dwell in heaven. And it was granted to him to make war with the saints and to overcome them. And authority was given him over every tribe, tongue, and nation. Rev. 13:4–7.

He shall come from heaven with glory, when the man of apostasy, who speaks strange things against the Most High, will venture to do unlawful deeds on the earth against us Christians. *Justin Martyr (c. 160, E), 1.253, 254.*

By means of the events that will occur in the time of the Antichrist, it is shown that he, being an apostate and a robber, is anxious to be worshipped as God. . . . For he is endowed with all of the power of the devil. He will come—not as a righteous king, nor as a legitimate king in subjection to God—but as an unholy, unjust, and lawless one. . . . He will set aside idols to persuade men that he himself is God. . . . Daniel, foresaw the end of the last kingdom (of the ten last kings), among whom the kingdom of those men will be partitioned and upon whom the son of perdition will come. *Irenaeus (c. 180, E/W), 1.553.*

When he comes, he will reign over the earth for three years and six months. *Irenaeus (c. 180, E/W), 1.554.*

Jeremiah does not merely point out the Antichrist's sudden coming, but he even indicates the tribe from which he will come, when he says, "We will hear the voice of his swift horses from Dan" [Jer. 8:16]. *Irenaeus (c. 180, E/W), 1.559.*

Once this Antichrist has devastated everything in this world, he will reign for three years and six months, and sit in the temple at Jerusalem. And then the Lord will come from heaven in the clouds. *Irenaeus (c. 180, E/W), 1.560.*

The deceiver seeks to liken himself in all things to the Son of God. . . . Christ is a king, so the Antichrist is also a king. The Savior appeared as a lamb. So he, too, in like manner, will appear as a lamb, though within he is a wolf. The Savior came into the world in the circumcision, and the Antichrist will come in the same manner. The Lord sent apostles among all the nations, and he in like manner will send false apostles. The Savior gathered together the sheep that were scattered abroad. And he, in like manner, will bring together a people who are scattered abroad. . . . The Savior raised up and showed His holy flesh like a temple, and he will raise a temple of stone in Jerusalem. *Hippolytus (c. 200, W), 5.206.*

He says, "Dan is a lion's whelp" [Deut. 33:22]. And in naming the tribe of Dan, he clearly declared the tribe from which the Antichrist is destined to spring. Just as Christ comes from the tribe of Judah, so the Antichrist is to come from the tribe of Dan. *Hippolytus (c. 200, W), 5.207.*

By the beast, then, coming up out of the earth, he means the kingdom of the Antichrist. And by the two horns, he means him and the false prophet after him. . . . He will act with vigor again and prove strong by reason of the laws established by him. And he will cause all those who will not worship the image of the beast to be put to death. . . . Being full of guile and exalting himself against the servants of God, he desires to afflict them and persecute them out of the world, for they do not give glory to him. He will order censers to be set up by everyone, everywhere, so that none of the saints may be able to buy or sell without first sacrificing. For this is what is meant by the mark received upon the right hand. And the phrase, "on their forehead," indicates that all are crowned and put on a crown of fire—of death, not of life. *Hippolytus (c. 200, W), 5.214.*

Let us look also at his actions. He will call together all the people to himself, out of every country of the Dispersion, making them his own, as though they were his own children. He will promise to restore their country and re-establish their kingdom and nation, in order that he may be worshipped by them as God. *Hippolytus (c. 200, W), 5.215.*

"After sixty-two weeks, the times will be fulfilled, and for one week he will make a covenant with many. And in the midst of the week, sacrifice and oblation will be removed." . . . For when the sixty-two weeks are fulfilled, and Christ has come, and the Gospel has been preached in every place, the times will then be accomplished. Then, there will remain only one week—the last—in which Elijah and Enoch will appear. And in the middle of it, the abomination of desolation will be manifested. This is the Antichrist, announcing desolation to the world. And when he comes, the sacrifice

and oblation will be removed, which now are offered to God in every place by the nations. *Hippolytus (c. 205, W), 5.182.*

The prophet sets forth these things concerning the Antichrist, who will be shameless, a war-monger, and a despot. Exalting himself above all kings and above every god, he will build the city of Jerusalem and restore the sanctuary. *Hippolytus (c. 205, W), 5.184.*

"For a time, times, and a half." By this, he indicated the three and a half years of the Antichrist. *Hippolytus (c. 205, W), 5.190.*

After the destruction of the Antichrist, there will be speedily transacted the great process of the resurrection. *Tertullian (c. 210, W), 3.565.*

He himself will divide the globe into three ruling powers, when Nero will be raised up from Hades. Elijah will first come to seal the beloved ones. At these things, the region of Africa and the northern nation, the whole earth on all sides, will tremble for seven years. But Elijah will occupy the half of the time; and Nero will occupy the other half. Then the embers of the whore Babylon, being reduced to ashes, will advance to Jerusalem. And the Latin conqueror will then say, "I am Christ, whom you always pray to." . . . He does many wonders, since the false prophet is his. That they may believe him, his image will speak. The Almighty has given it power to appear as such. The Jews, recapitulating Scriptures from him, exclaim at the same time to the highest that they have been deceived. *Commodianus (c. 240, W), 4.211.*

Celsus [the pagan critic] rejects the statements concerning the Antichrist (as he is called). That is because he has not read what is said of him in the Book of Daniel, nor in the writings of Paul, nor what the Savior has predicted in the Gospels about his coming. . . . Paul states the following: . . . "so that he sits in the temple of God, showing himself that he is God." This same fact is referred to in Daniel in the following manner: "And on the temple will be the abomination of desolations. And at the end of the time, an end will be put to the desolation" [Dan. 11:31]. *Origen (c. 248, E), 4.593, 594.*

Even the Antichrist, when he begins to come, will not be allowed to enter into the church just because he threatens. We will not yield to his arms and violence, even though he declares that he will destroy us if we resist. . . . They [i.e., the schismatics] endeavor to imitate the coming of the Antichrist, who is now approaching. *Cyprian (c. 250, W), 5.346.*

Beloved brethren, let none of you be so terrified by the fear of future persecution or the coming of the threatening Antichrist, so as not to be found armed for all things by the evangelical exhortations and precepts, as well as by the heavenly warnings. The Antichrist is coming. Yet, above him, comes Christ also. *Cyprian (c. 250, W), 5.349.*

The Antichrist will come as a man. Isaiah says, "This is the man who arouses the earth, who disturbs kings, who makes the whole earth a desert" [Isa. 14:16]. *Cyprian (c. 250, W), 5.556.*

"And I saw another angel ascending from the east, having the seal of the living God." He speaks of Elijah the prophet, who is the precursor of the times of the Antichrist—for the restoration and establishment of the churches from the great and intolerable persecution. *Victorinus (c. 280, W), 7.352.*

They must be slain by the Antichrist. . . . "And their dead bodies will lie in the streets of the great city, which spiritually is called Sodom and Egypt." He calls Jerusalem "Sodom and Egypt," for it will have become the heaping up of the persecuting people. *Victorinus (c. 280, W), 7.354, 355.*

By this name [666], we understand the Antichrist. Although he is cut off from the divine light and deprived of it, he nevertheless transforms himself into an angel of light, daring to call himself light. *Victorinus (c. 280, W), 7.356.*

But that king . . . will also be a prophet of lies. He will constitute and call himself God. And he will order himself to be worshipped as the Son of God. And power will be given him to do signs and wonders, the sight of which will entice men to worship him. . . . Then he will attempt to destroy the temple of God and persecute the righteous people. And there will be distress and tribulation, such as there never has been from the beginning of the world. All those who believe him and unite themselves to him will be marked by him as sheep. But those who refuse his mark will either flee to the mountains, or, being seized, will be slain with deliberate tortures. . . . Power will be given him to desolate the whole earth for forty-two months. . . . .

When these things happen, then the righteous and the followers of truth will separate themselves from the wicked and flee into solitary places. And when he hears of this, the unholy king, inflamed with anger, will come with a great army, and bringing up all his forces, will surround all the mountain in which the righteous are situated, so that he may seize them. But they . . . will call upon God with a loud voice. . . . And God will hear them and send from heaven a great king to rescue and free them. And He will destroy all the wicked with fire and sword. . . .

Christ will descend with a company of angels to the middle of the earth. And an unquenchable fire will go before Him. And the power of the angels will deliver into the hands of the just that multitude that has surrounded the mountain. . . . After all his forces have been destroyed, the wicked one will escape alone. His power will perish with him. Now, this is the one who is called the Antichrist. However, he will falsely call himself Christ and will fight against the truth. *Lactantius (c. 304–313, W), 7.215; extended discussion: 5.204–5.219, 4.593–4.595.*

SEE ALSO DANIEL, BOOK OF; ESCHATOLOGY; GREAT TRIBULATION; MARK OF THE BEAST; REVELATION, BOOK OF.

ANTIOCHUS EPIPHANES

Antiochus Epiphanes (215–163 B.C.) was the Seleucid king who attempted to turn Palestine into a Hellenistic Gentile province by forbidding the Jews to practice circumcision or to live under the tenets of the Mosaic law. He even erected a pagan altar in the temple in Jerusalem. However, his actions sparked the successful Maccabean revolt.

In this manner, too, Antiochus Epiphanes, the king of Syria, the descendant of Alexander of Macedonia, devised measures against the Jews. . . . And if one desires to inquire into it more accurately, he will find it recorded in the books of the Maccabees. *Hippolytus (c. 200, W), 5.214.*

Antiochus arose, surnamed Epiphanes, who was of the line of Alexander. And after he had reigned in Syria, and brought under him all of Egypt, he went up to Jerusalem and entered the sanctuary. He seized all the treasures in the house of the Lord—including the golden candlesticks, the table, and the altar. And he made a great slaughter in the land. Even as it was written: "And the sanctuary will be trodden under foot, unto evening and unto morning, a thousand and three hundred days." For it happened that the sanctuary remained desolate during that period ... until Judas Maccabeus arose after the death of his father, Matthias. *Hippolytus (c. 205, W), 5.180.*

SEE ALSO DANIEL, BOOK OF.

APOCALYPSE

SEE REVELATION, BOOK OF.

APOCRYPHA, NEW TESTAMENT

SEE PSEUDEPIGRAPHA, NEW TESTAMENT.

APOCRYPHA, OLD TESTAMENT

SEE DEUTEROCANONICAL BOOKS.

APOLOGETICS

SEE CHRISTIANITY (IV. DEFENSE OF CHRISTIANITY).

APOLOGISTS

SEE JUSTIN MARTYR; MINUCIUS FELIX; TERTULLIAN.

APOSTLES, TWELVE

Go therefore and make disciples of all the nations. Matt 28:19.

When He, the Spirit of truth, has come, He will guide you into all truth. John 16:13.

You will receive power when the Holy Spirit has come upon you; and you will be witnesses to Me in Jerusalem, and in Judea and Samaria, and to the end of the earth. Acts 1:8.

Now when they saw the boldness of Peter and John, and perceived that they were uneducated and untrained men, they marveled. And they realized that they had been with Jesus. Acts 4:13.

If, then, anyone who had attended on the elders came, I asked specifically what they said: what Andrew or Peter said, or what was said by Philip, Thomas, James, John, Matthew, or by any other of the Lord's disciples. *Papias (c. 120, E), 1.153.*

These twelve disciples went forth throughout the known parts of the world and continued to show His greatness with all modesty and uprightness. *Aristides (c. 125, E), 9.265.*

From Jerusalem there went out twelve men into the world. These men were uneducated and of no ability in speaking. But by the power of God, they proclaimed to every race of men that they were sent by Christ to teach the word of God to everyone. *Justin Martyr (c. 160, E), 1.175.*

When they had seen Him ascending into heaven, and had believed, and had received the power He sent upon them from heaven, they went to every race of men. And they taught these things and were called apostles. *Justin Martyr (c. 160, E), 1.179.*

Peter and Philip fathered children, and Philip gave his daughters in marriage. Furthermore, Paul did not hesitate to mention his "companion" in one of his epistles.... He says in his epistle, "Do I not have the right to take along a sister-wife, as do the other apostles?" However, the other apostles, in harmony with their particular ministry, devoted themselves to preaching without any distraction. Their spouses went with them, not as wives, but as sisters, in order to minister to housewives. *Clement of Alexandria (c. 195, E), 2.390, 391.*

He commanded equality with simplicity on the disciples, who were striving for the pre-eminence. *Clement of Alexandria (c. 195, E), 2.451.*

The man of God eats, drinks, and marries—not as the primary things of life, but as things that are necessary. I even mention marriage, ... for having become perfect, he has the apostles for examples. *Clement of Alexandria (c. 195, E), 2.543.*

Christ is said to have baptized Peter alone. And Peter baptized Andrew; Andrew, John. And the two of them baptized James and the rest. *Clement of Alexandria (c. 195, E), 2.578, as quoted by Moschus.*

To James the Just, John, and Peter, the Lord imparted knowledge after His resurrection. These imparted it to the rest of the apostles. And the rest of the apostles imparted it to the Seventy, of whom Barnabas was one. *Clement of Alexandria (c. 195, E), 2.579.*

His disciples also, spreading over the world, did as their Divine Master commanded them. *Tertullian (c. 197, W), 3.35.*

"When He, the Spirit of truth, will come, He will lead you into all truth." He thus shows that there was nothing of which they [the apostles] were ignorant, to whom He had promised the future attainment of all truth by the help of the Spirit of truth. *Tertullian (c. 197, W), 3.253.*

The apostles were ignorant of nothing and they preached nothing that contradicted one another. *Tertullian (c. 197, W), 3.254.*

When churches were advanced in the faith, much less would the apostles have withheld from them anything for the purpose of committing it separately to only a specific few. Even if we were to suppose that among intimate friends (so to speak) the apostles held various discussions, yet it is not believable that these discussions could have been of such a nature as to bring in some other rule of faith—differing from and contrary to that which they were proclaiming through the catholic churches. As if they spoke of one God in the church and another at home! *Tertullian (c. 197, W), 3.255.*

It is not believable that the apostles were either ignorant of the whole scope of the message which they had to declare, or failed to make known to all men the entire rule of faith. *Tertullian (c. 197, W), 3.256.*

You have the work of the apostles also predicted: "How beautiful are the feet of those who preach the gospel of peace, which brings good tidings of good"—not of war, nor evil tidings [Isa. 52:7]. In response to which is the Psalm, "Their sound is gone through all the earth, and their words to the ends of the world" [Ps. 19:5]. *Tertullian (c. 207, W), 3.340.*

In fact, he is expecting us to trust him as we do the prophets or the apostles, who had authority. *Origen (c. 228, E), 9.331.*

As a matter of fact, not all of the disciples are described in Acts as unlearned and ignorant, but only Peter and John. *Origen (c. 245, E), 9.421.*

On this account, the apostles left Israel and accomplished that which had been commanded them by the Savior: "Make disciples of all the nations." *Origen (c. 245, E), 9.426.*

It was by help of a divine power that these men taught Christianity and succeeded in leading others to embrace the word of God. For it was not any power of theirs of speaking . . . according to the arts of Grecian dialects or rhetoric that was the effective cause of converting their hearers. . . . For had the doctrine and the preaching consisted of the persuasive utterance and arrange-

ment of words, then faith, too, . . . would have been through the wisdom of men and not through the power of God. Now, on seeing fishermen and tax collectors (who had not acquired even the merest elements of learning) . . . discoursing boldly about faith in Jesus—not only among the Jews, but also preaching him with success among other nations—who would not inquire from where they derived this power of persuasion? *Origen (c. 248, E), 4.424.*

At the request of their Master and God, the disciples scattered over the world and gave forth His teachings for salvation. *Cyprian (c. 250, W), 5.468.*

I am also of the opinion that there were many persons of the same name with John the apostle, who by their love, admiration, and emulation of him . . . were induced to embrace the same name also. Just as we find many of the children of the faithful called by the names of Paul and Peter. *Dionysius of Alexandria (c. 262, E), 6.83.*

The apostles have overcome unbelief though powers, signs, portents, and mighty works. *Victorinus (c. 280, W), 7.353.*

The disciples, being dispersed throughout the provinces, laid the foundations of the church everywhere. They themselves did many and almost unbelievable miracles in the name of their divine Master. For at His departure, He had endowed them with power and strength—by which the system of their new announcement could be founded and confirmed. *Lactantius (c. 304–313, W), 7.123.*

They primarily attacked Paul and Peter, and the other disciples, as propagators of deceit. Yet, at the same time, they testified that these men were unskilled and unlearned. . . . Therefore, the desire of inventing and craftiness were absent from these men. For they were unskilled. . . . Yet, their teaching, because it is true, agrees in every place. It is altogether consistent with itself. On this account, it is persuasive, for it is based on a consistent plan. The apostles did not devise this religion for the sake of gain and advantage. *Lactantius (c. 304–313, W), 7.138.*

At that time [after the Ascension], his apostles were eleven in number. To them was added Matthias, in the place of the traitor Judas. And afterwards Paul was added. Then they were dispersed throughout all the earth to preach the gospel as the Lord their Master had commanded them. For the next twenty-five years (until the beginning of the reign of Emperor Nero), they busied themselves in laying the foundations of the church in every province and city. *Lactantius (c. 320, W), 7.301; see also 3.675.*

SEE ALSO ANDREW; CHRISTIANITY (II. GROWTH OF CHRISTIANITY); EVANGELISM; JOHN, THE APOSTLE; MATTHEW; PETER; SEVENTY, THE (DISCIPLES); THOMAS.

APOSTOLIC FAITH

When He, the Spirit of truth, has come, He will guide you into all truth. John 16:13.

But even if we, or an angel from heaven, preach any other gospel to you than what we have preached to you, let him be accursed. Gal. 1:18.

O Timothy! Guard what was committed to your trust. 1 Tim. 6:20.

The things that you have heard from me among many witnesses, commit these to faithful men who will be able to teach others also. 2 Tim. 2:2.

Avoid foolish and ignorant disputes, knowing that they generate strife. 2 Tim. 2:23.

Let that abide in you which you heard from the beginning. If what you heard from the beginning abides in you, you also will abide in the Son and in the Father. 1 John 2:24.

Contend earnestly for the faith which was once for all delivered to the saints. Jude 3.

You are fond of contention, brethren, and full of zeal about things which do not pertain to salvation. *Clement of Rome (c. 96, W), 1.17.*

Study, therefore, to be established in the doctrines of the Lord and the apostles. *Ignatius (c. 105, E), 1.64.*

I wish now to give you a more accurate demonstration of the historical periods, God helping me. I wish to do this so that you may see that our doctrine is not modern nor fabulous, but more ancient and true than all poets and authors who have written in uncertainty. *Theophilus (c. 180, E), 2.116.*

Nor will any one of the rulers in the churches teach doctrines different from these (however highly gifted he may be as to eloquence)—for no one is greater than the Master. Nor, on the other hand, will he who is deficient in power of expression inflict injury on the tradition. For the faith is ever one and the same. So he who is able to teach at great length regarding it makes no addition to it. Nor does he who can say but little, diminish it. *Irenaeus (c. 180, E/W), 1.331.*

It is unlawful to assert that the apostles preached before they possessed "perfect knowledge," as some do even venture to say, boasting themselves as being improvers of the apostles. For, after our Lord rose from the dead, the apostles were energized with power from on High when the Holy Spirit came down [upon them]. They were completely filled and had perfect knowledge. They departed to the ends of the earth, preaching the glad tidings of the good things sent to us from God. *Irenaeus (c. 180, E/W), 1.414.*

Let us suppose that the apostles had known hidden mysteries that they were in the habit of imparting to "the perfect" privily and apart from the rest. If that were true, they would have especially delivered such mysteries to those to whom they were also committing the churches themselves. For the apostles were desirous that these men should be very perfect and blameless in all things, whom also they were leaving behind as their successors. *Irenaeus (c. 180, E/W), 1.415.*

In this order, and by this succession, the ecclesiastical tradition from the apostles, and the preaching of the truth, have come down to us. And this is most abundant proof that there is one and the same life-giving faith, which has been preserved in the church from the apostles until now, and handed down in truth. *Irenaeus (c. 180, E/W), 1.416.*

It is not necessary to seek the truth among others, for it is easy to obtain it from the church. For the apostles lodged in her hands most abundantly all things pertaining to the truth—just like a rich man [depositing his money] in a bank. Therefore, every man who wants to can draw from her the water of life. *Irenaeus (c. 180, E/W), 1.416, 417.*

True knowledge is that which consists in the doctrine of the apostles and the ancient constitution of the church throughout all the world. It also consists in the distinctive manifestation of the body of Christ according to the succession of the bishops. For by this they have handed down that church which exists in every place and which has come down even unto us. She is guarded and preserved without any forging of Scriptures, by a very complete system of doctrine. She neither receives any addition to, nor does she allow any diminishing of, the truths which she believes. True knowledge also consists of reading the Word of God without falsification, but with a lawful and diligent exposition in harmony with the Scriptures—both without danger and without blasphemy. Above all, it consists in the pre-eminent gift of love, which is more precious than knowledge, more glorious than prophecy, and which excels all the other gifts of God. *Irenaeus (c. 180, E/W), 1.508.*

In the Lord's apostles, we possess our authority. For even they did not of themselves choose to introduce anything [new], but faithfully delivered to the nations the teaching that they had received from Christ. If, therefore, even "an angel from heaven should preach any other gospel" than theirs, he would be called accursed by us. *Tertullian (c. 197, W), 3.246.*

At the beginning, I lay down the fact that there is one definite thing taught by Christ. . . . You must "seek" only until you have found; once you have "found," you must believe. After that, you have nothing further to do but to keep what you have believed. . . . For nothing else is to be believed, and so nothing else is to be sought. *Tertullian (c. 197, W), 3.248.*

We hold communion with the apostolic churches because our doctrine is in no respect different than theirs. This is our witness of truth. *Tertullian (c. 197, W), 3.252, 253.*

The [heretics] usually tell us that the apostles did not know all things . . . exposing Christ to blame for having sent forth apostles who had either too much ignorance, or too little simplicity. What man of sound mind can possibly suppose that they were ignorant of anything, whom the Lord ordained to be teachers? . . . Was anything withheld from the knowledge of Peter, who is called the rock on which the church would be built? For he also obtained "the keys of the kingdom of heaven" with the power of binding and loosing in heaven and on earth." Again, was anything hidden from John, the Lord's most beloved disciple, who used to lean on His breast? *Tertullian (c. 197, W), 3.253.*

"When He, the Spirit of truth, will come, He will lead you into all truth." He thus shows that there was nothing of which the apostles were ignorant, to whom He had promised the future attainment of all truth by the help of the Spirit of truth. *Tertullian (c. 197, W), 3.253.*

When the churches were advanced in the faith, the apostles would not have kept anything back from them for the purpose of committing it separately to a select few persons. *Tertullian (c. 197, W), 3.255.*

No other teaching will have the right of being received as apostolic than that which is at the present day proclaimed in the churches of apostolic foundation. *Tertullian (c. 207, W), 3.286.*

I say that my Gospel is the true one. Marcion says that his is. I assert that Marcion's Gospel is adulterated. Marcion says that mine is. Now what can settle this matter for us—unless it is the principle of time. This principle maintains that the authority lies with that doctrine that is found to be more ancient. It assumes as a fundamental truth that corruption belongs to the side that is convicted of comparative lateness in its origin. For, inasmuch as error is falsification of truth, it must necessarily be that truth precedes error. *Tertullian (c. 207, W), 3.349.*

If that [doctrine] has existed from the beginning which has the apostles for its authors, then it will certainly be quite evident that the doctrine which comes down from the apostles is that which has been kept as a sacred deposit in the churches of the apostles. *Tertullian (c. 207, W), 3.349, 350.*

Such are the summary arguments that we use . . . maintaining both the order of time (which rules that a late date is the mark of forgers) and the authority of churches (which lends support to the tradition of the apostles). For truth must necessarily precede the forgery, and it must come directly from those by whom it has been handed down. *Tertullian (c. 207, W), 3.351.*

"For the hope that is laid up for you in heaven, of which you have heard before in the word of the truth of the gospel, has come unto you, just as it has unto all the world." . . . Now, if it is our gospel that has spread everywhere (rather than any heretical gospel, much less Marcion's), . . . then ours will be the gospel of the apostles. But even if Marcion's gospel succeeded in filling the whole world, it would not even then be entitled to be characterized as "apostolic." For the term "apostolic" . . . can only belong to that gospel which was the *first* to fill the world. *Tertullian (c. 207, W), 3.470.*

Wide are men's inquiries into uncertainties. Wider still are their disputes about conjectures. . . . To the Christian, however, only a few words are necessary for the clear understanding of the whole subject. For, in the few words, there always arises certainty to him. Nor is he permitted to give his inquiries a wider range than is necessary for their solution. For the apostle forbids "endless questions." *Tertullian (c. 210, W), 3.183.*

The teaching of the apostles in everything was surely according to the mind of God. They neither forgot nor omitted any part of the Gospel. *Tertullian (c. 212, W), 4.121.*

You [the church] lay down a rule that this faith has its solemnities appointed by either the Scriptures or the tradition of the forefathers, and that no further addition in the way of observance must be added, because innovation is unlawful. *Tertullian (c. 213, W), 4.111.*

From here on, in the following principle, we find a presumption of equal force against all heresies whatsoever: The principle is that whatever is first is true. Therefore, that which is later in date is spurious. *Tertullian (c. 213, W), 3.598.*

I now have to ascertain what those matters are which it is proper to discuss in the following pages—all in . . . agreement with the creed of the church. *Origen (c. 225, E), 4.262.*

Even in regards to those who . . . have not gone into these deep questions, we find that they believe in the Most High God and in His Only-Begotten Son (the Word and God). Furthermore, they often exhibit in their character a high degree of seriousness, purity, and integrity. *Origen (c. 248, E), 4.631.*

We must not at all depart from the evangelical precepts. Disciples should observe and do the same things that the Master both taught and did. . . . So, then, neither the apostle himself nor an angel from heaven can preach or teach anything other than what Christ has once taught and that His apostles have announced. Therefore, I wonder very much from where this practice has originated. For it is contrary to evangelical and apostolic discipline. *Cyprian (c. 250, W), 5.361.*

The secrets of God cannot be known. Therefore, our faith should be simple. We read in the first Epistle of Paul to the Corinthians: "We see now through the glass in an enigma, but then we will see face to face. Now I know partly; but

then I will known even as I am also known" [1 Cor. 13:12]. Also, in Solomon, in Wisdom: "And in simplicity of heart seek Him" [Wisd. 1:1]. . . . Also in Solomon: "Be not excessively righteous and do not reason more than is required" [Sir. 7:17]. . . . Also, in the Epistle of Paul to the Romans: "Oh the depth of the riches of the wisdom and knowledge of God! How incomprehensible are his judgments and how unsearchable are his ways!" *Cyprian (c. 250, W), 5.547.*

This is the doctrine of the holy prophets that we Christians follow. This is our wisdom, which those who worship frail objects . . . deride as folly and vanity. For we are not used to defending and asserting it in public. For God orders us to hide His secrets in quietness and silence. *Lactantius (c. 304–313, W), 7.10.*

Christ asks what business is it of yours to examine and inquire as to . . . the origin of souls, or who devised the causes of evil. . . . Leave those things to God. Allow *Him* to know what is, . . . where it had to have been or not, whether something always existed, or whether it was created at the beginning. . . .What *does* pertain to you is the salvation of your souls. And it is in jeopardy. *Arnobius (c. 305, E), 6.457.*

As Paul himself seems to tell us, and as we have also learned from the earlier account given in the Gospel, to introduce new preaching, teaching, evangelizing, or prophesying is not (in this life, at least) held out on the same terms to any person in the later times [after the apostles]. And if the opposite ever appears to be the case, that person can only be held to be a false prophet or a false Christ. *Disputation of Archelaus and Manes (c. 320, E), 6.210.*

Those who seek to set up any new dogma have the habit of very readily perverting into conformity with their own notions any proofs they care to take from the Scriptures. . . . The apostolic word marks out the case in these words, "If anyone preaches any other gospel to you other than that which you have received, let him be accursed." Consequently, in addition to what has been once committed to us by the apostles, a disciple of Christ should receive nothing new as doctrine. *Disputation of Archelaus and Manes (c. 320, E), 6.213, 214.*

SEE ALSO APOSTOLIC SUCCESSION; CHURCHES, APOSTOLIC; CREEDS, EARLY; TRADITION (III. APOSTOLIC TRADITION).

APOSTOLIC SUCCESSION

Many professing Christians view apostolic succession as a fundamental principle of Christianity. Other professing Christians deem apostolic succession to be a corruption and perversion of the gospel. Both sides may be surprised to discover what the term originally did—and did not—mean.

I. The succession of bishops and presbyters

II. The question of unworthy ministers

III. Can bishops change the apostolic faith?

I. The succession of bishops and presbyters

The things that you have heard from me among many witnesses, commit these to faithful men who will be able to teach others also. 2 Tim. 2:2.

For this reason I left you in Crete, that you should set in order the things that are lacking, and appoint elders in every city as I commanded you. Tit. 1:5.

Through our Lord Jesus Christ, our apostles knew that there would be strife over the office of oversight [episcopacy]. Accordingly, since they had obtained a perfect foreknowledge of this, they appointed those men already mentioned. And they afterwards gave instructions that when those men would fall asleep, other approved men should succeed them in their ministry. Therefore, we are of the opinion that those appointed by the apostles, or afterwards by other acclaimed men, with the consent of the whole church, and who have blamelessly served the flock of Christ in a humble, peaceable, and disinterested spirit, and have for a long time possessed the good opinion of all, cannot be justly dismissed from the ministry. *Clement of Rome (c. 96, W), 1.17.*

When we refer them to that tradition which originates from the apostles, which is preserved by means of the successions of presbyters in the churches, they object to tradition, saying that they themselves are wiser not merely than the presbyters, but than even the apostles. *Irenaeus (c. 180, E/W), 1.415.*

Therefore, it is within the power of all in every church who may wish to see the truth to examine clearly the tradition of the apostles manifested throughout the whole world. And we are in a position to reckon up those who were instituted bishops in the churches by the apostles, and the succession of these men to our own times. . . . For if the apostles had known

hidden mysteries, . . . they would have delivered them especially to those to whom they were also committing the churches themselves. For they were desirous that these men should be very perfect and blameless in all things, whom also they were leaving behind as their successors, delivering up their own place of government to these men. *Irenaeus (c. 180, E/W), 1.415.*

In this order, and by this succession, the ecclesiastical tradition from the apostles, and the preaching of the truth, have come down to us. And this is most abundant proof that there is one and the same life-giving faith, which has been preserved in the church from the apostles until now, and handed down in truth. *Irenaeus (c. 180, E/W), 1.416.*

It is necessary to obey the presbyters who are in the church—those who, as I have shown, possess the succession from the apostles. For those presbyters, together with the succession of the bishops, have received the certain gift of truth, according to the good pleasure of the Father. But we should hold in suspicion others who depart from the primitive succession and assemble themselves together in any place whatsoever. For they are either heretics of perverse minds, or else they are schismatics who are puffed up and self-pleasing. Or, perhaps, they are hypocrites, acting this way for the sake of money and vainglory. . . . Therefore, it behooves us to keep aloof from all such persons and to adhere to those who, as I have already observed, hold the doctrine of the apostles. For they, together with the order of presbyters, display sound speech and blameless conduct for the confirmation and correction of others. *Irenaeus (c. 180, E/W), 1.497.*

It behooves us to learn the truth from those who possess that succession of the church which is from the apostles, and among whom exists that which is sound and blameless in conduct, as well as that which is unadulterated and incorrupt in speech. . . . They expound the Scriptures to us without danger, neither blaspheming God, nor dishonoring the patriarchs, nor despising the prophets. *Irenaeus (c. 180, E/W), 1.498.*

True knowledge is the doctrine of the apostles and the ancient constitution of the church throughout all the world and the distinctive manifestation of the body of Christ according to the successions of the bishops, by which they have handed down that church which exists in every place. *Irenaeus (c. 180, E/W), 1.508.*

All these [heretics] are of much later date than the bishops to whom the apostles committed the churches. *Irenaeus (c. 180, E/W), 1.547.*

Let them [the heretics] produce the original records of their churches. Let them unfold the roll of their bishops, running down in due succession from the beginning in such a manner that the first bishop of theirs can show for his ordainer and predecessor one of the apostles or apostolic men—a man, moreover, who continued steadfast with the apostles. For this is the manner in which the apostolic churches transmit their registers. For example, the church of Smyrna records that Polycarp was placed there by John. Likewise, the church of Rome demonstrates Clement to have been ordained in like manner by Peter. In exactly the same way, the other churches similarly exhibit [their list of bishops], whom, as having been appointed to their episcopal places by apostles, they regard as transmitters of the apostolic seed. *Tertullian (c. 197, W), 3.258.*

No one will refute these [heretics] except the Holy Spirit bequeathed unto the church, which the Apostles—having received in the first instance—have transmitted to those who have rightly believed. But we, as being their successors and as participators in this grace, high priesthood, and office of teaching—as well as being reputed guardians of the church—must not be found deficient in vigilance. Nor should we be disposed to suppress correct teaching. *Hippolytus (c. 225, W), 5.10.*

We cling to the standard of the heavenly church of Jesus Christ according to the succession of the apostles. *Origen (c. 225, E), 4.357.*

He cannot be reckoned as a bishop who succeeds no one. For he has despised the evangelical and apostolic tradition, springing from himself. For he who has not been ordained in the church can neither have nor hold to the church in any way. . . . How can he be esteemed a pastor, who succeeds to no one, but begins from himself? For the true shepherd remains and presides over the church of God by successive ordination. Therefore, the other one becomes a stranger and a profane person, an enemy of the Lord's peace. *Cyprian (c. 250, W), 5.398.*

The power of remitting sins was given to the apostles and to the churches which they established (having been sent by Christ) and to the bishops who succeeded to them by vicarious ordination. However, the enemies of the one catholic church to which we belong, who are the enemies of those of us who have succeeded the apostles, claim for themselves unlawful priesthoods—in opposition to us. And they also set up profane altars. So what else are they other than Korah, Dathan, and Abiram? *Firmilian (c. 256, E), 5.394.*

The words of our Lord Jesus Christ are plain that He sent His apostles and gave to them alone the power that had been given to Him by His Father. And we have succeeded to them, governing the Lord's church with the same power. *Seventh Council of Carthage (c. 256, W), 5.572.*

Not everyone who wants to is ordained—as was the case with that counterfeit priesthood of the calves under Jeroboam. Rather, only he who is called of God is ordained. . . . A presbyter may not perform ordination. For it is not agreeable to holiness to have this order perverted. For "God is not the God of confusion." So subordinate persons should not tyrannically assume functions that belong to their superiors. . . . However, someone may accuse Philip, the deacon, or Ananias, the faithful brother. For the first one [i.e., Philip] baptized the eunuch; the other baptized Paul. However, such a person does not understand what we are saying. We are only saying that no one snatches the priestly dignity to himself. He either receives it from God—as did Melchizedek and Job—or from a high priest—as did Aaron from Moses. Now, Philip and Ananias did not ordain themselves, but were appointed by Christ, the High Priest. *Apostolic Constitutions (compiled c. 390, E), 7.499, 500.*

II. The question of unworthy ministers

Does episcopal succession prevent a congregation from removing an unworthy minister or separating itself from such a minister?

In the ordinations of priests, we should choose no one but unstained and upright ministers. In that way, the ministers who offer sacrifices to God with holy and worthy hands may be heard in the prayers that they make for the safety of the Lord's people. . . . On this account, a people obedient to the Lord's commandments, and fearing God, should separate themselves from a sinful prelate. They should not associate themselves with the sacrifices of a sacrilegious priest. This is especially so since they themselves have the power of either choosing worthy priests or of rejecting unworthy ones. *Cyprian (c. 250, W), 5.370.*

How can he who is himself unclean and in whom the Holy Spirit does not dwell, cleanse and sanctify the water [of baptism]? For the Lord says in the book of Numbers, "And whatever the unclean person touches will be unclean." . . . After all, what prayer can a priest who is impious and is a sinner offer for a baptized person? For it is written, "God does not hear a sinner" [John 9:31]. . . . Who can give what he himself does not have? How can he discharge spiritual functions who himself has lost the Holy Spirit? . . . There can be no spiritual anointing among heretics. For it is clear that the oil cannot be sanctified nor the Eucharist celebrated at all among them. *Cyprian (c. 250, W), 5.376.*

If any bishop uses the rulers of this world and by their means comes to be a bishop of a church, let him be deprived and suspended— together with all who communicate with him. *Apostolic Constitutions (compiled c. 390, E), 7.501.*

If any bishop, or even a presbyter or deacon, obtains that office through money, let him and the person who ordained him be deprived. And let him be entirely cut off from communion, as Simon Magus was by Peter. *Apostolic Constitutions (compiled c. 390, E), 7.501.*

III. Can bishops change the apostolic faith?

Nor will any one of the rulers in the churches teach doctrines different from these (however highly gifted he may be as to eloquence)—for no one is greater than the Master. Nor, on the other hand, will he who is deficient in power of expression influct injury on the tradition. For the faith is ever one and the same. So he who is able to teach at great length regarding it makes no addition to it. Nor does he who can say but little, diminish it. *Irenaeus (c. 180, E/W), 1.331.*

By this [succession], they have handed down that Church which exists in every place and which has come down even unto us. She is guarded and preserved without any forging of Scriptures, by a very complete system of doctrine. She neither receives any addition to,

nor does she allow any diminishing of the truths which she believes. *Irenaeus (c. 180, E/W), 1.508.*

Let the heretics contrive something of the same kind [i.e., a list of episcopal succession back to the apostles.] . . . However, even if they were to produce such a contrivance, they will not advance even one step. For when their very doctrine is compared with that of the apostles, its own diversity and discrepancy proves that it had neither an apostle nor an apostolic man for its authorship. *Tertullian (c. 197, W), 3.258.*

No other teaching will have the right of being received as apostolic than that which is at the present day proclaimed in the churches of apostolic foundation. *Tertullian (c. 207, W), 3.286.*

SEE ALSO APOSTOLIC FAITH; CHURCHES, APOSTOLIC; ORDINATION; TRADITION (II. APOSTOLIC TRADITION).

APPAREL

SEE CLOTHING.

AQUILA, TRANSLATION OF

Aquila, a Jewish proselyte who lived in the early second century, made a Greek translation of the Old Testament. Thereafter, the Jews used it in preference to the Septuagint, which had become the Old Testament of the Christians.

It is not as some allege, . . . "Behold, a *young woman* will conceive and bring forth a son"—as Theodotion the Ephesian has interpreted it and Aquila of Pontus, both of whom are Jewish proselytes. *Irenaeus (c. 180, E/W), 1.451.*

I have compared our own copies with theirs that have the confirmation of the versions never subjected to corruption of Aquila, Theodotion, and Symmachus. *Origen (c. 228, E), 9.371.*

Aquila, following the Hebrew reading, gives it in this manner. He has obtained a reputation among the Jews for having interpreted the Scriptures with no ordinary care. His version is most commonly used by those who do not know Hebrew, being the one that has been most successful. *Origen (c. 240, E), 4.386; see also 5.163–5.166.*

ARABIA

Arabia's pagan females will be your judges. For they not only veil the head, but the face also. *Tertullian (c. 207, W), 4.37.*

Among . . . the Arabians, not only is she who commits adultery put to death, but also her upon whom even the suspicion of adultery has come. *Bardesanes (c. 222, E), 8.731.*

It is but as yesterday since the Romans took possession of Arabia. They abolished all the laws previously existing there—particularly the circumcision that they practiced. *Bardesanes (c. 222, E), 8.733.*

You laugh because in ancient times the Persians worshipped rivers; . . . and the Arabians, an unshaped stone. *Arnobius (c. 305, E), 6.510.*

ARCHIMEDES

Archimedes (285–212 B.C.) was a Greek inventor and mathematician.

Look at that very marvelous piece of organic mechanism invented by Archimedes. I am referring to his hydraulic organ, with its many limbs, parts, bands, passages for the notes, outlets for their sounds, combinations for their harmony, and the array of its pipes. *Tertullian (c. 210, W), 3.193.*

Archimedes of Sicily was able to construct a likeness and representation of the universe in hollow brass. He arranged the sun and moon, just as they appear every day. . . . That sphere, while it revolved, demonstrated not only the rising and setting of the sun and the increase and diminishing of the moon, but also the unequal courses of the stars. *Lactantius (c. 304–313, W), 7.48.*

ARISTEAS

In tradition, Aristeas (3rd century B.C.) was an official of Ptolemy Philadelphus, the ruler who commissioned the translation of the Septuagint.

[Ptolemy] Philadelphus chose such a man for this responsibility and appointed him to the oversight of his most noble library. I speak of Aristeas, his confidential chamberlain, whom he also sent as his representative to Eleazar, with most magnificent gifts, in recognition of the translation of the sacred Scriptures. And this person also wrote the full history of the Seventy translators. *Theonas of Alexandria (c. 300, E), 6.160.*

See also Septuagint.

ARISTOBULUS

Aristobulus was a Jewish philosopher who lived in Alexandria during the second century B.C. He wrote commentaries on the Old Testament. Some of the early Christians believed that he was also one of the translators of the Septuagint.

According to Aristobulus, the fire [on Sinai] was seen while the whole multitude . . . were congregated around the mountain. *Clement of Alexandria (c. 195, E), 2.487.*

The eminent Aristobulus was one of the Seventy who translated the sacred and holy Scriptures of the Hebrews for Ptolemy Philadelphus and his father. *Anatolius (c. 270, E), 6.147.*

See also Septuagint.

ARISTOTLE

Aristotle (384–322 B.C.) was Plato's brightest pupil, who went on to develop his own system of philosophy and science.

In a book addressed to Alexander of Macedonia, Aristotle gives a comprehensive explanation of his own philosophy, and he clearly and manifestly overthrows the opinion of Plato. *Justin Martyr (c. 160, E), 1.275.*

To speak generally [of Aristotle's teachings], in everything the accidents are to be distinguished from the essence. *Clement of Alexandria (c. 195, E), 2.515.*

Aristotle, who was a pupil of this Plato, reduced philosophy to an art. He was distinguished more for his proficiency in logical science, supposing "substance" and "accident" to be the elements of all things. He says that there is one *substance* underlying all things, but that there are nine *accidents*. *Hippolytus (c. 225, W), 5.19.*

Was it an indictment against Plato that Aristotle, after being his pupil for twenty years, went away and attacked his doctrine of the immortality of the soul and called the ideas of Plato the merest trifling? *Origen (c. 248, E), 4.436.*

Aristotle thought that all philosophy consisted of theory and practice. He divided the practical into ethical and political. . . . He very clearly and skillfully showed that mathematics is part of philosophy. *Anatolius (c. 270, E), 6.152.*

Although he is at variance with himself, . . . Aristotle, upon the whole, bears witness that one Mind presides over the universe. *Lactantius (c. 304–313, W), 7.14.*

SEE ALSO PHILOSOPHERS, PHILOSOPHY; PLATO.

ARIUS, ARIANISM

Arius (c. 250–336) was a presbyter in Alexandria who taught that the Son of God was not of the same substance as the Father and that he was created out of nothing. His bishop, Alexander of Alexandria, strongly opposed Arius's teachings. Arius's heresy was condemned at the Council of Nicaea.

There was also a certain Arius, who wore the habit of piety and was similarly possessed with the ambition to be a teacher. *Phileas (c. 307, E), 6.164.*

Arius denies the Godhood of our Savior and preaches that He is only the equal of all others. Having collected all the passages that speak of His plan of salvation and His humiliation for our sake, . . . [his followers] ignore altogether the passages in which His eternal Godhood and unutterable glory with the Father is set forth. *Alexander of Alexandria (c. 324, E), 6.291.*

They drag us before the tribunals of the judges, by relations with silly and disorderly women, whom they have led into error. . . . On account of their concealment, their manner of life, and their unholy attempts, we have—by the common vote of everyone—cast them out of the congregation of the church, which adores the Godhood of Christ. *Alexander of Alexandria (c. 324, E), 6.291.*

I have stirred myself up to show you the faithlessness of these men, who say that there was a time when the Son of God was not. And that He who did not exist before came into existence afterwards—becoming such when at length He was made, even as every man is necessarily born. They say that God made all things from things that did not exist, including even the Son of God in the creation of all things rational and irrational. To this, they add that, as a consequence, He is of a changeable nature, capable of both virtue and vice. Having assumed these propositions, that He is made from things that did not exist, they overturn the sacred writings concerning His eternity. For they reveal the immutability and the Divinity of

Wisdom and the Word that are Christ. . . . They say that since God foreknew and had foreseen that His Son would not rebel against Him, He chose Him from all. For He did not choose Him as if by nature He had anything special beyond His other sons, or any peculiar properties of His own. For they say that no one is by nature a Son of God. Rather, God chose Him who was of a mutable nature, because of His careful life and practices. For He in no way turned to that which is evil. So, according to this, if Paul and Peter had striven for this, there would have been no difference between their sonship and His. *Alexander of Alexandria (c. 324, E), 6.292.*

You are not ignorant that this doctrine, which has recently raised its head against the piety of the church, is that of Ebion and Artemas. Nor is it anything else but an imitation of Paul of Samosata, bishop of Antioch. And he was put out of the church by the judgment and counsel of all the bishops. *Alexander of Alexandria (c. 324, E), 6.294.*

They boast that they are the only men who are wise and who are divested of worldly possessions. They pride themselves as being the sole discoverers of dogmas and that to them alone are those things revealed that have never before come into the mind of anyone else under the sun. *Alexander of Alexandria (c. 324, E), 6.295.*

They ignorantly declare that one of two things must necessarily be said: Either that He is from things that are not, or that there are two Unbegottens. These ignorant men do not know how great the difference is between the unbegotten Father and the things that He created out of nothing. Between these two—as holding the middle place—is the Only-Begotten nature of God the Word, by whom the Father formed all things out of nothing. He was begotten of the true Father Himself. *Alexander of Alexandria (c. 324, E), 6.295.*

They have been excommunicated and anathematized by the church. *Alexander of Alexandria (c. 324, E), 6.298.*

The words invented by them, and spoken contrary to the mind of Scripture, are as follows: "God was not always the Father." Rather, there was a time when God was not the Father. The Word of God was not always, but was made "from things that are not." . . . Therefore, there was a time when He was not. For the Son is a thing created and a thing made. Nor is he like the Father in substance. Nor is He the true and natural Word of the Father. Nor is He His true Wisdom. Rather, He is one of the things fashioned and made. . . . Someone asked them whether the Son of God could change, even as the devil changed. And they were not afraid to answer that He can. For, since He was made and created, he is of changeable nature. *Alexander of Alexandria (c. 324, E), 6.297.*

SEE ALSO CHRIST, DIVINITY OF; HERESIES, HERETICS; TRINITY.

ARK, NOAH'S

The remains of the ark can be seen to this day in the Arabian mountains. *Theophilus (c. 180, E), 2.117.*

SEE ALSO FLOOD, THE; NOAH.

ARK OF THE COVENANT

Then Bezaleel made the ark of acacia wood. . . . He made two cherubim of beaten gold; he made them of one piece at the two ends of the mercy seat. Exod. 37:1, 7.

The entire tabernacle of witness was made for the sake of the ark of the covenant. It was constructed in this manner: its length was two cubits and a half. Its width was one cubit and a half. And its height was one cubit and a half. *Irenaeus (c. 180, E/W), 1.394.*

Just as the ark was gilded both inside and out with pure gold, so likewise was the body of Christ pure and resplendent. *Irenaeus (c. 180, E/ W), 1.570.*

The ark is declared to be a type of the body of Christ, which is both pure and immaculate. *Irenaeus (c. 180, E/W), 1.576.*

Those golden figures, each of them with six wings, signify either the two bears (as some would have it) or rather the two hemispheres. For the name cherubim meant "much knowledge." . . . For He who prohibited the making of a graven image would never Himself have made an image in the likeness of holy things. *Clement of Alexandria (c. 195, E), 2.453.*

When forbidding the likeness to be made of all things that are in heaven, in earth, and in the waters, he declared also the reason: to prohibit all material display of an unseen idolatry. For He adds: "You will not bow down to them, nor

serve them." . . . The golden cherubim and seraphim were purely an ornament in the figured fashion of the ark. It was adapted to ornamentation for reasons totally remote from all condition of idolatry—the reason for which the making a likeness is prohibited. The cherubim are evidently not at variance with this law of prohibition, because they are not found in that form of likeness. *Tertullian (c. 207, W), 3.314.*

SEE ALSO IMAGES; TABERNACLE; TEMPLE, JEWISH.

ARMENIA

In the second year of Abgar's reign, all the districts of Armenia became vassals to the Romans. A command was given by the Emperor Augustus . . . to number all the people in every part. Roman commissioners were sent into Armenia for that purpose, and they carried there statues of the Emperor Augustus. They set them up in all the temples. *Moses of Chorene (date uncertain, E), 8.702.*

SEE ALSO ABGAR, KING.

ART, ARTS

On the other hand, of what are your other pictures? Small Pans, naked girls, drunken satyrs, and phallic symbols—all painted naked in pictures disgraceful for filthiness. And more than this: you are not ashamed in the eyes of all to look at representations of all forms of licentiousness that are portrayed in public places. Rather, you set them up and guard them with scrupulous care. *Clement of Alexandria (c. 195, E), 2.189.*

Let our seals be either a dove, a fish, a ship scudding before the wind, a musical lyre (which Polycrates used), or a ship's anchor (which Seleucus had engraved as a device). If there is anyone fishing, he will remember the apostle, and the children drawn out of the water. We are not to draw an outline of the faces of idols (since we are prohibited to cling to them), nor of a sword or a bow, since we follow peace. Nor should we draw an outline of . . . drinking cups, since we are temperate. *Clement of Alexandria (c. 195, E), 2.286.*

If we adduce the following statement [from Scripture], it will be clear that artistic and skillful invention is from God. . . . For good reason, therefore, the apostle has called the wisdom of God "manifold" [i.e., of many forms] [Eph. 3:10]. For His wisdom has manifested its power "in many departments and in many modes": by art, by knowledge, by faith, by prophecy. And all of this is for our benefit. As says the Wisdom of Jesus [i.e., Sirach], "For all wisdom is from the Lord, and is with Him forever." *Clement of Alexandria (c. 195, E), 2.304, 305.*

The thoughts of virtuous men are produced through the inspiration of God. *Clement of Alexandria (c. 195, E), 2.517.*

What is good in the arts . . . has its beginning from God. *Clement of Alexandria (c. 195, E), 2.518.*

Works of art cannot be sacred and divine. *Clement of Alexandria (c. 195, E), 2.530.*

The following quotation probably is referring to literature, not paintings: In the various arts, we make public property of our works for your benefit. *Tertullian (c. 197, W), 3.49.*

There are . . . certain special energies of this world—spiritual powers—that bring about certain effects, which persons have chosen to produce in virtue of their freedom of the will. . . . For example, there is a peculiar energy and power that is the inspirer of poetry. Another, of geometry. Similarly, there is a separate power to remind us of each of the arts and professions of this kind. Finally, many Greek writers have held the opinion that the art of poetry cannot exist without madness. For that reason, it is related several times in their histories that those whom they call poets were suddenly filled with a kind of spirit of madness. *Origen (c. 225, E), 4.335.*

That contemplative wisdom by which we are impelled to the arts . . . is the gift of God. If we have been created as rational creatures, we have received this. *Methodius (c. 290, E), 6.401.*

SEE ALSO ENTERTAINMENT; IMAGES; INSPIRATION; VESSELS, EUCHARISTIC.

ASCENSION OF CHRIST

SEE RESURRECTION OF CHRIST.

ASCETICISM

Now John was clothed with camel's hair and with a leather belt around his waist, and he ate locusts and wild honey. Mark 1:6.

Jesus said to him, "If you want to be perfect, go, sell what you have and give to the poor, and you will have treasure in heaven; and come, follow Me." Matt. 19:21.

If any one of you will entirely avoid luxury, he will, by a frugal upbringing, train himself for the endurance of involuntary labors [in persecution]. He will constantly use voluntary afflictions as training exercises for persecution. In that manner, when a person is faced with compulsory labors, fears, and griefs, he will not be untrained in endurance. *Clement of Alexandria (c. 195, E), 2.281.*

Are there not many who . . . seal themselves up to eunuchhood for the sake of the kingdom of God, spontaneously relinquishing a pleasure that is both honorable and authorized? Are there not some who prohibit to themselves the use of the very creation of God—abstaining from wine and meat, the enjoyments of which border upon no peril or concern? Rather, they sacrifice to God the humility of their soul even in the chastened use of food. *Tertullian (c. 198, W), 4.23.*

As he who treads a road is happier the lighter he walks, so happier is he in this journey of life who lifts himself along in poverty and does not breathe heavily under the burden of riches. *Mark Minucius Felix (c. 200, W), 4.195.*

SEE ALSO CHRISTIAN LIFE, THE; FASTING; PROSPERITY.

ASSEMBLIES, CHRISTIAN

They continued steadfastly in the apostles' doctrine and fellowship, in the breaking of bread, and in prayers. Acts 2:42.

Let us consider one another in order to stir up love and good works, not forsaking the assembling of ourselves together. Heb. 10:25.

Every day, you should seek out the faces of the saints, by word examining them and going to exhort them, meditating how to save a soul by the word. Or else, by your hands, you should labor for the redemption of your sins. You shall not hesitate to give, nor murmur when you give. *Barnabas (c. 70–130, E), 1.148.*

Every day, seek out the faces of the saints, so that you may be refreshed by their words. *Didache (c. 80–140, E), 7.378.*

For when you assemble frequently in the same place, the powers of Satan are destroyed. *Ignatius (c. 105, E), 1.55.*

Let your assembling together be of frequent occurrence. *Ignatius (c. 105, E), 1.94.*

But after we have baptized the one who has been convinced and who has agreed to our teaching, we bring him to the place where those who are called brothers are assembled. There, we offer heartfelt prayers in common both for ourselves and for the baptized person—and for all others in every place—so that we may be counted worthy. . . . Having ended the prayers, we greet one another with a kiss. Then there is brought to the president of the brethren bread and a cup of wine mixed with water. *Justin Martyr (c. 160, E), 1.185.*

And on the day called Sunday, all who live in cities or in the country gather together to one place. And the memoirs of the apostles or the writings of the prophets are read, as long as time permits. Then, when the reader has ceased, the president verbally instructs us and exhorts us to imitate these good things. Then we all rise together and pray. And, as we said before, when our prayer is ended, bread and wine and water are brought. Then, the president in like manner offers prayers and thanksgivings, according to his ability. And the people assent, saying "Amen." Then, [the Eucharist] is distributed to everyone, and everyone participates in [the bread and wine], over which thanks has been given. And a portion of it is sent by the deacons to those who are absent. *Justin Martyr (c. 160, E), 1.186.*

Rusticus, the prefect, said, "Where do you assemble?" Justin Martyr replied, "Where each one chooses and is able. Do you imagine that we all meet in the very same place? . . . Then Rusticus, the prefect, said, "Tell me where you assemble, or into what place do you collect your followers?" Justin Martyr replied, "I live above one Martinus, at the Timiotinian Bath. And during the whole time . . . I am unaware of any other meeting than his." *Martyrdom of the Holy Martyrs (c. 160, E), 1.305.*

It is said that we should go to the sacrifices and prayers washed, clean, and bright. It is said that this external adornment and purification are practiced for a sign. *Clement of Alexandria (c. 195, E), 2.435.*

Pliny [a Roman official] found in the religious services nothing but meetings at early morning for singing hymns to Christ and God, and sealing home their way of life by a united pledge to be faithful to their religion, forbidding murder, adultery, dishonesty, and other crimes. *Tertullian (c. 197, W), 3.18.*

We are a body knit together as such by a common religious profession, by unity of discipline, and by the bond of a common hope. We meet together as an assembly and congregation so that, offering up prayer to God with united force, we may wrestle with Him in our supplications. God delights in this "violence." We pray, too, for the emperors, for their ministers and for all in authority, for the welfare of the world, for the prevalence of peace, and for the delay of the final consummation. We assemble to read our sacred writings. *Tertullian (c. 197, W), 3.46.*

We assemble together with the same quietness with which we live as individuals. *Mark Minucius Felix (c. 200, W), 4.192.*

The following passage was addressed to Christians who were afraid of attracting persecution:

You say that the pagans are led to inquire about us—seeing that we assemble "without order," and assemble at the same time, and flock in large numbers to the church. You are alarmed that we may awaken their anxieties. *Tertullian (c. 212, W), 3.118.*

But you say, "How will we assemble together [if we do not pay tribute to avoid persecution]?" To be sure, just as the apostles also did—who were protected by faith, not by money. . . . Finally, if you cannot assemble by day, you have the night—the light of Christ luminous against its darkness. . . . Be content with a church of threes. It is better that you sometimes should not see the crowds [of other Christians], than to subject yourselves [to paying tribute]. *Tertullian (c. 212, W), 4.125.*

[SPOKEN AS A REBUKE:] Moreover, the women assemble as if they were about to enter the bath. They press closely and treat God's house as if it were a fair. . . . You speak in an undisciplined manner, as if God were absent. *Commodianus (c. 240, W), 4.218.*

First [the persecutors] drove us away. And although we were quite alone, pursued by everyone, and in danger of being killed, we kept our festival even at such a time. And every place that had been the scene of some of the continuing sufferings that befell any of us, it became a seat for our solemn assemblies— whether it was a field, desert, ship, inn, or prison. *Dionysius of Alexandria (c. 262, E), 6.108.*

When you call an assembly of the church . . . let the building be long, with its head to the east. . . . In the middle, let the bishop's chair be placed. On each side of him, let the presbyters sit down. And let the deacons stand near at hand. . . . Let the laity sit on the other side, with all quietness and good order. And let the women sit by themselves, they also keeping silence. In the middle, let the reader stand upon some high place. . . . Let the young persons sit by themselves, if there is a place for them. If not, let them stand upright. However, let those who are already stricken in years sit, in order. As to the children who stand, let their fathers and mothers take them to themselves. Let the younger women also sit by themselves, if there is a place for them. . . . Let the virgins, widows, and the older women stand or sit before all the rest. . . . In like manner, let the deacon oversee the people, that nobody may whisper, slumber, laugh, or nod. For, in the church, all souls stand wisely, soberly, and attentively, having their attention fixed upon the Word of the Lord. After this, let all rise up with one consent and looking towards the east—after the catechumens and penitents are gone out—pray to God eastward. . . .

As to the deacons, after the prayer is over, let some of them attend upon the oblation of the Eucharist, ministering to the Lord's body with fear. . . . Then let the men give the men, and the women give the women, the Lord's kiss. . . . After this, let the deacon pray for the whole church. . . . Finally, let the sacrifice follow, the people standing and praying silently. And when the oblation has been made, let every rank by itself partake of the Lord's body and precious blood, in order. Let them approach with reverence and holy fear—as to the body of their king. Let the women approach with their heads covered, as is becoming the order of women. But let the door be watched, lest any unbeliever, or one not yet initiated, come in. *Apostolic Constitutions (compiled c. 390, E), 7.421, 422.*

But assemble yourselves together every day, morning and evening, singing psalms and praying in the Lord's house. *Apostolic Constitutions (compiled c. 390, E), 7.423.*

Everyday, the Gentiles, when they arise from sleep, run to their idols to worship them. And before all their work and all their labors, they first of all pray to their idols. . . . Likewise, those who are falsely called Jews, when they have

worked six days, they rest on the seventh day and come together into their synagogue. . . . Therefore, if those who are not saved assemble together frequently, . . . what excuse will you make to the Lord God—you who forsake His church? *Apostolic Constitutions (compiled c. 390, E), 7.423.*

SEE ALSO EUCHARIST; LITURGY; WORSHIP, CHRISTIAN (II. CUSTOMS).

ASSOCIATION, CHRISTIAN

Evil company corrupts good habits. 1 Cor. 15:33.

Have no fellowship with the unfruitful works of darkness, but rather expose them. Eph. 5:11.

With whom, then, are we to associate? With the righteous. *Clement of Alexandria (c. 195, E), 2.289.*

If the presence of a good man, through the respect and reverence that he inspires, always improves him with whom he associates, with much more reason does not he who always holds uninterrupted conversation with God by knowledge, life, and thanksgiving grow at every step. *Clement of Alexandria (c. 195, E), 2.533.*

Follow associations and conversations that are worthy of God. Always remember that short verse, sanctified by the apostle's quotation of it: "Evil company corrupts good morals." *Tertullian (c. 205, W), 4.43.*

Let our most beloved brethren firmly reject the others. Let them avoid the words and conversations of those whose teaching creeps onwards like a cancer. As the apostle says, "Evil communications corrupt good manners." *Cyprian (c. 250, W), 5.346; see also 5.427.*

ASSUMPTION OF MOSES

The *Assumption of Moses* was a Jewish spiritual work, written prior to the time of Christ, purporting to contain prophecies of Moses and an account of his death. Only a few fragments of this work presently survive.

Yet Michael the archangel, in contending with the devil, when he disputed about the body of Moses, dared not bring against him a reviling accusation, but said, "The Lord rebuke you." Jude 9 (apparently quoting from the *Assumption of Moses*).

The work entitled *The Assumption of Moses* is a little treatise of which the apostle Jude makes mention in his epistle. In this work, the archangel Michael, when disputing with the devil regarding the body of Moses, says that the serpent, being inspired by the devil, was the cause of Adam and Eve's transgression. *Origen (c. 225, E), 4.328.*

SEE ALSO ASSUMPTIONS; MOSES; PSEUDEPIGRAPHA, OLD TESTAMENT.

ASSUMPTIONS

And Enoch walked with God; and he was not, for God took him. Gen. 5:24.

Then it happened, as they continued on and talked, that suddenly a chariot of fire appeared with horses of fire, and separated the two of them; and Elijah went up by a whirlwind into heaven. 2 Kings 2:11.

By faith Enoch was translated so that he did not see death. Heb. 11:5.

"And God planted a garden eastward in Eden, and there He placed the man whom He had formed." And then afterwards, when man proved disobedient, he was cast out from there into this world. For that reason, the elders who were disciples of the apostles tell us that those who were taken up [i.e., Enoch and Elijah] were transferred to that place. For Paradise has been prepared for righteous men, those who have the Spirit. Likewise, Paul the apostle, when he was caught up, heard words in this place that are unspeakable. . . . So it is there that those who have been taken up will remain until the consummation of all things, as a prelude to immortality. *Irenaeus (c. 180, E/W), 1.531.*

Enoch was no doubt taken up, and so was Elijah. Nor did they experience death. It was most certainly postponed. They are reserved for the suffering of death, that by their blood, they may extinguish the Antichrist. Even John underwent death, although there had prevailed an unfounded expectation concerning him that he would remain alive until the coming of the Lord. *Tertullian (c. 210, W), 3.227, 228.*

Enoch and Elijah, even now, without experiencing a resurrection, are learning to the full what it is for the flesh to be exempted from all humiliation, all loss, injury, and disgrace— transported as they have been from this world, and from this very cause, already candidates for everlasting life. *Tertullian (c. 210, W), 3.591.*

Concerning the soul of Elijah . . . the Scriptures say that he was taken up in the flesh. . . . For it is shown by his case that the body is sus-

ceptible of immortality, as was also proved by the assumption of Enoch. *Methodius (c. 290, E), 6.376, as quoted by Photius.*

The two prophets Enoch and Elijah have been taken up into some remote place so they might attend our Lord when He comes to judgment. *Lactantius (c. 320, W), 7.302.*

Now, if it had pleased Him that all men should be immortal, it was in His power. For He showed this in the examples of Enoch and Elijah, whom he did not allow to have any experience of death. *Apostolic Constitutions (compiled c. 390, E), 7.440.*

SEE ALSO ASSUMPTION OF MOSES; ELIJAH; ENOCH; ESCHATOLOGY.

ASTROLOGY

Do not learn the way of the Gentiles; do not be dismayed at the signs of heaven. Jer. 10:2.

Such are the demons. These are the ones who laid down the doctrine of Fate. Their fundamental principle was the placing of animals in the heavens. For they dignified the creeping things on the earth with celestial honor. . . . They did this so that they themselves might be thought to remain in heaven. By placing the constellations there, they attempt to make the irrational course of life on earth appear to be rational. . . . Let them have their Fate! I am not willing to worship wandering stars! *Tatian (c. 160, E), 2.68.*

The Egyptians were the first to introduce astrology among men. Similarly, the Chaldeans [practiced it]. *Clement of Alexandria (c. 195, E), 2.317.*

Astrologers should not even be mentioned. . . . As a result of thinking that we are predestined by the unchangeable arrangement of the stars, men think that God is not to be sought after. I lay down this one proposition: that those angels—the deserters from God, the lovers of women—were likewise the discoverers of this curious art. And on that account, they were also condemned by God. . . . For we know the mutual alliance of magic and astrology. *Tertullian (c. 200, W), 3.65.*

The interpreters of the stars, then, were the first to announce Christ's birth, the first to present Him gifts . . . However, that practice had been allowed [to the Gentiles] until the Gospel, in order that after Christ's birth no one should thereafter interpret any one's birth by the heavens. *Tertullian (c. 200, W), 3.65.*

After the Gospel, you will nowhere find either sophists, Chaldeans, enchanters, diviners, or magicians—except as clearly punished. . . . You know nothing, astrologer, if you do not know that you should be a Christian. If you did know it, you should have known this also—that you should have nothing more to do with that profession of yours. *Tertullian (c. 200, W), 3.66.*

The Marcionites are very strongly addicted to astrology. *Tertullian (c. 207, W), 3.284.*

Now, lest anyone suppose the opinions propounded by the Chaldeans respecting astrological doctrine to be trustworthy and secure, we will not hesitate to furnish a brief refutation respecting them—establishing that the futile art is calculated both to deceive and blind the soul. *Hippolytus (c. 225, W), 5.24.*

[The Chaldeans] frame an account concerning the action of the zodiacal signs, to which they say the persons who are born become similar to. . . . For example, they say that one born under Leo will be brave and that one born under Virgo will have long straight hair, be of a fair complexion, childless, and modest. However, these statements, and others similar to them, are more deserving of laughter than of serious consideration. *Hippolytus (c. 225, W), 5.27.*

We are not forced by any necessity to act either rightly or wrongly—which those persons think is the case who say that the courses and movements of the stars are the cause of human actions. *Origen (c. 225, E), 4.240.*

[The Chaldeans and Egyptians] say that the stars revolve around the nature of the twelve signs of the Zodiac. *Methodius (c. 290, E), 6.341.*

To do good or evil is in our own power; it is not decided by the stars. *Methodius (c. 290, E), 6.343; extended discussion: 5.24–5.34, 5.43–5.46.*

SEE ALSO FATE; SPIRITISM.

ATHEISM

SEE ATOMS; CREATION; DEISM; EVOLUTION; SOVEREIGNTY AND PROVIDENCE OF GOD.

ATOMS

According to Epicurus, the atoms and the void are indestructible, and it is by a definite arrange-ment and adjustment of the atoms as they come together that all other formations are produced, including the body itself. *Justin Martyr (c. 160, E), 1.173.*

Those who deny that this arrangement of the whole world was perfected by the divine Reason, but assert that it was heaped together by certain fragments casually adhering to each other, seem to me to have neither mind, nor sense, nor even sight itself. For what can possibly be so obvious, so confessed, and so evident, when you lift your eyes up to heaven and look into the things that are below and around us, than that there is some Deity of most excellent intelligence. *Mark Minucius Felix (c. 200, W), 4.182.*

For there are those who, giving the name of atoms to certain imperishable and most minute bodies that are supposed to be infinite in number, . . . allege that these atoms, as they were carried along by chance in the void, all clashed fortuitously against each other in an unregulated whirl. They thereby commingled with one another in a multitude of forms. Entering into combination with each other, they gradually formed this world and all objects in it. . . . This was the opinion of Epicurus and Democritus. *Dionysius of Alexandria (c. 262, E), 6.85.*

Who can bear to hear it said that this mighty habitation, which is composed of heaven and earth and is called the "cosmos," . . . was established in all its order and beauty by those atoms that hold their course devoid of order and beauty? Or, that this same state of disorder has grown into this true cosmos of order? *Dionysius of Alexandria (c. 262, E), 6.86.*

Truly we have here a most marvelous democracy of atoms, where friends welcome and embrace friends! Where all are eager to journey together in one habitation! By their own determination, some have rounded themselves off into that mighty luminary the sun! *Dionysius of Alexandria (c. 262, E), 6.87; extended discussion: 6.84–6.89, 7.87–7.88.*

SEE ALSO CREATION; EPICURUS; EVOLUTION.

ATONEMENT

I. Atonement through Christ

II. Recapitulation in Christ

I. Atonement through Christ

How can one enter a strong man's house and plunder his goods, unless he first binds the strong man? And then he will plunder his house Matt. 12:29.

The Son of Man did not come to be served, but to serve, and to give His life a ransom for many. Matt. 20:28.

I am the good shepherd. The good shepherd gives his life for the sheep. John 10:11.

God was in Christ reconciling the world to Himself. 2 Cor. 5:19.

You ... once were alienated and enemies in your mind by wicked works, yet now He has reconciled in the body of His flesh through death. Col. 1: 21, 22.

He Himself likewise shared in the same, that through death He might destroy him who had the power of death, that is, the devil, and release those who through fear of death were all their lifetime subject to bondage. Heb. 2:14, 15.

But this Man, after He had offered one sacrifice for sins forever, sat down at the right hand of God. Heb. 10:12.

He Himself is the propitiation for our sins, and not for ours only but also for the whole world. 1 John 2:2.

Because of the love He had for us, Jesus Christ our Lord gave His blood for us by the will of God. He gave His flesh for our flesh, and His soul for our souls. *Clement of Rome (c. 96, W), 1.18.*

I mean Him who crucified my sin, along with him [Satan] who was the inventor of it. Christ has condemned all the deceit and malice of the devil under the feet of those who carry Him in their hearts. *Ignatius (c. 105, E), 1.129.*

The Father Himself placed upon Christ the burden of our iniquities. He gave His own Son as a ransom for us: the holy one for the transgressors, the blameless One for the wicked. ... For what other thing was capable of covering our sins than His righteousness? ... O sweet exchange! O unsearchable operation! O benefits surpassing all expectation! That the wickedness of many should be hid in a single righteous One, and that the righteousness of One should justify many transgressors. *Letter to Diognetus (c. 125–200), 1.28.*

Jesus Christ "bore our sins in His own body on the tree." *Polycarp (c. 135, E), 1.35.*

He Himself purged away their sins, having suffered many trials and undergone many labors. For no one is able to dig without labor and toil. He Himself, then, having purged away the sins of the people, showed them the paths of life by giving them the law which He received from His Father. *Hermas (c. 150, W), 2.35.*

The whole human race will be found to be under a curse. ... The Father of all wished His Christ, for the whole human family, to take upon Him the curses of all, knowing that, after He had been crucified and was dead, He would raise Him up. ... His Father wished Him to suffer this, in order that by His stripes the human race might be healed. *Justin Martyr (c. 160, E), 1.247.*

My brothers, do not say any evil thing against the One who was crucified. Do not treat with scorn the stripes by which everyone may be healed, even as we [Christians] are healed. *Justin Martyr (c. 160, E), 1.268.*

Corruption became inherent in nature. So it was necessary that He who wished to save us would be someone who destroyed the essential cause of corruption. And this could not be done other than by the life that is according to nature being united to that which had received corruption. For this would destroy the corruption. At the same time, it would preserve the body that had received it with immortality for the future. Therefore, it was necessary that the Word would become possessed of a body. This was so He could deliver us from the death of natural corruption. For if, as you suggest, He had simply warded off death from us by a simple nod, indeed death would not have approached us—on account of His will. However, we would have again become corruptible, for we carried about in ourselves that natural corruption. *Justin Martyr (c. 160, E), 1.301, as quoted by Leontius.*

When our Lord arose from the place of the dead, and trampled death under foot, and bound the strong one, and set man free, then the whole creation saw clearly that for man's sake the Judge was condemned. *Melito (c. 170), 8.756.*

He suffered for the sake of those who suffer, and He was bound for the sake of Adam's race, which was imprisoned. *Melito (c. 170), 8.758.*

In place of Isaac the just, a ram appeared for slaughter, in order that Isaac might be liberated from his bonds. The slaughter of this animal redeemed Isaac from death. In like manner, the Lord, being slain, saved us. Being bound, He loosed us. Being sacrificed, He redeemed us. *Melito (c. 170), 8.759.*

When He became incarnate and was made man, he began anew the long line of human beings. And He furnished us . . . with salvation—so that what we had lost in Adam (namely, to be in the image and likeness of God), we might recover in Christ Jesus. *Irenaeus (c. 180, E/W), 1.446.*

Christ fought and conquered. That is because He was man, contending for the fathers. Through obedience, He completely did away with disobedience. For He bound the strong man and set free the weak. He endowed His own handiwork with salvation, by destroying sin. For He is a most holy and merciful Lord, and He loves the human race. Therefore, as I have already said, He caused man to cleave to and to become one with God. For unless man had overcome the enemy of man, the enemy would not have been legitimately conquered. *Irenaeus (c. 180, E/W), 1.447, 448.*

For by no other means could we have attained to incorruptibility and immortality, unless we had been united to incorruptibility and immortality. But how could we be joined to incorruptibility and immortality—unless, first, incorruptibility and immortality had become that which we also are, so that the corruptible might be swallowed up by incorruptibility. *Irenaeus (c. 180, E/W), 1.448, 449.*

For at the first, Adam became a vessel in his [Satan's] possession, whom he did also hold under his power. That is, by bringing sin on him unjustly, and under color of immortality, he brought death upon him. For, while promising that they should be as gods, which was in no way possible for him to be, he created death in them. For that reason, he who had led man captive, was justly captured in his turn by God. But man, who had been led captive, was loosed from the bonds of condemnation. *Irenaeus (c. 180, E/W), 1.456.*

Abraham, according to his faith, followed the command of the Word of God. With a ready mind, he delivered up, as a sacrifice to God, his only-begotten and beloved son. This was to demonstrate that God also might be pleased to offer up for all his seed His own beloved and only-begotten Son, as a sacrifice for our redemption. *Irenaeus (c. 180, E/W), 1.467.*

By means of our first [parents], we were all brought into bondage, by being made subject to death. So at last, by means of the New Man, all who from the beginning were His disciples, having been cleansed and washed from things pertaining to death, can come to the life of God. *Irenaeus (c. 180, E/W), 1.493.*

In the last times, the Son was made a man among men, and He re-formed the human race. However, He destroyed and conquered man's enemy. So He gave to His handiwork victory against the adversary. *Irenaeus (c. 180, E/W), 1.495.*

How will man pass into God, unless God had first passed into man? . . . Yet, how could He have subdued him who was stronger than men, who had not only overcome man, but also retained him under his power? How could He have conquered him who had conquered, while he set free mankind, who had been conquered? To do these things, He had to be greater than man who had been conquered in this manner. *Irenaeus (c. 180, E/W), 1.507.*

This very thing was proclaimed beforehand: that a new thing should come to renew and quicken mankind. *Irenaeus (c. 180, E/W), 1.511.*

In no other way could we have learned the things of God, unless our Master, existing as the Word, had become man. For no other being had the power of revealing to us the things of the Father. *Irenaeus (c. 180, E/W), 1.526.*

Redeeming us by His own blood in a manner in harmony with reason, He gave Himself as a redemption for those who had been led into captivity. . . . The apostasy tyrannically and unjustly ruled over us. And it alienated us contrary to nature (for we were by nature the property of the omnipotent God), rendering us its own disciples. However, the Word of God, powerful in all things (and not defective with regard to His own justice) did righteously turn against that apostasy, and redeem His own property from it. For the apostasy had obtained dominion over us at the beginning, when it insatiably snatched away what was not its own. Now, Christ did not do this by violent means, but by means of persuasion. This is becoming to a God of counsel, who does not use violent means to obtain what He desires. In this manner, neither would justice be infringed upon, nor would the ancient handiwork of God go to destruction. *Irenaeus (c. 180, E/W), 1.527.*

In this manner, the Lord has redeemed us through His own blood, giving His soul for our souls, and His flesh for our flesh. He has also poured out the Spirit of the Father for the union and communion of God and man, actually imparting God to men by means of the Spirit. On the other hand, He has joined man to God by His own incarnation. And He will truly and lastingly bestow immortality upon us at His coming—through communion with God. *Irenaeus (c. 180, E/W), 1.527.*

The Word of the Father and the Spirit of God had become united with the ancient substance of Adam's formation. So it rendered man living and perfect, receptive of the perfect Father, in order that as in the natural [Adam] we all were dead, so in the spiritual [Adam] we may all be made alive. *Irenaeus (c. 180, E/W), 1.527.*

To do away with that disobedience of man that had taken place at the beginning by means of a tree, "He became obedient unto death, even the death of the cross." He thereby rectified that disobedience that had occurred by reason of a tree, through that obedience that was upon the tree [i.e., the cross].... In the first Adam, we had offended God Himself. For Adam did not perform God's commandment. However, in the second Adam, we are reconciled to God, being made obedient even unto death. For we were debtors to no one else but to Him whose commandment we had transgressed at the beginning.... By transgressing [God's] commandment, we became His enemies. Therefore, in the last times, the Lord has restored us into friendship through His incarnation. He has become "the Mediator between God and men," propitiating indeed for us the Father against whom we had sinned. He has cancelled our disobedience by His own obedience. He also conferred upon us the gift of communion with, and subjection to, our Maker. *Irenaeus (c. 180, E/W), 1.544.*

He is the God who is proclaimed in the Scriptures, to whom we were debtors, having transgressed His commandment.... Since He is the same One against whom we had sinned in the beginning, He is the One who grants forgiveness of sins in the end.... And in what way can sins be truly forgiven, unless it be that He

against whom we have sinned has Himself granted forgiveness "through the bowels of mercy of our God," in which "He has visited us" through His Son? [Luke 1:78]. *Irenaeus (c. 180, E/W), 1.545.*

In His work of recapitulation, He has summed up all things. He has waged war against our enemy. He has crushed him who had in the beginning led us away captives in Adam, and trampled upon his head. *Irenaeus (c. 180, E/W), 1.548.*

Therefore, the Lord declares himself to be the Son of man. For He comprised in Himself that original man out of whom the woman was fashioned. He did this so that, as our species went down to death through a conquered man, so we may ascend to life again through a victorious one. *Irenaeus (c. 180, E/W), 1.549.*

[After Satan tempted Him,] Christ spurned Satan ... as having been conquered out of the Law. So, by the commandments of the Law, which the Son of man observed, there was done away with that breaking of God's commandment that had occurred in Adam. *Irenaeus (c. 180, E/W), 1.459, 550.*

It was necessary that through man himself Satan would, when conquered, be bound with the same chains with which he had bound man. This was so that man, being set free, could return to his Lord, leaving to Satan those bonds by which man himself had been fettered—that is, sin. For when Satan is bound, man is set free. For "no one can enter a strong man's house and spoil his goods, unless he first binds the strong man himself." *Irenaeus (c. 180, E/W), 1.550.*

Satan is justly led captive, for he had led men unjustly into bondage. At the same time, man, who had been led captive in times past, was rescued from the grasp of his possessor, according to the tender mercy of God the Father. For He had compassion on His own handiwork, and gave salvation to it. *Irenaeus (c. 180, E/W), 1.550.*

By His own passion, He rescued us from offenses and sins. *Clement of Alexandria (c. 195, E), 2.257.*

[CHRIST SPEAKING:] For you I contended with Death, and I paid your death, which you owed for your former sins and your unbelief towards God. *Clement of Alexandria (c. 195, E), 2.598.*

About to be offered up and giving himself a ransom, he left for us a new testament: My love

I give unto you. And what and how great is it? For each of us, He gave His life—the equivalent for all. *Clement of Alexandria (c. 195, E), 2.601.*

Christ became man in the midst of men, to re-create our Adam through Himself. [He is Lord of] things under the earth, because He was also reckoned among the dead, preaching the Gospel to the souls of the saints. By death, he overcame death. *Hippolytus (c. 200, W), 5.209.*

As a young bull, . . . such was Christ in submitting voluntarily to the death of the flesh. Yet, He was not overcome by death. Although as man He became one of the dead, He remained alive in the nature of divinity. For Christ is the bull—an animal, above all, strong, neat, and devoted to sacred use. And the Son is Lord of all power, who had no sin, but rather offered Himself for us, a savor of a sweet smell to his God and Father. *Hippolytus (c. 205, W), 5.164.*

He passed through every stage in life in order that he Himself might serve as a law for persons of every age, and that, by being present among us, He might demonstrate His own manhood as a model for all men. He also did this so that by himself He could prove that God made nothing evil and that man possesses the capacity of self-determination. For he is able to both will and not to will. And he is endowed with power to do both. *Hippolytus (c. 225, W), 5.152.*

God therefore sent down into the virgin's womb His Word, as the good brother, who would blot out the memory of the evil brother. Hence, it was necessary that Christ should come forth for the salvation of man in that same condition of flesh into which man had entered ever since his condemnation. *Tertullian (c. 210, W), 3.536.*

You have already been ransomed by Christ—and that at a great price! *Tertullian (c. 211, W), 3.101.*

Should you ransom with money a man whom Christ has ransomed with His blood? . . . Being numbered with the transgressors, He was delivered up to death, nay, the death of the cross. All this took place so that He might redeem us from our sins. The sun ceded to us the day of our redemption. Hades gave back the right it had on us. *Tertullian (c. 212, W), 4.123.*

When that which was delivered with so much authority has come to pass, it shows that God—

having really become man—delivered to men the doctrines of salvation. *Origen (c. 225, E), 4.351.*

We were not helped by His original life, sunk as we were in sin. Therefore, He came down into our deadness in order that, He having died to sin, we might then receive that life of His that is forever. For we bear about in our body the dying of Jesus. *Origen (c. 228, E), 9.316.*

[Christ] was made like a lamb who is dumb before her shearer, so that we might be purified by His death. For His death is given as a sort of medicine against the opposing power and also against the sin of those who open their minds to the truth. For the death of Christ reduced to weakness those powers that war against the human race. And it set the life of each believer free from sin through a power beyond our words. He takes away sin until every enemy will be destroyed and death last of all—in order that the whole world may be free from sin. Therefore, John pointed to Him and said, "Behold! The Lamb of God who takes away the sin of the world." . . . His taking away sin is still going on. He is taking it away from every individual in the world until sin is taken away from the whole world. *Origen (c. 228, E), 4.316, 317.*

Christ is our Redemption because we had become prisoners and needed ransoming. *Origen (c. 228, E), 9.318.*

He submitted to death, purchasing us back by His own blood from him who had got us into his power, sold under sin. *Origen (c. 228, E), 9.377.*

As death came through one man, so also the justification of life is through one man. Had He not assumed humanity, we could not have received such a benefit we have from the Logos. *Origen (c. 228, E), 9.384.*

A man could not give anything as an exchange for his own life, but God gave an exchange for the life of us all, "the precious blood of Christ Jesus." Accordingly, "we were bought with a price," "having been redeemed, not with corruptible things as silver or gold, but with precious blood." *Origen (c. 245, E), 9.465.*

The Son also gave Himself to death for us, so that He was delivered up—not only by the Father—but also by Himself. *Origen (c. 245, E), 9.479.*

There is in the nature of things (for certain mysterious reasons that are difficult to be understood by the multitude) such a virtue that one just man—dying a voluntary death for the common good—might be the means of removing wicked spirits who are the cause of plagues, famine, storms, or similar calamities. Let those persons, therefore, who would disbelieve the statement that Jesus died on the cross on behalf of men, tell us whether they also refuse to accept the many accounts prevalent among both Greeks and barbarians of persons who have laid down their lives for the public advantage—in order to remove those evils that had fallen upon cities and countries? *Origen (c. 248, E), 4.409, 410.*

Christ is to be contemplated in our captive brethren. He, who redeemed us from the peril of death, is to be redeemed from the peril of captivity. He took us out of the jaws of the devil. He abides and dwells in us. And He redeemed us by His cross and blood. Now, He Himself can be rescued and redeemed by a sum of money from the hands of barbarians. . . . The Lord in His Gospel says, "I was sick, and you visited me." *Cyprian (c. 250, W), 5.355.*

He who is freed owes obedience to his Deliverer. *Cyprian (c. 250, W), 5.432.*

This gift of His mercy He confers upon us—by overcoming death in the trophy of the cross, by redeeming the believer with the price of His blood, by reconciling man to God the Father, by quickening our mortal nature with a heavenly regeneration. *Cyprian (c. 250, W), 5.465.*

This is Christ, who, as the Mediator of the two, puts on man so that He may lead them to the Father. What man is, Christ was willing to be—so that man may also be what Christ is. *Cyprian (c. 250, W), 5.468.*

The Son was willing to be sent and to become the Son of man, so that He could make us sons of God. . . . He underwent death so that He could present immortality to mortals. . . . At His coming, the Lord cured those wounds that Adam had borne. He healed the old poisons of the serpent. Thereafter, He gave a law to the sound man and bade him to sin no more, lest a worse thing should befall the sinner. . . . Those sins that had been previously committed are purged by the blood and sanctification of Christ. *Cyprian (c. 250, W), 5.476.*

He desired to re-create that Adam by means of the week, and to bring aid to His entire creation. He accomplished these things through the birth of His Son Jesus Christ, our Lord. *Victorinus (c. 280, W), 7.343.*

For man's salvation, He was made man in order to overcome death and to set all men free. In that He offered himself as a victim to the Father on our behalf, he was called a calf. *Victorinus (c. 280, W), 7.348.*

The devil, the traitor angel, thought that all men alike would perish by death. However, because Christ was not born of [human] seed, He owed nothing to death. Therefore, the devil could not devour Him—that is, detain Him in death. For on the third day, He rose again. *Victorinus (c. 280, W), 7.355.*

With this purpose, the Word assumed the nature of man so that, having overcome the serpent, He might by himself destroy the condemnation that had come into being along with man's ruin. For it was fitting that the Evil One should be overcome by none other than man, whom he had deceived and of whom he was boasting that he held in subjection. For in no other way was it possible for sin and condemnation to be destroyed except by creating anew that same man on whose account it had been said, "Dust you are and to dust you will return." Only in this way could the sentence be undone that had gone forth on all because of [Adam]. So that "as in Adam" at first "all die," so likewise "in Christ," who assumed the [nature and position of] Adam, should "all be made alive." *Methodius (c. 290, E), 6.319.*

"As in Adam, all die, even so in Christ all will be made alive." For He bore flesh for no other reason than to set the flesh free and raise it up. *Methodius (c. 290, E), 6.368.*

The Word descended into our world and was incarnate of our body. He did this so that—having fashioned it to a more divine image—He might raise it incorruptible (even though it had been dissolved by time). *Methodius (c. 290, E), 6.378.*

In the teaching of the church, He gave Himself up for the remission of sins. *Alexander of Lycopolis (c. 300, E), 6.251.*

He sent his Son as an ambassador to men, so He could turn them from their unholy and vain worship to the knowledge and worship of the true God. He also sent Him so that He could turn their minds from foolishness to wisdom, and from wickedness to deeds of righteousness. *Lactantius (c. 304–313, W), 7.114.*

He Himself is virtue and He Himself is righteousness. Accordingly, He descended so that He could teach these things and mold the character of man. *Lactantius (c. 304–313, W), 7.117.*

He gained life for us by overcoming death. *Lactantius (c. 304–313, W), 7.122.*

For this reason, therefore, a Mediator came—that is, God in the flesh—that the flesh might be able to follow Him. It was also so that He might rescue man from death—which has dominion over the flesh. *Lactantius (c. 304–313, W), 7.127.*

His teaching was about to have such might that the nations throughout the world could be given life through the knowledge of the true light. Thereby, they could arrive at the rewards of immortality. For previously, they were estranged from God and subject to death. *Lactantius (c. 304–313, W), 7.128.*

When He had determined to set man free, God sent as His Ambassador to the earth a Teacher of virtue, who could train men to innocence by healthful commandments. He sent a Teacher who could open the way of righteousness by works and deeds performed before their eyes. *Lactantius (c. 304–313, W), 7.128.*

Our Lord Jesus Christ endured man's condition on our behalf, so that He could destroy all sin and furnish us with the provision necessary for our entrance into eternal life. *Phileas (c. 307, E), 6.162.*

God sent down from heaven His incorporeal Son to take flesh upon Him in the virgin's womb. Thus, He was made man—the same as you. He came to save lost man and to collect all His scattered members. When Christ joined manhood to His Person, he united that which death had dispersed by the separation of the body. So Christ suffered that we should live forever. . . . He suffered shame for man's sake, to set him free from death. *Alexander of Alexandria (c. 324, E), 6.300.*

When our Lord was suffering upon the cross, the tombs were burst open, exposing Hades. The souls leaped forth, the dead returned to life, and many of them were seen in Jerusalem. . . . You see, therefore, how great the effect of Christ's death was. For no creature endured His demise with equal mind, nor did the elements His Passion. Furthermore, the earth did not retain His body, nor Hades His Spirit. *Alexander of Alexandria (c. 324, E), 6.301.*

As we have said, when the body of the Lord was hung upon the cross, the tombs were opened, Hades was unlocked, the dead received life again, and the souls were sent back again into the world. For the Lord had conquered Hades, had trodden down death, and had covered the enemy with shame. It was for that reason that the souls came forth from Hades and the dead appeared upon the earth. *Alexander of Alexandria (c. 324, E), 6.301; see also 1.454.*

II. Recapitulation

Recapitulation refers to the "summing up" of all things in Christ through the incarnation. By becoming human and living a perfect life, the Son restored fallen mankind to communion with God and undid the evil caused by Satan in the Garden of Eden. Irenaeus particularly developed this theme in his writings.

In Him we have redemption through His blood, . . . having made known to us the mystery of His will, according to His good pleasure which He purposed in Himself, that in the dispensation of the fullness of the times He might gather together [recapitulate] in one all things in Christ, both which are in heaven and which are on earth. Eph. 1:10.

He came to save all by means of Himself. I am referring to all who through Him are born again to God: infants, children, boys, youth, and old men. He therefore passed through every age. He became an infant for infants, thus sanctifying infants. He became a child for children. . . . At last, he came to death itself, so that He might be "the first-born from the dead." *Irenaeus (c. 180, E/W), 1.391.*

The Lord took dust from the earth and formed man. For that reason, He who is the Word, desiring to recapitulate Adam in Himself, rightly received a birth. For this enabled Him to gather up Adam from Mary, who was as yet a virgin. . . . If the former [Adam] was taken from the dust, and God was his Maker, it was necessary that the second [Adam] also, making a recapitulation in Himself, should be formed as man by God. . . . For if He had not received the substance of flesh from a human being, He would have been neither man nor the son of man. And if He was not made into what we are, He did no great thing in what He suffered and endured. But everyone will allow that we are a body taken from the earth, and a soul receiving spirit from God. Therefore, the Word of God was made into this, too, thereby recapitulating in Himself His own handiwork. *Irenaeus (c. 180, E/W), 1.454.*

The Lord, coming to the lost sheep, made recapitulation of so comprehensive a dispensation. Seeking after his own handiwork, it was necessary for him to save that very man who had been created after his image and likeness—that is, Adam.... Man had been created by God so that he might live. Now what if, after losing life (by being injured by the serpent who had corrupted him), man would not any more return to life? What if he were utterly abandoned to death? It would mean that God would have been conquered! It would mean the wickedness of the serpent would have prevailed over the will of God. *Irenaeus (c. 180, E/W), 1.455.*

Luke points out that the genealogy that traces the lineage of our Lord back to Adam contains seventy-two generations. This connects the end with the beginning, and indicates that He has summed up in Himself all nations dispersed from Adam forward and that he has summed up all languages and generations of men, together with Adam himself. *Irenaeus (c. 180, E/W), 1.455.*

It was for this reason that the Son of God, although He was perfect, passed through the state of infancy in common with the rest of mankind. He partook of it thus not for His own benefit, but for that of the infantile stage of man's existence, in order that man might be able to receive Him. *Irenaeus (c. 180, E/W), 1.521.*

He would not have been one truly possessing flesh and blood, by which He redeemed us, unless He had summed up in Himself the ancient formation of Adam. *Irenaeus (c. 180, E/W), 1.527.*

Through the instrumentality of a tree, we were made debtors to God. So also, by means of a tree [i.e., the cross], we can obtain the remission of our debt. *Irenaeus (c. 180, E/W), 1.545.*

The Lord then was manifestly coming to His own things, and was sustaining them by means of that creation that is supported by Himself. He was making a recapitulation of that disobedience that had occurred in connection with a tree, through the obedience that was upon a tree. Furthermore, the original deception was to be done away with—the deception by which that virgin Eve (who was already espoused to a man) was unhappily misled. That this was to be overturned was happily announced through means of the truth by the angel to the virgin Mary (who was also [espoused] to a man).... So although Eve disobeyed God, Mary was persuaded to be obedient to God. In this way, the virgin Mary might become the helper of the virgin Eve. And thus, as the human race fell into bondage to death by means of a virgin, so is it rescued by a virgin. Virginal disobedience has been balanced in the opposite scale by virginal obedience. For in the same way, the sin of the first created man received amendment by the correction of the First-Begotten, and the cunning of the serpent was conquered by the harmlessness of the dove. *Irenaeus (c. 180, E/W), 1.547.*

Into this Paradise, the Lord has introduced those who obey His call, "summing up in Himself all things that are in heaven and that are on earth." ... These things, therefore, He recapitulated in Himself. By uniting man to the Spirit, and causing the Spirit to dwell in man, He is Himself made the head of the Spirit, and gives the Spirit to be the head of man.... In His work of recapitulation, He has summed up all things. He has waged war against our enemy. He has crushed the one who had in the beginning led us away captives in Adam, and trampled upon his head. *Irenaeus (c. 180, W), 1.548.*

Indeed the enemy would not have been fairly vanquished, unless it was a man [born] of a woman who conquered him. For it was by means of a woman that he got the advantage over man at first, setting himself up as man's opponent. *Irenaeus (c. 180, E/W), 1.549.*

At the beginning, it was by means of food that [the enemy] persuaded man to transgress God's commandments (although man was not suffering hunger). Similarly, in the end the enemy did not succeed in persuading Christ, who was hungry, to take that food which proceeded from God. *Irenaeus (c. 180, E/W), 1.549; see also 1.541.*

SEE ALSO BLOOD OF CHRIST; FALL OF MAN; INCARNATION; JESUS CHRIST; SALVATION.

ATTRIBUTES OF GOD

SEE GOD, ATTRIBUTES OF.

AUGUSTUS CAESAR

Julius Octavius (27 B.C.–A.D. 14), the grand-nephew of Julius Caesar, became the first emperor of Rome. Because of his wise rulership, the Roman Senate gave him the title "Augustus." He was the reigning emperor when Jesus Christ was born.

Augustus, the founder of the empire, would not even accept the title of lord. For that, too, is a name for deity. *Tertullian (c. 197, W), 3.43.*

[Cicero] had learned that . . . Julius Octavius was the destined Augustus, the suppressor and destroyer of civil conflicts. Yet, at the time, Octavius was still only a little boy, was in a private station, and was personally unknown to Cicero. *Tertullian (c. 210, W), 3.224, 225.*

It was by the law of Augustus that the empire of Rome was established. *Hippolytus (c. 200, W), 5.214.*

Octavius Sebastus, or, as the Romans call him, Augustus . . . on returning to Rome . . . where he was educated, took hold of the principal place in the government. *Julius Africanus (c. 245, E), 6.135.*

Up until the time of Herod, [the Jews] did appear to retain some semblance of a kingdom. It was under Augustus that the first census took place among them and that they began to pay taxes. *Disputation of Archelaus and Manes (c. 320, E), 6.219.*

SEE ALSO ROMAN EMPIRE, ROMANS.

BABEL, TOWER OF

SEE TOWER OF BABEL.

BABYLON THE GREAT

Come, I will show you the judgment of the great harlot who sits on many waters. . . . The woman was arrayed in purple and scarlet, and adorned with gold and precious stones and pearls, having in her hand a golden cup full of abominations and the filthiness of her fornication. And on her forehead a name was written: "Mystery, Babylon the Great, the mother of harlots and of the abominations of the earth." And I saw the woman, drunk with the blood of the saints and with the blood of the martyrs of Jesus. Rev. 17:1–6.

So, again, Babylon, in [the writings of] our own John, is a figure of the city Rome. For she is equally great and proud of her sway. *Tertullian (c. 197, W), 3.162.*

That powerful state that presides over the seven mountains and very many waters has merited from the Lord the designation of a prostitute. *Tertullian (c. 198, W), 4.24.*

By a similar usage, in the writings of our John, Babylon is a figure of the city of Rome. For Rome is like Babylon in being great and proud in royal power and in warring against the saints of God. *Tertullian (c. 207, W), 3.333.*

We are called away from even *dwelling* in that Babylon of John's Revelation. How much more so its pomp! *Tertullian (c. 212, W), 3.101.*

Tell me, blessed John—apostle and disciple of the Lord—what did you see and hear concerning Babylon? Arise and speak! For it [i.e., Rome] sent you into banishment. *Hippolytus (c. 200, W), 5.211.*

. . . the great overthrow of Babylon, that is, the Roman state. *Victorinus (c. 280, W), 7.352.*

SEE ALSO REVELATION, BOOK OF; ROMAN EMPIRE, ROMANS.

BAPTISM

I. Meaning of baptism

II. Mode and description of baptism

III. The question of infant baptism

IV. Who may baptize?

V. Baptism by heretics

I. Meaning of baptism

Jesus answered, "Most assuredly, I say to you, unless one is born of water and the Spirit, he cannot enter the kingdom of God." John 3:5.

Then Peter said to them, "Repent, and let every one of you be baptized in the name of Jesus Christ for the remission of sins; and you will receive the gift of the Holy Spirit." Acts 2:38.

Arise and be baptized, and wash away your sins, calling on the name of the Lord. Acts 22:16.

For as many of you as were baptized into Christ have put on Christ. Gal. 3:27.

According to His mercy He saved us, through the washing of regeneration and renewing of the Holy Spirit. Tit. 3:5.

Let us draw near with a true heart in full assurance of faith, having our hearts sprinkled from an evil conscience and our bodies washed with pure water. Heb. 10:22.

There is also an antitype which now saves us, namely baptism (not the removal of the filth of the flesh, but the answer of a good conscience toward God). 1 Pet. 3:21.

Concerning the water, indeed, it is written, in reference to the Israelites, that they should not receive that baptism which leads to the remission of sins, but should procure another for themselves. *Barnabas (c. 70–130, E), 1.144.*

Blessed are they who, placing their trust in the cross, have gone down into the water.... We indeed descend into the water full of sins and defilement. However, we come up, bearing fruit in our heart, having the fear [of God] and the trust in Jesus in our spirit. *Barnabas (c. 70–130, E), 1.144.*

He was born and baptized so that by His passion He could purify the water. *Ignatius (c. 105, E), 1.57.*

I heard, sir, some teachers maintain that there is no other repentance than that which takes place, when we descended into the water and received remission of our former sins. *Hermas (c. 150, W), 2.22.*

Before a man bears the name of the Son of God, he is dead. But when he receives the seal, he lays aside his deadness and obtains life. The seal, then, is the water. They descend into the water dead, and they arise alive. *Hermas (c. 150, W), 2.49.*

At our birth, we were born without our own knowledge or choice, but by our parents coming together.... In order that we may not remain the children of necessity and of ignorance, but may become the children of choice and knowledge, and may obtain in the water the remission of sins formerly committed, there is pronounced over him who chooses to be born again, and has repented of his sins, the name of God the Father and Lord of the universe.... And in the name of Jesus Christ ... and in the name of the Holy Spirit. *Justin Martyr (c. 160, E), 1.183.*

This washing of repentance and knowledge of God has been ordained on account of the transgression of God's people, as Isaiah cries. Accordingly, we have believed and testify that the very baptism which he announced is alone able to purify those who have repented. And this is the water of life.... For what is the use of that baptism which cleanses only the flesh and body? Baptize the soul from wrath and from covetousness, from envy, and from hatred. *Justin Martyr (c. 160, E), 1.201.*

We who have approached God through Him have received, not carnal, but spiritual circumcision, which Enoch and those like him

observed. And we have received it through baptism by God's mercy, since we were sinners. And all men alike may obtain it. *Justin Martyr (c. 160, E), 1.216.*

But there is no other [way] than this: to become acquainted with this Christ; to be washed in the fountain spoken of by Isaiah for the remission of sins; and for the rest, to live sinless lives. *Justin Martyr (c. 160, E), 1.217.*

Christ has redeemed us by being crucified on the tree and by purifying us with water. *Justin Martyr (c. 160, E), 1.242.*

The things proceeding from the waters were blessed by God, that this also could be a sign of men being destined to receive repentance and remission of sins, through the water and bath of regeneration—as many as come to the truth and are born again. *Theophilus (c. 180, E), 2.101.*

When we come to refute them [the Gnostics], we will show in its proper place that this class of men have been instigated by Satan to a denial of that baptism which is regeneration to God. Thus, they have renounced the whole faith.... For the baptism instituted by the visible Jesus was for the remission of sins. *Irenaeus (c. 180, E/W), 1.346.*

But there are some of them [Gnostics] who assert that it is unnecessary to bring persons to the water. Rather, they mix oil and water together, and they place this mixture on the heads of those who are to be initiated.... This they maintain to be the redemption.... Other [heretics], however, reject all these practices, and maintain that the mystery of the unspeakable and invisible power should not to be performed by visible and corruptible creatures. ...These claim that the knowledge of the unspeakable Greatness is itself perfect redemption. *Irenaeus (c. 180, E/W), 1.346.*

When [do we bear] the image of the heavenly? Doubtless when he says, "You have been washed," believing in the name of the Lord, and receiving His Spirit. *Irenaeus (c. 180, E/W), 1.537.*

Man, with respect to that formation which was after Adam, having fallen into transgression, needed the bath of regeneration. Therefore, the Lord said to [the blind man] after He had smeared his eyes with the clay, "Go to Siloam and wash." By this means, He restored to him both confirmation and that regeneration that takes place by means of the bath. *Irenaeus (c. 180, E/W), 1.543.*

[Scripture] says, "And he dipped himself seven times in the Jordan." It was not for nothing that Naaman of old, when suffering from leprosy, was purified upon his being baptized. Rather, this was a symbol for us. For as we are lepers in sin, we are made clean from our old transgressions by means of the sacred water and the invocation of the Lord. We are spiritually regenerated as new-born babes, just as the Lord has declared: "Unless a man is born again through water and the Spirit, he will not enter into the kingdom of heaven." *Irenaeus (c. 180, E/W), 1.574.*

Being baptized, we are illuminated. Illuminated, we become sons. . . . This work is variously called grace, illumination, perfection, and washing. Washing, by which we cleanse away our sins. Grace, by which the penalties accruing to transgressions are remitted. Illumination, by which that holy light of salvation is beheld, that is, by which we see God clearly. *Clement of Alexandria (c. 195, E), 2.215.*

If He was perfect, why was He, the perfect one, baptized? It was necessary, they say, to fulfill the profession that pertained to humanity. *Clement of Alexandria (c. 195, E), 2.215.*

Straightway, on our regeneration, we attained that perfection after which we aspired. For we were illuminated, which is to know God. *Clement of Alexandria (c. 195, E), 2.215.*

And he who has just been regenerated—as the name necessarily indicates—and has been enlightened, is immediately delivered from darkness, and instantly receives the light. . . . Thus also, we who are baptized, having wiped off the sins that obscure the light of the Divine Spirit, have the eye of the spirit free, unimpeded, and full of light, by which alone we contemplate the Divine, the Holy Spirit flowing down to us from above. *Clement of Alexandria (c. 195, E), 2.216.*

Our transgressions were taken away by one Poeonian medicine, the baptism of the Word. We are washed from all our sins, and are no longer entangled in evil. This is the one grace of illumination, that our characters are not the same as before our washing. *Clement of Alexandria (c. 195, E), 2.216, 217.*

In the same way, therefore, we also repent of our sins, renounce our iniquities, and are purified by baptism. Thereby, we speed back to the eternal light as children of the Father. *Clement of Alexandria (c. 195, E), 2.217.*

The union of the Logos with baptism is like the agreement of milk with water. For, of all liquids, milk alone receives water. It allows itself to be mixed with water for the purpose of cleansing—just as baptism does for the remission of sins. *Clement of Alexandria (c. 195, E), 2.222.*

John prophesied up until the baptism of salvation. *Clement of Alexandria (c. 195, E), 2.331.*

This is what was said, "unless you are converted and become as children" [Matt. 28:3]. That is, unless you become pure in flesh and holy in soul by refraining from evil deeds. This shows that He would have us to be such, as also He generated us from our mother—the water. *Clement of Alexandria (c. 195, E), 2.439.*

The three days may represent the mystery of the seal [i.e., baptism], in which God is really believed. *Clement of Alexandria (c. 195, E), 2.462.*

The sins committed before faith are accordingly forgiven by the Lord—not that they may be undone, but as if they had not been done. *Clement of Alexandria (c. 195, E), 2.437.*

We were drawn out from the calamities of this world in which we were tarrying, perishing with thirst. We were revived by "drinking" . . . of the baptismal water. *Tertullian (c. 197, W), 3.170.*

Happy is our sacrament of water, in that, by washing away the sins of our early blindness, we are set free and admitted into eternal life. . . . We, like little fishes, after the example of our ichthus, Jesus Christ, are born in water. *Tertullian (c. 198, W), 3.669.*

Oh, miserable unbelief that denies to God His own properties, simplicity, and power! What then? Is it not wonderful, too, that death should be washed away by washing? *Tertullian (c. 198, W), 3.669.*

We nevertheless proceed to address this question, "How foolish and impossible it is to be formed anew by water! Pray tell, in what respect has this material substance merited a position of such high dignity?" . . . [TERTULLIAN'S ANSWER:] Water was the first to produce that which had life, so that it would be no wonder in baptism if waters know how to give life. *Tertullian (c. 198, W), 3.670.*

Therefore, after the waters have been (in a manner) endowed with medicinal virtue through the intervention of the angel, the spirit is physically washed in the waters, and the flesh is spiritually cleansed in the same water. *Tertullian (c. 198, W), 3.671.*

[The waters] that used to remedy bodily defects, now heal the spirit. The waters that used to bring temporal health, now renew eternal health. The waters that set free but once in the year, now daily save people en masse, death being done away through washing of sins. Once the guilt is removed, the penalty is, of course, removed as well. . . . It is not that in the waters we obtain the Holy Spirit. Rather, in the water, under the angel, we are cleansed and prepared for the Holy Spirit. . . . Thus, too, does the angel, the witness of baptism, "make the paths straight" for the Holy Spirit. For He is about to come upon us. The "paths are made straight" by the washing away of sins, which faith obtains, sealed in the Father, the Son, and the Holy Spirit. *Tertullian (c. 198, W), 3.672.*

Now, the teaching is laid down that "without baptism, salvation is attainable by no one." This is based primarily on the ground of that declaration of the Lord, who says, "Unless one is born of water he has not life." However, when this is laid down, there immediately arise scrupulous (or rather, audacious) doubts on the part of some. *Tertullian (c. 198, W), 3.674, 675.*

"Unless a man has been born again of water and Spirit, he will not enter into the kingdom of the heavens." These words have tied faith to the necessity of baptism. Accordingly, all thereafter who became believers were baptized. So it was, too, that Paul, when he believed, was baptized. *Tertullian (c. 198, W), 3.676.*

We, then, enter the font once. Our sins are washed away once, for they should never be repeated. *Tertullian (c. 198, W), 3.676.*

Know that baptism is not rashly to be administered. . . . "Give not the holy thing to the dogs, nor cast your pearls before swine." *Tertullian (c. 198, W), 3.678.*

Easter [Gr. *pascha*] provides a more than usually solemn day for baptism—when the Lord's passion, in which we are baptized, was com-

pleted. Nor will it be incongruous to interpret figuratively the fact that, when the Lord was about to celebrate the last Passover, He said to the disciples who were sent to make preparation, "You will meet a man bearing water." . . . After that, Pentecost is a most joyous time for conferring baptisms. . . . However, every day is the Lord's. Every hour, every time, is appropriate for baptism. If there is a difference in the solemnity, there is no distinction in the grace. *Tertullian (c. 198, W), 3.678.*

Therefore, blessed ones, whom the grace of God awaits, when you ascend from that most sacred bath of your new birth and spread your hands for the first time in the house of your mother, together with your brethren, ask from the Father, ask from the Lord, that His own specialties of grace and distributions of gifts may be supplied to you. *Tertullian (c. 198, W), 3.679.*

Let not the fact that Jesus Himself did not baptize trouble anyone. For into what would He have baptized? Into repentance? Of what use, then, was His forerunner? Into remission of sins? But He gave this by a word. Into Himself, whom by humility He was concealing? Into the Holy Spirit, who had not yet descended from the Father? Into the church, which His apostles had not yet founded? *Tertullian (c. 198, W), 3.674.*

I do not deny that the divine benefit (that is, the putting away of sins) is in every way certain to those who are about to enter the [baptismal] water. But what we have to labor for is, that it may be granted us to attain that blessing. For who will grant to you—a man of such faithless repentance—one single sprinkling of any water whatever? . . . However, some think that God is under a necessity of bestowing what He has promised [to give] even on the unworthy. So they turn His liberality into His slavery! . . . For do not many afterwards fall out of [grace]? Is not this gift taken away from many? *Tertullian (c. 203, W), 3.661.*

That baptismal washing is a sealing of faith, which faith is begun and is commended by the faith of repentance. We are not washed in order that we may cease sinning, but because *we have ceased,* since in heart we have been bathed already. For the first baptism of a hearer is this: a perfect fear. . . . If it is only after the baptismal waters that we cease sinning, it is out of necessity, not of free will. *Tertullian (c. 203, W), 3.662.*

I see no coherence and consistency [in Marcion]. No, not even in the very sacrament of his faith! For what end does baptism serve, according to him? If it is the remission of sins, how will he demonstrate that he remits sins, when [his God] affords no evidence that He retains them? . . . Marcion therefore seals a man who had never been unsealed in respect of [his God]. He washes a man who had never been defiled so far as [his God] was concerned. And into the sacrament of salvation, he wholly plunges that flesh which is beyond the pale of salvation [according to Marcion]! No farmer will irrigate ground that will yield him no fruit in return—unless he is as silly as Marcion's God! *Tertullian (c. 207, W), 3.293.*

The cleansing of the Syrian [i.e., Naaman] rather portrayed to the nations of the world their own cleansing in Christ their Light. . . . For the virtue and fullness of the one baptism was thus solemnly imputed to Christ. For He alone was one day to establish on earth—not only revelation—but also a baptism endowed with bountiful power. *Tertullian (c. 207, W), 3.356.*

"Unless a man is born of water and of the Spirit, he cannot enter into the kingdom of God"—in other words, he cannot be holy. Every soul, then, by reason of its birth, has its nature in Adam until it is born again in Christ. Moreover, it is unclean all the time that it remains without this regeneration. And because it is unclean, it is actively sinful. *Tertullian (c. 210, W), 3.220.*

The flesh is the clothing of the soul. The uncleanness, indeed, is washed away by baptism. *Tertullian (c. 213, W), 3.646.*

The ropes that stretch around her [the ship of the church] are the love of Christ, which binds the church. The net that she bears with her is the bath of the regeneration that renews the believing, from which too are these glories. Just like the wind, the Spirit from heaven is present, by whom those who believe are sealed. *Hippolytus (c. 200, W), 5.217.*

Matthew alone adds the words, "to repentance," teaching us that the benefit of baptism is connected with the *intention* of the baptized person. To him who repents, it is saving. However, to him who comes to it without repentance, it will produce greater condemnation. *Origen (c. 228, E), 9.367.*

Regeneration did not take place with John [the Baptist]. However, with Jesus, through His disciples, it does occur. What is called the bath of regeneration takes place with renewal of the Spirit. For the Spirit, as well, now comes. It comes from God and is over and above the water. Yet, it does not come to all after the water. *Origen (c. 228, E), 9.367.*

"By the bath of regeneration," they were born as new-born babes. *Origen (c. 245, E), 9.491.*

It is the Holy Spirit who effects with water the second birth, as a certain seed of divine generation. It is a consecration of a heavenly birth and the pledge of a promised inheritance. *Novatian (c. 235, W), 5.641.*

In baptism, the coarse garment of your birth is washed. . . . You have once been washed. Shall you be able to be immersed again? *Commodianus (c. 240, W), 4.212.*

By the help of the water of new birth, the stain of former years had been washed away, and a light from above—serene and pure—had been infused into my reconciled heart. Then, by the agency of the Spirit breathed from heaven, a second birth had restored me to a new man. *Cyprian (c. 250, W), 5.276.*

. . . from that death which once the blood of Christ extinguished and from which the saving grace of baptism and of our Redeemer has delivered us. *Cyprian (c. 250, W), 5.332.*

By baptism, the Holy Spirit is received. . . . The Lord speaks to the Samaritan woman, saying, "Whoever drinks of this water will thirst again. But whoever drinks of the water that I will give him will not thirst forever." By this, He signified the very baptism of saving water, which indeed is once received and is not again repeated. . . . The Lord, when He came, manifested the truth of baptism . . . in commanding that this faithful water—the water of life eternal—should be given to believers in baptism. *Cyprian (c. 250, W), 5.360.*

From [baptism] springs the whole origin of faith, the saving access to the hope of life eternal, and the divine condescension for purifying and quickening the servants of God. For if anyone could be [truly] baptized by heretics, he certainly could also obtain remission of sins. *Cyprian (c. 250, W), 5.382.*

He who has been sanctified, his sins being put away in baptism, and has been spiritually reformed into a new man, has become fitted for receiving the Holy Spirit. *Cyprian (c. 250, W), 5.387.*

The blessed apostle sets forth and proves that baptism is that by which the old man dies and the new man is born, saying, "He saved us by the washing of regeneration." *Cyprian (c. 250, W), 5.388.*

One is not born by the imposition of hands when he receives the Holy Spirit. Rather, it is in baptism. Thereafter, being already born, he may receive the Holy Spirit. *Cyprian (c. 250, W), 5.388.*

Since in baptism, every person has his own sins remitted, the Lord proves and declares in His Gospel that sins can only be put away by those who have the Holy Spirit. *Cyprian (c. 250, W), 5.400.*

It is clear that the devil is driven out in baptism by the faith of the believer. And if that faith should fail afterwards, he returns. *Cyprian (c. 250, W), 5.402.*

They who still are of the earth by their first birth can begin to be of heaven by being born of water and of the Spirit. *Cyprian (c. 250, W), 5.452.*

In the bath of saving water, the fire of Gehenna is extinguished. *Cyprian (c. 250, W), 5.476.*

In the baptism of water, there is received the remission of sins. *Cyprian (c. 250, W), 5.497.*

The old baptism should cease and a new one should begin. . . . Also, according to John: "Unless a man is born of water and of the Spirit, he cannot enter into the kingdom of God." *Cyprian (c. 250, W), 5.511.*

Unless a man has been baptized and born again, he cannot attain unto the kingdom of God. In the Gospel according to John: "Unless a man is born again of water and the Spirit, he cannot enter into the kingdom of God." *Cyprian (c. 250, W), 5.542.*

All sins are put away in baptism. In the first Epistle of Paul to the Corinthians: . . . "And these things indeed you were. But you are washed; but you are sanctified in the name of our Lord Jesus Christ." *Cyprian (c. 250, W), 5.551.*

The second birth, which occurs in baptism, begets sons of God. *Firmilian (c. 256, E), 5.393.*

Nemesianus of Thubunae said: "The baptism that heretics and schismatics bestow is not the true one. . . . In the Gospel our Lord Jesus Christ spoke with His divine voice, saying, "Unless a man is born again of water and the Spirit, he cannot enter the kingdom of God." . . . Therefore, unless they receive saving baptism in the catholic church, which is one, they cannot be saved. Rather, they will be condemned with the carnal in the Judgment of the Lord Christ. *Seventh Council of Carthage (c. 256, W), 5.566.*

Munnulus of Girba said: "Brethren, the truth of our mother, the catholic church, has always remained and still remains with us—especially in the Trinity of baptism." *Seventh Council of Carthage (c. 256, W), 5.567.*

Our salvation is founded in the baptism of the Spirit, which for the most part is associated with the baptism of water. *Treatise on Re-Baptism (c. 257, W), 5.673.*

Thus, cleaving to the baptism of men, the Holy Spirit either goes before or follows it. Or failing the baptism of water, it falls upon those who believe. *Treatise on Re-Baptism (c. 257, W), 5.676.*

They ask that their reproach may be taken away—that is, that they might be cleansed from their sins. For the reproach is the original sin that is taken away in baptism. They then begin to be called Christians. *Victorinus (c. 280, W), 7.346.*

Christ willingly suffered death for her, that He might present the church to Himself glorious and blameless—having cleansed her by the bath. . . . For in this way, too, the command, "Be fruitful and multiply," is duly fulfilled. . . . For in no other way could the church conceive believers and give them the new birth through the bath of regeneration, except by Christ emptying Himself for their sake, so that He might be contained by them. *Methodius (c. 290, E), 6.319, 320.*

Those who are born again by the bath receive . . . of His holiness and of His glory. . . . The illuminated receive the Comforter, the Spirit of truth, and they are appropriately born again to incorruption. *Methodius (c. 290, E), 6.320.*

This denotes the faith of those who are cleansed from corruption in the bath [i.e., baptism]. *Methodius (c. 290, E), 6.336.*

Otherwise, we would not do wrong after baptism, for we would be entirely and absolutely free from sin. However, even after believing and after the time of being touched by the water of sanctification, we are oftentimes found in sin. *Methodius (c. 290, E), 6.365.*

Man is born mortal. He afterwards becomes immortal when he begins to live in conformity with the will of God. That is, he begins to follow righteousness.... And this takes place when man, purified in the heavenly bath, lays aside his infancy along with all the pollution of his past life. Then, having received an increase of divine vigor, he becomes a perfect and complete man. *Lactantius (c. 304–313, W), 7.201.*

In this we also have the instruction delivered by Peter ... and the faith of those present and their salvation by baptism. *Pamphilus (c. 309, E), 6.166.*

If he was not baptized, neither are any of us baptized. Yet, if there is no baptism, neither will there be any remission of sins. Rather, every man will die in his own sins. *Disputation of Archelaus and Manes (c. 320, E), 6.228.*

Black I was in sins, but I am comely. For I have repented and converted. I have put away that hateful hue in baptism. For He, the Savior of all creatures, has washed me in His innocent blood. *Canticle of Mar (date uncertain, E), 8.654.*

When they wish to repent, we receive the pagans into the church to hear the Word. However, we do not admit them to communion until they have received the seal of baptism and are made complete Christians. *Apostolic Constitutions (compiled c. 390, E), 7.414.*

He who out of contempt will not be baptized will be condemned as an unbeliever. He will be reproached as ungrateful and foolish. For the Lord says, "Unless a man is baptized of water and of the Spirit, he will by no means enter into the kingdom of heaven." And again: "He who believes and is baptized will be saved. But he who does not believe will be condemned." However, he may say, "When I am dying, I will be baptized, lest I should afterwards sin and defile my baptism." Such a person is ignorant of God, and he forgets his own mortal nature. For it is written, "Do not delay to turn unto the Lord, for you do not know what the next day will bring forth." Apostolic Constitutions (compiled c. 390, E), 7.457; see also 3.580; extended discussion: 3.669–3.679.

II. Mode and description of baptism

... baptizing them in the name of the Father and of the son and of the Holy Spirit. Matt. 28:19.

Now John also was baptizing in Aenon near Salim, because there was much water there. John 3:23.

Both Philip and the eunuch went down into the water, and he baptized him. Acts 8:38.

Concerning baptism, baptize in this manner: Having first said all these things, baptize into the name of the Father, the Son, and the Holy Spirit—in living water. But if you have no living water, baptize into other water. If you cannot baptize in cold water, baptize in warm. But if you do not have either, pour out water three times upon the person's head in the name of the Father, the Son, and the Holy Spirit. However, before the baptism, let the baptizer fast, and the one to be baptized, together with whoever else can. But you will instruct the one to be baptized to fast one or two days before [the baptism]. *Didache (c. 80–140, E), 1.379.*

The apostles themselves also gave them the seal of the preaching [i.e., baptism]. Accordingly, they descended with them into the water and ascended again. *Hermas (c. 150, W), 2.49.*

I will also relate the manner in which we dedicated ourselves to God when we had been made new through Christ.... As many as are persuaded and believe that what we teach and say is true, and undertake to be able to live accordingly, are instructed to pray and to entreat God with fasting, for the remission of their past sins. The rest of us pray and fast with them. They are brought up by us where there is water, and are regenerated in the same manner in which we were regenerated ourselves. They there receive the washing with water in the name of God (the Father and Lord of the universe), of our Savior Jesus Christ, and of the Holy Spirit. For Christ also said, "Unless you are born again, you will not enter into the kingdom of heaven." *Justin Martyr (c. 160, E), 1.183.*

I will turn to that highest authority of our "seal" itself. When entering the water, we make profession of the Christian faith in the words of its rule. We then bear public testimony that we have renounced the devil, his pomp, and his angels. *Tertullian (c. 197, W), 3.81.*

Do we not renounce and rescind that baptismal pledge, when we cease to bear its testimony? *Tertullian (c. 197, W), 3.89.*

With great simplicity, without pomp, without any considerable novelty of preparation, and without expense, a man is dipped in water. Amid the utterance of some few words, he is moistened, and then rises again, not much the [physically] cleaner. Because of that, the consequent attainment of eternity is esteemed the more incredible. *Tertullian (c. 198, W), 3.669.*

It makes no difference whether a man is washed in a sea or a pool, a stream or a fountain, a lake or a trough. . . . All waters . . . attain the sacramental power of sanctification. For the Spirit immediately supervenes from the heavens and rests over the waters, sanctifying them through Himself. And being thus sanctified, they acquire at the same time the power of sanctifying. *Tertullian (c. 198, W), 3.670, 671.*

When we have come from the font, we are thoroughly anointed with a blessed unction [i.e., oil]. This practice comes from the old discipline, where on entering the priesthood, men used to be anointed with oil from a horn. . . . In our case, the oil runs physically, but it profits us spiritually. It is similar to the act of baptism itself, which is also physical—in that we are plunged in water. Yet, its effect is spiritual, in that we are freed from sins. . . . Next, the hand is laid on us, invoking and inviting the Holy Spirit through a benediction. . . . This is derived from the old sacramental rite in which Jacob blessed his grandsons who were born of Joseph—Ephraim and Manasseh—with his hands laid on them and crossed. . . . Then that most Holy Spirit willingly descends from the Father over our cleansed and blessed bodies. *Tertullian (c. 198, W), 3.672, 673.*

Those who are about to enter baptism should pray with repeated prayers, fasts, and bendings of the knee—with all-night vigils and with the confession of all past sins. This way they may express the meaning even of the baptism of John. The Scripture says, "They were baptized, confessing their own sins." *Tertullian (c. 198, W), 3.678, 679.*

From our sacrament itself, we should draw our interpretation that practices of that kind are opposed to the faith. For how have we renounced the devil and his angels, if we make [idols to] them? *Tertullian (c. 200, W), 3.64.*

Marcion washes a man who had never been defiled so far as [his God] was concerned. And into the sacrament of salvation, he wholly plunges that flesh which is beyond the pale of salvation [according to him]! *Tertullian (c. 207, W), 3.293.*

According to Marcion, the flesh is not immersed in the water of the sacrament, unless it is in the state of virginity, widowhood, or celibacy. *Tertullian (c. 207, W), 3.293.*

Now the covenant you have made respecting [the devil] is to renounce him, his pomp, and his angels. Such is your agreement in this matter. Now . . . you must never think of getting back any of the things that you have renounced and have given back to him. Otherwise, he may summon you before God the Judge as a fraudulent man, and a transgressor of your agreement. *Tertullian (c. 210, W), 3.216.*

When we are going to enter the water, but a little before—in the presence of the congregation and under the hand of the president—we solemnly profess that we disown the devil, his pomp, and his angels. Upon that, we are immersed [Latin: *mergo*, to dip, to immerse] three times, making a somewhat ampler pledge than the Lord has appointed in the Gospel. Then, when we are taken up, we taste first of all a mixture of milk and honey. Then, from that day, we refrain from the daily bath for a whole week. [THE PRACTICE OF PARTAKING OF MILK AND HONEY AND REFRAINING FROM BATHING WERE APPARENTLY A LOCAL CUSTOM, AS NO OTHER WRITERS MAKE MENTION OF THIS PRACTICE.] *Tertullian (c. 211, W), 3.94.*

He commands them to baptize into the Father, the Son, and the Holy Spirit—not into a unipersonal God. And, indeed, it is not once only—but three times—that we are immersed into the three Persons, at the mention of each individual name. *Tertullian (c. 213, W), 3.623.*

It is required, then, that the water should first be cleansed and sanctified by the priest, so that it may wash away by its baptism the sins of the man who is baptized. For the Lord says by Ezekiel the prophet: "Then I will sprinkle clean water upon you, and you will be cleansed from all your filthiness." . . . The very question that is asked in baptism is a witness of the truth. For when we say, "Do you believe in eternal life and remission of sins through the holy church?" we are saying that remission of sins is not granted except in the church. *Cyprian (c. 250, W), 5.376.*

There is no ground for anyone . . . to oppose us in the name of Christ and to say, "All who are baptized everywhere, and in any manner, in the name of Jesus Christ, have obtained the grace of baptism." . . . The Son alone, without the Father (or against the Father) cannot be of advantage to anybody. It is the same as with the Jews. They boasted as to their having the Father. Yet, the Father would profit them nothing unless they believed on the Son whom He had sent. . . . There cannot be a hope of salvation except by knowing the two together. How, when God the Father is not known—nay, is even blasphemed—can they who among the heretics are said to be baptized in the name of Christ be judged to have obtained the remission of sins? . . . Christ Himself commands the pagans to be baptized in the full and united Trinity. *Cyprian (c. 250, W), 5.383.*

Someone may object, saying that Novatian . . . baptizes with the same symbol with which we baptize, knows the same God and Father, the same Christ the Son, the same Holy Spirit, and that for this reason he may claim the power of baptizing—namely, that he does not seem to differ from us as to the baptismal questions. *Cyprian (c. 250, W), 5.399.*

You have also asked, dearest son, what I thought of those who obtain God's grace in sickness and weakness. Are they to be considered legitimate Christians, for they have not been *bathed* with the saving water, but only *sprinkled?* On this point, my shyness and modesty prejudges no one. I prevent no one from feeling what he thinks right and from doing what he feels to be right. As far as my limited understanding conceives it, I think that the divine benefits can in no respect be mutilated and weakened. Nothing less can occur in that case where, with full and entire faith both of the giver and the receiver, what is drawn from the divine gifts is accepted. . . . In the sacraments of salvation, when necessity compels, and God bestows his mercy, the divine methods confer the whole benefit on believers. *Cyprian (c. 250, W), 5.400, 401.*

The dove, flying about through the air over the water, was sent out three times from the ark. This signified the sacraments of our church. *Treatise against Novatian (c. 255), 5.658.*

Those who are called antichrists cannot administer the grace of saving baptism. . . . Water sanctified in the church by the prayer of the priest washes away sins. . . . By the regeneration of baptism, they may then come to the promise of Christ. . . . Sins are not remitted except in the baptism of the church. . . . If there is anyone who says that the grace of baptism is with heretics, he must first show and prove that the church is among them. *Seventh Council of Carthage (c. 256, W), 5.567.*

. . . immediately they have descended into the water. *Treatise on Re-Baptism (c. 257, W), 5.676.*

He overturns faith and confession, which go before baptism. *Dionysius of Alexandria (c. 262, E), 6.103.*

[The bishop] . . . will anoint the head of those who are to be baptized (whether they are men or women) with the holy oil, as a representation of the spiritual baptism. After that, either you, the bishop, or a presbyter that is under you, will in the solemn form pronounce over them the Father, the Son, and the Holy Spirit, and will dip them in the water. And let a deacon receive the man and a deaconess the woman. . . . After that, let the bishop anoint with ointment those who are baptized. *Apostolic Constitutions (compiled c. 390, E), 7.431.*

You should anoint the person beforehand with the holy oil and then baptize him with the water. Finally, you should seal him with the ointment. This is so that the anointing with oil may be the participation of the Holy Spirit, that the water may be the symbol of death, and that the ointment may be the seal of the covenants. However, if there is neither oil nor ointment, water is sufficient both for the anointing and for the seal, as well as for the confession of Him who is dead, or in fact is dying together [with Christ]. However, before baptism, let the candidate fast. For even the Lord, when He was first baptized by John and lived in the wilderness, afterward fasted forty days and forty nights. Now, He fasted *after* baptism, because He Himself had no need of cleansing, fasting, or purgation. For He was by nature pure and holy. . . . But he who is to be initiated into His death should first fast, and then be baptized. *Apostolic Constitutions (compiled c. 390, E), 7.469.*

When the catechumen is to be baptized, let him learn what is involved in the renunciation of the devil and the joinder of himself to Christ.

For it is appropriate that he should first abstain from things contrary and then be admitted to the mysteries. He must beforehand purify his heart from all wickedness.... For even our Lord exhorted us in this manner, saying first, "Make disciples of all nations." But then he adds: "and baptize them into the name of the Father, the Son, and the Holy Spirit." Therefore, let the candidate for baptism declare his renunciation in this manner: "I renounce Satan, his works, his pomps, his worship, his angels, his falsehoods, and all things that are under him." And after his renunciation, let him make his public association, saying: "I associate myself to Christ and believe, and am baptized into one Unbegotten Being, the only true God Almighty . . ." [here follows the creed].

And after this vow, he comes next to the anointing with oil. Now, this is blessed by the high priest [i.e., bishop] for the remission of sins. It is the first preparation for baptism. For he calls upon the Unbegotten God, the Father of Christ, . . . that He will sanctify the oil in the name of the Lord Jesus and impart to it spiritual grace and efficacious strength.... After this, he comes to the water and blesses and glorifies the Lord God Almighty. . . . Next, when he has baptized the person in the name of the Father, the Son, and the Holy Spirit, he will anoint him with ointment.... After this, let him stand up and pray the prayer that the Lord taught us. Of necessity, he who is risen again should stand up and pray, for he that has been raised up stands upright. Therefore, let him who has been dead with Christ, and is raised up with Him, stand up. But let him pray towards the east. *Apostolic Constitutions (compiled c. 390, E), 7.477.*

If any bishop or presbyter does not perform the three immersions of the one initiation—but performs only one immersion into the death of Christ—let him be deprived. For the Lord did not say, "Baptize into my death." Rather, He said, "Go and make disciples of all nations, baptizing them into the name of the Father, the Son, and the Holy Spirit." Therefore, O bishops, baptize three times into one Father, and Son, and Holy Spirit, according to the will of Christ. *Apostolic Constitutions (compiled c. 390, E), 7.503.*

III. The question of infant baptism

He came to save all persons by means of Himself—all, I say, who through Him are born again to God—infants, children, boys, youth, and old men. *Irenaeus (c. 180, E/W), 1.391.*

And so, according to the circumstances, disposition, and even the age of each individual, the delay of baptism is preferable. This is particularly true in the case of little children. For why is it necessary—if baptism itself is not so necessary—that the sponsors likewise should be thrust into danger? . . . Let the children come, then, while they are growing up. Let them come while they are learning—while they are learning *where* to come. Let them become Christians when they have become able to know Christ. Why does the innocent period of life hasten to the remission of sins? . . . If anyone understands the weighty importance of baptism, he will fear its reception more than its delay. Sound faith is secure of salvation. *Tertullian (c. 198, W), 3.678.*

In respect of the case of the infants, you say that they should not be baptized within the second or third day after their birth—that the law of ancient circumcision should be regarded. So you think that one who has just been born should not be baptized and sanctified within the eighth day. However, we all thought very differently in our council.... Rather, we all believe that the mercy and grace of God is not to be refused to anyone born of man. . . . As far as we can, we must strive that no soul be lost, if at all possible. For what is lacking to him who has once been formed in the womb by the hand of God? *Cyprian (c. 250, W), 5.353, 354.*

Moreover, belief in divine Scripture declares to us that among all—whether infants or those who are older—there is the same equality of the divine gift. . . . Otherwise, it would seem that the very grace which is given to the baptized is given either more, or less, depending on the age of the receivers. However, the Holy Spirit is not given with measure. Rather, it is given alike to all, by the love and mercy of the Father. . . . For although the infant is still fresh from its birth, yet it is not such that anyone should shudder at kissing it in giving grace and in making peace. *Cyprian (c. 250, W), 5.354.*

Even to the greatest sinners and to those who have sinned much against God, when they subsequently believe, remission of sins is granted. Nobody is hindered from baptism and from grace. How much more should we shrink from hindering an infant. For he, being lately born, has not sinned—other than, in being born after the flesh according to Adam, he has contracted the contagion of the ancient death at its earliest birth. For this reason, he more easily approaches the reception of the forgiveness of sins. For to him are remitted—not his own sins—but the sins of another. Therefore, dearest brother, this was our opinion in council that no one should be hindered by us from baptism and from the grace of God. *Cyprian (c. 250, W), 5.354.*

Baptize your infants also and bring them up in the nurture and admonition of God. For He says, "Allow the little children to come unto me and do not forbid them." *Apostolic Constitutions (compiled c. 390, E), 7.457.*

IV. Who may baptize?

Of giving [baptism], the chief priest (who is the bishop) has the right. In the next place, the presbyters and deacons—yet, not without the bishop's authority, on account of the honor of the church. For when it is preserved, peace is preserved. In addition to these, laymen have the right. For what is equally received can be equally given. So, unless bishops, presbyters, or deacons are present at that location, other disciples are called to the work. . . . But how much more is the rule of reverence and modesty necessary to laymen—seeing that these powers belong to their superiors. . . . The most holy apostle has said, "all things are lawful, but not all expedient." *Tertullian (c. 198, W), 3.677.*

But the woman of audacity, who has usurped the power to teach, will surely not give birth for herself likewise to a right of baptizing! *Tertullian (c. 198, W), 3.677.*

[The bishop] has begotten you again to the adoption of sons by water and the Spirit. *Apostolic Constitutions (compiled c. 390, E), 7.410.*

[The bishops are] the ambassadors of God, who have regenerated you by water and endowed you with the fullness of the Holy Spirit. *Apostolic Constitutions (compiled c. 390, E), 7.412.*

[The bishop] . . . will anoint the head of those who are to be baptized (whether they are men or women) with the holy oil, as a representation of the spiritual baptism. After that, either you, the bishop, or a presbyter that is under you, will in the solemn form pronounce over them the

Father, the Son, and the Holy Spirit, and will dip them in the water. *Apostolic Constitutions (compiled c. 390, E), 7.431.*

V. Baptism by heretics

One Lord, one faith, one baptism. Eph. 4:4.

He adds, "For so will you pass through the water of another," reckoning heretical baptism not proper and true water. *Clement of Alexandria (c. 195, E), 2.322.*

Heretics, however, have no fellowship in our discipline. . . . I am not bound to recognize in them a thing that is commanded to me, because they do not have the same God as we do. Nor do they have the same Christ. Therefore, their baptism is not one with ours, either, for it is not the same. *Tertullian (c. 198, W), 3.676.*

When we were together in council, dearest brethren, we read your letter that you wrote to us concerning those who seem to be baptized by heretics and schismatics, asking whether—when they come to the catholic church, which is one—they should be baptized. . . . We put forward our opinion, but not as a new one. Rather, we join with you in equal agreement in an opinion long since decreed by our predecessors and observed by us. This opinion is namely . . . that no one can be baptized outside the church, for there is one baptism appointed in the holy church. . . . How can the person who baptizes give remission of sins to another when he himself—being outside the church—cannot put away his own sins? *Cyprian (c. 250, W), 5.375, 376.*

I know not by what presumption some of our colleagues are led to think that those who have been dipped by heretics should not be baptized when they come to us. The reason they give is that there is "one baptism." . . . He who of his own authority grants this advantage to the heretics yields and consents to them that the enemies and adversaries of Christ have the power of washing, purifying, and sanctifying a man. However, *we* say that those who come from them are not *re-baptized* by us, but are *baptized*. For, indeed, they did not receive anything there, where there is nothing. *Cyprian (c. 250, W), 5.377.*

Christ Himself commands the pagan to be baptized in the full and united Trinity. Are we to believe that someone who denies Christ is denied by Christ, but that he who denies his Father . . . is not denied? Are we to believe that he who blasphemes against Him whom Christ called His Lord and His God is rewarded by Christ? Are we to believe he obtains remission of sins and the sanctification of baptism? *Cyprian (c. 250, W), 5.383, 384.*

Someone might say, "What, then, becomes of those who were received from heresy into the church without baptism, in times past?" The Lord is able by His mercy to make allowances and not to separate from the gifts of His church those who through ignorance were admitted into the church and have since fallen asleep [in death] in the church. However, just because there was error at one time, it does not mean that there must always be error. *Cyprian (c. 250, W), 5.385.*

On the reading of [the letter from Stephen, bishop of Rome], you will more and more observe his error in endeavoring to maintain the cause of heretics against Christians. . . . For he judged the baptism of all heretics to be just and lawful. . . . If, therefore, it is either commanded in the Gospel, or contained in the Epistles or Acts of the apostles, that those who come from any heresy should not be baptized, but only have hands laid upon them to repentance, let this divine and holy tradition be observed. But if everywhere heretics are called nothing else than adversaries and antichrists, . . . no one should defame the apostles as if they had approved of the baptisms of heretics. *Cyprian (c. 250, W), 5.386.*

It is practiced and held by us that all who are converted from any heresy whatever to the church must be baptized by the only and lawful baptism of the church—with the exception of those who had previously been baptized in the church (and from there had passed over to the heretics). *Cyprian (c. 250, W), 5.389, 390.*

Just as a heretic may not lawfully ordain or lay on hands, so neither may he baptize. . . . What kind of thing is it that when we see that Paul, after John's baptism, baptized those disciples again, we are hesitating to baptize those who come to the church from heresy, after their unhallowed and profane dipping. *Firmilian (c. 256, E), 5.392.*

Who in the church is perfect and wise and can either defend or believe that the bare invocation of names [of the Trinity] is sufficient for the remission of sins and the sanctification of baptism? For these things are only of advantage when he who baptizes has the Holy Spirit. *Firmilian (c. 256, E), 5.392.*

If the baptism of heretics can have the regeneration of the second birth, those who are baptized among them must be considered to be children of God—not heretics. For the second birth, which occurs in baptism, begets sons of God. *Firmilian (c. 256, E), 5.393.*

[Stephen, bishop of Rome] says, "the name of Christ is of great advantage to faith and the sanctification of baptism. So whoever is anywhere baptized in the name of Christ, he immediately obtains the grace of Christ." . . . However, we join custom to truth. And we resist the Romans' custom with custom—the custom of truth. . . . It has always been observed here that we knew none but the one church of God. And we have deemed no baptism holy except that of the holy church. *Firmilian (c. 256, E), 5.395.*

Cyprian said: "We have determined over and over again that heretics who come to the church must be baptized and sanctified by the baptism of the church." *Seventh Council of Carthage (c. 256, W), 5.565.*

Primus of Misgirpa said: "I decide that every man who comes to us from heresy must be baptized. For in vain does he think that he has been baptized there. . . . Whatever is done outside the church has no effect towards salvation." *Seventh Council of Carthage (c. 256, W), 5.566.*

Crescens of Cirta said: "I judge that all heretics and schismatics who wish to come to the catholic church will not be allowed to enter without their having first been exorcised and baptized." *Seventh Council of Carthage (c. 256, W), 5.567.*

Pomponius of Dionysiana said: "It is evident that heretics cannot baptize and give remission of sins, seeing that they do not have power to be able to bind or loose anything on earth." *Seventh Council of Carthage (c. 256, W), 5.570.*

A divine and sacred provincial synod, gathered together at Rome by Stephen, the blessed martyr and father, excommunicated those who (in an African synod) had without reason concluded that those who came to the catholic church from any heresy should be re-baptized. *Roman Council of Stephen (c. 256, W), 5.653.*

According to the most ancient custom and ecclesiastical tradition, it would suffice that—after that baptism that they have received outside [the church] indeed, but still in the name of Jesus Christ our Lord—that only hands should be laid upon them by the bishop for their reception of the Holy Spirit. And this imposition of hands affords them the renewed and perfected seal of faith. *Treatise on Re-Baptism (c. 257, W), 5.667.*

Not without reason, we also in the present day may believe that men who are amended from their former error may be baptized in the Holy Spirit, who, although they were baptized with water in the name of the Lord, might have had a faith somewhat imperfect. *Treatise on Re-Baptism (c. 257, W), 5.671.*

As far as concerns the disciples themselves [prior to Pentecost], they are found to have had a faith that was neither sound nor perfect—as to the matters we have referred to. And what is much more serious, they baptized others, as it is written in the Gospel according to John. Besides, what will you say of those who are in many cases baptized by bishops of very bad character, who . . . are deprived of their office itself, or barred from communion? Or what will you say of those who may have been baptized by bishops whose opinions are unsound, or who are very ignorant? *Treatise on Re-Baptism (c. 257, W), 5.672.*

Outside the church, there is no Holy Spirit. Therefore, sound faith cannot exist—not just among heretics, but even among those who are established in schism. For that reason, those who repent and are amended by the doctrine of the truth . . . should be aided only by spiritual baptism—that is, by the imposition of the bishop's hands. *Treatise on Re-Baptism (c. 257, W), 5.673.*

What will you determine against the person who hears the Word . . . and has at once confessed and then been martyred before there was an opportunity for him to be baptized with water? . . . If you say that he has [eternally] perished, you will be opposed by the statement of the Lord, who says, "Whoever will confess me before men, I will confess him also before my Father who is in heaven." . . . All of this is not meant to be taken too liberally—as if it could be stretched to such a point that any heretic whatever can confess the name of Christ even though he denies Christ Himself. Nor does it apply to the person who believes on another Christ. *Treatise on Re-Baptism (c. 257, W), 5.673, 674.*

Heretics who are already baptized in water in the name of Jesus Christ must only be baptized with the Holy Spirit. . . . This is so even though, if they continue as they are, they cannot be saved, for they have not sought the Lord after the invocation of His name upon them. *Treatise on Re-Baptism (c. 257, W), 5.674.*

In the most considerable councils of the bishops, I hear it has been decreed that those who come from heresy should first be trained in [orthodox] doctrine and then should be cleansed by baptism. *Dionysius of Alexandria (c. 262, E), 6.102.*

Those who have been baptized by heretics are not initiated. Rather, they are polluted. They do not receive the remission of sins—but the bond of impiety. *Apostolic Constitutions (compiled c. 390, E), 7.456.*

If a bishop or presbyter rebaptizes someone who has had true baptism—or does not baptize one who has been polluted by the ungodly [baptism]—let him be deprived. *Apostolic Constitutions (compiled c. 390, E), 7.503; extended discussion: 5.375–5.402, 5.565–5.572.*

SEE ALSO BAPTISM FOR THE DEAD; BAPTISM OF FIRE; BAPTISM, HOLY SPIRIT; BAPTISM, JEWISH; BAPTISM, JOHN'S; CATECHUMENS; CHILDBIRTH; CHILDREN, INFANTS; MARTYRS, MARTYRDOM (III. BAPTISM OF BLOOD); NEW BIRTH; OIL, ANOINTING WITH; SACRAMENTS.

BAPTISM, JEWISH

When they come from the marketplace, they do not eat unless they wash. And there are many other things which they have received and hold, like the washing of cups, pitchers, copper vessels, and couches. Mark 7:4.

[ADDRESSED TO JEWS:] We Christians do not receive that useless baptism of cisterns, for it has nothing to do with our baptism of life. *Justin Martyr (c. 160, E), 1.203.*

The Jewish Israel bathes daily, because it is daily being defiled. *Tertullian (c. 198, W), 3.676.*

Even the Jewish nation had wicked heresies. . . . The Hemerobaptists do not eat unless daily they wash. And unless they cleanse their beds, tables, platters, cups, and seats, they do not use any of those things. *Apostolic Constitutions (compiled c. 390, E), 7.452.*

Do not seek after Jewish separations or perpetual washings. *Apostolic Constitutions (compiled c. 390, E), 7.464.*

BAPTISM, JOHN'S

He went into all the region around the Jordan, preaching a baptism of repentance for the remission of sins. Luke 3:3.

And he said to them, "Into what then were you baptized?" So they said, "Into John's baptism." Then Paul said, "John indeed baptized with a baptism of repentance." Acts 19:3, 4.

John was sent by the Lord to perform this work, but it was human in its nature. For it conveyed nothing heavenly. Rather, it was a forerunner of heavenly things. It was ordained for repentance, which is in man's power. . . . But if repentance is a human thing, its baptism must necessarily be of the same nature. Otherwise, if it had been heavenly, it would have given both the Holy Spirit and the remission of sins. *Tertullian (c. 198, W), 3.674.*

His disciples used to baptize, as ministers, with the selfsame "baptism of John," with which John had previously baptized as a forerunner. Let no one think it was with some other baptism, for no other baptism exists—except that which Christ subsequently ordained. *Tertullian (c. 198, W), 3.674.*

He desired that the baptism of repentance would lead the way. He did this with the view of first preparing those whom He was calling, by means of the sign and seal of repentance. *Tertullian (c. 203, W), 3.658.*

The Pharisees . . . came to the baptism without believing in him. They probably did so because they feared the crowds. So with their accustomed hypocrisy towards the crowds, they thought it better to undergo the washing—so as not to appear hostile to those who did believe in it. Their belief was actually that John derived his baptism from men and not from heaven. However, because of the crowds, they were afraid to say what they thought, lest they might be stoned. *Origen (c. 228, E), 9.365.*

The baptism of John was inferior to the baptism of Jesus, which was given through His dis-

ciples. Those persons in the Acts who were baptized with John's baptism and who had not heard if there was any Holy Spirit were baptized over again by the apostle. Regeneration did not take place with John. However, with Jesus, through His disciples, it does so. What is called the bath of regeneration takes place with renewal of the Spirit. For the Spirit now comes, as well. It comes from God and is over and above the water. Yet, it does not come to all after the water. *Origen (c. 228, E), 9.367.*

John the Baptist baptized for the remission of sins. *Origen (c. 248, E), 4.416; extended discussion: 3.673–3.674.*

SEE ALSO BAPTISM; JOHN THE BAPTIST.

BAPTISM FOR THE DEAD

Otherwise, what will they do who are baptized for the dead, if the dead do not rise at all? Why then are they baptized for the dead? 1 Cor. 15:29.

He asks, "What will they do who are baptized for the dead, if the dead do not rise?" . . . Do not then suppose that the apostle here indicates that some new god is the author and advocate of this practice. Rather, it was so that he could all the more firmly insist upon the resurrection of the body, in proportion as they who were baptized for the dead resorted to the practice from their belief of such a resurrection. We have the apostle in another passage defining "only one baptism." Therefore, to be "baptized for the dead" means, in fact, to be baptized for the body. For, as we have shown, it is the body that becomes dead. What, then, will they do who are baptized for the body, if the body does not rise again? *Tertullian (c. 207, W), 3.449, 450.*

Inasmuch as "some are also baptized for the dead," we will see whether there is a good reason for this. Now it is certain that they adopted this [practice] with a presumption that made them suppose that the vicarious baptism would be beneficial to the flesh of another in anticipation of the resurrection. For unless this is a bodily resurrection, there would be no pledge secured by this process of a bodily baptism. *Tertullian (c. 210, W), 3.581, 582.*

BAPTISM, HOLY SPIRIT

He who is coming after me is mightier than I, whose sandals I am not worthy to carry. He will baptize you with the Holy Spirit and fire. Matt. 3:11.

Jesus answered, "Most assuredly, I say to you, unless one is born of water and the Spirit, he cannot enter the kingdom of God." John 3:5.

You will be baptized with the Holy Spirit not many days from now. Acts 1:4, 5.

The Lord promised to send the Comforter, who should join us to God. For as a compacted lump of dough cannot be formed of dry wheat without fluid matter, . . . so in like manner, neither could we, being many, be made one in Christ Jesus without the water from heaven. . . . For our bodies have received unity among themselves by means of that bath [i.e., water baptism] which leads to incorruption. However, our souls receive it by means of the Spirit. For that reason, both are necessary, since both contribute towards the life of God. Our Lord comforted that erring Samaritan woman . . . by pointing out and promising to her living water. This water would enable her to thirst no more, nor occupy herself in acquiring the refreshing water obtained by labor. For she could have in herself water springing up to eternal life. The Lord received this as a gift from His Father, and He also confers it upon those who are partakers of Himself, sending the Holy Spirit upon all the earth. *Irenaeus (c. 180, E/W), 1.444, 445.*

That most Holy Spirit willingly descends from the Father over our cleansed and blessed bodies [after baptism]. . . . The dove of the Holy Spirit flies to earth, that is, to our flesh as it emerges from the font, . . . bringing us the peace of God, sent out from the heavens. *Tertullian (c. 198, W), 3.673*

"He will baptize you with the Holy Spirit and with fire." . . . "You will be baptized with the Holy Spirit not many days from now." . . . So John made a distinction. For he said that he indeed baptized in water, but that one would come who would baptize in the Holy Spirit, by the grace and power of God. And they are so baptized by the Spirit's bestowal and operation of hidden results. . . . The Lord said in the Gospel: "Unless a man is born again of water and of the Spirit, he cannot enter into the kingdom of heaven." From this, it is clear that the baptism that alone is profitable is that where the Holy Spirit can dwell. *Treatise on Re-Baptism (c. 257, W), 5.668.*

SEE ALSO BAPTISM; OIL, ANOINTING WITH.

BAPTISM OF BLOOD

SEE MARTYRDOM (III. BAPTISM OF BLOOD).

BAPTISM OF FIRE

One mightier than I is coming, whose sandal strap I am not worthy to loose. He will baptize you with the Holy Spirit and with fire. Luke 3:16.

True and stable faith is baptized with water, unto salvation. Pretended and weak faith is baptized with fire, unto judgment. *Tertullian (c. 198, W), 3.674.*

John said that we must be baptized in the Holy Spirit and in fire. Because he said "and fire," . . . very crafty men seek a way to thereby corrupt and violate—and even neutralize—the baptism of holiness. They derive the origin of their notion from Simon Magus, practicing it with manifold perversity through various errors. . . . However, those who are not ignorant of the nature of the Holy Spirit, understand that what is said about fire is said about the Spirit Himself. For in the Acts of the Apostles, . . . they were baptized with the Holy Spirit and with fire. That is, they were baptized with the Spirit. . . . This was similar to the fire that burned in the bush, but did not consume the bush. *Treatise on Re-Baptism (c. 257), 5.676, 677.*

BARBARIANS

There are four classes of men in this world: barbarians, Greeks, Jews, and Christians. *Aristides (c. 125, E), 9.264.*

Because they did not know God, the barbarians went astray among the elements. They began to worship created things instead of their Creator. For this purpose, they made images and enclosed them in shrines. *Aristides (c. 125, E), 9.265.*

I approve of the simplicity of the barbarians. Loving an unencumbered life, the barbarians have abandoned luxury. *Clement of Alexandria (c. 195, E), 2.277.*

This is the history of the oldest wise men and philosophers among the Greeks. And that most of them were barbarians by extraction, and were trained among barbarians, what need is there to say? *Clement of Alexandria (c. 195, E), 2.315.*

Barbarians were inventors not only of philosophy, but of almost every art. *Clement of Alexandria (c. 195, E), 2.317.*

BAR-COCHBA

Bar-Cochba was the leader of the Jewish uprising in Palestine, A.D. 132–135.

[The Jews] kill and punish us whenever they have the power, as you can well believe. For example, in the Jewish war that lately raged, Bar-Cochba, the leader of the revolt of the Jews, gave orders that Christians alone should be led to cruel punishments, unless they would deny Jesus Christ and utter blasphemy. *Justin Martyr (c. 160, E), 1.173.*

BARNABAS

The church in Jerusalem . . . sent out Barnabas to go as far as Antioch. . . . He was a good man, full of the Holy Spirit and of faith. Acts 11:22–24.

To James the Just, John, and Peter, the Lord imparted knowledge after His resurrection. These imparted it to the rest of the apostles. And the rest of the apostles imparted it to the Seventy, of whom Barnabas was one. *Clement of Alexandria (c. 195, E), 2.579.*

SEE ALSO BARNABAS, EPISTLE OF; SEVENTY, THE (DISCIPLES).

BARNABAS, EPISTLE OF

The Epistle of Barnabas is an early Christian writing, possibly written prior to A.D. 100. The work itself is anonymous. On the belief that it was written by the Barnabas of Acts, some persons in the early church viewed it as Scripture. However, most churches apparently did not include it in their canon. Eusebius describes it as one of the "disputed books."

The apostle Barnabas says, "From the portion I have received, I have done my diligence to send to you little by little." *Clement of Alexandria (c. 195, E), 2.354.*

Barnabas says mystically, "May God, who rules the universe, also vouchsafe wisdom to you." *Clement of Alexandria (c. 195, E), 2.366.*

The apostolic Barnabas (he was one of the Seventy and a fellow-worker of Paul) speaks in these words: "Before we believed in God, the dwelling-place of our heart was unstable." *Clement of Alexandria (c. 195, E), 2.372.*

Barnabas, too, who in person preached the Word along with the apostle in the ministry of the Gentiles, says, "I write to you most simply, that you may understand." *Clement of Alexandria (c. 195, E), 2.459.*

The same is declared by Barnabas in his Epistle, where he says there are two ways—one of light and one of darkness. *Origen (c. 225, E), 4.332.*

In the general Epistle of Barnabas, from which perhaps Celsus took the statement that the apostles were notoriously wicked men, it is recorded that "Jesus elected his own apostles as persons who were more guilty of sin than all other evildoers." And in the Gospel according to Luke, Peter says to Jesus, "Depart from me, O Lord, for I am a sinful man." *Origen (c. 248, E), 4.424; see also 2.355, 2.362.*

SEE ALSO BARNABAS; HEBREWS, EPISTLE TO THE.

BASILIDES

Basilides, one of the foremost Gnostic teachers, lived in Alexandria during the first half of the second century.

Basilides again, that he may appear to have discovered something more sublime and plausible, gives an immense development to his doctrines. He sets forth that Nous was the First-Born of the Unborn Father. Then he says that from him was born Logos; from Logos, Phronesis; from Phronesis, Sophia and Dynamis. *Irenaeus (c. 180, E/W), 1.349.*

[THE TEACHING OF BASILIDES:] The chief of the angels is he who is thought to be the God of the Jews. And inasmuch as he desired to render the other nations subject to his own people, that is, the Jews, all the other princes resisted and opposed him. Therefore, all other nations were at enmity with his nation. The Father without birth and without name, perceiving that they would be destroyed, sent his own First-Begotten Nous (He it is who is called Christ) to bestow deliverance on those who believe in Him, from the power of those who made the world. Christ appeared, then, on earth as a man, to the nations of these powers, and He worked miracles. For that reason, He did not himself suffer death, but Simon, a certain man of Cyrene, being forced, carried the cross in his place. Christ changed the appearance of this Simon, so that Simon might be thought to be Jesus. Therefore, Simon was crucified, through ignorance and error. In the meanwhile, Jesus himself took on the form of Simon, and, standing by, laughed at them. *Irenaeus (c. 180, E/W), 1.349.*

The hypothesis of Basilides says that the soul, having sinned previously in another life, endures punishment in this life. *Clement of Alexandria (c. 195, E), 2.424.*

It was later, in the time of Hadrian the king, that there arose those who invented the heresies. And they extended to the age of Antoninus the elder. One example is Basilides—although he claims Glaucias, the interpreter of Peter, was his master. *Clement of Alexandria (c. 195, E), 2.555.*

. . . contending with Marcion and Basilides that [the body of Christ] possessed no reality. *Tertullian (c. 210, W), 3.546.*

[Basilides says] the light . . . descended from the hebdomad upon Jesus, the son of Mary, and He had radiance imparted to Him by being illuminated with the light that shone upon Him. *Hippolytus (c. 225, W), 5.108; see also 2.355, 2.371–2.372, 2.423; extended discussion: 5.100–5.109.*

SEE ALSO GNOSTICS, GNOSTICISM; HERESIES, HERETICS; VALENTINUS, VALENTINIANS.

BATHS, PUBLIC

The baths are opened promiscuously to men and women. And there they strip for licentious indulgence (for from looking, men get to loving). It is as if their modesty had been washed away in the baths. Those who have not become utterly destitute of modesty shut out strangers. Yet, they bathe with their own servants and strip naked before their slaves. *Clement of Alexandria (c. 195, E), 2.279.*

We should not use the bath in such a way as to require a servant, nor are we to bathe constantly. *Clement of Alexandria (c. 195, E), 2.283.*

What of those [virgins] who patronize indecent baths? . . . They who disgracefully look at naked men and are seen naked by men—do they not themselves afford enticement to vice? . . . You make a show of the bath house. These places where you assemble are more foul than a theater. There, all modesty is put off. The honor and modesty of the body is laid aside along with the covering of garments. Virginity is exposed, to be pointed at and to be handled. And now, then, consider whether, when you are clothed, you are modest among men—after the boldness of nakedness has conduced to immodesty! For this reason, therefore, the church frequently mourns over her virgins. . . .

Therefore, let your baths be performed with women, among whom your bathing is modest. *Cyprian (c. 250, W), 5.435.*

Do we believe that a man is lamenting with his whole heart . . . who from the first day of his sin daily frequents the bathing places with women? *Cyprian (c. 250, W), 5.445.*

Women should also avoid that disorderly practice of bathing in the same place with men. *Apostolic Constitutions (compiled c. 390, E), 7.395; see also 2.282–2.283.*

BEARD

You will not shave around the sides of your head, nor will you disfigure the edges of your beard. Lev. 19:27.

. . . nor will they shave the edges of their beards. Lev. 21:5.

The philosophers perform no useful service. Yet, they are not even willing to wear a long beard without being paid for it! *Tatian (c. 160, E), 2.73.*

What great and wonderful things have your philosophers effected? They leave uncovered one of their shoulders. They let their hair grow long. They cultivate their beards. *Tatian (c. 160, E), 2.75.*

The hair of the chin showed him to be a man. *Clement of Alexandria (c. 195, E), 2.271.*

How womanly it is for one who is a man to comb himself and shave himself with a razor, for the sake of fine effect, and to arrange his hair at the mirror, shave his cheeks, pluck hairs out of them, and smooth them! . . . For God wished women to be smooth and to rejoice in their locks alone growing spontaneously, as a horse in his mane. But He has adorned man, like the lions, with a beard, and endowed him, as an attribute of manhood, with a hairy chest— a sign of strength and rule. *Clement of Alexandria (c. 195, E), 2.275.*

This, then, is the mark of the man, the beard. By this, he is seen to be a man. It is older than Eve. It is the token of the superior nature. . . . It is therefore unholy to desecrate the symbol of manhood, hairiness. *Clement of Alexandria (c. 195, E), 2.276.*

It is not lawful to pluck out the beard, man's natural and noble adornment. *Clement of Alexandria (c. 195, E), 2.277.*

Let the chin have the hair.... For an ample beard suffices for men. And if someone, too, shaves a part of his beard, it must not be made entirely bare, for this is a disgraceful sight.... The moustache similarly, which is dirtied in eating, is to be cut round, not by the razor (for that is not well bred), but by a pair of cropping scissors. But the hair on the chin is not to be disturbed. *Clement of Alexandria (c. 195, E), 2.286.*

This sex of ours acknowledges to itself deceptive trickeries of form peculiarly its own—such as to cut the beard too sharply, to pluck it out here and there, to shave around the mouth. *Tertullian (c. 198, W), 4.22.*

In their manners, there was no discipline. In men, their beards were defaced. *Cyprian (c. 250, W), 5.438.*

Although it is written, "You will not mar the figure of your beard," he plucks out his beard and dresses his hair! *Cyprian (c. 250, W), 5.445.*

The beard must not be plucked. "You will not deface the figure of your beard" [Lev. 19:32]. *Cyprian (c. 250, W), 5.553.*

The nature of the beard contributes in an incredible degree to distinguish the maturity of bodies, or to distinguish the sex, or to contribute to the beauty of manliness and strength. *Lactantius (c. 304–313, W), 7.288.*

Men may not destroy the hair of their beards and unnaturally change the form of a man. For the Law says, "You will not deface your beards." For God the Creator has made this decent for women, but has determined that it is unsuitable for men. *Apostolic Constitutions (compiled c. 390, E), 7.392.*

SEE ALSO GROOMING.

BEAST, THE

SEE ANTICHRIST; MARK OF THE BEAST; REVELATION, BOOK OF.

BEATITUDES

SEE MATT. 5:3–12.

"Blessed are the poor." ... It is not simply those who are poor that He pronounces blessed. Rather, it is those who have wished to become poor for righteousness' sake. It is those who have despised the honors of this world in order to attain "the good." *Clement of Alexandria (c. 195, E), 2.413.*

"Blessed are the meek, for they will inherit the earth." The meek are those who have quelled the battle of unbelief in the soul—the battle of wrath and lust—and the other forms that are subject to them. *Clement of Alexandria (c. 195, E), 2.415.*

SEE ALSO SERMON ON THE MOUNT.

BETHESDA, POOL OF

Now there is in Jerusalem by the Sheep Gate a pool, which is called in Hebrew, Bethesda, having five porches. In these lay a great multitude of sick people, blind, lame, paralyzed, waiting for the moving of the water. For an angel went down at a certain time into the pool and stirred up the water; then whoever stepped in first, after the stirring of the water, was made well of whatever disease he had. John 5:2–4.

"The Law and the Prophets were until John," and the fish pool of Bethesda was until the coming of Christ. Thereafter, it ceased curatively to remove infirmities of health from Israel. *Tertullian (c. 197, W), 3.171.*

An angel, by his intervention, used to stir the pool at Bethesda. Those who were complaining of poor health used to watch for him. For whoever was the first to descend into the pool, ceased to complain after his washing. The figure of physical healing foreshadowed a spiritual healing. *Tertullian (c. 198, W), 3.671, 672.*

BETHLEHEM

We perceive that now none of the race of Israel has remained in Bethlehem—ever since the edict was issued forbidding any of the Jews to linger in the confines of this very district. *Tertullian (c. 197, W), 3.169.*

SEE ALSO BIRTH OF JESUS.

BETHSAIDA, POOL OF

SEE BETHESDA, POOL OF.

BIBLE

SEE SCRIPTURES.

BINDING AND LOOSING

I will give you the keys of the kingdom of heaven, and whatever you bind on earth will be bound in heaven, and whatever you loose on earth will be loosed in heaven. Matt. 16:19.

Whatever you bind on earth will be bound in heaven, and whatever you loose on earth will be loosed in heaven. Matt. 18:18.

If you forgive the sins of any, they are forgiven them; if you retain the sins of any, they are retained. John 20:23.

In that dispute about the observance or non-observance of the Law, Peter was the first of all to be endowed with the Spirit. After making an introduction, he addressed the calling of the nations, saying, "And now why are you tempting the Lord, concerning the imposition upon the brothers of a yoke that neither we nor our fathers were able to bear?" . . . This proclamation both "loosed" those parts of the Law that were abandoned and "bound" those that were retained. Hence, the power of loosing and of binding given to Peter had nothing to do with the mortal sins of believers. *Tertullian (c. 212, W, Montanistic), 4.99.*

When one judges unrighteously and does not bind upon earth according to the Word of God, nor loose upon earth according to His will, the gates of Hades prevail against him. However, in the case of anyone against whom the gates of Hades do not prevail, this man judges righteously. As a result, that person had the keys of the kingdom of heaven, opening to those who have been loosed on earth that they may also be loosed in heaven, and set free. *Origen (c. 245, E), 9.459.*

Those who maintain the function of the episcopate make use of this word as Peter (having received the keys of the kingdom of heaven from the Savior). They teach that things bound by them (i.e., condemned) are also bound in heaven and that those who have obtained remission by them are also loosed in heaven. I must say that they speak wholesomely if they have the way of life on account of which it was said to that Peter, "You are Peter." And if they are such persons that upon them the church is built by Christ. . . . But if they are tightly bound with the cords of their sins, to no purpose do they bind and loose. . . . And if anyone who is not such a Peter, and does not possess the things spoken of here, yet he still imagines that as a Peter he will so bind on earth that the things bound are bound in heaven . . . he is puffed up, not understanding the meaning of the Scriptures. And being puffed up, he has fallen into the ruin of the devil. *Origen (c. 245, E), 9.459.*

"And whatever you will bind on the earth, etc." . . . It seems to be indicated that the things that had been granted earlier to Peter alone are here bestowed on all persons who give the three admonitions to someone who has sinned [i.e., Matt. 18:15–18]. The result is that, if they are not heard [by the sinner], they will bind on earth him who is judged to be as a Gentile and a tax-collector. For such a one has been bound in heaven. *Origen (c. 245, E), 9.494.*

Someone may delude us with the pretense of repentance. However, God is not mocked, and He looks into man's heart. So He will judge those things that we have imperfectly looked into. And the Lord will amend the sentence of his servants. *Cyprian (c. 250, W), 5.331.*

It is clear where and by whom remission of sins can be given. I speak of that which is given in baptism. For first of all the Lord gave that power to Peter, upon whom He built the church. He appointed and showed the source of unity—namely, the power that whatever he loosed on earth would be loosed in heaven. And after the resurrection, He spoke also to the apostles, saying, "As the Father has sent me, even so I send you. And when he had said this, He breathed on them and said unto them, 'Receive the Holy Spirit. Whosoever sins you remit, they are remitted unto them. And those whose sins you retain, they are retained.'" Therefore, we perceive that only those who are set over the church and established in the Gospel law, and in the ordinance of the Lord, are allowed to baptize and to give remissions of sins. However, outside the church, nothing can be either bound or loosed. For there is no one there who can bind or loose anything. *Cyprian (c. 250, W), 5.381.*

Communion is relaxed to heedless persons! But this is a vain and false peace! It is dangerous to those who grant it. And it probably avails nothing to those who receive it. *Cyprian (c. 250, W), 5.441.*

Let no one cheat himself. Let no one deceive himself. The Lord alone can have mercy. He alone can bestow pardon for sins that have been committed against Himself. . . . The Lord must be appeased by our atonement. For He has said that he who denies Him, He will deny. *Cyprian (c. 250, W), 5.442.*

Speak as one having authority to judge offenders. For to you, O bishops, it is said, "Whatever you will bind on earth will be bound in heaven; and whatever you will loose on earth will be loosed in heaven." *Apostolic Constitutions (compiled c. 390, E), 7.399.*

This peace and haven of tranquility is the church of Christ, into which you restore them, when you have loosed them from their sins. *Apostolic Constitutions (compiled c. 390, E), 7.405.*

SEE ALSO DISCIPLINE, CHURCH; PETER.

BIRTH CONTROL

SEE PROCREATION.

BIRTH OF JESUS

How, then, was He manifested to the world? A star shone forth in heaven above all the other stars. The light from this star was inexpressible, and its uniqueness struck men with astonishment. *Ignatius (c. 105, E), 1.57.*

At the time of His birth, Magi came from Arabia and worshipped Him. . . . When the Child was born in Bethlehem, since Joseph could not find an inn in that village, he took up his lodging in a certain cave near the village. While they were there, Mary brought forth the Christ and placed Him in a manger. Here the Magi who came from Arabia found Him. *Justin Martyr (c. 160, E), 1.237.*

Christ was born one hundred and fifty years ago under Cyrenius. *Justin (c. 160, E), 1.178.*

Therefore, from the birth of Christ to the death of Commodus are a total of one hundred ninety-four years, one month, and thirteen days. There are those who have calculated not only the *year* of our Lord's birth, but also the day. They say that it took place in the twenty-eighth year of Augustus, on the twenty-fifth day of Pachon [May 20]. . . . Others say that He was born on the twenty-fourth or twenty-fifth day of Pharmuthi [April 19 or 20]. *Clement of Alexandria (c. 195, E), 2.333.*

Jesus was from the native soil of Bethlehem, and from the house of David. For, among the Romans, Mary is described in the census, of whom is born Christ. *Tertullian (c. 197, W), 3.164.*

It was not any of the constellations existing in the sky that was made to be the star of the East. Rather, it was something of another order, appointed for this purpose and in the service of the knowledge of Jesus. *Origen (c. 228, E), 9.312.*

Let him know that, in conformity with the narrative in the Gospel regarding His birth, there is displayed at Bethlehem the cave where Jesus was born and the manger in the cave where He was wrapped in swaddling clothes. And this sight is greatly talked of in the surrounding places—even among the enemies of the faith. They say that in this cave was born that Jesus who is worshipped and reverenced by the Christians. *Origen (c. 248, E), 4.418.*

The star that was seen in the east we consider to have been a new star, unlike any of the other well-known planetary bodies. . . . Yet, it had the nature of those celestial bodies that appear at times, such as comets. . . . It has been observed that, on the occurrence of great events, and of mighty changes in earthly things, such stars are apt to appear, indicating either the removal of dynasties or the breaking out of wars. . . . There is a prophecy of Balaam recorded by Moses to this effect: "There will arise a star out of Jacob, and a man will rise up out of Israel." *Origen (c. 248, E), 4.422.*

POST-NICENE REFERENCES TO CHRISTMAS: 7.443, 7.495.

SEE ALSO CALENDAR, CHRISTIAN; EPIPHANY; HOLIDAYS, PAGAN; MAGI; VIRGIN BIRTH.

BIRTHDAYS

Now it came to pass on the third day, which was Pharaoh's birthday, that he made a feast for all his servants; and he lifted up the head of the chief butler and of the chief baker among his servants. Gen. 40:20.

But when Herod's birthday was celebrated, the daughter of Herodias danced before them and pleased Herod. Matt. 14:6.

Perpetua answered to his face and said, "Why do you not at least permit us to be refreshed, being as we are objectionable to the most noble Caesar, and having to fight on his birthday." *Passion of Perpetua and Felicitas (c. 205, W), 3.704.*

And on birthdays, when the lawless word reigns over them, they dance so that their movements please that word. Someone before us has observed what is written in Genesis about the birthday of Pharaoh and has said that the worthless man who loves things connected with birth keeps birthday festivals. And I, taking this suggestion from him, find nowhere in Scripture that a birthday was kept by a righteous man. For Herod was more unjust than that famous Pharaoh. For the latter killed a chief baker on his birthday feast. But the former killed John. *Origen (c. 245, E), 9.428.*

SEE ALSO HOLIDAYS, PAGAN.

BISHOP

I. Position, qualifications, and authority

II. Bishop of Rome

I. Position, qualifications, and authority

To all the saints in Christ Jesus who are in Philippi, with the bishops and deacons. Phil. 1:1.

This is a faithful saying: If a man desires the position of a bishop, he desires a good work. A bishop then must be blameless, the husband of one wife, temperate, sober-minded, of good behavior, hospitable, able to teach. 1 Tim. 3:1, 2.

A bishop must be blameless, as a steward of God, not self-willed, not quick-tempered, not given to wine, not violent, not greedy for money. Tit. 1:7.

Appoint, therefore, for yourselves, bishops and deacons worthy of the Lord: men who are meek, not lovers of money, truthful, and tested; for they also render to you the service of prophets and teachers. Do not despise them, therefore, for they are your honored ones, together with the prophets and teachers. *Didache (c. 80–140, E), 7.381.*

Preaching through countries and cities, the apostles appointed the first-fruits of their labors to be bishops and deacons of those who would believe afterwards. However, they first tested them by the Spirit. *Clement of Rome (c. 96, W), 1.16.*

Our apostles also knew, through our Lord Jesus Christ, that there would be strife on account of the office of oversight. For this reason, therefore, inasmuch as they had obtained a perfect foreknowledge of this, they appointed those already mentioned. Afterwards, they gave instructions, that when those men should fall asleep, other approved men should succeed them in their ministry. We are of opinion, therefore, that those appointed by the apostles,

or afterwards by other eminent men, with the consent of the whole church, and who have blamelessly served the flock of Christ in a humble, peaceable, and disinterested spirit, and have for a long time possessed the good opinion of all, cannot be justly dismissed from the ministry. *Clement of Rome (c. 96, W), 1.17.*

[IGNATIUS, BISHOP OF ANTIOCH:] I do not issue orders to you, as though I were some great person. . . . For now I begin to be a disciple, and I speak to you as fellow disciples with me. *Ignatius (c. 105, E), 1.50.*

Being subject to the bishop and the presbyters, you may in all respects be sanctified. *Ignatius (c. 105, E), 1.50.*

If the prayer of one or two persons possesses such power, how much more will that of the bishop and the whole church! . . . Therefore, in order that we may be subject to God, let us be careful not to set ourselves in opposition to the bishop. . . . It is clear, therefore, that we should look upon the bishop even as we would upon the Lord Himself. *Ignatius (c. 105, E), 1.51, 52.*

Obey the bishop and the presbyters with an undivided mind. *Ignatius (c. 105, E), 58.*

Now it becomes you also not to treat your bishop too familiarly on account of his youth, but to yield him all reverence. . . . It is therefore fitting that you should obey [your bishop], after no hypocritical fashion. *Ignatius (c. 105, E), 1.60.*

I exhort you to study to do all things with a divine harmony, while your bishop presides in the place of God, and your presbyters in the place of the assembly of the apostles, along with your deacons. *Ignatius (c. 105, E), 1.61.*

As therefore the Lord did nothing without the Father, being united to Him, . . . so neither should you do anything without the bishop and presbyters. *Ignatius (c. 105, E), 1.62.*

It is therefore necessary that you do nothing without the bishop (as you indeed already practice). Likewise, you should also be subject to the presbyters. *Ignatius (c. 105, E), 1.66, 67.*

[IGNATIUS, BISHOP OF ANTIOCH:] Shall I . . . reach such a height of pride that, although being a condemned man, I should issue commands to you as if I were an apostle? *Ignatius (c. 105, E), 1.67.*

[Ignatius, bishop of Antioch:] I do not, as Peter and Paul, issue commandments to you. They were apostles. *Ignatius (c. 105, E), 1.75.*

The Lord grants forgiveness to all those who repent, if they turn in penitence to the unity of God, and to communion with the bishop. *Ignatius (c. 105, E), 1.84.*

Let that be deemed a proper Eucharist if it is [administered] either by the bishop, or by one to whom he has entrusted it. . . . It is not lawful without the bishop either to baptize or to celebrate a love-feast. . . . Wherever the bishop appears, let the congregation be there also. . . . It is well to reverence both God and the bishop. He who honors the bishop has been honored by God. *Ignatius (c. 105, E), 1.89, 90.*

Those square white stones which fitted exactly into each other, are apostles, bishops, teachers, and deacons who have lived in godly purity and have acted chastely and reverently as bishops, teachers, and deacons. *Hermas (c. 150, W), 2.14.*

Those who believed were the following: bishops given to hospitality, who always gladly received into their houses the servants of God, without hypocrisy. And by their ministry, these bishops never failed to protect the widows and those who were in need. And they always maintained a holy life. *Hermas (c. 150, W), 2.52.*

It is within the power of all, therefore, in every church, who may wish to see the truth, to contemplate clearly the tradition of the apostles manifested throughout the whole world. And we are in a position to reckon up those who were by the apostles instituted bishops in the churches, and the succession of these men to our own times. . . . For if the apostles had known hidden mysteries . . . they would have delivered them especially to those to whom they were also committing the churches themselves. For they were desirous that these men should be very perfect and blameless in all things, whom also they were leaving behind as their successors, delivering up their own place of government to these men. *Irenaeus (c. 180, E/W), 1.415.*

It is incumbent to obey the presbyters who are in the church—those who, as I have shown, possess the succession from the apostles. Those who, together with the succession of the episcopate, have received the certain gift of truth, according to the good pleasure of the Father. *Irenaeus (c. 180, E/W), 1.497.*

Now all these [heretics] are of much later date than the bishops to whom the apostles committed the churches. *Irenaeus (c. 180, E/W), 1.548.*

Innumerable commands such as these are written in the Holy Scriptures pertaining to chosen persons—some to presbyters, some to bishops, some to deacons, others to widows, of whom we will have another opportunity of speaking. *Clement of Alexandria (c. 195, E), 2.294.*

[Clement of Alexandria] says that Peter, James, and John (after the Savior's ascension), although preeminently honored by the Lord, did not contend for glory. Rather, they appointed James the Just to be bishop of Jerusalem. *Clement of Alexandria (c. 195, E), 2.579, as cited by Eusebius.*

Looking to the bishop appointed, . . . John said, "This youth I commit to you in all earnestness." . . . And the presbyter took home the youth committed to him. *Clement of Alexandria (c. 195, E), 5.603.*

The following quotation was written by Tertullian after he had left the church (either literally or spiritually) and identified himself with the Montanist sect. It was addressed to either the bishop of Carthage or the bishop of Rome. Regardless of to whom it was addressed, it was written as a rebuke, for Tertullian sarcastically labelled this bishop with the pagan title *pontifex maximus.*

I hear that there has even been an edict set forth—and a dogmatic one too! The pontifex maximus—that is, the bishop of bishops—issues an edict: "I remit the sins of both adultery and fornication to those who have fulfilled repentance!" O edict, on which cannot be inscribed, "Good deed!" And where will this liberality be posted up? On the very spot, I suppose, on the very gates of the sensual appetites! *Tertullian (c. 212, W), 4.74.*

Among the characteristic qualifications of those who are called "bishops," Paul . . . lays down as a qualification that he should be able to convince those who contradict. . . . And he selects for the episcopate a man who has been once married—rather than he who has twice entered into the married state. Also, he must be a man of blameless life, rather than one who is liable to rebuke. *Origen (c. 248, E), 4.483.*

Our methods of discussion, however, are rather of a gentle kind. For we have learned that he who presides over the preaching of the Word should be able to confute ridiculers. *Origen (c. 248, E), 4.576.*

Our Lord, . . . describing the honor of a bishop and the order of His church, speaks in the Gospel and says to Peter: "I say unto you, 'You are Peter, and upon this rock I will build my church and the gates of Hades will not prevail against it.' " . . . From there, through the changes of times and successions, the ordering of bishops and the plan of the church flow onward. So that the church is founded upon the bishops. And every act of the church is controlled by these same rulers. Since this, then, is founded on the divine law, I marvel that some, with daring temerity, have chosen to write to me as if they wrote in the name of the church. For the church is established in the bishop, the clergy, and all who stand fast in the faith. *Cyprian (c. 250, W), 5.305.*

They need to acknowledge and understand that when a bishop is once made and approved by the testimony and judgment of his colleagues and the people, another one can by no means be appointed. *Cyprian (c. 250, W), 5.319.*

I find that you there, contrary to ecclesiastical order, contrary to evangelical law, contrary to the unity of the Catholic institution, had consented that another bishop should be made. But that is neither right nor allowable to be done. *Cyprian (c. 250, W), 5.321.*

Among our predecessors, some of the bishops here in our province thought that peace was not to be granted to adulterers, and they wholly closed the gate of repentance against adultery. Still, they did not withdraw from the assembly of their co-bishops. Nor did they break the unity of the catholic church by the persistence of their severity or censure. . . . While the bond of concord remains, and the undivided sacrament of the catholic church endures, every bishop disposes and directs his own acts. He will have to give an account of his purposes to the Lord. *Cyprian (c. 250, W), 5.332.*

[WRITTEN ABOUT NOVATIAN:] There have already been ordained in each city, and through all the provinces, bishops who are old in years. They are sound in faith, proved in trial, and have been banished in persecution. Nevertheless, he dares to create over them other false bishops. *Cyprian (c. 250, W), 5.333.*

It certainly behooves those over whom we are placed not to run about nor to break up the harmonious agreement of the bishops with their crafty and deceitful rashness. . . . Unless, perhaps, the authority of the bishops constituted in Africa seems to be too little to a few desperate and abandoned men! . . . Already their case has been examined; already sentence concerning them has been pronounced! *Cyprian (c. 250, W), 5.344.*

But deacons should remember that the Lord chose apostles—that is, bishops and overseers. But apostles appointed for themselves deacons after the ascension of the Lord into heaven, as ministers of their episcopacy and of the church. *Cyprian (c. 250, W), 5.366.*

You should know that the bishop is in the church, and the church is in the bishop. If anyone is not with the bishop, he is not in the church. *Cyprian (c. 250, W), 5.374, 375.*

We . . . do not impose a law upon anyone. For each prelate has in the administration of the church the exercise of his free will. For he will give an account of his conduct to the Lord. *Cyprian (c. 250, W), 5.379.*

When we had met together, being bishops of the province of Africa and of Numidia and numbering seventy-one, we established this same matter once more. *Cyprian (c. 250, W), 5.379.*

The episcopate is one, each part of which is held by each one for the whole. The church also is one, which is spread abroad far and wide. *Cyprian (c. 250, W), 5.423.*

It remains that upon this same matter each of us should bring forward what we think—judging no man. Nor should we reject anyone from the right of communion if he should think differently from us. For none of us sets himself up as a bishop of bishops. Nor by tyrannical terror does anyone compel his colleague to the necessity of obedience. For every bishop—according to the allowance of his liberty and power—has his own proper right of judgment. He can no more be judged by another than he himself can judge another. Rather, let us all wait for the judgment of our Lord Jesus Christ. He is the only one who has the power of both preferring us in the government of his church and of judging us in our conduct there. *Cyprian (c. 256, W), 5.565.*

He gave the power of baptizing to bishops, not to heretics. *Seventh Council of Carthage (c. 256, W), 5.567.*

[ADDRESSED TO STEPHEN, BISHOP OF ROME:] Understand, however, my brother that . . . all those at the head of the churches everywhere are of one mind. They all rejoice exceedingly because of the peace [from persecution] that has been restored beyond all expectation. I might mention Demetrianus in Antioch, Theoctistus in Caesaria; Mazabanes in Aelia, . . . Marinus in Tyre, Heliodorus in Laodicea, . . . Helenus in Tarsus (and with him all the churches of Cilicia), and Firmilian and all Cappadocia. Now, I have named only the more illustrious of the bishops, so as to not make my letter too long. *Dionysius of Alexandria (c. 262, E), 6.101, 102.*

We wrote to many of the bishops, even those who live at a distance, and urged them to give their help in relieving us from this deadly doctrine. Among those whom we addressed were Dionysius, the bishop of Alexandria, and Firmilian of Cappadocia—those men of blessed name. *Malchion (c. 270, E), 6.169.*

[SAID OF PAUL OF SAMOSATA:] He set up for himself a lofty tribunal and throne—so unlike a disciple of Christ. *Malchion (c. 270, E), 6.170.*

It has been established and settled that it is not lawful for any bishop to celebrate ordinations in other districts than his own. This is a law that is extremely important and wisely devised. . . . But you . . . have not considered the law of our sainted fathers and those who have been taken to Christ time after time. Nor do you consider the honor of our great bishop and father, Peter [bishop of Alexandria], on whom we all depend. . . . For you have ventured on subverting all things at once. . . . You should have waited for the judgment of the superior father [i.e., bishop Peter] and for his permission of this practice. *Phileas (c. 307, E), 6.164.*

They revealed to Meletius certain presbyters, who were then in hiding [because of persecution], to whom the blessed Peter [bishop of Alexandria] had given power to act as parish visitors. *Phileas (c. 307, E), 6.164.*

It is your duty, O bishop, neither to overlook the sins of the people, nor to reject those who are penitent. *Apostolic Constitutions (compiled c. 390, E), 7.402.*

As to a good shepherd, let the layman honor him, love him, and reverence him as his master, his high priest of God, and as a teacher of piety. For he that hears him, hears Christ. And he that rejects him, rejects Christ. *Apostolic Constitutions (compiled c. 390, E), 7.404.*

The bishop is the minister of the word, the keeper of knowledge, the mediator between God and you in the various parts of your divine worship. He is the teacher of piety. And, next after God, he is your father. For he has begotten you again to the adoption of sons by water and the Spirit. *Apostolic Constitutions (compiled c. 390, E), 7.410.*

It was not lawful for one of another tribe, who was not a Levite, to offer anything, or to approach the altar without the priest. Likewise, you should do nothing without the bishop. For if anyone does anything without the bishop, he does it to no purpose. For it will not be considered as of any avail to him. . . . So every person among the laity who does anything without the priest, labors in vain. *Apostolic Constitutions (compiled c. 390, E), 7.410.*

We do not permit the rest of the clergy to baptize: neither readers, singers, porters, nor ministers. Rather, we permit only the bishops and presbyters. . . . We do not permit presbyters to ordain deacons, deaconesses, readers, ministers, singers, or porters. Rather, we permit only bishops. For this is the ecclesiastical order and harmony. *Apostolic Constitutions (compiled c. 390, E), 7.429.*

A bishop should not leave his own district and jump to another, even if the crowd should compel him—unless there is some good reason. *Apostolic Constitutions (compiled c. 390, E), 7.501.*

If any bishop uses the rulers of this world and by their means comes to be a bishop of a church, let him be deprived and suspended—together with all who communicate with him. *Apostolic Constitutions (compiled c. 390, E), 7.501.*

Let a bishop or presbyter who takes no care of the clergy or people, and does not instruct them in piety, be separated. And if he continues in his negligence, let him be deprived. *Apostolic Constitutions (compiled c. 390, E), 7.503; extended discussion of qualifications: 7.396–7.398; extended discussion: 7.398–400, 7.433–7.434.*

Post-Nicene mention of archbishops: 7.502.

SEE ALSO CHURCH GOVERNMENT; COUNCILS, CHURCH; DEACON; PRESBYTER; TWICE-MARRIED.

II. Bishop of Rome

The blessed apostles, then, founded and built up the church [in Rome]. They committed the office of bishop into the hands of Linus. Of this Linus, Paul makes mention in the Epistles to Timothy. To him succeeded Anacletus. After him, in the third place from the apostles, Clement was allotted the office of bishop. *Irenaeus (c. 180, E/W), 1.416.*

When the blessed Polycarp was visiting in Rome in the time of [bishop] Anicetus, . . . they were at once well inclined towards each other. They were not willing that any quarrel should arise between them upon this matter. Anicetus could not persuade Polycarp to forego the observance [of his Easter customs]. For these things had been always observed by John the disciple of our Lord, and by other apostles with whom Polycarp had been conversant. Nor, on the other hand, could Polycarp succeed in persuading Anicetus to keep [Easter in his way]. For Anicetus maintained that he was bound to adhere to the usage of the presbyters who preceded him. And in this state of affairs, they held fellowship with each other. *Irenaeus (c. 180, E/W), 1.569.*

The heretics say that . . . the truth of Gospel preaching was preserved until the times of Victor, who was the thirteenth bishop in Rome from Peter, and that beginning with his successor, Zephyrinus, the truth was falsified. . . . Since the doctrine of the church, then, has been proclaimed so many years ago, how is it possible that men have preached in the manner claimed by these men, up to the time of Victor? And how are these [heretics] not ashamed to utter these calumnies against Victor? For they well know that Victor excommunicated Theodotus the tanner, the leader and father of this God-denying apostasy? *Eusebius, quoting Caius (c. 215, W), 5.601.*

At that time, Zephyrinus [bishop of Rome] imagined that he administered the affairs of the church. He was an uninformed and shamefully corrupt man. He, being persuaded by proffered gain, was accustomed to connive at those who were present for the purpose of becoming disciples of Cleomenes. But after a while, he himself was enticed away. So he hurried headlong into the same opinions [of Monarchianism]. And he had Callistus as his adviser and a fellow champion of these wicked tenets. . . . During their oversight, the school of these heretics continued to acquire strength and augmentation from the fact that Zephyrinus and Callistus [bishops of Rome] helped them to prevail. Never at any time, however, have I been guilty of collusion with them. Instead, I have frequently opposed them, refuted them, and have forced them reluctantly to acknowledge the truth. *Hippolytus (c. 225, W), 5.125.*

Callistus attempted to confirm this heresy [of Monarchianism]. He was a man cunning in wickedness. He was subtle where deceit was concerned, and he was goaded on by restless ambition to mount the episcopal chair [of Rome]. Now, this man molded to his purpose Zephyrinus, an ignorant and illiterate man— one unskilled in ecclesiastical definitions. Inasmuch as Zephyrinus was covetous and was accessible to bribes, Callistus was able to seduce him into whatever course of action he wanted—luring him through gifts and illicit demands. . . . But Callistus perverted Sabellius himself. And he did this, even though he had the ability of rectifying [his errors]. *Hippolytus (c. 225, W), 5.128.*

The impostor [i.e., Callistus, bishop of Rome], having ventured on such opinions, established a school in antagonism to the church. And he adopted the foregoing system of instruction. And he first invented the device of conniving with men in regard to their indulgence in pleasures, saying he could forgive the sins of everyone. For if anyone commits any transgression, they say the sin is not counted unto him—provided only he hurries off to the school of Callistus. This is true even if the person is in the habit of attending the congregation of anyone else. He only needs to be called a Christian. And many persons were gratified with his regulation. . . . However, some of them, in accordance with my condemnatory sentence, had been by me forcibly ejected from the church. Yet, they passed over to him and served to crowd his school. *Hippolytus (c. 225, W), 5.131.*

[Callistus, bishop of Rome,] propounded the opinion that if a bishop were guilty of any sin— even a sin unto death—he should not be deposed. About the time of this man, bishops, presbyters, and deacons who had been twice married—even thrice married—began to retain their place among the clergy. Furthermore, if anyone who was in holy orders became married, he permitted such a one to continue in holy orders as though he had not sinned. And, he alleged that what has been spoken by the apostle refers to such a person: "Who are you to judge another man's servant?" . . .

In contempt of God, [the hearers of bishop Callistus] do not place restraint on the commission of sin, alleging that they pardon those who acquiesce. For Callistus even also permitted the following to females: If they were unmarried and burned with passion at an age at all events unbecoming, or if they were not inclined to overturn their own dignity through a legal marriage, he permitted them to choose whomever they wanted as a bedfellow—whether slave or free. He said that, although they were not legally married, they could consider such a one as a husband. For that reason, women who were reputed believers began to resort to drugs for producing sterility. They also began to gird themselves around, so as to expel what was being conceived. For they did not wish to have a child by either a slave or by any paltry fellow—for the sake of their family and excessive wealth. Behold, into how great an impiety the lawless one has proceeded: inculcating adultery and murder at the same time! They have no shame. For, after such audacious acts, they attempt still to call themselves a catholic church! *Hippolytus (c. 225, W), 5.131.*

[FROM A LETTER WRITTEN TO CORNELIUS, BISHOP OF ROME:] Cyprian to Cornelius, his brother, greeting. I have thought it both obligatory on me and necessary for you, dearest brother, to write a short letter to the confessors who are there with you. *Cyprian (c. 250, W), 5.320.*

You intimated that you did not hold communion with Novatian. Rather, you followed my advice and held one common agreement with Cornelius our co-bishop. *Cyprian (c. 250, W), 5.327.*

Lest perhaps the number of bishops in Africa might seem unsatisfactory, we also wrote to Rome, to Cornelius, our colleague, concerning this thing. He himself was also holding a council with very many bishops, which had concurred in the same opinion as we had held. *Cyprian (c. 250, W), 5.328, 329.*

Cornelius was made bishop by the judgment of God and of His Christ. This was by the testimony of almost all the clergy, by the election of the people who were then present, and by the assembly of ancient priests and good men. . . . This occurred when the place of Fabian, that is, when the place of Peter and the degree of the priestly chair, was vacant. *Cyprian (c. 250, W), 5.329.*

[FROM A LETTER WRITTEN TO CORNELIUS, BISHOP OF ROME:] I have read your letter, dearest brother, which you sent by Saturus our brother, the acolyte. . . . But, dearest brother, ecclesiastical discipline is not on that account to be forsaken, nor priestly censure to be relaxed. *Cyprian (c. 250, W), 5.338, 339.*

[FROM A LETTER WRITTEN TO CORNELIUS, BISHOP OF ROME:] From the mutual love that we owe and that we manifest towards each other, I know, dearest brother, that you always read my letters to the very distinguished clergy who preside with you there and to your very holy and large congregation. Yet, now I both warn and ask you to do by my request what at other times you do of your own accord and courtesy. *Cyprian (c. 250, W), 5.346.*

Since we have one church, a united mind, and an undivided peace, what priest does not congratulate himself on the praises of his fellow-priest [i.e., Cornelius, bishop of Rome], as if on his own? *Cyprian (c. 250, W), 5.351*

Cyprian to his brother, Stephen [bishop of Rome], greetings! *Cyprian (c. 250, W), 5.367.*

Cornelius [bishop of Rome], our colleague, was a peaceable and righteous priest. . . . He had long ago decreed with us and with all the bishops appointed throughout the whole world that men of this sort . . . were prohibited from ordination to the clergy. *Cyprian (c. 250, W), 5.371.*

Peter—whom the Lord chose first and upon whom He built His church—did not insolently claim anything to himself. Nor did he arrogantly assume anything when Paul later disputed with him about circumcision. He did not say that he held the primacy and that he needed to be obeyed by novices and those lately come! *Cyprian (c. 250, W), 5.377.*

You have desired that what Stephen [bishop of Rome], our brother, replied to my letters should be brought to your knowledge. Therefore, I have sent you a copy of his reply. On the reading of it, you will more and more observe his error in endeavoring to maintain the cause of heretics against Christians. . . . For he judged the baptism of all heretics to be just and lawful. . . . He says, "Let nothing be innovated; rather, follow what has been handed down." But where is that tradition [he speaks of]? Where do we find this practice descending from the authority of the Lord and of the Gospel? Or where do we find it among the commandments and the epistles of the apostles? *Cyprian (c. 250, W), 5.386.*

[WRITTEN CONCERNING STEPHEN, BISHOP OF ROME:] We must consider . . . whether the account can be satisfactory in the day of judgment for a priest of God who maintains, approves, and acquiesces in the baptism of blasphemers. . . . Does he give glory to God, who does not hold the unity and truth that arise from the divine law, but maintains heresies against the church? Does he give glory to God, who—a friend of heretics and an enemy to Christians—thinks that the priests of God who support the truth of Christ and the unity of the church are to be excommunicated? . . . It happens by a love of presumption and of obstinacy that a man would rather maintain his own evil and false position than to agree in the right and true position that belongs to another. Foreseeing this, the blessed apostle Paul wrote to Timothy and warned him that a bishop must not be "quarrelsome or contentious, but gentle and teachable." . . . For it behooves a bishop not only to teach, but to learn. *Cyprian (c. 250, W), 5.388.*

Let these things that were done by Stephen [bishop of Rome] be passed by for the present. Otherwise, while we remember his audacity and pride, we might bring a more lasting sadness on ourselves from the things that he has wickedly done. *Firmilian (c. 256, E), 5.390.*

However, those who are at Rome do not always observe those things that were handed down from the beginning. Yet, they vainly pretend the authority of the apostles. Anyone may

know also from the fact that, concerning the celebration of Easter . . . he may see that there are some diversities. . . . Similarly, in very many other provinces, many things are varied because of the difference of the places and names. Nevertheless, there is no departure at all from the peace and unity of the catholic church on this account—such as Stephen has dared to make. *Firmilian (c. 256, E), 5.391.*

I am justly indignant at this open and manifest folly of Stephen [bishop of Rome]! He boasts of the place of his episcopate and contends that he holds the succession from Peter, on whom the foundations of the church were laid. Yet, he introduces many other rocks and establishes the new buildings of many [heretical] churches! . . . He does not understand that the truth of the Christian Rock is overshadowed—and, in some measure, abolished—by him when he betrays and deserts unity in this manner. . . . Stephen, who declares that he holds the chair of Peter by succession, is not stirred with zeal against heretics. For he concedes to them . . . the very greatest power of grace. *Firmilian (c. 256, E), 5.394.*

We join custom to truth. And we resist the Romans' custom with custom—the custom of truth. *Firmilian (c. 256, E), 5.395.*

The following passage was written against Stephen, bishop of Rome, by Firmilian, an eastern bishop. The occasion was that Stephen had excommunicated all the churches who would not follow his practice of accepting baptism performed by heretics (requiring only that the bishop lay hands upon such heretics when coming to the church).

How great a sin you have heaped up for yourself, when you cut yourself off from so many flocks! For it is you yourself that you have cut off. Do not deceive yourself. For the real schismatic is the one who has made himself an apostate from the communion of ecclesiastical unity. Although you think that everyone can be excommunicated by you, you have really excommunicated yourself alone from everyone else. Not even the teachings of an apostle have been able to mold you to the rule of truth and peace, although he warned and said, "I . . . beseech you to walk worthy of the calling by which you are called, with all lowliness and meekness." . . .

[SAID SARCASTICALLY:] How carefully has Stephen fulfilled these salutary commands and warnings of the apostle! How carefully he has first kept lowliness of mind and meekness! For what is more lowly or meek than to have disagreed with so many bishops throughout the whole world, breaking peace with each one of them in various kinds of conflict. At one time, he has broken with the eastern churches, as we are sure you know. At another time, he has broken with you who are in the south. . . . This is to have kept the unity of the Spirit in the bond of peace? He has cut himself off from the unity of love and made himself a stranger in all respects from his brethren. He has rebelled against the sacrament and the faith with the madness of rebellious dissension. *Firmilian (c. 256, E), 5.396.*

[ADDRESSED TO STEPHEN, BISHOP OF ROME:] Understand, however, my brother that all the churches located in the east . . . that were formerly in a state of division, are now made one again. *Dionysius of Alexandria (c. 262, E), 6.101.*

[LETTER TO SIXTUS II, BISHOP OF ROME:] Truly, brother, I have need of advice, and I desire your judgment. *Dionysius of Alexandria (c. 262, E), 6.103.*

The contention was between Victor, at that time bishop of the city of Rome, and Polycrates, who then appeared to hold the primacy among the bishops of Asia. And this contention was adjusted most rightfully by Irenaeus, who at that time was president of a part of Gaul. The result was that both parties kept to their own order and did not decline from the original custom of antiquity. *Anatolius (c. 270, E), 6.148, 149.*

SEE ALSO APOSTOLIC SUCCESSION; CHURCH GOVERNMENT; CHURCHES, APOSTOLIC; MONARCHIANISM; PRESBYTER.

BISHOP OF ROME

SEE BISHOP (II. BISHOP OF ROME).

BLOOD (AS FOOD)

But you will not eat flesh with its life, that is, its blood. Gen. 9:4.

For the life of the flesh is in the blood, and I have given it to you upon the altar to make atonement for your souls; for it is the blood that makes atonement for the soul. Therefore I said to the children of Israel, "No one among you will eat blood, nor will any stranger who sojourns among you eat blood." Lev. 17:11, 12.

It seemed good to the Holy Spirit, and to us, to lay upon you no greater burden than these necessary things: that you abstain from things offered to idols, from blood, from things strangled, and from sexual immorality. Acts 15:28, 29.

God permitted Noah, being a just man, to eat of every animal, but not of flesh with the blood. *Justin Martyr (c. 160, E), 1.204.*

The blood . . . is the bond of union between soul and body. *Irenaeus (c. 180, E/W), 1.529.*

When faint with hunger, [the Scythian] asks his horse for sustenance; and the horse offers his veins, and supplies his master with all he possesses—his blood. To the nomad, the horse is at once conveyance and sustenance. . . . Perish, then, the savage beast whose food is blood! For it is unlawful for men, whose body is nothing but flesh elaborated of blood, to touch blood. For human blood has become a partaker of the Word. *Clement of Alexandria (c. 195, E), 2.277.*

The apostle says, "All other things buy out of the meat market, asking no questions," with the exception of the things mentioned in the catholic epistle of all the apostles "with the consent of the Holy Spirit." This is written in the Acts of the Apostles, and it was conveyed to the faithful by the hands of Paul himself. For they indicated "that they must of necessity abstain from things offered to idols, from blood, from things strangled, and from fornication." *Clement of Alexandria (c. 195, E), 2.427.*

Blush for your vile ways before the Christians, who do not have even the blood of animals at their meals of simple and natural food. We abstain from things strangled and from things that die a natural death. . . . To clench the matter with a single example, you tempt Christians with sausages of blood, just because you are perfectly aware that the thing by which you thus try to get them to transgress they hold unlawful. *Tertullian (c. 197, W), 3.25.*

"But flesh in the blood of its own soul you will not eat." For even by this very fact, that He exempts from eating that flesh only the soul of which is not eliminated through blood, it is clear that He has conceded the use of all other flesh. *Tertullian (c. 213, W), 4.104.*

So much do we shrink from human blood, that we do not use the blood even of edible animals in our food. *Mark Minucius Felix (c. 200, W), 4.192.*

Scripture has also added its authority to a second opinion, when it says, "You will not eat the blood, because the life of all flesh is its blood. And you will not eat the life with the flesh." In this, it indicates most clearly that the blood of every animal is its life. *Origen (c. 225, E), 4.286.*

He, then, eats in faith who believes that the food to be eaten has not been sacrificed in the temples of idols and that it is not strangled, nor is it blood. But he who is in doubt about any of these things does not eat in faith. *Origen (c. 245, E), 9.441.*

It seemed good to the apostles of Jesus and the elders assembled together from Antioch (and also, as they themselves say, to the Holy Spirit) to write a letter to the Gentile believers, forbidding them to partake of those things from which alone they say it is necessary to abstain: namely, "things offered to idols, things strangled, and blood." . . . As to things strangled, we are forbidden by Scripture to partake of them because the blood is still in them. Now, blood is said to be the food of demons, especially the odor arising from blood. Perhaps, then, if we were to eat strangled animals, we might have such spirits feeding along with us. And the reason that forbids the use of strangled animals for food is also applicable to the use of blood. *Origen (c. 248, E), 4.650.*

[The soul] is contained in the material of the blood. *Lactantius (c. 304–313, W), 7.209.*

If any bishop, presbyter, or deacon (or indeed anyone of the priestly category) eats flesh with the blood of its life, or that which is torn by beasts, or which died of itself—let him be deprived. For the law itself has forbidden this. But if he is one of the laity, let him be suspended. *Apostolic Constitutions (compiled c. 390, E), 7.504.*

SEE ALSO JERUSALEM COUNCIL.

BLOOD OF CHRIST

Shepherd the church of God which He purchased with His own blood. Acts 20:28.

In Him we have redemption through His blood, the forgiveness of sins. Eph. 1:7.

Knowing that you were not redeemed with corruptible things, . . . but with the precious blood of Christ. 1 Pet. 1:18, 19.

To Him who loved us and washed us from our sins in His own blood. Rev. 1:5.

. . . that we could be sanctified through the remission of sins, which is brought about by His blood of sprinkling. *Barnabas (c. 70–130, E), 1.139.*

Let us look steadfastly to the blood of Christ, and see how precious that blood is to God, which, having been shed for our salvation, has set the grace of repentance before the whole world. *Clement of Rome (c. 96, W), 1.7.*

They made it manifest that redemption should flow through the blood of the Lord to all those who believe and hope in God. *Clement of Rome (c. 96, W), 1.8.*

Let us reverence the Lord Jesus Christ, whose blood was given for us. *Clement of Rome (c. 96, W), 1.11.*

We are established in love through the blood of Christ. *Ignatius (c. 105, E), 1.86.*

Those who do not believe in the blood of Christ will incur condemnation as a result. *Ignatius (c. 105, E), 1.88, 89.*

We are no longer purified by the blood of sheep and goats, by the ashes of a heifer, or by the offerings of fine flour. Rather, we are purified by faith through the blood of Christ. *Justin Martyr (c. 160, E), 1.200.*

We trust in the blood of salvation. *Justin Martyr (c. 160, E), 1.206.*

This signified that He would wash those who believe in Him with His own blood. *Justin Martyr (c. 160, E), 1.222.*

As the blood of the Passover saved those who were in Egypt, so also the blood of Christ will deliver from death those who have believed. *Justin Martyr (c. 160, E), 1.254.*

His Son Jesus Christ redeemed us from apostasy with His own blood, so that we could also be a sanctified people. *Irenaeus (c. 180, E/ W), 1.418.*

The Son of God died for us and redeemed us with His blood. *Irenaeus (c. 180, E/W), 1.444.*

The Lamb who was slain has redeemed us with His own blood. *Irenaeus (c. 180, E/W), 1.488.*

The Lord thus has redeemed us through His own blood, giving His soul for our souls. *Irenaeus (c. 180, E/W), 1.527.*

He redeemed us by His own blood, which His apostle declares. *Irenaeus (c. 180, E/W), 1.528.*

Christ, who was called the Son of God before the ages, was manifested in the fullness of time, in order that He could cleanse us through His blood. *Irenaeus (c. 180, E/W), 1.575.*

The Lord should fill us with joy, we who have been redeemed from corruption by the blood of the Lord. *Clement of Alexandria (c. 195, E), 2.215.*

He says, "The blood of Jesus Christ His Son cleanses us." For the doctrine of the Lord, which is very powerful, is called His blood. *Clement of Alexandria (c. 195, E), 2.575.*

"We are not our own, but bought with a price." And what kind of price? The blood of God. *Tertullian (c. 205, W), 4.46.*

After the regeneration, He who has redeemed us with His own blood assigns us to a holy angel. *Origen (c. 245, E), 9.491.*

... from that death which once the blood of Christ extinguished and from which the saving grace of baptism and of our Redeemer has delivered us. *Cyprian (c. 250, W), 5.332.*

The Lord's loving kindness, no less than His mercy, is great in respect of our salvation. For He was not content to only redeem us with His blood, but He also prayed for us. *Cyprian (c. 250, W), 5.455.*

This gift of His mercy He confers upon us—by overcoming death in the trophy of the cross, by redeeming the believer with the price of His blood. *Cyprian (c. 250, W), 5.465.*

Those sins that had been previously committed are purged by the blood and sanctification of Christ. *Cyprian (c. 250, W), 5.476.*

One who wants to gain eternal salvation should purchase the precious pearl—eternal life—at the price of the blood of Christ. *Cyprian (c. 250, W), 5.478.*

... to whom but to them, no doubt, whom he had redeemed at the great price of his blood. *Treatise against Novatian (c. 255, W), 5.661.*

He freed us by His blood from sin. . . . His antiquity is immortality and the fountain of majesty. *Victorinus (c. 280, W), 7.344.*

You are redeemed by the precious blood of Christ. *Apostolic Constitutions (compiled c. 390, E), 7.446.*

O Lord, save your people and bless your inheritance, which you have purchased with the precious blood of your Christ. *Apostolic Constitutions (compiled c. 390, E), 7.498.*

SEE ALSO ATONEMENT; SALVATION.

BOOK OF LIFE

Let them be blotted out of the book of the living, and not be written with the righteous. Ps. 69:28.

. . . and the rest of my fellow workers, whose names are in the Book of Life. Phil. 4:3.

He who overcomes will be clothed in white garments, and I will not blot out his name from the Book of Life. Rev. 3:5.

I know that if they will repent with all their hearts, they will be enrolled in the Books of Life with the saints. *Hermas (c. 150, W), 2.10.*

There is one Book of Life from which those who have proved unworthy to be in it are blotted out. For it is written: "Let them be blotted out of the book of the living." *Origen (c. 228, E), 9.348.*

BORN AGAIN

SEE BAPTISM; NEW BIRTH.

BRAHMANS

SEE HINDUS.

BRITAIN

Paul also obtained the reward of patient endurance, after being seven times thrown into captivity. . . . After preaching both in the east and west, he gained the illustrious reputation due to his faith, having taught righteousness to the whole world, and having come to the extreme limit of the west. [Britain was the westernmost province of the Roman Empire.] *Clement of Rome (c. 96, W), 1.6.*

After their languages were divided, men gradually began to multiply and spread over all the earth. And some of them tended towards the east to dwell there. And others went to parts of the great continent. Others went northwards, so as to go as far as Britain. *Theophilus (c. 180, E), 2.107.*

The compilers of narratives say that on the island of Britain there is a cave situated under a mountain with a chasm on its summit. When the wind rushes through the cave, . . . a sound is heard like cymbals clashing. *Clement of Alexandria (c. 195, E), 2.487, 488.*

By this time, . . . [the name of Christ has reached] the various confines of the Moors, all the limits of Spain, the diverse nations of the Gauls, and the haunts of the Britons—inaccessible to the Romans, but subjugated to Christ. *Tertullian (c. 197, W), 3.157, 158.*

Britain is deficient in sunshine, but it is refreshed by the warmth of the sea that flows around it. *Mark Minucius Felix (c. 200, W), 4.182.*

The next best pearls are those taken from the sea at Britain. *Origen (c. 228, E), 9.417.*

SEE ALSO CELTS; DRUIDS.

BROTHERS OF JESUS

SEE JESUS CHRIST (VI. BROTHERS OF JESUS).

BUDDHA

Some of the Indians obey the precepts of Buddha, too. On account of his extraordinary sanctity, they have raised him to divine honors. *Clement of Alexandria (c. 195, E), 2.316.*

SEE ALSO HINDUS.

BUILDINGS, CHURCH

SEE CHURCH BUILDINGS.

BURIAL AND FUNERAL PRACTICES OF CHRISTIANS

Then his disciples came and took away the body and buried it, and went and told Jesus. Matt. 14:12.

And devout men carried Stephen to his burial, and made great lamentation over him. Acts 8:2.

[SAID OF CHRISTIANS:] Whenever one of the poor among them passes from this world, each one of them gives heed to him, according to his ability, and carefully sees to his burial. . . . If any righteous man among them passes from this world, they rejoice and offer thanks to

God. They escort his body as if he were setting out from one place to go to another nearby. *Aristides (c. 125, E), 9.276, 277.*

We certainly buy no frankincense. If the Arabians complain of this, let the Sabaeans be well assured that their more precious and costly merchandise is expended as largely in the burying of Christians as in the fumigating of the gods. *Tertullian (c. 197, W), 3.49.*

I on my side must deride [the pagan custom] still more, especially when it burns up its dead with harshest inhumanity, only to pamper them immediately afterwards with gluttonous satiety, using the selfsame fires to honor them and to insult them. *Tertullian (c. 210, W), 3.545.*

Even this partial survival of the soul finds a place in the opinions of some men. And on this account, they will not have the body consumed by fire at its funeral. For they would spare the small residue of the soul. There is, however, another way of accounting for this pious treatment. Perhaps it is not meant to favor the relics of the soul, but to avert a cruel custom in the interest even of the body. For, being human, [the body] itself does not deserve the same end that is inflicted upon murderers. *Tertullian (c. 210, W), 3.228.*

It is on a like principle that embalmed corpses are set aside for burial in mausoleums and sepulchers—in order that they may be removed therefrom when the Master orders it. *Tertullian (c. 210, W), 3.565.*

When there had been some agitation about places of burial for our dead, the cry arose, "No burial grounds for the Christians." Yet, it came to pass that their own grounds—their threshing floors—were wanting, for they gathered in no harvests. *Tertullian (c. 212, W), 3.106.*

[PAGAN ANTAGONIST, SPEAKING OF CHRISTIANS:] You reserve ointments only for funeral rites. You even refuse garlands for your sepulchers. *Mark Minucius Felix (c. 200, W), 4.179.*

We do not, as you [pagans] believe, fear any loss from cremation. Rather, we adopt the ancient and better custom of burying in the earth. *Mark Minucius Felix (c. 200, W), 4.194.*

The pomp of death art is in error. As a servant of God, you should please Him even in death. Alas that the lifeless body should be adorned in death! O true vanity to desire honor for the dead! ... What will the pomp benefit the dead man? *Commodianus (c. 240, W), 4.217.*

We are not at all distressed by the assertion of [the pagan] Heraclitus . . . that "dead bodies are to be cast out as more worthless than dung." . . . For in harmony with those laws that are based upon the principles of equity, bodies are deemed worthy of burial, with the honors accorded on such occasions. So far as it can be helped, no insult should be offered to the soul that dwelt within, by casting out the body like that of an animal. *Origen (c. 248, E), 4.553.*

As a matter of the greatest importance, if the bodies of the martyrs and others are not buried, a considerable risk is incurred by those whose duty it is to perform this function. *Letter from the church in Rome to Cyprian (c. 250, W), 5.281.*

They took the bodies of their fellow saints on their upturned hands and on their bosoms and closed their eyes and shut their mouths. And carrying them in company, they lay them out decently. They clung to them, embraced them, and properly prepared them with washing and with clothes. *Dionysius of Alexandria, (c. 262, E), 6.109, as quoted by Eusebius.*

No one can fittingly describe the cruelty of this beast [i.e., Rome] that . . . not only tears in pieces the limbs of men, but also breaks their very bones and rages over their ashes—so that there will be no place for their burial. As though those who confess God aimed at this:

that their tombs would be visited, rather than that they themselves may reach the presence of God. What brutality it is! What fury, what madness! To deny light to the living and earth to the dead! *Lactantius (c. 304–313, W), 7.147.*

The last and greatest office of piety is the burying of strangers and the poor. . . . We will not allow the image and workmanship of God to lie exposed as a prey to beasts and birds. Rather, we will restore it to the earth, from which it had its origin. And even in the case of an unknown person, we will fulfill the office of relatives. . . . For in what does the nature of justice consist more, than to render to strangers through kindness whatever we would render to our own relatives through family love? *Lactantius (c. 304–313, W), 7.177.*

To all these charities, Marcellus added yet larger deeds of piety. With a large band of his own household, he went to oversee the burying of the bodies of those [captives] who had died on the march. He secured an appropriate burial for as many of them as he could find, in whatever condition. *Disputation of Archelaus and Manes (c. 320, E), 6.180.*

In the funerals of the departed, if they were faithful in Christ, accompany them with singing. For "precious in the sight of the Lord is the death of His saints" [Ps. 116:15]. *Apostolic Constitutions (compiled c. 390, E), 7.464.*

CAINITES

The Cainites were an early Gnostic sect who taught that Cain, Judas, and other ungodly persons were actually spiritual seekers who resisted the evil Creator.

Others declare that Cain derived his existence from the Power above. They acknowledge that Esau, Korah, the Sodomites, and all such persons are related to themselves. . . . They maintain that Judas the traitor was thoroughly acquainted with these things. . . . They produce a fictitious history of this kind, which they call the Gospel of Judas. *Irenaeus (c. 180, E/W), 1.358.*

A viper of the Cainite heresy . . . has carried away a great number of persons with her most venomous doctrine. She makes it her first goal to destroy baptism. *Tertullian (c. 199, W), 3.669; extended discussion: 1.358.*

SEE ALSO GNOSTICS, GNOSTICISM; HERESIES, HERETICS.

CALENDAR, CHRISTIAN

The word translated "Easter" in the following passages is literally Passover [Gr. pascha]. This does not refer to the Jewish Passover but to the Christian Passover.

[WRITTEN TO CHRISTIANS:] You have your own registers, your own calendar. You have nothing to do with the joys of the world. In fact, you are called to the very opposite—for "the world will rejoice, but you will mourn." *Tertullian (c. 212, W), 3.101.*

If the apostle has erased all devotion absolutely of "seasons, days, months, and years," why do we celebrate Easter by an annual rotation in the first month? Why in the fifty ensuing days do we spend our time in all exultation? Why do we devote to stations the fourth and sixth days of the week, and to fasts the Preparation Day [i.e., Good Friday]? Anyhow, you

sometimes continue your station even over the Sabbath—a day never to be kept as a fast except at the Easter season. *Tertullian (c. 213, W), 4.112.*

We ourselves are accustomed to observe certain days. For example, there is the Lord's Day, the Preparation, Easter, and Pentecost. . . . However, the majority of those who are accounted believers are not of this advanced class [i.e., those who focus on Christ every day]. Rather, they require some sensible memorials to prevent spiritual things from passing completely away from their minds. For they are either unable or unwilling to keep every day in this manner. *Origen (c. 248, E), 4.647, 648.*

Compare the festivals that are observed among us (which have been described above) with the public feasts of Celsus and the pagans. Would you not say that ours are much more sacred observances than those feasts in which the lust of the flesh runs riot and leads to drunkenness and debauchery? *Origen (c. 248, E), 4.648.*

[REFERRING TO THE EASTER VIGIL:] Then the middle of the heavens will be laid open in the dead and darkness of the night so that the light of the descending God may be manifest in all the world. . . . This is the night that is celebrated by us in watchfulness on account of the coming of our King and God. *Lactantius (c. 304–313, W), 7.215.*

The following passage was written near the close of the fourth century, revealing a much more detailed Christian calendar by that time.

Brethren, observe the festival days. First of all, there is the birthday that you are to celebrate on the twenty-fifth of the ninth month [i.e., December 25]. After that, let the Epiphany be to you the most honored, in which the Lord made to you a display of His own divinity. And let that feast take place on the sixth of the tenth month [i.e., January 6]. After that, the fast of Lent is to be observed by you as containing a memorial of our Lord's manner of life and teaching. But let this solemnity be observed before the fast of Easter, beginning from the second day of the week and ending at the Day of the Preparation. After those solemnities, breaking your fast, begin the holy week of Easter, all of you fasting in this week with fear and trembling. *Apostolic Constitutions, (compiled c. 390, E), 7.443.*

From [Easter], count forty days, from the Lord's day until the fifth day of the week, and celebrate the feast of the Ascension of the Lord. *Apostolic Constitutions (compiled c. 390, E), 7.448.*

A reference to the Post-Nicene calendar: 7.495.

SEE ALSO BIRTH OF JESUS; EASTER; EPIPHANY; HOLIDAYS, PAGAN; LORD'S DAY; PENTECOST.

CANDLES

Is that man to be thought in his senses who presents the light of candles and torches as an offering to Him who is the Author and Giver of light? The light that He requires from us is of another kind.... I mean, the light of the mind, ... which light no one can exhibit unless he has known God. But their gods, because they are of the earth, stand in need of lights, that they may not be in darkness. And their worshippers, because they have no taste for anything heavenly, are recalled to the earth by the very religious rites to which they are devoted. *Lactantius (c. 304–313, W), 7.163.*

CANNIBALISM

For men to partake of the flesh of men is a thing most hateful and abominable, and more detestable than any other unlawful and unnatural food or act. *Athenagoras (c. 175, E), 2.153.*

CANON, NEW TESTAMENT

The apostle writes, "O Timothy, keep that which is committed to your trust, avoiding the profane and vain babbling and opposition of falsely called knowledge." ... Convicted by this utterance, the heretics reject the Epistles to Timothy. *Clement of Alexandria (c. 195, E), 2.359.*

The second Epistle of John, which was written to virgins, is very simple. It was written to a Babylonian lady, by the name of Electa, and it indicates the election of the holy church. *Clement of Alexandria (c. 195, E), 2.576, 577.*

In the Sketches, in a word, [Clement of Alexandria] has made abbreviated narratives of the whole testamentary Scripture. And he has not passed over the disputed books—I mean Jude and the rest of the catholic Epistles, Barnabas, and what is called the Revelation of Peter. And he says that the Epistle to the Hebrews is Paul's. *Eusebius, citing Clement of Alexandria (c. 195, E), 2.579.*

Again, in the same books, Clement has set down a tradition which he had received from the elders before him, in regard to the order of the Gospels, to the following effect: He says that the Gospels containing the genealogies were written first, and that the Gospel according to Mark was composed in the following circumstances: Peter preached the word publicly at Rome. By the Spirit, he proclaimed the Gospel. Those who were present (who were numerous) urged Mark to write down what had been spoken. For he had attended Peter from an early period and remembered what had been said. On his composing the Gospel, Mark handed it to those who had urged him. When this came to Peter's knowledge, he neither hindered nor encouraged it. Now, John, the last of all, seeing that what was declared in the Gospels was primarily physical, at the request of his intimate friends and inspired by the Spirit, he composed a spiritual Gospel. *Eusebius, citing Clement of Alexandria (c. 195, E), 2.580.*

Although different matters are taught us in the various books of the Gospels, there is no difference as regards the faith of believers. For in all of them, everything was related under one imperial Spirit. *Muratorian Fragment (c. 200, W), 5.603.*

As to the epistles of Paul, ... he wrote first of all—and at considerable length—to the Corinthians, to curtail the schism of heresy; and then to the Galatians, to forbid circumcision; and then to the Romans on the rule of the Old Testament Scriptures, and also to show them that Christ is the first object in them. *Muratorian Fragment (c. 200, W), 5.603.*

Following the rule of his predecessor, John, the blessed apostle Paul writes to no more than seven churches by name, in this order: the first to the Corinthians, the second to the Ephesians, the third to the Philippians, the fourth to the Colossians, the fifth to the Galatians, the sixth to the Thessalonians, the seventh to the Romans. Moreover, though he writes twice to the Corinthians and Thessalonians for their correction, it is yet shown—i.e., by this seven-fold writing—that there is one church spread abroad through the whole world. . . . He wrote, besides these, one to Philemon, one to Titus, and two to Timothy, in simple personal affection and love indeed. Yet, these are hallowed in the esteem of the catholic church and in the regulation of ecclesiastical discipline. *Muratorian Fragment (c. 200, W), 5.603.*

The Epistle of Jude, indeed, and two belonging to the above-named John—or bearing the name of John—are reckoned among the catholic epistles. And the Book of Wisdom, written by the friends of Solomon in his honor. We receive also the Apocalypse of John and that of Peter, though some among us will not have this latter read in the church. *Muratorian Fragment (c. 200, W), 5.603, 604.*

Paul then briefly addresses his own conversion from a persecutor to an apostle. In doing so, he confirms the Acts of the Apostles. In that book, we can find the very subject of this epistle [to the Galatians]—how that certain persons objected and said that men should be circumcised and that the Law of Moses was to be observed. *Tertullian (c. 207, W), 3.432.*

Marcion rejected the two epistles to Timothy and the one to Titus, all of which deal with church discipline. His aim, was, I suppose, to carry out his interpolating process even to the number of epistles. *Tertullian (c. 207, W), 3.473, 474.*

The Acts of the Apostles, too, attests the resurrection. *Tertullian (c. 210, W), 3.573.*

If anyone should quote to us out of the little treatise entitled *The Teaching of Peter* . . . I have to reply, in the first place, that this work is not included among ecclesiastical books. For we can show that it was composed neither by Peter nor by any other person inspired by the Spirit of God. *Origen (c. 225, E), 4.241.*

Peter . . . left one epistle of acknowledged authenticity. Perhaps we can allow that he left a second. However, this is doubtful. *Origen (c. 228, E), 9.346.*

John, who left one Gospel, . . . also wrote the Apocalypse. . . . He also left an epistle of very few lines. Perhaps he also wrote a second and a third. However, not everyone declares those to be genuine. Regardless, the two together do not amount to a hundred lines. *Origen (c. 228, E), 9.346, 347.*

The Scriptures that are current in the churches of God do not speak of seven heavens. *Origen (c. 248, E), 4.582, 583.*

In none of the Gospels current in the churches is Jesus ever described as being a carpenter Himself. *Origen (c. 248, E), 4.589.*

Paul wrote to the Romans, the Corinthians, the Galatians, the Ephesians, the Thessalonians, the Philippians, and to the Colossians. Afterwards, he wrote to individual persons. *Victorinus (c. 280, W), 7.345.*

If anyone publicly reads in the church the spurious books of the ungodly, as if they were holy, to the destruction of the people and of the clergy, let him be deprived. *Apostolic Constitutions (compiled c. 390, E), 7.503.*

Our sacred books, that is, those of the New Testament, are these: the four gospels of Matthew, Mark, Luke, and John; the fourteen Epistles of Paul; two Epistles of Peter, three of John, one of James, one of Jude; two Epistles of Clement; and the Constitutions. *Apostolic Constitutions (compiled c. 390, E), 7.505.*

SEE ALSO BARNABAS, EPISTLE OF; CANON, OLD TESTAMENT; GOSPEL ACCORDING TO THE HEBREWS; HEBREWS, EPISTLE TO; HERMAS, SHEPHERD OF; PSEUDEPIGRAPHA, NEW TESTAMENT.

CANON, OLD TESTAMENT

Melito to his brother Onesimus, greeting. Prompted by your regard for the Word, you have often expressed a wish to have some extracts made from the Law and the Prophets concerning the Savior. . . . I accordingly proceeded to the East, and went to the very spot where these things were preached and took place. Having made myself accurately acquainted with the books of the Old Testament, I have set them down below, and herewith send you the list. Their names are as follows: The five books of Moses (Genesis, Exodus, Leviticus, Numbers, Deuteronomy), Joshua son of Nun, Judges, Ruth, the four books of Kings, the two of Chronicles, the

Psalms of David, the Proverbs of Solomon, also Wisdom, Ecclesiastes, the Song of Songs, Job, the prophets Isaiah and Jeremiah, the twelve [prophets] contained in a single book, Daniel, Ezekiel, and Esdras. From these, I have made my extracts, dividing them into six books. *Melito (c. 170, E), 8.759.*

[The Book of Enoch] may now seem to have been rejected by the Jews for that very reason—just like nearly all the other portions that speak of Christ. Nor, of course, is this fact surprising: that they did not receive some Scriptures that spoke of Him whom they did not receive. For they did not receive Him even when He was here in person, speaking in their presence. *Tertullian (c. 198, W), 4.16.*

These philosophers have also made their attacks upon those writings which are condemned by us under the title of spurious—certain as we are that nothing should be received that does not agree with the true system of prophecy, which has arisen in this present age. *Tertullian (c. 210, W), 3.182.*

The twenty-four elders are the twenty-four books of the Law and the Prophets, which give testimonies of the Judgment. . . . The books of the Old Testament that are received are twenty-four, which you will find in the epitomes of Theodore. *Victorinus (c. 280, W), 7.348, 349.*

Let the following books be considered venerable and holy by you, both of the clergy and the laity. Of the Old Testament: the five books of Moses (Genesis, Exodus, Leviticus, Numbers, and Deuteronomy); one of Joshua, the son of Nun; one of the Judges; one of Ruth; four of the Kings; two of the Chronicles; two of Ezra; one of Esther; one of Judith; three of the Maccabees; one of Job; one hundred and fifty Psalms; three books of Solomon (Proverbs, Ecclesiastes, and the Song of Songs); and sixteen Prophets. Besides these, take care that your young persons learn the Wisdom of the very learned Sirach. *Apostolic Constitutions (compiled c. 390, E), 7.505.*

See also Canon, New Testament; Deuterocanonical Books; Enoch, Book of; Pseudepigrapha, Old Testament.

CAPITAL PUNISHMENT

You have heard that it was said, "An eye for an eye and a tooth for a tooth." But I tell you not to resist an evil

person. But whoever slaps you on your right cheek, turn the other to him also. Matt. 5:28, 29.

He is God's minister to you for good. But if you do evil, be afraid; for he does not bear the sword in vain; for he is God's minister, an avenger to execute wrath on him who practices evil. Rom. 13:4.

When they know that we cannot endure even to see a man put to death, though justly, who of them can accuse us of murder? . . . We consider that to see a man put to death is much the same as killing him. Therefore, we have sworn away from such [gladiatorial] spectacles. We do not even look on, lest we might contract guilt and pollution. So how can we put people to death? *Athenagoras (c. 175, E), 2.147.*

Let us suppose that it is possible for anyone to succeed in working under the mere *name* of the public office, in whatever office, and that he neither sacrifices nor lends his authority to sacrifices. . . . Furthermore, suppose that he neither sits in judgment on anyone's life or character (for you might allow his judging about *money*). Suppose that he neither condemns nor indicts anyone. Suppose he neither chains, imprisons, nor tortures anyone. Can anyone believe that all this is possible? *Tertullian (c. 200, W), 3.72.*

Now, inquiry is made about whether a believer may enter into military service. Likewise, it is asked whether those in the military can be admitted into the faith—even the rank and file, or any inferior grade, to whom there is no necessity for taking part in sacrifices or capital punishments. *Tertullian (c. 200, W), 3.73.*

These barbarous sentences of death consign the criminal who has committed murder—while yet alive—to various wild beasts (which are selected and trained even against their nature for their horrible office). In fact, [the criminal] is hindered from too easily dying, by a contrivance that retards his last moment in order to aggravate his punishment. But even if his *soul* should have anticipated the sword's last stroke and departed, his *body* at any event does not escape the weapon. Retribution of his own crime is yet exacted by stabbing his throat and stomach, and piercing his side. After that, he is flung into the fire, so that his very grave may be cheated. In no other way, indeed, is a sepulcher allowed him. . . . In fact, no mercy is shown to his bones; no indulgence to his ashes. Even these are punished with exposure and nakedness. The vengeance that is inflicted among men upon the murderer is really as great as that which is imposed by nature. Who would not prefer the justice of the world, which, as the apostle himself testifies, "does not bear the sword in vain"? For it is an institution of religion when it severely avenges in defense of human life. When we contemplate, too, the penalties assigned to other crimes—gallows, burnings, sacks, harpoons, and precipices—who would not think it better to receive his sentence in the courts of Pythagoras and Empedocles? *Tertullian (c. 210, W), 3.214.*

Christians could not slay their enemies. Nor could they condemn those who had broken the Law to be burned or stoned, as Moses commands. . . . However, in the case of the ancient Jews, who had a land and a form of government of their own, to take from them the right of making war upon their enemies, of fighting for their country, of putting to death or otherwise punishing adulterers, murderers, or others who were guilty of similar crimes, would have been to subject them to sudden and utter destruction whenever the enemy fell upon them. *Origen (c. 248, E), 4.618.*

Christians do not attack their assailants in return, for it is not lawful for the innocent to kill even the guilty. *Cyprian (c. 250, W), 5.351.*

He who reckons it a pleasure that a man—though justly condemned—should be slain in his sight, pollutes his conscience as much as if he should become a spectator and a sharer of a murder that is secretly committed. Yet, they call these "sports," in which human blood is shed! *Lactantius (c. 304–313, W), 7.186.*

When God forbids us to kill, He not only prohibits us from the open violence that is not even allowed by the public laws, but He also warns us against doing those things that are esteemed lawful among men. Thus it will not be lawful for a just man to engage in warfare, since his warfare is justice itself. Nor is it lawful for him to accuse anyone of a capital crime. For it makes no difference whether you put a man to death by word or by the sword. For it is the act of putting to death itself that is prohibited. Therefore, with regard to this commandment of God, there should be no exception at all. Rather, it is always unlawful to put a man to death, whom God willed to be a sacred creature. *Lactantius (c. 304–313, W), 7.187.*

Not as if all killing were wicked, but only that of the innocent. However, the killing that is just is reserved to the magistrates alone. *Apostolic Constitutions (compiled c. 390, E), 7.466.*

SEE ALSO CRIME AND PUNISHMENT; PUBLIC OFFICE; WAR.

CAPTIVITY, THE

The captivity in Babylon befell them after the exodus from Egypt. The whole population, then, was transported. The city was made desolate, and the sanctuary was destroyed. It was then that the word of the Lord was fulfilled that He spoke by the mouth of the prophet Jeremiah, saying, "the sanctuary shall be desolate seventy years." *Hippolytus (c. 205, W), 5.178.*

CARPOCRATES

Carpocrates, a leading Gnostic teacher of the second century, lived in Alexandria.

Carpocrates and his followers claim that the world and the things that are in it were created by angels greatly inferior to the unbegotten Father. They also hold that Jesus was the son of Joseph and that he was just like other men. *Irenaeus (c. 180, E/W), 1.350.*

However, it is not for you [Simon Magus] alone that the reincarnation philosophy has fabricated this story. Carpocrates also makes equally good use of it. He was a magician and a fornicator like yourself, only he did not have a Helen. *Tertullian (c. 210, W), 3.216.*

Carpocrates states that the world and the things in it were made by angels, far inferior to the unbegotten Father. He says that Jesus was begotten of Joseph and that, although having been born similar to other men, He was more just than the rest. He says that His soul—inasmuch as it was made vigorous and undefiled—remembered the things seen by it in its conversation with the unbegotten God. *Hippolytus (c. 225, W), 5.113.*

[The disciples of Carpocrates] make counterfeit images of Christ, alleging that these were in existence at the time . . . and were fashioned by Pilate. *Hippolytus (c. 225, W), 5.114; extended discussion: 1.350, 351.*

SEE ALSO GNOSTICS, GNOSTICISM; HERESIES, HERETICS.

CATECHUMENS

In the early church, catechumens were persons undergoing instruction prior to baptism.

The Greeks, having arrested the slaves of Christian catechumens, used force against them. *Ecumenius, citing Irenaeus (c. 180, E/W), 1.570.*

The young catechumen is imbued with perception and thought. *Clement of Alexandria (c. 195, E), 2.510.*

To begin with, it is doubtful [among the heretics] who is a catechumen and who is a believer. They all have access alike, they hear alike, and they pray alike. *Tertullian (c. 197, W), 3.263.*

Let no one, then, falter because of being assigned to the new recruit classes of hearers—as if on that account he has a license now even to sin. As soon as you know the Lord, you should fear Him. As soon as you have gazed on Him, you should reverence Him. For what difference does your knowing Him make, if you continue in the same practices as in bygone days—when you did not know Him? Furthermore, what is it that distinguishes you from a perfected servant of God? Is there one Christ for the baptized and another for the hearers? *Tertullian (c. 203, W), 3.661, 662.*

It is good that learners *desire* baptism, but do not hastily *receive* it. For he who desires it, honors it. He who hastily receives it, disdains it. . . . Hasty reception is the portion of irreverence. It inflates the seeker; it despises the Giver. And thus it sometimes deceives, for it promises to itself the gift before it is due. *Tertullian (c. 203, W), 3.662.*

[INSTRUCTIONS TO CATECHUMENS:] I admonish all believers in Christ, who have forsaken idols, for your salvation. . . . Let the mind be watchful of good things. Beware that you do not fall into former sins. In baptism, the coarse garment of your birth is washed. For if any sinful catechumen is marked with punishment, let him live in the signs, although not without loss. The whole of the matter for you is this: always shun great sins. *Commodianus (c. 240, W), 4.212.*

You see in the congregation of what is more commonly called the church the catechumens dispersed behind those who are at the extreme end of it. *Origen (c. 245, E), 9.447.*

There are certain doctrines that are not made known to the multitude. Rather, they are [revealed to the few] after the outsiders have been taught. But this is not a peculiarity of Christianity alone, but also of philosophic systems. *Origen (c. 248, E), 4.399.*

Christians test beforehand the souls of those who wish to become their hearers. First, we instruct them in private. Once they appear to have sufficiently demonstrated their desire towards a virtuous life, then we introduce them [to other Christians]—but not before. Next, we privately form one class of those who are beginners. These are the ones who are receiving admission, but who have not yet obtained the mark of complete purification. And we form another class of those who have manifested to the best of their ability their intention to desire no other things than what are approved by Christians. Among these, there are certain persons appointed to make inquiries regarding the lives and behavior of those who join them—so that they can prevent those who commit acts of infamy from coming into their public assembly. However, those of a different character, they receive with their whole heart, in order that they may daily make them better. *Origen (c. 248, E), 4.484, 485.*

We do everything in our power to secure that our meetings should be composed of wise men. We then venture to bring forward publicly in our discussions those things among us that are especially excellent and divine. That is, when we have an abundance of intelligent hearers. However, we conceal and pass by in silence the truths of deeper importance when we see that our audience is composed of simpler minds, who need such instruction as is figuratively called milk. *Origen (c. 248, E), 4.485.*

He who acts as an initiator . . . will say to those who have been purified in heart: "He whose soul has, for a long time, been conscious of no evil—particularly since he yielded himself to the healing of the word—let such a person hear the doctrines that were spoken in private by Jesus to His genuine disciples." *Origen (c. 248, E), 4.488.*

The catechumen should now sin no longer. *Cyprian (c. 250, W), 5.554.*

If they have departed this life, they are considered to be in the number of those who have been catechumens among us, but who died before they were baptized. Of course, they had attained no small advantage of truth and faith by forsaking error. However, they were prevented by death from gaining the consummation of grace. *Firmilian (c. 256, E), 5.395.*

The church now declares these mysteries to you who are transferred from the roles of the catechumens. However, it is not her custom to declare them to the Gentiles. For we do not declare the mysteries concerning the Father, the Son, and the Holy Spirit to a Gentile. Neither do we speak of the mysteries plainly in the presence of the catechumens. *Disputation of Archelaus and Manes (c. 320, E), 6.235.*

Instruct the catechumens in the elements of religion and then baptize them. *Apostolic Constitutions (compiled c. 390, E), 7.457.*

Let him ... be instructed before his baptism in the knowledge of the unbegotten God, in the understanding of His Only Begotten Son, and in the assured acknowledgement of the Holy Spirit. *Apostolic Constitutions (compiled c. 390, E), 7.475.*

Let him who is to be a catechumen be a catechumen for three years. However, if anyone is diligent and has a good-will to his earnestness, let him be admitted [to baptism]. For it is not the length of time that is to be judged, but the course of life. *Apostolic Constitutions (compiled c. 390, E), 7.495; extended discussion of subjects to be taught to the catechumen: 7.475, 476.*

CATHOLIC CHURCH

SEE CHURCH, THE.

CELIBACY

In discussing celibacy, some of the early Christian writers refer to it as "chastity" or "sanctity." In the passages below, those words are rendered as "celibacy" when that is the apparent meaning.

But He said to them, "All cannot accept this saying, but only those to whom it has been given: For there are eunuchs who were born thus ... and there are eunuchs who have made themselves eunuchs for the kingdom of heaven's sake. He who is able to accept it, let him accept it." Matt. 19:11, 12.

But I say to the unmarried and to the widows: It is good for them if they remain even as I am; but if they cannot exercise self-control, let them marry. For it is better to marry than to burn. 1 Cor. 7:8, 9.

Then I looked, and behold, a Lamb standing on Mount Zion, and with Him one hundred and forty-four thousand, having His Father's name written on their foreheads. . . . These are the ones who were not defiled with women, for they are virgins. These are the ones who follow the Lamb wherever He goes. These were redeemed from among men, being first-fruits to God and to the Lamb. Rev. 14:1, 4.

If anyone is able in power to continue in purity, to the honor of the flesh of our Lord, let him continue to do so without boasting. If he boasts, he is undone. *Ignatius (c. 105, E), 1.100.*

Many who have been Christ's disciples from childhood—both men and women—remain pure at the age of sixty or seventy years. *Justin Martyr (c. 160, E), 1.167.*

Some women (even though they are not barren) abstain from sexual relations. Some of these women have remained virgins from the beginning. Others have become celibate later in life. We also see men who remain as virgins. *Justin Martyr (c. 160, E), 1.295.*

You would find many among us, both men and women, growing old unmarried, in hope of living in closer communion with God. *Athenagoras (c. 175, E), 2.146.*

Melito, the eunuch, performed all his actions under the influence of the Holy Spirit, and he lies at Sardis. *Polycrates (c. 190, E), 8.774.*

There are many who do so and seal themselves up to being eunuchs for the sake of the kingdom of God, spontaneously relinquishing a pleasure so honorable and permitted. *Tertullian (c. 198, W), 4.23.*

We read in no place at all that marriage is prohibited; for it is a "good thing." What, however, is *better* than this "good thing" we learn from the apostle—who indeed *permits* marrying, but *prefers* abstinence. . . . How far better is it neither to marry nor to burn. *Tertullian (c. 205, W), 4.40.*

How many are there who from the moment of their baptism set the seal [of virginity] on their flesh? How many, again, who by equal mutual consent cancel the debt of matrimony [and become] voluntary eunuchs for the sake of their yearning after the celestial kingdom? *Tertullian (c. 205, W), 4.42.*

We do not reject marriage, but simply refrain from it [voluntarily]. Nor do we prescribe celibacy as the rule, but only recommend it. We observe it as a good state—yes, even as the better state—if each man uses it carefully according to his ability. But, at the same time, we earnestly vindicate marriage. *Tertullian (c. 207, W), 3.294.*

This passage [of Scripture] I would treat in such a way as to maintain the superiority of the other and higher sanctity—preferring self-control and virginity to marriage. However, I would by no means prohibit the latter. For my hostility is directed against those who are for destroying the God of marriage, not against those who follow after chastity. *Tertullian (c. 207, W), 3.462.*

The first type [of celibacy] is virginity from one's birth. The second is virginity from one's second birth—that is, from the font, which either in the married state keeps pure by mutual agreement, or else perseveres in widowhood from choice. A third class remains—monogamy—when, after the interception of a marriage once contracted, there is thereafter a renunciation of sexual relations. *Tertullian (c. 212, W), 4.50.*

What else is virginity than the glorious preparation for the future life? Virginity is of neither sex. Virginity is the continuation of infancy. Virginity is the triumph over pleasures. *Novatian (c. 235, W), 5.589, formerly attributed to Cyprian.*

According to the Word of God, marriage was a gift, just as holy celibacy was a gift. . . . But a man wishes to put asunder what God has joined together, when, "falling away from the sound faith . . . forbidding . . . to marry," he dissolves even those who had been previously joined together by the providence of God. *Origen (c. 245, E), 9.506.*

The Savior teaches us that absolute chastity is a gift given by God. It is not merely the fruit of training. Rather, it is given by God with prayer. "All men cannot receive the saying, but only those to whom it is given." . . . But, "Ask and it shall be given you." . . . Therefore, God will give the good gift—perfect purity in celibacy and chastity—to those who ask Him with the whole soul, with faith, and in prayers without ceasing. *Origen (c. 245, E), 9.512.*

Certain ones among them—from a desire of exceeding chastity and a wish to worship God

with greater purity—abstain even from the permitted indulgences of love. *Origen (c. 248, E), 4.407.*

Among Christians, those who maintain a perpetual virginity do not do so for any human honors. Nor do they do so for any fee or reward, nor from any motive of vainglory. Rather, "as they choose to retain God in their knowledge," they are preserved by God in a spirit that is well-pleasing to Him. *Origen (c. 248, E), 4.631.*

While the world was still rough and void, we were propagated by the fruitful begetting of numbers. We increased, to the enlargement of the human race. However, now that the world is filled and the earth is cultivated, those who can receive celibacy—living after the manner of eunuchs—are made eunuchs unto the kingdom. The Lord does not *command* this, but He *exhorts* it. . . . When He says that in His Father's house, there are many mansions, He indicates there are dwellings of better habitation. You [virgins] are seeking those better habitations. *Cyprian (c. 250, W), 5.436.*

Of the benefit of virginity and of continence: . . . in the Gospel according to Matthew: "All men do not receive this word, but those to whom it is given." . . . "There are eunuchs who have made themselves eunuchs for the kingdom of heaven's sake. He who can receive it, let him receive it." . . . Also, in the first Epistle of Paul to the Corinthians: "it is good for a man not to touch a woman." . . . Also, in the same place: "An unmarried man thinks of those things that are the Lord's." . . . Also in the Apocalypse: "These are those who have not defiled themselves with women, for they have continued as virgins." *Cyprian (c. 250, W), 5.543, 544.*

"I wish that all men were even as I am." Pierius, when he was expounding and unfolding the meaning of the apostle and purposed to explain these words, added this remark: "In saying this, Paul clearly preaches celibacy." *Pierius (c. 275, E), 6.157, as cited by Jerome.*

Virginity is something supernaturally great, wonderful, and glorious. To speak plainly and in accordance with the Holy Scriptures, this best and noblest manner of life is alone the root of immortality—as well as its flower and firstfruits. And for this reason, the Lord promises that those who have made themselves eunuchs shall enter into the kingdom of heaven. . . .

Celibacy among humans is a very rare thing and difficult to attain.... For we must think of virginity as walking upon the earth—yet, also reaching up to heaven. *Methodius (c. 290, E), 6.310, 311.*

It is not enough to merely keep the *body* undefiled, ... but we must care for the *souls* of men as being the divinities of their bodies.... For all of the irrational appetites of a virgin are banished from the body by divine teaching. *Methodius (c. 290, E), 6.311.*

Virginity ... was not revealed to the first generations [of humans]. For the race of mankind was still very small in number. So it was necessary for mankind to first increase in number and then to be brought to perfection. *Methodius (c. 290, E), 6.311.*

Let us inquire as to the reason that none of the many patriarchs, prophets, and righteous men ... either praised or chose the state of virginity. The reason is that it was reserved for the Lord alone to be the first to teach this doctrine.... It was fitting that He who was the first and chief of priests, prophets, and angels should also be hailed as the first and chief of virgins. For in old times, man was not yet perfect. And for this reason, he was unable to receive perfection—which is virginity. *Methodius (c. 290, E), 6.312.*

John shows us, saying in the Book of Revelation, "And I looked, and lo, ... with Him a hundred and forty-four thousand.... These are those who were not defiled with women. For they are virgins. These are those who follow the Lamb wherever he goes." This shows that the Lord is the Leader of the choir of virgins. In addition to this, notice how very great in the sight of God is the dignity of virginity: "These were redeemed from among men, being the first-fruits unto God and to the Lamb." ... And he clearly intends by this to teach us that the number of virgins was, from the beginning, restricted to a certain number—a hundred and forty-four thousand. In contrast, the multitude of the other saints is innumerable. *Methodius (c. 290, E), 6.313.*

It is not given to all to attain that undefiled state of being a eunuch for the sake of the kingdom of heaven. Rather, it plainly is given only to those who are able to preserve the ever-blooming and unfading flower of virginity. *Methodius (c. 290, E), 6.316.*

It is clear to all, without any doubt, that to care for the things of the Lord and to please God is much better than to care for the things of the world and to please one's wife. *Methodius (c. 290, E), 6.322.*

In the Song of Songs, to anyone who is willing to see it, Christ Himself praises those who are firmly established in virginity, saying, "As the lily among thorns, so is my love among the daughters" [Cant. 2:2]. *Methodius (c. 290, E), 6.331.*

Let no one think that all the remaining company of believers are condemned, thinking that we alone who are virgins shall be led on to attain the promises.... The Lord does not profess to give the same honors to all.... He announces that the order and holy choir of the virgins shall first enter into company with Him into the rest of the new dispensation, as into a bridal chamber. For they are martyrs—not as bearing the pains of the body for a brief moment of time—but as enduring them throughout all of their life. *Methodius (c. 290, E), 6.332.*

Concerning virginity, we have received no commandment. Rather, we leave it to the power of those who are willing to maintain it, as a vow. *Apostolic Constitutions (compiled c. 390, E), 7.436; extended discussion: 6.309–6.355.*

SEE ALSO CHURCH GOVERNMENT (VIII. BE-GINNINGS OF CLERICAL CELIBACY); MAR-RIAGE; REVELATION, BOOK OF (II. INTERPRE-TATION OF SPECIFIC PASSAGES); VIRGINS, ORDER OF; WIDOWS, ORDER OF.

CELTS

The Celts were an ancient people who migrated to Europe centuries before the time of Christ. They inhabited Galatia, Gaul, Britain, and Ireland, among other places.

The Scythians, the Celts, the Iberians, and the Thracians—all of them are warlike races. And they are greatly addicted to intoxication, thinking that it is an honorable, happy pursuit to engage in. *Clement of Alexandria (c. 195, E), 2.245, 246.*

The Nasamones consult private oracles by frequent and lengthened visits to the sepulchers of their relatives.... And the Celts, for the same purpose, stay all night at the tombs of their brave chieftains. *Tertullian (c. 210, W), 3.234.*

It is plain that the province was called Galatia from the following circumstances: Upon their arrival in [the region], the Gauls [i.e., Celts] united themselves with the Greeks. Because of that, the region was called Gallogrecia, and later, Galatia. It is no wonder if he said those things concerning the Galatians and related how a people of the West traveled over so great a distance in the middle of the earth and settled in a region of the East. *Lactantius (c. 304–313, W), 7.323.*

SEE ALSO BRITAIN; DRUIDS.

CERINTHUS

Cerinthus was an early Gnostic teacher who flourished around A.D. 100.

Cerinthus, again, was a man who was educated in the wisdom of the Egyptians. He taught that the world was not made by the primary God, but by a certain Power far separated from Him. . . . He denied that Jesus was born of a virgin. Instead, he represented Him as being the son of Joseph and Mary. *Irenaeus (c. 180, E/W), 1.351, 352.*

There are also those who heard from [Polycarp] that John, the disciple of the Lord, went to bathe at Ephesus. But realizing that Cerinthus was within [the bath house], John rushed out of the bath house without bathing. Instead, he exclaimed, "Let us fly, lest even the bath house falls down, because Cerinthus, the enemy of the truth, is within." *Irenaeus (c. 180, E/W), 1.416.*

John, the disciple of the Lord, preached this faith. And he sought, through the proclamation of the Gospel, to remove that error that Cerinthus had disseminated among men. *Irenaeus (c. 180, E/W), 1.426.*

Cerinthus, too, through written revelations by a great apostle (as he would have us to believe!) brings before us fantastic things. And he pretends these things were shown him by angels. He alleges that after the resurrection, the kingdom of Christ is to be on earth and that the flesh dwelling in Jerusalem is again to be subject to desire and pleasures. And being an enemy to the Scriptures of God and wishing to deceive men, he says that there is to be a space of a thousand years for marriage festivals. *Eusebius, quoting Caius (c. 215, W), 5.601.*

A certain Cerinthus, himself being disciplined in the teaching of the Egyptians, asserted that the world was not made by the primal Deity, but by some virtue that was an offshoot from that Power. *Hippolytus (c. 225, W), 5.114.*

The doctrine taught by Cerinthus is this: that there will be an earthly reign of Christ. Since Cerinthus was himself a man devoted to the pleasures of the body, and completely carnal in his dispositions, he imagined that the kingdom would consist in those kinds of gratifications on which his own heart was set. *Dionysius of Alexandria (c. 262, E), 6.82.*

They are not to be heard who assure themselves that there is to be an earthly reign of a thousand years. They think like the heretic Cerinthus. For the kingdom of Christ is already eternal in the saints—even though the glory of the saints shall be manifested after the resurrection. *Victorinus (c. 280, W), 7.360; see also 5.147.*

SEE ALSO GNOSTICS, GNOSTICISM; HERESIES, HERETICS; MILLENNIUM.

CERTIFICATES OF SACRIFICE

During some of the persecutions in the early centuries, the Roman rulers would order all the inhabitants of a region to sacrifice to the gods. Upon doing so, a person was given a certificate of sacrifice. Some Christians sought to avoid prison or martyrdom by obtaining a certificate through bribery or influence, even though they had not actually sacrificed to the gods.

You must not think, dearest brother, as some do, that those who receive certificates [of sacrifice] are to be put on a par with those who have sacrificed. . . . The one who has received the certificate may say, "I . . . had been made aware by the discourse of the bishop that we must not sacrifice to idols. . . . So I either went or directed some other person to go to the magistrate to say that I am a Christian and that I am not allowed to sacrifice. Because I cannot come to the devil's altars, I shall pay a price for this purpose, that I may not do what is not lawful for me to do." Now, he who has received a certificate is stained. . . . He has learned from our admonitions that he should not even have done this. Although his hand is pure and no contact of deadly food has polluted his lips, yet his conscience is polluted. *Cyprian (c. 250, W), 5.330, 331.*

SEE ALSO LAPSED.

CHALICE

See Vessels, Eucharistic.

CHILDBIRTH

All [pagans] are brought to birth with idolatry for the midwife. The very wombs that bear them are still bound with the bands that have been wreathed before the idols, declaring their offspring to be consecrated to demons. For in childbirth, pagan women invoke the aid of Lucina and Diana. For a whole week, a table is spread in honor of Juno. On the last day, the fates of the horoscope are invoked. The infant's first step on the ground is sacred to the goddess Statina. After this, does anyone fail to devote to idolatrous service the entire head of his son? . . . Hence, in no case is there any birth that is free from idolatrous superstition. It was from this circumstance that the apostle said that, when either of the parents were sanctified, the children were holy. And this as much by the prerogative of the seed as by the discipline of the institution. He says, "Otherwise, the children would be unclean" by birth. I think he meant us to understand that the children of believers were designed for holiness, and thereby for salvation. This was in order that—by this pledge of hope—he might give his support to marriage, which he had determined to maintain in its integrity. Besides, he had certainly not forgotten what the Lord had so definitively stated: "Unless a man is born of water and of the Spirit, he cannot enter into the kingdom of God." In other words, he cannot be holy. *Tertullian (c. 210, W), 3.219, 220.*

See also Abortion, Infanticide; Conception; Procreation.

CHILDREN, INFANTS

Unless you are converted and become as little children, you will by no means enter the kingdom of heaven. . . . And whoever receives one little child like this in My name receives Me. Matt. 18:3–5.

But Jesus said, "Let the little children come to Me, and do not forbid them; for of such is the kingdom of heaven." Matt. 19:14.

They are as infant children, in whose hearts no evil originates. Nor did they know what wickedness is, but always remained as children. *Hermas (c. 150, W), 2.53.*

If only a just judgment were the cause of the resurrection, it would of course follow that those who had done neither evil nor good—namely, very young children—would not rise again. However, we see that all persons are to rise again, including those who have died in infancy. *Athenagoras (c. 175, E), 2.156.*

Who are they that have been saved and have received the inheritance? Those, doubtless, who believe God and who have continued in His love—as did Caleb of Jephuneh and Joshua of Nun—and innocent children, who have had no sense of evil. *Irenaeus (c. 180, E/W), 1.502.*

"No one is pure from defilement, not even if his life were but for one day" [Job. 14:4, 5, LXX]. *Clement of Alexandria (c. 195, E), 2.428.*

Why does the innocent period of life hasten to the remission of sins? *Tertullian (c. 198, W), 3.678.*

Behold, Christ takes infants and teaches how all should be like them, if they ever wish to be greater. However, [the Gnostics point out that] the Creator, in contrast, let loose bears against children, in order to avenge His prophet Elisha, who had been mocked by them. This antithesis is impudent enough, since it throws together things so different as "infants" and "children." The first is an age that is still innocent. The other is one already capable of discretion (able to mock, if not to blaspheme). Therefore, God is a just God. *Tertullian (c. 207, W), 3.386.*

Christ, by accepting praise out of the mouth of babes and sucklings, has declared that neither childhood nor infancy is without sensibility. The first class [children], when meeting Him with approving shouts, proved its ability to offer Him testimony. The other class [infants], by being slaughtered for His sake, of course knew what violence meant. *Tertullian (c. 210, W), 3.200.*

If you mean the [region in Hades of the] good, why should you judge the souls of infants and of virgins to be unworthy of such a resting place—those who by reason of their condition in life were pure and innocent? *Tertullian (c. 210, W), 3.233.*

For such was the charm of Jesus' words, that not only were *men* willing to follow him to the wilderness, but . . . *children* too. Children are [normally] totally unaffected by such emotions, so perhaps they were only following their parents. Or perhaps they were also attracted by His divinity. In order that it might be implanted with them, they became his followers along with their parents. *Origen (c. 248, E), 4.468.*

The prophets . . . tell us that a sacrifice for sin was offered even for new-born infants, as not being free from sin. They say, "I was shaped in iniquity and in sin did my mother conceive me." Also, "They are estranged from the womb." Which is followed by the singular expression, "They go astray as soon as they are born, speaking lies." *Origen (c. 248, E), 4.631.*

Infancy is still yet innocent and unconscious of worldly evil. *Cyprian (c. 250, W), 5.434.*

And that nothing might be lacking to aggravate the crime [of denying Christ in persecution], infants were either carried in the arms of their parents or conducted. So, while yet little ones, they lost what they had gained at the very beginning of their birth. *Cyprian (c. 250, W), 5.439.*

We should always have our hands over the young. That is, when they err, we should correct them with careful punishments. Otherwise, by useless affection and excessive indulgence, they will be trained to evil and nourished to vices. *Lactantius (c. 304–313, W), 7.185.*

SEE ALSO ABORTION, INFANTICIDE; AGE OF ACCOUNTABILITY; BAPTISM (III. THE QUESTION OF INFANT BAPTISM); CHILDBIRTH; FALL OF MAN; MAN, DOCTRINE OF.

CHILIASM

SEE MILLENNIUM.

CHOIR

[Paul of Samosata] put a stop to the psalms sung in honor of our Lord Jesus Christ, as being the recent compositions of contemporary men. Instead, he prepared women to sing psalms in honor of himself in the midst of the church, during the great day of the Paschal festival. One might shudder to hear such choristers! *Malchion (c. 270, E), 6.170.*

SEE ALSO HYMNS.

CHRISM

SEE OIL, ANOINTING WITH.

CHRIST, DIVINITY OF

I. Divinity of the Son

II. Begetting of the Son
   A. Begotten of His Father
   B. Before all worlds
   C. God of God
   D. Light of Light
   E. Begotten, not made
   F. Being of one substance with the Father
   G. By whom all things were made

III. Relationship of the Son to the Father
   A. Equality of nature (substance)
   B. Difference in personal attributes
   C. Difference in order

IV. The internal Logos and the external Son

V. Origen's understanding of the Son

I. Divinity of the Son

In the beginning was the Word, and the Word was with God, and the Word was God. John 1:1.

I and My Father are one. John 10:30.

He who has seen Me has seen the Father; so how can you say, "Show us the Father"? John 14:9.

And Thomas answered and said to Him, "My Lord and my God!" John 20:28.

But to the Son He says: "Your throne, O God, is forever and ever; a scepter of righteousness is the scepter of Your kingdom. You have loved righteousness and hated lawlessness; therefore God, Your God, has anointed You." Heb. 1:8, 9.

He is Lord of all the world, to whom God said at the foundation of the world, "Let us make man after our image, and after our likeness." *Barnabas (c. 70–130, E), 1.139.*

Let us reverence the Lord Jesus Christ, whose blood was given for us. *Clement of Rome (c. 96, W), 1.11.*

God Himself was manifested in human form for the renewal of eternal life. *Ignatius (c. 105, E), 1.58.*

Continue in intimate union with Jesus Christ, our God. *Ignatius (c. 105, E), 1.68.*

I pray for your happiness forever in our God, Jesus Christ. *Ignatius (c. 105, E), 1.96.*

The Christians trace the beginning of their religion to Jesus the Messiah. He is called the Son of the Most High God. It is said that God came down from heaven. He assumed flesh and clothed Himself with it from a Hebrew virgin.

And the Son of God lived in a daughter of man. *Aristides (c. 125, E), 9.265.*

Truly God Himself, who is Almighty, the Creator of all things, and invisible, has sent from heaven, and placed among men, the One who is the truth, and the holy and incomprehensible Word. . . . God did not, as one might have imagined, send to men any servant, angel, or ruler. . . . Rather, He sent the very Creator and Fashioner of all things—by whom He made the heavens. . . . As a king sends his son, who is also a king, so God sent Him. He sent Him as God. *Letter to Diognetus (c. 125–200), 1.27.*

Brethren, it is fitting that you should think of Jesus Christ as of God—as the Judge of the living and the dead. *Second Clement (c. 150), 7.517.*

We reasonably worship Him, having learned that He is the Son of the true God Himself, and holding Him in the second place. *Justin Martyr (c. 160, E), 1.166.*

The Word, . . . He is Divine. *Justin Martyr (c. 160, E), 1.166.*

The Father of the universe has a Son. And He, being the First-Begotten Word of God, is even God. *Justin Martyr (c. 160, E), 1.184.*

Next to God, we worship and love the Word who is from the unbeggoten and ineffable God. *Justin Martyr (c. 160, E), 1.193.*

For Christ is King, Priest, God, Lord, Angel, and Man. *Justin Martyr (c. 160, E), 1.211.*

[TRYPHO, A JEW:] You utter many blasphemies, in that you seek to persuade us that this crucified man was with Moses and Aaron, and spoke to them in the pillar of the cloud. *Justin Martyr (c. 160, E), 1.213.*

Moses . . . declares that He who appeared to Abraham under the oak in Mamre is God. He was sent with the two angels in His company to judge Sodom by another One, who remains ever in the supercelestial places, invisible to all men, holding personal contact with no one. We believe this other One to be the Maker and Father of all things. . . . Yet, there is said to be another God and Lord subject to the Maker of all things. And He is also called an Angel, because he announces to men whatsoever the Maker of all things—above whom there is no other God—wishes to announce to them. *Justin Martyr (c. 160, E), 1.223.*

He deserves to be worshipped as God and as Christ. *Justin Martyr (c. 160, E), 1.229.*

David predicted that He would be born from the womb before the sun and moon, according to the Father's will. He made Him known, being Christ, as God, strong and to be worshipped. *Justin Martyr (c. 160, E), 1.237.*

The Son ministered to the will of the Father. Yet, nevertheless, He is God, in that He is the First-Begotten of all creatures. *Justin Martyr (c. 160, E), 1.262.*

If you had understood what has been written by the prophets, you would not have denied that He was God, Son of the Only, Unbegotten, Unutterable God. *Justin Martyr (c. 160, E), 1.263.*

"Rejoice, O you heavens, with him, and let all the angels of God worship Him" [Deut. 32:43]. *Justin Martyr (c. 160, E), 1.264.*

He is forever the first in power. For Christ, being the First-Born of every creature, became again the chief of another race regenerated by Himself through water, faith, and wood. *Justin Martyr (c. 160, E), 1.268.*

Then did the whole creation see clearly that for man's sake the Judge was condemned, and the Invisible was seen, and the Illimitable was circumscribed, and the Impassible suffered, and the Immortal died, and the Celestial was laid in the grave. *Melito (c. 170, E), 8.756.*

God was put to death, the King of Israel slain! *Melito (c. 170, E), 8.758.*

There is the one God and the Logos proceeding from Him, the Son. We understand that the Son is inseparable from Him. *Athenagoras (c. 175, E), 2.137.*

God by His own Word and Wisdom made all things. *Theophilus (c. 180, E), 2.91.*

"Thy throne, O God, is forever and ever; the scepter of Your kingdom is a right scepter. You have loved righteousness and hated iniquity. Therefore, God, Your God, has anointed You." For the Spirit designates by the name of God— both Him who is anointed as Son, and He who anoints, that is, the Father. And again, "God stood in the congregation of the gods; He judges among the gods." Here he refers to the

Father and the Son, and those who have received the adoption. *Irenaeus (c. 180, E/W), 1.419.*

For He fulfills the bountiful and comprehensive will of His Father, inasmuch as He is Himself the Savior of those who are saved, and the Lord of those who are under authority, and the God of all those things that have been formed, the Only-Begotten of the Father. *Irenaeus (c. 180, E/W), 1.443.*

I have shown from the Scriptures that none of the sons of Adam are, absolutely and as to everything, called God, or named Lord. But Jesus is Himself in His own right, beyond all men who ever lived, God, Lord, King Eternal, and the Incarnate Word. . . . He is the Holy Lord, the Wonderful, the Counselor, the Beautiful in appearance, and the Mighty God. *Irenaeus (c. 180, E/W), 1.449.*

Thus He indicates in clear terms that He is God, and that His advent was in Bethlehem. . . . God, then, was made man, and the Lord did Himself save us. *Irenaeus (c. 180, E/W), 1.451.*

He is God, for the name Emmanuel indicates this. *Irenaeus (c. 180, E/W), 1.452.*

Christ Himself, therefore, together with the Father, is the God of the living, who spoke to Moses, and who was also manifested to the fathers. *Irenaeus (c. 180, E/W), 1.467.*

Now the father of the human race is the Word of God. *Irenaeus (c. 180, E/W), 1.505.*

How can they be saved unless it was God who worked out their salvation upon earth? Or how shall man pass into God, unless God has first passed into man? *Irenaeus (c. 180, E/W), 1.507.*

It is plain that He was Himself the Word of God, who was made the son of man. He received from the Father the power of remission of sins. He was man, and He was God. This was so that since as man He suffered for us, so as God He might have compassion on us. *Irenaeus (c. 180, E/W), 1.545.*

He is God in the form of man, stainless, the minister of His Father's will, the Word who is God, who is in the Father, who is at the Father's right hand. And with the form of God, He is God. *Clement of Alexandria (c. 195, E), 2.210.*

There is a suggestion of the divinity of the Lord in [Isaac's] not being slain. Jesus rose again after His burial, having suffered no harm—just like Isaac was released from being sacrificed. *Clement of Alexandria (c. 195, E), 2.215.*

O the great God! O the perfect child! The Son in the Father and the Father in the Son. . . . God the Word, who became man for our sakes. *Clement of Alexandria (c. 195, E), 2.215.*

The Father of all is alone perfect, for the Son is in Him and the Father is in the Son. *Clement of Alexandria (c. 195, E), 2.222.*

Our Instructor is the holy God Jesus, the Word. *Clement of Alexandria (c. 195, E), 2.223.*

Nothing, then, is hated by God, nor yet by the Word. For both are one—that is, God. For He has said, "In the beginning the Word was in God, and the Word was God." *Clement of Alexandria (c. 195, E), 2.225.*

He who has the Almighty God, the Word, is in want of nothing. *Clement of Alexandria (c. 195, E), 2.281.*

Pointing to the First-Begotten Son, Peter writes, accurately comprehending the statement, "In the beginning God made the heaven and the earth." And He is called Wisdom by all the prophets. This is He who is the Teacher of all created beings. *Clement of Alexandria (c. 195, E), 2.493.*

The best thing on earth is the most pious man. The best thing in heaven, the nearer in place and purer, is an angel, the partaker of the eternal and blessed life. But the nature of the Son, which is nearest to Him who is alone the Almighty One, is the most perfect, most holy, most potent, most princely, most kingly, and most beneficent. This is the highest excellence, who orders all things in accordance with the Father's will and holds the helm of the universe in the best way. . . . The Son of God is never displaced . . . being always everywhere and being contained nowhere. He is complete mind, complete paternal light. He is all eyes, seeing all things, hearing all things, knowing all things. . . . All the host of angels and gods are placed in subjection to Him. He, the paternal Word, exhibits the holy administration for Him who put [all things] in subjection to Him. *Clement of Alexandria (c. 195, E), 2.524.*

The Son is the cause of all good things, by the will of the Almighty Father. *Clement of Alexandria (c. 195, E), 2.525.*

He is the true Only-Begotten, the express image of the glory of the universal King and Almighty Father, who impresses on the man of God the seal of the perfect contemplation, according to His own image. So that there is now a third divine image, made as far as possible like the Second Cause, the Essential Life. *Clement of Alexandria (c. 195, E), 2.527.*

Nor do we differ from the Jews concerning God. We must make, therefore, a remark or two as to Christ's divinity. *Tertullian (c. 197, W), 3.34.*

Search, then, and see if the divinity of Christ is true. *Tertullian (c. 197, W), 3.36.*

To all He is equal, to all King, to all Judge, to all God and Lord. *Tertullian (c. 197, W), 3.158.*

Christ's name is extending everywhere, believed everywhere, worshipped by all the above-enumerated nations, reigning everywhere. *Tertullian (c. 197, W), 3.158.*

This opens the ears of Christ our God. *Tertullian (c. 200, W), 3.715.*

We who believe that God really lived on earth, and took upon Him the low estate of human form, for the purpose of man's salvation, are very far from thinking as those do who refuse to believe that God cares for anything. . . . Fortunately, however, it is a part of the creed of Christians even to believe that God did die, and yet that He is alive forevermore. *Tertullian (c. 207, W), 3.309.*

Christ is received in the person of Christ, because even in this manner is He our God. *Tertullian (c. 207, W), 3.319.*

He is not on this account to be regarded as an angel—as a Gabriel or a Michael. . . . Since He is the Spirit of God and the Power of the Highest, can He be regarded as lower than the angels? He who is truly God and the Son of God? *Tertullian (c. 210, W), 3.534.*

For so did the Father previously say to the Son: "Let us make man in our own image, after our likeness." *Tertullian (c. 210, W), 3.549.*

If God had willed not to be born, He would not have presented Himself in the likeness of man. *Tertullian (c. 210, W), 3.522.*

Christ never used that familiar phrase of all the prophets, "Thus saith the Lord." For He was Himself the Lord, who openly spoke by His own authority, prefacing his words with the phrase, "Truly, truly, *I* say unto you." *Tertullian (c. 210, W), 3.534.*

"Blessed is He that comes in the name of the Lord," that is to say, the Son in the Father's name. And as for the Father's names—God Almighty, the Most High, the Lord of Hosts, the King of Israel, the One Who Is—the Scriptures teach us and we say that they belonged suitably to the Son also. We say that the Son came under these designations and has always acted in them and has thus manifested them in Himself to men. He says, "All things that the Father has are mine." Then, why not His names also? *Tertullian (c. 213, W), 3.613.*

How is it that the Son suffered, yet the Father did not suffer with Him? [The answer is that] the Father is separate from the Son, though not separated from Him as God. For example, a river flows from a fountain identical in nature with it, and it is not separated from the fountain. Nevertheless, if the river is soiled with mire and mud, the injury that affects the stream does not reach to the fountain. To be sure, it is the water of the fountain that suffers downstream. Nevertheless, since it is not affected at the fountain (but only at the river) the fountain suffers nothing. *Tertullian (c. 213, W), 3.626.*

Although He endured the cross, yet as God He returned to life, having trampled upon death. For His God and Father addresses Him, and says, "Sit at my right hand." *Hippolytus (c. 205, W), 5.166, 167.*

By the Ancient of Days, he means none other than the Lord, God, and Ruler of all—even of Christ Himself, who makes the days old and yet does not become old Himself by times and days. "His dominion is an everlasting dominion." The Father, having put all things in subjection to His own Son—both things in heaven and things on earth—presented Him as the First-Begotten of God. He did this in order that, along with the Father, He might be approved before angels as the Son of God and be manifested as also the Lord of angels. *Hippolytus (c. 205, W), 5.189.*

Christ's body lay in the tomb, not emptied of divinity. Rather, while in Hades, He was in essential being with His Father. Yet, He was also in the body and in Hades. For the Son is not contained in space, just as the Father is not. And he comprehends all things in Himself. *Hippolytus (c. 205, W), 5.194.*

Who, then, was in heaven but the Word unincarnate—who was sent to show that He was upon earth and was also in heaven? *Hippolytus (c. 205, W), 5.225.*

Having been made man, He is still God forever. For to this effect, John also has said, "Who is, and who was, and who is to come—the Almighty." And he has appropriately called Christ "the Almighty." For in this, he has said only what Christ testifies of Himself. For Christ gave this testimony and said, "All things are delivered unto me by my Father." *Hippolytus (c. 205, W), 5.225.*

Besides, there are writings of certain brethren older than the times of Victor, which they wrote against the pagans in defense of the truth and against the heresies of their day. . . . For who is ignorant of the books of Irenaeus and Melito, and the rest, which declare Christ to be God and man? All the psalms, too, and hymns of brethren—which have been written from the beginning by the faithful—celebrate Christ the Word of God, ascribing divinity to Him. *Eusebius, quoting Caius (c. 215, W), 5.601.*

No one should be offended that the Savior is also God, seeing God is the Father. Likewise, since the Father is called Omnipotent, no one should be offended that the Son of God is also called Omnipotent. For in this way, the words will be true that He says to the Father: "All mine are yours, and yours are mine, and I am glorified in them." Now, if all things that are the Father's are also Christ's, certainly one of those things is the omnipotence of the Father. *Origen (c. 225, E), 4.250.*

"The works that the Father does, these the Son does likewise." And again He says that the Son cannot do anything of Himself, but only what He sees the Father do. For the Son in no way differs from the Father in the power of His works. The work of the Son is not a different thing from that of the Father. Rather, it is one and the same movement. . . . He therefore called Him a stainless mirror, that by such an expression it might be understood that there is no dissimilarity whatever between the Son and the Father. *Origen (c. 225, E), 4.251.*

Jesus Christ Himself is the Lord and Creator of the soul. *Origen (c. 225, E), 4.271.*

He Himself is everywhere and passes swiftly through all things. For we are no longer to understand Him as existing in those narrow limits in which He was once confined for our sakes. He is not in that circumscribed body that He occupied on earth, when dwelling among men—according to which He might be considered as enclosed in one particular place. *Origen (c. 225, E), 4.299.*

Every beginning of those families that have a relation to God as to the Father of all, took its beginning lower down with Christ, who is next to the God and Father of all, being thus the Father of every soul, as Adam is the father of all men. *Origen (c. 225, E), 4.370, 371.*

No one will logically think this Son of God, in respect of the Word being God, is to be contained in any place. . . . For it is absurd to say that Christ was in Peter and in Paul, but not in Michael the archangel, nor in Gabriel. And from this, it is distinctly shown that the divinity of the Son of God was not shut up in some place. *Origen (c. 225, E), 4.377.*

We might say of Christ, that by nature His first principle [Gr. *archē*] is deity. However, in relation to us, who cannot comprehend the whole truth about Him because of its very greatness, His first principle is His manhood. *Origen (c. 228, E), 9.307.*

If it is permitted to say this, I consider that the beginning of real existence was the Son of God, who says, "I am the beginning and the end, the Alpha and Omega, the first and the last." . . . Now, God is altogether one and simple. But, for many reasons, our Savior is made many things—since God set Him forth as a propitiation and a first fruits of the whole creation. . . . The whole creation, so far as it is capable of redemption, stands in need of Him. *Origen (c. 228, E), 9.308.*

Should anyone inquire whether all that the Father knows . . . is known to our Savior also, and should he—imagining that he will thereby glorify the Father—show that some things known to the Father are unknown to the Son . . . we must remind him that it is from His being the truth that He is Savior. Accordingly, if He is the complete truth, then there is nothing true that He does not know. Truth must not limp for the want of the things that—according to these persons—are known to the Father only. *Origen (c. 228, E), 9.313.*

One cannot be in the Father or with the Father except by ascending upwards from below and first coming to the divinity of the Son—through which one may be led by the hand and brought to the blessedness of the Father himself. *Origen (c. 228, E), 9.313.*

The arrangement of the sentences seem to indicate an order. First we have, "In the beginning was the Word." Next, "And the Word was with God." And thirdly, "And the Word was God." It was arranged this way so that it might be seen that it is the Word's being with God that makes Him God. *Origen (c. 228, E), 9.323.*

He is said to have a name written that no one knows but He Himself. For there are some things that are known to the Word alone. For the beings that come into existence after Him have a poorer nature than His. *Origen (c. 228, E), 9.327*

The Canaanite woman came and worshipped Jesus as God, saying, "Lord help me." *Origen (c. 245, E), 9.446.*

He is perceived as being the Word, for He was God in the beginning with God. He reveals the Father. *Origen (c. 245, E), 9.452.*

We now believe Jesus Himself, when He speaks respecting his divinity: "I am the way, the truth, and the life." *Origen (c. 248, E), 4.426.*

The Gospels do not consider Him who in Jesus said these words, "I am the way, the truth, and the life," to have been of so circumscribed a nature so as to have had an existence nowhere out of the soul and body of Jesus. . . . Jesus himself, in raising the minds of His disciples to higher thoughts of the Son of God, says: "Where two or three are gathered together in My name, there I am in the midst of you." . . . We quote these passages, making no distinction between the Son of God and Jesus. *Origen (c. 248, E), 4.434.*

The divinity of Jesus is established by these things: the existence of the churches of the saved, the prophecies uttered concerning Him, the cures brought about in His name, and the wisdom and knowledge that are in Him. *Origen (c. 248, E), 4.477.*

The Word that was in the beginning with God (who is also very God) may come to us. *Origen (c. 248, E), 4.499.*

Every prayer, supplication, intercession, and thanksgiving is to be sent up to the Supreme God through the High Priest—the living Word and God, who is above all the angels. And to the Word himself will we also pray, make intercessions, and offer thanksgiving. *Origen (c. 248, E), 4.544.*

Although we may call him a second God, let men know that by the term, "second God," we mean nothing else than a Virtue capable of including all other virtues, and a Reason capable of containing all reason. *Origen (c. 248, E), 4.561.*

These are not the words of Christians. Rather, they are of those who are altogether alienated from salvation and who neither acknowledge Jesus as Savior, nor God, nor Teacher, nor Son of God. *Origen (c. 248, E), 4.587.*

The architect of this world is the Son of God. His Father is the first God and Sovereign Ruler over all things. *Origen (c. 248, E), 4.595.*

"The people who sat in darkness (the Gentiles) saw a great light"—the God Jesus. *Origen (c. 248, E), 4.603.*

If the same question is put to us in regard to the worship of Jesus, we will show that the right to be honored was given to Him by God "so that all may honor the Son, even as they honor the Father." For the prophecies that preceded His birth were preparations for His worship. *Origen (c. 248, E), 4.642.*

[CELSUS SAYS:] "If these people worshipped one God alone and no other, they would perhaps have some valid argument against the worship of others. But they pay excessive reverence to one who has but lately appeared among men. And they think it is no offense against God if they worship His servant also." To this we reply, that if Celsus had known that saying, "I and My Father are one," and the words used in prayer by the Son of God, "As you and I are one," he would not have thought that we worship any others besides Him who is the Supreme God. For he says, "My Father is in Me and I in Him." . . . However, from these words, someone may be afraid of my joining those who deny that the Father and the Son are two persons. If so, let him weigh the following passage: "And the multitude of those who believed were of one heart and of one soul," so he may understand the meaning of the saying, "I and My Father are one." We therefore worship one God—the Father and the

Son—as I have explained. So our argument against the worship of other gods still continues valid. And we do not "reverence beyond measure one who has but lately appeared," as though He did not exist before. For we believe Him when He says, "Before Abraham was, I am.". . . We worship, therefore, the Father of truth and the Son, who is the truth. And although they are two Persons or Beings, they are one in unity of thought, harmony, and identity of will. So entirely are they one that he who has seen the Son . . . has seen in Him (who is the image of God) God Himself. . . . Accordingly, we worship with all our power the one God and His only Son—the Word and the image of God—by prayers and supplications. And we offer our petitions to the God of the universe through His Only-Begotten Son. To the Son, we first present them, and beseech Him, as "the propitiation for our sins," and our High Priest, to offer our desires, sacrifices, and prayers to the Most High. Our faith, therefore, is directed to God through His Son. *Origen (c. 248, E), 4.643, 644.*

To explain this fully, and to justify the conduct of the Christians in refusing homage to any object except the Most High God and the First-Born of all creation (who is His Word and is God), we must quote this from Scripture. *Origen (c. 248, E), 4.639.*

We sing hymns to the Most High alone and to his Only-Begotten, who is the Word and God. *Origen (c. 248, E), 4.665.*

Why, then, should man hesitate to call Christ "God," when he observes that He is declared to be God by the Father, according to the Scriptures? . . . Reasonably, then, whoever acknowledges Him to be God may find salvation in Christ as God. Whoever does not acknowledge Him to be God will lose salvation that he could not find elsewhere than in Christ as God. *Novatian (c. 235, W), 5.621.*

In what way do they [the heretics] receive Christ as God? For now they cannot deny Him to be God. Do they receive Him as God the Father or God the Son? If as the Son, why do they deny that the Son of God is God? If as the Father, why do they not follow those who appear to maintain blasphemies of that kind? *Novatian (c. 235, W), 5.621.*

This saying can be true of no *man:* "I and the Father are one." Christ alone declared this utterance out of the consciousness of His divin-

ity. Finally, the apostle Thomas, instructed in all the proofs and conditions of Christ's divinity, says in reply to Christ, "My Lord and my God." Besides, the Apostle Paul says, " . . . of whom Christ came according to the flesh, who is over all, God blessed forever." *Novatian (c. 235, W), 5.622.*

Therefore, He is not only man, but God also, since all things are by Him. . . . If Christ is only man, how is He present wherever He is called upon? For it is not the nature of man, but of God, to be present in every place. *Novatian (c. 235, W), 5.623.*

If Christ was only man, how did he say, "Before Abraham was, I am?" For no man can be before someone from whom he himself has descended. Nor can it be that anyone could have been prior to him of whom he himself has taken his origin. Yet, Christ, although He was born of Abraham, says that He is before Abraham. *Novatian (c. 235, W), 5.624, 625.*

How can it be said that "I and the Father are one," if He is not both God and the Son? *Novatian (c. 235, W), 5.625.*

He strongly refuted his adversaries by the example and witness of the Scriptures. He said, "If He called them gods, to whom the words of God were given, and the Scriptures cannot be broken, you say of Him whom the Father sanctified and sent into this world 'You blaspheme' because I said, 'I am the Son of God.'" By these words, He did not deny Himself to be God, but rather, He confirmed the assertion that He was God. . . . Nevertheless, He refuted the charge of blasphemy in a fitting manner with lawful tact. For He wished that He should be thus understood to be God, as the Son of God. He would not wish to be understood to be the Father Himself. . . . He is God, therefore, but God in such a manner as to be the Son, not the Father. *Novatian (c. 235, W), 5.625.*

All heavenly things, earthly things, and things under the earth are subjected to Christ—even the angels themselves, with all other creatures. And since many who are subjected to Christ are called gods, rightly also Christ is God. And if any angel at all subjected to Christ can be called god, and this, if it be said, is also professed without blasphemy, certainly much more can this be fitting for Christ Himself, the Son of God, to be called God. *Novatian (c. 235, W), 5.631.*

If Christ had been only man, He would have been spoken of as being in "the image of God," not "in the form of God." *Novatian (c. 235, W), 5.633.*

Jesus Christ, our Lord and God. *Cyprian (c. 250, W), 5.359.*

God the Father ordained His Son to be worshipped. The Apostle Paul, mindful of the divine command, lays it down and says, "God has exalted Him and given Him a name that is above every name, that in the name of Jesus every knee should bow—of things heavenly, and things earthly, and things beneath." And in the Apocalypse, the angel rebukes John . . . and says: "Worship Jesus the Lord." *Cyprian (c. 250, W), 5.491.*

Christ is God. . . . In Isaiah: . . . "For God is in you and there is no other God beside you. For you are God, and we knew it not, O God of Israel, our Savior." . . . Moreover, in Jeremiah, "This is our God, and no other will be esteemed beside Him, who has found all the way of knowledge and has given it to Jacob His son and to Israel, his beloved. After this, He was seen upon earth, and he conversed with men" [Baruch 3:35–37]. . . . Also, in the forty-fourth Psalm: "Your throne, O God, is forever and ever. . . . Therefore God, your God, has anointed you with the oil of gladness above your fellows. . . . Also, in the sixty-seventh Psalm: "Sing unto God, sing praises unto his name. Make a way for Him who goes up into the west. God is his name." . . .

Also, in the Gospel according to John: "In the beginning was the Word, and the Word was with God, and the Word was God." Also, . . . Thomas answered and said unto Him, "My Lord and my God." . . . Also, Paul said to the Romans: . . . "Christ came, who is God over all, blessed forever." Also, in the Apocalypse: "I am the Alpha and Omega, the beginning and the end. . . . He that overcomes will possess these things and their inheritance. And I will be his God and he will be my son." . . . Also in the Gospel according to Matthew: "And you will call His name Emmanuel, which is interpreted, 'God with us.'" *Cyprian (c. 250, W), 5.517, 518.*

Jesus Christ, our Lord and God, is the Son of God the Father and Creator. *Seventh Council of Carthage (c. 256, W), 5.567.*

"He is" because He endures continually. "He was," because with the Father, He made all things. *Victorinus (c. 280, W), 7.344.*

Since He truly was and is, being in the beginning with God, and being God, He is the chief Commander and Shepherd of the heavenly ones. *Methodius (c. 290, E), 6.318.*

These testimonies of the prophets foretold that it would come to pass that the Jews would lay hands upon their God and put Him to death. *Lactantius (c. 304–313, W), 7.121.*

We believe Him to be God. *Lactantius (c. 304–313, W), 7.139.*

Do these [pagans], then, hear with offended ears that Christ is worshipped and that He is accepted by us and regarded as a Divine Person? *Arnobius (c. 305, E), 6.423.*

You [pagans] say that we worship one who was born a human being. . . . Yet, in consideration of the many generous gifts He has bestowed on us, He should be called and be addressed as God. Since He is God in reality and without any shadow of doubt, do you think that we will deny that He is worshipped by us with all the fervor we are capable of. . . . "Is that Christ of yours a god, then?" some raving, angry, and excited man will say. "A God," we will reply, "And God of the inner powers." . . . He was sent to us by the King Supreme for a purpose of the very highest significance. *Arnobius (c. 305, E), 6.424.*

Christ performed all those miracles . . . by the inherent might of His authority. For this was the proper duty of true Divinity, as was consistent with His nature, as was worthy of Him. *Arnobius (c. 305, E), 6.425.*

Christ assisted both the good and the bad. . . . For this is the mark of true Divinity and of kingly power: to deny his bounty to none and not to consider who merits it or who does not. *Arnobius (c. 305, E), 6.426.*

He was God on high, God in His inmost nature, God from unknown realism, and He was sent by the Ruler of all as a Savior God. . . . When freed from the body—which He carried about as only a very small part of Himself—He allowed Himself to be seen. *Arnobius (c. 305, E), 6.428.*

If what we say is admitted to be true, He is proved to have been God by the confession of everyone. *Arnobius (c. 305, E), 6.429.*

We profess that Christ is not a mere man, but is God the Word and man, the Mediator between God and men. He is the High Priest of the Father. *Apostolic Constitutions (compiled c. 390, E), 7.454; extended discussion: 3.597–3.627, 5.515–5.520, 5.611–5.644.*

II. Begetting of the Son

One of the key tenets of Nicene orthodoxy is that the Son is begotten of the Father. The Nicene Creed states: "I believe . . . in one Lord Jesus Christ, the Only-Begotten Son of God; Begotten of His Father before all worlds; God of God, Light of Light, Very God of Very God; Begotten, not made; Being of one substance with the Father; By whom all things were made." As can be seen from the quotations that follow, each phrase of the Creed was taken verbatim from the writings of the pre-Nicene church.

A. Begotten of His Father

The Lord has said to Me, "You are My Son, today I have begotten You." Ps. 2:7.

My heart has uttered a good matter. Ps. 45:1 (LXX).

The Lord made me the beginning of his ways for his works. . . . Before the mountains were settled, and before all hills, he begets me. . . . When he prepared the heaven, I was present with him. . . . I was by him, suiting myself to him, I was that wherein he took delight. Prov. 8:22, 23 (LXX).

The Word . . . after God, who begat Him. *Justin Martyr (c. 160, E), 1.166.*

We assert that the Word of God was born of God in a peculiar manner, different from ordinary generation. *Justin Martyr (c. 160, E), 1.170.*

Jesus Christ is the only proper Son who has been begotten by God, being His Word, His First-Begotten, and His Power. *Justin Martyr (c. 160, E), 1.170.*

[Christians] call Him the Word, because He carries tidings from the Father to men. But they maintain that this Power is indivisible and inseparable from the Father, just as they say that the light of the sun on earth is indivisible and inseparable from the sun in the heavens. . . . They say that the Father, when He chooses, causes His Power to spring forth. And when He chooses, He makes it return to Himself. . . . This power, which the prophetic word calls God . . . is indeed something numerically distinct [from the Father]. . . . This Power was begotten from the Father by His power and will, but not by division, as if

the essence of the Father were divided. For all other things that are partitioned and divided are not the same after the partition as they were before they were divided. And, for the sake of example, I took the case of fires kindled from a fire, which we see to be distinct from the original fire. Yet, the fire from which many fires can be kindled is by no means made less, but remains the same. *Justin Martyr (c. 160, E), 1.264.*

God, then, having His own Word internal within His own bowels, begat Him, emitting Him along with His own Wisdom before all things. *Theophilus (c. 180, E), 2.98.*

When God wished to make all that He determined on, He begot this Word. He uttered the First-Born of all creation. However, He Himself was not emptied of the Word, but having begotten the Word, and always conversing with His Word. And hence the holy writings, and all the Spirit-bearing men, teach us this. One of these men, John, says, "In the beginning was the Word, and the Word was with God," showing that at first God was alone, and the Word was in Him. *Theophilus (c. 180, E), 2.103.*

If anyone, therefore, says to us, "How then was the Son produced by the Father?" we reply to him, that no man understands that production, or generation, or calling, or revelation—or by whatever other name one may describe His generation. For it is in fact altogether indescribable. *Irenaeus (c. 180, E/W), 1.401.*

The Son reveals the Father, who begat the Son. *Irenaeus (c. 180, E/W), 1.469.*

As He was born of Mary in the last days, so did He also proceed from God as the First-Begotten of every creature. *Irenaeus (c. 180, E/W), 1.576.*

The perfect Word born of the perfect Father was begotten in perfection. *Clement of Alexandria (c. 195, E), 2.215.*

The Father, by loving, became "feminine." The great proof of this is He whom He begot of Himself. *Clement of Alexandria (c. 195, E), 2.601.*

The Father begat the Word as the Author, Fellow-Counselor, and Framer of the things that have been created. He uttered the first Voice, begetting Him as Light of Light. And He sent Him forth to the world as its Lord. *Hippolytus (c. 205, W), 5.227.*

You will say to me, "How is He begotten?" . . . You cannot explain with accuracy the economy in His case. For you do not have it in your power to acquaint yourself with the skilful and indescribable art of the Maker, but only to see, understand, and believe that man is God's work. Moreover, you are asking an account of the generation of the Word, whom God the Father begat as He willed, in His good pleasure. . . . Is it not enough for you to learn that the Son of God has been manifested to you for salvation (if you believe)—but do you also inquire curiously how He was begotten after the spirit [i.e., His heavenly birth]? . . . Are you then so bold as to seek the account after the spirit, which the Father keeps with Himself, intending to reveal it then to the holy ones and those worthy of seeing His face? . . . For He speaks in this manner: "From the womb, before the morning star, I have begotten you." *Hippolytus (c. 205, W), 5.229.*

This solitary and supreme Deity, by an exercise of reflection, brought forth the Logos first. . . . Him alone did [the Father] produce from existing things. For the Father Himself constituted existence, and the Being born from him was the cause of all things that are produced. The Logos was in [the Father] Himself, bearing the will of His Begetter and not being unacquainted with the mind of the Father. *Hippolytus (c. 225, W), 5.150, 151.*

Now, we believe that Christ did ever act in the name of God the Father. . . . We believe that He was the Son of the Creator and that He was His Word. God made Him His Son by emitting Him from Himself. He thereafter set the Son over every dispensation of His will. *Tertullian (c. 207, W), 3.318.*

I am therefore of the opinion that the will of the Father should be sufficient by itself for the existence of whatever He wishes to exist. . . . And thus also the existence of the Son is generated by Him. For this point must above all others be maintained by those who allow nothing to be unbegotten—unborn—except God the Father only. And we must be careful not to fall into the absurdities of those who picture to themselves certain emanations, so as to divide the divine nature into parts. *Origen (c. 225, E), 4.248.*

There is a meaning of "beginning" [Gr. *archē*] referring to a matter of origin, as might appear in

the saying: "In the beginning, God made the heaven and the earth." . . . This meaning of the word "beginning" in the sense of "origin" will serve us also in the passage in which Wisdom speaks in the Proverbs. We read, "God created me the beginning of His ways, for His works." Here the term could be interpreted as in the first application we spoke of—that of a way. It says, "The Lord created me the beginning of His ways." One might assert with good reason that God Himself is the beginning of all things. And one could go on to say—as is plain—that the Father is the origin [*archē*] of the Son. The Creator is the beginning of the works of the Creator. In a word, God is the beginning of all that exists. This view is supported by "In the beginning, was the Word." In the Word, one may see the Son. And because He is in the Father, He may be said to be in the beginning. *Origen (c. 228, E), 9.306.*

No one can worthily know the One without genealogy, the First-Born of all created nature, who is like the Father who begat Him. Nor can anyone know the Father as does the living Word, His Wisdom, and Truth. *Origen (c. 248, E), 4.581.*

The same rule of truth teaches us to believe, after the Father, also on the Son of God—Christ Jesus. He is the Lord our God, but He is the Son of God, out of that God who is both one and alone. *Novatian (c. 235, W), 5.618.*

God the Father is the Founder and Creator of all things. He alone knows no origin [*archē*]. He is invisible, infinite, immortal, eternal, and is one God. To his greatness, majesty, or power, not only can nothing be *preferred*, nothing can be *compared*. The Son, the Word, was born of Him, when He [the Father] willed it. The Word is not received in the sound of the stricken air, or in the tone of voice forced from the lungs. Rather, He is acknowledged in the substance of the power put forth by God. The mysteries of His sacred and divine nativity have not been learned by any apostle, nor discovered by any prophet, nor known by any angel, nor comprehended by any creature. They are known to the Son alone, who has known the secrets of the Father. *Novatian (c. 235, W), 5.643.*

Thus, He could not make two Gods, because He did not make two beginnings. For from Him who has no beginning [*archē*], the Son received the source of His nativity before all time. *Novatian (c. 235, W), 5.644.*

Christ is the First-Born. He is the Wisdom of God, by whom all things were made. Solomon says in the Proverbs: "The Lord made me in the beginning of His ways, into His works. He founded me before the world. In the beginning, . . . the Lord begot me. . . . When He prepared the heaven, I was present with Him." . . . Also, in the same, in Ecclesiasticus: "I went forth out of the mouth of the Most High, First-Born before every creature." *Cyprian (c. 250, W), 5.515.*

I said that the plant . . . is different from the [seed or root] from which it sprouted. Yet, it is absolutely of the same nature. Similarly, a river flowing from a spring takes another form and name. For neither is the spring called the river, nor the river the spring. . . . The spring is the father, so to speak, and the river is the water from the spring. . . . God is the spring of all good things, but the Son is called the river flowing from Him. *Dionysius of Alexandria (c. 262, E), 6.92, 93, as quoted by Athanasius.*

I do not think that the Word was a thing made. Therefore, I do not say that God was His *Maker,* but rather his *Father.* Nevertheless, if at any time, in speaking about the Son, I may have casually said that God was His Maker, even this manner of speaking would not be without defense. For the wise men among the Greeks call themselves the "makers" of their books, although the same are "fathers" of their books. *Dionysius of Alexandria (c. 262, E), 6.93, as quoted by Athanasius.*

God was possessed of the greatest foresight for planning. . . . So before He commenced this business of the world, . . . He produced a Spirit like Himself, who could be endowed with the perfection of God the Father. God did this in order that goodness might spring as a stream from Him and might flow forth afar. *Lactantius (c. 304–313, W), 7.52.*

In the thirty-second Psalm: "By the word of God were the heavens made firm. And all their power by the breath of His mouth." And also again in the forty-fourth Psalm: "My heart has given utterance to a good word." . . . Solomon also shows that it is the Word of God, and no other, by whose hands these works of the world were made. He says, "I came forth out of the mouth of the Most High before all creatures. I caused the light that does not fail to arise in the heavens" [Sir. 24:3]. John also taught in this

manner: "In the beginning was the Word, and the Word was with God, and the Word was God." *Lactantius (c. 304–313, W), 7.107.*

In the 109th Psalm, David teaches the same, saying, "Before the morning star, I begot you." *Lactantius (c. 304–313, W), 7.113.*

Not that the Word is unbegotten. For the Father alone is unbegotten. Rather, the unexplainable subsistence of the Only-Begotten Son is beyond the understanding of the evangelists and perhaps also of the angels. For that reason, I do not think that he is to be considered pious who presumes to inquire into anything beyond these things. . . . To the Father alone belonged the knowledge of this most divine mystery. He says, "For no man knows the Son, but the Father." *Alexander of Alexandria (c. 324, E), 6.292, 293.*

Concerning Him we believe in this manner, even as the apostolic church believes: In one Father, unbegotten, who has the cause of His being from no one, who is unchangeable and immutable. . . . And in one Lord Jesus Christ, the Only-Begotten Son of God. He is not begotten of things that are not, but of Him who is the Father. He is not begotten in a physical manner, nor by excision or division (as Sabellius and Valentinus thought), but in a certain unexplainable and unspeakable manner. In the words of the prophet cited above: "Who will declare His generation?" Because of His subsistence, no begotten nature can investigate Him—just as no one can investigate the Father. The nature of rational beings cannot comprehend the knowledge of His divine generation by the Father. *Alexander of Alexandria (c. 324, E), 6.295.*

We believe . . . in one Lord Jesus Christ, the Son of God, begotten of the Father, only begotten, that is, of the substance of the Father; God of God; Light of Light; very God of very God; begotten, not made; being of one substance with the Father. *Nicene Creed (A.D. 325), 7.524; extended discussion: 4.245–4.251.*

B. Before all worlds
Out of you shall come forth to me the One to be ruler in Israel, whose goings forth have been from of old, from everlasting. Mic. 5:2.

Jesus said to them, "Most assuredly, I say to you, before Abraham was, I AM." John 8:58.

Jesus Christ was with the Father before the ages, and in the end, He was revealed. *Ignatius (c. 105, E), 1.61.*

The Son of God is older than all His creatures, so that He was a Fellow-Counselor with the Father in His work of creation. *Hermas (c. 150, W), 2.47.*

His Son . . . also was with Him and was begotten before the works, when at first He created and arranged all things by Him. *Justin Martyr (c. 160, E), 1.190.*

And Trypho [a Jew] said, "For some of it appears to me to be paradoxical, and wholly incapable of proof. For example, you say that this Christ existed as God before the ages." *Justin Martyr (c. 160, E), 1.219.*

This is He who existed before all, who is the eternal Priest of God, and King, and Christ. *Justin Martyr (c. 160, E), 1.247.*

We know Him to be the First-Begotten of God, and to be before all creatures. . . . Since we call Him the Son, we have understood that, before all creatures, He proceeded from the Father by His power and will. *Justin Martyr (c. 160, E), 1.249.*

"The Lord created me the beginning of His ways for His works. From everlasting He established me in the beginning, before He formed the earth." . . . You perceive . . . that the Scripture has declared that this Offspring was begotten by the Father before all things created. Now, everyone will admit that He who is begotten is numerically distinct from Him who begets. *Justin Martyr (c. 160, E), 1.264.*

This Being is perfect Reason, the Word of God. He was begotten before the light. He is Creator, together with the Father. He is the Fashioner of man. . . . He is God who is from God. He is the Son who is from the Father. He is Jesus Christ, the King for evermore. . . . This was the First-Born of God, who was begotten before the sun. *Melito (c. 170, E), 8.756, 757.*

Moreover, we are worshippers of His Christ, who is truly God the Word, existing before all time. *Melito (c. 170, E), 8.759.*

Being at once both God and perfect man, He gave us sure indications of His two natures. . . . He concealed the signs of His Deity, although he was the true God existing before all ages. *Melito (c. 170, E), 8.760.*

What is meant by the Son? I will state briefly that He is the first product of the Father. I do not mean that He was brought into existence. For, from the beginning, God, who is the eternal Mind, had the Logos in Himself. From eternity, He is instinct with Logos. However, [the Son is begotten] inasmuch as He came forth to be the Idea and energizing Power of all material things, which lay like a nature without attributes. . . . The prophetic Spirit also agrees with our statements. "The Lord," it says, "made me the beginning of His ways to His works." *Athenagoras (c. 175, E), 2.133.*

Each of those things to which divinity is ascribed is conceived of as having existed from the first. *Athenagoras (c. 175, E), 2.137.*

But what else is this voice but the Word of God, who is also His Son? Not as the poets and writers of myths talk of the sons of gods begotten from intercourse, but as truth expounds, the Word who always exists, residing within the heart of God. For before anything came into being, He had Him as a counsellor, being His own mind and thought. *Theophilus (c. 180, E), 2.103.*

But the Son has been eternally co-existing with the Father. From of old, yes, from the beginning, He always reveals the Father. *Irenaeus (c. 180, E/W), 1.406.*

For not only before Adam, but also before all creation, the Word glorified His Father, remaining in Him. *Irenaeus (c. 180, E/W), 1.478.*

For with Him were always present the Word and Wisdom, the Son and the Spirit, by whom and in whom, freely and spontaneously, He made all things. He speaks to this one, saying, "Let Us make man after Our image and likeness." . . . I have also largely demonstrated that the Word, namely the Son, was always with the Father. *Irenaeus (c. 180, E/W), 1.487, 488.*

He was with the Father from the beginning. *Irenaeus (c. 180, E/W), 1.489.*

He is prior to all creation. *Irenaeus (c. 180, E/W), 1.526.*

Solomon also says that before heaven, earth, and all existences, Wisdom had arisen in the Almighty. *Clement of Alexandria (c. 195, E), 2.512.*

The timeless and unoriginated First Principle and Beginning of existences—the Son—from whom we are to learn the remoter Cause of the universe, the Father, the most ancient and the most beneficent of all. *Clement of Alexandria (c. 195, E), 2.523.*

The presbyter explained what is meant by "from the beginning," to this effect: That the beginning of generation is not separated from the beginning of the Creator. For when he says, "That which was from the beginning," he refers to the generation of the Son, that is without beginning, for He is co-existent with the Father. There was, then, a Word signifying an unbeginning eternity. *Clement of Alexandria (c. 195, E), 2.574, excerpted from a post-Nicene translation made by Cassiodorus.*

He signifies by the title of Father, that the Son also existed always, without beginning. *Clement of Alexandria (c. 195, E), 2.574, excerpted from a post-Nicene translation made by Cassiodorus.*

He who was co-existent with His Father before all time, and before the foundation of the world, always had the glory proper to Divinity. *Hippolytus (c. 205, W), 5.167.*

He was born the Word, of the heart of the Father, before all. *Hippolytus (c. 205, W), 5.189.*

They killed the Son of their Benefactor, for He is co-eternal with the Father. *Hippolytus (c. 205, W), 5.220.*

We have always held that God is the Father of His Only-Begotten Son, who was born indeed of Him, and derives from Him what He is, but without any beginning—not only such as may be measured by any divisions of time, but even that which the mind alone can contemplate within itself. . . . And therefore we must believe that Wisdom was generated before any beginning that can either be comprehended or expressed. And since all the creative power of the coming creation was included in this very existence of Wisdom . . . does Wisdom say, in the words of Solomon, that she was "created the beginning of the ways of God." For she contained within herself either the beginnings, forms, or species of all creation. *Origen (c. 225, E), 4.246.*

Let him, then, who assigns a beginning to the Word or Wisdom of God take care that he is not guilty of impiety against the unbegotten Father himself. For he denies that He had always been a Father, or had always generated the Word, or

had possessed Wisdom in all preceding periods, whether they be called times or ages. *Origen (c. 225, E), 4.246, 247.*

The Father generates an uncreated Son and brings forth a Holy Spirit—not as if He had no previous existence, but because the Father is the origin and source of the Son or Holy Spirit. *Origen (c. 225, E), 4.270.*

John also indicates that "God is Light." . . . Since light could never exist without splendor, so neither can the Son be understood to exist without the Father. For He is called the "express image of His person" and the Word and Wisdom. How, then, can it be declared that there was once a time when He was not the Son? For that is nothing else than to say that there was once a time when he was not the Truth, nor the Wisdom, nor the Life. . . . Now, this expression that we use—"that there never was a time when He did not exist"—is to be understood with an allowance. For these very words—"when" and "never"—have a meaning that relates to time. However, the statements made regarding Father, Son, and Holy Spirit are to be understood as transcending all times, all ages, and all eternity. *Origen (c. 225, E), 4.377.*

It is not only the Greeks who consider the word "beginning" [Gr. *archē*] to have many meanings. Let anyone collect the Scripture passages in which the word occurs and . . . note what it stands for in each passage. He will find that the word has many meanings in sacred discourse, as well. *Origen (c. 228, E), 9.305.*

"You are My Son. This day have I begotten You." This is spoken to Him by God, with whom all time is today. For there is no evening with God . . . and there is no morning. There is nothing but time that stretches out, along with His unbeginning and unseen life. The day is today within Him in which the Son was begotten. Accordingly, the beginning of His birth is not found, nor is the day of it. *Origen (c. 228, E), 9.314.*

The Word was always with the Father. And so it is said, "And the Word was with God." . . . He was in the beginning at the same time when He was with God—neither being separated from the beginning, nor being bereft of His Father. And again, neither did He come to be in the beginning after He had not been in it. Nor did He come to be with God after not having been with him. For before all time and the remotest age, the Word was in the beginning, and the Word was with God. *Origen (c. 228, E), 9.322.*

He was in the beginning with God. The term "beginning" may be taken as the beginning of the world, so that we may learn from what is said that the Word was older than the things that were made from the beginning. *Origen (c. 228, E), 9.325.*

The Word was not *made* in the beginning. There was no time when the beginning was devoid of the Word. For that reason it is said, "In the beginning was the Word." *Origen (c. 228, E), 9.334.*

He is therefore God, because He was before the world, and held His glory before the world. *Novatian (c. 235, W), 5.626.*

Since He was begotten of the Father, He is always in the Father. In saying "always," I do not mean Him to be unborn, but born. Yet, He who is before all time must be said to have been always in the Father. For no time can be assigned to Him who is before all time. He is always in the Father, unless the Father is not always the Father. Yet, the Father also precedes him in a certain sense. For it is necessary, in some degree, that He should *be* before He is Father. For it is essential that He who knows no beginning must go before Him who has a beginning. Just as the Son is the less, as knowing that He is in the Father, having an origin because He is born. And He is of like nature with the Father in some measure because of His nativity. He has a beginning in that He is born, inasmuch as He is born of that Father who alone has no beginning. He, then, when the Father willed it, proceeded from the Father. He who was in the Father came forth from the Father. And He who was *in* the Father because He was *of* the Father, was subsequently *with* the Father, because He came forth from the Father. I am speaking of the Divine substance whose name is the Word. *Novatian (c. 235, W), 5.643.*

There certainly was not a time when God was not the Father. . . . Because the Son has existence from the Father, not from Himself, it does not mean that God afterwards begot the Son. . . . Being the brightness of the eternal Light, He Himself also is absolutely eternal. If the light is always in existence, it is manifest that its brightness also exists. . . . God is the eternal Light, which has neither had a beginning, nor will it ever fail. Therefore, the eternal

brightness shines forth before Him and co-exists with Him. Existing without a beginning, and always begotten, He always shines before Him. He is that Wisdom that says, "I was that in which He delighted, and I was daily his delight before his face at all times." *Dionysius of Alexandria (c. 262, E), 6.92, as quoted by Athanasius.*

Now, this word, "I am," expresses His eternal subsistence. For if he is the reflection of the eternal light, he must also be eternal Himself. For if the light subsists forever, it is evident that the reflection also subsists forever. *Dionysius of Alexandria (c. 262, E), 6.120.*

Neither are they less to be blamed who think that the Son was a creation, determining that the Lord was made—just as one of those things that really were made. For the divine declarations testify that He was *begotten* (as is fitting and proper), but not that He was *created* or made. It is therefore not a trifling thing—but a very great impiety—to say that the Lord was in any way made with hands. For if the Son was made, there was a time when He was not. However, He always was, if (as He Himself declares) He is undoubtedly in the Father. And if Christ is the Word, the Wisdom, and the Power (for the divine writings tell us that Christ is these, as you yourselves know), assuredly these are powers of God. Wherefore, if the Son was made, there was a time when these were not in existence. And thus there was a time when God was without these things, which is utterly absurd. *Dionysius of Rome (c. 265, W), 7.365, as quoted by Athanasius.*

He had neither recently attained to the relationship of Son, nor again, having begun before, had an end after this. Rather, He had previously been begotten, and He was to be, and was the same. But the expression, "This day I have begotten you," means that he willed that He who existed before the ages in heaven should be begotten on the earth. *Methodius (c. 290, E), 6.338.*

Since the Son is always with Him, the Father is always complete, being destitute of nothing as regards good. He has begotten His Only-Begotten Son—not in time, nor after an interval, nor from things that are not. How, then, is it not unholy to say that the Wisdom of God once was not. . . . Or that the Power of God once did not exist? . . . Therefore, one may see that the Sonship of our Savior has nothing at all in common with the sonship of the rest. *Alexander of Alexandria (c. 324, E), 6.293.*

How can He be made of things that are not, when the Father says, "My heart belched forth a good Word"? And, "From the womb, before the morning, I have begotten you"? Or how can He be unlike the substance of the Father—He who is the perfect image and brightness of the Father and who says, "He that has seen Me has seen the Father"? Furthermore, if the Son is the Word, Wisdom, and Reason of God, how can there be a time when he was not? It is the same as if they said there was a time when God was without reason and wisdom. *Alexander of Alexandria (c. 324, E), 6.297.*

C. God of God

In the beginning was the Word, and the Word was with God, and the Word was God. John 1:1.

No man has seen God at any time; the only begotten God, who is in the bosom of the Father, He has explained Him. John 1:18 (NAS).

I will give you another testimony . . . from Scriptures, that God begat before all creatures a Beginning, a certain rational Power . . . who is called by the Holy Spirit, sometimes the Glory of the Lord, sometimes the Son, again Wisdom, again an Angel, then God, and then Lord, and Logos. *Justin Martyr (c. 160, E), 1.227.*

Those persons hold a far more appropriate [view of Christ] than do those others who equate the begetting of the eternal Word of God to the begetting of words to which men give utterance. For they assign to Him a beginning and course of production, just as they do their own words. If that were true, in what respect would the Word of God—yes, God Himself, since He is the Word—differ from the words of men? For He would follow the same order and process of generation. *Irenaeus (c. 180, E/W), 1.488.*

As also the Lord said: "The only-begotten God, who is in the bosom of the Father, he has declared Him." *Irenaeus (c. 180, E/W), 1.491.*

He is Prince of the angelic powers, God of God, and Son of the Father. *Irenaeus (c. 180, E/W), 1.577.*

We have been taught that He proceeds forth from God, and in that procession He is generated. So that He is the Son of God, and is called God from unity of substance with God. For

God, too, is a Spirit. Even when the ray is shot from the sun, it is still part of the parent mass. The sun will still be in the ray, because it is a ray of the sun. There is no *division* of substance, but merely an extension of it. . . . Thus Christ is Spirit of Spirit, and God of God—just as light is kindled from light. The material root remains entire and unimpaired, even though you derive from it any number of offshoots possessed of its qualities. So, too, that which has come forth out of God is at once God and the Son of God, and the two are one. *Tertullian (c. 197, W), 3.34.*

The Word was in the beginning "with God," the Father. It was not the Father who was with the Word. For although the Word was God, he was *with* God, for He is God *of* God. *Tertullian (c. 213, W), 3.610.*

It indicates the return to the glory that He had by nature. If we understand it correctly, actually His glory is merely *restored* to Him. For, as the Only-Begotten Word of God, being God of God, He emptied himself, according to the Scriptures, humbling himself of His own will to that which He was not before. And He took upon Himself this vile flesh and appeared in the "form of a servant." And He "became obedient to God the Father, even unto death." So hereafter He is said to be "highly exalted." . . . He "receives the name that is above every name," according to the word of the blessed Paul. But the matter, in truth, was not a "giving"—as if for the first time—of what He did not have by nature. It is far otherwise. We must understand it as a return and restoration to that which existed in Him at the beginning, essentially and inseparably. *Hippolytus (c. 205, W), 5.167.*

There is a great risk of saying that the Savior of the human race was only human. . . . For this contempt shown by the heretics also attacks God the Father—as if God the Father could not beget God the Son. *Novatian (c. 235, W), 5.620.*

Nature itself has prescribed that he must be believed to be man who is of man. Likewise, he must be believed to be God who is of God. *Novatian (c. 235, W), 5.620.*

God, then, proceeded from God, causing a person second to the Father as being the Son. But He does not deprive the Father of that characteristic that the Father is one God. For if the Son had not been born—compared with Him who was unborn—an equality would be manifested in both. So, then, the addition of the

Son would make two unborn Beings. And this would make two Gods. If He had not been begotten—compared with Him who was not begotten—they would be found equal. If they were both not begotten, this would have reasonably given two Gods. If He had been formed without beginning, just as the Father, and if He Himself were the beginning of all things as is the Father—this would have made two beginnings. Consequently, this would have demonstrated two Gods to us, also. *Novatian (c. 235, W), 5.643.*

The Word that was in the beginning with God (who is also very God) may come to us. *Origen (c. 248, E), 4.499.*

How much more must we believe that the voice of God both remains forever and is accompanied with perception and power. It has derived this from God the Father like a stream from a fountain. Someone may be puzzled that God could be produced from God [the Father] by a putting forth of the voice and breath. However, if such a person is acquainted with the sacred utterances of the prophets, he will cease to wonder. *Lactantius (c. 304–313, W), 7.106.*

We believe in one Lord Jesus Christ, the Only-Begotten Son of God. He is not begotten of things that are not. Rather, He is begotten of Him who is the Father. *Alexander of Alexandria (c. 324, E), 6.295.*

James, the brother of Christ according to the flesh, but His servant as to His being the Only-Begotten God. *Apostolic Constitutions (compiled c. 390, E), 7.496.*

D. Light of Light

That was the true Light which gives light to every man who comes into the world. John 1:9.

[The Son is] the brightness of His glory. Heb. 1:3.

It is just as we see also happening in the case of a fire, which is not lessened when it has kindled [another fire]. Rather, it remains the same. And that which has been kindled by it likewise appears to exist by itself, not diminishing the fire from which it was kindled. The Word of Wisdom . . . is Himself this God, begotten of the Father. . . . "The Lord made me the beginning of His ways for His works. From everlasting he established me in the beginning, before He had made the earth." *Justin Martyr (c. 160, E), 1.227.*

God was in the beginning. But the beginning, we have been taught, is the power of the Logos. For the Lord of the universe, who is Himself the necessary ground of all being, was alone. For no creature was in existence yet. Nevertheless, inasmuch as He was all power, Himself the necessary ground of things visible and invisible, with Him were all things. The Logos Himself was in Him and subsists with Him by Logos-Power. And by His simple will, the Logos springs forth. So the Logos, not coming forth in vain, becomes the first-begotten work of the Father. We know the Logos to be the beginning of the world. But He came into being by participation, not by abscission. For what is cut off is separated from the original substance. However, that which comes by participation, making its choice of function, does not render the one deficient from whom he is taken. From one torch many fires are lighted, but the light of the first torch is not lessened by the kindling of many torches. It is the same with the Logos. His coming forth from the Logos-Power of the Father has not divested the Father who begat Him of the Logos-Power. *Tatian (c. 160, E), 2.67.*

God the Word, incarnate, is intellectual Light. *Clement of Alexandria (c. 195, E), 2.578.*

As the Author, Fellow-Counselor, and Framer of the things that have been created, God begat the Word. He uttered the first voice, begetting Him as Light of Light. And He sent Him forth to the world as its Lord. *Hippolytus (c. 205, W), 5.227.*

Thus there appeared another One beside Himself. But when I say "another," I do not mean that there are two Gods, but that it is only as light of light, or as water from a fountain, or as a ray from the sun. For there is but one Power, which is from the All. And the Father is the All, from whom comes this Power, the Word. *Hippolytus (c. 205, W), 5.227.*

God sent forth the Word, as the Paraclete also declares, just as the root puts forth the tree, the fountain the river, and the sun the ray. For these are emanations of the substances from which they proceed. I would not hesitate, indeed, to call the tree the son or offspring of the root, and the river the offspring of the fountain, and the ray the offspring of the sun. For every original source is a parent, and everything that issues from the origin is an offspring. Much more is this so of the Word of

God, who has actually received as His own peculiar designation the name of "Son." But still, the tree is not severed from the root, nor the river from the fountain, nor the ray from the sun. Nor, indeed, is the Word separated from God. *Tertullian (c. 213, W), 3.603.*

According to John, "God is light." The Only-Begotten Son, therefore, is the glory of this light. He proceeds inseparably from [God] Himself, as brightness proceeds from light, illuminating the whole of creation. *Origen (c. 225, E), 4.248.*

A thing is properly termed everlasting or eternal that neither had a beginning of existence, nor can ever cease to be what it is. And this is the idea conveyed by John when he says that "God is light." Now, His Wisdom is the splendor of that light, . . . so that His Wisdom is eternal and everlasting splendor. If this is fully understood, it clearly shows that the existence of the Son is derived from the Father—but not in time, nor from any other beginning, except (as we have said) from God himself. *Origen (c. 225, E), 4.251.*

The Savior is here called simply "Light." But in the catholic Epistle of this same John, we read that God is Light. This, it has been maintained, furnishes a proof that the Son is not different from the Father in substance. *Origen (c. 228, E), 9.336.*

The substance of the Son is not a substance devised extraneously. Nor is it one introduced out of nothing. Rather, it was born of the substance of the Father, as the reflection of light or as the stream of water. For the reflection is not the same as the sun itself. Likewise, the stream is not the water itself; but neither is it anything alien to it. The Son is an emanation from the substance of the Father. Yet the substance of the Father did not suffer any partition. The sun remains the same and suffers no diminution from the rays that are poured out by it. So likewise, neither did the substance of the Father undergo any change in having the Son as an image of itself. *Theognostus of Alexandria (c. 260, E), 6.155.*

Since the Father is eternal, the Son is also eternal, Light of Light. . . . Since, then, God is the Light, Christ is the Brightness. . . . Moreover, the Son alone, always co-existing with the Father and filled with Him who is, Himself also is, since He is of the Father. *Dionysius of Alexandria (c. 262, E), 6.92, as quoted by Athanasius.*

Life is begotten from life in the same way as the river has flowed forth from the spring and the brilliant light is ignited from the inextinguishable light. *Dionysius of Alexandria (c. 262, E), 6.93, as quoted by Athanasius.*

E. Begotten, not made

When the student of the Nicene Creed comes to the phrase "Begotten, not made," it often appears that here there is a divergence between the Creed and the pre-Nicene church. There is, however, actually no difference in belief. There is only a difference in phraseology. The Nicene Creed affirms that the Son of God was begotten; he was not made or created out of nothing. The pre-Nicene church firmly believed this.

Orthodoxy in the pre-Nicene church, however, focused on right concepts—not on using this word instead of that word. As Origen expressed it: "Let everyone, then, who cares for truth not be concerned about words and language. For in every nation there prevails a different usage of speech. Rather, let him direct his attention to the meaning conveyed by the words (rather than to the nature of the words that convey the meaning), especially in matters of such importance and difficulty" (ANF 4.376). From the writings of the pre-Nicene Christians, it is quite apparent that many of them used "begotten" [Gr. *gennētos*] and "created" [Gr. *genētos* and *ktizein*] as interchangeable terms. This was partially based on usage in Scripture. In describing the generation of Wisdom (which the pre-Nicene church universally understood to be referring to the generation of the Son), the eighth chapter of Proverbs in the Septuagint uses the term "create" [Gr. *ektisen*]. But in using the term *ktizein*, neither Scripture nor the pre-Nicene writers meant that the Son was made or created out of nothing. Rather, they understood *ktizein* to have a broad meaning that encompasses both "beget" and "create." This becomes quite clear when a person reads the totality of what each writer says.

God speaks in the creation of man with the very same design, in the following words: "Let us make man after our image and likeness." . . . From this, we can indisputably learn that God conversed with someone who was numerically distinct from Himself, and was also a rational Being. . . . For I would not say that the dogma of that heresy which is said to be among you Jews is true, or that the teachers of it can prove that God spoke to angels, or that the human frame was the workmanship of angels. But this Offspring, who was truly brought forth from the Father, was with the Father before all the creatures. And the Father communed with Him. It is even as the Scripture by Solomon has made clear, that He whom Solomon calls Wisdom was begotten as a Beginning before all His creatures. *Justin Martyr (c. 160, E), 1.228.*

Not one of the created and subject things shall ever be compared to the Word of God, by whom all things were made, who is our Lord Jesus Christ. *Irenaeus (c. 180, E/W), 1.421.*

The Logos alone of this One is from God Himself. For that reason also, He is God, being of the substance of God. In contrast, the world was made from nothing. Therefore, it is not God. *Hippolytus (c. 225, W), 5.151.*

It is monstrous and unlawful to compare God the Father, in the generation of His Only-Begotten Son, and in the substance of the same, to any man or other living thing. . . . Wisdom has her existence nowhere else but in Him who is the beginning of all things—from whom is also derived everything that is wise, for He Himself is the only One who is by nature a Son; He is therefore called the Only-Begotten. *Origen (c. 225, E), 4.247.*

Seeing that God the Father is invisible and inseparable from the Son, the Son is not generated from Him by extension, as some suppose. For if the Son is an extension of the Father, then, of necessity, both He from whom [the Son was] extended and He who was extended are corporeal. For we do not say, as the heretics suppose, that some part of the substance of God was converted into the Son. Or that the Son was begotten by the Father out of things that were non-existent—i.e., beyond His own substance, so that there was once a time when He did not exist. However, putting away all corporeal conceptions, we say that the Word and Wisdom were begotten out of the invisible and incorporeal without any corporeal sense. It is as if it were an act of the will proceeding from the understanding. *Origen (c. 225, E), 4.376.*

The Word of God, knowing the Father, reveals the Father whom He knows. For no created being can approach the Father without a guide. For no one knows the Father except the Son and he to whomever the Son reveals Him. *Origen (c. 228, E), 9.320.*

If Christ is only man, how could He say, "I proceeded forth and came from God"? For it is evident that man was *made* by God and did not *proceed forth* from Him. . . . Thus the Word of God proceeded, of whom it is said, "My heart has uttered forth a good Word." This Word, because it is from God, is obviously also *with* God. . . . Therefore, God proceeded from God, in that the Word who proceeded is God, who proceeded forth from God. *Novatian (c. 235, W), 5.624.*

Christ is called by the apostle "the First-Born of every creature." Now, how could He be the First-Born of every creature, unless it is because the Word proceeded from the Father, according to His divinity, before every creature? . . . Therefore, He is before every creature in order that He may be the First-Born of every creature. He is not, then, only man, because man is *after* every creature. *Novatian (c. 235, W), 5.632.*

"The Lord created me the beginning of His ways." For, as you know, there is more than one meaning of the word "created." In this place, "created" is the same as "set over" the works made by Himself—that is, made by the Son Himself. But this "created" is not to be understood in the same manner as "made." . . . Oh, reckless and rash men! Was then "the first-born of every creature" something made? . . . Finally, anyone may read in many parts of the divine utterances that the Son is said to have been begotten, but never that He was made. For which considerations, those who dare to say that His divine and inexplicable generation was a creation are openly convicted of thinking that which is false. *Dionysius of Rome (c. 265, W), 6.365, as quoted by Athanasius.*

Before He commenced this excellent work of the world, God begat a pure and incorruptible Spirit, whom He called His Son. And He afterwards created by Himself innumerable other beings, whom we call angels. However, this First-Begotten was the only One whom He considered worthy of being called by the divine name, as being powerful in His Father's excellence and majesty. . . . Since, therefore, He made Him first, and alone, and one only, he appeared to Him beautiful and most full of all good things. And He hallowed Him and altogether loved him as His own Son." . . . Assuredly, He is the very Son of God, who by that most wise King Solomon, full of divine inspiration, spoke these things that we have added: "God founded me in the beginning of His ways, in His work before the ages." *Lactantius (c. 304–313, W), 7.105.*

That the Son of God was not made from "things which are not" and that there was no "time when he was not," the evangelist John sufficiently shows. For he writes in this manner concerning Him: "The Only-Begotten Son, who is in the bosom of the Father." The divine teacher spoke of the Son as being in the bosom of the Father, intending to show that the Father and the Son are two things inseparable from each other. Furthermore, that the Word of God is not included in the number of things that were created out of nothing, the same John says, "All things were made by Him." . . . Now, if *all* things were made by Him, how can it be that He who gave them their existence was at one time non-existent Himself? *Alexander of Alexandria (c. 324, E), 6.292.*

[The Arians] ignorantly declare that one of two things must necessarily be said: Either that He is from things that are not, or that there are two Unbegottens. These ignorant men do not know how great the difference is between the unbegotten Father and the things that He created out of nothing. Between these two—as holding the middle place—is the Only-Begotten nature of God the Word, by whom the Father formed all things out of nothing. He was begotten of the true Father Himself. *Alexander of Alexandria (c. 324, E), 6.295.*

F. Being of one substance with the Father
In the beginning was the Word, and the Word was with God, and the Word was God. John 1:1.

That they all may be one, as You, Father, are in Me, and I in You; that they also may be one in Us. John 17:21.

For in Him all the fulness of Deity dwells in bodily form. Col. 2:9 [NAS].

The Word itself, that is, the Son of God, is one with the Father by equality of substance. He is eternal and uncreated. *Clement of Alexandria (c. 195, E), 2.574, excerpted from a post-Nicene translation made by Cassiodorus.*

When you do not deny that the Creator's Son and Spirit and substance is also His Christ, you necessarily allow that those who have not acknowledged the Father have failed likewise to acknowledge the Son, through the identity of their natural substance. *Tertullian (c. 207, W), 3.326.*

Surely I might venture to claim the very Word also as being of the Creator's substance. *Tertullian (c. 207, W), 3.356.*

This heresy [Monarchianism] supposes itself to possess the pure truth, in thinking that one cannot believe in only one God in any other way than by saying that the Father, the Son, and the Holy Spirit are the very selfsame Person. As if in this way also One were not All, in that All are of One, by unity of substance. Yet, they are of one substance, one condition, and one power—inasmuch as He is one God from whom these degrees, forms, and aspects are reckoned under the name of the Father, the Son, and the Holy Spirit. How they are susceptible of number without division will be shown. *Tertullian (c. 213, W), 3.598.*

How does it come to pass that God is thought to suffer division and severance in the Son and in the Holy Spirit, who have the second and the third places assigned to them, and who are so closely joined with the Father in His substance? . . . Do you really suppose that those, who are naturally members of the Father's own substance, pledges of His love, instruments of His might . . . are the overthrow and destruction thereof? You are not right in thinking so. . . . As for me, I derive the Son from no other source than from the substance of the Father. And I believe He does nothing without the Father's will and that He received all power from the Father. So how can I possibly be destroying the Monarchy from the faith, when I preserve it in the Son just as it was committed to Him by the Father? . . . Likewise with the third degree, for I believe the Spirit is from no other source than from the Father through the Son. *Tertullian (c. 213, W), 3.599.*

The Father is not the same as the Son, for they differ from each other in the manner of their being. For the Father is the entire substance. However, the Son is a derivation and portion of the whole. *Tertullian (c. 213, W), 3.604.*

Now, if He too is God, for according to John, "The Word was God," then you have two Beings—One who commands that the thing be made, and the other who creates. In what sense, however, you ought to understand Him to be another, I have already explained: on the ground of personality, not of substance. And in the way of distinction, not of division. I must everywhere hold only one substance, in three coherent and inseparable [persons]. *Tertullian (c. 213, W), 3.607.*

The Logos alone of this One is from God Himself. For that reason also, He is God, being of the substance of God. In contrast, the world was made from nothing. Therefore, it is not God. *Hippolytus (c. 225, W), 5.151.*

Whatever is a property of physical bodies cannot be attributed to either the Father or the Son. What belongs to the nature of deity is common to the Father and Son. *Origen (c. 225, E), 4.245.*

It is an attribute of the divine nature alone—of the Father, Son, and Holy Spirit—to exist without any material substance, and without partaking in any way with an adjoining body. Someone else may say that in the end, every bodily substance will be so pure and refined as to be like ether—of celestial purity and clearness. However, how things will be is known with certainty only to God. *Origen (c. 225, E), 4.262.*

The Son is not different from the Father in substance. *Origen (c. 228, E), 9.336.*

A discussion about "substance" would be protracted and difficult. This is especially so if it were a question whether that which is permanent and immaterial is even properly called "substance." . . . It is also a question for investigation, whether the "Only-Begotten" and "First-Born of every creature" is to be called "substance of substances," . . . while above all there is his Father and God. *Origen (c. 248, E), 4.602, 603.*

The substance of the Son is not a substance devised extraneously. Nor is it one introduced out of nothing. Rather, it was born of the substance of the Father, as the reflection of light or as the stream of water. For the reflection is not the same as the sun itself. Likewise, the stream is not the water itself; but neither is it anything alien to it. He is an emanation from the substance of the Father. Yet the substance of the Father did not suffer any partition. *Theognostus of Alexandria (c. 260, E), 6.155.*

I have also proved the falsehood of the charge which they bring against me—that I do

not maintain that Christ is consubstantial with God. For although I say that I have never either found or read this word in the sacred Scriptures, yet other reasonings . . . are in no way discrepant from this view. Moreover, I gave the illustration of human offspring, which is certainly of the same kind as the begetter. And I said that parents are essentially distinguished from their children only by the fact that they themselves are not their children. *Dionysius of Alexandria (c. 262, E), 6.92, as quoted by Athanasius.*

If, from the fact that there are three persons [Gr. *hypostases*], they say that they are divided, there are three whether they like it or not. Otherwise, let them get rid of the divine Trinity altogether. *Dionysius of Alexandria (c. 262, E), 6.94, as quoted by Athanasius.*

It would be just to dispute against those who destroy the monarchy by dividing and rending it . . . into three powers and distinct substances [Gr. *hypostases*] and deities. . . . In a certain manner, these men declare three Gods, in that they divide the Holy Unity into three different substances, absolutely separated from one another. *Dionysius of Rome (c. 265, W), 7.365, as quoted by Athanasius.*

With respect to the Father and the Son, [Pierius] sets forth his sentiments in a godly manner, except that he speaks of two substances and two natures. However, it is apparent from both what follows and what precedes this passage that he uses the terms "substance" and "nature" in the sense of person [Gr. *hypostasis*] and not in the sense put on it by the adherents of Arius. *Pierius (c. 275, E), 6.157, as cited by Photius.*

Since, therefore, the Father makes the Son, and the Son the Father, they both have one mind, one spirit, one substance. However, the Father is, as it were, an overflowing fountain. The Son is, as it were, a stream flowing forth from it. The Father is as the sun; the Son is, as it were, a ray extended from the sun. *Lactantius (c. 304–313, W), 7.132, 133.*

There is only one unchangeable substance—the divine substance, eternal and invisible, as is known to all, and as is also supported by this Scripture: "No man has seen God at any time, except the only begotten Son, who is in the bosom of the Father." *Disputation of Archelaus and Manes (c. 320, E), 6.205.*

Who can venture to speak of the substance of God, unless, it may be our Lord Jesus Christ alone? *Disputation of Archelaus and Manes (c. 320, E), 6.212.*

G. By whom all things were made

All things were made through Him, and without Him nothing was made that was made. John 1:3.

By Him all things were created that are in heaven and that are on earth, visible and invisible, whether thrones or dominions or principalities or powers. All things were created through Him and for Him. Col. 1:16.

The Logos, too, before the creation of men, was the Framer of the angels. *Tatian (c. 160, E), 2.67.*

The universe has been created and set in order through His Logos. . . . For we acknowledge also a Son of God. *Athenagoras (c. 175, E), 2.133.*

He had this Word as a Helper in the things that were created by Him. By Him God made all things. *Theophilus (c. 180, E), 2.98.*

"Let Us make man in Our image, after our likeness." Now, to no one else than to His own Word and Wisdom did He say, "Let Us make." *Theophilus (c. 180, E), 2.101.*

For the Creator of the world is truly the Word of God. And this is our Lord. *Irenaeus (c. 180, E/W), 1.546.*

He is God and Creator. "For all things were made by Him, and without him nothing was made." *Clement of Alexandria (c. 195, E), 2.234.*

He is the Lord's right hand, indeed His two hands, by which He worked and constructed the universe. *Tertullian (c. 200, W), 3.502.*

All the rest of the created things He did in like manner make, who made the former ones. I am referring to the Word of God, "through whom all things were made, and without whom nothing was made." *Tertullian (c. 213, W), 3.607.*

Christ is, in a manner, the Creator, to whom the Father says, "Let there be light." *Origen (c. 228, E), 9.307.*

III. Relationship of the Son to the Father

When western Christians read what the early church believed about the relationship of the Father and the Son, they are often quite surprised. Some well-meaning Christians mistakenly accuse the early church of being Arian. In

doing so, they obviously have not given deep thought to the matter. As we have already seen, the Nicene Creed is an encapsulation of what the pre-Nicene church believed about the Father and the Son. In accordance with the Nicene Creed, the early Christians taught that the Father and the Son are of the same substance and that the Son was not created out of nothing.

Of course, many Christians believe that the church grew into a better understanding of the Trinity in the centuries following the council of Nicaea. That position is a subject beyond the scope of this work. Before we can even discuss the development of the doctrine of the Trinity in a meaningful way, however, we must first thoroughly understand what the church originally taught about the Trinity, particularly concerning the relationship of the Father and the Son.

The key to understanding the pre-Nicene doctrine of the Trinity is comprehending the difference between "nature," "personal attributes," and "order." These terms refer to three very different things, yet many western Christians do not grasp this distinction. Arius certainly did not grasp it, which is what led to his heresy. In theology, "nature" or "substance" refers to the essence or class to which a person or creature belongs. All humans are of one nature or one substance, regardless of differing personal characteristics. In a genetic sense, no man or woman is any less human than anybody else. But humans are not of the same nature or substance as the angels. Now, the Nicene Creed affirms that the Father and the Son are of the same nature or substance. The Son is not something foreign to the Father; rather, He possesses the same nature as the Father. Both the Father and the Son are equally divine. If the Son were not of equal nature or substance as the Father, He would not be fully divine; He would not possess true Godhood. The quotations above reveal that the pre-Nicene church explicitly taught that the Son is fully divine.

"Personal attributes" are something altogether different. Personal attributes refer to the individual characteristics and differences between members of the same class or nature. To grasp this distinction, let us go back in time to the creation of man. According to Genesis, at one time there were only two humans on the earth, Adam and Eve. These two humans shared the same nature or substance. Adam was not more human than Eve, nor was Eve more human than Adam. They were equal in nature or substance. Now, does that mean that the first two humans were equal or identical in personal attributes? No, it does not. Adam was no doubt taller and stronger than Eve. Furthermore, Eve had come out of Adam, being formed from his rib. On the other hand, Eve had the ability to give birth to children and to breast-feed infants. Adam could do neither of these things. In short, there were personal attributes that made Adam and Eve different from each other—even though they were both equal in nature.

Likewise, the church has taught from the beginning that there are personal attributes that distinguish the Father from the Son. For example, the Father begets the Son, and, therefore, the Son has His origin [archē] in the Father. Does this make the Son less divine than the Father? Does this reduce the Son to being a demigod? Not at all! Being unbegotten is not an aspect of divinity; it is a personal attribute. Again, the early church believed that the Father could never become incarnate nor could he ever make himself visible to human eyes. To the early church, this would have been a denial of the Father's unique personhood. That is because the Father is the ultimate Source not only of the universe, but also of the Trinity. In saying this, the early church was not demoting the Son to being a demigod. Rather, it understood that such things are not attributes of divinity. Rather, those attributes are simply differing characteristics of the Father and the Son. So the early church affirmed that the Father is greater than the Son—as to personal attributes, but not as to nature. The Son (and the Holy Spirit) possess the full attributes of divinity, but the Father possesses unique personal attributes that make him greater than the Son and the Holy Spirit. As has been said, one of these characteristics is that the Father is the Begetter.

There is another sense, however, in which the early church taught that the Father is greater than the Son: in the sense of order. Here, "order" means chain of authority. Equality of nature does not mean equality of order. Returning to our illustration of Adam and Eve, we find that not only did the first two humans differ in personal attributes; they also differed in order. Although Adam and Eve were equal in nature, Adam was created first, and he was the head of Eve. Paul explains that

there is the exact same order within the Trinity, saying, "I want you to know that the head of every man is Christ, the head of woman is man, and the head of Christ is God" (1 Cor. 11:3). So the Father has authority over the Son. The Son is sent by the Father; the Son does the will of the Father; and the Son sits at the Father's right hand. This hierarchy of order cannot be reversed. Yet this hierarchy of order in no way diminishes the Son's divinity.

When Christians do not understand the difference between nature, personal attributes, and order, they end up with a confused understanding of the Trinity. They also misconstrue what the early Christians taught about the Father and the Son. The following passages illustrate how the early church understood the Scriptures regarding the nature, personal attributes, and order of the Father and the Son.

A. Equality of nature (substance)

In the beginning was the Word, and the Word was with God, and the Word was God. John 1:1.

That they all may be one, as You, Father, are in Me, and I in You. John 17:21.

In Him all the fulness of Deity dwells in bodily form. Col. 2:9 [NAS].

The quotations above under II.F. "Being of one substance with the Father" clearly show that the pre-Nicene church believed that there was an equality of nature between the Father and the Son. A few of those quotations are repeated here:

The Word itself, that is, the Son of God, is one with the Father by equality of substance. He is eternal and uncreated. *Clement of Alexandria (c. 195, E), 2.574, excerpted from a post-Nicene translation made by Cassiodorus.*

He is made a second in manner of existence—in position, not in nature. He did not withdraw from the original source, but went forth. *Tertullian (c. 197, W), 3.34.*

Now, if He too is God, for according to John, "The Word was God," then you have two Beings—One who commands that the thing be made, and the Other who creates. In what sense, however, you ought to understand Him to be another, I have already explained: on the ground of personality, not of substance. *Tertullian (c. 213, W), 3.607.*

The Logos alone of this One is from God Himself. For that reason also, He is God, being of the substance of God. *Hippolytus (c. 225, W), 5.151.*

Besides, He is in [the Father] and is truly and entirely made one with Him. . . . The Father of all things has made Him one with Himself . . . and honors Him with a power in all respects equal to His own, just as He also is honored. First and alone of all creatures who exist, He has had assigned Him this position. This is the Only-Begotten of the Father, who is in Him and who is God the Word. . . . He is the altogether perfect, living, and truly animate Word of the First Mind Himself. *Gregory Thaumaturgus (c. 255, E), 6.24.*

The substance of the Son is not a substance devised extraneously. Nor is it one introduced out of nothing. Rather, it was born of the substance of the Father. *Theognostus of Alexandria (c. 260, E), 6.155.*

B. Difference in personal attributes

But of that day and hour no one knows, neither the angels in heaven, nor the Son, but only the Father. Mark 13:32.

No man has seen God at any time; the only begotten God, who is in the bosom of the Father, he has explained Him. John 1:18 [NAS].

Most assuredly, I say to you, the Son can do nothing of Himself, but what He sees the Father do; for whatever He does, the Son also does in like manner. For the Father loves the Son, and shows Him all things that He Himself does. John 5:19, 20.

If you loved Me, you would rejoice because I said, "I am going to the Father," for My Father is greater than I. John 14:28.

I am ascending to My Father and your Father, and to My God and your God. John 20:17.

For us there is only one God, the Father, of whom are all things, and we for Him; and one Lord Jesus Christ, through whom are all things, and through whom we live. 1 Cor. 8:6.

Blessed be the God and Father of our Lord Jesus Christ. 2 Cor. 1:3.

He is the image of the invisible God, the firstborn over all creation. Col. 1:15.

He who is the blessed and only Potentate, the King of kings and Lord of lords, who alone has immortality, dwelling in unapproachable light, whom no man has

seen or can see, to whom be honor and everlasting power. 1 Tim. 6:15, 16.

[God] has in these last days spoken to us by His Son, whom He has appointed heir of all things, through whom also he made the worlds; who being the brightness of His glory and the express image of His person, and upholding all things by the word of His power, when He had by Himself purged our sins, sat down at the right hand of the Majesty on high, having become so much better than the angels, as He has by inheritance obtained a more excellent name than they. For to which of the angels did He ever say: "You are My Son, today I have begotten You"? And again: I will be to Him a Father, and He shall be to Me a Son"? But when He again brings the firstborn into the world, He says: "Let all the angels of God worship Him." And of the angels He says: "Who makes His angels spirits and His ministers a flame of fire." But to the Son He says: "Your throne, O God, is forever and ever; a scepter of righteousness is the scepter of Your kingdom. You have loved righteousness and hated lawlessness; therefore God, Your God, has anointed You." Heb. 1:2–9.

He who overcomes, I will make him a pillar in the temple of My God, and he shall go out no more. And I will write on him the name of My God and the name of the city of My God. Rev. 3:12.

The God and Father of our Lord Jesus Christ. *Polycarp (c. 135, E), 1.35.*

The Son foretells that He will be saved by the same God. He does not boast of accomplishing anything through His own will or might. For when on earth, He acted in the very same manner. He answered to man who addressed Him as "Good Master": "Why do you call me good? One is good, my Father who is in heaven." *Justin Martyr (c. 160, E), 1.249.*

You must not imagine that the Unbegotten God Himself came down or went up from any place. For the ineffable Father and Lord of everything neither has come to any place, nor walks, nor sleeps, nor rises up, but remains in His own place. . . . He is not moved or confined to a spot in the whole world, for He existed before the world was made. How, then, could He talk with anyone, or be seen by anyone, or appear on the smallest portion of the earth? . . . Therefore, neither Abraham, nor Isaac, nor Jacob, nor any other man saw the Father, who is the inexpressible Lord of all, including Christ. Rather, they saw One who was the Father's Son, according to the Father's will. The Son is also God and the Angel, for He ministered to His [Father's] will. *Justin Martyr (c. 160, E), 1.263.*

Even the Lord, the very Son of God, acknowledged that the Father alone knows the very day and hour of judgment. For He plainly declares, "But of that day and that hour no man knows, neither the Son, but the Father only." If, then, the Son was not ashamed to ascribe the knowledge of that day to the Father only (but declared what was true regarding the matter), neither let us be ashamed to reserve for God those greater questions that may occur to us. *Irenaeus (c. 180, E/W), 1.401.*

For if anyone asks about the reason why the Father, who has fellowship with the Son in all things, has been declared by the Lord alone to know the hour and the day, he will find at present no more suitable, becoming, or safe reason than this (since, indeed, the Lord is the only true Master): that we may learn through Him that the Father is above all things. For He says, "The Father is greater than I." The Father, therefore, has been declared by our Lord to excel with respect to knowledge. *Irenaeus (c. 180, E/W), 1.402.*

He is discovered to be the one only God who created all things, who alone is Omnipotent, and who is the only Father. He founded and formed all things.... He has fitted and arranged all things by His Wisdom. He contains all things, but He Himself can be contained by no one.... But there is one only God, the Creator. He is above every principality, power, dominion, and virtue. He is Father; He is God; He is Founder; He is Maker; He is Creator. He made those things by Himself, that is, through His Word and His Wisdom.... He is the God of Abraham, the God of Isaac, and the God of Jacob.... He is the Father of our Lord Jesus Christ. Through His Word, who is His Son, through Him, He is revealed and manifested to all to whom He is revealed. For [only] those know Him to whom the Son has revealed Him. But the Son, eternally co-existing with the Father, from of old, yes, from the beginning, always reveals the Father. *Irenaeus (c. 180, E/W), 1.406.*

Everyone saw the Father in the Son. For the Father is the invisible [archetype] of the Son. But the Son is the visible [image] of the Father. *Irenaeus (c. 180, E/W), 1.469.*

It is manifest that the Father is indeed invisible, of whom also the Lord said, "No man has seen God at any time".... As also the Lord said: "The only-begotten God, who is in the bosom of the Father, he has declared Him." *Irenaeus (c. 180, E/W), 1.491.*

He has a full faith in one God Almighty, *of* whom are all things; and in the Son of God, Jesus Christ our Lord, *by* whom are all things. *Irenaeus (c. 180, E/W), 1.508.*

John the apostle says: "No man has seen God at any time. The Only-Begotten God, who is in the bosom of the Father, He has declared Him." Here he calls invisibility and inexpressible glory "the bosom of God." ... No one can rightly express Him wholly. For on account of His greatness, He is ranked as the All. He is the Father of the universe.... If we name Him, we cannot do so properly. For example, we can call Him the One, or the Good, or Mind, or Absolute Being, or Father, or God, or Creator, or Lord.... For each one by itself does not express God. However, all together, they are indicative of the power of the Omnipotent.... But there is nothing prior to the Unbegotten. It is sufficient, then, that we understand the Unknown by divine grace and by the Word alone who proceeds from Him. *Clement of Alexandria (c. 195, E), 2.463, 464.*

The Unoriginated Being is one, the Omnipotent God. One, too, is the First-Begotten. *Clement of Alexandria (c. 195, E), 2.493.*

All benefit pertaining to life, in its highest reason, proceeds from the Sovereign God, the Father. He is over all. He is consummated by the Son, who also on this account "is the Savior of all men." ... This is in accordance with the command and injunction of the One who is nearest the First Cause, that is, the Lord. *Clement of Alexandria (c. 195, E), 2.518.*

From the Son, we are to learn the remoter Cause of the universe, the Father. He is the most ancient and the most beneficent of all. He is not capable of expression by the voice. Rather, He is to be worshipped with reverence, silence, and holy wonder, and to be supremely venerated. *Clement of Alexandria (c. 195, E), 2.523.*

The object of our worship is the One God, He who by His commanding Word, His arranging Wisdom, His mighty Power, brought forth from nothing this entire mass of our world. *Tertullian (c. 197, W), 3.31.*

For He who ever spoke to Moses was the Son of God Himself, who, too, was always seen. For no one ever saw God the Father and lived. *Tertullian (c. 197, W), 3.163.*

How can it be that anything—except the Father—could be older, and on this account indeed nobler, than the Son of God, the Only-Begotten and First-Begotten Word? *Tertullian (c. 200, W), 3.487.*

He calls Christ "the image of the invisible God." We, in like manner, say that the Father of Christ is invisible, for we know that it was the Son who was seen in ancient times. *Tertullian (c. 207, W), 3.470.*

The Father is not the same as the Son, for they differ from each other in the manner of their being. For the Father is the entire substance. However, the Son is a derivation and portion of the whole. He Himself acknowledges this: "My Father is greater than I." In the Psalm, His subordination is described as being "a little lower than the angels." Thus, the Father is distinct from the Son, being greater than the Son, inasmuch as He who begets is one, and He who is begotten is another. *Tertullian (c. 213, W), 3.604.*

You reply, "If He was God who spoke, and He was also God who created . . . two Gods are declared." If you are so venturesome and harsh, reflect awhile. . . . Listen to the Psalm in which two are described as God: "Thy throne, O God, is forever and ever. The scepter of Your kingdom is a scepter of righteousness. . . . Therefore, God, even your God, has anointed You." Now, since He here speaks to God, and affirms that God is anointed by God, He must have affirmed that Two are God. . . . "In the beginning was the Word, and the Word was with God, and the Word was God." A much more ancient testimony we have also in Genesis: "Then the Lord rained upon Sodom and upon Gomorrah brimstone and fire from the Lord out of heaven." . . . That there are, however, two Gods or two Lords, is a statement that at no time proceeds out of our mouths. I will therefore not speak of Gods at all, nor of Lords, but I will follow the apostle. So that if the Father and the Son are both to be invoked, I will call the Father "God" and invoke Jesus Christ as

"Lord." But when Christ alone [is spoken of], I will be able to call Him "God," as the same apostle says: "Of whom is Christ, who is over all, God blessed forever." For I should give the name of "sun" even to a sunbeam, when considered by itself. But if I were to mention the sun from which the ray emanates, I certainly should at once withdraw the name of sun from the mere beam. For although I do not make two suns, still I will reckon both the sun and its ray to be as much two things and two forms of one undivided substance—just as God and His Word, the Father and the Son. *Tertullian (c. 213, W), 3.608.*

It will therefore follow that by Him who is invisible we must understand the Father in the fullness of His majesty. At the same time, we recognize the Son as visible because of the dispensation of His derived existence. For example, it is not permitted us to contemplate the sun in the full amount of its substance which is in the heavens. Rather, we can only endure with our eyes a ray of the sun. *Tertullian (c. 213, W), 3.609.*

The Word was in the beginning "with God," the Father. It was not the Father who was with the Word. For although the Word was God, he was *with* God, for He is God *of* God. *Tertullian (c. 213, W), 3.610.*

Of the Father, however, he says to Timothy: "Whom no one among men has seen, nor indeed can see." And he adds to the description in still fuller terms: "Who alone has immortality and dwells in the light that no man can approach." It was of Him, too, that he had said in a previous passage: "Now unto the King eternal, immortal, invisible, to the only God." So that we might apply even the contrary qualities to the Son Himself. . . . It was the Son, therefore, who was always seen, and the Son who always conversed with men. This is the Son who has always worked by the authority and will of the father. For "the Son can do nothing of Himself, but what He sees the Father do." *Tertullian (c. 213, W), 3.611.*

[The Father] is named without the Son whenever He is defined as the Principle in the character of its First Person. In those situations, He had to be mentioned before the name of the Son. For it is the Father who is acknowledged in the first place. And after the Father, the Son is named. Therefore, "there is one God, the Father," and without Him, there is no one else. And when He Himself makes this declaration,

He does not deny the Son. . . . For as this Son in undivided and inseparable from the Father, so is He to be reckoned as being in the Father (even when He is not named). . . . Suppose the sun were to say, "I am the sun, and there is none other besides me, *except my ray.*" Would you not have remarked how useless such a statement was, as if the ray were not itself reckoned in the sun? *Tertullian (c. 213, W), 3.613.*

The Father, however, has no origin. For He proceeds from no one. Nor can He be seen, since He was not begotten. He who has always been alone could never have had order or rank. *Tertullian (c. 213, W), 3.614.*

Christ is also ignorant of the last day and hour, which is known to the Father only. He awards the kingdom to His disciples, as He says it had been appointed to Him by the Father. He has power to ask, if He wishes, legions of angels from the Father for His help. He exclaims that God had forsaken Him. *Tertullian (c. 213, W), 3.623.*

"This is God, and no other can be considered in comparison to Him." He said that rightly. For in comparison to the Father, who will be accounted of? . . . "He has found out all the way of knowledge and has given it unto Jacob His servant and to Israel His beloved." He spoke well. For who is Jacob His servant? Who is Israel His beloved? It is He of whom He cries, saying, "This is my beloved Son, in whom I am well pleased. Hear Him." So having received all knowledge from the Father, the perfect Israel (the true Jacob) afterwards showed himself upon earth. . . . This, then, is He to whom the Father has given all knowledge. *Hippolytus (c. 205, W), 5.225.*

"Then He Himself will also be subject to Him who put all things under Him, that God may be all in all." If, therefore, all things are put under Him with the exception of Him who put them under Him, the Son is Lord of all, and the Father is Lord of Him. Thereby, there is manifest in all one God, to whom all things are made subject together with Christ, to whom the Father has made all things subject—with the exception of Himself. And this, indeed, is said by Christ Himself, as when in the Gospel He confessed Him to be His Father and His God. For Christ speaks in this manner: "I go to my Father and your Father, and to my *God* and your God." *Hippolytus (c. 205, W), 5.226.*

The Father generates an uncreated Son and brings forth a Holy Spirit—not as if He had no previous existence, but because the Father is the origin and source of the Son and the Holy Spirit. *Origen (c. 225, E), 4.270.*

By His spiritual healing aids, the Son disposes all things to receive at the end the goodness of the Father. It was from His sense of that goodness that He answered him who addressed the Only-Begotten with the words, "Good Master." In reply, Jesus said, "Why do you call Me good? No one is good but one, God the Father." This we have discussed elsewhere, especially in dealing with the question of the One who is greater than the Creator. Christ we have taken to be the Creator, and the Father is the One who is greater than He. *Origen (c. 228, E), 9.318.*

The archetypal image, again, of all these images is the Word of God—who was in the beginning and who by being with God is at all times Divine, not possessing divinity of Himself, but by His being with the Father. . . . The Father is the fountain of divinity; the Son is the fountain of reason [Gr. *logos*]. *Origen (c. 228, E), 9.323.*

If all things were made (as in this passage also) *through* the Logos, then they were not made *by* the Logos—but by a stronger and greater than He. And who else could this be but the Father? *Origen (c. 228, E), 9.328.*

Life, in the full sense of the word, especially after what we have been saying on the subject, belongs perhaps to God and to no one but Him. . . . It says about God . . . "who alone has immortality." No living being besides God has life free from change and variation. Why should we be in further doubt? Even Christ did not share the Father's immortality. For He "tasted death for every man." *Origen (c. 228, E), 9.333.*

The Savior is here called simply "Light." But in the catholic Epistle of this same John, we read that God is Light. This, it has been maintained, furnishes a proof that the Son is not different from the Father in substance. Another student, however, looking into the matter more closely and with a sounder judgment, will say that the Light that shines in darkness and is not overtaken by it is not the same as the Light in which there is no darkness at all. The Light that shines in the darkness comes upon this darkness, as it were, and is pursued by it. Yet, in spite of attempts made upon it, it is not overtaken. But the Light in which there is no darkness at all neither shines on darkness, nor is at first pursued by it.... But in proportion as God, since He is the Father of truth, is more and greater than truth, and since He is the Father of wisdom, is greater and more excellent than wisdom. *Origen (c. 228, E), 9.336.*

Let no one suppose that we say this from any lack of piety towards the Christ of God. For as the Father alone has immortality and our Lord took upon Himself the death He died for us (out of His love of men), so also to the Father alone the words apply, "In Him there is no darkness," since Christ took upon Himself our darkness—out of His goodwill towards men. *Origen (c. 228, E), 9.338.*

"No one has seen God at any time. The Only-Begotten God, who is in the bosom of the Father, he has declared Him." *Origen (c. 228, E), 9.343.*

[John the Baptist] answers by exalting the superior nature of Christ—that He has such virtue as to be invisible in His deity, though present to every man and extending over the whole universe. *Origen (c. 228, E), 9.365, 366.*

The Father sent the One who is the God of the living.... The Father also alone is good, and He is greater than He who was sent by Him.... He who first of all was girded about with the whole creation, in addition to the Son's being in Him, granted to the Savior to pervade the whole creation. For He [the Word] was second after him and was God the Word. *Origen (c. 228, E), 9.370.*

Pay careful attention to what follows, where He is called God: "For your throne, O God, is forever and ever.... Therefore, God, even your God, has anointed you with the oil of gladness above your fellows." Observe that the prophet, speaking familiarly to God, ... says that this God had been anointed by a God who was His God. *Origen (c. 248, E), 4.421.*

We charge the Jews with not acknowledging Him to be God, to whom testimony was borne in many passages by the prophets. Those passages testify to the effect that He was a mighty Power and a God next to the God and Father of all things. For we maintain that it was to Him that the Father gave the command ... "Let there be light." ... We say that to Him were also addressed the words, "Let Us make man in Our own image and likeness." The Logos,

when commanded, obeyed all of the Father's will. *Origen (c. 248, E), 4.433.*

Our Lord and Savior, hearing himself on one occasion addressed as "Good Master," referred the person who used it to His own Father, saying, "Why do you call me good? There is no one good but one, that is, God the Father." It was in accordance with sound reason that this was said by the Son of His Father's love, for He was the image of the goodness of God. *Origen (c. 248, E), 4.548.*

Our Savior, also, does not partake of righteousness. Rather, being "Righteousness" Himself, he is partaken of *by* the righteous.... It is also a question for investigation, whether the "Only-Begotten" and "First-Born of every creature" is to be called "substance of substances," ... while above all there is his Father and God. *Origen (c. 248, E), 4.602, 603.*

But the God and Father of all things is not the only Being who is great in our judgment. For He has imparted Himself and His greatness to His Only-Begotten and First-Born of every creature, in order that He—being the image of the invisible God—might preserve, even in His greatness, the image of the Father. For it was not possible that there could exist a well-proportioned, so to speak, and beautiful image of the invisible God unless it also preserved the image of His greatness. *Origen (c. 248, E), 4.605.*

He to whom God bore testimony through the prophets, and who has done great things in heaven and earth, should receive on those grounds honor that is second only to that which is given to the Most High God. *Origen (c. 248, E), 4.634.*

Again Celsus [a pagan critic] proceeds: "If you were to tell the Christians that Jesus is not the Son of God, but that God is the Father of all, and that He alone should be truly worshipped, they would not consent to discontinue their worship of Him who is their leader in the sedition. And they call Him the Son of God, not out of any extreme reverence for God, but from an extreme desire to extol Jesus Christ." ... [ORIGEN'S REPLY:] There is nothing extravagant or unbecoming in the doctrine that He should have begotten such an only Son. And no one will persuade us that such a One is not a Son of the unbegotten God and Father.... He is the Son who has been most highly exalted by the Father. Granted, there may be some individuals among the multitudes of believers who are not in entire agreement with us [i.e., the Monarchists]. They incautiously assert that the Savior is the Most High God. However, we do not concur with them. Rather, we believe Him when He says, "The Father who sent me is greater than I." We would not, therefore, make him whom we call Father inferior to the Son of God—as Celsus accuses us of doing. *Origen (c. 248, E), 4.644.*

The rule of truth requires that we should first of all believe on God the Father and Lord Almighty. He is the absolutely perfect Founder of all things. . . . Over all these things, He has left room for no superior God (such as some people conceive). For He contains all things, having nothing vacant beyond Himself. . . . He is always unbounded, for nothing is greater than He. He is always eternal, for nothing is more ancient than He. For He who is without beginning can be preceded by no one, in that He has no time. On that account, He is immortal . . . and He excludes the mode of time. . . . If He could be understood, he would be smaller than the human mind that could conceive Him. *Novatian (c. 235, W), 5.611, 612.*

The Lord rightly declares Him alone to be good. . . . He is declared to be one, having no equal. *Novatian (c. 235, W), 5.614.*

Although He was in the form of God, He did not think of robbery—that He should be equal with God. For although He remembered that He was God from God the Father, He never either compared or associated Himself with God the Father. He was mindful that He was from His Father and that He possessed that very thing that He is because the Father had given it to Him. . . . He yielded all obedience to the Father and still yields it as ever. From that it is shown that He thought that the claim of a certain divinity would be robbery—to wit, that of equalling himself with God the Father. Rather, on the other hand, obedient and subject to all His Father's rule and will, He even was content to take on Himself the form of a servant. *Novatian (c. 235, W), 5.633.*

If He were not the Son . . . and if He were designated to be as great as the Father, He would have caused two Fathers. Thereby, He would have proved the existence of two Gods. Had He been invisible, as compared with the Invisible and thereby declared equal, He would have shown forth two Invisibles. Thus, once

again, He would have proved there to be two Gods. . . . But now, whatever He is, He is not of Himself, because He is not unborn. Rather, He is of the Father, because He is begotten. . . . He is not from any other source than the Father, as we have already said before. Owing His origin to His Father, He could not make a disagreement in the divinity by the number of two Gods. For His beginning was in being born of Him who is one God. . . . Therefore, He declared that God is one, in that He proved God to be from no source or beginning. Rather, He is the beginning and source of all things. Moreover, the Son does nothing of His own will, nor does He do anything of His own determination. Likewise, He does not come from Himself, but obeys all His Father's commands and precepts. So, although birth proves Him to be a Son, yet obedience even to death declares Him to be the Servant of the will of His Father, of whom He is. . . . He is indeed proved to be the Son of His Father. But He is found to be both Lord and God of all else. All things are put under Him and delivered to Him. For He is God, and all things are subjected to Him. Nevertheless, the Son refers all that He has received to the Father. He remits again to the Father the whole authority of His divinity. The true and eternal Father is manifested as the one God, from whom alone this power of divinity is sent forth. . . . So reasonably, God the Father is God of all. And He is the source, also, of His Son Himself, whom He begot as Lord. Moreover, the Son is God of all else, because God the Father put Him whom He begot over all. *Novatian (c. 235, W), 5.644.*

There are two types of formative power. . . . The one works by itself whatever it chooses . . . by its bare will, without delay, as soon as it wills. This is the power of the Father. The other [type of power] adorns and embellishes the things that already exist, by imitation of the first. This is the power of the Son, who is the Almighty and Powerful hand of the Father. *Methodius (c. 290, E), 6.381, as quoted by Photius.*

We must say that the Beginning, out of which the most upright Word came forth, is the Father and Maker of all things, in whom He was. And the words, "the same was in the beginning with God," seem to indicate the position of authority of the Word, which He had with the Father before the world came into existence. "Beginning" signifies His power. And so, after the unique unbeginning Beginning, who is the

Father, He is the Beginning of other things, by whom all things are made. *Methodius (c. 290, E), 6.381, as quoted by Photius.*

Someone may perhaps ask how we say that we worship only one God. For we declare that there are two—God the Father and God the Son. This declaration has driven many into the greatest error. . . . When we speak of God the Father and God the Son, we do not speak of them as different, nor do we separate them. Because the Father cannot exist without the Son, nor can the Son be separated from the Father. That is because the name of Father cannot be applied without the Son. Nor can the Son be begotten without the Father. Since, therefore, the Father makes the Son, and the Son the Father, they both have one mind, one spirit, one substance. However, the Father is, as it were, an overflowing fountain. The Son is, as it were, a stream flowing forth from it. The Father is as the sun; the Son is, as it were, a ray extended from the sun. And since the Son is both faithful to the Most High Father and beloved by Him, He is not separated from Him. Just as the stream is not separated from the fountain, nor the ray from the sun. For the water of the fountain is in the stream, and the light of the sun is in the ray. Similarly, the voice cannot be separated from the mouth, nor the strength or hand from the body. So, when He is also spoken of by the prophets as the Hand, the Strength, and Word of God, there is plainly no separation. . . .

We may use an example more closely connected with us. Suppose someone has a son whom he especially loves—who is still in the house and in the power of his father. Now although the father may give to him the name and power of a master, by civil law, the house is one. Only one person is called master. Likewise, this world is the one house of God. And the Son and the Father, who unanimously inhabit the world, are one God. For the one is as two and the two are as one. Nor is that unbelievable, for the Son is in the Father, as the Father loves the Son. And the Father is in the Son, for the Son faithfully obeys the will of the Father. He has never done, nor will He do, anything other than what the Father either willed or commanded. So the Father and the Son are but one God. . . . For there is one God alone—free, Most High, without any origin. For He Himself is the origin of all things. And in Him both the Son and all things are con-

tained. Therefore, since the mind and will of the one is in the other—or rather, since there is one in both—both are justly called one God. For whatever is in the Father flows on to the Son. And whatever is in the Son descends from the Father. Accordingly, that Highest and Matchless God cannot be worshipped except through the Son. He who thinks that he worships only the Father, and will not worship the Son—he does not even worship the Father. However, he who receives the Son and bears His name—he truly worships the Father together with the Son. For the Son is the Ambassador, Messenger, and Priest of the Most High Father. *Lactantius (c. 304–313, W), 7.132, 133.*

The following two quotations are from Alexander, bishop of Alexandria, who was the primary opponent of Arius leading up to the Council of Nicaea.

He is equally with the Father unchangeable and immutable, lacking in nothing. He is the perfect Son, and, as we have learned, He is like the Father. In this alone is He inferior to the Father: that He is not unbegotten. For He is the very exact image of the Father and differs from Him in nothing. . . . But let no one take the word "always" in a manner that raises suspicion that He is unbegotten. . . . For neither are the words, "he was," "always," or "before all worlds," equivalent to unbegotten. For the human mind cannot use any synonyms to signify "unbegotten." . . . For these words do not at all signify unbegotten. Rather, these words seem to denote simply a lengthening out of time. Still, they cannot properly signify the divinity and antiquity of the Only-Begotten. Nevertheless, they have been used by holy men, while each—according to his capacity—seeks to express this mystery, asking patience from the hearers and pleading a reasonable excuse, in saying, "This is as far as we can come." . . .

In short, whatever word we use is not equivalent to "unbegotten." Therefore, to the Unbegotten Father, indeed, we should preserve His proper dignity, in confessing that no one is the cause of His being. However, to the Son must be also given His fitting honor, in assigning to Him . . . a generation from the Father without beginning and assigning worship to Him. . . . We by no means reject His Godhood, but ascribe to him a likeness that exactly answers in every respect to the image and example of the

Father. Still, we must say that to the Father alone belongs the property of being unbegotten. For the Savior Himself said, "My Father is greater than I." *Alexander of Alexandria (c. 324, E), 6.294, 295.*

Concerning Him, we believe in this manner, even as the apostolic church believes: In one Father, unbegotten, who has the cause of His being from no one, who is unchangeable and immutable. He is always the same and can have no increase or diminution. He gave the Law to us, the Prophets, and the Gospels. He is Lord of the patriarchs, apostles, and all the saints. And we believe in one Lord Jesus Christ, the Only-Begotten Son of God. He is not begotten of things that are not, but of him who is the Father. *Alexander of Alexandria (c. 324, E), 6.295.*

C. Difference in order
To sit on My right hand and on My left is not Mine to give, but it is for those for whom it is prepared by My Father. Matt. 20:23.

When you lift up the Son of Man, then you will know that I am He, and that I do nothing of Myself; but as My Father taught Me, I speak these things. John 8:28, 29.

I have not spoken on My own authority; but the Father who sent Me gave me a command, what I should say and what I should speak. John 12:49, 50.

The God of Abraham, Isaac, and Jacob, the God of our fathers, glorified His Servant Jesus. Acts 3:13.

For truly against Your holy Servant Jesus, whom You anointed, both Herod and Pontius Pilate, with the Gentiles and the people of Israel, were gathered together. Acts 4:27.

I want you to know that the head of every man is Christ, the head of woman is man, and the head of Christ is God. 1 Cor. 11:3.

When all things are made subject to Him, then the Son Himself will also be subject to Him who put all things under Him, that God may be all in all. 1 Cor. 15:25–28.

The Revelation of Jesus Christ, which God gave Him to show His servants. Rev. 1:1.

The Lord did nothing without the Father, for He was united to Him. . . . [There is] one Jesus Christ, who came forth from one Father. He is with one Father, and He has gone to one Father. *Ignatius (c. 105, E), 1.62.*

Be the followers of Jesus Christ, even as He is of His Father. *Ignatius (c. 105, E), 1.84.*

He is the Lord of the people, having received all authority from His Father. *Hermas (c. 150, W), 2.35.*

They proclaim our madness to consist in this: that we give to a crucified man a place second to the unchangeable and eternal God, the Creator of all. For they do not discern the mystery that is herein. *Justin Martyr (c. 160, E), 1.167.*

He who is said to have appeared to Abraham, Jacob, and Moses, and who is called God, is distinct from the One who made all things. I mean, he is numerically distinct; He is not distinct in will. For I assert that He has never at anytime done anything that the One who made the world (above whom there is no other God) has not wished Him both to do and to engage Himself with. *Justin Martyr (c. 160, E), 1.224.*

I will repeat the whole Psalm, in order that you may hear His reverence for the Father. Listen to how He refers all things to Him, and prays to be delivered by Him from this death. . . . "O God, my God, attend to me: why have You forsaken me? . . . O my God, I will cry to you in the daytime." *Justin Martyr (c. 160, E), 1.248.*

The Son performs the good pleasure of the Father. For the Father sends, and the Son is sent, and comes. *Irenaeus (c. 180, E/W), 1.468.*

For His Offspring and His Image do minister to Him in every respect. That is, the Son and the Holy Spirit, the Word and Wisdom—whom all the angels serve and to whom they are subject. *Irenaeus (c. 180, E/W), 1.470.*

The Word Himself is the manifest mystery: God in man, and man in God. The Mediator executes the Father's will. For the Mediator is the Word, who is common to both man and God. He is the Son of God, but the Savior of men. He is God's Servant, but our Teacher. *Clement of Alexandria (c. 195, E), 2.271.*

We have heard it said, "The Head of Christ is the God and Father of our Lord Jesus Christ." . . . The Son sees the goodness of the Father. God the Savior works, for He is called the First Principle of all things. He first imaged forth from the invisible God, before the ages. He fashioned all things that came into being after Himself. *Clement of Alexandria (c. 195, E), 2.453.*

Xenocrates the Chalcedonian mentions the supreme Zeus and the subordinate Zeus. In doing so, he leaves an indication of the Father and the Son. *Clement of Alexandria (c. 195, E), 2.471.*

Jesus is the Lord of all and serves above all the will of the Good and Almighty Father. *Clement of Alexandria (c. 195, E), 2.524.*

He Himself proclaimed that He did not do His own will, but that of the Father. *Tertullian (c. 198, W), 3.682.*

However, with regard to the Father, the very gospel which is common to us will testify that He was never visible, according to the word of Christ. . . . He means that the Father is invisible, in whose authority and in whose name was He God who appeared as the Son of God. *Tertullian (c. 207, W), 3.319.*

In addition to the title of Son, He was the Sent One. The authority, therefore, of the Sender must necessarily have first appeared in a testimony of the Sent. That is because no one who comes in the authority of another declares things for himself, that is, on his own assertion. *Tertullian (c. 207, W), 3.321, 322.*

He Himself received from the Father the ability of uttering words in season: "The Lord has given to me the tongue of the learned, that I should know how to speak a word in season." However, Marcion introduces to us a Christ who is not subject to the Father. *Tertullian (c. 207, W), 3.415.*

No directive about the salvation of angels did Christ ever receive from the Father. And that which the Father neither promised nor commanded, Christ could not have undertaken. *Tertullian (c. 210, W), 3.533.*

The Son of God has faith's protection absolutely committed to Him. He beseeches it of the Father—from whom He receives all power in heaven and on earth. *Tertullian (c. 212, W), 4.117.*

No one, therefore, will impair [the monarchy of God] on account of admitting the Son. For it is certain that it has been committed to Him by the Father. Eventually, it has to be delivered up again by Him to the Father. *Tertullian (c. 213, W), 3.600.*

With us, however, the Son alone knows the Father, and has Himself unfolded the Father's bosom. He has also heard and seen all things with the Father. And what He has been commanded by the Father, that also is what He speaks. And it is not His own will, but the Father's that He has accomplished. He had known this fact most intimately, even from the beginning. . . . The Word, therefore, is both always *in* the Father (as He says, "I am in the Father") and is always *with* God (according to what is written, "And the Word was with God"). He is never separated from the Father, or different from the Father, since "I and the Father are one." *Tertullian (c. 213, W), 3.603.*

Consider whether the Son also is not indicated by these designations, who in His own right is God Almighty, in that He is the Word of Almighty God and has received power over all. He is the Most High, in that He is exalted at the right hand of God, as Peter declares in the Acts. He is the Lord of hosts, because all things are made subject to Him by the Father. *Tertullian (c. 213, W), 3.613.*

He accordingly says *Unum,* a neuter term, which does not imply singularity of number, but unity of essence, likeness, and conjunction. It implies affection on the Father's part, who loves the Son. And it implies submission on the Son's part, who obeys the Father's will. *Tertullian (c. 213, W), 3.618.*

It is the Father who commands, and the Son who obeys, and the Holy Spirit who gives understanding. The Father is *above* all, the Son is *through* all, and the Holy Spirit is *in* all. *Hippolytus (c. 205, W), 5.228.*

He is called the "image of the invisible God and the First-Born of every creature." "In Him all things were created, visible and invisible, . . . and He is before all things and by Him all things were made." So He is the head of all things, having God the Father alone as His head. For it is written, "The head of Christ is God." *Origen (c. 225, E), 4.281.*

He became obedient to the Father—not only by the death of the cross—but also in the end of the world. For He embraces in Himself all whom He subjects to the Father, and who by Him come to salvation. For He Himself (along with them, and in them) is said to also be subject to the Father. . . . Consequently, this is what the apostle says of Him: "And when all things will be subjected to Him, then will the Son also Himself be subject to Him that put all things under Him, that God may be all in all." Indeed, I do not know how the heretics—not understanding the meaning of the apostle in these words—consider the term "subjection" to be degrading when applied to the Son. . . . Now, according to their view, the language of the apostle means . . . that He who is not now in subjection to the Father will become subject to Him when the Father will have first subdued all things unto Him. However, I am astonished how it can be conceived that the meaning is that He who is not Himself in subjection at the present (when all things have *not* been subjected to Him) will later be made subject once all things have been subjected to Him. *Origen (c. 225, E), 4.343.*

Nor must we forget to mention the Word, who is God after the Father of all. *Origen (c. 228, E), 9.303.*

He will be at no loss to account for the Father's saying to Him, "You are My Servant," and a little further on, "It is a great thing that you should be called My Servant." For we do not hesitate to say that the goodness of Christ appears in a greater and more divine light . . . because "He humbled himself, becoming obedient unto death, even the death of the cross" than if He had judged it a thing to be grasped to be equal with God, and had shrunk from becoming a servant for the salvation of the world. He desires to teach us that in accepting this state of servitude, He had received a great gift from His Father. Hence, He says, "And My God will be My strength." *Origen (c. 228, E), 9.316.*

Just as Christ is our head, so God is His head. *Origen (c. 228, E), 9.318.*

The Word of God, who is called Faithful, is also called True. In righteousness, He judges and makes war. For He has received from God the faculty of judging. *Origen (c. 228, E), 9.326.*

The Unbegotten God commanded the First-Born of all creation, and they were created. *Origen (c. 228, E), 9.331.*

First, then, stands the Father, being without any turning or change. And then stands also His Word, always carrying on His work of salvation. *Origen (c. 228, E), 9.369.*

We say that the visible world is under the government of Him who created all things. We do thereby declare that the Son is not mightier than the Father—but subordinate to Him. And this belief we ground on the saying of Jesus himself, "The Father who sent me is greater than I." And none of us is so insane as to declare that the Son of man is Lord over God. But we regard the Savior as God the Word, and Wisdom, Righteousness, and Truth. And we certainly do say that He has dominion over all things that have been subjected to Him in this capacity. But we do not say that His domain extends over the God and Father who is Ruler over all. *Origen (c. 248, E), 4.645.*

Who does not acknowledge that the person of the Son is second after the Father? *Novatian (c. 235, W), 5.636.*

The divine Scripture (not so much of the Old as also of the New Testament) everywhere demonstrates Him to be born of the Father. By Him all things were made and without Him nothing was made. He always has obeyed and still obeys the Father. He always has power over all things—but these have been delivered, granted, or permitted to Him by the Father Himself. And what can be so evident proof that He is not the Father, but is the Son, than that He is shown as being obedient to God the Father. *Novatian (c. 235, W), 5.637.*

He declares that He was sanctified by His Father. Therefore, in receiving sanctification from the Father, He is secondary to the Father. Obviously, then, He who is secondary to the Father is not the Father, but the Son. For had He been the Father, He would have *given*, and not *received*, sanctification. . . . Besides, He says that He is *sent*. So in being obedient as to His coming, being sent, He proved to be the Son—not the Father. If he had been the Father, He would have done the sending. But being sent, He was not the Father. Otherwise, in being sent, the Father would be proved to be subjected to another God. *Novatian (c. 235, W), 5.638.*

He also is the image of God the Father. . . . And the Son is an imitator of all the Father's works. Therefore, everyone may regard it just as if he saw the Father, when he sees Him who always imitates the invisible Father in all His works. *Novatian (c. 235, W), 5.639.*

Christ received that very power by which we are baptized and sanctified from the same Father whom He called greater than Himself. This is the same Father by whom He desired to be glorified, whose will He fulfilled even unto the obedience of drinking the cup and undergoing death. *Cyprian (c. 250, W), 5.384.*

He who is called a confessor of Christ should imitate Christ whom he confesses. . . . For He Himself has been exalted by the Father. For, as the Word, the Strength, and the Wisdom of God the Father, He humbled Himself upon earth. . . . And He Himself received the highest name from the Father as the reward for His humility. *Cyprian (c. 250, W), 5.428.*

"I came down from heaven not to do my own will, but the will of Him that sent me." Now, if the Son was obedient to do His Father's will, how much more should the servant be obedient to do his Master's will. *Cyprian (c. 250, W), 5.451.*

Of this mercy and grace, the Word and Son of God is sent as the Dispenser and Master. . . . He is the Power of God. He is the Logos. He is His Wisdom and Glory. He enters into a virgin. Through the Holy Spirit, He is clothed with flesh. God is mingled with man. This is our God, this is Christ, who, as the Mediator of the two, puts on man that He may lead them to the Father. What man is, Christ was willing to be—so that man may also be what Christ is. *Cyprian (c. 250, W), 5.468.*

Assuredly, the will of the Son is not one thing, and the will of the Father another. For He who wills what the Father wills, is seen to have the Father's will. So He is speaking figuratively when He says, "Not my will, but yours." For it is not that He wishes the cup to be removed, but that He refers the correct issue of His passion to the Father's will. He thereby honors the Father as the First [Gr. *archē*]. *Dionysius of Alexandria (c. 262, E), 6.94, as quoted by Athanasius.*

On the head, the whiteness is shown. "But the head of Christ is God." *Victorinus (c. 280, W), 7.344.*

The prophets and apostles spoke more fully concerning the Son of God. They assigned to Him a divinity above other men. They did not refer their praises of Him to the teaching of angels, but to Him upon whom all authority and power depend. For it was fitting that He, who was greater than all things after the Father, should have the Father as His witness—who alone is greater than Himself. *Methodius (c. 290, E), 6.331.*

When God began the fabric of the world, He set over the whole work that first and greatest Son. He used Him at the same time as a Counsellor and Artificer, in planning, arranging, and accomplishing. For the Son is complete both in knowledge, judgment, and power. *Lactantius (c. 304–313, W), 7.53.*

Jesus displayed faith towards God. For He taught that there is but one God, and this one God alone should be worshipped. Nor did He at any time say that He Himself was [the] God. For He would not have maintained His faithfulness if He had introduced another God besides that One. For He was sent to abolish the false gods and to assert the existence of the one God. This would not have been to proclaim one God nor to do the work of Him who sent Him. . . . He was so faithful because He arrogated nothing at all to Himself. On account of this, in order to fulfill the commands of Him who sent Him, He received the dignity of everlasting Priest, the honor of supreme King, the authority of Judge, and the name of God. *Lactantius (c. 304–313, W), 7.114.*

We Christians are nothing else than worshippers of the Supreme King and Head, under our Master, Christ. *Arnobius (c. 305, E), 6.419.*

It will be revealed from what realms He has come, of what God He is the Minister. *Arnobius (c. 305, E), 6.426.*

He who does not receive Christ does not receive His God and Father. *Apostolic Constitutions (compiled c. 390, E), 7.404.*

Let the deacon minister to the bishop as Christ does to His Father. And let him serve him unblamably in all things. For Christ does nothing of Himself, but always does those things that please His Father. *Apostolic Constitutions (compiled c. 390, E), 7.410.*

Christ does nothing without his Father. . . . And as the Son is nothing without His Father, so is the deacon nothing without his bishop. And as the Son is subject to His Father, so is every deacon subject to his bishop. *Apostolic Constitutions (compiled c. 390, E), 7.411.*

He . . . blesses and glorifies the Lord God Almighty, the Father of the Only-Begotten God. *Apostolic Constitutions (compiled c. 390, E), 7.477; see also 2.227, 3.438.*

IV. The internal Logos and the external Son

The numerous quotations above make it clear that the early church believed the Logos of God to be eternal. The statements of some of the writers, however—when taken out of context or read carelessly—make it sound as though they thought the Son came into existence from nothing. They sometimes speak of God the Father having originally been alone. They sometimes also speak of the Father as begetting the Word or the Son at some time or interval. Yet those same writers state that the Father has always had his Logos or Wisdom with him. Upon more careful examination, one finds that those writers are distinguishing between the internal Logos and the external Word (who are one and the same person). They are saying that, technically speaking, the title of "Word" (and perhaps "Son") do not apply to the Logos until he went forth from the Father to create the universe. They will sometimes speak of this going forth from the Father as the begetting of the Son, distinguishing it from the eternal generation of the Logos from the Father. For example, the following passage from Tatian sounds quite Arian at first glance:

God was in the beginning. . . . For the Lord of the universe, who is Himself the necessary ground of all being, was alone. For no creature was in existence yet. *Tatian (c. 160, E), 2.67.*

When a person reads the entire passage, however, he or she soon realizes that Tatian believed the Logos to be eternal. But he distinguishes between the eternal existence of the Logos and the point at the beginning of time when the Logos went forth to create the universe:

Nevertheless, inasmuch as the Father was all power, Himself the necessary ground of things visible and invisible, with Him were all things. The Logos Himself was in Him and subsists with Him by Logos-Power. And by His simple will, the Logos springs forth. So the Logos, not coming forth in vain, becomes the first-begotten work of the Father. We know the Logos to be the beginning of the world. But He came into being by participation, not by abscission. For what is cut off is separated from the original substance. However, that which comes by participation, making its choice of function, does not render him deficient from whom he is taken. From one torch many fires are lighted, but the light of the first torch is not lessened by the kindling of many torches. It is the same

with the Logos. His coming forth from the Logos-Power of the Father has not divested Him who begat Him of the Logos-Power. *Tatian (c. 160, E), 2.67.*

In the following quotation, Tertullian says that there was a time when the Son did not exist. At first glance, this sounds like an Arian statement:

He could not have been the Father previous to the Son, nor a Judge previous to sin. There was, however, a time when neither sin existed with Him, nor the Son. *Tertullian (c. 200, W), 3.478.*

Again, however, when a person reads all of what Tertullian says about the Father and the Son (as illustrated in the passage that follows), it becomes clear that Tertullian was not Arian. Rather, in his view, the title of "Son" did not apply to the eternal Logos until He went forth from the Father to create the universe.

I am led to other arguments derived from God's own dispensation, in which He existed before the creation of the world, up to the generation of the Son. For before all things, God was alone—being in Himself and for Himself universe, space, and all things. Moreover, He was alone, because there was nothing external to Him but Himself. Yet, even then He was not [completely] alone. For He had with Him that which He possessed in Himself—that is to say, His own Reason. For God is rational, and Reason was first in Him. And so all things were from Himself. This Reason is His own Thought, which the Greeks call *logos,* by which term we also designate Word or Discourse. Therefore, it is now usual with our people—owing to the mere simple interpretation of the term—to say that the *Word* was in the beginning with God. Although it would be more suitable to regard *Reason* as the more ancient. For God did not have "Word" from the beginning. But He did have Reason even before the beginning. . . . For although God had not yet sent out His "Word," He still had Him within Himself, both in company with and included within His very Reason—as He silently planned and arranged within Himself everything that He was afterwards about to utter through His Word. Now, while He was thus planning and arranging with His own Reason, He was actually causing that to become Word. . . . I may therefore without rashness first lay this down that even then before the creation of the universe, God was not alone. For He had within Himself both

Reason, and, inherent in Reason, His Word, which He made second to Himself by agitating it within Himself. . . .

Now, as soon as it pleased God to [begin creation], . . . He first put forth the Word himself, having within Him His own inseparable Reason and Wisdom, in order that all things could be made through Him through whom they had been planned and disposed. . . . Then, therefore, does the Word also himself assume His own form and glorious garb, His own sound and vocal utterance, when God says, "Let there be light." This is the perfect nativity of the Word, when He proceeds forth from God—formed by Him first to devise and think out all things under the name of Wisdom—"The Lord created me as the beginning of His ways," then afterward begotten, to carry all into effect: "When He prepared the heaven, I was present with Him." He thus makes His Son equal to Him. For, by proceeding from Himself, He became His First-Begotten Son. For He was begotten before all things. And He is His Only-Begotten also, for He was alone begotten of God in a way peculiar to Himself, from the womb of [the Father's] own heart. This is just as the Father Himself testifies. He says, "My heart has emitted my most excellent Word." The Father took pleasure evermore in Him, who equally rejoiced with a mutual gladness in the Father's presence. "You are my Son. Today I have begotten you." *Tertullian (c. 213, W), 3.600, 601.*

We need not dwell any longer on this point, as if it were not the very Word Himself, who is spoken of under the name of both Wisdom and Reason, and of the entire Divine Soul and Spirit. He became also the Son of God and was begotten, when He proceeded forth from Him. *Tertullian (c. 213, W), 3.602.*

The following passage from Hippolytus illustrates this same concept of distinguishing between the eternal Logos (Reason) and his going forth from the Father as the Word of God.

God, subsisting alone, and having nothing contemporaneous with Himself, determined to create the world. . . . For us, then, it is sufficient simply to know that there was nothing contemporaneous with God. Beside Him, there was nothing. However, He—while existing alone—yet existed in plurality. For He was neither without Reason, nor Power, nor Counsel. And all things were in Him, and He was the All.

When He willed, and as He willed, He manifested His Word in the time determined by Him. And by Him He made all things. . . . And, as the Author, Fellow-Counselor, and Framer of the things that have been created, He begat the Word. He uttered the first voice, begetting Him as Light of Light. And He sent Him forth to the world as its Lord. *Hippolytus (c. 205, W), 5.227.*

V. Origen's understanding of the Son

It has become quite commonplace today for Origen to be singled out among the pre-Nicene writers as holding heterodox views of the Son. This is quite unjust, as Origen's teachings on the Son are essentially the same as the rest of the early church. This can clearly be seen from the many preceding quotations from Origen, which show that he held to a Nicene understanding of the deity of the Son. Of course, like the rest of the early Christians, Origen can be selectively quoted to make him appear either Arian, Monarchian, or anything else that is desired. One of the quotations that has often been misunderstood and misquoted is the following passage:

We next notice John's use of the article in these sentences [John 1:1]. He does not write without care in this respect. Nor is he unfamiliar with the subtleties of the Greek language. In some cases, he uses the article; and in some cases, he omits it. He adds the article before the word "Logos." But to the name, "God," he adds it only sometimes. That is, he uses the article when the word, "God," refers to the uncreated cause of all things [i.e., the Father]. But he omits it when the Logos is called "God." *Origen (c. 228, E), 9.323.*

At first glance, the passage above may sound as though Origen held to an Arian view of the Son. But Origen goes on to explain what he means:

There are many persons who are sincerely concerned about religion and who here fall into great perplexity. They are afraid that they may be proclaiming two Gods. As a result, their fear drives them into doctrines that are false and wicked. They sometimes deny that the Son has a distinct nature of His own, besides that of the Father. They thereby make Him whom they call the Son to be *the* God, all but in the name. Or else, they deny the divinity of the Son—giving Him a separate existence of His own and making His sphere of essence fall outside that of the Father, so that they are separable from each other. To such persons, we have to say that *the* God on the one hand is *Autotheos* [God of Himself]. For that reason, the Savior says in His prayer to the Father, "That they may know you, the only true God." But all other Persons beyond this *Autotheos* are made Divine [Gr. *theos*] by participation in His divinity. They are not to be simply called *"the* God" [Gr. *ho theos*], but rather, "God" [or "Divine" [Gr. *theos*]. *Origen (c. 228, E), 9.323.*

Furthermore, preceding the first passage quoted above, Origen had already stated:

The Word was always with the Father. And so it is said, "And the Word was with God." . . . He was in the beginning at the same time when He was with God—neither being separated from the beginning, nor being bereft of His Father. And again, neither did He come to be in the beginning after He had not been in it. Nor did He come to be with God after not having been with him. For before all time and the remotest age, the Word was in the beginning, and the Word was with God. *Origen (c. 228, E), 9.322.*

So in no sense can Origen be accused of holding to an Arian understanding of the Son. The passage that follows is sometimes also misunderstood in an Arian sense:

The Son of God, "the First-Born of all creation," although He seemed recently to have become incarnate, is not by any means recent on account of that. For the Holy Scriptures know Him to be the most ancient of all the works of creation. For it was to Him that God said regarding the creation of man, "Let us make man in our image, after our likeness." *Origen (c. 248, E), 4.560.*

Again, we must remember (as discussed above under II.E. "Begotten, not made") that most of the pre-Nicene writers used "begotten" [Gr. *gennētos*] and "created" [Gr. *ktizein*] interchangeably as synonyms. When Origen refers to the Son as a "work of creation," he does not mean it in the sense of the Son's being created out of nothing. He means it in the sense of begetting. As quoted above, Origen distinctly says that "the Word was always with the Father." The following passage shows that Origen was not including the Son among those things that were created out of nothing:

The Word of God, knowing the Father, reveals the Father whom He knows. For no cre-

ated being can approach the Father without a guide. For no one knows the Father except the Son and he to whomever the Son reveals Him. *Origen (c. 228, E), 9.320.*

SEE ALSO ARIUS, ARIANISM; FATHER, GOD THE; JESUS CHRIST; LOGOS; MESSIANIC PROPHECIES; MONARCHIANISM; THEOPHANIES; TRINITY; WISDOM; WORD OF GOD (CHRIST).

CHRIST, TITLES OF

SEE JESUS CHRIST (III. TITLES OF JESUS).

CHRIST, TWO ADVENTS OF

SEE JESUS CHRIST (II. TWO ADVENTS OF CHRIST).

CHRISTIAN

SEE CHRISTIANITY.

CHRISTIAN LIFE

I say to you, do not worry about your life, what you will eat or what you will drink; nor about your body, what you will put on. Is not life more than food and the body more than clothing? Matt. 6:25.

Let all bitterness, wrath, anger, clamor, and evil speaking be put away from you, with all malice. Eph. 4:31.

Finally, brethren, whatever things are true, whatever things are noble, whatever things are just, whatever things are pure, whatever things are lovely, whatever things are of good report, if there is any virtue and if there is anything praiseworthy—meditate on these things. Phil. 4:8.

Having food and clothing, with these we will be content. 1 Tim. 6:8.

Not conforming yourselves to the former lusts, as in your ignorance; but as he who called you is holy, you also be holy in all your conduct. 1 Pet. 1:14–16.

Do not love the world or the things in the world. If anyone loves the world, the love of the Father is not in him. For all that is in the world—the lust of the flesh, the lust of the eyes, and the pride of life—is not of the Father but is of the world. 1 John 2:6.

Let us honor the aged among us. *Clement of Rome (c. 96, W), 1.11.*

Let it be understood that those who are not found living as He taught are not Christians—even though they profess with the lips the teachings of Christ. *Justin Martyr (c. 160, E), 1.168.*

He says, "Take no anxious thought for tomorrow," meaning that the man who has devoted himself to Christ should be sufficient to himself, and servant to himself, and moreover lead a new life that provides for each day by itself. For it is not in war, but in peace, that we are trained. War needs great preparation, and luxury craves profusion. But peace and love, simple and quiet sisters, require no arms nor excessive preparation. The Word is their sustenance. *Clement of Alexandria (c. 195, E), 2.234, 235.*

There is discrimination to be employed in reference to food. It is to be simple, truly plain, suiting precisely simple and artless children—as ministering to life, not to luxury. *Clement of Alexandria (c. 195, E), 2.237.*

On the other hand, one does not have to be gloomy, only serious. For I certainly prefer a man to smile who has a stern countenance, rather than the reverse. . . . But even smiling must be disciplined. For we should not smile at what is disgraceful. Rather, we should blush, lest we seem to take pleasure in it by sympathy. *Clement of Alexandria (c. 195, E), 2.250.*

We ourselves must entirely abstain from filthy speaking. And we should stop the mouths of those who practice it by stern looks and averting the face. *Clement of Alexandria (c. 195, E), 2.250.*

Let us keep away from ribbing others. For this is the originator of insults. Strife, contention, and enmities burst forth from insults. As I have said, insult is the servant of drunkenness. So a man is not judged by his deeds alone, but also by his words. *Clement of Alexandria (c. 195, E), 2.251.*

He who sells or buys should not name two prices for what he buys or sells. Rather, he should state the net price and endeavor to speak the truth. *Clement of Alexandria (c. 195, E), 2.290.*

Our aim is to be free from disturbances. This is the meaning of the phrase, "Peace to you." . . . In a word, the Christian is characterized by composure, tranquility, calmness, and peace. *Clement of Alexandria (c. 195, E), 2.252, 253.*

Look to Elisha the Tishbite, for instance. In him, we have a beautiful example of frugality—when he sat down beneath the thorn, and the angel brought him food. "It was a cake of barley and a jar of water." *Clement of Alexandria (c. 195, E), 2.281.*

We must cast away the multitude of vessels, silver and gold drinking cups, and the crowd of domestic servants. For we have received from the Instructor the fair and grave attendants, Self-Help and Simplicity. *Clement of Alexandria (c. 195, E), 2.281.*

He who has adopted the true life, if he is to abandon luxury as something treacherous, must not only cultivate a simple mode of *living*, but also a style of speech that is free from verbosity and insincerity. *Clement of Alexandria (c. 195, E), 2.311.*

Those whose speech is evil are no better than those whose actions are evil. *Clement of Alexandria (c. 195, E), 2.331.*

Leaving his dwelling place and property without excessive emotion, the man of God embraces the mansion that is in heaven. He readily follows Him who leads him away from this present life. He by no means and on no occasion turns back. Rather, he gives thanks for his journey and blesses [God] for his departure. *Clement of Alexandria (c. 195, E), 2.440.*

We should not gnaw and consume the soul by idleness, nor by being vexed because things happen against our wishes. *Clement of Alexandria (c. 195, E), 2.451.*

The struggle for freedom, then, is waged not alone by the athletes of battles in wars. Rather, it is also waged in banquets, in bed, and in the tribunals by those who are anointed by the Word—who are ashamed to become the captives of pleasures. *Clement of Alexandria (c. 195, E), 2.506.*

Holding festival in our whole life, persuaded that God is present everywhere, we cultivate our fields, praising. We sail the sea, hymning. In all the rest of our life, we conduct ourselves according to discipline. *Clement of Alexandria (c. 195, E), 2.533.*

Such are they who are restrained by law and fear. For on finding a favorable opportunity, they defraud the law, by giving what is good the slip. But self-control, desirable for its own sake, . . . makes the man lord and master of himself. *Clement of Alexandria (c. 195, E), 2.542.*

The spiritual man certainly relieves the afflicted person, helping him with consolations, encouragements, and the necessities of life. He gives to all who need. Yet, he does not give equally, but justly—according to desert. Furthermore, he even gives to him who persecutes and hates. *Clement of Alexandria (c. 195, E), 2.542.*

The spiritual man rejoices exceedingly. All day and night, he speaks and does the Lord's commands. He does this not only on rising in the morning and at noon, but also when walking about, when asleep, and when dressing and undressing. He teaches his son, if he has a son. He is inseparable from the commandments and from hope. He is ever giving thanks to God. *Clement of Alexandria (c. 195, E), 2.546.*

He never remembers those who have sinned against him, but forgives them. *Clement of Alexandria (c. 195, E), 2.546.*

We are the same to emperors as to our ordinary neighbors. For we are equally forbidden to wish ill, to do ill, to speak ill, to think ill of any person. The things we must not do to an emperor, we must not do to anyone else. *Tertullian (c. 197, W), 3.45.*

It is mainly the deeds of a love so noble that lead many to put a brand upon us. They say, "See how they love one another!" . . . And they are angry with us, too, because we call each other brothers. *Tertullian (c. 197, W), 3.46.*

There is no law forbidding the mere places [i.e., the circus] to us. For the servant of God may enter without any peril of his religion not only the places for the shows, but even the temples—if he has only some honest reason for it, unconnected with their proper business and official duties. Why, even the streets, the market place, the baths, the taverns, and our very dwelling places are not altogether free from idols. Satan and his angels have filled the whole world. It is not by merely *being* in the world, however, that we lapse from God, but by touching and tainting ourselves with the world's sins. . . . The polluted things pollute us. *Tertullian (c. 197, W), 3.83.*

Shall you escape notice when you sign your bed or your body? When you blow away some impurity? When even by night you rise to pray? Will you not be thought to be engaged in some work of magic? . . . Render to Caesar, indeed, *money.* Render to God *yourself.* Other-

wise, what will be God's, if all things are Caesar's? *Tertullian (c. 200, W), 3.70.*

[CONCERNING MARRYING AN UNBELIEVER:] If a station is to be kept, the [unbelieving] husband makes an appointment with his wife at daybreak to meet him at the baths. If there are fasts to be observed, the husband holds a convivial banquet that same day. If a charitable expedition has to be made, never is family business more urgent. For who would permit his wife to go around from street to street to other men's . . . cottages, for the sake of visiting the brethren? What husband will willingly bear her being taken from his side for nocturnal meetings, if the need is there? Finally, who will without anxiety endure her absence all the night long at the Easter solemnities? Who will, without some suspicion of his own, dismiss her to attend that Lord's supper, which they defame? What husband will permit her to creep into prison to kiss a martyr's chains? Nay, truly, to meet any one of the brothers to exchange the kiss? Who will permit her to offer water for the saints' feet? . . . If a pilgrim brother arrives, what hospitality will there be for him in an alien home? If goods are to be distributed to any, the granaries and the storehouses are closed in advance. *Tertullian (c. 205, W), 4.46.*

Christ is an "object of envy" or emulation to the saints. For they aspire to follow His footsteps and conform themselves to His divine beauty. They aspire to make Him the pattern of their conduct, and thereby win their highest glory. *Hippolytus (c. 205, W), 5.167.*

He is called the resurrection. He raises a person from the dead not only at the moment when a man says, "We are buried with Christ through baptism and have risen again with Him." Rather, He also does this when a man, while still here—having laid off all around him that belongs to death—walks in the newness of life that belongs to Him, the Son. *Origen (c. 228, E), 9.312.*

Our Lord is a Teacher and an Interpreter for those who are striving towards godliness. On the other hand, He is a Master of those servants who have the spirit of bondage to fear. *Origen (c. 228, E), 9.314.*

This way is indeed narrow, for the majority of persons are lovers of their flesh and cannot bear to walk in it. *Origen (c. 228, E), 9.360.*

He who zealously imitates the prophetic life and attains to the spirit that was in the prophets must be dishonored in the world, and in the eyes of sinners. To them, the life of the righteous man is a burden. *Origen (c. 245, E), 9.426*

When false witnesses testified against our Lord and Savior, Jesus Christ, He remained silent. . . . For He believed that His whole life and conduct among the Jews were a better refutation than any answer to the false testimony. . . . And yet even now He continues silent before these charges and makes no audible answer. Rather, he places His defense in the lives of His genuine disciples, who are a pre-eminent testimony. *Origen (c. 248, E), 4.395.*

By His sufferings, Jesus brought no discredit upon that faith of which He is the object. Rather, he confirmed this faith among those who would approve of manly courage and among those who were taught by Him that what was truly and properly the happy life was not here below. Rather, it was to be found in that which was called (in His own words) the "coming world." In contrast, in what is called the "present world," life is a calamity—or at least the first and greatest struggle of the soul. *Origen (c. 248, E), 4.447, 448.*

From the very beginning, this was inculcated as a precept of Jesus among His hearers: men are to despise the life that is eagerly sought after by the multitude, and are to be earnest in living the life that resembles that of God. *Origen (c. 248, E), 4.449.*

According to the view of Celsus [a pagan critic], piety is not divine by its own nature, but by a certain arrangement and appointment of things. . . . According to this, the same individual will be regarded as acting piously according to one set of laws and impiously according to another. This is the most absurd result that can be conceived! *Origen (c. 248, E), 4.555.*

[Celsus, a pagan critic,] would have us believe that we and the interpreters of the mysteries equally teach the doctrine of eternal punishment and that it is an open question as to which side the truth lies on. Now I should say that the truth lies with those who are able to induce their hearers to live as men who are convinced of the truth of what they have heard. *Origen (c. 248, E), 4.657.*

When the Lord says that man should eat bread with groaning, what are you now doing—you who desire to live with joy? You seek to rescind the judgment uttered by the highest God, when He first formed man. . . . If the Almighty God has commanded you to live with sweat, you who are living in pleasure will already be a stranger to Him. The Scripture says that the Lord was angry with the Jews. Their sons, refreshed with food, rose up to play. Now, therefore, why do we follow these circumcised men? In what respect they perished, we should beware. Most of you obey them, for you are surrendered to luxuries. *Commodianus (c. 240, W), 4.214.*

The following passage was written concerning brethren who were captured by raiding barbarians:

Christ is to be contemplated in our captive brethren, and He is to be redeemed from the peril of captivity—He who redeemed us from the peril of death. . . . Our brotherhood, considering all these things according to your letter, and sorrowfully examining them, have all promptly, willingly, and liberally gathered together supplies of money for the brethren. *Cyprian (c. 250, W), 5.355.*

Christians used to sell houses and estates so that they might lay up for themselves treasures in heaven. They presented the proceeds from them to the apostles, to be distributed for the use of the poor. However, now, we do not even give the tenths from our patrimony! And while our Lord bids us to *sell*, we rather *buy* and increase our store. Thus has the vigor of faith dwindled away among us. Thus has the strength of believers grown weak. And, therefore, the Lord, looking to our days, says in His Gospel, "When the Son of man comes, do you think He will find faith on the earth?" We see that what He foretold has come to pass. *Cyprian (c. 250, W), 5.429.*

In Holy Scripture, discipline is frequently and everywhere prescribed. The whole foundation of religion and of faith springs from obedience and fear. *Cyprian (c. 250, W), 5.430.*

Nothing distinguishes the unrighteous from the righteous more than this: that in affliction, the unrighteous man impatiently complains and blasphemes. In contrast, the righteous man is proved by his patience. *Cyprian (c. 250, W), 5.489.*

The kingdom of God is not in the wisdom of the world, nor in eloquence, but in the faith of the cross and in virtue of living. *Cyprian (c. 250, W), 5.551.*

131

The sick are to be visited. In Solomon, in Ecclesiasticus, it says: "Do not be slow to visit the sick man." . . . Also in the Gospel: "I was sick and you visited me. I was in prison and you came to me." *Cyprian (c. 250, W), 5.555.*

The just man is neither at enmity with any human being, nor does he desire anything at all that is the property of another. For why should he take a voyage? What should he seek from another land—when his own is sufficient for him? Or why would he carry on war and mix himself with the passions of others—when his mind is engaged in perpetual peace with men? *Lactantius (c. 304–313, W), 7.153.*

The just man will omit no opportunity to do anything merciful. . . . He must not receive a gift from a poor man. That way, if he himself has given the poor man something, it will be good, for it was gratuitous. If anyone reviles the just man, he must answer him with a blessing. He himself must never revile, so that no evil word will proceed out of the mouth of a man who reverences the good Word. Moreover, he must also diligently take care lest by any fault of his he should at anytime make an enemy. *Lactantius (c. 304–313, W), 7.183.*

True things must be preferred to false; eternal things, to those that are temporary; useful things, to those that are pleasant. Let nothing be pleasing to the sight but that which you see to be done with piety and justice. Let nothing be agreeable to the hearing but that which nourishes the soul and makes you a better man. . . . If it is a pleasure to hear melodies and songs, let it be pleasant to sing and hear the praises of God. . . . For he who chooses temporal things will be without eternal things. He who prefers earthly things will not have heavenly things. *Lactantius (c. 304–313, W), 7.188.*

Whoever, then, prefers the life of the soul must despise the life of the body. He will in no other way be able to strive after that which is highest, unless he will have despised the things that are lowest. . . . However, he who prefers to live well for eternity will live badly for the present. He will be subjected to all sorts of troubles and labors as long as he is on earth—so that he may have divine and heavenly consolation. And he who prefers to live well for the present will live ill in eternity. For he will be condemned to eternal punishment by the sentence of God. *Lactantius (c. 304–313, W), 7.201.*

Follow your trades as secondary, as something necessary for earning a livelihood. However, make the worship of God your main business. *Apostolic Constitutions (compiled c. 390, E), 7.423.*

If the following persons come [to be baptized], whether they are man or woman, let them leave off their employments, or else be rejected: someone belonging to the theater, a charioteer, dueler, racer, player of prizes, a dance master, huckster, Olympic gamester, or one who plays at those games on the pipe, lute, or harp. *Apostolic Constitutions (compiled c. 390, E), 7.495; see also 2.291–2.295, 2.496–2.498, 2.533, 2.537.*

SEE ALSO CHRISTIANITY (I. DESCRIPTION OF CHRISTIANS); CLOTHING; GROOMING; LAWSUITS; MODESTY; NONRESISTANCE; PERFECTION, CHRISTIAN; SERMON ON THE MOUNT; WAR; WORLD, SEPARATION FROM.

CHRISTIAN LIVING
SEE CHRISTIAN LIFE.

CHRISTIANITY

I. Description of Christians

II. Growth of Christianity

III. Meaning of name

IV. True accusations against Christians

V. False accusations against Christians

VI. Defense of Christianity

VII. Christians as salt and light

I. Description of Christians
You are the light of the world. A city that is set on a hill cannot be hidden. . . . Let your light so shine before men, that they may see your good works and glorify your Father in heaven. Matt. 5:14, 16.

Beloved, I beg you as sojourners and pilgrims, abstain from fleshly lusts which war against the soul, having your conduct honorable among the Gentiles, that when they speak against you as evildoers, they may, by your good works which they observe, glorify God in the day of visitation. 1 Pet. 2:11, 12.

We know many among us who have given themselves up to bonds, in order that they might ransom others. Many, too, have surrendered themselves to slavery, that with the price that they received for themselves, they might provide food for others. *Clement of Rome (c. 96, W), 1.20.*

The Christians, O King, went about and searched, and they have found the truth. As I have learned from their writings, they have come nearer to truth and genuine knowledge than the rest of the nations. For they know and trust in God, the Creator of heaven and of earth, in whom and from whom are all things. . . . Therefore, they do not commit adultery or fornication. They do not bear false witness. They do not embezzle what is held in pledge, nor do they covet that which is not theirs. They honor father and mother and show kindness to those who are near to them. Whenever they are judges, they judge uprightly. They do not worship idols made in the likeness of man. Whatever they would not wish others to do to them, they do not do to others. They do not eat food that is consecrated to idols, for they are pure. They comfort their oppressors and make them their friends. They do good to their enemies.

Their women, O king, are pure as virgins, and their daughters are modest. Their men keep themselves from every unlawful union and from all uncleanness—in the hope of a reward in the world to come. Furthermore, if any of them have male or female slaves, or children, out of love towards them, they persuade them to become Christians. When they have done so, they call them brothers, without any distinction. They do not worship strange gods, and they go their way in all modesty and cheerfulness. Falsehood is not found among them. And they love one another. They do not turn away their care from widows, and they deliver the orphan from anyone who treats him harshly. He who has, gives to him who has not. And this is done without boasting.

When they see a stranger, they take him into their homes, and they rejoice over him as a very brother. For they do not call themselves brothers after the flesh, but brothers after the spirit and in God. Whenever one of the poor among them passes from this world, each one of them gives heed to him, according to his ability, and carefully sees to his burial. And if they hear that one of their number is imprisoned or afflicted because of the name of their Christ, all of them carefully attend to his needs. If it is possible to redeem him, they set him free. If there are any poor and needy among them, but if they have

no spare food to give, they fast two or three days in order to supply the necessary food to the needy.

They follow the commandments of their Christ with much care, living justly and seriously, just as the Lord their God commanded them. Every morning and every hour they give thanks and praise to God for His loving-kindnesses to them. They give thanksgiving to him for their food and drink. If any righteous man among them passes from this world, they rejoice and offer thanks to God. They escort his body as if he were setting out from one place to go to another nearby. And when a child has been born to any of them, they give thanks to God. *Aristides (c. 125, E), 9.276, 277.*

Christians are distinguished from other men neither by country, nor language, nor the customs which they observe. For they neither inhabit cities of their own, nor employ a peculiar form of speech, nor lead a life which is marked out by any singularity. . . . But inhabiting Greek as well as barbarian cities, according as the lot of each of them has determined, and following the customs of the inhabitants in respect to clothing, food, and the rest of their ordinary conduct, they display to us their wonderful and confessedly striking method of life. They dwell in their own countries only as sojourners. . . . They pass their days on earth, but they are citizens of heaven. They obey the prescribed laws, and at the same time, they surpass the laws by their lives. They love all men, and are persecuted by all. *Letter to Diognetus (c. 125–200), 1.26.*

With us there is no desire of vainglory, nor do we indulge in a variety of opinions. For having renounced the popular and earthly, obeying the commands of God, and following the law of the Father of immortality, we reject everything which rests upon human opinion. Not only do the rich among us pursue our philosophy, but the poor enjoy free instruction. For the things which come from God surpass the rewards of worldly gifts. Thus we accept all who desire to hear—even old women and youths. In short, persons of every age are treated by us with respect. *Tatian (c. 160, E), 2.78.*

Among us you will find uneducated persons, artisans, and old women. They may be unable in words to prove the benefit of our doctrine. However, by their deeds, they demonstrate the benefit arising from their accepting its truth.

They do not rehearse speeches, but exhibit good works. When struck, they do not strike again. When robbed, they do not go to law. They give to those who ask of them, and love their neighbors as themselves. *Athenagoras (c. 175, E), 2.134.*

On this account, too, according to age, we recognize some as sons and daughters. Others we regard as brothers and sisters. To the more advanced in life, we give the honor due to fathers and mothers. On behalf of those, then, to whom we apply the names of brothers and sisters, and other designations of relationship, we exercise the greatest care so that their bodies should remain undefiled and uncorrupted. *Athenagoras (c. 175, E), 2.146.*

[The spiritual man] is, then, the truly kingly man. He is the sacred high priest of God. . . . He, therefore, never surrenders himself to the rabble that rules supreme over the theaters. He gives no admittance even in a dream to the things that are spoken, done, and seen for the sake of alluring pleasures. Nor does he give himself to the pleasures of sight, nor other pleasures, . . . such as costly incense and fragrances that bewitch the nostrils. Nor is he given to the preparations of meats and indulgences in different wines that ensnare the palate, nor to fragrant bouquets of many flowers, which effeminate the soul through the senses. Instead, he always traces up to God the serious enjoyment of all things. So he offers the first-fruits of food, drink, and oil to the Giver of all, acknowledging his thanks in the gift and in the use of them by the Word given to him. He rarely goes to boisterous banquets of all and sundry, unless he is induced to go by the announcement in advance of the friendly and harmonious nature of the entertainment. For he is convinced that God knows and perceives all things—not just the words, but also the thoughts. *Clement of Alexandria (c. 195, E), 2.533.*

We are accused of being useless in the affairs of life. How in all the world can that be the case with people who are living among you, eating the same food, wearing the same attire, having the same habits, and enduring the same necessities of existence? We are not Indian Brahmans or Gymnosophists, who dwell in the woods and exile themselves from ordinary human life. . . . So we journey with you in the world, abstaining from neither forum, meat market, bath, booth, workshop, inn, weekly market, nor any other places of commerce. We sail with you, serve in the military with you, and cultivate the ground with you. . . . Even in the various arts, we make public property of our works for your benefit. *Tertullian (c. 197, W), 3.49.*

[ADDRESSED TO PAGANS:] Here we call your own acts to witness, you who daily are presiding at the trials of prisoners and are passing sentence upon crimes. Well, in your long lists of those accused of many and various atrocities, has any assassin, any purse-snatcher, any man guilty of sacrilege, seduction, or stealing bathers' clothes, ever had his name entered as also being a Christian? Or when Christians are brought before you on the mere basis of their name, is there ever found among them an evildoer of this sort? It is always with *your* people that the prison is steaming. . . . You find no Christian there, unless he is there for being a Christian. Or, if someone is there as something else, he is a Christian no longer. We alone, then, are without crime. *Tertullian (c. 197, W), 3.49, 50.*

Even among those who are not of his religion, the Christian is noted for his fidelity. *Tertullian (c. 197, W), 3.51.*

Our discipline carries its own evidence in itself. We are not betrayed by anything else than our own goodness, just as bad men also become conspicuous by their own evil. . . . For what mark do we exhibit except the prime wisdom that teaches us not to worship the frivolous works of the human hand? Our marks are the temperance by which we abstain from other men's goods, the chastity that we do not even pollute with a look, the compassion that prompts us to help the needy, the truth itself (which makes us give offense), and liberty, for which we have even learned to die. Whoever wishes to understand who the Christians are must seek these marks for their discovery. *Tertullian (c. 197, W), 3.112.*

As to your saying of us that we are a most shameful set—utterly steeped in luxury, avarice, and depravity—we will not deny that this is true of some. It is, however, a sufficient testimonial for our name that this cannot be said of all, not even of the greater part of us. It must happen that even in the healthiest and purest body that a mole may grow, a wart arise on it, or freckles disfigure it. . . . The goodness of the larger portion is well attested by the slender flaw. But although you prove that some of our people are evil, you do not thereby prove that they are Christians. . . . You have no right to call them Christians to whom the Christians themselves deny that name. *Tertullian (c. 197, W), 3.113.*

You are accustomed in conversation yourselves to say in disparagement of us, "Why is so-and-so deceitful, when the Christians are so self-denying? Why he is merciless, when they are so merciful?" You thus bear your testimony to the fact that this is not the character of Christians. For you ask in the way of a retort how men who are reputed to be Christians can be of such and such a disposition. *Tertullian (c. 197, W), 3.113.*

Of how much greater dignity and constancy is the assertion of Christian wisdom, before the very breath of which the whole host of demons is scattered! This wisdom of the school of heaven frankly denies the gods of this world, without reserve. . . . It does not corrupt youth, but instructs them in all goodness and moderation. And so it bears the unjust condemnation—not of one city only—but of all the world. *Tertullian (c. 210, W), 3.182.*

Although our numbers are so great—constituting all but the majority in every city—we conduct ourselves quietly and modestly. I might say that we are known more as individuals, than as organized communities. We are remarkable only for reforming our former vices. *Tertullian (c. 212, W), 3.106.*

We never deny the deposit placed in our hands. We never pollute the marriage bed. We deal faithfully with our wards. We give aid to the needy. We render evil for evil to no one. As for those who falsely pretend to belong to us—and whom we, too, repudiate—let them answer for themselves. In short, does anyone have a complaint to make against us on other grounds [except being a Christian]? To what else does the Christian devote himself, except the affairs of his own community? . . . It is for such a notable freedom from crime, for an honesty so great, for righteousness, for purity, for faithfulness, for truth, for the living God, that we are sentenced to the flames. *Tertullian (c. 212, W), 3.107.*

[Pagan antagonist]: All men must be indignant, all men must feel pain, that certain persons—and these unskilled in learning, strangers to literature, without knowledge even of sordid arts—should dare to teach with any certainty about nature at large and the divine majesty. . . . Is it not a thing to be lamented, that men . . . of

a reprobate, unlawful, and desperate faction should rage against the gods? These persons have gathered together from the lowest dregs the more unskilled men, along with women—credulous and by the facility of their sex, yielding—thereby establishing a herd of a profane conspiracy. This is linked together by nightly meetings, solemn fasts, and inhuman meats. . . . They despise the temples as dead houses. They reject the gods. They laugh at sacred things. Wretched, they pity the priests—if they are allowed. Half naked themselves, they despise honors and purple robes. Oh, unbelievable folly and incredible audacity! They scorn present torments, although they fear those that are uncertain and future. While they fear to die after death, they do not fear to die for the present. . . .

Look! A portion of you—and, as you declare, the larger and better portion—are in want, are cold, laboring in hard work and hunger. Yet, your God allows it. . . . So He either is not willing or not able to assist His people. . . . You do not visit exhibitions. You have no interest in public displays. You reject the public banquets and abhor the sacred contests. You refuse the meats previously tasted by (and the drinks made an offering upon) the altars. . . . You do not wreath your heads with flowers. You do not grace your bodies with perfume. You reserve ointments for funeral rites. You even refuse garlands for your sepulchers. . . .

[CHRISTIAN REPLY:] We do not, at once, stand on the level of the lowest of the people, simply because we refuse your honors and purple robes. . . . We do not distinguish our people by some small bodily mark (as you suppose) but easily enough by the sign of innocency and modesty. Thus we love one another (to your regret) with a mutual love, because we do not know how to hate. For that reason, we call one another (to your envy) brothers, as being men born of one God. . . . You [pagans] forbid, and yet commit, adulteries. We are born men only for our own wives. You punish crimes when committed. With us, even to *think* of crimes is to sin. . . . From your numbers the prison boils over. But there is no Christian there, unless he is accused on account of his religion, or else is an apostate. *Mark Minucius Felix (c. 200, W), 4.175–4.195.*

What will we say of the new race of us Christians—whom Christ at His coming planted in every country and in every region? Wherever we are, we are all called after the one name of Christ—Christians. On one day, the first of the week, we assemble ourselves together; and on the days of the readings, we abstain from food. The brethren in Gaul do not take males for wives, nor do those in Persia take two wives [things that were lawful in those countries]. Nor do those who are in Judea circumcise themselves. Nor do our sisters who are among the Geli consort with strangers. Nor do the brethren in Persia take their daughters for wives. Nor do those in Media abandon their dead, bury them alive, or give them as food to the dogs. Those in Edessa do not kill their wives or their sisters if they commit impurity. Rather, they withdraw from them and give them over to the judgment of God. Those who are in Hatra do not stone thieves to death. In short, wherever they are, and in whatever place they happen to be, the laws of various countries do not hinder them from obeying the law of their Christ. . . . On the other hand, sickness and health, riches and poverty—these befall them wherever they are, for such things are not within the scope of their freedom. *Bardesanes (c. 222, E), 8.733.*

When the churches of God . . . are carefully contrasted with the [pagan] assemblies of the districts in which they are situated, they are seen as beacons in the world. For who would not admit that even the inferior members of the church . . . are nevertheless more excellent than the majority of those who belong to the temples in the different districts? *Origen (c. 248, E), 4.476.*

The church of God that is at Athens is a meek and stable body—one that desires to please God. . . . And you may say the same things of the church of God at Corinth . . . or of the church of God at Alexandria. . . . In like manner, also, in comparing the council of the church of God with the council in any city, you would find that certain councilors of the church are worthy to rule in the city of God. . . . So you must compare the ruler of the church in each city with the ruler of the people of that city in order to observe that even among those councilors and rulers of the church of God who fall far short of their duty . . . it is still possible to discover a general superiority in what relates to the progress of virtue—in comparison with the councilors and rulers of the various cities. *Origen (c. 248, E), 4.476.*

The following passage is from a message by Cyprian, bishop of Carthage, rebuking his flock for the growing laxity in the church:

Each one was desirous of increasing his estate. Forgetting what believers had either done back in the times of the apostles, or always should do, they devoted themselves to the increase of their property with the insatiable ardor of covetousness. Among the priests, there was no devotion of religion. Among the ministers, there was no sound faith. In their works, there was no mercy. In their manners, there was no discipline. In men, their beards were defaced. In women, their complexion was dyed. Their eyes were falsified from what God's hand had made them. Their hair was stained with a falsehood. . . .

They united with unbelievers in the bond of marriage. . . . They would swear not only rashly, but even worse, would swear *falsely.* . . . A number of bishops, . . . despising their divine responsibility, became agents in secular business. They forsook their chair, deserted their people, wandered about over foreign provinces, and hunted the markets for profitable merchandise. In the meanwhile, brethren were starving in the church. . . . We deserve to suffer for sins of this kind. . . . Indeed, we still have not been converted to the fear of the Lord, so as to patiently and courageously undergo this, our correction and divine test. Immediately at the first words of the threatening foe, the majority of the brethren betrayed their faith. . . . What a thing unheard of! *Cyprian (c. 250, W), 5.438.*

It disturbs some Christians that the power of this disease attacks our people equally with the pagans. As if the Christian believed for the purpose that he might have the enjoyment of the world and of this life, free from the contact of ills. . . . It disturbs some that this mortality is common to us with others. . . . However, so long as we are here in the world, we are associated with the human race in fleshly equality (although we are separated in spirit). . . . Therefore, when the earth is barren with an unproductive harvest, famine makes no distinction. Likewise, when a city is taken with the invasion of an enemy, captivity at once desolates all. When the serene clouds withhold the rain, the drought is alike to all. Likewise, when the jagged rocks destroy the ship, the shipwreck is common to all, without exception to anyone who sails in her. Finally, the disease of the eyes, the attack of fevers, and the feebleness of all the limbs is common to us with others—so long as this common flesh of ours is borne by us in the world. *Cyprian (c. 250, W), 5.471.*

The following passage was written by a bishop after barbarians had raided a certain region. He denounces Christians who took advantage of the situation to loot the belongings of others. Some Christians even cooperated with the barbarian raiders.

Let no one deceive himself. Let him not pretend to have "found" such property. For it is not lawful, even for a man who has found anything, to enrich himself by it.... Others deceive themselves by fancying that they can retain the property of others by rationalizing that it is merely a substitution for their own property that had been taken.... Moreover, it has been reported to us that something has happened in your country that is surely unbelievable. If it is true, it is altogether the work of unbelievers and impious men.... We have heard that some have sunk to such a degree of cruelty and inhumanity that they are detaining by force certain captives who have escaped. *Gregory Thaumaturgus (c. 255, E), 6.19.*

[CONCERNING A SEVERE EPIDEMIC:] Very many of our brethren, in their exceeding love and brotherly kindness, did not spare themselves. Rather, they stayed by each other and visited the sick without thought of their own peril. They diligently ministered to them and treated them for their healing in Christ. They died from time to time most joyfully along with them, loading themselves with pains derived from others and drawing upon themselves their neighbors' diseases.... And many who had thus cured others of their sicknesses, and restored them to strength, died themselves. For they transferred to their own bodies the death of their neighbors.... Yes, the very best of our brethren have departed this life in this manner, including some presbyters and some deacons.... This form of death seems to equal martyrdom itself.... But among the pagans, everything was just the reverse. They pushed aside anyone who began to be sick and kept away even from their dearest friends. They threw the suffering out upon the public roads half dead, and left them unburied. *Dionysius of Alexandria (c. 262, E), 6.108, 109, as quoted by Eusebius.*

[ADDRESSED TO PAGANS:] Lay aside every evil thought from your hearts, and that golden age will at once return to you. For you cannot attain this by any other means than by beginning to worship the true God.... If only God were worshipped, there would not be dissensions and wars. For men would know that they are the sons of one God.... There would be no adulteries, debaucheries, and prostitution of women—if everyone knew that whatever is sought beyond the desire of procreation is condemned by God.... The males also would restrain their lust. The pious and religious contributions of the rich would provide for the destitute. As I have said, there would not be these evils on the earth if there were a general observance of the law of God by common consent. How happy and how golden would be the condition of human affairs, if gentleness, piety, peace, innocence, justice, temperance, and faith took up their abode throughout the world. In short, there would be no need of so many and varying laws to rule men. For the law of God alone would be sufficient for perfect innocence. In fact, there would be no need of prisons, the swords of rulers, or the terror of punishments. *Lactantius (c. 304–313, W), 7.143.*

[DESCRIBING PAGANS:] But these men, when they come to offer sacrifice, present to their gods nothing from within, nothing of their own—no uprightness of mind, no reverence or fear. Therefore, when the worthless sacrifices are finished, they leave their religion back in the temple.... They do not bring anything of their religion with them, nor do they take anything of it back with them. For that reason, their religious observances are neither able to make men good, nor to be firm and unchangeable.... In short, I see nothing else in it than a rite pertaining to the fingers only. But our religion is firm, solid, and unchangeable, because it teaches justice. It is always with us, for it has its existence altogether in the soul of the worshipper. It has the mind itself for a sacrifice. In their religion, nothing else is required but the blood of animals, the smoke of incense, and the senseless pouring out of drink offerings. But in our religion, there is required a good mind, a pure breast, and an innocent life. *Lactantius (c. 304–313, W), 7.157.*

II. Growth of Christianity

This gospel of the kingdom will be preached in all the world as a witness to all the nations, and then the end will come. Matt. 24:14.

These who have turned the world upside down have come here too. Acts 17:6.

The gospel which you heard, which was preached to every creature under heaven. Col. 1:23.

The whole world, along with Athens and Greece, has already become the domain of the Word. *Clement of Alexandria (c. 195, E), 2.203.*

We are but of yesterday, and we have filled every place among you—cities, islands, fortresses, towns, market places, the very camps, tribes, companies, palace, senate, forum—we have left nothing to you but the temples of your gods. *Tertullian (c. 197, W), 3.45.*

If such multitudes of men were to break away from you, and take themselves to some remote corner of the world, why, the very loss of so many citizens would cover the empire with shame—no matter what sort of people they were.... For now it is the immense number of Christians that makes your enemies so few. For almost all the inhabitants of your various cities are followers of Christ. *Tertullian (c. 197, W), 3.45.*

The more often we are mown down by you, the more in number we grow. The blood of Christians is seed.... For who that contemplates it, is not excited to inquire what is at the bottom of it? Who, after inquiry, does not embrace our doctrines? *Tertullian (c. 197, W), 3.55*

Day after day, indeed, you groan over the increasing number of Christians. Your constant cry is that the state is beset [by us]. You groan that Christians are in your fields, your camps, and in your islands. You grieve over it as a calamity that each sex, every age—in short, every rank—is passing over from you to us. ... I know very well with what answer you usually counter the argument from our rapid increase. You say that something should not be hastily accounted as a good thing simply because it converts a great number of persons. *Tertullian (c. 197, W), 3.109.*

Upon whom else have the universal nations believed, but upon the Christ who is already come? For whom have the nations believed—Parthians, Medes, Elamites, those who inhabit Mesopotamia, Armenia, Phrygia, Cappadocia, ... and all other nations? By this time, ... [the name of Christ has reached] the manifold confines of the Moors, all the limits of Spain, the diverse nations of the Gauls, and the haunts of the Britons—inaccessible to the Romans, but subjugated to Christ.... Furthermore, there are Germans, Scythians, and persons of many remote nations and provinces and islands—many to us unknown and which we can scarcely enumerate. In all these places, the name of Christ (who is already come) reigns. ... Christ's name is extending everywhere, believed everywhere, worshipped by all the above-enumerated nations, and is reigning everywhere. *Tertullian (c. 197, W), 3.157, 158.*

Although our numbers are so great—constituting all but the majority in every city—we conduct ourselves very quietly and modestly. *Tertullian (c. 212, W), 3.106.*

If we were to take it into our heads to do that very thing, what would you make of so many thousands—of such a multitude of men and women, persons of every sex, age, and rank—if they presented themselves before you? *Tertullian (c. 212, W), 3.107.*

Day by day the number of us in increased. However, this is not grounds for charging us with error. Rather, it is a testimony that claims praise. For, in a fair mode of life, our actual numbers both continue and abide undiminished; and strangers increase it. *Mark Minucius Felix (c. 200, W), 4.192.*

We observe how powerful the Word has become in a very few years, despite the fact that conspiracies were formed against those who acknowledged Christianity.... Despite the small number of its teachers, it was preached everywhere throughout the world. As a result, Greeks and barbarians, wise and foolish, gave themselves up to the worship that is through Jesus. We have no difficulty in saying that such a result is beyond human power. *Origen (c. 225, E), 4.350.*

Almost the entire world is better acquainted with what Christians preach than with the favorite opinions of the philosophers. For who is ignorant of the statement that Jesus was born of a virgin, that He was crucified, or that His resurrection is an article of faith among many? Who does not know that a general judgment is proclaimed to come, in which the wicked are to be punished according to their deserts and the righteous to be duly rewarded? *Origen (c. 248, E), 4.399.*

Could it have come to pass without divine assistance that Jesus ... could have been so successful that everywhere throughout the world, many persons—Greeks as well as barbarians, educated as well as ignorant—adopted His doctrine? In fact, they have even met death in its defense, rather than to deny it. No one has ever related the same thing to have been done for any other movement. *Origen (c. 248, E), 4.407.*

Among the multitude of converts to Christianity, the simple and ignorant necessarily outnumbered the more intelligent, since the former class always outnumbers the latter. *Origen (c. 248, E), 4.408.*

I assert that the whole inhabited world contains evidence of the works of Jesus, in the existence of those churches of God which have been founded through him by those who have been converted from the practice of innumerable sins. And the name of Jesus can still remove distractions from the minds of men, expel demons, and also take away diseases. Furthermore, it produces a marvelous meekness of spirit and complete change of character. *Origen (c. 248, E), 4.427.*

At the present day, indeed, there is a multitude of Christian believers. Not only rich men receive the teachers of Christianity, but also persons of rank, as well as refined and highborn ladies. So some will perhaps dare to say that it is for the sake of a little glory that certain individuals assume the office of Christian instructors. However, it is impossible to reasonably entertain such a notion about Christianity in its beginnings. For back then, the danger incurred was great—especially by its teachers. Even at the present day, the discredit attached to it among the rest of mankind is greater than any supposed honor to be enjoyed. *Origen (c. 248, E), 4.468.*

Their discourses . . . at once convert multitudes from a life of immorality to one of great discipline, from a life of wickedness to one that is better. . . . Why, then, should we not justly admire the power that they contain? For the words of those who initially assume the office of ambassadors, who gave their labors to raise up the churches of God . . . were accompanied with a persuasive power. . . . The demonstration that followed the words of the apostles of Jesus was given from God and was manifested by the Spirit and by power. Therefore, . . . the Word of God (through their instrumentality)

transformed many persons who had been sinners both by nature and habit. *Origen (c. 248, E), 4.491.*

This providence has extended the Christian religion day by day, so that it is now preached everywhere with boldness. And this is in spite of the numerous obstacles that oppose the spread of Christ's teaching in the world. However, since it was the purpose of God that the nations would receive the benefits of Christ's teaching, all the devices of men against Christians have been brought to nothing. For the more that kings, rulers, and peoples have persecuted them everywhere, the more they have increased in number and grown in strength. *Origen (c. 248, E), 4.621.*

Every form of worship will be destroyed except the religion of Christ, which alone will prevail. Indeed, it will one day triumph, for its principles take possession of the minds of men more and more every day. *Origen (c. 248, E), 4.666.*

[Christians] come out of all nations and from the whole world. *Cyprian (c. 250, W), 5.507.*

No nation is so uncivilized, no region so remote that either His passion or the height of His majesty is unknown. So, in His suffering, he stretched forth His hands and measured out the world—so that even then He might show that a great multitude (collected out of all languages and tribes, from the rising of the sun even to its setting) was about to come under His wings. *Lactantius (c. 304–313, W), 7.129.*

Our number is continually increased from the worshippers of gods. . . . The divine law has been received from the rising of the sun to its setting. And each sex, every age, nation, and country—with one and the same mind—obeys God. *Lactantius (c. 304–313, W), 7.148.*

In the times that followed [Valerian], during which many well-deserving rulers guided the helm of the Roman empire, the church suffered no violent assaults from her enemies. And she extended her hands unto the east and unto the west—so much so that at that time [in the second century] there was no remote corner of the earth to which the divine religion had not penetrated. There were no people of customs so barbaric that they did not become mild and gentle by being converted to the worship of God. *Lactantius (c. 320, W), 7.302.*

If the gods willed that the Germans and the Persians should be defeated because Christians dwelled among their tribes, how did those gods grant victory to the Romans? For Christians dwelled among their peoples also. Or, if the gods willed that mice and locusts would swarm forth in prodigious numbers in Asia and in Syria because Christians dwelled among their tribes, why was there likewise no such phenomenon in Spain and in Gaul? For innumerable Christians lived in those provinces also. If the gods sent drought and aridity on the crops of [certain African tribes], why did they also in that very same year give the most bountiful harvest to the Moors and nomads? After all, Christianity had its abode in these regions as well. . . . So, if we really are the cause of such evils, then no nation would have any blessings, for we are in all nations. *Arnobius (c. 305, E), 6.417.*

If the [Christian] record of events is false, as you say, how is it that in so short a time the whole world has been filled with such a religion? Or how could peoples dwelling widely apart and separated by climate . . . unite in one conclusion? *Arnobius (c. 305, E), 6.429.*

The [baptismal] oaths of this vast army have spread abroad over all the earth. Already, there are no people so backward and fierce that they have not been changed by His love. There are no people that have not subdued their fierceness and become mild in disposition, with a tranquility previously unknown. Men who are endowed with great abilities seek to learn these things—men such as orators, critics, rhetoricians, lawyers, physicians, and those who delve into the mysteries of philosophy. *Arnobius (c. 305, E), 6.435.*

His virtues have been made manifest to you, along with that unheard-of power over things . . . that was used over the whole world by those who proclaimed Him. It has subdued the fires of passion and caused races, peoples, and nations that are most diverse in character to hasten with one accord to accept the same faith. For the deeds can be listed and numbered that have been done in India and among the Seres, Persians, and Medes. They have also been done in Arabia, Egypt, and Syria in Asia, as well as among the Galatians, Parthians, and Phrygians. . . . And they have been done in all islands and provinces on which the rising and setting sun shines, and in Rome herself, the mistress of the world. *Arnobius (c. 305, E), 6.438.*

III. Meaning of name

The disciples were first called Christians in Antioch. Acts 11:26.

We are called Christians for this reason: because we are anointed with the oil of God. *Theophilus (c. 180, E), 2.92.*

The name *Christian,* however, so far as its meaning goes, bears the sense of anointing. Even when by a faulty pronunciation you call us "Chrestians" . . . you in fact lisp out the sense of pleasantness and goodness. *Tertullian (c. 197, W), 3.111.*

IV. True accusations against Christians

This is the sole accusation you can bring against us—that we do not reverence the same gods as you do, nor offer drink offerings and the aroma of fat to the dead, nor crowns for their statues. *Justin Martyr (c. 160, E), 1.171.*

You say, "You do not worship the gods, and you do not offer sacrifices for the emperors." Well, for the same reason that we do not offer sacrifices for ourselves, we do not offer them for others. That reason is that your gods are not at all the objects of our worship. Therefore, we are accused of sacrilege and treason. *Tertullian (c. 197, W), 3.26.*

Christians do not enter your temples even in the daytime. *Tertullian (c. 197, W), 3.30.*

We alone are prevented from having a religion of our own. Because we do not worship the gods of Rome, we give offense to the Romans, and we are excluded from the rights and privileges of Romans. *Tertullian (c. 197, W), 3.39.*

Therefore, when we are ordered to sacrifice, we resolutely refuse. *Tertullian (c. 197, W), 3.41.*

This is the reason why Christians are counted public enemies: that they pay no vain, false, or foolish honors to the emperor. *Tertullian (c. 197, W), 3.43.*

It becomes evident that the crime of which we are accused consists not of any sinful conduct, but lies wholly in our *name. Tertullian (c. 197, W), 3.111.*

When you direct against us the general charge of separating ourselves from the institutions of our forefathers, consider again and again whether you are not yourselves open to that accusation in common with us. *Tertullian (c. 197, W), 3.118.*

It is therefore against these things that our contest lies: against the institutions of our ancestors, the authority of tradition, the laws of our governors, and the reasonings of the "wise." It is against antiquity, custom, requirements, precedents, prodigies, and miracles. For all of these things have had their part in creating that spurious system of your gods. *Tertullian (c. 197, W), 3.129.*

[CELSUS, A PAGAN, SPEAKING:] "They also have a teaching to this effect: that we should not avenge ourselves on one who injures us. Or, as He expresses it: "Whoever will strike you on the one cheek, turn the other to him also." *Origen (c. 248, E), 4.634.*

[CELSUS:] They cannot tolerate temples, altars, or images. *Origen (c. 248, E), 4.635, 636.*

You argue against us that we turn away from the religion of the past. *Arnobius (c. 305, E), 6.459.*

You are in the habit of labelling us with a very serious charge of ungodliness for the following reasons: we do not construct temples for the ceremonies of worship, we do not set up statues and images of any god, and we do not build altars. Neither do we offer incense, sacrificial meals, or the blood of slain creatures. *Arnobius (c. 305, E), 6.506.*

V. False accusations against Christians

The Greeks, O King, follow debased practices in intercourse with males, or with mothers, sisters, and daughters. Yet, they, in turn, impute their monstrous impurity to the Christians. *Aristides (c. 125, E), 9.279.*

We are called atheists. And we admit that we are atheists—so far as gods of this kind are concerned. But we are not atheists with respect to the most true God. *Justin Martyr (c. 160, E), 1.164.*

Have you also believed about us that we eat humans? And do you believe that after our feasts, we extinguish the lights and engage in promiscuous sexual relations? *Justin Martyr (c. 160, E), 1.199.*

It is not *we* who eat human flesh. Those among you who claim such a thing have been bribed to be false witnesses. *Tatian (c. 160, E), 2.76.*

Three things are alleged against us: atheism, Thyestean feasts, and Oedipodean intercourse. And if these charges are true, spare none of us. Proceed at once against our crimes. If any Christian is found to really live like such animals, destroy us root and branch, with our wives and children. *Athenagoras (c. 175, E), 2.130.*

They have also made up stories against us about impious feasts and forbidden sexual relations between the sexes. *Athenagoras (c. 175, E), 2.145.*

Godless lips falsely accuse us, . . . alleging that we hold our wives in common and use them promiscuously. They even allege that we commit incest with our own sisters. And what is most unholy and barbarous of all, they say that we eat human flesh. *Theophilus (c. 180, E), 2.112.*

When they receive a true description of what a Christian is, hopefully the philosophers will condemn their own stupidity. For they have rashly and unthinkingly persecuted the name [of Christian] for no reason, saying that those who know the true God are ungodly. *Clement of Alexandria (c. 195, E), 2.523.*

In your ordinary judicial investigations, when a man confesses the crime of murder, sacrilege, incest, or treason (to take the points of which we are accused), you do not proceed at once to sentence. . . . Similarly, the falsehoods spread about us should receive the same investigation, so that it might be found how many murdered children each of us has tasted or how many incests each of us has hidden in the darkness. *Tertullian (c. 197, W), 3.18.*

You think that the Christian is a man guilty of every crime and that he is the enemy of the gods, the emperor, the laws, good morals, and all nature! . . . I have made these remarks by way of introduction, so that I can show in its true colors the injustice of the public hatred against us. I will now take my stand on our plea of innocence. And I will not only refute the things that we are accused of, but I will also throw them back against the accusers. *Tertullian (c. 197, W), 3.19–21.*

Monsters of wickedness! We are accused of observing a holy rite in which we kill a little child and then eat him. It is said that after the feast, we practice incest. . . . This is what is constantly laid to our charge. Yet, you take no pains to investigate the truth of what we have been accused of for so long. *Tertullian (c. 197, W), 3.23.*

Like some others, you are under the delusion that our god is an ass's head. Cornelius Tacitus first put this notion into people's minds. . . . Others believe that the sun is our god. *Tertullian (c. 197, W), 3.31.*

Lately, a new edition of our god has been given to the world in that great city [Rome]. It originated with a certain vile man who . . . displayed a picture with this inscription: "The God of the Christians, born of an ass." He had the ears of an ass, was hoofed in one foot, carried a book, and wore a toga. *Tertullian (c. 197, W), 3.31.*

The common people now have some knowledge of Christ. Yet, they think of Him as only a man—one indeed such as the Jews condemned. So naturally enough, some of them have thought that we are worshippers of a mere human being. *Tertullian (c. 197, W), 3.34.*

You choose to call us enemies of the human race. *Tertullian (c. 197, W), 3.45.*

They think the Christians are the cause of every public disaster and of every affliction that comes upon the people. If the Tiber river rises as high as the city walls, if the Nile does not send its waters up over the fields, if the heavens give no rain, if there is an earthquake, if there is famine or pestilence, immediately the cry is, "Away with the Christians to the lion!" *Tertullian (c. 197, W), 3.47.*

In our case alone are such things called "presumptuous speculations." In regard to the philosophers and poets, they are regarded as "sublime speculations" and "illustrious discoveries." They are men of wisdom; we are fools! They are worthy of all honor; we are persons to have the finger pointed at! *Tertullian (c. 197, W), 3.54.*

We are falsely charged with treason, although no one has ever been able to find followers of Albinus, Niger, or Cassius among Christians. *Tertullian (c. 212, W), 3.105.*

[PAGAN SPEAKER:] Those abominable shrines of an unholy assembly are growing throughout the whole world. Assuredly, this confederacy ought to be rooted out and destroyed. They know one another by secret marks and signs. They love one another almost before they know one another. There is also mingled among them everywhere a certain religion of lust. They promiscuously call one another brothers and sisters—so that even a normal debauchery can . . . become incestuous. . . . I hear that they worship the head of an ass. . . . Some say that they worship the genitals of their pontiff and priest, and adore the nature, as it were, of their common parent. I do not know whether these things are false. Suspicion rightfully attaches to secret and nocturnal rites. *Mark Minucius Felix (c. 200, W), 4.177.*

[PAGAN SPEAKER:] The story about the initiation of young novices is as much to be detested as it is well known. An infant covered over with flour (so that it may deceive the unwary) is placed before the one who is to be stained with their rites. This infant is slain by the young initiate, who has been urged on to make dark and secret wounds as if they were harmless blows on the surface of the flour. O horror, they then thirstily lick up its blood and eagerly divide its limbs. *Mark Minucius Felix (c. 200, W), 4.177, 178.*

[PAGAN SPEAKER:] On a solemn day, they assemble at the feast, with all their children, sisters, mothers: people of both sexes and of every age. After much feasting, when the fellowship has grown warm and the fervor of incestuous lust has grown hot with drunkenness, . . . the connections of abominable lust overtake them. *Mark Minucius Felix (c. 200, W), 4.178.*

The first accusation that Celsus brings forward (in his desire to discredit Christianity) is that Christians enter into secret associations with each other, contrary to law. . . . And his wish is to disparage what are called the "love feasts" of the Christians. . . . Celsus next proceeds to say that the system of doctrine upon which Christianity depends (that is, Judaism) was barbarous in its origin. *Origen (c. 248, E), 4.397.*

Notice also how Celsus tries to discredit our system of morals, alleging that it is only common to us with other philosophers. . . . After this, . . . Celsus asserts that it is by the names of certain demons and by the use of incantations that Christians appear to be possessed of [supernatural] power. *Origen (c. 248, E), 4.398.*

Since he frequently calls the Christian doctrine a secret system, we must refute him on this point, too. For almost the entire world is better acquainted with what Christians preach than with the favorite opinions of the philosophers. *Origen (c. 248, E), 4.399.*

He claims that certain persons (who do not wish to either give or receive a reason for their belief) keep saying, "Do not examine; just believe!" and "Your faith will save you." He claims that such persons also say, "The wisdom of this life is bad. However, foolishness is a good thing." To which we have to answer . . . that in the Christian system it will be found that there is . . . much investigation into articles of belief. *Origen (c. 248, E), 4.400.*

[Celsus] invents something altogether different. He somehow acknowledges the miraculous works done by Jesus, by means of which he persuaded the multitudes to follow him as the Christ. However, Celsus desires to discredit those works, saying they were done through magic, not by divine power. *Origen (c. 248, E), 4.413.*

[CELSUS SPEAKING:] The following are the rules laid down by them: "Let no one come to us who has been educated or who is wise or prudent. . . . However, if there are any ignorant, unintelligent, unlearned, or foolish persons, let them come with confidence." By such words, they acknowledge that only those kind of persons are worthy of their god. Furthermore, they clearly show that they desire and are able to win over only the silly, lowly, and stupid—along with women and children. *Origen (c. 248, E), 4.482.*

He accuses the Christian teachers of "seeking after the unintelligent." I answer, in reply, "Who do you mean by the 'unintelligent'?" To speak accurately, every wicked man is unintelligent. *Origen (c. 248, E), 4.493.*

[Celsus] appears to me, indeed, to have acted like those Jews who spread abroad false reports about the Gospel when Christianity first began to be preached. Some of those rumors were that Christians offered up an infant in sacrifice and partook of his flesh. Or, again, that those who practiced Christianity, wishing to do the works of darkness, used to extinguish the lights [in their assemblies] and each one had sexual relations with any woman whom he chanced to meet. These accusations have long influenced the minds of very many persons, even though they are unreasonable. They have led those who are strangers to the Gospel to believe that Christians are persons of such a character. Even at the present day, they mislead some and prevent them from entering into even a simple dialogue with those who are Christians. *Origen (c. 248, E), 4.585.*

This is often thrown in our teeth as a reproach: that we worship a man, and one who was punished and tormented with an extreme punishment. *Lactantius (c. 304–313, W), 7.116.*

I have found some persons who consider themselves very wise in their opinions, . . . who announced with all the authority of an oracle that from the time when the Christian people began to exist in the world, the universe has gone to ruin and the human race has been visited with evils of many kinds. *Arnobius (c. 305, E), 6.413.*

Because we approach the Head and Pillar of the universe with worshipful service, are we to be considered as "persons to be shunned" and as "godless ones" (to use the terms employed by you in reproaching us)? *Arnobius (c. 305, E), 6.420; see also 3.110.*

VI. Defense of Christianity

Examine more fully the life history of such an individual [i.e., Jesus]. . . . He was brought up in frugality and poverty. He did not receive a complete education. He had not studied systems and opinions. . . . How could such a person . . . have been able to teach in a manner not at all to be despised . . . so that not only rustic and ignorant persons were won by His words, but also many of those who were distinguished by their wisdom? . . . Now, would not anyone who investigated with ordinary care the nature of these facts be struck with amazement at this man's victory? . . . This man, in addition to His other merits, is an object of admiration for His wisdom, His miracles, and His power of government. *Origen (c. 248, E), 4.408, 409.*

Besides this, one may well wonder how it happened that the disciples . . . were not afraid to endure the same sufferings with their Master. Why were they not afraid to expose themselves to danger, and to leave their native country to teach the doctrine delivered to them by Him—according to the desire of Jesus? I think that no one who candidly examines the facts would say that these men would have devoted themselves to a life of danger for the sake of the doctrine of Jesus—unless they had a profound belief of the truth of what He had wrought in their minds. *Origen (c. 248, E), 4.409.*

Before I begin my reply, I must remark that the effort to prove any history—however true—to have actually existed and to produce an intelligent conception regarding it—is one of the most difficult undertakings that can be attempted. In some instances, it is impossible. *Origen (c. 248, E), 4.414.*

He led His disciples to believe in His resurrection. He so thoroughly persuaded them of its truth that they show to all men by their sufferings how they are able to laugh at all the troubles of life, beholding the life eternal and the resurrection clearly demonstrated to them both in word and deed. *Origen (c. 248, E), 4.463.*

VII. Christians as salt and light

It is said, "You are the salt of the earth." The rest of mankind is considered the "earth," and believers are their salt. It is because of their faith that the earth is preserved. For the end will come if the salt loses its savor. *Origen (c. 228, E), 9.380.*

Men of God are assuredly the salt of the earth. They preserve the order of the world. And society is held together as long as the salt is uncorrupted. *Origen (c. 248, E), 4.666.*

SEE ALSO APOSTLES, TWELVE; CHRISTIAN LIFE, THE; CHURCH, THE; EVANGELISM; CULTURE AND CHRISTIANITY; PERSECUTION.

CHRISTMAS

SEE BIRTH OF JESUS; CALENDAR, CHRISTIAN; HOLIDAYS, PAGAN.

CHRONOLOGY

In six days, that is, in six thousand years, all things will be completed. *Barnabas (c. 70–130, E), 1.146.*

Solomon the king built the temple in Judea 566 years after the exodus of the Jews from Egypt. . . . The temple was built in the twelfth year of the reign of Hiram. So the entire time from the building of the temple to the founding of Carthage was 143 years and 8 months. *Theophilus (c. 180, E), 2.117, 118.*

The flood came during Noah's life, in his 600th year. *Theophilus (c. 180, E), 2.118.*

All the years from the creation of the world amount to a total of 5698 years, plus the odd months and days. . . . Perhaps our knowledge of the whole number of the years is not quite accurate, because the odd months and days are not set down in the sacred books. *Theophilus (c. 180, E), 2.120.*

In as many days as this world was made, in so many thousand years will it be concluded. . . . For the day of the Lord is as a thousand years; and in six days created things were completed. It is evident, therefore, that they will come to an end at the sixth thousand year. *Irenaeus (c. 180, E/W), 1.557.*

In a similar work, Eupolemus says that all the years from Adam to the fifth year of Ptolemy Demetrius (who reigned twelve years in Egypt) come to 5149 years, when they are all added together. From the time that Moses brought the Jews out of Egypt up to the above-mentioned date (i.e., the fifth year of Ptolemy Demetrius), there were a total of 2580 years. Finally, from that date until the consulship in Rome of Caius Domitian and Casian, there were 120 years. *Clement of Alexandria (c. 195, E), 2.332.*

From Adam to the death of Commodus, there were 5784 years, 2 months, and 12 days. *Clement of Alexandria (c. 195, E), 2.333.*

The first appearance of our Lord in the flesh took place in Bethlehem, under Augustus, in the year 5500. And He suffered in the thirty-third year. And 6000 years has to be accomplished, in order that the Sabbath may come—the rest, the holy day "on which God rested from all His works." For the Sabbath is the type and emblem of the future kingdom of the saints, when they will reign with Christ, when He comes from heaven, as John says in his Apocalypse. For "a day with the Lord is as a thousand years." Since, then, in six days God made all things, it follows that 6000 years must be fulfilled. *Hippolytus (c. 205, W), 5.179.*

From the birth of Christ, then, we must include the 500 years that remain to make up the 6000, and then the end will come. *Hippolytus (c. 205, W), 5.179.*

These things Bardesanes computed when he desired to show that this world would stand only six thousand years. *Fragment concerning Bardesanes (c. 222, E), 8.734.*

According to Daniel, seventy weeks were fulfilled until Christ the Ruler. *Origen (c. 225, E), 4.353.*

I believe that the destruction of Jerusalem took place forty-two years after the date of the crucifixion of Jesus. *Origen (c. 248, E), 4.506.*

We will be immortal when six thousand years are completed. *Commodianus (c. 240, W), 4.209.*

The most famous exile that befell the Hebrews—when they were led captive by Nebuchadnezzar, king of Babylon—lasted seventy years, as Jeremiah had prophesied. *Julius Africanus (c. 245, E), 6.133.*

It is by calculating from Artaxerxes, therefore, up to the time of Christ that the seventy weeks are made up, according to the calendar of the Jews. *Julius Africanus (c. 245, E), 6.135.*

Six thousand years are now nearly completed since the devil first attacked man. *Cyprian (c. 250, W), 5.496.*

[Satan is bound] until the thousand years are completed—that is, what is left of the sixth day. *Victorinus (c. 280, W), 7.358.*

In the seventh thousand of years, we will resume immortality again and will celebrate the great feast of true tabernacles. *Methodius (c. 290, E), 6.344.*

This world will be terminated at the seventh thousand years. At that time, God will have completed the world and will rejoice in us. *Methodius (c. 290, E), 6.344.*

A thousand years are considered as one day in the sight of God. Now, since from the creation of the world to His rest is six days, so also to our time, six days are defined. . . . Therefore, they say that an age of six thousand years extends from Adam to our time. They also say that the Judgment will come on the seventh day, that is, in the seventh thousand years. *Methodius (c. 290, E), 6.381, as quoted by Photius.*

[The Jews] had tetrachs until the time of Herod, who ruled during the reign of Tiberius Caesar. In his fifteenth year, during the consulship of the two Gemini, on the 23rd day of March, the Jews crucified Christ. *Lactantius (c. 304–313, W), 7.109.*

In the latter days of the Emperor Tiberius, in the consulship of Ruberius Geminus and Rufius Geminus, on the seventh day before the first day of April [i.e., March 23], as I find it written, Jesus Christ was crucified by the Jews. *Lactantius (c. 304–313, W), 7.301. [Note: The text here is a bit ambiguous.]*

Let the philosophers—who enumerate thousands of ages from the beginning of the world—know that the six thousandth year is not yet completed. When this number is completed, the consummation must take place. And the condition of human affairs will be remodelled for the better. *Lactantius (c. 304–313, W), 7.211.*

Since all the works of God were completed in six days, the world must continue in its present state through six ages—that is, six thousand years. For the great day of God is limited by a circle of a thousand years. . . . As God labored during those six days in creating such great works, so His religion and truth must labor during these six thousand years (during which wickedness prevails and rules). And, again, since God rested on the seventh day and blessed it (having finished His works), so at the end of the six thousandth year all wickedness must be abolished from the earth. And righteousness will reign for a thousand years. And there must be tranquility and rest from the labors that the world now has long endured. *Lactantius (c. 304–313, W), 7.211; extended discussion: 2.118–2.121, 2.324–2.334, 3.158–3.160, 6.130–6.137.*

SEE ALSO DANIEL, BOOK OF; DAYS OF CREATION; NUMEROLOGY; REVELATION, BOOK OF; SEVENTH DAY OF CREATION.

CHURCH, THE

I also say to you that you are Peter, and on this rock I will build My church, and the gates of Hades will not prevail against it. Matt. 16:18.

Lo, I am with you always, even to the end of the age. Matt. 28:20.

Greet the church that is in their house. Rom. 16:5.

You are the body of Christ, and members individually. 1 Cor. 12:27.

There is one body and one Spirit. Eph. 4:4.

He, therefore, who does not assemble with the church, has even by this displayed his pride, and he has condemned himself. *Ignatius (c. 105, E), 1.51.*

Wherever the bishop appears, let the congregation be there also. Just as, wherever Jesus Christ is, there is the catholic church. *Ignatius (c. 105, E), 1.90.*

The church of God that sojourns at Smyrna, to the church of God sojourning in Philomelium—and to all of the congregations [Gr. *paroikiais*] of the holy and catholic church in every place. *Martyrdom of Polycarp (c. 135, E), 1.39.*

Our Lord Jesus Christ is the Savior of our souls, the Governor of our bodies, and the Shepherd of the catholic church throughout the world. *Martyrdom of Polycarp (c. 135, E), 1.43.*

Let us choose to be of the church of life, so that we may be saved. However, I suppose you are aware that the living church is the body of Christ. For the Scriptures say, "God made man, male and female" [Gen. 1:27]. The male is Christ, and the female is the church. And the books and the apostles declare that the church is not of the present, but is from the beginning. For she was spiritual. *Second Clement (c. 150), 7.521.*

He said, "It is the church." And I said to him, "Why, then, is she an old woman?" He replied, "Because she was created first of all. On this account she is old. And the world was made for her sake." *Hermas (c. 150, W), 1.12.*

Those who have believed on the Lord through His Son, and are clothed with these spirits, will become one spirit, one body. Furthermore, the color of their garments will be one. *Hermas (c. 150, W), 2.48.*

All the nations that dwell under heaven were called by hearing and believing upon the name of the Son of God. Having, therefore, received the seal, they had one understanding and one mind. And their faith became one, and their love one. *Hermas (c. 150, W), 2.50.*

The world is driven and tempest-tossed by sins. Therefore, God has given to it assemblies—we mean holy churches—in which survive the doctrines of the truth. *Theophilus (c. 180, E), 2.100.*

Although dispersed throughout the whole world, even to the ends of the earth, the church has received this faith from the apostles and their disciples. . . . The church received this preaching and this faith. Although she is scattered throughout the whole world, yet, she carefully preserves it, as if she occupied only one house. She also believes these points just as if she had only one soul, and one and the same heart. She proclaims these things, teaches them, and hands them down, with perfect harmony—as if she possessed only one mouth. For although the languages of the world are different, yet the significance of the tradition is one and the same. For the churches which have been planted in Germany do not believe or hand down anything different. Neither do those in Spain, Gaul, the East, Egypt, Libya, or in the central regions of the world. *Irenaeus (c. 180, E/W), 1.330, 331.*

To this cause also are due the various opinions that exist among the heretics, inasmuch as each one adopted errors just as he was capable. But the church throughout all the world, having its origin firm from the apostles, perseveres in one and the same opinion with regard to God and His Son. *Irenaeus (c. 180, E/W), 1.433.*

It is said, "In the church, God has set apostles, prophets, teachers," and all the other means through which the Spirit works. Those who do not join themselves to the church are not partakers of these things. Rather, they defraud themselves of life through their perverse opinions and infamous behavior. For where the church is, there is the Spirit of God. And where the Spirit of God is, there is the church, and every kind of grace. *Irenaeus (c. 180, E/W), 1.458.*

It will be God's good pleasure to take out a church that will be sanctified by fellowship with His Son. *Irenaeus (c. 180, E/W), 1.492.*

Some are believed to be presbyters by many. However, they serve their own lusts and do not place the fear of God supreme in their hearts. Rather, they conduct themselves with contempt towards others. They are puffed up with the pride of holding the chief seat, and they work evil deeds in secret. . . . From all such persons, it behooves us to keep aloof. We should adhere to those who, as I have already observed, hold the doctrine of the apostles and who, together with the order of presbyters, display sound speech and blameless conduct for the confirmation and correction of others. *Irenaeus (c. 180, E/W), 1.497.*

The church is the salt of the earth. It has been left behind within the confines of the earth, and it is subject to human suffering. And even though entire members are often taken away from it, the pillar of salt still endures. This typifies the foundation of the faith that makes [Christians] strong and sends children forward to their Father. *Irenaeus (c. 180, E/W), 1.505.*

The illustrious church is everywhere. The winepress is dug everywhere. For those who receive the Spirit are everywhere. *Irenaeus (c. 180, E/W), 1.515.*

But the path of those belonging to the church encircles the whole world, as possessing the sure tradition from the apostles. It enables us to see that the faith of all is one and the same. For all receive one and the same God the Father. All believe in the same dispensation regarding the incarnation of the Son of God. All are cognizant of the same gift of the Spirit and are familiar with the same commandments. All preserve the same form of ecclesiastical constitution and expect the same advent of the Lord. All await the same salvation of the complete man, that is, the soul and body. And undoubtedly the preaching of the church is true and steadfast, in which one and the same way of salvation is shown throughout the whole world. For the light of God is entrusted to her. *Irenaeus (c. 180, E/W), 1.548.*

The church preaches the truth everywhere, and she is the seven-branched candlestick that bears the light of Christ. Those, therefore, who desert the preaching of the church, call in question the knowledge of the holy presbyters. . . . It behooves us, therefore, to avoid their doctrines and to take careful heed lest we suffer any injury from them. So we should flee to the church, and be brought up in her bosom, and be nourished with the Lord's Scriptures. For the church has been planted as a garden in this world. *Irenaeus (c. 180, E/W), 1.548.*

The mother draws the children to herself; and we seek our mother, the church. *Clement of Alexandria (c. 195, E), 2.214.*

She alone remains to all generations, always rejoicing. She subsists as she does by the endurance of us believers, who are the members of Christ. *Clement of Alexandria (c. 195, E), 2.214.*

The Holy Spirit is one and the same everywhere, and one is the only virgin mother. I love to call her the church. *Clement of Alexandria (c. 195, E), 2.220.*

The Instructor, by transplanting us into His church, has united us to Himself. *Clement of Alexandria (c. 195, E), 2.295.*

The earthly church is the image of the heavenly. *Clement of Alexandria (c. 195, E), 2.421.*

Now, it is not the *place,* but the assemblies of the elect that I call the church. *Clement of Alexandria (c. 195, E), 2.530.*

I am demonstrating that the only truly holy and pious man is he who is truly one according to the rule of the church. *Clement of Alexandria (c. 195, E), 2.534.*

We must not in any way violate the canon of the church. *Clement of Alexandria (c. 195, E), 2.549.*

It is necessary to graciously respond to questions and to demonstrate from the Scriptures themselves how the heresies failed. It is necessary to show how in the truth alone and in the ancient church, there are both the most exact knowledge and the truly best set of principles. *Clement of Alexandria (c. 195, E), 2.550.*

It is evident from the high antiquity and perfect truth of the church that these later heresies (together with those even later in time) were new, falsified inventions. From what has been said, it is my opinion that the true church (the one that is really ancient) is one. In it are enrolled those who are just, according to God's purpose. . . . The one church is associated in a joint heritage in the nature of the One. But the schismatics strive to cut the church asunder into many sects. Therefore, we say that the ancient and catholic church is alone in substance, idea, origin, and pre-eminence. It collects as it does into the unity of the one faith . . . those already ordained. *Clement of Alexandria (c. 195, E), 2.555.*

The pre-eminence of the church is its oneness. It is the basis of union. In this, it surpasses all other things and has nothing like or equal to itself. *Clement of Alexandria (c. 195, E), 2.555.*

Wherever it will be manifest that the true Christian rule and faith are, there likewise will be the true Scriptures and the correct expositions thereof—and all the Christian traditions. *Tertullian (c. 197, W), 3.251, 252.*

The apostles, then, in like manner founded churches in every city, from which all the other churches—one after another—borrowed the tradition of the faith and the seeds of doctrine. And they are every day borrowing them, that they may become churches. Indeed, it is only on this account that they will be able to deem themselves apostolic—as being the offspring of apostolic churches. Every sort of thing must necessarily revert to its original mold for its classification. Therefore, the churches, although they are so many and so great, comprise but the one primitive church of the apostles—from which they all [spring]. In this way, all are primitive. And all are apostolic. And they are all proved to be one in unity by their peaceful communion, title of brotherhood, and bond of hospitality—privileges that no other rule directs than the one tradition of the selfsame mystery. *Tertullian (c. 197, W), 3.252.*

From this, therefore, do we draw up our rule. Since the Lord Jesus Christ sent the apostles to preach, no others should be received as preachers [i.e., founding teachers] than those whom Christ appointed. For "no man knows the Father except the Son, and he to whomever the Son will reveal Him." Nor does the Son seem to have revealed Him to any other than the apostles, whom He sent forth to preach.... Now, the message that they preached (in other words, what Christ revealed to them) can ... properly be proved in no other way than by those very churches which the apostles founded in person. For they declared the gospel to them directly themselves.... If, then, these things are so, it is equally clear that all doctrine that agrees with the apostolic churches—those molds and original sources of the faith—must be considered as truth, as undoubtedly containing the teaching that the said churches received from the apostles, the apostles from Christ, and Christ from God. *Tertullian (c. 197, W), 3.252.*

We hold communion with the apostolic churches because our doctrine is in no respect different than theirs. This is our witness of truth. *Tertullian (c. 197, W), 3.252, 253.*

It is not believable to say that the apostles were either ignorant of the whole scope of the message which they had to declare, or that they failed to make known to all men the entire rule of faith. Let us see, then, whether—even though the apostles proclaimed it simply and fully—the churches, through their own fault, proclaimed it differently than had the apostles. You will find that the heretics put forward all these suggestions of distrust.... Suppose, then, that all churches have erred. Suppose that the apostle was mistaken in giving his testimony. Suppose that the Holy Spirit had insufficient concern for

any one church as to lead it into truth—although He was sent for this reason by Christ.... Suppose also, that He, the Steward of God, the Vicar of Christ, neglected His office, permitting the churches for a time to understand differently—to believe differently—than what He Himself was preaching through the apostles. If so, is it likely that so many churches, and they so great, should have gone astray into one and the same faith? No accident distributed among many men leads to one and the same result. Error of doctrine in the churches must necessarily have produced various results. However, when that which is deposited among many is found to be one and the same—it is not the result of error, but of tradition. Can anyone, then, be reckless enough to say that the ones who handed on the tradition were in error? *Tertullian (c. 197, W), 3.256.*

Where the fear of God is, there is seriousness, an honorable and yet thoughtful diligence, an anxious carefulness, and a well-considered admission [to the ministry]. There is also a safely guarded communion, promotion [to leadership] after good service, and a scrupulous submission [to authority]. And there is a devout attendance, a modest gait, a united church, and God in all things. *Tertullian (c. 197, W), 3.264.*

Our lady mother, the church, makes provision from her bountiful breasts. And each brother, out of his private means, provides for your bodily needs in the prison. *Tertullian (c. 197, W), 3.693.*

The peace of God is sent out from the heavens, where the church is, the typified ark. *Tertullian (c. 198, W), 3.673.*

Let us see whether, after the type of the Ark, there will be in the church either raven, kite, dog, or serpent. In any event, an idolater is certainly not found in the type of the Ark. For no animal has been created to represent an idolater. Let there not be in the church anything that was not in the Ark. *Tertullian (c. 200, W), 3.76.*

In a company of two is the church. But the church is Christ. When, then, you cast yourself at the brethren's knees, you are handling Christ. You are entreating Christ. In like manner, when they shed tears over you, it is Christ who suffers, Christ who begs the Father for mercy. *Tertullian (c. 203, W), 3.664.*

His church is that very stone in Daniel, cut out of the mountain, which was to smite and crush the image of the secular kingdom. *Tertullian (c. 207, W), 3.326.*

It will be only right that you [Marcion] should hate the church also, for it is loved by Christ on the same principle. Yes, Christ loved the flesh even as the church. *Tertullian (c. 207, W), 3.469.*

As Adam was a figure of Christ, Adam's sleep foreshadowed the death of Christ (who was to sleep a mortal slumber). In like manner, from the wound inflicted on His side is typified the church, the true mother of the living. *Tertullian (c. 210, W), 3.222.*

Accordingly, where there is no joint session of the ecclesiastical order, you [the laity] offer, baptize, and are priest, alone for yourself. But where there are three, a church is—even if it is laity. *Tertullian (c. 212, W), 4.54.*

Our one Father, God, lives. And so does our mother, the church. *Tertullian (c. 217, W), 4.64.*

The sea is the world, in which the church is set. She is like a ship tossed in the deep, but not destroyed. For she has with her the skilled Pilot, Christ. She also carries in her midst the trophy over death—for she carries with her the cross of the Lord. Her prow is the east, her stern is the west, her hold is the south, and her tillers are the two Testaments. The ropes that stretch around her are the love of Christ, which bind the church. The net that she bears with her is the bath of the regeneration that renews the believing, from which too are these glories. Like the wind, the Spirit from heaven is present, and He seals those who believe. She also has anchors of iron accompanying her— the holy commandments of Christ Himself, which are as strong as iron. *Hippolytus (c. 200, W), 5.216, 217.*

[Said in disapproval:] Callistus alleged that the parable of the tares was uttered in reference to such a person, saying, "Let the tares grow along with the wheat"! Or, in other words, let those in the church who are guilty of sin, remain in it! *Hippolytus (c. 225, W), 5.131.*

For that reason, women who were reputed believers began to resort to drugs for producing sterility and to gird themselves around, so as to expel what was being conceived. . . . Behold, into how great an impiety the lawless one has proceeded: inculcating adultery and murder at the same time! Yet, after such audacious acts, they lose all sense of shame and attempt to call themselves a catholic church! *Hippolytus (c. 225, W), 5.131.*

We cling to the standard of the heavenly church of Jesus Christ according to the succession of the apostles. *Origen (c. 225, E), 4.357.*

Some persons desire that before the end of the age, and before the angels come to remove the wicked from among the righteous, there should not be evil persons of every kind in the dragnet. However, such a person seems not to have understood the Scripture. For he desires the impossible. Therefore, let us not be surprised if, before the removing of the wicked from among the righteous by the angels, . . . we see our gatherings filled with wicked persons. Let us hope that those who will be cast into the furnace of fire will not be greater in number than the righteous! *Origen (c. 245, E), 9.421.*

The soul that . . . is neither holy nor blameless because of wickedness . . . is not part of the church that Christ builds upon the rock. But if anyone wishes to embarrass us in regard to these things because of the great majority of those of the church who are thought to believe, it must be said to him that "many are called, but few chosen." . . . "Many, I say unto you, will seek to enter in and will not be able." You will understand that this refers to those who boast that they are of the church, but who live weakly and contrary to the Word. *Origen (c. 245, E), 9.457.*

We say that the Holy Scriptures declare the body of Christ, animated by the Son of God, to be the whole church of God. The members of this body—considered as a whole—consist of those who are believers. . . . The Word, arousing and moving the whole body, the church, to fitting action, awakens each individual member belonging to the church. Thereby, they do nothing apart from the Word. *Origen (c. 248, E), 4.595.*

The seed of the tares stands mingled in the church. . . . The Husbandman separates all those collected tares. *Commodianus (c. 240, W), 4.213.*

There is one God. Furthermore, Christ is one, and there is one church. There is also one chair founded upon the rock by the word of the Lord. Another altar cannot be constituted. A new priesthood cannot be made in addition to the one altar and the one priesthood. Whoever gathers elsewhere, scatters. *Cyprian (c. 250, W), 5.318.*

Although there seem to be tares in the church, yet neither our faith nor our charity should be hindered. Because we see that there are tares in the church, we ourselves should not withdraw from the church. Rather, we only should labor that we may be wheat. In that manner, when the wheat begins to be gathered into the Lord's barns, we may receive fruit for our labor. *Cyprian (c. 250, W), 5.327.*

Neither let the new heretics [i.e., the Novatianists] flatter themselves in this, that they say that they do not communicate with idolaters. . . . They say that one is polluted by another's sin. . . . However, with us, according to our faith and the given rule of divine preaching, the principle of truth agrees that everyone is personally held fast in his own sin. Nor can somebody become guilty for another. For the Lord forewarns us, saying, "The righteousness of the righteous will be upon him, and the wickedness of the wicked will be upon him." And again, "The fathers will not die for the children, and the children will not die for the fathers. Everyone will die for his own sin." *Cyprian (c. 250, W), 5.334.*

Since we have one church, a united mind, and an undivided peace, what priest does not congratulate himself on the praises of his fellow-priest, as if on his own? *Cyprian (c. 250, W), 5.351*

The house of God is one, and there can be no salvation to anyone except in the church. *Cyprian (c. 250, W), 5.358.*

Peter answered Him, "Lord, to whom will we go?" . . . Peter, on whom the church was to be built, . . . taught and showed in the name of the church that a rebellious and arrogant multitude may depart [from the church]. I speak of those who will not hear and obey. However, the church does not depart from Christ. And the church consists of those who are a people united to the priest. It is the flock that adheres to its pastor. Therefore, you should know that the bishop is in the church and the church is in the bishop. If anyone is not with the bishop, he is not in the church. . . . The church is catholic and is one. It is not cut or divided. Rather it is connected and bound together by

the cement of priests who cohere with one another. *Cyprian (c. 250, W), 5.374, 375.*

When we say, "Do you believe in eternal life and remission of sins through the holy church?" we mean that remission of sins is not granted except in the church. *Cyprian (c. 250, W), 5.376.*

The church resembles Paradise. She includes within her walls fruit-bearing trees. But that which does not bring forth good fruit is cut off and is cast into the fire. These trees she waters with four rivers—that is, with the four Gospels, with which, by a heavenly outpouring, she bestows the grace of saving baptism. *Cyprian (c. 250, W), 5.382.*

The faithful, saving, and holy water of the church cannot be corrupted and adulterated, for the church herself is also uncorrupted, chaste, and modest. If heretics are devoted to the church and are established in the church, they may use both her baptism and her other saving benefits. However, if they are not in the church—in fact, if they act *against* the church—how can they baptize with the church's baptism? *Cyprian (c. 250, W), 5.382.*

There is no salvation outside of the church. *Cyprian (c. 250, W), 5.384.*

Can he have God as his Father, before he has had the church for his mother? *Cyprian (c. 250, W), 5.388.*

Peter himself, showing and vindicating the unity, has commanded and warned us that we cannot be saved except by the one only baptism of the one church. He says, "In the ark of Noah, a few, that is, eight souls, were saved by water. Similarly, baptism will in like manner save you." . . . In that baptism of the world in which its ancient wickedness was washed away, he who was not in the ark of Noah could not be saved by water. Likewise, neither can he be saved by baptism who has not been baptized in the church. *Cyprian (c. 250, W), 5.389.*

The one ark of Noah was a type of the one church. *Cyprian (c. 250, W), 5.398.*

He who has not been ordained in the church can neither have nor hold to the church in any way. For the faith of the sacred Scripture sets forth that the church is not outside, nor can it be separated and divided against itself. Rather, it maintains the unity of an inseparable and undivided house. *Cyprian (c. 250, W), 5.398.*

The desire of schismatics is not in the law. For the law points out to us the one and only church in that ark—which was fashioned by the providence of God. . . . We find that there were enclosed [in the ark] not only clean animals, but also unclean ones. The ark alone was saved, along with those who were in it. On the other hand, the things that were not found in it perished in the deluge. *Treatise against Novatian (c. 255, W), 5.658.*

Anyone may observe that there are some diversities among the churches. For example, there are the practices concerning the celebration of Easter and concerning many other sacraments of divine matters. All things are not observed among them in the same manner, nor as they are observed at Jerusalem. Likewise, in very many other provinces, many things are varied because of the difference of the places and names. Nevertheless, there is no departure at all from the peace and unity of the catholic church on this account. *Firmilian (c. 256, E), 5.391.*

According to the Song of Songs, the church is a garden enclosed and a fountain sealed—a Paradise with the fruit of apples. . . . And the ark of Noah was nothing else than the sacrament of the church of Christ. All those who were outside the ark perished. Only those were kept safe who were within the ark. Therefore, we are clearly instructed to look to the unity of the church. *Firmilian (c. 256, E), 5.394.*

No controversy or discussion could have arisen at all if each one of us had been content with the venerable authority of all the churches and if, with fitting humility, each one had desired to innovate nothing. *Treatise on Re-Baptism (c. 257, W), 5.667.*

It is the very greatest disadvantage and damage to our most holy mother church, to now for the first time suddenly and without reason rebel against former decisions after so long a series of so many ages. *Treatise on Re-Baptism (c. 257, W), 5.570.*

The catholic church is one. *Victorinus (c. 280, W), 7.345.*

Christ is the Rock *by* which, and *on* which, the church is founded. *Victorinus (c. 280, W), 7.360.*

The church is formed out of His bones and flesh. And it was for this cause that the Word, leaving His Father in heaven, came down to be "joined to His wife." . . . And He willingly suf-

fered death for her, that He might present the church to Himself glorious and blameless—having cleansed her by the bath. *Methodius (c. 290, E), 6.319.*

The church swells and travails in birth until Christ is formed in us, so that each of the saints, by partaking of Christ, has been born as a "christ" [i.e., an anointed one]. *Methodius (c. 290, E), 6.337.*

He says that the church [Gr. *ecclēsia*] is given that designation because it is being called out with respect to pleasures. *Post-Nicene writer citing Methodius (c. 290, E), 6.381.*

The church, which is the true temple of God, does not consist of walls. Rather, it consists of the heart and faith of the men who believe on Him and are called faithful. *Lactantius (c. 304–313, W), 7.113.*

All the prophets declared concerning Christ that . . . He would build an eternal temple in honor of God, which is called the church. They declared that He would assemble all nations to the true worship of God. This is the faithful house. This is the everlasting temple. If anyone has not sacrificed in this, he will not have the reward of immortality. . . . And there can be no approach to the shrine of the temple and to the sight of God, except through Him who built the temple. *Lactantius (c. 304–313, W), 7.113.*

When they are called Phrygians, Novatians, Valentinians, Marcionites . . . or by any other name, they have ceased to be Christians. They have lost the name of Christ and have assumed human and external names. It is the catholic church alone that retains true worship. This is the fountain of truth. This is the house of the faith. This is the temple of God. If anyone will not enter into this, he is estranged from the hope of life and eternal salvation. *Lactantius (c. 304–313, W), 7.133.*

All the separate assemblies of heretics call themselves Christians in preference to others. They think that theirs is the catholic church. Therefore, it must be known that the true catholic church is that in which there is confession and repentance, a church which treats in a wholesome manner the sins and wounds to which the weakness of the flesh is liable. *Lactantius (c. 304–313, W), 7.134.*

The catholic church is the plantation of God; it is His beloved vineyard. It contains those who have believed in His unerring divine religion. These are the ones who are the heirs by faith of His everlasting kingdom and who are partakers of His divine influence and of the communication of the Holy Spirit. These are the ones who are armed through Jesus and have received his fear into their hearts. They enjoy the benefit of the sprinkling of the precious and innocent blood of Christ. They have free liberty to call Almighty God, "Father." They are fellow-heirs and joint-partakers of his beloved Son. *Apostolic Constitutions (compiled c. 390, E), 7.391.*

SEE ALSO APOSTOLIC FAITH, THE; APOSTOLIC SUCCESSION; BAPTISM (V. BAPTISM BY HERETICS); BISHOP; CHURCH AND STATE; CHURCH BUILDINGS; CHURCH GOVERNMENT; CHURCHES, APOSTOLIC; MOTHER, SPIRITUAL; PARABLES OF JESUS; WOMAN CLOTHED WITH THE SUN.

CHURCH AND STATE

Render therefore to Caesar the things that are Caesar's, and to God the things that are God's. Matt. 22:21.

Then Peter and the other apostles answered and said: "We ought to obey God rather than men." Acts 5:29.

Let every soul be subject to the governing authorities. For there is no authority except from God, and the authorities that exist are appointed by God. Rom. 13:1.

I exhort first of all that supplications, prayers, intercessions, and giving of thanks be made for all men, for kings and all who are in authority, that we may lead a quiet and peaceable life in all godliness and reverence. 1 Tim. 2:2.

Fear God. Honor the king. 1 Pet. 2:17.

We are taught to give all due honor . . . to the powers and authorities that are ordained of God. *Martyrdom of Polycarp (c. 135, E), 1.41.*

To God alone we render worship. However, in other things we gladly serve you, acknowledging you as kings and rulers of men, and praying that with your kingly power you will be found also to possess sound judgment. *Justin Martyr (c. 160, E), 1.168.*

In a sense, the king's government is committed to him by God. . . . Accordingly, honor the king, be subject to him, and pray for him with loyal mind. If you do this, you will do the will of God. *Theophilus (c. 180, E), 2.92.*

Paul the apostle also says upon this same subject: "Be subject to all the higher powers; for there is no power but of God." . . . Now, he spoke these words, not in regard to angelic powers, nor of invisible rulers (as some venture to expound the passage) but of those actual human authorities. *Irenaeus (c. 180, E/W), 1.552.*

And of civil government, it says: "Render to Caesar the things that are Caesar's; and unto God, the things that are God's." *Clement of Alexandria (c. 195, E), 2.293.*

We offer prayer to the eternal, the true, the living God for the safety of our princes. *Tertullian (c. 197, W), 3.42.*

For all our emperors, we offer prayer without ceasing. We pray for prolonged life, for security to the empire, for protection to the imperial house, for brave armies, a faithful senate, a virtuous people, the world at rest—whatever an emperor would wish, as man or Caesar. *Tertullian (c. 197, W), 3.42.*

You, then, who think that we do not care for the welfare of Caesar, look into God's revelations, examine our sacred books. We do not keep these in hiding. In fact, many circumstances put them into the hands of those who are not of us. Learn from them that a large benevolence is enjoined upon us, even so far as to supplicate God for our enemies and to request blessings on our persecutors. . . . Most clearly, the Scripture says, "Pray for kings, rulers, and powers, that all may be peace with you." *Tertullian (c. 197, W), 3.42.*

There is also another and a greater necessity for our offering prayer on behalf of the emperors—in fact, for the complete stability of the empire and for Roman interests in general. For we know that a mighty shock impending over the whole earth—in fact, the very end of all things threatening dreadful woes—is only retarded by the continued existence of the Roman empire. We have no desire, then, to be overtaken by these dire events. In praying that their coming may be delayed, we are lending our aid to Rome's duration. *Tertullian (c. 197, W), 3.42, 43.*

We respect in the emperors the ordinance of God, who has set them over the nations. We know that in them there is that thing which God has willed. *Tertullian (c. 197, W), 3.43.*

Why dwell any longer on the reverence and sacred respect of Christians to the emperor? We cannot help but to look upon him as someone called by our Lord to his office. Therefore, on valid grounds, I can say that Caesar is more ours than yours, for our God has appointed him. *Tertullian (c. 197, W), 3.43.*

Hippias [a pagan] was put to death for laying plots against the state. No Christian ever attempted such a thing on behalf of his brethren, even when persecution was scattering them abroad with every atrocity. *Tertullian (c. 197, W), 3.51.*

No conspiracy has ever broken out from our body. No Caesar's blood has ever fixed a stain upon us in the senate or even in the palace. No assumption of the purple has ever in any of the provinces been affected by us. *Tertullian (c. 197, W), 3.125.*

Indeed, render to Caesar *money*. Render to God, *yourself*. Otherwise, what will be God's, if all things are Caesar's? *Tertullian (c. 200, W), 3.70.*

As to what relates to the honors due to kings or emperors, we have a sufficient commandment. According to the apostle's commandment, it behooves us all to be in obedience, "subject to magistrates, princes, and powers." We honor them within the confines of our discipline—that is, so long as we keep ourselves free from idolatry. . . . Daniel was submissive to Darius in all other matters. He rendered his duty so long as it was free from danger to his religion. *Tertullian (c. 200, W), 3.71.*

"Render unto Caesar the things that are Caesar's, and unto God the things that are God's." What will be "the things that are God's"? Such things as are parallel to Caesar's denarius. That is to say, His image and likeness. Therefore, what God commands to be rendered unto God the Creator is man himself. For man has been stamped with His image, likeness, name, and substance. *Tertullian (c. 207, W), 3.413.*

All the powers and dignities of this world are not only alien to, but are enemies of, God. Through them, punishments have been determined against God's servants. Through them, too, penalties prepared for the impious are ignored. *Tertullian (c. 212, W), 3.73.*

Treason is falsely laid to our charge, though no one has ever been able to find followers of Albinus, Niger, or Cassius among Christians. . . . A Christian is enemy to no one—least of all to the emperor of Rome, whom he knows to be appointed by his God. So he cannot help but to love and honor him. And the Christian must necessarily desire his well-being, along with that of the empire over which he reigns—so long as the world will stand, for so long as that will Rome continue. To the emperor, therefore, we render such reverential homage as is lawful for us and good for him. We regard him as the human being next to God, who from God has received all his power. He is less only than God. . . . Being only less than the true God, he is greater than all others. *Tertullian (c. 212, W), 3.105, 106.*

Far be it from us to take it badly that we have laid on us the very things that we wish [i.e., martyrdom], or in any way to plot vengeance at our own hands. For we expect vengeance to come from God. *Tertullian (c. 212, W), 3.106.*

No doubt the apostle admonishes the Romans to be subject to all powers, for there is no power but of God. . . . Then he goes on to show also how he wishes you to be subject to the powers, exhorting you to pay "tribute to whom tribute is due, custom to whom custom [is due]." In other words, give the things that are Caesar's back to Caesar, and the things that are God's to God. But man is the property of God alone. Similarly, Peter, no doubt, had said that the king indeed must be honored. But he means that the king is honored only when he keeps to his own sphere—that is, when he is far from claiming divine honors. *Tertullian (c. 213, W), 3.647, 648.*

When it is not opposed to the law of God, it is a proper thing for citizens not to abandon the written law, under the pretext that is a foreign custom. However, what if the law of nature—that is, the law of God—commands what is opposed to the written law? Does not reason tell us to bid a long farewell to the written code . . . and to give ourselves up to the Legislator, God? This is so even if in doing so it may be necessary to encounter dangers, countless labors, and even death and dishonor. *Origen (c. 248, E), 4.560.*

Celsus [a pagan critic] would have us obey such laws and to propitiate the demons. If he means laws enacted in states, he must show that they are in agreement with the divine laws. However, if this cannot be done, . . . these laws must therefore either be no laws at all (in the proper sense of the word) or else must be the enactments of wicked men. And we must not obey such men, for "we must obey God rather than men." *Origen (c. 248, E), 4.649.*

Celsus goes on to say: "They must make their choice between two alternatives. If they refuse to render due service to the gods and to respect those who are set over this service, . . . let them depart at once with all speed and leave no posterity behind them, so that such a race may become extinct from the face of the earth." . . . To this, we reply that there is to us no good reason for our leaving this world, except when piety and virtue require it. Such an example would be when those who are set as judges and think that they have power over our lives, place before us the alternative either to live in violation of the commands of Jesus or to die if we continue obedient to them. *Origen (c. 248, E), 4.660.*

We are to scorn trying to ingratiate ourselves with kings or any other men—not only if their favor is to be won by murders, licentiousness, or deeds of cruelty—but even if it involves impiety towards God, or any servile expressions of flattery and fawning. For those things are unworthy of brave and high-principled men. . . . However, although we do nothing that is contrary to the law and Word of God, we are not so insane as to [purposefully] stir up against us the wrath of kings and rulers. For they will bring upon us sufferings, tortures, or even death. We read, "Let every soul be subject to the higher powers. For there is no power but of God." . . . However, we will never swear by "the fortune of the king," nor by anything else that is considered equivalent to God. For if the word "fortune" is nothing but an expression for the uncertain course of events (as some say) . . . we do not swear by that . . . lest we bind ourselves by an oath to things that have no existence. *Origen (c. 248, E), 4.664.*

We deny that all things that are on the earth have been given to the king, or that whatever we receive in this life we receive from him. For whatever we rightly and honorably receive, we receive from God. . . . For kings are not appointed by the son of Saturn . . . but by God, who governs all things and who wisely arranges whatever belongs to the appointment of kings. *Origen (c. 248, E), 4.665.*

Celsus also urges us to "take office in the government of the country, if that is necessary for the maintenance of the laws and the support of religion." However, we recognize in each state the existence of another national organization that was founded by the Word of God. And we exhort those who are mighty in word and of blameless life to rule over churches. . . . So it is not for the purpose of escaping public duties that Christians decline public offices. Rather, it is so they may reserve themselves for a more divine and necessary service in the church of God—for the salvation of men. *Origen (c. 248, E), 4.668.*

When his sovereignty was in a prosperous position and when affairs were turning out according to his wish, Decius oppressed those holy men who interceded with God on behalf of his peace and his welfare. Consequently, . . . he also persecuted the prayers offered in his own behalf. *Dionysius of Alexandria (c. 262, E), 6.106, as quoted by Eusebius.*

Consider every command of the emperor that does not offend God as though it has proceeded from God Himself. And obey it in love as well as in fear, with all cheerfulness. *Theonas of Alexandria (c. 300, E), 6.159.*

God might have bestowed upon His people [i.e., the Christians] both riches and kingdoms, as he had given previously to the Jews, whose successors and posterity we are. However, He would have Christians live under the power and government of others, lest they should become corrupted by the happiness of prosperity, slide into luxury, and eventually despise the commandments of God. For this is what our ancestors did. *Lactantius (c. 304–313, W), 7.160.*

When men command us to act in opposition to the law of God, and in opposition to justice, we should not be deterred by any threats or punishments that come upon us. For we prefer the commandments of God to the commandments of man. *Lactantius (c. 304–313, W), 7.182.*

SEE ALSO GOVERNMENT; NONRESISTANCE; PUBLIC OFFICE; TAXES; WAR; WORLD, SEPARATION FROM.

CHURCH BUILDINGS

Jesus answered and said to them, "Destroy this temple, and in three days I will raise it up." . . . But He was speaking of the temple of His body. John 2:19, 21.

God, who made the world and everything in it, since He is Lord of heaven and earth, does not dwell in temples made with hands. Acts 17:24.

Likewise greet the church that is in their house. Rom. 16:5.

You are the temple of the living God. 2 Cor. 6:16.

The Word, prohibiting all sacrifices and the building of temples, indicates that the Almighty is not contained in anything. *Clement of Alexandria (c. 195, E), 2.462.*

We refuse to build lifeless temples to the Giver of all life.... Our bodies are the temple of God. If anyone defiles the temple of God by lust or sin, he will himself be destroyed for acting impiously towards the true temple. Of all the temples spoken of in this sense, the best and most excellent was the pure and holy body of our Savior Jesus Christ.... He said to them, "Destroy this temple, and in three days I will raise it again. This He said of the temple of His body.".... When they reproach us for not deeming it necessary to worship the divine Being by raising lifeless temples, we set before them our temples. *Origen (c. 248, E), 4.646.*

You say that we build no temples to [the gods] and do not worship their images. . . . Well, what greater honor or dignity could we ascribe to them than that we put them in the same position as the Head and Lord of the universe! . . . Do we honor Him with shrines and by building temples? *Arnobius (c. 305, E), 6.507.*

Some were swift to slaughter [the Christians]. For example, there was a certain individual in Phrygia who burned a whole assembly of Christians, together with their place of meeting. *Lactantius (c. 304-313, W), 7.147.*

[Emperor Daia] secretly procured addresses from different cities, requesting that no Christian church be built within their walls. . . . The function of those [Roman] officers was to make daily sacrifices to all of their gods and . . . to prevent Christians from erecting churches. *Lactantius (c. 304–313, W), 7.315.*

While it was yet hardly light, the [Roman] prefect, together with chief commanders . . . came to the church in Nicomedia. The gates having been forced open, they searched everywhere for an image of the Divinity. The books of the Holy Scriptures were found, and they were committed to the flames. The utensils and furniture of the church were abandoned to pillage. *Lactantius (c. 320, W), 7.305.*

Constantius . . . permitted the demolition of churches, which are mere walls and capable of

being built up again. However, he preserved entire that true temple of God, which is the human body. *Lactantius (c. 320, W), 7.306.*

Moreover, with respect to the Christians, we formerly gave certain orders concerning the places set aside for their religious assemblies. However, now we resolve that all persons who have purchased such places, either from our treasurer, or from anyone else, must restore them to the Christians, without money demanded or price claimed. . . . All those places are, by your intervention, to be immediately restored to the Christians. And it appears that, in addition to the places set aside for religious worship, the Christians possessed other places (which belonged to the society in general, not to individuals). These we include in the aforesaid regulations. *Lactantius (c. 320, E), 7.320, quoting from the Edict of Milan.*

Let the building be long, with its head to the east, with its vestries on both sides at the east end—so it will be like a ship. *Apostolic Constitutions (compiled c. 390, E), 7.421.*

SEE ALSO EDICT OF MILAN.

CHURCH GOVERNMENT

I. References to twofold order of leadership

II. References to threefold order of leadership

III. Interchangeable uses of "bishop" and "presbyter"

IV. Authority and duties of church leadership

V. Qualifications of and counsel to the clergy

VI. Material support of the clergy

VII. References to married clergy

VIII. The beginnings of clerical celibacy

IX. Clergy and laity distinctions

X. Priesthood of church leaders

XI. Priesthood of all believers

I. References to twofold order of leadership

To all the saints in Christ Jesus who are in Philippi, with the bishops and deacons. Phil. 1:1.

A bishop then must be blameless, the husband of one wife, temperate.... Likewise deacons must be reverent, not double-tongued. 1 Tim. 2:2, 8.

Therefore, appoint for yourselves bishops and deacons worthy of the Lord. *Didache (c. 80–140, E), 7.381.*

Preaching throughout countries and cities, the apostles appointed the first-fruits of their labors to be bishops and deacons of those who would believe afterwards. However, they first tested them by the Spirit. This was no new thing. Indeed, many ages before, it had been written concerning bishops and deacons. For the Scriptures say in a certain place, "I will appoint their bishops in righteousness and their deacons in faith" [Isa. 60:17, LXX]. *Clement of Rome (c. 96, W), 1.16.*

It is necessary to abstain from all of these things, being subject to the presbyters and deacons, as unto God and Christ. *Polycarp (c. 135, E), 1.34.*

II. References to threefold order of leadership

I have had the privilege of seeing you, through Damas, your most worthy bishop, and through your worthy presbyters, Bassus and Apollonius, and through my fellow servant, the deacon Sotio. *Ignatius (c. 105, E), 1.59.*

I exhort you to study to do all things with a divine harmony, while your bishop presides in the place of God, and your presbyters in the place of the assembly of the apostles, along with your deacons. *Ignatius (c. 105, E), 1.61.*

. . . with your most admirable bishop, and the well-formed spiritual crown of your presbytery, and the deacons, who are according to God. *Ignatius (c. 105, E), 1.64.*

There is one bishop, along with the presbyters and deacons, my fellow servants. *Ignatius (c. 105, E), 1.81.*

Innumerable commands like these are written in the Holy Scriptures, pertaining to chosen persons: some to presbyters, some to bishops, some to deacons. *Clement of Alexandria (c. 195, E), 2.294.*

According to my opinion, the grades here in the church, of bishops, presbyters, and deacons, are imitations of the angelic glory, and of that arrangement which (the Scriptures say) awaits those who, following the footsteps of the apostles, have lived in perfection of righteousness according to the Gospel. *Clement of Alexandria (c. 195, E), 2.505.*

What if a bishop, a deacon, a widow, a virgin, a teacher, or even a martyr has fallen from the rule? On that account, will heresies appear to possess the truth? *Tertullian (c. 197, W), 3.244.*

And so it came to pass that [among the heretics] today one man is their bishop, tomorrow another. Today he is a deacon who tomorrow is a reader. Today he is a presbyter who tomorrow is a layman. For even on laymen do they impose the functions of priesthood. *Tertullian (c. 197, W), 3.263.*

Cyprian, to the presbyters and deacons, brethren abiding at Rome. *Cyprian (c. 250, W), 5.281.*

Cyprian, to the presbyters and deacons, his beloved brethren. *Cyprian (c. 250, W), 5.282.*

Caldonius to Cyprian and his fellow presbyters abiding at Carthage. *Letter to Cyprian (c. 250, W), 5.297.*

To Caecilius Cyprian, bishop of the church of Carthage, Moyses and Maximus, presbyters, and Nicostratus and Rufinius, deacons. *Letter to Cyprian (c. 250, W), 5.302.*

Deacons should remember that the *Lord* chose apostles—that is, bishops and overseers. In contrast, the *apostles* appointed deacons for themselves. *Cyprian (c. 250, W), 5.366.*

To all our fellows in the ministry throughout the world—bishops, presbyters, and deacons—and to the whole catholic church under heaven. *Malchion (c. 270, E), 6.169.*

All these bishops, presbyters, and deacons had suffered martyrdom in the prison at Alexandria. *Phileas (c. 307, E), 6.164.*

Archelaus [a bishop] sends greeting to the presbyter Diodorus, his honorable son. My dearly beloved friend, the receipt of your letter has caused me to rejoice exceedingly. *Disputation of Archelaus and Manes (c. 320, E), 6.215.*

Paul himself has laid our foundation, that is, the foundation of the church. And he has put us in trust of the law—ordaining deacons, presbyters, and bishops. *Disputation of Archelaus and Manes (c. 320, E), 6.229.*

For [the bishops] are your high priests, as the presbyters are your priests. You have the deacons in place of the Levites. . . . But He who is above all these is *the* High Priest [Christ]. *Apostolic Constitutions (compiled c. 390, E), 7.410.*

When [Moses] made constitutions and divine laws, he distinguished among the things to be performed by the high priests, the priests, and the Levites. He distributed to each one his proper and suitable office in the divine service. The priests were not to meddle with the things that were allotted for the high priests. And the Levites were not to meddle with the things allotted to the priests. . . . Being taught by the Lord this series of things, [the apostles] allotted the functions of the high-priesthood to the bishops, those of the priesthood to the presbyters, and the ministries under both of them to the deacons. *Apostolic Constitutions (compiled c. 390, E), 7.499.*

Those who are called by us bishops, presbyters, and deacons were made such by prayer and by the laying on of hands. The difference of their names shows the difference of their duties. . . . For it is not lawful for a deacon to offer the sacrifice, to baptize, or to give either the greater or the lesser blessing. A presbyter many not perform ordination. For it is not agreeable to holiness to have this order perverted. For "God is not the God of confusion." So subordinate persons should not tyrannically assume functions that belong to their superiors. . . . However, someone may accuse Philip the deacon or Ananias, the faithful brother, [of doing this]. For the one baptized the eunuch; the other baptized Paul. However, such an accuser does not understand what we are saying. We are only saying that no one snatches the priestly dignity to himself. He either receives it from God—as did Melchizedek and Job—or from a high priest—as did Aaron from Moses. So Philip and Ananias did not ordain themselves, but were appointed by Christ, the High Priest. *Apostolic Constitutions (compiled c. 390, E), 7.499, 500.*

Do not receive any stranger—whether bishop, presbyter, or deacon—without commendatory letters. And when such are offered, let them be examined. *Apostolic Constitutions (compiled c. 390, E), 7.502.*

III. Interchangeable uses of "bishop" and "presbyter"

Sometimes the early Christian writers used the terms "bishop" and "presbyter" interchangeably.

From Miletus he sent to Ephesus and called for the elders of the church. And when they had come to him, he said to them: . . . "Take heed to yourselves and to all the flock, among which the Holy Spirit has made you overseers [bishops], to shepherd the church of God." Acts 20:17, 18, 28.

Do not neglect the gift that is in you, which was given to you by prophecy with the laying on of the hands of the presbytery. 1 Tim. 4:14.

The elders [presbyters] who are among you I exhort, I who am a fellow elder and a witness of the sufferings of Christ, and also a partaker of the glory that will be revealed: Shepherd the flock of God which is among you, serving as overseers [bishops]. 1 Pet. 5:1, 2.

Our sin will not be small if we eject from oversight [or, from the episcopate] those who have blamelessly and holily fulfilled its duties. Blessed are those presbyters who have obtained a fruitful and perfect departure, having finished their course before now. *Clement of Rome (c. 96, W), 1.17.*

We refer them to that tradition which originates from the apostles and is preserved by the successions of presbyters in the churches. . . . The faith preached to men comes down to our time by means of the successions of the bishops. *Irenaeus (c. 180, E/W), 1.415.*

The church nourishes such presbyters, of whom also the prophet says: "I will give your rulers in peace, and your bishops in righteousness." *Irenaeus (c. 180, E/W), 1.498.*

Now, all these heretics are of much later date than the bishops to whom the apostles committed the churches. . . . Therefore, those who desert the preaching of the church, call into question the knowledge of the holy presbyters. *Irenaeus (c. 180, E/W), 1.547, 548.*

Polycarp, too, was instructed by apostles, and he spoke with many who had seen Christ. Furthermore, the apostles in Asia appointed him bishop of the church in Smyrna. *Irenaeus (c. 180, E/W), 1.416.*

Compare the above passage by Irenaeus with the following excerpt from another work of his:

Those presbyters who preceded us, and who were conversant with the apostles, did not hand down those opinions to you. For, while I was yet a body, I saw you in Lower Asia with Polycarp. *Irenaeus (c. 180, E/W), 1.568.*

Anicetus [bishop of Rome] maintained that he was bound to adhere to the usage of the presbyters who preceded him. *Irenaeus (c. 180, E/W), 1.569.*

Looking to the appointed bishop, . . . John said, "This [youth] I commit to you in all earnestness." . . . And the presbyter took home the youth committed to him. *Clement of Alexandria (c. 195, E), 5.603.*

In respect of that which our fellow presbyters . . . wrote to me, I have not been able to reply by myself, since, from the first commencement of my episcopacy, I made up my mind to do nothing on my own private opinion. *Cyprian (c. 250, W), 5.283.*

Caldonius to Cyprian and his fellow presbyters abiding at Carthage. *Letter to Cyprian (c. 250, W), 5.297.*

You will hear everything most fully from Primitivus, our co-presbyter. *Cyprian (c. 250, W), 5.319.*

IV. Authority and duties of church leadership

We urge you, brethren, to recognize those who labor among you, and are over you in the Lord and admonish you, and to esteem them very highly in love for their work's sake. 1 Thess. 5:12.

Obey those who rule over you, and be submissive, for they watch out for your souls, as those who must give account. Heb. 13:17.

My child, remember night and day the one who speaks the word of God to you. Honor him as the Lord, for wherever His Lordship is taught, there the Lord is. *Didache (c. 80–140, E), 7.378.*

Let us honor those who have the rule over us. *Clement of Rome (c. 96, W), 1.11.*

Let everyone reverence the deacons as an appointment of Jesus Christ; and the bishop as Jesus Christ, who is the Son of the Father; and the presbyters as the Sanhedrin of God and assembly of the apostles. Apart from these, there is no church. *Ignatius (c. 105, E), 1.67.*

He who does anything apart from the bishop, the presbyters, and the deacons, such a man is not pure in his conscience. *Ignatius (c. 105, E), 1.69.*

It is necessary to abstain from all of these things, being subject to the presbyters and deacons, as unto God and Christ. *Polycarp (c. 135, E), 1.34.*

Of giving [baptism], the chief priest (who is the bishop) has the right. In the next place, the presbyters and deacons have the right. Yet, they should not do so without the bishop's

authority, on account of the honor of the church. For when it is preserved, peace is preserved. *Tertullian (c. 198, W), 3.677.*

We must rise when a bishop or a presbyter comes. In Leviticus, it says: "You will rise up before the face of the elder and you will honor the person of the presbyter" [Lev. 19:32]. *Cyprian (c. 250, W), 5.553.*

If the sinner sees that the bishop and deacons are innocent and unblamable and that the flock is pure, he will not venture to despise their authority. *Apostolic Constitutions (compiled c. 390, E), 7.399.*

Neither a presbyter nor a deacon should ordain anyone from the laity into the clergy. Rather, the presbyter is only to teach, to offer, to baptize, and to bless the people. And the deacon is to minister to the bishop and to the presbyters. *Apostolic Constitutions (compiled c. 390, E), 7.432.*

It is not lawful for them, if they are unmarried when they are ordained, to be married afterwards. . . . We do not permit any of the clergy to take a wife who is a prostitute, a servant, a widow, or one who is divorced. *Apostolic Constitutions (compiled c. 390, E), 7.457.*

Let the bishop bless the water or the oil. But if he is not there, let the presbyter bless it, the deacon standing by. *Apostolic Constitutions (compiled c. 390, E), 7.494.*

V. Qualifications of and counsel to the clergy

A bishop then must be blameless, the husband of one wife, temperate, sober-minded, of good behavior, hospitable, able to teach; not given to wine, not violent, not greedy for money, but gentle, not quarrelsome, not covetous. 1 Tim. 3:2, 3.

Likewise deacons must be reverent, not double-tongued, not given to much wine, not greedy for money. 1 Tim. 3:8.

You will tell those who preside over the church to direct their ways in righteousness, so that they will receive in full the promises with great glory. *Hermas (c. 150, W), 2.11.*

Those square white stones which fitted exactly into each other, are apostles, bishops, teachers, and deacons, who have lived in godly purity, and have acted as bishops, teachers, and deacons chastely and reverently. *Hermas (c. 150, W), 2.14.*

But when persons in authority themselves—I mean, the very deacons, presbyters, and bishops—take flight, how will a layman be able to discern? *Tertullian (c. 212, W), 4.122.*

If certain teachers relax individual commandments to you, while looking for your gifts or fearing your persons, . . . I am compelled to speak the truth. . . . You trust the gift by which the teachers shut up their mouths and become silent, not telling you the divine commands. *Commodianus (c. 240, W), 4.214.*

The apostle bids that such persons should be teachers. Let him be a patient ruler. Let him know when he may relax the reins. Let him terrify at first, and then anoint with honey. And let him be the first to practice what he teaches. *Commodianus (c. 240, W), 4.216.*

We exhort those who are mighty in word and of blameless life to rule over churches. We reject those who are ambitious to rule. . . . And if those who govern in the church . . . rule well, they rule in accordance with the divine commands and never allow themselves to be led astray by worldly policy. *Origen (c. 248, E), 4.668.*

In respect of that which our fellow presbyters . . . wrote to me, I have not been able to reply by myself, since, from the first commencement of my episcopacy, I made up my mind to do nothing on my own private opinion, without your advice [i.e., the advice of the presbyters and deacons] and without the consent of the people. *Cyprian (c. 250, W), 5.283.*

The following passage is from a letter that concerns certain presbyters who had rashly granted peace to the lapsed in Cyprian's absence.

What danger should we not fear from the Lord's displeasure, when some of the presbyters, remembering neither the Gospel nor their own place . . . nor the bishop now placed over them, claim to themselves entire authority—a thing that was never in any way done under our predecessors . . . ? *Cyprian (c. 250, W), 5.289.*

In the meanwhile, let those certain [presbyters] among you who are rash, incautious, and boastful . . . be suspended from offering [the Eucharist]. *Cyprian (c. 250, W), 5.290.*

[Cornelius] was not one who suddenly attained to the episcopacy. Rather, he was promoted through all the ecclesiastical offices. Having often deserved well of the Lord in divine administrations, he ascended by all the grades of religious service to the lofty summit of the priesthood. . . . He was quiet, meek, and of the type who are chosen of God to this office, having regard to the modesty of his virgin continence. *Cyprian (c. 250, W), 5.329.*

Those, therefore, who have brought grievous sins upon themselves—that is, who, by sacrificing to idols, have offered sacrilegious sacrifices—cannot claim to themselves the priesthood of God, nor make any prayer for their brethren in His sight. *Cyprian (c. 250, W), 5.364.*

In the ordinations of priests, we should choose no one but unstained and upright ministers. In that way, the ministers who offer sacrifices to God with holy and worthy hands, may be heard in the prayers that they make for the safety of the Lord's people. . . . On this account, a people obedient to the Lord's commandments, and fearing God, should separate themselves from a sinful prelate. They should not associate themselves with the sacrifices of a sacrilegious priest. This is especially so since they themselves have the power of either choosing worthy priests or of rejecting unworthy ones. *Cyprian (c. 250, W), 5.370.*

It is evident that men of that kind may neither rule over the church of Christ, nor ought to offer sacrifices to God. This is especially so since Cornelius also, our colleague, a peaceable and righteous priest [bishop of Rome] . . . has long ago decreed with us and with all the bishops appointed throughout the whole world that men of this sort might indeed be admitted to repentance, but were prohibited from ordination to the clergy or to priestly honor. *Cyprian (c. 250, W), 5.371.*

How can he who is himself unclean and in whom the Holy Spirit does not dwell, cleanse and sanctify the water [of baptism]? For the Lord says in the book of Numbers, "And whatever the unclean person touches will be unclean." . . . After all, what prayer can a priest who is impious and is a sinner offer for a baptized person? For it is written, "God does not hear a sinner" [John 9:31]. . . . Who can give what he himself does not have? How can he discharge spiritual functions who himself has lost the Holy Spirit? *Cyprian (c. 250, W), 5.376.*

Any presbyters or deacons who have been previously ordained in the catholic church but have subsequently left as traitors and rebels . . . can be received when they return—only on the condition that they thereafter communicate as laymen. *Cyprian (c. 250, W), 5.379.*

Beloved, we know that the bishop and all the clergy should be an example in all good works to the people. *Malchion (c. 270, E), 6.170.*

It is not right either that those of the clergy who have deserted of their own accord and have lapsed, but have taken up the contest anew, should remain any longer in their sacred office. *Peter of Alexandria (c. 310, E), 6.274.*

If a presbyter comes from another parish, let him be received to communion by the presbyters. Let a deacon be received by the deacons. If he is a bishop, let him sit with the bishops. *Apostolic Constitutions (compiled c. 390, E), 7.422.*

Let not a bishop, priest, or a deacon cast off his own wife under the pretense of piety. . . . Let not a bishop, priest, or deacon undertake the cares of this world. If he does, let him be deprived. *Apostolic Constitutions (compiled c. 390, E), 7.500.*

He who has taken a widow, a divorced woman, a harlot, a servant, or someone belonging to the theater cannot be a bishop, priest, deacon, or indeed any one of the priestly category. *Apostolic Constitutions (compiled c. 390, E), 7.501.*

Of those who come into the clergy unmarried, we permit only the readers and singers to marry afterwards, if they so desire. *Apostolic Constitutions (compiled c. 390, E), 7.501.*

If a bishop, presbyter, or deacon indulges himself in dice or drinking, he must either leave off those practices or else let him be deprived. *Apostolic Constitutions (compiled c. 390, E), 7.502.*

Let not the presbyters and deacons do anything without the consent of the bishop. For it is he who is entrusted with the people of the Lord and will be required to give an account of their souls. *Apostolic Constitutions (compiled c. 390, E), 7.502.*

We do not permit slaves to be ordained into the clergy without their masters' consent. For this would grieve those who owned them. . . . However, if at any time a slave appears worthy to be ordained into a high office (such as Onesimus

appeared to be), and if his master allows it and gives him his freedom, dismissing him from his house—let him be ordained. *Apostolic Constitutions (compiled c. 390, E), 7.505.*

VI. Material support of the clergy

For it is written in the law of Moses, "You will not muzzle an ox while it treads out the grain." Is it oxen God is concerned about? Or does He say it altogether for our sakes? For our sakes, no doubt, this is written. . . . The Lord has commanded that those who preach the gospel should live from the gospel." 1 Cor. 9:9, 10, 14.

No one engaged in warfare entangles himself with the affairs of this life, that he may please him who enlisted him as a soldier. . . . The hard-working farmer must be first to partake of the crops. 2 Tim. 2:4, 6.

Let him who is taught the word share in all good things with him who teaches. Gal. 6:6.

Natalius was persuaded by them to let himself be chosen bishop of this heresy, on the understanding that he would receive from them a salary of a hundred and fifty denarii a month. . . . He gave little heed to the visions, being ensnared by the distinction of presiding over them and by that sordid lust of gain that ruins very many. *Eusebius, quoting Caius (c. 215, W), 5.602.*

It was decreed in a council of the bishops that no one should appoint any of the clergy and the ministers of God as an executor or guardian in his will. For everyone honored by the divine priesthood, and ordained in the clerical service, should serve only the altar and sacrifices and should have time for prayers and supplications. For it is written: "No man that wars for God entangles himself with the affairs of this life." . . . But in the honor of the brethren who contribute—receiving as it were the tenths of the fruits—they should not withdraw from the altars and sacrifices. *Cyprian (c. 250, W), 5.367.*

Let the bishop view such food and clothing sufficient as meets necessity and decency. Let him not make use of the Lord's goods as another's. Rather, let him use them moderately, "for the laborer is worthy of his reward." Let him not be luxurious in diet or fond of idle furniture. . . . Let him use as a man of God those tithes and first-fruits that are given according to the command of God. *Apostolic Constitutions (compiled c. 390, E), 7.408.*

Those who attend upon the church should be maintained by the church—as being priests, Levites, presidents, and ministers of God. *Apostolic Constitutions (compiled c. 390, E), 7.409.*

As much as is given to each one of the elder women, let double that amount be given to the deacons, in honor of Christ. Let also a double portion be set apart for the presbyters. . . . If there is a reader, let him receive a single portion. *Apostolic Constitutions (compiled c. 390, E), 7.411.*

VII. References to married clergy

Do we have no right to take along a believing wife, as do also the other apostles, the brothers of the Lord, and Cephas? 1 Cor. 9:5.

A bishop then must be blameless, the husband of one wife. . . . Let deacons be the husbands of one wife, ruling their children and their own houses well. 1 Tim. 3:2, 12.

I am greatly grieved for Valens, who was once a presbyter among you. . . . I am deeply grieved, therefore, brethren, for him and his wife. May the Lord grant true repentance to them. *Polycarp (c. 135, E), 1.35.*

In fact, Paul completely approves of the man who is the husband of one wife—whether he is a bishop, presbyter, deacon, or layman—so long as he conducts his marriage beyond reproach. *Clement of Alexandria (c. 195, E), 2.398.*

Let not a bishop, priest, or a deacon cast off his own wife under the pretense of piety. *Apostolic Constitutions (compiled c. 390, E), 7.500.*

If any bishop, presbyter, or deacon (or indeed anyone of the priestly category) abstains from marriage, meat, and wine not for his own discipline but because he abominates these things, he forgets that "all things were very good" and that "God made man male and female." So he blasphemously abuses the creation. Therefore, either let him reform, or else let him be deprived and be cast out of the church. The same is true for any of the laity. *Apostolic Constitutions (compiled c. 390, E), 7.503.*

VIII. The beginnings of clerical celibacy

If also, however, anyone who is in holy orders should become married, he [Callistus, bishop of Rome] permitted such a one to continue in holy orders as if he had not sinned. And he alleges that what has been spoken by the apostle

refers to such a person: "Who are you to judge another man's servant?" *Hippolytus (c. 225, W), 5.131.*

Of those who come into the clergy unmarried, we permit only the readers and singers to marry afterwards, if they so desire. *Apostolic Constitutions (compiled c. 390, E), 7.501.*

IX. Clergy and laity distinctions

The English word "clergy" comes from the Greek word *klēros*, which means a "lot." After the ascension of Christ, Matthias was selected by casting lots. Eventually, the term *klēros* came to mean the person selected for a ministerial office—whether or not by casting lots. The English word "laity" comes from the Greek word *laos*, which simply means "people."

My brethren, let not many of you become teachers, knowing that we will receive a stricter judgment. Jas. 3:1.

And so it came to pass that [among the heretics] today one man is their bishop, tomorrow another. Today he is a deacon who tomorrow is a reader. Today he is a presbyter who tomorrow is a layman. For even on laymen they impose the functions of priesthood. *Tertullian (c. 197, W), 3.263.*

Among *us,* the commandment is more fully and more carefully laid down, that they who are chosen into the priestly order must be men of one marriage. This rule is so rigidly observed that I remember some who were removed from their office for a second marriage. But you will say, "then all others may [remarry], whom he excepts." Vain will we be if we think that what is not lawful for priests is lawful for laity. Are not even we laymen priests? *Tertullian (c. 212, W, Montanistic), 4.54.*

But when persons in authority themselves—I mean, the very deacons, presbyters, and bishops—take flight, how will a layman be able to see? *Tertullian (c. 212, W), 4.122.*

He rolled not only beneath the feet of the clergy, but those even of the laity, moving the pity of the compassionate church of the merciful Christ by his weeping. *Eusebius, quoting Caius (c. 215, W), 5.602.*

[Demetrius] has added to his letter that this is a matter that was never heard of before, and has never been done: that laymen should take part in public speaking when there are bishops present. However, in this assertion, he has evidently departed far from the truth. . . . For, indeed, wherever there are found persons capable of profiting the brethren, such persons are exhorted by the holy bishops to address the people. *Alexander of Cappadocia (c. 250, E), 6.154.*

X. Priesthood of church leaders

I have written very boldly to you on some points, so as to remind you again, because of the grace that was given me from God, to be a minister of Christ Jesus to the Gentiles, ministering as a priest the gospel of God. Rom. 15:15, 16.

Every first-fruit, therefore, of the products of wine-press and threshing-floor, of oxen and of sheep, you will take and give to the prophets, for they are your high priests. *Didache (c. 80–140, E), 7.381.*

[AMONG THE HERETICS:] Today he is a presbyter who tomorrow is a layman. For even on laymen do they impose the functions of priesthood. *Tertullian (c. 197, W), 3.263.*

Of giving [baptism], the chief priest (who is the bishop) has the right. In the next place, the presbyters and deacons—yet, not without the bishop's authority, on account of the honor of the church. When it is preserved, peace is preserved. *Tertullian (c. 198, W), 3.677.*

Those who devote themselves to the divine Word and have no other employment but the service of God may not unnaturally . . . be called our Levites and priests. And those who fulfill a more distinguished office than their kinsmen will perhaps be high priests, according to the order of Aaron (but not that of Melchizedek). Here someone may object that it is somewhat too bold to apply the name of "high priests" to men. For Jesus Himself is spoken of in many a prophetic passage as the one great priest. . . . For that reason, we say that men can be high priests according to the order of Aaron. However, as to the order of Melchizedek, only the Christ of God can be High Priest. *Origen (c. 228, E), 9.298.*

He immediately received the presbyterate and the priesthood. *Pontius the deacon (c. 258, W), 5.267.*

What kind of people do you think they are who are the enemies of the priests and are rebels against the catholic church? . . . Heresies have arisen and schisms have originated from no other source than this: that God's priest is not obeyed. *Cyprian (c. 250, W), 5.340.*

If we are priests of God and of Christ, I do not know anyone whom we ought rather to follow than God and Christ. *Cyprian (c. 250, W), 5.363.*

Give to the priest those things that are due to him—the first-fruits of your [threshing] floor and of your wine-press, along with sin offerings. For he is as a mediator between God and those who stand in need of purgation and forgiveness. *Apostolic Constitutions (compiled c. 390, E), 7.413.*

XI. Priesthood of all believers

I beseech you therefore, brethren, by the mercies of God, that you present your bodies a living sacrifice, holy, acceptable to God, which is your reasonable service. Rom. 12:1.

You also, as living stones, are being built up a spiritual house, a holy priesthood, to offer up spiritual sacrifices acceptable to God through Jesus Christ. 1 Pet. 2:5.

Blessed and holy is he who has part in the first resurrection. Over such the second death has no power, but they shall be priests of God and of Christ. Rev. 20:6.

David had been appointed as a priest by God, although Saul persecuted him. For all of the righteous possess the priestly rank. And all the disciples of the Lord are priests, for they inherit here neither lands nor houses. Rather, they serve God and the altar continually. . . . His disciples had a priesthood of the Lord. So, for them it was lawful when hungry to eat the ears of corn. *Irenaeus (c. 180, E/W), 1.471.*

In the preceding book, I have shown that all the disciples of the Lord are Levites and priests, . . . but they are blameless. *Irenaeus (c. 180, E/W), 1.564.*

The spiritual man is, then, the truly kingly man. He is the sacred high priest of God. *Clement of Alexandria (c. 195, E), 2.533.*

"But you are a chosen race, a royal priesthood." That we are a chosen race by the election of God is abundantly clear. He says "royal" because we are called to sovereignty and belong to Christ. He says "priesthood" because of the oblation that is made by prayers and instructions, through which souls are gained. *Clement of Alexandria (c. 195, E), 2.572.*

We are the true worshippers and the true priests who, praying in the spirit, offer a sacrifice in spirit: prayer, which is a proper and acceptable victim to God. *Tertullian (c. 198, W), 3.690.*

Vain will we be if we think that what is not lawful for priests is lawful for laity. Are not even we laymen priests? It is written: "He has made us a kingdom also and priests to His God and Father." It is the authority of the church, and the honor that has acquired sanctity through the body of ecclesiastical order, that has established the difference between the ordained and the laity. Accordingly, where there is no body of the ecclesiastical order, you [the layman] offer, baptize, and are priest, alone for yourself. For where there are three persons—even if they are laity—there is a church. . . . If you have the *right* of a priest in your own persons in cases of necessity, it behooves you to have likewise the *discipline* of a priest whenever it may be necessary to have the right of a priest. If you are twice-married, do you baptize? If you are twice-married, do you offer? How much more wrong is it for a twice-married layman to act as a priest, when the priest himself, if he becomes twice-married, is deprived of the power of acting as a priest! But you say, "to necessity, indulgence is granted." *Tertullian (c. 212, W), 4.54.*

[Demetrius] has added to his letter that this is a matter that was never heard of before, and has never been done: that laymen should take part is public speaking when there are bishops present. However, in this assertion, he has evidently departed far from the truth. . . . For, indeed, wherever there are found persons capable of profiting the brethren, such persons are exhorted by the holy bishops to address the people. *Alexander of Cappadocia (c. 250, E), 6.154.*

For he who will have kept the undertaking of virginity completely and will have faithfully fulfilled the precepts of the Decalogue . . . he is the true priest of Christ. *Victorinus (c. 280, W), 7.359.*

Let him who teaches, teach. This is true even if he is one of the laity—if he is skillful in the Word and serious in his living. *Apostolic Constitutions (compiled c. 390, E), 7.495.*

See also Alms, Almsgiving; Apostles, Twelve; Bishop; Celibacy; Church, The; Deacon; Minor Orders; Ordination; Presbyter; Reader; Tithes, Tithing; Twice-Married.

CHURCH LEADERSHIP

See Church Government.

CHURCHES, APOSTOLIC

I. Definition, function, and importance

II. Church at Antioch

III. Church at Corinth

IV. Church at Ephesus

V. Church at Philippi

VI. Church at Rome

I. Definition, function, and importance

For how does the case stand? Suppose there arises a dispute relative to some important question among us? Should we not have recourse to the most ancient churches with which the apostles had constant communication? Should we not learn from them what is certain and clear in regard to the question at hand? For how would it be if the apostles themselves had not left us writings? Would it not be necessary to follow the course of the tradition that they handed down to those to whom they did commit the churches? To which course, many nations of those barbarians who believe in Christ do agree. *Irenaeus (c. 180, E/W), 1.417.*

[The apostles] founded churches in every city, from which all the other churches—one after another—derived the tradition of the faith, and the seeds of doctrine. In fact, they are every day deriving them, so that they may become churches. Indeed, it is only on this account that they will be able to deem themselves apostolic—as being the offspring of apostolic churches. . . . Therefore, although the churches are so many and so great, they comprise but the one primitive church of the apostles. *Tertullian (c. 197, W), 3.252.*

Let the heretics contrive something of the same kind [i.e., a list of episcopal succession back to the apostles]. . . . However, even if they were to produce such a contrivance, they will not advance even one step. For when their very doctrine is compared with that of the apostles, its own diversity and discrepancy proves that it had neither an apostle nor an apostolic man for its authorship. . . . The heretics will be put to this test by those churches, who, although they do not have as their founder the apostles or apostolic men (as being of much later date, for churches are in fact being founded daily), yet, since they agree in the same faith, they are considered to be no less apostolic because they are alike in doctrine. Therefore, let all the heresies, when challenged to these two tests [i.e., episcopal succession and apostolic doctrine] by our apostolic church, offer their proof of how they consider themselves to be apostolic.... They are not admitted to peaceful relations and communion by the churches that are in any way connected with the apostles. For the heretics are in no sense themselves apostolic because of their diversity as to the mysteries of the faith. *Tertullian (c. 197, W), 3.258.*

Run over the apostolic churches, in which the very chairs of the apostles are still pre-eminent in their places, in which their own authentic writings are read.... Achaia is very near you, where you find Corinth. Since you are not far from Macedonia, you have Philippi. You also have the Thessalonians. Since you are able to cross to Asia, you have Ephesus, as well. Finally, since you are close to Italy, you have Rome, from which there comes into our own hands [i.e., in Carthage] the very authority [of the apostles]. *Tertullian (c. 197, W), 3.260.*

No other teaching will have the right of being received as apostolic than that which is at the present day proclaimed in the churches of apostolic foundation. You will, however, find no church of apostolic origin other than those who place their Christian faith in the Creator. But if the churches can be proved to have been corrupt from the beginning, where will the pure ones be found? Will it be among the adversaries of the Creator? Show us, then, one of your churches that can trace its descent from an apostle, and you will have gained the day. *Tertullian (c. 207, W), 3.286.*

If that [doctrine] has existed from the beginning which has the apostles for its authors, then it will certainly be quite evident that [the doctrine] which comes down from the apostles is that which has been kept as a sacred deposit in the churches of the apostles. Let us see what milk the Corinthians drank from Paul. Let us see to what rule of faith the Galatians were brought for correction. Let us see what the Philippians, the Thessalonians, and the Ephesians read. What utterance also do the Romans give, so very near [to Carthage], to whom Peter and Paul jointly bequeathed the Gospel, even sealing it with their own blood. We have also John's foster churches. *Tertullian (c. 207, W), 3.349, 350.*

In the same manner, the excellent source of the other churches is recognized. I say, therefore, that the Gospel of Luke that we are defending with all our might has stood its ground from its very first publication in them. It has stood, not simply in those churches that were founded by apostles, but in all of the churches that are united with them in the fellowship of the mystery of the gospel of Christ.... The same authority of the apostolic churches will afford defense of the other Gospels also, which we possess equally through their means, and according to their usage. *Tertullian (c. 207, W), 3.350.*

I have proposed [as models] those churches which were founded by apostles or apostolic men. *Tertullian (c. 207, W), 4.28.*

II. Church at Antioch

The disciples were first called Christians in Antioch. Acts 11:26.

Your prayer has reached to the church that is at Antioch in Syria.... Your church should elect some worthy delegate so that he, travelling to Syria, may congratulate them that they are at peace [from persecution] and are restored to their proper greatness. *Ignatius (c. 105, E), 1.91.*

III. Church at Corinth

To the church of God which is at Corinth.... I thank my God always concerning you for the grace of God which was given to you by Christ Jesus, that you were enriched in everything by Him in all utterance and all knowledge. 1 Cor. 1:1, 4.

The church of God that sojourns at Rome, to the church of God sojourning at Corinth.... What person has dwelled even for a short time among you, and did not find your faith to be as fruitful of virtue as it was firmly established? Who did not admire the sobriety and moderation of your godliness in Christ? Who did not proclaim the magnificence of your habitual hospitality? And who did not rejoice over your perfect and well-grounded knowledge? For you did all things without respect of persons, being obedient to those who had the rule over you. *Clement of Rome (c. 96, W), 1.5.*

It is disgraceful, beloved, yes, highly disgraceful and unworthy of your Christian profession, that such a thing should be heard of as that the most steadfast and ancient church of the Corinthians should ... engage in sedition against its presbyters. *Clement of Rome (c. 96, W), 1.18.*

... the churches that were planted by Peter and Paul, that of the Romans and that of the Corinthians. For both Peter and Paul came to our Corinth, and taught us in the same way as they taught you. *Dionysius of Corinth (c. 170), 8.765.*

In the time of this Clement, no small dissension occurred among the brethren at Corinth. So the church in Rome dispatched a most powerful letter to the Corinthians, exhorting them to peace, renewing their faith, and declaring the tradition which it had lately received from the apostles. *Irenaeus (c. 180, E/W), 1.416.*

Likewise, the Corinthians themselves understood him in this manner. In fact, at this very day, the Corinthians do veil their virgins. What the apostles taught, their disciples approve. *Tertullian (c. 207, W), 4.33.*

IV. Church at Ephesus

I also, after I heard of your faith in the Lord Jesus and your love for all the saints, do not cease to give thanks for you. Eph. 1:15.

To the angel of the church of Ephesus write, ... "I know your works, your labor, your patience, and that you cannot bear those who are evil. And you have tested those who say they are apostles and are not, and have found them liars; and you have persevered and have patience, and have labored for My name's sake and have not become weary. Nevertheless I have this against you, that you have left your first love. Rev. 2:1–4.

... to the church that is at Ephesus, in Asia, deservedly most happy, being blessed in the greatness and fullness of God the Father, and predestined before the beginning of time that it would have an enduring and unchangeable glory. *Ignatius (c. 105, E), 1.49.*

The church in Ephesus was founded by Paul, and John remained among them permanently until the times of Trajan. It is a true witness of the tradition of the apostles. *Irenaeus (c. 180, E/W), 1.416.*

V. Church at Philippi

Polycarp and the presbyters with him, to the church of God sojourning at Philippi: ... I have greatly rejoiced with you in our Lord Jesus Christ because you have followed the example of true love ... and because the strong root of your faith (spoken of in days long gone by) endures even until now. *Polycarp (c. 135, E), 1.33.*

If a man does not keep himself from covetousness, he shall be defiled by idolatry and shall be judged as one of the Gentiles.... However, I have neither seen nor heard of any such thing among you [Philippians], in the midst of whom the blessed Paul labored. In fact, you are commended in the beginning of his epistle. For he boasts of you among all those churches which alone then knew the Lord. *Polycarp (c. 135, E), 1.35.*

VI. Church at Rome

To all who are in Rome, beloved of God, called to be saints.... I thank my God through Jesus Christ for you all, that your faith is spoken of throughout the whole world. Rom. 1:1, 8.

The church of God that sojourns at Rome, to the church of God sojourning at Corinth.... We have been somewhat tardy in turning our attention to the points respecting which you consulted us. *Clement of Rome (c. 96, W), 1.5.*

... to the church that has obtained mercy, through the majesty of the Most High Father and Jesus Christ, His Only-Begotten Son. To the church that is beloved and enlightened by the will of Him who wills all things, ... which also presides in the place of the region of the Romans, worthy of God, worthy of honor, worthy of the highest happiness, worthy of praise, worthy of obtaining her every desire, worthy of being deemed holy, and which presides over love. *Ignatius (c. 105, E), 1.73.*

For this has been your custom from the beginning, to do good to all the brethren in various ways, and to send resources to many churches which are in every city. You thus refreshed the poverty of the needy, and you granted subsidies to the brethren who are in the mines. Through the resources which you have sent from the beginning, you Romans keep up the custom of the Romans handed down by the fathers. Your blessed bishop Soter has not only preserved this custom, but he has added to it. For he sent a splendid gift to the saints, and he exhorted with blessed words those brethren who go up to Rome, as an affectionate father his children. *Dionysius of Corinth (c. 170), 8.765.*

Therefore you also have by such admonition joined in close union the churches that were planted by Peter and Paul, that of the Romans and that of the Corinthians. For both Peter and Paul came to our Corinth, and taught us in the same way as they taught you when they went to

Italy. And having taught you, they suffered martyrdom at the same time. *Dionysius of Corinth (c. 170), 8.765.*

Since, however, it would be very tedious in such a volume as this to reckon up the successions of all the churches, we put to confusion all those who, in whatever manner (whether by an evil self-pleasing by vainglory, or by blindness and perverse opinion), assemble in unauthorized meetings. [We do this] by indicating that tradition derived from the apostles, of the very great, the very ancient, and universally known church founded and organized at Rome by the two most glorious apostles, Peter and Paul. We do this also [by pointing out] the faith preached to men, which comes down to our time by means of the successions of the bishops. For it is a matter of necessity that every church should agree with this church, on account of its pre-eminent authority, that is, the faithful everywhere. For the apostolic tradition has been preserved continuously by those who exist everywhere. The blessed apostles, then, having founded and built up the church, committed into the hands of Linus the office of the episcopate. Of this Linus, Paul makes mention in the epistles to Timothy. . . . And this is most abundant proof that there is one and the same vivifying faith, which has been preserved in the church from the apostles until now, and handed down in truth. *Irenaeus (c. 180, E/W), 1.415, 416.*

In the third place from the apostles, Clement was allotted the bishopric. This man, as he had seen the blessed apostles, and had been conversant with them, might be said to have the preaching of the apostles still echoing and their traditions before his eyes. Nor was he alone, for there were many still remaining who had received instructions from the apostles. In the time of this Clement, no small dissension occurred among the brethren at Corinth. The church in Rome dispatched a most powerful letter to the Corinthians, exhorting them to peace, renewing their faith, and declaring the tradition which it had lately received from the apostles. *Irenaeus (c. 180, E/W), 1.416.*

But Polycarp also was not only instructed by apostles, and conversed with many who had seen Christ, but was also, by apostles in Asia, appointed bishop of the church in Smyrna. . . . He it was who, coming to Rome in the time of Anicetus, caused many to turn away

from the aforesaid heretics to the church of God. *Irenaeus (c. 180, E/W), 1.416.*

Run over the apostolic churches, in which the very chairs of the apostles are still pre-eminent in their places. . . . Since you are able to cross to Asia, you have Ephesus. Since, moreover, you are close to Italy, you have Rome, from which there comes even into our own hands [in Carthage] the very authority [of the apostles]. How happy is its church, on which apostles poured forth all their doctrine along with their blood! Here is where Peter endured a passion like his Lord's. Here is where Paul won his crown in a death like John's. Here is where the Apostle John was first plunged, unhurt, into boiling oil. From there, he was sent to his island of exile. See what she has learned, what she has taught, what fellowship has had with even churches in Africa. *Tertullian (c. 197, W), 3.260.*

I can show the trophies of the apostles. For if you choose to go to the Vatican or to the Ostian Road, you will find the trophies of those who founded this church. *Eusebius, quoting Caius (c. 215, W), 5.601.*

Cyprian, to his brothers, the presbyters and deacons assembled at Rome, greeting. *Cyprian (c. 250, W), 5.294.*

The presbyters and deacons abiding at Rome, to father Cyprian, greetings. Beloved brother, we carefully read your letter that you had sent by Fortunatus, the subdeacon. *Letter from the Roman clergy to Cyprian (c. 250, W), 5.307.*

This is read among us as the ancient rigor, the ancient faith, the ancient discipline. For the apostle would not have published such praise about us (when he said, "your faith is spoken of throughout the whole world"), unless that vigor had already borrowed the roots of faith from those times. And it is a very great crime to have become degenerate from such praise and glory. For it is less of a disgrace never to have attained to the heraldry of praise, than to have fallen from the height of praise. . . . It is less discredit to have lain without the announcement of virtues, to be lowly without praise, than to have lost our proper praises, being disinherited of the faith. For the things that are proclaimed to the glory of someone can puff him up into the odium of the greatest crime. So they must be maintained with anxious and careful pains. *Letter from the Roman clergy to Cyprian (c. 250, W), 5.308.*

From her greatness, Rome plainly should take precedence over Carthage. Therefore, he therefore committed still greater and graver crimes. *Cyprian (c. 250, W), 5.325.*

They still dare . . . to set sail and to bear letters from schismatic and profane persons to the chair of Peter and to the chief church from which priestly unity takes its source! They forget that these were the Romans whose faith was praised in the preaching of the apostle, to whom faithlessness could have no access. *Cyprian (c. 250, W), 5.344.*

SEE ALSO APOSTOLIC FAITH, THE; BISHOP (II. BISHOP OF ROME); CHURCH, THE; TRADITION (II. APOSTOLIC TRADITION).

CICERO

Marcus Tullius Cicero (106–43 B.C.) was a prominent Roman statesman, orator, and Stoic philosopher.

Cicero's eminence was foreseen by his nurse, while he was still a little boy. *Tertullian (c. 210, W), 3.225.*

Cicero, following and imitating [Plato] in many instances, frequently acknowledges God and calls Him supreme. . . . [HE WRITES:] "Nothing is superior to God. Therefore, the world must be governed by Him." *Lactantius (c. 304–313, W), 7.15.*

Marcus Tullius was not only an accomplished orator, but also a philosopher (for he alone was an imitator of Plato). . . . He did not hesitate to say that those gods who were publicly worshipped were men. *Lactantius (c. 304–313, W), 7.27.*

It is a well-known saying of Cicero: "I wish that I could as easily find out what is true as I can refute what is false." *Lactantius (c. 304–313, W), 7.44*

[SAID OF CICERO:] That greatest imitator of Plato among our [Roman] writers thought that philosophy was not for the multitudes. *Lactantius (c. 304–313, W), 7.95.*

What does Marcus Tullius say in his books on *Offices*? Does he not advise that almsgiving should not be employed at all? . . . If Cicero were now alive, I would certainly exclaim: "Here, Marcus Tullius—here you have erred from true justice! *Lactantius (c. 304–313, W), 7.174, 175.*

Cicero says . . . : "It is highly becoming that the houses of illustrious men should be open to illustrious guests." Here he has committed the same error as before. . . . For the house of a just and wise man should not be open to the illustrious, but to the lowly and downcast. *Lactantius (c. 304–313, W), 7.176.*

CIRCUMCISION

He is not a Jew who is one outwardly, nor is that circumcision which is outward in the flesh; but he is a Jew who is one inwardly, and circumcision is that of the heart. Rom. 2:28, 29.

Indeed I, Paul, say to you that if you become circumcised, Christ will profit you nothing. And I testify again to every man who becomes circumcised that he is a debtor to keep the whole law. Gal. 5:2, 3.

He declared that circumcision was not of the flesh. Rather, [the Jews] transgressed because an evil angel deluded them. . . . But you will say, "Yes, truly the people are circumcised for a seal." Yet, so is every Syrian, Arab, and all the priests of idols, as well. So are these people, then, also within the bond of His covenant? In fact, the Egyptians practice circumcision, too. *Barnabas (c. 70–130, E), 1.142.*

The inability of the female sex to receive fleshly circumcision proves that circumcision was given for a sign. It was not given as a work of righteousness. *Justin Martyr (c. 160, E), 1.206.*

[SPEAKING TO JEWS:] Your first circumcision was and is performed by iron instruments, for you remain hard-hearted. However, our circumcision is the second circumcision, because it has been instituted after yours. It circumcises us from idolatry and from absolutely every form of wickedness. *Justin Martyr (c. 160, E), 1.256.*

God gave circumcision as a sign, not as the completion of righteousness. *Irenaeus (c. 180, E/W), 1.480.*

We do not follow the Jews in their peculiarities in regard to food, nor in their sacred days, nor even in their well-known bodily sign. *Tertullian (c. 197, W), 3.34.*

Let the one who contends that . . . circumcision on the eighth day is still to be observed because of the threat of death, . . . prove to us that in ancient times righteous men kept the Sabbath or practiced circumcision, and were thereby made "friends of God." God created

Adam uncircumcised and non-observant of the Sabbath. Why did God not circumcise him—even after his sinning—if circumcision purges? . . . Furthermore, God freed from the deluge Noah, who was uncircumcised and did not observe the Sabbath. Enoch, too, God transported from this world, even though that most righteous man was uncircumcised and did not observe the Sabbath. . . . Melchizedek also, "the priest of the most high God," although uncircumcised and not observing the Sabbath, was chosen to the priesthood of God. *Tertullian (c. 197, W), 3.153.*

Therefore, for all those who had been delivered from the yoke of slavery, he would earnestly have to obliterate circumcision, the very mark of slavery. *Tertullian (c. 207, W), 3.437.*

Celsus [a pagan critic] does not condemn circumcision as practiced by the Jews. Rather, he claims that this practice was derived from the Egyptians. He thus believes the Egyptians rather than Moses, who says that Abraham was the first among men to practice this rite. . . . However, the rite of circumcision began with Abraham and was discontinued by Jesus, who desired that His disciples should not practice it. *Origen (c. 248, E), 4.405.*

Probably [circumcision] was performed on account of the hostility of some angel towards the Jewish nation, who had the power to injure those of them who were not circumcised. Yet, he was powerless against those who had undergone the rite. This may be said to appear from what is written in the book of Exodus, where the angel was able to work against Moses before the circumcision of Eliezer, but could not do anything after his son was circumcised. . . . However, this power lasted only so long as Jesus had not assumed a human body. But when He had become human and had undergone the rite of circumcision in His own person, all the power of the angel was abolished over those persons who practice the same worship, but are not circumcised. For Jesus reduced it to nothing by His unspeakable divinity. Therefore, His disciples are forbidden to circumcise themselves. They are reminded: "If you become circumcised, Christ will profit you nothing." *Origen (c. 248, E), 4.564.*

Concerning the abolishing of circumcision, Isaiah prophesied in this manner: . . . "Circum-cise yourselves to the Lord your God and take away the foreskins of your heart." *Lactantius (c. 304–313, W), 7.118.*

The circumcision of the flesh is plainly irrational. For, if God had so willed it, he could have formed man from the beginning without a foreskin. However, [fleshly circumcision] was a figure of this second circumcision, signifying . . . that we should live with an open and simple heart. *Lactantius (c. 304–313, W), 7.119.*

I, who have been made rich by the grace of God, and who have obtained the circumcision of the heart, cannot by any means stand in need of that most profitless circumcision. And, yet, having said that, it does not follow that I should call it evil. Far be it from me to do so! *Disputation of Archelaus and Manes (c. 320, E), 6.218; see also 3.153–3.155.*

SEE ALSO JEWISH CHRISTIANITY; LAW, MOSAIC.

CLASS DISTINCTIONS
SEE EQUALITY OF MANKIND.

CLEMENT OF ALEXANDRIA
Clement of Alexandria (c. 150–200) was the head of the catechetical school in the church at Alexandria. His most famous pupil was Origen.

Besides, there are writings of certain brethren older than the times of Victor, which they wrote against the pagans in defense of the truth and against the heresies of their day. I mean Justin, Miltiades, Tatian, Clement, and many others. In all their writings, divinity is ascribed to Christ. *Eusebius, quoting Caius (c. 215, W), 5.601.*

I have sent . . . this letter by the hand of the blessed presbyter Clement, a man virtuous and well tried, whom you already know. [This may or may not be a reference to Clement of Alexandria.] *Alexander of Cappadocia (c. 250, E), 6.154.*

We are well acquainted with those blessed fathers who have trodden the course before, and to whom we too will soon go: namely, Pantaenus, the truly blessed man, my master; and also the holy Clement, who was once my master and my benefactor. *Alexander of Cappadocia (c. 250, E), 6.154.*

Our predecessors, men most learned in the books of the Hebrews and Greeks (I refer to Isidore, Jerome, and Clement), . . . come harmoniously to one and the same most exact determination of Easter. *Anatolius (c. 270, E), 6.146.*

CLEMENT OF ROME

Clement of Rome (c. 30–100) was a bishop in the church at Rome and was probably a disciple of both Peter and Paul. He may have been the person referred to in Philippians 4:3:

I urge you also, true companion, help these women who labored with me in the gospel, with Clement also, and the rest of my fellow workers, whose names are in the Book of Life. Phil. 4:3.

Therefore, you will write two books, and you will send the first to Clement and the other to Grapte. And Clement will send his to foreign countries, for permission has been granted to him to do so. *Hermas (c. 150, W), 2.12.*

In the third place from the apostles, Clement was allotted the bishopric. Since he had seen the blessed apostles and had been conversant with them, this man might be said to have the preaching of the apostles still echoing in his ears and their traditions still before his eyes. Nor was he alone. For there were many others still remaining who had received instructions from the apostles. In the time of this Clement, no small dissension occurred among the brethren at Corinth. So the church in Rome dispatched a most powerful letter to the Corinthians, exhorting them to peace, renewing their faith, and declaring the tradition which it had lately received from the apostles. *Irenaeus (c. 180, E/W), 1.416.*

Now Clement, in his Epistle to the Corinthians, while expounding the differences of those who are approved according to the church, says expressly, "One may be a believer; one may be powerful in uttering knowledge." *Clement of Alexandria (c. 195, E), 2.308.*

In the Epistle to the Corinthians, the apostle Clement . . . says, "For who that has sojourned among you has not proved your perfect and firm faith?" *Clement of Alexandria (c. 195, E), 2.428.*

Clement, in the Epistle to the Corinthians, says, "The greater someone seems to be, the more humble he should be." *Clement of Alexandria (c. 195, E), 2.495.*

Clement, indeed a disciple of the apostles, makes mention of those whom the Greeks called *Antichthones*, and other parts of the earth, to which none of our people can approach. *Origen (c. 225, E), 4.273.*

But from what Clement seems to indicate when he says, "The ocean is impassable to men, and those worlds which are behind it," speaking in the plural number of the worlds, . . . he wished the globe of the sun or moon—and of the other bodies called planets—to each be called "worlds." *Origen (c. 225, E), 4.274.*

Paul bears witness to the faithful Clement . . . when he says, "With Clement also, and the others, my fellow workers, whose names are in the book of life." *Origen (c. 228, E), 9.377.*

Clement, the bishop and citizen of Rome, was the disciple of Paul. *Apostolic Constitutions (compiled c. 390, E), 7.453.*

Papias of Hierapolis, the illustrious, was a disciple of the apostle who leaned on the bosom of Christ. He was also a disciple of Clement. *Anastasius Sinaita, post-Nicene writer, 1.155; see also 2.429.*

CLERGY
See Church Government.

CLERGY, SECOND MARRIAGES OF
See Twice-Married.

CLOTHING

I. Exhortations on simple and modest clothing

II. Dyeing of clothing

I. Exhortations on simple and modest clothing

A woman will not wear anything that pertains to a man, nor will a man put on a woman's garment, for all who do so are an abomination to the Lord your God. Deut. 22:5.

In like manner also, [I desire] that the women adorn themselves in modest apparel, with propriety and moderation, not with braided hair or gold or pearls or costly clothing. 1 Tim. 2:9, 10.

Do not let your beauty be that outward adorning of arranging the hair, of wearing gold, or of putting on fine apparel. 1 Pet. 3:3.

A virgin meets me, adorned as if she were proceeding from the bridal chamber, clothed entirely in white, and with white sandals, and veiled up to her forehead, and her head was covered by a hood. *Hermas (c. 150, W), 2.18.*

By no means are women to be allowed to uncover and exhibit any part of their bodies, lest both fall—the men by being incited to look, and the women by attracting to themselves the eyes of the men. *Clement of Alexandria (c. 195, E), 2.246.*

Neither are we to provide for ourselves costly clothing. *Clement of Alexandria (c. 195, E), 2.263.*

I say, then, that man requires clothes for nothing else than the covering of the body, for defense against excess of cold and intensity, lest the inclemency of the air injure us. And if this is the purpose of clothing, see that one kind is not assigned to men and another to women. For it is common to both to be covered, as it is to eat and drink.... And if some accommodation is to be made, women may be permitted to use softer clothes, provided they avoid fabrics that are foolishly thin and of curious texture in weaving. They should also bid farewell to embroidery of gold and Indian silks. *Clement of Alexandria (c. 195, E), 2.265.*

Luxurious clothing that cannot conceal the shape of the body is no more a covering. For such clothing, falling close to the body, takes its form more easily. Clinging to the body as though it were the flesh, it receives its shape and outlines the woman's figure. As a result, the whole make of the body is visible to spectators, although they cannot see the body itself. Dyeing of clothes is also to be rejected.... But for those persons who are white and unstained within, it is most suitable to use white and simple garments. *Clement of Alexandria (c. 195, E), 2.265.*

Neither is it seemly for the clothes to be above the knee. *Clement of Alexandria (c. 195, E), 2.266.*

Buying, as they do, a single dress at the price of ten thousand talents, they prove themselves to be of less use and less value than cloth. *Clement of Alexandria (c. 195, E), 2.267.*

Women should for the most part wear shoes. For it is not suitable for the foot to be shown naked. Besides, woman is a tender thing, easily hurt. But for a man, bare feet are quite in keeping, except when he is on military service. *Clement of Alexandria (c. 195, E), 2.267.*

Those who glory in their looks—not in their hearts—dress to please others. *Clement of Alexandria (c. 195, E), 2.273.*

The wearing of gold and the use of softer clothing is not to be entirely prohibited. Nevertheless, irrational cravings must be curbed. ... The Instructor permits us, then, to use simple clothing, that of a white color, as we said before.... As in the case of the soldier, the sailor, and the ruler, so also the proper dress of the temperate man is what is plain, becoming, and clean. *Clement of Alexandria (c. 195, E), 2.284.*

Let a woman wear a plain and becoming dress, but softer than what is suitable for a man. Yet, it should not be immodest or entirely steeped in luxury. And let the garments be suited to age, person, figure, nature, and pursuits. *Clement of Alexandria (c. 195, E), 2.285.*

It is never suitable for women whose lives are framed according to God to appear in public clothed in things bought from the market. Rather, they should be clothed in their own homemade work. For a most beautiful thing is a thrifty wife, who clothes both herself and her husband. *Clement of Alexandria (c. 195, E), 2.287.*

Woman and man are to go to church decently attired, with natural step, embracing silence.... Let the woman observe this, further: Let her be entirely covered, unless she happens to be at home. For that style of dress is serious and protects from being gazed at. And she will never fall, who puts before her eyes modesty and her veil. Nor will she invite another to fall into sin by uncovering her face. For this is the wish of the Word, since it is becoming for her to pray veiled. *Clement of Alexandria (c. 195, E), 2.290.*

What reason is there in the Law's prohibition against a man wearing woman's clothing? Is it not that it would have us to be masculine and not to be effeminate in either person or actions? *Clement of Alexandria (c. 195, E), 2.365.*

In His Law, it is declared that the man is cursed who wears female garments. So what must His judgment be of the pantomime, who is even trained to act the part of a woman? *Tertullian (c. 197, W), 3.89.*

Concerning modesty of dress and embellishments, indeed, the commandment of Peter is likewise plain, restraining as he does with the same mouth ... the glory of garments, the pride of gold, and the showy elaboration of the hair. *Tertullian (c. 198, W), 3.687.*

First, then, blessed sisters, take heed that you do not admit to your use flashy and sluttish garbs and clothing. *Tertullian (c. 198, W), 4.22.*

But it is argued by some, "Let not the Name be blasphemed in us, if we make any derogatory change from our old style and dress." Let us, then, not abolish our old vices! Let us maintain the same character! ... And then the nations will not blaspheme! *Tertullian (c. 198, W), 4.24.*

I find no dress cursed by God except when a woman's dress is on a man. For he says, "Cursed is every man who clothes himself in woman's attire." *Tertullian (c. 200, W), 3.71.*

The dress of a modest woman should be modest. A believer should not be conscious of adultery even in the mixture of colors. *Novatian (c. 235, W), 5.591, formerly attributed to Cyprian.*

But self-control and modesty do not consist only in purity of the flesh, but also in seemliness and in modesty of dress and adornment. *Cyprian (c. 250, W), 5.431; extended discussion: 5.430–5.436.*

II. Dyeing of clothing

As we said before, the Instructor permits us to use simple clothing, and those of a white color. . . . White colors are befitting to seriousness. *Clement of Alexandria (c. 195, E), 2.284.*

What legitimate honor can garments derive from adulteration with illegitimate colors? That which He Himself has not produced is not pleasing to God—unless He was unable to order sheep to be born with purple and sky-blue fleeces! If He was *able*, then plainly He was *unwilling*. What God did not will, of course should not be fashioned. *Tertullian (c. 198, W), 4.17.*

God neither made the sheep scarlet nor purple, nor taught the extracts of herbs and shellfish to dye and color wool. *Cyprian (c. 250, W), 5.434.*

SEE ALSO COSMETICS; GROOMING; JEWELRY; MODESTY; PERFUME; VEIL; WORLD, SEPARATION FROM.

COMMUNION

SEE EUCHARIST.

COMMUNITY OF GOODS

Now all who believed were together, and had all things in common, and sold their possessions and goods, and divided them among all, as anyone had need. Acts 2:44, 45.

Now the multitude of those who believed were of one heart and one soul; neither did anyone say that any of the things he possessed was his own, but they had all things in common. Acts 4:32.

You will share all things with your neighbor. You will not call things your own. For if you are partakers in common of things that are incorruptible, how much more [should you be] of those things which are corruptible. *Barnabas (c. 70–130, E), 1.148.*

We who used to value above everything the acquisition of wealth and possessions, now bring what we have into a common stock, and share with everyone in need. *Justin Martyr (c. 160, E), 1.167.*

All things therefore are common, and not for the rich to appropriate an undue share. Therefore, the expression, "I possess and possess in abundance; why then should I not enjoy?" is suitable neither to the man, nor to society. But more worthy of love is this: "I have; why should I not give to those who need?" ... I know very well that God has given to us the liberty of use. But only so far as is necessary. And He has determined that the use should be common. For it is monstrous for one to live in luxury, while many are in need. *Clement of Alexandria (c. 195, E), 2.268.*

[ADDRESSED TO PAGANS:] Family possessions, which usually destroy brotherhood among *you*, create fraternal bonds among *us*. Being one in mind and soul, we do not hesitate to share our earthly goods with one another. All things are common among us, except our wives. *Tertullian (c. 197, W), 3.46.*

SEE ALSO ALMS, ALMSGIVING; CHRISTIAN LIFE.

CONCEPTION

If men fight, and hurt a woman with child, so that she gives birth prematurely, . . . if any lasting harm follows, then you will give life for life, eye for eye, tooth for tooth. Ex. 21:22–24.

[ADDRESSED TO EXPECTANT MOTHERS:] Tell us whether you feel in the embryo within you any vital force other than your own. For your bowels tremble, your sides shake, your entire womb throbs, and the burden that affects you constantly changes its position. Are not these movements a joy to you and a positive removal of anxiety? Does this not make you confident that your infant both possesses vitality and enjoys it? If his restlessness stopped, your first fear would be for him. *Tertullian (c. 210, W), 3.205.*

Life begins with conception, for we contend that the soul also begins from conception. Life takes its commencement at the same place and time that the soul does. *Tertullian (c. 210, W), 3.207.*

Nature should be to us an object of reverence, not of blushes. It is lust—not natural usage—that has brought shame on the intercourse of the sexes. It is the *excess*, not the normal state, that is immodest and unchaste. The normal condition has received a blessing from God, and is blessed by Him. *Tertullian (c. 210, W), 3.208.*

Now the entire process of sowing, forming, and completing the human embryo in the womb is no doubt regulated by some power, which ministers therein to the will of God— regardless of what may be the method that it is appointed to employ.... We, on our part, believe the angels to officiate herein for God. The embryo, therefore, becomes a human being in the womb from the moment that its form is completed. *Tertullian (c. 210, W), 3.217.*

The flesh and the soul have a simultaneous birth, without any calculable difference in time. *Tertullian (c. 210, W), 3.578.*

If we become injured in the womb, this is a loss suffered by what is already a human being. *Tertullian (c. 210, W), 3.589.*

The soul is not introduced into the body after birth, as some philosophers think. Rather, it is introduced immediately after conception, when the divine necessity has formed the offspring in the womb. *Lactantius (c. 304–313, W), 7.297.*

SEE ALSO ABORTION, INFANTICIDE; CHILDBIRTH; PROCREATION.

CONFESSION OF SINS

Confess your trespasses to one another, and pray for one another, that you may be healed. Jas. 5:16.

If we confess our sins, he is faithful and just to forgive us our sins. 1 John 1:9.

In the congregation, confess your sins; do not come to your prayer with an evil conscience. *Didache (c. 80–140, E), 7.378.*

The Lord . . . desires nothing of anyone, except that confession be made to Him. *Clement of Rome (c. 96, W), 1.19.*

I took courage, bent my knees, and once again confessed my sins to God, just as I had done before. *Hermas (c. 150, W), 2.12.*

His wife, a woman of remarkable beauty, became a victim both in mind and body to this magician. For a long time, she travelled about with him. At last, when, with no small difficulty, the brethren had converted her, she spent her whole time in the exercise of public confession, weeping over and lamenting the defilement which she had received from this magician. *Irenaeus (c. 180, E/W), 1.335.*

By the confession of all past sins, they may express the meaning even of the baptism of John. For the Scripture says: "They were baptized, confessing their own sins." To us, it is a matter for thankfulness if we now do publicly confess our iniquities or our depravities. For, by mortification of our flesh and spirit, we make satisfaction for our former sins. At the same time, we lay in advance the foundation of defenses against the temptations that will closely follow. *Tertullian (c. 198, W), 3.678, 679.*

In smaller sins, sinners may do penance for a set time and come to public confession according to the rules of discipline. *Cyprian (c. 250, W), 5.290.*

I entreat you, beloved brethren, that each one should confess his own sins while he is still in this world—while his confession can still be received and while the satisfaction and remission made by the priests are still pleasing to the Lord. *Cyprian (c. 250, W), 5.445.*

SEE ALSO ABSOLUTION; DISCIPLINE, CHURCH (III. PENITENTIAL DISCIPLINE); FORGIVENESS OF SINS.

CONFESSORS

A "confessor" was a person who endured imprisonment, torture, or some other form of suffering (short of martyrdom) because of publicly confessing the name of Christ. Some confessors were later martyred.

Whoever confesses me before men, him I will also confess before My Father. Matt. 10:32.

Remember the prisoners as if chained with them, and those who are mistreated, since you yourselves are in the body also. Heb. 13:3.

Moreover, let a more earnest care be bestowed upon the glorious confessors. I know that very many of them have been maintained by the vow and by the love of the brethren. Still, if there are any who are in need of either clothing or care, let them be supplied. . . . Only let them know from you and be instructed and learn what the discipline of the church requires of them, according to the authority of Scripture. Let them know that they should be humble, modest, and peaceable. They should maintain the honor of their name, so that those who have achieved glory by what they have testified may achieve glory also by their characters. . . . For there remains more than what is yet seen to be accomplished. For it is written, "Praise not any man before his death." And again, "Be faithful unto death, and I will give you a crown of life." And the Lord also says, "He that endures to the end, the same will be saved."

Let them imitate the Lord, who at the very time of His passion was not more proud, but more humble. For then He washed his disciples' feet, saying, "If I, your Lord and master, have washed your feet, you also should wash one another's feet." . . . Let them also follow the example of the apostle Paul, who, after often-repeated imprisonment, after scourging, after exposures to wild beasts, continued to be meek and humble in everything. Even after his rapture to the third heaven and Paradise, he did not proudly arrogate anything to himself. . . . For I am grieved when I hear that some of the confessors run about wickedly and proudly and give themselves up to follies or to discords. I hear that members of Christ, and even members who have confessed Christ, are defiled by unlawful concubinage and cannot be ruled by either deacons or by presbyters. Because of the wicked and evil characters of a few, the honorable glories of the many good confessors are tarnished. They should fear, lest, being condemned by their testimony and judgment, they are excluded from their fellowship. *Cyprian (c. 250, W), 5.283.*

Cyprian, to the presbyter, Rogatian, and to the other confessors, his brethren. . . . I exhort you by our common faith, by the true and simple love of my heart towards you, that, having overcome the adversary in this first encounter, you should hold fast your glory with a brave and persevering virtue. . . . But I hear that some infect your number and destroy the praise of a distinguished name by their corrupt lifestyle. You yourselves, even as being lovers and guardians of your own praise, should rebuke, restrain, and correct. For what a disgrace is suffered by your name when one spends his days in intoxication and debauchery. *Cyprian (c. 250, W), 5.283, 284.*

I have heard that you have received the ministry of the purpled ones [i.e., confessors and martyrs]. Oh, happy are you, even sleeping on the ground, to obtain your wishes that you have always desired! You have desired to be sent into prison for His name's sake, which now has come to pass. *Letter to Lucian (c. 250, W), 5.298.*

The dignity of martyrdom was not the less in the case of the three youths, . . . simply because they came forth the same from the fiery furnace. . . . Among confessors of Christ, deferred martyrdoms do not diminish the merits of confession. Rather, they demonstrate the greatness of divine protection. *Cyprian (c. 250, W), 5.352.*

Confession is the beginning of glory, not the full desert of the crown. *Cyprian (c. 250, W), 5.428; see also 5.282, 5.295.*

SEE ALSO LAPSED; MARTYRS, MARTYRDOM.

CONFIRMATION

SEE HANDS, LAYING ON OF; OIL, ANOINTING WITH.

CONSTANTINE

Emperors Constantine (c. 274–337) and Licinius issued the Edict of Milan in 313, giving full legal recognition to Christianity for the first time. Constantine convened the Council of Nicaea in 325 and began the process that eventually led to the full union of church and state. He was baptized on his deathbed. The following quotations are all from Lactantius, whom Constantine summoned to tutor his son, Crispus.

We now commence this work under the auspices of your name, O mighty Emperor Constantine, who was the first of the Roman rulers to repudiate errors and to acknowledge and honor the majesty of the one and only true

God. For when that most happy day had shone upon the world, in which the Most High God raised you to the prosperous height of power, you entered upon a dominion that was both salutary and desirable for all. *Lactantius (c. 304–313, W), 7.10.*

All fictions have now been hushed, most holy Emperor—ever since the time when the great God raised you up for the restoration of the house of justice and for the protection of the human race. For while you rule the Roman state, we worshippers of God are no longer regarded as accursed and impious.... The providence of the supreme Deity has raised you to the imperial dignity so that you might, with true piety, rescind the injurious decrees of others. ... The powerful right hand of God protects you from all dangers. He bestows on you a quiet and tranquil reign, with the highest congratulations of all men. And not undeservedly has the Lord and Ruler of the world chosen you in preference to all others, by whom He might renew His holy religion. ... We supplicate Him with daily prayers that He may especially guard you, whom He has wished to be the guardian of the world. *Lactantius (c. 304–313, W), 7.221, 222.*

Constantius also had a son, Constantine. He was a young man of very great worth and well deserving the high station of Caesar. The distinguished comeliness of his figure, his strict attention to all military duties, his virtuous demeanor and singular friendliness—all these had endeared him to the troops and made him the choice of every individual. *Lactantius (c. 320, W), 7.308.*

Constantine Augustus, having assumed the government, made it his first task to restore Christians to the exercise of their worship and to their God. *Lactantius (c. 320, W), 7.311.*

Constantine was directed in a dream to cause the heavenly sign to be outlined on the shields of his soldiers and so to proceed to battle. He did as he had been commanded. And he marked on their shields the letter X, with a perpendicular line drawn through it and turned round at the top—being the monogram of Christ. *Lactantius (c. 320, W), 7.318.*

SEE ALSO DIOCLETIAN; EDICT OF MILAN.

CONVERSION

I. Christianity changes lives

II. Testimonies of conversion

I. Christianity changes lives

Assuredly, I say to you, unless you are converted and become as little children, you will by no means enter the kingdom of heaven. Matt. 18:3.

Repent therefore and be converted, that your sins may be blotted out, so that times of refreshing may come from the presence of the Lord. Acts 3:19.

Some persons wonder that those whom they had known to be unsteady, worthless, or wicked before they bore this name have suddenly been converted to virtuous courses. Yet, unfortunately, they are better at wondering at it than at attaining it. *Tertullian (c. 197, W), 3.112.*

In Greek, the word for repentance is formed—not from the confession of a sin—but from a change of mind. *Tertullian (c. 207, W), 3.316.*

The Logos of instruction takes hold of those who are most intemperate and savage and brings about a transformation, so that the alteration and change for the better is most extensive. *Origen (c. 225, E), 4.304.*

The multitude of the church is astonished at beholding transformations that have taken place from very great evils to that which is better. *Origen (c. 245, E), 9.447.*

No improvement ever takes place among men without divine help. How much more confidently will a person make the same assertion regarding Jesus, when he compares the former lives of many converts to His doctrine with their later conduct. This is especially so if he reflects on what acts of licentiousness, injustice, and covetousness they formerly indulged in.... Yet, these same persons, from the time that they adopted [Christianity], have become in some way meeker, more religious, and more consistent. *Origen (c. 248, E), 4.407.*

The name of Jesus ... produces a marvelous meekness of spirit and a complete change of character. *Origen (c. 248, E), 4.427.*

Observe whether the principles of our faith, harmonizing with the general ideas implanted in our minds at birth, do not produce a change upon those who listen candidly to its statements. *Origen (c. 248, E), 4.480.*

II. Testimonies of conversion

When I was delighting in the doctrines of Plato, I heard Christians being slandered. Yet, I saw that they were fearless in death and unafraid of all other things that are considered fearful. And I realized that it was impossible that they could be living in wickedness and pleasure. For what sensual or intemperate person . . . could welcome death, which would deprive him of his enjoyments? Such a person would prefer to continue always in the present life. *Justin Martyr (c. 160, E), 1.192.*

When this Christian had spoken these and many other things (which there is no time for mentioning at present) he went away, exhorting me to attend to them. And I have not seen him since. But immediately a flame was kindled in my soul—and I was possessed by a love of the prophets and of those men who are friends of Christ. *Justin Martyr (c. 165, E), 1.198.*

Retiring by myself, I sought how I might be able to discover the truth. And, while I was giving my most earnest attention to the matter, I happened to meet with certain barbaric writings, too old to be compared with the opinions of the Greeks—yet too divine to be compared with their errors. And I was led to put faith in them by the unpretentious nature of the language, the candid character of the writers, the foreknowledge displayed of future events, the excellent quality of the teachings, and the declaration that the government of the universe is centered in one Being. *Tatian (c. 160, E), 2.77.*

I myself also used to disbelieve that this would take place. However, now, having taken these things into consideration, I believe. At the same time, I met with the sacred Scriptures of the holy prophets. By the Spirit of God, they foretold the things that have already happened, just as they came to pass. [They also predicted] the things now occurring . . . and future things in the order in which they will be accomplished. Acknowledging this proof of events happening just as they were predicted, I no longer disbelieve, but believe. *Theophilus (c. 180, E), 2.9*

I used to indulge my sins as if they were actually parts of me and native to me. But after that, by the help of the water of new birth, the stain of former years had been washed away, and a light from above—serene and pure—had been infused into my reconciled heart. Then, by the agency of the Spirit breathed from heaven, a second birth had restored me to a new man. . . . I was enabled to acknowledge that what had been previously living in the practice of sins (being born of the flesh) was of the earth and

was earthly. But now it had begun to be of God and was enlivened by the Spirit of holiness. *Cyprian (c. 250, W), 5.275, 276.*

Like some spark lighting upon our inmost soul, love was kindled and burst into flame with us—a love for the holy Word, the most lovely object of all, who attracts everyone irresistibly toward Himself. *Gregory Thaumaturgus (c. 255, E), 6.28.*

SEE ALSO BAPTISM; CHRISTIANITY (II. GROWTH OF CHRISTIANITY); EVANGELISM; NEW BIRTH.

CORBAN

But you say, "If a man says to his father or mother, 'Whatever profit you might have received from me is Corban'" . . . you no longer let him do anything for his father or his mother. Mark 7:11.

The Pharisees and scribes promulgated in opposition to the Law a tradition that is found rather obscurely in the Gospel. I myself would have never thought of this tradition if a Hebrew man had not given to me the following facts relating to the passage. He says that sometimes when money lenders argued with stubborn debtors who were able, but not willing, to pay their debts, the lenders dedicated what was owed them to the account of the poor. . . . Therefore, they sometimes said to their debtors in their own language, "that which you owe to me is Corban"—that is, a gift—"for I have consecrated it to the poor, to the account of piety towards God." Then, the debtor was trapped, for he was no longer in debt to men, but to God. . . .

What, then, the money lender did to the debtor, some sons did the same to their parents. They said to them, "Whatever profit you might have received from me, father or mother, know that you will receive this from Corban," that is, from the account of the poor who are consecrated to God. Upon hearing that the thing that should have been given to them was Corban (consecrated to God), the parents, then, no longer wished to take it from their sons, even though they were in extreme need of the necessities of life. . . . The Savior condemns this tradition. . . . And the Pharisees, as lovers of money, promoted the tradition in order that under the pretext of being "the poor" they might receive that which should have been given to the parents. *Origen (c. 245, E), 9.438; extended discussion: 9.437–9.439.*

CORINTH, CHURCH AT

See Churches, Apostolic (III. Church at Corinth).

COSMETICS

Do not let your beauty be that outward adorning of arranging the hair, of wearing gold, or of putting on fine apparel. 1 Pet. 3:3.

He takes away anxious care for clothes, food, and all luxuries as being unnecessary. What are we to imagine, then, should be said about love of embellishments, the dyeing of wool, and the variety of colors? What should be said about the love of gems, exquisite working of gold, and still more, of artificial hair and wreathed curls? Furthermore, what should be said about staining the eyes, plucking out hairs, painting with rouge and white lead, dyeing of the hair, and the wicked arts that are employed in such deceptions? *Clement of Alexandria (c. 195, E), 2.264.*

Those women who wear gold imitate the Egyptians. They occupy themselves with curling their locks. They are busy anointing their cheeks, painting their eyes, dyeing their hair, and practicing the other pernicious arts of luxury. The truth is that they deck the covering of their flesh in order to attract their infatuated lovers. *Clement of Alexandria (c. 195, E), 2.272.*

If anyone were to refer to these women as prostitutes, he would make no mistake. For they turn their faces into masks. *Clement of Alexandria (c. 195, E), 2.274.*

What does God think of spurious beauty, rejecting utterly as He does all falsehood? *Clement of Alexandria (c. 195, E), 2.274.*

But there are circumstances in which this strictness may be relaxed. For allowance must sometimes be made in favor of those women who have not been fortunate in falling in with chaste husbands, and so they adorn themselves in order to please their husbands. But let desire for the admiration of their husbands alone be proposed as their objective. *Clement of Alexandria (c. 195, E), 2.285.*

Nor are the women to smear their faces with the ensnaring devices of wily cunning. But let us show to them the decoration of sobriety. *Clement of Alexandria (c. 195, E), 2.286.*

They [the wicked angels] conferred properly—and as it were, peculiarly—upon women that instrumental means of womanly ostentation: the radiances of jewels, ... the medicaments of orchil with which wools are dyed, and that black powder itself with which the eyelids and eyelashes are made prominent. *Tertullian (c. 198, W), 4.14, 15.*

No wife is ugly to her own husband. She pleased him enough when she was selected [to be his wife]. Let none of you think that, if she abstains from beautifying herself, she will incur the hatred and aversion of her husband. Every husband is the exacter of *chastity*. But a believing husband does not require *beauty*. For we are not captivated by the same graces that the Gentiles think are graces. *Tertullian (c. 198, W), 4.20.*

These suggestions [against cosmetics] are not made to you, of course, to be developed into an entire crudity and wildness of appearance. Nor am I seeking to persuade you that squalor and slovenliness are good. Rather, I am seeking to persuade you of the limit, norm, and just measure of cultivation of the person. *Tertullian (c. 198, W), 4.20.*

For those women sin against God when they rub their skin with ointments, stain their cheeks with rouge, and make their eyes prominent with antimony. To them, I suppose, the artistic skill of God is displeasing! *Tertullian (c. 198, W), 4.20.*

Whatever is *born* is the work of God. So whatever is *plastered on*, is the devil's work. . . . How unworthy of the Christian name it is to wear a fictitious face—you on whom simplicity in every form is enjoined! You, to whom lying with the tongue is not lawful, are lying in appearance. *Tertullian (c. 198, W), 4.21.*

What purpose, again, does all the labor spent in arranging the hair render to salvation? Why is no rest allowed to your hair? First, it must be bound, then loosed, then cultivated, then thinned out? Some are anxious to force their hair into curls. *Tertullian (c. 198, W), 4.21.*

I will then see whether you will rise [at the resurrection] with your ceruse and rouge and saffron—and in all that parade of headgear. I will then see whether it will be women thus decked out whom the angels carry up to meet Christ in the air! If these things are now good, and of God, they will then also present themselves to the rising bodies. *Tertullian (c. 198, W), 4.22.*

It was the fact that Tamar had painted out and adorned herself that led Judah to regard her as a harlot. *Tertullian (c. 198, W), 4.24.*

Draw your whiteness from simplicity, your ruddy hue from modesty. Paint your eyes with bashfulness, and your mouth with silence. Implant in your ears the words of God and place around your necks the yoke of Christ. *Tertullian (c. 198, W), 4.25.*

What will I say of the fact that these [young women] of ours confess their change of age even by their garb! As soon as they have understood themselves to be women, . . . they lay aside their former selves. They change their hair and fasten their hair with more wanton pins, professing obvious womanhood with their hair parted from the front. The next thing, they consult the mirror to aid their beauty. They thin down their over-exacting face with washing. Perhaps they even dress it up with cosmetics. They toss their mantle about them with an air, fit tightly into the multiform shoe, and carry down more ample appliances to the baths. *Tertullian (c. 207, W), 4.35.*

"Now Susannah was a very delicate woman." This does not mean that she had flashy adornments on herself or eyes painted with various colors—as Jezebel had. Rather, it means she had the adornment of faith, chastity, and sanctity. *Hippolytus (c. 205, W), 5.193.*

She is not a modest woman who strives to stir up the fancy of another—even though her physical chastity is preserved. Away with those who do not really adorn their beauty, but prostitute it instead. For anxiety about beauty is not only the wisdom of an evil mind, but belongs to deformity. . . . Why is the color of hair changed? Why are the edges of the eyes darkened? Why is the face molded by art into a different form? *Novatian (c. 235, W), 5.591, formerly attributed to Cyprian.*

You wish, O Christian woman, that the matrons should be as the ladies of the world. You surround yourself with gold, or with the modest silken garment. . . . You affect vanity with all the pomp of the devil. You are adorned at the mirror, with your curled hair turned back from your brow. Moreover, with evil purpose, you put on false cosmetics. You put antimony on your pure eyes, with painted beauty. Or you dye your hair, so that it will always be black. . . . But these things are not necessary for modest women. *Commodianus (c. 240, W), 4.214.*

To a wife approved by her husband, let it suffice that she is so, not by her dress, but by her good disposition. . . . O good matrons, flee from the adornment of vanity. Such attire is fitting for women who haunt the brothels. Overcome the evil one, O modest women of Christ! *Commodianus (c. 240, W), 4.214.*

It is not right before God that a faithful Christian woman should be adorned. . . . God's heralds . . . condemn as being unrighteous those women who adorn themselves in such a manner. You stain your hair. You paint the opening of your eyes with black. You lift up your hair, one by one, on your painted brow. You anoint your cheeks with some sort of reddish color laid on. . . . You are rejecting the law when you wish to please the world. *Commodianus (c. 240, W), 4.215.*

All of these things [i.e., the making of jewelry] the sinning and apostate angels put forth by their arts, when, lowered to the contagions of earth, they forsook their heavenly vigor. They also taught women to paint the eyes with blackness drawn around them in a circle and to stain the cheeks with a deceitful red. *Cyprian (c. 250, W), 5.434.*

Both sexes alike should be admonished that the work of God and His fashioning and formation should in no manner be adulterated—either with the application of yellow color, black dust, rouge, or with any kind of cosmetic. . . . God says, "Let us make man in our image and likeness." Does anyone dare to alter and change what God has made? *Cyprian (c. 250, W), 5.434.*

In their manners, there was no discipline. . . . In women, their complexion was dyed. Their eyes were falsified from what God's hand had made them. Their hair was stained with a falsehood. *Cyprian (c. 250, W), 5.438.*

Did he send souls . . . to seek after cosmetics with which to cover their bodies and to darken their eyes with henna? *Arnobius (c. 305, E), 6.450.*

Do not paint your face, which is God's workmanship. For there is no part of you that lacks beauty. For God has made all things very good. But the wanton extra adorning of what is already good is an affront to the Creator's work. *Apostolic Constitutions (compiled c. 390, E), 7.395; extended discussion: 5.432–5.436.*

SEE ALSO ANGEL, ANGELS (III. WICKED ANGELS); CLOTHING; GROOMING; JEWELRY; MODESTY; PERFUME.

COUNCILS, CHURCH

But some of the sect of the Pharisees who believed rose up, saying, "It is necessary to circumcise them, and to command them to keep the law of Moses." So the apostles and elders came together to consider this matter. Acts 15:6, 7.

Throughout the provinces of Greece, there are held in definite localities those councils gathered out of the universal churches. By means of these councils, not only are all the deeper questions handled for the common good, but the actual representation of the whole Christian name is celebrated with great veneration. *Tertullian (c. 213, W), 4.111.*

If, at any time, any subject of investigation among us should not be clear, let us go to Jesus with all unanimity in regard to the question in dispute. For he is present where two or three are gathered together in His name. He is ready by His presence with power to illuminate the hearts of those who truly desire to become his disciples. *Origen (c. 245, E), 9.483.*

We should deal with the problem of the lapsed by gathering together for counsel an assembly with bishops, presbyters, deacons, confessors, and the laity who stand fast. *Cyprian (c. 250, W), 5.310.*

When the persecution had quieted, and opportunity of meeting was afforded, a large number of bishops ... met together.... And lest perhaps the number of bishops in Africa might seem unsatisfactory, we also wrote to Rome concerning this thing, to Cornelius, our colleague. He himself was also holding a council with very many bishops, which had concurred in the same opinion as we had held. *Cyprian (c. 250, W), 5.328, 329.*

It is evident that men of that kind may not rule over the church of Christ.... This is especially so since Cornelius also, our colleague, a peaceable and righteous priest [bishop of Rome] ... has long ago decreed with us and with all the bishops appointed throughout the whole world that men of this sort ... were prohibited from ordination. *Cyprian (c. 250, W), 5.371.*

Dearest brethren, when we were together in council, we read your letter. *Cyprian (c. 250, W), 5.375.*

We have thought it necessary for the arranging of certain matters, dearest brother, and for their investigation by the examination of a common council, to gather together and to hold a council, at which many priests were assembled at once. *Cyprian (c. 250, W), 5.378.*

When we had met together, being bishops of the province of Africa and of Numidia and numbering seventy-one, we established this same matter once more. *Cyprian (c. 250, W), 5.379.*

Just as a heretic may not lawfully ordain or lay on hands, so neither may he baptize, nor do anything that is holy or spiritual.... All of which we confirmed some time ago in Iconium, which is a place in Phrygia, when we were assembled together with those who had gathered from Galatia, Cilicia, and other neighboring countries. *Firmilian (c. 256, E), 5.392.*

On the first of September, a great many bishops from the provinces of Africa, Numidia, and Mauritania met together at Carthage, together with the presbyters and deacons. And a considerable part of the congregations were also present. *Seventh Council of Carthage (c. 256, W), 5.565.*

A divine and sacred provincial synod, gathered together at Rome by Stephen, the blessed martyr and father, which excommunicated those in an African synod. *Roman Council of Stephen (c. 256, W), 5.653.*

In the most considerable councils of the bishops, I hear it has been decreed that those who come from heresy should first be trained in [orthodox] doctrine and then should be cleansed by baptism. *Dionysius of Alexandria (c. 262, E), 6.102.*

Let a synod of bishops be held twice a year. Let them ask one another the doctrines of piety, and let them resolve the ecclesiastical disputes that happen. *Apostolic Constitutions (compiled c. 390, E), 7.502.*

SEE ALSO JERUSALEM COUNCIL.

COVENANTS OF GOD

Marcion and the Gnostics argued that the differences between the old covenant and the new prove that these covenants came from two different Gods. Most of the quotations below were written by Christians who were refuting this false premise.

. . . which things are symbolic. For these are the two covenants. Gal. 4:24.

In that he says, "A new covenant," He has made the first obsolete. Heb. 8:13.

For this reason, four principal covenants were given to the human race: The first was under Adam, prior to the deluge. The second was the one after the deluge, under Noah. The third was the giving of the Law under Moses. The fourth is that which renovates man, and sums up all things in itself by means of the Gospel. *Irenaeus (c. 180, E/W), 1.429.*

As in the Law, therefore, and in the Gospel, the first and greatest commandment is to love the Lord God with the whole heart. Next, there follows a commandment like it: to love one's neighbor as one's self. The Author of the Law and the Gospel is shown to be one and the same for the teachings of an absolutely perfect life, since they are the same in each covenant. *Irenaeus (c. 180, E/W), 1.476.*

In both covenants, there is the same righteousness of God. *Irenaeus (c. 180, E/W), 1.501.*

If it appears that conflicting dogmas draw some away, these must be taken out of the way . . . by explaining the truth by the connection of the covenants. *Clement of Alexandria (c. 195, E), 2.552, 553.*

Indeed, I do allow that one order did run its course in the old dispensation under the Creator, and that another is on its way in the new one under Christ. I do not deny that there is a difference in the language of their documents, in their commandments of virtue, and in their teachings of the law. Yet all this diversity is consistent with one and the same God. *Tertullian (c. 207, W), 3.345, 346.*

God thus shows that the ancient covenant is temporary only, when He indicates its change. Also, when He promises that it will be followed by an eternal one. *Tertullian (c. 207, W), 3.346.*

Still, we make this concession: that there is a separation [of the two covenants] by reformation, amplification, and progress. To illustrate, fruit is separated from the seed, although the fruit comes from the seed. Likewise, the Gospel is separated from the Law even though it is developed from the Law. It is a different thing from it, but not an alien one. It is distinct from it, but it is not inimical to it. *Tertullian (c. 207, W), 3.361.*

The epistle that we also allow to be the most decisive against Judaism, is that in which the apostle instructs the Galatians. For we fully admit the abolition of the ancient Law. We hold that it actually proceeds from the dispensation of the Creator. . . . Christ marks the period of the separation when He says, "The Law and the Prophets were until John." He thus made the Baptist the boundary between the two dispensations of the old things that were then terminating and the new things that were then beginning. *Tertullian (c. 207, W), 3.431; see also 3.157.*

SEE ALSO LAW, MOSAIC; SABBATH.

CREATION

On the fourth day, the luminaries were made. This was because God, who possesses foreknowledge, knew the follies of the vain philosophers. He knew that they were going to say that the things that grow on the earth are produced from the heavenly bodies. For in this way, the philosophers exclude God. Therefore, in order that the truth might be obvious, the plants and seeds were produced prior to the heavenly bodies. For that which is later cannot produce that which precedes it. *Theophilus (c. 180, E), 2.90.*

Any person who sees a ship on the sea rigged and in sail, and heading for the harbor, will no doubt infer that there is a pilot in her who is steering her. Likewise, we must perceive that God is the Pilot of the whole universe, although He is not visible to the eyes of the flesh. For He is incomprehensible. *Theophilus (c. 180, E), 2.90.*

God formed Adam, not as if He stood in need of man, but so that He might have [someone] upon whom to confer His benefits. *Irenaeus (c. 180, E/W), 1.478.*

For with Him were always present the Word and Wisdom, the Son and the Spirit, by whom and in whom, freely and spontaneously, He made all things. He speaks to Him, saying, "Let Us make man after Our image and likeness." *Irenaeus (c. 180, E/W), 1.488.*

The other works of creation He made by the word of command alone. But man He framed by Himself, by His own hand. *Clement of Alexandria (c. 195, E), 2.210.*

How could creation take place in time, seeing time was born along with things that exist. *Clement of Alexandria (c. 195, E), 2.513.*

God completed all His works in a specified order. At first, He laid them out in their unformed elements, so to speak. Then He arranged them in their finished beauty. For He did not inundate the light all at once with the splendor of the sun. Nor did he immediately temper darkness with the moon's soothing beam. He did not adorn the heaven all at once with constellations and stars. Nor did He at once fill the seas with their teeming monsters. He did not endow the earth all at once with its various kinds of vegetation. Rather, He first gave it existence; then He filled it. *Tertullian (c. 200, W), 3.493.*

The truth is, a great matter was in progress—out of which the creature under consideration was being fashioned. . . . Imagine God wholly employed and absorbed in it—in His hand, His eye, His labor, His purpose, His wisdom, His providence, and above all, in His love. All of these things were dictating the lineaments [of man]. For, whatever was the form and expression that was then given to the clay, it was in His thoughts that Christ would one day become man. *Tertullian (c. 210, W), 3.549.*

This is also part of the church's teaching: that the world was made and took its beginning at a certain time and that it is to be destroyed on account of its wickedness. But there is no clear statement in the teaching of the church regarding what existed before this world or what will exist after it. . . . Insofar as the credibility of Scripture is concerned, the declarations on this matter are easy to prove. Even the heretics (although having widely differing opinions on many other things) appear to be of one mind on this, yielding to the authority of Scripture. Concerning the creation of the world, what portion of Scripture can give us more information regarding it than the account that Moses has transmitted about its origin? It contains matters of profounder significance than the mere histori-

cal narrative appears to indicate. Furthermore, it contains very many things that are to be spiritually understood. When discussing profound and mystical subjects, it uses literal language as a type of veil. Nevertheless, the language of the narrator reveals that all visible things were created at a certain time. *Origen (c. 225, E), 4.340, 341.*

It may be said that the family of lions, bears, leopards, wild boars, and similar animals has been given to us in order to call into exercise the elements of the manly character that exist within us. *Origen (c. 248, E), 4.532.*

We should admire the divine nature that gave even irrational animals the capacity . . . of imitating rational beings, perhaps with a view of putting rational beings to shame. For example, by looking upon ants, men might become more industrious and more thrifty in the management of their goods. Likewise, by considering the bees, they might place themselves in subjection to their ruler and take their respective parts in those constitutional duties that are of use in ensuring the safety of cities. *Origen (c. 248, E), 4.533.*

The *immediate* Creator, and, as it were, the very Maker of the world was the Word, the Son of God. By commanding His own Son, the Word, to create the world, the Father of the Word is the *primary* Creator. *Origen (c. 248, E), 4.601.*

When all things had been settled with a wonderful arrangement, He determined to prepare for Himself an eternal kingdom and to create innumerable souls, on whom He might bestow immortality. Then He made for Himself a figure endowed with perception and intelligence—that is, after the likeness of His own image. . . . So He formed man out of the dust of the ground. *Lactantius (c. 304–313, W), 7.58.*

It cannot be said that God made the world for His own sake. For He can exist without the world. . . . It is evident, therefore, that the world was constructed for the sake of living beings, since living beings enjoy those things that it consists of. *Lactantius (c. 304–313, W), 7.198.*

God designed the world for the sake of man. But He formed man himself for His own sake. Man was, as it were, a priest of a divine temple, a spectator of God's works and of heavenly objects. For he is the only [earthly] being who is able to understand God, for he is intelligent and capable of reason. . . . On this account, he alone of all the other living creatures has been made with an upright body and stance. So it seems that he was raised up for the contemplation of his Parent. For this reason also, he alone has received language . . . so that he may be able to declare the majesty of his Lord. . . . So it is plainly most just that man should worship Him who bestowed such great gifts upon him. He should also love his fellow man, who is united with him in the participation of the divine justice. *Lactantius (c. 314, W), 7.271.*

He made man . . . destitute of those things that are given to the other animals, because wisdom is able to supply those things that the condition of nature has denied to him. *Lactantius (c. 314, W), 7.282.*

When he sees that even elephants (with their vast bodies and strength) are subservient to man, can anyone, then complain about God . . . simply because man has received only moderate strength and a small body? *Lactantius (c. 314, W), 7.284; see also 4.182; extended discussion: 4.268–4.275, 6.84–6.89, 7.286–7.291.*

SEE ALSO ATOMS; DAYS OF CREATION; EVOLUTION; FLOOD, THE; SOVEREIGNTY AND PROVIDENCE OF GOD.

CREATIVE DAYS

SEE DAYS OF CREATION.

CREEDS, EARLY

Therefore, stop your ears when anyone speaks to you contrary to Jesus Christ, who was descended from David, and was also of Mary; who was truly born and did eat and drink. He was truly persecuted under Pontius Pilate. He was truly crucified and died—in the sight of beings in heaven, on earth, and under the earth. He was also truly raised from the dead, His Father raising Him to life—in the same manner as His Father will also raise us up, we who believe in Him by Christ Jesus. *Ignatius (c. 105, E), 1.69.*

The church, though dispersed throughout the whole world, even to the ends of the earth, has received from the apostles and their disciples this faith: [We believe] in one God, the Father Almighty, Maker of heaven and earth, and the sea, and all things that are in them. And in one Christ Jesus, the Son of God, who became incarnate for our salvation. And in the Holy Spirit, who proclaimed through the prophets the dispensations of God, and the advents, and the birth from a virgin, and the passion, and the

resurrection from the dead, and the ascension into heaven in the flesh of the beloved Christ Jesus, our Lord. And we believe in His manifestation from heaven in the glory of the Father to gather all things into one, and to raise up anew all flesh of the whole human race—in order that to Christ Jesus, our Lord, God, Savior, and King, according to the will of the invisible Father, "every knee should bow, of things in heaven, and things in earth, and things under the earth, and that every tongue should confess" Him. And we believe that He will execute just judgment towards all, so that He may send spiritual evils and the angels who transgressed and became apostates—together with the ungodly, and unrighteous, and wicked, and profane among men—into everlasting fire. And we believe that He will, in the exercise of his grace, confer immortality on the righteous, the holy, those who have kept His commandments, and those who have persevered in His love—some from the beginning and others from the time of their repentance. We believe He will surround them with everlasting glory. *Irenaeus (c. 180, E/W), 1.330, 331.*

To which course, many nations of those barbarians who believe in Christ do assent, having salvation written in their hearts by the Spirit, without paper or ink, and carefully preserving the ancient tradition: believing in one God, the Creator of heaven and earth, and all things therein, by means of Christ Jesus, the Son of God, who, because of His surpassing love towards His creation, humbled Himself to be born of the virgin, He Himself uniting man through Himself to God. And having suffered under Pontius Pilate, and rising again, and having been received up in splendor, He will come in glory, the Savior of those who are saved, and the Judge of those who are condemned. He will send into eternal fire those who transform the truth and despise His Father and His advent. *Irenaeus (c. 180, E/W), 1.417.*

This rule of faith . . . is that there is only one God, and that He is none other than the Creator of the world, who produced all things out of nothing through His own Word, first of all sent forth. That this Word is called His Son, and, under the name of God, was seen "in diverse manners" by the patriarchs, heard at all times in the prophets, at last brought by the Spirit and Power of the Father down into the virgin Mary. He was made flesh in her womb, and, being born of her, went forth as Jesus

Christ. Thereafter, He preached the new land and the new promise of the kingdom of heaven, and He worked miracles. Having been crucified, He rose again on the third day. Having ascended into the heavens, He sat at the right hand of the Father. He sent in place of Himself the power of the Holy Spirit to lead those who believe. He will come with glory to take the saints to the enjoyment of everlasting life and of the heavenly promises, and to condemn the wicked to everlasting fire. This will take place after the resurrection of both these classes, together with the restoration of their flesh. *Tertullian (c. 197, W), 3.249.*

The church acknowledges one Lord God, the Creator of the universe, and Christ Jesus born of the virgin Mary—the Son of God the Creator; and in the resurrection of the flesh. The church unites the Law and the Prophets into one volume, with the writings of evangelists and apostles, from which she drinks in her faith. This she seals with the water [of baptism], arrays with the Holy Spirit, feeds with the Eucharist, and cheers with martyrdom. Against such a discipline thus maintained, she admits no deniers. *Tertullian (c. 197, W), 3.260, 261.*

The rule of faith, indeed, is altogether one, alone immoveable and irreformable. The rule is: to believe in only one God Almighty, the Creator of the universe, and His Son Jesus Christ, born of the virgin Mary, crucified under Pontius Pilate, raised again the third day from the dead, received in the heavens, sitting now at the right [hand] of the Father, destined to come to judge the living and the dead through the resurrection of the flesh. *Tertullian (c. 207, W), 4.27.*

We profess our belief that [the flesh of Christ] is sitting at the right hand of the Father in heaven. And we further declare that it will come again from there in all the grandeur of the Father's glory. *Tertullian (c. 210, W), 3.535.*

We . . . believe that there is only one God, but under the following dispensation or "economy" [Gr. *oikonomia*], as it is called: that this one only God also has a Son, His Word, who proceeded from Himself, by whom all things were made, and without whom nothing was made. We believe Him to have been sent by the Father into the virgin, and to have been born of her—being both man and God, the son of man and the Son of God, and to have been called by the name of Jesus Christ. He suffered, died, and was buried, according to the Scriptures.

And, after He had been raised again by the Father and taken back to heaven, He has been sitting at the right hand of the Father. We believe that He will come to judge the living and the dead. And He sent also from heaven from the Father, according to His own promise, the Holy Spirit, the Paraclete, the sanctifier of the faith of those who believe in the Father, the Son, and the Holy Spirit. This rule of faith has come down to us from the beginning of the gospel, even before any of the older heretics. *Tertullian (c. 213, W), 3.598.*

Regarding Him, then, we will state, in the fewest possible words, the contents of our creed—rather than the assertions that human reason is inclined to advance. *Origen (c. 225, E), 4.282.*

The rule of truth requires that we should first of all believe on God the Father and Lord Almighty. *Novatian (c. 235, W), 5.611.*

We confess the Father Almighty and His Son Christ, who was begotten by the Father before the beginning of the world. He was made man in very soul and body, both of them having overcome misery and death. When He was received with His body into heaven by the Father, He sent forth the Holy Spirit, the gift and pledge of immortality. He [the Son] was announced by the prophets, was described by the Law, was God's hand, and was the Word of the Father from God. He is Lord over all and founder of the world. This is the reed and the measure of faith. No one worships at the holy altar except he who confesses this faith. *Victorinus (c. 280, W), 7.354.*

Concerning Him we believe in this manner, even as the apostolic church believes: In one Father, unbegotten, who has the cause of His being from no one, who is unchangeable and immutable. He is always the same and can have no increase or diminution. He gave the Law to us, the Prophets, and the Gospels. He is Lord of the patriarchs, apostles, and all the saints. And in one Lord Jesus Christ, the Only-Begotten Son of God. He is not begotten of things that are not, but of Him who is the Father. . . .

And besides the pious opinion concerning the Father and the Son, we confess one Holy Spirit, as the divine Scriptures teach us. He has inspired both the holy men of the Old Testament and the divine teachers of that which is called the New. And, in addition, [we believe] one only catholic and apostolic church, which can never be destroyed. . . . After this, we know of the resurrection of the dead, the first-fruits of which was our Lord Jesus Christ, who in very deed (and not merely in appearance) carried a body, which was of Mary, the God-bearer. He, in the end of the world, came to the human race to put away sin, was crucified and died. (Yet He did not thereby receive any loss of His divinity.) He was raised from the dead, taken up into heaven, and seated at the right hand of majesty. *Alexander of Alexandria (c. 324, E), 6.295, 296.*

I believe and am baptized into one unbegotten Being, the only true God Almighty, the Father of Christ, the Creator and Maker of all things, from whom are all things. And into the Lord Jesus Christ, His Only-Begotten Son, the First-Born of the whole creation, who before the ages was begotten by the good pleasure of the Father, by whom all thing were made, both those in heaven and those on earth, visible and invisible; who in the last days descended from heaven and took flesh, and was born of the holy virgin Mary, and did live righteously according to the laws of His God and Father. He was crucified under Pontius Pilate, and died for us, and rose again from the dead after His passion on the third day, and ascended into the heavens, and sits at the right hand of the Father. He will come again at the end of the world with glory to judge the living and the dead, of whose kingdom there will be no end. And I am baptized into the Holy Spirit, that is, the Comforter, who worked in all the saints from the beginning of the world, but was afterwards sent to the apostles by the Father, according to the promise of our Savior and Lord, Jesus Christ. And after the apostles, He was sent to all those who believe in the holy catholic church. I believe in the resurrection of the flesh, the remission of sins, the kingdom of heaven, and the life of the world to come. *Apostolic Constitutions (compiled c. 390, E), 7.476.*

We believe in one God, the Father Almighty, Maker of all things, visible and invisible; And in one Lord Jesus Christ, the Son of God, begotten of the Father, only begotten, that is, of the substance of the Father; God of God; Light of Light; very God of very God; begotten, not made; being of one substance with the Father, by whom all things were made, both things in heaven and things in earth; who for us men and for our salvation came down and was

incarnate and was made man; He suffered and rose again the third day; And ascended into heaven; And He will come again to judge the living and the dead; And in the Holy Spirit; etc. *Nicene Creed (A.D. 325), 7.524.*

SEE ALSO APOSTOLIC FAITH, THE.

CRIME AND PUNISHMENT

For he is God's minister to you for good. But if you do evil, be afraid; for he does not bear the sword in vain; for he is God's minister, an avenger to execute wrath on him who practices evil. Rom. 13:4.

The punishment of criminals, consummated in the highways, is not for children to see. The man of God . . . cannot possibly learn anything from such spectacles or be delighted with them. *Clement of Alexandria (c. 195, E), 2.544.*

It is good, no doubt, to have the guilty punished. Who but the criminal himself will deny that? And yet the innocent can find no pleasure in another's sufferings. He rather mourns that a brother has sinned so heinously as to need a punishment so dreadful. But how am I guaranteed that it is always the guilty who are thrown to the wild beasts, or to some other doom? How can I be guaranteed that the innocent never suffer from the revenge of the judge, the weakness of the defense, or the pressure of the torture rack? How much better, then, is it for me to remain ignorant of the punishment inflicted on the wicked. *Tertullian (c. 197, W), 3.87.*

In our case you actually conduct trials contrary to the usual form of judicial process against criminals. For when culprits are brought up for trial, if they deny the charge, you press them for a confession by tortures. However, when Christians confess without compulsion, you apply torture to induce them to *deny. Tertullian (c. 197, W), 3.110.*

[EXAMPLES OF VARIOUS GENTILE LAWS:] If a man drove out his father by force of arms, the Falcidian and Sempronian law would bind the murderer of his father in a sack with beasts. If a man violated his sisters, the Papinian law would punish the outrage with all penalties, limb by limb. If a man invaded another's wedlock, the Julian law would visit its adulterous violator with the death penalty. If a man defiled freeborn boys, the Cornelian law would condemn with novel severities the crime of transgressing the sexual bond. *Tertullian (c. 200, W), 3.150.*

183

Shall the Christian apply the chain, the prison, the torture, and the punishment—he who is not the avenger even of his own wrongs? *Tertullian (c. 211, W), 3.99.*

Pregnant women are not allowed to be publicly punished. *Passion of Perpetua and Felicitas (c. 205, W), 3.703.*

There are many places, too, in the kingdom of Persia where men kill their wives, brothers, and children—yet incur no penalty. In contrast, among the Romans and the Greeks, he who kills one of these incurs capital punishment, the severest of penalties. *Bardesanes (c. 222, E), 8.730.*

Among the Romans, he who commits a small theft is whipped and sent about his business. *Bardesanes (c. 222, E), 8.731.*

Although a judge may be angry with [criminals] without incurring blame, let us, however, suppose that he should be of a sedate mind when he sentences the guilty to punishment. For he is the executor of the *laws*, not of his own spirit or power. *Lactantius (c. 304–313, W), 7.274.*

SEE ALSO CAPITAL PUNISHMENT.

CROSS

I. The cross and its significance

II. Prefigured in the Old Testament

III. Shape of the cross seen in nature and in human activities

I. The cross and its significance

The message of the cross is foolishness to those who are perishing, but to us who are being saved it is the power of God. 1 Cor. 1:18.

He has taken it out of the way, having nailed it to the cross. Col. 2:14.

The cross was to express grace by the letter "T." *Barnabas (c. 70–130, E), 1.143.*

By means of a tree, we were made debtors to God. Likewise, by means of a tree [the cross], we can obtain the remission of our debt. *Irenaeus (c. 180, E/W), 1.545.*

We neither worship nor wish for crosses. *Mark Minucius Felix (c. 200, W), 4.191.*

II. Prefigured in the Old Testament

And so it was, when Moses held up his hand, that Israel prevailed; and when he let down his hand, Amalek prevailed. But Moses' hands became heavy; so they took a stone and put it under him, and he sat on it. And Aaron and Hur supported his hands, one on one side, and the other on the other side; and his hands were steady until the going down of the sun. Ex. 17:11,12.

Go through the midst of Jerusalem, and set a mark [Gr. tau] on the foreheads of the men that groan and that grieve for all the iniquities that are done in the midst of them. Ezek 9:4 (LXX). [NOTE: THE GREEK LETTER *TAU*, EQUIVALENT TO THE ENGLISH CAPITAL "T," IS IN THE SHAPE OF A CROSS.]

The Spirit spoke to the heart of Moses, that he should make a figure of the cross. . . . Moses therefore placed one weapon above another in the midst of the hill, and standing upon it, so as to be higher than all the people, he stretched forth his hands, and thus again Israel acquired the mastery. *Barnabas (c. 70–130, E), 1.145.*

The lamb, which is roasted, is roasted and dressed up in the form of the cross. For one spit pierces right through from the lower parts up to the head, and another one pierces the lamb across the back, to which are attached the legs of the lamb. *Justin Martyr (c. 160, E), 1.215.*

Moses himself prayed to God, stretching out both hands, and Hur with Aaron supported them during the whole day. . . . For if he gave up any part of this sign, which was an imitation of the cross, the people were beaten. *Justin Martyr (c. 160, E), 1.244.*

Why, again, did the same Moses—after the prohibition of any "likeness of anything"—display a bronze serpent, placed on a tree in a hanging posture? . . . In this case he was displaying the Lord's cross on which the [real] serpent, the devil, was made a show of. *Tertullian (c. 197, W), 3.166.*

"He said unto him, 'Pass through the midst of Jerusalem and write the sign Tau on the foreheads of the men who groan and grieve over all the enormities that are done in their midst.'" . . . Now the mystery of this sign was in various ways predicted, in which the foundation of life was prepared for mankind. *Tertullian (c. 197, W), 3.168.*

Jacob also signified [Christ] by placing his hands crossed upon his sons. . . . From placing his hands in this manner, he thus foreshadowed the figure and form of the future passion. *Novatian (c. 235, W), 5.631.*

By this sign of the cross, Amalek was also conquered by Jesus through Moses. . . . "And it came to pass that when Moses lifted up his hands, Israel prevailed. But when Moses had let down his hands, Amalek prevailed." . . . In this sign of the cross, there is salvation for all the people who are marked on their foreheads. In Ezekiel, the Lord says: "Pass through the midst of Jerusalem, and you will mark the sign upon the men's foreheads who groan and grieve for the iniquities that are done." *Cyprian (c. 250, W), 5.525.*

Moses, when he was attacked, stretched forth his hands and fought against Amalek. And when we were attacked and were perishing by the violence of that sinning spirit who still works in the unrighteous, Jesus stretched forth His hands upon the cross and gave us salvation. *Disputation of Archelaus and Manes (c. 320, E), 6.220.*

III. Shape of the cross seen in nature and in human activities

This shows no other form than that of the cross. . . . The power of this form is shown by your own symbols on what are called banners and trophies. *Justin Martyr (c. 160, E), 1.181.*

Concerning the Son of God, in the *Timaeus* of Plato, he says, "He placed him crosswise in the universe." . . . And Moses, by the inspiration and influence of God, took brass, and made it into the figure of a cross. *Justin Martyr (c. 160, E), 1.183.*

If any of you think we render superstitious adoration to the cross, in that adoration he is a sharer with us. . . . The camp religion of the Romans is thoroughly a worship of the standards, for the standards are set above all gods. *Tertullian (c. 197, W), 3.31*

In its material, a cross is a sign of wood. Among yourselves the object of worship is also a wooden figure. The difference between us is that with you [Romans] the figure is a human one. With us, the wood is its own figure. *Tertullian (c. 197, W), 3.122.*

Every piece of timber that is fixed in the ground in an erect position is a part of a cross, and indeed the greater portion of its mass. But an entire cross is attributed to us, with its transverse beam, of course, and its projecting seat. *Tertullian (c. 197, W), 3.122; see also 1.545, 3.165–166.*

SEE ALSO SERPENT, BRONZE; SIGNING; WORSHIP, CHRISTIAN (II. WORSHIP CUSTOMS).

CROWNS

The following passages about "crowns" refer to wreaths made of flowers, laurel leaves, or other materials, worn on various occasions by pagans and also used to adorn various objects.

It is unfit for a man of temperance to adorn himself with "a crown woven from the fresh mead," and to wear it at home. For it is not suitable to fill the loose hair with rose-leaves, violets, lilies, or other such flowers. *Clement of Alexandria (c. 195, E), 2.255.*

How, then, will I crown myself, anoint with ointment, or offer incense to the Lord? It is said, "An odor of a sweet fragrance is the heart that glorifies Him who made it" [Ps. 51:17]. Such hearts are the crowns and sacrifices, aromatic odors, and flowers of God. *Clement of Alexandria (c. 195, E), 2.293.*

[ADDRESSED TO PAGANS:] I do not buy a crown for my head. Yet, what concern is it of yours how I use them—if nevertheless I purchase the flowers? *Tertullian (c. 197, W), 3.49.*

The tribune at once put the question to the Christian, "Why are you so different in your attire?" He declared that he had no liberty to wear the crown with the rest. *Tertullian (c. 211, W), 3.93.*

In short, what patriarch, what prophet, what Levite, what priest, or what leader—or at a later period, what apostle, preacher of the gospel, or bishop—do you ever find wearing a crown? I do not think that even the temple of God itself was crowned. Neither was the ark of the covenant, nor the tabernacle of witness. *Tertullian (c. 211, W), 3.98.*

Marriage, too, decks the [pagan] bridegroom with its crown. Therefore, we will not have pagan brides, lest they seduce us even to the idolatry with which marriage is initiated among them. *Tertullian (c. 212, W), 3.101.*

Much less may the Christian put the service of idolatry on his own head . . . since Christ is the head of the Christian man. . . . But even the head that is bound to have the veil, I mean woman's head, . . . is not open also to a wreath. She has the burden of her own humility to bear. If she should not appear with her head uncovered on account of the angels, how much more—by wearing a crown on it—will she offend those who are perhaps already wearing crowns above. *Tertullian (c. 212, W), 3.102.*

[PAGAN ANTAGONIST, SPEAKING OF CHRISTIANS:] You do not wreath your heads with flowers. *Mark Minucius Felix (c. 200, W), 4.179.*

Pardon us that we do not crown our heads. We are accustomed to receive the scent of a sweet flower in our nostrils, not to inhale it with the back of our heads or with our hair. Nor do we crown the dead. *Mark Minucius Felix (c. 200, W), 4.197.*

SEE ALSO HOLIDAYS, PAGAN; WREATHS.

CULTURE AND CHRISTIANITY

When you level against us the general charge of divorcing ourselves from the institutions of our forefathers, consider again and again whether you are not yourselves open to that accusation in common with us. *Tertullian (c. 197, W), 3.118.*

It is therefore against these things that our contest lies: against the institutions of our ancestors, against the authority of tradition, against the laws of our governors, and against the reasonings of the "wise." It is against antiquity, custom, requirements, precedents, prodigies, miracles—all of which things have had their part in constructing that spurious system of your gods. *Tertullian (c. 197, W), 3.129.*

Will you prefer to follow antiquity or reason? . . . If you prefer reason, you must abandon the institutions and authority of our ancestors. For nothing is right but that which reason prescribes. *Lactantius (c. 304–313, W), 7.50.*

SEE ALSO CHRISTIAN LIFE; CHRISTIANITY; CHURCH AND STATE; WORLD, SEPARATION FROM.

CYPRIAN

Cyprian was bishop of Carthage from about 248 to 258. A vast amount of the correspondence both from him and to him has been preserved. This gives the modern reader considerable insight into church life in the middle of the third century. During the Decian persecution, Cyprian continued his ministry underground. When the Valerian persecution broke out a few years later, however, he was captured and beheaded.

Immediately as the first burst of the disturbance arose, and the people with violent clamor repeatedly demanded me, I withdrew for a while—as the Lord's commandment teaches. I was not considering so much my own safety as I was the public peace of the brethren. Otherwise, by my overly bold presence, the tumult that had begun might be incited even more. Nevertheless, although absent in body, I was not lacking either in spirit, or in act. *Cyprian (c. 250, W), 5.294.*

It is no wonder, brother Cyprian, that you should do this, who—with your usual modesty and innate industriousness—have wished us to be not so much judges of, but sharers in, your counsels. *Letter from the clergy of Rome to Cyprian (c. 250, W), 5.308.*

Yet Stephen [bishop of Rome] is not ashamed . . . to call Cyprian "a false Christ, a false apostle, and a deceitful worker." *Firmilian (c. 256, E), 5.397.*

[A DESCRIPTION OF CYPRIAN:] Neither poverty nor pain broke him down. The persuasion of his wife did not influence him. The dreadful suffering of his own body did not shake his firmness. . . . His house was open to every comer. No widow returned from him with an empty apron. No blind man was unguided by him as a companion. . . . Who is sufficient to relate the manner in which he bore himself? What compassion was his! What vigor! How great his mercy! How great his strictness! So much sanctity and grace beamed from his face that it confounded the minds of the beholders. *Pontius the deacon (c. 258, W), 5.268, 269.*

Cyprian was distinguished above all other [Christian writers] and famous persons. For [prior to his conversion,] he had sought great glory for himself from the profession of public speaking. And he wrote very many things that are worthy of admiration in their particular genre. For he had a mind that was ready, copious, agreeable . . . plain, and open. So a person would be hard-pressed to say whether he was more embellished in speech, or more ready in explanation, or more powerful in persuasion. *Lactantius (c. 304–313, W), 7.136.*

I have not shrunk from this labor that I might complete the subject, which Cyprian did not fully carry out in that discourse in which he endeavored to refute Demetrian. *Lactantius (c. 304–313, W), 7.140; extended discussion: 5.267–5.274.*

DAN, TRIBE OF

Jeremiah does not merely point out [the Antichrist's] sudden coming, but he even indicates the tribe from which he will come. For he says, "We will hear the voice of his swift horses from Dan" [Jer. 8:16].... This, too, is the reason that this tribe is not included in the Apocalypse along with those who are saved. *Irenaeus (c. 180, E/W), 1.559.*

He says, "Dan is a lion's whelp" [Deut. 33:22]. And in naming the tribe of Dan, he clearly identified the tribe from which the Antichrist is destined to spring. Just as Christ comes from the tribe of Judah, so the Antichrist is to come from the tribe of Dan. *Hippolytus (c. 200, W), 5.207.*

But of the fathers who will judge, the patriarch Jacob says, "Dan himself will also judge the people among his brethren, even as one of the tribes in Israel" [Gen. 49:16]. *Victorinus (c. 280, W), 7.349.*

DANCING

"Praise with the timbrel and the dance." This refers to the church mediating on the resurrection of the dead in the resounding skin. *Clement of Alexandria (c. 195, E), 2.248.*

Outside [of church], they foolishly amuse themselves with impious playing, . . . occupied with flute playing, dancing, intoxication, and all kinds of foolishness. *Clement of Alexandria (c. 195, E), 2.290.*

You are rejecting the law when you wish to please the world. You dance in your houses. Instead of psalms, you sing love songs. *Commodianus (c. 240, W), 4.215.*

The dancing of Herodias was opposed to that holy dancing with which those who have not danced will be reproached when they hear the words, "We piped unto you, and you did not dance." And on birthdays, when the lawless word reigns over them, they dance so that their movements please that word. *Origen (c. 245, E), 9.428.*

We turn women away from an immoral life . . . and from all mad desires after theaters and dancing. *Origen (c. 248, E), 4.486.*

The fact that David led the dances in the presence of God is no sanction for faithful Christians to occupy seats in the public theater. For David did not twist his limbs about in obscene movements. He did not depict in his dancing the story of Grecian lust. *Cyprian (c. 250, W), 5.576.*

Another crowd of souls is led in their wantonness to abandon themselves to clumsy motions, to dance and sing, and form rings of dancers. Finally, raising their haunches and hips, they float along with a tremulous motion of the loins. *Arnobius (c. 305, E), 6.450.*

See also Entertainment; Music, Musical Instruments.

DANIEL, BOOK OF

I. Seventy weeks

II. Explanation of other passages

I. Seventy weeks

Seventy weeks are determined for your people and for your holy city. . . . Know therefore and understand, that from the going forth of the command to restore and build Jerusalem until Messiah the Prince, there will be seven weeks and sixty-two weeks. . . . And after the sixty-two weeks Messiah will be cut off. Dan. 9:24–26.

Christ became King of the Jews, reigning in Jerusalem in the fulfillment of the seven weeks. In the sixty and two weeks, all of Judea was quiet and without wars. . . . In those "sixty and two weeks," as the prophet said, and "in the one week," He was Lord. The half of the week, Nero held sway. In the holy city Jerusalem he placed the abomination. And in the half of the week he was taken away, followed by Otho, Galba, and Vitellius. And Vespasian rose to the supreme power and destroyed Jerusalem and desolated the holy place. *Clement of Alexandria (c. 195, E), 2.329.*

Daniel says that "both the holy city and the holy place are exterminated together with the coming Leader, and that the pinnacle is destroyed unto ruin." Therefore, we must inquire into the times of the coming of Christ, the Leader. We will trace those times in [the book of] Daniel.... Therefore, we demonstrate that Christ came within the sixty-two and one-half weeks. *Tertullian (c. 197, W), 3.158, 159.*

By showing "the number of the years, and the time of the sixty-two and one-half completed weeks," we have proved that Christ came. That is, He was born at the time predicted. *Tertullian (c. 197, W), 3.168.*

He says, "And for one week he will make a covenant with many, and it will be that in the midst of the week, my sacrifice and oblation will cease." By "one week," therefore, he meant the last week that is to be at the end of the whole world. In that week, the two prophets, Enoch and Elijah, will take up the half. For they will preach 1260 days clothed in sackcloth, proclaiming repentance to the people and to all the nations. *Hippolytus (c. 200, W), 5.213.*

"Unto Christ the Prince will be seven weeks," which make forty-nine years. It was in the twenty-first year that Daniel saw these things in Babylon. Hence, the forty-nine years added to the twenty-one, make up the seventy years, of which the blessed Jeremiah spoke: "The sanctuary will be desolate seventy years." ... Now, who is this Christ that he speaks of? Is it not Jesus [i.e., Joshua the high priest] the son of Josedech, who returned at that time along with the people and offered sacrifice according to the Law, in the seventieth year, when the sanctuary was built? *Hippolytus (c. 205, W), 5.180.*

He says, "And after seven weeks there are other sixty and two weeks." This period embraces the space of 434 years. For, after the return of the people from Babylon under the leadership of Jesus the son of Josedech, Ezra the scribe, and Zerubbabel the Son of Shealtiel (of the line of David), there were 434 years until the coming of Christ. *Hippolytus (c. 205, W), 5.180.*

"After sixty-two weeks, the times will be fulfilled, and for one week he will make a covenant with many. And in the midst of the week, sacrifice and oblation will be removed." ... For when the sixty-two weeks are fulfilled, and Christ has come, and the Gospel is preached in every place, the times will then be accomplished. Then, there will remain only one week (the last), in which Elijah and Enoch will appear. And in the middle of it, the abomination of desolation will be manifested. This is the Antichrist, announcing desolation to the world. And when he comes, the sacrifice and oblation will be removed, which now are offered to God in every place by the nations. *Hippolytus (c. 205, W), 5.182.*

II. Explanation of other passages

He whom Daniel foretells would have dominion for a time, and times, and an half, is even already at the door. He is about to speak blasphemous and daring things against the Most High. *Justin Martyr (c. 160, E), 1.210.*

[Daniel] said that there were two thousand three hundred days from the time that the abomination of Nero stood in the holy city, until its destruction. For thus the declaration, which is added, shows: "How long will be the vision, the sacrifice taken away, the abomination of desolation?" *Clement of Alexandria (c. 195, E), 2.334.*

As these things, then, are in the future—and as the ten toes of the image are equivalent to democracies, and the ten horns of the fourth beast are distributed over ten kingdoms—let us look at the subject a little more closely. ... The golden head of the image and the lioness denoted the Babylonians. The shoulders and arms of silver, and the bear, represented the Medes and Persians. The belly and thighs of brass, and the leopard, signified the Greeks, who held the sovereignty from Alexander's time. The legs of iron, and the dreadful and terrible beast, represented the Romans, who presently hold the sovereignty. The toes of the feet that were part clay and part iron, and the ten horns, were emblems of the kingdoms that are yet to rise. The other little horn that grows up among them meant the Antichrist in their midst. The stone that smites the earth and brings judgment upon the world was Christ. *Hippolytus (c. 200, W), 5.209, 210.*

War was again made by Ptolemy against Antiochus, and Antiochus met him. For the Scripture says, "And the king of the South will stand up against the king of the North, and her seed will stand up against him." *Hippolytus (c. 205, W), 5.183.*

So Daniel has spoken of two abominations. The first is of destruction. The other is of desolation. What is the abomination of destruction, but that which Antiochus established there at the time? And what is the abomination of desolation, but that which will be universal when the Antichrist comes? *Hippolytus (c. 205, W), 5.184; extended discussion: 1.553–1.555, 3.158–3.160, 5.177–5.191, 5.208–5.210, 5.178–5.191.*

SEE ALSO ANTICHRIST; ANTIOCHUS EPIPHANES; CHRONOLOGY; ESCHATOLOGY; NUMEROLOGY; REVELATION, BOOK OF.

DAYS OF CREATION

With the Lord one day is as a thousand years, and a thousand years as one day. 2 Pet. 3:8.

In six days, God made the works of his hands. On the seventh day, he made an end, rested on it, and sanctified it. *Barnabas (c. 70–130, E), 1.146.*

In the day that they did eat, in the same day did they die, and became death's debtors. For it was one day of the creation. It is said, "There was made in the evening, and there was made in the morning, one day." Now in this same day that they did eat, in that day they also died. . . . From this it is clear that the Lord suffered death, in obedience to His Father, upon that same day on which Adam died while he disobeyed God. *Irenaeus (c. 180, E/W), 1.551.*

In as many days as this world was made, in so many thousand years will it be concluded. . . . For the day of the Lord is as a thousand years. In six days created things were completed. It is evident, therefore, that they will come to an end at the sixth thousand year. *Irenaeus (c. 180, E/W), 1.557.*

What are the hundred-fold [rewards] in this world? . . . These are in the times of the kingdom, that is, upon the seventh day, which has been sanctified. This is the day in which God rested from the works He had created. It is the true Sabbath of the righteous. *Irenaeus (c. 180, E/W), 1.562.*

No man can give a sufficient explanation of this six days' work, nor can he describe all of its parts. He could not do this even if he had ten thousand tongues. *Theophilus (c. 180, E), 2.99.*

Not even the Law and the commandments totally convey what is agreeable to reason. For who that has understanding would think that the first, second, and third day—and the evening and the morning—existed without a sun, moon, and stars? Or, too, who would think that the first day was, as it were, without a sky? . . . I do not suppose that anyone doubts that these things figuratively indicate certain mysteries—the history having taken place in appearance, and not literally. *Origen (c. 225, E), 4.365.*

The first seven days in the divine arrangement contain seven thousand years. *Cyprian (c. 250, W), 5.503. [This is not necessarily talking about the days of creation.]*

God produced that entire mass for the adornment of His majesty in six days. On the seventh day, He consecrated it with a blessing. *Victorinus (c. 280, W), 7.341.*

The creation of the world in six days was still recent. *Methodius (c. 290, E), 6.333.*

God made heaven and earth and the things that are in them in six days. *Methodius (c. 290, E), 6.339.*

After God had made the world and all the things in it in the span of six days, he rested on the seventh day from all His works. *Disputation of Archelaus and Manes (c. 320, E), 6.203.*

Clement, Irenaeus, and Justin the martyr and philosopher, comment with exceeding wisdom on the number six of the sixth day. They declare that the intelligent soul of man and his five susceptible senses were the six works of the sixth day. *Anastasius, post-Nicene writer, citing Justin Martyr (c. 160, E), 1.302; see also 2.98, 99; extended discussion: 7.341–7.342.*

SEE ALSO CREATION; SEVENTH DAY OF CREATION.

DEACON

Therefore, brethren, seek out from among you seven men of good reputation, full of the Holy Spirit and wisdom, whom we may appoint over this business. Acts 6:3.

To all the saints in Christ Jesus who are in Philippi, with the bishops and deacons. Phil. 1:1.

Likewise deacons must be reverent, not double-tongued, not given to much wine, not greedy for money. 1 Tim. 3:8.

Appoint, therefore, for yourselves, bishops and deacons worthy of the Lord—men who are meek, truthful and tested, and are not lovers of money. For they also render to you the service of prophets and teachers. Therefore, do not despise them, for they are your honored ones, together with the prophets and teachers. *Didache (c. 80–140, E), 7.381.*

And thus preaching through countries and cities, they appointed the first-fruits [of their labors], having first tested them by the Spirit, to be bishops and deacons of those who would afterwards believe. *Clement of Rome (c. 96, W), 1.16.*

It is fitting also that the deacons, as being [the ministers] of the mysteries of Jesus Christ, should in every respect be pleasing to all. *Ignatius (c. 105, E), 1.67.*

It would behoove you, as a church of God, to elect a deacon to act as the ambassador of God. *Ignatius (c. 105, E), 1.85.*

The deacons should be blameless before the face of His righteousness. They must be the servants of God and Christ, not of men. They must not be slanderers, double-tongued, or lovers of money. Rather, they must be temperate in all things—compassionate, industrious, walking according to the truth of the Lord. *Polycarp (c. 135, E), 1.34.*

Stephen was chosen the first deacon by the apostles. *Irenaeus (c. 180, E/W), 1.434.*

There were present there Tertius and Pomponius, the blessed deacons who ministered to us, and who had arranged by means of a gratuity that we might be refreshed by being sent out for a few hours into a more pleasant part of the prison. *Passion of Perpetua and Felicitas (c. 205, W), 3.700.*

Those who have received certificates from the martyrs ... if they should be seized with any misfortune and peril of sickness, ... and if a presbyter cannot be found and death begins to be imminent, they can make confession of their sin before even a deacon. Thereby, with the imposition of hands upon them for repentance, they can come to the Lord with the peace that the martyrs have desired. *Cyprian (c. 250, W), 5.293.*

If a poor man, or one of low birth, or a stranger, comes upon you—whether he is young or old—and there is no place for him, the deacon will find a place for him. *Apostolic Constitutions (compiled c. 390, E), 7.422.*

You who are deacons, it is your duty to visit all those who stand in need of visitation. *Apostolic Constitutions (compiled c. 390, E), 7.432.*

A deacon does not bless.... He also does not baptize and does not offer [the Eucharist]. However, when a bishop or presbyter has offered, the deacon distributes to the people. He does this, not as a priest, but as one who ministers to the priests. But it is not lawful for any of the other clergy [i.e., the minor orders] to do the work of a deacon. *Apostolic Constitutions (compiled c. 390, E), 7.494.*

SEE ALSO BISHOP; CHURCH GOVERNMENT; PRESBYTER.

DEACONESS

... also your readers, your signers, your porters, your deaconesses, your widows, your virgins, and your orphans. *Apostolic Constitutions (compiled c. 390, E), 7.410.*

Let not any woman address herself to the deacon or bishop without the deaconess. *Apostolic Constitutions (compiled c. 390, E), 7.410.*

Ordain also a deaconess who is faithful and holy for the ministrations towards women. For sometimes the bishop cannot send a deacon (who is a man) to the women, on account of unbelievers. You should therefore send a woman, a deaconess, on account of the imaginations of the bad. For we stand in need of a woman, a deaconess, for many necessities. For example, in the baptism of women, the deacon will anoint only their forehead with the holy oil. And after him, the deaconess will anoint them. For there is no necessity that the women should be seen by the men. *Apostolic Constitutions (compiled c. 390, E), 7.431.*

Let the deaconess be a pure virgin. Or, at the minimum, let her be a widow who has been married only once and who is faithful and well-esteemed. *Apostolic Constitutions (compiled c. 390, E), 7.457.*

A deaconess does not bless, nor does she perform anything belonging to the office of presbyters or deacons. Rather, she is only to keep the doors and to minister to the presbyters in the baptizing of women, for the sake of decency. *Apostolic Constitutions (compiled c. 390, E), 7.494.*

Prayers for appointment of a deaconess: 7.492.

SEE ALSO VIRGINS; WIDOWS.

DEAD, ABODE OF THE

SEE DEAD, INTERMEDIATE STATE OF THE.

DEAD, INTERMEDIATE STATE OF THE

The intermediate state of the dead refers to the condition of the dead between the time of death and the resurrection from the dead.

Come, my people, enter your chambers, and shut your doors behind you; hide yourself, as it were, for a little moment, until the indignation is past. Isa. 26:20.

So it was that the beggar died, and was carried by the angels to Abraham's bosom. The rich man also died and was buried. And being in torments in Hades, he lifted up his eyes and saw Abraham afar off, and Lazarus in his bosom. Luke 16:22, 23.

Jesus said to him, "Assuredly, I say to you, today you will be with Me in Paradise." Luke 23:43.

Jesus of Nazareth . . . whom God raised up, having loosed the pains of death, because it was not possible that he should be held by it. For David says concerning him: . . . "You will not leave my soul in Hades." Acts 2:22–27.

When the Chief Shepherd appears, you will receive the crown of glory that does not fade away. 1 Pet. 5:4.

Peter, through unrighteous envy [of his persecutors], endured not one or two, but numerous labors. And when he had at length suffered martyrdom, he departed to the place of glory due to him. . . . Paul also obtained the reward of patient endurance, after being seven times thrown into captivity . . . and suffering martyrdom under the prefects. In that manner, he was removed from the world and went into the holy place. *Clement of Rome (c. 96, W), 1.6.*

All the generations from Adam even unto this day have passed away. However, those who, through the grace of God, have been made perfect in love, now possess a place among the godly. And they will be made manifest at the revelation of the kingdom of Christ. For it is written, "Enter into your secret chambers for a little time, until my wrath and fury pass away. And I will remember a propitious day, and will raise you up out of your graves." *Clement of Rome (c. 96, W), 1.18.*

[IN REFERENCE TO SOME FAITHFUL MARTYRS:] They are in their due place in the presence of the Lord, with whom they also suffered. *Polycarp (c. 135, E), 1.35.*

But [the martyrs] were revealed by the Lord to them, inasmuch as they were no longer men, but had already become angels. *Martyrdom of Polycarp (c. 135, E), 1.39.*

After we have departed from the world, no further power of confessing or repenting will belong to us. *Second Clement (c. 150, W), 7.519.*

The souls of the godly remain in a better place, while those of the unjust and wicked are in a worse place, waiting for the time of judgment. *Justin Martyr (c. 160, E), 1.197.*

You may have fallen in with some [Gnostics] who are called Christians. However, they do not admit this [intermediate state], and they venture to blaspheme the God of Abraham. . . . They say there is no resurrection of the dead. Rather, they say that when they die, their souls are taken to heaven. Do not imagine that they are Christians. *Justin Martyr (c. 160, E), 1.239.*

[Christ's enemies] imagined they would put Him to death, and that He, like some common mortal, would remain in Hades. *Justin Martyr (c. 160, E), 1.248.*

It is likely enough that they themselves are now lamenting in Hades and repenting with a repentance that is too late. *Justin Martyr (c. 160, E), 1.288.*

If they believe that there is nothing after death, but declare that those who die pass into insensibility, then they become our benefactors when they set us free from sufferings. *Justin Martyr (c. 160, E), 1.182.*

Having been born, and through death existing no longer, and seen no longer, I will exist again, just as before I was not, but was afterwards born. *Tatian (c. 160, E), 2.67.*

The soul is not in itself immortal, O Greeks, but mortal. Yet it is possible for it not to die. If, indeed, it does not know the truth, it dies. It is dissolved with the body, but rises again at last at the end of the world with the body, receiving death by punishment in immortality. But, again, if it acquires the knowledge of God, it does not die, although for a time it is dissolved. *Tatian (c. 160, E), 2.70, 71.*

[The Gnostics] are in all points inconsistent with themselves when they declare that all souls do not enter into the intermediate place, but only those of the righteous. *Irenaeus (c. 180, E/W), 1.403.*

The Lord has taught with very great fullness that souls continue to exist. They do not do this by passing from body to body. Rather, they preserve the same form as that of the body to which they were adapted. . . . The Lord states that the rich man recognized Lazarus after death, as well as Abraham. . . . From these things, then, it is plainly declared that souls continue to exist, that they do not pass from body to body, that they possess the form of a man (so that they may be recognized), and that they retain the memory of things in this world. Moreover, it is plain that the gift of prophecy was possessed by Abraham and that each class receives a habitation such as it has deserved, even before the judgment. *Irenaeus (c. 180, E/W), 1.411.*

The heretics . . . do not acknowledge the salvation of their flesh . . . but claim that immediately upon their death, they will pass above the heavens and the Demiurge [Creator] and go to the Mother or to that Father whom they pretend exists. . . . For they do not choose to understand, that if these things are as they say, the Lord Himself, in whom they profess to believe, did not rise again upon the third day. Rather, immediately upon His expiring on the cross, He undoubtedly departed on high, leaving His body to the earth. . . . The Lord observed the law of the dead so that He might become the First-Begotten from the dead. And He waited until the third day "in the lower parts of the earth." . . . [Accordingly,] these men [the Gnostics] must be put to confusion, who allege that "the lower parts" refer to this world of ours, but that their inner man, leaving the body here, ascends into the super-celestial place . . . .

The Lord "went away in the midst of the shadow of death," where the souls of the dead were. However, afterwards, He arose in the body. And after the resurrection, He was taken up [into heaven]. From this, it is clear that the souls of His disciples also (upon whose account the Lord underwent these things) will go away into the invisible place allotted to them by God. And they will remain there until the resurrection, awaiting that event. Then receiving their bodies, and rising in their entirety (that is, bodily), just as the Lord arose, they will come in that manner into the presence of God. *Irenaeus (c. 180, E/W), 1.560.*

"No disciple is above the Master." . . . Our Master, therefore, did not at once depart, taking flight [to heaven]. Rather, He awaited the time of His resurrection, as determined by the Father. . . . Likewise, we also should await the time of our resurrection determined by God. *Irenaeus (c. 180, E/W), 1.560, 561.*

If, then, the Lord descended to Hades for no other reason but to preach the Gospel (as He did descend), it was either to preach the Gospel to *all*, or else to the Hebrews only. If, accordingly, He preached to all, then all who believe will be saved on making their profession there—even though they may be Gentiles. For God's punishments are saving and disciplinary, leading to conversion. He desires the repentance, rather than the death, of a sinner. This is especially so since souls, although darkened by passions, when released from their bodies, are able to perceive more clearly. For they are no longer obstructed by the paltry flesh. *Clement of Alexandria (c. 195, E), 2.490, 491.*

So I think it is demonstrated that God (being good) and the Lord (being powerful) both save with a righteousness and equality that extends to all who turn to God, whether here or elsewhere. For it is not here alone that the active power of God is present. Rather, it is everywhere and is always at work. . . . For it is not right that those persons [who died before Christ] should be condemned without trial, and that those alone who lived after His coming should have the advantage of the divine righteousness. *Clement of Alexandria (c. 195, E), 2.491.*

We speak of Paradise, the place of divine bliss appointed to receive the spirits of the saints. There, the saints are cut off from the knowledge of this world by that fiery zone, as by a sort of enclosure. So, the Elysian plains have taken possession of their faith. *Tertullian (c. 197, W), 3.52.*

[The Marcionites] say that the Creator is the Judge who commits to prison and allows no release out of it without the payment of the very last cent. *Tertullian (c. 207, W), 3.399.*

Our answer to this is that the Scripture itself ... expressly distinguishes between Abraham's bosom (where the poor man dwells) and Hades. Hades means one thing; and "Abraham's bosom," another. A great gulf is said to separate those regions and to hinder a passage from one to the other. *Tertullian (c. 207, W), 3.406.*

It must therefore be evident to every man of intelligence who has ever heard of the Elysian fields, that there is some determinate place called Abraham's bosom. It is designed for the reception of the souls of Abraham's children—even from among the Gentiles. . . . This region, therefore, I call Abraham's bosom. Although it is not in heaven, it is yet higher than Hades. And it is appointed to afford an interval of rest to the souls of the righteous until the consummation of all things completes the resurrection of all men with the full recompense of their reward. . . . By Abraham's bosom is meant some temporary receptacle of faithful souls, wherein is even now foreshadowed an image of the future, and where is given some foresight of the glory of both judgments. *Tertullian (c. 207, W), 3.406.*

When the soul, by the power of death, is released from its bond to the flesh, it is by the very release cleansed and purified. . . . And then it finds itself enjoying its freedom from matter. And by virtue of its liberty, it recovers its divinity. It is just as one who awakes out of sleep passes from dreams to realities. Then the soul declares what it sees. Then it either exults or it fears as soon as it sees the very angel's face—depending on what lodging it discovers has been prepared for it. *Tertullian (c. 210, W), 3.230.*

There is not a soul that can at all procure salvation, unless it believes while it is still in the flesh. For it is an established truth that the flesh is the very condition on which salvation hinges. *Tertullian (c. 210, W), 3.551.*

As [the soul] has acted in each individual instance, so proportionably does it suffer in Hades, being the first to taste of judgment. For it was the first to induce to the commission of sin. Nevertheless, it is still waiting for the flesh. . . . This, in short, will be the process of that judgment that is postponed to the last great day. It is delayed until then, so that by the exhibition of the flesh, the entire course of the divine vengeance may be accomplished. Besides, if it were destined for souls alone, there would be no reason to delay until the end that doom which souls are already tasting in Hades. *Tertullian (c. 210, W), 3.557.*

When we read, "Go, my people, enter into your closets for a little season, until my anger passes away," we understand the closets to be graves, in which will rest for a little while those who—at the end of the world—have departed this life in the last furious onset of the power of the Antichrist. *Tertullian (c. 210, W), 3.565.*

For who is there that will not desire, while he is in the flesh, to put on immortality? Who would not desire to continue his life by a happy escape from death through the transformation that must be experienced instead of [death]—without also encountering that Hades which will exact the very last farthing? *Tertullian (c. 210, W), 3.575.*

The remaining quotations from Tertullian apparently reflect more of a Montanist view of Paradise and Hades.

"We are indeed confident and deem it good rather to be absent from the body and present with the Lord." . . . Observe how he here also ascribes to the excellence of martyrdom a contempt for the body. For no one, on becoming absent from the body, is at once a dweller in the presence of the Lord—unless by the prerogative of martyrdom he gains a lodging in Paradise, not in Hades. *Tertullian (c. 210, W), 3.576.*

In Hades, the soul of a certain man is in torment, punished in flames, suffering excruciating thirst, and pleading for the relief of a drop of water for his tongue, from the finger of a happier soul. Do you suppose that this end of the blessed poor man and the miserable rich man is only imaginary? Then, why is the name of Lazarus given in this narrative—if the account is not of a real occurrence? But even if it is to be regarded as a parable, it will still be a testimony to truth and reality.... But what is that which is removed to Hades after the separation of the body? What is detained there? What is reserved until the Day of Judgment? To what did Christ also descend, on dying? I imagine it is the souls of the patriarchs. But for what purpose are they retained there—if the soul is not a bodily substance. For whatever is incorporeal is incapable of being kept and guarded in any way. It is also exempt from either punishment or refreshment.... Therefore, whatever amount of punishment or refreshment the soul tastes in Hades—in its prison or lodging, in the fire or in Abraham's bosom—it gives proof thereby of its own corporeality. *Tertullian (c. 210, W), 3.187.*

If you are inclined to apply the term "adversary" to the devil, you are advised by injunction "while you are on the way with him" to make even with him such a covenant as may be deemed compatible with the requirements of your true faith. Now the covenant you have made concerning him is to renounce him, his pomp, and his angels. So ... you must never think of getting back any of the things that you have renounced and have given back to him. Otherwise, he may summon you before God the Judge as a fraudulent man, and a transgressor of your covenant. And this Judge may deliver you over to the angel who is to execute the sentence. And he may commit you to the prison of Hades, out of which there will be no dismissal until even the smallest of your delinquencies is paid off in the period before the resurrection. What can be a more fitting sense than this? What can be a truer interpretation? *Tertullian (c. 210, W), 3.216.*

Hades is not supposed by us to be a bare cavity, nor some subterranean sewer of the world. Rather it is a vast deep space in the interior of the earth.... For we read that Christ in His death spent three days in the heart of the earth. ... He did not ascend into the heights of heaven before descending into the lower parts of the earth. This was so that He might there [in Hades] make the patriarchs and prophets partakers of Himself. You must believe Hades is a subterranean region. You should keep at arm's length those [Gnostics] who are too proud to believe that the souls of the faithful deserve a place in Hades. These persons—who are servants above their Lord, and disciples above their Master—would no doubt spurn to

receive the comfort of the resurrection, if they must expect it in Abraham's bosom. But it was for this purpose, they say, that Christ descended into Hades—that we might not ourselves have to descend there. Well, then, what difference is there between pagans and Christians, if the same prison awaits them all when dead? How, indeed, will the soul mount up to heaven, where Christ is already sitting at the Father's right hand? For the archangel's trumpet has not yet been heard by the command of God. ... To no one is heaven opened. ... When the world, indeed, will pass away, *then* the kingdom of heaven will be opened. *Tertullian (c. 210, W), 3.231.*

Shall we then have to sleep high up in ether? ... No, but in Paradise, you tell me. This is where the patriarchs and prophets have already been transported, from Hades in the retinue of the Lord's resurrection. How is it, then, that the region of Paradise displays no other souls as in it besides the souls of the martyrs? For it was revealed to John in the Spirit as lying "under the altar." How is it that the most heroic martyr Perpetua on the day of her martyrdom saw only her fellow martyrs there—in the revelation which she received of Paradise? ... The sole key to unlock Paradise is your own life's blood. *Tertullian (c. 210, W), 3.231.*

You have a treatise by us, in which we have established the position that every soul is detained in safe-keeping in Hades until the day of the Lord. There arises the question of whether this takes place immediately after the soul's departure from the body. Are some souls detained in the meantime here on earth for special reasons? Is it permitted them of their own accord, or by the intervention of authority, to be removed from Hades at some subsequent time? *Tertullian (c. 210, W), 3.231, 232.*

You will say that it is all the wicked souls that are banished to Hades. I must compel you to determine which of its two regions—the region of the good or that of the bad. If you mean the bad, even now the souls of the wicked deserve to be consigned to those abodes. If you mean the good, why should you judge the souls of infants and of virgins—those which, by reason of their condition in life were pure and innocent—to be unworthy of such a resting place? *Tertullian (c. 210, W), 3.233.*

The fact that Hades is not in any case opened for [the release] of any soul has been firmly established by the Lord in the person of Abraham—in His representation of the poor man at rest and the rich man in torment. No one could possibly be sent from those abodes to report to us how matters went in the lower regions. *Tertullian (c. 210, W), 3.234.*

All souls, therefore, are shut up within Hades. Do you admit this? [It is true, whether] you say yes or no. Moreover, there are already experienced there punishments and consolations. And there you have a poor man and a rich. . . . Why, then, cannot you suppose that the soul undergoes punishment and consolation in Hades in the interval, while it awaits its alternative of judgment, in a certain anticipation either of gloom or of glory? You reply: "Because in the judgment of God, this matter should be sure and safe and there should be no inkling beforehand of the award of his sentence—and also because it should first be covered by its vestment of the restored flesh." . . . What, then, is to take place in that interval? Shall we sleep? But souls do not sleep even when men are alive. It is indeed the business of *bodies* to sleep, to which also belongs death itself. *Tertullian (c. 210, W), 3.234, 235.*

Full well, then, does the soul even in Hades know how to rejoice and to sorrow even without the body. . . . It is therefore quite in keeping with this order of things that this part of our nature [i.e., the soul] should be the first to have the recompense and reward to which they are due on account of its priority. In short, inasmuch as we understand "the prison" pointed out in the gospel to be Hades, and as we also interpret "the uttermost farthing" to mean the very smallest offense which has to be recompensed there before the resurrection, no one will hesitate to believe that the soul undergoes in Hades some compensatory discipline, without prejudice to the full process of the resurrection—when the recompense will be administered through the flesh as well. The Paraclete has also pressed home this point on our attention in most frequent admonitions, whenever any of us have admitted the force of His words from a knowledge of His promised spiritual disclosures. *Tertullian (c. 210, W), 3.235.*

A person of old used to say that only those who are instructed in the knowledge of divine things descend alive into Hades. For he who has not tasted of the words of life is already dead. *Hippolytus (c. 205, W), 5.202.*

Now we must speak of Hades, in which the souls both of the righteous and the unrighteous are detained. Hades is a place in the created system, rude, a locality beneath the earth, in which the light of the world does not shine. And since the sun does not shine in this place, there is necessarily perpetual darkness there. This place has been destined to be, as it were, a guardhouse for souls. The angels are stationed there as guards distributing temporary punishments for characters, according to each one's deeds. And in this locality there is a certain place set apart by itself, a lake of unquenchable fire, into which we suppose no one has ever yet been cast. . . . But the righteous (who will obtain the incorruptible and unfading kingdom) are indeed presently detained in Hades, but not in the same place with the unrighteous. For to this locality there is one descent, at the gate of which we believe an archangel is stationed with an army. And when those who are conducted by the angels who are appointed unto the souls have passed through this gate, they do not all proceed down one and the same path. Rather, the righteous are conducted in the light toward the right. And being hymned by the angels stationed at the place, they are brought to a locality full of light. And there all the righteous persons from the beginning dwell. They are not ruled by any necessity. Rather, they perpetually enjoy the contemplation of the blessings that are in their view. Also, they delight themselves with the expectation of other blessings, ever new. In fact, they consider the new blessings as ever better than the first ones. And that place brings no labors for them. In that locale, there are neither fierce heat, cold, nor thorns. But the faces of the fathers and the righteous are seen to be always smiling, as they wait for the rest and eternal revival in heaven that follow this location. And we call this place by the name of "Abraham's bosom."

However, the unrighteous are dragged toward the left by angels who are ministers of punishment. These souls no longer go of their own accord. Rather, they are dragged as prisoners by force. And the angels appointed over them hurry them along, reproaching them and threatening them with an eye of terror, forcing them down into the lower parts. And when the souls are brought there, those appointed to that task drag them on to the vicinity of Gehenna. And those who are so near [to Gehenna] hear incessantly its agitation, and they feel the hot smoke. And when that vision is so near, as they see the terrible and excessively glowing spectacle of the fire, they shudder in horror at the expectation of the future judgment, already feeling the power of their punishment. And again, when they see the place of the fathers and the righteous, they also suffer punishment merely from seeing this. For a deep and vast abyss is set there in the midst, so that neither can any of the righteous in sympathy think to cross it, nor do any of the unrighteous dare to cross it.

I think I have said enough on the subject of Hades, in which all souls are detained until the time that God has determined. And then He will accomplish a resurrection of all—not by transferring souls into other bodies—but by raising the bodies themselves. *Hippolytus (c. 205, W), 5.222.*

Those here who die according to the death common to all are—in consequence of the deeds done here—arranged in a way so as to obtain different places according to the proportion of their sins—if they are deemed worthy of the placed called Hades. *Origen (c. 225, E), 4.372.*

What lies beneath the earth is not itself void of distributed and arranged powers. For there is a place where the souls of the just and the unjust are taken, conscious of the anticipated dooms of future judgment. *Novatian (c. 235, W), 5.612.*

Those who had sacrificed [to idols] should be assisted at death, [if repentant,] for there is no confession in Hades. *Cyprian (c. 250, W), 5.331.*

Do not think, dearest brother, that either the courage of the brethren will be lessened, or that martyrdoms will fail for this cause—that repentance is relaxed to the lapsed. . . . It is one thing to stand for pardon. It is another thing to attain to glory. It is one thing, when cast into prison, not to go out from it until one has paid the last coin. It is another thing at once to receive the wages of faith and courage. It is one thing, tortured by long suffering for sins, to be cleansed and long purged by fire. It is another to have all sins purged by suffering. It is one thing to be in suspense until the sentence of God at the day of judgment. It is another to be crowned at once by the Lord. *Cyprian (c. 250, W), 5.332.*

When you have once departed yonder, there is no longer any place for repentance. And there is no possibility of making satisfaction. *Here* life is either lost or saved. Here eternal

safety is provided for by the worship of God and the fruits of faith. Do not let anyone be restrained from coming to obtain salvation, either by his sins or by his years. To him who still remains in this world, no repentance is too late. *Cyprian (c. 250, W), 5.465.*

In Hades there is no repentance. . . . So while the way of mercy is open, brethren, let us entreat God with full atonements. *Treatise against Novatian (c. 255, W), 5.662, 663.*

After the death of a man in this position, there cannot be added to him anything at all. He cannot be supplemented. Nor can anything avail him in the Day of Judgment. Treatise on Re-Baptism (c. 257, W), 5.671. The "bronze altar" refers to the earth, under which is Hades. This is a region away from punishments and fires. It is a place of rest for the saints. Here, indeed, the wicked see the righteous, but they cannot be carried across to them. *Victorinus (c. 280, W), 7.351.*

If we ask concerning the tongue, the finger, Abraham's bosom, and the reclining there, it may perhaps be that the soul receives in the change a form similar in appearance to its coarse and earthly body. *Methodius (c. 290, E), 6.377, as quoted by Photius.*

The rich man was in torment and the poor man was comforted in the bosom of Abraham. The one was to be punished in Hades, and the other was to be comforted in Abraham's bosom. Yet, they are both spoken of as *before* the [second] coming of the Savior and before the end of the world. Therefore, their condition is before the resurrection. *Methodius (c. 290, E), 6.377, as quoted by Photius.*

A second life is not granted to us. It is not as though if we seek wisdom in this life, we will be wise in the next one. Each result must be brought about in this life. It should be quickly found in order that it may be quickly embraced. *Lactantius (c. 304–313, W), 7.85.*

Let no one imagine that souls are immediately judged after death. For all are detained in one and a common place of confinement—until the arrival of the time in which the great Judge will make an investigation of their deserts. Those whose piety will have been approved will receive the reward of immortality. However, those whose sins and crimes will have been brought to light—these will not rise again. Rather, they will be hidden in the same darkness with the wicked, being destined to certain punishment. *Lactantius (c. 304–313, W), 7.217.*

What about the punishment in Hades, of which we have heard, which assumes also many forms of torture? *Arnobius (c. 305, E), 6.445.*

When man afterwards had inclined to death, because of the fall, it was necessary that man's form should be recreated anew to salvation by the same Maker. For the form [i.e., the body] lay rotting in the ground. However, that inspiration that had been as the breath of life—it was detained separately from the body in a dark place that is called Hades. So there was a separation of the soul from the body. The soul was banished to Hades while the body was returned back to dust. *Alexander of Alexandria (c. 324, E), 6.300; extended discussion: 3.231–3.235.*

SEE ALSO DEATH; DESCENT INTO HADES; ESCHATOLOGY; ETERNAL PUNISHMENTS AND REWARDS; RESURRECTION OF THE DEAD.

DEAD, PRAYERS FOR THE

SEE PRAYER (VI. SHOULD CHRISTIANS PRAY FOR THE DEAD?)

DEAD, STATE OF THE

SEE DEAD, INTERMEDIATE STATE OF THE; RESURRECTION OF THE DEAD.

DEAD, WORSHIP OF THE

This is the sole accusation you can bring against us—that we do not reverence the same gods as you do, nor offer drink offerings and the aroma of fat to the dead, nor crowns for their statues. *Justin Martyr (c. 160, E), 1.171.*

We know that the names of the dead are nothing, as are their images. But we know well enough, too, when images are set up, who carry on their wicked work under their names. We know who exult in the homage rendered to the dead and who pretend to be divine. It is none other than the accursed spirits. *Tertullian (c. 197, W), 3.84.*

Offerings to propitiate the dead were regarded as belonging to the class of funeral sacrifices. And these are idolatry. In fact, idolatry is a type of homage to the departed. The one as well as the other is a service to dead men. Moreover, demons have their abode in the images of the dead. . . . Therefore, we make no funeral oblations to the departed. *Tertullian (c. 197, W), 3.85.*

What, indeed, do you perform in honoring your gods that you do not equally perform to your dead? . . . You slay the same victims and burn the same odors for your dead as you do for your gods. *Tertullian (c. 197, W), 3.119.*

SEE ALSO GODS, PAGAN; IMAGES; PRAYER (VII. SHOULD CHRISTIANS PRAY TO THE DEAD?).

DEATH

I. What is death?

II. Why humans die

III. Christian attitude towards death

I. What is death?

According to the general sentiment of the human race, we declare death to be the debt of nature. This much has been settled by the voice of God. *Tertullian (c. 210, W), 3.227.*

The operation of death is plain and obvious: it is the separation of body and soul. *Tertullian (c. 210, W), 3.228.*

We define the first death in this manner: death is the dissolution of the nature of living beings. Or we can say that death is the separation of body and soul. *Lactantius (c. 304–313, W), 7.61.*

II. Why humans die

If a vessel being molded has some flaw in it, it is remolded or re-made, so that it can become new and entire. So also it happens to man by death. For somehow or other he is broken up, that he may rise in the resurrection whole. I mean, spotless, righteous, and immortal. *Theophilus (c. 180, E), 2.104, 105.*

God set a limit to man's sin, by interposing death. For death causes sin to cease. It puts an end to it by the dissolution of the flesh. This dissolution should take place in the earth, so that man, ceasing at length to live to sin, and dying to it, might begin to live to God. *Irenaeus (c. 180, E/ W), 1.457.*

Although the body is dissolved at the appointed time, because of that original disobedience, it is placed, as it were, in the crucible of the earth, to be re-cast again. When it is re-cast, it will not be as this corruptible [body]. Rather, it will be pure, and no longer subject to decay. To each body, its own soul will be restored. *Irenaeus (c. 180, E/W), 1.570.*

We boldly assert and persistently maintain that death happens not by way of natural consequence to man, but owing to a fault and defect that is actually unnatural. . . . If man had been directly designed to die as the condition of his creation, then, of course, death must be imputed to nature. However, that he was *not* thus appointed to die is proved by the very law that made his condition dependent on a warning. And death resulted from man's arbitrary choice. Indeed, if he had not sinned, he certainly would not have died. *Tertullian (c. 210, W), 3.229.*

An eminent artisan once created a noble statue, made of gold. It was beautifully proportioned in all of its members—exquisite to look upon. But there was an evil man who was so jealous over this beautiful statue that he could no longer bear to see its beauty. So in his envy, he mutilated the statue, destroying its elegance. Upon discovering this, the artificer decided to cast the statue over again. For he had bestowed much pain, labor, and care upon the statue. And he wanted it to be free from defect. So his only choice was to melt the statue down and then remold it to its original beauty. Now, God's plan seems to be similar. Upon seeing man, his most beautiful work, corrupted by envious treachery, he could not bear to leave man in such a condition. For he loved man, and he did not want man to remain blemished forever and to carry blame for all eternity. So he dissolves man again back to his original materials. In this way, by remolding man, all of man's blemishes can waste away and disappear. So the melting down of the statue corresponds to the death and dissolution of the body. And the remolding of the statue corresponds to the resurrection after death. *Condensed from Methodius (c. 290, E), 6.365.*

If death were appointed at a fixed age, man would become most arrogant and would be destitute of all humanity. For almost all the rights of humanity—by which we are united with one another—arise from fear [of death] and the consciousness of frailty. *Lactantius (c. 304–313, W), 7.285.*

III. Christian attitude towards death

Let not your heart be troubled, neither let it be afraid. You have heard Me say to you, "I am going away and coming back to you." If you loved Me, you would rejoice because I said, "I am going to the Father," for My Father is greater than I. John 14:27, 28.

For to me, to live is Christ, and to die is gain. Phil. 1:21.

I do not want you to be ignorant, brethren, concerning those who have fallen asleep, lest you sorrow as others who have no hope. 1 Thess. 4:13.

We are not concerned when men cut us off. For death is a debt which must at all events be paid. *Justin Martyr (c. 160, E), 1.166.*

Men, after the loss of immortality, have conquered death by submitting to death in faith. *Tatian (c. 160, E), 2.71.*

Since, then, there is certainty as to the resurrection of the dead, grief for death is needless. . . . For why should you grieve, if you believe that your loved one has not perished? . . . We wound Christ when we do not accept with equanimity the summoning out of this world of anyone by Him, as if they were to be pitied. *Tertullian (c. 200, W), 3.713.*

Although the death of children leaves grief for the heart, it is not right to either go forth in black garments, or to bewail them. The Lord prudently says that you must grieve with the mind, not with outward show. . . . Are you not ashamed to lament your children without restraint, like the Gentiles do? You tear your face, beat your breast, and take off your garments. Do you not fear the Lord, whose kingdom you desire to behold? *Commodianus (c. 240, W), 4.217.*

When the dear ones whom we love depart from the world, we should rejoice rather than grieve. Remembering this truth, the blessed apostle Paul in his epistle lays it down, saying, "To me, to live is Christ and to die is gain." *Cyprian (c. 250, W), 5.470.*

How preposterous and absurd it is, that while we ask that the will of God should be done, yet when God calls and summons us from this world, we do not at once obey the command of His will. . . . Do we wish to be honored with heavenly rewards by Him to whom we come *unwillingly?* Why, then, do we pray and ask that the kingdom of heaven may come, if the captivity of earth delights us? *Cyprian (c. 250, W), 5.473.*

Our brethren who are freed from this world by the Lord's summons are not to be lamented. For we know that they are not lost. Rather, they are sent before us. Departing from us, they precede us as travellers—as navigators are accustomed to do. They should be envied, not bewailed! The black garments should not be taken upon us *here*, when they have already taken white garments *there*.... The Gentiles can deservedly and rightly criticize us that we mourn as though our dead were extinct and lost. For, we say they are alive with God.... There is no advantage in setting forth virtue by our words, but then destroying the truth by our deeds.... The Holy Spirit teaches by Solomon that those who please God are taken from here sooner and are more quickly set free. Otherwise, while they are delaying longer in this world, they might be polluted with the pollution of the world ....

When the day of our summons arrives, we should come without delay. We should come without resistance to the Lord, when He Himself calls us. Although this should always be done by God's servants, it should much more be done now—now that the world is collapsing. ... We should ever and a day reflect that we have renounced the world and are in the meantime living here as guests and strangers.... Who would not hurry to return to his own country, if he has been placed in foreign lands? Who that is hurrying to return to his friends would not eagerly desire a prosperous gale so that he might embrace those dear to him even sooner. We regard Paradise as our country. We have already begun to consider the patriarchs as our parents. Why do we not hasten and run so that we may behold our country? Why do we not hurry to greet our parents? For a great number of our dear ones are awaiting us there. *Cyprian (c. 250, W), 5.474, 475.*

No one should be made sad by death. In living, there is labor and peril. In dying, there is peace and the certainty of the resurrection.... According to John: "If you loved me, you would rejoice because I go to the Father; for the Father is greater than I." *Cyprian (c. 250, W), 5.548; see also 4.346; extended discussion: 5.469–5.475.*

SEE ALSO ASSUMPTIONS; DEAD, INTERMEDIATE STATE OF THE; PRAYER (VI. SHOULD CHRISTIANS PRAY FOR THE DEAD?); ESCHATOLOGY; FALL OF MAN; UNCORRUPTED BODIES.

DECALOGUE

If anyone does not observe the Decalogue, he has no salvation. *Irenaeus (c. 180, E/W), 1.479.*

Preparing man for this life, the Lord Himself did speak the words of the Decalogue in His own person to all alike. Therefore, in like manner, do these commandments remain permanently with us. Because of His advent in the flesh, they have received extension and increase, but not abrogation. *Irenaeus (c. 180, E/W), 1.482.*

We have the Decalogue given by Moses. Using elementary principles (ones that are simple and limited to one thing), it defines the designation of sins in a way that is conducive to salvation. *Clement of Alexandria (c. 195, E), 2.292.*

For he who will have kept the undertaking of virginity completely and will have faithfully fulfilled the precepts of the Decalogue ... he is the true priest of Christ. *Victorinus (c. 280, W), 7.359.*

O virgins, the ten horns and stings ... are the ten opposites to the Decalogue. *Methodius (c. 290, E), 6.340; see also 2.512–2.515; extended discussion: 2.511–2.515.*

SEE ALSO LAW, MOSAIC.

DECIUS, EMPEROR

Decius (201–251) instituted the first empire-wide persecution against Christians, in 250.

He did not understand the wickedness of Decius.... When his sovereignty was in a prosperous position and when affairs were turning out according to his wish, he oppressed those holy men who interceded with God on behalf of his peace and his welfare. *Dionysius of Alexandria (c. 262, E), 6.106, as quoted by Eusebius.*

Decius appeared in the world as an accursed wild beast to afflict the church. *Lactantius (c. 320, W), 7.302.*

SEE ALSO CHURCH AND STATE.

DEFENSE OF CHRISTIANITY

SEE CHRISTIANITY.

DEIFICATION OF MAN

As used in the early church, deification of man refers to the Christians' union with God in this life and to their becoming partakers of the divine nature after the resurrection.

God stands in the congregation of the mighty; He judges among the gods. Ps. 82:1.

I do not pray for these alone, but also for those who will believe in Me through their word; that they all may be one, as You, Father, are in Me, and I in You; that they also may be one in Us. John 17:20, 21.

We have become partakers of Christ if we hold the beginning of our confidence steadfast to the end. Heb. 3:14.

. . . through these you may be partakers of the divine nature, having escaped the corruption that is in the world through lust. 2 Pet. 1:4.

We have learned that only those who have lived close to God in holiness and virtue are deified. *Justin Martyr (c. 160, E), 1.170.*

Neither, then, immortal nor yet mortal did He make man. Rather, as we have said above, man was capable of both. If he would incline to the things of immortality, keeping the commandment of God, he would receive immortality as a reward from Him. And he would become divine. *Theophilus (c. 180, E), 2.105.*

And again, "God stood in the congregation of the gods; He judges among the gods." He refers to the Father and the Son, and to those who have received the adoption. *Irenaeus (c. 180, E/W), 1.419.*

As I have already said, He caused man to cleave to and to become one with God. . . . Unless man had been joined to God, he could never have become a partaker of incorruptibility. *Irenaeus (c. 180, E/W), 1.448.*

How will man pass into God, unless God had first passed into man? *Irenaeus (c. 180, E/W), 1.507.*

Humans are not uncreated. But by their being in existence throughout a long course of ages, they will receive a faculty of the Uncreated. This will be through the free bestowal of eternal existence upon them by God. . . . But being in subjection to God is continuance in immortality, and immortality is the glory of the uncreated One. *Irenaeus (c. 180, E/W), 1.521.*

It must be that you should partake of the nature of man at the outset, and then afterwards partake of the glory of God. *Irenaeus (c. 180, E/W), 1.523.*

Our Lord Jesus Christ, through His transcendent love, became what we are, so that He might bring us to be even what He Himself is. *Irenaeus (c. 180, E/W), 1.526.*

The Lord thus has redeemed us through His own blood, giving His soul for our souls, and His flesh for our flesh. He has also poured out the Spirit of the Father for the union and communion of God and man. He indeed imparts God to men by means of the Spirit. On the other hand, He has attached man to God by His own incarnation. He bestowed true and enduring immortality upon us at His coming— by means of communion with God. *Irenaeus (c. 180, E/W), 1.527.*

Being baptized, we are illuminated. Illuminated, we become sons. Being made sons, we are made perfect. Being made perfect, we are made immortal. He says, "I have said that you are gods, and all are sons of the Highest." *Clement of Alexandria (c. 195, E), 2.215.*

In this way, it is possible for the man of God already to have become divine. "I said, you are gods, and sons of the highest." *Clement of Alexandria (c. 195, E), 2.437.*

The man of God is consequently divine and is already holy. He is God-bearing and God-borne. *Clement of Alexandria (c. 195, E), 2.547.*

It would be impossible that another God could be admitted, when it is permitted to no other being to possess anything of God. Well, then, you say, at that rate we ourselves possess nothing of God. But indeed we do, and will continue to do so. Only, it is from *Him* that we receive it, and not from *ourselves.* For we will be even gods, if we deserve to be among those of whom He declared, "I have said, 'You are gods,'" and "God stands in the congregation of the gods." But this comes of His own grace, not from any property in us. For it is He alone who can make gods. *Tertullian (c. 200, W), 3.480.*

You will be a companion of God, and a co-heir with Christ, no longer enslaved by lusts or passions and wasted by disease. For you have become divine. . . . God has promised to bestow these upon you, for you have been deified and begotten unto immortality. *Hippolytus (c. 225, W), 5.153.*

I am of the opinion that the expression, "God will be all in all," means that He will be "all" in each individual person. Now, He will be "all" in each individual in this way: when everything that one can either feel, understand, or think will be wholly God. This will be when a person has been cleansed from the dregs of every sort of vice, and has every cloud of wickedness completely swept away. . . . It is when God will be the measure and standard of all movements. Thus, God will be "all," for there will no longer be any distinction of good and evil—for evil will exist nowhere. *Origen (c. 225, E), 4.345.*

It is one and the same thing to have a share in the Holy Spirit, which is of the Father and the Son. For the nature of the Trinity is one and incorporeal. And what we have said regarding the participation of the soul is to be understood also of angels and heavenly powers . . . because every rational creature needs a participation in the Trinity. *Origen (c. 225, E), 4.379.*

They see that from Him there began the union of the divine with the human nature. This was so that the human—by communion with the divine—might rise to be divine. This not only happened in Jesus, but also in all those who not only believe, but enter upon the life that Jesus taught. *Origen (c. 248, E), 4.475.*

These are honored by God—through His Only-Begotten Word—by participation in His divinity and thereby also in His name. *Origen (c. 248, E), 4.479.*

What man is, Christ was willing to be—so that man may also be what Christ is. *Cyprian (c. 250, W), 5.468.*

What Christ is, we Christians will be, if we imitate Christ. *Cyprian (c. 250, W), 5.469; see also 1.463, 1.522, 1.533.*

SEE ALSO ATONEMENT; ETERNAL PUNISHMENTS AND REWARDS; GODS (PSALM 82).

DEISM

Deism is the belief that God exists and that he created the world, but that he exercises no providential care or control over either people or the material universe.

The philosophers try to persuade us that God takes care of the universe, along with its genera and species. However, they say He does not take care of you and me, individually. Otherwise, they say we would surely not need to pray to Him night and day. *Justin Martyr (c. 160, E), 1.194.*

The Epicureans regarded God as apathetic and inert. Essentially, then, He is a non-entity to them. *Tertullian (c. 197, W), 3.130.*

Epicurus said that there was indeed a God, . . . but that there was no providence. *Lactantius (c. 304–313, W), 7.264.*

SEE ALSO ATOMS; CREATION; EPICURUS; EVOLUTION; SOVEREIGNTY AND PROVIDENCE OF GOD.

DELPHI, ORACLE OF

SEE ORACLES, PAGAN.

DEMONS, DEMON POSSESSION

I. Origin and nature of the demons

II. Worship of demons

III. Demon activities and possession

IV. The Christian's authority over demons

I. Origin and nature of the demons

There were giants on the earth in those days, and also afterward, when the sons of God came in to the daughters of men and they bore children to them. Those were the mighty men who were of old, men of renown. Gen. 6:4.

The angels transgressed this appointment and were captivated by love of women. And they begat children, who are those who are called demons. *Justin Martyr (c. 160, E), 1.190.*

None of the demons possess flesh. Their structure is spiritual, like that of fire or air. And only by those whom the Spirit of God dwells in and fortifies are the bodies of the demons easily seen, not at all by others. *Tatian (c. 160, E), 2.71.*

The demons who rule over men are not the souls of men. *Tatian (c. 160, E), 2.72.*

The demons were driven forth to another abode. *Tatian (c. 160, E), 2.74.*

These angels, then, who have fallen from heaven, and haunt the air and the earth, and are no longer able to rise to heavenly things, and the souls of the giants, who are the demons who wander about the world, perform similar actions. *Athenagoras (c. 175, E), 2.142.*

The philosophers acknowledge there are demons. *Tertullian (c. 197, W), 3.36.*

Furthermore, we are instructed by our sacred books how from certain angels, who fell of their own free will, there sprang a more wicked demon brood, condemned of God along with the authors of their race. . . . Their great business is the ruin of mankind. So, from the start, spiritual wickedness sought our destruction. Accordingly, they inflict upon our bodies diseases and other grievous calamities. And by violent assaults, they hurry the soul into sudden and extraordinary excesses. . . . By an influence equally obscure, demons and angels breathe into the soul, and rouse up its corruptions with furious passions and vile excesses. *Tertullian (c. 197, W), 3.36.*

Every spirit is possessed of wings. This is a common property of both angels and demons. So they are everywhere in a single moment. The whole world is as one place to them. *Tertullian (c. 197, W), 3.36.*

From dwelling in the air, and their nearness to the stars, and their familiarity with the clouds, the demons have means of knowing the preparatory processes going on in these upper regions. By this means, they can give promise of the rains that they already feel. No doubt, they are very kind, too, in regard to the healing of diseases! For, first of all, they make you ill. Then, to get a miracle out of it, . . . they withdraw their hurtful influence. Supposedly, then, they have wrought a cure! *Tertullian (c. 197, W), 3.37.*

There are some insincere and vagrant spirits who have been degraded from their heavenly vigor by earthly stains and lusts. Now that these spirits . . . are ruined themselves, they never cease to ruin others. Being depraved themselves, they infuse into others the error of their depravity. . . . The poets know that these spirits are demons. The philosophers speak of them, too. *Mark Minucius Felix (c. 200, W), 4.189.*

From the seed [of the fallen angels and women], giants are said to have been born. By them, arts were made known in the earth. They taught the dyeing of wool and everything that is done. When they died, men erected images to them. Yet, because they were of an evil seed, the Almighty did not approve of their being brought back from death when they had died. For that reason, they wander and they now subvert many bodies. And it is these whom you [pagans] presently worship and pray to as gods. *Commodianus (c. 240, W), 4.203.*

In my opinion, it is certain wicked demons (so to speak, of the race of Titans or giants) who have been guilty of impiety towards the true God and towards the angels in heaven. They have fallen from it, and they haunt the denser parts of bodies. They also frequent unclean places on the earth. Since they are without bodies of earthly material, they possess some power

of foretelling future events. So they engage in works of this kind, desiring to lead the human race away from the true God. They also secretly enter the bodies of the more predatory, savage, and wicked of animals and stir them up to do whatever they choose, whenever they choose. They can turn the fancies of these animals to make flights and movements of various kinds, in order to entrap men by such power of divination. *Origen (c. 248, E), 4.538.*

The term "demons" is always applied to those wicked powers, who are freed from the encumbrance of a grosser body. They lead men astray and fill them with distractions. They drag them down from God and from heavenly thoughts to things here below. *Origen (c. 248, E), 4.545.*

It is true of all demons that they were not originally demons. Rather, they became so in departing from the true way. Accordingly, the name "demon" is given to those beings who have fallen away from God. *Origen (c. 248, E), 4.638.*

Among angels, some are angels of God, and others are angels of the devil. But among demons, there is no such distinction. For they are all said to be wicked. *Origen (c. 248, E), 4.648, 649.*

However, those who were born from [the relations of angels with women]—because they were neither angels nor men, but had a mixed nature—were not admitted into Hades [when they died]. Similarly, their fathers had not been admitted into heaven, either. Thus there came to be two kinds of demons: one of heaven, the other of the earth. The latter are the wicked spirits, who are the authors of all the evils that are done. This same devil is their prince. . . . However, grammarians say that the reason they are called demons . . . is because they are skilled and acquainted with matters. For the grammarians think they are gods. In truth, the demons are acquainted with *some* future events, but not with all. For He has not permitted them to know entirely the counsel of God . . . .

As I was saying, these contaminated and abandoned spirits wander over the whole earth. They console their own ruin by destroying others. Therefore, they fill every place with snares, deceits, frauds, and errors. For they cling to individuals and even occupy whole houses, from door to door. . . . And since spirits are without physical substance and cannot be held, they slink into the bodies of men. Secretly working in their inward parts, they corrupt the health of these persons, bring on diseases, terrify their souls with dreams, and harass their minds with frenzies. They do this so that by these evils, they may cause men to come to them for aid. *Lactantius (c. 304–313, W), 7.64; extended discussion: 4.328–4.334.*

II. Worship of demons

I say that the things which the Gentiles sacrifice they sacrifice to demons and not to God, and I do not want you to have fellowship with demons. 1 Cor. 10:20.

But the rest of mankind . . . did not repent of the works of their hands, that they should not worship demons, and idols of gold, silver, brass, stone, and wood. Rev. 9:20.

Not knowing that these spirits were demons, they called them "gods," and gave to each the name which each of the demons chose for himself. *Justin Martyr (c. 160, E), 1.164.*

The poets and mythologists did not know that it was the [wicked] angels, and those demons who had been begotten by them, who did the various things to men, women, cities, and nations that the poets and mythologists wrote about. So they ascribed them to God Himself and to those who were considered to be His very offspring. . . . For they called them by whatever name each of the angels had given to himself and to his children. *Justin Martyr (c. 160, E), 1.190.*

The demons, as you call them, received their structure from matter and obtained the spirit which is inherent in it. As a result, they became intemperate and greedy. . . . O Greeks, you worship these beings, produced from matter, but very remote from right conduct. *Tatian (c. 160, E), 2.70.*

[When exorcised by Christians,] these beings admit that they are not gods. And they confess to you that there is no God, except one—the God whom we worship. *Tertullian (c. 197, W), 3.38.*

As is shown by the Magi, the philosophers, and Plato, these impure spirits (the demons) lurk under the statues and images that are consecrated to them. In the meantime, they are breathed into the [pagan] prophets. They dwell in the shrines, and they sometimes animate the fibers of the entrails. They control the flights of birds, direct the lots, and are the cause of oracles involved in many falsehoods. *Mark Minucius Felix (c. 200, W), 4.190.*

When they are adjured, those most wicked spirits confess that they are demons. Yet, when they are worshipped, they falsely say that they are gods, in order to lead men into errors. *Lactantius (c. 304–313, W), 7.130.*

III. Demon activities and possession

They brought to him all sick people who were afflicted with various diseases and torments, and those who were demon-possessed. Matt. 4:24.

Now it happened, as we went to prayer, that a certain slave girl possessed with a spirit of divination met us, who brought her masters much profit by fortune-telling. Acts 16:16.

It is the practice of some men to capture persons and then to restore them to their friends for a ransom. Similarly, those who are considered to be gods invade the bodies of certain persons. They then produce a sense of their presence by dreams. Then, when they have taken their fill of the things of this world, these "gods" command them to come forth into public. In the sight of all, they then fly away from the sick, destroying the disease which they had produced. They thereby restore men to their former state. *Tatian (c. 160, E), 2.73.*

Secretly creeping into human bodies with subtlety (as being spirits), they simulate diseases, alarm the minds, and wrench about the limbs. They do this so that they may constrain men to worship them. . . . By remitting what they had bound, they seem to have cured it. *Mark Minucius Felix (c. 200, W), 4.190.*

I could show him . . . many other things in natural connection with the soul. For instance, there is demon possession. I could point out possession not only of one [demon]—as in the case of Socrates' own demon—but of seven spirits. Such was the case of the Magdalene. I can point to a legion in number, as in the Gadarene. *Tertullian (c. 210, W), 3.206.*

Holy Scripture teaches us that there are certain invisible enemies that fight against us. And it commands us to arm ourselves against them. From that, the more simple among the believers in the Lord Christ are of the opinion that all the sins that men have committed are caused by the persistent efforts of these opposing powers exerted upon the minds of sinners. . . . In other words, they think that if there were no devil, no single human being would go astray. We, however, who see the reason more clearly, do not hold this opinion. For we take into account those [sins] that clearly originate as a necessary consequence of our bodily constitution.... The devil is obviously not the cause of our feeling hunger and thirst. Likewise, neither is he the cause of that desire that naturally arises at the time of maturity—the desire of sexual intercourse. *Origen (c. 225, E), 4.329, 330.*

We receive certain initial elements and (as it were) seeds of sins from those things that we use agreeably to nature. However, when we have indulged them beyond what is proper and have not resisted the first movements to intemperance, then the hostile powers seize the occasion of this first transgression. They incite and press us hard in every way. They seek to extend our sins over a wider field and to furnish us human beings with opportunities and beginnings of sins. *Origen (c. 225, E), 4.330.*

Now, of wicked spirits, there is a twofold mode of operations. Sometimes they take complete and entire possession of the mind, so as not to allow their captives the power of either understanding or feeling. For example, this is the case with those who are commonly called "possessed," whom we see to be deprived of reason.... At other times, [these forces] use their wicked suggestions to deprave a conscious and intelligent soul with thoughts of various kinds—persuading it to do evil. Judas is an illustration of this. *Origen (c. 225, E), 4.336.*

[Celsus, a pagan] next returns to the subject of the seven ruling demons. However, their names are not found among Christians. Rather, I think they are accepted by the Ophites. *Origen (c. 248, E), 4.586.*

We must determine whether the Logos of God, who governs all things, has appointed wicked demons for certain employments. This would be similar to the way that executioners are appointed in states, or that other officers are appointed with cruel, but necessary, duties to discharge.... Or perhaps the demons (who are scattered as it were in troops in different parts of the earth) have chosen for themselves a chief under whose command they may plunder and pillage the souls of men. *Origen (c. 248, E), 4.639.*

The Psalmist bears witness that divine justice employs certain evil angels to inflict calamities upon men: "He cast upon them the fierceness of His anger, wrath, indignation, and trouble, sent by evil angels" [Ps. 78:49]. *Origen (c. 248, E), 4.651.*

Sometimes a wicked spirit has foresight and perceives that there will be an earthquake. So he pretends that he will accomplish what he already foresees will happen. By such lies and boasting, [one demon] subdued the minds of various persons. As a result, they obeyed him and did whatever he commanded. They also went wherever he led them. He would also make a certain woman walk in the dead of winter with bare feet over frozen snow. Yet, she was not troubled or hurt in any degree by doing this. *Cyprian (c. 250, W), 5.393.*

These [wicked spirits] were the inventors of astrology, soothsaying, divination, ... those productions that are called oracles, necromancy, the art of magic, and whatever other evil things that men practice either openly or in secret. *Lactantius (c. 304–313, W), 7.65.*

IV. The Christian's authority over demons

When He had come to the other side, to the country of the Gergesenes, there met him two demon-possessed men, coming out of the tombs, exceedingly fierce, so that no one could pass that way. And suddenly they cried out, saying, "What have we to do with You, Jesus, You Son of God? Have You come here to torment us before the time?" Matt. 8:28, 29.

Then the seventy returned with joy, saying, "Lord, even the demons are subject to us in Your name." Luke 10:17.

We do continually beseech God by Jesus Christ to preserve us from the demons.... When they are exorcised in the name of Jesus Christ, ... they are overcome. And thus it is demonstrated to all, that His Father has given Him such great power. For, by virtue of this power, demons are subdued by His name. *Justin Martyr (c. 160, E), 1.209.*

Even to this day, the demon-possessed are sometimes exorcised in the name of the living and true God. And these spirits of error themselves confess that they are the demons who used to inspire these writers [i.e., the pagan poets]. *Theophilus (c. 180, E), 2.97.*

The whole power of demons and kindred spirits is subject to us. Nevertheless, ill-disposed slaves sometimes join disobedience with fear. Such slaves delight in injuring those of whom they also stand in awe. So it is with the demons. *Tertullian (c. 197, W), 3.41.*

Of how much greater dignity and constancy is the assertion of Christian wisdom. Before the very breath of it, the whole host of demons is scattered! *Tertullian (c. 210, W), 3.182.*

God, Creator of the universe, has no need of odors or of blood. These things are the food of devils. But we not only reject those wicked spirits, we overcome them. We daily hold them up to contempt. We exorcise them from their victims, as multitudes can testify. *Tertullian (c. 212, W), 3.106.*

Do you fear man, O Christian? You should be feared by the angels, since you are to judge angels! You should be feared by evil spirits, since you have received power also over evil spirits! *Tertullian (c. 212, W), 4.122.*

Even at the present time, the demons and other unseen powers show that they either fear the name of Jesus as that of a Being of superior power, or else they reverentially accept Him as their lawful ruler. For if the commendation had not been given Him by God, the demons would not have withdrawn from those whom they had attacked. For they withdrew in obedience at the mere mention of His name. *Origen (c. 248, E), 4.479.*

We do not deny that there are many demons upon earth. However, we maintain that they exist and exercise power among the wicked, as a punishment for their wickedness. But they have no power over those who "have put on the whole armor of God," who have received strength to "withstand the wiles of the devil" [Eph. 6:11]. *Origen (c. 248, E), 4.652.*

A Christian—I mean a true Christian, who has submitted to God and His Word—will suffer nothing from demons. For he is mightier than demons. The Christian will suffer nothing, for "the angel of the Lord will encamp around them who fear Him and will deliver them" [Ps. 34:7]. *Origen (c. 248, E), 4.653.*

The obstinate wickedness of the devil prevails even up to the saving water [of baptism]. However, in baptism, a person loses all the poison of his wickedness. ... When they come to the water of salvation and to the sanctification of baptism, we should know and trust that there

the devil is beaten down. And the man, being dedicated to God, is set free by the divine mercy. ... So also, the wicked spirits are called scorpions and serpents. Yet, they are trodden under foot by us, by the power given us by the Lord. They cannot remain any longer in the body of a man who is baptized and sanctified, in whom the Holy Spirit is beginning to dwell. *Cyprian (c. 250, W), 5.402.*

In fact, [the demons] do injure some—but only those by whom they are feared. For the powerful and lofty hand of God does not protect such ones, for they have not been initiated in the sacrament of truth. However, the demons fear the righteous, the worshippers of God. When adjured by the name of God, they depart from the bodies. ... They cannot speak falsely either to God (by whom they are adjured) or to the righteous, by whose voice they are tormented. Therefore, oftentimes they have uttered the greatest howls. They cry out that they are beaten and are on fire. ... So whom can they injure, other than those whom they have in their own power? *Lactantius (c. 304–313, W), 7.65.*

SEE ALSO ANGEL, ANGELS (III. WICKED ANGELS); EXORCISM; GODS, PAGAN; SATAN; SPIRITISM.

DEPRAVITY OF MAN
SEE FALL OF MAN; MAN, DOCTRINE OF.

DESCENT INTO HADES
For David says concerning Him: ... You will not leave my soul in Hades, nor will You allow Your Holy One to see corruption. Acts 2:25, 27.

Now this, "He ascended"—what does it mean but that He also first descended into the lower parts of the earth? Eph. 4:9.

He went and preached to the spirits in prison, who formerly were disobedient, when once the longsuffering of God waited in the days of Noah. 1 Pet. 3:19.

For this reason the gospel was preached also to those who are dead, that they might be judged according to men in the flesh, but live according to God in the spirit. 1 Pet. 4:6.

These apostles and teachers preached the name of the Son of God. After falling asleep in the power and faith of the Son of God, the apostles not only *preached* it to those who were asleep, but they themselves also gave them the seal of the preaching [i.e., baptism].

Accordingly, the apostles descended with them into the water and ascended again.... For such ones slept in righteousness and in great purity. Only, they did not have this seal. *Hermas (c. 150, W), 1.49.*

Christ rose from the place of the dead, and raised up the race of Adam from the grave below. *Melito (c. 170, E), 8.757.*

The Lord was made "the First-Begotten of the dead." Receiving into His bosom the ancient fathers, He has regenerated them into the life of God. *Irenaeus (c. 180, E/W), 1.455.*

For their benefit, "He also descended into the lower parts of the earth," to behold with His eyes the state of those who were resting from their labors.... For Christ did not come merely for those who believed on Him in the time of Tiberius Caesar. Nor did the Father exercise His providence only for the men who are presently alive. Rather, He exercised it for all men altogether, who from the beginning ... have both feared and loved God. *Irenaeus (c. 180, E/W), 1.494.*

It was for this reason, too, that the Lord descended into the regions beneath the earth, preaching His advent there also. And He [declared] the remission of sins received by those who believe in Him. *Irenaeus (c. 180, E/W), 1.499.*

He gathered from the ends of the earth into His Father's fold the children who were scattered abroad. And He remembered His own dead ones, who had previously fallen asleep. He came down to them so that He might deliver them. *Irenaeus (c. 180, E/W), 1.506.*

For three days He dwelt in the place where the dead were, as the prophet said concerning Him. "And the Lord remembered His dead saints who slept formerly in the land of the dead. And He descended to them to rescue and save them." The Lord Himself said, "As Jonah remained three days and three nights in the whale's belly, so will the Son of man be in the heart of the earth." *Irenaeus (c. 180, E/W), 1.560.*

The Lord preached the Gospel to those in Hades.... Do not [the Scriptures] show that the Lord preached the Gospel to those who perished in the flood, or rather had been chained, as to those kept in ward and guard? And it has been shown also ... that the apostles, following the Lord, preached the Gospel to those in Hades.... If, then, the Lord descended to Hades for no other reason but to preach the Gospel (as He did descend), it was either to preach the Gospel to *all,* or else to the Hebrews only. If, accordingly, He preached to all, then all who believe will be saved on making their profession there—even though they may be Gentiles. For God's punishments are saving and disciplinary, leading to conversion. He desires the repentance, rather than the death, of a sinner. This is especially so since souls, although darkened by passions, when released from their bodies, are able to perceive more clearly. For they are no longer obstructed by the paltry flesh.... Did not the same dispensation obtain in Hades? For even there, all the souls, on hearing the proclamation, could either exhibit repentance, or confess that their punishment was just, because they did not believe. And it was not arbitrary that they could obtain either salvation or punishment. For those who had departed before the coming of the Lord had not had the Gospel preached to them. So they had been given no opportunity to either believe or not believe. *Clement of Alexandria (c. 195, E), 2.490, 491.*

He preached the Gospel to those in the flesh so that they would not be condemned unjustly. So how is it conceivable that He did not for the same reason preach the Gospel to those who had departed this life before His coming? *Clement of Alexandria (c. 195, E), 2.492.*

The Shepherd, speaking plainly of those who had fallen asleep, recognizes certain righteous ones among Gentiles and Jews, not only before the appearance of Christ, but before the Law.... He adds, "They gave them the seal of preaching. Therefore, they [the apostles] descended with them into the water, and again ascended." *Clement of Alexandria (c. 195, E), 2.357.*

"For this cause was the Gospel preached also to the dead"—namely, to us, who were at one time unbelievers. *Clement of Alexandria (c. 195, E), 2.572.*

However, [He saves] with dignity of honor others who voluntarily follow. This is so "that every knee should bow to Him, of things in heaven, and things on earth, and things under the earth"—that is, angels, men, and souls who had departed from this temporal life before His coming. *Clement of Alexandria (c. 195, E), 2.575.*

[Christ is Lord of] things under the earth, because He was also reckoned among the dead. For He preached the Gospel to the souls of the saints. Through death, He overcame death. *Hippolytus (c. 200, W), 5.209.*

[John the Baptist] also first preached to those in Hades, becoming a forerunner there when he was put to death by Herod. So even there, too, John revealed that the Savior would descend to ransom the souls of the saints from the hand of death. *Hippolytus (c. 200, W), 5.213.*

Christ delivered the first man of earth from the lowest Hades, when he was lost and bound by the chains of death. . . . This is He who was to become the preacher of the gospel to the dead. *Hippolytus (c. 205, W), 5.170.*

The jailers of Hades trembled when they saw Him. And the gates of brass and the bolts of iron were broken. For, look! The Only-Begotten, God the Word, had entered Hades with a soul—a soul among souls. *Hippolytus (c. 205, W), 5.194.*

Hades is not supposed by us to be a bare cavity, nor some subterranean sewer of the world. Rather it is a vast deep space in the interior of the earth. . . . For we read that Christ in His death spent three days in the heart of the earth. . . . He did not ascend into the heights of heaven before descending into the lower parts of the earth. This was so that He might there [in Hades] make the patriarchs and prophets partakers of Himself. *Tertullian (c. 210, W), 3.231.*

It was the same among the dead. Christ was the only free person there, and His soul was not left in Hades. As a result, then, He is the first and the last. *Origen (c. 228, E), 9.315.*

After this, I think, He descended into Hades to the dead as a "free person among the dead." *Origen (c. 245, E), 9.451.*

When Christ became a soul, without the covering of the body, He dwelled among those souls who were also without bodily covering. And He converted those of them who were willing. *Origen (c. 248, E), 4.448.*

Now, it had been foretold by the prophets that He would not remain in Hades, but would rise again on the third day. David says in the fifteenth Psalm: "You will not leave my soul in Hades. Neither will you suffer your holy one

to see corruption." Also, in the third Psalm: "I laid me down to sleep, took my rest, and rose again, for the Lord sustained me" [Ps. 3:5]. *Lactantius (c. 304–313, W), 7.122.*

Christ was not in the lower regions more than two days. *Lactantius (c. 304–313, W), 7.131.*

Meanwhile, Hades was resplendent with light. For the Star had descended to there. Actually, the Lord did not descend into Hades in His *body*, but in His *spirit*. In short, He is working everywhere. For while He raised the dead by His body, by His spirit He was liberating souls. . . . For the Lord had conquered Hades, had trodden down death. *Alexander of Alexandria (c. 324, E), 6.301; see also 1.510.*

SEE ALSO DEAD, INTERMEDIATE STATE OF THE.

DEUTEROCANONICAL BOOKS

The deuterocanonical books (often called the Apocrypha) are the books of the Old Testament that were included in the Septuagint but that the Jews deleted from their canon at the close of the first century.

I. Early Christian quotations from the deuterocanonical books

II. Why the Jews deleted these works

III. The early church's position towards these works

I. Early Christian quotations from the deuterocanonical books

The Ante-Nicene Fathers contain over 300 quotations from and references to the deuterocanonical books. The following quotations are only a few examples.

The prophet also says, "The stone that the builders rejected, the same has become the head of the corner" [Isa. 50:7]. . . . What does the prophet say again? "The assembly of the wicked surrounded me; they encompassed me as bees do a honeycomb," and "upon my garments they cast lots" [Ps. 22:17, 19]. Therefore, since He was about to be manifested and to suffer in the flesh, His suffering was predicted. For the prophet speaks against Israel, "Woe to their soul, because they have counseled an evil counsel against themselves, saying, "Let us bind the just one, because he is displeasing to us" [Wis. 2:12]. *Barnabas (c. 70–130), 1.140.*

"Do not be a stretcher forth of the hands to receive and a drawer back of them when it is time to give" [Sir. 4:31]. *Didache (c. 80–140, E), 7.378.*

When you can do good, defer it not, because "alms delivers from death" [Tobit 4:10; 12:9]. *Polycarp (c. 135, E), 1.35.*

Cyrus, king of the Persians, said to Daniel, the prophet, "Why do you not worship Bel?" Daniel replied, saying, "Because I do not worship idols made with hands" [Dan. 14, also known as Bel and the Dragon]. *Irenaeus (c. 180, E/W), 1.467.*

For that reason, the Scripture most strenuously exhorts, "Do not introduce everyone into your house, for the snares of the crafty are many" [Sir. 11:29]. *Clement of Alexandria (c. 195, E), 2.278.*

The Wisdom of Jesus [i.e., Sirach] says, "For all wisdom is from the Lord, and is with Him forever" [Sir. 1:1]. *Clement of Alexandria (c. 195, E), 2.305.*

Esther and Mordecai lived during the captivity. Their book is still extant—as is also the book of the Maccabees. . . . Tobias married Sarah through the assistance of the angel Raphael. For the demon had killed her first seven suitors. After the marriage of Tobias, his father, Tobit, recovered his eyesight. *Clement of Alexandria (c. 195, E), 2.328.*

Our instruction comes from the porch of Solomon, who had himself taught that "the Lord should be sought in simplicity of heart" [Wis. 1:1]. *Tertullian (c. 197, W), 3.246.*

Who is this but Christ? They say, "Come, let us remove the righteous one, because he is hateful to us; he sets himself contrary to our doings" [Wis. 2:12]. *Tertullian (c. 207, W), 3.340.*

We find that the blessed Daniel prophesied in Babylon and appeared as the vindicator of Susannah. *Hippolytus (c. 205, W), 5.178.*

They are all clearly described in the books of the Maccabees. *Hippolytus (c. 205, W), 5.180.*

He shows also that when Susannah prayed to God and was heard, the angel was then sent to help her—just as was the case in the matter of Tobias and Sarah. . . . The angel Raphael was sent to heal them both. *Hippolytus (c. 205, W), 5.193.*

As in the person of the Jews, Solomon speaks again of this righteous one, who is Christ, in this way: "He was made to reprove our thoughts, and he makes his boast that God is his Father. Let us see, then, if his words are true. . . . For if the just man is the Son of God, God will help him and deliver him from the hand of his enemies. Let us condemn him with a shameful death" [Wis. 2:14–20]. *Hippolytus (c. 205, W), 5.221.*

That we may believe on the authority of Holy Scripture that such is the case, hear how in the Book of Maccabees, where the mother of seven martyrs exhorts her sons to endure torture, this truth is confirmed. *Origen (c. 225, E), 4.270*

That certain thoughts are suggested to men's hearts either by good or evil angels is shown both by the angel who accompanied Tobias and by the language of the prophet. *Origen (c. 225, E), 4.332.*

Holy Scripture instructs us, saying, "Prayer is good with fasting and almsgiving" [Tobit 20:8]. *Cyprian (c. 250, W), 5.456.*

Be a father to your children as was Tobias. Give useful and saving teachings to your pledges, just as he gave to his son. What he commanded his son, command your children. *Cyprian (c. 250, W), 5.481.*

Although under a royal and tyrannical slavery, Tobias was free in spirit and feeling. He maintained his confession to God. He sublimely announced both the divine power and majesty, saying: "In the land of my captivity, I confess to him, and I show forth His power in a sinful nation" [Tobias 13:6]. What, indeed, do we find in the Maccabees of the seven brothers? They were all equally alike in their lot of birth and virtues. They filled up the number seven in the sacraments of a perfected completion. Seven brothers were therefore associated together in martyrdom. *Cyprian (c. 250, W), 5.503.*

Of this same thing in the Maccabees: "It is just to be subjected to God and that a mortal should not think things equal to God" [2 Macc. 9:12]. *Cyprian (c. 250, W), 5.533.*

Zechariah says, "Be converted unto me, and I will be turned unto you" [Zech. 1:3]. . . . Also, in Ecclesiasticus: "Turn to the Lord and forsake your sins" [Sir. 17:26]. . . . Also, in the second Epistle of the blessed Paul to the Corinthians: "For the sorrow that is according to God works a steadfast repentance unto salvation" [2 Cor. 7:10]. *Exhortation to Repentance (c. 255, W), 5.594.*

In the Book of Wisdom, a book full of all virtue, the Holy Spirit sings in this manner, now openly drawing His hearers to celibacy and chastity: "It is better to have no children and to have virtue. For the memorial thereof is immortal" [Wis. 4:1, 2]. *Methodius (c. 290, E), 6.312.*

The Book of Wisdom confirms this, saying, "For God created all things that they might have their being" [Wis. 1:14]. *Methodius (c. 290, E), 6.365.*

The Book of Wisdom says, "For God created man to be immortal and made him to be an image of His own eternity" [Wis. 2:23]. *Methodius (c. 290, E), 6.367.*

They caught Manasseh in bonds, and they bound him in chains of brass, bringing him to Babylon. . . . And he prayed to the Lord, saying, "O Lord, Almighty God of our fathers Abraham, Isaac, and Jacob, and of their righteous seed" [Prayer of Manasseh 1:1]. *Apostolic Constitutions (compiled c. 390, E), 7.407.*

II. Why the Jews deleted these works

But I am far from putting reliance in your [Jewish] teachers, who refuse to admit that the interpretation made by the seventy elders who were with Ptolemy of the Egyptians is a correct one [i.e., the LXX]. . . . I wish you to observe, that they have altogether taken away many Scriptures from the translations effected by those seventy elders who were with Ptolemy, and by which this very man who was crucified is proved to have been set forth expressly as God and man. *Justin Martyr (c. 160, E), 1.234.*

I have not attempted to establish proof about Christ from the passages of Scripture which are not admitted by you [Jews]—which I quoted from the words of Jeremiah the prophet, Esdras, and David. But [I have proved this] from those which you even now admit. And, if your teachers had comprehended them, be well assured they would have deleted them, too—just as they did those [writings] about the death of Isaiah, whom you sawed asunder with a wooden saw. *Justin Martyr (c. 160, E), 1.259.*

We read that every Scripture suitable for edification is divinely inspired. So it may now seem to have been rejected by the Jews for that very reason—just like nearly all the other portions [of Scripture] that speak of Christ. Nor, of course, is this fact surprising: that they did not receive some Scriptures that spoke of Him whom they did not receive. For they did not receive Him even when He was here in person, speaking in their presence. *Tertullian (c. 198, W), 4.16.*

There was a learned Hebrew, who was said to be the son of a wise man and to have been specially trained to succeed his father. I had conversations with him on many subjects. I remember hearing from him the names of those elders [mentioned in the account of Susanna]. This indicated that he did not reject the history of Susanna. *Origen (c. 240, E), 4.388.*

Probably you will reply, "Why, then, is the history [of Susanna] not in their Daniel—if, as you say, their wise men hand down such stories by tradition?" The answer is that they hid from the knowledge of the people as many of the passages as they could that contained any scandal against the elders, rulers, and judges. Some of these have been preserved in hidden writings. *Origen (c. 240, E), 4.388.*

Let us now see if in these cases we are not forced to the conclusion that, while the Savior gives a true account of [certain events], none of the Scriptures are to be found that could prove what He speaks of. . . . "If we had been in the days of our fathers, we would not have been partakers with them in the blood of the prophets." In the blood of *what* prophets, can anyone tell me? For where do we find anything like this written of Isaiah, Jeremiah, Daniel, or any of the twelve [minor prophets]? What about Zachariah, the son of Barachiah, who was slain between the temple and the altar? We learn this only from Jesus, not knowing it otherwise from any Scripture. Accordingly, I think no other supposition is possible than that those who had the reputation of wisdom, along with the rulers and elders, took away from the people every passage that might bring the elders into discredit among the people. We should not be surprised, then, that this history of the evil scheme of the licentious elders against Susanna is true. Yet, it was removed from the Scriptures by men who themselves were not very far removed from the counsel of such elders. *Origen (c. 240, E), 4.389.*

III. The early church's position towards these works

If this word "matter" should happen to occur in any other passage, it will never be found, in my opinion, to have the meaning of which we are now seeking—unless perhaps in the book that is called the Wisdom of Solomon, a work that is certainly not esteemed authoritative by all. *Origen (c. 225, E), 4.379.*

Greeting, my lord and son, most worthy Origen, from Africanus. In your sacred discussion with Agnomon, you referred to that prophecy of Daniel that is related of his youth. At that time . . . I accepted this as genuine. However, now I cannot understand how it escaped you that this part of the book is spurious. . . . A more fatal objection is that this section, along with the other two at the end of it, is not contained in the Daniel received among the Jews. . . . Moreover, the style is different. I have struck the blow; do you give the reply? Answer and instruct me. *Julius Africanus (c. 240, E), 4.385; see also 5.191–5.194.*

Origen to Africanus, . . . greeting. From your letter, I learned what your thoughts are as to the Susanna in the Book of Daniel, which is used in the churches. . . . In answer to this, I have to tell you what it is necessary for us to do in the cases of not only the history of Susanna, but also of thousands of other passages that I found in many places when, with my little strength, I was collating the Hebrew copies of Scripture with our copies. Susanna is found in every church of Christ in that Greek copy that the Greeks use. Yet, it is not in the Hebrew. Likewise, the two other passages you mention at the end of the book, containing the history of Bel and the Dragon, are not in the Hebrew copy of Daniel. . . . In many of the other sacred books, I sometimes found more in our copies [i.e., in the LXX] than in the Hebrew; sometimes, I found less. . . . When we notice such things, are we to abruptly reject as spurious the copies in use in our churches? Should we command the brotherhood to put away the sacred books that are currently used among them? Should we coax the Jews and persuade them to give us copies that will be free from tampering and forgery? Are we to suppose that the Providence that has ministered to the edification of all the churches of Christ in the sacred Scriptures, had no concern for those who were bought with a price, the ones for whom Christ died? *Origen (c. 240, E), 4.386, 387.*

The Jews do not use Tobit. It is not even found in the Hebrew hidden writings, as I learned from the Jews themselves. However, since the churches use Tobit, you must know that even in the captivity, some of the captives were rich and well to do. *Origen (c. 240, E), 4.391; extended discussion: 4.385–4.392.*

Commentary on Susannah: 5.191–5.194.

SEE ALSO CANON, OLD TESTAMENT; JUDITH; MACCABEES; PSEUDEPIGRAPHA, OLD TESTAMENT; SEPTUAGINT.

DEVIL, THE

SEE SATAN.

DIDACHE

It is such a person that the Scripture calls a thief. For that reason it is said, "Son, do not be a liar; for lying leads to theft." *Clement of Alexandria (c. 195, E), 2.324, quoting from Didache 3.5.*

DIOCLETIAN

Diocletian (240–316) was the Roman emperor who instituted the last great persecution against Christians.

The emperor himself, though not yet attached to the Christian religion, has entrusted the care of his life and person to these same Christians as his more faithful servants. *Theonas of Alexandria (c. 300, E), 6.158.*

When Diocletian—that author of ill and deviser of misery—was ruining all things, he could not withhold his insults, not even against God. This man . . . overturned the Roman empire. For he selected three persons to share the government with him. The empire was sectioned into quarters, and so armies were multiplied. Each of the four rulers strove to maintain a greater military force than any single emperor had done in times past. Eventually, there were less men who paid taxes than there were who received wages. As a result, the estate of the farmer was exhausted by enormous taxes. Farms were abandoned; cultivated grounds became woodlands. Universal dismay prevailed. *Lactantius (c. 320, W), 7.303.*

DIOGENES

Diogenes (412–323 B.C.) was a Greek Cynic philosopher who rejected conventional society norms.

Diogenes, who made such a parade of his independence with his barrel, was seized with an intestinal attack from eating a raw polypus. So he lost his life through gluttony. *Tatian (c. 160, E), 1.65.*

In the house of a bad man, Diogenes found the inscription, "Hercules, for victory famed, dwells here. Let nothing bad enter." So Diogenes remarked, "So how will the master of the house go in?" *Clement of Alexandria (c. 195, E), 2.529.*

Long ago, indeed, there was a Greek philosopher who preferred a state of poverty. Yet, he exhibited the pattern of a happy life. He thereby showed that he was not excluded from happiness, even though he possessed nothing. So he termed himself a Cynic. *Origen (c. 248, E), 4.586.*

DISASTERS

Why can they not take it in, that their evils come from the Being whose goodness they have failed to recognize? They suffer at the hands of Him to whom they have been ungrateful. And, for all that is said, if we compare the calamities of former times, they fall on us more lightly now, since God gave Christians to the world. For from that time, virtue put some restraint on the world's wickedness, and men began to pray for the averting of God's wrath. *Tertullian (c. 197, W), 3.48.*

In a word, when the summer clouds give no rain, and the season is a matter of anxiety, you indeed offer up to Jupiter your rain sacrifices. Yet, you are full of feasting day by day, and ever eager for the banquet, baths, taverns, and brothels, being always busy. It is true that you force barefoot processions on the people. You seek heaven at the Capitol, and you look up to the temple ceilings for the longed for clouds. Yet, God and heaven are not in all your *thoughts.* In contrast, we [Christians] are dried up with fasting. Our passions are tightly bound up. We hold back from all the ordinary enjoyments of life, as long as possible. We roll in sackcloth and ashes and assail heaven with our cries. Thereby, we touch God's heart. Yet, once we have extorted divine compassion, why, Jupiter gets all the honor! *Tertullian (c. 197, W), 3.48.*

SEE ALSO SOVEREIGNTY AND PROVIDENCE OF GOD.

DISCIPLESHIP

SEE CHRISTIAN LIFE.

DISCIPLINE, CHURCH

I. Excommunication, rebuking, and shunning

II. Penitential discipline

If he refuses to hear them, tell it to the church. But if he refuses even to hear the church, let him be to you like a heathen and a tax collector. Matt. 18:17.

I have written to you not to keep company with anyone named a brother, who is a fornicator, or covetous, or an idolater, or a reviler, nor a drunkard, or an extortioner—not even to eat with such a person. 1 Cor. 5:11.

Do you not know that a little leaven leavens the whole lump? 1 Cor. 5:6.

If anyone does not obey our word in this epistle, note that person and do not keep company with him, that he may be ashamed. 2 Thess. 3:14.

Those who are sinning rebuke in the presence of all, that the rest also may fear. 1 Tim. 5:20.

If anyone comes to you and does not bring this doctrine, do not receive him into your house nor greet him; for he who greets him shares in his evil deeds. 2 John 10:11.

I. Excommunication, rebuking, and shunning

It is fitting, therefore, that you should keep aloof from such persons [i.e., the Gnostics]. You should not speak to them either in private or in public. *Ignatius (c. 105, E), 1.89.*

All of those who separate from the church and give heed to old wives' tales, like these persons, are truly self-condemned. Paul commands us "to avoid [these men] after a first and second admonition." Furthermore, John, the disciple of the Lord, has intensified their condemnation. For he desires us not even to address them with the salutation of "Godspeed." He says, "He who bids them Godspeed is a partaker with their evil deeds." *Irenaeus (c. 180, E/W), 1.341, 342.*

Cerdon, too, was Marcion's predecessor. . . . Having been denounced for corrupt teaching, he was excommunicated from the assembly of the brethren. *Irenaeus (c. 180, E/W), 1.417.*

From all such persons [heretics and false shepherds], it behooves us to keep aloof. *Irenaeus (c. 180, E/W), 1.497.*

"Therefore, do not be partakers with them." Back then, the condemnation of sinners extended to others who approved of them and joined in their society. And the case at present is still the same, for "a little leaven leavens the whole lump." *Irenaeus (c. 180, E/W), 1.500.*

If one must censure, it is necessary also to rebuke. For it is the time to wound the apathetic soul. I do not mean mortally, but salutarily, securing exemption from everlasting death by a little pain. *Clement of Alexandria (c. 195, E), 2.228.*

The physician is not evil to the sick person because he tells him of his fever. For the physician is not the *cause* of the fever; he only points out the fever. Likewise, he who reproves is not ill-disposed towards him who is diseased in soul. For he is not the cause of the transgressions on him. He only reveals the sins that are there. *Clement of Alexandria (c. 195, E), 2.231.*

God does not punish, for punishment is retaliation for evil. Rather, He *chastises*—for the purpose of good. *Clement of Alexandria (c. 195, E), 2.553.*

He forbids us either to salute such persons or to receive them to our hospitality. Yet, this is not harsh in the case of a man of this sort. But he admonishes Christians neither to confer nor dispute with those who are not able to handle divine things with intelligence, lest through them they be seduced from the doctrine of truth. *Clement of Alexandria (c. 195, E), 2.577.*

In the same place also, exhortations are made. Rebukes and sacred censures are administered. That is because the work of judging is carried on among us with great seriousness.... And you have the most notable example of judgment to come when anyone has sinned so grievously as to require his severance from us in prayer, in the congregation, and in all sacred matters. *Tertullian (c. 197, W), 3.46.*

But it will be said that some of us, too, depart from the rules of our discipline. In that case, however, we count such persons no longer as Christians. *Tertullian (c. 197, W), 3.51.*

[ADDRESSED TO PAGANS:] Persons of this doubtful mold do not assemble with us. Neither do they belong to our communion. By their delinquency, they become yours once more. For we are unwilling to mix even with those whom your violence and cruelty have compelled to recant. Yet, we should, of course, be more ready to have included among us those who have unwillingly forsaken our discipline, than willful

apostates. However, you have no right to call them Christians to whom Christians themselves deny that name. *Tertullian (c. 197, W), 1.113.*

These evidences, then, of a stricter discipline existing among us, are an additional proof of truth. *Tertullian (c. 197, W), 3.264.*

In this example of a leper ... [the Law] prohibited any contact with a person who was defiled with sin. The apostle also forbids us even to eat food with such a one. For the taint of sins can be communicated as if contagious, wherever a man mixes himself with the sinner. *Tertullian (c. 207, W), 3.355.*

[Marcion] rejected the two epistles to Timothy and the one to Titus, all of which deal with church discipline. *Tertullian (c. 207, W), 3.473.*

All the other frenzies of passions beyond the laws of nature—impious toward both the bodies and the sexes—we banish not only from the threshold, but from all shelter of the church. For they are not *sins*, but *monstrosities*. *Tertullian (c. 212, W), 4.77.*

The Montanists taught that there is no forgiveness for major postbaptismal sins. Writing as a Montanist in the following two passages, Tertullian criticizes the bishops of the church for extending mercy to repentant adulterers, etc.

You [the bishops of the church] reply that communion is indeed denied to sinners—particularly those who have been polluted by the flesh. But you say it is only for the present. You say they are to be restored as a result of penitential pleading, in accordance with the clemency of God that prefers a sinner's repentance to his death. *Tertullian (c. 212, W), 4.94.*

Here they [the bishops of the church] go so far as to interpret "destruction of the flesh" to be the office of repentance. In other words, by fasts, squalor, and every species of neglect and studious ill-treatment devoted to the extermination of the flesh, it seems to make satisfaction to God. So they argue that the fornicator (or rather, that incestuous person) was delivered to Satan by the apostle—not with a view of ruin, but with a view to correction.... On account of the "destruction of the flesh," he obtained pardon. *Tertullian (c. 213, W), 4.87.*

And how are they not ashamed to utter these calumnies against Victor? For they know full well that Victor excommunicated Theodotus the tanner, the leader and father of this God-denying apostasy. *Caius (c. 215, W), 5.601.*

"If your brother sins against you, go and lay bare his fault between you and him alone." . . . Some understand these words to be limited in their application to lesser sins. . . . They say that even in the case of the least of the sins of men, he who has not repented after the public announcement of the sin is to be considered as a Gentile and a tax collector. That is, with regard to sins that are "not unto death." Or as the Law has described them in the Book of Numbers, not "death bringing." However, this seems to be very harsh. For I do not think that anyone will readily be found who has not been censured three times for the same form of sin. For example, I am referring to the reviling with which revilers abuse their neighbors, or being carried away by passion, or drinking in excess, or using false and idle words—or any of those things that exist in the masses. . . . However, Christ does not say *what* he will suffer if he does not hear the church. . . . Therefore, he is not altogether gained, nor will he altogether perish. But what at all he will suffer, . . . only God knows. For we do not pronounce the judgment, because we follow the commandment, "Do not judge, lest you be judged." *Origen (c. 245, E), 9.492, 493.*

Christians lament as dead those who have been conquered by immorality or any other sin. For they are lost and dead to God. At some future time [if they repent], they receive them as being risen from the dead. However, this is after a greater interval than in the case of those who were admitted at first [i.e., the period of testing a catechumen]. However, those who have lapsed and fallen *after* professing the Gospel are not placed in any office or post of rank in the church of God. *Origen (c. 248, E), 4.485.*

Truly, such evil practices do not at all prevail among Christians—if you properly examine what constitutes a Christian. Or, if any persons of that kind are discovered, they are at least not to be found among those who frequent the assemblies and come to the public prayers—without their being excluded from them. *Origen (c. 248, E), 4.508.*

For this reason, I beg you that you will designate by name in the certificate [of communion] only those whom you yourselves witness, whom you have known, whose penitence you see to be very near to full satisfaction. *Cyprian (c. 250, W), 5.292.*

Those who have received certificates from the martyrs . . . if they should be seized with any misfortune and peril of sickness, . . . and if a presbyter cannot be found and death begins to be imminent, they can make confession of their sin before even a deacon. Thereby, with the imposition of hands upon them for repentance, they can come to the Lord with the peace that the martyrs have desired. *Cyprian (c. 250, W), 5.293.*

How can the medicine of permissiveness profit anyone? What if a physician hides the wound and does not allow the necessary remedy of time to close the scar? To not require repentance makes the way easy for new dangers. To do that is not *curing* someone. If we are honest, it is *slaying* him. *Cyprian (c. 250, W), 5.309.*

Felicissimus has rushed forth with many more and has declared himself as a leader of a faction. . . . Let him receive the sentence that he first of all imposed—that he may know that he is excommunicated by us. For he has added the crime of adultery to his crimes of fraud and plunder. . . . All of these things we will judicially examine when, with the Lord's permission, we will assemble in one place with many of our colleagues. . . . Moreover, whoever will ally himself with that man's conspiracy and faction, let him know that he will not communicate in the church with us, since he has preferred to be separated from the church of his own accord. *Cyprian (c. 250, W), 5.316.*

Those persons cannot remain in God's church who have not maintained its divine and ecclesiastical discipline—either in the manner of their life or in the peace of their character. *Cyprian (c. 250, W), 5.325.*

We should give our assistance, our healing art, to those who are wounded. Let us not think of them as dead. . . . In them, there is that, which, by subsequent repentance, may be strengthened into faith. . . . If someone is harshly and cruelly separated from the church, he may turn himself to Gentile ways and to worldly works . . . or pass over to heretics and schismatics. *Cyprian (c. 250, W), 5.331.*

If we reject the repentance [of the lapsed], . . . it will be attributed to us in the day of judgment. For we have not cared for the wounded sheep. And, on account of a single wounded one, we have lost many sound ones. *Cyprian (c. 250, W), 5.331.*

Do not think, dearest brother, that either the courage of the brethren will be lessened, or that martyrdoms will fail for this cause—that repentance is relaxed to the lapsed. . . . It is one thing to stand for pardon. It is another thing to attain to glory. It is one thing, when cast into prison, not to go out from it until one has paid the last coin. It is another thing at once to receive the wages of faith and courage. It is one thing, tortured by long suffering for sins, to be cleansed and long purged by fire. It is another to have all sins purged by suffering. It is one thing to be in suspense until the sentence of God at the day of judgment. It is another to be crowned at once by the Lord. *Cyprian (c. 250, W), 5.332.*

Among our predecessors, some of the bishops here in our province thought that peace was not to be granted to adulterers. So they wholly closed the gate of repentance against adultery. *Cyprian (c. 250, W), 5.332.*

How do we teach or provoke them to shed their blood in confession of His name, if we deny the blood of Christ to those who are about to enter on the warfare? Or how do we make them fit for the cup of martyrdom, if we do not first admit them to drink in the church the cup of the Lord by the right of communion? *Cyprian (c. 250, W), 5.337.*

No banquets nor conferences should be entertained with the wicked. Rather we should be as much separated from them as they are deserters from the church. For it is written, "If he will neglect to hear the church, let him be unto you as a heathen man and a tax collector." . . . If they come with prayers and atonements, let them be heard. If they heap together curses and threats, let them be rejected. *Cyprian (c. 250, W), 5.347.*

If they obstinately persevere and do not mutually separate themselves, let them know that they can never be admitted by us into the church with their immodest obstinacy. . . . They should not think that the way of life or of salvation is still open to them, if they have refused to obey the bishops and priests. For in Deuteronomy, the Lord God says, "And the man that will do presumptuously and will not listen to the priest or judge . . . that man will die" [Deut. 17:12, 13]. *Cyprian (c. 250, W), 5.358.*

The proud and disobedient are slain with the sword of the Spirit, in that they are cast out of the church. For they cannot live out of it, since the house of God is one. And there can be no salvation to anyone except in the church. *Cyprian (c. 250, W), 5.358.*

It behooves you to write a very lengthy letter to our fellow bishops appointed in Gaul. Exhort them not to allow Marcian any longer to insult our assembly, simply because he does not appear to have been excommunicated by us. For he is stubborn and haughty, and he is hostile to the divine mercy and to the salvation of the brotherhood. *Cyprian (c. 250, W), 5.368.*

"Do not be partakers with them." We must withdraw. Nay, rather, we must flee—from those who fall away. *Cyprian (c. 250, W), 5.429.*

Contrary to the vigor of the Gospel, contrary to the law of the Lord and God, . . . communion is relaxed to heedless persons! But this is a vain and false peace! It is dangerous to those who grant it. And it probably avails nothing to those who receive it. For they are not seeking the patience necessary to [spiritual] health, nor the genuine medicine that is derived from atonement. Penitence is driven forth from their breasts. The memory of their very grave and extreme sin is taken away. . . . Returning from the altars of the devil, they draw near to the holy place of the Lord! . . . With jaws still breathing their crime . . . they intrude on the body of the Lord. . . . All these warnings are scorned and disdained. They do violence to His body and blood—before their sin is expiated, before confession of their crime has been made! [They receive His body and blood] before their conscience has been purged by sacrifice and by the hand of the priest! *Cyprian (c. 250, W), 5.441.*

We must separate from a believer who lives irregularly and contrary to discipline. Paul [said] to the Thessalonians: "But we have commanded you, in the name of Jesus Christ, that you depart from all brethren who walk disorderly and not according to the tradition that you have received from us." *Cyprian (c. 250, W), 5.551.*

The sinner must be publicly reproved. In the first Epistle of Paul to Timothy, it says: "Rebuke those who sin, in the presence of all." *Cyprian (c. 250, W), 5.552.*

We should not speak with heretics. He said to Titus: "A man that is a heretic, avoid after one rebuke." . . . Of this same thing, it is written in the Epistle of John: "They went out from among us, but they were not of us." *Cyprian (c. 250, W), 5.552.*

Covetousness is a great evil. . . . Robbery is declared to be a horrible thing, something to be abhorred. Yet, the covetous mind in general is likewise condemned. . . . And all persons of that spirit are excommunicated from the church of God. *Gregory Thaumaturgus (c. 255, E), 6.18.*

Concerning those who have joined the barbarians and . . . have become such thorough barbarians as even to put to death those of their own race, . . . it is necessary for you to bar such persons from even being listeners in the public assemblies. *Gregory Thaumaturgus (c. 255, E), 6.19.*

Some Christians have been so audacious as to pilfer the houses of [those taken captive by barbarians]. If they have already been put on trial and convicted, they should not be considered fit to even be listeners in the public assembly. However, if they have declared themselves and made restitution, they should be placed in the ranks of the penitent. *Gregory Thaumaturgus (c. 255, E), 6.19.*

Therefore, we have been compelled to excommunicate this man . . . who refuses submission, and to appoint another bishop in his place. *Malchion (c. 270, E), 6.170.*

If anyone is convicted of having done a wicked action . . . that causes the whole body of the church and its teaching to be blasphemed, . . . the bishop must boldly reject such a person upon proof—unless the person changes his course of life. *Apostolic Constitutions (compiled c. 390, E), 7.399.*

In the present world, the righteous and the wicked are mingled together in the common affairs of life—but not in the holy communion. *Apostolic Constitutions (compiled c. 390, E), 7.401.*

Sin that passes by without correction grows worse and worse and spreads to others. For "a little leaven infects the whole lump." . . . Likewise, one diseased sheep, if not separated from those who are well, infects the rest. . . . Therefore, if we neglect to separate the transgressor from the church of God, we will make the "Lord's house a den of thieves." For it is the

bishop's duty not to be silent in the case of offenders. *Apostolic Constitutions (compiled c. 390, E), 7.403.*

A righteous man unjustly slain by anyone will be in rest with God forever. The same is true of anyone who is separated by his bishop without cause. He who has cast him out as a wicked fellow when he was innocent, is more furious than a murderer. *Apostolic Constitutions (compiled c. 390, E), 7.406.*

If anyone hardens himself, "tell it to the church. However, if he refuses to listen to the church, let him be to you as a Gentile and a tax–collector." In other words, receive him no longer into the church as a Christian, but reject him as a pagan. However, if he is willing to repent, receive him. For the church does not receive a pagan or a tax–collector to communion. . . . As to those who are convicted of any wicked action and have not repented—you should view them as tax collectors or pagans. However, if they later repent and turn from their error, . . . we permit such ones to enter [the church]—but only to hear, until they show the fruits of repentance. . . . However, do not let them be admitted to communion in prayer. Rather, let them depart after the reading of the Law, the Prophets, and the Gospel—that by such departure they may be made better in their course of life. *Apostolic Constitutions (compiled c. 390, E), 7.414.*

If anyone prays with a person who has been excommunicated—even in the house—let him be suspended. *Apostolic Constitutions (compiled c. 390, E), 7.501; extended discussion: 7.402–7.406.*

II. Penitential discipline

Whatever you bind on earth will be bound in heaven, and whatever you loose on earth will be loosed in heaven. Matt. 18:15.

If you forgive the sins of any, they are forgiven them; if you retain the sins of any, they are retained. John 20:23.

Those who fall into sin after baptism are those who are subjected to discipline. For the deeds done before baptism are remitted [in baptism]. However, those committed after baptism are purged [through discipline]. *Clement of Alexandria (c. 195, E), 2.438.*

It is irksome to add mention of a second—nay, in that case, the *last*—hope. Lest, by treating of a remedial repenting yet in reserve, we seem to be pointing to a yet further space for sinning. ... Let no one be less good because God is more so. Let no one repeat his sin as often as he is forgiven. Otherwise, be sure he will find an end of escaping, when he will not find an end to sinning. We have escaped once. Thus far and no farther let us commit ourselves to perils, even if we seem likely to escape a second time. *Tertullian (c. 203, W), 3.662.*

Although the gate of forgiveness has been shut and fastened up with the bar of baptism, God has permitted it still to stand somewhat open. In the vestibule, He has stationed the second repentance for opening to those who knock. But now it is *once for all*—because now it is for the second time. It will not be repeated, if the last time it was in vain. For is not even this once enough? You have what you did not deserve, for you lost what you had received. If the Lord's indulgence grants you the means of restoring what you had lost, be thankful for the benefit renewed. *Tertullian (c. 203, W), 3.663.*

This act [penance] is more usually expressed and commonly spoken of under a Greek name, *exomologesis.* Through it, we confess our sins to the Lord. ... Penance is a discipline for man's prostration and humiliation, requiring a demeanor calculated to bring mercy. With regard also to the very dress and food, it commands the penitent to lie in sackcloth and ashes, to cover his body in mourning ... to know no food and drink but such as is plain—not for the stomach's sake, but for the soul's. *Tertullian (c. 203, W), 3.664.*

While it abases the man, it raises him. While it covers him with squalor, it renders him more clean. ... Yet most men either shun this work, as being a public exposure of themselves, or else postpone from day to day. I presume that they are more mindful of embarrassment than of salvation. ... However, I give no place to bashfulness when I am a gainer by its loss. ... Is it better to be damned in secret than absolved in public? *Tertullian (c. 203, W), 3.664.*

Let him say, "I have sinned against God and am in peril of eternally perishing. And so now I am drooping, and wasting and torturing myself, so that I may reconcile God to myself, whom by sinning I have offended." ...

Since you know that after the first bulwarks of the Lord's baptism, there still remains for you, in penance a second reserve of aid against

Gehenna, why do you desert your own salvation? Why are you slow to approach what you know heals you? *Tertullian (c. 203, W), 3.665.*

Repentance and her handmaid, penance, he had cast away. *Tertullian (c. 203, W), 3.666.*

As the quotations above demonstrate, Tertullian originally supported the church's position that it could extend God's forgiveness even for serious sins such as adultery—if the sinner were truly repentant. After adopting the teachings of the Montanists, however, Tertullian rejected any forgiveness for such serious sins, as demonstrated by the following quotations, where he derides the bishop of either Carthage or Rome, sarcastically labelling him with the pagan title *pontifex maximus.*

I hear that there has even been an edict set forth—and a dogmatic one too. The pontifex maximus—that is, the bishop of bishops—issues an edict: "I remit the sins of both adultery and fornication to those who have fulfilled repentance!" O edict, on which cannot be inscribed, "Good deed!" And where will this liberality be posted up? On the very spot, I suppose, on the very gates of the sensual appetites! *Tertullian (c. 212, W), 4.74.*

When bringing the repentant adulterer into the church, for the purpose of softening the brotherhood by his prayers, do you yourself lead him into the midst and prostrate him? There he is, all in haircloth and ashes, a compound of disgrace and horror, before the widows, before the presbyters, begging for the tears of all, licking the footprints of all, clasping the knees of all. *Tertullian (c. 212, W), 4.86.*

He rose early in the morning and threw himself, clothed with sackcloth and covered with ashes, before Zephyrinus, the bishop, with great haste and many tears. He rolled not only beneath the feet of the clergy, but those even of the laity. By his weeping, he moved the pity of the compassionate church of the merciful Christ. And after trying many a prayer and showing the welts left by the blows that he had received [from angels], he was at length with difficulty admitted to communion. *Eusebius, quoting Caius (c. 215, W), 5.602.*

You have become a penitent. Pray night and day. But do not depart far from your mother [i.e., the church]. For then, the Highest will be able to be merciful to you. The confession of your fault will not be in vain. In your state of accusation, learn to weep manifestly. *Commodianus (c. 240, W), 4.212.*

He who is of lowly mind does not by any means humble himself in an unseemly or inauspicious manner—falling down upon his knees, casting himself headlong on the ground, putting on the dress of the miserable, or sprinkling himself with dust.... If there are some, however, who through their ignorance have not clearly understood the doctrine of humiliation (but act as they do), it is not our teaching that is to be blamed. *Origen (c. 248, E), 4.580.*

In smaller sins, sinners may do penance for a set time and come to public confession in accordance with the rules of discipline. By imposition of the hand of the bishop and clergy, they receive the right of communion. *Cyprian (c. 250, W), 5.290.*

Before penitence was fulfilled, before confession even of the gravest and most heinous sin was made, before hands were placed upon the repentant person by the bishops and clergy, they dare to offer on their behalf and to give them the Eucharist! *Cyprian (c. 250, W), 5.291.*

We have decided that those who do not repent, nor give evidence of sorrow for their sins with their whole heart, and with manifest profession of their lamentation, are to be absolutely restrained from the hope of communion and peace, even if they begin to beg for them in the middle of sickness and peril. For what drives them to ask is not the repentance for sin, but the fear of imminent death. *Cyprian (c. 250, W), 5.333.*

Do we believe that a man is lamenting with his whole heart, that he is entreating the Lord with fasting, weeping, and mourning—if from the first day of his sin he daily frequents the bathing places with women? Is he lamenting if he feeds at rich banquets and (stuffed with too many dainties) vomits the contents of his stomach the next day? Is he lamenting if he does not forego his meat and drink in order to help the needs of the poor? ... Or does she groan and lament if she has time to put on the clothing of precious garments? Does she lament if she receives valuable jewelry and expensively made necklaces—instead of bewailing the loss of divine and heavenly adornment? *Cyprian (c. 250, W), 5.445.*

Even as we have sinned greatly, let us lament.... You must cling close to the ashes and be surrounded with sackcloth and dirt. After losing the garment of Christ, you must be willing now to have austere clothing. After the devil's meat, you must prefer fasting. Be earnest in righteous works, by which sins may be purged. Frequently apply yourself to almsgiving, by which souls are freed from death.... Let good works be done without delay. *Cyprian (c. 250, W), 5.447.*

No one can be so prudent and so cautious as not at some time to slip. Therefore, God, knowing our weakness, out of His compassion has opened a harbor of refuge for man—that the medicine of repentance might aid this necessity to which our frailty is liable. *Lactantius (c. 304–313, W), 7.191.*

The present canons address those who have in the persecution denied the faith and are doing penance. The first canon decrees that those who, after many torments, have sacrificed to the gods—not being able to persevere because of frailty—and who have passed three years in penance, another forty days should be enjoined—and then they can be admitted into the church. *Peter of Alexandria (c. 310, E), 6.269.*

Let a penalty of six months' penance be imposed upon them. *Peter of Alexandria (c. 310, E), 6.271.*

When he does repent and has submitted to his chastisement, receive him, remembering that our Lord has said, "There is joy in heaven over one sinner who repents." *Apostolic Constitutions (compiled c. 390, E), 7.400.*

SEE ALSO ABSOLUTION; BINDING AND LOOSING; LAPSED; REPENTANCE.

DISCRIMINATION

SEE EQUALITY OF HUMANKIND.

DIVINATION

SEE SPIRITISM.

DIVORCE

For the Lord God of Israel says that He hates divorce. Mal. 2:16.

He said to them, "Moses, because of the hardness of your hearts, permitted you to divorce your wives, but from the beginning it was not so. And I say to you, whoever divorces his wife, except for sexual immorality, and marries another, commits adultery;

and whoever marries her who is divorced commits adultery." Matt. 19:9.

A wife is not to depart from her husband. But even if she does depart, let her remain unmarried or be reconciled to her husband. And a husband is not to divorce his wife. 1 Cor. 7:10, 11.

And I said to him, "Sir, if anyone has a wife who trusts in the Lord, and if he detects her in adultery, does the man sin if he continues to live with her?" And he said to me, "As long as he remains ignorant of her sin, the husband commits no transgression in living with her. But if the husband knows that his wife has gone astray, and if the woman does not repent, but persists in her fornication, and yet the husband continues to live with her, he also is guilty of her crime, and a sharer in her adultery." And I said to him, "What then, sir, is the husband to do, if his wife continues in her vicious practices?" And he said, "The husband should put her away, and remain by himself. But if he puts his wife away and marries another, he also commits adultery."

And I said to him, "What if the woman who has been put away should repent, and wishes to return to her husband? Shall she not be taken back by her husband?" And he said to me, "Assuredly. If the husband does not take her back, he sins. And he brings a great sin upon himself. For he should take back the sinner who has repented. But not repeatedly. For there is but one repentance to the servants of God. In case, therefore, that the divorced wife may repent, the husband should not marry another after his wife has been put away. In this matter, man and woman are to be treated exactly in the same way. Moreover, adultery is committed not only by those who pollute their flesh, but also by those who imitate the pagans in their actions. For that reason, if anyone persists in such deeds, and does not repent, withdraw from him, and cease to live with him, otherwise you are a sharer in his sin." *Hermas (c. 150, W), 2.21.*

All who have been twice married by human law, are sinners in the eye of our Master. *Justin Martyr (c. 160, E), 1.167.*

She considered it wicked to live any longer as a wife with a husband who tried to indulge in every kind of pleasure contrary to the law of nature. . . . So she desired to be divorced from him. But she changed her mind because of her [Christian] friends, who advised her to remain with him, with the thought that some time or other her husband might give some hope of change. *Justin Martyr (c. 160, E), 1.189.*

The Lord also showed that certain provisions were enacted for them by Moses on account of their hardness. . . . It was for that reason that they received from Moses this law of divorce, adapted to their hard nature. *Irenaeus (c. 180, E/W), 1.480.*

That the Scripture counsels marriage and allows no release from the union is expressly contained in the law, "You will not put away your wife, except for the cause of fornication." And it regards as fornication the marriage of those separated while the other is alive. . . . "He who takes a woman who has been put away commits adultery." *Clement of Alexandria (c. 195, E), 2.379.*

Where is that happiness of married life, ever so desirable, that distinguished our earlier [Roman] manners? As the result of that, for about 600 years there was not among us [Romans] a single divorce. Now, [Roman] women have every member of the body heavy laden with gold; . . . and as for divorce, they long for it as though it were the natural consequence of marriage. *Tertullian (c. 197, W), 3.23.*

The Lord holds it more pleasing that marriage should not be contracted, than that it should at all be dissolved. In short, He prohibits divorce, except for the cause of fornication. *Tertullian (c. 205, W), 4.45.*

Christ prohibits divorce, saying, "Whoever puts away his wife and marries another, commits adultery. And whoever marries her who is put away from her husband also commits adultery." In order to forbid divorce, He makes it unlawful to marry a woman who has been put away. *Tertullian (c. 207, W), 3.404.*

I maintain, then, that there was a condition in the prohibition that He now made of divorce: the case at hand was that a man put away his wife for the express purpose of marrying another. . . . That is, [she was put away] for the reason for which a woman should not be dismissed—to obtain another wife. . . . Permanent is the marriage that is not rightly dissolved. Therefore, to marry while marriage is undissolved is to commit adultery. Since, therefore, His prohibition of divorce was a conditional one, He did not prohibit it absolutely. And what He did not absolutely forbid, He permitted on some occasions—when there is an absence of the cause why He gave His prohibition. *Tertullian (c. 207, W), 3.405.*

Well, then, what is a husband to do in your sect [the Marcionites] if his wife commits adultery? Shall he keep her? But your own apostle [i.e., Paul], you know, does not permit the members of Christ to be joined to a harlot. Divorce, therefore, when justly deserved, has even a defender in Christ. *Tertullian (c. 207, W), 3.405.*

In whatever direction you try to escape, you will find Christ also protecting marriage. He prohibits divorce when He will have the marriage inviolable. He permits divorce when the marriage is spotted with unfaithfulness. *Tertullian (c. 207, W), 3.405.*

Christ plainly forbids divorce; Moses unquestionably permits it. . . . Even Christ, however, when He commands "the wife not to depart from her husband, or if she departs, to remain unmarried or be reconciled to her husband," both permitted divorce (which indeed he never *absolutely* prohibited) and confirmed marriage (by first prohibiting its dissolution). If separation had taken place, He wished the marriage bond to be resumed by reconciliation. *Tertullian (c. 207, W), 3.443.*

The reason why He has abolished divorce, which "was not from the beginning," was in order to strengthen that thing which "was from the beginning"—the permanent joinder of two into one flesh. . . . So He permits divorce for no cause, except one. . . . So true is it that divorce "was not from the beginning," that among the Romans, it was not until after the six hundredth year from the building of the city [of Rome] that this type of "hard-heartedness" began to be permitted. . . . To us, even if we do divorce them [i.e., adulterous spouses], marriage will not be lawful. *Tertullian (c. 217, W), 4.66.*

She must necessarily persevere in that peace with him whom she will no longer have the power to divorce. Not that she would have been marriageable—even if she had been able to divorce him. *Tertullian (c. 217, W), 4.67.*

We gladly abide by the bond of a single marriage. In the desire of procreating, we know either one wife, or none at all. *Mark Minucius Felix (c. 200, W), 4.192.*

When being inquired of, Christ gave this judgment: He said that a wife must not be put away, except for the cause of adultery. . . . Laws are prescribed to married women, who are so bound that they cannot thence be separated. *Novatian (c. 235, W), 5.589, formerly attributed to Cyprian.*

Some of the laws were written—not as excellent—but as by way of accommodation to the weakness of those to whom the Law was given. For something of this kind is indicated in the words, "Moses, because of your hardness of heart, allowed you to put away your wives." *Origen (c. 245, E), 9.510.*

Our Savior does not at all permit the dissolution of marriages for any other sin than fornication alone, when detected in the wife. . . . But someone might ask if He allows a man to put away a wife for any other reasons besides her being caught in fornication. For example, what about poisoning [her husband]? Or what if, during the absence of her husband from the home, she destroys an infant born to them? Or what about any form of murder whatever? . . . Sins of such heinousness seem to be worse than adultery or fornication. To endure them would appear to be irrational. However, on the other hand, to act contrary to the design of the teaching of the Savior, everyone would acknowledge to be impious. *Origen (c. 245, E), 9.511.*

The husband can cause his own wife to commit adultery in other ways than by putting her away. For example, he can allow her to do what she wishes beyond what is fitting, and stooping to friendship with what men she wishes. . . . And even he who withholds himself from his wife oftentimes makes her to be an adulteress when he does not satisfy her desires. This is true even though he does it under the appearance of greater seriousness and self-control. *Origen (c. 245, E), 9.511.*

A wife must not depart from her husband. Or, if she should depart, she must remain unmarried. *Cyprian (c. 250, W), 5.553.*

He who marries a woman divorced from her husband is an adulterer. So is he who divorced a wife for any cause other than adultery, in order to marry another. *Lactantius (c. 304–313, W), 7.190, translated from the Latin.*

Do not let it be considered lawful after marriage to put her away who is without blame. For He says, "You will take care to your spirit and will not forsake the wife of your youth" [Mal. 2:14, 15].... And the Lord says, "What God has joined together, let no man put asunder." For the wife is the partner of life, united by God into one body from two. However, he who divides back into two that body that has become one—he is the enemy of the creation of God and the adversary of His providence. Similarly, he who retains her who is corrupted [by adultery] is a transgressor of the law of nature. For "he who retains an adulteress is foolish and impious" [Pro. 18:22]. Also, He says, "Cut her off from your flesh" [Sir. 25:26]. For she is no longer a helpmate, but a snare, having turned her mind from you to another. *Apostolic Constitutions (compiled c. 390, E), 7.456.*

If a layman divorces his own wife and takes another—or if he marries one divorced by another—let him be suspended. *Apostolic Constitutions (compiled c. 390, E), 7.503; extended discussion: 9.505–9.511.*

SEE ALSO REMARRIAGE; TWICE-MARRIED.

DOCETISTS

SEE GNOSTICS, GNOSTICISM.

DOCTRINE

SEE APOSTOLIC FAITH; CREEDS, EARLY.

DOMITIAN

Domitian (51–96) was the ruthless Roman emperor under whose reign the apostle John was sent to the isle of Patmos.

When John said these things, he was on the island of Patmos, condemned by Caesar Domitian to labor in the mines. When John had grown old, he thought that he would eventually meet his end through suffering. However, Domitian was killed and all his judgments were thrown out. *Victorinus (c. 280, W), 3.353.*

After an interval of some years from the death of Nero, there arose another tyrant [Domitian], who was no less wicked. His government was exceedingly hateful. For a very long time, he oppressed his subjects and reigned in security—until at length he stretched forth his unholy hands against the Lord. Having been instigated by evil demons to persecute the righteous people, he was then delivered into the power of his enemies and suffered due punishment. That he was murdered in his own palace was not suf-

ficient vengeance; the very memory of his name was erased. *Lactantius (c. 320, W), 7.302.*

DREAMS

In the ancient world, most persons believed that dreams were caused by the wandering of the soul while the body was sleeping. The early Christians generally held to the common view of their day.

I will go further and say that the soul does not even fall into sleep along with the body, nor does it even lie down in rest with its companion. For it is agitated in dreams. *Tertullian (c. 210, W), 3.558.*

Where do dreams come from? The fact is, [the soul] cannot rest or be altogether idle, nor does it confine its immortality to the still hours of sleep. Instead, it shows that it possesses a constant motion. It travels over land and sea. It trades. It is excited. It labors. It plays. *Tertullian (c. 210, W), 3.222, 223.*

Indeed, in these dreams, good actions are useless; and crimes are harmless. For we will no more be condemned for imaginary acts of sin, than we will be crowned for imaginary martyrdom. But you will ask, "How can the soul remember its dreams, when it is said to be without any mastery over its own operations?" This memory must be a special gift of the ecstatic condition. *Tertullian (c. 210, W), 3.224.*

Likewise in sleep, revelations are made of high honors and eminent talents. Remedies are also discovered, thefts brought to light, and treasure indicated. Thus Cicero's eminence was foreseen by his nurse, while he was still a little boy.... How many commentators and chroniclers vouch for this phenomenon! *Tertullian (c. 210, W), 3.225.*

Dreams are inflicted on us mainly by demons, although they sometimes turn out to be true and even to be favorable to us.... But all those visions that are honest, holy, prophetic, inspired, instructive, and inviting to virtue ... must be regarded as emanating from God. For He has promised, indeed, to pour out the grace of the Holy Spirit upon all flesh.... It was, indeed, by an inspiration from God that Nebuchadnezzar dreamed his dreams.... The third class of dreams will consist of those that the soul apparently creates for itself from an intense application to special circumstances. *Tertullian (c. 210, W), 3.225, 226.*

220

They say that dreams are more sure and clear when they happen towards the end of the night, for then the vigor of the soul emerges and heavy sleep departs. *Tertullian (c. 210, W), 3.226.*

As for those persons who suppose that infants do not dream, . . . they should observe attentively their tremors, nods, and bright smiles as they sleep. From such facts, they should realize that they are the emotions of their soul. *Tertullian (c. 210, W), 3.226, 227.*

In dreams, I am still occupied with what the soul has seen and handled in the day. *Gregory Thaumaturgus (c. 238, E), 6.38.*

It is a matter of belief that in dreams, impressions have been brought before the minds of many. Some relate to divine things; others, to future events of this life. This may be with clearness or in a symbolic manner. *Origen (c. 248, E), 4.416.*

SEE ALSO HEARING FROM GOD; SLEEP; VISIONS.

DRESS

SEE CLOTHING.

DRUIDS

The Druids were the priests of the ancient Celts.

The Druids among the Celts . . . devoted themselves to philosophic pursuits. *Hippolytus (c. 225, W), 5.9.*

The Celtic Druids investigated to the utmost the Pythagorean philosophy. . . . The Celts esteem the Druids as prophets and seers, on account of their foretelling to them certain events, from calculations and numbers of the Pythagorean art. . . . The Druids resort to magical rites as well. *Hippolytus (c. 225, W), 5.22.*

SEE ALSO BRITAIN; CELTS.

DYEING OF CLOTHING

SEE CLOTHING (III. DYEING OF CLOTHING).

DYEING OF THE HAIR

SEE GROOMING (II. DYEING OF THE HAIR).

EARTH

During the period of the pre-Nicene writings, many learned persons believed that the earth was round. Others thought differently. Both views are represented in the writings of the early Christians.

The world, being made spherical, is confined within the circles of heaven. *Athenagoras (c. 175, E), 2.132.*

Without a doubt, the world is beautiful. It excels as well in its magnitude as in the arrangement of its parts—both those in the oblique circle and those about the north, and also in its spherical form. Yet we must not worship the world, but rather its Artificer. *Athenagoras (c. 175, E), 2.136.*

There was a time when the whole globe underwent change, because it was overrun by all waters. . . . Even now, her shape undergoes local changes. *Tertullian (c. 200, W), 4.6.*

Let us first lay bare . . . the theory of the Chaldeans and the Egyptians. They say that the circumference of the universe is likened to the turnings of a well-rounded globe, the earth being a central point. They say that since its outline is spherical, . . . the earth should be the center of the universe, around which the heaven is whirling. . . . They say that surely the earth originally consisted in a state of chaos and disorganization. *Methodius (c. 290, E), 6.340.*

The philosophers fancied that the universe is round like a ball. They also thought that heaven revolves in accordance with the motion of the heavenly bodies. . . . For that reason, they constructed brass globes, as though after the figure of the universe. They engraved upon them certain monstrous images that they said were constellations. . . . But if this were so, the earth itself must be like a globe. . . . However, if you ask those who defend these marvelous fictions why everything does not fall into that lower part of the heavens, they reply that such is the nature of things. They say that heavenly bodies are carried to the middle and that they are all joined together towards the middle, just like spokes in a wheel. . . . I am at a loss as to what to say concerning those who, once they have erred, continue in their folly, defending one vain thing by another vain thing. *Lactantius (c. 304–313, W), 7.94, 95.*

In the first place, indeed, the world itself is neither right nor left. It has neither upper nor lower regions, nor front nor back. For whatever is round and bounded on every side by the circumference of a solid sphere, has no beginning or end. . . . Accordingly, when we speak of the right or the left side, we are not referring to anything in the world, which is everywhere very much the same. Rather, we refer to our own place and position. *Arnobius (c. 305, E), 6.477.*

SEE ALSO ATOMS; CREATION.

EAST

Now when Daniel knew that the writing was signed, he went home. And in his upper room, with his windows open toward Jerusalem, he knelt down on his knees three times that day and prayed. Dan. 6:10.

The Scripture says, "His name shall rise up above the sun." And again, Zechariah says, "His name is the East." *Justin Martyr (c. 160, E), 1.260.*

Corresponding to the manner of the sun's rising, prayers are made looking towards the sunrise, in the east. *Clement of Alexandria (c. 195, E), 2.535.*

Others . . . believe that the sun is our god. The idea no doubt has originated from our being known to turn to the east in prayer. *Tertullian (c. 197, W), 3.31.*

Others . . . suppose that the sun is the god of the Christians, for it is a well-known fact that we pray towards the east. *Tertullian (c. 197, W), 3.123.*

He also established two parts of the earth that are opposite to one another, and of a different character. I speak of the east and the west. Of these, the east is assigned to God, for He Himself is the Fountain of light and the Enlightener of all things. Furthermore, He makes us rise to eternal life. However, the west is ascribed to that disturbed and depraved mind, for it conceals the light. It always brings on darkness, and it makes men die and perish in their sins. *Lactantius (c. 304–313, W), 7.57.*

Let the building be long, with its head to the east, with its vestries on both sides at the east end—so it will be like a ship. *Apostolic Constitutions (compiled c. 390, E), 7.421.*

SEE ALSO PRAYER (II. PRAYER POSTURES AND CUSTOMS).

EASTER

The day that English-speaking Christians refer to as "Easter" was called Passover [Gr. *pascha*] by the early Christians. To avoid confusion with the Jewish Passover, pascha is rendered as "Easter" in this work. The term "Easter" did not begin to be used, however, until centuries after the Council of Nicaea.

When Servilius Paulus was proconsul of Asia, at the time that Sagaris suffered martyrdom, there arose a great controversy at Laodicea concerning the date of Easter, which had fallen due at that time. *Melito (c. 170, E), 8.758.*

When the blessed Polycarp was visiting in Rome in the time of Anicetus [c. 155], . . . they were at once well inclined towards each other, not willing that any quarrel should arise between them upon this matter [the observance of Easter]. For Anicetus could not persuade Polycarp to forego the observance [of his Easter customs] inasmuch as these things had been always observed by John the disciple of our Lord, and by other apostles with whom he had been conversant. *Irenaeus (c. 180, E/W), 1.569.*

In Alexandria, too, they observe the festival on the same day as ourselves. For the Paschal letters are sent from us to them, and from them to us. *Theophilus of Caesarea (c. 180, E), 8.774.*

In Asia great luminaries have gone to their rest, who will rise again on the day of the coming of the Lord. . . . These all kept Easter on the fourteenth day, in accordance with the Gospel. *Polycrates (c. 190, E), 8.773, 774.*

Finally, [what unbelieving husband] will without anxiety endure her absence all the night long at the Easter solemnities? *Tertullian (c. 205, W), 4.46.*

We consider fasting or kneeling in worship on the Lord's Day to be unlawful. We rejoice in the same privilege also from Easter to Pentecost. *Tertullian (c. 211, W), 3.94.*

If it were true that the apostle has erased all devotion absolutely of "seasons, days, months, and years," why do we celebrate Easter by an annual rotation in the first month? *Tertullian (c. 213, W), 4.112.*

They will assemble together at Easter, that most blessed day of ours. And let them rejoice! *Commodianus (c. 240, W), 4.218.*

We ourselves are accustomed to observe certain days. For example, there is . . . Easter. . . . He who considers that "Christ our Passover was sacrificed for us," and that it is his duty to keep the feast by eating of the flesh of the Word, never ceases to keep the paschal feast. For *pascha* means a "passover." So he is ever striving in all his thoughts, words, and deeds to pass over in all from the things of this life to God. *Origen (c. 248, E), 4.647.*

You have sent to me, most faithful and accomplished son, in order to inquire what is the proper hour for bringing the fast to a close on the day of Easter. You say that there are some of the brethren who hold that it should be done at cockcrow. However, others say that it should end at nightfall. . . . It will be cordially acknowledged by all that those who have been humbling their souls with fasting should immediately begin their festal joy and gladness at the same hour as the resurrection. . . . However, no precise account seems to be offered in [Scripture] as to the hour at which He rose. *Dionysius of Alexandria (c. 262, E), 6.94.*

We make the following statement and explanation to those who seek an exact account of the specific hour, half-hour, or quarter of an hour at which it is proper to begin their rejoicing over our Lord's rising from the dead: Those who are too hasty and give up even before midnight, we reprove as irresponsible and intemperate. *Dionysius of Alexandria (c. 262, E), 6.95.*

The other party keeps the day of the Lord's passion as one replete with sadness and grief. They hold that it would not be lawful to celebrate the Lord's mystery of the Passover at any other time but on the Lord's Day. *Anatolius (c. 270, E), 6.148, 149.*

[Paul of Samosata] . . . trained women to sing psalms in honor of himself in the midst of the church, during the great day of the Paschal festival. One would shudder to hear such choristers. *Malchion (c. 270, E), 6.170.*

It is your duty, brethren . . . to observe the days of Easter exactly. . . . No longer be concerned about keeping the feast with the Jews, for we now have no communion with them. In fact, they have been led astray in regard to the calculation itself. . . . You should not, through ignorance, celebrate Easter twice in the same year, or celebrate this day of the resurrection of our Lord on any day other than a Sunday. *Apostolic Constitutions (compiled c. 390, E), 7.447.*

Break your fast when it is daybreak of the first day of the week, which is the Lord's Day. From the evening until the cock-crows, keep awake; assemble together in the church; watch and pray; entreat God. When you sit up all night, read the Law, the Prophets, and the Psalms—until cock-crowing. Baptize your catechumens and read the Gospel with fear and trembling. And speak to the people such things as will assist their salvation. . . . And from that point on [i.e., cock-crowing], leave off your fasting and rejoice! Keep a festival, for Jesus Christ, the pledge of our resurrection, is risen from the dead! *Apostolic Constitutions (compiled c. 390, E), 7.447.*

SEE ALSO LENT; PASCHAL CONTROVERSY; QUARTODECIMANS.

EBIONITES

The Ebionites were a heretical sect who believed Jesus was the Jewish Messiah. They did not accept his divinity, however, and they continued to keep the Mosaic law.

Those who are called Ebionites agree that the world was made by God. But their opinions with respect to the Lord are similar to those of Cerinthus and Carpocrates. They use only the Gospel according to Matthew. They repudiate the apostle Paul, maintaining that he was an apostate from the Law. . . . They practice circumcision and persevere in the observance of those customs that are commanded in the Law. They are so Jewish in their style of life, that they even adore Jerusalem as if it were the house of God. *Irenaeus (c. 180, E/W), 1.352.*

The Ebionites, who use only Matthew's Gospel, are refuted out of this very same work, making false suppositions with regard to the Lord. *Irenaeus (c. 180, E/W), 1.428.*

[The passage] is not as some allege . . . "Behold, a *young woman* will conceive and bring forth a son." For this is as Theodotion the Ephesian has interpreted it, and Aquila of Pontus—both of whom are Jewish proselytes. The Ebionites, following these men, assert that He was begotten by Joseph. *Irenaeus (c. 180, E/W), 1.451.*

Vain also are the Ebionites, who do not receive by faith into their soul the union of God and man. Rather, they remain in the old leaven of [the natural] birth. They do not choose to understand that the Holy Spirit came upon Mary, and the power of the Most High overshadowed her. *Irenaeus (c. 180, E/W), 1.527.*

In his epistle, John especially designates those as antichrists who "denied that Christ had come in the flesh," and who refused to think that Jesus was the Son of God. Marcion maintained the first teaching; Hebion [i.e., the Ebionites] maintained the second one. *Tertullian (c. 197, W), 3.259.*

Again, there is an answer to Ebion in the Scripture, "Born, not of blood, nor of the will of the flesh, nor of the will of man, but of God." *Tertullian (c. 210, W), 3.541, 542.*

The Ebionites . . . conform to the customs of the Jews, alleging that they are justified according to the Law. They say that Jesus was justified by fulfilling the Law. They also say that it was because of this that He was called Jesus and the Christ of God, for no one else had observed the Law completely. . . . In short, they assert that our Lord Himself was a man in a like sense with all of us. *Hippolytus (c. 225, W), 5.114.*

I do not understand this expression as do the Ebionites, who are poor in understanding. They think that the Savior came especially to the carnal Israelites. *Origen (c. 225, E), 4.371.*

The physical Jews, and the Ebionites (who differ little from them), reproach us for transgressing the commandments about clean and unclean meats. *Origen (c. 245, E), 9.440.*

The word *ebion* signifies "poor" among the Jews. And those Jews who have received Jesus as Christ are called by the name of Ebionites. *Origen (c. 248, E), 4.429.*

There are some of them who accept Jesus, and, because of that, they consider themselves Christians. However, they regulate their lives in accordance with the Jewish Law, like the Jewish multitude. There are two sects of Ebionites. One of these sects acknowledges with us that Jesus was born of a virgin. The other sect denies this and maintains that He was begotten like other human beings. *Origen (c. 248, E), 4.570.*

There are certain heretical sects that do not receive the epistles of the apostle Paul—such as the two sects of Ebionites, as well as those who are called Encratites. *Origen (c. 248, E), 4.571.*

The Ebionites maintain that the Son of God was a mere man, begotten by human pleasure from the joinder of Joseph and Mary. *Apostolic Constitutions (compiled c. 390, E), 7.452; see also 1.439, 1.507.*

SEE ALSO HERESIES, HERETICS; JEWISH CHRISTIANITY.

ECONOMY OF GOD

SEE TRINITY.

EDESSA

Edessa, a small kingdom lying at the eastern edge of the Roman Empire, became a center for eastern, Aramaic Christianity. It was eventually absorbed into the Roman Empire and later into the Persian empire.

After Jesus was risen from the abode of the dead and was received into heaven, Thomas the apostle . . . by an impulse from God, sent Thaddaeus . . . to Edessa to be a preacher and proclaimer of the teaching of Christ. And the promise of Christ was fulfilled through him. You have in writing the evidence of these things, which are taken from the book of records that was at Edessa. For at that time, the kingdom was still standing. *Eusebius (c. 315, E), 8.651.*

SEE ALSO ABGAR, KING; SEVENTY, THE (DISCIPLES).

EDICT OF MILAN

The Edict of Milan, described below, was issued by Licinius and Constantine in 313. It gave Christianity formal legal recognition for the first time.

When [Licinius] and Constantine were consuls for the third time, he [Licinius] commanded the following edict for the restoration of the church, directed to the president of each province, for him to promulgate:

> When we, Constantine and Licinius, emperors, had a conference at Milan, and conferred together with respect to the well-being and security of the commonwealth, it seemed to us that . . . it was proper that the Christians, and all others, should have liberty to follow that manner of religion which to each one appeared best. So that God, who is seated in heaven, might be benign and favorable to us and to everyone under our government. . . .
>
> Moreover, with respect to the Christians, we formerly gave certain orders concerning the places set aside for their religious assemblies. However, now we resolve that all persons who have purchased such places, either from our treasurer, or from anyone else, must restore them to the Christians, without money demanded or price claimed. . . . All those places are, by your intervention, to be immediately restored to the Christians. And it appears that, in addition to the places set aside for religious worship, the Christians possessed other places (which belonged to the society in general, not to individuals). These we include in the aforesaid regulations.

Lactantius (c. 320, E), 7.320.

SEE ALSO CONSTANTINE.

EDUCATION

You [Romans] have learned geometry from the Egyptians, astronomy from the Babylonians, and the methods of healing from the Thracians. The Assyrians have also taught you many things. However, for the laws that are consistent with truth and your understandings of God, you are indebted to the Hebrews. *Clement of Alexandria (c. 195, E), 2.192.*

To the spiritual man, knowledge is the principal thing. As a consequence, he applies himself to the subjects that provide training for knowledge. He takes from each branch of study its contribution to the truth. So he studies the proportion of harmonies in music. In arithmetic, he notes the increasing and decreasing of numbers and their relations to one another. . . .

Studying geometry, which is abstract logic, he comprehends a continuous distance and an unchanging essence that is different from these bodies. Again, through astronomy, he is mentally raised from the earth; he is elevated along with the heavens. *Clement of Alexandria (c. 195, E), 2.498.*

He who culls what is useful for the advantage of the catechumens—and especially when they are Greeks—must not (like an irrational animal) abstain from learning. Rather, he must collect together as many aids as is possible for his hearers. Yet, he should not linger over those studies, unless solely for the advantage accruing from them. Once they are grasped, . . . he may be able to take his departure home to the true philosophy—[Christianity]. *Clement of Alexandria (c. 195, E), 2.500.*

We must inquire, likewise, concerning school teachers. . . . It is necessary for them to preach the gods of the nations, to express their names, genealogies, honorable distinctions—all and singular. Further, they must observe the solemnities and festivals of the gods. . . . The schools must be wreathed with flowers. . . . Who will think that these things are befitting to a Christian teacher? . . . We know it may be said, "If teaching literature is not lawful to God's servants, neither will learning be, either." . . . Let us see, then, the necessity of literary learning. Let us consider that, on the one hand, it should not be allowed; yet, on the other hand, it cannot be avoided. In short, *learning* literature is allowable for believers, but not *teaching* it. *Tertullian (c. 200, W), 3.66.*

It is not that *no* wise men according to the flesh [receive Christ], but that not *many* who are wise according to the flesh. *Origen (c. 228, E), 9.345.*

Greetings in God, my most excellent sir and venerable son, Gregory, from Origen. . . . Your natural talents might make of you a finished Roman lawyer or a Greek philosopher. . . . But I am anxious that you should devote all the strength of your natural talents to Christianity for your end. To this end, I wish to ask you to extract from the philosophy of the Greeks what may serve as a course of study or a preparation for Christianity. And from geometry and astronomy, take what will serve to explain the sacred Scriptures. *Origen (c. 240, E), 4.393.*

Celsus has claimed that it is a saying of many Christians that "the wisdom of this life is a bad thing, but that foolishness is good." I have to answer that he slanders the Gospel, not quoting the words as they actually occur in the writings of Paul. . . . By the term, "the wisdom of this world," we mean every *false* system of philosophy. According to the Scriptures, they are brought to nothing. However, we do not indiscriminately say that foolishness is good. Rather, we say this only when a man becomes foolish as to *this world*. *Origen (c. 248, E), 4.402.*

Some have been led to think that no one who is educated, wise, or prudent, embraces the Gospel. Now, in answer to such a person, I would say that it has not been stated that "*no* wise man according to the flesh," but that "not *many* wise men according to the flesh" are called. *Origen (c. 248, E), 4.483.*

Truly, it is no evil to have been educated. For education is the way to virtue. . . . It is no hindrance to the knowledge of God to have been educated. Rather, it is a help. *Origen (c. 248, E), 4.484.*

If, therefore, it should happen that a believer in Christ is called to this same office [librarian for the emperor], he should not despise the secular literature and those Gentile intellects that please the emperor. The poets are to be praised for the greatness of their genius. . . . Furthermore, the orators and the philosophers are to be praised, in their own class. . . . On occasion, also, he will endeavor to praise the divine Scriptures . . . Sometimes, too, the Gospel and the apostles will be praised for their divine oracles. And there will be an opportunity to speak of Christ. *Theonas of Alexandria (c. 300, E), 6.160.*

Sometimes, the common people have more wisdom. For they are only wise as far as is necessary. If you ask them whether they know something or not, they will say that they know the things that they truly know. But they will admit that they are ignorant of the things they do not know. . . . What then is wisdom? It consists in thinking neither that you know all things (for that is the property of God) nor that you are ignorant of all things (which is the property of the beasts). *Lactantius (c. 304–313, W), 7.73.*

Great attention should be give to the grammarians, so that you can know the right method of speaking. That should occupy many years. Nor should you be ignorant of rhetoric, for it enables you to say and express the things that you have learned. Furthermore, geometry, music, and astronomy are necessary. *Lactantius (c. 304–313, W), 7.95.*

SEE ALSO WORLD, SEPARATION FROM THE.

EGYPTIANS

Because they are more menial and ignorant than every other people who are on the earth, the Egyptians have erred more than everyone else. For the gods of the barbarians and Greeks were not sufficient for them. So they introduced gods in the nature of animals and said that these were gods. . . . From ancient times, they also worshipped Isis. They say that she is a goddess whose husband was her brother, Osiris. . . . Some of them worship sheep; others worship a calf. Still others worship the pig, the herring, the crocodile, the hawk, the fish, the ibis, the vulture, the eagle, and the raven. Some of them worship the cat . . . and others, the dog. Some worship the adder and some, the asp. . . . Great then is the error into which the Egyptians have strayed. In fact, it is greater than that of any people who are upon the face of the earth. *Aristides (c. 125, E), 9.272–274.*

O Greeks, do not be hostile towards the barbarians. Do not look on their opinions with ill will. For which of your institutions has not been derived from the barbarians? . . . To the Babylonians you owe astronomy; . . . to the Egyptians, geometry. *Tatian (c. 160, E), 2.65.*

The Egyptians were the first to introduce astrology among men. . . . The Egyptians first invented the burning of lamps. They were the first to divide the year into twelve months, to prohibit intercourse with women in the temples, and to enact that no man should enter the temples from a woman without bathing. Again, they were the inventors of geometry. *Clement of Alexandria (c. 195, E), 2.317.*

The best of the philosophers . . . culled tenets from other barbarians—primarily, the Egyptians. This is particularly true of transmigration of the soul. For the Egyptians pursue a philosophy of their own. This is principally shown by their sacred ceremonial. *Clement of Alexandria (c. 195, E), 2.488.*

The Egyptians, in the purifications practiced among them, do not allow the priests to feed on meat. *Clement of Alexandria (c. 195, E), 2.532.*

The Egyptians themselves have been permitted [by the Romans] the legal use of their ridiculous superstition. They have freedom to make gods of birds and beasts. In fact, they have freedom to condemn to death anyone who kills one of their gods. *Tertullian (c. 197, W), 3.39.*

In that prophet [Isaiah], Egypt is sometimes understood to mean the whole world. *Tertullian (c. 197, W), 3.162.*

Do not you [Romans] adore and feed Apis the ox, along with the Egyptians? You do not condemn their sacred rites instituted in honor of serpents, crocodiles, and other beasts! *Mark Minucius Felix (c. 200, W), 4.191.*

Such a person appears to me to act very much like someone who had merely *visited* Egypt, . . . yet imagined that he was acquainted with the whole circle of Egyptian knowledge—even though he had learned only from the ignorant and had never associated with any of the priests or had learned the mysteries of the Egyptians from any other source. *Origen (c. 248, E), 4.401.*

The Egyptians were guilty of error. For they, indeed, had solemn enclosures around the buildings they considered as their temples. However, within them, there was nothing except apes, crocodiles, goats, serpents, or some other animal. *Origen (c. 248, E), 4.610.*

The Egyptians are a people who went as far as possible in degrading the Divine Being to the level of brute beasts. They did this either from superstition or from some other form of delusion. *Origen (c. 248, E), 4.659.*

SEE ALSO GODS, PAGAN.

EIGHTH DAY

Sunday, the first day of the week, was also referred to as the "eighth day" by Christians.

I will make a beginning of the eighth day, that is, a beginning of another world. For that reason, also, we keep the eighth day with joyfulness, the day also on which Jesus rose again from the dead. *Barnabas (c. 70–130, E), 1.147.*

The eighth day possessed a certain mysterious significance, which the seventh day did not possess. It was promulgated by God through these rites. *Justin Martyr (c. 160, E), 1.206.*

Our Lord Jesus Christ rose from the dead on the first day after the Sabbath. Although the first day after the Sabbath remains the first of all the days, it is nevertheless also called the eighth. *Justin Martyr (c. 160, E), 1.215.*

Righteous Noah . . . with his own wife, his three sons and their wives—being eight in number—were a symbol of the eighth day. *Justin Martyr (c. 160, E), 1.268.*

Concerning the observance of the eighth day in the Jewish circumcision of the flesh, a sacrament was given beforehand in shadow and in usage. But when Christ came, it was fulfilled in truth. For the eighth day (that is, the first day after the Sabbath) was to be that day on which the Lord would rise again, enliven us, and give us the circumcision of the spirit. The eighth day (that is, the first day after the Sabbath), the Lord's day, was foreshadowed. *Cyprian (c. 250, W), 5.354.*

They foreshadowed the circumcision of the spiritual eighth day. *Methodius (c. 290, E), 6.333.*

SEE ALSO LORD'S DAY; SABBATH.

ELECT

SEE FREE WILL AND PREDESTINATION.

ELDERS

SEE CHURCH GOVERNMENT.

ELIJAH

Then it happened, as they continued on and talked, that suddenly a chariot of fire appeared with horses of fire, and separated the two of them; and Elijah went up by a whirlwind into heaven. 2 Kings 2:11.

Behold, I will send you Elijah the prophet before the coming of the great and dreadful day of the Lord. Mal. 4:5.

"I will give power to my two witnesses, and they will prophesy one thousand two hundred and sixty days, clothed in sackcloth." . . . *If anyone wants to harm them, fire proceeds from their mouth and devours their enemies.* . . . *These have power to shut heaven, so that no rain falls in the days of their prophecy.* Rev. 11:3–6.

Elijah, too, was taken up when he was yet in the substance of the [natural] form. *Irenaeus (c. 180, E/W), 1.530.*

In that week, the two prophets, Enoch and Elijah, will take up the half. For they will preach 1260 days clothed in sackcloth, proclaiming repentance to the people and to all the nations. *Hippolytus (c. 200, W), 5.213.*

Of the removal of a man from earth to heaven, the Creator has afforded us an example in Elijah. *Tertullian (c. 207, W), 3.456.*

But Elijah is to come again, not after quitting life, but after his assumption. It is not for the purpose of being restored to the body from which he had not departed, but for the purpose of revisiting the world from which he was taken up. It will not be by way of resuming a life that he had laid aside, but by way of fulfilling prophecy. He will really and truly be the same man, both in respect to his name, his designation, and his unchanged humanity. Therefore, in what sense could John be Elijah? You have your answer in the angel's announcement, who said: "And he will go before the people in the *spirit* and *power* of Elijah"—not in his body and soul. *Tertullian (c. 210, W), 3.217.*

However, it is likely that before the second and more divine coming of Christ, John or Elijah will come to bear witness about life. *Origen (c. 228, E), 9.345.*

"And I saw another angel ascending from the east, having the seal of the living God." He speaks of Elijah the prophet, who is the precursor of the times of the Antichrist—for the restoration and establishment of the churches from the great and intolerable persecution. . . . The aid of the great eagle's wings is the gift of the [two] prophets, which is given to that catholic church. In the end times, a hundred and forty-four thousand men will believe on the preaching of Elijah. . . . The "two great wings" are the two prophets—Elijah and the prophet who will be with him. *Victorinus (c. 280, W), 7.352.*

SEE ALSO ANTICHRIST; ASSUMPTIONS; ENOCH; ESCHATOLOGY.

EMMAUS

SEE SIMON AND CLEOPHAS.

EMPEROR WORSHIP

To God alone we render worship. However, in other things we gladly serve you, acknowledging you as kings and rulers of men. *Justin Martyr (c. 160, E), 1.168.*

You will say to me, then, "Why do you not worship the king?" The answer is that he is not made to be *worshipped,* but to be reverenced with lawful *honor.* For he is not a god, but a man appointed by God to judge justly, not to be worshipped. *Theophilus (c. 180, E), 2.92.*

Let him be satisfied with bearing the name of "emperor." That, too, is a great name of God's giving. But to call him "god" is to rob him of his title. If he is not a man, he cannot be an emperor.... Augustus, the founder of the empire, would not even accept the title "lord." ... Far less should the emperor have the name of "god." ... Give all reverence to God, if you wish Him to be propitious to the emperor. Give up all worship of, and belief in, any other being as divine. Cease from giving the sacred name to him who has need of God himself. *Tertullian (c. 197, W), 3.43.*

We are charged with being irreligious towards [the Caesars] since we neither pray to their images nor swear by their genius. *Tertullian (c. 197, W), 3.125.*

Peter had said that the king indeed must be honored. But he means that the king is honored only when he keeps to his own sphere—that is, when he is far from claiming divine honors. *Tertullian (c. 213, W), 3.647,648.*

We read, "Let every soul be subject to the higher powers. For there is no power but of God." ... However, we will never swear by "the fortune of the king," nor by anything else that is considered equivalent to God. *Origen (c. 248, E), 4.664.*

SEE ALSO GODS, PAGAN.

EMPLOYMENT

Go to the ant, you sluggard! Consider her ways and be wise. Prov. 6:6.

Do not labor for the food which perishes, but for the food which endures to everlasting life. John 6:27.

Let him who stole steal no longer, but rather let him labor, working with his hands what is good. Eph. 4:28.

Whatever you do, do it heartily, as to the Lord and not to men. Col. 3:23.

If a prophet desires to abide with you, and if he is a tradesman, let him work and eat. However, if he has no trade, according to your understanding see to it that as a Christian, he will not live with you idle. *Didache (c. 80–140, E), 7.381.*

Refrain from much business, and you will never sin. For those who are occupied with much business also commit many sins. For they are distracted about their affairs and are not at all serving their Lord. *Hermas (c. 150, W), 2.33.*

Grant now that there may be some righteousness in business, secure from the duty of watchfulness against covetousness and falsehood.... I acknowledge that I cannot exercise the trade of pandering, or keep that kind of place for my neighbor's benefit. So, too, the prohibition of murder shows me that a trainer of gladiators is also excluded from the church. *Tertullian (c. 200, W), 3.67.*

If he will pass through temples, with what mouth will a Christian seller of frankincense ... spit down upon and blow out the smoking altars? After all, he himself has supplied it [with incense]? ... Therefore, no art, no profession, and no trade that assists the equipping or forming of idols can be free from the title of idolatry. *Tertullian (c. 200, W), 3.68.*

If anyone alleges the pretense of his own work [as his excuse for neglecting worship], he is a despiser, "offering pretenses for his sins." Let such a person know that the trades of the faithful are our secondary employment. The worship of God is our primary vocation. Therefore, follow your trades as you are able, in order to maintain your livelihood. However, make the worship of God your main business. As our Lord said, "Do not labor for the meat that perishes, but for that which endures unto everlasting life." *Apostolic Constitutions (compiled c. 390, E), 7.423.*

Attend to your employment with all appropriate seriousness, so that you will always have sufficient funds to support both yourselves and those who are needy. In that way, you will not burden the church of God.... Some of us are fishermen, tentmakers, and farmers, so that we may never be idle. Solomon says, "Go to the ant, you sluggard; consider her ways diligently and become wiser than she." *Apostolic Constitutions (compiled c. 390, E), 7.424; extended discussion: 3.64–3.68.*

ENCRATITES

The Encratites were a heretical sect known for their ascetic practices.

The Encratites have sprung from Saturninus and Marcion. They preach against marriage.

They have thereby set aside the original creation of God. So they indirectly blame Him, for He made the male and female for the propagation of the human race. Some of their leaders have also instituted abstinence from animal food. They thereby show themselves to be ungrateful to God, who made all things. Furthermore, they deny the salvation of the first created man [Adam]. However, it is only recently that this last opinion has been introduced among them. A certain man named Tatian first introduced this blasphemy. *Irenaeus (c. 180, E/W), 1.353.*

Others, however, call themselves Encratites. They acknowledge some things concerning God and Christ in the same manner as the church. However, as to their manner of life, they spend their days puffed up with pride. They imagine that they make themselves better by foods. So they abstain from animal foods and drink only water. They forbid their people to marry. For the rest of their lives, they devote themselves to ascetic practices. But persons of this description should be considered Cynics rather than Christians. For they do not pay attention to the words spoken against them through the apostle Paul. For he foretold the novelties that would later be introduced by certain ones, saying, "The Spirit speaks expressly that in the latter times certain ones will depart from sound doctrine, giving heed to seducing spirits and doctrines of devils . . . forbidding to marry, abstaining from meats that God has created to be partaken of with thanksgiving." *Hippolytus (c. 225, W), 5.124.*

There are certain heretical sects that do not receive the epistles of the apostle Paul—such as the two sects of Ebionites, as well as those who are termed Encratites. *Origen (c. 248, E), 4.571.*

SEE ALSO HERESIES, HERETICS; TATIAN.

END OF THE WORLD

SEE ESCHATOLOGY.

ENOCH

And Enoch walked with God; and he was not, for God took him. Gen. 5:24.

By faith Enoch was translated so that he did not see death. Heb. 11:5.

Let us take (for instance) Enoch. He, being found righteous in obedience, was taken up,

and he was never known to have experienced death. *Clement of Rome (c. 96, W), 1.7.*

Enoch, too, pleased God without circumcision. He performed the office of God's envoy to the angels, even though he was a man. He was taken up, and he is preserved until now as a witness of the just judgment of God. *Irenaeus (c. 180, E/W), 1.429.*

When he had pleased God, Enoch was taken up in the same body in which he had pleased Him. *Irenaeus (c. 180, E/W), 1.530.*

Enoch was no doubt taken up, and so was Elijah. Neither of them experienced death. Rather, it was most certainly postponed. They are reserved for the suffering of death, that by their blood, they may extinguish the Antichrist. Even John underwent death, although there had prevailed an unfounded expectation concerning him that he would remain alive until the coming of the Lord. *Tertullian (c. 210, W), 3.227, 228.*

SEE ALSO ANTICHRIST; ASSUMPTIONS; ENOCH, BOOK OF; ESCHATOLOGY.

ENOCH, BOOK OF

The following New Testament passages refer to events described in the book of Enoch:

God did not spare the angels who sinned, but cast them down to hell and delivered them into chains of darkness, to be reserved for judgment. 2 Pet. 2:4.

The angels who did not keep their proper domain, but left their own habitation, He has reserved in everlasting chains under darkness for the judgment of the great day. Jude 6.

Now Enoch, the seventh from Adam, prophesied about these men also, saying, "Behold, the Lord comes with ten thousands of His saints, to execute judgment on all, to convict all who are ungodly among them of all their ungodly deeds." Jude 14 [quoting from Enoch 1:9].

For the Scripture says, "And it will come to pass in the last days, that the Lord will deliver up the sheep of His pasture, their sheepfold, and their tower to destruction" [*Enoch* 89:56–66]. *Barnabas (c. 70–130, E), 1.147.*

Jude says, "Enoch also, the seventh from Adam, prophesied of these." In these words, he verifies the prophecy. *Clement of Alexandria (c. 195, E), 2.573.*

I am aware that the Scripture of *Enoch*, which has assigned this order of action to angels, is not received by some. For it is not admitted into the Jewish canon, either. I suppose they did not think that, having been written before the deluge, it could have safely survived that worldwide calamity, the destroyer of all things. If that is the reason for rejecting it, let them remember that Noah, who survived the deluge, was the great-grandson of Enoch himself. . . . There is still this consideration to warrant our assertion of the genuineness of this Scripture: [Noah] could equally have rewritten it, under the Spirit's inspiration, if it had been destroyed by the violence of the deluge. *Tertullian (c. 198, W), 4.15.*

Since in the same Scripture, Enoch has preached similarly concerning the Lord, nothing at all must be rejected by us that pertains to us. We read that every Scripture suitable for edification is divinely inspired. So it may now seem to have been rejected by the Jews for that very reason—just like nearly all the other portions that speak of Christ. . . . To these considerations is added the fact that Enoch possesses a corroboration in the apostle Jude. *Tertullian (c. 198, W), 4.16.*

Enoch had preceded [Moses], predicting that "the demons and the spirits of the apostate angels would turn all the elements into idolatry." . . . In short, the same Enoch condemns in advance by a general denunciation both idol worshippers and idol makers. . . . And why should I, a man of limited memory, suggest anything further? Why recall anything more from the Scriptures? *Tertullian (c. 200, W), 3.62, 63.*

In the book of *Enoch*, we also have similar descriptions. *Origen (c. 225, E), 4.252.*

However, perhaps someone will inquire whether we can obtain out of Scripture any basis for such an understanding of the subject. Now, I think such a view is indicated in the Psalms, when the prophet says, "My eyes have seen your imperfection." . . . Enoch, also, in his book, speaks as follows, "I have walked on even to imperfection." . . . It is written in the same book of *Enoch*, "I saw the whole of matter." *Origen (c. 225, E), 4.380.*

That the first month among the Hebrews is around the equinox, is clearly shown also by what is taught in the book of *Enoch. Anatolius (c. 270, E), 6.147.*

SEE ALSO ENOCH; PSEUDEPIGRAPHA, OLD TESTAMENT.

ENTERTAINMENT

References below to the "circus" refer to the chariot races, not to what is known as a circus today.

I have hated the congregation of evildoers, and will not sit with the wicked. Ps. 26:5.

Therefore gird up the loins of your mind, be sober, . . . not conforming yourselves to the former lusts, as in your ignorance; but as He who called you is holy, you also be holy in all your conduct. 1 Pet. 1:13–15.

In regard to these, they think it strange that you do not run with them in the same flood of dissipation, speaking evil of you. 1 Pet. 4:4.

[WRITTEN TO PAGANS:] They utter ribaldry in pretentious tones, and they act out indecent movements. Your daughters and your sons watch them giving lessons in adultery on the stage. . . . Admirable, too, are your lying poets, who beguile their listeners from the truth through their fictions! . . . And the boxers meet in single combat, for no reason whatever. . . . Are such exhibitions to your credit? He who is chief among you collects a legion of blood-stained murderers [i.e., gladiators], engaging to maintain them. . . . And he who misses the murderous exhibition is grieved, for he was not doomed to be a spectator of wicked, impious, and abominable deeds! *Tatian (c. 160, E), 2.75.*

Neither may we watch the other spectacles [i.e., the theaters], lest our eyes and ears be defiled by participating in the utterances that are sung there. For if one should speak of cannibalism, in these spectacles the children of Thyestes and Tereus are eaten. And as for adultery, both in the case of men and of gods, whom they celebrate in elegant language for honors and prizes, this is made the subject of their dramas. *Theophilus (c. 180, E), 2.115.*

The Instructor will not, then, bring us to public spectacles. Not inappropriately, one might call the racecourse and the theater "the seat of plagues." . . . Let spectacles, therefore, and plays that are full of indecent language and abundant gossip, be forbidden. For what base action is there that is not exhibited in the theaters? *Clement of Alexandria (c. 195, E), 2.289, 290.*

We renounce all your spectacles. . . . Among us nothing is ever said, seen, or heard that has anything in common with the madness of the circus, the immodesty of the theater, the atrocities of the arena, or the useless exercise of the wrestling ground. Why do you take offense at us because we differ from you in regard to your pleasures? *Tertullian (c. 197, W), 3.46.*

We do not go to your spectacles. As for the merchandise that is sold there, if I need them, I will obtain them more readily at their proper places. *Tertullian (c. 197, W), 3.49.*

Everyone [i.e., among the pagans] is ready with the argument that all things, as we teach, were created by God and given to man for his use. Therefore, they must be good, since they all come from so good a source. [They say] that among them are found the various constituent elements of the public shows—such as the horse, the lion, bodily strength, and musical voice.... How skillful a pleader seems human wisdom to herself, especially if she has the fear of losing any of her delights! *Tertullian (c. 197, W), 3.79, 80.*

Fortified by this knowledge against pagan views, let us turn instead to the unworthy reasonings of our own people. Now, the faith of some is either too simple or too scrupulous. For it demands direct authority from Scripture for giving up the shows. They say the issue is an uncertain one, for such abstinence is not clearly and in [plain] words imposed upon God's servants. *Tertullian (c. 197, W), 3.80.*

It will be made clear that the entire apparatus of the shows is based upon idolatry. *Tertullian (c. 197, W), 3.81.*

See, Christian, how many impure names have taken possession of the circus! You have nothing to do with a sacred place that is inhabited by such multitudes of diabolic spirits. *Tertullian (c. 197, W), 3.83.*

Now let me address the kind of performances peculiar to the circus exhibitions. In former days, equestrianism was practiced in a simple way on horseback. Certainly, its ordinary use had nothing sinful in it. But when it was dragged into the games, it passed from the service of God into the employment of demons. *Tertullian (c. 197, W), 3.83.*

We will now direct our discourse from there to the theater, beginning with the place of exhibition. At first, the theater was actually a temple of Venus. And, to speak briefly, it was because of

this that stage performances were allowed to escape censure. That is how they got a foothold in the world. For oftentimes the censors, in the interests of morality, put down the rising theaters. *Tertullian (c. 197, W), 3.84.*

Since all passionate excitement is forbidden to us, we are barred from every kind of spectacle, and especially from the circus.... The spectators fly into rages, passions, arguments, and all kinds of things that they who are consecrated to peace should never indulge in. Next, there are curses and reproaches, with no [rational] cause of hatred. There are cries of applause, with nothing [genuinely] to merit them. *Tertullian (c. 197, W), 3.86.*

Are we not, in like manner, commanded to put away from us all immodesty? On this ground, again, we are excluded from the theater, which is immodesty's own peculiar abode. ... The very harlots, too, victims of the public lust, are brought upon the stage.... Let the Senate, let all ranks, blush for very shame! ... Is it right to *look* on what it is disgraceful to *do*? How is it that the things that defile a man in going out of his mouth, are not regarded as doing so when they go in his eyes and ears? *Tertullian (c. 197, W), 3.86, 87.*

If, again, we despise the teaching of secular literature as being foolishness in God's eyes, our duty is plain enough in regard to those spectacles that come from this source: the tragic and comic plays. Tragedies and comedies are the bloody, wanton, impious, and licentious inventors of crimes and lusts. Yet, it is not good for us to dwell on anything that is atrocious or vile. What you reject in deed, you are not to welcome in word. *Tertullian (c. 197, W), 3.87.*

If you argue that the racecourse is mentioned in Scripture, I grant it at once. But you will not refuse to admit that the things that are done there are not for you to look upon: the blows, kicks, cuffs, and all the recklessness of hand. *Tertullian (c. 197, W), 3.87*

The father who carefully protects and guards his virgin daughter's ears from every polluting word, takes her to the theater himself—exposing her to all its vile words and attitudes. Again, in the streets, a man will either apprehend or scold a brawling fighter. However, in the arena, the same man gives complete encouragement to combats of a much more serious kind. *Tertullian (c. 197, W), 3.88.*

Does it then remain for us to appeal to the pagans themselves? Let them tell us whether it is right for Christians to frequent the shows. Why, the rejection of these amusements is the chief sign to them that a man has adopted the Christian faith. *Tertullian (c. 197, W), 3.89.*

Seated where there is nothing of God, will one be thinking of his Maker? Will there be peace in his soul when there is eager strife there for a charioteer? . . . When the athletes are hard at struggle, will he be ready to proclaim that there must be no striking back? *Tertullian (c. 197, W), 3.89.*

The Lord Himself is our witness that we have the case of the woman who went to the theater and came back demon-possessed. In the exorcism, when the unclean creature was upbraided for having dared to attack a believer, he firmly replied, "And in truth I did it most lawfully, for I found her in my domain." . . . Grant that you have there things that are pleasant—things both agreeable and innocent in themselves. You even have some things that are excellent. Nobody dilutes poison with gall and hellebore [bitter potions]. Rather, the poison is put into well seasoned and sweet-tasting mixtures. Similarly, the devil puts things of God (things most pleasant and most acceptable) into the deadly drink that he prepares. *Tertullian (c. 197, W), 3.90.*

Simply because God has given to man the horse, the panther, and the power of speech, it does not follow that a Christian should attach himself to the frenzies of the racecourse, the atrocities of the arena, or the degradation of the stage. *Tertullian (c. 198, W), 4.17.*

[SPEAKING TO PAGANS:] We are evaluated by our character and our modesty. Therefore, for good reason, we abstain from evil pleasures, and from your pomps and exhibitions. We know the origin in connection with religious things, and we condemn their mischievous enticements. For in the chariot games, who does not shudder at the madness of the people brawling among themselves? Who does not wince at the teaching of murder in the gladiatorial games? In the drama games, the madness is not less. Rather, the debauchery is more prolonged. For now a mime either expounds or acts out adulteries. . . . The same actor provokes your tears with pretended sufferings, with vain gestures and expressions. *Mark Minucius Felix (c. 200, W), 4.196.*

Men who claim for themselves the authority of the Christian name are not ashamed . . . to find a defense in the heavenly Scriptures for the vain superstitions associated with the public exhibitions of the pagans. . . . They say, "Where are there such Scriptures? Where are these things prohibited? On the contrary, both Elijah was a charioteer of Israel and David himself danced before the ark. We read of psalteries, horns, trumpets, drums, pipes, harps, and choral dances. . . . Why, then, may not a faithful Christian man gaze upon that which the divine pen might write about?" . . . However, the fact that Elijah was the charioteer of Israel is no defense for gazing upon the public games. For he did not run his race in a circus. And the fact that David led the dances in the presence of God is no sanction for faithful Christians to occupy seats in the public theater. For David did not twist his limbs about in obscene movements. *Novatian (c. 235, W), 5.575, 576, formerly attributed to Cyprian.*

Idolatry . . . is the mother of all the public amusements. . . . A man has no shame if he exorcises demons in the church, but then praises their delights in the public shows. A Christian has once for all renounced [Satan]. However, he disregards what he has renounced in baptism if he goes to the devil's exhibitions after coming to Christ. In doing so, he renounces Christ just as much as [he had previously renounced] the devil. *Novatian (c. 235, W), 5.576, formerly attributed to Cyprian.*

As often happens, a Christian hurries to the public spectacle when dismissed from the Lord's [assembly]—still bearing inside him the Eucharist. Such an unfaithful man has carried about the holy body of Christ among the filthy bodies of harlots. . . . But now I will pass from this to the shameless corruption of the stage. I am ashamed to talk about the things that are said there. In fact, I am even ashamed to denounce the things that are done—the tricks of arguments, the cheating of adulterers, the immodesty of women, the indecent jokes. . . . People flock there to the public disgrace of the brothel, for the teaching of obscenity. *Novatian (c. 235, W), 5.577, formerly attributed to Cyprian.*

The Christian has nobler exhibitions if he desires them. . . . He has that beauty of the world to look upon and admire—to say nothing of those pleasures he cannot yet contemplate. He may gaze upon the sun's rising and on its setting . . . and on the troops of shining stars and those that glitter from on high with extreme mobility. . . . I say, let these and other divine works be the exhibitions for faithful Christians. What theater built by human hands could ever be compared to works such as these? *Novatian (c. 235, W), 5.578, formerly attributed to Cyprian.*

You are going to vain shows with the crowd of the evil one, where Satan is at work in the circus with din. You persuade yourself that everything that pleases you is lawful. You are the offspring of the highest; yet, you mingle with the sons of the devil! . . . Love not the world, nor the things in it! *Commodianus (c. 240, W), 4.214.*

Turn your attention to the abominations of another kind of spectacle that is not less to be deplored [than the gladiator contests]. In the theaters also, you will behold what may well cause you grief and shame. . . . The old horrors of parental murders and incest are unfolded in action calculated to resemble reality. . . . Things that have now ceased to be actual deeds of vice become examples. . . . Adultery is learned while it is seen. . . . The matron who has perhaps gone to the spectacle as a modest woman, returns from it immodest. What a degradation of morals it is! What a stimulus to abominable deeds, what food for vice! *Cyprian (c. 250, W), 5.277.*

The following letter was written concerning a former actor who had become a Christian and was now teaching drama to others.

How much greater is the crime, not only to take women's garments, but also to express sordid, effeminate, and luxurious gestures through the teaching of an immodest art. Let no one excuse himself on the grounds that he personally has given up the theater—if he is still teaching the art to others. . . . But if such a man uses poverty [as an excuse], . . . his needs can be met along with the others who are maintained by the support of the church. That is, if he is content with very simple, but innocent food. . . . However, if your church does not have the means to do this—to afford support for those in need—he may transfer himself to us and receive here the needed food and clothing. *Cyprian (c. 250, W), 5.356.*

I am inclined to think that the corrupting influence of the stage is more contaminating than [the gladiator combats]. That is because the subject of comedies is the dishonoring of virgins or the loves of harlots. And the more eloquent they are who have written the narratives of these disgraceful actions, the more they persuade others by the elegance of their words. . . . In like manner, the tragedies place before the eyes [of the audience] the incests and parental murders of wicked kings. They also portray dire crimes. . . . And what effect do the immodest gestures of the actors produce, except to teach and incite lust? The actors' weakened bodies are rendered effeminate after the gait and dress of women. They imitate unchaste women by their disgraceful gestures. Why should I even mention the mimes, who instruct others in corrupting influences. They teach adulteries while they act them out. By pretended actions, they train their audience to do those actions that are real. What can young men or virgins do when they see that these things are practiced without shame and are willingly watched by all? *Lactantius (c. 304–313, W), 7.187.*

Abstain from all pagan books. For what have you to do with such alien discourses, laws, or false prophets? For these subvert the faith of the unstable. *Apostolic Constitutions (compiled c. 390, E), 7.393.*

Avoid indecent shows. I mean the theaters and the ceremonies of the pagans. *Apostolic Constitutions (compiled c. 390, E), 7.424.*

A Christian who is faithful should neither repeat a pagan hymn nor sing an obscene song. *Apostolic Constitutions (compiled c. 390, E), 7.442; extended discussion: 3.79–3.91, 5.575–5.578.*

SEE ALSO CHRISTIAN LIFE; GAMBLING; GLADIATORS; SPORTS; WORLD, SEPARATION FROM THE.

EPHESUS, CHURCH AT

SEE CHURCHES, APOSTOLIC (IV. CHURCH AT EPHESUS).

EPICURUS

Epicurus (342–270 B.C.) was a Greek philosopher who taught that the goal of man should be a life of pleasure, regulated by moderation. He also taught that the universe came into existence by the spontaneous joinder of atoms and that there is no afterlife.

Epicurus himself not only teaches atheism, but teaches along with it incest with mothers and sisters. . . . Epicurus and the Stoics teach incest and sodomy, with which doctrines they have filled libraries. *Theophilus (c. 180, E), 2.112.*

Epicurus, too, very greatly preferred pleasure to truth. He supposed that faith was a preconception of the mind. *Clement of Alexandria (c. 195, E), 2.350.*

The Christian view . . . is more worthy of honor than the Epicurean, for it preserves you from annihilation. *Tertullian (c. 197, W), 3.177.*

The Epicureans hold the opinion that the soul dies. *Tertullian (c. 197, W), 3.246.*

Epicurus, indeed, in his fairly widely known doctrine, has asserted that death does not concern us. He says that whatever is dissolved lacks sensation, and that which is without sensation is of no concern to us. *Tertullian (c. 210, W), 3.221.*

Epicurus, however, propagated an opinion almost contrary to everyone. He believed atoms and the vacuum to be the originating principles of all things. He believed the vacuum to be the place that would contain the things that will exist. And he believed atoms to be the matter out of which all things could be formed. He also believed that God and all of the elements derived their existence from the concourse of atoms. . . . He says that God does not have providential care of anything. In fact, he says that there is no such thing at all as providence or fate. Rather, he says that all things happen by chance. *Hippolytus (c. 225, W), 5.21.*

Epicurus saw that good people are always subject to adversities, poverty, labors, exile, and loss of dear friends. In contrast, he saw that the wicked were happy, were exalted with influence, and were loaded with honors. . . . Therefore, when Epicurus reflected on these things, . . . he decided there can be no Providence. *Lactantius (c. 304–313, W), 7.86.*

I cannot here be prevented from again showing the folly of Epicurus. For all of the ravings of Lucretius belong to him. . . . Epicurus saw in the bodies of animals the skill of a divine plan. However, in order to be consistent with that which he had imprudently assumed before [i.e., that there was no Creator], he added another absurdity on top of the first. That is, he

said that the eyes were not produced for seeing, nor the ears for hearing, . . . since these members were produced before there was the use of sight and hearing. *Lactantius (c. 304–313, W), 7.287; see also 1.192, 1.274, 2.374, 2.485, 6.437, 7.198.*

SEE ALSO ATOMS; DEISM; EVOLUTION; PHILOSOPHERS, PHILOSOPHY.

EPIPHANY

The followers of Basilides hold the day of His baptism as a festival, spending the night before it in readings. And they say that [His baptism] was in the fifteenth year of Tiberius Caesar, on the fifteenth day of the month of Tubi [i.e., January 6]. But some say that it was on the eleventh of the same month. *Clement of Alexandria (c. 195, E), 2.333.*

POST-NICENE REFERENCE TO EPIPHANY: 7.495.

SEE ALSO BIRTH OF JESUS.

EQUALITY OF HUMANKIND

In truth I perceive that God shows no partiality. But in every nation whoever fears Him and works righteousness is accepted by Him. Acts 10:34, 35.

There is neither Jew nor Greek, there is neither slave nor free, there is neither male nor female; for you are all one in Christ Jesus. Gal. 3:28.

Both slave and free must philosophize equally—whether male or female in sex. *Clement of Alexandria (c. 195, E), 2.409.*

Know that all persons are born alike, with a capacity and ability of reasoning and feeling—without preference of age, sex, or class. *Mark Minucius Felix (c. 200, W), 4.181.*

Are you elevated by nobility of birth? Do you praise your parents? Yet, we are all born with one lot. It is only by virtue that we are distinguished. *Mark Minucius Felix (c. 200, W), 4.196.*

God does not reject any of His servants as being unworthy of the divine mysteries. He does not value the rich man more highly than the poor. He does not despise the poor man because of his poverty. He does not disdain the barbarian, nor does He reject the eunuch as being no man. He does not hate the female because of the woman's act of disobedience in the beginning. Nor does He reject the male because of the man's transgression. Rather, He seeks everyone and desires to save everyone. *Hippolytus (c. 200, W), 5.205.*

Such, indeed, was the abounding love that He had for men, that he gave to the more learned a theology capable of raising the soul far above all earthly things. Yet, with no less consideration, He comes down to the weaker capacities of ignorant men, of simple women, of slaves, and, in short, of all those who from Jesus alone could have received that help for the better regulation of their lives. These are supplied by his instructions in regard to the Divine Being, adapted to their needs and capacities. *Origen (c. 248, E), 4.627.*

When the Word of God, our Lord Jesus Christ, came unto all, He gathered alike the learned and unlearned. He published the teachings of salvation to each sex and every age. He made a concise summary of His teachings, so that the memory of the scholars might not be burdened by the heavenly learning, but could quickly learn what was necessary to a simple faith. *Cyprian (c. 250, W), 5.455.*

We call everyone together to the heavenly pasture, without any distinction either of sex or of age. *Lactantius (c. 304–313, W), 7.10.*

God, who produces and gives breath to men, willed that all should be equal, that is, equally matched. He has imposed the same condition of living on all. He has opened wisdom to all. He has promised immortality to all. No one is cut off from His heavenly benefits. . . . In His sight, no one is a slave; no one is a master. For if all have the same Father, by an equal right we are all children. No one is poor in the sight of God but he who is without justice. No one is rich, but he who is full of virtues. . . . For this reason, neither the Romans nor the Greeks could possess justice. For they had men differing from one another by many degrees: the poor and the rich, the humble and the powerful, private persons and the highest authorities of kings. However, where all persons are not equally matched, there is no justice. And, by its nature, inequality excludes justice. . . .

However, someone will say, "Are there not among you some who are poor and others who are rich? Are not some servants and others masters? Is there not some difference between individuals?" There is none. Nor is there any other cause why we mutually bestow upon each other

the name of brothers, except that we believe ourselves to be equal. We measure all human things by the spirit, not by the body. Although the condition of our bodies is different, yet we have no servants. For we both regard and speak of them as brothers in spirit and as fellow-servants in religion. . . . Therefore, in lowliness of mind, we are on an equality: the free with the slaves and the rich with the poor. Nevertheless, in the sight of God we are distinguished only by virtue. . . . The person who has conducted himself not only as an equal, but even as an inferior, he will plainly obtain a much higher rank of dignity in the judgment of God. *Lactantius (c. 304–313, W), 7.150, 151.*

[The philosophers] do not allow anyone to enter upon their way [of enlightenment] except boys and young men, because the arts are learned at these ages. On the other hand, we lead those of each sex, every age, and every race into this heavenly path. For God, who is the Guide of that way, denies immortality to no human being. *Lactantius (c. 304–313, W), 7.165.*

If we all derive our origin from one man whom God created, we are clearly of one blood. Therefore, it must be considered the greatest wickedness to hate a man—even if he is guilty. . . . For, if we are all animated and enlivened by one God, what else are we than brothers? *Lactantius (c. 304–313, W), 7.172, 173.*

SEE ALSO CHRISTIANITY (I. DESCRIPTION OF CHRISTIANS); HANDICAPPED; SLAVES; WOMEN.

ESCHATOLOGY

This gospel of the kingdom will be preached in all the world as a witness to all the nations, and then the end will come. Matt. 24:14.

Then comes the end, when He delivers the kingdom to God the Father, when He puts an end to all rule and all authority and power. 1 Cor. 15:24.

For that Day will not come unless the falling away comes first, and the man of sin is revealed, the son of perdition. 2 Thess. 2:3.

But the day of the Lord will come as a thief in the night, in which the heavens will pass away with a great noise, and the elements will melt with fervent heat; both the earth and the works that are in it will be burned up. . . . Nevertheless we, according to His promise, look for new heavens and a new earth in which righteousness dwells. 2 Pet. 3:10, 13.

Behold, He is coming with clouds, and every eye will see Him, and they also who pierced Him. And all the tribes of the earth will mourn because of Him. Rev. 1:7.

And I will give power to my two witnesses, and they will prophesy one thousand two hundred and sixty days, clothed in sackcloth. Rev. 11:3.

Now when the thousand years have expired, Satan will be released from his prison and will go out to deceive the nations. Rev. 20:7, 8.

So also will it be at the end time. There will be a flood of fire, and the earth will be burned up, together with its mountains. Mankind, too, will be burned up, along with the idols which they have made.... But the just will be preserved from His anger. *Melito (c. 170, E), 8.755, 756.*

But why do we speak of Jerusalem? After all, the desires of the whole world must also pass away, when the time for its end has come. This must take place so that the fruit can be gathered into the granary, but the chaff, left behind, may be consumed by fire. *Irenaeus (c. 180, E/W), 1.466.*

There is also another and a greater necessity for our offering prayer on behalf of the emperors. In fact, we should pray for the complete stability of the empire, and for Roman interests in general. That is because we know that a mighty cataclysm hangs over the whole earth. In fact, the very end of all things threatens dreadful woes. And this is only held back by the continued existence of the Roman empire. We have no desire, then, to be overtaken by these dire events. In praying that their coming may be delayed, we are lending our aid to Rome's duration. *Tertullian (c. 197, W), 3.42, 43.*

But what a spectacle is that fast-approaching return of our Lord! For He will now be acknowledged by all; He will now be highly exalted; He will now be a triumphant One! What an exultation of the angelic hosts there will be! What a glorious rising of the saints! What a kingdom of the just there will be thereafter! How great will be the city of New Jerusalem! Yes, and there are other sights: that last Day of Judgment. *Tertullian (c. 197, W), 3.91.*

The belief that everything was made from nothing will be impressed upon us by that ultimate dispensation of God which will bring back all things to nothing. For "the very heavens will be rolled together as a scroll." In fact, they will come to nothing, along with the earth itself. *Tertullian (c. 200, W), 3.496.*

"The stars too will fall from heaven." ... "The mountains will melt like wax." ... Even "the sea will be no more." Now, if any person were to go so far as to suppose that all these passages should be figuratively interpreted, he will still be unable to deprive them of the true fulfillment of those issues that must come to pass, just as they have been written. For figurative speech necessarily arises out of realities. *Tertullian (c. 200, W), 3.497.*

After its thousand years are over (within which period is completed the resurrection of the saints, who rise sooner or later according to their deserts), there will follow the destruction of the world and the burning of all things at the judgment. We will then be instantly changed into the substance of angels, by being clothed with an incorruptible nature. And we will be removed to that kingdom in heaven. *Tertullian (c. 207, W), 3.343.*

"Jerusalem was to be trodden down by the Gentiles until the times of the Gentiles would be fulfilled"—meaning, of course, those who were to be chosen of God and gathered in with the remnant of Israel. *Tertullian (c. 210, W), 3.560.*

Jesus was questioned by His disciples concerning when those things were to come to pass that He had said about the destruction of the temple. So He first spoke to them about the order of Jewish events until the overthrow of Jerusalem. Then, he spoke about the things that will concern all nations—up to the very end of the world.... Therefore, although there is presently a sprouting in the acknowledgement of all this mystery, yet it is only in the actual presence of the Lord that the flower will be developed and the fruit will be borne.... Who has yet beheld Jesus descending from heaven in a manner similar to how the apostles saw Him ascend?.... Up to the present moment, no one has smitten their breasts, tribe by tribe, looking on Him whom they pierced. No one has yet fallen in with Elijah. No one has yet escaped from the Antichrist. No one has yet had to bewail the downfall of Babylon. *Tertullian (c. 210, W), 3.561.*

"For that day will not come, unless indeed there first comes a falling away." He means indeed this present empire.... What obstacle is there but the Roman state, the falling away of which, by being scattered into ten kingdoms, will usher in the Antichrist? *Tertullian (c. 210, W), 3.563.*

After the casting of the devil into the bottomless pit for a while, the blessed prerogative of the first resurrection may be ordained from the thrones. And then again, after the consignment of him to the fire, the judgment of the final and universal resurrection may be determined out of the books. *Tertullian (c. 210, W), 3.563.*

[Enoch and Elijah] are reserved for the suffering of death, that by their blood, they may extinguish the Antichrist. *Tertullian (c. 210, W), 3.227, 228.*

There will be reclining at the feast in the kingdom of God. There will be sitting on Christ's thrones. There will be standing at last on His right hand and his left, and eating of the tree of life. Now, what are all these things but most certain proofs of a bodily appointment and destination? *Tertullian (c. 210, W), 3.571.*

As to the burning up of the world, it is a foolish error to deny that fire will fall upon it in an unforeseen way, or to deny that the world will be destroyed by fire. . . . Who would question the fact that all things that have had a beginning will perish? All created things must come to an end. *Mark Minucius Felix (c. 200, W), 4.194.*

For when the sixty-two weeks are fulfilled, and Christ has come, and the Gospel has been preached in every place, the times will then be accomplished. There will remain only one week—the last—in which Elijah and Enoch will appear. And in the midst of it, the abomination of desolation will be manifested—the Antichrist, announcing desolation to the world. And when he comes, the sacrifice and oblation will be removed, which now "are offered to God in every place by the nations." *Hippolytus (c. 205, W), 5.182.*

When at length the Judge of judges and the King of kings comes from heaven, He will overturn the whole dominion and power of the Adversary. He will also consume all of them with the eternal fire of punishment. But to His servants, prophets, and martyrs, and to all those who fear Him, He will give an everlasting kingdom. *Hippolytus (c. 205, W), 5.190.*

I have pointed out in the preceding pages those questions that must be set forth in clear, dogmatic propositions—as I think has been

done to the best of my ability when speaking of the Trinity. But on the present occasion, my exercise is to be conducted as best I can—in the style of a disputation rather than of strict definition. The end of the world, then, and the final consummation will take place when everyone will be subjected to punishment for his sins. This is a time that God alone knows, when He will bestow on each one what he deserves. *Origen (c. 225, E), 4.260.*

Jacob is the first one who provides any information about the end of the world. . . . Our Lord and Savior . . . says, "Heaven and earth will pass away, but My word will not pass away." So He points out that the [heavens and earth] are perishable and must come to an end. *Origen (c. 225, E), 4.341.*

He is taking sin away from every individual in the world until sin is taken away from the whole world. Then, the Savior delivers the prepared and completed kingdom to the Father—a kingdom in which no sin is left at all. That kingdom is, therefore, ready to accept the Father as its king. *Origen (c. 228, E), 4.317.*

However, it is likely that before the second and more divine coming of Christ, John or Elijah will come to bear witness about life. *Origen (c. 228, E), 9.345.*

The world is so established by a bonded union that no force can dissolve it—except when He alone who made it commands it to be dissolved. He will do this for the purpose of bestowing other things (which are greater) upon us. *Novatian (c. 235, W), 5.612.*

I will add something about the Day of Judgment, on account of the unbelievers. Again, the fire of the Lord sent forth will be appointed. . . . Another newness of sky and of everlasting earth is arranged. Afterwards, those who deserve it are sent away to the second death; but the righteous are placed in inner dwelling places. *Commodianus (c. 240, W), 4.212.*

This has pleased Christ, that the dead should rise again. Yes, they will rise with their bodies. And those, too, will rise again who have been burned with fire in this world. This will happen when six thousand years have been completed, and the world has come to an end. In the meantime, the heavens will be changed with an altered course, for then the wicked are burned up with divine fire. The creature burns with groaning in the anger of the Highest God.

Those who are more worthy . . . live again in the world for a thousand years, according to God's command. However, this is so that they may serve the saints and the High One under a servile yoke. . . . What is more, they will be judged again when the reign is finished. Those who treat God as of no account will perish by fire when the thousandth year is finished. . . . All flesh in the monuments and tombs will be restored according to its deeds. They will be plunged into Gehenna. They bear their punishments in the world. *Commodianus (c. 240, W), 4.218.*

The end of the world comes suddenly. *Cyprian (c. 250, W), 5.553.*

When the three years and six months are completed in the preaching of Elijah, [Satan] will be cast down from heaven. For up until that time he had had the power of ascending. And all the apostate angels, as well as the Antichrist, must be roused up from Hades. . . . "And I saw a beast rising up from the sea, like a leopard." This signifies the kingdom of that time of the Antichrist and the people mingled with the variety of nations. *Victorinus (c. 280, W), 7.356.*

It is not satisfactory to say that the universe will be utterly destroyed and that the sea, earth, and sky will no longer exist. For the whole world will be deluged with fire from heaven and burned for the purpose of purification and renewal. However, it will not come to complete ruin and corruption. . . . God did not work in vain. *Methodius (c. 290, E), 6.365.*

He says the creation was made subject to vanity, but he looks for it to be set free from such servitude. . . . For in reality, God did not establish the universe in vain or only for it to be destroyed, as those weak-minded men say. Rather, He made it to exist, to be inhabited, and to continue. For that reason, the earth and the heaven must exist again after the burning and shaking of all things. *Methodius (c. 290, E), 6.366.*

There is no contradiction nor absurdity in Holy Scripture. For it is not "the world" that passes away, but the *"fashion* of this world." . . . So we can look for creation to pass away, as if it were to perish in the burning, in order for it to be renewed. In that manner, we who are renewed may dwell in a renewed world without taste of sorrow. However, it will not be destroyed. . . . Now, since the earth is to exist

after the present age, there must also be inhabitants for it. These persons will no longer be subject to death. They will not marry, nor beget children. Rather, they will live in all happiness without change or decay, like the angels. *Methodius (c. 290, E), 6.366.*

This unrighteous age, having run the course of its appointed times, should come to an end. *Lactantius (c. 304–313, W), 7.196.*

At that time [during the days of Moses], the people of God were one. And so only one nation, Egypt, was struck. However, now the people of God are collected out of all languages and dwell among all nations. And they are oppressed by those who rule over them. Therefore, it must come to pass that all nations (that is, the whole world) will be beaten with heavenly stripes. As a result, the righteous people, who are worshippers of God, will be set free. Back then, signs were given to announce the coming destruction to the Egyptians. Likewise, at the last day, wonderful phenomena will take place throughout all the parts of the world, by which the impending destruction will be understood by all nations. Therefore, as the end of this world approaches, the condition of human affairs will undergo a change. Through the prevalence of wickedness, things will become worse. As a result, these times of ours—in which iniquity and impiety have increased even to the highest degree—will then be considered as having been happy. They will seem as almost golden times in comparison to that incurable evil. For righteousness will greatly decrease, and impiety, avarice, desire, and lust will greatly increase. . . .

At that time, there will be no faith among men, nor peace, kindness, shame, or truth. As a result, there will be no security, no government, nor any rest from evils. The entire earth will be in a state of tumult. Wars will rage everywhere. All nations will be in arms and will oppose one another. . . . Egypt will pay the penalties for her foolish superstitions and will be covered with blood as if with a river. . . . The cause of this desolation and confusion will be this: the Roman name, by which the world is now ruled, will be taken away from the earth, and the government will return to Asia. And the East will again bear rule. The West will be reduced to servitude. *Lactantius (c. 304–313, W), 7.212.*

At that time, civil discords will perpetually be sown. There will be no rest from deadly wars, until ten kings arise at the same time. These kings will divide the world—not to govern it, but to consume it. . . . Then a most powerful enemy will suddenly arise against them from the extreme boundaries of the northern region. Having destroyed three of that number who will then possess Asia, he will be admitted into an alliance by the others. And he will be made the ruler of all. He will harass the world with an intolerable rule. He will mingle divine things with human things. . . . He will change the laws and appoint his own. He will contaminate, plunder, spoil, and put to death.

Then, in truth, a detestable and abominable time will come, in which life will be pleasant to no men. Cities will be utterly overthrown and will perish. . . . The atmosphere will be tainted and become corrupt and pestilential. At one time, there will be unseasonable rains. At another, there will be barren drought. At times, it will be cold; then excessively hot. The earth will not give its fruit to man. No field, tree, or vine will produce anything. . . . Fountains will also be dried up, together with the rivers. . . . On account of these things, beasts will fail on the land, birds in the air, and fishes in the sea. Awe-inspiring signs in heaven will confound the minds of men with the greatest terrors: the trails of comets, the darkness of the sun, the color of the moon, and the sweep of the falling stars. . . .

Stars will fall in great numbers, so that all the heavens will appear dark without any lights. The loftiest mountains will also fall and be lev-elled with the plains. The sea will be rendered unnavigable. And that nothing may be lacking to evils of men and the earth, the trumpet will be heard from heaven. . . . And then everyone will tremble and quake at that mournful sound. . . . Then they will call upon God, but He will not hear them. Death will be desired, but it will not come. . . . For the human race will be so consumed, that scarcely the tenth part of mankind will be left. . . . Two-thirds of the worshippers of God will perish as well. But the third part, which will have been proved faithful, will remain. *Lactantius (c. 304–313, W), 7.214.*

When the end of the times draw near, a great prophet will be sent from God to turn men to the knowledge of God. And he will receive the power of doing miraculous things. Wherever men will not hear him, he will close heaven and

cause it to withhold its rains. He will turn their water into blood. . . . When his works have been accomplished, another king will arise out of Syria, born from an evil spirit. . . . He will fight against the prophet of God and will over-come and slay him. And he will allow him to lie unburied. But after the third day, the prophet will come to life again. And, while all look on and wonder, he will be caught up to heaven. *Lactantius (c. 304–313, W), 7.214.*

After these things, the lower regions will be opened and the dead will rise again. The same King and God will pass judgment on the dead. . . . However, not all men will be judged by God at that time. Rather, only those who have practiced the religion of God. Sentence cannot be passed to acquit those who have not known God. They are already judged and con-demned. For the Holy Scriptures testify that the wicked will not rise to condemnation [Ps. 1:5]. Therefore, only those who have known God will be judged. And their deeds, that is, their evil works, will be compared and weighed against their good ones. . . . But when He will have judged the righteous, He will also test them with fire. Those persons whose sins will exceed [their good works] either in weight or in number will be scorched by the fire and burned. However, those who are filled with complete justice and maturity will not feel this fire. For they have something of God in them that repels and rejects the violence of the flame. *Lactantius (c. 304–313, W), 7.216, 217.*

When the thousand years of the kingdom have ended—that is, seven thousand years [from the creation of the world]—Satan will be loosed again. Being sent forth from prison, he will go forth and assemble all the nations, which will then be under the dominion of the righteous. . . . Then the last anger of God will come upon the nations and will utterly destroy them. . . . The whole race of the wicked will utterly perish. There will no longer be any nation in this world except the nation of God. . . . Thereafter, there will be no war—only peace and everlasting rest. But when the thou-sand years are completed, the world will be renewed by God and the heavens will be folded together. The earth will be changed and God will transform men into the likeness of angels. . . . At the same time, the second and general resurrection of all mankind will take place. In this, the unrighteous will be raised to everlasting punishments. *Lactantius (c. 304–313, W), 7.221.*

SEE ALSO ANTICHRIST; CHRONOLOGY; DANIEL, BOOK OF; ETERNAL PUNISHMENTS AND REWARDS; GENTILE TIMES; JUDGMENT, LAST; LAST DAYS; MILLENNIUM; RESURRECTION OF THE DEAD; REVELATION, BOOK OF; SECOND COMING OF CHRIST.

ESSENES

The Essenes were an ascetic Jewish sect that lived in Palestine from the second century B.C. to the second century A.D.

[The Essenes] practice a more devotional life, being filled with mutual love and being temperate. They turn away from every act of inordinate desire, being unwilling even to hear things of this sort. They also renounce marriage. However, they take in the boys of others and thus have an offspring begotten for them. And they lead these boys into an observance of their own peculiar customs. . . . However, they do not admit women, even though some women may be disposed to adhere to the same course of life. . . . They disdain wealth and do not turn away from sharing with those who are destitute. No one among them has a greater amount of riches than another. A rule with them is that an individual coming forward to join the sect must sell his possessions and present [the price] to the community. . . . And they continue in an orderly manner. With perseverance, they pray from early dawn. And they do not speak a word unless they have praised God in a hymn. And in this way, they each go forth and engage in whatever employment they please. And after having worked up to the fifth hour, they leave off. They come together once again into one place. They gird themselves with linen girdles, for the purpose of concealing their private parts. And in this manner they perform washings in cold water. *Hippolytus (c. 225, W), 5.134.*

With oaths . . . the Essenes bind those who come forward. If, however, anyone is condemned for any sin, he is expelled from the order. One who has been excommunicated sometimes perishes by an awful death. For, since he is bound by the oaths and rites, he is not able to partake of the food in use among other people. . . . Over the course of time, the Essenes have undergone divisions, and they do

not preserve their system of training after a similar manner. For they have been split up into four parties. Some of them discipline themselves above what is necessary. Those ones will not even handle a current coin of the country, saying that they should neither carry, look at, nor make an image. For that reason, none of them goes into a city, lest he should enter through a gate at which there are statues. For they regard it as a violation of the Law to pass beneath images. . . .

If anyone would even torture persons of this description—in order to induce any among them to either speak evil of the Law or eat what is offered in sacrifice to an idol—it will be to no effect. For they submit to death and endure torment rather than to violate their consciences. Now the doctrine of the resurrection has also found support among them. For they acknowledge both that the flesh will rise again and that it will be immortal. *Hippolytus (c. 225, W), 5.136.*

There is another order of the Essenes who use the same customs . . . but make an alteration from these others in one respect: marriage. . . . However, they make a trial of their betrothed women for a period of three years. . . . And the women likewise undergo washings in a similar manner, and are themselves also arrayed in linen garments. *Hippolytus (c. 225, W), 5.137.*

There are also those who separate themselves from all of these [i.e., the Pharisees and Sadducees] and observe the laws of their fathers. These people are the Essenes. *Apostolic Constitutions (compiled c. 390, E), 7.452; extended discussion: 5.134–5.137.*

SEE ALSO JEW, JEWS; PHARISEES; SADDUCEES.

ETERNAL PUNISHMENTS AND REWARDS

Then the King will say to those on His right hand, "Come, you blessed of My Father, inherit the kingdom prepared for you from the foundation of the world." . . . Then He will also say to those on the left hand, "Depart from Me, you cursed, into the everlasting fire prepared for the devil and his angels." . . . And these will go away into everlasting punishment, but the righteous into eternal life. Matt. 25:34, 41, 46.

If your eye is your downfall, tear it out! Better for you to enter the kingdom of God with one eye than to be thrown with both eyes into Gehenna, where "the worm dies not and the fire is never extinguished." Mark 9:47, 48 [NA].

In My Father's house are many mansions; if it were not so, I would have told you. I go to prepare a place for you. And if I go and prepare a place for you, I will come again and receive you to Myself; that where I am, there you may be also. John 14:2.

The sea gave up the dead who were in it, and Death and Hades delivered up the dead who were in them. And they were judged, each one according to his works. Then Death and Hades were cast into the lake of fire. This is the second death. And anyone not found written in the Book of Life was cast into the lake of fire. Rev. 20:14, 15.

He who overcomes will inherit all things, and I will be his God and he will be My son. But the cowardly, unbelieving, abominable, murderers, sexually immoral, sorcerers, idolaters, and all liars will have their part in the lake which burns with fire and brimstone, which is the second death. Rev. 21:7, 8.

They will see His face, and His name will be on their foreheads. And there will be no night there: They need no lamp nor light of the sun, for the Lord God gives them light. And they will reign forever and ever. Rev. 22:4, 5.

The way of darkness is crooked, and it is full of cursing. It is the way of eternal death with punishment. *Barnabas (c. 70–130, E), 1.149.*

You should fear what is truly death, which is reserved for those who will be condemned to the eternal fire. It will afflict those who are committed to it even to the end. *Letter to Diognetus (c. 125–200), 1.29.*

They despised all the torments of this world, redeeming themselves from eternal punishment by the suffering of a single hour.... For they kept before their view escape from that fire which is eternal and will never be quenched. *Martyrdom of Polycarp (c. 135, E), 1.39.*

He will enjoy the immortal fruit of the resurrection.... A blessed time waits for him. He will be joyful for an eternity without grief, living again above with the fathers. *Second Clement (c. 150), 7.523.*

Sinners will be consumed because they sinned and did not repent. *Hermas (c. 150, W), 2.33.*

Those who have not known God and do evil are condemned to death. However, those who have known God and have seen His mighty works, but still continue in evil, will be chastised doubly, and will die forever. *Hermas (c. 150, W), 2.50.*

As the presbyters say, those who are deemed worthy of a habitation in heaven will go there, others will enjoy the delights of Paradise, and others will possess the splendor of the city. For everywhere the Savior will be seen according to the worthiness of those who see Him.... There is a distinction between the habitation of those who produce a hundred-fold, and the habitation of those who produce sixty-fold, and the habitation of those who produce thirty-fold. For the first class will be taken up into the heavens. The second class will dwell in Paradise. And the last will inhabit the city. It is for that reason that the Lord said, "In my Father's house are many mansions." *Papias (c. 120, E), 1.154, as quoted by Eusebius.*

He goes to the everlasting punishment of fire. *Justin Martyr (c. 160, E), 1.166.*

But if you pay no regard to our prayers and frank explanations, we will suffer no loss. For we believe ... that every man will suffer punishment in eternal fire according to the merits of his deed.... Sensation remains to all who have ever lived, and eternal punishment is laid up. *Justin Martyr (c. 160, E), 1.168, 169.*

Gehenna is a place where those who have lived wickedly are to be punished. *Justin Martyr (c. 160, E), 1.169.*

Christ foretold that Satan would be sent into the fire with his host, along with the men who follow him, and they will be punished for an endless duration. *Justin Martyr (c. 160, E), 1.172.*

The unjust and intemperate will be punished in eternal fire. *Justin Martyr (c. 160, E), 1.188.*

Some are sent to be punished unceasingly into judgment and condemnation of fire. Others will exist in immortality, with freedom from suffering, from corruption, and from grief. *Justin Martyr (c. 160, E), 1.217.*

We know from Isaiah that the members of those who have transgressed will be consumed by the worm and unquenchable fire, remaining immortal. As a result, they become a spectacle to all flesh. *Justin Martyr (c. 160, E), 1.264, 265.*

We who are now easily susceptible to death, will afterwards receive immortality with either enjoyment or with pain. *Tatian (c. 160, E), 1.71.*

Rusticus the prefect said, "Do you suppose, then, that you will ascend into heaven to receive some recompense?" Justin replied, "I do not suppose it, but I know and am fully persuaded of it." *Martyrdom of the Holy Martyrs (c. 160), 1.306.*

We are persuaded that when we are removed from the present life we will live another life, better than the present one. It will be a heavenly life, not an earthly one. For we will abide near God, and with God, free from all change or suffering in the soul. We will not abide as flesh (even though we will have flesh), but as heavenly spirit. . . . Or, if they fall with the rest, they will endure a worse [life], one in fire. For God has not made us as sheep or beasts of burden, who are mere by-products. For animals perish and are annihilated. On these grounds, it is not likely that we would wish to do evil. *Athenagoras (c. 175, E), 2.146.*

We are persuaded that nothing will escape the scrutiny of God. Rather, even the body that has ministered to the irrational impulses of the soul, and to its desires, will be punished along with it. Therefore, it is not likely that any of us will commit even the smallest sin. *Athenagoras (c. 175, E), 2.148.*

He . . . will examine all things, and will judge righteous judgment, rendering merited awards to each. To those who seek immortality by patient endurance in well-doing, He will give life everlasting, joy, peace, rest, and an abundance of good things. To the unbelieving and despisers, who do not obey the truth, but are obedient to unrighteousness, when they will have been filled with adulteries and fornications, . . . there will be anger and wrath, tribulation and anguish. At the end, everlasting fire will possess such men. *Theophilus (c. 180, E), 2.93.*

He who acts righteously will escape the eternal punishments, and he will be thought worthy of the eternal life from God. *Theophilus (c. 180, E), 2.108.*

And the Sibyl, who was a prophetess among the Greeks, . . . reproaches the race of men, saying: . . . "Therefore, burning fire will come upon you, and you will daily burn in flames forever. You will be ashamed forever of your useless god. But those who worship the eternal God, they will inherit everlasting life." *Theophilus (c. 180, E), 2.108, 109.*

Eternal fire is prepared for sinners. The Lord has plainly declared this, and the rest of the Scriptures demonstrate it. *Irenaeus (c. 180, E/W), 1.401.*

Those who, in this brief temporal life, have shown themselves ungrateful to Him who bestowed life, they will justly not receive from Him length of days forever and ever. *Irenaeus (c. 180, E/W), 1.412.*

He will send into eternal fire those who transform the truth and who despise His Father and His coming. *Irenaeus (c. 180, E/W), 1.417.*

Eternal fire was not originally prepared for man, but for him who beguiled man and caused man to sin. I say, it was prepared for him who is the chief of the apostasy, as well as for those angels who became apostates along with him. Indeed, those angels will justly feel that fire, too. For, like him, they continue in works of wickedness, without repentance, and without turning back. *Irenaeus (c. 180, E/W), 1.456.*

But why do we speak of Jerusalem? After all, the desires of the whole world must also pass away, when the time for its end has come. This must take place so that the fruit can be gathered into the granary, but the chaff, left behind, may be consumed by fire. *Irenaeus (c. 180, E/W), 1.466.*

To such, He has assigned everlasting damnation by cutting them off from life. *Irenaeus (c. 180, E/W), 1.475.*

Those who believe in Him will be incorruptible and will not be subject to suffering. They will receive the kingdom of heaven. *Irenaeus (c. 180, E/W), 1.495.*

The unrighteous, the idolaters, and the fornicators all perished. So is it also now. For . . . the Lord declares that such persons are sent into eternal fire. *Irenaeus (c. 180, E/W), 1.500.*

The Lord will say, "Depart from me, you cursed ones, into everlasting fire." These persons will be damned forever. However, to others He will say, "Come, you blessed of my Father. Inherit the kingdom prepared for you for eternity." These ones receive the kingdom forever, and they make constant advancement in it. *Irenaeus (c. 180, E/W), 1.501.*

He has prepared darkness suitable to persons who oppose the light, and He has inflicted an appropriate punishment upon those who try to avoid being subject to Him. . . . He has prepared the eternal fire for the ringleader of the apostasy—the devil—and for those who revolted with him. The Lord has declared that those who have been set apart by themselves on His left hand will be sent into this fire. *Irenaeus (c. 180, E/W), 1.523.*

Those, therefore, who cast away these afore-mentioned things because of apostasy are in fact destitute of all good. So, they experience every kind of punishment. . . . Now, good things are eternal and without end with God, and therefore the loss of these things is also eternal and never-ending. *Irenaeus (c. 180, E/W), 1.556.*

"And death and Hades were sent into the lake of fire, the second death." Now this is what is called Gehenna, which the Lord called "eternal fire." *Irenaeus (c. 180, E/W), 1.566.*

When this world passes away, and man has been renewed, and flourishes in an incorruptible state, so as to preclude the possibility of becoming old, there will be the new heaven and the new earth, in which the new man will remain, always holding fresh communion with God. . . . As the presbyters say, those who are deemed worthy of an abode in heaven will go there, others will enjoy the delights of Paradise, and others will possess the splendor of the city. For everywhere the Savior will be seen—depending on the worthiness of those who see him. There is this distinction between the habitation of those who produce a hundred-fold, and those who produce sixty-fold, and those who produce thirty-fold. For the first will be taken up into the heavens, the second will dwell in Paradise, the last will inhabit the city. It was on this account the Lord declared, "In My Father's house are many mansions." . . .

The presbyters, the disciples of the apostles, affirmed that this is the gradation and arrangement of those who are saved, and that they advance through steps of this nature. The presbyters also said that [the righteous] ascend through the Spirit to the Son, and through the Son to the Father. In due time, the Son will yield up His work to the Father, even as it is said by the apostle. . . . "And when all things will be subdued unto Him, then will the Son also Himself be subject unto Him who put all things under Him, that God may be all in all." *Irenaeus (c. 180, E/W), 1.567.*

The same work, then, is different, depending on what prompted it. Was it because of fear, or was it accomplished because of love, faith, or knowledge? Rightly, therefore, their rewards are different. *Clement of Alexandria (c. 195, E), 2.430.*

The Lord says, "And other sheep there are also which are not of this fold." These are deemed worthy of another fold and mansion, in proportion to their faith. *Clement of Alexandria (c. 195, E), 2.505.*

There are various abodes according to the worth of those who have believed. *Clement of Alexandria (c. 195, E), 2.506.*

It leads us to the eternal and perfect end, teaching us beforehand the future life that we will lead, according to God and with gods. This is after we are freed from all punishment and penalty that we undergo in consequence of our sins for the purpose of salutary discipline. After this redemption, the reward and the honors are assigned to those who have become perfect. This is when they have completed purification and ceased from all service—even though it is holy service and among saints. Then, becoming pure in heart and near to the Lord, restoration to everlasting contemplation awaits them. *Clement of Alexandria (c. 195, E), 2.539.*

All souls are immortal, even those of the wicked. Yet, it would be better for them if they were not deathless. For they are punished with the endless vengeance of quenchless fire. Since they do not die, it is impossible for them to have an end put to their misery. *Clement of Alexandria (c. 195, E), 2.580, from a fragment in a post-Nicene manuscript.*

We receive our awards under the judgment of an all-seeing God, and we Christians anticipate eternal punishment from Him for sin. Therefore, we alone make a real effort to attain a blameless life. We do this under the influence of . . . the magnitude of the threatened torment. For it is not merely long-enduring; rather, it is everlasting. *Tertullian (c. 197, W), 3.50.*

If we threaten Gehenna, which is a reservoir of secret fire under the earth for purposes of punishment, we likewise have derision heaped upon us. *Tertullian (c. 197, W), 3.52.*

After the [Last Judgment], there is neither death nor repeated resurrections. But we will be the same as we are now, and still unchanged. That is, we will be the servants of God, ever with God, clothed with the proper substance of eternity. But the profane, and all who are not true worshippers of God, in like manner will be consigned to the punishment of everlasting fire. That fire, from its very nature indeed, directly attends to their incorruptibility. . . . There is a distinction between ordinary fire and a secret fire. That which is in common use is far different from that which we see in divine judgments. . . . For [the secret fire] does not consume what it scorches. Instead, it repairs while it burns. . . . A notable proof that this fire is eternal is that . . . the mountains burn and yet last. How will it be with the wicked and the enemies of God? *Tertullian (c. 197, W), 3.54.*

Governors of provinces, too, who persecuted the Christian name, [will be] in fires more fierce than those with which in the days of their pride they raged against the followers of Christ. The world's wise men will be alongside them. . . . They will then be covered with shame before their poor deluded ones, as the same fire consumes them! *Tertullian (c. 197, W), 3.91.*

By the sentence of the judgment, we say that the wicked will have to spend an eternity in endless fire. The godly and innocent will spend it in a region of bliss. *Tertullian (c. 197, W), 3.127.*

We maintain that, after life has passed away, you still remain in existence and anticipate a day of judgment. Furthermore, according to your deserts, you are assigned either to misery or to bliss. Either way, it will be forever. . . . .If you have no power of suffering after death, if no feeling remains, if (in a word) severance from the body is merely annihilation, . . . why do you fear death at all? There is nothing after death to be feared if there is nothing to be felt. *Tertullian (c. 197, W), 3.177.*

We, however, so understand the soul's immortality as to believe it to be "lost"—not in the sense of destruction—but of punishment, that is, in Gehenna. *Tertullian (c. 210, W), 3.569.*

If, therefore, anyone will violently suppose that the destruction of the soul and the flesh in Gehenna amounts to a final annihilation of the two substances—and not to their penal treatment—let him recollect that the fire of Gehenna is eternal. *Tertullian (c. 210, W), 3.570.*

Since, then, after the resurrection, the body has to be "killed" by God in Gehenna (along with the soul), . . . its killing is eternal. Otherwise, it would be most absurd if the flesh were to be raised up and destined to the killing in Gehenna in order to be brought to an end. For it would suffer such an annihilation if it were not raised again at all! *Tertullian (c. 210, W), 3.571.*

How will there be many mansions in our Father's house if it is not according to a variety of deserts? How will one star differ from another star in glory, unless it is because of a disparity in their rays. *Tertullian (c. 213, W), 3.639.*

I am not ignorant that many [pagans], in the consciousness of what they deserve, would prefer to believe that they will become nothing after death. For they would rather be altogether extinguished, rather than to be restored for the purpose of punishment. *Mark Minucius Felix (c. 200, W), 4.194.*

There is neither limit nor termination of these torments. There, the intelligent fire burns the limbs and restores them. It feeds on them and nourishes them. . . . That penal fire is not fed by the waste of those who burn, but is nourished by the unexhausted eating away of their bodies. However, no one except a profane man hesitates to believe that those who do not know God are deservedly tormented as impious, as unrighteous persons. *Mark Minucius Felix (c. 200, W), 4.195.*

Those who eat will receive eternal life and will enjoy the tree of life in Paradise, with Adam and all the righteous. But the souls of the unrighteous meet an untimely expulsion from the presence of God, who will leave them to remain in the flame of torment. *Hippolytus (c. 205, W), 5.173.*

To the lovers of wickedness, there will be given eternal punishment. And the fire that is unquenchable and without end awaits these latter ones. So does a certain fiery worm that does not die and that does not consume the body, but continues bursting forth from the body with unending pain. No sleep will give them rest. No night will soothe them. No death will deliver them from punishment. No voice of interceding friends will profit them. For the righteous are not seen by them any longer, nor are they worthy of remembrance. Rather, the righteous will remember only the righteous deeds by which they reached the heavenly kingdom—in which there is neither sleep, nor pain, nor corruption, nor worry, nor night, nor day measured by time. . . . There will be no more heaven inaccessible to men. The way of its ascent will no longer be impossible to find. And there will be no more earth uncultivated or toilsome for men. Rather, it will be one that produces fruit spontaneously in beauty and order. There will be no more generation of wild beasts again, nor the bursting substance of other creatures. Nor with man will there be birth again. For the number of the righteous remains perfect with the righteous angels and spirits. *Hippolytus (c. 205, W), 5.222, 223.*

By means of this knowledge, you will escape the approaching threat of the fire of judgment and the sunless scenery of gloomy Tartarus, where there never shines a beam from the irradiating voice of the Word. You will also escape the boiling flood of Gehenna's eternal lake of fire, and the eye ever fixed in menacing glare of the angels who are chained in Tartarus as punishment for their sins. And you will also escape the worm that endlessly coils for food around the body whose scum has bred it. Now these things you will avoid by being instructed in a knowledge of the true God. And you will possess an immortal body, even one placed beyond the possibility of corruption, just like the soul. And you will receive the kingdom of heaven. . . . And you will be a companion of God, and a co-heir with Christ, no longer enslaved by lusts or passions, or wasted by disease. For you will have become divine. . . . God has promised to bestow these things upon you, for you have been deified and begotten unto immortality. *Hippolytus (c. 225, W), 5.153.*

The apostolic teaching is that the soul . . . after its departure from the world, will be recompensed according to its deserts. It is destined to obtain either an inheritance of eternal life and blessedness (if its actions will have procured this for it) or to be delivered up to eternal fire and punishments (if the guilt of its crimes will have brought it down to this). *Origen (c. 225, E), 4.240.*

If anyone imagines that at the end, bodily nature will be entirely destroyed, he and I have different views. For how can beings so numerous and powerful be able to live and to exist without bodies? It is an attribute of the divine nature alone—of the Father, Son, and Holy Spirit—to exist without any material substance, and without partaking in any way with an adjoining body. Someone else may say that in the end, every bodily substance will be so pure and refined as to be like ether—of celestial purity and clearness. However, how things will be is known with certainty only to God. *Origen (c. 225, E), 4.262.*

To those who will deserve to obtain an inheritance in the kingdom of heaven, that germ of the body's restoration . . . by God's command restores a spiritual body out of the earthly and animal body. It restores a body capable of inhabiting the heavens. At the same time, to each one of those who may be of inferior merit, or of more abject condition, or even the lowest on the scale, . . . there is yet given—in proportion to the dignity of his life and soul—a glory and dignity of body. However, even the resurrected body of those who are destined to everlasting fire or to severe punishments is by the very change of the resurrection so incorruptible that it cannot be corrupted and dissolved even by severe punishments. . . .

Let us see now what is the meaning of the threatening of eternal fire. We find in the prophet Isaiah, that the fire with which each one is punished is described as his own. For he says, "Walk in the light of your own fire, and in the flame which you have kindled" [Isa. 50:2]. By these words, it seems to be indicated that every sinner kindles for himself the flame of his own fire. He is not plunged into some fire that has been already kindled by another, or was in existence before him. Of this fire, the fuel and food are our sins, which are called by the apostle Paul "wood, hay, and stubble." . . .

So, when the soul has gathered together a multitude of evil works, and an abundance of sins against itself, at the appropriate time all that assembly of evils boils up to punishment and is set on fire to chastisements. The mind itself . . . will see exposed before its eyes a type of history (as it were) of all the foul, shameful, and unholy deeds that it has done. Then will the conscience itself be harassed—pierced by its own goads—and will become an accuser and a witness against itself. . . . From this it is understood that around the substance of the soul certain tortures are produced by the hurtful affections of sins themselves. . . . We can draw some parallels from the evil effects of those passions that are inclined to befall some souls—such as when a soul is consumed by the fire of love, or wasted away by zeal or envy, or when the passion of anger is kindled, or when someone is consumed by the greatness of his madness or his sorrow. On these occasions some have deemed it more tolerable to submit to death than to perpetually endure torture of such a kind, finding the excess of these evils unbearable. *Origen (c. 225, E), 4.294, 295.*

There are also many other things that escape our notice and are known to Him alone, who is the physician of our souls. To illustrate, on account of those bad effects that we bring upon ourselves by eating and drinking, we deem it necessary for the health of the body to make use of some unpleasant and painful drug. If the nature of the disease demands it, it sometimes even requires the severe cure of the amputating knife. And if the virulence of the disease transcends even these remedies, the evil has at last to be burned out by fire. Now, how much more is it to be understood that God our Physician desires to remove the defects of our souls, which they have contracted from their different sins and crimes. How much more should He use penal measures of this sort—and might even apply the punishment of fire to those who have lost their soundness of mind! Pictures of this method of procedure are also found in the Holy Scriptures. *Origen (c. 225, E), 4.295.*

In my opinion, the outer darkness is not to be understood so much to be some dark atmosphere without any light. Rather, it refers to those persons who, being plunged in the darkness of profound ignorance, have been placed beyond the reach of any light of understanding. *Origen (c. 225, E), 4.296.*

To those who possess in this life a sketchy outline of truth and knowledge, there will be added the beauty of a perfect image in the future. I believe that some such desire was indicated by [Paul]. . . . He knew that when he returned to Christ he would then know more clearly the reasons of all things that are done on earth. . . . From all of this, we can surmise that not a little time will pass by until the reason of all these things upon the earth are pointed out to the worthy and deserving, after their departure from life. As a result, by the knowledge of all these things and by the grace of full knowledge, they may enjoy an unspeakable joy. . . . I think, therefore, that all the saints who depart from this life will remain in some place situated in the earth, which Holy Scripture calls Paradise. I think it will be, so to speak, a classroom or school of souls, in which they are to be instructed regarding all the things that they had seen on earth. I think they will also receive some information respecting things that are to follow in the future. . . . If anyone indeed is pure in heart, holy in mind, and more practiced in perception, he will—by making rapid progress—quickly ascend to a place in the air and reach the kingdom of heaven through those mansions, so to speak, in the various places that the Greeks have called spheres or globes, but which Holy Scripture has called heavens. *Origen (c. 225, E), 4.299.*

When, then, the saints will have reached the celestial abodes, . . . He will show to them, as to children, the causes of things and the power of His creation. He will explain why that star was placed in that particular quarter of the sky and why it was separated from another by so great an interval of space. . . . And, then, when they have finished all those matters that are connected with the stars and with the heavenly revolutions, they will come to those that are not seen and to those of whom we have only heard their names. *Origen (c. 225, E), 4.299, 300.*

The more simple among those who profess to belong to the church have believed that there is no Deity greater than the Creator—being right in so thinking. However, they imagine such things regarding Him as would not be believed of the most savage and unjust of mankind. In all of these points previously enumerated, the cause of the false opinions and of the impious statements or ignorant assertions about God appear to be nothing else than not understanding Scripture according to its spiritual meaning. It comes from interpreting according to the mere letter. *Origen (c. 225, E), 4.357.*

To those who say that no one is delivered by Jesus to the tormentors, it must be said, "Please, explain to us, good sirs, who is the king who delivered the wicked servant to the tormentors?" *Origen (c. 245, E), 9.504.*

Almost the entire world is better acquainted with what Christians preach than with the favorite opinions of the philosophers. For who is ignorant . . . that a general judgment is proclaimed to come, in which the wicked are to be punished according to their deserts and the righteous are to be duly rewarded? *Origen (c. 248, E), 4.399.*

We defend our own procedure when we say that our object is to reform the human race. This can be done either by the threats of punishments (which we are persuaded are necessary for the whole world, and which perhaps are not without use to those who are to endure them) or else by the promises made to those who have lived virtuous lives. In these promises are contained the statements regarding the blessed rest that is to be found in the kingdom of God, reserved for those who are worthy of becoming His subjects. *Origen (c. 248, E), 4.501.*

If, on the contrary, the works of the wicked man are spoken of figuratively under the names of "wood, hay, or stubble," why does it not immediately occur to them [to wonder] in what sense the word "fire" is to be taken, since it consumes "wood" of that kind. . . . He enters in as a "refiner's fire," to refine the rational nature, which has been filled with the lead of wickedness. *Origen (c. 248, E), 4.502.*

We say that God brings fire upon the world—not like a cook—but like a God who is the benefactor of those who stand in need of the discipline of fire. This will be testified by the prophet Isaiah. *Origen (c. 248, E), 4.549.*

"All the rest of the race will be completely burned up, and the [Christians] alone will remain." It is not to be wondered at, indeed, if such thoughts have been entertained by those among us who are called in Scripture the "foolish things." To those whom the Word calls "the foolish things of the world," . . . the just and obvious meaning of the passages relating to punishments is suitable. For they cannot receive any other mode of conversion than that which is by fear and the threat of punishment. Thus they are saved from many evils. . . . Some persons, according to their deserts, will require the administration of punishment by fire. They will incur these sufferings with a view to an end that is suitable for God to bring upon those who have been created in His image, but who have lived in opposition to the will of that nature. *Origen (c. 248, E), 4.550.*

After the troubles and struggles that we suffer here in order to reach the highest heavens, we hope . . . that we will be united there with those waters that are said to be above the heavens and that praise His name. *Origen (c. 248, E), 4.582.*

The Scriptures that are current in the churches of God do not speak of seven heavens, or of any definite number at all. Rather, they do appear to teach the existence of "heavens," whether that means the spheres of those bodies that the Greeks call "planets," or something more mysterious. *Origen (c. 248, E), 4.582, 583.*

If someone wishes to obtain the means for a more profound contemplation of the entrance of souls into divine things, . . . let him study the visions at the end of Ezekiel's prophecies. I speak of the visions that were beheld by the prophet in which gates of different kinds are listed. These obscurely refer to the different modes in which divine souls enter into a better world. Let him also study what is related of the city of God in the Apocalypse of John. *Origen (c. 248, E), 4.583.*

Let them rest assured that punishment will be inflicted on the wicked and that rewards will be bestowed upon the righteous by Him who deals with everyone just as he deserves. He will proportion His rewards to the good that each has done, according to the account of himself that he is able to give. *Origen (c. 248, E), 4.659.*

To him who has lived well, there is advantage after death. You, however, when one day you die, you will be taken away to an evil place. But those who believe in Christ will be led into a good place. . . . Luxury and the short-lived joys of the world are ruining you. As a result, you will be tormented in Gehenna for all time. *Commodianus (c. 240, W), 4.207.*

You will wail in Gehenna. Certainly God lives, who makes the dead to live, that He may give worthy rewards to the innocent and to the good. But to the fierce and impious, He gives the cruel Gehenna. . . . You seek to recklessly live without God, believing that death is merely extinction and that it is absolute. But God has not arranged it as you think, you who believe that the dead are forgetful of what they have previously done. . . . You will not escape from God. He will distribute punishments according to your deeds. So I would have you be careful that you do not come to the burning of fire. Give yourself up at once to Christ. . . . Otherwise, you will be taken where it will grieve you to be. There the spiritual punishment, which is eternal, is undergone. There is always wailing there, for you do not absolutely die in it. *Commodianus (c. 240, W), 4.208.*

There the eternal flame will torment on the day decreed. *Commodianus (c. 240, W), 4.213.*

He has prepared heaven, but He has also prepared Gehenna. He has prepared places of refreshment, but he has also prepared eternal punishment. He has prepared the light that no one can approach, but He has also prepared the vast and eternal gloom of perpetual night. *Cyprian (c. 250, W), 5.311.*

. . . considering the eternal punishments of Gehenna. *Cyprian (c. 250, W), 5.346.*

How great will that Day be at its coming, beloved brethren. The Lord will begin to count up His people and to recognize the deserts of each one by the inspection of His divine knowledge. He will send the guilty to Gehenna. He will set on fire our persecutors with the perpetual burning of a penal fire. However, He will pay us the reward of our faith and devotion. How great will be the glory, and how great will be the joy, to be admitted to see God! . . . When that revelation comes, when that glory of God shines upon us, we will be as happy and joyful . . . as the others will remain guilty and wretched. For as either deserters from God or as rebels against Him, they have done the will of the devil. Therefore, it will be necessary for them to be tormented with the devil himself in unquenchable fire. *Cyprian (c. 250, W), 5.350.*

Did he not previously ordain eternal punishments for those who deny Him, and saving rewards for those who confess Him? *Cyprian (c. 250, W), 5.439.*

The Lord prophesies that the aliens will be burned up and consumed. He refers to those who are aliens from the divine race—the profane, those who are not spiritually new-born, nor made children of God. Only those can escape who have been born anew and signed with the sign of Christ. . . . Believe Him who will give to all believers the reward of eternal life. Believe Him who will call down on unbelievers eternal punishments in the fires of Gehenna. . . . An ever-burning Gehenna will burn up the condemned—a punishment that devours with living flames. Nor will there be any means by which at any time they can have either rest or an end to their torments. Souls with their bodies will be reserved in infinite tortures for suffering. . . . This is in accord with the truth of Holy Scriptures, which says, "Their worm will not die and their fire will not be quenched." . . . The pain of punishment will then be without the fruit of penitence. Weeping will be useless and prayer ineffectual. Too late, those persons will believe in eternal punishment who would not believe in eternal life. *Cyprian (c. 250, W), 5.464, 465.*

On your departure from this world, God promises to you immortality and eternity. And do you doubt? *Cyprian (c. 250, W), 5.470.*

A person may fear to die, who from this death will pass over to a second death. He may fear to die, whom on his departure from this world eternal flames will torment with never-ending punishments. *Cyprian (c. 250, W), 5.472.*

The highest heaven is the heaven of wisdom. The second, of understanding. The third, of counsel. The fourth, of might. The fifth, of knowledge. The sixth, of piety. The seventh, of God's fear. *Victorinus (c. 280, W), 7.342.*

The Lord does not profess to give the same honors to all. Rather, to some He promises that they will be numbered in the kingdom of heaven. To others, they are promised the inheritance of the earth. And to still others, there is promised [the privilege] to see the Father. *Methodius (c. 290, E), 6.332.*

Immortal beings are not all of one order, . . . but there are differences of race and tribe. The cherubim do not depart from their own nature and assume the form of angels. Nor, again, do angels assume the form of the others. . . . Moreover, man was appointed by the original order of things to inhabit the world and to rule over all that is in it. So when he is immortal, he will never be changed from being a man into the form either of angels or any other. . . . For Christ at his coming did not proclaim that the human nature would be remolded or transformed into another nature once it is immortal. . . . Why, then, did He make man instead of angels, if He wished men to be angels and not men? . . . He intended man to be man; that is why He originally made him so. . . . For He did not say "they will *be* angels," but only that "they will be *like* angels." *Methodius (c. 290, E), 6.366, 367.*

The force of this is not that it altogether annihilates the souls of the unrighteous, but subjects them to everlasting punishment. We call that punishment the second death, which is also perpetual, the same as immortality. We define the first death in this manner: it is the dissolution of the nature of living beings. Or we say that death is the separation of body and soul. But we define the second death in this manner: It is the suffering of eternal pain. It is the condemnation of souls to eternal punishments, to receive their deserts. *Lactantius (c. 304–313, W), 7.61, 62.*

Death is to be weighed in accordance with the past actions of life. So it comes to pass that if life has been spent in the service of God, death is not an evil thing. For it is a transplanting to immortality. But if life has not been spent this way, death must necessarily be something evil. For it then transports men to everlasting punishment. *Lactantius (c. 304–313, W), 7.90.*

He has prepared everlasting fire for the wicked spirits. And, by His prophets, He Himself threatens this to the ungodly and the rebellious. *Lactantius (c. 304–313, W), 7.155.*

We speak better and more truly who say that the two ways belong to heaven and Hades, for immortality is promised to the righteous, and everlasting punishment is threatened to the unrighteous. *Lactantius (c. 304–313, W), 7.164.*

[Immortality] does not come unless it is given to man by God. Otherwise, there would be no difference between the just and the unjust— since every man who is born would become immortal. So immortality is not the consequence of nature, but the reward and recompense of virtue.... Man is born mortal. He afterwards becomes immortal when he begins to live in conformity with the will of God. That is, when he begins to follow righteousness. *Lactantius (c. 304–313, W), 7.201.*

When the times that God has appointed for death are completed, death itself will be terminated. Since temporal death follows temporal life, it follows that souls rise again to everlasting life. For temporal death has come to an end. The life in which the soul receives the divine and indescribable fruits of its immortality is an eternal one. So, likewise, the death in which the soul suffers perpetual punishments and infinite torments for its sins, must be eternal.... Death, therefore, does not extinguish man, but admits him to the reward of virtue. However, he who has contaminated himself . . . with vices and crimes and has been the slave of pleasure, he will be truly condemned. And he will suffer eternal punishment. The sacred writings call this the second death, which is both eternal and full of the severest torments. *Lactantius (c. 304–313, W), 7.207.*

Although they are immortal, souls are nevertheless capable of suffering at the hand of God.... The sacred writings inform us in what manner the wicked are to undergo punishment. Since they have committed sins in their bodies, they will be clothed with flesh again. And they will pay for their sins in their bodies. However, it will not be in that flesh with which God [originally] clothed man.... Rather, it will be in indestructible flesh. This flesh will abide forever so that it can hold out against tortures and everlasting fire, the nature of which is different from this fire of ours.... That same divine fire, with one and the same force and power, will

both burn the wicked and then form them again. It will replace as much of their bodies as it will consume.... Thus, without any wasting of bodies, ... it will only burn and affect them with a sense of pain. *Lactantius (c. 304–313, W), 7.217.*

Do you dare to laugh at us when we speak of Gehenna, and fires that cannot be quenched— into which we have learned that souls are cast. . . . They are cast in, and being annihilated, they pass away vainly in everlasting destruction. For theirs is an in-between state [i.e., between mortal and immortal], as has been learned from Christ's teaching. Hence, on the one hand, they can perish if they have not known God. On the other hand, they can be delivered from death if they have given heed to His warnings and favors. And to proclaim what is unknown, this is man's real death—that which leaves nothing behind. For that which is seen by the eyes is the separation of the soul from the body. It is not the last end—annihilation. This, I say, is man's real death: when souls who do not know God will be consumed in long-protracted torment with raging fire, which certain fiercely cruel beings will cast them into. *Arnobius (c. 305, E), 6.439, 440.*

Our salvation is not necessary to Him, such that He would gain something or suffer some loss if He either made us divine, or allowed us to be annihilated and destroyed by corruption. *Arnobius (c. 305, E), 6.459.*

He casts them into everlasting fire, even though they do not cease to direct their entreaties to Him. *Disputation of Archelaus and Manes (c. 320, E), 6.212.*

SEE ALSO DEAD, INTERMEDIATE STATE OF THE; DEIFICATION OF MAN; ESCHATOLOGY; ETERNAL PUNISHMENTS AND REWARDS; GEHENNA; JUDGMENT, LAST.

ETERNAL SECURITY

SEE SALVATION (VI. CAN THOSE WHO ARE SAVED EVER BE LOST?)

ETERNITY

Eternity, for instance, presents in an instant the future, the present, and also the past of time. *Clement of Alexandria (c. 195, E), 2.313.*

Eternity has no time. It is itself all time. *Tertullian (c. 207, W), 3.276.*

This is spoken to Him by God, with whom all time is today. For there is no evening with God, . . . and there is no morning. There is nothing but time that stretches out, along with His unbeginning and unseen life. *Origen (c. 228, E), 9.314.*

Our resurrection is the beginning of the future age and the end of this one. For in that age, there is neither past nor future, but only the present. *Methodius (c. 290, E), 6.378.*

SEE ALSO ESCHATOLOGY; ETERNAL PUNISHMENTS AND REWARDS.

ETHIOPIAN EUNUCH

So he arose and went. And behold, a man of Ethiopia, a eunuch of great authority under Candace the queen of the Ethiopians. Acts 8:27.

Immediately after Philip had baptized him, the eunuch departed from him. For nothing else was lacking to him who had already been instructed by the prophets. He was not ignorant of God the father, nor of the rules as to the [proper] manner of life. Rather, he was merely ignorant of the coming of the Son of God. After he had learned of this, in a brief while, he went on his way rejoicing, to become the herald in Ethiopia of Christ's coming. *Irenaeus (c. 180, E/W), 1.495.*

If Philip so easily baptized the chamberlain, let us reflect that there had been interposed a manifest and conspicuous evidence that the Lord deemed him worthy. *Tertullian (c. 198, W), 3.677, 678.*

SEE ALSO PHILIP.

EUCHARIST

I. Doctrine of the Eucharist

II. How the Eucharist was celebrated

III. Letters of communion

IV. The Eucharist as a spiritual sacrifice

V. Other spiritual sacrifices

VI. Other interpretations of "body" and "blood"

VII. Unworthy participation

I. Doctrine of the Eucharist

As they were eating, Jesus took bread, blessed it and broke it, and gave it to the disciples and said, "Take, eat; this is My body." Then He took the cup, and gave thanks, and gave it to them, saying, "Drink from it, all of you. For this is My blood of the new covenant, which is shed for many for the remission of sins." Matt. 26:26–28.

This is the bread which comes down from heaven, that one may eat of it and not die. I am the living bread which came down from heaven. If anyone eats of this bread, he will live forever; and the bread that I will give is My flesh, which I will give for the life of the world. . . . Most assuredly, I say to you, unless you eat the flesh of the Son of Man and drink His blood, you have no life in you. Whoever eats My flesh and drinks My blood has eternal life, and I will raise him up at the last day. For My flesh is food indeed, and My blood is drink indeed. He who eats My flesh and drinks My blood abides in Me, and I in him. John 6:51–55.

The cup of blessing which we bless, is it not the communion of the blood of Christ? The bread which we break, is it not the communion of the body of Christ? 1 Cor. 10:16.

The Lord Jesus on the same night in which He was betrayed took bread; and when He had given thanks, He broke it and said, "Take, eat; this is My body which is broken for you; do this in remembrance of me." In the same manner, he also took the cup after supper, saying, "This cup is the new covenant in My blood. This do, as often as you drink it, in remembrance of me." For as often as you eat this bread and drink this cup, you proclaim the Lord's death till he comes. Therefore whoever eats this bread or drinks this cup of the Lord in an unworthy manner will be guilty of the body and blood of the Lord. 1 Cor. 11:23–27.

You gave food and drink to men for enjoyment, that they might give thanks to you. But to us you freely gave spiritual food and drink and life eternal through your Servant. *Didache (c. 80–140, E), 1.380.*

. . . breaking one and the same bread, which is the medicine of immortality, and the antidote to prevent us from dying, so that we should live forever in Jesus Christ. *Ignatius (c. 105, E), 1.58.*

I desire the bread of God, the heavenly bread, the bread of life—which is the flesh of Jesus Christ, the Son of God. . . . And I desire the drink of God, namely His blood, which is incorruptible love and eternal life. *Ignatius (c. 105, E), 1.77.*

Take heed, then, to have only one Eucharist. For there is one flesh of our Lord Jesus Christ, and one cup to the unity of His blood. *Ignatius (c. 105, E), 1.81.*

They [the Gnostics] abstain from the Eucharist and from prayer, because they do not believe the Eucharist to be the flesh of our Savior Jesus Christ.... Those, therefore, who speak against this gift of God, incur death. *Ignatius (c. 105, E), 1.89.*

We do not receive these as common bread and common drink. Rather, Jesus Christ our Savior, having been made flesh by the Word of God, had both flesh and blood for our salvation. So, likewise, we have been taught that the food which is blessed by the prayer of His word, and from which our blood and flesh by transmutation are nourished, is the flesh and blood of that Jesus who was made flesh. *Justin Martyr (c. 160, E), 1.185.*

This prophecy refers to the bread which our Christ gave us to eat, in remembrance of His being made flesh for the sake of His believers, for whom also He suffered. And it refers to the cup which He gave us to drink, in remembrance of His own blood, with giving of thanks. *Justin Martyr (c. 160, E), 1.234.*

How can they [the Gnostics] be consistent with themselves [when they say] that the bread over which thanks has been given is the body of their Lord and that the cup is His blood—if they do not call Him the Son of the Creator? ... Then, again, how can they say that the flesh, which is nourished with the body of the Lord and with His blood, goes to corruption and does not partake of life? *Irenaeus (c. 180, E/W), 1.486.*

Our opinion is in accordance with the Eucharist, and, in turn, the Eucharist establishes our opinion. For we offer to Him His own, announcing consistently the fellowship and union of the flesh and spirit. For the bread, which is produced from the earth, when it receives the invocation of God, is no longer common bread, but the Eucharist—consisting of two realities, earthly and heavenly. So also our bodies, when they receive the Eucharist, are no longer corruptible, having the hope of the resurrection to eternity. *Irenaeus (c. 180, E/W), 1.486.*

If the Lord belonged to another Father, how could He, with any justice, have acknowledged the bread to be His body and declared the mixed cup to be His blood, while He took it from that creation to which we belong? *Irenaeus (c. 180, E/W), 1.507.*

But if [the flesh] indeed does not obtain salvation, then neither did the Lord redeem us with His blood, nor is the cup of the Eucharist the communion of His blood, nor the bread which we break the communion of His body. *Irenaeus (c. 180, E/W), 1.528.*

He has acknowledged the cup (which is a part of the creation) as His own blood, from which He refreshes our blood. And the bread (also a part of the creation) He has established as His own body, from which He gives increase to our bodies. When, therefore, the mingled cup and the baked bread receive the Word of God, and the Eucharist of the blood and the body of Christ is made (from which things the substance of our flesh is increased and supported), how can they [the Gnostics] maintain that the flesh is incapable of receiving the gift of God? *Irenaeus (c. 180, E/W), 1.528.*

[The wine and bread] having received the Word of God, become the Eucharist, which is the body and blood of Christ. *Irenaeus (c. 180, E/W), 1.528.*

These slaves had nothing to say that would meet the wishes of their tormentors, except that they had heard from their masters that the divine communion was the body and blood of Christ. Now, imagining that it was actually flesh and blood, those slaves gave their inquisitors answer to that effect. *Irenaeus (c. 180, E/W), 1.570.*

The vine produces wine, as the Word produces blood. And both of them drink health to men: wine for the body; blood for the spirit. *Clement of Alexandria (c. 195, E), 2.213.*

To drink the blood of Jesus is to become partaker of the Lord's immortality.... As wine is blended with water, so is the Spirit with man.... And the mixture of both—of the water and of the Word—is called the Eucharist, renowned and glorious grace. Those who by faith partake of it are sanctified both in body and soul. *Clement of Alexandria (c. 195, E), 2.242.*

Melchizedek, king of Salem, priest of the Most High God, gave bread and wine, providing consecrated food as a type of the Eucharist. *Clement of Alexandria (c. 195, E), 2.439.*

Christ is our Bread, because Christ is Life, and bread is life. He says, "I am the Bread of life." . . . Then, too, we find that His body is reckoned in bread: "This is my body." *Tertullian (c. 198, W), 3.683.*

Touching the days of stations [i.e., fast days], most think that they must not be present at the sacrificial prayers, on the ground that the station would be dissolved by reception of the Lord's body. Does, then, the Eucharist cancel a service devoted to God—or does it bind it more to God? Will not your station be more solemn if you have stood at God's altar? When the Lord's body has been received and reserved, each point is secured—both the participation of the sacrifice and the discharge of duty [i.e., fasting]. *Tertullian (c. 198, W), 3.687.*

Will not your [unbelieving] husband know what it is that you secretly taste before any food? And if he knows it to be bread, does he not believe it to be that which it is said to be? *Tertullian (c. 205, W), 4.46, 47.*

He declared plainly enough what He meant by the bread, when He called the bread His own body. He likewise, when mentioning the cup and making the new testament to be sealed in His blood, affirmed the reality of His body. *Tertullian (c. 207, W), 3.418.*

Even those very hands deliver to others what they have contaminated! Idol makers are chosen even into the ecclesiastical order! Oh wickedness! The Jews laid hands on Christ only once. These persons mangle his body daily. . . . What hands [deserve] more to be amputated than those in which scandal is done to the Lord's body? *Tertullian (c. 200, W), 3.64.*

We also eat the bread presented to us. And this bread becomes by prayer a sacred body, which sanctifies those who sincerely partake of it. *Origen (c. 248, E), 4.652.*

We have a symbol of gratitude to God in the bread that we call the Eucharist. *Origen (c. 248, E), 4.661.*

These, disregarding the honor that the blessed martyrs maintain for me with the confessors, . . . communicate with the lapsed and offer and give them the Eucharist. . . . Those presbyters, contrary to the Gospel law . . . before penitence was fulfilled . . . dare to offer on their behalf and to give them the Eucharist. That is, they dare to profane the sacred body of the Lord. However, it is written, "Whoever will eat the bread and drink the cup of the Lord unworthily,

will be guilty of the body and blood of the Lord." *Cyprian (c. 250, W), 5.291.*

. . . but may fortify them with the protection of Christ's body and blood. For the Eucharist is appointed for this very purpose. *Cyprian (c. 250, W), 5.337.*

They drink the cup of Christ's blood daily, for the reason that they themselves also may be able to shed their blood for Christ. *Cyprian (c. 250, W), 5.347.*

Let us also arm the right hand with the sword of the Spirit, that it may bravely reject the deadly sacrifices. Thereby, mindful of the Eucharist, the hand that has received the Lord's body may embrace the Lord Himself. *Cyprian (c. 250, W), 5.350.*

There can be no spiritual anointing among heretics. For it is clear that the oil cannot be sanctified nor the Eucharist celebrated at all among them. *Cyprian (c. 250, W), 5.376.*

Returning from the altars of the devil, they draw near to the holy place of the Lord! . . . With jaws still breathing their crime . . . they intrude on the body of the Lord. . . . All these warnings are scorned and disdained. They do violence to His body and blood! *Cyprian (c. 250, W), 5.441.*

He says that whoever will eat of His bread will live forever. So it is clear that those who partake of His body and receive the Eucharist by the right of communion are living. On the other hand, we must fear and pray lest anyone who is separate from Christ's body—being barred from communion—should remain at a distance from salvation. For He Himself warns and says, "Unless you eat the flesh of the Son of man and drink His blood, you have no life in you." *Cyprian (c. 250, W), 5.452.*

The hand must not be spotted with the sword and blood—not after the Eucharist is carried in it. *Cyprian (c. 250, W), 5.488.*

I do not think they will themselves be rash enough in such a condition to either approach the holy table or to touch the body and blood of the Lord. *Dionysius of Alexandria (c. 262, E), 6.96.*

I did not dare to renew afresh, after all, one who had heard the giving of thanks and who had answered "Amen" with others. He had stood at the holy table and had stretched forth his hands to receive the blessed food and had received it. And for a very long time, he had been a partaker of the body and blood of our Lord Jesus Christ. *Dionysius of Alexandria (c. 262, E), 6.103.*

The church increases daily in greatness, beauty, and numbers by the union and communion of the Word, who now still comes down to us and falls into a trance [like the first Adam] by the remembrance of His passion. *Methodius (c. 290, E), 6.319.*

But to those who have been delivered up and have fallen . . . and have been tormented and thrown into prison, it is right with joy . . . to communicate to them in all things—both in prayer and in partaking of the body and blood of Christ. *Peter of Alexandria (c. 310, E), 6.272; extended discussion: 5.358–5.363.*

II. How the Eucharist was celebrated

Now concerning the Eucharist [Thanksgiving], give thanks in this manner: First, concerning the cup: "We thank you, our Father, for the holy vine of David your servant, which you made known to us through Jesus your Servant; to you be the glory forever." And concerning the broken [bread]: "We thank you, our Father, for the life and knowledge which you made known to us through Jesus your Servant. To you be the glory forever. Even as this broken bread was scattered over the hills, and was gathered together and became one, so let your church be gathered together from the ends of the earth into your kingdom. For yours is the glory and the power through Jesus Christ forever." But let no one eat or drink of your Eucharist but those who have been baptized into the name of the Lord. For concerning this also the Lord has said, "Do not give that which is holy to the dogs." But after you are filled, give thanks in this manner. *Didache (c. 80–140, E), 1.379, 380.*

Let that be deemed a proper Eucharist, which is [administered] either by the bishop, or by one to whom he has entrusted it. *Ignatius (c. 105, E), 1.89, 90.*

Having ended the prayers, we greet one another with a kiss. Then there is brought to the president of the brethren bread and a cup of wine mixed with water. He takes them and gives praise and glory to the Father of the universe. . . . And when the president has given thanks, and all the people have expressed their assent, those whom we call deacons give to each of those present the bread and wine mixed with water over which the thanksgiving was pronounced, to partake of. And they carry away a portion to those who are absent. And this food is called among us the Eucharist [Thanksgiving]. And no one is allowed to partake of it but the one who believes that the things which we teach are true, and who has been washed with the washing that is for the remission of sins, and unto regeneration, and who is living as Christ has commanded. *Justin Martyr (c. 160, E), 1.185.*

And on the day called Sunday, all who live in cities or in the country gather together to one place. And the memoirs of the apostles or the writings of the prophets are read, as long as time permits. Then, when the reader has ceased, the president verbally instructs us and exhorts us to imitate these good things. Then we all rise together and pray. And, as we said before, when our prayer is ended, bread and wine and water are brought. Then, the president in like manner offers prayers and thanksgivings, according to his ability. And the people assent, saying "Amen." Then, [the Eucharist] is distributed to everyone, and everyone participates in that over which thanks have been given. And a portion of it is sent by the deacons to those who are absent. *Justin Martyr (c. 160, E), 1.186.*

According to custom, in the dispensing of the Eucharist, some direct that each one of the people individually should take his part. *Clement of Alexandria (c. 195, E), 2.300.*

Those heresies employ bread and water in the oblation, not according to the canon of the church. For there are those [heretics] who celebrate the Eucharist with mere water. *Clement of Alexandria (c. 195, E), 2.322.*

When the Lord's Body has been received and reserved, each point is secured. *Tertullian (c. 198, W), 3.687.*

Surely your [unbelieving] husband will know what it is that you secretly taste before eating any food. And if he knows it to be bread, no doubt he will believe it to be that which it is rumored to be. *Tertullian (c. 205, W), 4.46,47.*

In congregations before daybreak, we take from the hand of no one but the presidents the sacrament of the Eucharist—which the Lord both commanded to be eaten at mealtimes and commanded to be taken by all alike. . . . We feel pained should any wine or bread fall on the ground—even if it is our own. *Tertullian (c. 211, W), 3.94.*

Some, either by ignorance or simplicity, in sanctifying the cup of the Lord and in ministering to the people, do not do that which Jesus Christ, our Lord and God . . . did and taught. . . . When anything is prescribed by the inspiration and command of God, it is necessary that a faithful servant should obey the Lord. . . . Know, then, that I have been admonished that, in offering the cup, the tradition of the Lord must be observed. Nothing must be done by us but what the Lord first did on our behalf. So the cup that is offered in remembrance of Him should be offered mingled with wine. For when Christ says, "I am the true vine," the blood of Christ is assuredly not water, but wine. Neither can His blood by which we are redeemed and quickened appear to be in the cup—when there is no wine in the cup. . . .

We find in Genesis also, in respect of the sacrament in Noah, this same thing was to them a precursor and figure of the Lord's passion. He drank wine and became drunk. . . . Also in the priest Melchizedek we see prefigured the sacrament of the sacrifice of the Lord. . . . It says, "And Melchizedek, king of Salem, brought forth bread and wine." . . . By baptism, the Holy Spirit is received. Therefore, those who are baptized and have received the Holy Spirit are allowed to drink of the Lord's cup. . . . The cup should be mingled with a mixture of wine and water. . . . The cup that the Lord offered was mixed, and it was wine that He called His blood. Therefore, it appears that the blood of Christ is not offered if there is no wine in the cup. The Lord's sacrifice is not celebrated with a legitimate consecration unless our oblation and sacrifice correspond to His passion. . . .

As often as we drink it in remembrance of the Lord, we do the same thing that the Lord also did. So we find that we are not observing what was commanded unless we also do what the Lord did. By mixing the Lord's cup in like manner, we do not depart from the divine teaching. For we must not at all depart from the evangelical precepts. And disciples should also observe and do the same things that the Master both taught and did. . . . Neither the apostle himself, nor an angel from heaven, can preach or teach anything other than what Christ has once taught and His apostles have announced.

Therefore, I very much wonder where this practice has originated. That is, contrary to evangelical and apostolic discipline, in some places water is offered in the Lord's cup. But water by itself cannot represent the blood of Christ. The Holy Spirit also is not silent in the Psalms on the sacrament of this thing, when He makes mention of the Lord's cup and says, "Your inebriating cup, how excellent it is." Now the cup that inebriates is certainly mingled with wine. For water cannot inebriate anybody. And the cup of the Lord inebriates in the same way as Noah also was intoxicated by drinking wine, in Genesis. However, the intoxication of the Lord's cup and blood is not the same as is the intoxication of the world's wine. . . . The Lord's cup inebriates those who drink it in such a manner as to make them sober. It restores their minds to spiritual wisdom. . . . The cup of salvation having been drunk, the memory of the old man is laid aside. And there arises an oblivion of the former worldly life. . . .

Therefore, in consecrating the cup of the Lord, water alone cannot be offered, even as wine alone cannot be offered. For if anyone offers wine only, the blood of Christ is dissociated from us. Yet, if the water is alone, the people are dissociated from Christ. But when both are mingled and are joined with one another by a close union, there is a complete spiritual and heavenly sacrament. Thus the cup of the Lord is indeed neither water alone, nor wine alone. . . . Certainly that priest truly discharges the office of Christ who imitates that which Christ did. He then offers a true and full sacrifice in the church to God the Father, when he proceeds to offer it according to what he sees Christ Himself to have offered. . . . Does anyone perhaps flatter himself with this notion: that although in the morning, water alone is seen to be offered, yet when we come to supper, we offer the mingled cup? However, when we come together for supper [i.e., the love feast], we cannot call the people together to our banquet, so as to celebrate the truth of the sacrament in the presence of all the brotherhood. Nevertheless, it was not in the morning, but after supper, that the Lord offered the mingled cup. Should we then celebrate the Lord's cup after supper, so that by continual repetition of the Lord's supper we may offer the mingled cup? It behooved Christ to offer about the evening of the day, so that the very hour of sacrifice might reveal the setting . . . "And all the people of the synagogue of the children of Israel will kill it in the evening." . . . However, we celebrate the resurrection of the Lord in the morning. *Cyprian (c. 250, W), 5.359–5.363.*

The boy ran for the presbyter. But it was night and the presbyter was sick and was, as a result, unable to come. However, I had issued an injunction that persons at the point of death, if they requested it, . . . should be absolved in order that they might depart this life in cheerful hope. So the presbyter gave the boy a small portion of the Eucharist, telling him to steep it in water and drop it into the old man's mouth. *Dionysius of Alexandria (c. 262, E), 6.101.*

[The bishops are] the ambassadors of God, who have . . . imparted to you the saving body and precious blood of Christ, . . . who have made you partakers of the holy and sacred Eucharist. *Apostolic Constitutions (compiled c. 390, E), 7.412.*

When they wish to repent, we receive the pagans into the church to hear the Word. However, we do not receive them to communion until they have received the seal of baptism and are made complete Christians. *Apostolic Constitutions (compiled c. 390, E), 7.414.*

After this, let the sacrifice follow, the people standing and praying silently. And when the oblation has been made, let every rank by itself partake of the Lord's body and precious blood, in order. Let them approach with reverence and holy fear—as to the body of their king. Let the women approach with their heads covered, as is becoming the order of women. But let the door be watched, lest any unbeliever, or one not yet initiated, should come in. *Apostolic Constitutions (compiled c. 390, E), 7.421, 422.*

III. Letters of communion

For this reason, I beg you that you will designate by name in the certificate [of communion] only those whom you yourselves witness, whom you have known, whose penitence you see to be very near to full satisfaction. *Cyprian (c. 250, W), 5.292.*

We have communicated this fact to you in order that you may write him and receive letters of communion from him. *Malchion (c. 270, E), 6.171.*

If any brother—man or woman—comes in from another parish and brings recommenda-

tory letters, let the deacon be the judge of that affair. *Apostolic Constitutions (compiled c. 390, E), 7.422.*

IV. The Eucharist as a spiritual sacrifice

In every place incense shall be offered to My name, and a pure offering; for My name shall be great among the nations. Mal. 1:11.

If you bring your gift to the altar, and there remember that your brother has something against you, leave your gift there before the altar, and go your way. First be reconciled to your brother. Matt. 5:23, 24.

Therefore by Him let us continually offer the sacrifice of praise to God, that is, the fruit of our lips, giving thanks to his name. Heb. 13:15.

But every Lord's Day, gather yourselves together, and break bread, and give thanksgiving after having confessed your transgressions, that your sacrifice may be pure. But let no one that is at variance with his fellow man come together with you, until they are reconciled, so that your sacrifice may not be profaned. For this is the thing that was spoken of by the Lord: "'In every place and time offer to me a pure sacrifice; for I am a great King,' the Lord says, 'and my name is wonderful among the nations.'" *Didache (c. 80–140, E), 7.381.*

He then speaks of those Gentiles, namely us, who in every place offer sacrifices to Him, i.e., the bread of the Eucharist, and also the cup of the Eucharist. *Justin Martyr (c. 160, E), 1.215.*

God anticipated all the sacrifices which we offer through this name, and which Jesus the Christ enjoined us to offer—i.e., in the Eucharist of the bread and the cup, which are presented by Christians in all places throughout the world. So He bears witness that they are well-pleasing to Him. . . . Now, that prayers and giving of thanks, when offered by worthy men, are the only perfect and well-pleasing sacrifices to God, I also admit. For Christians have undertaken to offer only these, and in the remembrance effected by their solid and liquid food, by which the suffering of the Son of God which He endured is brought to mind. *Justin Martyr (c. 160, E), 1.257.*

He took that created thing, bread, and gave thanks, saying, "This is My body." And the cup likewise, which is part of that creation to which we belong, He confessed to be His blood. And He taught the new oblation of the new covenant, which the church receiving from the apostles, offers to God throughout all the world. . . . Concerning this, Malachi, who is among the twelve [minor] prophets, spoke beforehand in this manner: . . . "'In every place incense is offered to My name, and a pure sacrifice. For great is My name among the Gentiles,' says the Lord Omnipotent." By these words, He indicated in the plainest manner that the former people [the Jews] will indeed cease to make offerings to God, but that in every place sacrifice will be offered to him, and that it will be a pure one. *Irenaeus (c. 180, E/W), 1.484.*

The oblation of the church, which the Lord gave instructions to be offered throughout all the world, is considered by God to be a pure sacrifice, and it is acceptable to Him. . . . For by the gift, both honor and affection are shown forth towards the King. And the Lord, wishing us to offer it in all simplicity and innocence, did express Himself in this manner, "Therefore, when you offer your gift upon the altar, and there remember that your brother has anything against you, leave your gift before the altar, and go your way. First be reconciled to your brother, and then return and offer your gift." We are bound, therefore, to offer to God the first-fruits of His creation. *Irenaeus (c. 180, E/W), 1.484.*

Therefore, sacrifices do not sanctify a man. For God does not stand in any need of sacrifices. Instead, it is the conscience of the offerer that sanctifies the sacrifice when it is pure. This moves God to accept it as from a friend. . . . It behooves us to make an oblation to God and in all things to be found grateful to God our Maker. We should do this in a pure mind, in faith without hypocrisy, in well-grounded hope, in fervent love, offering to Him the first-fruits of His own created things. And the church alone offers this pure oblation to the Creator. *Irenaeus (c. 180, E/W), 1.485.*

The oblation of the Eucharist is not a carnal one, but a spiritual one. And in this respect, it is pure. For we make an oblation to God of the bread and the cup of blessing, giving Him thanks in that He has commanded the earth to bring forth these fruits for our nourishment. And then, when we have perfected the oblation, we invoke the Holy Spirit, that He may exhibit this sacrifice, both the bread (the body of Christ) and the cup (the blood of Christ) in order that those who receive these antitypes may obtain remission of sins and life eternal. *Irenaeus (c. 180, E/W), 1.574.*

You, however, have no cause for appearing in public, except such as is serious. Either some brother who is sick is visited, or else the sacrifice is offered, or else the word of God is dispensed. *Tertullian (c. 198, W), 4.24.*

In the priest Melchizedek, we see the sacrament of the sacrifice of the Lord prefigured. . . . It says, "And Melchizedek, king of Salem, brought forth bread and wine." Now, Melchizedek was a priest of the Most High God, and he blessed Abraham. The Holy Spirit declares in the Psalms that Melchizedek was a type of Christ. *Cyprian (c. 250, W), 5.359.*

Certainly, only the priest who imitates that which Christ did [i.e., using wine mixed with water] is the one who truly discharges the office of Christ. He only offers a true and full sacrifice in the church to God the Father when he proceeds to offer it in the manner that he sees Christ Himself to have offered it. *Cyprian (c. 250, W), 5.362.*

Learn what occurred when I myself was present and a witness. Some parents who were fleeing [persecution] left an infant daughter under the care of a wet nurse. The nurse turned the forsaken child over to the magistrates. They gave the child bread mingled with wine in the presence of an idol where the people flocked. . . . Later, the mother recovered her child. But the girl was unable to speak or indicate the crime that had been committed. . . . When we were sacrificing, the mother brought the daughter in with her. . . . When the solemnities were finished, the deacon began to offer the cup to those present. When the rest had received it and her turn approached, the little child—by the instinct of the divine majesty—turned away her face, shut her mouth tight with resisting lips, and refused the cup. Still, the deacon persisted . . . and forced on her some of the sacrament of the cup. There then followed a sobbing and vomiting. The Eucharist could not remain in a profane body and mouth. The drink, sanctified in the blood of the Lord, burst forth from the polluted stomach. . . .

Another woman tried with unworthy hands to open her box in which was the holy [sacrament] of the Lord. However, she was deterred by fire rising from it—because of her daring to touch it. And another person, who was also defiled, dared to secretly receive a part of the sacrifice celebrated by the priest, along with the rest. However, when he opened his hands, he found he had a cinder instead. Thus, by the experience of one, it was demonstrated that the Lord withdraws when He is denied. That which is received does not benefit unto salvation those who are undeserving. For the saving grace is changed by the departure of the sanctity into a cinder. *Cyprian (c. 250, W), 5.444.*

The Eucharist is to be received with fear and honor. In Leviticus it says, "But whatever soul will eat of the flesh of the sacrifice of salvation, which is the Lord's, and his uncleanness is still upon him—that soul will perish from his people" [Lev. 7:20]. Also, in the first letter to the Corinthians: "Whoever will eat the bread or drink the cup of the Lord unworthily, will be guilty of the body and blood of the Lord." *Cyprian (c. 250, W), 5.554.*

In our religion, there is no place even for a slight and ordinary offense. And if anyone comes to a sacrifice without a sound conscience, he hears what threats God denounces against him. *Lactantius (c. 304–313, W), 7.157.*

V. Other spiritual sacrifices

I beseech you therefore, brethren, by the mercies of God, that you present your bodies a living sacrifice, holy, acceptable to God, which is your reasonable service. Rom. 12:1.

The noblest sacrifice to him is for us to know who stretched out and vaulted the heavens and who fixed the earth in its place.... Yet, indeed, it does behoove us to offer a bloodless sacrifice and the "service of our reason." *Athenagoras (c. 175, E), 2.135.*

It is not by earthly sacrifices, but by spiritual, that offering is to be made to God. Therefore, we read ... "Offer to God a sacrifice of praise, and render to the Highest your vows." Thus, accordingly, the spiritual "sacrifices of praise" are pointed to. *Tertullian (c. 197, W), 3.156.*

He who cultivates innocence, supplicates God. He who cultivates justice, makes offerings to God. He who abstains from fraudulent practices, propitiates God. He who snatches man from danger, slaughters the most acceptable victim. These are our sacrifices; these are our rites of God's worship. *Mark Minucius Felix (c. 200, W), 4.193.*

"My name will be great among the Gentiles. And in every place sacrifice will be offered unto my name, and a pure offering"—such as the ascription of glory, blessing, praise, and hymns. *Tertullian (c. 207, W), 3.341.*

That which is incorporeal must be offered to God, for he accepts this. His offering is innocency of soul. His sacrifice is praise and hymns. For, if God is not seen, he should be worshipped with things that are not seen. *Lactantius (c. 304–313, W), 7.193.*

VI. Other interpretations of "body" and "blood"

As can be seen from the preceding quotations, the early church understood Jesus' words about eating his body and drinking his blood to be primarily referring to the Eucharist. Many of these same writers, however, also believed there were additional interpretations of Jesus' words.

Christ did this when He appeared as a man, that we, being nourished, as it were, from the breath of His flesh, and having, by such a course of milk-nourishment, become accustomed to eat and drink the Word of God, may be able also to contain in ourselves the Bread of immortality, which is the Spirit of the Father. ... The apostle had the power to give them strong meat. For those upon whom the apostles had laid hands received the Holy Spirit. And He is the Food of life. *Irenaeus (c. 180, E/W), 1.521.*

Elsewhere the Lord, in the Gospel according to John, brought this out by symbols, when He said: "Eat my flesh and drink my blood," describing distinctly by metaphor the drinkable properties of faith. *Clement of Alexandria (c. 195, E), 2.219.*

You will certainly find nothing else more nourishing, or sweeter, or whiter than milk. In every respect, accordingly, it is like spiritual nourishment, which is wet through grace, nourishing as life, and bright as the day of Christ. The blood of the Word has been also exhibited as milk. *Clement of Alexandria (c. 195, E), 2.219.*

He says, "Eat my flesh and drink my blood." Such is the suitable food that the Lord ministers. ... The flesh figuratively represents to us the Holy Spirit; for the flesh was created by Him. The blood indicates to us the Word, for as rich blood the Word has been infused into life. *Clement of Alexandria (c. 195, E), 2.220.*

To Christ, the fulfilling of His Father's will was food. And to us infants, who drink the milk of the Word of the heavens, Christ Himself is food. . . . But He said, "And the bread that I will give is My flesh." Now, flesh is moistened with blood, and blood is figuratively called wine. *Clement of Alexandria (c. 195, E), 2.221.*

"Take, drink. This is my blood," the blood of the vine. He figuratively calls the Word "shed for many, for the remission of sins" the holy stream of gladness. *Clement of Alexandria (c. 195, E), 2.246.*

The following passage may, or may not, be a reference to the Eucharist:

I am He who feeds you, giving Myself as bread, of which he who has tasted experiences death no more. I supply day by day the drink of immortality. *Clement of Alexandria (c. 195, E), 2.598.*

The Jews lose heavenly blessings by confining their hopes to earthly ones—being ignorant of the promise of heavenly bread, of the oil of God's anointing, the wine of the Spirit, and that water of life that has its vigor from the vine of Christ. *Tertullian (c. 210, W), 3.564.*

They thought His discourse was harsh and intolerable, for they thought that He had really and literally directed them to eat his flesh. . . . His word is spirit and life. So He likewise called His flesh by the same description. Since the Word has become flesh, we should desire Him in order that we may have life. We should devour Him with the ear and feed on Him with our understanding. We should digest Him by faith. *Tertullian (c. 210, W), 3.572.*

He says that, not only is He the vine, but that He is also the Bread of life. Bread nourishes and makes strong. . . . On the other hand, wine pleases, rejoices, and relaxes man. So perhaps it can be said that ethical studies are the bread of life, for they bring life to him who learns them and practices them. . . . On the other hand, secret and mystical speculations are called the juice of the true vine, because they flow from it and gladden the heart, causing those to feel inspired who take them in. *Origen (c. 228, E), 9.314.*

"Unless you eat the flesh of the Son of Man, and drink his blood, you have no life in you." . . . We eat the flesh of the Lamb, with bitter herbs and unleavened bread, when we repent of our sins and grieve with godly sorrow. *Origen (c. 228, E), 9.390.*

The bread signifies His body. For He Himself is the food and the life of all who believe in the flesh that He bore. *Lactantius (c. 304–313, W), 7.121.*

VII. Unworthy participation

He who eats and drinks in an unworthy manner eats and drinks judgment to himself, not discerning the Lord's body. For this reason many are weak and sick among you, and many sleep. 1 Cor. 11:29, 30.

Writing to the Corinthians, who had various sicknesses, the apostle says, "For this reason, many among you are weak and sickly, and not a few sleep." In these words, hear him knitting a band and pleating it with different types of sin. In his analogy, the first group are "weak." However, others are "sickly," which is more serious than the "weak." Finally, others "sleep," in comparison to the first two. . . . Those who "sleep" are the ones who are not taking notice and watching with their souls, as they should be doing. Rather, they . . . are drowsy in their reflections. *Origen (c. 245, E), 9.430.*

That which is sanctified through the word of God and by prayer does not (by its own nature) sanctify the one who uses it. Otherwise, it would sanctify even him who eats unworthily of the bread of the Lord. In that case, no one on account of this food would become weak, sickly, or asleep. . . . Accordingly, in the case of the bread of the Lord, there is an advantage to him who uses it only when he partakes of the bread with undefiled mind and pure conscience. *Origen (c. 245, E), 9.443.*

Those presbyters, contrary to the Gospel law, . . . before penitence was fulfilled . . . dare to offer on their behalf and to give them the Eucharist. That is, they dare to profane the sacred body of the Lord. However, it is written, "Whoever eats the bread and drinks the cup of the Lord unworthily, will be guilty of the body and blood of the Lord." *Cyprian (c. 250, W), 5.291.*

What a crime is theirs who rashly seize communion and touch the body and blood of the Lord . . . even though their foulness is not washed away by the laver of the church. For it is written, "Whoever eats the bread or drinks the cup of the Lord unworthily will be guilty of the body and blood of the Lord." *Cyprian (c. 250, W), 5.395.*

SEE ALSO ASSEMBLIES, CHRISTIAN; LITURGY; VESSELS, EUCHARISTIC; VESTMENTS, RELIGIOUS; WORSHIP, CHRISTIAN (II. WORSHIP CUSTOMS).

EVANGELISM

And this gospel of the kingdom will be preached in all the world as a witness to all the nations, and then the end will come. Matt 24.14.

Go therefore and make disciples of all the nations. Matt 28:19.

The gospel which you heard . . . was preached to every creature under heaven. Col. 1:23.

From Jerusalem, twelve men went out into the world. These were uneducated and of no ability in speaking. But by the power of God, they proclaimed to every race of men that they were sent by Christ to teach the word of God to everyone. *Justin Martyr (c. 160, E), 1.175.*

"His blood I will require at your hand. But if you warn him, you will be innocent." For this reason, out of fear, we are very earnest in desiring to witness according to the Scriptures—but not from love of money, of glory, or of pleasure. *Justin Martyr (c. 160, E), 1.240.*

There is not one single race of men, whether barbarians, or Greeks, or whatever they may be called—whether nomads, vagrants, or herdsmen living in tents—among whom prayers and giving of thanks are not offered through the name of the crucified Jesus. *Justin Martyr (c. 160, E), 1.258.*

The church having received this preaching and this faith, although scattered throughout the whole world, yet, as if occupying but one house, carefully preserves it. . . . For the churches which have been planted in Germany do not believe or hand down anything different, nor do those in Spain, nor those in Gaul, nor those in the East, nor those in Egypt, nor those in Libya, nor those which have been established in the central regions of the world. But just as the sun, that creation of God, is one and the same throughout the whole world, so also the preaching of the truth shines everywhere, and enlightens all men who are willing to come to a knowledge of the truth. *Irenaeus (c. 180, E/W), 1.330, 331.*

After our Lord rose from the dead, the apostles were empowered from on high when the Holy Spirit came down [upon them]. They were completely filled and had perfect knowledge. They departed to the ends of the earth, preaching the glad tidings of the good things sent from God to us. *Irenaeus (c. 180, E/W), 1.414.*

To which course, many nations of those barbarians who believe in Christ do assent, having salvation written in their hearts by the Spirit. Without paper or ink, they carefully preserve the ancient tradition. . . . Those who have believed this faith without any written documents are barbarians as to language. But as to doctrine, manner, and tenor of life, they are, because of faith, very wise indeed. *Irenaeus (c. 180, E/W), 1.417.*

The word of our Teacher did not remain in Judea alone—as philosophy did in Greece. Rather, it was diffused over the whole world, over every nation, village, and town. *Clement of Alexandria (c. 195, E), 2.520.*

His disciples also, spreading over the world, did as their Divine Master commanded them. *Tertullian (c. 197, W), 3.35.*

We see that the voice of the apostles of Jesus has gone forth into all the earth, and their words to the end of the world. *Origen (c. 248, E), 4.424.*

[Celsus, the pagan critic] says, "If all men wished to become Christians, the latter would not desire such a result." Now, that this statement is false is clear from this: that Christians do not neglect (as far as in them lies) to take steps to disseminate their doctrine throughout the whole world. Accordingly, some of them have made it their business to travel not only through cities, but even to villages and rural houses in order to make converts to God. And no one would claim that they did this for the sake of gain. For sometimes they would not accept even necessary sustenance. Or, if at any time they were pressed by a necessity of this sort, they were content with the mere supplying of their needs. *Origen (c. 248, E), 4.468.*

We *do* desire to instruct all men in the word of God, so as to give to young men the exhortations that are appropriate to them. We desire to show to slaves how they may recover freedom of thought and be ennobled by the Word. And those among us who are the ambassadors of Christianity sufficiently declare that they are "debtors to Greeks and barbarians, to wise men and fools." *Origen (c. 248, E), 4.485.*

The Word of God declares that the preaching is not sufficient to reach the human heart (even though it may be true and worthy of belief), unless a certain power is imparted to the speaker from God. *Origen (c. 248, E), 4.573.*

There are some who are capable of receiving nothing more than an exhortation to believe. To these, that is all we address. However, we approach others, to the extent possible, in the way of demonstration by means of questions and answers. *Origen (c. 248, E), 4.577.*

SEE ALSO APOSTLES, TWELVE; CHRISTIANITY (II. GROWTH OF CHRISTIANITY); CONVERSION.

EVE

Then the rib which the Lord God had taken from man he made into a woman, and he brought her to the man. Gen. 2:22.

Adam was formed first, then Eve. And Adam was not deceived, but the woman being deceived, fell into transgression. 1 Tim. 2:13, 14.

God had formed Eve into a wife for him out of his rib. . . . He did this lest it would be supposed that one God made the man and another God made the woman. Therefore, He made them both. And God made the woman together with the man, not only so that thereby the mystery of God's sole government might be displayed, but also so that their mutual love might be greater. *Theophilus (c. 180, E), 2.105.*

This Eve, on account of her having been deceived in the beginning by the serpent, became the author of sin. *Theophilus (c. 180, E), 2.105.*

But Eve was disobedient. For she did not obey when as yet she was a virgin. Although she did, indeed, have a husband, Adam, she was nevertheless still a virgin. For in Paradise "they were both naked, and were not ashamed," inasmuch as they had been created a short time previously and had no understanding of the procreation of children. For it was necessary that they should first come to adult age, and then multiply from that time onward. Having become disobedient, she was made the cause of death, both to herself and to the entire human race. *Irenaeus (c. 180, E/W), 1.455.*

That deception was done away with, by which that virgin Eve (who was already espoused to a man) was unhappily misled. [Its overturning] was happily announced by means of the truth through the angel to the virgin Mary, who was [espoused] to a man. . . . And if Eve did disobey God, yet Mary was persuaded to be obedient to God. This was in order that the virgin Mary might become the advocate of the virgin Eve. And thus, as the human race fell into bondage to death by means of a virgin, so is it rescued by a virgin. *Irenaeus (c. 180, E/W), 1.547.*

She did not endure to have been met alone. Instead, in the presence of Adam, not yet her husband, not yet bound to lend her his ears, she was impatient to keep silent. So she made him the transmitter of that which she had imbibed from the Evil One. *Tertullian (c. 200, W), 3.710.*

For Adam was formed first, and the woman came far behind him, for Eve was formed later. Her flesh was for a long time without specific form. Yet, she was even then herself a living being—for I should regard her at that time in [Adam's] soul as even a portion of Adam. Besides, God's breath would have enlivened her as well, if there had not been in the woman a transmission from Adam of his soul also as well as of his flesh. *Tertullian (c. 210, W), 3.217.*

Furthermore, if Eve is intended by the apostle to refer to the church, it is not surprising that Cain, who was born of Eve, and everyone after him . . . should be types of the church. For, in a pre-eminent sense, they are all descended from the church. *Origen (c. 225, E), 4.371.*

SEE ALSO ADAM; FALL OF MAN; TREE OF KNOWLEDGE; TREE OF LIFE.

EVENING PRAYER

SEE MORNING AND EVENING PRAYER.

EVIL, PROBLEM OF

The Lord said to Satan, "Behold, he is in your hand, but spare his life." Then Satan went out from the presence of the Lord and struck Job with painful boils. Job 2:6, 7.

No temptation has overtaken you except such as is common to man; but God is faithful, who will not allow you to be tempted beyond what you are able. 1 Cor. 10:13.

My brethren, count it all joy when you fall into various trials, knowing that the testing of your faith produces patience. Jas. 1:2.

Let no one say when he is tempted, "I am tempted by God"; for God cannot be tempted by evil, nor does He himself tempt anyone. But each one is tempted when he is drawn away by his own desires and enticed. Jas. 1:14.

The Lord is not slack concerning His promise, as some count slackness, but is longsuffering toward us, not willing that any should perish but that all should come to repentance. 2 Pet. 3:9.

This, therefore, was the [object of the] longsuffering of God: that man may always live in a state of gratitude to the Lord. For, having passed through all types of trials, then acquiring the knowledge of moral discipline, then attaining to the resurrection from the dead and learning through experience who is the Source of his deliverance, and finally having obtained from Him the gift of incorruptibility, man might love Him the more. *Irenaeus (c. 180, E/W), 1.450.*

Those who flee from the eternal light of God (which contains all good things in itself) are their own cause of inhabiting eternal darkness, which is destitute of good things. *Irenaeus (c. 180, E/W), 1.523.*

Evil has sprung from voluntary apostasy. Yet, it is the greatest achievement of divine providence not to allow this evil to remain useless. . . . For it is the work of the divine wisdom . . . to ensure that whatever happens through the evils hatched by someone, a good and useful result will come of it. *Clement of Alexandria (c. 195, E), 2.320.*

Although disease, accident, and . . . death come upon the spiritual man, . . . by the power of God they become the medicine of salvation. Through discipline, they benefit those who are difficult to reform. They are allotted according to what is deserved by providence, which is truly good. *Clement of Alexandria (c. 195, E), 2.540.*

He deals with all sorts of men alike, so that all men together share His favors and reproofs. His will is that both the elect and the outcasts should have adversities and prosperities in common. In that way, we will all experience both His goodness and His severity. Having learned these things from His own lips, we love His goodness and fear His wrath. *Tertullian (c. 197, W), 3.48.*

While morbidly brooding over the question of the origin of evil, [Marcion's] perception became blunted by the very irregularity of his researches. . . . So he concluded from other arguments (which are satisfactory only to a perverted mind) that God is the author of evil. *Tertullian (c. 207, W), 3.272.*

These are the bones of contention, which you are perpetually gnawing: If God is good and foreknows the future, and is able to avert evil, why did He permit man, the very image and likeness of Himself, . . . to be deceived by the devil, and fall from obedience of the law into death? . . . In reply, we must first vindicate those attributes in the Creator that are called into question. . . . I find, then, that God constituted man to be free, master of his own will and power. *Tertullian (c. 207, W), 3.300, 301.*

The liberty of man will—after a second thought—show us that man's liberty alone can be charged with the fault that it committed itself. . . . Therefore, the necessary consequence was that God had to separate His foreknowledge and power from the liberty that He had once for all bestowed upon man. He did this even though He might have prevented man's falling into danger when attempting to enjoy his liberty wrongly. Yet, if God had intervened, He would have rescinded the liberty of man's will, which He had permitted for a specific purpose. *Tertullian (c. 207, W), 3.303.*

If man failed to make the most of the good gift he had received, he must see how that he was himself guilty in respect of the law that he did not choose to keep. *Tertullian (c. 207, W), 3.303.*

As, therefore, God designed for man a condition of life, so man brought on himself a state of death. And this was neither through infirmity nor through ignorance. *Tertullian (c. 207, W), 3.303.*

By allowing a permission for the operation of [Satan's] designs, God acted consistently with the purpose of His own goodness. He deferred the devil's destruction for the very same reason that He postponed the restitution of man. For He afforded room for a conflict, wherein man might crush his enemy with the same freedom of his will as had made him succumb to Satan. This proves that the fault was all his own, not God's. [And it enables man] to worthily recover his salvation by a victory. In this way, also, the devil receives a more bitter punishment, by being vanquished by him whom he had previously injured. By these means, God is discovered to be so much the more good. For He has waited for man to return from his present life to a more glorious Paradise, with a right to eat of the tree of life. *Tertullian (c. 207, W), 3.306.*

If it is His will that men should do the things they are commanded, why did He not create men in such a manner that they could not be able to do wrong? . . . God, in His goodness, chose not to make man [like the inanimate objects]. Rather, by his freedom, He exalted man above many of His creatures. *Bardesanes (c. 222, E), 8.723, 724.*

God also knows the secret things of the heart and foresees future events. In His long-suffering, He permits things to happen. And by means of those things that happen outside ourselves, He reveals the secret evil within a person in order to cleanse him. . . . For God governs souls not with reference . . . to the fifty years of the present life, but with reference to an unlimited age. *Origen (c. 225, E), 4.314.*

It might be maintained that if all things were made through the Logos, and evil is a part of all things, then the whole matter of sin—and everything that is wicked—were also made through the Logos. But we must regard this as false. . . . In respect that he is the devil, he is not the work of God. Yet, he who is the devil is a created being. Since there is no other Creator but our God, he is a work of God. It is as if we should say that a murderer is not a work of God. However, we would also say that as to his being a man, God made him. He received his existence as a *man* from God. However, we do not say that he received his existence as a *murderer* from God. *Origen (c. 228, E), 9.330, 331.*

A person should inquire instead why it was not possible for God . . . to create men who needed no improvement, but who were of themselves virtuous and perfect. Why is it not possible for evil to be completely non-existent? These questions may perplex ignorant and foolish individuals, but not someone who sees into the nature of things. For if you take away the spontaneity of virtue, you destroy its essence. *Origen (c. 248, E), 4.498.*

On the other hand, we maintain that evil, wickedness, and the actions that proceed from them were not created by God. For if God created that which is truly evil, how is it possible that the proclamation regarding the Judgment should be confidently announced? For it informs us that the wicked are to be punished for their evil deeds in proportion to the amount of their wickedness. At the same time, those who have lived a virtuous life, or performed virtuous actions, will have the enjoyment of blessedness and will receive rewards from God. I am well aware that those who would daringly assert that these evils were created by God will quote certain expressions of Scripture, for we are not able to show one consistent series of passages. For, although Scripture blames the wicked and approves of the righteous, it nevertheless contains some statements which—although comparatively few in number—seem to disturb the minds of ignorant readers of Holy Scripture. *Origen (c. 248, E), 4.598.*

[CELSUS, THE PAGAN CRITIC:] "All things are ordered according to God's will. His providence governs all things. Is not everything that happens in the universe regulated by the law of the Most High God—whether it is the work of God, angels, demons, or heroes?" . . . [ORIGEN'S REPLY:] We must inquire into the meaning of the statement, "all things are ordered according to God's will." We must determine if Celsus means that sins are included among the things that God orders. For if God's government extends to sins, . . . it follows that all sins and all their consequences are ordered by the will of God. And this is a different thing than saying that they come to pass with God's *permission.* . . . When we say that "the providence of God regulates all things," we utter a great truth if we attribute to that providence nothing but what is just and right. But if we attribute to the providence of God all things whatever—however unjust they may be—then it is no longer true that the providence of God regulates all things. . . . We cannot say that transgressors follow the law of God when they transgress. *Origen (c. 248, E), 4.638.*

Many men have expressed opinions on the origin of evil. Prior to you and me, no doubt, there have been many capable men who have made the most searching inquiry into the matter. *Methodius (c. 290, E), 6.358.*

Now, these [evil] things are produced by men. Men, therefore, are the authors of them and the causes of their existing or not existing. *Methodius (c. 290, E), 6.360.*

Man, after his creation, received a commandment from God. And from this, evil quickly arose. For man did not obey the divine command. And this alone is evil: disobedience, which had a beginning. *Methodius (c. 290, E), 6.362.*

God did not make evil. Nor is He at all in any way the Author of evil. But whoever failed to keep the law ... after being created by God with the faculty of free will ... is called evil. *Methodius (c. 290, E), 6.364.*

Death was appointed by God for the sinner, so that evil might not remain forever. *Methodius (c. 290, E), 6.370, as quoted by Photius.*

Someone will say, "Then why does God permit these [evil] things to be done? Why does He not apply a remedy to such disastrous errors?" [He permits them] so that evils may be contrasted with the good. So that vices may be contrasted with virtues. The result is that He will have some whom He will punish and others whom He will honor. For He has determined at the last times to pass judgment on the living and the dead.... So He delays this until the end of the times has come. *Lactantius (c. 304–313, W), 7.66, 67.*

God arranged that there would be this distinction between good and evil things so that we can know the value of the good from [observing] that which is evil. We can also recognize the meaning of evil from [observing] the good. The nature of either one cannot be fully comprehended if the other one is taken away. So in order that the nature of virtue could be evident, God did not banish evil. For how could patient endurance have any meaning and name if there were nothing that we were forced to endure? How could faith ... deserve praise, unless there were someone who wished to turn us away from God? For this reason, God permitted the unjust to be more powerful ... and to be more numerous, so that virtue might be precious on account of its rarity. *Lactantius (c. 304–313, W), 7.142.*

Reason itself and necessity require that both good and evil things should be set before man: good things that he can use, and evil things that he can guard against and avoid. *Lactantius (c. 304–313, W), 7.199.*

Someone may ask, "From where did sins extend to man? Or what perversion distorted the rule of the divine institution to worse things?" ... God permitted the evil for this reason: that the good might also shine forth. *Lactantius (c. 304–313, W), 7.272.*

For this reason God does not immediately punish everyone who is guilty: so that man may have the opportunity of correcting himself, coming to a right mind. *Lactantius (c. 304–313, W), 7.277.*

They will ask, "Why, then, does not the Almighty God take away these evils? Why does he allow them to exist and to go on without ceasing through all the ages?" ... We must answer that we do not know these things. *Arnobius (c. 305, E), 6.454; extended discussion: 6.356–363.*

SEE ALSO FALL OF MAN; FOREKNOWLEDGE OF GOD; FREE WILL AND PREDESTINATION; MAN, DOCTRINE OF; SOVEREIGNTY AND PROVIDENCE OF GOD; SATAN.

EVIL SPIRITS

SEE ANGELS (III. WICKED ANGELS); DEMONS; EXORCISM; SPIRITISM.

EVOLUTION

It is commonly believed that evolution is a relatively new theory introduced by Charles Darwin in the 1800s. As can be seen from the passages below, however, many of the basic tenets of evolution were taught thousands of years ago by the Greek philosophers Epicurus and Democritus.

The heavens declare the glory of God; and the firmament shows His handiwork. Ps. 19:1.

For since the creation of the world His invisible attributes are clearly seen, being understood by the things that are made. Rom. 1:20.

Every house is built by someone, but He who built all things is God. Heb. 3:4.

According to Epicurus, the atoms and the void are indestructible. Epicurus says that it was by a definite arrangement and adjustment of the atoms as they came together that all formations have been produced, including the body itself. *Justin Martyr (c. 160, E), 1.173.*

Man is not merely a rational animal, who happens to be capable of understanding and knowledge—as the croaking philosophers say. *Tatian (c. 160, E), 2.71.*

Any person who sees a ship on the sea rigged and in sail, and making for the harbor, will no doubt infer that there is a pilot in her who is steering her. Likewise, we must recognize that God is the Pilot of the whole universe, though He is not visible to the eyes of the flesh, since He is incomprehensible. *Theophilus (c. 180, E), 2.90.*

I cannot understand how so many distinguished men have been of the opinion that matter . . . was uncreated. That is, it was not formed by God Himself, who is the Creator of all things. Rather, they say that its nature and power were the result of chance, . . . thinking that so great a work as the universe could exist without an architect or overseer. *Origen (c. 225, E), 4.269.*

Celsus [a pagan critic] harbors a secret desire to discredit the Mosaic account of the Creation. It teaches that the world is not yet ten thousand years old, but, in fact, is very much under that. *Origen (c. 248, E), 4.404.*

Let Celsus then say distinctly that the great diversity among the products of the earth is not the work of providence, but that a certain fortuitous concurrence of atoms gave birth to qualities that are so diverse. Let him say that it was due to chance that so many kinds of plants, trees, and herbs resemble one another. Let him say that no governing Reason gave existence to them and that they do not derive their origin from an understanding that is beyond all admiration. In contrast, we Christians feel grateful for these things, for we are devoted to the worship of the only God, who created them. *Origen (c. 248, E), 4.531.*

It is false that [as Celsus claims] "in the beginning, men were captured and devoured by wild beasts, while wild beasts were very seldom caught by men." . . . God did not subject men to wild beasts, but gave wild beasts to be a prey to the understanding of man. . . . For it was not without the help of God that men acquired for themselves the means of protection against wild beasts and of securing the mastery over them. *Origen (c. 248, E), 4.533.*

[Celsus] does his utmost to reduce the human race to a still lower position and to bring them to the level of the irrational animals. *Origen (c. 248, E), 4.535.*

Celsus has also expressed his opinion that the narrative of the creation of man is "exceedingly silly." . . . He makes the statements about the days of creation as his grounds for accusation. . . . For some of them elapsed before the creation of light, heaven, sun, moon, and stars. And some of them elapsed after the creation of these things. I will only make this observation: Moses must then have forgotten that he had said a little before that "in six days the creation of the world had been finished"! And in consequence of this act of forgetfulness, he adds to these words the following: "This is the book of the creation of man, in the *day* when God made the heaven and the earth." However, it is not in the least bit believable that after what he had said concerning the six days, Moses would immediately have added, without a special meaning, the words, "in the *day* that God made the heavens and the earth." *Origen (c. 248, E), 4.596.*

What greater injury can befall a man than that he should be unable—amid the order of the world—to see Him who has made it? And what worse affliction can come to anyone than the blindness of mind that prevents him from seeing the Creator and Father of every soul? *Origen (c. 248, E), 4.653.*

For there are those who, giving the name of atoms to certain imperishable and most minute bodies that are supposed to be infinite in number, . . . allege that these atoms, as they were carried along by chance in the void, all clashed fortuitously against each other in an unregulated whirl. They thereby commingled with one another in a multitude of forms. Entering into combination with each other, they gradually formed this world and all objects in it. . . . This was the opinion of Epicurus and Democritus. . . . How will we bear with these men who assert that all those wise . . . constructions are only the works of common chance? . . . But truly these men do not reflect on the analogies even of small, familiar things that might come under their observation at any time. For, from such things, they could learn that no object that has any value—and that is fitted to be serviceable—is made without design. *Dionysius of Alexandria (c. 262, E), 6.85.*

When a house or a city is built, it does not take on its stones, as though some of them placed themselves spontaneously upon the foundations and other stones lifted themselves up to the various stories. Rather, the builder carefully places the skillfully prepared stones in their proper positions. In contrast, if the structure happens to give way, the stones are separated, cast down, and scattered about. *Dionysius of Alexandria (c. 262, E), 6.85.*

Who can bear to hear it said that this mighty habitation, which is composed of heaven and earth and is called the "cosmos," ... was established in all its order and beauty by those atoms that hold their course—devoid of order and beauty? Or, that this same state of disorder has grown into this true cosmos of order? *Dionysius of Alexandria (c. 262, E), 6.86.*

Truly we have here a most marvelous democracy of atoms, where friends welcome and embrace friends! Where all are eager to travel together in one domicile! By their own determination, some have rounded themselves off into that mighty luminary the sun! ... Even though men like these may choose not to admit it, there is a mighty Lord who made the sun. And, indeed, these are miserable men, regardless of how righteous they may believe themselves to be.... O you blind ones, do these atoms of yours bring you the winter season and the rains, in order that the earth may yield food for you? *Dionysius of Alexandria (c. 262, E), 6.87.*

How did that little seed of generation draw together the many atoms that were to constitute Epicurus? ... How did it frame and adapt the many members and parts? ... For of all these things, there is not one that is either idle or useless. Not even the smallest of them— such as the hair and the nails. They all have their function to perform.... Was Epicurus made, as they say, by the irrational multitude of atoms? No, the conjunction of atoms could not mold even an image of clay! ... And if even these representations and models cannot be made without the aid of wisdom, how can the genuine and original patterns of these copies have come into existence spontaneously? *Dionysius of Alexandria (c. 262, E), 6.88, 89.*

It is dangerous to wholly disdain the literal meaning ... particularly of Genesis, where the unchangeable decrees of God for the constitution of the universe are set forth. *Methodius (c. 290, E), 6.317.*

There is no one so uncivilized and of such an uncultivated disposition, who, when he raises his eyes to heaven ... does not understand from the very magnitude of the objects— from their motion, arrangement, constancy, usefulness, beauty, and temperament—that

there is some providence and that the things that exist with such wonderful arrangement must have been created by some greater Intelligence. *Lactantius (c. 304–313, W), 7.11.*

It is more believable that matter was made by God (because He is All-Powerful) than to believe that the world was *not* made by God. For nothing can be made without mind, intelligence, and design. *Lactantius (c. 304–313, W), 7.55.*

If you had been brought up in a well-built and nicely furnished house, but had never seen a workshop, would you have supposed that your house was not built by some man, just because you did not know *how* it was built? *Lactantius (c. 304–313, W), 7.56.*

I cannot omit here that some erring philosophers say that men and the other animals arose from the earth without any Maker. *Lactantius (c. 304–313, W), 7.59.*

If nothing can be done or produced without design, it is plain that there is a divine providence, to which that which is called "design" peculiarly belongs. *Lactantius (c. 304–313, W), 7.61.*

If there is no providence, how is it that the bodies of animals are arranged with such foresight? How is it that the various members are designed in a wonderful manner and each serve their own functions individually? ... If there is no providence, why do rains fall, fruits spring up, and trees put forth leaves? *Lactantius (c. 304–313, W), 7.87.*

If we all derive our origin from one man whom God created, we are clearly of one blood. *Lactantius (c. 304–313, W), 7.172, 173.*

Some [unbelievers] say that the first men spent a nomadic life among the woods and plains. Men were not united by any mutual bond of speech or justice. They had leaves and grass for their beds, and they used caves and grottos for their dwellings. Furthermore, they were prey to the beasts and stronger animals. Later, those who had either escaped (having been torn by beasts) ... had recourse to other men. They begged protection from them. At first, they made their wishes known by nods. Then they tried the beginnings of conversation. By attaching names to each object, they, little by little, completed the system of language. However, when they saw that numbers alone were not sufficient protection from the beasts, they began to build towns. . . . O minds unworthy of men, which produced these foolish trifles! . . . These things are by no means true. Men were not born from the ground around the world, as though sprung from the teeth of some dragon, as the poets relate. Rather, one man was formed by God. And from that one man all the earth was filled with the human race. . . . There were never men on the earth who could not speak (except for those who are infants). *Lactantius (c. 304–313, W), 7.173.*

God completed the world and this admirable work of nature in the space of six days, as is contained in the secrets of Holy Scripture. *Lactantius (c. 304–313, W), 7.211.*

Epicurus said that . . . the world itself was not ordered by any plan, art, or workmanship. Instead, he said that the universe was made up of certain minute and indivisible seeds. *Lactantius (c. 304–313, W), 7.264.*

Those who do not admit that the world was made by divine providence, either say that it is composed of atoms coming together at random, or that it suddenly came into existence naturally. *Lactantius (c. 314, W), 7.265.*

I cannot be prevented here from again showing the folly of Epicurus. For all the ravings of Lucretius belong to him. He is accustomed to say that animals are not produced by any design of the Divine Mind, but by chance. And in order that he can show this, he says that in the beginning of the world, innumerable other animals of wonderful form and magnitude were produced. However, he says that they were unable to be permanent, because either the power of taking food, or the method of uniting and procreating, had failed them. *Lactantius (c. 314, W), 7.287.*

Epicurus saw in the bodies of animals the skill of a divine plan. However, that he might carry into effect that which he had imprudently assumed before, he added another absurdity to agree with the former. He said that the eyes were not produced for seeing, nor the ears for hearing, nor the feet for walking. Instead, these members were produced before there were the functions of seeing, hearing, and walking. So all the uses of these members developed after they had already come into being. . . . It is evident that he who has lost the main point itself of the truth must always be in error. For if all things

are produced by a fortuitous meeting together of atoms, rather than by Providence, why does it never happen by chance that those first principles meet together in such a way as to make an animal of such a kind that it might rather hear with its nostrils, smell with its eyes, or see with its ears? *Lactantius (c. 314, W), 7.287.*

Does it not occur to you to reflect and to examine in whose domain you live? On whose property you are? Whose is that earth that you cultivate? Whose is that air that you inhale and return again in breathing? Whose fountains do you abundantly enjoy? Whose water? . . . O greatest, O Supreme Creator of things invisible, . . . you are truly worthy—if only mortal tongue may speak of you. All breathing and intelligent nature should never cease to feel and to return thanks. *Arnobius (c. 305, E), 6.421.*

Of those who have given themselves to philosophizing, we have heard that some deny the existence of any divine power. Others ask daily whether there is [a God] or not. Still others would construct the entire fabric of the universe by chance accidents and by random collision [of atoms]. They fashion it by the flowing together of atoms of different shapes. *Arnobius (c. 305, E), 6.421; extended discussion: 6.84–6.89, 7.87–7.88.*

SEE ALSO CREATION; EPICURUS.

EXCOMMUNICATION
SEE DISCIPLINE, CHURCH.

EXOMOLOGESIS
SEE DISCIPLINE, CHURCH (II. PENITENTIAL DISCIPLINE).

EXORCISM
Many will say to Me in that day, "Lord, Lord, have we not . . . cast out demons in Your name." . . . And then I will declare to them, "I never knew you; depart from Me, you who practice lawlessness!" Matt. 7:22.

He was casting out a demon, and it was mute. . . . If I cast out demons with the finger of God, surely the kingdom of God has come upon you. Luke 11:19, 20.

God worked unusual miracles by the hands of Paul, so that even handkerchiefs or aprons were brought from his body to the sick, and the diseases left them and the evil spirits went out of them. Then some of the itinerant Jewish exorcists took it upon themselves to call the name of the Lord Jesus over those who had evil spirits, saying, "We adjure you by the Jesus whom Paul preaches." Acts 19:11–13.

Resist the devil and he will flee from you. Jas. 4:7.

Throughout the whole world, and in your city, many of our Christian men have healed numerous demon-possessed persons, exorcising them in the name of Jesus Christ. *Justin Martyr (c. 160, E), 1.190.*

We call Him Helper and Redeemer. Even the demons fear the power of His name. At this day, when they are exorcised in the name of Jesus, . . . they are defeated. *Justin Martyr (c. 160, E), 1.209.*

He said, "I give unto you power to tread on serpents and on scorpions." . . . And now we have all the demons and evil spirits subjected to us, when we exorcise them. *Justin Martyr (c. 160, E), 1.236.*

Every demon, when exorcised in the name of this very Son of God . . . is overcome and subdued. *Justin Martyr (c. 160, E), 1.241.*

Even to this day, the demon-possessed are sometimes exorcised in the name of the living and true God. *Theophilus (c. 180, E), 2.97.*

[ADDRESSED TO PAGANS:] Let a person be brought before your tribunals who is plainly under demon possession. The wicked spirit, ordered to speak by a follower of Christ, will as readily make the truthful confession that he is a demon, as elsewhere he has falsely asserted that he is a god. *Tertullian (c. 197, W), 3.37.*

[ADDRESSED TO PAGANS:] Why, all the authority and power we have over them is from our naming the name of Christ and reminding them of the woes with which God threatens them at the hands of Christ as Judge. For they realize that one day these woes will overtake them. Fearing Christ in God, and God in Christ, they become subject to the servants of God and Christ. So, overwhelmed by the thought and realization of those judgment fires, at our touch, our breath, and our command, they leave the bodies they have entered— unwilling and distressed. For before your very eyes, they are put to an open shame. You believe them when they lie. So why not give credit to them when they speak the truth about themselves? . . . [When exorcised by Christians,] these beings admit that they are not

gods. And they confess to you that there is no God, except one—the God whom we worship. *Tertullian (c. 197, W), 3.38.*

The Lord Himself is witness that we have the case of the woman who went to the theater and came back possessed. Accordingly, in the exorcism, when the unclean creature was rebuked for having dared to attack a believer, he firmly replied, "And in truth I did it most lawfully, for I found her in my domain." *Tertullian (c. 197, W), 3.90.*

We say that there are demons—as though, in the simple fact that we alone expel them from the bodies of men, we did not also prove their existence. *Tertullian (c. 197, W), 3.176.*

We daily hold them up to contempt. We exorcise them from their victims, as multitudes can testify. *Tertullian (c. 212, W), 3.106.*

How many men of rank have been delivered from devils and healed of diseases! *Tertullian (c. 212, W), 3.107.*

The demons themselves confess concerning themselves as often as they are driven by us from bodies by the torments of our words and by the fires of our prayers. . . . Since they themselves are witnesses to the fact that they are demons, believe them when they confess the truth about themselves. For when renounced by the only and true God, the wretched beings unwillingly shudder in their bodies and either at once leap forth—or else vanish by degrees. *Mark Minucius Felix (c. 200, W), 4.190.*

Celsus [a pagan] asserts that it is by the names of certain demons and by the use of incantations that Christians appear to be possessed of power. . . . But it is not by incantations that Christians seem to prevail, but by the name of Jesus, accompanied by the pronouncement of the narratives that relate to him. For the repetition of these has frequently been the means of driving demons out of men, especially when those who repeated them did so in a sound and genuinely believing spirit. Indeed, the name of Jesus possesses such power over evil spirits that there have been instances where it was effective even when it was pronounced by bad men. Jesus Himself foretold this when He said, "Many will say to Me in that day, did we not cast our devils in your name?" *Origen (c. 248, E), 4.398, 399.*

A similar philosophy of names applies also to our Jesus. His name has already been seen in an unmistakable manner to have expelled myriads of evil spirits from souls and bodies. This demonstrates how great the power was that was exerted upon those from whom the spirits were driven out. *Origen (c. 248, E), 4.406.*

What spirit must it be that fills her mind and clouds her judgment with darkness? Must it not be one of the same order with those demons that many Christians cast out of persons possessed with them? And this, we may observe, they do without the use of any incantations or curious arts of magic. Rather, they use only prayer and simple adjurations that the plainest person can use. In fact, for the most part, it is unlettered persons who perform this work. *Origen (c. 248, E), 4.612.*

This is also done in the present day. For the devil is scourged, burned, and tortured by exorcists—by the human voice and by divine power. Although he often promises that he is going out and will leave the [unbaptized] men of God, yet he lies in what he says. He repeats the same thing that was done before by Pharaoh, with the same obstinate and fraudulent deceit. However, when they come to the water of salvation, . . . we can know and trust that there the devil is beaten down and the man who is dedicated to God is set free by the divine mercy. *Cyprian (c. 250, W), 5.402.*

Oh, if you could only hear and see them when they are adjured by us. For they are tortured with spiritual scourges and are cast out from the possessed bodies with tortures of words. Howling and groaning at the voice of man and the power of God, they feel the stripes and blows and confess the judgment to come. Come and acknowledge that what we say is true. And since you say that you worship these ones as gods, believe even those whom you worship! *Cyprian (c. 250, W), 5.462.*

Now His followers banish the same polluted spirits from men, in the name of their Master, and by the sign of His passion [i.e., the sign of the cross]. *Lactantius (c. 304–313, W), 7.129.*

The same demons, when adjured by the name of the true God, immediately flee. *Lactantius (c. 304–313, W), 7.130.*

As long as there is peace among the people of God, these spirits flee from the righteous and fear them. And when they seize the bodies of men and harass their souls, they are adjured by [Christians] and are put to flight at the name of the true God. *Lactantius (c. 304–313, W), 7.159.*

An exorcist is not ordained. For it is a work of voluntary goodness, a work of the grace of God through Christ, by the inspiration of the Holy Spirit. *Apostolic Constitutions (compiled c. 390, E), 7.493.*

SEE ALSO DEMONS, DEMON POSSESSION; SPIRITISM.

FAITH

The righteousness of God is revealed from faith to faith; as it is written, "The just will live by faith." Rom. 1:17.

If you have faith as a mustard seed, you will say to this mountain, "Move from here to there," and it will move; and nothing will be impossible for you. Matt. 17:20.

Faith is the substance of things hoped for, the evidence of things not seen. Heb. 11:1.

Faith is a voluntary anticipation, the assent of piety. However, the Greeks disparage faith, considering it futile and barbarous. *Clement of Alexandria (c. 195, E), 2.349.*

Faith is something superior to knowledge and is its criterion. Conjecture, which is only a feeble supposition, is a counterfeit faith. *Clement of Alexandria (c. 195, E), 2.350.*

Now he is faithful who keeps inviolably what is entrusted to him. And we are entrusted with the utterances concerning God and the divine words, the commandments. *Clement of Alexandria (c. 195, E), 2.353.*

We have discovered faith to be the first movement towards salvation. After faith, fear, hope, and repentance (accompanied by temperance and patience) lead us to love and knowledge. *Clement of Alexandria (c. 195, E), 2.354.*

"If you have faith as a grain of mustard, you will remove the mountain." And again, "According to your faith, let it be to you." And one is cured, receiving healing by faith. And a dead person is raised up because of the power of one believing that he would be raised. *Clement of Alexandria (c. 195, E), 2.358*

Faith is power for salvation and strength to eternal life. *Clement of Alexandria (c. 195, E), 2.360.*

We say, then, that faith must not be inert and alone. Rather, it should be accompanied with investigation. For I do not say that we are not to inquire at all. *Clement of Alexandria (c. 195, E), 2.446.*

Trusting is more than faith. For when one has believed that the Son of God is our Teacher, he trusts that His teaching is true. *Clement of Alexandria (c. 195, E), 2.464.*

Faith, so to speak, is a comprehensive knowledge of the essentials. And knowledge is the strong and sure demonstration of what is received by faith. It is built upon faith by the Lord's teaching. *Clement of Alexandria (c. 195, E), 2.539.*

In my opinion, the faith they possessed was firm, for it was followed by works of faith. *Clement of Alexandria (c. 195, E), 2.541.*

"If you have faith as a grain of mustard seed, you will say to this mountain . . ." The mountains here spoken of are, in my opinion, the hostile powers that have their being in a flood of great wickedness. . . . Whenever, then, anyone has all faith so that he no longer disbelieves in any things that are contained in the Holy Scriptures, . . . he has all faith as a grain of mustard seed. *Origen (c. 245, E), 9.479.*

The following passage was written in response to Celsus, a pagan critic, who ridiculed unlearned persons who came to believe in Christ because of a genuine, but simple, faith.

Let us ask the following question with respect to the great multitude of believers, who have washed away the mire of wickedness in which they formerly wallowed. Was it better for them to believe without a reason and so to have become reformed and improved in their habits? . . . Or, would it have been better not to have allowed themselves to be converted on the strength of faith alone, but [to have waited] until they could give themselves to a thorough examination of the reasons? *Origen (c. 248, E), 4.400.*

Who enters on a voyage, contracts a marriage, becomes the father of children, or sows seed into the ground—without believing that better things will result from doing so? . . . If the hope and belief of a better future is the support of life in every uncertain enterprise, . . . why should not this faith rather be rationally accepted by him who believes on better grounds . . . in the existence of a God who was the Creator of all these things? *Origen (c. 248, E), 4.401.*

[WRITTEN TO CHRISTIANS FACING MARTYR-DOM:] It is written that the just live by faith. If you are just and live by faith—if you truly believe in Christ—why do you not embrace the assurance that you are called to Christ? Why do you not rejoice that you are freed from the devil? For you are about to be with Christ and are secure of the Lord's promise. *Cyprian (c. 250, W), 5.470.*

SEE ALSO APOSTOLIC FAITH; LOVE; SALVATION (II. ROLE OF GRACE AND FAITH IN SALVATION).

FALL OF MAN

Through one man sin entered the world, and death through sin, and thus death spread to all men, because all sinned. Rom. 5:12.

Our old man was crucified with Him, that the body of sin might be done away with, that we should no longer be slaves of sin. Rom. 6:6.

I know that in me (that is, in my flesh) nothing good dwells. Rom. 7:18.

The human race . . . from Adam had fallen under the power of death and the guile of the serpent. Each one had committed personal transgression. *Justin Martyr (c. 160, E), 1.243.*

The whole human race will be found to be under a curse. For it is written in the Law of Moses, "Cursed is everyone who does not continue in all things that are written in the book of the Law to do them." And no one has accurately done them all. *Justin Martyr (c. 160, E), 1.247.*

As Satan had deceived Adam, so he hoped that he could contrive some mischief against Christ also. *Justin Martyr (c. 160, E), 1.251.*

God ordained that, if man kept this, he would partake of immortal existence. However, if he transgressed it, his lot would be just the opposite. Having been made in this manner, man soon went towards transgression. And so he naturally became subject to corruption. Therefore, corruption became inherent in nature. So it was necessary that He who wished to save us would be someone who destroyed the essential cause of corruption. . . . For if, as you suggest, He had simply warded off death from us by a simple nod, indeed death would not have approached us—on account of His will. However, we would have again become corruptible, for we carried about in ourselves that natural corruption. *Justin Martyr (c. 160, E), 1.301, as quoted by Leontius.*

Because of his disobedience, man extracted, as from a fountain, labor, pain, and grief. At last, he fell prey to death. God showed great kindness to man in this, for He did not allow him to remain in sin forever. Instead, by a kind of banishment, as it were, He cast man out of Paradise. God did this so that man could expiate his sin through punishment, within an appointed time. Having been disciplined, man could afterwards be restored. *Theophilus (c. 180, E), 2.104.*

But man received, as the punishment for his transgression, the toilsome task of tilling the earth, to eat bread in the sweat of his face, and to return to the dust from where he was taken. Similarly also did the woman receive toil, labor, groans, the pangs of childbirth, and a state of subjection. That is, she would serve her husband. All of this was so that they would neither perish altogether (as would have happened if they had been cursed by God), nor, by remaining unreprimanded, would they be led to despise God. *Irenaeus (c. 180, E/W), 1.456.*

By means of our first parents, we were all brought into bondage by being made subject to death. *Irenaeus (c. 180, E/W), 1.493.*

That God was true, and the serpent a liar, was proved by the result. For death came upon those who had eaten. Along with the fruit, they fell under the power of death, because they ate in disobedience. And disobedience to God entails death. For that reason, they came under the penalty of death. From that [moment], they were handed over to it. Thus, then, in the day that they ate, in the same day they died. For they became death's debtors. And it was one day of the creation. *Irenaeus (c. 180, E/W), 1.551.*

Although the body is dissolved at the appointed time, because of that original disobedience, it is placed, as it were, in the crucible of the earth, to be re-cast again. When it is re-cast, it will not be as this corruptible [body]. Rather, it will be pure, and no longer subject to decay. To each body, its own soul will be restored. *Irenaeus (c. 180, E/W), 1.570.*

It is evident that no one during this period of life has been able to comprehend God clearly. But "the pure in heart will see God," when they arrive at the final perfection. Now, since the soul became too enfeebled to apprehend realities, we needed a divine Teacher. *Clement of Alexandria (c. 195, E), 2.446.*

He says, "Woe unto them! For they have gone in the way of Cain." For so also we lie under Adam's sin because of similarity of sin. *Clement of Alexandria (c. 195, E), 2.573.*

In the beginning, the corrupting and God-opposing angel overthrew the virtue of man— the work and image of God, the possessor of the earth. So Satan has entirely changed man's nature into his own state of wicked enmity against his Maker. For it was created, like his own, for perfect sinlessness. . . . [Satan did this so] he could make man guilty in God's eyes and set up his own supremacy. *Tertullian (c. 197, W), 3.80.*

You have Satan constantly upon your lips. Yet, he is the very one we hold to be the angel of evil, the source of error, the corrupter of the whole world. Because of him, in the beginning man was trapped into breaking the commandment of God. And the entire human race went over to death on account of his sin. For they were tainted in their descent from him. They were made a channel for transmitting his condemnation. *Tertullian (c. 197, W), 3.177.*

Fallen as the soul is, it is the victim of the great adversary's machinations. Yet, it does not forget its Creator. *Tertullian (c. 197, W), 3.178.*

When once he succumbed to impatience, man entirely ceased to be of sweet savor to God. He completely ceased to be able to endure heavenly things. Thereafter, he became a creature given to earth and ejected from the sight of God. He began to be easily turned by impatience into every use that was offensive to God. *Tertullian (c. 200, W), 3.710.*

So many and so great sins of human temerity have been committed. They were begun by the first of the race, Adam, after the condemnation of man. This became the dowry of the world, after man's ejection from Paradise and his subjection to death. However, after that, when God had hurried back to His own mercy, He did from that time onward inaugurate "repentance" in His own self. He [did this] by rescinding the sentence of His first wrath, granting pardon to His own work and image. *Tertullian (c. 203, W), 3.657.*

Man was condemned to death for tasting the fruit of one poor tree. From that, there proceeded sins with their penalties. And now all are perishing, even though they have never seen a single sod of Paradise. *Tertullian (c. 207, W), 3.287.*

Since God placed on man a condition for life, so man brought on himself a state of death. And this was neither through infirmity nor through ignorance. *Tertullian (c. 207, W), 3.303.*

Woman was at once condemned to bring forth in sorrow, and to serve her husband. Previously, she had heard the increase of her race proclaimed with the blessing, "Increase and multiply," without pain. Previously, she had been designed to a be a helper, not a slave, to her male partner. Immediately, the earth was also cursed, even though it had previously been blessed. . . . Immediately arose sweat and labor for bread. Previously, every tree yielded spontaneous food. . . . Thus God's prior goodness was from nature. His subsequent severity was from a cause. The one was innate; the other, caused by external factors. The one was His own; the other was admitted by Him. *Tertullian (c. 207, W), 3.306.*

Yet, when evil afterwards broke out—and the goodness of God began now to have an adversary to contend with, God's justice also acquired another function: that of directing His goodness according to men's supplication for it. The result is that the divine goodness . . . is now dispensed according to the deserts of every man. It is offered to the worthy; denied to the unworthy. *Tertullian (c. 207, W), 3.307.*

Accordingly, He did not actually curse Adam and Eve, for they were candidates for restoration. Furthermore, they had been relieved by confession. *Tertullian (c. 207, W), 3.317.*

The irrational element [in man], however, we must understand to have accrued later. It proceeded from the instigation of the serpent—the very fruit of transgression. From then on, it became inherent in the soul, and it grew with the soul's growth. *Tertullian (c. 210, W), 3.194.*

The attributes that belong to its own proper condition are namely immortality, rationality, sensibility, intelligence, and freedom of the will. All of these endowments of the soul are bestowed on the soul at birth. Yet, they are obscured and corrupted by the malignant being who, in the beginning, regarded them with envious eye. As a result, they are never seen in their spontaneous action, nor are they used as they should be. *Tertullian (c. 210, W), 3.219.*

Every soul, then, by reason of its birth, has its nature in Adam until it is born again in Christ. Moreover, it is unclean all the time that it remains without this regeneration. And because it is unclean, it is actively sinful. *Tertullian (c. 210, W), 3.220.*

It was necessary that Christ would come forth for the salvation of man in that same condition of flesh into which man had entered ever since his condemnation. *Tertullian (c. 210, W), 3.536.*

The transgression that caused man's ruin was committed just as much by the instigation of the soul in lusting as it was by the action of the flesh in actual doing. Therefore, it has marked the entire man [i.e., body and soul] with the sentence of transgression. It has therefore rendered him deservedly amenable to ruin. *Tertullian (c. 210, W), 3.569.*

Now the fall took place in Paradise, for Adam fell there. *Hippolytus (c. 200, W), 5.218.*

Still, God indulgently tempered his punishment by cursing—not so much [Adam] himself—but his labors upon earth. *Novatian (c. 235, W), 5.612.*

The only food for the first men was fruit and the other produce of the trees. But afterwards, man's sin transferred his need from the fruit trees to the produce of the earth. . . . And since now it was no more a Paradise to be tended, but a whole world to be cultivated, the more robust food of meat was offered to men. *Novatian (c. 235, W), 5.646.*

The animals were not condemned by their Creator because of man's guilt. In fact, men can be instructed by the animals to return to the unspotted nature of their own creation. *Novatian (c. 235, W), 5.647.*

Adam was the first man who fell. . . . And he conferred on us also what he did, whether of good or of evil. For he was the chief of all who were born from him. As a result, we die through his means. For he, receding from the divine, became an outcast from the Word. *Commodianus (c. 240, W), 4.209.*

In baptism, the coarse garment of your birth is washed. *Commodianus (c. 240, W), 4.212.*

In the beginning of the world and of the human race, Adam . . . received God's judgment. . . . We are all tied and bound with the chain of this sentence until we depart from this life. At that time, death is expunged. We must spend the days of our lives in sorrow and groaning. It is necessary that we eat our bread with sweat and labor. *Cyprian (c. 250, W), 5.487.*

"Then I went down to the potter's house. And, look, he wrought a work on the wheels. But the vessel that he made of clay was marred in the hand of the potter. So he made it again into another vessel, as seemed good to the potter to make it" [Jer. 18:3, 4]. Now, Adam was formed out of clay. However sin ruined him while he was still soft and moist, for sin flowed and dropped down upon him like water on soft clay. Adam was not yet like a tile, which is hard and incorruptible. Therefore, God, moistened him afresh and formed anew the same clay to His honor. He first hardened it and fixed it in the virgin's womb, uniting and mixing it with the Word. He then brought it forth into life no longer soft and broken. *Methodius (c. 290, E), 6.318.*

In no other way was it possible for sin and condemnation to be destroyed except by creating anew that same man on whose account it had been said, "Dust you are and to dust you will return." Only in this way could the sentence be undone that had gone forth on everyone because of [Adam]. So that "as in Adam" at first "all die," so likewise "in Christ," who assumed the [nature and position of] Adam, should "all be made alive." *Methodius (c. 290, E), 6.319.*

"For I know that in me—that is, in my flesh— no good thing dwells." And this is rightly said. For remember how it has been already shown that from the time when man went astray and disobeyed the law, from then on sin dwelled in him. It received its birth from his disobedience. As a result, a commotion was stirred up. We were filled with agitations and foreign imaginations. We were emptied of the divine inspiration and filled with carnal desires, which the cunning serpent infused into us. For that reason, God invented death for our sakes—that he might destroy sin. Otherwise, if we were immortal and sin rose up in us, sin would be immortal as well. *Methodius (c. 290, E), 6.372, as quoted by Photius.*

Thus the life of man became limited in duration. Nevertheless, his life span was still long, for it was extended to a thousand years. . . . However, when the earth was dry [after the Flood], . . . God gradually diminished the age of man by each successive generation, so that the length of man's life would not again be a cause of evils. And he placed a limit [on man's life] at a hundred and twenty years, which we are not permitted to exceed. *Lactantius (c. 304–313, W), 7.63.*

When man afterwards by his fall had inclined to death, it was necessary that his form would be recreated anew to salvation. *Alexander of Alexandria (c. 324, E), 6.300.*

Man went forth from Paradise to a region that was the dregs of unrighteousness, fornication, adultery, and cruel murder. And there he found his destruction. For all things conspired towards his death. They all worked toward the ruin of him who had barely entered there. *Alexander of Alexandria (c. 324, E), 6.300; see also 2.102, 103.*

SEE ALSO ADAM; ATONEMENT; DEATH; EVE; EVIL, PROBLEM OF; FLESH; FREE WILL AND PREDESTINATION; MAN, DOCTRINE OF; SALVATION; TREE OF KNOWLEDGE.

FALLEN ANGELS

SEE ANGEL, ANGELS (III. FALLEN ANGELS).

FASTING

Is this not the fast that I have chosen; to loose the bonds of wickedness, to undo the heavy burdens, to let the oppressed go free, and that you break every yoke? Is it not to share your bread with the hungry? Isa. 58:6, 7.

When you fast, anoint your head and wash your face, so that you do not appear to men to be fasting, but to your Father who is in the secret place; and your Father who sees in secret will reward you openly. Matt. 6:17.

This kind can come out by nothing but prayer and fasting. Mark 9:29.

But before the baptism, let the baptizer fast, and the baptismal candidate, and whoever else can. But you will order the baptismal candidate to fast one or two days before [the baptism]. But do not let your fasts be with the hypocrites; for they fast on the second and fifth day of the week. But you should fast on the fourth day [Wednesday] and the Preparation [Friday]. *Didache (c. 80–140, E), 1.379.*

Every prayer should be accompanied with humility. Fast, therefore, and you will obtain from the Lord what you plead for. *Hermas (c. 150, W), 2.16.*

He says, "You do not know how to fast unto the Lord; this useless fasting which you observe to Him is of no value." . . . "I say to you," he continued, "that the fasting which you think you observe is not a fasting. But I will teach you what is a full and acceptable fast to the Lord: . . . Do no evil in your life, and serve the Lord with a pure heart. Keep His commandments, walking in His precepts, and let no evil desire arise in your heart. . . . If you guard against these things, your fasting will be perfect." . . . Having fulfilled what is written, in the day on which you fast, you will taste nothing but bread and water. Then, reckon up the price of the meals of that day that you intended to have eaten, and give that amount to a widow, an orphan, or some person in need. *Hermas (c. 150, W), 2.33, 34.*

What is a fast, then? "Look, this is the fast that I have chosen, says the Lord. Loose every band of wickedness." *Clement of Alexandria (c. 195, E), 2.293.*

"Fasting with prayer is a good thing." Now fasting signifies abstinence from all evils whatsoever: in action, word, and even in thought. *Clement of Alexandria (c. 195, E), 2.503.*

He knows also the enigmas of the fasting of those days—I mean the Fourth [Wednesday] and the Preparation [Friday]. . . . He fasts, then, according to the law, abstaining from bad deeds. *Clement of Alexandria (c. 195, E), 2.544.*

At the time of some religious observance [i.e., fasting], our prayer ascends with more acceptability. *Tertullian (c. 198, W), 3.686.*

On the day of the Passover, when the religious observance of a fast is general (and as it were public), we justly forego the kiss [of peace], not worrying about concealing a fast that we keep in common with all.... Concerning the days of stations [i.e., special fast days], most think that they must not be present at the sacrificial prayers, on the grounds that the station would be dissolved by reception of the Lord's body. Does the Eucharist, then, cancel a service devoted to God? Or, rather, does it bind it more to God? Will not your station be more solemn if you have stood at God's altar? *Tertullian (c. 198, W), 3.687.*

At fasts, moreover, and stations, no prayer should be made without kneeling and the other customary marks of humility. For we are not only *praying,* but pleading and making satisfaction to God our Lord. *Tertullian (c. 198, W), 3.689.*

In the first place, fasting is the affliction of the flesh. It makes an offering to the Lord of mourning garments and scantiness of food, content with a simple diet and the pure drink of water. It is a victim able to appease the Lord by means of the sacrifice of humiliation.... This bodily patience adds grace to our prayers for good, a strength to our prayers against evil. *Tertullian (c. 200, W), 3.715.*

We consider fasting or kneeling in worship on the Lord's Day to be unlawful. We rejoice in the same privilege also from Easter to Pentecost. *Tertullian (c. 211, W), 3.94.*

When, indeed, have droughts not been put away by our kneelings and our fastings? *Tertullian (c. 212, W), 3.107.*

The next six passages were written by Tertullian after he had adopted the Montanist practices. The Montanists made various fasts obligatory, and they usually continued their fasts past the ninth hour (3:00 p.m.)—in contrast to the church. These passages reveal much about the church's practice of fasting.

[The majority of Christians think] that fasting is to be indifferently observed. They say it is part of the new discipline of choice—not command. They say it should be observed according to the times and needs of each individual.

Furthermore, they say that this had been the observance of the apostles, imposing no other yoke of definite fasts to be observed by all Christians in general—nor similarly of the stations—which have, besides, days of their own.... They say that the stations do not extend beyond the last hour of the day, since even prayers were generally concluded at the ninth hour, according to Peter's example, which is recorded in Acts. *Tertullian (c. 213, W), 4.103.*

[The church] hurls in our teeth the fact that Isaiah also has authoritatively declared, "Not such a fast has the Lord elected"—that is, not abstinence from food, but the works of righteousness. *Tertullian (c. 213, W), 4.103.*

[The majority say] that this duty of the stations also should be observed by free choice and that it should not continue beyond the ninth hour. All of this comes, of course, from their own practice.... If this is from the fact that we read that Peter and he who was with him entered the temple "at the ninth [hour], the hour of prayer," who will prove to me that they had that day been performing a station, so as to interpret the ninth hour as the hour for the conclusion and discharge of the station? *Tertullian (c. 213, W), 4.108.*

It is not that we [Montanists] slight the ninth hour. For, on the fourth and sixth days of the week, we most highly honor them. *Tertullian (c. 213, W), 4.109.*

It is a customary practice for the bishops to issue mandates for fasts to the universal commonalty of the church. I do not mean fasts for the special purpose of collecting contributions of alms, as your beggarly fashion has it. Rather, I am referring to fasts sometimes enacted because of some particular cause of ecclesiastical concern. *Tertullian (c. 213, W), 4.111.*

If the apostle has erased all devotion absolutely of "seasons, days, months, and years," why do we ... devote to stations the fourth and sixth days of the week, and to fasts the Preparation day? Anyhow, you sometimes continue your station even over the Sabbath—a day never to be kept as a fast except at the Easter season. *Tertullian (c. 213, W), 4.112.*

We fast even to the ninth hour, or even to the evening. There may even be a passing over to the next day. *Victorinus (c. 280, W), 7.341.*

On this day also, because of the passion of the Lord Jesus Christ, we make either a station to God, or a fast. . . . On the former day we are accustomed to fast rigorously, so that on the Lord's Day we may go forth to our bread with thanksgiving. And let this become a rigorous fast, lest we would appear to observe any Sabbath with the Jews. *Victorinus (c. 280, W), 7.341.*

No one will find fault with us for observing the fourth day of the week [Wednesday] and the Preparation [Friday], on which it is reasonably directed for us to fast according to the tradition. We fast on the fourth day, indeed, because on it the Jews took counsel for the betrayal of the Lord. And we fast on the sixth day, because Christ Himself suffered for us on it. *Peter of Alexandria (c. 310, E), 6.278.*

He commanded us to fast on the fourth and sixth days of the week. The former was on account of His being betrayed. The latter was on account of His passion. *Apostolic Constitutions (compiled c. 390, E), 7.445.*

Before baptism, let him (the one who is to be baptized) fast. For even the Lord, when He was first baptized by John and lived in the wilderness, afterward fasted for forty days and forty nights. *Apostolic Constitutions (compiled c. 390, E), 7.469.*

Do not let your fasts be with the hypocrites. For they fast on the second and fifth days of the week. But you should either fast the entire five days—or else fast on the fourth day of the week and on the day of the Preparation [Friday]. For on the fourth day, the condemnation went out against the Lord, Judas promising on that day to betray Him for money. And you must fast on the day of the Preparation because the Lord suffered the death of the cross under Pontius Pilate on that day. *Apostolic Constitutions (compiled c. 390, E), 7.469.*

He who fasts on the Lord's Day will be guilty of sin, for it is the day of the resurrection. He who fasts during the time of Pentecost will also be guilty. Or, in general, whoever is sad on a festival day to the Lord will be guilty. *Apostolic Constitutions (compiled c. 390, E), 7.449.*

If any member of the clergy is found to fast on the Lord's Day, or on the Sabbath day, excepting one only [i.e., the Saturday before Easter], let him be deprived. However, if he is one of the laity, let him be suspended. *Apostolic Constitutions (compiled c. 390, E), 7.504.*

If any bishop, presbyter, deacon, reader, or singer does not fast the fast of forty days [i.e., Lent] or the fourth day of the week [Wednesday] and the day of the Preparation [Friday], let him be deprived, unless he is hindered by weakness of body. But if he is one of the laity, let him be suspended. *Apostolic Constitutions (compiled c. 390, E), 7.504; see also 1.138, 1.141, 1.202.*

SEE ALSO CALENDAR, CHRISTIAN; LENT; LORD'S DAY.

FATE

The demons introduced fate, a flagrant injustice. They teach that the judge and the judged are made so by fate. The murderers and the murdered, the wealthy and the needy—they are all the offspring of the same fate. *Tatian (c. 160, E), 2.68.*

According to our [Christian] notions, the primary powers are the Lord God and His adversary the devil. But according to men's general opinion about providence, they are fate and necessity. *Tertullian (c. 210, W), 3.201.*

There are others [the Chaldeans] who say that men are governed by the decree of fate. As a result, sometimes men act wickedly, and other times, they act well. *Bardesanes (c. 222, E), 8.727.*

You say that those beings who are plainly cruel are gods. And you say that creation assigns the fates to you. . . . If the fates give the generations, why do you pray to the gods? *Commodianus (c. 240, W), 4.205.*

If God harmoniously orders the whole circular motion of the stars, . . . and if the stars produce the qualities of virtue and vice in human life, . . . then God is the cause and giver of evils. However, God is the cause of injury to no one. Therefore, fate is not the cause of all things. *Methodius (c. 290, E), 6.342.*

If fate causes men to injure one another and to be injured by one another, what need is there for laws? . . . To do good or evil is in our own power, and it is not decided by the stars. *Methodius (c. 290, E), 6.343.*

If [the gods] are unable to turn aside the course of events and to change what has been appointed by fate, what reason, what cause, is there to want to weary and deafen the ears of those [gods]? For you cannot trust in their help in your utmost need. *Arnobius (c. 305, E), 6.521.*

SEE ALSO ASTROLOGY; FOREKNOWLEDGE OF GOD; FREE WILL AND PREDESTINATION.

FATHER, GOD THE

His greatness is unsearchable. Ps. 145:3.

The Word became flesh and dwelt among us, and we beheld His glory, the glory as of the only begotten of the Father. John 1:14.

No one has seen God at any time. The only begotten Son, who is in the bosom of the Father, He has declared Him. John 1:18.

For us there is only one God, the Father, of whom are all things, and we for Him; and one Lord Jesus Christ, through whom are all things, and through whom we live. 1 Cor. 8:6.

Who alone has immortality, dwelling in unapproachable light, whom no man has seen or can see, to whom be honor and everlasting power. 1 Tim. 6:16.

Follow the only Unbegotten God through His Son. *Justin Martyr (c. 160, E), 1.167.*

He who has but the smallest intelligence will not venture to assert that the Maker and Father of all things, having left all supercelestial matters, was visible on a little portion of the earth. *Justin Martyr (c. 160, E), 1.227.*

He really exists, and by His power everything subsists. This Being is in no sense made, nor did He ever come into existence. Rather, He has existed from eternity, and He will continue to exist forever and ever. *Melito (c. 170, E), 8.751.*

No eye can see Him, nor thought apprehend Him, nor language describe Him. And those who love Him speak of Him in this way: as "Father" and the "God of Truth." *Melito (c. 170, E), 8.751.*

He conceals Himself in His power from all His works. For it is not permitted for any being who is subject to change to see Him who changes not. *Melito (c. 170, E), 8.755.*

If I call Him Father, I speak of all things as being from Him. *Theophilus (c. 180, E), 2.90.*

He is without beginning, because He is unbegotten. And He is unchangeable, because He is immortal. And He is called God. *Theophilus (c. 180, E), 2.90.*

He says, "No man has seen God at anytime except the Only-Begotten Son of God, who is in the bosom of the Father, He has declared [Him]." For He, the Son who is in His bosom, declares to everyone the Father who is invisible. For that reason, they know Him to whom the Son reveals Him. *Irenaeus (c. 180, E/W), 1.427.*

He whom the Law proclaimed as God, the same did Christ point out as the Father. *Irenaeus (c. 180, E/W), 1.550.*

It is a difficult task to discover the Father and Maker of this universe. Yet, having found Him, it is impossible to declare Him to all. For He is by no means capable of expression. . . . The apostle will testify: "I know a man in Christ, caught up into the third heaven, and thence into Paradise, who heard unutterable words that it is not lawful for a man to speak." He thereby indicates the impossibility of expressing God. He indicates that what is Divine is unutterable by human power. *Clement of Alexandria (c. 195, E), 2.462, 463.*

So far as a human being can form a definition of God, I present one that the conscience of all men will also acknowledge—that God is the great Supreme, existing in eternity, unbegotten, unmade, without beginning, without end. *Tertullian (c. 207, W), 3.273.*

Although no one is able to speak with certainty of God the Father, it is nevertheless possible for some knowledge of Him to be gained by means of the visible creation and the natural feelings of the human mind. Moreover, it is possible for such knowledge to be confirmed from the sacred Scriptures. *Origen (c. 225, E), 4.252.*

He called the Most High God the Ancient of days, whose age and origin cannot be comprehended. For He alone was from generations, and He will always be to generations. *Lactantius (c. 304–313, W), 7.111.*

You are illimitable, unbegotten, immortal, enduring forever, God Yourself alone! No bodily shape can represent you, nor any outline delineate you. Your virtues are inexpressible, and your greatness is indefinable. You are unrestricted as to locality, movement, and condition. In short, concerning you, nothing can be clearly expressed by the meaning of man's words. *Arnobius (c. 305, E), 6.421.*

By the unanimous judgment of all, and by the common admission of the human race, the Omnipotent God is regarded as having never been born. He has never been brought forth to new light. He has never begun to exist at any time or century. For He Himself is the source of all things, the Father of ages and of seasons. For those things do not exist of themselves. Rather, from His everlasting perpetuity, they move on in an unbroken and ever endless flow. *Arnobius (c. 305, E), 6.421, 422.*

SEE ALSO CHRIST, DIVINITY OF (III. RELATIONSHIP OF THE SON TO THE FATHER); GOD; TRINITY.

FATHER (TERM OF ADDRESS)

Now Elisha saw it, and he cried out, "My father, my father, the chariot of Israel and its horsemen!" 2 King 2:12.

Do not call anyone on earth your father; for One is your Father, He who is in heaven. And do not be called teachers; for One is your Teacher, the Christ. Matt. 23:9, 10.

Though you might have ten thousand instructors in Christ, you do not have many fathers; for in Christ Jesus I have begotten you through the gospel. 1 Cor. 4:15.

But you know his proven character, that as a son with his father he served with me in the gospel. Phil. 2:22.

Was not Abraham our father justified by works? JAS. 2:21; see also Luke 16:24, 25; Acts 7:2; 22:1.

I said, "But father, the Deity cannot be seen merely by the eyes." *Justin Martyr (c. 165, E), 1.196.*

When any person has been taught from the mouth of another, he is called the son of his instructor. And the instructor is called his father. *Irenaeus (c. 180, E/W), 1.524.*

I intend to leave good children to posterity. This is the case with children of our bodies. But words are the offspring of the soul. Hence, we call those who have instructed us, fathers. *Clement of Alexandria (c. 195, E), 2.299.*

The holy apostles—Peter, James, John, and Paul—the sons receiving it from the fathers (but few were like the fathers). *Clement of Alexandria (c. 195, E), 2.301.*

He refers to the perfect as "fathers." They "have known what was from the beginning" and have received it with understanding. *Clement of Alexandria (c. 195, E), 2.575.*

When John advanced, he recognized him and began to run, being ashamed. John followed him with all his might . . . , crying, "Why, my son, do you flee from me, your father?" *Clement of Alexandria (c. 195, E), 2.603.*

And we went forth, and I saw before the entrance, Optatus, the bishop, at the right hand. And I saw Aspasius, the presbyter, a teacher, at the left hand, separate and sad. . . . And we said to them, "Are you not our father, and you our presbyter?" *Passion of Perpetua and Felicitas (c. 205, W), 3.703.*

This very one [the perfect man] the [pagan] Phrygians also call "papa," because he tranquillized all things which . . . were confusedly and dissonantly moved. For he says that the name "papa" belongs simultaneously to all creatures. *Hippolytus (c. 225, W), 5.54.*

The Savior says, "Call no man Teacher upon the earth." However, the apostle says that teachers have been appointed in the church. Accordingly, these latter persons will not be "teachers" in the strict sense of the language of the Gospel. *Origen (c. 228, E), 9.299.*

We have been informed by Crementius the subdeacon, who came to us from you, that the blessed father Cyprian has withdrawn for a certain reason. *Letter from the church in Rome to Cyprian (c. 250, W), 5.280.*

All the confessors, to father Cyprian. *Letter to Cyprian from the confessors (c. 250, W), 5.296.*

The presbyters and deacons abiding at Rome, to father Cyprian. *Letter from the Roman clergy to Cyprian (c. 250, W), 5.307.*

His Gospel has bidden us to call "no man our father upon earth, because there is to us one Father, who is in heaven." And to the disciple who had made mention of his dead father, he replied, "Let the dead bury their dead." For he had said that his father was dead, while the Father of believers is living. *Cyprian (c. 250, W), 5.450.*

We are well acquainted with those blessed fathers who have trodden the course before, and to whom we too will soon go. I am referring to Pantaenus, the truly blessed man, my master; and also the holy Clement, who was once my master and my benefactor. *Alexander of Cappadocia (c. 250, E), 6.154.*

The meats are no burden to us, most holy father. *Gregory Thaumaturgus (c. 255, E), 6.18.*

But you, . . . not considering the law of our sainted fathers . . . nor the honor of our great bishop and father, Peter [bishop of Alexandria], on whom we all depend, . . . have ventured on subverting all things at once. . . . You should have waited for the judgment of the superior father [i.e., bishop Peter] and for his allowance of this practice. *Phileas (c. 307, E), 6.164.*

Diodorus sends greeting to bishop Archelaus: I wish you to know, most pious father, that in these days there has arrived in our parts a certain person named Manes. *Disputation of Archelaus and Manes (c. 320, E), 6.213.*

And, next after God, the bishop is your father. For he has begotten you again to the adoption of sons by water and the Spirit. *Apostolic Constitutions (compiled c. 390, E), 7.410.*

Love and honor him [your bishop]. For, after God, he has become a father to you. *Apostolic Constitutions (compiled c. 390, E), 7.412.*

Ordain bishops worthy of the Lord, along with presbyters and deacons. . . . Honor them as your fathers, as your lords, as your benefactors, as the mentors of your well-being. *Apostolic Constitutions (compiled c. 390, E), 7.471; see also 5.308.*

FATHERS

You, fathers, do not provoke your children to wrath, but bring them up in the training and admonition of the Lord. Eph. 6:4.

A bishop then must be blameless, . . . one who rules his own house well, having his children in submission with all reverence. 1 Tim. 3:2, 4.

Make known these words to all your children and to your wife, who is to be your sister. *Hermas (c. 150, W) 2.11.*

Some fathers have approached the trial [of martyrdom] on behalf of all their family, protecting their wife, children, and their whole family by themselves undergoing the danger. *Cyprian (c. 250, W), 5.330.*

You fathers, educate your children in the Lord. Bring them up in the nurture and admonition of the Lord. . . . Do not be afraid to reprove them and to teach them wisdom with severity. For your corrections will not kill them; rather, they will preserve them. . . . When they reach an age appropriate for marriage, join them in wedlock. *Apostolic Constitutions (compiled c. 390, E), 7.435, 436.*

FEAR OF GOD

The fear of the Lord is the beginning of knowledge. Prov. 1:7.

Fear Him who is able to destroy both soul and body in hell. Matt. 10:28.

Let us cleanse ourselves from all filthiness of the flesh and spirit, perfecting holiness in the fear of God. 2 Cor. 7:1.

Now "the fear of the Lord is the beginning of wisdom." The recognition of sin leads to repentance, and God bestows His compassion upon those who are repentant. *Irenaeus (c. 180, E/W), 1.457.*

There is a twofold species of fear. The first kind is accompanied with reverence. This is the type of fear that citizens show towards good rulers, and that we show towards God. Right-minded children show this fear towards their fathers. . . . The other kind of fear is accompanied with hatred. This is the type of fear that slaves feel towards harsh masters and that the Hebrews felt. For they made God a Master, not a Father. *Clement of Alexandria (c. 195, E), 2.231.*

Cautious fear is therefore shown to be reasonable, being the avoidance of what hurts. From this, arises repentance for sins previously committed. "For the fear of the Lord is the beginning of wisdom; good understanding is to all who do it." He calls wisdom a doing, which is the fear of the Lord paving the way for wisdom. *Clement of Alexandria (c. 195, E), 2.355.*

He says, "Let us then perfect holiness in the fear of God." Although fear begets pain, he says, "I rejoice, not that you were made sorry, but that you showed susceptibility to repentance." *Clement of Alexandria (c. 195, E), 2.433.*

Where the fear of God is, there is seriousness and an honorable and yet thoughtful diligence. *Tertullian (c. 197, W), 3.264.*

"Do not be deceived; God is not to be mocked." But Marcion's God can be mocked.

For he does not know how to be angry, or how to take vengeance. *Tertullian (c. 207, W), 3.438; see also 2.229, 2.543.*

SEE ALSO SALVATION.

FEETWASHING

SEE FOOTWASHING.

FILIOQUE

Filioque is Latin for "and the Son." It refers to the addition made in the sixth century in the West to the Nicene-Constantinopolitan Creed, saying that the Holy Spirit proceeds from the Father and the Son. The eastern church has vigorously opposed this addition, as it implies two sources of the Trinity.

When the Helper comes, whom I will send to you from the Father, the Spirit of truth who proceeds from the Father, He will testify of Me. John 15:26.

I believe the Spirit to proceed from no other source than from the Father through the Son. *Tertullian (c. 213, W), 3.599.*

The Holy Spirit, through whom all things are sanctified, proceeds from the Father. *Origen (c. 225, E), 4.344.*

The Father generates an uncreated Son and brings forth a Holy Spirit—not as if He had no previous existence, but because the Father is the origin and source of the Son and Holy Spirit. *Origen (c. 225, E), 4.270.*

. . . to the Holy Spirit (through whom all things are sanctified). He proceeds from the Father, to whom be glory forever and ever. *Origen (c. 225, E), 4.344.*

It is one and the same thing to have a share in the Holy Spirit, which is of the Father and the Son, since the nature of the Trinity is one and incorporeal. *Origen (c. 225, E), 4.379.*

Many of the pre-Nicene Christians used "begotten" [Gr. *gennētos*] and "created" [Gr. *genētos* and *ktizein*] as interchangeable terms. For example, in the passage below, Origen used the verb *ktizein* to describe the generation of the Spirit. He does not mean, however, that the Spirit was created out of nothing. Rather, as Origen states below and in other places, the Holy Spirit shares in the one essence of the Father, through the Son.

We have seen that all things were made through Him [the Son]. Accordingly, we have to inquire if the Holy Spirit also was generated through Him. It appears to me that those who hold the Holy Spirit to be generated, and who also admit that "all things were made through Him" must necessarily assume that the Holy Spirit was made through the Logos, the Logos accordingly being older than He. And he who shrinks from allowing the Holy Spirit to have been made through Christ must—if he admits the truth of the statements of this Gospel [of John]—assume the Spirit to be ungenerated. . . . We consider, therefore, that there are three Persons: the Father, the Son, and the Holy Spirit. At the same time, we believe nothing to be unbegotten but the Father. We, therefore, as the more pious and the truer course, admit that all things were made by the Logos and that the Holy Spirit is the most excellent and the first in order of all that was made by the Father through Christ. And this, perhaps, is the reason why the Spirit is not said to be God's own Son. The Only-Begotten is the only One who is by nature and from the beginning a Son. The Holy Spirit seems to have need of the Son to administer to Him His essence—so as to enable Him not only to exist, but to be wise, reasonable, and just. *Origen (c. 228, E), 9.328.*

How can the Holy Spirit be the Mother of Christ when He was Himself brought into being through the Word? *Origen (c. 228, E), 9.329.*

The source of the entire Holy Spirit remains in Christ, so that from Him could be drawn streams of gifts and works, while the Holy Spirit dwelled richly in Christ. *Novatian (c. 235, W), 5.641.*

Methodius thinks that the following are types of the holy and consubstantial Trinity. He says the innocent and unbegotten Adam is a type and resemblance of God the Father Almighty, who is uncaused and the cause of all. . . . He says Eve, who proceeded forth from Adam, signifies the person and procession of the Holy Spirit. *Reference to Methodius (c. 290, E), 6.402, from a post-Nicene writer.*

[I believe in the Holy Spirit], who proceeds from the Father, who with the Father and the Son together is worshipped and glorified. *Creed of Constantinople (A.D. 381), 7.524.*

SEE ALSO HOLY SPIRIT; TRINITY.

FISH SYMBOL

In the early years of Christianity, the fish became a symbol of Christ, of newly baptized Christians, and of the Eucharist. The symbol may be derived from the acrostic "Jesus Christ, Son of God, Savior," taken from the letters of the Greek word for fish, *ichthus.*

Follow Me, and I will make you fishers of men. Matt. 4:19.

He took the five loaves and the two fish, and looking up to heaven, He blessed and broke and gave the loaves to the disciples. Matt. 14:17.

Let our seals be either a dove, a fish, or a ship scudding before the wind. . . . If there is anyone fishing, he will remember the apostle, and the children drawn out of the water. *Clement of Alexandria (c. 195, E), 2.285, 286.*

We, little fishes, after the example of our fish, Jesus Christ, are born in water. *Tertullian (c. 198, W), 3.669.*

[IN REFERENCE TO MATT. 17:24–27:] This coin was not in the house of Jesus. Rather, it was in the sea, in the mouth of a fish of the sea. In my opinion, the fish was benefited when it came up and was caught in the net of Peter, who became a fisher of men. For in that net was that which is figuratively called a fish. *Origen (c. 245, E), 9.481.*

FLESH

Those who are in the flesh cannot please God. Rom. 8:8.

Flesh and blood cannot inherit the kingdom of God. 1 Cor. 15:50.

The flesh lusts against the spirit and the spirit against the flesh; the two are directly opposed. This is why you do not do what your will intends. Gal. 5:17 [NA].

"Flesh and blood cannot inherit the kingdom of God." He means the works of the flesh and blood, which . . . deprive men of the kingdom of God. *Tertullian (c. 207, W), 3.451.*

"Those who are in the flesh cannot please God." Now, when will we be able to please God except while we are in this flesh? There is, I suppose, no other time when a man can work. However, even though we are even naturally living in the flesh, if we nevertheless renounce the *deeds* of the flesh, then we will not be "in the flesh." *Tertullian (c. 207, W), 3.451.*

What has the flesh alone, without the soul, ever done in operations of virtue, righteousness, endurance, or chastity? What absurdity, however, it is to attribute sin and crime to that substance to which you do not assign any good actions or character of its own! *Tertullian (c. 210, W), 3.220.*

When it is written that "flesh and blood cannot inherit the kingdom of God," it is not the *substance* of the flesh that is condemned . . . but only the guilt of the flesh. *Novatian (c. 235, W), 5.620.*

We possess the body from the earth and the spirit from heaven. So we ourselves are both earth and heaven. And we pray that God's will may be done in both body and spirit. For there is a struggle between the flesh and the spirit. *Cyprian (c. 250, W), 5.451.*

There are two motions in us, the desire of the flesh and the desire of the soul. And these differ from each other. For that reason, they have received two names: virtue and vice. *Methodius (c. 290, E), 6.343.*

"Flesh and blood cannot inherit the kingdom of God." . . . By "flesh," he did not mean the flesh itself, but the irrational impulse towards the immoral pleasures of the soul. *Methodius (c. 290, E), 6.374, as quoted by Photius.*

If the soul (which has its origin from God) gains the mastery, it is immortal and lives in perpetual light. On the other hand, if the body overpowers the soul and is subject to its rule, it is in everlasting darkness and death. *Lactantius (c. 304–313, W), 7.61.*

The flesh is earthly and therefore mortal. It pulls down the spirit linked to it and leads it from immortality to death. *Lactantius (c. 304–313, W), 7.127.*

Man is formed of different and opposing elements: soul and body, that is, heaven and earth. He possesses both . . . that which is eternal and that which is temporal. He possesses that which has sensibility and that which is beyond the senses. He possesses that which is filled with light and that which is dark. *Lactantius (c. 304–313, W), 7.199.*

When a separation will have been made between the body and the soul, then evil will be disunited from good. And as the body perishes and the soul remains, so evil will perish and good will be permanent. Then man, having received the garment of immortality, will be wise and free from evil, as God is. *Lactantius (c. 304–313, W), 7.202.*

We are composed of two substances equally opposed to one another: soul and body. One of these is assigned to heaven. . . . The other is assigned to the earth. . . . Therefore, good clings to the one and evil to the other. Hence there arose among men the corruption of their nature, so that it was necessary that a law should be established by which vices could be prohibited and the duties of virtue could be admonished. *Lactantius (c. 304–313, W), 7.272.*

SEE ALSO FALL OF MAN; MAN, DOCTRINE OF; SOUL (III. TRIPARTITE DISTINCTION OF BODY, SOUL, AND SPIRIT).

FLOOD, THE

We have explained the things about Noah, who is called by some Deucalion. . . . After the flood, there was again a beginning of cities and kings. *Theophilus (c. 180, E), 2.107.*

For Plato . . . when he had demonstrated that a deluge had happened, said that it did not extend over the whole earth. Rather, he said it extended only over the plains and that those who fled to the highest hills saved themselves. But others say that there existed Deucalion and Pyrrha, and that they were preserved in a chest. *Theophilus (c. 180, E), 2.116.*

There was a time when the whole globe underwent change, because it was overrun by all waters. To this day, marine shells and tritons' horns lay as foreign objects on the mountains—eager to prove to Plato that even the heights have been undulated. Eventually, by ebbing out, the globe again underwent a change of form. *Tertullian (c. 200, W), 4.6.*

Xenophanes [a Greek philosopher] is of the opinion that there had been a mixture of the earth with the sea. . . . He alleges that he could produce such proofs as the following: that shells are discovered in the middle of the earth and in mountains. Also, he asserts that in the quarries of Syracuse, the print of a fish and of seals were found. . . . Furthermore, in Melita, parts of all sorts of marine animals were found. And he says that these were produced when all things originally were embedded in mud, and that an impression of them was dried in the mud. He says that all men had perished when the earth—

being precipitated into the sea—was converted into mud. *Hippolytus (c. 225, W), 5.17.*

[Celsus, a pagan critic] continues as follows: "They speak in the next place of a deluge and of a monstrous ark, . . . falsifying and recklessly altering the story of Deucalion." *Origen (c. 248, E), 4.516.*

Why should we not rather admire a structure [i.e., the ark] that resembled an extensive city, if its measurements are taken to mean what they are capable of meaning. *Origen (c. 248, E), 4.516.*

It is agreed by all that the deluge took place for the destruction of wickedness and for its removal from the earth. Now, philosophers, poets, and writers of ancient history all assert the same. . . . But it is plain that they have corrupted this, too, as they did the former account. For they were ignorant both of the date of the flood on the earth and who it was who deserved to be saved on account of his righteousness. *Lactantius (c. 304–313, W), 7.59.*

You say that the Mother of the gods was produced from the stones that Deucalion and Pyrrha threw. . . . Did the Mother of the gods, then, not exist at all except because of the deluge? Would there have been no cause or beginning of her birth had not violent storms of rain swept away the whole race of men? . . . Varro, that famous Roman who was noted for his learning and for his untiring research into ancient times, . . . shows by careful calculations that from the time of the deluge (which we mentioned before) down to the consulship of Hirtius and Pansa [c. 43 B.C.], there were not quite 2000 years. *Arnobius (c. 305, E), 6.492, 493.*

SEE ALSO ARK, NOAH'S; NOAH; TOWER OF BABEL.

FOOD

But as the days of Noah were, so also will the coming of the Son of Man be. For as in the days before the flood, they were eating and drinking, marrying and giving in marriage, until the day that Noah entered the ark, and did not know until the flood came and took them all away, so also will the coming of the Son of Man be. Matt. 24:37–39.

Many walk, of whom I have told you often, and now tell you even weeping, that they are the enemies of the cross of Christ; whose end is destruction, whose god is their belly, and whose glory is in their shame—who set their mind on earthly things. Phil. 3:18, 19.

There is discrimination to be employed in reference to food. It is to be simple, truly plain, suiting precisely simple and artless children—as ministering to life, not to luxury. *Clement of Alexandria (c. 195, E), 2.237.*

They emasculate plain food, namely bread. For they strain off the nourishing part of the grain, so that the necessary part of food becomes a matter of reproach to luxury. *Clement of Alexandria (c. 195, E), 2.237, 238.*

It is the part of a temperate man also, in eating and drinking, to take a small portion, taking it deliberately, not eagerly. . . . A temperate man, too, must rise before the general company, and retire quietly from the banquet. *Clement of Alexandria (c. 195, E), 2.252.*

"All were under the cloud and partook of spiritual meat and drink." . . . The Savior's teaching is to us spiritual food and drink that knows no thirst. *Clement of Alexandria (c. 195, E), 2.554.*

Faith, free in Christ, owes no abstinence from particular meats—even to the Jewish Law. For the apostle has allowed the whole range of the meat market to everyone. *Tertullian (c. 213, W), 4.103.*

In the beginning, indeed, it had only been the food of herbs and trees that God had assigned to man. . . . Later, however, after explaining to Noah the subjection of all beasts of the earth and fowls of the heaven, . . . He says, "They will be to you for food." *Tertullian (c. 213, W), 4.104.*

Nothing has so restrained intemperance as has the Gospel. Nor has anyone given such strict laws against gluttony as has Christ. *Novatian (c. 235, W), 5.649.*

Although in the Gospel the use of meats is universally given to us, yet it is understood to be given to us only within the law of frugality and self-control. *Novatian (c. 235, W), 5.649.*

Too great a lust for food is not to be desired. . . . In Exodus, "And the people sat down to eat and drink and rose up to play." *Cyprian (c. 250, W), 5.550; see also 2.237–2.242.*

SEE ALSO BLOOD (AS FOOD); FASTING.

FOOTWASHING

Peter said to Him, "You will never wash my feet!" Jesus answered him, "If I do not wash you, you have no part with Me." Simon Peter said to Him, "Lord, not my feet only, but also my hands and my head!" Jesus said to him, "He who is bathed needs only to wash his feet, but is completely clean." John 13:8–10.

Do not let a widow under sixty years old be taken into the number, and not unless she has been the wife of one man, . . . if she has washed the saints' feet. 1 Tim. 5:9, 10.

Now in the last days, when the fullness of the time of liberty had arrived, the Word Himself did by Himself "wash away the filth of the daughters of Zion," when He washed the disciples' feet with His own hands. . . . In the beginning, by means of our first [parents], we were all brought into bondage, by being made subject to death. Accordingly, at last, by means of the New Man, all who were His disciples from the beginning were cleansed and washed from things pertaining to death. Thereby, they can come to the life of God. For He who washed the feet of the disciples sanctified the entire body, and rendered it clean. *Irenaeus (c. 180, E/W), 1.493.*

"If she has washed the feet of saints"—that is, if she has performed without shame the lowest offices for the saints. *Clement of Alexandria (c. 195, E), 2.579.*

[What unbelieving husband will permit his wife] to offer water for the saints' feet? *Tertullian (c. 205, W), 4.46.*

FOREKNOWLEDGE OF GOD

. . . being delivered by the determined counsel and foreknowledge of God. Acts 2:23.

For whom He foreknew, He also predestined to be conformed to the image of His Son, that He might be the firstborn among many brethren. Rom. 8:29.

To the pilgrims of the Dispersion, . . . elect according to the foreknowledge of God the Father. 1 Pet. 1:1, 2.

The Lord knows the heart and foreknows all things. *Hermas (c. 150, W), 2.22.*

He foreknows that some are to be saved by repentance, some even that are perhaps not yet born. *Justin Martyr (c. 160, E), 1.172.*

Lest some suppose, from what has been said by us, that we say that whatever happens, happens by a fatal necessity, because it is foretold as known beforehand, this too we explain. *Justin Martyr (c. 160, E), 1.177.*

And this prophecy proves that we [Gentiles] will behold this very King with glory.... For the people foreknown to believe in Him were foreknown to pursue diligently the fear of the Lord. *Justin Martyr (c. 160, E), 1.234.*

For if this is not the case, God will be slandered, as having no foreknowledge. *Justin Martyr (c. 160, E), 1.246.*

If the Word of God foretells that some angels and men will be certainly punished, it did so because it foreknew that they would be unchangeable [i.e., would remain wicked]. However, this is not because God had created them so. For all who wish for it can obtain mercy from God if they repent. *Justin Martyr (c. 160, E), 1.270.*

The power of the Logos has in itself a faculty to foresee future events. Yet, these events are not fated, but take place by the choice of free agents. For the Logos foretold from time to time the issues of things to come. *Tatian (c. 160, E), 2.67, 68.*

The Lord has plainly declared, and the rest of the Scriptures have demonstrated, that eternal fire is prepared for sinners. God foreknew that this would happen. The Scriptures do in like manner demonstrate this. For He prepared eternal fire from the beginning for those who were [afterwards] to transgress. *Irenaeus (c. 180, E/W), 1.401.*

When the number is completed which He had predetermined in His own counsel, all those who have been enrolled for life will rise again.... So the number of mankind, corresponding to the fore-ordination of God, will be completed. Thereby, they may fully realize the design formed by the Father. *Irenaeus (c. 180, E/W), 1.411.*

God predestined that the first man would be of an animal nature. He did it with the view that he might be saved by the spiritual One. *Irenaeus (c. 180, E/W), 1.445.*

Our God, one and the same, is also their God. He knows hidden things, and He knows all things before they can come to pass. *Irenaeus (c. 180, E/W), 1.493.*

God knows the number of those who will not believe (since He foreknows all things). He has given them over to unbelief and turned away His face from men of this mold. *Irenaeus (c. 180, E/W), 1.502.*

He had prepared the marriage for His Son from the beginning. *Irenaeus (c. 180, E/W), 1.516.*

By His foreknowledge, He knew the infirmity of human beings, and the consequences that would flow from it. *Irenaeus (c. 180, E/W), 1.522.*

God, foreknowing all things, prepared fit habitations for both. *Irenaeus (c. 180, E/W), 1.523.*

Christ predestined, according to the foreknowledge of the Father, that we, who had as yet no existence, might come into being. *Irenaeus (c. 180, E/W), 1.527.*

Even before his birth, he was manifested to the Lord, who knew the martyr's choice. *Clement of Alexandria (c. 195, E), 2.411.*

Not only the believer, but even the unbeliever, is judged most righteously. For since God knew in virtue of His foreknowledge that this person would not believe, He nevertheless, in order that he might receive his own perfection, gave him philosophy. However, He gave it to him previous to faith. *Clement of Alexandria (c. 195, E), 2.505.*

He has dispensed His kindness both to Greeks and barbarians, even to those of them who were predestined, and who in due time were called the faithful and elect. *Clement of Alexandria (c. 195, E), 2.524.*

Those were already ordained, whom God predestined. For He knew before the foundation of the world that they would be righteous. *Clement of Alexandria (c. 195, E), 2.555.*

As God, He foresaw both what He would be asked and what each one would answer Him. *Clement of Alexandria (c. 195, E), 2.593.*

But what will I say of His foreknowledge, which has for its witnesses as many prophets as it inspired? After all, what title to foreknowledge do we look for in the Author of the universe? For it was by this very attribute that He foreknew all things when he appointed their places to them.... There is sin itself. If He had not foreknown this, He would not have proclaimed a warning against it under the penalty of death. *Tertullian (c. 207, W), 3.301.*

God, however, foreknew that man would make a bad use of his created constitution. Yet, what can be so worthy of God as His earnestness of purpose? *Tertullian (c. 207, W), 3.303.*

Saul is chosen, for he is not yet the despiser of the prophet Samuel. Solomon is rejected, for he has now become a prey to foreign women and a slave to the idols of Moab and Sidon. What must the Creator do, in order to escape the censure of the Marcionites? Must He prematurely condemn men who are thus far correct in their conduct—because of future delinquencies? Yet, it is not the mark of a good God to condemn beforehand persons who have not yet deserved condemnation. *Tertullian (c. 207, W), 3.315.*

God is fully acquainted with whatever is about to take place, for He has foreknowledge. *Hippolytus (c. 225, W), 5.150.*

. . . the unbelief of the Corinthians and of the good-will of God towards them, according to foreknowledge revealed to Paul. *Pamphilus (c. 309, E), 6.168; see also 1.501.*

SEE ALSO EVIL, PROBLEM OF; FREE WILL AND PREDESTINATION; SOVEREIGNTY AND PROVIDENCE OF GOD.

FORGIVENESS OF SINS
SEE ABSOLUTION.

FREE WILL AND PREDESTINATION

I. Free will in humans and angels

II. The elect

III. Predestination

IV. Synergism

I. Free will in humans and angels

I call heaven and earth as witnesses today against you, that I have set before you life and death, blessing and cursing; therefore choose life, that both you and your descendants may live. Deut. 30:19, 20.

Because they hated knowledge and did not choose the fear of the Lord, they would have none of my counsel and despised all my reproof, therefore they will eat the fruit of their own way. Prov. 1:29–31.

If you are willing and obedient, you shall eat the good of the land; but if you refuse and rebel, you shall be devoured by the sword. Isa. 1:19, 20.

He has shown you, O man, what is good; and what does the Lord require of you but to do justly, to love mercy, and to walk humbly with your God? Mic. 6:8.

Not everyone who says to Me, "Lord, Lord," will enter the kingdom of heaven, but he who does the will of My Father in heaven. . . . Therefore whoever hears these sayings of Mine, and does them, I will liken him to a wise man who built his house on the rock. Matt. 7:21, 24.

Because you have kept My command to persevere, I also will keep you from the hour of trial which will come upon the whole world, to test those who dwell on the earth. Behold, I come quickly! Hold fast what you have, that no one may take your crown. He who overcomes, I will make him a pillar in the temple of My God. Rev. 3:10–12.

In the beginning, He made the human race with the power of thought and of choosing the truth and doing right, so that all men are without excuse before God. *Justin Martyr (c. 160, E), 1.172.*

Lest some suppose, from what has been said by us, that we say that whatever occurs happens by a fatal necessity, because it is foretold as known beforehand, this too we explain. We have learned from the prophets, and we hold it to be true, that punishments, chastisements, and good rewards, are rendered according to the merit of each man's actions. Now, if this is not so, but all things happen by fate, then neither is anything at all in our own power. For if it is predetermined that this man will be good, and this other man will be evil, neither is the first one meritorious nor the latter man to be blamed. And again, unless the human race has the power of avoiding evil and choosing good by free choice, they are not accountable for their actions. *Justin Martyr (c. 160, E), 1.177.*

Neither do we maintain that it is by fate that men do what they do, or suffer what they suffer. Rather, we maintain that each man acts rightly or sins by his free choice. . . . Since God in the beginning made the race of angels and men with free will, they will justly suffer in eternal fire the punishment of whatever sins they have committed. *Justin Martyr (c. 160, E), 1.190.*

It was God's desire for both angels and men, who were endowed with free will . . . that if they chose the things acceptable to Him, He would keep them free from death and from punishment. However, if they did evil, He would punish each as He sees fit. *Justin Martyr (c. 160, E), 1.243.*

He created both angels and men free to do that which is righteous. And He appointed periods of time during which He knew it would be good for them to have the exercise of free will. *Justin Martyr (c. 160, E), 1.250.*

I have proved in what has been said that those who were foreknown to be unrighteous, whether men or angels, are not made wicked by God's fault. Rather, each man is what he will appear to be through his own fault. *Justin Martyr (c. 160, E), 1.269.*

Each of these two orders of creatures [men and angels] was made free to act as it pleased. They did not have the nature of good, which again is with God alone. However, it is brought to perfection in men through their freedom of choice. In this manner, the bad man can be justly punished, having become depraved through his own fault. Likewise, the just man can be deservedly praised for his virtuous deeds, since in the exercise of his free choice, he refrained from transgressing the will of God. . . . And the power of the Logos has in itself a faculty to foresee future events. He foretold from time to time the issues of things to come—not as fated, but as taking place by the choice of free agents. *Tatian (c. 160), 2.67, 68.*

We were not created to die. Rather, we die by our own fault. Our free will has destroyed us. We who were free have become slaves. We have been sold through sin. Nothing evil has been created by God. We ourselves have manifested wickedness. But we, who have manifested it, are able again to reject it. *Tatian (c. 160), 2.69, 70.*

There is, therefore, nothing to hinder you from changing your evil manner of life, because you are a free man. *Melito (c. 170, E), 8.754.*

If, on the other hand, he would turn to the things of death, disobeying God, he would himself be the cause of death to himself. For God made man free, and with power of himself. *Theophilus (c. 180), 2.105.*

Concerning subjection to authorities and powers, and prayer for them, the divine word gives us instructions so that "we may lead a quiet and peaceable life." Furthermore, it teaches us to render all things to all, "honor to whom honor, fear to whom fear, tribute to whom tribute; to owe no man anything, but to love all." *Theophilus (c. 180), 2.115.*

But man, being endowed with reason, and in this respect similar to God, having been made free in his will, and with power over himself, is himself his own cause that sometimes he becomes wheat, and sometimes chaff. *Irenaeus (c. 180, E/W), 1.466.*

God has always preserved freedom and the power of self-government in man. Yet, at the same time, He issued His own exhortations, in order that those who do not obey Him would be righteously judged because they have not obeyed Him. And those who have obeyed and believed on Him should be honored with immortality. *Irenaeus (c. 180, E/W), 1.480.*

[The Marcionites] say, "But God hardened the heart of Pharaoh and of his servants." Now those who allege such difficulties do not read in the Gospel the passage where the Lord replied to the disciples, when they asked Him, "Why do you speak in parables?" He replied: "Because it is given to you to know the mystery of the kingdom of heaven. However, I speak to them in parables so that seeing they may not see and hearing they many not hear." . . . So God knows the number of those who will not believe, since He foreknows all things. So He has given them over to unbelief and turned His face away from men of this character, leaving them in the darkness that they have chosen for themselves. So what is baffling if He gave Pharaoh and those who were with him over to their unbelief? For they would never have believed. *Irenaeus (c. 180, E/W), 1.502.*

This expression . . . sets forth the ancient law of human liberty. For God made man free from the beginning, possessing his own power, even as he does his own soul, to obey the commandments of God voluntarily, and not by compulsion of God. For there is no coercion with God. . . . And in man, as well as in angels (for angels are rational beings), He has placed the power of choice, so that those who had yielded obedience might justly possess what is good—given indeed by God, but preserved by themselves. *Irenaeus (c. 180, E/W), 1.518.*

Those who work it will receive glory and honor, because they have done that which is good when they had it in their power not to do it. But those who do not do it will receive the just judgment of God, because they did not work good when they had it in their power to do so. But if some had been made by nature bad, and others good, these latter would not be deserving of praise for being good, for they were created that way. Nor would the former be reprehensible, for that is how they were made. However, all men are of the same nature. They are all able to hold fast and to do what is good. On the other hand, they have the power to cast good from them and not to do it. For that reason, some justly receive praise. *Irenaeus (c. 180, E/W), 1.519.*

"Let your light so shine before men, that they may see your good deeds".... And "Why call me, Lord, Lord, and do not do the things that I say?".... All such passages demonstrate the independent will of man.... For it is in man's power to disobey God and to forfeit what is good. *Irenaeus (c. 180, E/W), 1.519*

If, then, it were not in our power to do or not to do these things, what reason did the apostle have, and much more the Lord Himself, to give us counsel to *do* some things, and to *abstain* from others? But because man is possessed of free will from the beginning, and God is possessed of free will (in whose likeness man was created), advice is always given to him to hold fast to the good, which is done through obedience to God. God has preserved the will of man free and under his own control. This is not merely in works, but also in faith. *Irenaeus (c. 180, E/W), 1.519.*

Nor, again, does God exercise compulsion upon anyone unwilling to accept the exercise of His skill.... They have been created free agents and possessed of power over themselves. *Irenaeus (c. 180, E/W), 1.523.*

Those who believe, do His will agreeably to their own choice. Likewise, agreeably to their own choice, the disobedient do not consent to His doctrine. It is clear that His Father has made everyone in a like condition, each person having a choice of his own and a free understanding. *Irenaeus (c. 180, E/W), 1.556.*

We ... have believed and are saved by voluntary choice. *Clement of Alexandria (c. 195, E), 2.217.*

Each one of us who sins with his own free will, chooses punishment. So the blame lies with him who chooses. God is without blame. *Clement of Alexandria (c. 195, E), 2.226.*

It is by one's own fault that he does not choose what is best. God is free of blame. *Clement of Alexandria (c. 195, E), 2.300.*

Neither praises nor censures, neither rewards nor punishments, are right if the soul does not have the power of inclination and disinclination and if evil in involuntary.... In no respect is God the author of evil. But since free choice and inclination originate sins, ... punishments are justly inflicted. *Clement of Alexandria (c. 195, E), 2.319.*

We have heard by the Scriptures that self-determining choice and refusal have been given by the Lord to men. Therefore, we rest in the infallible criterion of faith, manifesting a willing spirit, since we have chosen life. *Clement of Alexandria (c. 195, E), 2.349.*

To obey or not is in our own power, provided we do not have the excuse of ignorance. *Clement of Alexandria (c. 195, E), 2.353.*

Sin, then, is voluntary on my part. *Clement of Alexandria (c. 195, E), 2.362.*

The Lord clearly shows sins and transgressions to be in our own power, by prescribing modes of cure corresponding to the maladies. *Clement of Alexandria (c. 195, E), 2.363.*

Their estrangement is the result of free choice. *Clement of Alexandria (c. 195, E), 2.426.*

It is not possible to attain it without the exercise of free choice. However, the whole does not depend on our own purpose, as for example, what is destined to happen. *Clement of Alexandria (c. 195, E), 2.445.*

Perhaps the Father Himself draws to Himself every one who has led a pure life and who has reached the conception of the blessed and incorruptible nature. Or, perhaps the free will that is in us, by reaching the knowledge of the good, leaps and bounds over the barriers (as the gymnasts say). Either way, it is not without eminent grace that the soul is winged, soars, and is raised above the higher spheres. *Clement of Alexandria (c. 195, E), 2.464.*

Wisdom, which is given by God (being the power of the Father), rouses indeed our free will and allows faith. It repays the application of the elect with its crowning fellowship. *Clement of Alexandria (c. 195, E), 2.464.*

God's will is especially obeyed by the free will of good men. *Clement of Alexandria (c. 195, E), 2.517.*

Believing and obeying are in our own power. *Clement of Alexandria (c. 195, E), 2.527.*

Nor will he who is saved be saved against his will, for he is not inanimate. But above all, he will speed to salvation voluntarily and of free choice. *Clement of Alexandria (c. 195, E), 2.534.*

Whenever, then, one is righteous—not from necessity or out of fear or hope—but from free choice, this is called the royal road. *Clement of Alexandria (c. 195, E), 2.544.*

Choice depended on the man as being free. But the gift depended on God as the Lord. And He gives to those who are willing, are exceedingly earnest, and who ask. So their salvation becomes their own. For God does not compel. *Clement of Alexandria (c. 195, E), 2.593.*

This is the mind and judgment of man, which has freedom in itself and self-determination in the treatment of what is assigned to it. *Clement of Alexandria (c. 195, E), 2.595.*

If one chooses to continue in pleasures and to sin perpetually, . . . let him no longer blame either God, riches, or his having fallen. Rather, let him blame his own soul, which voluntarily perishes. *Clement of Alexandria (c. 195, E), 2.604.*

I find, then, that man was constituted free by God. He was master of his own will and power. . . . For a law would not be imposed upon one who did not have it in his power to render that obedience which is due to law. Nor again, would the penalty of death be threatened against sin, if a contempt of the law were impossible to man in the liberty of his will. . . . Man is free, with a will either for obedience or resistance. *Tertullian (c. 207, W), 3.300, 301.*

As to fortune, it is man's freedom of will. *Tertullian (c. 210, W), 3.201.*

This will be the power of the grace of God—more potent indeed than nature—exercising its sway over the faculty that underlies itself within us: even the freedom of our will. . . . We define the soul as having sprung from the breath of God. It is immortal . . . [and] free in its determinations. *Tertullian (c. 210, W), 3.202.*

You must necessarily correspond to the seed from which you sprang—if indeed it is true that

the originator of our race and our sin, Adam, willed the sin which he committed. *Tertullian (c. 212, W), 4.51.*

On the contrary, men are not governed like [the plants and animals]. . . . In matters pertaining to their minds, they do whatever they choose—as those who are free, endowed with power, and in the likeness of God. *Bardesanes (c. 222, E), 8.726.*

God, who created [the world], did not, nor does not, make evil. . . . Now, man (who was brought into existence) was a creature endowed with a capacity of self-determination, yet he did not possess a sovereign intellect. . . . Man, from the fact of his possessing a capacity of self-determination, brings forth what is evil. . . . Since man has free will, a law has been given him by God, for a good purpose. For a law will not be laid down for an animal that is devoid of reason. Only a bridle and a whip will be given it. In contrast, man has been given a commandment to perform, coupled with a penalty. *Hippolytus (c. 225, W), 5.151.*

The Word promulgated the divine commandments by declaring them. He thereby turned man from disobedience. He summoned man to liberty through a choice involving spontaneity—not by bringing him into servitude by force of necessity. *Hippolytus (c. 225, W), 5.152.*

Christ passed through every stage in life in order that He Himself could serve as a law for persons of every age, and that, by being present among us, He could demonstrate His own manhood as a model for all men. Furthermore, through Himself He could prove that God made nothing evil and that man possesses the capacity of self-determination. For man is able to both will and not to will. He is endowed with power to do both. *Hippolytus (c. 225, W), 5.152.*

This also is clearly defined in the teaching of the church, that every rational soul has free will and volition. Furthermore, each soul has a struggle to maintain against the devil, his angels, and other opposing powers. For those powers strive to burden it with sins. . . . We understand that we are not subject to necessity. We are not compelled by various means to do either good or evil, even against our will. For if we are our own masters, some influences may perhaps impel us to sin, and others may help us to salvation. However, we are not forced by any necessity to act either rightly or wrongly. *Origen (c. 225, E), 4.240.*

Every rational creature, therefore, is capable of earning praise and censure. If in conformity to the reason that he possesses, he advances to better things, he is worthy of praise. If he falls away from the plan and course of rectitude, he is worthy of condemnation. And for this reason, he is justly liable to pains and penalties. *Origen (c. 225, E), 4.256, 257.*

It seems a possible thing that rational natures, from whom the faculty of free will is never taken away, may be again subjected to movements of some kind. *Origen (c. 225, E), 4.272.*

Since those rational creatures themselves . . . were endowed with the power of free will, this freedom of the will incited each one to either progress (by imitation of God), or else it reduced a person to failure through negligence. And this, as we have already stated, is the cause of the diversity among rational creatures. It does not derive its origin from the will or judgment of the Creator, but from the freedom of the individual will. Now God deemed it just to arrange His creatures according to their merit. . . . Divine Providence continues to regulate each individual according to the variety of his movements, or of his feelings and purpose. On which account, the Creator will not appear to be unjust in distributing to everyone according to his merits. Nor will the happiness or unhappiness of each one's birth (or whatever is the condition that falls to his lot) be considered accidental. *Origen (c. 225, E), 4.292.*

In the preaching of the church, there is included the doctrine concerning a just judgment of God. When this teaching is believed to be true, it incites those who hear it to live virtuously and to shun sin by all means. For they clearly acknowledge that things worthy of praise and blame are within our own power. *Origen (c. 225, E), 4.302.*

It is *our* responsibility to live virtuously. God asks this of us as being our own doing—not as being dependent on Him, nor on any other, nor on Fate (as some think). The prophet Micah proves this when he says: "If it has been announced to you, O man, what is good, or what does the Lord require of you, except to do justice and to love mercy?" Moses, too, said: "I have placed before your face the way of life and the way of death. Choose what is good and

walk in it." Isaiah also said: "If you are willing and hear me, you will eat the good of the land." . . . And the Savior also, when He commands, "But I say to you, resist not evil." . . . And by any other commandments that He gives, He declares that it lies with us to keep what is commanded and that we will reasonably be liable to condemnation if we transgress. *Origen (c. 225, E), 4.305, 306.*

In the following lengthy discussion of free will, Origen counters the arguments being made by certain Gnostics, who said that humans have a ruined nature because of being created by the inferior Demiurge. These Gnostics taught that, as a result of these ruined natures, salvation was purely a matter of grace and election by the Father of Jesus.

Let us observe how Paul, too, addresses us as having freedom of the will and as being ourselves the cause of ruin or salvation. He says, "You are treasuring up for yourself wrath on the day of wrath and the revelation of the righteous judgment of God—who will render to everyone according to his works." . . . There are, indeed, innumerable passages in the Scriptures that establish with exceeding clarity the existence of freedom of the will. But, since certain declarations of the Old Testament and of the New lead to the opposite conclusion—namely, that it does not depend on ourselves to keep the commandments and to be saved, or to transgress them and to be lost—let us examine them one by one and see the explanations. . . . The statements regarding Pharaoh have troubled many, respecting whom God declared several times, "I will harden Pharaoh's heart." For if he is hardened by God and commits sin because of being hardened, he is not the cause of sin to himself. If so, then Pharaoh does not possess free will. . . . There is also the declaration in Ezekiel, "I will take away their stony hearts and will put in them hearts of flesh so that they may walk in My precepts and keep My commandments." This might lead someone to think that it was God who gave the power to walk in His commandments and to keep His commandments—by His withdrawing the hindrance (the stony heart) and implanting a better heart of flesh. And let us look also at the passage in the Gospel . . . "That seeing they might not see and hearing they may hear and not understand. Lest they would be converted and their sins be forgiven them."

There is also the passage in Paul: "It is not of him that wills, nor of him that runs, but of God who shows mercy." Furthermore, there are declarations in other places that "both to will and to do are of God" and "that God has mercy upon whom He will have mercy; and whom He wishes, He hardens." . . . And also, "But who are you, O man, to talk back to God? Will the thing formed say to him who formed it, 'Why have you made me like this?' Does the potter not have power over the clay—from the same lump to make one vessel unto honor, and another unto dishonor?" Now, these passages are sufficient of themselves to trouble the multitude—as if man were not possessed of free will, but as if it were God who saves and destroys whom He wills. Let us begin, then, with what is said about Pharaoh—that he was hardened by God so that he would not send the people away. . . . Some of those who hold different opinions [i.e., the Gnostics] misuse these passages. They essentially destroy free will by introducing ruined natures incapable of salvation and by introducing others as being saved in such a way that they cannot be lost. . . . Let us now see what these passages mean. For we will ask them if Pharaoh was of a fleshly nature. And when they answer, we will say that he who is of a fleshly nature is altogether disobedient to God. And if he is disobedient, what need is there for his heart to be hardened—not only once, but frequently? Unless we are to think that . . . God needs him to be disobedient to a greater degree in order that He could manifest His mighty deeds for the salvation of the multitude. Therefore, God hardens his heart. This will be our answer to them in the first place.

Since we consider God to be both good and just, let us see how the good and just God could harden the heart of Pharaoh. Perhaps by an illustration used by the apostle in the Epistle to the Hebrews, we may be able to show that, by the same operation, God can show mercy on one man while he hardens another, although not intending to harden. . . . "The earth," he says, "drinks in the rain that often comes upon it and produces crops to those for whom it is farmed, receiving the blessing from God. But that which produces thorns and briers is worthless, and is in danger of being cursed. Its end is to be burned." . . . It may seem profane for the One who produces rain to say, "I produced both the fruit and the thorns that are in the earth." Yet, although seemingly profane, it is true. If the rain had not fallen, there would have

been neither fruit nor thorns. . . . The blessing of the rain, therefore, fell even on the unproductive land. But since it was neglected and uncultivated, it yielded thorns and thistles. In the same way, the wonderful acts of God are like the rain. The differing purposes are like the cultivated and the neglected land. . . . If the sun had a voice, it might say, "I both liquefy and dry up." Although liquefying and drying are opposite things, the sun would not speak falsely on this point. For wax is melted and mud is dried up by the same heat. In the same way, the operation performed through the instrumentality of Moses, on the one hand, hardened Pharaoh (because of his own wickedness), and it softened the mixed Egyptian multitude, who departed with the Hebrews. . . . Now, suppose that the words the apostle addressed to sinners had been addressed to Pharaoh. Then, the announcements made to him will be understood to have been made with particular application. It is as to one who—according to his hardness and unrepentant heart—was treasuring up wrath for himself. For his hardness would not have been demonstrated nor made manifest unless miracles had been performed, particularly miracles of such magnitude and importance. . . .

If it is not we who do anything towards the production within ourselves of the heart of flesh—but if it is [all] God's doing—it would not be our own act to live agreeably to virtue. Rather, it would be altogether an act of divine grace. This would be the statements of one who from the mere words annihilates free will. But we will answer, saying that we should understand these passages in this way: It is like a man who happens to be ignorant and uneducated. On perceiving his own defects—either because of an exhortation from his teacher, or in some other way—he spontaneously gives himself up to an instructor whom he believes can educate him and teach him virtue. Now, on his yielding himself up, his instructor promises that he will take away the man's ignorance and implant instruction. Yet, it is not as if the student contributed nothing to his own training. . . . In the same way, the Word of God promises to take away wickedness (which it calls a stony heart) from those who come to Him. But not if they are unwilling to come. It is only if they submit themselves to the Physician of the sick. . . .

After this, there is the passage from the Gospel where the Savior said, . . . "Seeing, they may not see, and hearing, they may not understand. Lest they would be converted and their sins be forgiven them." Now, our opponent [the Gnostics] will say . . . it is not within the power of such ones to be saved. If that were so, we are not possessed of free will as regards salvation and destruction. . . . In the first place, then, we must notice the passage in its bearing on the heretics, who . . . daringly assert the cruelty of the Creator of the world. . . . They say that goodness does not exist in the Creator. . . . Come, then, and let us (to the best of our ability) furnish an answer to the question submitted to us. . . . The Savior . . . had foreseen them as persons who were not likely to prove steady in their conversion, even if they heard the words that were spoken more clearly. For that reason, they were treated this way by the Savior. . . . Otherwise, after a rapid conversion and healing through obtaining remission of sins, they would despise the wounds of their wickedness, as being slight and easy to heal. As a result, they would again quickly relapse into them. . . .

"Shall the thing formed say to him who formed it, "Why have you made me this way?" Has not the potter power over the clay, of the same lump to make one vessel unto honor, and another unto dishonor?" . . . Now we must ask the person who uses these passages whether it is possible to conceive that the apostle contradicts himself. I presume that no one will venture to say it is. If, then, the apostle does not utter contradictions, how can he, according to the person who so understands him, justly find fault with anyone? How could he condemn the individual at Corinth who had committed fornication, or those who had fallen away? . . . And how could he bless those whom he praises as having done well? . . . It is not consistent for the same apostle to blame the sinner as worthy of censure and to praise him who had done well as deserving of approval—but yet, on the other hand, to say (as if nothing depended on ourselves) that the cause was in the Creator for the one vessel to be formed to honor and the other to dishonor. . . . The power that is given us to enable us to conquer may be used—in accordance with our faculty of free will—either in a diligent manner (in which case, we prove victorious) or in a slothful manner (in which case, we are defeated). For if such a power were wholly given us in such a way that we would always prove victorious and never

be defeated, what further reason would there be for a struggle—for such a one could not be overcome? Or what merit would there be in a victory, if the power of successful resistance is taken away? However, if the possibility of conquering is equally conferred on all of us—and if it is in our own power how to use this possibility (either diligently or slothfully)—then the defeated can be justly censured and the victor can be deservedly praised. *Origen (c. 225, E), 4.331.*

When a malignant power has begun to incite us to evil, it is quite within our power to cast the wicked suggestions away from us. . . . Similarly, when a divine power calls us to better things, it is possible for us not to obey the call. Our freedom of will is preserved in either case. *Origen (c. 225, E), 4.332.*

A soul is always in possession of free will—both when it is in the body and when it is outside of it. *Origen (c. 225, E), 4.337.*

To such an interpretation, all the Scriptures are opposed. They emphasize the freedom of the will. They condemn those who sin, and they approve those who do right. . . . We are responsible for our being good and worthy of being called [honorable] vessels. Likewise, we are responsible for being bad and worthy of being cast outside. For it is not the nature in us that is the cause of the evil; rather, it is the voluntary choice that works evil. Likewise, our nature is not the cause of righteousness, as though it were incapable of admitting unrighteousness. *Origen (c. 245, E), 9.419.*

You can always find evil men coming from wickedness to virtue. And you can always find righteous men returning from progress towards virtue to the flood of wickedness. . . . Now, from the parable of the dragnet, the heretics introduce the doctrine of different natures. Let them tell us in regard to the wicked man who afterwards turned aside from all the wickedness . . . what nature he was when he was wicked? *Origen (c. 245, E), 9.419*

In the case of souls, it is our free will (and actions and habits of such a kind) that furnish the reason why one is great, little, or of middle height [i.e., spiritually speaking]. And it is our free will to increase our size, by advancing in stature, or else to be short, by not advancing. *Origen (c. 245, E), 9.490.*

Would [Celsus] then have ... God fill the minds of men with new ideas, immediately removing the wickedness and implanting virtue? ... Where, then, is our free will? And what credit is there in agreeing to the truth? Or how is it praiseworthy to reject what is false? *Origen (c. 248, E), 4.498.*

When He had given man all things for his service, he willed that man alone should be free. And lest an unbounded freedom would lead man into peril, He laid down a command, in which man was taught that there was no evil in the fruit of the tree. Rather, he was forewarned that evil would arise if man were to exercise his free will in contempt of the law that had been given him. ... As a result, he could receive either worthy rewards or a just punishment. For he had in his own power that which he might choose to do. *Novatian (c. 235, W), 5.612.*

The liberty of believing or of not believing is placed in free choice. In Deuteronomy, it says: "Look! I have set before your face life and death, good and evil. Choose for yourself life, that you may live." Also in Isaiah: "And if you are willing and hear me, you will eat the good of the land." *Cyprian (c. 250, W), 5.547.*

Some persons decide that man is not possessed of free will. Rather, they assert that he is governed by the unavoidable necessities of fate and her unwritten commands. Such persons are guilty of impiety towards God Himself. For they make Him out to be the cause and author of human evils. *Methodius (c. 290, E), 6.342.*

To do good or evil is in our own power, and it is not decided by the stars. For there are two motions in us, the desire of the flesh and the desire of the soul. And these differ from each other. For that reason, they have received two names: virtue and vice. *Methodius (c. 290, E), 6.343.*

Man was made with a free will ... on account of his capacity of obeying or disobeying God. For this was the meaning of the gift of free will. *Methodius (c. 290, E), 6.362.*

Man received power and enslaved *himself*— not because he was overpowered by the irresistible tendencies of his nature. ... For if he had been made as any of the elements of creation, ... he would cease to receive a reward befitting deliberate choice. Instead, he would be like an instrument of the Maker. And it would be unreasonable for him to suffer blame for his wrong-doings. For the real author of them would be the one by whom he is used. ... Therefore, I say that God—purposing to honor man in this manner and to grant him an understanding of better things— has given man the power of being able to do what he wishes. He commends the use of his power for better things. However, it is not that God deprives man again of free will. Rather, He wishes to point out the better way. For the power is present with man, and he receives the commandment. But God exhorts him to turn his power of choice to better things. *Methodius (c. 290, E), 6.362.*

I do not think that God urges man to obey His commandments, but then deprives him of the power to obey or disobey. ... He does not give a command in order to take away the power that he has given. Rather, He gives it in order to bestow a better gift ... in return for his having rendered obedience to God. For man had power to withhold it. I say that man was made with free will. *Methodius (c. 290, E), 6.362.*

[Methodius] says that it is in our power to do, or to avoid doing, evil. Otherwise, we would not be punished for doing evil nor be rewarded for doing good. However, the presence or absence of evil thoughts does not depend upon ourselves. *Methodius (c. 290, E), 6.370, as quoted by Photius.*

He who gives commandments for life should remove every method of excuse—so he can impose upon men the necessity of obedience. Not by any constraint, but by a sense of shame. Yet, he should do it in a way to leave them freedom, so that a reward may be appointed for those who obey. That is because it was in their power not to obey if they so wished. And he can give a punishment for those who do not obey—for it was in their power to obey if they so wished. ... But how can one practice what he teaches, unless he is like the teacher? For if the teacher is subject to no passion, a man may answer the teacher in this manner: "It is my wish not to sin. However, I am overpowered. For I am clothed with frail and weak flesh. It is this that covets, is angry, and fears pain and death. And thus I am led on against my will. So I sin, not because it is my wish, but because I am compelled. I realize that I sin. Yet, the necessity imposed by my frailty (which I am unable to resist) impels me. Now, what will that teacher of righteousness say in reply to these things? How will he refute and convict a man who alleges the frailty of the flesh as an excuse for his faults—unless he himself will also be clothed with flesh—so that he can show that even the flesh is capable of virtue? *Lactantius (c. 304–313, W), 7.125.*

If your "wisdom" is so great that you consider the things that are offered by Christ to be ridiculous and absurd, why should He keep on inviting you? For His only duty is to make the enjoyment of His gift dependent upon your own free choice. *Arnobius (c. 305, E), 6.458.*

Rational creatures have been entrusted with free will. Because of this, they are capable of converting [i.e., from bad to good]. *Disputation of Archelaus and Manes (c. 320, E), 6.189.*

All the creatures that God made, he made very good. And he gave to every individual the sense of free will, in accordance with which standard He also instituted the law of judgment. To sin is ours, and that we sin not is God's gift. For our will is made to choose either to sin or not to sin. . . . Certainly, whoever wishes to may keep the commandments. And whoever will despise them and turn aside to what is contrary to them, he will yet undoubtedly have to face this law of judgment. . . . All persons will not follow the example of [Satan's] fall and ruin. For everyone is given liberty of will. *Disputation of Archelaus and Manes (c. 320, E), 6.204, 205.*

Since both sides admit that there will be a judgment, it is necessarily involved in that admission that every person is shown to have free will. And since this is clearly brought out, there can be no doubt that every person—in the exercise of his own proper power of will—may shape his course in whatever direction he pleases. *Disputation of Archelaus and Manes (c. 320, E), 6.206.*

Natural will is the free faculty of every intelligent nature, as having nothing involuntary pertaining to its essence. *Alexander of Alexandria (c. 324, E), 6.299; see also 1.520, 1.525; extended discussions: 2.319–2.321, 4.302–4.328, 6.362–6.363.*

II. The elect

Therefore, as the elect of God, holy and beloved, put on tender mercies. Col. 3:12.

To the pilgrims of the Dispersion, . . . elect according to the foreknowledge of God the Father. 1 Pet. 1:2.

Day and night, you were anxious for the whole brotherhood, so that the number of God's elect might be saved. *Clement of Rome (c. 96, W), 1.5.*

God removes the heavens, mountains, hills and seas, so that all things become plain to His elect, so that He may bestow on them the blessing which He has promised them. *Hermas (c. 150, W), 2.10.*

The white part is the age that is to come, in which the elect of God will dwell. For those who are elected by God to eternal life will be spotless and pure. *Hermas (c. 150, W), 2.18.*

When the number is completed that He had predetermined in His own counsel, all those who have been enrolled for life will rise again. *Irenaeus (c. 180, E/W), 1.411.*

Therefore, all having been called, those who are willing to obey have been named "the called." For there is no unrighteousness with God. . . . To these, prophecy says, "If you are willing and hear me, you will eat the good things of the land," proving that choice or refusal depends on ourselves. *Clement of Alexandria (c. 195, E), 2.321.*

The teachings of both the Old and the New Testaments are unnecessary if a person is saved by nature (as Valentinus would have it) and is a believer and an elect man by nature (as Basilides thinks). *Clement of Alexandria (c. 195, E), 2.444, 445.*

It is no longer seemly that the friend of God, whom "God has foreordained before the foundation of the world" to be enrolled in the highest adoption, should fall into pleasures or fears and be occupied with the repression of lusts. For I venture to declare that as he is predestined through what he shall do and what he shall obtain, so also has he predestined himself by reason of what he knew and whom he loved. *Clement of Alexandria (c. 195, E), 2.497.*

[When] the predestined number of men will be fulfilled, men will afterwards abstain from the generation of children. *Methodius (c. 290, E), 6.313.*

III. Predestination

The Gentiles and the people of Israel, were gathered together to do whatever Your hand and Your purpose determined before to be done. Acts 4:27, 28.

For whom He foreknew, He also predestined to be conformed to the image of His Son. Rom. 8:29.

He chose us in Him before the foundation of the world, that we should be holy and without blame before him in love, having predestined us to adoption as sons by Jesus Christ to Himself. Eph. 1:4, 5.

He, then, who faultlessly acts the drama of life that God has given him to play, knows both what is to be done and what is to be endured. *Clement of Alexandria (c. 195, E), 2.541.*

"Twice dead," he says ... according to the predestined judgments of God. *Clement of Alexandria (c. 195, E), 2.573.*

We have been predestined by God, before the world was, to [appear] in the extreme end of the times. And so we are trained by God for the purpose of chastising ... the world. *Tertullian (c. 198, W), 4.23.*

Neither let anyone take comfort from—or apologize for what happens from—fate. . . . For what else is fate than what God has spoken of each one of us? Since He can foresee our constitution, He determines also the fates for us, according to the deserts and the qualities of individuals. Thus, in our case, it is not the star under which we are born that is punished. Rather, the particular nature of our disposition is blamed. *Mark Minucius Felix (c. 200, W), 4.195.*

God is good and wise. He does what is best. Therefore, there is no fixed destiny. *Methodius (c. 290, E), 6.343.*

Even the Jewish nation had wicked heresies. . . . There are the Pharisees, who ascribe the practice of sinners to fortune and fate. *Apostolic Constitutions (compiled c. 390, E), 7.452.*

IV. Synergism

Synergism is the doctrine that the human will can and must cooperate with the Holy Spirit in order for a person to be saved. According to this belief, God's grace is not irresistible.

[God] "will render to each one according to his deeds"; eternal life to those who by patient continuance in doing good seek for glory, honor, and immortality;

but to those who are self-seeking and do not obey the truth, but obey unrighteousness—indignation and wrath. Rom. 2:6, 7.

Moreover, brethren, I declare to you the gospel . . . by which also you are saved, if you hold fast that word which I preached to you—unless you believed in vain. 1 Cor. 15:1, 2.

See that you do not refuse Him who speaks. For if they did not escape who refused Him who spoke on earth, much more shall we not escape if we turn away from Him who speaks from heaven. Heb. 12:25.

Blessed is the man who endures temptation; for when he has been proved, he will receive the crown of life which the Lord has promised to those who love Him. Let no one say when he is tempted, "I am tempted by God"; for God cannot be tempted by evil, nor does he Himself tempt anyone. But each one is tempted when he is drawn away by his own desires and enticed. Jas. 1:12, 13.

The Lord is not slack concerning His promise, as some count slackness, but is longsuffering toward us, not willing that any should perish but that all should come to repentance. 2 Pet. 3:9.

When you are desirous to do well, God is also ready to assist you. *Ignatius (c. 105, E), 1.91.*

The man who has the Lord in his heart can also be lord of all, and of every one of these commandments. However, as to those who have the Lord only on their lips, whose hearts are hardened, and who are far from the Lord—the commandments are hard and difficult. *Hermas (c. 150, W), 2.29.*

"I hope, sir, to be able to keep all these commandments which you have commanded to me, the Lord strengthening me." "You will keep them," he says, "if your heart is pure towards the Lord." *Hermas (c. 150, W), 2.30.*

To those whose heart He saw would become pure and obedient to Him, He gave power to repent with the whole heart. But to those whose deceit and wickedness He perceived, and seeing that they intended to repent hypocritically, He did not grant repentance. *Hermas (c. 150, W), 2.41.*

If you bear His name but do not possess His power, it will be in vain that you bear His name. *Hermas (c. 150, W), 2.48.*

God ministers eternal salvation to those who cooperate for the attainment of knowledge and good conduct. Since what the commandments direct are in our own power, along with the performance of them, the promise is accomplished. *Clement of Alexandria (c. 195, E), 2.536.*

A man by himself working and toiling at freedom from passion achieves nothing. But if he plainly shows himself very desirous and earnest about this, he attains it by the addition of the power of God. For God conspires with willing souls. But if they abandon their eagerness, the Spirit who is bestowed by God is also restrained. For to save the unwilling is the part of one exercising compulsion. But to save the willing is that of one showing grace. *Clement of Alexandria (c. 195, E), 2.597.*

"Unless the Lord builds the house, they labor in vain who build it. Except the Lord keep the city, the watchman watches in vain." This is not said to persuade us against building. Nor does it teach us not to keep watch in order to guard the city of our soul. Rather, it shows that what is built without God (and therefore does not receive His protection) is built in vain. . . . If we were to say that such a building is not the work of the builder, but of God, . . . we would be correct. Yet, it is understood that something had also been done by human means. Nevertheless, the benefit is gratefully referred to God, who brought it to pass. The human desire is not sufficient to attain the end. Likewise, the running of those who are (as it were) athletes does not enable them to gain the prize of the high calling of God in Christ Jesus. For these things are accomplished only with the assistance of God. Therefore, it is appropriately said that "it is not of him who wills, nor of him who runs, but of God who shows mercy." *Origen (c. 225, E), 4.322.*

"I planted, Apollos watered; and God gave the increase. So then neither is he that plants anything, nor he that waters; but God, who gives the increase." Now, we could not correctly assert that the production of full crops was the work of the farmer, or of him that watered. Rather, it is the work of God. Likewise, our own perfection is not brought about as if we ourselves did nothing. Yet, it is not completed by us. Rather, God produces the greater part of it. . . . In the matter of our salvation, what is done by God is infinitely greater than what is done by ourselves. For that reason, I think, it is said that "it is not of him who wills, nor of him who runs, but of God, who shows mercy." For if that statement means

what they [the Gnostics] imagine it means, . . . then the commandments are unnecessary. Furthermore, it would be in vain that Paul himself blames some persons for having fallen away and praises others for having remained upright. It was in vain that he enacted laws for the churches. . . . However, it was *not* in vain that Paul gave such advice, censuring some and approving others. *Origen (c. 225, E), 4.322, 323.*

The apostle in one place does not purport that becoming a vessel to honor or dishonor depends upon God. Rather, he refers everything back to ourselves, saying, "If, then, a man purges himself, he will be a vessel to honor, sanctified, fit for the Master's use, and prepared for every good work." Elsewhere, he does not even purport that it is dependent upon ourselves. Rather, he appears to attribute everything to God, saying, "The potter has power over the clay, of the same lump to make one vessel to honor and another to dishonor." Since his statements are not contradictory, we must reconcile them and extract one consistent statement from both. Our own power—when separated from the knowledge of God—does not enable us to make progress. On the other hand, the knowledge of God [does not enable us to make progress, either,] unless we ourselves also contribute something to the good result. . . . And these observations are sufficient to have been made by us on the subject of free will. *Origen (c. 225, E), 4.328.*

"God is faithful, who will not allow you to be tempted beyond what you are able to bear." That is, each one is tempted in proportion to the amount of his strength or power of resistance. Now, although we have said that it is by the just judgment of God that everyone is tempted according to the amount of his strength, we are not therefore to suppose that he who is tempted will by all means prove victorious in the struggle. It is similar to a man who contends in the arena. Although he is paired with his adversary on a just principle of arrangement, he does not necessarily prove to be the winner. Yet, unless the powers of the combatants are equal, the prize of the victor will not be justly won. Nor will blame justly attach to the loser. . . . It is not written that, in temptation, He will make a way of escape so that we *will* bear it. Rather, He makes a way of escape so that we can be *able* to bear it. However, it depends upon ourselves to use this power that He has given us either with energy or with feebleness. There is no doubt that under every temptation we have a power of endurance—if we properly use the strength that is granted us. However, possessing the *power* to conquer is not the same thing as actually *being* victorious. The apostle himself has shown this in his very careful language, saying, "God will make a way to escape so that you may be *able* to bear it"—not that you *will* bear it. *Origen (c. 225, E), 4.331.*

Those who hear the word powerfully proclaimed are filled with power. They manifest this both by their dispositions and their lives. And they show this by struggling even to death on behalf of the truth. However, others are altogether empty, even though they profess to believe in God through Jesus. Not possessing any divine power, they have only the appearance of being converted to the word of God. *Origen (c. 248, E), 4.424.*

We maintain that human nature is in no way able to seek after God or to attain a clear knowledge of Him—without the help of Him whom it seeks. He makes Himself known to those who, after doing all that their powers will allow, confess that they need help from Him. For He reveals Himself to those whom He approves. *Origen (c. 248, E), 4.628.*

SEE ALSO ANGEL, ANGELS; EVIL, PROBLEM OF; FATE; FOREKNOWLEDGE OF GOD; MAN, DOCTRINE OF; SALVATION; SOVEREIGNTY AND PROVIDENCE OF GOD.

FREEDOM OF RELIGION

SEE LIBERTY, RELIGIOUS.

FUNERAL PRACTICES, CHRISTIAN

SEE BURIAL AND FUNERAL PRACTICES OF CHRISTIANS.

GALATIA

It is plain that from the following circumstances the province was called Galatia: Upon their arrival in it, the Gauls [i.e., Celts] united themselves with the Greeks. From that event, the region was called Gallogrecia, and later, Galatia. It is no wonder if he said what he did concerning the Galatians and related how a people of the West traveled over so great a distance in the middle of the earth and settled in a region of the East. *Lactantius (c. 304–313, W), 7.323.*

GAMBLING

The game of dice is to be prohibited, as is also the pursuit of gain, especially by dicing, which many follow intently. *Clement of Alexandria (c. 195, E), 2.289.*

If a bishop, presbyter, or deacon indulges himself in dice or drinking, he must either leave off those practices or else let him be deprived. If a subdeacon, a reader, or a singer does the same, he must either cease to do so or else let him be suspended. And the same is true for one of the laity. *Apostolic Constitutions (compiled c. 390, E), 7.390.*

SEE ALSO ENTERTAINMENT.

GEHENNA

Geenna is one of three Greek words that are translated as "hell" in the King James Version. The other two are *hadēs* and *tartaros*. This confusion of terms in the King James Version has led to a considerable amount of misunderstanding as to what the Scriptures teach about the afterlife. To the early church, Gehenna and Hades were two very different places. Gehenna is the lake of fire, the place of eternal punishment after the resurrection. Hades is the intermediate place where souls await the resurrection.

If your right eye causes you to sin, pluck it out and cast it from you; for it is more profitable for you that one of your members perish, than for your whole body to be cast into hell [Gr. geenna]. Matt. 5:29.

Then Death and Hades were cast into the lake of fire. This is the second death. Rev. 20:14.

"And death and Hades were sent into the lake of fire, the second death." Now this is what is called Gehenna, which the Lord called "eternal fire." *Irenaeus (c. 180, E/W), 1.566.*

If we threaten Gehenna, which is a reservoir of secret fire under the earth for purposes of punishment, we have in the same way derision heaped on us. *Tertullian (c. 197, W), 3.52.*

Consider Gehenna in your heart, which penance will extinguish for you. First imagine the magnitude of the *penalty*, so that you will not hesitate to adopt the *remedy*. What do we think this storehouse of eternal fire is—when small vent holes of it rouse such blasts of flames that neighboring cities either no longer exist, or are in daily expectation of the same fate? . . . This proves to us the perpetuity of the judgment. Although they are torn asunder, although they are devoured, they never come to an end. *Tertullian (c. 203, W), 3.665.*

I found that Gehenna was mentioned in the Gospel as a place of punishment. So I searched to see whether it is mentioned anywhere in the ancient Scriptures. I did this particularly because the Jews use the word, too. I ascertained the places where the valley of the son of Hinnom was mentioned in the Hebrew Scriptures. It was called both the valley of Hinnom and also Gehenna. Continuing my research, I found that what was called Gehenna or the valley of Hinnom was included in the lot of the tribe of Benjamin, in which Jerusalem also was situated. . . . I found a certain confirmation of what is said regarding the place of punishment, intended for the purification of such souls as are to be purified by torments, in accord with the saying: "The Lord comes like a refiner's fire, and like fullers' soap. And he will sit as a refiner and purifier of silver and of gold." It is in the precincts of Jerusalem, then, that punishments will be inflicted upon those who undergo the process of purification. These are those who have received the elements of wickedness into the substance of their souls. . . . But the remarks that might be made on this topic are neither to be made to everyone, nor to be spoken on the present occasion. For there is some danger to committing to writing the explanation of such subjects. For the multitude need no further instruction than that which relates to the punishment of sinners. To ascend beyond this is not expedient, on account of those who are restrained with difficulty from plunging into any degree of wickedness—even by the fear of eternal punishment. *Origen (c. 248, E), 4.584, 585.*

An ever-burning Gehenna will burn up the condemned—a punishment that devours with living flames. Nor will there be any means by which at any time they can have either rest or an end to their torments. Souls with their bodies will be reserved in infinite tortures for suffering. . . . This is in accord with the truth of Holy Scripture, which says, "Their worm will not die and their fire will not be quenched." . . . The pain of punishment will then be without the fruit of penitence. Weeping will be useless and prayer ineffectual. Too late, they will believe in eternal punishment who would not believe in eternal life. *Cyprian (c. 250, W), 5.464, 465.*

A horrible place it is, of which the name is Gehenna. There is there an awful murmuring and groaning of bewailing souls. There are flames belching forth through the horrid darkness of thick night. It is always breathing out the raging fires of a smoking furnace. . . . There are many different degrees of its violence, as it gathers into itself whatever tortures the consuming fire of the emitting heat can supply. Those who have been rejected by the voice of the Lord, those who scorned His rule, it punishes with different dooms. *Treatise on the Glory of Martyrdom (c. 255, W), 5.584.*

SEE ALSO DEAD, INTERMEDIATE STATE OF THE; ETERNAL PUNISHMENTS AND REWARDS.

GENESIS

SEE ADAM; CREATION; EVE; FALL OF MAN; FLOOD, THE; TOWER OF BABEL.

GENTILE TIMES

SEE ESCHATOLOGY; ISRAEL OF GOD; JEW, JEWS.

GENTILES

SEE ISRAEL OF GOD.

GERMANS

[The name of Christ has reached] the various confines of the Moors, all the limits of Spain, the diverse nations of the Gauls, and the haunts of the Britons—inaccessible to the Romans, but subjugated to Christ. . . . Furthermore, there are Germans, Scythians, and persons of many remote nations and provinces and islands— many to us unknown and which we can scarcely enumerate. In all these places, the name of Christ (who is already come) reigns. *Tertullian (c. 197, W), 3.158.*

All the Germans die by strangulation, except those who are killed in battle. *Bardesanes (c. 222, E), 8.732.*

If the gods willed that the Germans and the Persians would be defeated because Christians dwelled among their tribes, why did the gods grant victory to the Romans? For Christians dwelled among their peoples also. *Arnobius (c. 305, E), 6.417.*

GIFTS OF THE SPIRIT

And it will come to pass afterward that I will pour out My Spirit on all flesh; your sons and your daughters will prophesy, your old men will dream dreams, your young men will see visions. Joel 2:28.

Many will say to Me in that day, "Lord, Lord, have we not prophesied in Your name, cast out demons in Your name, and done many wonders in Your name?" And then I will declare to them, "I never knew you; depart from Me, you who practice lawlessness!" Matt. 7:22, 23.

But you will receive power when the Holy Spirit has come upon you; and you will be witnesses to me. Acts 1:8.

There are diversities of gifts, but the same Spirit. There are differences of ministries, but the same Lord. . . . For to one is given the word of wisdom through the Spirit, to another the word of knowledge through the same Spirit, to another faith by the same

Spirit, to another gifts of healing by the same Spirit, to another the working of miracles, to another prophecy, to another discerning of spirits, to another different kinds of tongues, to another the interpretation of tongues. 1 Cor. 12:4, 5, 8–10.

Love never fails. But whether there are prophecies, they will fail; whether there are tongues, they will cease; whether there is knowledge, it will vanish away. 1 Cor. 13:8.

Tongues are for a sign, not to those who believe but to unbelievers; but prophesying is not for unbelievers but for those who believe. 1 Cor. 14:22.

Seeing that the divine fruits of righteousness abound among you, I rejoice exceedingly and above measure in your happy and honored spirits. For you have received the engrafted spiritual gift with such effect. *Barnabas (c. 70–130, E), 1.137.*

Let everyone be subject to his neighbor, according to the special gift bestowed upon him. *Clement of Rome (c. 96, W), 1.15.*

Grace, widely spread, increases in the saints. It furnishes understanding, reveals mysteries, announces times, and rejoices over the faithful. *Letter to Diognetus (c. 125–200), 1.29.*

Daily some are becoming disciples in the name of Christ, . . . who are also receiving gifts, each as he is worth. These are illumined through the name of this Christ. For one receives the spirit of understanding, another of counsel, another of strength, another of healing, another of fore-knowledge, another of teaching, and another of the fear of God. *Justin Martyr (c. 160, E), 1.214.*

It was prophesied that, after the ascent of Christ to heaven, He would deliver us from error and give us gifts. . . . Accordingly, we . . . have received gifts from Christ. *Justin Martyr (c. 160, E), 1.214.*

The prophetical gifts remain with us, even to the present time. And hence you should understand that [the gifts] formerly among your nation have been transferred to us. *Justin Martyr (c. 160, E), 1.240.*

It was necessary that such gifts would cease from you [Jews] and . . . would again, as had been predicted, become gifts which, from the grace of His Spirit's power, He would impart to those who believe in Him, according as He deems each man worthy of it. . . . Now, it is

possible to see among us women and men who possess gifts of the Spirit of God. *Justin Martyr (c. 160, E), 1.243.*

For the Lord . . . "gave gifts to men," and bestowed on those who believe in Him the power "to tread upon serpents and scorpions," that is, of the leader of apostasy. [Eph. 4:8; Luke 10:19]. *Irenaeus (c. 180, E/W), 1.388.*

Those also will be thus confuted who belong to Simon and Carpocrates [heretical teachers], and if there are any others who are said to perform miracles. For they perform what they do neither through the power of God, nor in connection with the truth, nor for the well-being of men. . . . They can neither confer sight on the blind, nor hearing on the deaf, nor expel all sorts of demons—except those who are sent into others by themselves (if they can even do this much). . . . And so far are they from being able to raise the dead, that they do not even believe this can possibly be done. However, the Lord raised the dead, and the apostles did so by means of prayer, and this has been frequently done in the brotherhood on account of some necessity. When the entire church in that particular locality entreated God with much fasting and prayer, the spirit of the dead man has returned, and he has been bestowed in answer to the prayers of the saints. *Irenaeus (c. 180, E/W), 1.407.*

It behooves us to flee from them [the Gnostics] as we would from Satan. The greater the display with which they are said to perform miracles, the more carefully should we watch them, as having been endowed with a greater spirit of wickedness. *Irenaeus (c. 180, E/W), 1.407.*

Those who are truly His disciples, receiving grace from Him, . . . perform [works] in His name, in order to promote the welfare of others, according to the gift that each one has received from Him. Some truly and certainly cast out devils. The result is that those who have been cleansed from evil spirits frequently both believe and join themselves to the church. Others have foreknowledge of things to come. They see visions, and they utter prophetic expressions. Still others heal the sick by laying their hands upon them, and the sick are made whole. What is more, as I have said, even the dead have been raised up and remained among us for many years. What more can I say? It is not possible to name the number of the gifts which the church throughout the whole world has received from God, in the name of Jesus

Christ, who was crucified under Pontius Pilate, and which she exerts day by day for the benefit of the Gentiles, neither practicing deception upon any, nor taking any reward from them. For, just as she has received without charge from God, so does she minister without charge. Nor does she perform anything by means of angelic invocations, incantations, or any other wicked curious art. . . . Calling upon the name of our Lord Jesus Christ, she has worked miracles for the benefit of mankind, and not to lead them into error. The name of our Lord Jesus Christ even now confers benefits. It cures thoroughly and effectively all who anywhere believe on Him. *Irenaeus (c. 180, E/W), 1.409.*

The following passage was written about the Montanists, who thought only they—not the church—had the spirit of prophecy.

Wretched men, indeed! They wish to be pseudo-prophets, for they exclude the gift of prophecy from the church. . . . They hold themselves aloof from the communion of the brethren. We must conclude, moreover, that these men cannot admit the apostle Paul, either. For, in his letter to the Corinthians, he speaks expressly of prophetical gifts. And he recognizes men and women prophesying *in the church. Irenaeus (c. 180, E/W), 1.429.*

For this reason, the apostle declares, "We speak wisdom among those who are perfect," calling those persons "perfect" who have received the Spirit of God, and who through the Spirit of God do speak in all languages, as he himself also used to speak. In like manner, we also hear many brethren in the church who possess prophetic gifts, and who through the Spirit speak all kinds of languages, and bring to light for the general benefit the hidden things of men. *Irenaeus (c. 180, E/W), 1.531.*

"The manifestation of the Spirit is given for our profit. To one is given the word of wisdom by the Spirit. To another, the word of knowledge." . . . Such being the case, the prophets are perfect in prophecy; the righteous, in righteousness; the martyrs, in confession; and others, in preaching. It is not that they are not sharers in the common virtues. Rather, they are proficient in those to which they are appointed. . . . Each has his own proper gift of God—one in one way, another in another. But the apostles were perfected in all. If you choose to look, you will find in their acts and writings knowledge,

life, preaching, righteousness, purity, and prophecy. *Clement of Alexandria (c. 195, E), 2.434.*

What is nobler than to tread under foot the gods of the nations, to exorcise evil spirits, to perform cures, to seek divine revelations, and to live to God? These are the pleasures—these are the spectacles—that befit Christian men. *Tertullian (c. 197, W), 3.91.*

[If the church were in error, as the Gnostics claim,] during the interval, so many thousands were wrongly baptized; so many works of faith were wrongly wrought; so many miraculous gifts and so many spiritual endowments were wrongly set in operation. *Tertullian (c. 197, W), 3.256.*

The heretics will, besides, add a great deal respecting the high authority of each teacher of heresy—how these teachers mightily strengthened belief in their own doctrine, how they raised the dead, restored the sick, foretold the future. They say this so that they might deservedly be regarded as apostles. As if this warning were not also in the written record: that many would come who were to work even the greatest miracles, in defense of the deception of their corrupt preaching. *Tertullian (c. 197, W), 3.264, 265.*

When you ascend from that most sacred bath of your new birth and spread your hands for the first time in the house of your mother, together with your brethren, ask from the Father, ask from the Lord, that His own specialties of grace and distributions of gifts may be supplied to you. *Tertullian (c. 198, W), 3.679.*

He declared that many would come and "display great signs and wonders," so as to turn aside the very elect. Yet, despite that, Christ would not receive them. So He showed how rash it was to believe in signs and wonders, for they would be so very easy to accomplish, even by false christs. *Tertullian (c. 207, W), 3.322.*

"In the last days, I will pour out of my Spirit upon all flesh, and their sons and their daughters will prophesy." . . . So, then, the Creator promised the gift of His Spirit in the latter days. And since Christ has in these last days appeared as the dispenser of spiritual gifts, . . . it evidently follows in connection with this prediction of the last days, that this gift of the Spirit belongs to Him who is the Christ of the predictors. *Tertullian (c. 207, W), 3.446.*

[THE FOLLOWING QUOTATION REFLECTS THE MONTANISTIC PRACTICE OF ECSTATIC PROPHECY:] Let Marcion then exhibit, as gifts of his God, some prophets—such as have not spoken by human sense, but with the Spirit of God—such as have both predicted things to come and have made manifest the secrets of the heart. Let him produce a psalm, a vision, a prayer—only let it be by the Spirit, in an ecstasy (that is, in a rapture) whenever an interpretation of tongues has occurred to him. Let him show to me also that any woman of boastful tongue in his community has ever prophesied from among those special "holy sisters" of his. Now, all these signs are forthcoming from my side without any difficulty. *Tertullian (c. 207, W), 3.446, 447.*

From Him also is sought the spirit of wisdom, at whose disposal is enumerated that sevenfold distribution of the spirit of grace by Isaiah. *Tertullian (c. 207, W), 3.465.*

The apostle most assuredly foretold that there were to be spiritual gifts in the church. *Tertullian (c. 210, W), 3.188.*

[Paul's] reason for saying so was so that the could re-assert his apostolic authority. For apostles have the Holy Spirit properly. They have Him fully in the operations of prophecy, the efficacy of virtues, and the evidences of tongues. They do not have Him partially as all other do. *Tertullian (c. 212, W), 4.53.*

The apostles left the grounds of their statements to be examined into by those who would deserve the excellent gifts of the Spirit—and who, particularly by means of the Holy Spirit Himself—would obtain the gift of language, wisdom, and knowledge. *Origen (c. 225, E), 4.239.*

The spiritual meaning that the Law conveys is not known to all—but only to those on whom the grace of the Holy Spirit is bestowed in the word of wisdom and knowledge. *Origen (c. 225, E), 4.241.*

When a gift (the word of wisdom, word of knowledge, or any other gift that has been given) has been bestowed upon a man either by baptism or by the grace of the Spirit, but has not been rightly used, . . . the gift of the Spirit will certainly be withdrawn from his soul. *Origen (c. 225, E), 4.296.*

Being purified by lengthened abstinence and filled with holy and religious training, through

these means they assume a portion of divinity and earn the grace of prophecy and other divine gifts. *Origen (c. 225, E), 4.336.*

I consider that the Holy Spirit supplies the material of the gifts (which come from God) to those who—through Him and through participation in Him—are called saints. As a result, the said substance of the gifts is made powerful by God, is ministered by Christ, and owes its actual existence in men to the Holy Spirit. I am led to this view of the *charismata* by the words of Paul, which he writes somewhere, "There are diversities of gifts, but the same Spirit." *Origen (c. 228, E), 9.329.*

If there are those who have obtained the gift of accurate comprehension of these things, they know what they should do. But as for me, I acknowledge that I fall short of the ability to see into the depth of the things signified here. . . . Therefore, I do not venture to commit it to writing. *Origen (c. 245, E), 9.502.*

Traces of those signs and wonders are still preserved among those who regulate their lives by the teachings of the Gospel. *Origen (c. 248, E), 4.397, 398.*

He who is adorned with the spiritual gift that is called the "word of wisdom," he will explain also the reason of the heavens opening and the dove appearing. *Origen (c. 248, E), 4.415.*

There are still preserved among Christians traces of that Holy Spirit that appeared in the form of a dove. They expel evil spirits, perform many cures, and foresee certain events. *Origen (c. 248, E), 4.415.*

The name of Jesus can still remove distractions from the minds of men, expel demons, and also take away diseases. Furthermore, it produces a marvelous meekness of spirit and a complete change of character. *Origen (c. 248, E), 4.427.*

The Jews no longer have prophets or miracles. Yet, traces of those things are still found among Christians to a considerable extent. Some of these miracles are more remarkable than any that existed among the Jews. I have witnessed these myself. *Origen (c. 248, E), 4.433.*

Down to the present time, those whom God wills are healed by His name. This fact demonstrates the nobility of the work of Jesus. *Origen (c. 248, E), 4.445.*

Jesus says that even some who lead wicked lives will perform miracles in the name of Jesus and expel demons out of men.... We see, then, that it is possible for someone who makes use of His name, and who is moved upon by some power in an unknown way, to make the pretence that he is the Christ and to seem to perform miracles like those of Jesus. Others, through His name, would perform works resembling those of His genuine disciples. *Origen (c. 248, E), 4.450.*

The works of the antichrists, and of those who pretend that they can work miracles as though they were the disciples of Christ, are said to be lying signs and wonders. They prevail among those who perish with all of the deceit of unrighteousness. In contrast, the works of Christ and his disciples did not have deceit for their fruits. Rather, they had the salvation of human souls. Who would rationally assert that an improved moral life—one that daily lessened the number of a man's sins—could proceed from a system of deceit?... So if we once acknowledge ... that some works can be found among men that proceed from divine power, why would we not test those who profess to perform them? Why not test them by their lives, morals, and the consequences of their miracles? Do they result in the injury of men or in the reformation of conduct? *Origen (c. 248, E), 4.451.*

We can clearly show a countless multitude of Greeks and barbarians who acknowledge the existence of Jesus. And some give evidence of their having received through this faith a marvelous power by the cures which they perform, invoking no other name over those who need their help than that of the God of all things, and of Jesus—along with a mention of His history. For by these means, I, too, have seen many persons freed from grievous calamities, from distractions of mind, madness, and countless other ills that could not be cured by either men or devils. *Origen (c. 248, E), 4.473.*

Not a few cures are brought about in the name of Jesus, and certain other manifestations of no small significance have taken place. *Origen (c. 248, E), 4.475.*

Paul, too, in the list of *charismata* bestowed by God, placed first "the word of wisdom." Secondly, as being inferior to it, there is "the word of knowledge." Thirdly, and lower down, there is "faith." And because he regarded "the word"

as higher than miraculous powers, he for that reason placed workings of miracles and gifts of healing in a lower place than the gifts of the word. *Origen (c. 248, E), 4.483.*

Divine wisdom ... is the first of the so-called *charismata* of God. The second after it—in the estimation of those who know how to distinguish such things accurately—is what is called knowledge. And the third is faith—seeing that even the more simple class of men adhere to the service of God. Therefore, Paul says, "To one is given by the Spirit the word of wisdom; to another, the word of knowledge by the same Spirit; to another, faith by the same Spirit." Therefore, it is no ordinary individuals whom you will find to have participated in the divine wisdom. Rather, it is the more excellent and distinguished among those who have given their adherence to Christianity. *Origen (c. 248, E), 4.579.*

It is not the part of a divine spirit to drive the prophetess into such a state of ecstasy and madness that she loses control of herself. For he who is under the influence of the Divine Spirit would be the first to receive the beneficial effects.... Moreover, when a person is in close contact with the Deity, it should be the time of clearest perception. *Origen (c. 248, E), 4.612.*

The Holy Spirit gave signs of His presence at the beginning of Christ's ministry. And after His ascension, He gave still more. But since that time, these signs have diminished, although there are still traces of His presence in a few who have had their souls purified by the Gospel, and their actions regulated by its influence. *Origen (c. 248, E), 4.614.*

This is He who places prophets in the church, instructs teachers, directs tongues, gives powers and healing, does wonderful works, offers discrimination of spirits, affords powers of government, suggests counsels, and orders and arranges whatever other gifts there are of the *charismata. Novatian (c. 235, W), 5.641.*

By His own Power, He not only performed those miraculous deeds, ... but He has permitted many others to attempt them and to perform them by the use of His name.... He chose fishermen, artisans, peasants, and unskilled persons of a similar kind, so that they, being sent through various nations, would perform all those miracles without any fraud and without any material aids. *Arnobius (c. 305, E), 6.427.*

Even if you were to work signs and wonders, or even raise the dead, or even present to us the very representation of Paul himself, you would still remain accursed. For we have been instructed beforehand concerning you. . . . For we already know that the devil himself is to be transformed into an angel of light and that his servants are to make their appearance in a similar manner. We know that they will perform signs and wonders—so much so that if it were possible, they would deceive the very elect. *Disputation of Archelaus and Manes (c. 320, E), 6.209, 210.*

In that first Epistle to the Corinthians, Paul speaks in the following terms of the perfection that is to come: "Whether there are prophecies, they will fail. Whether there are tongues, they will cease. Whether there is knowledge, it will be destroyed. For we know in part, and we prophesy in part. But when that which is perfect will come, then that which is in part will be done away." . . . Let this man [Manes, a heretic] tell us what prophecy of the Jews or Hebrews he has done away with. Or what tongues he has caused to cease—whether of the Greeks or of others who worship idols. Or what alien dogmas has he destroyed—whether of a Valentinus, Marcion, Tatian, or a Sabellius—or of any others of those who have constructed for themselves their peculiar systems of knowledge? *Disputation of Archelaus and Manes (c. 320, E), 6.211.*

[Upon the coming of] my Lord Jesus Christ, who is the truly perfect one, . . . where there are prophecies or the books of prophets, they will fail. Where there are the tongues of the whole race, they will cease. For men will no longer need to feel anxiety or to care about those things that are necessary for life. Where there is knowledge—regardless of what teachers possess it, it also will be destroyed. For none of these things will be able to survive the coming of that mighty King. *Disputation of Archelaus and Manes (c. 320, E), 6.211.*

It is not necessary that every one of the faithful should cast out demons, raise the dead, or speak with tongues. But only such a one who has been graciously given this gift—for the purpose that it may be advantageous to the salvation of the unbelievers. . . . We say these things

so that those who have received such gifts may not exalt themselves against those who have not received them. We are referring to those gifts pertaining to the working of miracles. Otherwise, there is no man who has believed in God through Christ who has not received some spiritual gift. For it is a gift of God to have been delivered from the impiety of polytheism and to have believed in God the Father through Christ. . . . Therefore, do not let anyone who works signs and wonders judge any of the faithful who is not given the same. For there are various gifts of God that are bestowed by Him through Christ. And one man receives one gift, and another man, another. Perhaps one has the word of wisdom. Another, the word of knowledge. Another, the discerning of spirits. Another, foreknowledge of things to come. Another, the word of teaching. Another, longsuffering. And another, celibacy according to the law. . . .

Therefore, let none of you exalt himself against his brother—even though you may be a prophet or a worker of miracles. For if it happens that there are no longer any unbelievers, all the power of signs will afterwards be unnecessary. To be godly is from one's own good disposition. But to work wonders is from the power of Him that works them by us. Now, godliness concerns ourselves. However, to work wonders, concerns God. . . . To be a Christian is in our own power. But to be an apostle, bishop, or to be in any other such office—this is not in our own power. Rather, it is at the disposal of God, who bestows the gifts. . . . Furthermore, every person who prophesies is not holy. Every person who casts out devils is not religious. For even Balaam the prophet, the son of Beor, prophesied, although he was himself ungodly. So did Caiaphas, the falsely named high priest. In fact, the devil foretells many things about God, and so do the demons. Yet, despite that, there is not even a spark of godliness in them. . . . It is obvious, therefore, that the ungodly—even if they prophesy—do not cover their own impiety by their prophesying. And those who cast out demons are not sanctified by the fact that demons are made subject to them. *Apostolic Constitutions (compiled c. 390, E), 7.479–7.481; extended discussion: 7.479–7.481.*

SEE ALSO EXORCISM; HEALING, DIVINE; HEARING FROM GOD; HOLY SPIRIT; MIRACLES; PRAYER (IV. PRAYING IN THE SPIRIT); PROPHECY, PROPHETS.

GLADIATORS

The robber commits murder for the sake of plunder, but the rich man purchases gladiators for the sake of their being killed. *Tatian (c. 160, E), 2.75.*

When they know that we cannot endure even to see a man put to death, though justly, who of them can accuse us of murder or cannibalism? Who does not reckon among the things of greatest interest the contests of gladiators and wild beasts, especially those which are given by you? But we have renounced such spectacles, deeming that to see a man put to death is much the same as killing him. *Athenagoras (c. 175, E), 2.147.*

We are forbidden so much as to witness shows of gladiators, lest we become partakers and abettors of murders. *Theophilus (c. 180, E), 2.115.*

Some of [the Gnostics] do not even keep away from that bloody spectacle that is hateful both to God and men. I speak of the spectacle in which gladiators either fight with wild beasts or else fight each other in single combat. *Irenaeus (c. 180, E/W), 1.324.*

It remains for us to examine the spectacle most noted of all [i.e., the gladiator fights]. . . . Formerly, in the belief that the souls of the departed were appeased by human blood, the Romans were in the habit of buying captives or slaves of wicked disposition and burning them in their funeral ceremonies. Afterwards, they thought it would be good to throw the veil of pleasure over their iniquity. Therefore, those whom they had provided for the combat, they killed at the places of burial on the funeral day. First, they trained them in arms as best they could, only so that they could learn to die. *Tertullian (c. 197, W), 3.85.*

We will now see how the Scriptures condemn the amphitheater. . . . Gladiators who are not charged with crime are offered in sale for the games, so that they may become the victims of the public pleasure. Even in the case of those who are judicially condemned to the amphitheater, what a monstrous thing it is. For, in undergoing their punishment, they advance from some less serious crime to the crime of homicide. I am addressing those remarks to the pagans. As to Christians, I will not insult them by adding another word as to the aversion with which they should regard this sort of exhibition. *Tertullian (c. 197, W), 3.87.*

The prohibition of murder shows me that a trainer of gladiators is also to be excluded from the church. *Tertullian (c. 200, W), 3.67.*

In the chariot games, who does not shudder at the madness of the people brawling among themselves? Who does not shudder at the teaching of murder in the gladiatorial games? . . . Thus you demand murder in *reality*, although you weep at it in *fiction*. *Mark Minucius Felix (c. 200, W), 4.196.*

The gladiator games are prepared so that blood may gladden the lust of cruel eyes. . . . Training is undergone to acquire the power to murder. The achievement of murder is its glory. *Cyprian (c. 250, W), 5.277.*

Did He send souls . . . to build amphitheaters for themselves—places of blood and open wickedness? In one, they watch men devoured and torn in pieces by wild beasts. At others, they slay men for no purpose except to please and gratify the spectators. Did He send souls, on the very days in which such wicked deeds are done, to spend those days in general enjoyment—having a celebration with festive gaiety? *Arnobius (c. 305, E), 6.450.*

Yet, they call these "sports," in which human blood is shed! . . . I now ask whether they can be just and pious men, who, when they see men placed under the stroke of death and pleading for mercy, not only *allow* them to be put to death, but also *demand* it! They give cruel and inhuman votes for their death, for they are not satisfied with mere wounds or the shedding of blood. . . . They are even angry with the combatants unless one of the two is quickly slain. As though they thirsted for human blood, they hate delays. . . . Filled with this practice, they have lost their humanity! *Lactantius (c. 304–313, W), 7.187.*

If, then, it is in no way permitted to commit homicide, it is not allowed for us to be present at all—lest any bloodshed should reach our conscience. *Lactantius (c. 304–313, W), 7.187; see also 3.88.*

SEE ALSO ENTERTAINMENT; SPORTS.

GLUTTONY

SEE FOOD.

GNOSTICS, GNOSTICISM

The primary heresy the pre-Nicene church faced was Gnosticism. There were numerous Gnostic teachers and sects, with varying teachings. There were some basic teachings, however, that all Gnostic sects had in common. Among these was the teaching that mankind and the earth were not created by the Father of Jesus. Rather, the Demiurge, who was either a wicked angel or a lesser deity, created mankind and the earth. Because of the imperfections of the Demiurge, all material things (including man's flesh) are inherently flawed and incapable of salvation. The Gnostics taught that the God of the Old Testament was harsh and cruel and that he was this Demiurge. Some Gnostics labelled him as the "just God," in contrast to Jesus' Father, who is the "good God." Feeling pity on mankind, the ultimate God, the Father of Jesus, sent his Son to show humans the way to salvation. Since the flesh is inherently corrupt, the Son never actually became man. Some Gnostics, called Docetists, taught that the Son took on only the illusion of flesh. Other Gnostic teachers said that there was an actual man named Jesus, whose body the Son of God possessed and used—only to abandon Jesus at the crucifixion.

Most Gnostic teachers rejected the physical sacraments of baptism and communion as being inefficacious. They also rejected the teaching of the resurrection of the body, along with the intermediate state of the dead. Gnostic teachers often claimed that the apostles had secretly revealed their teachings to a few close followers. Without this revealed knowledge (gnōsis), humans cannot be saved. Some Gnostic groups taught that there were numerous lesser divinities, and most Gnostics believed in both male and female deities. Some Gnostic sects practiced a strict asceticism; others were notoriously licentious. Among the leading Gnostic teachers of the second century were Basilides, Carpocrates, Cerinthus, and Valentinus. Another leading second-century heretic, Marcion, held to some of the basic Gnostic tenets.

I. Basic Gnostic tenets

II. Female deities of the Gnostics

I. Basic Gnostic tenets

O Timothy! Guard what was committed to your trust, avoiding the profane and vain babblings and contradictions of what is falsely called knowledge [gno-sis]—by professing it, some have strayed concerning the faith. 1 Tim. 6:20, 21.

Every spirit that does not confess that Jesus Christ has come in the flesh is not of God. And this is the spirit of the Antichrist, which you have heard was coming, and is now already in the world. 1 John 4:3.

The unbelieving say that He only *seemed* to suffer. *Ignatius (c. 105, E), 1.70.*

How does anyone benefit me if he praises me, but blasphemes my Lord—not confessing that He was possessed of a body? *Ignatius (c. 105, E), 1.88.*

[The Gnostics] abstain from the Eucharist and from prayer, because they do not confess the Eucharist to be the flesh of our Savior Jesus Christ. . . . Those, therefore, who speak against this gift of God, incur death. *Ignatius (c. 105, E), 1.89.*

You may have fallen in with some [Gnostics] who are called Christians, but who do not admit this. For they venture to blaspheme the God of Abraham . . . and say there is no resurrection of the dead, and that their souls, when they die, are taken to heaven. Do not imagine that they are Christians. *Justin Martyr (c. 160, E), 1.239.*

Those who maintain the wrong opinion say that there is no resurrection of the flesh. *Justin Martyr (c. 160, E), 1.294.*

There are some who maintain that even Jesus himself appeared only as a spiritual Being, and not in the flesh. *Justin Martyr (c. 160, E), 1.295.*

When the sacred band of apostles had in various ways completed their lives' work, and when the [next] generation of men had passed away (to whom it had been vouchsafed to personally listen to the godlike wisdom), then did the confederacy of godless error take its rise through the treachery of false teachers. For upon seeing that none of the apostles were living any longer, they at length attempted with bare and uplifted head to oppose the preaching of the truth by preaching "knowledge falsely so called." *Hegesippus (c. 170), 8.764.*

They deny that the Son assumed anything material. For [according to them] matter is indeed incapable of salvation. . . . At every pagan festival celebrated in honor of the idols, these men are the first to assemble. . . . Some of them do not even keep away from that bloody spectacle that is hateful both to God and men, in which gladiators either fight with wild beasts or fight each other in single combat. *Irenaeus (c. 180, E/W), 1.324.*

Valentinus adapted the principles of the heresy known as "Gnostic" to the distinctive character of his own school. *Irenaeus (c. 180, E/W), 1.332.*

[The Gnostics use] the above-named invocations so that the persons referred to [upon their deaths] may become incapable of being seized or seen by the principalities and powers. They also use them so that their inner man may ascend on high in an invisible manner. They believe that their body is left among created things in this world, while their soul is sent forward to the Demiurge. And they instruct their disciples, on their reaching the principalities and powers, to make use of these words: "I am a son from the Father—the Father who had a pre-existence, and I am a son in Him who is pre-existent. I have come to behold all things, both those which belong to myself and others, although, strictly speaking, they do not belong to others, but to Achamoth, who is female in nature, and made these things for herself". . . . And they maintain that, by saying these things, the dead person escapes from the spiritual powers. He then advances to the companions of the Demiurge, and addresses them in this manner: "I am a vessel more precious than the female who formed you. If your mother is ignorant of her own descent, I know myself, and I am aware from where I am. And I call upon the incorruptible Sophia, who is in the Father, and is the Mother of your mother." *Irenaeus (c. 180, E/W), 1.346.*

Saturnus [a Gnostic teacher] presented it as a truth that the Savior was without birth, without body, and without form. Rather, he only *appeared* to be a visible man. Saturnus asserted that the God of the Jews was one of the angels. It was for this reason that Christ came to destroy the God of the Jews: because all the powers wished to destroy His Father. . . . This heretic was the first to declare that two kinds of men were created by the angels—one kind who are wicked and the other who are good. . . . Furthermore, He did not suffer death Himself. Rather, Simon, a certain man of Cyrene, under compulsion carried the cross in his place. Now Jesus changed the appearance of this Simon so that everyone would think he was Jesus. Through ignorance and error, Simon was cru-

cified, while Jesus Himself took on the form of Simon and stood by and laughed at everyone. *Irenaeus (c. 180, E/W), 1.349.*

Carpocrates and his followers maintain that the world and all the things in it were created by angels greatly inferior to the unbegotten Father. They also hold that Jesus was the son of Joseph. They say He was just like other men, differing from them only in this respect: that inasmuch as his soul was steadfast and pure, he perfectly remembered those things which he had witnessed within the sphere of the unbegotten God. *Irenaeus (c. 180, E/W), 1.350.*

So unbridled is their madness, that they declare they have in their power all things that are irreligious and ungodly. And they are at liberty to practice them. For they maintain that things are evil or good simply because of human opinion. They deem it necessary, therefore, that by means of transmigration from body to body, souls should experience every kind of life. *Irenaeus (c. 180, E/W), 1.351.*

Others of them employ outward marks, branding their disciples inside the lobe of the right ear. From among these ones, there also arose Marcellina, who came to Rome under [the episcopate of] Anicetus. Holding these doctrines, she led multitudes astray. They call themselves Gnostics. They also possess images, some of them painted, and others formed from different kinds of material. They maintain that a likeness of Christ was made by Pilate at that time when Jesus lived among them. *Irenaeus (c. 180, E/W), 1.351.*

In my first book, which immediately precedes this, exposing "knowledge falsely so called," I showed you, my very dear friend, that the whole [Gnostic] system developed in divergent and opposite ways. . . . I mentioned, too, the multitude of those Gnostics . . . and the points of difference between them. I explained their various doctrines, and the order of their succession. I have also described all those heresies which have originated with them. Moreover, I showed that all these heretics who introduce impious and irreligious doctrines take their beginning from Simon [Magus]. *Irenaeus (c. 180, E/W), 1.359.*

Those, moreover, who say that the world was formed by angels, or by another other Maker of it, contrary to the will of Him who is the

Supreme Father, err first of all in this very point. *Irenaeus (c. 180, E/W), 1.361.*

[The Gnostics] possess no proof of their system, which has but recently been invented by them. Sometimes they rest upon certain numbers; sometimes, on syllables; and still other times, on names. *Irenaeus (c. 180, E/W), 1.401.*

But the rest, who are called Gnostics, take their rise from Menander, Simon's disciple, as I have shown. And each one of them appeared to be both the father and the high priest of that doctrine into which he has been initiated. *Irenaeus (c. 180, E/W), 1.417.*

Some, however, make the assertion, that this dispensational Jesus did become incarnate, and did suffer. They represent Him as having passed through Mary just as water passes through a duct. But others allege him to be the Son of the Demiurge, upon whom the dispensational Jesus descended. However, still others say that Jesus was born from Joseph and Mary, but that the Christ from above descended upon him. For Christ Himself was without flesh and was impassible. However, none of the heretics acknowledge that the Word of God was made flesh. *Irenaeus (c. 180, E/W), 1.427.*

This [Father] is the Maker of heaven and earth, as is shown from his words. He is not the false Father who has been invented by Marcion, Valentinus, Basilides, Carpocrates, Simon, or the rest of the falsely called Gnostics. *Irenaeus (c. 180, E/W), 1.468.*

Supposing that He was not flesh [as the Gnostics say], but was a man merely in appearance, how could He have been crucified and how could blood and water have issued from His pierced side? *Irenaeus (c. 180, E/W), 1.507.*

I have proved already that it is the same thing to say that He merely *seemed* to appear and to say that He received nothing from Mary. For He would not have been a human, truly possessing flesh and blood (by which He redeemed us), unless He had summed up in Himself the ancient formation of Adam. *Irenaeus (c. 180, E/W), 1.527.*

Those persons who invent the existence of another Father beyond the Creator, and who call him "the good God," deceive themselves. *Irenaeus (c. 180, E/W), 1.530.*

The heretics . . . do not admit the salvation of their flesh. . . . Instead, they claim that immedi-

ately upon their death, they will pass above the heavens and the Demiurge [Creator] and go to the Mother or to that Father whom they have invented. . . . For they do not choose to understand, that if these things are as they say, the Lord Himself, in whom they profess to believe, did not rise again on the third day. Rather, immediately upon His expiring on the cross, He undoubtedly departed on high, leaving His body to the earth. *Irenaeus (c. 180, E/W), 1.560.*

The Lord observed the law of the dead so that He could become the First-Begotten from the dead. And he tarried until the third day "in the lower parts of the earth." . . . Accordingly, how must these men not be put to confusion, who allege that "the lower parts" refer to this world of ours, but that their inner man, leaving the body here, ascends into the super-celestial place! *Irenaeus (c. 180, E/W), 1.560.*

I wonder how some dare to call themselves "perfect" and "Gnostics." They are inflated and boastful, viewing themselves above the apostle. For Paul himself acknowledged about himself: "Not that I have already attained or am already perfect" [Phil. 3:15]. *Clement of Alexandria (c. 195, E), 2.222.*

Let not the above-mentioned people call us "natural men," by way of reproach. *Clement of Alexandria (c. 195, E), 2.426.*

[The Gnostics] . . . are very anxious to shake that belief in the resurrection that was firmly settled before the appearance of our modern Sadducees. As a result, they even deny that the expectation thereof has any relation whatever to the flesh. . . . For they cannot but be apprehensive that, if it is once determined that Christ's flesh was human, a presumption would immediately arise in opposition to them that our flesh must by all means rise again. For it has already risen in Christ. *Tertullian (c. 210, W), 3.521.*

Here they discover humanity mingled with divinity—so they deny the manhood [of Christ]. *Tertullian (c. 210, W), 3.535.*

They distort into some imaginary sense even the most clearly described doctrine of the resurrection of the dead, alleging that even death itself must be understood in a spiritual sense. They say that the thing which is commonly supposed to be death (that is, separation of body and soul) is not really so. They say that it is instead simply the ignorance of God. Because of this ignorance, they say man is dead to God and is buried in error (similarly to being buried in the grave). *Tertullian (c. 210, W), 3.558.*

These doctrines, then, the Naasseni attempt to establish, calling themselves Gnostics. *Hippolytus (c. 225, W), 5.58.*

[The Docetists say] the Son assumed thirty forms from the thirty Aeons. And for this reason, that eternal One existed for thirty years on the earth. *Hippolytus (c. 225, W), 5.120.*

We refute those who think that the Father of our Lord Jesus Christ is a different God from Him who gave the answers of the Law to Moses, or commissioned the prophets. *Origen (c. 225, E), 4.275.*

From the New Testament, they gather together words of compassion and piety (through which the disciples are trained by the Savior). From these words, it seems to be declared that no one is good except God the Father only. And by this means, they have ventured to designate the Father of the Savior Jesus Christ as the "Good God." However, they say that the "God of this world" [i.e., the Creator] is a different one. *Origen (c. 225, E), 4.278.*

Those belonging to heretical sects read . . . [such statements as] "I am a jealous God, visiting the iniquities of the fathers upon the children," . . . and "An evil spirit from the Lord plagued Saul" and countless other passages like these. . . . They believe them to be [words] of the Demiurge, whom the Jews worship. They think that since the Demiurge was an imperfect and unloving God, the Savior had come to announce a more perfect Deity. *Origen (c. 225, E), 4.356, 357.*

How can John [the Baptist] be the beginning of the Gospel if they suppose he belongs to a different God? For he belongs to the Demiurge and (as they hold) is not acquainted with the new Deity. *Origen (c. 228, E), 9.305.*

I see the heretics attacking the holy church of God in these days, under the pretense of having "higher wisdom." They bring forth works in many volumes in which they offer expositions of the evangelical and apostolic writings. . . . Therefore, it seems to me that it is necessary for someone to refute those dealers of "falsely called knowledge." Someone who is able to present the doctrine of the church in a genuine manner should take a stand against these histor-ical fictions and oppose them with the true and lofty evangelical message. *Origen (c. 228, E), 9.348; see also 1.539–1.541, 2.445; extended discussion: 5.47–5.58, 5.100–5.110, 5.117–5.120.*

II. Female deities of the Gnostics

They also call this Mother by the names of Ogdoad, Sophia, Terra, Jerusalem, Holy Spirit, and (with a masculine reference) Lord. Her place of habitation is an intermediate one. *Irenaeus (c. 180, E/W), 1.323.*

They also declare that there were manifested the Mother, the Father, and the Son. . . . Next, they assert that, from the first angel, . . . the Holy Spirit has been sent forth, whom they also call Sophia and Prunicus. . . . The Father and the Son thus both had relations with the woman, whom they also call the Mother of the living. . . . Their only Son, Christ, who belonged to the right side and was ever moving to what was higher, was immediately caught up with His Mother to form an incorruptible Aeon. *Irenaeus (c. 180, E/W), 1.354.*

They declare that, at the consummation of all things, their Mother will re-enter the Pleroma, and receive the Savior as her consort. *Irenaeus (c. 180, E/W), 1.402.*

They maintain that, according to nature and substance, three sorts [of beings] were produced by the Mother. *Irenaeus (c. 180, E/W), 1.403.*

What work, then, will they point to as having been accomplished through themselves by the Savior, or by their Mother? *Irenaeus (c. 180, E/W), 1.404.*

They imagine a lofty [mystery] about their Mother, whom they represent as having been begotten without a father, that is, with God, a female from a female. *Irenaeus (c. 180, E/W), 1.460.*

This world belongs to Him and was made by Him, according to the Father's will. It was not made by angels, . . . nor by any power of Prunicus, whom certain of them also call "the Mother." *Irenaeus (c. 180, E/W), 1.546.*

[According to the Gnostics,] He [begets] by means of Monoganes Nus, a male-female [Aeon], for there is this variation of statement about the Father's sex. *Tertullian (c. 200, W), 3.509.*

Although they say that Achamoth devised these forms in honor of the Aeons, they yet transfer this work to Soter as its author. For they say that he operated through her, so far as to give her the very image of the invisible and unknown Father. *Tertullian (c. 200, W), 3.513.*

Meanwhile, [to be one of them] you must believe that Sophia has the surnames of Earth and of Mother—"Mother Earth," of course—and . . . even Holy Spirit. In this way they have conferred all honor on that female. *Tertullian (c. 200, W), 3.514.*

I would not tarry a moment longer on this point were it not for those heretics who introduce into the soul some spiritual germ (which passes my comprehension) conferred upon the soul by the secret generosity of her Mother, Sophia, without the knowledge of the Creator. *Tertullian (c. 210, W), 3.191.*

Sophia, however, was outside the Pleroma. She was searching for Christ, who had given form to her and to the Holy Spirit. She was terrified that she would perish if He separated from her. For He had given her form and consistency. She was seized with grief, and fell into a state of considerable perplexity. . . . During the utterance of her entreaties, Christ, who is within the Pleroma, had mercy upon her. *Hippolytus (c. 225, W), 5.87.*

Marcus asserts that the Tetrad came to him in the form of a woman, for he says the world could not bear the male form of this Tetrad. He says that she revealed who she was, and explained to him alone the creation of the universe, which she had never revealed to anyone else—to neither gods nor men. *Hippolytus (c. 225, W), 5.93.*

[According to the Gnostics,] Jesus possesses this inexpressible generation. For from the Mother of the universe (I mean the first Tetrad), there proceeded forth the second Tetrad, in the manner of a daughter. *Hippolytus (c. 225, W), 5.97.*

They allege that the first four elements were created by the Mother. They say these four elements are fire, water, earth, and air. *Hippolytus (c. 225, W), 5.98; see also 1.386.*

SEE ALSO BASILIDES; CARPOCRATES; CERINTHUS; DEAD, INTERMEDIATE STATE OF THE; HERESIES, HERETICS; MANES, MANICHAEANS; MARCION; SIMON MAGUS; VALENTINUS, VALENTINIANS.

GOD

God is not born, nor made. He is of an everabiding nature without beginning and without end. He is immortal, perfect, and incomprehensible. Now, when I say that He is "perfect," I mean that there is no defect in Him and that He is not in need of anything. Rather, all things are in need of Him. . . . He has no name, for everything that has a name is related to created things. He has no form, nor any bodily members. . . . He is neither male nor female. The heavens do not limit him. *Aristides (c. 125, E), 9.264.*

Our God did not begin to be in time. He alone is without beginning, and He Himself is the beginning of all things. *Tatian (c. 160, E), 2.66.*

Christ did not stand in need of our service when he ordered us to follow Him. Rather, He thereby bestowed salvation upon us. For to follow the Savior is to be a partaker of salvation. . . . Thus, also, service to God profits God nothing; nor has God any need of human obedience. Rather, He grants to those who follow and serve Him life, incorruption, and eternal glory. He bestows benefits upon those who serve Him because they have served Him. He bestows benefits on His followers, because they follow Him. However, He Himself does not receive any benefit from them. For he is rich, perfect, and in need of nothing. *Irenaeus (c. 180, E/W), 1.478.*

When He perceived . . . that they imagined that God could be propitiated by sacrifices and the other typical observances, Samuel spoke to them even then, saying, "God does not desire whole burnt-offerings and sacrifices. . . . Behold, a ready obedience is better than sacrifice." *Irenaeus (c. 180, E/W), 1.482.*

He did not reject their sacrifices because He was angry, as many venture to say, as though he were like a man. Rather, it was out of compassion for their blindness. It was with the view of suggesting to them the true sacrifice . . . so that they could receive life from Him. *Irenaeus (c. 180, E/W), 1.483.*

With God, there is nothing without purpose. *Irenaeus (c. 180, E/W), 1.493.*

God's resting is not, then, as some conceive, that God ceased from doing. For, being good, if He should ever cease from doing good, then He would cease to be God, which is a sacrilege even to say. *Clement of Alexandria (c. 195, E), 2.513.*

Neither by sacrifices nor offerings—nor, on the other hand, by glory and honor—is the Deity won over. Nor is He influenced by any such things. *Clement of Alexandria (c. 195, E), 2.527.*

We maintain, then, that the name, *God,* always existed with Himself and in Himself. However, the title, *Lord,* has not eternally been. For the condition of the one is not the same as that of the other. God is the designation of the substance itself—that is, of the Divinity. But Lord is the title, not of substance, but of power. I maintain that the substance existed always with its own name, which is God. But the title Lord was afterwards added. . . . He was not Lord previous to [the creation of] those things over which he was to be the Lord. *Tertullian (c. 200, W), 3.478.*

What must be the condition of the great Supreme Himself? Surely it must be that nothing is equal to Him, i.e., that there is no other great Supreme. For, if there were, He would have an equal. And if He had an equal, He would be no longer the great Supreme. . . . Since, then, God is the great Supreme, our Christian truth has rightly declared, "God is not, if He is not one." *Tertullian (c. 207, W), 3.273.*

Whatever other god, then, you may introduce, you will at least be unable to maintain his divinity under any other guise, than by ascribing to him too these properties of Godhood: both eternity and supremacy over all. How, therefore, can two great Supremes co-exist? For it is the attribute of the Supreme Being to have no equal—an attribute which belongs to One alone, and can by no means exist in two. *Tertullian (c. 207, W), 3.273.*

God, moreover, is as independent of beginning and end as He is of time. *Tertullian (c. 207, W), 3.276.*

God is both a perfect Father and a perfect Master. He is a father in His mercy, but a master in His discipline. He is a father in the mildness of His power, but a master in its severity. He is a father who must be loved with dutiful affection. Yet, He is also a master who must be feared. He is to be loved, for He prefers mercy to sacrifice. Yet, he should be feared because he dislikes sin. He should be loved because He prefers the sinner's repentance over his death. Yet, he is to be feared, for He dislikes the sinners who do not repent. *Tertullian (c. 207, W), 3.308.*

Whatever is a property of physical bodies cannot be attributed to either the Father or the Son. What belongs to the nature of deity is common to the Father and Son. Even the Son Himself did not say in the Gospel that no one has *seen* the Father except the Son. Nor did He say that no one has *seen* the Son except the Father. Rather, His words are: "No one *knows* the Son, except the Father; nor does anyone *know* the Father, except the Son." From this, it is evident that the aspect of physical bodies that is called "seeing" and "being seen," is called "knowing" and "being known" as between the Father and the Son. *Origen (c. 225, E), 4.245.*

The more simple among those who profess to belong to the church have believed that there is no Deity greater than the Creator—being right in so thinking. However, they imagine such things regarding Him as would not be believed of the most savage and unjust of mankind. In all of these points previously enumerated, the cause of the false opinions and of the impious statements or ignorant assertions about God appear to be nothing else than not understanding Scripture according to its spiritual meaning. It comes from interpreting according to the mere letter. *Origen (c. 225, E), 4.357.*

Indeed, if one considers the multitude of speculation and knowledge about God, then one may know how God is surrounded with darkness. For He is beyond the power of human nature to comprehend. Perhaps He is beyond the power of all originated beings except Christ and the Holy Spirit. *Origen (c. 228, E), 9.339.*

God can do everything that it is possible for Him to do without ceasing to be God, and good, and wise. . . . So neither is God able to commit wickedness, for the power of doing evil is contrary to His deity and His omnipotence. *Origen (c. 248, E), 4.492.*

Since God is not known by wicked men, He desires to make Himself known. This is not because He thinks that He meets with less than His due, but because the knowledge of

Him will free the possessor from unhappiness. *Origen (c. 248, E), 4.499.*

However, we do not back ourselves into a most absurd corner, saying that with God *all* things are possible. For we know how to understand this word "all." It does not refer either to things that are non-existent or that are inconceivable. For example, we maintain that God cannot do what is disgraceful, for then He would be capable of ceasing to be God. For if He does anything that is disgraceful, he is not God. *Origen (c. 248, E), 4.553.*

He cannot be seen—He is too bright for vision. He cannot be comprehended, for He is too pure for our discernment. He cannot be estimated, for He is too great for our perception. And, therefore, we are only worthily estimating Him when we say that He is inconceivable. . . . He is one, and He in His entirety is everywhere diffused. *Cyprian (c. 250, W), 5.467.*

He is a heretic who believes on another God, or receives a Christ other than Him whom the Scriptures of the Old and New Testament clearly declare. They announce without any obscurity the Father Omnipotent, Creator of all things, and His Son. *Treatise on Re-Baptism (c. 257, W), 5.675.*

The secret of the Most High God, who created all things, cannot be attained by our own ability and perceptions. If human thought could reach to the counsels and arrangements of that eternal majesty, there would be no difference between God and man. *Lactantius (c. 304–313, W), 7.9.*

Why should I mention that this highest power and divine energy is altogether incapable of division? For whatever is capable of division must also of necessity be liable to destruction. However, if destruction is far removed from God, since He is incorruptible and eternal, it follows that the divine power is incapable of division. *Lactantius (c. 304–313, W), 7.12.*

God, who is immortal, has no need of difference of sex, nor of succession. . . . What need is there of the female sex, since God, who is Almighty, is able to produce sons without the agency of the female? *Lactantius (c. 304–313, W), 7.18.*

If the honor paid to Him is shared by others, He altogether ceases to be worshiped, for His religion requires us to believe that He is the one and only God. *Lactantius (c. 304–313, W), 7.32.*

We are all bound to love Him because He is our Father and to reverence Him because He is our Lord. We are bound both to pay Him honor (because He is generous) and to fear Him (because He is strict). Each quality in Him is worthy of reverence. *Lactantius (c. 304–313, W), 7.279.*

When we speak of Him we use a masculine word. However, let no thoughtless person raise the false accusation against us as though we believed the God whom we worship to be a man. Let him understand that it is not gender that is expressed, but rather His name, its meaning according to custom, and the way in which we customarily use words. For the Deity is not male. However, His name is of the masculine gender. In contrast, you Romans cannot say the same thing about your ceremonies. For in your prayers you are accustomed to say "whether you are god or goddess," . . . showing that you attribute gender to the gods. *Arnobius (c. 305, E), 6.466.*

SEE ALSO ANTHROPOMORPHISMS; CHRIST, DIVINITY OF; FATHER, GOD THE; GOD, ATTRIBUTES OF; GOD, NAME OF; HOLY SPIRIT; TRINITY.

GOD, ATTRIBUTES OF

I. General attributes

II. Omnipresence of God

III. Omniscience of God

IV. Impassibility of God

I. General attributes

The Lord, the Lord God, merciful and gracious, longsuffering, and abounding in goodness and truth. Ex. 34:6.

He is the Rock, His work is perfect; for all His ways are justice, a God of truth and without injustice; righteous and upright is He. Deut. 32:4.

He who does not love does not know God, for God is love. 1 John 4:8.

Nothing is impossible with God, except to lie. . . . All things are open before Him. Nothing can be hidden from His counsel. *Clement of Rome (c. 96, W), 1.12.*

He is Lord because He rules over the universe. He is Father because he is before all things. He is Fashioner and Creator, because He is Creator and Maker of the universe. He is the Highest, because He is above all. He is Almighty because he Himself rules and embraces everything. The heights of heaven and the depths of the abysses, as well as the ends of the earth, are in His hand. *Theophilus (c. 180, E), 2.90.*

God is not involuntarily good, the way a fire is involuntarily hot. Rather, in Him, the imparting of good things is voluntary. . . . Therefore, God does not do good by necessity, but He benefits others from His free choice. *Clement of Alexandria (c. 195, E), 2.534.*

He cannot be seen—He is brighter than light. Nor can He be grasped—He is purer than touch. He cannot be estimated, for He is greater than all perceptions. He is infinite and immense. His greatness is known to Himself alone. But our heart is too limited to understand Him. . . . He who thinks he knows the magnitude of God is diminishing His magnitude. *Mark Minucius Felix (c. 200, W), 4.182.*

According to strict truth, God is incomprehensible and incapable of being measured. For whatever the knowledge is that we are able to obtain about God—either by perception or by reflection—we must of necessity believe that He is far better by many degrees than what we perceive Him to be. *Origen (c. 225, E), 4.243.*

Nothing is impossible to the Omnipotent. Nor is anything incapable of restoration to its Creator. *Origen (c. 225, E), 4.347.*

Is anyone greater than God, or more merciful than God's goodness? *Cyprian (c. 250, W), 5.443.*

By His providence, He designed. By His energy, He established. And by His judgment, He completed works that are great and wonderful. Even now He sustains them by His Spirit, and He governs them by His power. He is incomprehensible and unspeakable. He is fully known to no one other than Himself. *Lactantius (c. 304–313, W), 7.18; extended discussion: 1.10–1.16, 4.242–4.245.*

II. Omnipresence of God

Behold, heaven and the heaven of heavens cannot contain You. 1 Ki. 8:27.

This is the attribute of God, the Highest and Almighty, and the living God: not only to be everywhere present, but also to see all things and to hear all things. He is by no means to be confined in a place. For if he were, then the place containing Him would be greater than He. . . . For God is not contained, but is Himself the place of all. *Theophilus (c. 180, E), 2.95.*

They are ignorant as to what the expression means, that heaven is His throne and earth His footstool. For they do not know what God is. Rather, they imagine that He sits after the fashion of a man. They think He is contained within bounds, but does not contain. *Irenaeus (c. 180, E/W), 1.465.*

God is not in darkness or in place, but He is above both space and time, and qualities of objects. For that reason, neither is He at any time in a particular part—either as containing it or as being contained, either by limitation or by section. . . . Though heaven is called His throne, not even there is He contained. *Clement of Alexandria (c. 195, E), 2.348.*

Such a person is persuaded that God is always beside him. He does not suppose that He is confined in certain limited places. *Clement of Alexandria (c. 195, E), 2.533.*

Where is God afar off, when all things heavenly and earthly . . . are known to God, are full of God? Everywhere He is not only very near to us, but He is infused into us. Accordingly, look upon the sun once more. It is fixed steadfast in the heaven, yet it is diffused over all lands equally. . . . How much more is God. *Mark Minucius Felix (c. 200, W), 4.193.*

If in created beings there is any portion of space anywhere void of God, the void clearly will be of a false deity. *Tertullian (c. 207, W), 3.279.*

The God of the universe may, through His own power, descend with Jesus into the life of men. The Word that was in the beginning with God (who is also very God) may come to us. However, He does not give up His place or vacate His own seat, in doing so. It is not that one place becomes empty of Him. Or that another place that did not formerly contain Him is now filled. *Origen (c. 248, E), 4.499.*

We do not ask the question, "How will we go to God?" as though we thought that God existed in some place. God is of too excellent a nature for any place. He holds all things in His power, and He Himself is not confined by anything whatever. *Origen (c. 248, E), 4.624.*

III. Omniscience of God

There is no creature hidden from His sight, but all things are naked and open to the eyes of Him to whom we must give account. Heb. 4:13.

God is greater than our heart, and knows all things. 1 John 3:20.

He knows all things beforehand, and He is acquainted with what is in our hearts. *Second Clement (c. 150), 7.519.*

They are unaware that God is in every country, and in every place. He is never absent, and there is nothing done that He does not know. *Melito (c. 170, E), 8.755.*

God knows all things. He not only knows those things that presently exist, but also those things that *will* exist. He knows how each thing will be. *Clement of Alexandria (c. 195, E), 2.517.*

That Guardian of the world and Ruler of the universe knows all things. Nothing is concealed from His divine eyes. *Lactantius (c. 304–313, W), 7.65.*

IV. Impassibility of God

By the "impassibility of God," the early Christians meant that God is not affected by human passions.

[The Gnostics] endow God with human affections and emotions. However, if they had known the Scriptures, and had been taught by the truth, they would have known beyond doubt that God is not like men. His thoughts are not like the thoughts of men. For the Father of all is at a vast distance from those dispositions and passions that operate among men. *Irenaeus (c. 180, E/W), 1.374.*

"Be perfect as your father, perfectly," by forgiving sins, forgetting injuries, and living in the habit of passionlessness. *Clement of Alexandria (c. 195, E), 2.549.*

We maintain that God is altogether impassible and is to be regarded as wholly free from all affections of this kind. *Origen (c. 225, E), 4.277.*

We will not serve God as though He stood in need of our service, or as though He would be made unhappy if we ceased to serve Him. Rather, we do it because we are ourselves benefited by the service of God. And we do it because we are freed from griefs and troubles by serving the Most High God through His Only-Begotten Son, the Word and Wisdom. *Origen (c. 248, E), 4.642.*

Our salvation is not necessary to Him, such that He would gain something or suffer some loss if He either made us divine, or allowed us to be annihilated and destroyed by corruption. *Arnobius (c. 305, E), 6.459.*

SEE ALSO ANGER OF GOD; FOREKNOWLEDGE OF GOD; GOD; SOVEREIGNTY AND PROVIDENCE OF GOD.

GOD, NAME OF

God has no name, for everything that has a name is related to created things. *Aristides (c. 125, E), 9.264.*

He has as many virtues as are distinctive to a God who is called by no proper name. *Justin Martyr (c. 160, E), 1.165.*

To the Father of all, who is unbegotten, there is no name given.... These words—Father, God, Creator, Lord, and Master—are not names. Rather, they are appellations derived from His good deeds and functions. *Justin Martyr (c. 160, E), 1.190.*

As to the name of God the Father and Lord of the universe,... if anyone dares to say that there is a name, he raves with a hopeless madness. *Justin Martyr (c. 160, E), 1.183.*

God cannot be called by any proper name. For names are given to mark out and distinguish various subject matters, because these matters are many and diverse. However, no one existed before God who could give Him a name, nor did He Himself think it right to name Himself. For He is one and unique.... On this account, He said to Moses, "I am the Being." By the participle *being*, He taught the difference between the God who is and the gods who are not. *Justin Martyr (c. 160, E), 1.281.*

However, the [Gnostics] object that, in the Hebrew language, diverse expressions occur in the Scriptures, such as *Sabaoth, Eloë,* and *Adonai,* and all other such terms. From this they try to prove that there are different powers and gods. However, let them learn that all expressions of this kind are but announcements and appellations of one and the same Being. ... These are not the names and titles of a succession of different beings, but of one and the same, by means of which the one God and Father is revealed. *Irenaeus (c. 180, E/W), 1.412, 413.*

If we name Him, we do not do so properly. We can call Him either the One, or the Good, or Mind, or Absolute Being, or Father, or God, or Creator, or Lord. But we are not speaking as though supplying His name. Rather, for lack of an alternative, we use good names in order that the mind may have these as points of reference, so as not to err in other respects. For each one by itself does not express God; but all together are indicative of the power of the Omnipotent. *Clement of Alexandria (c. 195, E), 2.464.*

The soul may be under the oppressive bondage of the body. . . . It may be in slavery to false gods. Nevertheless, whenever the soul comes to itself, such as out of a . . . sleep or sickness, and attains something of its natural soundness, it speaks of God. It uses no other word, because this is the peculiar name of the true God. "God is great and good." *Tertullian (c. 197, W), 3.32.*

The name of God the Father had been published to no one. *Tertullian (c. 198, W), 3.682.*

Neither must you ask for a name of God. God is His name. We have need of names when a multitude are to be separated into individuals. . . . To God, who is alone, the name "God" is the whole. *Mark Minucius Felix (c. 200, W), 4.183.*

We say that the name *Sabaoth, Adonai,* and the other names treated with so much reverence among the Hebrews, do not apply to any ordinary created things. Rather, they belong to a secret theology concerning the Framer of all things. *Origen (c. 248, E), 4.406.*

We defend the conduct of the Christians when they struggle even to death to avoid calling God by the name of Zeus, or to give Him a name from any other language. For they use the common name of God—either by itself or with some such addition as that of the "Maker of all things." *Origen (c. 248, E), 4.407.*

Christians in prayer do not even use the precise names that divine Scripture applies to God. Rather, the Greeks use Greek names. The Romans use Latin names. And everyone prays and sings praises to God as best he can in his mother tongue. For the Lord of all the languages of the earth hears those who pray to Him in each different language. *Origen (c. 248, E), 4.653.*

God's own name also cannot be declared, for He cannot be conceived. . . . For the name is the significance of whatever thing can be comprehended from a name. *Novatian (c. 235, W), 5.615.*

Neither must you ask the name of God. God is His name. Where a multitude is to be distinguished by the appropriate characteristics of names, there is a need of names. However, to God—who alone is—belongs the whole name of God. *Cyprian (c. 250, W), 5.467.*

As I have shown in the beginning, God does not need a name, since He is alone. *Lactantius (c. 304–313, E), 7.65.*

SEE ALSO GOD; JEHOVAH; TETRAGRAMMATON.

GODPARENTS

For why is it necessary—if (baptism itself) is not so necessary—that the sponsors likewise should be thrust into danger? For, because of mortality, they may fail to fulfill their promises. Or they may be disappointed by the development of an evil disposition in those for whom they stood. *Tertullian (c. 198, W), 3.678.*

SEE ALSO BAPTISM (III. THE QUESTION OF INFANT BAPTISM).

GODS, PAGAN

This Paul has persuaded and turned away many people, saying that they are not gods which are made with hands. Acts 19:26.

When you did not know God, you served those which by nature are not gods. Gal. 4:8.

I. Character, nature, and absurdities of the gods

II. Origin of the gods

I. Character, nature, and absurdities of the gods

[The Greeks] have introduced many fictitious gods. They have presented some of them as males and others as females. Some of their gods are adulterers. Others of them committed murder. Some were deluded; others were envious, wrathful, and lustful. Some murdered their parents; others were thieves and robbers. They say that some of them were crippled and they limped. Some were sorcerers; others actually went insane. . . . Therefore, [from them], mankind has received examples to commit adultery and fornication, to steal, and to practice everything that is offensive, hated, and abhorred. After all, if those who are called their gods practiced all of these things, how much more should humans practice them! *Aristides (c. 125, E), 9.268, 269.*

When the Greeks made laws, they did not realize that they condemned their own gods by their laws. For if their laws are righteous, their gods are unrighteous. That is because the gods broke those laws. *Aristides (c. 125, E), 9.275.*

As to the other complaint, that we do not pray to and believe in the same gods as the cities, it is an exceedingly silly one. Why, the very men who charge us with atheism for not admitting the same gods as they acknowledge, are not agreed among themselves concerning the gods. *Athenagoras (c. 175, E), 2.135.*

Why should I recount further the vast array of such names and genealogies? For all the authors and poets, and those called philosophers, are wholly deceived. Likewise, those who give heed to them are deceived. For they plentifully composed fables and foolish stories about their gods, and did not exhibit them as gods, but as men. Not only that, they described them as men who were drunks, fornicators and murderers. *Theophilus (c. 180, E), 2.97.*

For after they had said that these are gods, they again made them of no account. For some said that they were composed of atoms, . . . and they say that the gods have no more power than men. *Theophilus (c. 180, E), 2.112, 113.*

I can readily demonstrate that humans are better than these gods of yours—who are but demons. *Clement of Alexandria (c. 195, E), 2.183.*

The Greeks represent the gods as possessing human forms and human passions. Each of them depict their forms similar to themselves. *Clement of Alexandria (c. 195, E), 2.529.*

You demand a price for the privilege of standing on temple ground and for access to the sacred services. There is no gratuitous knowledge of your divinities permitted. You must buy their favors with a price. *Tertullian (c. 197, W), 3.29.*

Nor indeed do either tragic or comic writers shrink from setting forth the gods as the origin of all family calamities and sin. . . . Others of your writers, in their wantonness, even minister to your pleasures by vilifying the gods. *Tertullian (c. 197, W), 3.30.*

How will those gods who are thereby in Caesar's power . . . give *to* Caesar what they more readily get *from* him? *Tertullian (c. 197, W), 3.41.*

It would be a far worthier thing if I believed in no god, rather than in one that is open to doubt, is full of shame, or is the object of arbitrary selection. *Tertullian (c. 197, W), 3.130.*

Men have their respective gods in their brothels, their kitchens, and even in their prisons. Therefore, heaven is crowded with innumerable gods of its own—not only these but also others belonging to the Romans. *Tertullian (c. 197, W), 3.145.*

These, then, are the actions of [the gods], which we will consider first: births, lurkings, ignorance, parricides, adulteries, and obscenities. However, such things are committed, not by gods, but by most impure and savage human beings. *Tertullian (c. 200, W), 3.150.*

How much more truly do dumb animals naturally assess your gods? Mice, swallows, and kites know that they have no feeling. They gnaw them, trample on them and sit upon them. And unless you drive them off, they build their nests in the very mouths of your gods. *Mark Minucius Felix (c. 200, W), 4.187.*

If anyone desires to inquire further into the matter, let him assemble those who are skilled in calling forth spirits from the dead. Let them call forth Jupiter, Neptune, Vulcan, Mercury, Apollo, and finally Saturn, the father of all. All of them will answer from the lower regions. Being questioned, they will speak and confess respecting themselves and God. After these things, let them call up Christ. He will not be present; He will not appear. *Lactantius (c. 304–313, W), 7.130, 131.*

Temples have been erected with lofty roofs to cats, beetles, and heifers. Yet, the powers of these insulted deities are silent. *Arnobius (c. 305, E), 6.420.*

You have placed Liber in the assembly of the gods because he discovered the use of wine. Ceres, because she discovered the use of bread. Aesculapius, because he discovered the use of [medicinal] herbs. Minerva, because she produced the olive. And Triptolemus, because he invented the plow. *Arnobius (c. 305, E), 6.423.*

Etruria declares . . . that souls become divine and are freed from the law of death if the blood of certain animals is offered to certain deities. But these are empty delusions! *Arnobius (c. 305, E), 6.457.*

With you, certain gods have fixed offices, privileges, and powers. You do not ask something from any of them when it is not in his power or permitted to him. . . . You believe that father Bacchus can give a good vintage, but he cannot give relief from sickness. You believe that Ceres can brings good crops; Aesculapius, health; Neptune, one thing; and Venus, another. *Arnobius (c. 305, E), 6.459.*

You worship so great and so innumerable gods. You build temples to them, fashion images of god, sacrifice herds of animals, and heap up boxfuls of incense on the already loaded altars. *Arnobius (c. 305, E), 6.463.*

You might, perhaps, have been able to attract us to the worship of these deities you mention, had you not been the first yourselves, with repugnant and improper imaginations, to devise such tales about them! These tales do not merely stain their honor, but . . . prove that they never existed at all. *Arnobius (c. 305, E), 6.465.*

Call us impious as much as you please. Call us scorners of religion and atheists. But you will never make us believe in gods of sexual love and war. . . . For, if they do the things that you say, they are obviously not gods! *Arnobius (c. 305, E), 6.471.*

The same theologians say that there are four Vulcans, three Dianas, three Aesculapii, five Dionysi, six Hercules, four Venuses, three sets of Castors and Muses, three winged Cupids, and four gods named Apollo. *Arnobius (c. 305, E), 6.480.*

We wish to hear or learn from you something befitting the gods. However, on the contrary, you bring forward to us the cutting off of breasts, the lopping off of men's members, ragings, blood, frenzies, the self-destruction of maidens, and flowers and trees that spring up from the blood of the dead! *Arnobius (c. 305, E), 6.495; extended discussion: 2.91–2.92, 2.138– 2.141, 2.143–2.145, 3.25–3.30, 3.39, 3.119, 3.135–3.146, 3.149, 150, 4.184–4.190, 9.268– 9.275.*

II. Origin of the gods

I will further write and show, as far as my ability goes, how and for what causes images were made to kings and tyrants, and how they came to be regarded as gods. The people of Argos made images to Hercules, because he belonged to their city. Furthermore, he was strong, and by his valor, he slew noxious beasts. Besides that, they were afraid of him. For he was subject to no control, and he carried off the wives of many. His lust was great, like that of Zuradi the Persian, his friend. Again, the people of Acte worshipped Dionysius, a king, because he had recently planted the vine in their country. The Egyptians worshipped Joseph the Hebrew, who was called Serapis, because he supplied them with corn during the years of famine. *Melito (c. 170, E), 8.752.*

I maintain, then, that it was Orpheus, Homer, and Hesiod who gave both genealogies and names to those whom they call gods. Such, too, is the testimony of Herodotus. "My opinion," he says, "is that Hesiod and Homer preceded me by four hundred years, and no more. And it was they who framed a theogony for the Greeks, and gave the gods their names. It was they who assigned them their various honors and functions, and described their forms." *Athenagoras (c. 175, E), 2.136.*

The gods, as they affirm, were not from the beginning. Rather, every one of them has come into existence just like ourselves. *Athenagoras (c. 175, E), 2.137.*

Not one of your gods is earlier than Saturn. From him, you trace all your deities, even those of higher rank and greater fame. . . . Yet, none of the writers about sacred antiquities have ventured to say that Saturn was anything but a man. *Tertullian (c. 197, W), 3.26.*

As you cannot deny that these deities of yours once were men, you have taken it on yourselves to assert that they were made gods after their deaths. *Tertullian (c. 197, W), 3.27.*

As we have already shown, every god depended on the decision of the senate for his deity. *Tertullian (c. 197, W), 3.29.*

That those are no gods whom the common people worship, is known from this: They were formerly kings. On account of their royal memory, they subsequently began to be adored by their people even in death. Later, temples were founded to them. Next, images were sculptured to retain the faces of the deceased by such likenesses. Later, men sacrificed victims and celebrated festal days to give them honor.

Finally, those rites became sacred to posterity—although at first they had been adopted as a consolation. *Cyprian (c. 250, W), 5.465.*

Since it is evident from these things that they were men, it is not difficult to see how they began to be called gods. For apparently there were no kings before Saturn or Uranus. Rather, men existed in small numbers, and they lived a rural life without any ruler. Undoubtedly, then, in those days, men began to exalt the king himself and his whole family with the highest praises and with new honors—so that they even called them gods. *Lactantius (c. 304–313, W), 7.26.*

Different people privately honored the founders of their nation or city with the highest veneration—whether they were men distinguished for bravery, or women admirable for chastity. So the Egyptians honored Isis; the Moors, Juba; . . . the Romans, Quirinus. In the same exact manner, Athens worshipped Minerva; Samos, Juno; Paphos, Venus; . . . and Delos, Apollo. And thus various sacred rites were undertaken among different peoples and countries. For men desire to show gratitude to their rulers. . . . Moreover, the piety of their successors contributed largely to this error. For, in order that they might appear to be born from a divine origin, men paid divine honors to their parents. *Lactantius (c. 304–313, W), 7.27.*

[Others, however,] not only admit that gods have been made from men, but even boast of it as a subject of praise. [Such humans have been deified] either because of their valor (as in the case of Hercules), or because of their gifts (as Ceres and Liber), or because of the arts that they discovered (as Aesculapius or Minerva). But how foolish these things are! How unworthy of being the causes of why men should contaminate themselves with inexpiable guilt, and become enemies of God. For it is in contempt of Him that they make offerings to the dead. *Lactantius (c. 304–313, W), 7.30.*

We can show that all those whom you represent to us as gods, and whom you call gods, were actually men. We can do this by quoting either Euhererus of Acragas . . . or Nicanor the Cyprian. *Arnobius (c. 305, E), 6.486.*

SEE ALSO DEMONS, DEMON POSSESSION; IDOLATRY; IMAGES; MOTHER, GREAT; MYSTERY RELIGIONS; SUN WORSHIP; WORSHIP, PAGAN.

GODS (PSALM 82)

God stands in the congregation of the mighty; He judges among the gods. Ps. 82:1.

I said "You are gods, and all of you are children of the Most High. But you will die like men. Ps. 82:6.

"God stood in the congregation of the gods; he judges in the midst of the gods." Who are these "gods"? They are those humans who are superior to pleasure, who rise above the passions. . . . It is those who are greater than the world. *Clement of Alexandria (c. 195, E), 2.374.*

"God stands in the assembly of the gods; and in the midst, God distinguishes between the gods." Accordingly, since Christ stood at various times in the synagogue, He stood in the synagogue as God, judging between the gods, . . . accusing the men of the synagogue with not practicing just judgments. *Novatian (c. 235, W), 5.631.*

Concerning the bishop and others like him, God pronounces, "I have said, 'You are gods; and you are all children of the Most High.'" *Apostolic Constitutions (compiled c. 390, E), 7.410.*

SEE ALSO DEIFICATION OF MAN.

GOSPEL ACCORDING TO THE HEBREWS

The Gospel according to the Hebrews (not to be confused with the New Testament Epistle to the Hebrews) was a first- or second-century work that purports to contain sayings of Jesus not recorded in the four canonical Gospels. It was apparently written in Aramaic by a Jewish Christian.

In the Gospel to the Hebrews, it is written, "He who wonders will reign, and he who has reigned will rest." *Clement of Alexandria (c. 195, E), 2.358.*

If anyone should lend credence to the Gospel according to the Hebrews, where the Savior Himself says, "My mother, the Holy Spirit, took me just now by one of my hairs and carried me off to the great Mount Tabor," he will have to face the difficulty of explaining how the Holy Spirit can be the mother of Christ. *Origen (c. 228, E), 9.329.*

Papias [c. 120] gives another story of a woman who was accused of many sins before the Lord. This story is to be found in the Gospel according to the Hebrews. *Eusebius (c. 320, E), 1.155.*

GOSPELS

The Ebionites, who use only Matthew's Gospel, are refuted out of this very same work, making false suppositions with regard to the Lord. But Marcion, mutilating the Gospel according to Luke, is still proved to be a blasphemer of the only existing God, from those passages which he still retains. Those, again, who separate Jesus from Christ, alleging that Christ remained impassible, but that it was Jesus who suffered, prefer the Gospel by Mark. However, if they read it with a love of truth, they would have their errors rectified. Those persons, moreover, who follow Valentinus, make copious use of the Gospel according to John to illustrate their conjunctions. However, they, too, will be proved to be totally in error. *Irenaeus (c. 180, E/W), 1.428.*

It is not possible that the Gospels can be either more or fewer in number than they are. For, there are four zones of the world in which we live, and four principal winds. Now, the church is scattered throughout all the world, and the "pillar and ground" of the church is the Gospel. Therefore, it is fitting that she should have four pillars, breathing out immortality on every side, and renewing men afresh. *Irenaeus (c. 180, E/W), 1.428.*

All who destroy the form of the Gospel are vain, unlearned, and also audacious. I speak of those who represent the number of the Gospel as being either more in number than as aforesaid, or, on the other hand, fewer. The first group purport to have discovered more than what is true; the latter group wish to set the dispensations of God aside. *Irenaeus (c. 180, E/W), 1.429.*

These things are written in the Gospel according to Mark—and likewise in all of the other Gospels, correspondingly. Although the expressions may vary slightly in each Gospel, they all show identical agreement in meaning. *Clement of Alexandria (c. 195, E), 2.592.*

We lay it down as our first position that the evangelical instrument has apostles for its authors. For to them, the Lord Himself assigned this office of publishing the gospel. Since, however, there are apostolic men also, they are still not alone. Rather, they appear with apostles and after apostles. . . . Of the apostles, therefore, John and Matthew first instill faith into us. While of apostolic men, Luke and Mark renew it afterwards. . . . Never mind if there

does occur some variation in the order of their narratives, provided that there is agreement in the essential substance of the faith. *Tertullian (c. 207, W), 3.347.*

I say, therefore, that in those [apostolic] churches, the Gospel of Luke that we are defending with all our might has stood its ground from its very first publication. And it has stood its ground not simply in those churches that were founded by apostles, but in all the churches that are united with them in the fellowship of the mystery of the gospel of Christ. . . . The same authority of the apostolic churches will afford defense of the other Gospels also, which we possess equally through their means, and according to their usage. I mean the Gospels of John and Matthew—while that which Mark published may be affirmed to be Peter's, whose interpreter Mark was. For men usually ascribe Luke's form of the Gospel to Paul. *Tertullian (c. 207, W), 3.350*

It is even more believable that the Gospels existed from the very beginning. For, being the work of apostles, they were prior, and co-equal in origin with the churches themselves. For how would it have come to pass—if the apostles had published nothing—that their disciples were more forward in such a work? For they could not have been disciples without any instruction from their masters. *Tertullian (c. 207, W), 3.350.*

Now, the Gospels are four. These four are, as it were, the building blocks of the faith of the church. *Origen (c. 228, E), 9.299.*

Concerning the four Gospels which alone are uncontroverted in the church of God under heaven, I have learned by tradition that the Gospel according to Matthew (who was at one time a tax collector and afterwards an apostle of Jesus Christ) was written first. He composed it in the Hebrew tongue and published it for the converts from Judaism. The second one written was that according to Mark, who wrote it according to the instruction of Peter. For Peter, in his general epistles, acknowledged Mark as a son, saying, "The church that is in Babylon, elect together with you, salutes you. And so does Mark, my son." And third, was the one according to Luke, which he composed for the converts from the Gentiles. This is the Gospel commended by Paul. Last of all, there is the one according to John. *Origen (c. 245, E), 9.412.*

We have confidence also in the intentions of the writers of the Gospels, observing their godliness and conscientiousness. This is manifested in their writings, which contain nothing spurious, deceptive, false, or cunning. . . . I am of the opinion that it was on this account that Jesus wished to employ such persons as teachers of His doctrines: that there could be no grounds for any suspicion of plausible sophistry. Rather, it would be clear to all who were capable of understanding that the guileless purpose of the writers—marked with great simplicity—was deemed worthy of being accompanied by a more divine power. *Origen (c. 248, E), 4.480.*

The four living creatures are the four Gospels. . . . The lion designates Mark, in whom is heard the voice of the lion roaring in the desert. And in the figure of a man, Matthew strives to declare to us the genealogy of Mary, from whom Christ took flesh. . . . Therefore, his announcement sets forth the image of a man. Luke, in narrating the priesthood of Zachariah as he offered a sacrifice for the people, . . . bore the likeness of a calf. John the evangelist is like an eagle speeding on uplifted wings to greater heights. For he writes about the Word of God. *Victorinus (c. 280, W), 7.348.*

Four Gospels have been given because God has four times given the gospel to the human race. And He has instructed them by four laws. *Methodius (c. 290, E), 6.348; extended discussion: 9.299–9.304.*

SEE ALSO CANON, NEW TESTAMENT; GOSPELS, HARMONY OF; JOHN, GOSPEL OF; LUKE, GOSPEL OF; MARK, GOSPEL OF; MATTHEW, GOSPEL OF.

GOSPELS, HARMONY OF

If the historians desired to teach us what they have seen in their minds, using an image, their meaning would be found . . . to exhibit no disagreement. And we must understand that it is no different with the four evangelists. . . . In some places, they tack on to their writing language apparently implying things of sense, but describing things made manifest to them in a purely spiritual way. I do not condemn them if they even sometimes dealt freely with things that to the eye of history happened differently. Or if they changed them so as to serve the mystical aims they had in view. For example, they

may speak of a thing that happened in a certain place as though it had happened in another. *Origen (c. 228, E), 9.383.*

So much I have said of the apparent discrepancies in the Gospels and of my desire to have them treated in the way of spiritual interpretation. *Origen (c. 228, E), 9.384.*

I believe it is impossible for those who admit nothing more than the history in their interpretation to show that these discrepant statements [regarding the last week before the Crucifixion] are in harmony with each other. If anyone thinks that I have not given a sound exposition, let him write a reasoned rebuttal to this declaration of mine. *Origen (c. 228, E), 9.393; see also 2.581; extended discussion: 9.382–9.387.*

SEE ALSO GOSPELS; SCRIPTURES (V. SCRIPTURE DIFFICULTIES).

GOSSIP

You shall not go about as a talebearer among your people. Lev. 19:16.

A talebearer reveals secrets, but he who is of a faithful spirit conceals a matter. Prov. 11:13.

Remind them . . . to speak evil of no one. Tit. 3:2.

Speak evil of no one, nor listen with pleasure to anyone who speaks evil of another. But if you listen, you will partake of the sin of the one who speaks evil—if you believe the slander which you hear. *Hermas (c. 150, W), 2.20.*

We should keep pure from calumnious reports. To such things, the ears of those who have believed in Christ should be inaccessible. It appears to me that it is for this reason that the Instructor does not permit us to say anything that is unseemly. *Clement of Alexandria (c. 195, E), 2.251.*

And let not men, therefore, spend their time in barbers' shops and taverns, babbling nonsense. And let them give up hunting for the women who sit near, and ceaselessly talking slander against many in order to raise a laugh. *Clement of Alexandria (c. 195, E), 2.289.*

Tale-bearers are accursed. *Cyprian (c. 250, W), 5.555.*

GOVERNMENT

Render therefore to Caesar the things that are Caesar's, and to God the things that are God's. Matt. 22:21.

Jesus answered, "You could have no power at all against Me unless it had been given you from above." John 19:11.

Let every soul be subject to the governing authorities. For there is no authority except from God, and the authorities that exist are appointed by God. Rom. 13:1.

I exhort first of all that supplications, prayers, intercessions, and giving of thanks be made for all men, for kings and all who are in authority, that we may lead a quiet and peaceable life in all godliness and reverence. 1 Tim. 2:2.

Fear God. Honor the king. 1 Pet. 2:17.

Christians obey the prescribed laws. In fact, they actually surpass the laws by their lives. *Letter to Diognetus (c. 125–200), 1.27.*

My opinion is this: that in this way a kingdom may be governed in peace—when the sovereign is acquainted with the God of truth. That is, if the ruler withholds from doing wrong to his subjects out of fear of God, and he judges everything with equity. . . . For, if the sovereign abstains from doing wrong to those who are under his rule, and they abstain from doing wrong to him and to each other, it is evident that the whole country will dwell in peace. Many blessings, too, will be enjoyed there, because among all of them the name of God will be glorified. For what blessing is greater than for a sovereign to deliver the people that are under his rule from error, and by this good deed render himself pleasing to God? *Melito (c. 170, E), 8.755.*

Who are more deserving to obtain the things they ask for than those who, like us, pray for your government? We pray that you may receive the kingdom, the son receiving it from the father (as is most equitable). We pray that your empire may receive increase and addition—and that all men may become subject to your sway. And this is also for our advantage, that we may lead a peaceable and quiet life and may readily perform all that is commanded us. *Athenagoras (c. 175, E), 2.148.*

Satan declared, "All these things are delivered unto me, and to whomever I will I give them." However, this statement proceeded from him when he was puffed up with pride. For the creation is *not* subjected to his power. For he is himself but one among created things. Nor will he give away human rulership to men. Rather, all human affairs and all other things are arranged according to God the Father's disposal. . . . Satan certainly did not speak truth, but a lie, when he said, "For all these things are delivered to me." *Irenaeus (c. 180, E/W), 1.551.*

It is not Satan who has appointed the kingdoms of this world, but God. . . . And the Word also says by Solomon, "By me, kings reign and princes administer justice." *Irenaeus (c. 180, E/W), 1.552.*

God imposed upon mankind the fear of man, for mankind did not acknowledge the fear of God. So He did this in order that, being subjected to the authority of men, and kept under restraint by their law, mankind might obtain some degree of justice. They might exercise mutual forbearance through dread of the sword. . . . Earthly rule, therefore, has been appointed by God for the benefit of nations. It was not appointed by the devil. . . . This is so that under the fear of human rulers, men may not eat each other up like fishes. Rather, through the establishment of laws, men may keep down an excess of wickedness among the nations. Considered from this point of view, those who exact tribute from us are "God's ministers, serving for this very purpose." Therefore, since "the existing powers are ordained of God," it is clear that the devil lied when he said, "These have been delivered unto me and to whomever I will, I give them." *Irenaeus (c. 180, E/W), 1.552.*

By the counsels of holy men, states are managed well. *Clement of Alexandria (c. 195, E), 2.370.*

The Caesars too would have believed on Christ, if either the Caesars had not been necessary for the world, or if Christians could have been Caesars. *Tertullian (c. 197, W), 3.35.*

Examine then, and see if God is not the dispenser of kingdoms. For He is Lord both of the world that is ruled and of the man who rules. See if He has not ordained the changes of dynasties, with their appointed seasons. . . . See if the rise and fall of states are not His work, under whose sovereignty the human race once existed without states at all. *Tertullian (c. 197, W), 3.40.*

We offer prayer for the safety of our rulers to the eternal, true and living God. . . . We offer prayer without ceasing for all of our emperors. We pray for their prolonged lives and for security to the empire. We pray for protection of the imperial house, for brave armies, a faithful senate, a virtuous people, and a world at peace. *Tertullian (c. 197, W), 3.42.*

In us, all ardor in the pursuit of glory and honor is dead. So we have no pressing inducement to take part in your public meetings. Nor is there anything more entirely foreign to us than affairs of state. *Tertullian (c. 197, W), 3.45.*

He is the same One who dispenses kingdoms and has put the supremacy of them into the hands of the Romans. *Tertullian (c. 197, W), 3.146, 147.*

When the turn of worldly lots varied, God next favored the Romans. *Tertullian (c. 200, W), 4.5.*

In the Holy Scriptures, we find that there are princes over individual nations. For example, in Daniel, we read that there was a prince of the kingdom of Persia.... Likewise, in the prophecies of Ezekiel, the prince of Tyre is unmistakably shown to be a type of spiritual power. *Origen (c. 225, E), 4.335.*

Christ also restored the laws of rulership and government that had been corrupted. By subduing all enemies under His feet, He might teach rulers themselves moderation in their government. *Origen (c. 225, E), 4.343.*

The prince of this world says concerning the powers that are in the sphere of the invisible (the kingdoms that are set up against men): "All these things I will give you, if you will fall down and worship me." *Origen (c. 245, E), 9.480.*

God prepared the nations for His teaching, so that they could be under one ruler, the king of the Romans. He did not want it to be more difficult for the apostles of Jesus to accomplish the task given them by their Master. And it would have been difficult on account of the lack of unity among the nations, caused by the existence of many kingdoms.... The existence of many kingdoms would have been a hindrance to the spread of the doctrine of Jesus throughout the entire world. This is not only for the reason mentioned, but also because of the necessity of men everywhere engaging in war, and fighting on behalf of their native country, which was the case before the times of Augustus. *Origen (c. 248, E), 4.444.*

For example, let him tell us whether the laws of the Scythians—which permit the murder of parents—are upright laws. Or those of the Persians, which permit the marriages of sons with their mothers or of daughters with their own fathers.... For example, is it an act of impiety to do away with those laws that prevail in the Tauric Chersonese, regarding the offering up of strangers in sacrifice to Diana? Or what about the sacrifice of children to Saturn by certain of the Libyan tribes? *Origen (c. 248, E), 4.554.*

Those persons are more severely judged who in this world have had more power. Solomon says: "The hardest judgment will be made on those who govern" [Wis. 6:6]. *Cyprian (c. 250, W), 5.556.*

Civil law is one thing, which varies everywhere according to customs. However, justice is another thing—which God has set forth uniformly and simply to all. *Lactantius (c. 304–313, W), 7.171.*

[DECREE OF EMPEROR GALERIUS:] Because of our toleration, it will be the duty of the Christians to pray to God for our welfare and for that of the populace, as well as for their own welfare. *Emperor Galerius, as quoted by Lactantius (c. 304–313, W), 7.315.*

You cruelly break up our meetings, in which prayer is made to the Supreme God and in which peace and pardon are asked for all those in authority—for soldiers, kings, friends, and enemies. *Arnobius (c. 305, E), 6.488.*

Be subject to all royal power and dominion in things that are pleasing to God.... Render to everyone the fear that is due to him: all offerings, all customs, all honor, gifts, and taxes. *Apostolic Constitutions (compiled c. 390, E), 7.436.*

Whoever abuses the king or the governor unjustly, let him suffer punishment. If he is a clergyman, let him be deprived. However, if he is a layman, let him be suspended. *Apostolic Constitutions (compiled c. 390, E), 7.505.*

SEE ALSO CHURCH AND STATE; PATRIOTISM; PUBLIC OFFICE; TAXES; TOWER OF BABEL (II. ANGELIC DIVISION OF THE NATIONS); WAR.

GRACE

SEE SALVATION (II. ROLE OF GRACE AND FAITH IN SALVATION).

GREAT COMMISSION

SEE CHRISTIANITY (II. GROWTH OF CHRISTIANITY); EVANGELISM.

GREAT TRIBULATION

Then there will be great tribulation, such as has not been since the beginning of the world until this time, no, nor ever will be. Matt. 24:21.

These are the ones who come out of the great tribulation, and washed their robes and made them white in the blood of the Lamb. Rev. 7:14.

Happy are you who endure the great tribulation that is coming. And happy are they who will not deny their own life. *Hermas (c. 150, W), 2.11.*

This beast is a type of the great tribulation that is coming. If then you prepare yourselves, repent with all your heart, and turn to the Lord, it will be possible for you to escape it. *Hermas (c. 150, W), 2.18.*

"There will be tribulation such as has not been since the beginning, neither will be." For this is the last contest of the righteous, in which they are crowned with incorruption—when they overcome. *Irenaeus (c. 180, E/W), 1.558.*

"The woman was given two wings of the great eagle, so that she could fly into the wilderness, where she is nourished for a time, and times, and half a time, from the face of the serpent." That refers to the one thousand two hundred and sixty days during which the tyrant is to reign and persecute the church, which flees from city to city, and seeks concealment in the wilderness among the mountains. For she possesses no other defense than the two wings of the great eagle, that is to say, the faith of Jesus Christ. *Hippolytus (c. 200, W), 5.217.*

When the times are fulfilled, and the ten horns spring from the beast in the last days, then the Antichrist will appear among them. When he makes war against the saints and persecutes them, then we can expect the manifestation of the Lord from heaven. *Hippolytus (c. 205, W), 5.179.*

At that time, there will be great trouble, such as has not been from the beginning of the world. For men will be sent through every city and country to destroy the faithful—some in one direction, and others in another. And the saints will travel from the west to the east and will be driven in persecution from the east to the south. But other saints will conceal themselves in the mountains and caves. And the abomination will war against them everywhere. By his decree, he will cut the saints off by sea and by land. By all available means, he will attempt to destroy them out of the world. And no one will be able any longer to sell his own property or to buy from strangers—unless he keeps and carries with him the name of the beast, or bears its mark upon his forehead. *Hippolytus (c. 205, W), 5.190.*

When we read, "Go, my people, enter into your closets for a little season, until my anger passes away," we understand the closets to be graves, in which will rest for a little while those who (at the end of the world) have departed this life in the last furious onset of the power of the Antichrist. *Tertullian (c. 210, W), 3.565.*

Those persons will also come who overcame cruel martyrdom under the Antichrist. And they themselves live for the whole time and receive blessings because they have suffered evil things. *Commodianus (c. 240, W), 4.212.*

SEE ALSO ANTICHRIST; ESCHATOLOGY; MARK OF THE BEAST; RAPTURE; REVELATION, BOOK OF.

GREEK LANGUAGE

As matters stand, to you Greeks alone does it happen that you do not even speak alike in common conversation. For the way of speaking among the Dorians is not the same as that of the people of Attica. Nor do the Aeolians speak like the Ionians. And since such a discrepancy exists where it should not, I am at a loss as to whom to call a Greek. The strangest thing of all is that you hold foreign expressions in honor. By the intermixture of barbarian words, you have made your language a medley. *Tatian (c. 160, E), 2.65.*

For there is among the Greeks one definition of *logos* which means "the principle that thinks." There is also another definition that means "the instrument by means of which thought is expressed." . . . But God is all Mind and all Logos. So He speaks exactly what He thinks. *Irenaeus (c. 180, E/W), 1.400.*

We have neither practiced nor do we study how to express ourselves in pure Greek. For this suits those who seduce the multitude from the truth. . . . In my opinion, he who is solicitous about truth should not frame his language with artfulness and care. Rather, he should only try to express his meaning as best he can. For those who are particular about words, and devote their time to them, miss the point of the whole picture. *Clement of Alexandria (c. 195, E), 2.347.*

In Greek, the word for repentance is formed—not from the confession of a sin—but from a change of mind. *Tertullian (c. 207, W), 3.316.*

It is our [Latin] custom to call our *wives* our "women"—however improper this may linguistically be. In fact, the Greeks, too, use the name of "woman" even more often in the sense of "wife." This is even though they have other names appropriate to "wife." *Tertullian (c. 207, W), 4.30.*

What we call in Latin *mundus*, is called in Greek *cosmos*. And *cosmos* signifies not only a world, but also adornment. *Origen (c. 225, E), 4.273.*

The Holy Spirit, who is called the Paraclete, is called this because of His work of consolation. For *paraclesis* is called in Latin *consolatio*. For if anyone has deserved to participate in the Holy Spirit by the knowledge of His inexpressible mysteries, he undoubtedly obtains comfort and joy of heart. . . . Our Savior is also called the Paraclete in the Epistle of John, when he says, "If anyone sins, we have a Paraclete with the Father, Jesus Christ the righteous, and He is the propitiation for our sins" [1 John 2:1]. Let us consider whether this term "Paraclete" has one meaning when applied to the Savior and another when applied to the Holy Spirit. "Paraclete," when spoken of the Savior, seems to mean intercessor. For in Greek, *paraclesis* has both meanings: intercessor and comforter. *Origen (c. 225, E), 4.286.*

[The Gospel of John] has been committed to the earthly treasure house of common speech—a writing that anybody can read. And, when it is read aloud, it can be understand by anyone. *Origen (c. 228, E), 9.300.*

"Gospel" [Gr. *euangelion*] is a word that either implies the actual presence to the believer of something that is good—or else promises the arrival of something good that is expected. *Origen (c. 228, E), 9.300.*

It is not only the Greeks who consider the word "beginning" [Gr. *archē*] to have many meanings. Let anyone collect the Scripture passages in which the word occurs and . . . note what it stands for in each passage. He will find

that the word has many meanings in sacred discourse, as well. *Origen (c. 228, E), 9.305.*

On the question of what is meant in Scripture by the word "world" [Gr. *kosmos*], I think it is proper to repeat this: I am aware that a certain scholar understands "world" to mean the church alone. For the church is the adornment of the world and is said to be the light of the world. . . . If those who hold the view in question cannot show this, then let them consider if my interpretation is not a sound one: that the light is the church and the "world" refers to those others who call on the Name. *Origen (c. 228, E), 9.380.*

The word *cosmos* is used in itself and absolutely in the passage, "He was in the world and the world knew Him not." . . . In the Book of Esther, speaking of her, it is written that she stripped off all her *cosmos*. The word *cosmos* simply is not the same as the *cosmos* of heaven, or the *cosmos* of Esther. *Origen (c. 245, E), 9.487; extended discussion of "beginning" [Gr. archē]: 9.305–9.309.*

SEE ALSO GREEKS; HEBREW LANGUAGE.

GREEKS

Jews request a sign, and Greeks seek after wisdom; but we preach Christ crucified, to the Jews a stumbling block and to the Greeks foolishness. 1 Cor. 1:22, 23.

The excellent ones among the Greeks worshipped the same God as we do, but they had not learned by perfect knowledge that which was delivered by the Son. *Clement of Alexandria (c. 195, E), 2.489.*

He made a new covenant with us. For what belonged to the Greeks and Jews is old. But we, who worship Him in a new way, in the third form, are Christians. For I think he clearly showed that the one and only God was known by the Greeks in a Gentile way, by the Jews in a Jewish way, and by us, in a new and spiritual way. Clement of Alexandria (c. 195, E), 2.489.

To those who were righteous according to philosophy, not only was faith in the Lord necessary, but also the abandonment of idolatry. *Clement of Alexandria (c. 195, E), 2.490.*

GREGORY THAUMATURGUS

Gregory (c. 210–260) was born of upper-class pagan parents, but he was converted to Christianity by Origen, to whom he had gone for studies. Gregory later became bishop of Neocaesarea, and he was instrumental in converting much of the population of that city to Christianity. After his death, legends began to abound concerning his miracles, and he was given the surname Thaumaturgus, meaning "wonderworker."

From the time of my birth onwards, I was under the hand of my parents. And the manner of life in my father's house was one of error. It was of a kind from which no one, I imagine, expected that we would be delivered. . . . Then followed the loss of my father and my becoming an orphan. *Gregory Thaumaturgus (c. 255, E), 6.25; extended discussion: 6.25–6.33.*

GRIEF

SEE DEATH (III. CHRISTIAN ATTITUDE TOWARDS DEATH).

GROOMING

I. General admonition

II. Dyeing of the hair

III. Wigs

I. General admonition

In like manner also, [I desire] that the women adorn themselves in modest apparel, with propriety and moderation, not with braided hair or gold or pearls or costly clothing. 1 Tim. 2:9.

Do not let your beauty be that outward adorning of arranging the hair, of wearing gold, or of putting on fine apparel. 1 Pet. 3:3.

Let the head of men be clipped, unless they have curly hair. But let the chin have the hair. . . . Cutting is to be used, not for the sake of elegance, but on account of the necessity of the case . . . so that it may not grow so long as to come down and interfere with the eyes. *Clement of Alexandria (c. 195, E), 2.286.*

It is enough for women to protect their locks, and bind up their hair simply along the neck with a plain hair-pin, nourishing chaste locks with simple care to true beauty. *Clement of Alexandria (c. 195, E), 2.286.*

This [male] sex of ours acknowledges to itself deceptive trickeries of form peculiarly its own. I am referring to things such as cutting the beard too sharply, plucking it out here and there, shaving around about the mouth,

arranging the hair, and disguising its hoariness by dyes. *Tertullian (c. 198, W), 4.22.*

A woman should not be adorned in a worldly fashion. . . . "Let your women be such as adorn themselves with shamefacedness and modesty, not with twisted hair, nor with gold, nor with pearls, or precious garments." *Cyprian (c. 250, W), 5.544.*

[INSTRUCTIONS TO CHRISTIAN SERVANTS OF CAESAR:] All of you should also be elegant and tidy in person and dress. At the same time, your dress should not in any way attract attention because of extravagance or artificiality. Otherwise, Christian modesty may be scandalized. *Theonas of Alexandria (c. 300, E), 6.160.*

Though in the form of men, they . . . curl their hair with curling pins, make the skin of the body smooth, and they walk with bare knees. In every other type of wantonness, they lay aside the strength of their masculinity and grow effeminate in women's habits and luxury. *Arnobius (c. 305, E), 6.450.*

Do not adorn yourself in such a manner that you might entice another woman to you. . . . Do not further enhance the beauty that God and nature has bestowed on you. Rather, modestly diminish it before others. Therefore, do not permit the hair of your head to grow too long. Rather, cut it short. . . . Do not wear overly fine garments, either. . . . Nor should you put a gold ring on your fingers. *Apostolic Constitutions (compiled c. 390, E), 7.392.*

If you desire to be one of the faithful and to please the Lord, O wife, do not add adornments to your beauty, in order to please other men. Do not wear fine embroidery, garments, or shoes, to entice those who are allured by such things. It may be that you do not do these wicked things for the purpose of sinning yourself—but only for the sake of adornment and beauty. Nevertheless, you still will not escape future punishment for having compelled another to look so close at you as to lust after you. *Apostolic Constitutions (compiled c. 390, E), 7.395.*

II. Dyeing of the hair

The Ancient of Days was seated; his garment was white as snow. Dan. 7:9.

You cannot make one hair white or black. Matt. 5:36.

Silly women who dye their gray hair and anoint their locks, grow speedily grayer by the perfumes they use. For they are of a drying nature. *Clement of Alexandria (c. 195, E), 2.255.*

Prophecy has called him the "Ancient of days." And the prophet says, "the hair of His head was as pure wool." The Lord says, "And no one can make the hair white or black." See, then, how these godless ones work in rivalry with God, or rather violently oppose Him! For they change the hair that has been made white by Him. *Clement of Alexandria (c. 195, E), 2.275.*

Neither is the hair to be dyed, nor gray hair to have its color changed. . . . Old age, which conciliates trust, is not to be concealed. *Clement of Alexandria (c. 195, E), 2.286.*

I see some women turn the color of their hair with saffron. They are ashamed even of their own nation, ashamed that their birth did not assign them to Germany or to Gaul. To there, as it is, they transfer their hair. Ill, most ill, do they predict for themselves with their flame-colored head. *Tertullian (c. 198, W), 4.21.*

God says, "Who of you can make a white hair black, or out of a black a white?" And so they refute the Lord! They say, "Behold! Instead of white or black, we make it *yellow*." *Tertullian (c. 198, W), 4.21.*

You dye your hair, so that it will always be black. . . . But these things are not necessary for modest women. *Commodianus (c. 240, W), 4.214.*

Although it is written of the Lord, "His head and His hair were white like wool or snow,"

you curse that whiteness. You hate the hoariness that is like the Lord's head. *Cyprian (c. 250, W), 5.434.*

III. Wigs

Additions of other people's hair are entirely to be rejected. It is a most sacrilegious thing for spurious hair to shade the head, covering the skull with dead locks. For on whom does the presbyter lay his hand? Whom does he bless? *Clement of Alexandria (c. 195, E), 2.286.*

If you feel no shame at the enormity [of wearing a wig], feel some at the pollution. You should fear that you may be fitting on a holy and Christian head the excess of someone else's head—perhaps unclean, perhaps guilty and destined to Gehenna. *Tertullian (c. 198, W), 4.21.22.*

A tuft of hair is not to be worn on the head. In Leviticus: "You will not make a tuft from the hair of your head" [Lev. 19:27 LXX]. *Cyprian (c. 250, W), 5.553; see also 2.275–2.277.*

SEE ALSO BEARD; CLOTHING; COSMETICS; JEWELRY; MODESTY.

GYMNASIUM

The gymnasium is sufficient for boys, even if a bath is within reach. And even for men to prefer gymnastic exercises by far to the baths, is perhaps not bad. . . . When this is done without dragging a man away from better employments, it is pleasant, and not unprofitable. *Clement of Alexandria (c. 195, E), 2.283; see also 2.284.*

SEE ALSO SPORTS.

HADES

SEE DEAD, INTERMEDIATE STATE OF THE.

HADRIAN

Hadrian (76–138), the Roman emperor, is remembered today primarily for his construction of Hadrian's Wall across the then northern frontier of Britain.

Here follows the defense that Aristides the philosopher made before Hadrian the king. *Aristides (c. 125, E), 9.263.*

It was later, in the time of Hadrian the king, that there arose those who invented the heresies. And they extended to the age of Antoninus the elder. One example is Basilides—although he claims for his master, Glaucias, the interpreter of Peter. *Clement of Alexandria (c. 195, E), 2.555.*

Letter of Hadrian: 1.186.

HAIR

SEE GROOMING.

HAM

Another mystery was accomplished and predicted in the days of Noah, of which you are not aware. This mystery is in the blessings by which Noah blessed his two sons and in the curse he pronounced on his son's son [i.e., Ham's son]. For the Spirit of prophecy would not curse the son who had been blessed by God along with [his brothers]. *Justin Martyr (c. 160, E), 1.269.*

HANDICAPPED

If any of the clergy mocks at a lame, deaf, or a blind man—or one who is maimed in his feet—let him be suspended. And the same goes for the laity. *Apostolic Constitutions (compiled c. 390, E), 7.504.*

If anyone is maimed in an eye or lame in his leg, but is worthy of the episcopal dignity, let him be made a bishop. For it is not a blemish of the body that defiles a person, but the pollution of the soul. However, if he is deaf *and* blind, do not make him a bishop. We say this not because he is a defiled person, but so that the ecclesiastical affairs will not be hindered. *Apostolic Constitutions (compiled c. 390, E), 7.504.*

SEE ALSO EQUALITY OF HUMANKIND.

HANDS, CUTTING OFF

If your right eye causes you to sin, pluck it out and cast it from you. . . . And if your right hand causes you to sin, cut it off and cast it from you; for it is more profitable for you that one of your members perish, than for your whole body to be cast into hell. Matt. 5:29, 30.

Someone in the whole body of the congregations of the church may have the designation of a "hand" because of his practical gifts. Nevertheless, if he should change and become a hand causing stumbling, let the eye say to such a hand, "I have no need of you," and, after saying it, let him cut it off and cast it from him. . . . It is also possible to apply these words to our nearest kinfolk. . . . For let us cut off from ourselves—as a hand, foot, or an eye—a father or mother who wishes us to do that which is contrary to godliness. The same can be said of a son or daughter who . . . would have us revolt from the church of Christ and the love of Him. Even if the wife of our bosom, or a friend who is kindred in soul, become stumbling blocks to us, let us not spare them. Rather, let us cut them out from ourselves and cast them outside of our soul. . . . Also, anyone is saved with one eye who has cut out the eye of his own house—his wife—if she commits fornication. Lest having two eyes, he may go away into Gehenna. *Origen (c. 245, E), 9.489, 490.*

HANDS, LAYING ON OF

And they chose Stephen, a man full of faith and the Holy Spirit, and Philip, . . . whom they set before the apostles; and when they had prayed, they laid hands on them. Acts 6:5, 6.

Then they laid hands on them, and they received the Holy Spirit. Acts 8:17.

Having fasted and prayed, and laid hands on them, they sent them away. Acts 13:3.

Do not lay hands on anyone hastily. 1 Tim. 5:22.

Leaving the discussion of the elementary principles of Christ, let us go on to perfection, not laying again the foundation of repentance, . . . of the doctrine of baptisms, of laying on of hands. Heb. 6:1.

For on whom does the presbyter lay his hand? Whom does he bless? *Clement of Alexandria (c. 195, E), 2.286.*

Next, the hand is laid on us, invoking and inviting the Holy Spirit, through benediction. *Tertullian (c. 198, W), 3.672.*

In the Acts of the Apostles, the Holy Spirit was given by the imposition of the apostles' hands in baptism. *Origen (c. 225, E), 4.252.*

It is of little consequence to "lay hands on them so that they may receive the Holy Spirit," unless they receive also the baptism of the church. For they can be fully sanctified and be the sons of God only when they are born of each sacrament. For it is written, "Unless a man is born again of water *and* of the Spirit, he cannot enter into the kingdom of God." We find this also in the Acts of the Apostles. *Cyprian (c. 250, W), 5.378.*

Prayer being made for [the Samaritans whom Philip baptized] and hands being imposed on them, the Holy Spirit was invoked and poured out upon them. This same thing is now done among us, too. Those who are baptized in the church are brought to the prelates of the church. And by our prayers and by the imposition of hands, they obtain the Holy Spirit and are perfected with the Lord's seal. *Cyprian (c. 250, W), 5.381.*

If a man is not baptized by a bishop (so as to have had the imposition of hands at once) and should yet die before having received the Holy Spirit, would you judge him to have received salvation or not? . . . Even as also the Samaritans, when they were baptized by Philip,

waited until the apostles . . . went down to them to lay hands upon them and conferred on them the Holy Spirit by the imposition of hands. *Treatise on Re-Baptism (c. 257, W), 5.669.*

The Ethiopian eunuch, when he was returning from Jerusalem . . . had at the Spirit's suggestion heard the truth from Philip the deacon. He believed and was baptized. And when he had gone up out of the water, the Spirit of the Lord took away Philip, and the eunuch saw him no more. For he went on his way rejoicing, although, as you observe, hands were not laid on him by the bishop in order to receive the Holy Spirit. *Treatise on Re-Baptism (c. 257, W), 5.669.*

Furthermore, as you know, the Holy Spirit is found to have been given by the Lord to men who believed, without baptism of water. This is contained in the Acts of the Apostles in this manner: "While Peter was still speaking these words, the Holy Spirit fell upon all of them who heard the word. . . . Then Peter answered, 'Can any man forbid them to be baptized, who have received the Holy Spirit as well as us.'" . . . So they received the grace of the promise both without the imposition of the apostle's hands and without the bath, which they attained afterwards. Their hearts being purified, God bestowed upon them remission of sins at the same time, in virtue of their faith. The result is that the subsequent baptism conferred upon them this benefit alone: that they received also the invocation of the name of Jesus Christ. This way, nothing might appear to be wanting to the integrity of their service and faith. *Treatise on Re-Baptism (c. 257, W), 5.670.*

How dare any man speak against his bishop, by whom the Lord gave the Holy Spirit among you through the laying on of his hands. *Apostolic Constitutions (compiled c. 390, E), 7.412.*

By the laying on of hands, the Holy Spirit was given to believers. *Apostolic Constitutions (compiled c. 390, E), 7.415.*

SEE ALSO ABSOLUTION; BAPTISM; OIL, ANOINTING WITH.

HANDS, LIFTING IN PRAYER

SEE PRAYER (III. LIFTING HANDS IN PRAYER).

HANDS, WASHING

SEE ABLUTION; PRAYER (II. PRAYER POSTURES AND CUSTOMS).

HANNAH

Hannah, in the First Book of Kings, was a type of the church. She . . . prayed to God, not with clamorous petition, but silently and modestly—within the very recesses of her heart. She spoke with hidden prayer, but with manifest faith. She spoke with her heart, not her voice. *Cyprian (c. 250, W), 5.448.*

HARLOT, GREAT

SEE BABYLON THE GREAT.

HEAD COVERING

SEE VEIL.

HEALING, DIVINE

These twelve Jesus sent out and commanded them, saying . . . "Heal the sick, cleanse the lepers, raise the dead, cast out demons. Matt. 10:5.

Great multitudes followed Him, and he healed them all. Matt. 12:15.

They brought the sick out into the streets and laid them on beds and couches, that at least the shadow of Peter passing by might fall on some of them. Also a multitude gathered from the surrounding cities to Jerusalem, bringing sick people and those who were tormented by unclean spirits, and they were all healed. Acts 5:15, 16.

To another gifts of healing by the same Spirit. 1 Cor. 12:9.

Disease, accident, and . . . death come upon the spiritual man, too. *Clement of Alexandria (c. 195, E), 2.540.*

Were not the eyes of the blind opened? Did not the tongue of the dumb recover speech? Did not the weak hands and palsied knees become strong, and the lame leap like the hart? We are accustomed, no doubt, to give a spiritual meaning also to these statements of prophecy, according to the analogy of the physical diseases which were healed by the Lord. But, still, they were all fulfilled literally. *Tertullian (c. 210, W), 3.559.*

See how many men of rank have been delivered from devils and healed of diseases! *Tertullian (c. 212, W), 3.107.*

We have faith for a defense . . . in immediately making the sign and adjuring. . . . We often aid in this manner even the pagan, seeing that we have been endowed by God with that power

that the apostle first used when he despised the viper's bite. *Tertullian (c. 213, W), 3.633.*

Some persons provide evidence of their having received through this faith a marvelous power by the cures which they perform. They invoke no other name over those persons who need their help than the name of the God of all things, and of Jesus, along with a mention of His history. By these means, I, too, have seen many persons freed from grievous calamities, from distractions of mind, madness, and countless other ills that could not be cured by either men or devils. *Origen (c. 248, E), 4.473.*

It disturbs some that the power of this disease attacks our people equally with the pagans—as if the Christian believed for the purpose that he could have the enjoyment of the world and of this life, free from the contact of ills. *Cyprian (c. 250, W), 5.470.*

The disease of the eyes, the attack of fevers, and the feebleness of all the limbs is common to us with others—so long as this common flesh of ours is borne by us in the world. *Cyprian (c. 250, W), 5.471.*

He who has received the gift of healing is declared by revelation from God. The grace which is in him is manifest to all. *Apostolic Constitutions (compiled c. 390, E), 7.493.*

SEE ALSO GIFTS OF THE SPIRIT; MEDICINE, MEDICAL SCIENCE.

HEARING FROM GOD

I received no report from any man. Rather, the Spirit proclaimed these words: "Do nothing without the bishop. Keep your bodies as the temples of God. Love unity. Avoid divisions. Be the followers of Jesus Christ, even as He is of His Father." *Ignatius (c. 105, E), 1.83, 84.*

To those who ask questions, there is given from the Scriptures the gift of the God-given knowledge. *Clement of Alexandria (c. 195, E), 2.558.*

Be constant in both prayer and reading. Now speak with God; then let God speak with you. Let Him instruct you in His teachings, let Him direct you. *Cyprian (c. 250, W), 5.279, 280.*

By the kindness of the Lord instructing me, I am very often instigated and warned. *Cyprian (c. 250, W), 5.347.*

After the lapse of four days, God gave me instructions to leave. And He opened the way for me. *Dionysius of Alexandria (c. 262, E), 6.104.*

SEE ALSO DREAMS; PROPHECY, PROPHETS; VISIONS.

HEAVEN

SEE ETERNAL PUNISHMENTS AND REWARDS.

HEAVENLY BODIES

It is impossible that the sun could be a god, for it is the work of God. The same is true of the moon and stars. *Aristides (c. 125, E), 9.268.*

You pagans suppose that power and dominion belong to the elements. However, they are only slaves and functionaries. . . . They have been appointed in the manner of a law for their revolutions of time and for directing the guidance of time. From observing their conditions and the faithfulness of their operations, can you fail to be convinced . . . that a governing power presides over them? *Tertullian (c. 197, W), 3.134.*

According to the opinion of some, the moon is itself without light. It receives its light from the sun. *Alexander of Lycopolis (c. 300, E), 6.250.*

SEE ALSO CREATION; EARTH; ORIGEN; SUN WORSHIP.

HEBREW LANGUAGE

The Hebrew dialect, like all the rest, has certain properties, consisting in a mode of speech that exhibits the national character. *Clement of Alexandria (c. 195, E), 2.510.*

If we translate the word *Israel* into Greek, or any other language, we will produce no result. . . . We may say the same also of the pronunciation of *Sabaoth,* a word that is frequently employed in incantations. For if we translate the term into "Lord of hosts," or "Lord of armies," or "Almighty," we will accomplish nothing. Whereas, if we retain the original pronunciation, we will . . . produce some effect. And the same thing holds true of *Adonai. Origen (c. 248, E), 4.563.*

Indeed, the language of the Jews, in which the prophets wrote the books that have come down to us, has a grace of expression peculiar to the genius of the Hebrew tongue. *Origen (c. 248, E), 4.634.*

SEE ALSO GREEK LANGUAGE.

HEBREWS, EPISTLE TO

By the style of writing, Luke may be recognized both to have composed the Acts of the Apostles and to have translated Paul's Epistle to the Hebrews. *Clement of Alexandria (c. 195, E), 2.573.*

And Clement says that the Epistle to the Hebrews is Paul's, and was written to the Hebrews in the Hebrew language. But he says that Luke, having carefully translated it, gave it to the Greeks. For that reason, the same style of expression is exhibited in this Epistle and in the Acts. The name, "Paul, an apostle," was very properly not prefixed to the work. For Clement says that, writing to the Hebrews (who were prejudiced against Paul and suspicious), he with great wisdom did not repel them in the beginning by putting down his name. *Eusebius, citing Clement of Alexandria (c. 195, E), 2.579.*

And now, as the blessed presbyter [Clement] used to say, the Lord, as the Apostle of the Almighty, was sent to the Hebrews. However, Paul was sent to the Gentiles. Therefore, Paul did not subscribe himself as apostle to the Hebrews, out of modesty and reverence for the Lord. Furthermore, because he was the herald and apostle to the Gentiles, his writing to the Hebrews was something over and above [his assigned function.] *Eusebius, citing Clement of Alexandria (c. 195 E), 2.579.*

There is extant an Epistle to the Hebrews under the name of Barnabas—a man sufficiently accredited by God, as being one whom Paul had stationed next to himself in the uninterrupted observance of abstinence. . . . And, of course, this epistle of Barnabas is more generally received among the churches than that apocryphal *Shepherd* of adulterers. . . . "For it is impossible that those who have once been illuminated, and have tasted the heavenly gift, and have participated in the Holy Spirit, and have tasted the Word of God and found it sweet, when they . . . have fallen away, would be again recalled to repentance." *Tertullian (c. 212, W), 4.97.*

I think it is sufficient to quote this one testimony of Paul from the Epistle to the Hebrews. *Origen (c. 225, E), 4.239.*

Someone hard pressed by this argument may have recourse to the opinion of those who reject this Epistle [to the Hebrews] as not being

Paul's. Against such ones, I must at some other time use other arguments to prove that it is Paul's. *Origen (c. 240, E), 4.388.*

SEE ALSO CANON, NEW TESTAMENT.

HEBREWS, GOSPEL ACCORDING TO THE

SEE GOSPEL ACCORDING TO THE HEBREWS.

HELL

SEE DEAD, INTERMEDIATE STATE OF THE; ETERNAL PUNISHMENTS AND REWARDS; GEHENNA.

HERESIES, HERETICS

I. Heretics and the church's response

II. Descriptions of specific heretics and sects

III. Examples of heretical doctrines

IV. How the heretics misuse Scripture

I. Heretics and the church's response

There must also be factions [or heresies] among you, that those who are approved may be recognized among you. 1 Cor. 11:19.

Now the works of the flesh are evident, which are . . . selfish ambitions, dissensions, heresies, envy, murders, drunkenness, revelries, and the like; of which I tell you beforehand, just as I also told you in time past, that those who practice such things will not inherit the kingdom of God. Gal. 5:19–21.

The time will come when they will not endure sound doctrine, but according to their own desires, because they have itching ears, they will heap up for themselves teachers; and they will turn their ears away from the truth, and be turned aside to fables. 2 Tim. 4:3, 4.

There will be false teachers among you, who will secretly bring in destructive heresies, even denying the Lord who bought them, and bring on themselves swift destruction. And many will follow their destructive ways, because of whom the way of truth will be blasphemed. 2 Pet. 2:1.

Keep yourselves away from those evil plants that Jesus Christ does not tend. For they are not the planting of the Father. For as many as are of God and of Jesus Christ are also with the bishop. . . . If anyone walks according to a strange opinion, he does not agree with the Passion. *Ignatius (c. 105, E), 1.80.*

Therefore, it is fitting that you should keep aloof from such persons [i.e., heretics] and not to speak of them either in private or in public. *Ignatius (c. 105, E), 1.89.*

How much more will this be the case with anyone who by wicked doctrine corrupts the faith of God, for which Jesus Christ was crucified! Such a one becomes defiled. He will go away into everlasting fire, and so will everyone that listens to him. *Ignatius (c. 105, E), 1.56.*

They were hypocrites, and introducers of strange doctrines. They were also subverters of the servants of God, especially of those who had sinned. For they did not require them to repent, but persuaded them by foolish doctrines. *Hermas (c. 150, W), 2.41.*

[The heretics] taught them to both speak and do ungodly and blasphemous things. These persons are called by us after the name of the men from whom each doctrine and opinion had its origin. *Justin Martyr (c. 160, E), 1.212.*

The church was called a virgin, for she had not as yet been corrupted by worthless teaching. Thebulis it was who, displeased because he was not made a bishop, first began to corrupt the church by stealth. . . . From these men have come false Christs, false prophets, false apostles—men who have split up the one church into parts through their corrupting doctrines. *Hegesippus (c. 170), 8.764.*

Handing mixed cups to the women, [Marcus, a heretic] instructs them to consecrate them in his presence. . . . He devotes himself especially to women, and particularly to those women who are well-bred, elegantly attired, and of great wealth. *Irenaeus (c. 180, E/W), 1.334.*

Marcion met Polycarp on one occasion, and he said, "Do you know me?" Polycarp replied, "I do know you, the first-born of Satan!" Such was the horror that the apostles and their disciples had against holding even verbal communication with any corrupters of the truth. As Paul also says, "Reject a man who is a heretic, after the first and second, knowing that he who is such is subverted, and sins, being condemned of himself." *Irenaeus (c. 180, E/W), 1.416.*

The Ebionites, who use only Matthew's Gospel, are refuted out of this very same work, making false suppositions with regard to the Lord. But Marcion, mutilating the Gospel according to Luke, is still proved to be a blasphemer of the only existing God, from those passages which he still retains. Those, again, who separate Jesus from Christ, alleging that Christ remained impassible, but that it was Jesus who suffered, prefer the Gospel by Mark. However, if they read it with a love of truth, they would have their errors rectified. Those, moreover, who follow Valentinus, make copious use of the Gospel according to John to illustrate their conjunctions. However, they, too, will be proved to be totally in error. *Irenaeus (c. 180, E/W), 1.428.*

Alienated from the truth, they deservedly wallow in all error, tossed to and fro by it. They think differently in regard to the same things at different times. And they never attain to a well-grounded knowledge.... They always have the excuse of searching after truth (for they are blind), but they never succeed in finding it. *Irenaeus (c. 180, E/W), 1.458.*

We pray for these things on their behalf, loving them better than they seem to love themselves. For our love, inasmuch as it is true, is salutary to them, if they will only receive it. *Irenaeus (c. 180, E/W), 1.460.*

It is incumbent to obey the presbyters who are in the church—those who, as I have shown, possess the succession from the apostles. These men, together with the succession of the bishops, have received the certain gift of truth, according to the good pleasure of the Father. But we should hold in suspicion others who depart from the primitive succession, and assemble themselves together in any place whatsoever—either as heretics of perverse minds, or as schismatics puffed up and self-pleasing. Or they may be hypocrites, acting this way for the sake of money and vainglory. For all of those persons have fallen from the truth. The heretics bring strange fire to the altar of God—namely, strange doctrines. So they shall be burned up by the fire from heaven, as were Nadab and Abihu. And those persons who rise up in opposition to the truth and exhort others against the church of God shall remain among those in the pit of Hades, being swallowed up by an earthquake, even as those who were with Korah, Nadab, and Abihu. *Irenaeus (c. 180, E/W), 1.497.*

Therefore, it behooves us to keep aloof from all such persons, and to adhere to those who, as I have already observed, hold to the doctrine of the apostles. It is these who, together with the order of presbyters, display sound speech and blameless conduct for the strengthening and correction of others. *Irenaeus (c. 180, E/W), 1.497.*

The heretics, as many as they are, all depart [from each other], holding so many opinions as to one thing. They bear about their "clear notions" in secret within themselves. Therefore, if they ever agree among themselves as to the things predicted in the Scriptures, then we will also refute them. Meanwhile, in addition to holding wrong opinions, they also convict themselves, for they are not of one mind with regard to the same words. *Irenaeus (c. 180, E/W), 1.514.*

Now all these heretics are of much later date than are the bishops to whom the apostles committed the churches.... It follows, then, as a matter of course, that these aforementioned heretics—since they are blind to the truth and deviate from the way—will walk in diverse roads. Therefore, the footsteps of their doctrines are scattered here and there without agreement or connection. In contrast, the path of those belonging to the church circumscribes the whole world, as possessing the sure tradition from the apostles. *Irenaeus (c. 180, E/W), 1.548.*

Those, therefore, who desert the preaching of the church, call into question the knowledge of the holy presbyters.... Now, all the heretics are such persons. So are those who imagine that they have hit upon something further beyond the truth.... They do not always keep to the same opinions with regard to the same things. So as blind men who are led by the blind, they will deservedly fall into the ditch of ignorance. *Irenaeus (c. 180, E/W), 1.548.*

They therefore form opinions on what is beyond the limits of understanding. For this cause also the apostle says, "Be not wise beyond what is fitting to be wise, but be wise prudently" [Rom. 12:3]. *Irenaeus (c. 180, E/W), 1.548.*

"He has forsaken the way of his own vineyard and wandered in the tracks of his own husbandry." Such are the sects that deserted the primitive church. Now he who has fallen into heresy passes through an arid wilderness, abandoning the only true God. As a result, he is destitute of God. *Clement of Alexandria (c. 195, E), 2.322.*

[The pagans] make this objection to us, saying that they do not believe [on Christ] because of the discord of the sects. For the truth is warped when some teach one set of dogmas, and others teach another. We reply to them, "Among you who are Jews, and among the most famous of the Greek philosophers, very many sects have sprung up. Yet, you do not say that one should hesitate to philosophize or to Judaize because of the lack of agreement of your sects between themselves. Furthermore, that heresies would be sown among the truth, as 'tares among the wheat' was foretold by the Lord." *Clement of Alexandria (c. 195, E), 2.549.*

Therefore, on account of the heresies, the toil of discovery must be undertaken. Yet, we must not at all abandon [the truth]. Suppose that fruit were set before us. Some of it was real and ripe, and some was made of wax. However, the wax fruit was as much like the real as is possible. Would we abstain from both kinds of fruit merely because of the similarity? . . . Among garden-grown vegetables, weeds also spring up. Are the gardeners, then, to desist from gardening? *Clement of Alexandria (c. 195, E), 2.550.*

This may be seen in all the heresies, when you examine the iniquities of their dogmas. For when they are overturned by our clearly showing that they are opposed to the Scriptures, those who defend the [heretical] teaching do one of two things: They either despise the consistency of their own dogmas, or else they despise the prophecy itself. . . . They go to the extreme of ungodliness by disbelieving the Scriptures—rather than to be removed from the honors of the heresy and the boasted first seat in their churches. *Clement of Alexandria (c. 195, E), 2.552.*

We call those heretics "empty," for they are destitute of the counsels of God and of the traditions of Christ. Their dogmas originate with themselves and are therefore bitter—like the wild almond. *Clement of Alexandria (c. 195, E), 2.552.*

We have learned that voluptuousness, which is to be attributed to the Gentiles, is one thing. But wrangling, which is preferred among the heretical sects, is another. *Clement of Alexandria (c. 195, E), 2.553.*

They do not have the key of entrance, but rather a false or counterfeit key. With this, they do not enter in, as we do. For we enter through the tradition of the Lord. . . . The human assemblies that they held were later in origin than the catholic church. It does not require many words to show this. . . . Such being the case, it is evident, from the high antiquity and perfect truth of the church, that these later heresies—and those even later in time—were new, falsified inventions. . . . The one church is associated in a joint heritage in the nature of the One. But they strive to cut [the church] asunder into many sects. *Clement of Alexandria (c. 195, E), 2.554, 555.*

Heresies would have no power if men would cease to wonder that they have such power. For it either happens that, while men wonder, they fall into a snare. Or, because they are ensnared, they cherish their surprise—as if heresies were so powerful because of some truth which belonged to them. *Tertullian (c. 197, W), 3.243, 244.*

Heresies derive what strength as they have from the infirmities of individuals. For heresies have no strength whenever they encounter a truly powerful faith. *Tertullian (c. 197, W), 3.244.*

Some ask, "How did it come to pass that this woman or that man, who were the most faithful, the most prudent, and the most approved in the church, have gone over to the other side?" . . . However, what if a bishop, a deacon, a widow, a virgin, a teacher, or even a martyr has fallen from the rule? Will heresies on that account appear to possess the truth? Do we prove the faith by the persons, or the persons by the faith? *Tertullian (c. 197, W), 3.244.*

Let us rather be mindful of the sayings of the Lord, and of the letters of the apostles. For they have all told us beforehand that there will be heresies. And, in anticipation, they have given us warnings to avoid them. *Tertullian (c. 197, W), 3.244.245.*

At the present time, heresies will no less tear the church apart by their perversion of doctrine than will the Antichrist persecute her at that day. . . . Therefore, "heresies need to be in order that those who are approved might be made manifest"—both those who remained steadfast under persecution and those who did not wander off the way into heresy. For the apostle does not mean that those persons should be deemed approved who exchange their creed for heresy. *Tertullian (c. 197, W), 3.245.*

Of these, the practical effects are false doctrines, called in Greek *heresies*. This word is used in the sense of the *choice* that a man makes when he either teaches [false doctrines] or takes up with them. It is for this reason that he calls the heretic self-condemned, for the heretic has himself chosen that for which he is condemned. *Tertullian (c. 197, W), 3.245, 246.*

Your object in seeking was to find.... Now, because so many other things have been taught by various persons, are we on that account obliged to go on seeking?... When will the seeking ever end? Where is the finality of belief? Where is the completion in finding? *Tertullian (c. 197, W), 3.248.*

Away with the man who is ever seeking, for he never finds. He seeks in places where nothing can be found. *Tertullian (c. 197, W), 3.249.*

This heresy of yours does not accept certain Scriptures. And those Scriptures it does receive, it perverts by means of additions and diminutions. It does this to accomplish its own purpose. And such Scriptures as it does receive, it does not receive in their entirety. But even when it does receive any Scripture up to a certain point as entire, it nevertheless perverts even them by the contrivance of diverse interpretations. Truth is just as much opposed by an adulteration of its meaning as it is by a corruption of its text. *Tertullian (c. 197, W), 3.251.*

The heretics insist that [the apostles] did not reveal everything to all men. Rather, they say that the apostles proclaimed some things openly and to all the world, but that they disclosed other things only in secret and to a few. *Tertullian (c. 197, W), 3.254, 255.*

It is inconceivable that the apostles were either ignorant of the whole scope of the message which they had to declare, or that they failed to make known to all men the entire rule of faith. Indeed, the apostles proclaimed it simply and fully. So let us see, then, whether the churches, through their own fault, set it forth otherwise than the apostles had done. All these suggestions of distrust you may find put forward by the heretics. *Tertullian (c. 197, W), 3.256.*

In the apostolic times, those heresies were in a crude form. They are now found to be the same heresies—only in a much more polished version. *Tertullian (c. 197, W), 3.260.*

I must not omit an account of the conduct also of the heretics. How frivolous it is! How worldly, how merely human, without seriousness. It is without authority, without discipline, as suits their creed. To begin with, it is doubtful who is a catechumen and who is a believer. They all have access alike, they hear alike, they pray alike—even pagans, if any such happen to come among them.... All are puffed up, all offer you knowledge. Their catechumens are complete before they are fully taught. The very women of these heretics, how wanton they are! For they are bold enough to teach, to dispute, to enact exorcisms, to undertake cures—it may be even to baptize.... Their ordinations are carelessly administered, capricious, changeable. At one time, they put novices in office. At another time, [they ordain] men who are tied to some secular employment.... Nowhere is promotion easier than in the camp of these rebels.... And so it comes to pass that today one man is their bishop, tomorrow another. Today he is a deacon who tomorrow is a reader. Today he is a presbyter who tomorrow is a layman. For even on laymen do they impose the functions of priesthood.... But what will I say concerning the ministry of the word, since they make it their business not to convert the pagan, but to subvert our people?... They undermine our edifices, so that they may erect their own. *Tertullian (c. 197, W), 3.263.*

All heresies, when thoroughly looked into, are found to harbor dissent in many particulars—even from their own founders. The majority of them do not even have churches. Motherless, houseless, creedless outcasts—they wander about in their own essential worthlessness.... In their discipline, we have a measure of their doctrine. They say that God is not to be feared. Therefore, all things are in their view free and unchecked. *Tertullian (c. 197, W), 3.264.*

In addition, they will add a good deal respecting the high authority of each teacher of heresy. They will relate how that these men strengthened belief in their own doctrine through mighty works, how that they raised the dead, restored the sick, foretold the future—so that they might deservedly be regarded as apostles. As if this warning were not also in the written record: that many would come who were to work even the greatest miracles, in defense of the deception of their corrupt preaching. *Tertullian (c. 197, W), 3.264, 265.*

We are accustomed, for the purpose of short-ening argument, to lay down the rule against heretics of the *lateness* of their date. For accord-ing to our rule, priority in time indicates the truth. The truth also foretold that there would be heresies. Therefore, all later teachings must be prejudged as heresies—since the more ancient rule of truth already predicted them to happen. *Tertullian (c. 200, W), 3.477.*

There is even within the confines of God's church a sect that is more nearly allied to the Epicureans than to the prophets. *Tertullian (c. 210, W), 3.546.*

Just as a heretic may not lawfully ordain or lay on hands, so neither may he baptize, nor do anything holy or spiritual. *Firmilian (c. 256, E), 5.392.*

In addition to all these things, there is also this evil: that the priests of the devil dare to cele-brate the Eucharist. *Seventh Council of Carthage (c. 256, W), 5.566.*

We must regard it as most impious to search into those things that God wished to be kept secret. *Lactantius (c. 304–313, W), 7.56.*

We should know that both He Himself and His ambassadors foretold that there must be numerous sects and heresies, which would break the unity of the sacred body. So they admonished us to be on our guard with the greatest prudence. *Lactantius (c. 304–313, W), 7.133.*

Some of [the heretics] teach that humans should not marry and that they must abstain from meat and wine. In other words, they assert that marriage, the begetting of children, and the eating of certain foods are abominable.... Some of them absolutely prohibit the eating of any meat, saying that it is not the flesh of brute animals, but of creatures that have a rational soul.... Others of them declare that we should only abstain from pork. However, such ones say that we may eat of any of the meats that are clean by the Law. They also say that we should be circumcised according to the Law. They believe Jesus to be only a holy man and a prophet. Others teach that humans should be bold in sin, abusing the flesh.... Now, all of these are the instruments of the devil. They are the children of wrath. *Apostolic Constitutions (compiled c. 390, E), 7.453, 454.*

II. Descriptions of specific heretics and sects

Of the heresies, some receive their appellation from a name—as that which is called after Val-entinus, and that after Marcion, and that after Basilides.... Some take their designation from a place, as the Peratici. Some take it from a nation, as that of the Phrygians. Some from an action, as that of the Encratites. And some take it from peculiar dogmas, as that of the Docetists. *Clement of Alexandria (c. 195, E), 2.555.*

Apelles ... forsook the continence of Marcion by resorting to the company of a woman. And he withdrew to Alexandria, out of sight of his most temperate master. He returned from there after some years. However, he had not improved, except that he was no longer a Mar-cionite. He now clung to another woman, the maiden Philumene.... She herself later became an infamous prostitute. Having been imposed on by her vigorous spirit, he commit-ted to writing the revelations that he had learned from her. *Tertullian (c. 197, W), 3.257.*

It will be appropriate also to say this to every-one who has fallen away from the doctrines of God and the words of the church.... For example, I mean those who accept as true the teachings of Basilides, Valentinus, or Mar-cion—or anyone else who teaches the things of men as though they were the things of God. *Origen (c. 245, E), 9.463.*

I know of no others who have altered the Gospel, except the followers of Marcion, Val-entinus, and, I think, Lucian. *Origen (c. 248, E), 4.443.*

There are certain Marcellians, so called from Marcellina. And there are Harpocratians from Salome. There are still others who derive their name from Mariamne, and others from Mar-tha. *Origen (c. 248, E), 4.570.*

They have gone astray with regard to one of the three Persons of the Trinity. For example, some say, like Sabellius, that the Almighty per-son of the Father Himself suffered. Others say, like Artemas, that the person of the Son only *appeared* to be born and manifested. Still others contend, like the Ebionites, that the prophets spoke of the person of the Spirit. As to Marcion and Valentinus, ... it is better not even to make mention. *Methodius (c. 290, E), 6.338.*

What alien dogmas has he destroyed—whether he is a Valentinus, Marcion, Tatian, or a Sabellius—or of any others of those who have constructed for themselves their peculiar systems of knowledge. *Disputation of Archelaus and Manes (c. 320, E), 6.211.*

III. Examples of heretical doctrines

Now the Spirit expressly says that in latter times some will depart from the faith, giving heed to deceiving spirits and doctrines of demons, . . . forbidding to marry, and commanding to abstain from foods which God created to be received with thanksgiving. 1 Tim. 4:1–3.

[They] have strayed concerning the truth, saying that the resurrection is already past; and they overthrow the faith of some. 2 Tim. 2:18.

Every spirit that does not confess that Jesus Christ has come in the flesh is not of God. 1 John 4:3.

I add a review of the [heretical] doctrines themselves, which, existing as they did in the days of the apostles, were both exposed and denounced by the said apostles. . . . Paul, in his first epistle to the Corinthians, sets his mark on certain ones who denied and doubted the resurrection. This opinion was the special property of the Sadducees. A part of it, however, is maintained by Marcion, Apelles, Valentinus, and all other impugners of the resurrection. Writing also to the Galatians, Paul denounces those men who observed and defended circumcision and the Law. Thus runs Hebion's [i.e., the Ebionites'] heresy. Those who "forbid to marry," he reproaches in his instructions to Timothy. Now, this is the teaching of Marcion and his followers. *Tertullian (c. 197, W), 3.259.*

The apostle delivers a similar blow against those who said that "the resurrection was already past." Such an opinion did the Valentinians assert. *Tertullian (c. 197, W), 3.259.*

A better god has been discovered [by the heretics]: one who never takes offense, is never angry, never inflicts punishments, has prepared no fire in Gehenna, and requires no gnashing of teeth in the outer darkness! He is purely and simply "good." He indeed forbids all delinquency—but only in word. He is in you, if you are willing to pay him homage. This is for the sake of appearances, so that you may *seem* to honor God. For He does not want your fear. *Tertullian (c. 207, W), 3.292.*

After all this, we must turn our attention also to those Scriptures that prevent our believing in such a resurrection as is held by your [heretics]. . . . I mean a resurrection that is either to be assumed to be taking place now (as soon as men come to the knowledge of the truth), or else that it is accomplished immediately after their departure from this life. *Tertullian (c. 210, W), 3.560.*

Marcion, I suppose, took sound words in a wrong sense, when he rejected Jesus' birth from Mary and declared that, as to Jesus' divine nature, He was not born of Mary. Hence, he boldly deleted from the Gospel the passages that have this effect. And a like fate seems to have overtaken those who make away with his humanity and receive only His deity. And then there are those of the opposite extreme, who cancel His deity and assert Him to be only a holy man and the most righteous of all men. *Origen (c. 228, E), 9.384.*

IV. How the heretics misuse Scripture

Paul, according to the wisdom given to him, has written to you, as also in all his epistles, speaking in them of these things, in which are some things hard to understand, which those who are untaught and unstable twist to their own destruction, as they do also the rest of the Scriptures. 2 Pet. 3:16.

It comes to this, therefore, that these men accept neither Scripture nor tradition. Such are the adversaries with whom we have to deal. *Irenaeus (c. 180, E/W), 1.415.*

Those who give themselves up to pleasures, twist Scripture in accordance with their lusts. . . . Such people, in consequence of falling away from the right path, err in most individual points. As you might expect, they do not have the faculty for judging what is true and false. . . . For if they had, they would have obeyed the Scriptures. . . . We also give a complete explanation of the Scriptures from the Scriptures themselves. From faith, we are persuaded by demonstration. However, when those who follow heresies venture to avail themselves of the prophetic Scriptures, [they do the following]: In the first place, they do not use *all* the Scriptures. Secondly, they do not quote them *entirely.* Finally, they do not quote them as the body and context of prophecy prescribes. Rather, selecting ambiguous expressions, they twist them to suit their own opinions, gathering a few expressions here and there. Instead of looking to the sense, they make use of the mere words. *Clement of Alexandria (c. 195, E), 2.551.*

They actually quote the Scriptures and recommend [their beliefs] out of the Scriptures. Of course they do! From what other source could they derive arguments concerning the things of the faith? *Tertullian (c. 197, W), 3.250.*

Where diversity of doctrine is found, there, then, must there be corruption both of the Scriptures and the explanations of them. *Tertullian (c. 197, W), 3.261.*

One man perverts the Scriptures with his hand. Another perverts their meaning by his exposition. For although Valentinus seems to use the entire volume [of Scripture], he has none the less laid violent hands on the truth. Only, he has done it with a more cunning mind and skill than Marcion. Marcion expressly and openly used the knife, rather than the pen. For he made excisions of the Scriptures to suit his own subject matter. *Tertullian (c. 197, W), 3.262.*

As is usual with heretics, they have found their opportunity in wresting the plain meaning of certain words. *Tertullian (c. 200, W), 3.488.*

In this manner, heretics either wrest plain and simple words to any sense they choose by their conjectures—or else, they violently resolve by a literal interpretation words that imply a conditional interpretation and are incapable of a literal solution. *Tertullian (c. 207, W), 3.377.*

Indeed, take way from the heretics the wisdom that they share with the pagans, and let them support their inquiries from the Scriptures alone. They will then be unable to hold their ground. *Tertullian (c. 210, W), 3.547.*

They [the heretics] would have the entire revelation of both Testaments yield to these three passages. However, the only proper course is to understand the few statements in the light of the many. But, in their contention, they are only following the principle of all heretics. For, inasmuch as only a few testimonies are to be found in the general mass, they obstinately set off the few against the many. *Tertullian (c. 213, W), 3.615.*

He cites these words without understanding what precedes them. For whenever they wish to attempt anything underhanded, they mutilate the Scriptures. Instead, let him quote the passage as a whole! *Hippolytus (c. 205, W), 5.224.*

They have boldly falsified the sacred Scriptures, rejected the canons of the ancient faith, and ignored Christ. Instead of inquiring what

the sacred Scriptures say, they laboriously seek to discover what form of syllogism might be contrived to establish their impiety. *Caius (c. 215, W), 5.602, as quoted by Eusebius.*

As to those men who abuse the arts of the unbelievers to establish their own heretical doctrine, what need is there to say that these are not near the faith? By their craft, these ungodly ones adulterate the simple faith of the divine Scriptures. For this reason, they have boldly laid their hands upon the divine Scriptures, alleging that they have corrected them. *Caius (c. 215, W), 5.602, as quoted by Eusebius.*

Those who seek to set up some new dogma have the habit of very readily perverting into a conformity with their own notions any proofs they care to take from the Scriptures. . . . Consequently, in addition to what has been once committed to us by the apostles, a disciple of Christ should receive nothing new as doctrine. *Disputation of Archelaus and Manes (c. 320, E), 6.213, 214.*

SEE ALSO ARIUS, ARIANISM; BAPTISM (V. BAPTISM BY HERETICS); BASILIDES; CARPOCRATES; CERINTHUS; EBIONITES; ENCRATITES; GNOSTICS, GNOSTICISM; HERMENEUTICS; MANES, MANICHEANS; MARCION; MENANDER, THE HERETIC; MONARCHIANISM; MONTANISTS; NICOLAITANS; SCHISM; SIMON MAGUS; VALENTINUS, VALENTINIANS.

HERETICS

SEE HERESIES, HERETICS.

HERMAS, SHEPHERD OF

The work entitled The Shepherd, written by Hermas, is an orthodox work that is included in *The Ante-Nicene Fathers.* It was widely read among the early Christians, and some Christians viewed it as canonical Scripture.

The Shepherd, the angel of repentance, says to Hermas about the false prophet: "For he speaks some truths." *Clement of Alexandria (c. 195, E), 2.319.*

Divinely, therefore, the power that spoke to Hermas by revelation said, "The visions and revelations are for those who are of double mind." *Clement of Alexandria (c. 195, E), 2.341.*

The Shepherd, speaking plainly of those who had fallen asleep, recognizes certain righteous ones among Gentiles and Jews—not only before the appearance of Christ—but before the Law. . . . He adds, "They gave them the seal of preaching. They descended, therefore, with them into the water and again ascended." *Clement of Alexandria (c. 195, E), 2.357.*

As the Shepherd says, "The virtue, then, that encloses the church in its grasp is faith." *Clement of Alexandria (c. 195, E), 2.360.*

For instance, the Shepherd says: "You will escape the energy of the wild beast if your heart becomes pure and blameless." *Clement of Alexandria (c. 195, E), 2.422.*

Did not the power that appeared to Hermas in the vision in the form of the church, give for transcription the book that she wished to be made known to the elect? *Clement of Alexandria (c. 195, E), 2.510.*

What if that Hermas, whose writing is generally inscribed with the title *The Shepherd,* had not sat down after finishing his prayer? *Tertullian (c. 198, W), 3.686.*

Moreover, Hermas wrote *The Shepherd* very recently in our times in the city of Rome, while his brother, bishop Pius, sat in the chair of the church in Rome. And therefore it also should be read. However, it cannot be published in the church to the people. Nor can it be placed among the Prophets, for their number is complete. *Muratorian Fragment (c. 200, W), 5.604.*

The Montanists were opposed to *The Shepherd* because it allowed mercy to be given to repentant persons who had committed serious sins such as adultery. This opposition is reflected in the next two passages from Tertullian:

I would yield my ground to you, if the scripture of *The Shepherd*—which is the only one that favors adulterers [i.e., allows forgiveness to adulterers]—had deserved to find a place in the divine canon. However, it has been habitually judged by every council of churches among apocryphal and false works. *Tertullian (c. 212, W), 4.85.*

And, of course, that epistle of Barnabas [i.e., the *Epistle According to the Hebrews*] is more generally received among the churches than that apocryphal *Shepherd* of adulterers. *Tertullian (c. 212, W), 4.97.*

Even in that little treatise called *The Shepherd* or *Angel of Repentance,* composed by Hermas, we have the following: "First of all, believe that

there is one God who created and arranged all things." *Origen (c. 225, E), 4.252.*

That we may believe on the authority of Holy Scripture that such is the case, hear how in the Book of Maccabees. . . . In the book of *The Shepherd,* also, in the first commandment, he speaks as follows: "First of all believe that there is one God who created and arranged all things, and made all things to come into existence out of a state of nothingness." Perhaps, also, the expression in the Psalms has reference to this. *Origen (c. 225, E), 4.270*

The book of *The Shepherd* declares the same, saying that each individual is attended by two angels. Whenever good thoughts arise in our hearts, they are suggested by the good angel. But when those of a contrary kind arise, they are the instigation of the evil angel. *Origen (c. 225, E), 4.332.*

We deduce this also from a book, *The Shepherd,* which is despised by some, in respect of the command given to Hermas to write two books. *Origen (c. 225, E), 4.359.*

We believe that God made the things that exist out of nothing, as the mother of the seven martyrs in the Maccabees teaches, and as the angel of repentance in *The Shepherd* taught. *Origen (c. 228, E), 9.306, 307.*

If someone should desire to soften down a teaching of this kind and should venture to use a Scripture that is in circulation in the church, but is not acknowledged by all to be divine, the passage might be taken from *The Shepherd,* concerning some who are put in subjection to Michael as soon as they believe. *Origen (c. 245, E), 9.509; see also 2.348.*

SEE ALSO CANON, NEW TESTAMENT.

HERMENEUTICS

I. General principles of hermeneutics

II. Interpretation of prophecy and parables

I. General principles of hermeneutics

Since I am entirely convinced that no Scripture contradicts another, I will rather acknowledge that I do not understand what is written. *Justin Martyr (c. 160, E), 1.230.*

Perhaps you are not aware of this, my friends, that there were many sayings written obscurely, parabolically, and mysteriously. There are also symbolic actions. *Justin Martyr (c. 160, E), 1.232.*

Therefore, having the truth itself as our rule, and the testimony concerning God set clearly before us, we should not, by running after numerous and diverse answers to questions, cast away the firm and true knowledge of God. *Irenaeus (c. 180, E/W), 1.399.*

Even with respect to creation, there are some things known only to God. Other things come within the range of our own knowledge. So what ground is there for complaint? For, by the grace of God, we are able to explain some of the things that we investigate in the Scriptures (which are throughout spiritual). We must leave other things in the hands of God. *Irenaeus (c. 180, E/W), 1.399.*

It is fitting, therefore, to leave the knowledge of this matter [eternal fire] to God, even as the Lord does of the day and hour and not to rush to such an extreme of danger. . . . But when we investigate points which are above us, and with respect to which we cannot reach satisfaction, [it is absurd] for us to display such an extreme amount of presumption as to unveil God and things that are not yet discovered. *Irenaeus (c. 180, E/W), 1.401.*

Every word will also seem consistent to him if he diligently reads the Scriptures in company with those who are presbyters in the church, among whom is the apostolic doctrine. *Irenaeus (c. 180, E/W), 1.506.*

The Word . . . is not committed to those who have been reared in the arts of all kinds of words and in the power of inflated attempts at proof. For such minds are already pre-disposed; they have not been previously emptied. *Clement of Alexandria (c. 195, E), 2.300, 301.*

We know full well that the Savior teaches nothing in a merely human way. Rather, He teaches all things to His own people with divine and mystic wisdom. Therefore, we must not listen to His utterances carnally. Instead, we should listen with due investigation and intelligence. We must search out and learn the meaning hidden in them. *Clement of Alexandria (c. 195, E), 2.592.*

Divine Scripture has ever far-reaching applications. After the immediate sense has been exhausted, it fortifies the practice of the religious life in all directions. *Tertullian (c. 197, W), 3.81.*

We may understand a thing as spoken generally, even when it requires a certain special interpretation to be given to it. For some things spoken with a *special* reference contain in them *general* truth. *Tertullian (c. 197, W), 3.81.*

Some, when they have come across a very normal form of prophetic statement—generally expressed in figure and allegory (though not always)—distort it. In fact, they distort into some imaginary sense even the most clearly described doctrine of the resurrection of the dead. *Tertullian (c. 210, W), 3.558.*

It cannot but be right (as we have shown above) that uncertain statements should be determined by certain ones, and obscure ones by those that are clear and plain. *Tertullian (c. 210, W), 3.560.*

There are, again, some statements so plainly made as to be free from all obscurity of allegory. Yet, they strongly require their very simplicity to be interpreted. *Tertullian (c. 210, W), 3.565.*

Things that are destined for the body should be carefully understood in a bodily sense—not in a spiritual sense. *Tertullian (c. 210, W), 3.569.*

They [the heretics] would have the entire revelation of both Testaments yield to these three passages. However, the only proper course is to understand the few statements in the light of the many. But, in their contention, they are only following the principle of all heretics. For, inasmuch as only a few testimonies are to be found in the general mass, they obstinately set off the few against the many. *Tertullian (c. 213, W), 3.615.*

He cites these words without understanding what precedes them. For whenever they wish to attempt anything underhanded, they mutilate the Scriptures. Instead, let him quote the passage as a whole! *Hippolytus (c. 205, W), 5.224.*

The more simple among those who profess to belong to the church have believed that there is no Deity greater than the Creator. And they are right in so thinking. However, they imagine things regarding Him as would not be believed about the most savage and unjust of mankind. In all of these points previously enumerated, the cause of the false opinions and of the ungodly statements (or ignorant assertions) about God appear to be nothing else than not understanding Scripture according to its spiritual meaning. It comes from literally interpreting the mere letter. *Origen (c. 225, E), 4.357.*

What need is there to speak about the prophecies—which we all know to be filled with enigmas and obscure sayings? And if we come to the Gospels, the exact understanding of them, too, (since they are the mind of Christ) requires the grace that was given to him who said, "But we have the mind of Christ." . . . And who, on reading the revelations made to John, would not be amazed at the unspeakable mysteries concealed therein? . . . And to what person who is skillful in investigating words would the epistles of the apostles seem to be clear and easy to understand? For even in them there are countless numbers of most profound ideas that . . . allow no quick comprehension. *Origen (c. 225, E), 4.358.*

I have not yet spoken of the observance of everything that is written in the Gospels. For each one of these observances contains many teachings difficult to be understood—not merely by the multitude, but even by certain of the more intelligent. *Origen (c. 248, E), 4.472.*

To such a degree does the gospel desire that there should be wise men among believers that—for the sake of exercising the understanding of its hearers—it has spoken certain truths in enigmas . . . and others in parables. *Origen (c. 248, E), 4.482.*

Paul says, "But our sufficiency is of God, who has also made us able ministers of the new testament, not of the letter, but of the spirit. For the letter kills, but the spirit gives life." By the "letter," he means the explanation of Scripture that is apparent to the senses. By the "spirit," he means the explanation that is the object of the "understanding." *Origen (c. 248, E), 4.605.*

It is a dangerous to wholly disdain the literal meaning . . . particularly of Genesis, where the unchangeable decrees of God for the constitution of the universe are set forth. . . . Yet, Paul is not to be despised when he passes over the literal meaning and shows that the words extend to Christ and the church. *Methodius (c. 290, E), 6.317.*

II. Interpretation of prophecy and parables

The disciples came and said to Him, "Why do You speak to them in parables?" He answered and said to them, "Because it has been given to you to know the mysteries of the kingdom of heaven, but to them it has

not been given. . . . Therefore I speak to them in parables, because seeing they do not see, and hearing they do not hear, nor do they understand." Matt. 13:13, 14.

Philip ran to him, and heard him reading the prophet Isaiah, and said, "Do you understand what you are reading?" And he said, "How can I, unless someone guides me?" And he asked Philip to come up and sit with him. Acts 8:30, 31.

What the prophets said and did they veiled by parables and types . . . so that it was not easy for all persons to understand most [of what they wrote]. For they concealed the truth by these means, that those who are eager to find out and learn it could do so with much labor. *Justin Martyr (c. 160, E), 1.244.*

Would you suppose, gentlemen, that we could ever have understood these matters in the Scriptures, if we had not received grace to discern by the will of Him whose pleasure it was? *Justin Martyr (c. 160, E), 1.258.*

A sound mind . . . will eagerly meditate upon those things that God has placed within the power of mankind, and has subjected to our knowledge. Such a mind will make advancement in them, rendering the knowledge of them easy to him by means of daily study. These things are such as fall under our observation and are clearly and unambiguously in express terms set forth in the Sacred Scriptures. And therefore the parables should not to be adapted to ambiguous expressions. *Irenaeus (c. 180, E/W), 1.398.*

If, therefore, according to the rule that I have stated, we leave some questions in the hands of God, we will both preserve our faith uninjured, and will continue without danger. And all Scripture, which has been given to us by God, will be found by us perfectly consistent. And the parables will harmonize with those passages that are perfectly plain. And those statements that have a clear meaning will serve to explain the parables. *Irenaeus (c. 180, E/W), 1.400.*

All prophecies, before their fulfillment, are to men enigmas and ambiguities. But when the time has arrived and the prediction has come to pass, then the prophecies have a clear and certain exposition. *Irenaeus (c. 180, E/W), 1.496.*

It is therefore more certain, and less hazardous, to await the fulfillment of the prophecy, than to make surmises. *Irenaeus (c. 180, E/W), 1.559.*

Prophecy does not employ figurative forms in its expressions simply for the sake of beautiful diction. Rather, it uses these forms because the truth does not pertain to all. It is veiled in various ways, causing the light to arise only on those who are initiated into knowledge, who seek the truth through love. *Clement of Alexandria (c. 195, E), 2.510.*

The figurative expression is used, "reading according to the letter." In contrast, the revealed unfolding of the Scriptures—when faith has already reached an advanced state—is likened to "reading according to the syllables." *Clement of Alexandria (c. 195, E), 2.510.*

The prophecies and oracles are spoken in enigmas. *Clement of Alexandria (c. 195, E), 2.449.*

Rightly, therefore, the divine apostle says, "By revelation, the mystery was made known to me." *Clement of Alexandria (c. 195, E), 2.458.*

For neither prophecy nor the Savior Himself announced the divine mysteries simply so as to be easily understood by any person whatever. Rather, they expressed them in parables. . . . For that reason, the holy mysteries of the prophecies are veiled in the parables. They are preserved for chosen men, selected to knowledge because of their faith. For the style of the Scriptures is allegorical. *Clement of Alexandria (c. 195, E), 2.509.*

It was appropriate and necessary that the things spoken of old by the prophets should be sealed to the unbelieving Pharisees (who thought that they understood the letter of the Law) and be opened to the believing [saints]. The things, therefore, that had been formerly sealed are now all open to the saints by the grace of God the Lord. *Hippolytus (c. 205, W), 5.181.*

Let me dispel at once the basic premise on which they rest. They assert that the prophets make *all* their announcements in figures of speech. . . . Indeed, if *all* are figures, where will be the reality of which they are the figure? How can you hold up a mirror to your face, if the face nowhere exists? So, in truth, all are not figures. Rather, there are also literal statements. . . . For it was not figurative that the virgin conceived in her womb. . . . Even granting that He was figuratively to take the power of Damascus and the spoils of Samaria, still it was literal that He was to "enter into judgment

with the elders and princes of the people." . . . This shows that the prophets foretold both senses [literal and figurative]—except that very many of their words can only be taken in a pure and simple sense, free from all allegorical obscurity, as when we hear of the downfall of nations and cities. . . . Thus, then, the allegorical style is not used in all parts of the prophetic record—although it occasionally occurs in certain portions of it. *Tertullian (c. 210, W), 3.559, 560.*

The Prophets, in particular, are full of acknowledged difficulties and of declarations that are obscure to the multitude. . . . Even I myself, who have devoted much study to these writings, would not say that I was acquainted with everything. *Origen (c. 248, E), 4.401.*

It belongs only to those who are wise in the truth of Christ . . . to unfold the connection and meaning of even the obscure parts of prophecy, "comparing spiritual things with spiritual," and interpreting each passage according to the usage of the writers of Scripture. *Origen (c. 248, E), 4.615.*

SEE ALSO HERESIES, HERETICS (IV. HOW THE HERETICS MISUSE SCRIPTURE); LAW, MOSAIC (II. SPIRITUAL INTERPRETATION OF THE LAW); ORIGEN; SCRIPTURES; TYPE, TYPOLOGY.

HEROD

Herod had laid hold of John and bound him, and put him in prison for the sake of Herodias, his brother Philip's wife. For John had said to him, "It is not lawful for you to have her." Matt. 14:3, 4.

The Lord . . . hurled His denunciation against Herod in the form of unlawful marriages and of adultery. For he pronounced as an adulterer even the man who married a woman who had been put away by her husband. He said this in order the more severely to load Herod with guilt. For Herod had taken his brother's wife after she had been loosed from her husband—by death rather than by divorce. For he had been impelled thereto by his lust—not by the commandment of the Law. For his brother had left a daughter. Therefore, the marriage with his widow could not be lawful. *Tertullian (c. 207, W), 3.405, 406.*

When the last of the prophets was unlawfully killed by Herod, the king of the Jews was deprived of the power of putting to death. For, if Herod had not been deprived of it, Pilate would not have condemned Jesus to death. *Origen (c. 245, E), 9.428.*

Herod did this [i.e., the slaying of John] for the sake of Herodias, the wife of his brother Philip. For John said unto him, "It is not lawful for you to have her." Now this Philip was tetrarch of the region of Ituraea and of Trachonitis. Some, then, suppose that, when Philip died leaving a daughter, Herodias, Herod married his brother's wife. [They point out that] the Law permitted such a marriage only when there were no children. Nevertheless, as I find no clear evidence anywhere that Philip was dead, I conclude that a still greater transgression was committed by Herod: namely, he had induced his brother's wife to revolt from her husband while he was still living. *Origen (c. 245, E), 9.428; extended discussion: 6.135–6.136, 9.427–9.476.*

HEXAPLA

The Hexapla was a sixfold parallel edition of the Old Testament prepared by Origen. It included the Hebrew text, a Greek transliteration of the Hebrew, and four Greek translations (including Aquila and the Septuagint).

I do not say this because I shun the labor of investigating the Jewish Scriptures or of comparing them with ours—noticing their various readings. . . . For I have already done this to a great extent, to the best of my ability. I have labored hard to get at the meaning in all the editions and various readings. I paid particular attention to the interpretation of the Seventy [i.e., the LXX], lest I might be found accrediting any forgery to the churches that are under heaven. *Origen (c. 240, E), 4.387.*

SEE ALSO AQUILA, TRANSLATION OF; SEPTUAGINT.

HINDUS

The Indian gymnosophists are also in the number, as are the other barbarian philosophers. And of these there are two classes; some of them are called Sarmanae, and others are called Brahmins. . . . Some, too, of the Indians obey the precepts of Buddha. On account of his extraordinary sanctity, they have raised him to divine honors. *Clement of Alexandria (c. 195, E), 2.316.*

The philosophy of the Indians, too, has been celebrated. Alexander of Macedonia, having taken ten of the Indian Gymnosophists, who seemed the best and most perceptive, proposed to them problems. *Clement of Alexandria (c. 195, E), 2.488.*

The Brahmans, among the Hindus, of whom there are many thousands and tens of thousands, have a law forbidding to kill at all, or to pay reverence to idols, to commit immorality, to eat flesh, or to drink wine. . . . Yet, there is also another law in India, and in the same area, that prevails among those who are not of the caste of the Brahmans. And they do not embrace the Brahman teaching. Instead, they teach the people to serve idols, commit immorality, kill, and do other bad things. *Bardesanes (c. 222, E), 8.730.*

The Hindus, when they die, are all burned with fire, and many of their wives are burned along with them alive. *Bardesanes (c. 222, E), 8.732.*

The Brahmins among the Indians . . . devoted themselves to philosophic pursuits. *Hippolytus (c. 225, W), 5.9.*

There is also with the Indians a sect composed of those philosophizing among the Brahmans. They spend a contented existence. They abstain from both living creatures and all cooked food, being satisfied with fruits. They do not gather these from the trees, but carry off only those that have fallen to the ground. They subsist upon them, drinking the water of the river Tazabena. But they pass their life naked, teaching that the body has been constituted a covering to the soul by the Deity. These assert that God is light. *Hippolytus (c. 225, W), 5.21; see also 2.412, 2.418, 4.401.*

SEE ALSO BUDDHA.

HISTORY

Who, then, among those called sages, poets, and historians, could tell us truly of these things? For they were born much later. . . . Therefore, it is proved that all others have been in error and that we Christians alone have possessed the truth. For we are taught by the Holy Spirit, who spoke in the holy prophets. *Theophilus (c. 180, E), 2.107.*

HOLIDAYS, CHRISTIAN

SEE CALENDAR, CHRISTIAN; HOLIDAYS, PAGAN.

HOLIDAYS, PAGAN

[ADDRESSING PAGANS:] On your day of gladness, we [Christians] neither cover our doorposts with wreaths, nor intrude upon the day with lamps. At the call of public festivity, you consider it a proper thing to decorate your house like some new brothel. . . . We are accused of a lower sacrilege because we do not celebrate along with you the holidays of the Caesars in a manner forbidden alike by modesty, decency, and purity. *Tertullian (c. 197, W), 3.44.*

The Roman traitors clad their doorposts with green and branching laurels. They smoked up their porches with lofty and brilliant lamps. *Tertullian (c. 197, W), 3.44.*

Furthermore, you Christians have no acquaintance with the festivals of the Gentiles. *Tertullian (c. 198, W), 4.24.*

What less of a defilement does he incur on that ground than does a business . . . that is publicly consecrated to an idol? The Minervalia are as much Minerva's as the Saturnalia is Saturn's. Yes, it is Saturn's day, which must necessarily be celebrated even by little slaves at the time of the Saturnalia. Likewise, New Year's gifts must be caught at. The Septimontium must be kept. And all the presents of Midwinter and the Feast of Dear Kinsmanship must be exacted. The schools must be wreathed with flowers. . . . The same thing takes place on an idol's birthday. Every ceremony of the devil is frequented. Who will think that these things are befitting to a Christian teacher? *Tertullian (c. 200, W), 3.66.*

We must now address the subject of holidays and other extraordinary festivities. We sometimes excuse these to our wantonness, sometimes to our timidity—in opposition to the common faith and discipline. The first point, indeed, on which I will join issue is this: whether a servant of God should share with the very nations themselves in matters of this kind—either in dress, food, or in any other kind of festivity. . . . "There is no communion between light and darkness," between life and death. Or else, we should rescind what has been written, "The world will rejoice, but you will grieve" [John 16:20]. . . . When the world rejoices, let us grieve. And when the world afterward grieves, we will rejoice. . . . There are certain gift days, by which some adjust the claim of honor; or with others, the debt of wages. . . . If men have consecrated for themselves this custom from superstition, why do you . . . participate in festivities consecrated to idols? As for you, there is no law about a day (short of the observance of a particular day) to prevent your paying or receiving what you owe a man, or what is owed you by a man. *Tertullian (c. 200, W), 3.68, 69.*

The next three passages are written as rebukes to worldly minded Christians:

However, the majority [of Christians] have by this time convinced themselves in their minds that it is pardonable when they do what the pagan does at anytime, for fear that [otherwise] "the Name might be blasphemed." *Tertullian (c. 200, W), 3.69.*

The Saturnalia, New Year, Midwinter festivals, and Matronalia are frequented by us! Presents come and go! There are New Year's gifts! Games join their noise! Banquets join their din! The pagans are more faithful to their own sect. . . . For, even if they had known them, they would not have shared the Lord's Day or Pentecost with us. For they would fear lest they would appear to be Christians. Yet, we are not apprehensive that we might appear to be pagans! *Tertullian (c. 200, W), 3.70.*

Nowadays, you will find more doors of heathens without lamps and laurel wreaths than of Christians. . . . If it is for an idol's honor, without doubt an idol's honor is idolatry. Yet, even if it is for a man's sake, . . . let us again consider that all idolatry is worship done to men. *Tertullian (c. 200, W), 3.70.*

And among these, [the wife of an unbelieving husband] will be agitated by the odor of incense on all the memorial days of demons, at all solemnities of kings, at the beginning of the year, and at the beginning of the month. She will leave to exit by a gate wreathed with laurel and hung with lanterns, as from some new meeting place of public lusts. *Tertullian (c. 205, W), 4.47.*

You Christians have your own registers, your own calendar. You have nothing to do with the festivities of the world. In fact, you are called to the very opposite—for "the world will rejoice, but you will mourn." *Tertullian (c. 212, W), 3.101.*

It would follow as a consequence that we could take part in public feasts, if it were proved that the public feasts had nothing wrong in them and were grounded upon true views of the character of God. . . . However, the so-called public festivals can in no way be shown to harmonize with the service of God. Rather, on the contrary, they prove to have been devised by men for the purpose of commemorating some human events—or to set forth certain qualities of water, earth, or the fruits of the earth. Accordingly, it is clear that those who wish to offer an enlightened worship to the Divine Being will act according to sound reason and not take part in the public feasts. *Origen (c. 248, E), 4.647.*

Humans have birthdays, so the pagans believe that the powers of heaven have birthdays, too. *Arnobius (c. 305, E), 6.532.*

We may not join in their feasts, which are celebrated in honor of demons. *Apostolic Constitutions (compiled c. 390, E), 7.424.*

SEE ALSO CALENDAR, CHRISTIAN; WORLD, SEPARATION FROM THE; WREATHS.

HOLINESS

SEE CHRISTIAN LIFE; PERFECTION, CHRISTIAN; WORLD, SEPARATION FROM THE.

HOLY KISS

SEE KISS, HOLY.

HOLY SPIRIT

I. Work and operation of the Holy Spirit

II. Divinity of the Holy Spirit

I. Work and operation of the Holy Spirit

It is to your advantage that I go away; for if I do not go away, the Helper will not come to you; but if I depart, I will send Him to you. And when He has come, He will convict the world of sin, and of righteousness. John 16:7, 8.

When He, the Spirit of truth, has come, He will guide you into all truth; for He will not speak on His own authority, but whatever He hears He will speak; and He will tell you things to come. John 16:13.

Do not quench the Spirit. 1 Thess. 5:19.

If you are patient, the Holy Spirit that dwells in you will be pure. He will not be darkened by any evil spirit, but, dwelling in a broad region, he will rejoice and be glad. . . . But if any outburst of anger takes place, immediately the Holy Spirit, who is sensitive, is constricted. For He does not have a pure place, and He seeks to depart. For he is choked by the vile spirit. *Hermas (c. 150, W), 2.23.*

Do not crush the Holy Spirit who dwells in you. Otherwise, He may entreat God against you and withdraw from you. *Hermas (c. 150, W), 2.27.*

The Father's Offspring and His Image minister to Him in every respect. That is, the Son and the Holy Spirit, the Word and Wisdom—whom all the angels serve and to whom they are subject. *Irenaeus (c. 180, E/W), 1.470.*

For with Him were always present the Word and Wisdom, the Son and the Spirit, by whom and in whom, freely and spontaneously, He made all things. This is to whom also He speaks, saying, "Let Us make man after our image and likeness." *Irenaeus (c. 180, E/W), 1.488.*

I have also largely demonstrated that the Word, namely the Son, was always with the Father. And that Wisdom also, who is the Spirit, was present with Him before all creation. He declares this by Solomon: "By Wisdom, God founded the earth, and by understanding He has established the heavens." . . . There is therefore one God, who by the Word and Wisdom created and arranged all things. *Irenaeus (c. 180, E/W), 1.488.*

So now let us, receiving the Spirit, walk in newness of life, obeying God. Inasmuch, therefore, as without the Spirit of God we cannot be saved, the apostle exhorts us through faith and chaste conversation to preserve the Spirit of God. *Irenaeus (c. 180, E/W), 1.535.*

The breath of life, which also rendered man an animated being, is one thing, and the life-giving Spirit is another. *Irenaeus (c. 180, E/W), 1.537.*

He is Himself made the head of the Spirit, and He provides the Spirit to be the head of man. *Irenaeus (c. 180, E/W), 1.548.*

The mouth of the Lord, the Holy Spirit, has spoken these things. *Clement of Alexandria (c. 195, E), 2.195.*

Suppose . . . that the Holy Spirit had no such respect for any one church as to lead it into truth, although sent with this view by Christ. . . . Suppose, also, that He, the Steward of God, the Vicar of Christ, neglected His office. . . . [If so,] is it likely that so many churches—and ones so great—would have gone astray into one and the same faith? *Tertullian (c. 197, W), 3.256.*

You would have been refuted in this matter by the Gospel of John, when it declares that the Spirit descended in the body of a dove and sat upon the Lord. When the said Spirit was in this condition, He was as truly a dove as He was also a spirit. Nor did He destroy His own proper substance by the assumption of an extraneous substance. *Tertullian (c. 210, W), 3.523.*

By whom has Christ ever been explored without the Holy Spirit? By whom has the Holy Spirit ever been attained without the mysterious gift of faith? *Tertullian (c. 210, W), 3.181.*

Indeed, some of our predecessors have observed that in the New Testament, whenever the Spirit is named without that adjunct that denotes quality, the Holy Spirit is to be understood. For example, this is so in the expression, "Now the fruit of the Spirit is love, joy, and peace." *Origen (c. 225, E), 4.252.*

At the time of the Flood, when all persons had corrupted their way before God, it is recorded that God spoke in this manner, concerning undeserving men and sinners: "My Spirit will not abide with those men forever, because they are flesh." By this it is clearly shown that the Spirit of God is taken away from all who are unworthy. *Origen (c. 225, E), 4.254.*

I am of the opinion that every rational creature—without any distinction—receives a share of [the Holy Spirit] in the same way as of the Wisdom and of the Word of God. I observe, however, that the chief coming of the Holy Spirit is declared to men after the ascension of Christ to heaven—rather than before His coming into the world. Before that, the gift of the Holy Spirit was conferred upon the prophets alone and upon a few individuals. *Origen (c. 225, E), 4.285.*

We must therefore know that the Paraclete is the Holy Spirit, who teaches truths that cannot be uttered in words. *Origen (c. 225, E), 4.285.*

The Holy Spirit, who is called the Paraclete, is called this because of His work of consolation. For *paraclesis* is called in Latin *consolatio*. For if anyone has deserved to participate in the Holy Spirit by the knowledge of His inexpressible

mysteries, he undoubtedly obtains comfort and joy of heart. *Origen (c. 225, E), 4.286.*

There are some passages in which the Spirit is placed above Christ.... In the Gospel, Christ declares that there is forgiveness for the sin committed against Himself, but that for blasphemy against the Holy Spirit there is no forgiveness—either in this age or in the age to come. What is the reason for this? Is it because the Holy Spirit is of more worth than Christ? Is this why the sin against Him cannot be forgiven? Rather, is it not that ... only those persons who have been found worthy of it have part in the Holy Spirit. As a result, there appropriately cannot be any forgiveness for those who fall away into evil—despite such a great and powerful co-operation. For they defeat the counsels of the Spirit who is in them. *Origen (c. 228, E), 9.329.*

The Holy Spirit Himself receives instruction. This is clear from what is said about the Paraclete and the Holy Spirit: "He will take of mine and will declare it to you." Does He, then, from these instructions, take in everything that the Son Himself knows, gazing at the Father from the first? *Origen (c. 228, E), 9.334.*

God is perpetually bestowing His own Spirit on those who are capable of receiving Him. However, it is not by way of division and separation that He dwells in the deserving. Nor, in our opinion, is the Spirit a "body," any more than fire is a "body." *Origen (c. 248, E), 4.605.*

In the Spirit, there are different kinds of ministrations. For, at times, there is a different order of occasions. Yet, on this account, He who discharges these offices is not different.... He is therefore one and the same Spirit who was in the prophets and in the apostles. The only difference is that as to the former, He was in them *occasionally;* in the latter, he was in them *always. Novatian (c. 235, W), 5.640.*

The Lord has taught us most plainly by His words about the liberty and power of the Holy Spirit ... saying, "The Spirit breathes where He will." ... Now, the same Spirit is sometimes found to be upon those who are unworthy of Him. This is certainly not in vain or without reason. Rather, it is for the sake of some needful operation. For example, He was upon Saul, upon whom the Spirit of God came, and Saul prophesied. *Treatise on Re-Baptism (c. 257, W), 5.676.*

He said that in His right hand He had seven stars, because the Holy Spirit of seven-fold agency was given into His power by the Father. *Victorinus (c. 280, W), 7.345; see also 1.536; extended discussion: 4.251–4.256.*

II. Divinity of the Holy Spirit

The following passages reveal that the early church believed in the divinity of the Holy Spirit. They also reveal that, while believing in the consubstantiality of all three persons of the Trinity, the early church also believed in a hierarchy of order among the members of the Trinity.

The Holy Spirit Himself, who operates in the prophets, we assert to be an effluence of God, flowing from Him, and returning back again like a beam of the sun. *Athenagoras (c. 175, E), 2.133.*

He [Isaiah] attributes the Spirit as unique to God, whom in the last times He pours forth upon the human race by the adoption of sons. But that breath [of life] was common throughout the creation, and he points it out as something created. Now that which has been made is a different thing from the one who makes it. The breath, then, is temporal, but the Spirit is eternal. *Irenaeus (c. 180, E/W), 1.538.*

God here assumed the likeness, not of man, but of a dove, for He wished, by a new apparition of the Spirit in the likeness of a dove, to declare His simplicity and majesty. *Clement of Alexandria (c. 195, E), 2.578.*

You would have been refuted in this matter by the Gospel of John, when it declares that the Spirit descended in the body of a dove and sat upon the Lord. When the said Spirit was in this condition, He was as truly a dove as He was also a spirit. Nor did He destroy His own proper substance by the assumption of an extraneous substance. *Tertullian (c. 210, W), 3.523.*

He says, "I will pray the Father, and He will send you another Comforter—even the Spirit of truth," thus making the Paraclete distinct from Himself, even as we say that the Son is also distinct from the Father. So He showed a third degree in the Paraclete. For we believe the second degree is in the Son, by reason of the order observed in the "Economy." *Tertullian (c. 213, W), 3.604.*

He has received from the Father the promised gift, and has shed it forth, even the Holy Spirit—the third name in Divinity, and the third degree of the Divine Majesty. *Tertullian (c. 213, W), 3.627.*

The apostles related that the Holy Spirit was associated in honor and dignity with the Father and the Son. But in His case it is not clearly distinguished whether He is to be regarded as born or unborn—or also as a Son of God or not. *Origen (c. 225, E), 4.240.*

In the Acts of the Apostles, the Holy Spirit was given by the imposition of the apostles' hands in baptism. From which we learn that the person of the Holy Spirit was of such authority and dignity that saving baptism was not complete except by the authority of the most excellent Trinity of them all. . . . Who, then, is not amazed at the exceeding majesty of the Holy Spirit when he hears that he who speaks a word against the Son of man may hope for forgiveness, but that he who is guilty of blasphemy against the Holy Spirit has no forgiveness—either in the present world or in that which is to come. *Origen (c. 225, E), 4.252.*

Up to the present time, we have been able to find no statement in Holy Scripture in which the Holy Spirit could be said to be made or created—not even in the way in which we have shown above that the Divine Wisdom is spoken of by Solomon. *Origen (c. 225, E), 4.252.*

We must understand, therefore, that as the Son (who alone knows the Father) reveals Him to whom He wills, so the Holy Spirit (who alone searches the deep things of God) reveals God to whom He wills. "For the Spirit blows where He wills." We are not, however, to suppose that the Spirit derives His knowledge through revelation from the Son. *Origen (c. 225, E), 4.253.*

It was not by progressive advancement that He came to be the Holy Spirit. . . . For if this were the case, the Holy Spirit would never be counted in the unity of the Trinity—along with the unchangeable Father and His Son—unless He had always been the Holy Spirit. Indeed, when we use such terms as "always," or "was," or any other designation of time, they are not to be taken absolutely, but with due allowance. *Origen (c. 225, E), 4.253.*

Let no one indeed suppose that we . . . give a preference to the Holy Spirit over the Father and the Son, or assert that His dignity is greater, which certainly would be a very illogical conclusion. *Origen (c. 225, E), 4.254, 255.*

The Gospel shows Him to be of such power and majesty that—until the coming of the Holy Spirit—it says the apostles could not yet receive those things that the Savior wished to teach them. For, pouring Himself into their souls, He might enlighten them regarding the nature and faith of the Trinity. *Origen (c. 225, E), 4.285.*

The Paraclete has received from Christ what He may declare. But if He has received from Christ what He may declare to us, Christ is greater than the Paraclete. For the Paraclete would not receive from Christ unless He were less than Christ. But the very fact that the Paraclete is less than Christ proves Christ to be God. So the testimony of Christ's divinity is immense in the Paraclete being found to be less than Christ in this economy. *Novatian (c. 235, W), 5.625, 626.*

The source of the entire Holy Spirit remains in Christ, so that from Him could be drawn streams of gifts and works, while the Holy Spirit dwelled richly in Christ. *Novatian (c. 235, W), 5.641.*

SEE ALSO CHRIST, DIVINITY OF; FILIOQUE; GIFTS OF THE SPIRIT; FATHER, GOD THE; SIN (II. UNFORGIVABLE SIN); TRINITY; VICAR OF CHRIST; WISDOM.

HOLY WEEK

Holy Week refers to the week preceding Easter.

He therefore charged us Himself to fast these six days on account of the impiety and transgression of the Jews, commanding us to also bewail over them and lament for their ruin. . . . He appointed us to break our fast on the seventh day at the cock-crowing, but to fast on the Sabbath day. Not that the Sabbath day is a day of fasting (being the rest from the creation) but because we should fast on this one Sabbath only—when on this day the Creator was under the earth. *Apostolic Constitutions (compiled c. 390, E), 7.445.*

Fast on the days of Easter, beginning from the second day of the week [Tuesday] until the Preparation [Friday], and then the Sabbath—for a total of six days. Make use of only bread, salt, herbs, and water for your drink. Abstain on these days from wine and meat, for they are days of lamentation and not of feasting. Those who are able, should fast the days of the Preparation and the Sabbath day entirely—tasting nothing until the cock-crowing of the night. . . . For the Lord says, . . . "When the bridegroom will be taken away from them, in those days they will fast." *Apostolic Constitutions (compiled c. 390, E), 7.447.*

There is only one Sabbath to be observed by you during the whole year—that of our Lord's burial. On that day, men should keep a fast, rather than a festival. *Apostolic Constitutions (compiled c. 390, E), 7.469.*

SEE ALSO CALENDAR, CHRISTIAN; EASTER; LENT.

HOMER

Homer (c. 800 B.C.) was the ancient Greek poet who has been credited in tradition with writing the Iliad and the Odyssey. His writings played a major role in the development of Greek religious thought.

Not only Plato, but also Homer, received similar enlightenment in Egypt. . . . This poet transferred to his own poem much of what is contained in the divine writings of the prophets. First, he borrowed what Moses had related about the beginning of the creation of the world. For Moses had written in this manner: "In the beginning, God created the heaven and the earth," then the sun, moon, and stars. Now, having learned this in Egypt and having been impressed with what Moses had written in his Genesis of the world, Homer fabricated the story that Vulcan . . . had made a type of representation of the creation of the world. *Justin Martyr (c. 160, E), 1.284, 285.*

Stop the song, O Homer! It is not beautiful. It teaches adultery, and we are prohibited from polluting our ears with hearing about adultery. *Clement of Alexandria (c. 195, E), 2.189.*

[ADDRESSED TO PAGANS:] I will begin with that enthusiastic fondness which you lavish on him from whom every depraved writer gets his dreams. By this description, I am referring to Homer. You ascribe as much honor to him as you show to your gods. You magnify the very man who made sport of the gods. In my opinion, it is he who has treated the majesty of the Divine Being on the low level of human condition. He has portrayed the gods as having the same sins and passions as humans. He has even pitted them against each other. *Tertullian (c. 197, W), 3.120.*

Ennius dreamed that Homer remembered that he was once a peacock. However, I cannot for my part believe poets, even when they are wide awake. *Tertullian (c. 210, W), 3.214.*

Homer was not able to give us any information relating to the truth, for he wrote of human things rather than divine things. *Lactantius (c. 304–313, W), 7.14; see also 2.95.*

SEE ALSO POETS, PAGAN.

HOMILY

SEE PREACHING.

HOMOSEXUALITY

Do you not know that the unrighteous will not inherit the kingdom of God? Do not be deceived. Neither fornicators, . . . nor homosexuals, nor sodomites. 1 Cor. 6:9, 10.

You shall not commit adultery; you shall not commit pederasty. *Didache (c. 80–140, E), 7.377.*

It is well that they should be cut off from the lusts of the world, since "every lust wars against the spirit" and "neither fornicators, nor homosexuals . . . will inherit the kingdom of God." *Clement of Rome (c. 96, W), 1.34.*

Some polluted themselves by lying with males. *Aristides (c. 125, E), 9.269.*

The Greeks, O King, follow debased practices in intercourse with males, or with mothers, sisters, and daughters. Yet, they, in turn, impute their monstrous impurity to the Christians. *Aristides (c. 125, E), 9.279.*

Paederasty is condemned by the barbarians. However, by the Romans it is honored with certain privileges. In fact, they try to collect herds of boys like grazing horses. *Tatian (c. 160, E), 2.77.*

They do not abstain even from males, males with males committing shocking abominations, outraging all the noblest and comeliest bodies in all sorts of ways. *Athenagoras (c. 175, E), 2.143.*

Show me yourself whether you are not an adulterer, a fornicator, a thief, a robber, or a thief. Show me that you do not corrupt boys. . . . For God is not manifest to those who do these things. *Theophilus (c. 180, E), 2.89.*

Men play the part of women, and women that of men, contrary to nature. Women are at once both wives and husbands. . . . O miserable spectacle! Horrible conduct! *Clement of Alexandria (c. 195, E), 2.276.*

The whole earth has now become full of fornication and wickedness. I admire the ancient legislators of the Romans. These men detested effeminacy of conduct. The giving of the body to feminine purposes, contrary to the law of nature, they judged worthy of the most extreme penalty. *Clement of Alexandria (c. 195, E), 2.77.*

The fate of the Sodomites was judgment to those who had done wrong, and instruction to those who hear. The Sodomites had fallen into uncleanness through much luxury. They practiced adultery shamelessly, and they burned with insane love for boys. *Clement of Alexandria (c. 195, E), 2.282.*

The Christian man confines himself to the female sex. *Tertullian (c. 197, W), 3.51.*

I find no dress cursed by God except a woman's dress on a man. For he says, "Cursed is every man who clothes himself in woman's attire." *Tertullian (c. 200, W), 3.71.*

The coupling of two males is a very shameful thing. *Tertullian (c. 200, W), 3.509.*

Such sins are committed by fornicators, adulterers, abusers of themselves with men, effeminate men, idolaters, and murderers. *Origen (c. 245, E), 9.500.*

The sin of Sodom is contrary to nature. *Apostolic Constitutions (compiled c. 390, E), 7.463.*

HOROSCOPE

SEE ASTROLOGY.

HOSPITALITY

Do not let a widow under sixty years old be taken into the number, and not unless she has been the wife of one man, well reported for good works: if she has brought up children, if she has lodged strangers. 1 Tim. 5:9, 10.

She who emulates Sarah is not ashamed of that highest of ministries, helping travellers. *Clement of Alexandria (c. 195, E), 2.283.*

SEE ALSO CHRISTIAN LIFE; CHRISTIANITY (I. DESCRIPTION OF CHRISTIANS).

HUNDRED AND FORTY-FOUR THOUSAND

SEE REVELATION, BOOK OF.

HUSBANDS

Husbands, love your wives, just as Christ also loved the church and gave himself for it. Eph. 5:25.

Husbands, love your wives and do not be bitter toward them. Col. 3:19.

Let deacons be the husbands of one wife, ruling their children and their own houses well. 1 Tim. 3:12.

Likewise you husbands, dwell with them with understanding, giving honor to the wife, as to the weaker vessel, and as being heirs together of the grace of life, that your prayers may not be hindered. 1 Pet. 3:7.

The family cannot be afflicted at all, unless you, the head of the house, be afflicted. For when you are afflicted, of necessity they also suffer affliction. *Hermas (c. 150, W), 2.38.*

What man who marries lawfully does not spurn mother and father, and his whole family connection, and all his household? Who does not cleave to and become one with his own wife, fondly preferring her? Often, for the sake of their wives, some men submit even to death. *Theophilus (c. 180, E), 2.105.*

I speak particularly of those who are in our own power: such as slaves, children, wives, and pupils. When we see them offend, we are incited to restrain them. *Lactantius (c. 304–313, W), 7.274.*

Let the husband not be insolent or arrogant towards his wife. But let him be compassionate, generous, willing to please his own wife. Let him treat her honorably and obligingly, trying to be agreeable to her. *Apostolic Constitutions (compiled c. 390, E), 7.392.*

In like manner, you husbands love your own wives as your own members, as partners in life, and as fellow-helpers for the procreation of children. . . . Love them, therefore, as your own members, as your very bodies. *Apostolic Constitutions (compiled c. 390, E), 7.463.*

SEE ALSO FATHERS; MARRIAGE; UNBELIEVING SPOUSE; WIFE, WIVES.

HYMNS

When they had sung a hymn, they went out to the Mount of Olives. Matt. 26:30.

. . . speaking to one another in psalms and hymns and spiritual songs. Eph. 5:19.

[SAID FIGURATIVELY:] Your justly renowned presbytery, worthy of God, is fitted as exactly to the bishop as are the strings on a harp. Therefore, in your agreement and harmonious love, Jesus Christ is sung. You should work together as a choir, so that being harmonious in love and taking up the song of God in unison, you may with one voice sing to the Father through Jesus Christ. *Ignatius (c. 105, E), 1.50,51.*

We offer thanks for our creation by invocations and hymns. *Justin Martyr (c. 160, E), 1.166.*

All our women are chaste. And the maidens at their work sing of divine things more nobly than that woman of yours. *Tatian (c. 160, E), 2.79.*

Let love songs be banished far away. But let our songs be hymns to God. *Clement of Alexandria (c. 195, E), 2.249.*

We cultivate our fields, praising. We sail the sea, singing hymns. *Clement of Alexandria (c. 195, E), 2.533.*

An unworthy opinion of God preserves no piety—whether in hymns, discourses, writings, or dogmas. *Clement of Alexandria (c. 195, E), 2.533.*

His sacrifices are prayers, praises, and readings in the Scriptures before meals—and psalms and hymns during meals and before bed. *Clement of Alexandria (c. 195, E), 2.537.*

After washing the hands and the bringing in of lights, each is asked to stand forth and sing, as he can, a hymn to God—either one from the Holy Scriptures or one of his own composing. *Tertullian (c. 197, W), 3.47.*

Wisdom is praised in hymns, in the places of egress. For the death of martyrs is also praised in song. *Tertullian (c. 213, W), 3.639.*

For who is ignorant of the books of Irenaeus and Melito, and the rest, which declare Christ to be God and man? All the psalms, too, and hymns of the brethren—which have been written from the beginning by the faithful—celebrate Christ as the Word of God, ascribing divinity to Him. *Eusebius, quoting Caius (c. 215, W), 5.601.*

... both by day and by night the holy laws are declared and hymns, songs, and spiritual words are heard. *Gregory Thaumaturgus (c. 238, E), 6.37, 38.*

We sing hymns to the Most High alone and to his Only-Begotten, who is the Word and God. *Origen (c. 248, E), 4.665.* ONE OF THE EARLIEST CHRISTIAN HYMNS: ANF 2.295, 296.

SEE ALSO ASSEMBLIES, CHRISTIAN; CHOIR; MUSIC, MUSICAL INSTRUMENTS.

HYPOCRITES

This is how those who are consecrated to Christ should appear. And they should frame themselves in their whole of life just as they fashion themselves in the church—for the sake of gravity. They should seek to actually be meek, pious, and loving—not merely to *seem* to be so. However, I cannot understand how people change their fashions and manners, depending on the place. It is said that polypi become assimilated to the rocks to which they adhere and become one in color with the rocks. Similarly, [some Christians] lay aside the inspiration of the assembly. And after their departure from it, they become like others with whom they associate. Nay, in laying aside the artificial mask of solemnity, they are proved to be what they secretly were. After having paid reverence to the discourse about God, they leave behind what they have heard. Outside of the assembly, they foolishly amuse themselves with ungodly playing and romantic quavering, occupied with flute-playing, dancing, intoxication, and all kinds of frivolity. *Clement of Alexandria (c. 195, E), 2.290.*

HYPOSTATIC UNION

SEE INCARNATION.

ICHTHUS

SEE FISH SYMBOL.

ICON

SEE ART, ARTS; IMAGES.

IDOLATRY

My beloved, flee from idolatry. 1 Cor. 10:14.

What agreement has the temple of God with idols? For you are the temple of the living God. 2 Cor. 6:16.

Little children, keep yourselves from idols. 1 John 5:21.

Those who draw men to idols are the aforementioned demons.... They are always ready to lead men into error.... They take possession of their thoughts, and they cause empty visions to flow into the mind as though coming from the idols and the statues. *Athenagoras (c. 175, E), 2.143.*

We abstain from both kinds of idolatry [i.e., the gods and the dead]. Nor do we dislike the temples less than the monuments [to the dead]. We have nothing to do with either altar. And we adore neither image. We do not offer sacrifices to the gods, and we make no funeral oblations to the departed. *Tertullian (c. 197, W), 3.85.*

The principal crime of the human race, the highest guilt charged upon the world, the whole procuring cause of judgment—is idolatry. *Tertullian (c. 200, W), 3.61.*

Most men regard idolatry as being limited to these practices alone: burning incense, immolating a victim, giving a sacrificial banquet, or being bound to some sacred functions or priesthoods.... [However, idolatry] can be practiced outside of a temple and without an idol. *Tertullian (c. 200, W), 3.62.*

God prohibits an idol as much to be *made* as to be *worshipped. Tertullian (c. 200, W), 3.62.*

The zeal of faith will direct its pleadings to this matter. It bewails that a Christian would come from idols into the church. It bewails that he would come from an adversary workshop into the house of God. It bewails that he would raise to God the Father hands that are the mothers of idols.... In fact, those very hands deliver to others what they have contaminated. For idol makers are chosen even into the ecclesiastical order! Oh wickedness! The Jews laid hands on Christ only once. However, these mangle His body daily.... What hands [deserve] more to be amputated than those in which scandal is done to the Lord's body? *Tertullian (c. 200, W), 3.64.*

No art, then, no profession, no trade that administers either to equipping or forming idols can be free from the title of idolatry. *Tertullian (c. 200, W), 3.68.*

It is for this reason, too, that the example of the three [Hebrew] brethren has run before us. For they, who in other respects were obedient toward King Nebuchadnezzar, rejected with all firmness the honor to his image. This demonstrates that whatever is extolled beyond the measure of human honor, and begins to resemble divine majesty, is idolatry. *Tertullian (c. 200, W), 3.71.*

It is a mark of timidity, when some other man binds you in the name of his gods, by the making of an oath, ... and you, out of fear of discovery, remain quiet.... One who has been initiated into Christ will not endure to be blessed in the name of the gods of the nations. *Tertullian (c. 200, W), 3.74.*

When forbidding the likeness to be made of all things that are in heaven, in earth, and in the waters, he declared also the reasons: to prohibit all material display of an unseen idolatry. For He adds: "You will not bow down to them, nor serve them." The form of the bronze serpent that the Lord afterwards commanded Moses to make, afforded no excuse for idolatry. *Tertullian (c. 207, W), 3.314.*

He has, from His abhorrence of idols, framed a series of curses too: "Cursed is the man who makes a graven or a molten image." . . . Therefore, it is evident that from the beginning this kind of worship has both been forbidden and has never been engaged in without punishment. For example, witness the commands so numerous and weighty. . . . No offense is counted by God so presumptuous as a trespass of this sort. *Tertullian (c. 213, W), 3.635, 636.*

They, too, are not less insane who think that images—fashioned by men of worthless and sometimes most wicked character—confer any honor upon genuine divinities. *Origen (c. 248, E), 4.494.*

What folly to hope for protection from those things that are unable to protect themselves. . . . Whatever is subjected to the eyes and to the hands, being perishable, is inconsistent with the whole subject of immortality. It is in vain, therefore, that men distinguish and adorn their gods with gold, ivory, and jewels—as though they were capable of deriving any pleasure from these things. *Lactantius (c. 304–313, W), 7.45.*

That which is incorporeal must be offered to God, for He accepts this. His offering is innocency of the soul. His sacrifice is praise and hymns. For if God is not seen, He should be worshipped with things that are not seen. *Lactantius (c. 304–313, W), 7.193.*

It has been sufficiently shown . . . how vain it is to form images. *Arnobius (c. 305, E), 6.518; see also 3.122, 9.274; extended discussion: 3.61–3.76.*

SEE ALSO GODS, PAGAN; HOLIDAYS, PAGAN; IMAGES; SERPENT, BRONZE; WORSHIP, PAGAN.

IGNATIUS

Ignatius (c. 35–105) was a bishop of Antioch and a personal disciple of the apostle John. He was martyred in Rome about 105. On his way to Rome, under custody, he wrote to various churches letters that were preserved by Polycarp.

You have seen before your eyes—not only in the case of the blessed Ignatius, Zosimus, and Rufus—but also in others among yourselves. . . . They are in their due place in the presence of the Lord, with whom they also suffered. *Polycarp (c. 135, E), 1.35.*

As a certain man of ours [Ignatius] said when he was condemned to the wild beasts because of his testimony with respect to God: "I am the wheat of Christ, and am ground by the teeth of the wild beasts, that I may be found the pure bread of God." *Irenaeus (c. 180, E/W), 1.557.*

ILLUMINATION

SEE BAPTISM.

IMAGES

You will not make for yourself a carved image—any likeness of anything that is in heaven above, or that is in the earth beneath, or that is in the water under the earth; you will not bow down to them nor serve them. Ex. 20:4, 5.

Therefore, . . . flee from idolatry. 1 Cor. 10:14.

For we walk by faith, not by sight. 2 Cor. 5:7.

Little children, keep yourselves from idols. 1 John 5:21.

This is the sole accusation you can bring against us—that we do not . . . offer drink offerings and the aroma of fat to the dead, nor crowns for their statues. *Justin Martyr (c. 160, E), 1.171.*

It is asserted by some pagans that, although these are only images, yet there exist gods in honor of whom they are made. They say that the prayers and sacrifices presented to the images are to be referred to the gods, and are in fact made to the gods. *Athenagoras (c. 175, E), 2.137.*

They call themselves Gnostics. They also possess images, some of them painted, and others formed from different kinds of material. They maintain that a likeness of Christ was made by Pilate at that time when Jesus lived among them. They crown these images, and set them up along with the images of the philosophers of the world. That is to say, they place them with the images of Pythagoras, Plato, Aristotle, and the rest. They have also other modes of honoring these images, after the same manner of the Gentiles. *Irenaeus (c. 180, E/W), 1.351.*

It is with a different kind of spell that art deludes you. . . . It leads you to pay religious honor and worship to images and pictures. *Clement of Alexandria (c. 195, E), 2.188.*

We are not to draw the faces of idols, for we are prohibited to cling to them. *Clement of Alexandria (c. 195, E), 2.286.*

The Law itself exhibits justice. It teaches wisdom by abstinence from visible images and by inviting us to the Maker and Father of the universe. *Clement of Alexandria (c. 195, E), 2.365.*

Ages before, Moses expressly commanded that neither a carved, nor molten, nor molded, nor painted likeness should be made. This was so that we would not cling to things of sense, but pass to spiritual objects. For familiarity with the sense of sight disparages the reverence of what is divine. *Clement of Alexandria (c. 195, E), 2.451.*

Those golden figures, each of them with six wings, signify either the two bears (as some would have it) or rather the two hemispheres. For the name cherubim meant "much knowledge." . . . For He who prohibited the making of a graven image would never Himself have made an image in the likeness of holy things. *Clement of Alexandria (c. 195, E), 2.452, 453.*

Works of art cannot be sacred and divine. *Clement of Alexandria (c. 195, E), 2.530.*

In a word, if we refuse our homage to statues and frigid images, . . . does it not merit praise instead of penalty that we have rejected what we have come to see is error? *Tertullian (c. 197, W), 3.28.*

We know that the names of the dead are nothing, as are their images. But when images are set up, we know well enough, too, who carry on their wicked work under these names. We know who exult in the homage rendered to the images. We know who pretend to be divine. It is none other than accursed spirits. *Tertullian (c. 197, W), 3.84.*

Demons have their abode in the images of the dead. *Tertullian (c. 197, W), 3.85.*

"Not that an idol is anything," as the apostle says, but that the homage they render to it is to demons. These are the real occupants of these consecrated images—whether of dead men or (as they think) of gods. *Tertullian (c. 197, W), 3.85.*

Pompey the Great, after conquering the Jews and capturing Jerusalem, entered the temple.

But he found nothing in the shape of an image, even though he examined the place carefully. *Tertullian (c. 197, W), 3.121.*

We are charged with being irreligious towards [the Caesars] since we neither propitiate their images nor swear by their genius. *Tertullian (c. 197, W), 3.125.*

[Hermogenes the heretic] despises God's law in his painting, and he maintains repeated marriages. Although he purports to follow the law of God in defense of his lust, he despises it in respect of his art. *Tertullian (c. 200, W), 3.477.*

How could [Peter] have known Moses and Elijah except in the Spirit? People could not have had their images, statues, or likenesses. For the Law forbade that. *Tertullian (c. 207, W), 3.383.*

[The disciples of Carpocrates] make counterfeit images of Christ, alleging that these were in existence at the time . . . and were fashioned by Pilate. *Hippolytus (c. 225, W), 5.114.*

These different tribes erected temples and statues to those individuals I have previously enumerated. In contrast, we have refrained from offering to the Divinity honor by any such means, seeing that they are better adapted to demons. *Origen (c. 248, E), 4.477.*

Neither painter nor image-maker existed in the nation of Israel, for the Law expelled all such persons from it. In that way, there was no pretext for the construction of images. For image-making is an art that attracts the attention of foolish men. It drags the eyes of the soul down from God to earth. Accordingly, there was among them a Law to the following effect: "Do not transgress the Law and make to yourselves a carved image, or any likeness of male or female." *Origen (c. 248, E), 4.510.*

Celsus, the pagan critic, had accused Christians of being "uneducated, servile, and ignorant." The following passage is Origen's reply:

We, on the other hand, deem those [pagans] to be "uneducated" who are not ashamed to address inanimate objects, to ask for health from those who have no strength, to ask the dead for life, and to entreat the helpless for assistance. Some may say that these objects are not gods—but only representations and symbols of real divinities. Nevertheless, these very individuals, in imagining that the hands of lowly artisans can frame representations of divinity, are "uneducated, servile, and igno-rant." *Origen (c. 248, E), 4.579.*

[CELSUS, THE PAGAN CRITIC:] "They cannot tolerate temples, altars, or images. In this, they are like the Scythians." . . . [ORIGEN:] To this, our answer is that if the Scythians . . . cannot bear the sight of temples, altars, and images, it does not follow that our reason for objecting to these things is the same as theirs—even though we cannot tolerate them anymore than they can. . . . The Scythians, the nomadic Libyans, the godless Seres, and the Persians agree in this with the Christians and Jews. However, they are actuated by very different principles. For none of these other groups abhor altars and images on the ground that they are afraid of degrading the worship of God and reducing it to the worship of material things. . . . It is not possible at the same time to know God and to address prayers to images. *Origen (c. 248, E), 4.635–4.637.*

To explain this fully, and to justify the conduct of the Christians in refusing homage to any object except the Most High God, and the First-Born of all creation (who is His Word and is God), we must quote this from Scripture. *Origen (c. 248, E), 4.639.*

[The pagan gods] were once kings. But on account of their royal memory, they subsequently began to be adored by their people even in death. Afterwards, . . . images were sculptured to retain the faces of the deceased by the likeness. Later, men sacrificed victims and celebrated festal days, to give them honor. Finally, those rites became sacred to posterity—even though they had originally been adopted as a consolation. *Cyprian (c. 250, W), 5.465.*

In the book on the Passover and on Hosea, Pierius discusses both the pillar of Jacob and the cherubim made by Moses. In these passages, he admits the actual construction of those things, but propounds the foolish theory that they were given economically and that they were in no respect like other things that are made. *Pierius (c. 275, E), 6.157, as cited by Photius (c. 850).*

What madness is it, then, either to form those objects that they themselves may afterwards fear, or to fear the things that they have formed? However, they say, "We do not fear the images themselves, but those beings after whose likeness they were formed, and to whose names they are dedicated." No doubt you fear them for this reason: because you think that they are in heaven. For if they are gods, the case cannot be otherwise. So why, then, do you not raise your eyes to *heaven*? Why do you not invoke their names and offer sacrifices in the open air? Why do you look to walls, wood, and stone—rather than to the place where you believe them to be? What is the meaning of temples and altars? What, in short, is the meaning of the images themselves, which are memorials either of the dead or of the absent? For the idea of making likenesses was invented by men for this reason: that it might be possible to retain the memory of those who had either been removed by death or else separated by absence. *Lactantius (c. 304–313, W), 7.41.*

The likeness of a man appears to be necessary at that time when he is far away. But it will become unnecessary when he is at hand. However, in the case of God, whose spirit and influence are diffused everywhere, and can never be absent, it is plain that an image is always unnecessary. *Lactantius (c. 304–313, W), 7.42.*

How much better, therefore, is it, to leave vain and insensible objects and, instead, to turn our eyes in that direction where is the seat and dwelling place of the true God. *Lactantius (c. 304–313, W), 7.47.*

It is also supernatural that the statue of Fortune, in the form of a woman, is reported to have spoken more than once. Also, that the statue of Juno Moneta, when . . . one of the soldiers . . . jokingly asked whether she wished to transfer to Rome, answered that she wished it. *Lactantius (c. 304–313, W), 7.51.*

I have shown that the religious ceremonies of the gods are in vain for three reasons. In the first place, those images that are worshipped are representations of men who are dead. And it is a wrong and inconsistent thing that the image of a man should be worshipped by the image of God. For he who worships is naturally lower and weaker than that which is worshipped. Furthermore, it is an unforgivable crime to desert the living in order to serve memorials for the dead. For the dead can give neither life nor light to anyone. For they are themselves without it. . . . Secondly, the sacred images themselves, to which most senseless men render service, are destitute of all perception. For they are earth. *Lactantius (c. 304–313, W), 7.67.*

Without a doubt, there is no religion wherever there is an image. For religion consists of divine things, and there is nothing divine except in heavenly things. So it follows that images are without religion. For there can be nothing heavenly in something that is made from the earth. *Lactantius (c. 304–313, W), 7.68.*

While it was yet hardly light, the prefect, together with chief commanders . . . came to the church in Nicomedia. The gates having been forced open, they searched everywhere for an image of the Divinity. However, the books of the Holy Scriptures were found, and they were committed to the flames. The utensils and furniture of the church were abandoned to pillage. *Lactantius (c. 320, W), 7.305.*

You say that we rear no temples to [the gods] and do not worship their images. . . . Well, what greater honor or dignity could we ascribe to them than that we put them in the same position as the Head and Lord of the universe! . . . Do we honor him with shrines and by building temples? *Arnobius (c. 305, E), 6.507.*

Do you perhaps say that under these images of deities there is displayed to you their presence, as it were? That because it has not been give you to see the gods, they are worshipped in this manner and the duties owed to them are paid? A person who says and asserts this does not believe that the gods exist. And he is proved not to put faith in his own religion, to whom it is necessary to see what he may hold. *Arnobius (c. 305, E), 6.509.*

You [pagans] say, "But you err and are mistaken. For we do not consider either copper, gold, silver, or those other materials of which statues are made to be in themselves gods and sacred deities. Rather, in them we worship and venerate those beings whom their dedication as sacred items cause to dwell in those statues made by workmen." *Arnobius (c. 305, E), 6.514.*

The advocates of images are accustomed to saying that the ancients knew well that images have no divine nature and that there is no sense in them. Yet, they say that they still formed them profitably and wisely, for the sake of the unmanageable and ignorant crowds. This was so that . . . they might from fear shake off their crude natures, supposing that they were acting in the presence of the gods. *Arnobius (c. 305, E), 6.516.*

It has been sufficiently shown . . . how vain it is to form images. *Arnobius (c. 305, E), 6.518.*

SEE ALSO ARK OF THE COVENANT; IDOLATRY; SERPENT, BRONZE.

IMPASSIBILITY OF GOD

SEE GOD, ATTRIBUTES OF.

IMPUTATION OF RIGHTEOUSNESS

[ADDRESSED TO JEWS:] If they repent, all who wish for it can obtain mercy from God. The Scripture foretells that they shall be blessed, saying, "Blessed is the man to whom the Lord does not impute sin." That is, after repenting of his sins, such a man can receive remission of those sins from God. It is not as you deceive yourselves and some others who resemble you in this. For you say that even though they are sinners, the Lord will not impute sin to them, for they know God. *Justin Martyr (c. 160, E), 1.270.*

SEE ALSO SALVATION.

INCARNATION

The Word became flesh and dwelt among us, and we beheld His glory, the glory as of the only begotten of the Father. John 1:14.

When the fullness of the time had come, God sent forth His Son, born of a woman, born under the law. Gal. 4:4.

God was manifested in the flesh. 1 Tim. 3:16.

There is one Physician who is possessed both of flesh and spirit. He is both made and not made. He is God existing in flesh, true Life in death. He is both of Mary and of God. *Ignatius (c. 105, E), 1.52.*

He is both the Son of man and the Son of God. *Ignatius (c. 105, E), 1.58.*

Jesus Christ . . . was truly born, and did eat and drink. . . . He was truly crucified and died. *Ignatius (c. 105, E), 1.70.*

He was truly of the seed of David according to the flesh, and the Son of God according to the will and power of God. He was truly born of a virgin. *Ignatius (c. 105, E), 1.86.*

It is said that God came down from heaven. He assumed flesh and clothed Himself with it from a Hebrew virgin. And the Son of God lived in a daughter of man. *Aristides (c. 125, E), 9.265.*

The holy, pre-existent spirit Person who created every creature, God made to dwell in flesh, which He chose. *Hermas (c. 150, W), 2.35.*

[TRYPHO, A JEW:] You say that this Christ existed as God before the ages. You say that He then submitted to being born and becoming man. Yet, you say that He is not man of man. Now, this appears to me to be not merely paradoxical, but also foolish. *Justin Martyr (c. 160, E), 1.219.*

The First-Begotten of all creation would become incarnate by the virgin's womb, and be a child. *Justin Martyr (c. 160, E), 1.241.*

In a unique manner, He was begotten by the Father as the Word and Power. Later, He became man through the virgin. *Justin Martyr (c. 160, E), 1.251.*

The goat that was sent away presented a type of Him who takes away the sins of men. But the two goats contained a representation of the one economy of God incarnate. *Justin Martyr (c. 160, E), 1.301.*

We do not act as fools, O Greeks, nor utter idle tales, when we announce that God was born in the form of man. *Tatian (c. 160, E), 2.74.*

Though the Son was incorporeal, He formed for Himself a body after our fashion. He appeared as one of the sheep; yet, He still remained the Shepherd. He was esteemed a servant; yet, He did not renounce the Sonship. He was carried in the womb of Mary, yet arrayed in the nature of His Father. He walked upon the earth, yet He filled heaven. He appeared as an infant, yet He did not discard the eternity of His nature. He was invested with a body, but it did not circumscribe the unmixed simplicity of His Divinity. . . . He needed sustenance inasmuch as He was man; yet, He did not cease to feed the entire world inasmuch as He is God. He put on the likeness of a servant, while not impairing the likeness of His Father. *Melito (c. 170, E), 8.756.*

Being at once both God and perfect man, He gave us sure indications of His two natures. . . . He concealed the signs of His Deity, although he was the true God existing before all ages. *Melito (c. 170, E), 8.760.*

Christ Jesus, the Son of God, because of His surpassing love towards His creation, humbled Himself to be born of the virgin. He Himself united man to God through Himself. *Irenaeus (c. 180, E/W), 1.417.*

Inasmuch as the Word of God was man from the root of Jesse, and son of Abraham, in this respect the Spirit of God rested upon Him and anointed Him to preach the Gospel to the lowly. But inasmuch as Christ was God, Christ did not judge according to glory, nor reprove after the manner of speech. *Irenaeus (c. 180, E/W), 1.423.*

He took up man into Himself. Thereby, the invisible became visible; the incomprehensible was made comprehensible; the impassible became capable of suffering. So the Word was made man and thereby summed up all things in Himself. *Irenaeus (c. 180, E/W), 1.443.*

He received testimony from everyone that He was very man and that He was very God. *Irenaeus (c. 180, E/W), 1.469.*

His advent according to the flesh was the thing by which the blending and communion of God and man took place. *Irenaeus (c. 180, E/W), 1.488.*

[The Gnostics], therefore, who allege that He took nothing from the virgin, do greatly err. In order that they may cast away the inheritance of the flesh, they also reject the analogy [between Him and Adam]. . . . For if He did not receive the substance of flesh from a human being, He neither was made man nor the Son of man. And if He was not made what we were, He did no great thing in what He suffered and endured. . . . For why did He come down into her [Mary] if He was to take nothing of her? *Irenaeus (c. 180, E/W), 1.454.*

I have proved already that it is the same thing to say that He merely seemed to appear and to say that He received nothing from Mary. For He would not have been one truly possessing flesh and blood, by which He redeemed us, unless He had summed up in Himself the ancient formation of Adam. *Irenaeus (c. 180, E/W), 1.527.*

Vain also are the Ebionites, who do not receive by faith into their soul the union of God and man. Rather, they remain in the old leaven of [the natural] birth. For they do not choose to understand that the Holy Spirit came upon

Mary, and the power of the Most High did overshadow her. *Irenaeus (c. 180, E/W), 1.527.*

Nor did the Son truly redeem us by His own blood, if He did not really become man. *Irenaeus (c. 180, E/W), 1.528.*

The same apostle [Paul] has in every place adopted the phrase "flesh and blood" with regard to the Lord Jesus Christ. Paul does this partly to establish His human nature (for Christ Himself spoke of Himself as the "Son of man"), and partly so that he could confirm the salvation of our flesh. *Irenaeus (c. 180, E/W), 1.541.*

The Son of God—He who made the universe—assumed flesh and was conceived in the virgin's womb. *Clement of Alexandria (c. 195, E), 2.509.*

The loving Lord became man for us. *Clement of Alexandria (c. 195, E), 2.543.*

This ray of God, then, as it was always foretold in ancient times, descended into a certain virgin, and made flesh in her womb. He is in His birth God and man united. *Tertullian (c. 197, W), 3.34, 35.*

While He lived on earth, He Himself declared who He is, of what God He is the Son, and of what substance He is man and God. *Tertullian (c. 197, W), 3.252.*

God suffers Himself to be conceived in a mother's womb, and awaits the time for birth. And, when born, He bears the delay of growing up. . . . Furthermore, He is baptized by His own servant. *Tertullian (c. 200, W), 3.708.*

You yourselves have now come to the belief that God moved about in the form and in all other characteristics of man's nature. . . . For if [your Marcionite] God, even from His higher condition, prostrated the supreme dignity of His majesty to such a lowliness as to undergo death, even the death of the cross—why can you not suppose that some humiliations are becoming to our God also? *Tertullian (c. 207, W), 3.318.*

It is the Son who has been seen, heard, and encountered. He is the Witness and Servant of the Father, uniting in Himself man and God. In mighty deeds, He is God. In weak ones, He is man. This is so that He can give to man as much as He takes from God. *Tertullian (c. 207, W), 3.319.*

He who remitted sins was both God and man. *Tertullian (c. 207, W), 3.359.*

On this account, therefore, the Son was sent in the "likeness of sinful flesh," so that He could redeem this sinful flesh by a like substance—even a fleshly one—which bore a resemblance to sinful flesh, although it was itself free from sin. *Tertullian (c. 207, W), 3.459.*

As He was found to be God by His mighty power, so was He found to be man by reason of His flesh. *Tertullian (c. 207, W), 3.473.*

You [Gnostics] should not worry that, if He had been born and truly clothed Himself with man's nature, He would have ceased to be God. You should not worry that He would lose what He was—while becoming what He was not. For God is in no danger of losing His own state and condition. *Tertullian (c. 210, W), 3.523.*

Was not God really crucified? And, having been really crucified, did He not really die? And, having indeed really died, did He not really rise again? *Tertullian (c. 210, W), 3.525*

Christ could not be described as being man without flesh, nor the Son of man without any human parent. Just as he is not God without the Spirit of God, nor the Son of God without having God for His Father. Thus the origin of the two substances displayed Him as man and God. In one respect, He was born; in the other respect, He was unborn. In one respect, fleshly; in the other, spiritual. In one sense, weak; in the other, exceedingly strong. In one sense, dying; in the other sense, living. This property of the two states—the divine and the human—is distinctly asserted with equal truth of both natures alike. *Tertullian (c. 210, W), 3.525.*

The flesh of Christ, which committed no sin itself, resembled that which had sinned. I mean, it resembled it in its nature, but not in the corruption it received from Adam. For that reason, we also affirm that there was in Christ the same flesh as that whose nature in man is sinful. In the flesh, therefore, we say that sin has been abolished, for (in Christ) that same flesh was maintained without sin—which in man is *not* maintained without sin. *Tertullian (c. 210, W), 3.535.*

However, a word of caution must be addressed to all who refuse to believe that our flesh was in Christ, on the grounds that it did not come from the seed of a human father. Let them remember that Adam himself received this flesh of ours without the seed of a human father. *Tertullian (c. 210, W), 3.536.*

[The heretics] contend ... that just as the Word of God became flesh without the seed of a human father, so likewise there was no flesh of the virgin mother.... However, if that were the case, a virgin did *not* conceive and did *not* bring forth. For whatever she brought forth from the conception of the Word would not have been her own flesh. *Tertullian (c. 210, W), 3.539.*

Concerning Christ, ... the property of each nature is so wholly preserved that the Spirit on the one hand did all things in Jesus suitable to itself—such as miracles, mighty deeds, and wonders. On the other hand, the flesh exhibited the affections that belong to it. It was hungry under the devil's temptation, thirsty with the Samaritan woman, wept over Lazarus, was troubled even unto death, and at last it actually died.... Inasmuch, however, as the two substances acted distinctly, each in its own character, there necessarily accrued to them individually their own operations and their own issues. *Tertullian (c. 213, W), 3.624.*

We are not guilty of blasphemy against the Lord God, for we do not maintain that He died after the *divine* nature—but only after the *human*. *Tertullian (c. 213, W), 3.626.*

Whereas the Word of God was without flesh, He took upon Himself the holy flesh by the holy virgin, and prepared a robe which He wove for Himself, like a bridegroom, in the sufferings of the cross. He did this in order that by uniting His own power with our mortal body, and by mixing the incorruptible with the corruptible, and the strong with the weak, He might save perishing man. *Hippolytus (c. 200, W), 5.205.*

Christ is the perfect male child of God, who is declared to be God and man. *Hippolytus (c. 200, W), 5.217.*

Although as man He became one of the dead, he remained alive in the nature of His divinity. *Hippolytus (c. 205, W), 5.164.*

When He came into the world, He was manifested as God and man. It is easy to recognize the human nature in Him, when He hungers and shows exhaustion and is weary and thirsty. ... On the other hand, the divine in Him is equally manifest, when he is worshiped by angels, ... and at a marriage makes wine of water, ... and raises Lazarus after he was dead for four days. *Hippolytus (c. 205, W), 5.170.*

"She has mingled her wine" in the bowl. By this is meant that the Savior, uniting His divinity, like pure wine, with the flesh in the virgin, was born of her—being both God and man without confusion of the one in the other. *Hippolytus (c. 205, W), 5.175.*

Christ takes the common name for tender affection among men in being called the Son. When He was by Himself and prior to the incarnation, He was not yet perfect Son (although He was perfect Word, the Only-Begotten). Nor could the flesh subsist by itself apart from the Word, for it has its subsistence in the Word. *Hippolytus (c. 205, W), 5.229.*

Let us believe, then, dear brethren, according to the tradition of the apostles, that God the Word came down from heaven into the holy virgin Mary, in order that by taking the flesh from her and assuming also a human soul (by which I mean a rational soul) and thus becoming all that man is (with the exception of sin), He could save fallen man and confer immortality on men who believe on His name.... In the same manner also, He came and manifested Himself—being made a new man by the virgin and the Holy Spirit. He had the heavenly nature of the Father (as the Word) and the earthly nature, as taking to Himself the flesh from the old Adam through the medium of the virgin. Coming forth into the world, He now was manifested as God in a body, coming forth too as a perfect man. For it was not in mere appearance or by conversion, but in reality that He became man. *Hippolytus (c. 205, W), 5.230.*

The Logos received a body from a virgin, and He remodelled the old man by a new creation. He passed through every period of life, so that He Himself could serve as an example for every age.... For if He were not of the same nature as ourselves, it would be in vain that He commands us to imitate Him as the Teacher. For if He were of a different substance than us, why did He give commandments to us that were similar to those He had received? Would that be the act of One who is good and just? *Hippolytus (c. 225, W), 5.152.*

For who is ignorant of the books of Irenaeus and Melito, and the rest, which declare Christ to be God and man? All the psalms, too, and hymns of the brethren—which have been written from the beginning by the faithful—celebrate Christ as the Word of God, ascribing divinity to Him. *Eusebius, quoting Caius (c. 215, W), 5.601.*

After He had been the minister of the Father in the creation of all things ("for by Him all things were made"), He in the last times divested Himself and became a man, and was incarnate although still God. While He was made a man, He remained the God that He was. He assumed a body like our own, differing in only one respect: that the body was born of a virgin and of the Holy Spirit. This Jesus Christ was truly born, truly suffered, . . . and truly died. *Origen (c. 225, E), 4.240.*

After the consideration of questions of such importance concerning the being of the Son of God, we are lost in the deepest amazement that such a nature—pre-eminent above all others—would have divested itself of its condition of majesty and would have become man. *Origen (c. 225, E), 4.281.*

We see in Him some things so human that they appear to differ in no respect from the common frailty of mortals. We also see some things so divine that they can appropriately belong to nothing else than to the primal and ineffable nature of Deity. . . . The truth of both natures may be clearly shown to exist in one and the same Being. This was so that nothing unworthy or unbecoming could be perceived in that divine and ineffable substance, nor yet those things that were done be thought to be the illusions of imaginary appearances. To utter these things in human ears, and to explain them in words, far surpasses the powers either of our rank, or of our intellect and language. I think that it surpasses the power even of the holy apostles. Nay, the explanation of that mystery may perhaps be beyond the grasp of the entire creation of celestial powers. *Origen (c. 225, E), 4.282.*

More truly indeed of this than of any other can the statement be affirmed that "the two will become one flesh. And they are no longer two, but one flesh." For the Word of God is to be considered as being more in one flesh with the soul than a man with his wife. *Origen (c. 225, E), 4.282.*

It cannot be doubted that the nature of His soul was the same as that of all others. Otherwise, it could not be called a soul—were it not truly one. But since the power of choosing good and evil is within the reach of all, this soul that belonged to Christ elected to love righteousness. So then in proportion to the immensity of its love, it clung to it unchangeably and inseparably. Firmness of purpose and immensity of affection . . . destroyed all susceptibility for alteration and change. . . . So we must believe that there existed in Christ a human and rational soul, without supposing that it had any feeling or possibility of sin. *Origen (c. 225, E), 4.283.*

The nature of the incarnation will render unnecessary any inquiry into the soul of Christ. For just as He truly possessed flesh, so He also truly possessed a soul. *Origen (c. 225, E), 4.287.*

With respect to the bodily advent and incarnation of the Only-Begotten Son of God, we are not to suppose that all the majesty of His divinity was confined within the limits of His slender body, so that all the Word, Wisdom, essential truth, and life of God were either torn asunder from the Father or restrained and confined within the narrowness of His bodily person. . . . So it should not be believed that anything of divinity was lacking in Christ, nor that any separation at all was made from the essence of the Father, which is everywhere. *Origen (c. 225, E), 4.377.*

It was as a man that He is Christ—in respect of His soul, which was human and liable to be troubled and sorely vexed. However, He was conceived as king because of the divinity in Him. *Origen (c. 228, E), 9.313.*

[John the Baptist] answers by exalting the superior nature of Christ—that He has such virtue as to be invisible in His deity, though present to every man and extending over the whole universe. *Origen (c. 228, E), 9.365, 366.*

It is true to call Him man, and to call Him not man. Man, because He was capable of death; not man, on account of His being more divine than man. *Origen (c. 228, E), 9.384.*

If such were the life of Jesus, how could anyone . . . not believe according to the promise that He was God, who appeared in human form to do good for our race? *Origen (c. 248, E), 4.427.*

Moreover, Celsus says that this charge is brought against the Jews by the Christian converts: that they have not believed in Jesus as in God. Now on this point, we have in the preceding pages offered a preliminary defense, showing at the same time in what respects we understand him to be God, and in what sense we take him to be man. *Origen (c. 248, E), 4.432.*

In other dead bodies, the blood congeals, and pure water does not flow forth. However, the miraculous feature in the case of the dead body of Jesus was that blood and water flowed forth from the side, around the dead body. *Origen (c. 248, E), 4.446.*

He whom we regard and believe to have been from the beginning God, and the Son of God, is the very Logos, the very Wisdom, and the very Truth. With respect to His mortal body and the human soul that it contained, we assert by their unity and intermixture (not merely by their communion with Him), they received the highest powers, and after participating in His divinity, were changed into God. *Origen (c. 248, E), 4.480.*

With respect to His having descended among men, He was "previously in the form of God," but through benevolence, He divested himself so He could be capable of being received by men. *Origen (c. 248, E), 4.503.*

Nor is it at all incredible that we maintain that the soul of Jesus is made one with so great a Son of God through the highest union with Him, being no longer in a state of separation from Him. For the sacred language of Holy Scripture knows of other things also, which, although dual in their own nature, are considered to be, and really are, one in respect to one another. For example, this is said of husband and wife.... And if this is so, then the soul of Jesus and God the Word—the First-born of every creature—are no longer two. *Origen (c. 248, E), 4.595.*

Just as the soul of Jesus is joined in a perfect and inconceivable manner with the very Word, so the person of Jesus, generally speaking, is not separated from the Only-Begotten and First-Born of all creation, and is not a different Being from Him. *Origen (c. 248, E), 4.595.*

Of this Being and His nature, we must judge and reason in a way quite different from that in which we judge the man who was seen in Jesus Christ. You will find no Christian, however simple he may be, and however little versed in critical studies he may be, who would say that He who died was "the Truth, "the Way," "the Life," "the living Bread that came down from heaven," or "the Resurrection." There is no one among us, I say, so extravagant as to state that "the Life died," or "the Resurrection died." *Origen (c. 248, E), 4.617.*

In his statements on this subject, there is one point alone in which Celsus is correct. It is that in which he says ... "It involves that which is wicked and impious—namely, that the great God should become a slave or suffer death." But that which is predicted by the prophets *is* worthy of God: that He who is the brightness and express image of the divine nature should come into the world with the holy human soul that was to animate the body of Jesus, to sow the seed of His Word, which might bring all who received and cherished it into union with the Most High God.... He was to be in [the body and soul of man], but not in such a way as to confine in them all the rays of His glory.... If, then, we consider Jesus in relation to the divinity that was in Him, the things that He did in this capacity present nothing to offend our ideas of God.... And if we consider him as man, ... He suffered as one who was wise and perfect. *Origen (c. 248, E), 4.617.*

Scripture ... has as much described Jesus Christ to be man as it has also described Christ the Lord to be God. *Novatian (c. 235, W), 5.620.*

If weaknesses in Him prove human frailty, majesties in Him affirm Divine power. For the risk is, in reading of both [natures], to believe only one of the two, instead of both. *Novatian (c. 235, W), 5.621.*

We know that the Word of God was invested with the substance of flesh, and that He again was divested of the same bodily material, which again He took up in the resurrection and resumed as a garment. *Novatian (c. 235, W), 5.632.*

What of it if the divinity in Christ did not die, but rather only the substance of the flesh was destroyed? After all, in other men also (who are not only flesh, but flesh and soul) only the flesh suffers the effects of wasting and death. But the soul is uncorrupted and beyond the laws of destruction and death. *Novatian (c. 235, W), 5.636.*

He enters into a virgin. Through the Holy Spirit, He is clothed with flesh. God is mingled with man. *Cyprian (c. 250, W), 5.468.*

Although from the beginning He had been the Son of God, yet He had to be begotten again according to the flesh. In the second Psalm: "The Lord said unto me, 'You are my son. This day I have begotten you. Ask of me, and I will give you the nations for your inheritance." *Cyprian (c. 250, W), 5.519.*

Christ is both man and God, compounded of both natures, so that He could be a Mediator between us and the Father. In Jeremiah: "And he is man, and who will know him?" Also, in Numbers: "A Star will arise out of Jacob and a man will rise up from Israel." *Cyprian (c. 250, W), 5.519.*

Moreover, in what respect does he [Paul of Samosata] mean to allege that the formation of Christ is different and diverse from ours? For we hold that His constitution differs from ours in only one significant thing: that what in us is the inner man [i.e., the soul] is in Him the Logos. *Synod of Antioch (c. 270, E), 6.171.*

He, being God, was pleased to put on human flesh, so that we, beholding the divine Pattern of our life as on a tablet, should also be able to imitate Him who painted it. *Methodius (c. 290, E), 6.312.*

It was fitting that the First-Born of God, the First Shoot, the Only-Begotten, even the Wisdom of God, should be joined to the first-formed man [as the second Adam] ... and should become incarnate. *Methodius (c. 290, E), 6.318.*

Although He was the Son of God from the beginning, He was born again a second time according to the flesh. *Lactantius (c. 304–313, W), 7.106.*

He became both the Son of God through the Spirit and the Son of man through the flesh—that is, both God and man. The power of God was displayed in Him through the works that He performed. The frailty of man was displayed by the passion that He endured.... We learn from the predictions of the prophets that He was both God and man, composed of both natures. *Lactantius (c. 304–313, W), 7.112.*

They say, in short, that it was unworthy of God to be willing to become man and to bur-

den Himself with the infirmity of flesh. It was unworthy of Him to willingly become subject to sufferings, pain, and death.... However, these things were done by a great and wonderful plan. And the person who understands this will cease to wonder that God was tortured by men. *Lactantius (c. 304–313, W), 7.124.*

If anyone gives men commandments for living and molds the characters of others, ... he is obligated himself to practice the things that he teaches.... Otherwise, [the student] will answer his teacher in this way: "I am not able to do the things that you command, for they are impossible.... Or, if you are so entirely convinced that it is possible to resist nature, you yourself practice the things you teach, so I can know that they are possible." ... But how can one practice what he teaches, unless he is like the teacher? For if the teacher is subject to no passion, a man may answer the teacher in this manner: "It is my wish not to sin. However, I am overpowered. For I am clothed with frail and weak flesh." ... Now, what will that teacher of righteousness say in reply to these things? How will he refute and convict a man who alleges the frailty of the flesh as an excuse for his faults—unless he himself will also be clothed with flesh—so that he can show that even the flesh is capable of virtue? ... You see, therefore, how much more perfect is a teacher who is mortal, for he is able to be a guide to one who is mortal. ... Therefore, let men learn and understand why the Most High God—when He sent His Ambassador and Messenger to instruct mortals with the commandments of His righteousness—willed for Him to be clothed with mortal flesh, to be afflicted with torture, and to be sentenced to death.... For if he had been God only, He would not have been able to provide man with an example of goodness. *Lactantius (c. 304–313, W), 7.124–7.126.*

God was the Father of Jesus' spirit, without a mother. Likewise, a virgin was the mother of His body, without a father. He was therefore both God and man, being placed in the middle between God and man. From this, the Greeks call Him *Mesites* [Mediator], for He is able to lead man to God—that is, to immortality. *Lactantius (c. 304–313, W), 7.126; extended discussion: 3.521–3.542; 4.281–4.284.*

SEE ALSO CHRIST, DIVINITY OF; MARY; TRINITY; VIRGIN BIRTH.

INCENSE

The smoke of the incense, with the prayers of the saints, ascended before God from the angel's hand. Rev. 8:4.

God has no need of streams of blood, libations, and incense. *Justin Martyr (c. 160, E), 1.166.*

The Framer and Father of this universe does not need blood, nor the odor of burnt-offerings, nor the fragrance of flowers and incense, for He is Himself perfect fragrance. *Athenagoras (c. 175, E), 2.134, 135.*

"In every place incense is offered to my name, and a pure sacrifice" [Mal. 1:11–14]. As John declares in the Apocalypse: "The incense is the prayers of the saints." *Irenaeus (c. 180, E/W), 1.574.*

How, then, will I crown myself, anoint with ointment, or offer incense to the Lord? It is said, "An odor of a sweet fragrance is the heart that glorifies Him who made it" [Ps. 51:17]. These are the crowns and sacrifices, aromatic odors, and flowers of God. *Clement of Alexandria (c. 195, E), 2.293.*

The sacrifice of the church is the word breathing as incense from holy souls. Both the sacrifice and the whole mind are unveiled to God at the same time. . . . And will they not believe us when we say that the righteous soul is the truly sacred altar and that the incense arising from it is holy prayer? *Clement of Alexandria (c. 195, E), 2.531.*

That blended incense that is mentioned in the Law is that which consists of many tongues and voices in prayer. *Clement of Alexandria (c. 195, E), 2.532.*

I offer to Him at His own requirement that costly and noble sacrifice of prayer dispatched from the chaste body, an unstained soul, a sanctified spirit. I do not offer the few grains of incense that a small coin buys (incense being the tears of an Arabian tree). Nor do I offer a few drops of wine, or the blood of some worthless ox. *Tertullian (c. 197, W), 3.42.*

We certainly buy no frankincense. *Tertullian (c. 197, W), 3.49.*

The [theater and the arena] resemble each other also in their ceremony, having the same procession to the scene of their display from temples and altars, and that mournful profusion of incense and blood. *Tertullian (c. 197, W), 3.84.*

You slay the same victims and burn the same odors for your dead as you do for your gods. *Tertullian (c. 197, W), 3.119.*

Most persons regard idolatry as being limited to these practices alone: burning incense or immolating a victim. *Tertullian (c. 200, W), 3.62.*

[As a Christian], you worship—not with the spirit of some worthless perfume—but with your own. *Tertullian (c. 200, W), 3.64.*

The Magi therefore offered frankincense, myrrh, and gold to the then infant Lord. This was to be, as it were, the end of worldly sacrifice and glory, which Christ was about to do away with. *Tertullian (c. 200, W), 3.65, 66.*

Even now, for the most part, idolatry is perpetrated without the idol—merely by the burning of aromas. The frankincense seller is more serviceable to demons. For idolatry is more easily carried on without the idol than without the goods of the frankincense seller. *Tertullian (c. 200, W), 3.67.*

The handmaid of God dwells amid alien labors [if she is married to an unbelieving husband]. And among these, she will be agitated by the odor of incense on all the memorial days of demons, at all solemnities of kings, at the beginning of the year, and at the beginning of the month. *Tertullian (c. 205, W), 4.47.*

If the smell of some place or other offends me, I burn the Arabian product myself—but not with the same ceremony, nor in the same dress, nor with the same ceremony, with which it is done to idols. *Tertullian (c. 211, W), 3.99.*

God, the Creator of the universe, has no need of odors or of blood. These things are the food of devils. *Tertullian (c. 212, W), 3.106.*

God is not appeased by incense, victims, or costly offerings. For these things are all corruptible. Rather, he is appeased by a reform of the morals. *Lactantius (c. 304–313, W), 7.277.*

You say that we erect no temples to [the gods] and do not worship their images. You say that we do not slay victims in sacrifice and that we do not offer incense and offerings of wine. Well, what greater honor or dignity could we ascribe to them than that we put them in the same position as the Head and Lord of the universe! . . . Do we honor him with shrines and by building temples? Do we slay victims to Him? Do we give Him those other things? *Arnobius (c. 305, E), 6.507.*

With respect to that very incense that you [pagans] use, we ask this of you: from where or at what time did you become acquainted with it? . . . For if without incense the performance of a religious service is imperfect, and if a quantity of it is necessary to make the gods gentle and propitious to men, the ancients fell into sin, . . . for they carelessly neglected to offer it. . . . However, if in ancient times neither men nor gods sought for this incense, it is proved that today it is also offered uselessly and in vain. *Arnobius (c. 305, E), 6.528.*

SEE ALSO WORSHIP, PAGAN.

INFANT BAPTISM

SEE BAPTISM (III. THE QUESTION OF INFANT BAPTISM).

INFANTICIDE

SEE ABORTION, INFANTICIDE.

INFANTS

SEE CHILDREN, INFANTS.

INFANTS, ABANDONMENT OF

SEE ABORTION, INFANTICIDE.

INFANTS, EXPOSURE OF

SEE ABORTION, INFANTICIDE.

INSPIRATION

SEE SCRIPTURES (III. INSPIRATION OF THE SCRIPTURES).

INTEREST

SEE USURY.

INTERMEDIATE STATE

SEE DEAD, INTERMEDIATE STATE OF THE.

INVENTIONS

For a discussion of primitive inventors, see 2.317, 318.

SEE ALSO WRITING, ORIGIN OF.

IRENAEUS

Irenaeus (c. 130–200) was probably a native of Smyrna, for he had been taught by Polycarp as a boy. He eventually settled in Gaul, in the city of Lyons, where he eventually became bishop.

These have been already produced . . . in carefully written volumes, by so many eminently holy and excellent men. . . . For instance, . . . there is Irenaeus, that very exact inquirer into all doctrines. *Tertullian (c. 200, W), 3.505, 506.*

The blessed presbyter Irenaeus has powerfully and elaborately refuted the opinions of these [heretics]. *Hippolytus (c. 225, W), 5.99.*

Besides, there are writings of certain brethren older than the times of Victor, which they wrote against the pagans in defense of the truth and against the heresies of their day. . . . For who is ignorant of the books of Irenaeus and Melito, and the rest, which declare Christ to be God and man? *Eusebius, quoting Caius (c. 215, W), 5.601.*

The contention was between Victor, at that time bishop of the city of Rome, and Polycrates, who then appeared to hold the primacy among the bishops of Asia. And this contention was adjusted most rightfully by Irenaeus, at that time president of a part of Gaul. The result was that both parties kept to their own order and did not decline from the original custom of antiquity. *Anatolius (c. 270, E), 6.148, 149.*

Now this custom took its rise from apostolic times, as the blessed Irenaeus, the martyr and bishop of Lyons, declares in his treatise *On Easter. Eusebius (c. 125, E), 1.569.*

Clement, Irenaeus, and Justin the martyr and philosopher comment with exceeding wisdom on the number six of the sixth day. *Anastasius, post-Nicene writer, 1.302.*

SEE ALSO POLYCARP.

ISRAEL

SEE ISRAEL OF GOD; JEW, JEWS.

ISRAEL IN PROPHECY

SEE ISRAEL OF GOD; JEW, JEWS.

ISRAEL OF GOD

I will shake all nations, and they will come to the Desire of All Nations, and I will fill this temple with glory. Hag. 2:7.

Now it shall come to pass in the latter days that the mountain of the Lord's house shall be established on the top of the mountains, and shall be exalted above the hills; and people shall flow to it. Many nations shall come and say, "Come, and let us go up to the mountain of the Lord, to the house of the God of Jacob; He will teach us His ways, and we shall walk in His paths." For out of Zion the law shall go forth, and the word of the Lord from Jerusalem. Mic. 4:1, 2.

From the rising of the sun, even to its going down, My name will be great among the Gentiles. Mal. 1:11.

Do not think to say to yourselves, "We have Abraham as our father." For I say to you that God is able to raise up children to Abraham from these stones. Matt. 3:9.

I say to you that many will come from east and west, and sit down with Abraham, Isaac, and Jacob in the kingdom of heaven. Matt. 8:11.

I say to you, the kingdom of God will be taken from you and given to a nation bearing the fruits of it. Matt. 21:43.

For he is not a Jew who is one outwardly, nor is that circumcision which is outward in the flesh; but he is a Jew who is one inwardly. Rom. 2:28, 29.

They are not all Israel who are of Israel, nor are they all children because they are the seed of Abraham. Rom. 9:6, 7.

There is neither Jew nor Greek, . . . for you are all one in Christ Jesus. Gal. 3:28.

In Christ Jesus neither circumcision nor uncircumcision avails anything, but a new creation. And as many as walk according to this rule, peace and mercy be upon them, and upon the Israel of God. Gal. 6:15, 16.

Let us see if this people [the Christians] are the heirs, or if it is the former [the Jews]. Let us see if the covenant belongs to us or to them. *Barnabas (c. 70–130, E), 1.145.*

When He said, "Rejoice, you barren one who bears not," He referred to us [Gentiles]. For our church was barren before children were given to her. . . . And when He said, "For she that is desolate has many more children than she that has a husband," He meant that our people seemed to be outcast from God, but now, through believing, have become more numerous than those who are considered to possess God. *Second Clement (c. 150), 7.517.*

It was said by the same Isaiah, that the Gentile nations who were not looking for Him would worship Him. *Justin Martyr (c. 160, E), 1.179.*

Christians from among the Gentiles are both more numerous and more true than those from among the Jews and Samaritans. *Justin Martyr (c. 160, E), 1.180.*

For the true spiritual Israel, and descendants of Judah, Jacob, Isaac, and Abraham (who in uncircumcision was approved of and blessed by God on account of his faith, and called the father of many nations), are we who have been led to God through this crucified Christ. *Justin Martyr (c. 160, E), 1.200.*

[It had been foretold] that the Gentiles would repent of the evil in which they had led erring lives. This would happen when they heard the doctrine preached by His apostles from Jerusalem and when they learned from them. Let me demonstrate this to you by quoting a short statement from the prophecy of Micah, . . . "In the last days, the mountain of the Lord will be manifest . . . and many nations will go and say, 'Come, let us go up to the mountain of the Lord. . . . And they will enlighten us in His way and we will walk in His paths. For out of Zion will go forth the law, and the word of the Lord from Jerusalem.'" *Justin Martyr (c. 160, E), 1.253.*

Along with Abraham, we will inherit the holy land, when we will receive the inheritance for an endless eternity, being children of Abraham through a similar faith. *Justin Martyr (c. 160, E), 1.259.*

God blesses this people [i.e., Christians], and calls them Israel, and declares them to be His inheritance. So why is it that you [Jews] do not repent of the deception you practice on yourselves, as if you alone were the Israel? *Justin Martyr (c. 160, E), 1.261.*

All who through Him have fled for refuge to the Father constitute the blessed Israel. But you [Jews] have understood none of this. And you are not prepared to understand. Rather, since you are the children of Jacob after the fleshly seed, you expect that you will be assuredly saved. *Justin Martyr (c. 160, E), 1.262.*

By these words, he declares that we, the nations, rejoice with His people. For His people are Abraham, Isaac, Jacob, and the prophets, and in short, all people who are well-pleasing to God. *Justin Martyr (c. 160, E), 1.264.*

Those who were selected out of every nation have obeyed His will through Christ.... So, then, as I mentioned fully before, these persons must be Jacob and Israel. *Justin Martyr (c. 160, E), 1.265.*

We, who have been quarried out from the bowels of Christ, are the true Israelite race.... So it is necessary for us here to observe that there are two seeds of Judah, and two races, just as there are two houses of Jacob. The one is begotten by blood and flesh. The other is begotten by faith and the Spirit. *Justin Martyr (c. 160, E), 1.267.*

God ... introduces Abraham to the kingdom of heaven, through Jesus Christ. He also introduces Abraham's seed, that is, the church. For upon it were conferred the adoption and the inheritance promised to Abraham. *Irenaeus (c. 180, E/W), 1.471.*

Malachi, who was among the twelve [minor] prophets, spoke beforehand in this manner: "I have no pleasure in you, says the Lord Omnipotent, and I will not accept sacrifice at your hands. For from the rising of the sun, unto the going down, My name is glorified among the Gentiles, and in every place incense is offered to My name, and a pure sacrifice; for great is My name among the Gentiles, says the Lord Omnipotent." Here, He stated in the plainest manner, by these words, that the former people [the Jews] will indeed cease to make offerings to God, but that in every place sacrifice will be offered to him, and it will be a pure sacrifice. *Irenaeus (c. 180, E/W), 1.484.*

The elder nation rejected Him, saying, "We have no king but Caesar." But in Christ every blessing [is summed up], and therefore the latter people have snatched away the blessings of the former from the Father—just as Jacob took away the blessing of Esau. For this reason, Jacob suffered the plots and persecutions of a brother, just as the church suffers this self-same thing from the Jews. *Irenaeus (c. 180, E/W), 1.493.*

The Jews have rejected the Son of God and cast Him out of the vineyard when they slew Him. Therefore, God has justly rejected them and has given to the Gentiles outside the vineyard the fruits of its cultivation. *Irenaeus (c. 180, E/W), 1.515.*

The promise of God that He gave to Abraham remains steadfast.... For his seed is the church, which receives the adoption to God through the Lord, as John the Baptist said: "For God is able from the stones to raise up children to Abraham." Thus also the apostle says in the Epistle to the Galatians: "Now we, brethren, just as Isaac was, are the children of the promise." *Irenaeus (c. 180, E/W), 1.561.*

In this manner, the "lesser" people—that is, the later people—have overcome the "greater" people. For they acquire the grace of divine favor, from which Israel has been divorced. *Tertullian (c. 197, W), 3.152.*

We, who "were not the people of God" in days bygone, have been made His people, by accepting the aforementioned new law. *Tertullian (c. 197, W), 3.155.*

Should not the worshippers of the true God be of greater antiquity than all the Chaldeans, Egyptians, and Greeks? For we must bear in mind that the father of those Gentiles was born from this Japheth. He received the name of Javan, and he became the forefather of the Greeks and Ionians. *Hippolytus (c. 225, W), 5.150.*

Many of the present Egyptians and Idumeans who came near to Israel ... will enter into the church of the Lord, being no longer considered as Egyptians and Idumeans but as having become Israelites. *Origen (c. 225, E), 4.327.*

I do not understand this expression as do the Ebionites, who are poor in understanding. They think that the Savior came especially to the carnal Israelites. *Origen (c. 225, E), 4.371.*

It appears to me that the whole people of Christ, when we regard it in the aspect of the hidden man of the heart, have in a more mystic way the characteristics of the [twelve] tribes. For these people are called "Jews inwardly," and they are circumcised in the spirit. This may be more plainly gathered from John in his Apocalypse.... However, the number of believers who belong to Israel according to the flesh is small. One might venture to assert that they would not nearly be a hundred and forty-four thousand of them. It is evident, therefore, that the hundred and forty-four thousand ... must be made up of those who have come to the divine Word out of the Gentile world. *Origen (c. 228, E), 9.297.*

Those who are fully and truly sons of Abraham are sons of his actions (spiritually understood) and of the knowledge that was made manifest to him. *Origen (c. 228, E), 9.351.*

In the Gospel, we find that "children of Abraham are raised from stones," that is, gathered from the Gentiles. *Cyprian (c. 250, W), 5.359.*

According to what had been foretold in advance, the Jews had departed from God. They had lost God's favor, which had been given them in times past and had been promised them for the future. Instead, the Christians have succeeded to their place, deserving well of the Lord by faith. They come out of all nations and from the whole world. *Cyprian (c. 250, W), 5.507.*

Two peoples were foretold: the elder and the younger. The elder people are the Jews. The younger one consists of us. In Genesis it says, "And the Lord said unto Rebekah, 'Two nations are in your womb.'" . . . The church, which had been barren before, is to have more children from among the Gentiles than what the synagogue had had before. . . . The Jews were to lose, while we were to receive the bread and the cup of Christ and all His grace. The new name of Christians is to be blessed in the earth. . . . So the Gentiles, rather than the Jews, attain to the kingdom of heaven. In the Gospel, the Lord says, "Many will come from the east and from the west, and will lie down with Abraham, Isaac, and Jacob in the kingdom of heaven." *Cyprian (c. 250, W), 5.512, 513.*

Our ancestors were the patriarchs of the Hebrews. *Lactantius (c. 304–313, W), 7.108.*

To you, the converted Gentiles, is opened the gate of life. You were formerly not loved, but you are now beloved—a people ordained for the possession of God. *Apostolic Constitutions (compiled c. 390, E), 7.445.*

SEE ALSO JERUSALEM; JEW, JEWS.

JAMES, APOSTLE

After six days Jesus took Peter, James, and John his brother, brought them up on a high mountain by themselves, and was transfigured before them. Matt. 17:1, 2.

Herod the king stretched out his hand to harass some from the church. Then he killed James the brother of John with the sword. Acts 12:1, 2.

[Clement of Alexandria] says that Peter, James, and John, although preeminently honored by the Lord, did not contend for glory after the Savior's ascension, but made James the Just the bishop of Jerusalem. *Eusebius, citing Clement of Alexandria (c. 195, E), 2.579.*

And of this James, Clement also relates an anecdote worthy of remembrance in the seventh book of the *Sketches,* from a tradition of his predecessors. He says that the man who brought him to trial, on seeing him bear his testimony, was moved, and confessed that he was now a Christian himself. Accordingly, he says, they were both led away together. On the way, the other man asked James to forgive him. And after brief consideration, James said, "Peace be to you," and kissed him. And so both were beheaded together. *Eusebius, citing Clement of Alexandria (c. 195, E), 2.579.*

SEE ALSO APOSTLES, TWELVE; JAMES, BROTHER OF THE LORD.

JAMES, BROTHER OF THE LORD

This James is often referred to as James the Just, to distinguish him from the apostle James.

Is not His mother called Mary? And His brothers James, Joses, Simon, and Judas? Matt. 13:55.

After they had become silent, James answered, saying, "Men and brethren, listen to me." Acts 15:13.

I saw none of the other apostles except James, the Lord's brother. Gal. 1:19.

James, Cephas, and John, who seemed to be pillars. Gal. 2:9

James, a bondservant of God and of the Lord Jesus Christ. Jas. 1:1.

[Clement of Alexandria] says that Peter, James, and John (after the Savior's ascension), although preeminently honored by the Lord, did not contend for glory, but made James the Just the bishop of Jerusalem. *Eusebius, citing Clement of Alexandria (c. 195, E), 2.579.*

To James the Just, John, and Peter, the Lord imparted knowledge after His resurrection. These imparted it to the rest of the apostles. And the rest of the apostles to the Seventy, of whom Barnabas was one. *Eusebius, citing Clement of Alexandria (c. 195, E), 2.579.*

James is he whom Paul says in the Epistle to the Galatians that he saw: "But I saw no other of the apostles, except James, the Lord's brother." And this James rose to so great a reputation for righteousness among the people, that Flavius Josephus . . . said that these things happened to the Jews as a result of God's wrath because of the things they had dared to do against James, the brother of Jesus who is called Christ. *Origen (c. 245, E), 9.424.*

Paul, a genuine disciple of Jesus, says that he regarded this James as a brother of the Lord, not so much on account of their relationship by blood, or because they were brought up together, but more so because of his virtue and doctrine. If, then, Josephus says that it was on account of James that the desolation of Jerusalem came upon the Jews, would it not be more in accordance with reason to say that it happened on account of Jesus Christ? *Origen (c. 248, E), 4.416.*

We honor the blessed James the bishop and the holy Stephen, our fellow deacon. These men are considered blessed by God and are honored by holy men. For they were pure from all transgressions and were immoveable when tempted with sin. *Apostolic Constitutions (compiled c. 390, E), 7.442.*

James, the bishop of Jerusalem, the brother of our Lord. *Apostolic Constitutions (compiled c. 390, E), 7.477.*

James, the brother of Christ according to the flesh . . . [was] appointed bishop of Jerusalem by the Lord Himself and the apostles. *Apostolic Constitutions (compiled c. 390, E), 7.496.*

SEE ALSO JESUS CHRIST (VI. BROTHERS OF JESUS); JOSEPHUS; JUDE.

JAMES THE JUST

SEE JAMES, BROTHER OF THE LORD.

JEHOVAH

That mystic name that is called the Tetragrammaton, by which those alone who had access to the Holy of Holies were protected, is pronounced Jehovah. It means, "Who is and who will be." *Clement of Alexandria (c. 195, E), 2.585, from a Latin translation.*

SEE ALSO GOD, NAME OF.

JEPHTHAH'S DAUGHTER

Jephthah offered his freshly slaughtered virgin daughter as a sacrifice to God, like a lamb. *Methodius (c. 290, E), 6.352.*

JERUSALEM

I. Jerusalem under Roman dominion

II. Jerusalem in prophecy

I. Jerusalem under Roman dominion

O Jerusalem, Jerusalem, the one who kills the prophets and stones those who are sent to her! How often I wanted to gather your children together, as a hen gathers her brood under her wings, but you were not willing! See! Your house is left to you desolate. Luke 13:34.

But when you see Jerusalem surrounded by armies, then know that its desolation is near. Luke 21:20.

The whole nation from that time was strictly forbidden to set foot in the region around Jerusalem. This was by the formal decree and enactment of Hadrian, who commanded that they should not even look on their native soil from a distance. *Aristo of Pella (c. 140, E), 8.750.*

In such a way, therefore, did Daniel predict . . . that, after the passion of the Christ, this city had to be exterminated. *Tertullian (c. 197, W), 3.158.*

II. Jerusalem in prophecy

The Jerusalem above is free, which is the mother of us all. Gal. 4:26.

Then I, John, saw the holy city, New Jerusalem, coming down out of heaven from God, prepared as a bride adorned for her husband. Rev. 21:2.

[TRYPHO, A JEW:] "Do you really admit that this place, Jerusalem, is to be rebuilt? Do you expect your people to be gathered together, and made joyful with Christ, the patriarchs, and the prophets—both the men of our nation, and other proselytes who joined them before your Christ came?" . . . [JUSTIN'S REPLY:] I admitted to you formerly, that I and many others are of this opinion, and [believe] that such will take place. Of this, you assuredly are aware. On the other hand, I indicated to you that many who belong to the pure and pious faith, and are true Christians, think otherwise." *Justin Martyr (c. 160, E), 1.239.*

In the times of the kingdom, the earth will be called again [to its original state] by Christ. And Jerusalem will be rebuilt after the pattern of the Jerusalem above. *Irenaeus (c. 180, E/W), 1.565*

This will be (after the resurrection for a thousand years) in the divinely-built city of Jerusalem, which is "let down from heaven." The apostle also calls it "our mother from above." And, by declaring that our citizenship is in heaven, he indicates that it is really a city in heaven. Ezekiel had knowledge of this, and the Apostle John beheld it. *Tertullian (c. 207, W), 3.342*

As for you, you are a foreigner in this world, a citizen of Jerusalem, the city above. Our citizenship, the apostle says, is in heaven. *Tertullian (c. 212, W), 3.101.*

Whatever, therefore, is predicted of Jerusalem, and spoken of it, . . . we must understand the Scriptures to be speaking of the heavenly city, and of the whole territory included within the cities of the holy land. . . . If, therefore, the prophecies relating to Judea, Jerusalem, Israel,

Judah, and Jacob are not understood by us in a literal sense, . . . it will follow also that the predictions concerning Egypt and the Egyptians, Babylon and the Babylonians, Tyre and the Tyrians, Sidon and the Sidonians, or the other nations, are spoken not only of these physical Egyptians, Babylonians, Tyrians, and Sidonians, but also of their spiritual [counterparts]. *Origen (c. 225, E), 4.371, 372.*

We are not to take the interpretation of the promises recorded in the prophets—especially those of Isaiah—as though we were to look for their fulfillment in connection with the Jerusalem on earth. For this is fitting only for old wives or Jews. Certain remarkable things connected with the building of the temple and the restoration of the people from the captivity are spoken of as happening *after* the captivity and the destruction of the temple. Therefore, we must say that *we* are now the temple and the people who were carried captive but are to return to Judea and Jerusalem, and to be built with the precious stones of Jerusalem. *Origen (c. 228, E), 9.406; see also 1.566.*

SEE ALSO ESCHATOLOGY; ISRAEL OF GOD; JAMES, BROTHER OF THE LORD; JEW, JEWS; MILLENNIUM; MOTHER, SPIRITUAL.

JERUSALEM, NEW

SEE JERUSALEM (II. JERUSALEM IN PROPHECY).

JERUSALEM COUNCIL

It seemed to the Holy Spirit, and to us, to lay upon you no greater burden than these necessary things: that you abstain from things offered to idols, from blood, from things strangled, and from sexual immorality. Acts 15:28, 29.

The apostle says, "All other things buy out of the meat market, asking no questions," with the exception of the things mentioned in the catholic epistle of all the apostles "with the consent of the Holy Spirit." That epistle was written in the Acts of the Apostles and was conveyed to the faithful by the hands of Paul himself. For they indicated "that they must of necessity abstain from things offered to idols, from blood, from things strangled, and from fornication." *Clement of Alexandria (c. 195, E), 2.427.*

Since there was some obscurity about this matter [i.e., the Mosaic Law], and further explanation was needed, it seemed good to the apostles of Jesus, to the elders assembled from

Antioch, and to the Holy Spirit (as they themselves say) to write a letter to the Gentile believers. In this letter, they forbid them to partake only of those things from which they say it is necessary to abstain: namely, "things offered to idols, things strangled, and blood." *Origen (c. 248, E), 4.650.*

According to the decree and judgment of the apostles, the Gentiles who believe should not be circumcised. Here, also, is the epistle of the apostles themselves to those from among the Gentiles. *Pamphilus (c. 309, E), 6.167.*

SEE ALSO BLOOD (AS FOOD); MEAT SACRIFICED TO IDOLS.

JESUS, BROTHERS OF

SEE JESUS CHRIST (VI. BROTHERS OF JESUS).

JESUS CHRIST

I. Genealogy of Jesus

II. Two advents of Christ

III. Titles of Jesus

IV. Mediator between God and man

V. What did Jesus look like?

VI. Brothers of Jesus

I. Genealogy of Jesus

Eliud begot Eleazar, Eleazar begot Matthan, and Matthan begot Jacob. And Jacob begot Joseph the husband of Mary, of whom was born Jesus who is called Christ. Matt. 1:15, 16.

Now Jesus himself began his ministry at about thirty years of age, being (as was supposed) the son of Joseph, the son of Heli, the son of Matthat, the son of Levi, the son of Melchi, the son of Janna, the son of Joseph. Luke 3:23, 24.

If he had actually been the son of Joseph, He could not be either king or heir, according to Jeremiah. For Joseph is shown to be the son of Joachim and Jechoniah, as Matthew sets forth in his genealogy. Yet, Jechoniah and all his descendants were disinherited from the kingdom. *Irenaeus (c. 180, E/W), 1.453.*

Accordingly, neither of the evangelists [Matthew or Luke] is in error. For one of them reckons by nature, and the other by law. For the various generations—those descending from Solomon and those from Nathan—were very intermingled by the raising up of children to the childless, by second marriages, and by the raising up of seed. So the same persons are quite justly treated as belonging at one time to the one, and at another to the other. In other words, they are considered the sons of both their reputed fathers and their actual fathers. So both of these [genealogical] accounts are true. Both come down to Joseph—indeed, with considerable intricacy, but yet quite accurately. *Julius Africanus (c. 245, E), 6.126.*

Matthan, who was descended from Solomon, begat Jacob. Upon Matthan's dying, Melchi (who was descended from Nathan) begat Heli by the same wife. Therefore, Heli and Jacob are uterine brothers [i.e., having the same mother, but different fathers]. Upon Heli dying childless, Jacob raised up seed to him and begat Joseph. So Joseph was Jacob's son by nature, but the son of Heli by law. Thus, Joseph was the son of both. *Julius Africanus (c. 245, E), 6.127.*

In [Celsus's] finding fault with our Lord's genealogy, there are certain points that cause some difficulty even to Christians. Some put forth arguments against their correctness, because of the discrepancy between the genealogies. *Origen (c. 248, E), 4.444.*

Matthew strives to declare to us the genealogy of Mary, from whom Christ took flesh. *Victorinus (c. 280, W), 7.348; see also 1.155, probably spurious; extended discussion: 3.377–3.378.*

II. Two advents of Christ

He is despised and rejected by men, a Man of sorrows and acquainted with grief. Isa. 53:3.

Behold, he is coming with clouds, and every eye will see Him, and they also who pierced Him. And all the tribes of the earth will mourn because of Him. Rev. 1:7.

The prophets have announced two advents of Christ. In the first one, which has already past, He came as a dishonored and suffering man. However, in the second advent, according to prophecy, He will come from heaven with glory, accompanied by His angelic host. At that time, He will raise the bodies of all men who have lived. *Justin Martyr (c. 160, E), 1.180.*

It was prophesied by Jacob the patriarch that there would be two advents of Christ. In the first, He would suffer. And after His coming, there would be neither prophet nor king in your nation. *Justin Martyr (c. 160, E), 1.221.*

Two advents of Christ have been announced. In the first one, He is set forth as suffering, inglorious, dishonored, and crucified. However, in the other, He will come from heaven with glory, when the man of apostasy . . . speaks strange things. *Justin Martyr (c. 160, E), 1.253.*

It was declared by symbol, even in the time of Moses, that there would be two advents of this Christ. . . . [This is indicated] from the symbol of the goats presented for sacrifice during the fast. *Justin Martyr (c. 160, E), 1.254.*

All the prophets announced His two advents. . . . In the second one, He will come on the clouds, bringing on the Day which burns as a furnace. *Irenaeus (c. 180, E/W), 1.506.*

Two comings of Christ have been revealed to us: . . . a second one, which impends over the world, now near its close. In it, all the majesty of Deity will be unveiled. *Tertullian (c. 197, W), 3.35.*

Jesus is still sitting there at the right hand of the Father. He is man, yet also God. He is the last Adam; yet, He is also the primary Word. He is flesh and blood, yet purer than ours, and He will "descend in like manner as He ascended into heaven." That is, He will be the same both in substance and in form (as the angels affirmed). For He will even be recognized by those who pierced Him. *Tertullian (c. 197, W), 3.584.*

We affirm two characters of the Christ demonstrated by the prophets and as many advents. . . . In Zechariah, . . . Christ is described in a twofold garment, which prefigures his advents. First, He was clad in "sordid attire," which represents the lowliness of changeable and mortal flesh. . . . Next, the sordid garments were removed, and he was adorned with a robe down to his feet, along with a turban and a clean miter. This represents the second advent. *Tertullian (c. 197, W), 3.172.*

We maintain that the two conditions described by the prophets about Christ signify the same number of advents. The first one was to be in lowliness, when He was led as a sheep to be slain as a victim. . . . Now, these indications of humility fit His first coming. But the aspects of His majesty belong to His second advent. *Tertullian (c. 207, W), 3.326.*

The Scriptures indicate there will be two advents of our Lord and Savior. The one is

His first advent in the flesh, which took place without honor. . . . However, His second advent is foretold as being glorious, when He will come from heaven with the host of angels. *Hippolytus (c. 200, W), 5.213.*

III. Titles of Jesus

His name will be called Wonderful, Counselor, Mighty God, Everlasting Father, Prince of Peace. Isa. 9:6.

Christ the power of God and the wisdom of God. 1 Cor. 1:24.

He is the image of the invisible God, the firstborn over all creation. . . . And He is the head of the body, the church, who is the beginning, the firstborn from the dead, that in all things he may have the preeminence. Col. 1:16, 18.

I am the Alpha and the Omega, the Beginning and the End, the First and the Last. Rev. 22:13.

He desired to lead us to trust in His kindness and to esteem Him as our Nourisher, Father, Teacher, Counselor, Healer, Wisdom, Light, Honor, Glory, Power, and Life. *Letter to Diognetus (c. 125), 1.28.*

For Christ is King, Priest, God, Lord, Angel, and Man. *Justin Martyr (c. 160, E), 1.211.*

Again in Isaiah, if you have ears to hear it, God calls Christ "Jacob" and "Israel," speaking in parables. *Justin Martyr (c. 160, E), 1.261.*

Jesus is Himself in His own right, beyond all men who ever lived, God, Lord, King Eternal, and the Incarnate Word. . . . He is the Holy Lord, the Wonderful, the Counselor, the Beautiful in appearance, and the Mighty God. *Irenaeus (c. 180, E/W), 1.449.*

He is the circle of all powers rolled and united into one unity. For that reason, the Word is called the Alpha and the Omega, of whom alone the end becomes the beginning. . . . For that reason, also, to believe in Him and by Him, is to become a unity, being indissolubly united in Him. *Clement of Alexandria (c. 195, E), 2.438.*

[It is necessary] to inquire in what sense Christ is to be understood to be the Door, and in what sense He is the Vine, and why He is called the Word. *Origen (c. 228, E), 9.310.*

Our Lord is a Teacher and an Interpreter to those who are striving towards godliness. On the other hand, He is a Master to those servants who have the spirit of bondage to fear. *Origen (c. 228, E), 9.314.*

The Savior, then, is the First and the Last—not that He is not what lies between. *Origen (c. 228, E), 9.315.*

He is called His Servant by the God of all things, and Israel, and Light of the Gentiles. *Origen (c. 228, E), 9.316.*

How could He ever be the Advocate, and the Atonement, and the Propitiation without the power of God that makes an end of our weakness? *Origen (c. 228, E), 9.317.*

His Son is God the Word, and Wisdom, and Truth, and Righteousness, and everything else that the sacred Scriptures call Him when speaking of God. *Origen (c. 248, E), 4.541.*

Also, Paul wrote to the Colossians: "Who is the image of the invisible God, the First-Born of every creature." . . . In the Apocalypse, too: "I am the Alpha and Omega, the beginning and the end." . . . That He is also both the Wisdom and the Power of God, Paul proves in his first Epistle to the Corinthians: . . . "Christ, the Power of God and the Wisdom of God." *Cyprian (c. 250, W), 5.516.*

Christ is called a Sheep and a Lamb who was to be slain. . . . Christ is also called a Stone. . . . He Himself is both Judge and King. *Cyprian (c. 250, W), 5.521–5.527.*

The Champion and Savior of our souls is His First-Born Word, the Maker and Ruler of all things. . . . For He Himself is the Truth, the Wisdom, and the Power of the Father of the universe. *Gregory Thaumaturgus (c. 255, E), 6.24.*

His name, which the supreme Father gave Him from the beginning, is known to no one but Himself. For He has one name among the angels, but another among men. Among men, He is called Jesus. For Christ is not a proper name, but a *title* of power and dominion. In fact, the Jews were accustomed to call their kings by this title. . . . And as now the robe of purple is a sign of the assumption of royal dignity among the Romans, so with [the Jews] the anointing with the holy oil conferred the title and power of king. . . . On this account, we call Him Christ, that is, the Anointed. In Hebrew he is called the Messiah. *Lactantius (c. 304–313, W), 7.106.*

He was never called Emmanuel, but Jesus. In Latin, He is called Saving, or Savior, because He comes to bring salvation to all nations. So by this name [of Emmanuel], the prophet declared that God incarnate was about to come to men. For Emmanuel means "God with us." Because He was born of a virgin, men should confess that God was with them—that is, on the earth and in mortal flesh. *Lactantius (c. 304–313, W), 7.110.*

He is the Deliverer, Judge, Avenger, King, and God—whom we call Christ. *Lactantius (c. 304–313, W), 7.215; extended discussion: 5.515–5.527.*

IV. Mediator between God and man

For there is one God and one Mediator between God and men, the man Christ Jesus. 1 Tim. 2:5.

He is the Mediator of the new covenant. Heb. 9:15.

Unless man had been joined to God, he could never have become a partaker of incorruptibility. For it was incumbent upon the Mediator between God and men to bring both parties to friendship and harmony, through His relationship to both. He presented man to God, and He revealed God to man. *Irenaeus (c. 180, E/W), 1.448.*

When, then, you cast yourself at your brethren's knees, you are handling Christ. You are entreating Christ. In like manner, when they shed tears over you, it is Christ who suffers, Christ who prays the Father for mercy. *Tertullian (c. 203, W), 3.664.*

A man, once a sinner, but afterwards purified from the stains thereof by the Word of God, was obligated to offer unto God in the temple a gift—even prayer and thanksgiving in the church. This is through Christ Jesus, who is the Universal Priest of the Father. *Tertullian (c. 207, W), 3.357.*

We seek a Being who is intermediate between all created things and God—a Mediator. This is whom the apostle Paul calls the "First-Born of every creature." *Origen (c. 225, E), 4.281.*

We are lost in reverential wonder at Jesus, who has recalled our minds from all earthly things . . . and elevated them to honor the God who is over all, with prayers and a righteous life. We offer this to Him as being an Intermediary between the nature of the uncreated and that of all created things. He bestows upon us the benefits that come from the Father and

who, as High Priest, conveys our prayers to the supreme God. *Origen (c. 248, E), 4.478.*

We offer our petitions to the God of the universe through His Only-Begotten Son. To the Son, we first present them. We beseech Him, as "the propitiation for our sins," and as our High Priest, to offer our desires, sacrifices, and prayers to the Most High. Our faith, therefore, is directed to God through His Son. *Origen (c. 248, E), 4.643, 644.*

Our duty is to pray to the Most High God alone, and to the Only-Begotten—the First-Born of the whole creation—and to ask him as our High Priest to present the prayers that ascend to Him from us. That is, we ask Him to send them to his God and our God, to His Father and the Father of those who direct their lives according to his Word. *Origen (c. 248, E), 4.649.*

He who is declared as being made the "Mediator between God and man" is revealed to have associated in Himself both God and man. *Novatian (c. 235, W), 5.632.*

Christ is the High Priest of His Father, who presents our prayers to Him. *Julius Africanus (c. 245, E), 6.125.*

In His second birth, which was in the flesh, He was born of a virgin's womb without the agency of a father. So, bearing a middle substance between God and man, He is able, as it were, to take by the hand this frail and weak nature of ours, and raise it to immortality. *Lactantius (c. 304–313, W), 7.112.*

Neither may we address ourselves to Almighty God, but only through Christ. *Apostolic Constitutions (compiled c. 390, E), 7.411.*

V. What did Jesus look like?

He has no form or comeliness; and when we see Him, there is no beauty that we should desire Him. Isa 53:2.

Our Lord Jesus Christ . . . did not come in the pomp of pride or arrogance, although He might have done so. Rather, He came in a lowly condition, as the Holy Spirit had declared regarding Him. For he says . . . "He has no form nor glory. Yes, we saw Him, and He had no form nor comeliness. But His form was without eminence, yes, deficient in comparison with the [ordinary] form of men." *Clement of Rome (c. 96, W), 1.9.*

Our Christ appeared without comeliness and inglorious. *Justin Martyr (c. 160, E), 1.241.*

"There was not in Him attractiveness or glory. We saw Him, and he had no attractiveness or grace. Rather, His manner was unhonored, deficient in comparison with the sons of men." *Tertullian (c. 197, W), 3.172.*

That first [advent] was in lowliness, when he . . . was not handsome to look upon. *Tertullian (c. 207, W), 3.326; see also 1.244, 1.249, 3.337.*

VI. Brothers of Jesus

While He was still talking to the multitudes, behold, His mother and brothers stood outside, seeking to speak with Him. Then one said to Him, "Look, Your mother and Your brothers are standing outside, seeking to speak with You." Matt. 12:46–50.

Is not His mother called Mary? And His brothers, James, Joses, Simon, and Judas? Matt. 13:55.

Do we have no right to take along a believing wife, as do also the other apostles, the brothers of the Lord, and Cephas? 1 Cor. 9:5.

There still survived some of the kindred of the Lord. These were the grandsons of Jude, who according to the flesh was called His brother. These were informed against, as belonging to the family of David, and Evocatus brought them before Domitian Caesar. For that emperor dreaded the advent of Christ, as Herod had done. *Hegesippus (c. 170), 8.763.*

Jude, who wrote the catholic Epistle, was the brother of the sons of Joseph. And he was very religious. Although experiencing the near relationship of the Lord, yet he did not say that he himself was His brother. But what did he say? "Jude, a servant of Jesus Christ"—of Him as Lord; but "the brother of James." For this was true. Jude was his brother, through Joseph. *Clement of Alexandria (c. 195, E), 2.573.*

"Who is my mother or my brothers?" . . . He was justly indignant, that persons so very near to Him "stood *outside,*" while strangers were *inside* hanging on His words. This is particularly so since his mother and brothers wanted to call Him away from the solemn work he had in hand. He did not so much *deny* them as *disavow* them. Therefore, to the previous question, "Who is my mother, and who are my brothers?" He added the answer, "No one but those who hear my words and do them." He thereby transferred the names of blood relationship to others whom He judged to be more closely related to Him by reason of their faith. . . . It was no great matter that He preferred people of faith to his own kindred, who did not possess that faith. *Tertullian (c. 207, W), 3.378.*

There are some grounds for thinking that Christ's answer [about his mother and brothers] denies His mother and brothers for the present. Even Apelles might learn this. For "the Lord's brothers had not yet believed in Him." This is contained in the Gospel—which was published before Marcion's time. There is also a lack of evidence of His mother's adherence to Him. In contrast, the Marthas and the other Marys were in constant attendance on Him. Indeed, in this very passage, the unbelief [of his family] is evident. Jesus was teaching the way of life, preaching the kingdom of God . . . but, meanwhile, while strangers were intent on Him, His very nearest relatives were absent. . . . They preferred to interrupt Him, and they wished to call Him away from His great work. *Tertullian (c. 210, W), 3.528.*

In whatever sense He adopted as His own those who adhered to Him, in that did He deny as His those who kept aloof from Him. . . . How strange, then, would it certainly have been, if, while he was teaching others not to esteem mother, or father, or brothers, as highly as the Word of God, He Himself were to leave the Word of God as soon as His mother and brothers were announced to Him. He denied his parents, then, in the sense in which He has taught us to deny ours—for God's work. But there is also another view of the case: In the denied mother, there is a figure of the synagogue. In the unbelieving brothers, there is a type of the Jews. In the person [of Christ's nearest kin], Israel remained outside. On the other hand, the new disciples who kept close to Christ within—hearing and believing Him—represented the church. For He called the church "mother" in a preferable sense and a worthier brotherhood, with the repudiation of the fleshly relationship. *Tertullian (c. 210, W), 3.529.*

Some say, basing it on a tradition in the *Gospel According to Peter* (as it is entitled), or the *Book of James* [i.e., the spurious *Protevangelium of James*], that the brothers of Jesus were sons of Joseph by a former wife, whom he married before Mary. *Origen (c. 245, E), 9.424.*

The messenger came inopportunely to my Lord Jesus Christ and brought the report about His mother and His brothers unseasonably. For the messenger came just when Christ was fighting against ills that had attacked the very fortress of the heart and when He was healing those who for a long time had been under the power of diverse infirmities. . . . Truly that man might have [deservedly] met with a rebuke like the one pronounced on Peter. . . . However, the hearing of the name of His mother and His brothers drew forth His clemency. *Disputation of Archelaus and Manes (c. 320, E), 6.225; extended discussion: 6.125–6.127.*

SEE ALSO BIRTH OF JESUS; CHRIST, DIVINITY OF; INCARNATION; JAMES, BROTHER OF THE LORD; JUDE; LOGOS; MARY; MESSIANIC PROPHECIES; PARABLES OF JESUS; SECOND COMING OF CHRIST; THEOPHANIES; TRINITY; WISDOM; WORD OF GOD (CHRIST).

JEW, JEWS

I. Description and beliefs

II. Persecution of Christians

III. Rejection by God

IV. Restoration of Israel?

I. Description and beliefs

The Jews imitate God by the philanthropy that prevails among them. For they have compassion on the poor. They release the captives, bury the dead, and do other things like these that are acceptable before God. . . . However, they, too, have erred from true knowledge. In their imagination, they think that it is God whom they serve. Actually, by their type of worship, they render their service to the angels and not to God. I am speaking of their celebrations of Sabbaths, the beginning of the months, the feasts of unleavened bread, the great fast, fasting, circumcision, and the purification of meats. However, they do not observe these things perfectly. *Aristides (c. 125, E), 9.275, 276.*

Their scrupulosity concerning meats, their superstition as respects the Sabbaths, their boasting about circumcision, and their fancies about fasting and the new moons, . . . are utterly ridiculous and unworthy of notice. *Letter to Diognetus (c. 125–200), 1.26.*

[TRYPHO THE JEW:] We [Jews] all expect that Christ will be a man [born] of men. We believe that Elijah, when he comes, will anoint him. *Justin Martyr (c. 160, E), 1.219.*

To this day, in short, it is Christ that they are looking for, not Jesus. And they interpret Elijah to be Christ, rather than Jesus. *Tertullian (c. 207, W), 3.334.*

The doctrine among all Jews on the subject of religion is fourfold: theological, natural, moral, and ceremonial. They affirm that there is one God and that He is Creator and Lord of the universe. They believe that He has formed all these glorious works that had no previous existence. . . . They also believe that there are angels, and that these were brought into being for ministering unto the creation. They also say that there is a sovereign Spirit who always continues beside God for glory and praise. . . . The ceremonial service that has been adapted to divine [worship] in a dignified manner has been practiced among them with the highest degree of elaboration. It is easy for those who so desire to ascertain the superiority of their rituals [over the pagans]—provided they read the book that furnishes information on these points. With solemnity and sanctity, they offer unto God the first-fruits of the gifts bestowed by Him for the use and enjoyment of men. . . .

All of them alike expect the Messiah, since the Law and the Prophets preached beforehand that he was about to be present. However, inasmuch as the Jews did not recognize the period of His advent, there remains the supposition that the declarations concerning His coming have not been fulfilled. . . . They say that [the Messiah's] birth will be from the stock of David. But he will not be from a virgin and the Holy Spirit, but from a woman and a man. . . . And they allege that this one will be king over them—a warlike and powerful individual. After having gathered together the entire people of the Jews, and having done battle with all the nations, he will restore Jerusalem the royal city for them. And into this city he will collect together their entire race and bring it back once more into the ancient customs. *Hippolytus (c. 225, W), 5.138.*

For instance, now that the Romans rule, and the Jews pay the half-shekel to them, what great power the ethnarch has, by the concession of Caesar. So that I, who have experienced it, know that the ethnarch differs little from a true king. Private trials are held according to the

Law, and some are condemned to death. And though there is not full license for this, still it is not done without the knowledge of the ruler. I learned this and was convinced of it when I spent much time in the country of that people. *Origen (c. 240, E), 4.392.*

A Jew, however, will not admit that any prophet used the expression that the "Son of God" would come. For the term they use is that the "Christ of God" will come. Indeed, many times they directly question us about the "Son of God," saying that no such Being exists or was ever the subject of prophecy. *Origen (c. 248, E), 4.418.*

On account of their unbelief and the other insults that they heaped upon Jesus, the Jews will not only suffer more than others in that judgment that is believed to impend over the world, but have even already endured such sufferings. For what nation is in exile from their own metropolis and from the place sacred to the worship of their fathers, except the Jews alone. *Origen (c. 248, E), 4.433.*

So far as can be accomplished among mortals, everything that was not of advantage to the human race was withheld from the Jews. And only those things that are useful were bestowed upon them. For this reason, they had no gymnastic contests, nor dramas, nor horse races. There were no women among them who sold their beauty to anyone who wished to have sexual relations without offspring—thereby casting contempt upon the nature of human generation.... And how great was the advantage that they enjoyed in being instructed almost from their birth (at least, as soon as they could speak) in the immortality of the soul, in the existence of courts of justice under the earth, and in the rewards provided for those who have lived righteous lives. *Origen (c. 248, E), 4.562.*

Although [the pagan] Celsus will not admit it, the Jews are nevertheless possessed of a wisdom superior not only to that of the multitude, but also to those who have the appearance of philosophers. *Origen (c. 248, E), 4.562.*

Up to that time, the genealogies of the Hebrews had been registered in the public archives—even those that were traced back to the proselytes.... However, Herod, knowing that the lineage of the Israelites contributed nothing to him, and goaded by the conscious-

ness of his ignoble birth, burned the registers of their families. This he did, thinking that he would appear to be of noble birth. For no one else could trace back his descent by the public register to the patriarchs. *Julius Africanus (c. 245, E), 6.127.*

Let it shame the Jews that they do not perceive the deep things of the Scriptures. For they think that only outward things are contained in the Law and the Prophets. Being intent upon earthly things, they esteem the riches of the world more than the wealth of the soul. *Methodius (c. 290, E), 6.345.*

II. Persecution of Christians

Then [Herod] killed James the brother of John with the sword. And because he saw that it pleased the Jews, he proceeded further to seize Peter also. Acts 12:2, 3.

Now when the Gentiles heard this, they were glad and glorified the word of the Lord.... But the Jews stirred up the devout and prominent women and the chief men of the city, raised up persecution against Paul and Barnabas, and expelled them from their region. Acts 13:48, 50.

With these sayings they could scarcely restrain the multitudes from sacrificing to them. Then Jews from Antioch and Iconium came there; and having persuaded the multitudes, they stoned Paul. Acts 14:18, 19.

The multitudes immediately gathering together wood and fagots out of the shops and baths [to burn Polycarp]. As was their custom, the Jews especially were eager to assist them in it. *Martyrdom of Polycarp (c. 135, E), 1.42.*

[The Jews] kill and punish us whenever they have the power, as you can well believe. For in the Jewish war that recently raged, Barchocheba, the leader of the Jewish revolt, gave orders that Christians alone should be led to cruel punishments. *Justin Martyr (c. 160, E), 1.173.*

The circumcision according to the flesh, which is from Abraham, was given for a sign. It was given so that you [Jews] may be separated from other nations, and from us. It was also given so that you alone may suffer that which you now justly suffer.... Accordingly, these things have happened to you in fairness and justice, for you have slain the Just One, and His prophets before Him. Now, you reject those who hope in Him, ... cursing in your synagogues those who believe on Christ.... For other nations have not inflicted on us and on Christ this wrong to such an extent as you have. *Justin Martyr (c. 160, E), 1.202, 203.*

You curse in your synagogues all those who are called from Him Christians. . . . And in addition to all this, we pray for you that Christ may have mercy upon you. *Justin Martyr (c. 160, E), 1.247.*

Even when your city is captured and your land ravaged, you do not repent. Rather, you dare to utter curses on Him and all who believe in Him. Nevertheless, we do not hate you. *Justin Martyr (c. 160, E), 1.253.*

The crowd believed this infamous Jew. For what other set of men have been the seed-plot of all the attacks against us? *Tertullian (c. 197, W), 3.123; see also 1.265, 266.*

III. Rejection by God

Do not think to say to yourselves, "We have Abraham as our father." For I say to you that God is able to raise up children to Abraham from these stones. Matt. 3:9.

I say to you, the kingdom of God will be taken from you and given to a nation bearing the fruits of it. Matt. 21:43.

For he is not a Jew who is one outwardly, nor is that circumcision which is outward in the flesh; but he is a Jew who is one inwardly. Rom. 2:28, 29.

They are not all Israel who are of Israel, nor are they all children because they are the seed of Abraham. Rom. 9:6, 7.

There is neither Jew nor Greek, . . . for you are all one in Christ Jesus. Gal. 3:28.

Now we, brethren, as Isaac was, are children of promise. But, as he who was born according to the flesh then persecuted him who was born according to the Spirit, even so it is now. Gal. 4:28.

I will make those of the synagogue of Satan, who say they are Jews and are not, but lie—indeed I will make them come and worship before your feet, and to know that I have loved you. Rev. 3:9.

Their covenant was broken so that the covenant of the beloved Jesus could be sealed upon our heart, in the hope that flows from believing in Him. *Barnabas (c. 70–130, E), 1.139.*

Trypho [a Jew] remarked, "What is this you say? That none of us will inherit anything on the holy mountain of God?" And I replied, "I do not say so. However, it is true that those who have persecuted and do persecute Christ, if they do not repent, will not inherit anything on the holy mountain. But the Gentiles, who have believed on Him, and have repented of the sins which they have committed, they will receive the inheritance along with the patriarchs and the prophets." *Justin Martyr (c. 160, E), 1.207.*

They beguile themselves and you. For they suppose that the everlasting kingdom will be assuredly given to those of the dispersion who are of Abraham after the flesh—even though they are sinners, are faithless, and are disobedient towards God. However, the Scriptures have proved this is not the case. . . . Otherwise, our Lord . . . would not have said, "They will come from the east, and from the west, and will sit down with Abraham, Isaac, and Jacob in the kingdom of heaven. But the children of the kingdom will be cast out into outer darkness." *Justin Martyr (c. 160, E), 1.269.*

This is He who was put to death. And where was He put to death? In the midst of Jerusalem. By whom? By Israel. . . . O Israel, transgressor of the Law, why have you committed this new iniquity? *Melito (c. 170, E), 8.757.*

The church alone offers this pure oblation to the Creator, offering to Him from His own creation, with thanksgiving. But the Jews do not offer in this manner. For their hands are full of blood, because they have not received the Word. *Irenaeus (c. 180, E/W), 1.485.*

Inasmuch as the former [the Jews] have rejected the Son of God, and cast Him out of the vineyard when they slew Him, God has justly rejected them. He has given to the Gentiles (outside the vineyard) the fruits of its cultivation. *Irenaeus (c. 180, E/W), 1.515.*

"The Lord was not known by the people" who erred. For they were not circumcised in understanding. Their darkness was not enlightened, they knew not God, and they denied the Lord. So they forfeited the place of the true Israel. *Clement of Alexandria (c. 195, E), 2.256.*

You Romans once honored the God of Judea with victims. You honored Judea's temple with gifts, and its people with treaties. It would never have been beneath your scepter but for that last and crowning offense against God, in rejecting and crucifying Christ. *Tertullian (c. 197, W), 3.40.*

Thus has the "lesser" people—that is, the elder people—overcome the "greater" people. For [the lesser] have acquired the grace of divine favor, from which Israel has been divorced. *Tertullian (c. 197, W), 3.152.*

Let the Jews recognize their own fate—a fate which was constantly foretold as destined to occur after the advent of the Christ. This fate was on account of the impiety with which they despised and slew Him. . . . Thereafter, God's grace desisted among them. And "the clouds were commanded not to rain a shower upon the vineyard of Sorek,"—the clouds being celestial benefits. *Tertullian (c. 197, W), 3.171.*

It is manifest that it is on Christ's account that these things have befallen the Jews. *Tertullian (c. 197, W), 3.172.*

The Jews had formerly been in covenant with God. But being afterwards cast off on account of their sins, they began to be without God. *Tertullian (c. 197, W), 3.247.*

Although Israel were to daily wash all his limbs over, yet he is never clean. His hands, at any event, are ever unclean, eternally dyed with the blood of the prophets and of the Lord Himself. *Tertullian (c. 198, W), 3.685.*

You [Marcionites] join the Jews in denying that their Christ has come. Accordingly, recollect what is that end which they were predicted as about to bring upon themselves after the time of Christ—for their impiety in both rejecting and slaying Him. . . . And so in this manner "the Law and the Prophets were until John," but the dews of divine grace were withdrawn from the nation. After John's time, their madness still continued, and the name of the Lord was blasphemed by them. . . . And in the interval from Tiberius to Vespasian, they did not learn repentance. Therefore, "their land has become desolate, their cities are burned with fire, and strangers are devouring their country before their own eyes." *Tertullian (c. 207, W), 3.341.*

Inquire concerning the Jews in the books of Flavius Josephus, . . . and you will know that by their wickedness, they deserved this fortune. *Mark Minucius Felix (c. 200, W), 4.194.*

However, He does not say that the Jews are to be cut off. For that reason, their race still subsists and the succession of their children is continued. . . . However, they continue only as those who have been rejected and cast down from the honor of which of old they were deemed worthy by God. *Hippolytus (c. 205, W), 5.202.*

"Let their eyes be darkened, that they may not see." And surely you have been darkened in the eyes of your soul with a darkness utter and everlasting. For now that the true light has arisen, you [Jews] wander as in the night. You stumble on places with no roads and fall headlong. For you have forsaken the Way who says, "I am the way." Furthermore, hear this yet more serious word: "And their back do you bend always." This means, in order that they may be slaves to the nations—not four hundred and thirty years as in Egypt, nor seventy as in Babylon—but, he says, bend them to perpetual servitude. *Hippolytus (c. 205, W), 5.220.*

I produce now the prophecy of Solomon, which speaks of Christ, and announces clearly and specifically things concerning the Jews. And those are things that not only are befalling them at the present time, but that will also befall them in the future age. For those things are on account of the disobedience and audacity which they exhibited toward the Prince of Life. *Hippolytus (c. 205, W), 5.220.*

Perhaps those who are now Israelites—not having lived worthily of their heritage—will be deprived of their rank, being changed, as it were, from vessels of honor into those of dishonor. *Origen (c. 225, E), 4.327.*

And His citizens who did not wish Him to reign over them when He was a citizen in the world in respect to His incarnation are perhaps Israel who disbelieved Him and perhaps also the Gentiles who disbelieved Him. *Origen (c. 245, E), 9.503.*

Christ . . . did not put away His former wife, so to speak (that is, the former synagogue) for any other cause than that his wife committed fornication. For she was made an adulteress by the evil one. Along with him, she plotted against her husband and slew Him. . . . It was she, therefore, who herself revolted. *Origen (c. 245, E), 9.506.*

We will say that the mother of the people separated herself from Christ, her husband, without having received the bill of divorcement. However, afterwards, when there was found in her an unseemly thing, and she did not find favor in his sight, the bill of divorcement was written out for her. For when the new covenant called those of the Gentiles to the house of Him who had cast away his former wife, it virtually gave the bill of divorcement to her. . . . A sign that she has received the bill of divorcement is this: that Jerusalem was destroyed along with what they called the sanctuary. *Origen (c. 245, E), 9.507.*

It should be noted that the words are not "let this cup depart from Me." Rather, the whole expression is marked by a tone of piety and reverence: "Father, *if it is possible,* let this cup depart from Me." I know, indeed, that there is another explanation of this passage to the following effect: The Savior foresaw the sufferings that the Jewish people and the city of Jerusalem were to undergo in punishment for the wicked deeds that the Jews had dared to perpetrate upon Him. So He said this from no other motive than that of the purest love towards them and from a desire that they might escape the impending calamities. *Origen (c. 248, E), 4.442.*

We . . . take our stand against the Jews on those Scriptures that they believe to be divine, which show that He who was spoken of in prophecy *has* come and that they have been abandoned on account of the greatness of their sins. *Origen (c. 248, E), 4.508.*

As a nation wholly given to sin, when it became necessary for them to be brought back by their sufferings to their God, they were abandoned—sometimes for a longer period, sometimes for a shorter period. Finally, in the time of the Romans, having committed the greatest of sins in putting Jesus to death, they were completely deserted. *Origen (c. 248, E), 4.511.*

Since the coming of Christ, no prophets have arisen among the Jews. For they have confessedly been abandoned by the Holy Spirit because of their impiety towards God and towards Him of whom their prophets spoke. *Origen (c. 248, E), 4.614.*

The vineyard of the Lord of hosts was the house of Israel. But Christ taught and showed that the people of the Gentiles should succeed them and that by the merit of faith we should subsequently attain to the place that the Jews had lost. *Cyprian (c. 250, W), 5.361.*

"You have forsaken the Lord. You have provoked the Holy One of Israel to anger." In repudiation of these [Jews], when we Christians pray, we say "*Our* Father." For He has begun to be ours. But he has ceased to be the Father of the Jews, who have forsaken Him. *Cyprian (c. 250, W), 5.450.*

There is need of continual prayer and supplication so that we do not fall away from the heavenly kingdom, as the Jews fell away, to whom this promise had first been given. *Cyprian (c. 250, W), 5.451.*

"But the children of the kingdom will be cast out into outer darkness. There will be weeping and gnashing of teeth." He shows that the Jews were previously children of the kingdom—so long as they continued also to be children of God. However, after the name of the Father ceased to be recognized among them, the kingdom also ceased. *Cyprian (c. 250, W), 5.451.*

God had determined, as the last time drew near, to send from heaven a great Leader. He would reveal to foreign nations the thing that was taken away from a treacherous and ungrateful people. *Lactantius (c. 304–313, W), 7.102.*

Unless they did this [i.e., repent], laid aside their vanities, and returned to their God, it would come to pass that He would change His covenant. That is, He would bestow the inheritance of eternal life upon foreign nations. And He would collect to Himself a more faithful people out of those who were aliens by birth. . . . Because of these impieties of theirs, He cast them off forever. Therefore, He ceased to send prophets to them. Rather, He commanded His own Son . . . to descend from heaven so that He could transfer the sacred religion of God to the Gentiles—that is, to those who were ignorant of God. He did this so that He could teach them righteousness, which the unfaithful people had cast aside. He had long before forewarned that He would do this. The prophet Malachi shows this, saying: "The Lord says, 'I have no pleasure in you, and I will not accept an offering from your hands. For from the rising of the sun even unto its setting, my name will be great among the Gentiles.'" *Lactantius (c. 304–313, W), 7.109.*

Since God is kind and merciful to His people, He sent Him to those very persons whom He detested, that He might not close the way of salvation against them forever. Rather, He desired to give them a free opportunity to follow God. So, they could either gain the reward of life if they followed Him . . . or else they would incur the penalty of death by their own fault if they rejected their King. *Lactantius (c. 304–313, W), 7.110.*

On account of His humility, they did not recognize their God. So they entered into the detestable plan of depriving Him of life—He who had come to give them life. *Lactantius (c. 304–313, W), 7.118.*

Having suffered death for us, Christ made us heirs of His everlasting kingdom—the people of the Jews being deprived and disinherited. . . . However, it is plain that the house of Judah does not signify the Jews, whom He cast off. Rather, it signifies us, who have been called by Him out of the Gentiles and have succeeded to their place by adoption. And they are called sons of the Jews. *Lactantius (c. 304–313, W), 7.123.*

But I will have a separate chapter against the Jews, in which I will convict them of error and guilt. *Lactantius (c. 304–313, W), 7.195.*

The wicked synagogue is now cast off by the Lord God. He has rejected His own house. As He says: "I have forsaken my house; I have left my inheritance." *Apostolic Constitutions (compiled c. 390, E), 7.451; see also 7.108.*

IV. Restoration of Israel?

For if their being cast away is the reconciling of the world, what will their acceptance be but life from the dead? . . . For I do not desire, brethren, that you should be ignorant of this mystery, lest you should be wise in your own opinion, that hardening in part has happened to Israel until the fullness of the Gentiles has come in. And so all Israel will be saved. Rom. 11:15, 25, 26.

You [Jews] deceive yourselves. For you think that because you are the seed of Abraham after the flesh, you will fully inherit the good things announced to be bestowed by God through Christ. *Justin Martyr (c. 160, E), 1.216.*

[SAID IN SARCASM TO THE MARCIONITES:] Besides, your [Marcionite] Christ promises to the Jews their primitive condition, with the recovery of their country. And after this life's course is over, He promises rest in Hades in Abraham's bosom. Oh, most excellent God! He restores in amnesty that which He took away in wrath! Oh, what a God is yours! . . . As for the restoration of Judea, even the Jews themselves

(induced by the names of places and countries) hope for it just as it is described. However, it would be tedious to state at length how the figurative interpretation is spiritually applicable to Christ and His church. *Tertullian (c. 207, W), 3.342.*

"Jerusalem was to be trodden down by the Gentiles, until the times of the Gentiles would be fulfilled"—meaning, of course, those who were to be chosen of God and gathered in with the remnant of Israel. *Tertullian (c. 210, W), 3.560.*

[CONCERNING THE PARABLE OF THE PRODIGAL SON:] It will be no speech of a Jew to the Father: "Behold, how many years I have served you and your precepts I have never transgressed." For when has the Jew *not* been a transgressor of the Law? . . . Likewise, it will be no speech of the Father to the Jew: "You are always with me and everything I have is yours." For the Jew is declared to be an apostate son. . . . He has had every tasty morsel torn from his throat, not to mention the very land of paternal promise. As a result, at the present day, the Jew (no less than the younger son) is a beggar in alien territory, having squandered God's substance. Even until now, the Jew serves . . . the rulers of this world. . . . Much more aptly would the Christian have fit the elder son and the Jew the younger son. . . . However, the conclusion would preclude this interpretation. For it would be fitting for the Christian to rejoice at the restoration of Israel, and not to grieve—if it is true that our whole hope is intimately entwined with the remaining expectation of Israel. *Tertullian (c. 212, W), 4.82.*

As there is a bodily race of Jews, so also is there a race of those who are Jews inwardly—the soul having acquired this nobility for certain mysterious reasons. Now, there are many prophecies that predict things regarding Israel and Judah, concerning what is about to befall them. Do not these promises that are written concerning them need a mystical interpretation? For they are rather lowly in expression, manifesting no elevation [of thought] or anything worthy of the promise of God? *Origen (c. 225, E), 4.370.*

It says that the former husband who sent her away will not be able to turn back and take her to be a wife to himself after she has been defiled. For such a thing "is an abomination." . . . But these things will not seem to be consistent with this: "If the fullness of the Gentiles comes in, all Israel will be saved." However, consider if it can be said . . . that He who gives the law has power to give it "until a time of reformation" and to change the law. *Origen (c. 245, E), 9.508, 509.*

There is one fact that proves that Jesus was something divine and sacred. It is this: the Jews have suffered severe calamities now for a lengthened time on His account. And we say with confidence that they will never be restored to their former condition. For they committed a crime of the most unholy kind. *Origen (c. 248, E), 4.506.*

It is by the fall [of the Jews] that salvation has come to the Gentiles . . . until the fullness of the Gentiles comes. And after that, the whole of Israel . . . may be saved. *Origen (c. 248, E), 4.610.*

The Jews both confess and hope for His second advent. But they hope in vain. For He must return to the bewilderment of those for whom He had come before. For those who treated Him impiously with violence in His humiliation, will experience Him in His power as a conqueror. God repaying them, they will suffer all those things that they read and do not understand. For, being polluted with all sin, and moreover sprinkled with the blood of the Holy One, they were devoted to eternal punishment by that very One on whom they laid wicked hands. *Lactantius (c. 304–313, W), 7.195.*

SEE ALSO ANTICHRIST; BAPTISM, JEWISH; CAPTIVITY, THE; DAN, TRIBE OF; ESCHATOLOGY; ESSENES; ISRAEL OF GOD; JEWISH CHRISTIANITY; JOSEPHUS; LAW, MOSAIC; PHARISEES; SADDUCEES; SYNAGOGUE; TABERNACLE; TEMPLE, JEWISH.

JEWELRY

The daughters of Zion are haughty, and walk with outstretched necks and wanton eyes, walking and mincing as they go, making a jingling with their feet. . . . In that day the Lord will take away the finery: the jingling anklets, the scarves, and the crescents; the pendants, the bracelets, and the veils; the headdresses, the leg ornaments, and the headbands; the perfume boxes, the charms, and the rings. Isa. 3:16–21.

Do not let your beauty be that outward adorning of arranging the hair, of wearing gold, or of putting on fine apparel. But let it be the hidden person of the heart. 1 Pet. 3:3.

The woman [Babylon the Great] was arrayed in purple and scarlet, and adorned with gold and precious stones and pearls. Rev. 17:4.

Such is the case with the stones that silly women wear fastened to chains and set in necklaces. *Clement of Alexandria (c. 195, E), 2.267.*

These women, who do not comprehend the symbolism of Scripture, gape all they can for jewels. And they use the astounding argument: "Why can I not use what God has exhibited?" *Clement of Alexandria (c. 195, E), 2.268*

How much wiser to spend money on human beings, than on jewels and gold. . . . For women should be adorned within, and show the inner woman beautiful. *Clement of Alexandria (c. 195, E), 2.268.*

Let not their ears be pierced, contrary to nature, in order to attach to them earrings. *Clement of Alexandria (c. 195, E), 2.270.*

Love of dainties and love of wine, though great vices, are not of such magnitude as is fondness for finery. "A full table and repeated cups" are enough to satisfy gluttony. But to those who are fond of gold, purple, and jewels, neither the gold that is above the earth nor below it is sufficient. *Clement of Alexandria (c. 195, E), 2.273.*

To such an extent, then, has luxury advanced, that not only is the female sex deranged about this frivolous pursuit, but men also are infected with the disease. *Clement of Alexandria (c. 195, E), 2.275.*

The wearing of gold and the use of softer clothing is to be entirely prohibited. Irrational impulses must be curbed. *Clement of Alexandria (c. 195, E), 2.284.*

The Word prohibits us from doing violence to nature by boring the lobes of the ears. *Clement of Alexandria (c. 195, E), 2.285.*

Women who wear gold seem to me to be afraid, lest, if one strip them of their jewelry, they would be mistaken for servants, without their adornments. . . . But there are circumstances in which this strictness may be relaxed. For allowance must sometimes be made in favor of those women who have not been fortunate in falling in with chaste husbands. So they adorn themselves in order to please their husbands. But let desire for the admiration of their husbands alone be proposed as their aim. *Clement of Alexandria (c. 195, E), 2.285.*

Where is that happiness of married life, ever so desirable, that distinguished our earlier manners? For the result of it was that for about 600 years there was not among us [Romans] a single divorce. Nowadays, women have every member of their bodies heavy laden with gold. *Tertullian (c. 197, W), 3.23.*

[Was it] God who introduced the fashion of finely-cut wounds for the ears? Did he set so high a value upon the tormenting of His own work and the tortures of innocent infancy? For they learn to suffer with their earliest breath, in order that from those scars of the body . . . should hang I know not what. *Tertullian (c. 198, W), 4.23.*

Why are the necks oppressed and hidden by outlandish stones? The prices of these—without any workmanship—exceed the entire estate of many persons. *Novatian (c. 235, W), 5.591, formerly attributed to Cyprian.*

Moreover, earrings hang down with very heavy weight! You bury your neck with necklaces! With gems and gold, you bind hands with an evil omen—hands that are worthy of God. Why should I speak of your dresses, or of the whole pomp of the devil? You are rejecting the law when you wish to please the world. *Commodianus (c. 240, W), 4.215.*

The characteristics of jewelry, garments, and the allurements of beauty are not fitting for anyone except prostitutes and immodest women. *Cyprian (c. 250, W), 5.433.*

Has God willed that wounds should be made in the ears, by which infancy—as yet innocent and unconscious of worldly evil—may be put to pain? Has He willed this so that, at a later time, precious beads may hang from the scars and holes of the ears? . . . All of these things the sinning and apostate angels put forth by their arts, when, lowered to the contagions of earth, they forsook their heavenly vigor. *Cyprian (c. 250, W), 5.434.*

Did He send souls so that, forgetting their importance and dignity as something divine, they would acquire gems, precious stones, and pearls—all at the expense of their purity? Did he send them to entwine their necks with such

things, pierce the tips of their ears, and bind their foreheads with bands? *Arnobius (c. 305, E), 6.450; see also 2.267–2.270, 4.16–4.17, 4.23.*

SEE ALSO CLOTHING; COSMETICS; GROOMING; PERFUME; RING.

JEWISH CHRISTIANITY

They said to him, "You see, brother, how many myriads of Jews there are who have believed, and they are all zealous for the law." Acts 21:20.

[TRYPHO THE JEW SPEAKING TO A CHRISTIAN:] "But if some, even now, wish to live in the observance of the institutions given by Moses, can they also be saved? I speak of ones who also believe in this Jesus who was crucified, who recognize Him to be the Christ of God, and believe that it is given to Him to be the absolute Judge of all, and who believe that His is the everlasting kingdom." . . . I [Justin] said, "In my opinion, Trypho, such a one will be saved, if he does not strive in every way to persuade other men—I mean those Gentiles who have been circumcised from error by Christ—to observe the same things as himself, telling them that they will not be saved unless they do so." . . . Trypho then replied, "Why then have you said, 'in my opinion, such a one will be saved,' unless there are some who think that such persons will not be saved?" I [Justin] answered, "There are such people, Trypho, and these do not venture to have any dealings with or to extend hospitality to such persons. However, I do not agree with them." *Justin Martyr (c. 160, E), 1.218.*

The number of believers who belong to Israel according to the flesh is small. One might venture to assert that they would not nearly make up the number of a hundred and forty-four thousand. It is evident, therefore, that the hundred and forty-four thousand who have not defiled themselves with women must be made up of those who have come to the divine word out of the Gentile world. *Origen (c. 228, E), 9.298.*

Ebion signifies "poor" among the Jews. And those Jews who have received Jesus as Christ are called by the name of Ebionites. In fact, Peter himself seems to have observed for a considerable time the Jewish observances commanded by the Law of Moses. For he had not yet learned from Jesus to ascend from the Law that is regulated according to the letter, to that which is interpreted according to the spirit. *Origen (c. 248, E), 4.429.*

Certainly it was quite consistent that those persons who were sent to minister to the circumcision should not abstain from the observance of Jewish customs. Those who "seemed to be pillars" gave the right hand of fellowship to Paul and Barnabas, in order that, while devoting themselves to the circumcision, the latter might preach to the Gentiles.... Paul himself "became as a Jew to the Jews, that he might gain the Jews." For that reason, in the Acts of the Apostles, it is related that he even brought an offering to the altar so that he could satisfy the Jews that he was no apostate from their Law. *Origen (c. 248, E), 4.429, 430.*

SEE ALSO ISRAEL OF GOD; JEW, JEWS.

JOB

In the Book of Job, which is older even than Moses himself, the devil is distinctly described as presenting himself before God and asking for power against Job—so that he might involve him in trials of the most painful kind. *Origen (c. 248, E), 4.593.*

JOBS

SEE EMPLOYMENT.

JOHN, APOSTLE

Then Peter, turning around, saw the disciple whom Jesus loved following, who also had leaned on His breast at the supper.... This is the disciple who testifies of these things. John 21:20, 24.

I, John, both your brother and companion in tribulation, and in the kingdom and patience of Jesus Christ, was on the island that is called Patmos for the word of God and for the testimony of Jesus Christ. Rev. 1:9.

John, the disciple of the Lord, who also had leaned upon His breast, did himself publish a Gospel during his residence at Ephesus in Asia. *Irenaeus (c. 180, E/W), 1.414.*

There are also those who heard from [Polycarp] that John, the disciple of the Lord, went to bathe at Ephesus. But realizing that Cerinthus was within [the bath house], John rushed out of the bath house without bathing. Instead, he exclaimed, "Let us fly, lest even the bath house fall down, because Cerinthus, the enemy of the truth, is within." *Irenaeus (c. 180, E/W), 1.416.*

The church in Ephesus was founded by Paul, and John remained among them permanently until the time of Trajan. It is a true witness of the tradition of the apostles. *Irenaeus (c. 180, E/W), 1.416.*

John, who reclined on the Lord's breast, became a priest wearing the *petalon*, a martyr, and a teacher. He rests at Ephesus. *Polycrates (c. 190, E), 8.773* [SEE NOTE UNDER VESTMENTS, RELIGIOUS.]

To James the Just, John, and Peter, the Lord imparted knowledge after His resurrection. These imparted it to the rest of the apostles. And the rest of the apostles to the Seventy, of whom Barnabas was one. *Clement of Alexandria (c. 195, E), 2.579.*

Listen to a tale, which is not a tale but a narrative, handed down and committed to the custody of memory, about the apostle John. On the tyrant's death, John returned to Ephesus from the isle of Patmos. He then travelled to the adjoining territories of the nations, being invited, here to appoint bishops, there to set in order whole churches, there to ordain such men as were marked out by the Spirit. *Clement of Alexandria (c. 195, E), 2.603.*

Was anything, again, concealed from John, the Lord's most beloved disciple? For he used to lean on His breast. To him alone, the Lord pointed Judas out as the traitor. It was John whom He commended to Mary as a son in His own place. *Tertullian (c. 197, W), 3.253.*

Rome ... is where the apostle John was first plunged into boiling oil, but was unhurt. He was then banished to his island of exile. *Tertullian (c. 197, W), 3.260.*

What are we to say of him who leaned on Jesus' breast—namely, John? He left one Gospel, although he declared that he could make so many that the world could not contain them. *Origen (c. 228, E), 9.346.*

Again, in the second epistle, which is ascribed to John the apostle, and in the third epistle—though they are indeed brief—John is not set before us by name. Rather, we simply find the anonymous name, "the elder." *Dionysius, Bishop of Alexandria (c. 262, E), 6.83.*

I am also of the opinion that there were many persons of the same name with the apostle John, who were moved to choose the same name because of their admiration and emulation of him. *Dionysius, Bishop of Alexandria (c. 262, E), 6.83.*

They themselves also received the rule from an unimpeachable authority—the evangelist John. This is he who leaned on the Lord's breast and drank in spiritual instructions without doubt. They did not acquiesce on this matter with the authority of some—namely, the successors of Peter and Paul. *Anatolius (c. 270, E), 6.148, 149.*

It is plain, therefore, that to John—armed as he was with superior virtue [as an apostle]—this was not necessary. *Victorinus (c. 280, W), 7.353.*

When John said these things [in Revelation], he was on the island of Patmos, condemned by Caesar Domitian to labor in the mines. Therefore, it was there that he saw the Apocalypse. When he had grown old, he thought that he would eventually meet his end through suffering. However, Domitian was killed and all his judgments were thrown out. After he was released from the mines, John later delivered [to the churches] this same Apocalypse that he had received from God. . . . He later wrote the Gospel of the complete faith for the sake of our salvation. For when Valentinus, Cerinthus, Ebion, and others of the school of Satan were scattered abroad throughout the world, all the bishops assembled together to John from the neighboring provinces and compelled him to draw up his testimony. *Victorinus (c. 280, W), 7.353, 354; see also 2.603, 604.*

SEE ALSO APOSTLES, TWELVE; CANON, NEW TESTAMENT; JOHN, GOSPEL OF; JOHN, PRESBYTER; PASCHAL CONTROVERSY; REVELATION, BOOK OF.

JOHN THE BAPTIST

John was a prophet among your [Jewish] nation. After him, no other prophet appeared among you. *Justin Martyr (c. 160, E), 1.219.*

The blessed John, despising the locks of sheep as savoring of luxury, chose camel's hair, and was clad in it. So he became an example of frugality and simplicity of life. *Clement of Alexandria (c. 195, E), 2.266.*

Two forerunners were indicated. The first was John the son of Zachariah, who appeared in all things as a forerunner and herald of our Savior. . . . He, on hearing the salutation addressed to Elizabeth, leaped with joy in his mother's womb. For he recognized God the Word conceived in the womb of the virgin. Thereafter, he came forward preaching in the wilderness, proclaiming the baptism of repentance to the people. . . . He also first preached to those in Hades, becoming a forerunner there when he was put to death by Herod. For He wanted there, too, to reveal that the Savior would descend to ransom the souls of the saints from the hand of death. *Hippolytus (c. 200, W), 5.213.*

There is nothing absurd in believing that John, "in the spirit and power of Elijah," turned the hearts of the fathers to the children, and that it was on account of this spirit that he was called "Elijah who was to come." . . . For he who was called John was not the Elijah who had been taken up. *Origen (c. 228, E), 9.356; extended discussion: 9.474–9.476.*

SEE ALSO BAPTISM, JOHN'S.

JOHN, GOSPEL OF

The fourth Gospel is that of John, one of the disciples. When his fellow-disciples and bishops entreated him, he said, "Fast now with me for the space of three days, and let us recount to each other whatever may be revealed to each of us." On the same night, it was revealed to Andrew, one of the apostles, that John should narrate all things in his own name—as they called them to mind. *Muratorian Fragment (c. 200, W), 5.603.*

What a mind, then, we must have to enable us to interpret this work [the Gospel of John] in a worthy manner. This is so even though it has been committed to the earthly treasure house of common speech. It is a writing that anyone can read. And it can be understood by anyone when it is read aloud. *Origen (c. 228, E), 9.300.*

Furthermore, on the ground of difference in diction, it is possible to prove a distinction between the Gospel and the Epistle on the one hand, and the Revelation on the other. For the former are written—not only without actual errors as regards the Greek language—but they were also written with the greatest elegance. . . . As to the author of the latter, however . . . his dialect and language are not of the precise Greek type. He even uses barbarous idioms. *Dionysius of Alexandria (c. 262, E), 6.85.*

SEE ALSO GOSPELS; JOHN, APOSTLE.

JOHN, PRESBYTER

Which things are said by Aristion and presbyter John, the disciples of the Lord. *Papias (c. 120, E), 1.153, as quoted by Eusebius.*

It is said that there were two monuments in Ephesus and that each of them bears the name of John. *Dionysius of Alexandria (c. 262, E), 6.83.*

Moreover, Papias asserts that he heard Aristion and the presbyter John in person. *Eusebius (c. 320, E), 1.154.*

SEE ALSO JOHN, APOSTLE; REVELATION, BOOK OF.

JOSEPHUS

You men of Greece, these things about the antiquity of Moses have been recorded in writing by men who were not of our religion. And they said that they learned all of these things from the Egyptian priests. Moses was not only born among those Egyptians, but he was also thought worthy of receiving the education of the Egyptians. For he had been adopted by the king's daughter as her son. For the same reason, he was considered worthy of great attention. The wisest of the historians have related these things, for they have chosen to record his life and actions, as well as the rank of his lineage. I am speaking of Philo and Josephus. For, in their account of the history of the Jews, these men say that Moses was descended from the race of the Chaldeans and was born in Egypt. *Justin Martyr (c. 160, E), 1.277.*

I have told you things that you can also learn from others—and especially from those wise and esteemed men, Philo and Josephus, who have written about these things. *Justin Martyr (c. 160, E), 1.278, 279.*

So then let what has been said be sufficient for the testimony of the Phoenicians and Egyptians . . . and also Josephus, who wrote about the Jewish war, which they waged with the Romans. *Theophilus (c. 180, E), 2.118.*

Josephus says that when Moses had been brought up in the royal palaces, he was chosen as a general against the Ethiopians. And having proved victorious, he obtained in marriage the daughter of that king. *Irenaeus (c. 180, E/W), 1.573.*

Flavius Josephus, the Jew, who composed the history of the Jews, computed the various periods of time. He says that from Moses to David there were five hundred and eighty-five years. *Clement of Alexandria (c. 195, E), 2.334.*

Their critic, the Jew Josephus, the native vindicator of the ancient history of his people, either authenticates or refutes the others. *Tertullian (c. 197, W), 3.33.*

If you are better pleased with the Roman writings, inquire concerning the Jews in the books of Flavius Josephus or Antoninus Julianus, to say nothing of various ancient documents. From these books, you will know that because of their wickedness, the Jews deserved this fortune. *Mark Minucius Felix (c. 200, W), 4.194.*

This James rose to so great a reputation for righteousness among the people, that Flavius Josephus, who wrote the *Antiquities of the Jews* in twenty books, when wishing to present the cause why the people suffered such great misfortunes that even the temple was razed to the ground, said that these things happened to them as a result of God's wrath. This was because of the things they had dared to do against James, the brother of Jesus who is called Christ. And the surprising thing is that, although he did not accept Jesus as Christ, Josephus still gave testimony that the righteousness of James was so great. Josephus says that the people thought they had suffered these things because of James. *Origen (c. 245, E), 9.424.*

Anyone who chooses to may read what Flavius Josephus has recorded in his two books on the *Antiquity of the Jews.* In it, he brings together a sizeable collection of writers. They all bear witness to the antiquity of the Jewish people. *Origen (c. 248, E), 4.403.*

The existence of John the Baptist . . . is related by a man who lived not very long after John [the Baptist] and Jesus. In the Eighteenth Book of his *Antiquities of the Jews,* Josephus bears witness to John as having been a Baptist. . . . Now, this writer, although not believing in Jesus as the Christ, in seeking after the cause of the fall of Jerusalem . . . says . . . that these disasters happened to the Jews as a punishment for the death of James the Just, who was a brother of Jesus. *Origen (c. 248, E), 4.416.*

This may be learned from what Philo, Josephus, and Musaeus have written. *Anatolius (c. 270, E), 6.147.*

JUDE

Is not His mother called Mary? And His brothers, James, Joses, Simon, and Judas? Matt. 13:55.

There still survived some of the kindred of the Lord. These were the grandsons of Jude, who according to the flesh was called His brother. These were informed against, as belonging to the family of David, and Evocatus brought them before Domitian Caesar. For that emperor dreaded the advent of Christ, as Herod had done. *Hegesippus (c. 170), 8.763.*

Jude, who wrote the catholic Epistle, was the brother of the sons of Joseph. And he was very religious. Although experiencing the near relationship of the Lord, yet he did not say that he himself was His brother. But what did he say? "Jude, a servant of Jesus Christ"—of Him as Lord; but "the brother of James." For this was true. Jude was his brother, through Joseph. *Clement of Alexandria (c. 195, E), 2.573.*

It is true that Jude wrote a letter of only a few lines. However, it is filled with the healthful words of heavenly grace. He said in the preface, "Jude, the servant of Jesus Christ and the brother of James." *Origen (c. 245, E), 9.424.*

SEE ALSO JAMES, BROTHER OF THE LORD; JESUS CHRIST (VI. BROTHERS OF JESUS).

JUDGMENT, LAST

When the Son of Man comes in His glory, and all the holy angels with Him, then He will sit on the throne of His glory. All the nations will be gathered before Him, and he will separate them one from another, as a shepherd divides his sheep from the goats. Matt. 25:31, 32.

The hour is coming in which all who are in the graves will hear His voice and come forth—those who have done good, to the resurrection of life, and those who have done evil, to the resurrection of condemnation. John 5:28, 29.

We shall all stand before the judgment seat of Christ. Rom. 14:10–12.

And I saw the dead, small and great, standing before God, and books were opened. And another book was opened, which is the Book of Life. And the dead were judged according to their works, by the things which were written in the books. Rev. 21:12.

He who receives [alms] when he does not have the need will pay the penalty, being asked why he received and for what purpose. Coming into confinement, he will be examined concerning the things that he has done. And he will not escape from there until he pays back the last coin. *Didache (c. 80–140, E), 7.377.*

"We must all appear at the judgment seat of Christ, and we must each give an account of himself." Therefore, let us serve Him in fear and with all reverence. *Polycarp (c. 135, E), 1.34.*

We gain conviction respecting [the resurrection] from the arguments taken from providence. I am referring to the reward or punishment due to each man in accordance with just judgment, and from the end of human existence. *Athenagoras (c. 175, E), 2.156.*

The robber, ruler, or tyrant who has unjustly put to death myriads on myriads, could not by one death make restitution for these deeds. *Athenagoras (c. 175, E), 2.160.*

He . . . will examine all things, and will judge righteous judgment, rendering merited awards to each one. *Theophilus (c. 180, E), 2.93.*

The advent of the Son comes indeed alike to all. However, it is for the purpose of judging and separating the believing from the unbelieving. *Irenaeus (c. 180, E/W), 1.556.*

We get ourselves laughed at for proclaiming that God will one day judge the world. For, like us, the poets and philosophers set up a judgment seat in the realms below. *Tertullian (c. 197, W), 3.52.*

When even the outward fashion of the world itself . . . passes away, then the whole human race will be raised again. This is in order to have its dues meted out, according to what it has merited in the period of good or evil. Thereafter, it will have these paid out through the immeasurable ages of eternity. *Tertullian (c. 197, W), 3.54.*

A judgment has been ordained by God according to the merits of every man. *Tertullian (c. 197, W), 3.127.*

"We must all appear before the judgment seat of Christ, so that everyone may receive the things done in his body, according as he has done either good or bad." Since, however, there is then to be a satisfaction according to men's merits, how will anyone be able to reckon with God? By mentioning both the judgment seat and the distinction between good and bad works, he sets before us a Judge who is to award both sentences. He has thereby affirmed that all will have to be present at the tribunal in their bodies. *Tertullian (c. 207, W), 3.456.*

God's judgment will be more full and complete, for it will be pronounced at the very last. It will be an eternal, irrevocable sentence—either of punishment or of blessing. *Tertullian (c. 210, W), 3.215.*

Since the entire man consists of the union of the two natures [body and soul], he must therefore appear in both natures. For it is right that a man should be judged in his entirety. . . . Therefore, as he lived, he must also be judged. *Tertullian (c. 210, W), 3.555.*

He has appointed an eternal judgment, when both the thankful and unthankful will have to stand before His court. *Tertullian (c. 212, W), 3.105.*

Everyone—righteous and unrighteous alike—will be brought before God the Word. For the Father has committed all judgment to Him. . . . He, in administering the righteous judgment of the Father to everyone, assigns to each person what is righteous according to his works. . . . "Righteousness is Your judgment." Of which voice the justification will be seen by awarding to each person that which is just. Those who have done good will be justly assigned eternal bliss. To the lovers of wickedness, there will be given eternal punishment. *Hippolytus (c. 205, W), 5.222.*

There is no doubt that at the Day of Judgment, the good will be separated from the bad, and the just from the unjust. And all will be distributed according to their deserts, by the sentence of God, throughout those places of which they are worthy. *Origen (c. 225, E), 4.293*

"If you do not forgive, neither will your Father who is in heaven forgive you your sins." There remains no ground of excuse in the day of judgment—when you will be judged according to your own sentence. And whatever you have done, that you will also suffer. *Cyprian (c. 250, W), 5.454.*

Believe that everyone will be judged individually in the future and that every man will receive the just compensation for his deeds—whether they are good or evil. *Gregory Thaumaturgus (c. 260, E), 6.17.*

SEE ALSO ESCHATOLOGY; ETERNAL PUNISHMENTS AND REWARDS; MERIT; RESURRECTION OF THE DEAD; REVELATION, BOOK OF.

JUDGMENT DAY

SEE JUDGMENT, LAST.

JUDITH

Judith is the heroine of the book of Judith. When Jerusalem was besieged, she went into the enemy camp, pretending to be romantically attracted to Holofernes, the general. After acquiring his trust, she killed him in his sleep—causing the retreat of the invading army.

The blessed Judith, when her city was besieged, asked permission from the elders to go forth into the camp of the strangers. Exposing herself to danger, she went out for the love that she had for her country and for the people who were then besieged. And the Lord delivered Holofernes into the hands of a woman. *Clement of Rome (c. 96, W), 1.20.*

Judith, too, became perfect among women. In the siege of the city, at the entreaty of the elders, she went forth into the strangers' camp, despising all danger for her country's sake. *Clement of Alexandria (c. 195, E), 2.431.*

SEE ALSO DEUTEROCANONICAL BOOKS.

JUSTIFICATION BY FAITH

SEE SALVATION (II. ROLE OF GRACE AND FAITH IN SALVATION).

JUSTIN MARTYR

Justin Martyr (c. 110–165) was a philosopher who converted to Christianity and became a tireless evangelist. He died as a martyr during the reign of Marcus Aurelius.

I gave no thought to any of my people, that is, the Samaritans, when I communicated in writing with Caesar. Rather, I stated that they were in error to trust in the magician Simon. *Justin Martyr (c. 160, E), 1.260.*

The most admirable Justin has rightly denounced them as robbers. *Tatian (c. 160, E), 2.73.*

Crescens [a pagan philosopher] professed to despise death. However, he was so afraid of death that he endeavored to inflict the punishment of death on Justin (and indeed on me) as something evil. For, by proclaiming the truth, Justin convicted the philosophers of being gluttons and cheats. *Tatian (c. 160, E), 2.73.*

In his book against Marcion, Justin well says, "I would not have believed the Lord himself if He had announced any other [God] than He who is our Framer, Maker, and Nourisher." *Irenaeus (c. 180, E/W), 1.468.*

Truly has Justin remarked that before the Lord's appearance, Satan never dared to blaspheme God, inasmuch as Satan did not yet know his own sentence. *Irenaeus (c. 180, E/W), 1.555.*

These have been already produced . . . in carefully written volumes, by so many eminently holy and excellent men. . . . For instance, there is Justin, the philosopher and martyr. *Tertullian (c. 200, W), 3.505, 506.*

Besides, there are writings of certain brethren that are older than the times of Victor. They wrote these things against the pagans in defense of the truth and against the heresies of their day. I am referring to Justin, Miltiades, Tatian, Clement, and many others. In all their writings, divinity is ascribed to Christ. *Eusebius, quoting Caius (c. 215, W), 5.601.*

Although Tatian was himself a disciple of Justin the Martyr, he did not entertain similar opinions with his master. *Hippolytus (c. 225, W), 5.122.*

Clement, Irenaeus, and Justin the martyr and philosopher comment with great wisdom on the number six of the sixth day. *Anastasius, post-Nicene writer, citing Justin Martyr (c. 160, E), 1.302.*

KEYS OF THE KINGDOM

I will give you the keys of the kingdom of heaven, and whatever you bind on earth will be bound in heaven, and whatever you loose on earth will be loosed in heaven. Matt. 16:19.

Though you think heaven is still shut, remember that the Lord left the keys of it to Peter, and through him, to the church. And everyone who has here been put to the question [of being a Christian] and has also made confession [of Christ when faced with martyrdom] will carry these keys with him. *Tertullian (c. 213, W), 3.643.*

"I will give unto you the keys of the kingdom of heaven." . . . I think that for every virtue of knowledge, certain mysteries of wisdom corresponding to the type of that virtue are opened up to him who has lived according to virtue. To those who are not mastered by the gates of Hades, the Savior gives as many keys as there are virtues. *Origen (c. 245, E), 9.458.*

There are certain things that seem to be common to both Peter [Matt. 16:19] and to those who have admonished their brother three times [Matt. 18:18]. However, if we were to pay careful attention to the evangelical writings, we would all find that there is a great difference and a pre-eminence between the things said to Peter and those said to the second class. For it is no small difference that Peter received the keys, not of one heaven, but of more. . . . For they do not reach so high a stage with power as Peter to bind and loose in *all* the heavens. *Origen (c. 245, E), 9.494.*

SEE ALSO BINDING AND LOOSING; PETER.

KINGDOM OF GOD

In the days of these kings the God of heaven will set up a kingdom which shall never be destroyed; and the kingdom shall not be left to other people; it shall break

in pieces and consume all these kingdoms, and it shall stand forever. Dan. 2:44.

Indeed, the kingdom of God is within you. Luke 17:21.

My kingdom is not of this world. If My kingdom were of this world, My servants would fight, so that I should not be delivered to the Jews. John 18:36.

He has delivered us from the power of darkness and translated us into the kingdom of the Son of His love. Col 1:13.

When you hear that we look for a kingdom, you imagine—without making any inquiry—that we are speaking of a human kingdom. *Justin Martyr (c. 160, E), 1.166.*

He says, "The kingdom of God comes not with observation. Neither do they say, Look here! Or, Look there! For, behold, the kingdom of God is within you." Now, who will not interpret the words "within you" to mean in your hand, within your power? That is, if you hear and do the commandment of God. *Tertullian (c. 207, W), 3.409.*

That person is already in the kingdom of the heavens who lives according to the virtues. Accordingly, the saying, "Repent, for the kingdom of heaven is at hand," refers to deeds and disposition—not to a certain time. Christ, who is all virtue, has come. For this reason, He says that the kingdom of God is within His disciples—not here or there. *Origen (c. 245, E), 9.458.*

The Christ of God shows His superiority to all rulers by entering into their various provinces and summoning men out of them to be subject to Himself. *Origen (c. 248, E), 4.641.*

Such a person cannot be induced to combine the service of any other with the service of God—nor to serve two masters. There is, therefore, nothing seditious or factious in the language of those who hold these views and who refuse to serve more masters than one. To them, Jesus Christ is an all-sufficient Lord. He Himself instructs them so that when they are fully instructed, He may form them into a kingdom worthy of God and present them to God the Father. However, they presently, in a sense, separate themselves and stand aloof from those who are aliens from the kingdom of God and strangers to his covenants. They do this in order that they may live as citizens of heaven. *Origen (c. 248, E), 4.641.*

The Word rules over no one against that person's will. For there are still wicked beings—not only men, but also angels and all demons—over whom we say that in a sense He does not rule. For they do not yield Him a willing obedience. However, in another sense of the word, He rules even over them—in the same way as we say that man rules over the irrational animals. In other words, He does not rule them by persuasion, but as one who tames and subdues lions and beasts of burden. Nevertheless, He leaves no means untried to persuade even those who are still disobedient to submit to His authority. *Origen (c. 248, E), 4.645.*

Dearest brethren, Christ himself may be the kingdom of God, whom we day by day desire to come.... The kingdom of God may be understood to be Himself, since in Him we will reign. But we do well in seeking the kingdom of God—that is, the heavenly kingdom. For there is also an earthly kingdom. But he who has already renounced the world, is already greater than its honors and its kingdom. *Cyprian (c. 250, W), 5.451.*

On account of the goodness and faithfulness that He displayed towards God on earth, there was given to Him a kingdom, and glory, and dominion. And all peoples, tribes, and languages will serve Him.... And this is understood in two ways. First, even now He has an everlasting dominion—when [people of] all nations and languages adore His name, confess His majesty, follow His teaching, and imitate his goodness.... Second, when He comes again with majesty and glory to judge every soul and to restore the righteous to life, then He will truly have the dominion of the whole earth. *Lactantius (c. 304–313, W), 7.111.*

SEE ALSO ISRAEL OF GOD.

KISS, HOLY

Greet one another with a holy kiss. Rom. 16:16.

Greet one another with a kiss of love. 1 Pet. 5:14; see also 1 Cor. 16:20; 2 Cor. 13:12; and 1 Thess. 5:26.

Having ended the prayers, we salute one another with a kiss. *Justin Martyr (c. 160, E), 1.185.*

On behalf of those, then, to whom we apply the names of brothers and sisters (and other designations of relationship), we exercise the greatest care that their bodies should remain undefiled and uncorrupted. For the Logos again says to us, "If anyone kisses a second time because it has given him pleasure, [he sins]." He also adds, "Therefore the kiss, or rather the salutation, should be given with the greatest care, since, if there are mixed with it the least defilement of thought, it excludes us from eternal life." *Athenagoras (c. 175, E), 2.146.*

Love is not proved by a kiss, but by kindly feeling. But there are those who do nothing but make the churches resound with a kiss, not having love itself within. For this very thing, the shameless use of a kiss (which should be mystical), causes foul suspicions and evil rumors. The apostle calls the kiss holy. When the kingdom is worthily tested, we express the affection of the soul with a chaste and closed mouth. *Clement of Alexandria (c. 195, E), 2.291.*

On the way [to be martyred], the other man asked James to forgive him. And after brief consideration, James said, "Peace be to you," and kissed him. And so both were beheaded together. *Eusebius, citing Clement of Alexandria (c. 195, E), 2.579.*

Another custom has now become prevalent. Those who are fasting withhold the kiss of peace (which is the seal of prayer) after prayer made with brethren. But when is peace more to be concluded with brethren than when, at the time of some religious observance, our prayer ascends with more acceptability?... What prayer is complete if separated from the holy kiss? *Tertullian (c. 198, W), 3.687.*

[What unbelieving husband] will permit her to creep into prison to kiss a martyr's chains? Will he permit her to meet any of the brethren to exchange the kiss? *Tertullian (c. 205, W), 4.46.*

All of a sudden, Archelaus appeared among them and embraced Diodorus, saluting him with a holy kiss. *Disputation of Archelaus and Manes (c. 320, E), 6.221.*

Then let the men give the men, and the women give the women, the Lord's kiss. But let no one do it with deceit, as Judas betrayed the Lord with a kiss. *Apostolic Constitutions (compiled c. 390, E), 7.422.*

KISS OF PEACE

SEE KISS, HOLY.

KNEELING

SEE PRAYER (II. PRAYER POSTURES AND CUSTOMS).

LAITY

SEE CHURCH GOVERNMENT (IX. CLERGY AND LAITY DISTINCTIONS; XI. PRIESTHOOD OF ALL BELIEVERS).

LAKE OF FIRE

SEE ETERNAL PUNISHMENTS AND REWARDS; GEHENNA.

LAPSED

The "lapsed" were those Christians who denied Christ, sacrificed to the gods, or compromised in some other way during persecution.

Whoever denies Me before men, him I will also deny before My Father who is in heaven. Matt. 10:33.

He who overcomes shall be clothed in white garments, and I will not blot out his name from the Book of Life; but I will confess his name before My Father and before His angels. Rev. 3:5.

The church stands in faith, even though some persons have been driven to fall by very terror. This may be because they were persons of eminence, or because they were afraid with the fear of man, when they were seized. However, we did not abandon them, even though they were separated from us. Rather, we exhorted them and do exhort them to repent—if in any way they may receive pardon from Him who is able to grant it. For if they were deserted by us, they would become worse. You see, then, brethren, that you also should do the same. So that even those who have fallen may amend their minds by your exhortation. Perhaps if they are seized once more, they may confess [Christ] and thereby make amends for their previous sin. *Letter from the church in Rome to Cyprian (c. 250, W), 5.281.*

If any of those [i.e., the lapsed] who have fallen into this temptation begin to be taken with sickness and repent of what they have done and desire communion, it should in any way be granted to them. Or if you have widows or bedridden people who are unable to maintain themselves—or those who are in prisons or are excluded from their own dwellings—they should in all cases have someone to minister to them. *Letter from the church in Rome to Cyprian (c. 250, W), 5.281.*

Contrary to the Gospel law, . . . before penitence was fulfilled, before confession even of the gravest and most heinous sin was made, before hands were placed upon the repentant by the bishops and clergy, those presbyters dare to offer the Eucharist on their behalf and to give the lapsed the Eucharist! So they profane the sacred body of the Lord, although it is written, "Whoever will eat the bread and drink the cup of the Lord unworthily, will be guilty of the body and blood of the Lord." *Cyprian (c. 250, W), 5.291.*

Indeed, pardon may be granted to the lapsed in respect of this thing. . . . But it is the duty of those placed over them to keep the ordinance. . . . For to concede those things that tend to destruction is to deceive. The lapsed person is not raised up in this manner. Rather, by offending God, he is more urged on to ruin. *Cyprian (c. 250, W), 5.291.*

Cherish also by your presence the rest of the people who are lapsed, and cheer them by your consolation—that they may not fail of the faith and of God's mercy. *Cyprian (c. 250, W), 5.293.*

Therefore, hands polluted with impious sacrifices must be purified with good works. And wretched mouths defiled with accursed food must be purged with words of true penitence. And the spirit must be renewed and consecrated in the recesses of the faithful heart. Let the frequent groanings of the penitents be heard. Let faithful tears be shed from the eyes, not only once—but again and again. *Letter to Cyprian (c. 250, W), 5.304.*

If any unrestrained and impetuous person, whether of our presbyters or deacons or of strangers, should dare, before our decree, to communicate with the lapsed, let him be expelled from our communion. He can then plead the cause of his rashness before all of us when, by the Lord's permission, we will assemble together again. *Cyprian (c. 250, W), 5.306.*

When the persecution had quieted, and opportunity of meeting was afforded, a large number of bishops . . . met together. The divine Scriptures being brought forward on both sides, we balanced the decision with wholesome moderation. We felt that hope of communion and peace should not be wholly denied to the lapsed, lest they should fail still more. . . . On the other hand, neither should the condemnation of the Gospel be relaxed, enabling them to rashly rush to communion. Rather, repentance should be long protracted and the paternal clemency be sorrowfully sought after. . . . And lest perhaps the number of bishops in Africa might seem unsatisfactory, we also wrote to Rome, to Cornelius, our colleague, concerning this thing. He himself was also holding a council with very many bishops, which had concurred in the same opinion as we had held: that is, we should apply gravity balanced with wholesome moderation. *Cyprian (c. 250, W), 5.328, 329.*

We must not place on the same level one who has at once leapt forward with eagerness to the abominable sacrifice, and one who, after long struggle and resistance, has reached that fatal result under compulsion. *Cyprian (c. 250, W), 5.330.*

Do not think, dearest brother, that either the courage of the brethren will be lessened, or that martyrdoms will fail for this cause—that repentance is relaxed to the lapsed. *Cyprian (c. 250, W), 5.332.*

I wonder that some are so obstinate as to think that repentance is not to be granted to the lapsed. *Cyprian (c. 250, W), 5.332.*

You, O Novatian, judge and declare that the lapsed have no hope of peace and mercy. You do not incline your ear to the rebuke of the apostle, when he said, "Who are you, who judges another man's servant? To his own master he stands or falls." *Treatise against Novatian (c. 255, W), 5.660, 661.*

There was with us a certain Serapion, an aged believer. He had spent his long life blamelessly, but had fallen in the time of trial. . . . No one gave heed to him, for he had sacrificed to the idols. . . . However, an injunction had been issued by me that persons at the point of death, if they then requested it . . . should be absolved in order that they might depart this life in cheerful hope. *Dionysius of Alexandria (c. 262, E), 6.101.*

Let us not thrust from us those who seek a penitent return. Rather, let us receive them gladly and number them once more with the steadfast. Let us restore again what is defective in them. *Dionysius of Alexandria (c. 262, E), 6.120.*

In the case of those who have been arrested, thrown into prison, and have endured unbearable torments and intolerable stripes, . . . yet afterwards have been betrayed by the frailty of the flesh, . . . some are now bewailing their fault for the third year. I say it is sufficient that from the time of their submissive approach [three years ago] another forty days should be enjoined upon them, to keep them in remembrance of these things. . . . However, as for those who have suffered none of these things, and have shown no fruit of faith, but of their own accord have gone over to wickedness—being betrayed by fear and cowardice—but now come to repentance, it is necessary and appropriate to propose the parable of the unfruitful fig tree. . . . Keeping this before their eyes, and showing forth fruit worthy of repentance, after so long an interval of time, they will be profited. *Peter of Alexandria (c. 310, E), 6.269, 270.*

Other Christians have used deception—like David, who pretended to be mad. . . . These have mocked the snares of their enemies—either passing by the altars, or giving a writing, or sending an unbeliever to sacrifice instead of themselves. . . . With the greatest caution, they have avoided touching the fire with their own hands or to offer incense to the impure demons. Nevertheless, inasmuch as they escaped the notice of their persecutors by doing this, let a penalty of six months' penance be imposed upon them. . . . Still others have sent Christian slaves to offer sacrifice for them. The slaves . . . being threatened by their masters . . . and having lapsed, will during the year display the works of penitence, learning for the future to do the will of Christ, as the slaves of Christ. . . . However, the masters will be tried by penance for three years—both for their deception and for having forced their fellow-servants to offer sacrifice. *Peter of Alexandria (c. 310, E), 6.271.*

It is not right either that those of the clergy who have deserted of their own accord and have lapsed, but have taken up the contest anew, should remain any longer in their sacred office. . . . Instead, therefore, let them take heed to spend their life in humility, ceasing from vainglory. For communion is sufficient for them, which is granted them with diligence. *Peter of Alexandria (c. 310, E), 6.274.*

Let us be mindful of the many labors and distresses that the lapsed have endured for the name of Christ. Since they have themselves also repented and have bewailed that which was done by them, . . . let us pray together with them and plead for their reconciliation. *Peter of Alexandria (c. 310, E), 6.276.*

No accusation can be brought against those who have given money so that they could be entirely undisturbed by evil. For they have sustained the loss and sacrifice of their goods in order that their souls would not be hurt or destroyed. In these things, then, they have shown themselves to be the servants of God. For they have hated, trodden under foot, and despised money. . . . Neither is it now lawful to accuse those who have abandoned all and have fled for the safety of their lives. *Peter of Alexandria (c. 310, E), 6.276, 277; see also 5.335; extended discussion: 5.437–5.447.*

SEE ALSO CERTIFICATES OF SACRIFICE; DISCIPLINE, CHURCH; MARTYRS, MARTYRDOM.

LAST DAYS

God, who at various times and in different ways spoke in times past to the fathers by the prophets, has in these last days spoken to us by His Son. Heb. 1:1, 2.

He indeed was foreordained before the foundation of the world, but was manifest in these last times for you. 1 Pet. 1:20.

Little children, it is the last hour; and as you have heard that the Antichrist is coming, even now many antichrists have come, by which we know that it is the last hour. 1 John 2:18.

We take earnest heed in these last days. *Barnabas (c. 70–130, E), 1.139.*

Attend, my children, to the meaning of this expression, "He finished it in six days." This implies that the Lord will finish all things in six thousand years, for a day is with Him a thousand years. *Barnabas (c. 70–130, E), 1.146.*

The last times are come upon us. *Ignatius (c. 105, E), 1.54.*

When the tower is finished and built, then comes the end. And I assure you it will be finished soon. *Hermas (c. 150, W), 2.16.*

The advent of the Son of God took place in these last times—that is, in the end, rather than in the beginning. *Irenaeus (c. 180, E/W), 1.331.*

But now, since the last times are [upon us], evil is spread abroad among men. *Irenaeus (c. 180, E/W), 1.462.*

In as many days as this world was made, in so many thousand years will it be concluded. . . . For the day of the Lord is as a thousand years; and in six days created things were completed. It is evident, therefore, that they will come to an end at the sixth thousand year. *Irenaeus (c. 180, E/W), 1.557.*

Two comings of Christ have been revealed to us: . . . a second coming, which impends over the world, now near its close. In it, all the majesty of Deity will be unveiled. *Tertullian (c. 197, W), 3.35.*

We are those "upon whom the ends of the ages have met, having ended their course." *Tertullian (c. 198, W), 4.23.*

As the conquering power of things, evil is on the increase—which is the evidence of the last times. *Tertullian (c. 212, W), 4.74.*

. . . turning to the religion that in the last days has shone forth through Jesus Christ. *Origen (c. 248, E), 4.558.*

These things have been foretold as about to happen at the end of the world. And it was predicted by the voice of the Lord and by the testimony of the apostles that now the world is failing, and the Antichrist is drawing near, all good things will fail. However, evil and adverse things will prosper. Yet, in the last days, evangelic vigor has not failed in the church of God. *Cyprian (c. 250, W), 5.371.*

Wars continue frequently to prevail; death and famine accumulate anxiety; health is shattered by raging diseases; and the human race is wasted by the desolation of pestilence. Know that all this was foretold. For evils are to be multiplied in the last times. *Cyprian (c. 250, W), 5.459.*

Since now the end of the world is at hand, turn your minds to God, in the fear of God. *Cyprian (c. 250, W), 5.464.*

Beloved brethren, the kingdom of God is nearly at hand! The reward of life, the rejoicing of eternal salvation, and the perpetual gladness and possession of Paradise that were lately lost—are all now coming with the passing away of the world. Already heavenly things are taking the place of earthly. *Cyprian (c. 250, W), 5.469.*

What a grandeur of spirit it is to struggle with all the powers of an unshaken mind against so many onslaughts of devastation and death! What sublimity, to stand erect amid the desolation of the human race and not to lie prostrate with those who have no hope in God—but, rather, to rejoice. *Cyprian (c. 250, W), 5.472.*

The world is collapsing and is oppressed with the storms of mischievous ills. This is so that we who see that terrible things have begun— and know that still more terrible things are imminent—may regard it as the greatest advantage to depart from it as quickly as possible. *Cyprian (c. 250, W), 5.475.*

The ending and completion of the world, the hateful time of the Antichrist, is already beginning to draw near. *Cyprian (c. 250, W), 5.496.*

It was necessary that, as the end of the world approached, the Son of God would descend to the earth. *Lactantius (c. 304–313, W), 7.108.*

The voices also of the prophets of the world, agreeing with the heavenly, announce the end and overthrow of all things after a brief time. They describe the last old age of the wearied and wasting world, so to speak. *Lactantius (c. 304–313, W), 7.212.*

I have already shown above that when six thousand years are completed, this change must take place. So the last day of the extreme conclusion is now drawing near. . . . All expectation does not exceed the limit of two hundred years [before the completion of this six thousand years]. The subject itself declares that the fall and ruin of the world will shortly take place. How-

ever, while the city of Rome remains, it appears that nothing of this kind is to be feared. But when the capital of the world will have fallen, . . . who can doubt that the end has now arrived to the affairs of men and the whole world? It is that city, and only that city, that still sustains all things. *Lactantius (c. 304–313, W), 7.220.*

SEE ALSO ANTICHRIST; ESCHATOLOGY; GREAT TRIBULATION; SECOND COMING OF CHRIST.

LAST JUDGMENT

SEE JUDGMENT, LAST.

LAW, MOSAIC

I. Christians are not under the Law

II. Spiritual interpretation of the Law

III. Purpose and benefits of the Law

I. Christians are not under the Law

I will cause all her mirth to cease, her feast days, her New Moons, her Sabbaths—all her appointed feasts. Hos. 2:11.

For Christ is the end of the law for righteousness to everyone who believes. Rom. 10:4.

He Himself is our peace, . . . having abolished in His flesh the enmity, that is, the law of commandments contained in ordinances. Eph. 2:15.

Having wiped out the handwriting of requirements that was against us, which was contrary to us. And He has taken it out of the way, having nailed it to the cross. Col. 2:13, 14.

If we still live according to the Jewish Law, we acknowledge that we have not received grace. *Ignatius (c. 105, E), 1.62.*

If anyone preaches the Jewish Law to you, do not listen to him. For it is better to listen to Christian doctrine from a man who has been circumcised than to listen to Judaism from one who is uncircumcised. *Ignatius (c. 105, E), 1.82.*

The Christians do not observe the same forms of divine worship as do the Jews. *Letter to Diognetus (c. 125–200), 1.26.*

Is there any other matter, my [Jewish] friends, in which we Christians are blamed, than this: that we do not live after the Law, and are not circumcised in the flesh as your forefathers were, and do not observe Sabbaths as you do? *Justin Martyr (c. 160, E), 1.199.*

He gathered into the one faith of Abraham those persons from both covenants who are eligible for God's building. . . . For, as I have shown, this faith existed in Abraham prior to circumcision, as it also did in the rest of the righteous who pleased God. . . . But circumcision and the Law of works occupied the intervening period. *Irenaeus (c. 180, E/W), 1.496.*

The gifts granted through a faithful servant are not equal to those bestowed by the true Son. If, then, the Law of Moses had been sufficient to confer eternal life, it was to no purpose for the Savior Himself to come and suffer for us. *Clement of Alexandria (c. 195, E), 2.593.*

We do not follow the Jews in their peculiarities in regard to food, nor in their sacred days, nor even in their well-known bodily sign. *Tertullian (c. 197, W), 3.34.*

Paul blames [the Galatians] for maintaining circumcision, and observing times, days, months, and years, according to those Jewish ceremonies. For they should have known those things were now abrogated, according to the new dispensation. . . . Thus it was said by Hosea: "I will also cause all her mirth to cease, her feast days, her new moons, and her Sabbaths." . . . The Creator had long before discarded all these things, and the apostle was now proclaiming them to be worthy of renunciation. *Tertullian (c. 207, W), 3.285, 286.*

The following passage was written against Marcion, who claimed that Jesus came in opposition to the God of the Old Testament:

At the very outset of His ministry, He came not to destroy the Law and the Prophets, but rather to fulfill them. . . . "His word was with power." However, this was not because He taught in opposition to the Law and the Prophets. *Tertullian (c. 207, W), 3.352, 353.*

The same God, therefore, who prohibited meats also restored the use of them. For He had indeed originally allowed them. *Tertullian (c. 207, W), 3.445.*

We do not now deal with the Law any further than [to remark] that the apostle here teaches clearly how it has been abolished—by passing from shadow to substance. That is, it has passed from figurative types to the reality, which is Christ. *Tertullian (c. 207, W), 3.471.*

Deuteronomy is called, as it were, the second Law. . . . It was especially transmitted by Moses

to his successor Joshua. Now, Joshua is certainly believed to embody a type of our Savior. And it is by our Savior's "second law" (that is, the commandments of the Gospel) that all things are brought to perfection. *Origen (c. 225, E), 4.375.*

We do not regulate our lives like the Jews. For we are of the opinion that the literal following of the laws is not the thing that conveys the real meaning of this legislation. We maintain that "when Moses is read, the veil is upon their heart." For the meaning of the Law of Moses has been concealed from those who have not welcomed the way that is by Jesus Christ. *Origen (c. 248, E), 4.569.*

Jesus wished to lead all men by His teachings about the pure worship and service of God. He was anxious not to place any hindrance in the way of many who might be benefited by Christianity. So he did not impose a burdensome code of rules in regard to food. *Origen (c. 248, E), 4.650.*

But now Christ has come, who is the end of the Law. He has revealed all of the obscurities of the Law, all those things that antiquity had covered with the clouds of mysteries. *Novatian (c. 235, W), 5.648.*

From these things, it is plain that all those things [i.e., clean and unclean animals] are returned to their original blessedness now that the Law is finished. *Novatian (c. 235, W), 5.648.*

The lofty One despises your Sabbaths and altogether rejects your universal monthly feasts according to the Law. *Commodianus (c. 240, W), 4.210.*

The former Law that had been give by Moses was about to cease. And a new law was to be given. Another dispensation and a new covenant were to be given. The old baptism was to cease and a new one to begin. *Cyprian (c. 250, W), 5.508.*

The yoke of the Law was heavy, which is cast off by us. And the Lord's yoke is easy, which is taken up by us. . . . In the Gospel according to Matthew, it says: "Come unto me you who labor and are burdened and I will give you rest." . . . Also, in the Acts of the Apostles: "It seemed good to the Holy Spirit and to us, to impose upon you no other burden than those things that are of necessity: that you should abstain from idolatries, from shedding of blood, and from fornication." *Cyprian (c. 250, W), 5.556, 557.*

The first laws, which were published in the times of Adam, Noah, and Moses, were unable to give salvation to man. Rather, the evangelical law alone has saved everyone. *Methodius (c. 290, E), 6.349.*

The [Jewish religious leaders] alleged other causes for their anger . . . namely, that Jesus destroyed the obligation of the Law given by Moses. That is, He did not rest on the Sabbath, but labored for the good of men. Furthermore, He abolished circumcision, and He took away the necessity of abstaining from the flesh of pigs. . . . However, he did not do this by His own judgement, but according to the will of God. *Lactantius (c. 304–313, W), 7.118.*

As to the assertion that the Sabbath has been abolished, we deny that He has plainly abolished it. For He was Himself also Lord of the Sabbath. . . . And, again, He did not actually reject circumcision. Rather, we should say that He received in Himself and in our place the cause of circumcision, relieving us by what He Himself endured. Thereby, He permitted us not to have to suffer any pain to no purpose. . . . Accordingly, by a brief path, He opened up to us the ways of the fullest life. . . . This is quite in accordance with the truth that we have now learned—that if anyone prevails in the keeping of the two commandments, he fulfills the whole Law and the Prophets. *Disputation of Archelaus and Manes (c. 320, E), 6.217.*

Although my Lord Jesus Christ excels Moses in glory—as any lord excels his servant—it does not follow from this that the glory of Moses is to be scorned. *Disputation of Archelaus and Manes (c. 320, E), 6.218.*

When you read the Law, do not think yourself to be bound to observe the additional commandments. . . . Read them only for the sake of history, in order to learn about them and to glorify God that He has delivered you from such great and so numerous bonds. *Apostolic Constitutions (compiled c. 390, E), 7.393.*

If any persons keep to the Jewish customs and observances concerning nocturnal emissions, natural discharges, and lawful conjugal acts, let them tell us whether in those hours or days that those things happen, if they refuse to pray, to touch the sacred books, or partake of the Eucharist. . . . For neither lawful conjugal acts, nor childbearing, nor menstrual purgation, nor nocturnal emissions can defile the nature of a person or separate the Holy Spirit from him. Only ungodliness and unlawful practices can do that. *Apostolic Constitutions (compiled c. 390, E), 7.462; see also 2.338–341, 2.366–368.*

II. Spiritual interpretation of the Law

We know that the law is spiritual. Rom. 7:14.

For it is written in the law of Moses, "You shall not muzzle an ox while it treads out the grain." Is it oxen God is concerned about? Or does He say it altogether for our sakes? For our sakes, no doubt, this is written, that he who plows should plow in hope, and he who threshes in hope should be partaker of his hope. 1 Cor. 9:9, 10.

Moreover, brethren, I do not want you to be unaware that all our fathers were under the cloud, all passed through the sea, all were baptized into Moses in the cloud and in the sea, all ate the same spiritual food, and all drank the same spiritual drink. For they drank of that spiritual Rock that followed them, and that Rock was Christ. 1 Cor. 10:1–4.

Until this day the same veil remains unlifted in the reading of the Old Testament, because the veil is taken away in Christ. But even to this day, when Moses is read, a veil lies on their heart. Nevertheless when one turns to the Lord, the veil is taken away. 2 Cor. 3:14–16.

The law, having a shadow of the good things to come, and not the very image of the things. Heb. 10:1.

Is there then not a commandment of God that they should not eat [such things]? Yes, there is; however, Moses spoke spiritually. For this reason, he named the pig, meaning, "You shall not join yourself to persons who resemble pigs." For when such persons live in pleasure, they forget their Lord. However, when they are in need, then they remember the Lord. Similarly, when the pig has just eaten, it does not acknowledge its master. However, when it is hungry, it cries out. Nevertheless, on receiving food, the pig is quiet again. Moses also says, "Neither shall you eat the eagle, hawk, kite, nor raven." By this, he means, "You shall not join yourself to the type of persons who do not know how to earn food for themselves by labor and sweat. For those persons prey on the goods of others in their iniquity. Although appearing innocent outwardly, they are on the watch to plunder others." Likewise, those birds [of prey], when they are sitting idle, are seeking how they might devour the flesh of others. *Barnabas (c. 70–130), 1.143.*

[ADDRESSED TO JEWS:] This is the symbolic significance of unleavened bread: that you do not commit the old deeds of wicked leaven. However, you have understood all these things in a carnal sense. *Justin Martyr (c. 160, E), 1.201.*

The Passover was a type of Christ. . . . And the offering of fine flour . . . was a type of the bread of the Eucharist, the celebration of which our Lord Jesus Christ commanded. . . . Moreover, the requirement that twelve bells be attached to the robe of the high priest (which hung down to the feet) was a symbol of the twelve apostles. *Justin Martyr (c. 160, E), 1.215.*

Now all these teachings . . . were not those of someone doing away with the Law, but of someone fulfilling, extending, and widening it among us. *Irenaeus (c. 180, E/W), 1.478.*

When at this present time the Law is read to the Jews, it is like a fable. For they do not possess the explanation of all things pertaining to the coming of the Son of God, which took place in human nature. But when it is read by the Christians, it is a treasure, hid indeed in a field, but brought to light by the cross of Christ. *Irenaeus (c. 180, E/W), 1.496.*

The sense of the Law is to be taken in three ways: either as exhibiting a symbol, laying down a commandment for right conduct, or as uttering a prophecy. But I well know that it belongs to adult men to distinguish and declare these things. For the whole Scripture is not in its meaning a single "Myconos" (as the proverbial expression has it). Rather, those who hunt after the connection of the divine teaching must approach it with the utmost perfection of the logical faculty. *Clement of Alexandria (c. 195, E), 2.341.*

All these commandments had been given carnally, in previous times, to the people of Israel. So it follows that afterwards there was to supervene a time when the commandments of the ancient Law and of the old ceremonies would cease. There would come the promise of the new law, and the recognition of spiritual sacrifices, and the promise of the New Covenant. *Tertullian (c. 197, W), 3.157.*

I will not be sorry to meet him, and before anything else, to point out to him the force of

the Law when figuratively interpreted. In the symbol of a leper, . . . the Law prohibited any contact with a person who was defiled with sin, with whom the apostle also forbids us even to eat food. For the taint of sins is communicated as if contagious, if a man should mix himself with a sinner. The Lord, therefore, wished that the Law should be more profoundly understood as signifying spiritual truths through material facts. In that manner, He does not destroy, but builds up, that Law. *Tertullian (c. 207, W), 3.355, 356.*

He says, "You will not muzzle the ox that treads out the corn," and adds, "Is God concerned about oxen?" Yes, of oxen, for the sake of men. For he says, "It is written for our sakes." Thus Paul showed that the Law had a symbolic reference to ourselves, and that it gives its sanction in favor of those who live by the gospel. *Tertullian (c. 207, W), 3.444.*

The Scriptures were written by the Spirit of God. They have not only the meaning that is apparent at first sight, but also another meaning that escapes the notice of most people. For those written passages are the forms of certain mysteries and are the images of divine things. Concerning these, there is one opinion throughout the whole church that the *whole* Law is indeed spiritual. However, the spiritual meaning that the Law conveys is not known to all. It is known only to those on whom the grace of the Holy Spirit is bestowed in the word of wisdom and knowledge. *Origen (c. 225, E), 4.241.*

These things serve as a pattern and a shadow of the heavenly ones that we have spoken of. Yet, not only are such things as food, drink, new moons, and Sabbaths a shadow of the things to come, but the festivals are shadows, too. *Origen (c. 228, E), 9.389.*

Certainly, the introduction of Christianity is through the Mosaic worship and the prophetic writings. But after that introduction, progress takes place through the interpretation and explanation of these things. . . . Those who advance in the knowledge of Christianity do not, as you allege, treat the things written in the Law with disrespect. On the contrary, they bestow upon them greater honor, showing what depth of wise and mysterious reasons is contained in these writings—which are not fully comprehended by the Jews. . . . Just because [John the Baptist] was a Jew, it does not follow that every believer, whether a convert from paganism or from Judaism, must literally obey the Law of Moses. *Origen (c. 248, E), 4.431.*

First of all, we must avail ourselves of that passage "that the Law is spiritual." And if they deny it to be spiritual, they assuredly blaspheme. *Novatian (c. 235, W), 5.645.*

The characters, doings, and wills of men are depicted in the animals. They are clean if they chew the cud—that is, if they always have the divine teachings in their mouth as food. They divide the hoof, if with the firm step of innocency they tread the ways of righteousness and of every virtue of life. . . . Thus, by the Law, a certain mirror of human life is established in the animals—by which men may consider the images of penalties. *Novatian (c. 235, W), 5.647.*

When it forbids pigs to be taken for food, it assuredly reproves a life that is filthy, dirty, and delighting in the garbage of vice. . . . Who would use the body of the weasel for food? The purpose here is that [the Law] reproves theft. . . . Who would eat the hawk, kite, or the eagle? But the Law hates plunderers and violent people who live by crime. *Novatian (c. 235, W), 5.647.*

According to the apostle, the Law is spiritual. It contains the representations of future good things. So, then, come and let us take off the veil of the letter that is spread over it and consider its naked and true meaning. *Methodius (c. 290, E), 6.328.*

The prohibition on eating the flesh of pigs also has the same purpose. When God commanded the Jews to abstain from this, He wished for them to especially understand that they should abstain from sins and impurities. For this animal is filthy and unclean. It never looks up to heaven, but prostrates itself to the earth with its whole body and face. It is always the slave of its appetite and food. During its life, it can provide no useful service, as the other animals do. The others provide a means of transportation, aid in the plowing of the fields, pull wagons by their neck, carry burdens on their back, furnish a covering with their skins, abound with a supply of milk, or keep watch to guard our houses. For this reason, he forbade them to use the flesh of the pig for food. That is, they were not to imitate the life of a pig, which is nourished only for death. . . . Thus, all

the commandments of the Jewish Law have for their purpose the setting forth of righteousness. For they are given in a figurative manner, so that under the figure of physical things, those that are spiritual might be known. *Lactantius (c. 304–313, W), 7.119; see also 2.452–2.454, 2.458–2.460.*

III. Purpose and benefits of the Law

The law was our tutor to bring us to Christ, that we might be justified by faith. But after faith has come, we are no longer under a tutor. Gal. 3:24, 25.

Most of the passages below were written against Marcion and the Gnostics, all of whom claimed that the God who gave the Law was a different God from the Father of Jesus. Some of these heretics referred to the God of the Old Testament as the "just God" and the God of the New Testament as the "good God."

The Law, since it was laid down for those in bondage, used to instruct the soul by means of those physical objects that were of an external nature. It drew the soul, as if by a bond, to obey its commandments, so that man might learn to serve God. . . . It followed as a matter of course, that the bonds of slavery should be removed, to which man had now become accustomed, so that man would follow God without fetters. Moreover, it was intended that the laws of liberty would be extended and that subjection to the King would be increased, so that no one who is converted would appear unworthy to Him who set him free. Rather, it was intended that the piety and obedience due to the Master of the household would be equally rendered both by servants and children. *Irenaeus (c. 180, E/W), 1.477.*

The Israelites turned themselves to make a calf and went back in their minds to Egypt, desiring to be slaves instead of free men. Therefore, they were placed for the future in a state of servitude suited to their wish. This servitude [i.e., the Law] did not indeed cut them off from God, but it subjected them to the yoke of bondage. *Irenaeus (c. 180, E/W), 1.479.*

Why, then, did the Lord not form the covenant for the patriarchs? Because "the law was not established for righteous men." But the righteous patriarchs had the meaning of the Decalogue written in their hearts and souls. That is, they loved the God who made them and did no injury to their neighbor. There was, therefore, no occasion for them to be cautioned by prohibitory commandments, because they had the righteousness of the Law in themselves. But when this righteousness and love of God had passed into oblivion and became extinct in Egypt, God did [give commandments]. *Irenaeus (c. 180, E/W), 1.481.*

But the Law given to us commands us to shun the things that are truly bad. . . . How, then, is the Law still said to be "not good" by certain heresies? For they clamorously appeal to the apostle, who says, "For by the Law is the knowledge of sin." To whom we say, the Law did not *cause* sin, but *exposed* it. *Clement of Alexandria (c. 195, E), 2.355.*

How, then, can it be maintained that the Law is not humane, and is not the teacher of righteousness? *Clement of Alexandria (c. 195, E), 2.366.*

But what parts of the Law can I defend as good, with a greater confidence than those which heresy has shown such a longing for? There is the statute of retaliation, requiring eye for eye, tooth for tooth, and stripe for stripe. Now there is not here any hint of a permission to do mutual injury. Rather, on the whole, there is a provision for restraining violence. To a people who were very obstinate and lacking in faith towards God, it might seem tedious, and even impossible, to wait on God for that vengeance that was subsequently to be declared by the prophet: "Vengeance is mine; I will repay, says the Lord." Therefore, in the meanwhile, the commission of wrong was to be curtailed by the fear of an immediate retribution. *Tertullian (c. 207, W), 3.311.*

He says, "I will not eat the flesh of bulls." And in another passage, "The everlasting God will neither hunger nor thirst." He had respect for the offerings of Abel, and smelled a sweet savor from the burnt offering of Noah. Nevertheless, what pleasure could He receive from the flesh of sheep, or the odor of burning victims? And yet the simple and God-fearing mind of those who offered what they were receiving from God . . . was favorably accepted before God. *Tertullian (c. 207, W), 3.314.*

We affirm that this was the function of the Law as preparatory to the Gospel. It was utilized to form the faith, through gradual stages, of those who would learn the perfect light of the Christian discipline. *Tertullian (c. 207, W), 3.373.*

How agreeable to sound reason, and unattended with injury either to master or slave, was the law that a person of the same faith should not be allowed to continue in slavery more than six years. *Origen (c. 248, E), 4.562.*

It is for this reason, therefore, that the Law is called a "ministration of death," because it delivered sinners and transgressors over to death. But for those who observed it, it defended them from death. It also established them in glory, by the help and aid of our Lord Jesus Christ. *Disputation of Archelaus and Manes (c. 320, E), 6.203.*

I understand, then, that the primary effort [of Manes, a heretic] was directed at proving that the Law of Moses is not harmonious with the law of Christ. . . . However, we proved that the whole Old Testament agrees with the New Testament and is in perfect harmony with it. . . . Do you not think that a boy who is brought to the teachers of knowledge by his pedagogue should later view that pedagogue in dishonor after he has grown up to adulthood? Should he dishonor him simply because he no longer needs his services, but can make his way to the schools without any assistance from that custodian? *Disputation of Archelaus and Manes (c. 320, E), 6.215.*

I will demonstrate that Jesus neither said nor did anything that was contrary to Moses. First, let us address the saying, "An eye for an eye and a tooth for a tooth." This speaks of justice. Now, Jesus' commandment is that a man, when struck on the one cheek, should also offer the other one. This speaks of goodness. Well, then, are justice and goodness opposed to each other? Far from it! Rather, there has merely been an advance from simple justice to positive goodness. *Disputation of Archelaus and Manes (c. 320, E), 6.216.*

SEE ALSO CIRCUMCISION; DECALOGUE; JEW, JEWS; MOSES; SABBATH; TYPE, TYPOLOGY.

LAW, NATURAL

When Gentiles, who do not have the law, by nature do the things contained in the law, these, although not having the law, are a law to themselves, who show the work of the law written in their hearts, their conscience also bearing witness. Rom. 2:14, 15.

Those who did that which is universally, naturally, and eternally good are pleasing to God. Therefore, in the resurrection, they will be saved through this Christ. They will be saved equally with those righteous men who were before them—namely, Noah, Enoch, Jacob, and whoever else there may be—along with those who have known this Christ. *Justin Martyr (c. 160, E), 1.217.*

For God sets before every race of mankind that which is always and universally just, as well as all righteousness. Every race knows that adultery, fornication, homicide, and similar things are sinful. And though they all commit such practices, yet they do not escape from the knowledge that they act unrighteously whenever they do so. *Justin Martyr (c. 160, E), 1.246.*

However, God exercises a providence over all things. Therefore, He also gives counsel. When giving counsel, He is present with those who attend to moral discipline. It follows, of course, that the subjects who are watched over and governed should be acquainted with their ruler.... For this reason, some of the Gentiles who were less addicted to allurements and immorality (and were not led away to such a degree of superstition concerning idols) were somewhat moved by His providence. Therefore, they were convinced that they should call the Maker of this universe the Father, for He exercises a providence over all things and arranges the affairs of our world.... Therefore, the God who benevolently causes His sun to rise upon everyone and sends rain upon both the just and the unjust, will judge those who, although enjoying His equally distributed kindness, have led lives not corresponding to the dignity of His generosity. *Irenaeus (c. 180, E/W), 1.459.*

At the most, the Greeks have received certain scintillations of the divine Word. For that reason, they have made some utterances of truth. Therefore, they bear witness that the force of truth is not hidden. Yet, at the same time, they expose their own weakness in not having arrived at the end. *Clement of Alexandria (c. 195, E), 2.193.*

I contend that, before the Law of Moses was written on stone tablets, there was an unwritten, natural law that was habitually understood and that the fathers habitually kept. *Tertullian (c. 197, W), 3.152.*

Although good and evil are each known by nature, yet life is not thereby spent under the discipline of God. *Tertullian (c. 207, W), 3.372.*

Both the people [of Israel], by their transgression of His laws, and the whole race of mankind, by their neglect of natural duty, had sinned and rebelled against the Creator. *Tertullian (c. 207, W), 3.438, 439.*

The Lord Himself says, "If I had not come and spoken unto them, they would have no sin. But now they have no cloak for their sin." The only sense we can find in His words is that the Logos [Reason] Himself says that persons are not chargeable with sin to whom He has not fully come. However, those who have had part in Him—but act contrary to the ideas by which He declares His full presence in us—are guilty if they sin. Only when read in that manner is the saying true.... However, if the words are applied to the *visible* Christ (as many think that they should), then is it really true that those had no sin to whom He did not come? If so, then all who lived before the coming of the Savior were free from sin. For Jesus, as seen in the flesh, had not yet come. What is more, all those to whom He has never been preached will have no sin. And if they have no sin, then it is clear they are not liable to judgment. However, our whole race has part in the logos [reason] in man.... For before the consummation of logos [reason] comes, there is nothing in man except what is blameworthy. All is imperfect and defective. *Origen (c. 228, E), 9.320.*

It is no matter of surprise that the same God would have sown in the hearts of all men those truths that he taught by the prophets and the Savior. This was so that at the divine Judgment every man will be without excuse, having the "requirements of the law written upon his heart." *Origen (c. 248, E), 4.398.*

Plato ... in one of his epistles talks about the "chief good" and says, "The chief good can by no means be described in words. Rather, it is produced by long habit, and it bursts forth suddenly as a light in the soul." ... On hearing these words, we then admit that they are well said. For it is God who revealed to men these and other noble expressions. It is for this reason that those who have entertained correct ideas regarding God—but who have not offered to him a worship in harmony with the truth—are liable to the punishments that fall on sinners. *Origen (c. 248, E), 4.574.*

I imagine that He signified by the "sixty queens" [Cant. 6:8, 9] those persons who had pleased God—from the first man who was created, down to Noah. The reason is that these men had no need of commandments and laws for their salvation. For the creation of the world in six days was still recent. . . . These men had great honor, being associated with the angels and often seeing God manifested visibly, and not in a dream. Reflect on the confidence that Seth had towards God—and Abel, Enosh, Enoch, Methuselah, and Noah. These were the first lovers of righteousness. *Methodius (c. 290, E), 6.333.*

Since we often see that the worshippers of other gods themselves confess and acknowledge the Supreme God, what pardon can they hope for their impiety? For they do not acknowledge the worship of Him whom man cannot altogether be ignorant of. For in swearing, in expressing a wish, and in giving thanks, they do not name Jupiter, or a number of gods, but only "God." The truth, of its own accord, entirely breaks forth by the force of nature even from unwilling breasts! *Lactantius (c. 304–313, W), 7.40.*

If anyone is tossed about on the sea, the wind being furious, it is this God whom he invokes. If anyone is harassed by any violence, he implores His aid. . . . Thus, they never remember God unless it is when they are in trouble. When fear has left them, and the dangers have subsided, then in fact they quickly hasten to the temples of the gods. . . . But to God, whom they called on in their necessity itself, they do not give thanks even in word. *Lactantius (c. 304–313, W), 7.41.*

Cicero says, . . . "Among men themselves, there is no nation either so uncivilized or so savage that does not know that some conception of Deity should be contemplated, even if they are ignorant of proper conceptions of Him." *Lactantius (c. 304–313, W), 7.78.*

Is there any human being who has not entered on the first day of his life with an idea of that Great Ruler? Is there anyone in whom it has not been implanted by nature . . . that God is King and Lord, the Ruler of all things? *Arnobius (c. 305, E), 6.421.*

From where, then, did righteous Abel and all those succeeding worthies (who are enrolled among the righteous) derive their righteousness? For there was as yet no Law of Moses. . . . Were they not constituted righteous in virtue of their fulfilling the law—"everyone of them

showing the work of the law written in their hearts." . . . For when a man "who does not have the Law does naturally the things contained in the Law, he, not having the Law, is a law unto himself." *Disputation of Archelaus and Manes (c. 320, E), 6.201.*

SEE ALSO FALL OF MAN; FREE WILL AND PREDESTINATION; MAN, DOCTRINE OF; SOVEREIGNTY AND PROVIDENCE OF GOD.

LAW, ROMAN

As they bound him with thongs, Paul said to the centurion who stood by, "Is it lawful for you to scourge a man who is a Roman, and uncondemned?" When the centurion heard that, he went and told the commander, saying, "Take care what you do, for this man is a Roman." Acts 22:25, 26.

Those who are brought before you for trial, though they may be arraigned on the gravest charges, have no fear, because they know that you will inquire respecting their previous life. They know you will not be influenced by names if they mean nothing, nor by the charges contained in the indictments, if they are false. They accept with equal satisfaction, as regards its fairness, the sentence whether of condemnation or of acquittal. *Athenagoras (c. 175, E), 2.130.*

In the case of a pregnant woman being condemned to death, the Romans do not allow her to undergo punishment until she has delivered. *Clement of Alexandria (c. 195, E), 2.368.*

When the charges made against us are made against others, they are permitted to make use of their own lips and of hired advocates to show their innocence. They have full opportunity of answer and debate. In fact, to condemn anybody undefended and unheard is against the law. *Tertullian (c. 197, W), 3.18.*

What has become of the laws that repressed expensive and ostentatious ways of living? . . . Or the laws that closed down the theaters as quickly as they arose to debauch the manners of the people? . . . In regard to women, those laws of your fathers used to be an encouragement to modesty and sobriety. At that time, a woman wore no gold upon her except on the finger—that being the bridal ring by which her husband had sacredly pledged her to himself. But those laws have fallen into disuse. *Tertullian (c. 197, W), 3.22.*

You are barred by the rule that makes it illegal to allege crimes which no legal action discusses, no indictment specifies, no sentence enumerates. Only in a case that is submitted to the judge, inquired into against the defendant, responded to by him or denied, and cited from the bench—do I acknowledge a legal charge. *Tertullian (c. 197, W), 3.111.*

In the case of all other crimes that are similarly forbidden and punished by the laws, the penalty is not inflicted until it is sought by regular process. Take for instance, the case of a murderer or an adulterer. An examination is ordered concerning the particulars of the crime. *Tertullian (c. 197, W), 3.113.*

An unjust law secures no respect. In my opinion, however, there is a suspicion among you that some of these laws are unjust. For not a day passes by without your modifying their severity and iniquity by fresh deliberations and decisions. *Tertullian (c. 197, W), 3.114.*

It is in fact your own maxim that no one should determine a cause without hearing both sides of it. *Tertullian (c. 197, W), 3.127.*

The man of no philosophical system who abstains from adultery when the opportunity comes to him does so generally from dread of the law and its penalties. *Origen (c. 248, E), 4.636.*

Anyone who whispers any evil about your kings is accused of treason among you. You have made it a crime to degrade a magistrate or to use insulting language to a senator. To do so incurs the severest punishment. *Arnobius (c. 305, E), 6.487.*

To the debauched scoffers at the gods [i.e., actors and/or poets], gifts and presents are ordained—together with leisure and freedom from public burdens. *Arnobius (c. 305, E), 6.488.*

SEE ALSO CAPITAL PUNISHMENT; CRIME AND PUNISHMENT; ROMAN EMPIRE, ROMANS.

LAWSUITS

If anyone wants to sue you and take away your tunic, let him have your cloak also. Matt. 5:40.

Dare any of you, having a matter against another, go to law before the unrighteous, and not before the saints? . . . If then you have judgments concerning things pertaining to this life, do you appoint those who are least esteemed by the church to judge? I say this to your shame. Is it so, that there is not a wise man among

you, not even one, who will be able to judge between his brethren? But brother goes to law against brother, and that before unbelievers! Now therefore, it is already an utter failure for you that you go to law against one another. Why do you not rather accept wrong? Why do you not rather let yourselves be defrauded? 1 Cor. 6:1, 4–7.

We have learned not to return blow for blow, nor to go to law with those who plunder and rob us. *Athenagoras (c. 175, E), 2.129.*

When robbed, they do not go to law. *Athenagoras (c. 175, E), 2.134.*

"Do any of you, having a matter against the other, dare to go to law before the unrighteous and not before the saints?" . . . He teaches that the man of God does not remember injuries. Christ does not even allow him to pray against the man who has done wrong to him. . . . To say, then, that the man who has been injured goes to law before the unrighteous is nothing else than to say that he shows a wish to retaliate, and a desire to injure the other person in return. But this is also to do wrong himself. *Clement of Alexandria (c. 195, E), 2.547, 548.*

Shall the son of peace take part in the battle when it does not become him even to sue at law? *Tertullian (c. 211, W), 3.99*

Believers who differ among themselves should not go to a Gentile judge. *Cyprian (c. 250, W), 5.545.*

If by any management or temptation, a dispute arises with anyone, . . . let it not come before a pagan tribunal. . . . However, if brothers have lawsuits with one another (which God forbid), you who are the rulers should learn from it that such persons do not act as brothers in the Lord. Rather, they act as public enemies. . . . Let not the unbeliever know of your differences among one another. You should not receive unbelievers as witnesses against yourselves—nor be judged by them. . . . Let your adjudications be held on the second day of the week. That way, if any controversy arises concerning your decision, you will have a period of time until the Sabbath. That may enable you to set the controversy right and to bring the contestants to peace with one another in time for the Lord's Day. Let the deacons and presbyters be present at your adjudications. They should judge without respect of persons. Instead, they should judge with righteousness, as men of God. *Apostolic Constitutions (compiled c. 390, E), 7.417.*

SEE ALSO CHRISTIAN LIFE; NONRESISTANCE; SERMON ON THE MOUNT; WAR.

LAYING ON OF HANDS
SEE HANDS, LAYING ON OF.

LENT
Lent is the period of fasting that precedes Easter. In the early church, the length of this fast varied from region to region, being anywhere from one day to forty days in length.

The [paschal] controversy concerns not only the day, but also as regards the form itself of the fast. For some consider themselves bound to fast one day, others two days, others still more. In fact, others fast forty days. . . . And this variety among the observers [of the fasts] did not have its origin in our time, but long before in that of our predecessors. Some of our predecessors, perhaps not being very accurate in their observance of it, handed down to posterity the custom as it had been [introduced], through simplicity or private fancy. Nevertheless, all these churches lived in peace with one another. . . . In fact, the difference of the fast establishes the harmony of our faith. *Irenaeus (c. 180, E/W), 1.568, 569.*

You have sent to me, most faithful and accomplished son, in order to inquire what is the proper hour for bringing the fast to a close on the day of Easter. You say that there are some of the brethren who hold that it should be done at cockcrow, but others who say that it should end at nightfall. . . . It will be cordially acknowledged by all that those who have been humbling their souls with fasting should immediately begin their festal joy and gladness at the same hour as the resurrection. . . . However, no precise account seems to be offered in [Holy Scripture] as to the hour at which He rose. *Dionysius of Alexandria (c. 262, E), 6.94.*

We make the following statement and explanation to those who seek an exact account of the specific hour, half-hour, or quarter of an hour at which it is proper to begin their rejoicing over our Lord's rising from the dead. Those who are too hasty and give up even before midnight, we reprove as irresponsible and intemperate. . . . And those who hold out and continue for a very long time and persevere

even on to the fourth watch . . . we receive as noble and hardworking disciples. However, let us not come down harshly on those who pause and refresh themselves in the interim as they are able or feel the need. For all do not carry out the six days of fasting either equally or alike. Some observe even all the days as a fast, remaining without food through the whole period. Others take only two days. Others, three; and others, four. But some do not take even one. *Dionysius of Alexandria (c. 262, E), 6.95.*

Paul allows "by permission" one who is in such a condition to contract a second marriage. . . . To illustrate, suppose that in the fast that prepares us for the Easter celebration, one offers food to another who is dangerously ill, saying, "In truth, my friend, it would be fitting and good that you should bravely hold out like us and participate in the same things—for it is forbidden even to think of food today. However, since you are held down and weakened by disease and cannot bear it, therefore, 'by permission' we advise you to eat food. Otherwise, you might perish, being quite unable to hold out against your desire for food because of your sickness." *Methodius (c. 290, E), 6.321.*

If any bishop, presbyter, deacon, reader, or singer does not fast the fast of forty days, or the fourth day of the week and the day of the Preparation, let him be deprived, unless he is hindered by weakness of body. But if he is one of the laity, let him be suspended. *Apostolic Constitutions (compiled c. 390, E), 7.504.*

SEE ALSO CALENDAR, CHRISTIAN; EASTER; FASTING.

LETTERS OF COMMUNION
SEE EUCHARIST (III. LETTERS OF COMMUNION).

LIBERTY, RELIGIOUS
Choose for yourselves this day whom you will serve, whether the gods which your fathers served that were on the other side of the River, or the gods of the Amorites, in whose land you dwell. But as for me and my house, we will serve the Lord. Josh. 24:15.

Where the spirit of the Lord is, there is liberty. 2 Cor. 3:17.

See that you [the Romans] do not give a further reason for the charge of irreligion—by taking away religious liberty and forbidding free choice of deity. You say that I may no longer worship according to my inclination but am compelled to worship against it. Not even a human being would care to have unwilling homage rendered to him. And so even the Egyptians have been permitted the legal use of their ridiculous superstition. *Tertullian (c. 197, W), 3.39.*

With you, liberty is given to worship any god but the true God—as though He were not the God that all should worship, to whom all belong. *Tertullian (c. 197, W), 3.39.*

It was easily seen to be unjust to compel free men to offer sacrifice against their will. For even in other acts of religious service, a willing mind is required. Therefore, it should be counted quite absurd for one man to compel another to do honor to the gods. *Tertullian (c. 197, W), 3.41.*

It is a fundamental human right, a privilege of nature, that every man should worship according to his own convictions. One man's religion neither harms nor helps another man. It is certainly no part of religion to compel religion [on another]. Free will, and not force, should lead us. *Tertullian (c. 212, W), 3.105.*

Who is so arrogant, so high and mighty, to forbid me to raise my eyes to heaven? Who can impose upon me the necessity either of worshipping that which I am unwilling to worship—or of abstaining from the worship of Him whom I wish to worship? . . . No one will accomplish this, so long as we have any courage to despise death and pain. *Lactantius (c. 304–313, W), 7.149.*

There is no occasion for violence and injury. For religion cannot be imposed by force. *Lactantius (c. 304–313, W), 7.156.*

Religion is to be defended—not by putting to death—but by dying. Not by cruelty, but by patient endurance. Not by guilt, but by good faith. For the former belongs to evil, but the latter to the good. . . . For if you wish to defend religion by bloodshed, tortures, and guilt, it will no longer be defended. Rather, it will be polluted and profaned. For nothing is so much a matter of free will as religion. If the mind of the worshipper is disinclined to it, religion is at once taken away and ceases to exist. . . . We, on the contrary, do not require that anyone should be compelled to worship our God, whether he is willing or unwilling. . . . Nor are we angry if anyone does not worship Him. For we trust in

the majesty of Him who has power to avenge contempt shown towards Himself. . . . And, therefore, when we suffer such impious things, we do not resist even in word. Rather, we leave vengeance to God. We do not act as those persons who would have it appear that they are defenders of their gods, who rage without restraint against those who do not worship them. *Lactantius (c. 304–313, W), 7.157, 158.*

SEE ALSO MARTYRS, MARTYRDOM; PERSECUTION.

LIFE, BOOK OF
SEE BOOK OF LIFE.

LIFE, CHRISTIAN
SEE CHRISTIAN LIFE.

LIFE, TREE OF
SEE TREE OF LIFE.

LINUS

Linus was the first man appointed by the apostles to serve as bishop of the church in Rome.

Do your utmost to come before winter. Eubulus greets you, as well as Pudens, Linus, Claudia, and all the brethren. 2 Tim. 4:21.

The blessed apostles, then, having founded and built up the church, committed into the hands of Linus the office of the bishop. Of this Linus, Paul makes mention in the epistles to Timothy. *Irenaeus (c. 180, E/W), 1.416.*

SEE ALSO CLEMENT OF ROME; CHURCHES, APOSTOLIC (VI. CHURCH AT ROME).

LITURGY

Liturgy [Gr. *leitourgia*] refers to the public worship of Christians.

As they ministered [Gr. leitourgounton*] to the Lord and fasted, the Holy Spirit said, "Now separate to me Barnabas and Saul for the work to which I have called them."* Acts 13:2.

Now concerning the Eucharist, give thanks in this manner: First, concerning the cup: "We thank you, our Father, for the holy vine of David your servant, which you made known to us through Jesus your Servant. To you be the glory forever." And concerning the broken [bread]: "We thank you, our Father, for the life and knowledge which you made known to us through Jesus your Servant. To you be the glory forever. Even as this broken bread was scattered over the hills, and was gathered together and became one, so let your church be gathered together from the ends of the earth into your kingdom. For yours is the glory and the power through Jesus Christ forever." *Didache (c. 80–140, E), 7.379, 380.*

But after you are filled, give thanks in this manner: "We thank you, holy Father, for your holy name which you caused to tabernacle in our hearts, and for the knowledge and faith and immortality, which you made known to us through Jesus your Servant. To you be the glory forever. You, Almighty Master, created all things for your name's sake. You gave food and drink to men for enjoyment, so that they might give thanks to you. But to us, you freely gave spiritual food and drink and life eternal through your Servant. Before all things, we thank you that you are mighty. To you be the glory forever. Remember, Lord, your church, to deliver it from all evil and to make it perfect in your love, and gather it from the four winds, sanctified for your kingdom which you prepared for it. For yours is the power and the glory forever. Let grace come, and let this world pass away. Hosanna to the God of David! If anyone is holy, let him come; if anyone is not so, let him repent. Maranatha. Amen." But permit the prophets to make thanksgiving as much as they desire. *Didache (c. 80–140, E), 7.380.*

And on the day called Sunday, all who live in cities or in the country gather together to one place. And the memoirs of the apostles or the writings of the prophets are read, as long as time permits. Then, when the reader has ceased, the president verbally instructs us and exhorts us to imitate these good things. Then we all rise together and pray. And, as we said before, when our prayer is ended, bread and wine and water are brought. Then, the president in like manner offers prayers and thanksgivings, according to his ability. And the people assent, saying "Amen." Then, [the Eucharist] is distributed to everyone, and everyone participates in [the bread and wine], over which thanks has been given. And a portion of it is sent by the deacons to those who are absent. *Justin Martyr (c. 160, E), 1.186.*

Let him pass many sleepless nights for you, interceding for you with God, influencing the Father with the power of familiar litanies. *Clement of Alexandria (c. 195, E), 2.603.*

In the reading of the Scriptures, in the chanting of psalms, in the preaching of sermons, and in the offering up of prayers—in all of these religious services, matter and opportunity are afforded to her of seeing visions. *Tertullian (c. 210, W, Montanistic), 3.188.*

In the middle, let the reader stand upon some high place. Let him read the books of Moses, of Joshua the son of Nun, of the Judges, Kings, Chronicles, and those written after the return from the captivity. In addition, let him read the books of Job and of Solomon, and of the sixteen prophets. But when there have been two lessons individually read, let some other person sing the hymns of David. Then let the people join at the conclusions of the verses. Afterwards, let our Acts be read, and the Epistles of Paul our fellow-worker, which he sent to the churches under the conduct of the Holy Spirit. And afterwards, let a deacon or a presbyter read the Gospels—both those that Matthew and John have delivered to you, and those that the fellow-workers of Paul (Luke and Mark) received and left to you. And while the Gospel is read, let all the presbyters, deacons, and all the people stand up in great silence. . . . In the next place, let the presbyters one by one, not all together, exhort the people—and the bishop in the last place, as being the leader. . . .

After this, let all rise up with one consent and, looking towards the east—after the catechumens and penitents are gone out—pray to God eastward. . . . After the prayer is over, let some of the deacons attend upon the oblation of the Eucharist, ministering to the Lord's body with fear. Let others of them watch the multitude and keep them silent. And let the deacon who is at the high priest's hand say to the people, "Let no one have any quarrel against another. Let no one come in hypocrisy." Then let the men give the men, and the women give the women, the Lord's kiss. . . . After this, let the deacon pray for the whole church, the whole world, and the individual parts and fruits of it. Let him also pray for the priests and rulers, for the high priest and king, and for the peace of the world. After this, let the high priest pray for peace upon the people and bless them (as Moses commanded the priests to bless the people) in these words: "The Lord bless you and keep you. The Lord make his face to shine upon you and give you peace." Let the bishop pray for the people and say: "Save our people, O Lord, and bless your inheritance, which you have obtained with the precious blood of your Christ and have called a royal priesthood and a holy nation." After this, let the sacrifice follow, the people standing and praying silently. And when the oblation has been made, let every rank by itself partake of the Lord's body and precious blood, in order. Let them approach with reverence and holy fear—as to the body of their king. Let the women approach with their heads covered, as is becoming the order of women. But let the door be watched, lest any unbeliever, or one not yet initiated, should come in. *Apostolic Constitutions (compiled c. 390, E), 7.421, 422.*

Post-Nicene forms of early liturgies: 7.486–7.491, 7.537–7.550, 7.551–7.560, 7.561–7.568.

SEE ALSO ASSEMBLIES, CHRISTIAN; CALENDAR, CHRISTIAN; EUCHARIST; MORNING AND EVENING PRAYER; SURSUM CORDA; WORSHIP, CHRISTIAN (II. WORSHIP CUSTOMS).

LIVING, CHRISTIAN

SEE CHRISTIAN LIFE.

LOGOS

The Greek word logos is usually translated in English Bibles as "word." Although this is one of the meanings of logos, it also means "reason" and "mind." Where English-speaking persons think of the Son as being the Word of God, the early Christians were often thinking of Him as being the Reason of God.

The Logos existed in the very beginning, the Logos was with God, the Logos was divine. John 1:1 (Moffatt).

He is clad in a robe dipped in blood (his name is called THE LOGOS OF GOD). Rev. 19:13 (Moffatt).

The Son of God is the Logos of the Father, in idea and in operation. For all things were made after the pattern of Him and by Him—the Father and the Son being one. The Son is in the Father and the Father is in the Son, in oneness and power of spirit. The Understanding and Reason of the Father is the Son of God. *Athenagoras (c. 175, E), 2.133.*

Among the Greeks, there is one definition of *logos* which means "the principle that thinks." There is also another definition that means "the instrument by means of which thought is

expressed." ... But God is all Mind and all Word. So He speaks exactly what He thinks. *Irenaeus (c. 180, E/W), 1.400.*

He was the Logos of God, that primordial First-begotten Word. *Tertullian (c. 197, W), 3.35.*

He is also called the Logos [i.e., Reason], because He takes away from us all that is irrational and makes us truly reasonable. *Origen (c. 228, E), 9.319, 320.*

According to [the pagan] Celsus, God Himself is the Reason [Gr. *logos*] of all things. However, according to our view, it is God's Son. Of Him we say ... "In the beginning was the Logos, and the Logos was with God, and the Logos was God." *Origen (c. 248, E), 4.553.*

The Greeks speak of Him as the Logos, more appropriately than we [Romans] do as the "Word" or "Speech." For *logos* means both speech and reason. And He is both the Voice and the Wisdom of God. *Lactantius (c. 304–313, W), 7.107; extended discussion: 9.319–9.328.*

SEE ALSO CHRIST, DIVINITY OF; JESUS CHRIST; TRINITY; WISDOM; WORD OF GOD (CHRIST).

LORD

SEE GOD.

LORD'S DAY

What today is commonly referred to as Sunday was usually called the Lord's Day by the early Christians.

Now on the first day of the week, when the disciples came together to break bread, Paul, ready to depart the next day, spoke to them. Acts 20:7.

On the first day of the week let each one of you lay something aside, storing up as he may prosper. 1 Cor. 16:2.

I was in the Spirit on the Lord's Day. Rev. 1:10.

But every Lord's Day, gather yourselves together, and break bread, and give thanksgiving after having confessed your transgressions, so that your sacrifice may be pure. *Didache (c. 80–140, E), 7.381.*

No longer observing the Sabbath, but living in the observance of the Lord's Day. *Ignatius (c. 105, E), 1.62.*

And on the day called Sunday, all who live in cities or in the country gather together to one place, and the memoirs of the apostles or the writings of the prophets are read. . . . But Sunday is the day on which we all hold our common assembly, because it is the first day on which God . . . made the world. And Jesus Christ our Savior rose from the dead on that same day. *Justin Martyr (c. 160, E), 1.186.*

In fulfillment of the commandment according to the Gospel, a person keeps the Lord's Day—when he abandons an evil disposition and assumes the disposition of the spiritual man, glorifying the Lord's resurrection in himself. *Clement of Alexandria (c. 195, E), 2.545.*

Christ rose on the third day, which fell on the first day of the weeks of harvest, on which the Law prescribed that the priest should offer up the sheaf. *Clement of Alexandria (c. 195, E), 2.581.*

We devote Sunday to rejoicing for a far different reason than sun worship. *Tertullian (c. 197, W), 3.31.*

Others . . . suppose that the sun is the god of the Christians . . . because we make Sunday a day of festivity. *Tertullian (c. 197, W), 3.123.*

You who reproach us with the sun and Sunday should consider your proximity to us. We are not far off from your Saturn and your days of rest. *Tertullian (c. 197, W), 3.123.*

Prayer is also subject to diversity of observance in the matter of kneeling, through the act of a few persons who abstain from kneeling on the Sabbath [i.e., Saturday]. . . . We, however, have received this practice: that we refrain from kneeling only on the day of the Lord's resurrection. In fact, we not only refrain from kneeling, but also from every posture and office of solicitude. We even postpone our businesses, lest we give any place to the devil. *Tertullian (c. 198, W), 3.689*

We consider fasting or kneeling in worship on the Lord's Day to be unlawful. We rejoice in the same privilege also from Easter to Pentecost. *Tertullian (c. 211, W), 3.94.*

We ourselves are accustomed to observe certain days. For example, there is the Lord's Day. . . . To the perfect Christian, who is ever serving his natural Lord—God the Word—in his thoughts, words, and deeds, all his days are the Lord's. So he is always keeping the Lord's Day. *Origen (c. 248, E), 4.647.*

It should not be lawful to celebrate the Lord's mystery of Easter at any other time but on the Lord's Day, the day on which the Lord's resurrection from death took place. *Anatolius (c. 270, E), 6.148, 149.*

On the former day [Saturday], we are accustomed to fast rigorously, so that on the Lord's Day we may go forth to our bread with thanksgiving. *Victorinus (c. 280, W), 7.341, 342.*

We celebrate the Lord's Day as a day of joy. For on it, He rose again. We have received it as a custom not even to bow the knee on that day. *Peter of Alexandria (c. 310, E), 6.278.*

On the day of our Lord's resurrection, which is the Lord's Day, you should meet more diligently, sending praise to God who made the universe by Jesus. . . . Otherwise, what apology will a person make to God who does not assemble on that day to hear the saving Word concerning the resurrection? On this day, we pray three times, standing in memory of Him who rose in three days. On this day, there is the reading of the Prophets, the preaching of the Gospel, the oblation of the sacrifice, and the gift of the holy food. *Apostolic Constitutions (compiled c. 390, E), 7.423.*

Break your fast when it is daybreak of the first day of the week, which is the Lord's Day. *Apostolic Constitutions (compiled c. 390, E), 7.447.*

He will be guilty of sin who fasts on the Lord's Day, for it is the day of the resurrection. *Apostolic Constitutions (compiled c. 390, E), 7.449.*

Keep the Sabbath and the Lord's Day festival. The first is the memorial of the creation; the second is the memorial of the resurrection. *Apostolic Constitutions (compiled c. 390, E), 7.469.*

On the day of the resurrection of the Lord, that is, the Lord's Day, assemble yourselves together without fail, giving thanks to God and praising Him. *Apostolic Constitutions (compiled c. 390, E), 7.471.*

Let the slaves work five days. But on the Sabbath day and the Lord's Day, let them have rest to go to church for instruction in godliness. We say the Sabbath, on account of creation, and the Lord's Day, on account of the resurrection. *Apostolic Constitutions (compiled c. 390, E), 7.495.*

If anyone of the clergy is found to fast on the Lord's Day, or on the Sabbath day, excepting one only [i.e., the Saturday before Easter], let him be deprived. However, if he is one of the laity, let him be suspended. *Apostolic Constitutions (compiled c. 390, E), 7.504.*

SEE ALSO EIGHTH DAY; EUCHARIST; LITURGY; SABBATH.

LORD'S PRAYER

He said to them, "When you pray, say: Our Father in heaven, hallowed be your name . . ." Luke 11:2.

Do not pray as the hypocrites. Rather, as the Lord commanded in His Gospel, pray this way: "Our Father who is in heaven, hallowed be your name. Your kingdom come. Your will be done, as in heaven, so on earth. Give us today our daily bread, and forgive us our debts as we also forgive our debtors. And bring us not into temptation, but deliver us from evil; for yours is the power and the glory forever." Three times during the day, pray in this manner. *Didache (c. 80–140, E), 1.379.*

In this prayer is contained a summary of the whole Gospel. *Tertullian (c. 198, W), 3.681.*

When we say, "Hallowed be your name," we mean this: that it may be hallowed *in us* who are in Him. . . . "Your will be done in the heavens and on the earth": this does not mean that there is some opposing power that prevents God's will from being done. So we are not praying for His successful achievement of His will. Rather, we pray for His will to be done *in everyone. Tertullian (c. 198, W), 3.682.*

"Your kingdom come" also has reference . . . to *us.* For when does God not reign? For in His hand is the heart of all kings. *Tertullian (c. 198, W), 3.683.*

How gracefully has the Divine Wisdom arranged the order of the prayer. After things heavenly, . . . it also gives earthly necessities room for a petition! *Tertullian (c. 198, W), 3.683.*

In petitioning for "daily bread," we ask for perpetuity in Christ and indivisibility from His body. *Tertullian (c. 198, W), 3.683.*

He teaches us to plead "to have our debts remitted us." Now, a petition for pardon is a full confession. For he who begs for pardon fully admits his guilt. . . . Moreover, in the Scriptures, debt is a figure of guilt, because it is equally due to the sentence of judgment and is exacted by it. *Tertullian (c. 198, W), 3.684.*

"Lead us not into temptation." This means, do not allow us to be led into it by him who tempts. For far be the thought that the Lord should seem to tempt us—as if He either were ignorant of the faith of someone, or else were eager to overthrow it. *Tertullian (c. 198, W), 3.684.*

Jesus Himself gave us a form of praying. He Himself advised and instructed us as to what we should pray for. . . . What can be a more spiritual prayer than that which was given to us by Christ, by whom the Holy Spirit was also given to us. . . . So to pray in another way than what He taught is not merely ignorance—it is sin. For He Himself has established and said, "You reject the commandments of God so that you may keep your own traditions." Therefore, beloved brethren, let us pray as God our Teacher has taught us. . . . How much more effectually do we obtain what we ask in Christ's name, if we ask for it in His own prayer! *Cyprian (c. 250, W), 5.448.*

From the other writings of Cyprian, it is evident that in the preceding quotation, Cyprian does not mean that Christians can never pray extemporaneously or offer other prayers of the church. Instead, he means that we should not offer other prayers *in place of* the Lord's Prayer.

The Teacher of peace . . . does not want prayer to be made singly and individually—such as when someone prays for himself alone. For we do not say, "*My* Father, who is in heaven," nor "Give *me* this day *my* daily bread." . . . Our prayer is public and communal. When we pray, we do not pray for one person, but for the whole people. *Cyprian (c. 250, W), 5.449.*

The new man, born again and restored to his God through His grace, can say "Father" at the beginning, for he has now begun to be a son. *Cyprian (c. 250, W), 5.449.*

After this, we say, "Hallowed be Your name." It is not that we wish for God to be hallowed by *our* prayers. Rather, we beseech Him that His name may be hallowed in *us.* . . . We ask and entreat that we, who were sanctified in baptism, may continue in that which we have begun to be. And we pray daily for this. For we have need of daily sanctification—that we who daily fall away may wash out our sins by continual sanctification. *Cyprian (c. 250, W), 5.450.*

There follows in the prayer, "Your kingdom come." We ask that the kingdom of God may be set forth to *us*, in the same sense that we also ask for His name to be sanctified in us. For when does God not reign? *Cyprian (c. 250, W), 5.450.*

We also say, "Your will be done, as in heaven so in earth." . . . We pray and ask that God's will may be done in *us. Cyprian (c. 250, W), 5.451.*

It becomes a contradiction and a repugnant thing for us to seek to live long in this world. For we ask that the kingdom of God should come quickly. *Cyprian (c. 250, W), 5.452.*

As the prayer goes forward, we ask and say, "Give us this day our daily bread." This may be understood both spiritually and literally. [CYPRIAN GOES ON TO EXPLAIN HOW THESE WORDS CAN BE APPLIED TO THE EUCHARIST.] . . . But it may also be understood that we who have renounced the world and have cast away its riches and pomps in the faith of spiritual grace should ask for ourselves only food and sustenance. For the Lord teaches us and says, "Whoever does not forsake all that he has cannot be my disciple." So he who has begun to be Christ's disciple and renounces all things according to the word of his Master, should ask only for his *daily* food. He should not extend the desires of his prayer to a long period. *Cyprian (c. 250, W), 5.452.*

Daily bread cannot be lacking to the righteous man. . . . To those who seek God's kingdom and righteousness, he promises that all things will be added. *Cyprian (c. 250, W), 5.453.*

After this, we pray for our sins, saying, "And forgive us our debts, as we also forgive our debtors." After the supply of food, pardon of sin is then asked for. This is so that he who is fed by God may live in God. And not only the present and temporal life is to be provided for, but the eternal also—to which we may come if our sins are forgiven. *Cyprian (c. 250, W), 5.453.*

He who taught us to pray for our debts and sins has promised that His fatherly mercy and pardon will follow. . . . And that which we seek for our own sins cannot be obtained unless we ourselves have acted in a similar way in respect to our debtors. . . . The servant who, after having had all his debt forgiven him by his master, but would not forgive his fellow servant, was cast back into prison. *Cyprian (c. 250, W), 5.453.*

"And allow us not to be led into temptation." In these words, it is shown that the adversary can do nothing against us unless God has previously permitted it. *Cyprian (c. 250, W), 5.454.*

When we ask that we may not come into temptation, we are reminded of our infirmity and weakness, in that we need to ask this. Otherwise, someone may insolently vaunt himself or proudly and arrogantly assume anything to himself. *Cyprian (c. 250, W), 5.454.*

When we say, "Deliver us from evil," there remains nothing further that we should ask. . . . For what fear is there in this life to the man whose guardian in this life is God? *Cyprian (c. 250, W), 5.455.*

In the daily prayer, we ask, "Your will be done on earth as in heaven." *Cyprian (c. 250, W), 5.539.*

When we pray, the Lord has taught us to say to His Father: "Your will be done on earth as in heaven." Now, the heavenly creatures of the spiritual powers all glorify God with one accord. So, likewise, upon earth, may all men glorify with one mouth and one purpose the only, the one, and the true God, by Christ, His Only-Begotten. *Apostolic Constitutions (compiled c. 390, E), 7.420; extended discussion: 3.681–3.684, 5.447–5.457.*

SEE ALSO PRAYER.

LORD'S SUPPER

SEE EUCHARIST; LOVE FEAST.

LOT

With respect to those actions [in the Old Testament] on which the Scriptures pass no censure, but which are simply set down, we should not become the accusers. For we are not more exact than God, nor can we be superior to our Master. . . . Thus, the daughters [of Lot] spoke according to their simplicity and innocence, imagining that all mankind had perished, even as the Sodomites had done. They thought that the anger of God had come down upon the whole earth. For that reason, they are to be held excusable, since they supposed that only they, along with their father, were left for the preservation of the human race. *Irenaeus (c. 180, E/ W), 1.504, 505.*

Lot's daughters intoxicated their father, so that they might become mothers by him. However, let us, in a few words, soften down the repulsive features of the history. . . . When the young maidens, who had heard of the burning of the world, saw fire devastating their city and country, they supposed that the only means left of rekindling the flame of human life was in their father and themselves. On that supposition, they devised the plan so that the world would continue. Now, will their conduct be deemed worse than that of the wise man who—according to the teachings of the Stoics—acts correctly in having relations with his daughter in the situation already supposed—i.e., that all men have been destroyed? I am aware, of course, that some have taken offense at the desire of Lot's daughters and have regarded their conduct as very wicked. They have said that two accursed nations—Moab and Ammon—have sprung from that unhallowed intercourse. Yet, truly, sacred Scripture is nowhere found to distinctly approve of their conduct as good, nor to pass sentence upon it as blameworthy. *Origen (c. 248, E), 4.518.*

LOVE

This is My commandment, that you love one another as I have loved you. John 15:12.

Though I bestow all my goods to feed the poor, and though I give my body to be burned, but have not love, it profits me nothing. 1 Cor. 13:3.

And now abide faith, hope, love, these three; but the greatest of these is love. 1 Cor. 13:13.

He that has love is far from every sin. *Polycarp (c. 135, E), 1.34.*

We [Gentiles] who used to hate and destroy one another, and would not live with men of a different tribe because of their different manners, now, since the coming of Christ, live familiarly with them, and pray for our enemies. *Justin Martyr (c. 160, E), 1.167.*

Jesus commanded us to love even our enemies, as was predicted by Isaiah in many passages. *Justin Martyr (c. 160, E), 1.242.*

All of us pray for you, and for all men, as our Christ and Lord taught us to do. For He commanded us to pray even for our enemies, and to love those who hate us, and to bless those who curse us. *Justin Martyr (c. 160, E), 1.266.*

Loving one's enemies does not mean loving wickedness, ungodliness, adultery, or theft. Rather, it means loving the thief, the ungodly person, and the adulterer. Not as far as he sins (in respect of the actions by which he stains the name of man), but as he is a man and is the work of God. *Clement of Alexandria (c. 195, E), 2.426.*

Fear works abstinence from what is evil. But love exhorts to the doing of good, by building up to the point of spontaneity. *Clement of Alexandria (c. 195, E), 2.546.*

One gains immortality by the very exercise of loving the Father to the extent of one's might and power. For the more one loves God, the more he enters within God. . . . In both of the commandments, then, He introduces love. Yet, He distinguishes these loves in order. The first requirement of love He assigns us to give to God. The second He allots to our neighbor. *Clement of Alexandria (c. 195, E), 2.599.*

We are therefore to love Jesus equally with God. And he loves Christ Jesus who does His will and keeps His commandments. *Clement of Alexandria (c. 195, E), 2.599.*

Our religion commands us to love even our enemies, and to pray for those who persecute us. . . . For everyone loves those who love them. It is unique to Christians to love those who hate them. *Tertullian (c. 212, W), 3.105.*

What else is the preservation of humanity than to love a man because he is a man and the same as ourselves? . . . If it is contrary to nature to injure a man, it must be in accordance with nature to benefit a man. And he who does not do this deprives himself of the title of a man. *Lactantius (c. 304–313, W), 7.174; see also 2.426.*

SEE ALSO NONRESISTANCE; SERMON ON THE MOUNT; WAR.

LOVE FEAST

Therefore when you come together in one place, it is not to eat the Lord's Supper. For in eating, each one takes his own supper ahead of others; and one is hungry and another is drunk. 1 Cor. 11:20, 21.

They are spots and blemishes, carousing in their own deceptions while they feast with you. 2 Pet. 2:13.

These are spots in your love feasts, while they feast with you without fear. Jude 12.

It is not lawful without the bishop either to baptize or to celebrate a love feast. *Ignatius (c. 105, E), 1.90.*

Some, speaking with unbridled tongue, dare to apply the name *agape* to pitiful suppers, redolent of savor and sauces. . . . The supper is made for love, but the supper is not love. *Clement of Alexandria (c. 195, E), 2.238.*

The apostle, restraining those who transgress in their conduct at entertainments, says, "For everyone takes beforehand in eating his own supper. And one is hungry, and another drunk." *Clement of Alexandria (c. 195, E), 2.240.*

[The heretics] eagerly embrace that convivial couch of honor in the *agape*, falsely so called. *Clement of Alexandria (c. 195, E), 2.552.*

You [Romans] attack also our humble feasts on the grounds that they are extravagant as well as infamously wicked. You make it seem that the saying of Diogenes applies to us: "The people of Megara feast as though they were going to die tomorrow." . . . Yet, you make a great ado only about the modest supper room of the Christians. Our feast explains itself by its name. The Greeks call it *agape*, i.e., love. Whatever the meal costs, our outlay in the name of piety is gain. For we aid the needy with the good things of the feast. . . .

Before reclining, the participants first taste of prayer to God. Only as much is eaten as satisfies the cravings of hunger. Only as much is drunk as befits the chaste. . . . The participants talk as those who know that the Lord is one of their hearers. After washing the hands and the bringing in of lights, each is asked to stand forth and sing, as he can, a hymn to God—either one from the Holy Scriptures or one of his own composing. This is proof of the [temperate] measure of our drinking. Just as the feast began with prayer, so it is closed with prayer. We depart from the feast, not like troops of mischief-doers, . . . but as ones who have as much care for our modesty and chastity as though we had been at a school of virtue, rather than a banquet. *Tertullian (c. 197, W), 3.47.*

[What unbelieving husband], without some suspicion of his own, will dismiss her to attend that Lord's supper that they defame? *Tertullian (c. 205, W), 4.47.*

We practice sharing in our banquets, which are not only modest, but also sober. For we do not indulge in entertainments, nor do we prolong our feasts with wine. Rather, we temper our joyousness with seriousness, with chaste discourse, and with bodies even more chaste. *Mark Minucius Felix (c. 200, W), 4.192.*

In that last meal, which they call the free meal, they were partaking as far as they could, not of a free supper, but of an *agape*. *Passion of Perpetua and Felicitas (c. 205, W), 3.704.*

SEE ALSO ASSEMBLIES, CHRISTIAN; CHRISTIANITY (V. FALSE ACCUSATIONS AGAINST CHRISTIANS); EUCHARIST.

LUCIFER

How you are fallen from heaven, O Lucifer, son of the morning! How you are cut down to the ground, you who weakened the nations! Isa. 14:12.

Concerning another opposing power, we are taught the following by the prophet Isaiah: The prophet says, "How is Lucifer, who used to arise in the morning, fallen from heaven!" . . . Most evidently by these words a being is shown to have fallen from heaven—he who formerly was Lucifer, and who used to arise in the morning. For if he originally had a nature of darkness (as some think), how is it said that Lucifer existed this way before? Or how could he arise in the morning—if he had in himself nothing of the light? Nay, even the Savior Himself teaches us, saying of the devil, "Behold, I see Satan fallen from heaven like lightning." For at one time he was light. *Origen (c. 225, E), 4.259.*

Lucifer, star of the morning, fell from heaven to be warred against and destroyed by Jesus. *Origen (c. 228, E), 9.304.*

SEE ALSO SATAN.

LUKE

Luke also, the companion of Paul, recorded the Gospel in a book. *Irenaeus (c. 180, E/W), 1.414.*

He himself clearly shows that this Luke was inseparable from Paul. He was his fellow worker in the Gospel. *Irenaeus (c. 180, E/W), 1.437.*

By the style of writing, Luke may be recognized both to have composed the Acts of the Apostles and to have translated Paul's Epistle to the Hebrews. *Clement of Alexandria (c. 195, E), 2.573.*

The third book of the Gospel is that according to Luke. . . . Now, he himself did not see the Lord in the flesh. And he, according as he was able to accomplish it, began his narrative with the birth of John. . . . Moreover, the Acts of all the apostles are comprised by Luke in one book . . . because these different events took place when he was personally present. The principle on which he wrote was to write only of what fell under his own notice. And he shows this clearly by the omission of the martyrdom of Peter, and also of the journey of Paul, when Paul went from the city of Rome to Spain. *Muratorian Fragment (c. 200, W), 5.603.*

Now, of the authors whom we possess, Marcion seems to have singled out Luke for his mutilating process. Luke, however, was not an apostle, but only an apostolic man. He was not a master, but a disciple. *Tertullian (c. 207, W), 3.347.*

SEE ALSO GOSPELS.

LUST

I say to you that whoever looks at a woman to lust for her has already committed adultery with her in his heart. And if your right eye causes you to sin, pluck it out and cast it from you; for it is more profitable for you that one of your members perish, than for your whole body to be cast into hell. Matt. 5:28, 29.

We are so far from practicing promiscuous intercourse, that it is not lawful among us to indulge even a lustful look. "For," He says, "he that looks on a woman to lust after her has committed adultery already in his heart." *Athenagoras (c. 175, E), 2.146.*

Concerning chastity, the Holy Word teaches us not only not to sin in *act,* but not even in *thought.* We are not even in the heart to think of any evil, nor look on another man's wife with our eyes to lust after her. *Theophilus (c. 180, E), 2.115.*

Much more must we keep pure from shameful deeds. On the one hand, we must not exhibit and expose parts of the body that we should not. And on the other hand, we should not look at what is forbidden. *Clement of Alexandria (c. 195, E), 2.251.*

Above all, it seems right that we turn away from the sight of women. For it is sin not only to touch, but to look. *Clement of Alexandria (c. 195, E), 2.291.*

The Christian husband has nothing to do with any woman but his own wife. . . . A Christian with grace-healed eyes is sightless in this matter. He is mentally blind against the assaults of passion. *Tertullian (c. 197, W), 3.51.*

Just as there is a lust for money, rank, eating, impure enjoyment, and glory—so is there also a lust for pleasure. *Tertullian (c. 197, W), 3.85.*

He defines as an adulterer not only the man who has actually invaded another's marriage bed, but also the man who has contaminated her by the lust of his gaze. *Tertullian (c. 203, W), 3.659.*

You must not say, "What harm is there in the eyes? For he who looks will not necessarily be perverted." . . . The reason is that he who looks upon a woman—even though he escapes the temptation—does not come away pure from all lustful thoughts. . . . Figuratively speaking, he keeps a fire in his breast if he permits an impure thought to dwell in his heart. *Hippolytus (c. 205, W), 5.173.*

He who forbade adultery now forbids all unlawful lust. *Apostolic Constitutions (compiled c. 390, E), 7.460.*

SEE ALSO MODESTY.

LUXURY

SEE MATERIALISM; PROSPERITY.

MACCABEES

The Maccabees were a heroic Jewish family that led the fight to free the Jews from their Greek rulers in the second century B.C.

Also, in the times of the Maccabees, they bravely fought on the Sabbaths and routed their foreign enemies. *Tertullian (c. 197, W), 3.156.*

What will we say of the cruel tortures of the blessed martyrs in the Maccabees, and the various sufferings of the seven brethren? What will we say of the mother comforting her children in their agonies, herself dying also with her children? *Cyprian (c. 250, W), 5.349.*

SEE ALSO DEUTEROCANONICAL BOOKS.

MAGI

Before the child shall have knowledge to cry "My father" and "My mother," the riches of Damascus and the spoil of Samaria will be taken. Isa. 8:4.

Now after Jesus was born in Bethlehem of Judea in the days of Herod the king, behold, wise men [Gr. magoi] from the East came to Jerusalem. Matt. 2:1.

When the Child was born in Bethlehem, since Joseph could not find a lodging in that village, he took up his quarters in a certain cave near the village. While they were there, Mary brought forth the Christ and placed Him in a manger, and here the Magi who came from Arabia found Him. *Justin Martyr (c. 160, E), 1.237.*

For the Magi, who were held in bondage for the commission of all evil deeds through the owner of that demon, by coming to worship Christ, showed that they had revolted from that dominion which held them captive. *Justin Martyr (c. 160, E), 1.238.*

Another Scripture says, "Behold a man! The East is His name" [Zech. 6:12, LXX]. Accord-

ingly, when a star arose in heaven at the time of His birth—as is recorded in the memoirs of His apostles—the Magi from Arabia recognized the sign by this. And they came and worshipped Him. *Justin Martyr (c. 160, E), 1.252.*

The Greeks consider intercourse with a mother as unlawful. However, this practice is considered most becoming by the Persian Magi. *Tatian (c. 160, E), 2.77.*

The Magi of the Persians foretold the Savior's birth and came into the land of Judea, guided by a star. *Clement of Alexandria (c. 195, E), 2.316.*

Those who composed the *Persics* relate that in the highlands, in the country of the Magi, three mountains are situated on an extended plain. Those who travel through the locality, on coming to the first mountain, hear a confused sound as if of several legions shouting in battle array. *Clement of Alexandria (c. 195, E), 2.488.*

Let those Eastern magi be believed, endowing with gold and incense the infancy of Christ as a king. *Tertullian (c. 197, W), 3.162.*

The East, on the one hand, generally held the Magi to be kings. . . . Now, the Magi themselves, on recognizing Him, honored Him with gifts, and adored Him on bended knee as Lord and King. They did this on the evidence of the guiding and indicating star. Accordingly, they became "the spoils of Samaria," that is, of idolatry—by believing, namely, on Christ. *Tertullian (c. 197, W), 3.162.*

The Magi therefore offered to the then infant Lord that frankincense, myrrh, and gold. This was to be, as it were, the end of worldly sacrifice and glory, which Christ was about to do away with. *Tertullian (c. 200, W), 3.65, 66.*

Now it was in this [figurative] style that He called the Magi by the name of "Samaritans," for they practiced idolatry, just as the Samaritans did. *Tertullian (c. 207, W), 3.332.*

Notice the blunder of one who cannot distinguish between Magi and Chaldeans, nor recognize that what they profess is different. *Origen (c. 248, E), 4.422.*

The Magi, being on familiar terms with evil spirits, and invoking them for such purposes as their knowledge and wishes extend to, bring about only such results as apparently do not exceed the superhuman power and strength of the evil spirits.... However, if some greater manifestation of divinity is made, then the powers of the evil spirits are overthrown, being unable to resist the light of divinity.... The Magi, accordingly, wishing to produce the customary results, ... knew the reason of their failure, conjecturing the cause to be a great one. Beholding a divine sign in the heaven, they desired to learn its significance.... Accordingly, they came to Judea, persuaded that some king had been born.... However, He was Divine, the Savior of the human race, raised far above all those angels that minister to men. Accordingly, an angel rewarded the piety of the Magi for their worship of him, by making known to them that they were not to go back to Herod. *Origen (c. 248, E), 4.423.*

The Magi ... are from whom the art of magic derived its name. Through them, it has been transmitted to other nations, to the corruption and destruction of those who use it. *Origen (c. 248, E), 4.609, 610.*

But the master and president of the Magi of Egypt prevailed on him to abandon that course and urged him to slay and persecute those pure and holy men. *Dionysius of Alexandria (c. 262, E), 6.106, 107, as quoted by Eusebius.*

The Magi claim that they have intercessory prayers to win over certain powers, to make the way easy for those who are striving to climb to heaven. *Arnobius (c. 305, E), 6.457.*

SEE ALSO BIRTH OF JESUS.

MAGIC

SEE SPIRITISM.

MAJOR ORDERS

SEE BISHOP; CHURCH GOVERNMENT; DEACON; PRESBYTER.

MAMMON OF UNRIGHTEOUSNESS

SEE ALMS, ALMSGIVING (III. MAKING FRIENDS WITH UNRIGHTEOUS MAMMON).

MAN, DOCTRINE OF

I. Man created in the image of God

II. Free will and man's fallen nature

III. Man's mortality and immortality

I. Man created in the image of God

Then God said, "Let Us make man in Our image, according to Our likeness." Gen. 1:26.

Man is not, as the croaking philosophers say, merely a rational animal, capable of understanding and knowing.... Rather, man alone is the image and likeness of God. *Tatian (c. 160, E), 2.71.*

God ... willed to make man by whom He might be known. Therefore, He prepared the world for man. *Theophilus (c. 180, E), 2.98.*

Man is far from destitute of a divine idea. For, as it is written in Genesis, man partook of inspiration, being endowed with a purer essence than the other living creatures. *Clement of Alexandria (c. 195, E), 2.465.*

The victim of that seduction [i.e., Adam] was free and master of himself. And, as being the image and likeness of God, he was stronger than any angel. And, as being also the breath of the Divine Being, he was nobler than that material spirit of which angels were made.... He would not have made all things subject to man, if he had been too weak for such dominion, or if he were inferior to the angels, to whom He assigned no such subjects. *Tertullian (c. 207, W), 3.304.*

Since He is Himself the invisible image of the invisible God, He invisibly conveyed a share in Himself to all His rational creatures. So each one obtained a part of Him exactly proportioned to the amount of affection with which he regarded Him.... Agreeably to the faculty of free will, variety, and diversity that characterizes individual souls, one person is attached with a warmer love to the Author of its being, and another with a more feeble and weaker regard for Him. *Origen (c. 225, E), 4.282.*

II. Free will and man's fallen nature

I call heaven and earth as witnesses today against you, that I have set before you life and death, blessing and cursing; therefore choose life, that both you and your descendants may live. Deut. 30:19, 20.

Behold, I was brought forth in iniquity, and in sin my mother conceived me. Ps. 51:5.

The wicked are estranged from the womb; they go astray as soon as they are born. Ps. 58:3.

Our old man was crucified with Him, that the body of sin might be done away with, that we should no longer be slaves of sin. Rom. 6:6.

I know that in me (that is, in my flesh) nothing good dwells. Rom. 7:18.

Therefore, the prophets used to exhort men to what was good, to act justly and to work righteousness . . . because it is in our power to do so. *Irenaeus (c. 180, E/W), 1.519.*

It was possible for God Himself to have made man perfect [i.e., complete] from the first. However, man could not receive this, being as yet an infant. And for this cause, our Lord, in these last times, when He had summed up all things into Himself, came to us, not as He might have come, but as we were capable of beholding Him. *Irenaeus (c. 180, E/W), 1.521.*

After His great kindness, He graciously conferred good upon mankind. He created men like Himself—that is, in their own power. At the same time, through His foreknowledge, He knew the infirmity of human beings and the consequences that would flow from it. *Irenaeus (c. 180, E/W), 1.522.*

God has created us naturally social and just. *Clement of Alexandria (c. 195, E), 2.307.*

Sin, then, is voluntary on my part. *Clement of Alexandria (c. 195, E), 2.362.*

Now it is in our power . . . to philosophize or not, to believe or disbelieve. So, then, we are equally masters of each of the opposites. So what depends on us is found possible. *Clement of Alexandria (c. 195, E), 2.437.*

Let them not then say that he who does wrong and sins, transgresses because of demons. For then he would be guiltless. Instead, a person *becomes* a demoniac man by choosing the same things as do the demons: by sinning and being unstable, frivolous, and fickle in his desires—just like a demon. Now he who is bad (having become sinful by nature, because of evil) becomes depraved. He has what he has

chosen. And, being sinful, he sins also in his actions. Likewise, the good man does right. *Clement of Alexandria (c. 195, E), 2.502.*

He is the true servant of God who spontaneously subjects himself to His commands. And he who is already pure in heart (not through the commandments, but through knowledge itself) is the friend of God. For neither are we born by nature possessing virtue, nor after we are born does it grow naturally, as do certain parts of the body. For then it would be neither voluntary nor praiseworthy. *Clement of Alexandria (c. 195, E), 2.528.*

Entire freedom of will, therefore, was conferred upon man in both tendencies. So that, as master of himself, he might constantly encounter good by spontaneous observance of it, and evil by its spontaneous avoidance. . . . But the recompense for good or evil could not be given to the man who is found to have been either good or evil through necessity, and not choice. *Tertullian (c. 207, W), 3.302.*

Now, who is so faultless among men, that God could always have him in His choice, and never be able to reject him? On the other hand, who is so void of any good work, that God could reject him forever, and never be able to choose him? Show me, then, the man who is always good, and he will not be rejected. Show me, too, him who is always evil, and he will never be chosen. *Tertullian (c. 207, W), 3.315.*

It is clear that sins, lusts of the flesh, unbelief, and anger are ascribed to the common nature of all mankind. However, the devil has led that nature astray, which he has already infected with the implanted germ of sin. *Tertullian (c. 207, W), 3.466.*

"Unless a man is born of water and of the Spirit, he cannot enter into the kingdom of God." In other words, he cannot be holy. Every soul, then, by reason of its birth, has its nature in Adam until it is born again in Christ. Moreover, it is unclean all the while that it remains without this regeneration. And because it is unclean, it is actively sinful. *Tertullian (c. 210, W), 3.220.*

The flesh of Christ, which committed no sin itself, resembled the flesh that had sinned. I mean, it resembled it in its *nature,* but not in the *corruption* it received from Adam. For that reason, we also declare that there was in Christ the same flesh as that whose nature in man is sinful. *Tertullian (c. 210, W), 3.535.*

Is not [the doctrine of the Gnostics] from the beginning and everywhere an invective against the flesh? Their doctrine is against its origin, its substance, its casualties, and the invariable end that awaits it. According to them, it is unclean from its first formation of the dregs of the ground. It is even more unclean afterwards from the mire of its own seminal transmission. According to them, it is worthless, weak, covered with guilt, laden with misery, full of trouble. *Tertullian (c. 210, W), 3.548.*

The corruption of our nature is another nature having a god and father of its own—namely, the author of corruption. Still, there is a portion of good in the soul, of that original, divine, and genuine good, which is its proper nature. For that which is derived from God is *obscured*, rather than *extinguished*. It can indeed be obscured, because it is not God. However, it cannot be extinguished, for it comes from God. . . . Thus some men are very bad, and some are very good. Yet, the souls of everyone are all of one nature. Even in the worst person, there is something good. And even in the best person, there is something bad. . . . Just as no soul is without sin, so neither is any soul without seeds of good. *Tertullian (c. 210, W), 3.220, 221.*

Faith admits no plea of necessity. They are under no necessity to sin. Their only necessity is that they must not sin. *Tertullian (c. 211, W), 3.100.*

Avida [a pagan] said to him, "Those things you have said are very good. However, the commands which have been given to men are severe, and men cannot perform them." . . . [BARDESAN'S ANSWER:] Who is the man who is too weak to avoid stealing, lying, immorality, hatred, and deception? For all these things are under the control of man's mind. They are not dependent on the strength of the body, but on the will of the soul. For even if a man is poor, sick, old, and disabled in his limbs, he is able to avoid doing all these things. . . . For they are easy, and there are no circumstances that can hinder their performance. We are not commanded to carry heavy loads of stones. . . . Instead, in accordance with the goodness of God, commandments with no harshness in

them have been given to us. Any living man whoever can rejoice to do them. *Bardesanes (c. 222, E), 8.725.*

This also is clearly defined in the teaching of the church, that every rational soul is possessed of free will and volition and that it has a struggle to maintain against the devil, his angels, and other opposing powers. For those powers strive to burden it with sins. Yet, if we live rightly and wisely, we can endeavor to shake ourselves free of a burden of that kind. *Origen (c. 225, E), 4.240.*

It is evident from all this that no one is pure either by essence or by nature. And no one is polluted by nature. The consequence of this is that it lies within ourselves and in our own actions to either possess happiness and holiness, or by sloth and negligence to fall from happiness into wickedness and ruin. . . . In the Trinity alone, which is the author of all things, does goodness exist in virtue of *essential being*. In contrast, others possess it as an acquired and perishable quality. They only enjoy blessedness when they participate in holiness, wisdom, and divinity itself. *Origen (c. 225, E), 4.260.*

There is no rational creature that is not capable of both good and evil. *Origen (c. 225, E), 4.265.*

A man may possess an acquired righteousness, from which it is possible for him to fall away. *Origen (c. 225, E), 4.266.*

On the other hand, to blame the mere constitution of the body is absurd. . . . Reason, therefore, demonstrates that external events do not depend on us. Rather, it is our own business to use them in this way or the opposite—having received reason as a judge and as an investigator of the manner in which we should meet those external events. *Origen (c. 225, E), 4.304, 305.*

Certain men who hold different opinions [i.e., heretics] misuse these passages. They essentially destroy free will by introducing ruined natures incapable of salvation and by introducing others as being saved in such a way that they cannot be lost. *Origen (c. 225, E), 4.308.*

Let us use the following illustration from the Gospel. There is a certain rock with only a little surface soil. If seeds fall upon it, they quickly spring up. But not having any root, when they spring up, they are burned and withered when the sun rises. Now, this rock is a human soul, hardened on account of its neglect. It has become stone because of its wickedness. For no one receives from God a heart created of stone. Rather, it becomes such a heart because of wickedness. *Origen (c. 225, E), 4.314.*

Let us next look at the passage: "So, then, it is not of him who wills, nor of him who runs, but of God who shows mercy." Those who find fault say . . . that salvation does not depend upon ourselves, but upon the arrangement made by Him who has formed us the way we are. . . . If they [the Gnostics] say that it is virtuous to desire what is good and to run after what is good, we will ask them how a perishing nature desires better things. For then it is like an evil tree producing good fruit—since it is a virtuous act to desire better things. *Origen (c. 225, E), 4.320, 321.*

With respect to the thoughts that proceed from our hearts . . . we find that they sometimes proceed from ourselves and sometimes they originate from the opposing powers. Furthermore, frequently they are also suggested by God or by the holy angels. *Origen (c. 225, E), 4.331.*

Our whole race has part in the logos [reason] in man. . . . For before the consummation of logos [reason] comes, there is nothing in man but what is blameworthy. All is imperfect and defective. *Origen (c. 228, E), 9.320.*

It clearly appears that all men are inclined to sin by nature—and some, not only by nature, but by practice. However, not all men are incapable of an entire transformation. For there are found in every philosophical group, and in the Word of God, persons who . . . underwent so great of a change that they may be proposed as a model of excellence of life. *Origen (c. 248, E), 4.490.*

We, however, who know of only one nature in every rational soul, maintain that no one has been created evil by the Author of all things. Rather, many have *become* wicked through education, perverse example, and surrounding influences. *Origen (c. 248, E), 4.491.*

[Celsus, the pagan] alleges . . . that "those who are without sin are partakers of a better life." . . . [ORIGEN'S REPLY:] Of those who were so from the beginning of their lives, there cannot possibly be any. While those who are so after a transformation are found to be few in

number—being those who have become so after giving their allegiance to the saving Word. *Origen (c. 248, E), 4.492.*

The prophets . . . tell us that a sacrifice for sin was offered even for new-born infants, as not being free from sin. They say, "I was shaped in iniquity and in sin did my mother conceive me." Also, "They are estranged from the womb." These are followed by the singular expression, "They go astray as soon as they are born, speaking lies." *Origen (c. 248, E), 4.631.*

How much more should we shrink from hindering an infant. For he, being lately born, has not sinned—other than, in being born after the flesh according to Adam, he has contracted the contagion of the ancient death at its earliest birth. Therefore, on this very account, he approaches the more easily to the reception of the forgiveness of sins. For to him are remitted—not his own sins—but the sins of another. *Cyprian (c. 250, W), 5.354.*

While the body still lives . . . sin must also live with it, for it has its roots concealed within us. This is so, even though it is outwardly held in check by the wounds inflicted by corrections and warnings. Otherwise, we would not do wrong after baptism, for we would be entirely and absolutely free from sin. However, even after believing and after the time of being touched by the water of sanctification, we are oftentimes found in sin. *Methodius (c. 290, E), 6.365.*

Jesus was baptized by the prophet John in the river Jordan, so that He might wash away in the spiritual bath—not His own sins (for it is evident that He had none)—but those of the flesh that He bore. *Lactantius (c. 304–313, W), 7.115.*

A master and teacher of virtue should most closely resemble man. That is so that by overpowering sin, he may teach man that sin may be overpowered by him. However, if the teacher is immortal, he can by no means be an example to man. For there will stand forth someone maintaining his opinion, saying, "You indeed do not sin, for you are free from this body." . . . [But if he is mortal,] the teacher can answer, "See, I do them myself. Yet, I am clothed with flesh, and it is the property of flesh to sin. I, too, bear the same flesh; yet, sin does not rule over me. . . . I overcome those very things that you fear, so that I can make you victorious over pain and death. I go before you through those things that you allege that it is impossible to endure. If you cannot follow the *directions* I give you, then follow my *example.*" In this way, all excuse is taken away. Then you must confess that man is unjust through his own fault. *Lactantius (c. 304–313, W), 7.126.*

The Son clothed himself with flesh so that—the desires of the flesh being subdued—He might teach us that to sin was not the result of necessity, but of man's purpose and will. *Lactantius (c. 304–313, W), 7.127.*

No one can be without defect as long as he is burdened with a covering of flesh. For the infirmity of flesh is subject to the dominion of sin in a threefold manner: in deeds, words, and thoughts. *Lactantius (c. 304–313, W), 7.178.*

Nobody can be born vicious. Instead, if we make a bad use of the affections, they become vices. If we use them well, they become virtues. *Lactantius (c. 304–313, W), 7.181.*

[God created] an infinite multitude of souls, being at first united with frail and feeble bodies. He did this so He might place [man] in the middle between good and evil. Composed of both natures, man could observe the virtue placed before him. *Lactantius (c. 304–313, W), 7.200.*

He clothed and covered man's spirit with an earthly body, so that—being composed of different and opposite materials—man might be susceptible to both good and evil. *Lactantius (c. 304–313, W), 7.200.*

We are prone to err, and to yield to various lusts and appetites through the fault of our innate weakness. *Arnobius (c. 305, E), 6.419.*

III. Man's mortality and immortality

Of the tree of the knowledge of good and evil you shall not eat, for in the day that you eat of it you shall surely die. Gen. 2:17.

Through one man sin entered the world, and death through sin, and thus death spread to all men, because all sinned. Rom. 5:12.

And God transferred him from the earth, out of which he had been produced, into Paradise. He gave him means of advancement, in order that, maturing and becoming perfect, and being even declared a god, he might thus ascend into heaven in possession of immortality. For man had been made a middle nature, neither wholly

mortal, nor altogether immortal, but capable of either. *Theophilus (c. 180, E), 2.104.*

Man was by nature neither mortal nor immortal. For if God had made him immortal from the beginning, He would have made him God. Again, if He had made him mortal, God would seem to be the cause of his death. Neither, then, immortal nor yet mortal did He make him, but, as we have said above, capable of both. *Theophilus (c. 180, E), 2.105.*

We possess eternal duration from the excelling power of this Being, not from our own nature. *Irenaeus (c. 180, E/W), 1.528.*

The good man stands as the boundary between an immortal and a mortal nature. *Clement of Alexandria (c. 195, E), 2.365.*

It appears to me that man is like a Centaur, . . . compounded of a rational and irrational part—of soul and body. *Clement of Alexandria (c. 195, E), 2.410.*

When man inclines to corruption, he becomes corrupt and mortal. When he inclines to incorruption, he becomes incorrupt and immortal. For he is placed midway between the tree of life and the tree of the knowledge of good and evil, the fruit of which he tasted. So man was changed into the nature of the latter tree. He himself is neither a tree of life nor a tree of corruption. Rather, he is shown to be mortal through his participation in . . . corruption. Likewise, he is shown to be incorrupt and immortal by his connection with and participation in life. *Methodius (c. 290, E), 6.319; see also 3.302.*

SEE ALSO ATONEMENT; EVIL, PROBLEM OF; FALL OF MAN; FLESH; FREE WILL AND PREDESTINATION; NEW BIRTH; SALVATION; SINLESSNESS; SOUL.

MAN WITHIN
SEE SOUL.

MANES, MANICHAEANS

Manes (c. 216–276), also known as Mani and Manichaeus, founded a religious sect in Persia that incorporated many Gnostic elements, particularly dualism. It spread throughout the east as a distinct religion, but it emerged in the west primarily as a Christian heresy.

He whom they call Mani was a Persian by race. . . . He laid down two principles, God and Matter. He called God good; and Matter he declared to be evil. . . . God deliberated how to avenge Himself upon Matter. . . . So he sent the power that we call the soul into Matter to entirely permeate it. . . . They abstain from those things that have [animal] life. So they feed upon vegetables and everything that is void of sense. They abstain also from marriage, the rites of Venus, and the procreation of children. . . . These things are the principal beliefs that they say and think. And they particularly honor the sun and moon—not as gods—but as the way by which it is possible to attain unto God. *Alexander of Lycopolis (c. 300, E), 6.241, 242.*

They do acknowledge Christ, also. . . . They say that it only appeared that the Divine Virtue in matter was affixed to the cross. They say that He Himself did not undergo this punishment, since it was impossible for Him to suffer this. *Alexander of Lycopolis (c. 300, E), 6.251.*

The honorable report of the name [of Marcellus, an orthodox Christian] was carried into the territory of Persia. In this country dwelled a man named Manes. . . . He handed [his disciple] a letter and told him to depart and convey it to Marcellus. . . . On receiving the letter, Marcellus opened it and read it in the presence of Archelaus, the bishop of the place. And the following is a copy of what it contained: "Manichaeus, an apostle of Jesus Christ, and all the saints who are with me. . . . I was exceedingly delighted to observe the love cherished by you, which truly is of the largest measure. But I was distressed at your faith, which is not in accordance with the right standard. . . . I have considered it necessary to send this letter to you . . . to protect you against erroneous opinions, particularly against notions such as . . . the belief that good and evil have the same origin. . . . How can such persons be so bold as to call God the maker and inventor of Satan and his wicked deeds?" *Disputation of Archelaus and Manes (c. 320, E), 6.181, 182.*

The Manichaeans have also declared that the Only-Begotten Christ, who has descended from the bosom of the Father, is the son of a certain woman, Mary, and that He was born of flesh and blood. *Disputation of Archelaus and Manes (c. 320, E), 6.182.*

[Manes] worships two deities—both unoriginated, self-existent, eternal, and opposed to one another. He teaches that the one is good and the other is evil. The first deity is called Light, and the other is called Darkness. He also teaches that the soul in men is a portion of the light, but that the body . . . is part of the darkness. . . . The good Father, then, realizing that the darkness had come to sojourn on His earth, put forth from Himself a power that is called the Mother of Life. . . . The good Father also sent his Son forth from his own bosom into the heart of the earth. . . . He sent His own beloved Son for the salvation of the soul. . . . And the Son came and transformed himself into the likeness of man and appeared to men as a man, and men supposed that He was begotten. However, he was not a man. *Disputation of Archelaus and Manes (c. 320, E), 6.182–184.*

[MANES:] It is a thing not without peril, therefore, for anyone of you to teach the New Testament along with the Law and the Prophets, as if they were of one and the same origin. . . . You will find that the Creator of man is not the Lord, but another Being, who is himself also of an unbegotten nature. . . . He has been produced by his own malice alone. *Disputation of Archelaus and Manes (c. 320, E), 6.188.*

[MANES:] If man is fashioned of the evil nature, it is manifest that he is such a fruit, whether he sins or does not sin. From this, the name and race of men are once for all and absolutely of this character. *Disputation of Archelaus and Manes (c. 320, E), 6.191.*

How will we credit the professions of this Manes, who comes from Persia and declares himself to be the Paraclete? . . . You will not in this fashion divert us from the faith of Christ. Yes, this is so even if you were to work signs and wonders or even if you were to raise the dead! *Disputation of Archelaus and Manes (c. 320, E), 6.209.*

Archelaus said: "Are you not, then, of the opinion that He was born of the virgin Mary?" Manes replied: "God forbid that I should admit that our Lord Jesus Christ came down to us through the natural womb of a woman." *Disputation of Archelaus and Manes (c. 320, E), 6.223.*

[ARCHELAUS:] If your allegation is true that He was not born, then it will follow undoubtedly that He did not suffer. For it is not possible for someone to suffer who was not also born. However, if He did not suffer, then the name of the cross is done away with. And if the cross was not endured, then Jesus did not rise from the dead. And if Jesus did not rise from the dead, then no other person will rise again, either. And if no one will rise again, then there will be no judgment. *Disputation of Archelaus and Manes (c. 320, E), 6.225.*

Manes is neither the first nor the only originator of this type of doctrine. Rather, the founder and leader of this sect was a certain man belonging to Scythia, bearing the name of Scythianus, who lived in the time of the apostles.... This Scythianus, then, was the person who introduced this self-contradictory dualism. And for that, he was also himself indebted to Pythagoras. *Disputation of Archelaus and Manes (c. 320, E), 6.229; extended discussion: 6.181–6.233, 6.241–6.252.*

SEE ALSO GNOSTICS, GNOSTICISM; HERESIES, HERETICS; PERSIA, PERSIANS.

MARCION

Marcion, who founded his own church, was one of the leading heretical teachers of the second century. His teaching incorporated many Gnostic elements, including the belief that the God of the Old Testament was a different God from the Father of Jesus. Marcion accepted only the Gospel of Luke and the writings of Paul for his New Testament canon, and he was forced to alter even these to fit his teachings.

There is Marcion, a man of Pontus, who is even at this day alive. He teaches his disciples to believe in some other God greater than the Creator. *Justin Martyr (c. 160, E), 1.171.*

Marcion of Pontus . . . advanced the most daring blasphemy against Him who is proclaimed as God by the Law and the Prophets. Marcion says that this God is the author of evils, takes delight in war, is infirm of purpose, and is even contrary to Himself. He says that Jesus was derived from that Father who is above the God that made the world. . . . He says that Jesus was manifested in the form of a man to those who were in Judea, abolishing the Prophets and the Law, and all the works of that God who made the world. *Irenaeus (c. 180, E/W), 1.352.*

Besides this, Marcion mutilated the Gospel which is according to Luke, removing all that was written concerning the generation of the Lord. He also deleted a large amount of the teaching of the Lord. . . . In like manner, too, he dismembered the epistles of Paul, remov-

ing all that the apostle said concerning the God who made the world. . . . Marcion says that salvation will be the attainment only of those souls who have learned his doctrine. However, he says the body, being taken from the earth, is incapable of sharing in salvation. *Irenaeus (c. 180, E/W), 1.352.*

Marcion met Polycarp on one occasion, and said, "Do you know me?" Polycarp replied, "I do know you, the first-born of Satan." Such was the horror that the apostles and their disciples had against holding even verbal communication with any corrupters of the truth. *Irenaeus (c. 180, E/W), 1.416.*

With regard to those [i.e., the Marcionites] who allege that Paul alone knew the truth and that to him the mystery was manifested by revelation, let Paul himself convict them. *Irenaeus (c. 180, E/W), 1.436.*

By dividing God into two, declaring that one is "good" and the other is "just," Marcion actually puts an end to Deity altogether. *Irenaeus (c. 180, E/W), 1.459.*

Vain, too, are Marcion and his followers when they exclude Abraham from the inheritance. *Irenaeus (c. 180, E/W), 1.470.*

The spiritual man will also examine the doctrine of Marcion—how he holds that there are two Gods, separated from each other by an infinite distance. *Irenaeus (c. 180, E/W), 1.506, 507.*

The followers of Marcion and those who are like them maintain that the prophets were from another God. *Irenaeus (c. 180, E/W), 1.511.*

Where was Marcion then, that shipmaster of Pontus, the zealous student of Stoicism? . . . For it is evident that those heretics lived not so long ago . . . and that they at first were believers in the doctrine of the catholic church. They were in the church of Rome under the episcopate of the blessed Eleutherus. However, because of their ever restless curiosity, . . . they were expelled more than once. In fact, Marcion was expelled with the two hundred sesterces that he had brought into the church. And, when banished at last to a permanent excommunication, these men scattered abroad the poison of their doctrines. It is true that, afterwards, Marcion professed repentance, and he agreed to the conditions granted to him. Those conditions were that he would receive reconciliation if he restored to the church all the others whom he had been training for perdition. However, he was prevented by death from doing this. *Tertullian (c. 197, W), 3.257.*

Since Marcion separated the New Testament from the Old, it is obvious that he is subsequent in time to that which he separated. For it was only in his power to separate what had previously been united. *Tertullian (c. 197, W), 3.257.*

In his epistle, John especially designates those as antichrists who "denied that Christ was come in the flesh," and who refused to think that Jesus was the Son of God. The first dogma Marcion maintained; the second one Hebion taught. *Tertullian (c. 197, W), 3.259.*

One man perverts the Scriptures with his hand. Another perverts their meaning by his exposition. For although Valentinus seems to use the entire volume [of Scripture], he has nonetheless laid violent hands on the truth. Only, he has done it with a more cunning mind and skill than Marcion. Marcion expressly and openly used the knife, rather than the pen. For he made excisions of the Scriptures to suit his own subject matter. *Tertullian (c. 197, W), 3.262.*

The heretic of Pontus introduces two Gods. *Tertullian (c. 207, W), 3.272.*

Marcion makes his Gods unequal. One is judicial, harsh, and mighty in war. The other is mild, placid, and simply good and excellent. *Tertullian (c. 207, W), 3.275.*

The only resource left to the Marcionites is to divide things into the two classes of visible and invisible, with two Gods for their authors. And so they claim the invisible for their own God. *Tertullian (c. 207, W), 3.282.*

The Marcionites are very strongly addicted to astrology. *Tertullian (c. 207, W), 3.284.*

Marcion's special and principal work is the separation of the Law and the Gospel. And his disciples will not deny that in this point they have their very best pretext for initiating and confirming themselves in his heresy. There are Marcion's *Antitheses,* or contradictory propositions, which aim at showing the Gospel to be at variance with the Law. The purpose is that by showing the diversity of the two documents that contain the Law and the Gospel, they may argue that there is a diversity of Gods also.... The Marcionites allege that Marcion did not so much *innovate* on the rule [of faith] by his separation of the Law and the Gospel, as *restore* it after it had been previously adulterated. *Tertullian (c. 207, W), 3.285.*

Marcion ... has removed from his God all the severity and energy of the judicial character.... A better God has been discovered, who never takes offense! He is never angry, never inflicts punishment, has prepared no fire in Gehenna! There will be no gnashing of teeth in the outer darkness! For He is purely and simply good. He indeed forbids all delinquency, but only in word.... For He does not want your fear. And so satisfied are the Marcionites with such pretenses, that they have no fear of their God at all. They say it is only a bad man who will be feared, a good man will be loved. *Tertullian (c. 207, W), 3.290–292.*

According to Marcion, the flesh should not be immersed in the water of the sacrament, unless it is in virginity, widowhood, or celibacy—or has purchased by divorce a title to baptism.... Now, such a scheme as this must no doubt involve the prohibition of marriage. *Tertullian (c. 207, W), 3.293.*

This leads me to remark of Marcion's God, that in reproaching marriage as an evil and unchaste thing, He is really prejudicing the cause of that very sanctity that He seems to serve.... For if there is no marriage, there is no sanctity. *Tertullian (c. 207, W), 3.294.*

Similarly on other points also, you [Marcion] reproach the God of the Law with fickleness and instability for contradictions in His commandments. For example, He forbade work to be done on Sabbath days. However, at the siege of Jericho, He ordered the ark to be carried around the walls for eight days—which would, of course, include a Sabbath. You do not, however, understand the law of the Sabbath: it is *human* works that it prohibits—not divine. *Tertullian (c. 207, W), 3.313.*

The Marcionites are those whom the apostle John designated as antichrists, for they deny that Christ has come in the flesh.... Now, the more firmly the antichrist Marcion had seized this assumption, the more prepared was he, of course, to reject the bodily substance of Christ. *Tertullian (c. 207, W), 3.327.*

"In every place, sacrifice shall be offered to my name, and a pure offering"—such as the ascription of glory, blessing, praise, and hymns. Now, inasmuch as all these things are also found among you—together with the sign upon the forehead, the sacraments of the church, and the offerings of the pure sacrifice—you ought now to burst forth and declare that the Spirit of the Creator prophesied of your Christ. For, since you join the Jews in denying that their Christ has come, recollect also what is that end which they were predicted as about to bring on themselves. *Tertullian (c. 207, W), 3.341.*

Besides, your [Marcionite] Christ promises to the Jews their primitive condition, with the recovery of their country. And after this life's course is over, he gives rest in Hades in Abraham's bosom. Oh, most excellent God, when He restores in amnesty that which He took away in wrath! Oh, what a God is yours! *Tertullian (c. 207, W), 3.342.*

You must know that Marcion, on the other hand, ascribes no author to his Gospel. . . . Now, of the authors whom we possess, Marcion seems to have singled out Luke for his mutilating process. Luke, however, was not an apostle, but only an apostolic man. He was not a master; but a disciple. . . . Now, even if Marcion had published his Gospel in the name of Paul himself, the single authority of the document (destitute of all support from preceding authorities) would not be a sufficient basis for our faith. There would still be lacking that gospel which Paul found in existence, to which he yielded his belief. *Tertullian (c. 207, W), 3.347, 348.*

In the scheme of Marcion, . . . the mystery of the Christian religion begins from the discipleship of Luke. . . . On finding the Epistle of Paul to the Galatians (wherein Paul rebukes even apostles for not walking uprightly according to the truth of the gospel), Marcion labors very hard to destroy the character of those Gospels that are published as genuine. *Tertullian (c. 207, W), 3.348.*

In contrast, Marcion's Gospel is not known to most people, and to no one whatever is it known without its likewise being condemned. It too, of course, has its churches, but specially its own—as late as they are spurious. And should you want to know their pedigree, you will more easily discover *apostasy* in it than *apostolicity*—with either Marcion or one of Marcion's swarm as their founder. Even wasps make combs. So also these Marcionites make churches. *Tertullian (c. 207, W), 3.350.*

Marcion has laid down the position that Christ was revealed by a previously unknown God for the salvation of all nations, in the days of Tiberius. Marcion says this Christ is a different Being from the one who is ordained by God the Creator for the restoration of the Jewish state, and who is yet to come. Between these two Christs, he interposes the separation of a great and absolute difference. *Tertullian (c. 207, W), 3.351.*

This shows that at the very outset of Christ's ministry, Christ came not to destroy the Law and the Prophets, but rather to fulfill them. But Marcion has erased that passage as an interpolation. *Tertullian (c. 207, W), 3.352, 353.*

Marcion does not unite the nuptial bond. Nor, when contracted, does he allow it. He baptizes no one but a celibate or a eunuch. For all others, he reserves baptism until death or divorce. *Tertullian (c. 207, W), 3.361.*

If, however, you [Marcionites] deny that divorce is in any way permitted by Christ, how is it that you on your side destroy marriage? You do not unite man and woman. Nor do you permit the sacrament of baptism and of the Eucharist to those who have been united in marriage anywhere else—unless they should agree together to repudiate the fruit of their marriage. *Tertullian (c. 207, W), 3.405.*

Marcion, however, violently turns the passage [of the rich man and Lazarus] to another end. He decides that both the torment and the comfort are retributions of the Creator. They are reserved in the next life for those who have obeyed the Law and the Prophets. Meanwhile, he defines the heavenly bosom and harbor to belong to Christ and his own God. *Tertullian (c. 207, W), 3.406.*

The opinion of the heretics [i.e., Marcionites] is splintered to pieces, who say that there is no salvation of the flesh. *Tertullian (c. 207, W), 3.412.*

It would contribute very well to the support of Marcion's theory of a phantom body, that bread should have been crucified! *Tertullian (c. 207, W), 3.418.*

"Be not deceived; God is not to be mocked." But Marcion's God can be mocked. For He does not know how to be angry, or how to take vengeance. *Tertullian (c. 207, W), 3.438.*

We must now encounter the subject of marriage, which Marcion (more continent than the apostle!) prohibits. . . . Now, when Marcion wholly prohibits all sexual intercourse to the faithful (for we will say nothing about his catechumens), and when he prescribes repudiation of all engagements before marriage, whose teaching is he following—that of Moses or that of Christ? *Tertullian (c. 207, W), 3.443.*

Marcion does not in any way admit the resurrection of the flesh. Rather, it is only the salvation of the soul that he promises. *Tertullian (c. 207, W), 3.450.*

The latter method has been adopted by Marcion. He reads the passage that follows—"in whom the god of this world"—as if it described the Creator as the "god of this world." He does this in order that he may (by these words) imply that there is another God for the other world. *Tertullian (c. 207, W), 3.453.*

The serious gaps Marcion had made in this epistle [to the Romans], especially by withdrawing whole passages at his will, can be clear from the unmutilated text of our own copy. *Tertullian (c. 207, W), 3.457.*

As our heretic is so fond of his pruning-knife, I do not wonder when syllables are expunged by his hand, seeing that entire pages are usually the matter on which he practices his effacing process. *Tertullian (c. 207, W), 3.467.*

Let Marcion know that the fundamental principle of his creed comes from the school of Epicurus. . . . But how remote is our truth from the work of this heretic. For [our faith] fears to arouse the anger of God, and it firmly believes that He produced all things out of nothing. It believes that He promises to us a restoration from the grave of the same flesh, and our faith holds without a blush that Christ was born of the virgin's womb. *Tertullian (c. 207, W), 3.471.*

. . . contending with Marcion and Basilides that [the body of Christ] possessed no reality. *Tertullian (c. 210, W), 3.546.*

Marcion, a native of Pontus, was far more frantic than these [Gnostics]. He omitted the majority of the tenets of the greater number [of Gnostics], advancing into a doctrine still more unabashed. He supposed there to be two originating causes of the universe. He alleged one of

them to be a certain good God, but the other one to be an evil One. *Hippolytus (c. 225, W), 5.110.*

Does Marcion, then, maintain the Trinity? Does he then declare the same Father—the Creator—that we do? Does he know the same Son, Christ born of the virgin Mary, who as the Word was made flesh? *Cyprian (c. 250, W), 5.380; see also 2.356, 9.348, 9.463, 9.504; extended discussion: 5.110–5.113.*

SEE ALSO GNOSTICS, GNOSTICISM; HERESIES, HERETICS.

MARCUS AURELIUS

Marcus Aurelius (121–180) was an able Roman emperor, although a persecutor of Christians. He was also a devoted adherent of Stoicism. The apologetic works of Athenagoras and Theophilus were addressed to him.

You will see by examining the letters of Marcus Aurelius, that most serious of emperors, in which he bears his testimony that a certain Germanic drought was ended by the rains obtained through the prayers of the Christians. *Tertullian (c. 197, W), 3.22.*

Marcus Aurelius, also, in his expedition to Germany, received rain in that well-known drought by the prayers his Christian soldiers offered to God. *Tertullian (c. 212, W), 3.107.*

SEE ALSO STOICS, STOICISM.

MARK, GOSPEL OF

Having become the interpreter of Peter, Mark wrote down accurately whatever he remembered. However, he did not relate the sayings or deeds of Christ in exact order. For he neither heard the Lord nor accompanied Him. But afterwards, as I said, he accompanied Peter. Now, Peter accommodated his instructions to the necessities [of his hearers], but with no intention of giving a regular narrative of the Lord's sayings. Accordingly, Mark made no mistake in thus writing some things as he remembered them. For one thing, he took special care not to omit anything he had heard, and not to put anything fictitious into the statements. *Papias (c. 120, E), 1.155, as quoted by Eusebius.*

After their departure, Mark, the disciple and interpreter of Peter, also handed down to us in writing what had been preached by Peter. *Irenaeus (c. 180, E/W), 1.414.*

Mark, the interpreter and follower of Peter, begins his Gospel narrative in this manner. *Irenaeus (c. 180, E/W), 1.425.*

Mark was the follower of Peter. Peter publicly preached the gospel at Rome before some of Caesar's equestrian knights, and adduced many testimonies to Christ. In order that thereby they might be able to commit to memory what was spoken by Peter, Mark wrote entirely what is called the Gospel according to Mark. *Clement of Alexandria (c. 195, E), 2.573.*

Such a ray of godliness shone forth on the minds of Peter's hearers, that they were not satisfied with a single hearing or with the unwritten teaching of the divine proclamation. So, with all manner of entreaties, they pleaded with Mark, to whom the Gospel is ascribed (he being the companion of Peter) to leave in writing a record of the teaching that had been delivered to them verbally. And they did not let the man alone until they had prevailed upon him. And so to them, we owe the Scripture called the "Gospel of Mark." On learning what had been done, through the revelation of the Spirit, it is said that the apostle was delighted with the enthusiasm of the men and approved the composition for reading in the churches. Clement gives the narrative in the sixth book of the *Sketches. Eusebius, citing Clement of Alexandria (c. 195, E), 2.579.*

SEE ALSO GOSPELS.

MARK OF THE BEAST

In both the Greek and Roman systems of letters and numbers, there were no special characters (such as 1, 2, or 3) for numbers. Rather, letters of the alphabet served also as numbers. For example, in the Roman system, "I" represented a character of the alphabet; yet, it also represented the number one. Similarly, "V" was both a letter of the alphabet and also the number five. Accordingly, every person's name had a numerical equivalent. It was in this sense, then, that the early Christians understood the passage of Revelation that speaks of the "number of [the beast's] name."

He causes all, both small and great, rich and poor, free and slave, to receive a mark on their right hand or on their foreheads, and that no one may buy or sell except one who has the mark or the name of the beast, or the number of his name. Here is wisdom. Let him who has understanding calculate the number of the beast, for it is the number of a man: His number is 666. Rev. 13:16–18.

Let no one imagine that the Antichrist performs these wonders by divine power. Rather, he does it by the working of magic. And we must not be surprised that he performs wonders through demonic means. For the demons and apostate spirits are at his service. By these wonders, he leads the inhabitants of the earth astray. . . . And the number is six hundred and sixty-six. That is, six times a hundred, six times ten, and six units. This represents a summing up of the whole of that apostasy that has taken place during six thousand years. *Irenaeus (c. 180, E/W), 1.557.*

Fittingly, therefore, will his name possess the number six hundred and sixty-six. For he sums up in his own person all the mixture of wickedness that took place previous to the deluge, due to the apostasy of the angels. For Noah was six hundred years old when the deluge came upon the earth. . . . Thus, then, the six hundred years of Noah . . . prefigure the number of the name of that man in whom is concentrated the whole apostasy of six thousand years. *Irenaeus (c. 180, E/W), 1.558.*

This number is found in all the most approved and ancient copies [of Revelation]. Furthermore, those men who saw John face to face give their testimony to it. Reason also leads us to conclude that the number of the name of the beast, according to the Greek mode of calculation by the letters contained in it, will amount to six hundred and sixty and six. *Irenaeus (c. 180, E/W), 1.558.*

If there are many names found possessing this number [666], it will be asked which of them will the coming man bear. I do not say this because of a lack of names that contain the number of that name. Rather, I say it out of fear of God and zeal for the truth. For the name "Evanthas" contains the required number, but I make no allegation regarding it. Then also "Lateinos" has the number. . . . "Teitan," too, . . . is rather worthy of credit. For it has in itself the predicted number. . . . However, I will not incur the risk of dogmatically announcing the name of the Antichrist. For if it were necessary that his name should be distinctly revealed in this present time, it would have been announced by him who beheld the apocalyptic vision. *Irenaeus (c. 180, E/W), 1.559.*

[The Antichrist] will order censers to be set up by everyone, everywhere, so that no one among the saints may be able to buy or sell without first sacrificing. For this is what is meant by the mark received upon the right hand. And the phrase, "on their forehead," indicates that all are crowned. That is, they put on a crown of fire. This is a crown of death, not of life. *Hippolytus (c. 200, W), 5.214.*

With respect to his name, it is not in our power to explain it exactly—not as the blessed John understood it and was instructed about it. Rather, we can only conjecture about it. For when [the Antichrist] appears, the blessed one will show us what we seek to know. Yet, as far as our doubtful apprehension of the matter goes, we may speak. Indeed, we find many names for which the letters equate to this number. For example, there is the name Teitan, an ancient and notable name. Or Evanthas, for it too makes up the same number. And many others can be found. . . . It is evident to everyone that those who at present time hold power are the Lateinos. If, then, we take the name as the name of a single man, it becomes "Latinus." However, we should neither give it out as if this were certainly his name, nor again should we ignore the fact that he may not be otherwise designated. But having the mystery of God in our heart, we should in fear keep faithfully what has been told us by the blessed prophets. That way, when those things come to pass, we may be prepared for them and not deceived. *Hippolytus (c. 200, W), 5.215.*

As they have it figured from the Greek characters, they thus find it among many to be *Teitan*. For *Teitan* has this number, which the Gentiles call Sol and Phoebus. And it is figured in Greek in this manner: *t,* three hundred, *e,* five; *i,* ten; *t,* three hundred; *a,* one; *n,* fifty. When these are totaled together, they add up to six hundred and sixty-six. To the extent it belongs to the Greek letters, they fill up this number and name. If you wish to turn this name into Latin, it is understood by the word "Diclux." These letters are figured in this manner: *D,* five hundred; *I,* one; *C,* one hundred; *L,* fifty; *V,* five; and *X,* ten. By counting up these letters, it likewise totals six hundred and sixty-six. *Victorinus (c. 280, W), 7.356.*

SEE ALSO ANTICHRIST; ESCHATOLOGY; GREAT TRIBULATION; RAPTURE; REVELATION, BOOK OF.

MARRIAGE

I. Admonition and counsel on marriage

II. Marriage to unbelievers

I. Admonition and counsel on marriage

He answered and said to them, "Have you not read that He who made them at the beginning made them male and female, and said, 'For this reason a man shall leave his father and mother and be joined to his wife, and the two shall become one flesh'? So then, they are no longer two but one flesh. Therefore what God has joined together, let not man separate." Matt. 19:4–6.

Now the Spirit expressly says that in latter times some will depart from the faith, . . . forbidding to marry. 1 Tim. 4:1, 3.

Marriage is honorable among all, and the bed undefiled; but fornicators and adulterers God will judge. Heb. 13:4.

Speak to my sisters, that they love the Lord and be satisfied with their husbands, both in the flesh and in the spirit. In like manner also, exhort my brothers, in the name of Jesus Christ, that they love their wives, even as the Lord loves the church. . . . It becomes both men and women who marry to form their union with the approval of the bishop, that their marriage may be according to God, and not after their own lust. *Ignatius (c. 105, E), 1.100.*

For everyone is not to marry, nor are all times appropriate. But there is a time in which it is suitable. . . . Neither should everyone take a wife, nor is it every woman that one is to take. . . . But it is only for him who is in certain circumstances and such a one and at such time as is requisite, and for the sake of children. *Clement of Alexandria (c. 195, E), 2.377.*

Marriage is a help in the case of those advanced in years, by furnishing a spouse to take care of one, and by rearing children of her to nourish one's old age. *Clement of Alexandria (c. 195, E), 2.378.*

Legislators, moreover, do not allow those who are unmarried to perform the highest magisterial offices. . . . The renowned Plato orders the man who has not married to pay a wife's maintenance into the public treasury, and to give to the magistrates a suitable sum of money as expenses. For if they will not beget children, not having married, they produce . . . a scarcity of men. And this ruins states [according to Plato]. *Clement of Alexandria (c. 195, E), 2.378.*

The marriage of other people is often a license for indulgence. However, for one who loves wisdom, marriage leads to the agreement that is in accordance with reason. Such an agreement bids wives to adorn themselves not in outward appearance, but in character. It directs husbands not to treat their wedded wives as mistresses, making fleshly wantonness their goal. Rather, it directs them to take advantage of marriage for help in the whole of life, and for the best self-restraint. *Clement of Alexandria (c. 195, E), 2.378.*

Therefore, the spiritual man will prefer neither children, nor marriage, nor parents to his love for God and righteousness in life. To such a man of God, after conception, his wife is as a sister and is treated as if of the same father. *Clement of Alexandria (c. 195, E), 2.503.*

Peter called very encouragingly and comfortingly, addressing his wife by name, saying "Remember the Lord!" Such was the marriage of the blessed and their perfect disposition towards those dearest to them. Thus also the apostle says, "He who marries should be as though he married not." *Clement of Alexandria (c. 195, E), 2.541.*

The spiritual man also eats, drinks, and marries—not as principal ends of existence, but as necessary. I name marriage even. . . . For having become perfect, the spiritual man has the apostles for examples. One is not really shown to be a man in the choice of the single life. Rather, he surpasses [single men]—he who, disciplined by marriage, procreation of children, and care for the house . . . has been inseparable from God's love and withstood all temptation arising through children, wife, servants, and possessions. *Clement of Alexandria (c. 195, E), 2.543.*

It is not only fornication itself that is called fornication, but also the premature giving in marriage. I am referring to when a girl who is not yet of a developed age is given to a husband—either of her own accord or that of her parents. *Clement of Alexandria (c. 195, E), 2.581.*

Even on earth, children do not rightly and lawfully wed without their fathers' consent. *Tertullian (c. 205, W), 4.48.*

[In contrast to marriage to an unbeliever,] what kind of yoke is that of two believers? It is of one hope, one desire, one discipline, and one and the same service. Both are brethren; both are fellow servants. There is no difference of spirit or of the flesh. Rather, they are truly two in one flesh. Where the flesh is one, the spirit is one too. Together they pray; together they prostrate themselves. They perform their fasts together, mutually teaching, mutually exhorting, mutually sustaining. They are both equally in the church of God; equally at the banquet of God; equally in straits, in persecutions, in refreshments. Neither has to hide from the other; neither shuns the other; neither is troublesome to the other. With complete freedom, the sick are visited and the poor are relieved. . . . There is no stealthy signing, no trembling greeting, no mute benediction. Psalms and hymns echo between the two. And they mutually challenge each other as to which one will better chant to their Lord. Christ rejoices when He sees and hears such things! *Tertullian (c. 205, W), 4.48.*

We must now encounter the subject of marriage, which Marcion (more continent than the apostle!) prohibits. For the apostle, although preferring the grace of celibacy, yet permits the contracting of marriage and the enjoyment of it. He advises the continuance therein, rather than the dissolution thereof. *Tertullian (c. 207, W), 3.443.*

The apostles had permission to marry and lead wives about. They also had permission to "live by means of the Gospel." However, when the occasion required it, Paul did not use these rights. And he incites us to imitate his own example. *Tertullian (c. 212, W), 4.55.*

Wives are to be loved by their husbands even as Christ loved the church. And wives should love their husbands also as the church loves Christ. *Novatian (c. 235, W), 5.589, formerly attributed to Cyprian.*

"If two of you will agree on earth as regarding anything that they will ask, it will be done for them." . . . By the two, whom the Word desires to agree on earth, we must understand the husband and wife. For it is they who, by agreement, deprive each other of bodily intercourse so that they may give themselves unto prayer. If they pray for anything, they will receive whatever they will ask—the request being granted to them by the Father in heaven of Jesus Christ on the ground of such agreement. *Origen (c. 245, E), 9.495, 496.*

Describing what should be in the case of those who are joined together by God, so that they may be joined together in a manner worthy of God, the Savior adds, "So that they are no longer two [but one flesh]." Wherever there is true concord, unison, and harmony between husband and wife—when he is as ruler and she is obedient to the saying, "He will rule over you," then of such persons we may truly say, "they are no more two." *Origen (c. 245, E), 9.506.*

According to the Word of God, marriage was a gift, just as holy celibacy was a gift. . . . But a man wishes to put asunder what God has joined together, when, "falling away from the sound faith . . . forbidding . . . to marry," he dissolves even those who had been previously joined together by the providence of God. *Origen (c. 245, E), 9.506.*

"The two shall be one flesh." For the husband and wife are one in nature, in consent, in union, in disposition, and the conduct of life. However, they are separated in sex and number. *Apostolic Constitutions (compiled c. 390, E), 7.466.*

II. Marriage to unbelievers

In these days, a certain woman removed her marriage from the pale of the church and united herself to a Gentile. And when I remembered that this had been done by others in times past, . . . I said, "I wonder if they flatter themselves on the ground of that passage of the first letter to the Corinthians, where it is written: "If any of the brothers has an unbelieving wife, and she consents to the marriage, let him not dismiss her." . . . It may be that, by interpreting this admonition regarding married believers too broadly, they think that permission is thereby granted to marry even unbelievers. God forbid! . . . Rather, it is clear that this Scripture points to those believers who may have been found by the grace of God already in a Gentile marriage. *Tertullian (c. 205, W), 4.44, 45.*

Let her marry whom she wishes, "only in the Lord." . . . That Holy Spirit, therefore, who prefers that widows and unmarried women should persevere in their integrity . . . prescribes no other manner of repeating marriage except "in the Lord." *Tertullian (c. 205, W), 4.45.*

If these things are so, it is certain that believers contracting marriages with Gentiles are guilty of fornication and are to be excluded from all communication with the brotherhood—in accordance with the letter of the apostle. For he says that with persons of that kind, there is to be not even the taking of food. *Tertullian (c. 205, W), 4.45.*

Each and every believing woman must of necessity obey God. How can she serve two lords—the Lord, and her husband (a Gentile, to boot)? For in obeying a Gentile, she will carry out Gentile practices: personal attractiveness, dressing of the head, worldly elegancies, more sordid blandishments, and the very secrets of matrimony tainted. *Tertullian (c. 205, W), 4.46.*

He commands that marriage should be "only in the Lord," so no Christian should intermarry with a pagan. In doing so, Paul maintains a previous law of the Creator, who everywhere prohibits marriage with strangers. *Tertullian (c. 207, W), 3.443, 444.*

Marriage, too, decks the [pagan] bridegroom with its crown. Therefore, we will not have pagan brides, lest they seduce us even to the idolatry with which among them marriage is initiated. You have the law from the patriarchs. You have the apostle admonishing people to marry "in the Lord." *Tertullian (c. 211, W), 3.101.*

They united with unbelievers in the bond of marriage! They prostituted the members of Christ to the Gentiles! *Cyprian (c. 250, W), 5.438.*

Marriage is not to be contracted with Gentiles. In Tobias: "Take a wife from the seed of your parents. Do not take a strange woman who is not of the tribe of your parents" [Tob. 4:12]. Also, in the first Epistle of Paul to the Corinthians: . . . "If he dies, she is free to marry whom she will—only in the Lord." . . . Also in the second letter to the Corinthians: "Do not be joined together with unbelievers." *Cyprian (c. 250, W), 5.550, 551.*

SEE ALSO CELIBACY; DIVORCE; POLYGAMY; PROCREATION; REMARRIAGE; TWICE-MARRIED; UNBELIEVING SPOUSE; VIRGINS, ORDER OF; WIDOWS, ORDER OF.

MARRIAGE FEAST OF THE LAMB

SEE PARABLES OF JESUS (II. C. MARRIAGE FEAST).

MARTYRS, MARTYRDOM

I. Descriptions and exhortations of martyrdom

He who loves his life will lose it, and he who hates his life in this world will keep it for eternal life. John 12:25.

For me, to live is Christ, and to die is gain. . . . I am hard pressed between the two, having a desire to depart and be with Christ, which is far better. Nevertheless to remain in the flesh is more needful for you. Phil. 1:21.

I am already being poured out as a drink offering, and the time of my departure is at hand. I have fought the good fight, I have finished the race, I have kept the faith. Finally, there is laid up for me the crown of righteousness, which the Lord, the righteous Judge, will give to me on that Day. 2 Tim. 4:6–8.

You hold fast to My name, and did not deny My faith even in the days in which Antipas was My faithful martyr, who was killed among you. Rev. 2:13.

When He opened the fifth seal, I saw under the altar the souls of those who had been slain for the word of God and for the testimony which they held. And they cried with a loud voice, saying, "How long, O Lord, holy and true, until You judge and avenge our blood on those who dwell on the earth?" Rev. 6:9, 10.

Allow me to become food for the wild beasts, through whose instrumentality it will be granted me to attain to God. I am the wheat of God; so let me be ground by the teeth of the wild beasts—so that I may be found to be the pure bread of Christ. *Ignatius (c. 105, E), 1.75.*

All the martyrdoms were blessed and noble, and they took place according to the will of God. . . . The martyrs despised all the torments of this world, redeeming themselves from eternal punishment by [the suffering of] a single hour. *Martyrdom of Polycarp (c. 135, E), 1.39.*

Though threatened with death, we do not deny His name. *Justin Martyr (c. 160, E), 1.209.*

It is evident that no one can terrify or subdue us. For, throughout all the world, we have believed in Jesus! It is clear that, although beheaded, and crucified, and thrown to wild beasts . . . and fire, and all other kinds of torture, we do not give up our confession. But the more such things happen, the more do other persons and in larger numbers become faithful believers and worshippers of God through the name of Jesus. *Justin Martyr (c. 160, E), 1.254.*

The prophets . . . also foretold this, that all those on whom the Spirit of God should rest and who would obey the word of the Father and serve Him according to their ability would suffer persecution and be stoned and slain. *Irenaeus (c. 180, E/W), 1.509.*

We have exhibited before our eyes every day abundant sources of martyrs who are burned, impaled, and beheaded. The fear inspired by the Law (leading as a pedagogue to Christ) trained all of them so as to manifest their piety by their blood. *Clement of Alexandria (c. 195, E), 2.374.*

In love to the Lord, the spiritual man will most gladly depart from this life—perhaps giving thanks both to him who afforded the cause of his departure from here, and to him who laid the plot against him. . . . With good courage, then, he goes to the Lord, his friend, for whom he voluntarily gave his body. *Clement of Alexandria (c. 195, E), 2.411.*

We call martyrdom perfection, not because the man comes to the end of his life as others, but because he has exhibited the perfect work of love. *Clement of Alexandria (c. 195, E), 2.411.*

Now some of the heretics who have misunderstood the Lord, have at once an impious and cowardly love of life, saying that the true martyrdom is the knowledge of the only true God . . . and that a man is a self-murderer and a suicide if he makes confession by death. . . . Now we, too, say that those who have rushed into death . . . banish themselves without being martyrs, even though they are punished publicly. *Clement of Alexandria (c. 195, E), 2.412.*

The church is full of those persons—chaste women as well as men—who all of their life have contemplated the death that rouses up to Christ. *Clement of Alexandria (c. 195, E), 2.419.*

Although threatened with death at a tyrant's hands, and brought before the tribunals, and all his substances imperilled, the free man will by no means abandon piety. Nor will the wife who dwells with a wicked husband, or the son if he has a bad father, or the servant if he has a bad master, ever fail in holding nobly to virtue. But as it is noble for a man to die for virtue, for liberty, and for himself, so also is it for a woman. For this is not peculiar to the nature of males, but to the nature of the good. Accordingly, both the old man, the young, and the servant will live faithfully, and if need be, die (which is to really be made alive by death). So we know that children, women, and servants have often reached the highest degree of excellence—against their fathers', masters', and husbands' will. *Clement of Alexandria (c. 195, E), 2.421.*

On martyrdom, the Lord has spoken explicitly . . . "But I say unto you, Whoever confesses Me before men, the Son of man also will confess before the angels of God; but whoever denies Me before men, him will I deny before the angels." *Clement of Alexandria (c. 195, E), 2.421.*

When, again, He says, "When they persecute you in this city, flee to another," He does not advise flight as if persecution were an evil thing. Nor does He command them to avoid death by flight—as if in dread of death. Rather, He wishes us to be neither the authors nor abettors of any evil to anyone—either to ourselves or to the persecutor and murderer. *Clement of Alexandria (c. 195, E), 2.423.*

If he who kills a man of God sins against God, he also who [voluntarily] presents himself before the judgment seat becomes guilty of his death. And such is also the case with him who does not avoid persecution, but out of daring, presents himself for capture. Such a one—as far as in him lies—becomes an accomplice in the crime of the persecutor. *Clement of Alexandria (c. 195, E), 2.423.*

They say, "If God cares for you, why are you persecuted and put to death? Has He abandoned you to this?" No, we do not suppose that the Lord wishes us to be involved in calamities. . . . So that it was not that He wished us to be persecuted, but He indicated beforehand what we will suffer by His prediction of what would take place, training us to endurance. *Clement of Alexandria (c. 195, E), 2.423.*

He who is truly brave, with the peril arising from the hostility of the multitude before his eyes, courageously awaits whatever comes. In this way, he is distinguished from others who are called martyrs. For some furnish occasions for themselves and rush into the heart of dangers. . . . In contrast, those who are in accordance with right reason protect themselves. Then, upon God *really* calling them, they promptly surrender themselves and confirm the call. *Clement of Alexandria (c. 195, E), 2.541, 542.*

On the way [to be martyred], the other man asked James to forgive him. And after brief consideration, he said, "Peace be to you," and kissed him. And so both were beheaded together. *Eusebius, citing Clement of Alexandria (c. 195, E), 2.579.*

If the spiritual man is pointed out [as a Christian], he glories in it. If he is accused, he offers no defense. When questioned, he makes voluntary confession. When condemned, he gives thanks. *Tertullian (c. 197, W), 3.18.*

No one suffers willingly, since suffering necessarily implies fear and danger. Yet, . . . it is our battle to be summoned to your tribunals—so that there, under fear of execution, we may battle for the truth. But the day is won when the object of the struggle is gained. This victory of ours gives us the glory of pleasing God and the spoils of life eternal. . . . Therefore, we conquer in dying; we go forth victorious at the very time we are subdued. *Tertullian (c. 197, W), 3.54.*

The more often we are mown down by you, the more in number we grow. The blood of Christians is seed. . . . For who that contemplates it, is not excited to inquire what is at the bottom of it? Who, after inquiry, does not embrace our doctrines? And when he has embraced them, who does not desire to suffer so that he may become a partaker of the fullness of God's grace, that he may obtain from it complete forgiveness, by giving his blood in exchange? For [martyrdom] secures the forgiveness of all offenses. *Tertullian (c. 197, W), 3.55*

The rest of your charge of obstinacy against us you sum up in this indictment: that we boldly refuse neither your swords, your crosses, your wild beasts, fires, or tortures—such is our obstinacy and contempt of death. . . . All our obstinacy, however, is with you a foregone conclusion, based on our strong convictions. For we take for granted a resurrection of the dead.

Hope in this resurrection amounts to a contempt of death. *Tertullian (c. 197, W), 3.126, 127.*

The following two passages are addressed to Christians who were in prison, awaiting possible martyrdom.

Other things . . . may have accompanied you as far as the prison gate, to which also your relatives may have attended you. There and thenceforth you were severed from the world. . . . Do not let this separation from the world alarm you. For if we reflect that the world is more really the prison, we will see that you have gone *out* of a prison rather than *into* one. . . . Wherefore O blessed, you may regard yourselves as having been transported from a prison to—we may say—a place of safety. It is full of darkness, but you yourselves are light. It has chains, but God has made you free. Unpleasant exhalations are there, but you are an odor of sweetness. *Tertullian (c. 197, W), 3.693.*

O blessed ones, count whatever is hard in this lot of yours as a discipline of your powers of mind and body. You are about to pass through a noble struggle, in which the living God acts the part of superintendent, in which the Holy Spirit is your trainer, and in which the prize is an eternal crown of angelic essence—citizenship in the heavens, glory everlasting. *Tertullian (c. 197, W), 3.694.*

Christians always, and now more than ever, pass their times not in gold, but in iron. The stoles of martyrdom are now preparing. The angels who are to carry us are now being awaited. Go forth to meet them already arrayed in the cosmetics and adornments of prophets and apostles—drawing your whiteness from simplicity, your ruddy hue from modesty, painting your eyes with bashfulness, and your mouth with silence, implanting in your ears the words of God, fitting around your necks the yoke of Christ. *Tertullian (c. 198, W), 4.25.*

With this strength of patience, Isaiah is cut asunder, but ceases not to speak concerning the Lord. Stephen is stoned and prays for pardon for his foes. *Tertullian (c. 200, W), 3.716.*

Come, tell me what is your opinion of the flesh, when it has to contend for the name of Christ? . . . What is your view of it when, at length before the public view, it is racked by every kind of torture that can be devised, and when finally it is spent beneath its agonies, struggling to render its last turn for Christ by dying for Him, frequently upon His own cross

(not to mention by still more atrocious devices of torture). Most blessed, truly, and most glorious, must be the flesh that can repay its Master Christ so vast a debt—and so completely—that the only obligation remaining due to Him is, that it should cease [by death] to owe Him more. *Tertullian (c. 210, W), 3.551.*

In the Revelation of John, again, the order of these times is spread out to view, which the souls of the martyrs are taught to wait for beneath the altar, while they earnestly pray to be avenged and judged. *Tertullian (c. 210, W), 3.563.*

Condemnation gives us more pleasure than acquittal. *Tertullian (c. 212, W), 3.105.*

When Arrius Antoninus was driving things hard in Asia, all of the Christians of the province—in one united band—presented themselves before his judgment seat. On ordering a few persons to be led forth to execution, he said to the rest, "O miserable men, if you wish to die, you have precipices or nooses!" If we were to take it into our heads to do that very thing, what would you make of so many thousands— of such a multitude of men and women, persons of every sex, age, and rank—if they presented themselves before you? *Tertullian (c. 212, W), 3.107.*

I stoutly maintain that martyrdom is good. It is required by the God by whom likewise idolatry is forbidden and punished. *Tertullian (c. 213, W), 3.637.*

It remains for us to review the modern Christian system, lest ancient times may perhaps appear to have had this sacrament [of martyrdom] exclusively for their own. *Tertullian (c. 213, W), 3.641.*

It will be to no purpose to say, "Though I will deny that I am a Christian, I will not be denied by Christ, for I have not denied *Him*." . . . However, by denying he is a Christian, a person has also denied Christ. *Tertullian (c. 213, W), 3.642.*

The souls of the martyrs peacefully rest in the meantime under the altar, and they support their patience by the assured hope of vengeance. . . . The flesh is the clothing of the soul. The uncleanness, indeed, is washed away by baptism. However, the stains are changed into dazzling whiteness by martyrdom. *Tertullian (c. 213, W), 3.646.*

[PAGAN ANTAGONIST:] Oh, unbelievable folly and incredible audacity! Christians despise present torments, although they fear those that are uncertain and future. While they fear to die after death, they do not fear to die for the present. *Mark Minucius Felix (c. 200, W), 4.177.*

[PAGAN ANTAGONIST:] Look! For you, there are threats, punishments, tortures, and crosses. . . . Where is that God who is able to help you when you come to life again, if He cannot help you while you are in this life? *Mark Minucius Felix (c. 200, W), 4.179.*

How beautiful is the spectacle to God when a Christian does battle with pain! When he is drawn up against threats, punishments, and tortures! When, mocking the noise of death, he treads under foot the horror of the executioner! . . . When, triumphant and victorious, he tramples upon the very man who has pronounced sentence against him! For the person who has obtained the thing for which he contends is a conqueror. *Mark Minucius Felix (c. 200, W), 4.196.*

Boys and young women among us scorn crosses and tortures, wild beasts, and all the horrors of punishments, with the inspired patience of suffering. And do you not perceive, O wretched men, that there is nobody who either is willing to undergo punishment without purpose, or is able without God to bear tortures? *Mark Minucius Felix (c. 200, W), 4.196.*

Christ's blood was poured out upon the earth when the soldier pierced His side. For we will not lose all memory of that passion, even if it is our lot someday to come to that highest and supreme contemplation of the Logos. Nor will we forget the truth that our confession was brought about by His sojourning in our body. *Origen (c. 228, E), 9.327.*

Everyone who bears testimony to the truth—whether he supports it by words or by deed, or in any way whatever—may properly be called a witness [Gr. *martur*]. However, it has come to be the custom of the brotherhood to keep the name of witness more properly for those who have borne witness to the mystery of godliness by shedding their blood for it. For the brotherhood are struck with admiration for those who have contended to the death for truth and valor. Still, the Savior gives the name of witness [Gr. *martur*] to everyone who bears witness to the truth. *Origen (c. 228, E), 9.343.*

It was God's will that we should rather endure all the dreadful reproaches connected with confessing him as God than escape for a short time from such sufferings by allowing ourselves to conform to the will of the enemies of the truth, through our words. *Origen (c. 228, E), 9.377.*

The letter teaches us to withdraw as far as it is in our power from those who persecute us and from expected conspiracies through words. To do so is to act according to prudence. To go to meet critical situations when one can keep outside of them is rash and headstrong. For who would still hesitate about avoiding such things when not only did Jesus retreat in view of what happened to John, but also taught and said, "If they persecute you in this city, flee into the other." When a trial comes that is not in our power to avoid, we must endure it with exceeding nobleness and courage. But when it is in our power to avoid it, not to do so is rash. *Origen (c. 245, E), 9.429.*

Many also of our contemporaries, knowing well that if they made a confession of Christianity, they would be put to death—but that if they denied it, they would be liberated and their property restored—despised life and voluntarily selected death for the sake of their religion. *Origen (c. 248, E), 4.439.*

We have learned from the Gospel neither to relax our efforts in times of peace and to give ourselves up to leisure, nor, when the world makes war upon us, to become cowards and apostatize from the love of the God of all things, which is in Jesus Christ. *Origen (c. 248, E), 4.470.*

We think it is both reasonable in itself and well-pleasing to God to suffer pain for the sake of virtue, to undergo torture for the sake of piety, and even to suffer death for the sake of holiness. For "precious in the sight of God is the death of his saints." So we maintain that to overcome the love of life is to enjoy a great good. *Origen (c. 248, E), 4.660.*

I grieve for you, seeing that out of so great a people, none is crowned in the contest. Certainly, even if he does not personally fight [i.e., as a martyr], he should at least give encouragement to others. . . . However, those of you who are stuffed with wealth neither fight nor place yourself by the martyr's side when he is fighting. O fool, do you not perceive that one person is warring on behalf of many? The whole church is suspended on such a one if he conquers. *Commodianus (c. 240, W), 4.215.*

Since you desire martyrdom, O son, listen. ... You indeed desire that which is a matter suited for the blessed. However, first of all overcome the evil one with your good acts by living well. ... Many indeed err, saying, "With our blood we have overcome the wicked one." Yet, if they are not called to martyrdom, they are unwilling to overcome. ... Even now, if you have conquered by good deeds, you are a martyr [witness] in Him. You, therefore, who seek to extol martyrdom with your word, in peace [i.e., when there is no persecution], clothe yourself with good deeds and be secure. *Commodianus (c. 240, W), 4.215.*

Cyprian, to the martyrs and confessors in Christ our Lord and in God the Father, everlasting salvation. ... You were not kept back from the struggle by fear of tortures. ... Bravely and firmly, you have returned with ready devotion to contend in the most extreme contest. Of you, I find that some are already crowned. Others are even now within reach of the crown of victory. ... The multitude of those who were present saw with admiration the heavenly contest—the contest of God, the spiritual contest, the battle of Christ. They saw that His servants stood with free voice. *Cyprian (c. 250, W), 5.287, 288.*

Precious is the death that has bought immortality at the cost of its blood, which has received the crown from the consummation of its virtues. How Christ rejoiced therein! How willingly did He both fight and conquer in such servants of His! ... You are fighting under the eyes of a present Lord, whom you are attaining by the confession of His name to His own glory. He is not someone who only *looks* on His servants. Rather, He Himself also wrestles in us; He Himself is engaged in the struggle. *Cyprian (c. 250, W), 5.289.*

We say again, brother Cyprian, that we have received great joy, comfort, and refreshment in your description—with glorious and deserved praises—of the glorious *immortalities* (I won't say deaths) of the martyrs. ... From your letter, we saw those glorious triumphs of the martyrs. To some degree, with our eyes we have followed them as they went to heaven and have thought about them seated among the angels, powers, and dominions of heaven. We have in some manner sensed with our ears the Lord

giving them the promised testimony in the presence of the Father. *Letter of Moyses and various confessors to Cyprian (c. 250, W), 5.302.*

An assorted group of people, following your example, have confessed alike with you. ... Of these, there is no lack of virgins in whom the hundredfold is added to the fruit of sixtyfold. ... In boys, also, a courage greater than their age has surpassed their years in the praise of the confession. Accordingly, each sex and every age adorns the blessed flock of your martyrdom. *Cyprian (c. 250, W), 5.404.*

Did he not previously ordain eternal punishment for those who deny Him? Did he not ordain saving rewards for those who confess Him? *Cyprian (c. 250, W), 5.439.*

But someone may perhaps object and say, "The present pestilence saddens me in this: ... that I am deprived of martyrdom, for I may die first." ... However, God is the searcher of the affections and the heart. ... He sees you and praises and approves you. ... In God's servants among whom confession is purposed and martyrdom conceived in the mind, the intention dedicated to good is crowned by God the Judge. *Cyprian (c. 250, W), 5.473.*

Although this mortality [i.e., a plague] conferred nothing else, it has achieved this benefit to Christians and to God's servants—that we begin gladly to desire martyrdom, as we learn not to fear death. *Cyprian (c. 250, W), 5.473.*

If it is glorious for soldiers of this world to return in triumph to their country when the enemy is defeated, how much more excellent and greater is the glory to return in triumph to Paradise, when the devil is overcome? To bring back victorious trophies to that place from which Adam was ejected as a sinner. *Cyprian (c. 250, W), 5.506.*

If a Christian were to deny the Lord, he would incur guilt on His behalf. For he should have overcome. Therefore, it is essential that He should ... bear all things—even in suffering—to whom the victory is due. *Treatise on the Glory of Martyrdom (c. 255, W), 5.580.*

What is as illustrious and sublime ... as to preserve all the vigor of faith in the midst of so many weapons of executioners? What is as great and honorable as—in the midst of so many swords of the surrounding guards—to profess again and again, in repeated words, the Lord of one's liberty and the author of one's salvation? *Treatise on the Glory of Martyrdom (c. 255, W), 5.581.*

Surrounded as you are with the knives of the executioners and the instruments of probing tortures, stand sublime and strong! . . . Our hands are bound with tightened bonds. Heavy links fastened around our necks oppress us with their solid weight. Our bodies that were strained on the rack now hiss on the red-hot plates. All these things are not for the sake of seeking our blood—but for the sake of testing us. *Treatise on the Glory of Martyrdom (c. 255, W), 5.582.*

The cruel hands of the persecutors were wrenching asunder the martyr's limbs and the furious torturer was plowing up his lacerated muscles. Still, they could not overcome him. I know this from the words of those who stood around. "This is a great matter. I do not understand what it is—that he is not conquered by suffering, that he is not broken down by heavy torments." *Treatise on the Glory of Martyrdom (c. 255, W), 5.583.*

It would be a needless task for me to mention by name our [martyr] friends. . . . Only understand that they include men and women, both young men and old, both maidens and elderly matrons, both soldiers and private citizens. *Dionysius of Alexandria (c. 262, E), 6.96.*

People see that Christian men are lacerated by various kinds of tortures. Yet, those men retain their forbearance unsubdued—while the executioners are wearied. Seeing this, the crowd realizes (as is really the case) that neither the agreement of so many persons nor the constancy of the dying is without meaning. They realize that endurance alone could not overcome such great tortures, without the aid of God. After all, robbers and men of robust frame are unable to endure lacerations of this kind. . . . But in our case, boys and delicate women (not to speak of men) in silence overpower their torturers. Even the fire is unable to extort a groan from them. . . . Behold! The weak sex and fragile age endure to be lacerated in the whole body and to be burned. They do not endure this out of necessity, for it is permitted them to escape if they wished to do so [by denying Christ]. Rather, they endure out of their own will, because they put their trust in God. *Lactantius (c. 304–313, W), 7.149.*

To choose to be tortured and slain, rather than to take incense in three fingers and throw it upon the fire, appears to the pagans as foolish. *Lactantius (c. 304–313, W), 7.155.*

It is a virtue to despise death. It is not that we seek death, or of our own accord inflict it upon ourselves, . . . which is a wicked and impious thing. Rather, if we are compelled to desert God and to betray our faith, we would prefer to undergo death. . . . Thus, with lofty and invincible minds, we trample upon those things that others fear—pain and death. This is virtue! This is true constancy, to be steadfast and unmoving in this one thing alone: that no terror nor any violence can turn us away from God! *Lactantius (c. 304–313, W), 7.183.*

They devoted themselves to God and considered it as but a small sacrifice to surrender their bodies to you and to give their flesh to be mangled. *Arnobius (c. 305, E), 6.429.*

To narrate their virtue and their manly endurance under every torment, what language would suffice? For everyone who wanted to was free to abuse them. Some beat them with wooden clubs; others with rods; still others, with scourges, thongs, and ropes. The spectacle of these modes of torture had great variety in it and displayed extreme malice. Some had their hands bound behind them and were suspended on the rack. They then had every limb in their body stretched with a certain kind of pulley. *Phileas (c. 307, E), 6.162.*

When they were commanded to make their choice between these alternatives—namely, either to put their hand to the unholy sacrifice . . . or else to refuse to sacrifice and expect the judgment of death to be executed on them— they never hesitated. Rather, they went cheerfully to death. For they knew the sentence declared for us of old by the Holy Scriptures: "He that sacrifices to other gods will be utterly destroyed." *Phileas (c. 307, E), 6.163.*

He who denies being a Christian so that he may not be hated of men, and so loves his own life more than he does the Lord, . . . is wretched and miserable. . . . If we are allied to martyrdom, let us be steadfast to confess His precious name. And if we are punished on this account, let us rejoice, as hastening to immortality. *Apostolic Constitutions (compiled c. 390, E), 7.438, 439.*

II. Rewards for martyrdom

Precious in the sight of the Lord is the death of His saints. Ps. 116:15.

A faithful witness [Gr. martur] shall deliver a soul from evil. Prov. 14:25 (lxx).

Whoever confesses Me before men, him I will also confess before My Father who is in heaven. But whoever denies me before men, him I will also deny before My Father who is in heaven. Matt. 10:32, 33.

So they departed from the presence of the council, rejoicing that they were counted worthy to suffer shame for His name. Acts 5:41.

Do not fear any of those things which you are about to suffer. . . . Be faithful until death, and I will give you the crown of life. Rev. 2:10.

When He opened the fifth seal, I saw under the altar the souls of those who had been slain for the word of God and for the testimony which they held. Rev. 6:9.

I asked, "What have they borne?" She replied: "Scourges, prisons, great tribulations, crosses, and wild beasts for God's name's sake. On this account, there is assigned to them the portion of sanctification on the right hand. This is for everyone who will suffer for God's name. To the rest, there is assigned the division on the left. Nevertheless, there are the same gifts and promises for both those who sit on the right and those who sit on the left. Only, those ones sit on the right, and they have some glory." *Hermas (c. 150, W), 2.13.*

All who once suffered for the name of the Lord are honorable before God. And the sins of all of them were forgiven, because they suffered for the name of the Son of God. . . . Your sins were heavy. In fact, if you had not suffered for the name of the Lord, you would have died to God on account of your sins. *Hermas (c. 150, W), 2.52, 53.*

The next two passages may reflect more a Montanistic view of martyrdom than a general view held by the church.

"We are indeed confident and deem it good rather to be absent from the body and present with the Lord." . . . Observe how he here also ascribes to the excellence of martyrdom a contempt for the body. For no one, on becoming absent from the body, is at once a dweller in the presence of the Lord—unless if by the preroga-tive of martyrdom, he gains a lodging in Paradise, rather than in Hades. *Tertullian (c. 210, W), 3.576.*

How is it, then, that the region of Paradise (which, as revealed to John in the Spirit, lays under the altar) displays no other souls in it besides the souls of the martyrs? How is it that the most heroic martyr Perpetua on the day of her martyrdom saw only her fellow martyrs there—in the revelation which she received of Paradise? . . . The sole key to unlock Paradise is in your own life's blood. *Tertullian (c. 210, W), 3.231.*

[ADDRESSED TO PAGANS:] The greater our conflicts, the greater our rewards. Your cruelty is our glory. *Tertullian (c. 212, W), 3.107.*

The Lord desired that we should rejoice and leap for joy in persecutions. For when persecutions occur, then are given the crowns of faith. Then the soldiers of God are proved. Then the heavens are opened to martyrs. . . . We should not fear to be slain, for we are sure to be crowned when we are slain. *Cyprian (c. 250, W), 5.348.*

See the lofty and great contest, which is glorious with the reward of a heavenly crown. For God looks upon us as we struggle. . . . God looks upon us in the warfare and conflict in the encounter of faith. His angels look on us, and Christ looks on us. How great is the dignity! And How great is the happiness of the glory, to fight in the presence of God and to be crowned, with Christ for a judge! *Cyprian (c. 250, W), 5.349, 350.*

The first fruit for the martyrs is a hundredfold. *Cyprian (c. 250, W), 5.436.*

As to the benefits of martyrdom, in the Proverbs of Solomon, it says: "The faithful martyr deliverers his soul from evils" [Prov. 14:25]. *Cyprian (c. 250, W), 5.537*

Heaven lies open to our blood! The dwelling place of Gehenna gives way to our blood! And among all the attainments of glory, the title of blood is sealed as the fairest—and its crown is designated as the most complete. *Treatise on the Glory of Martyrdom (c. 255, W), 5.581.*

Martyrs rejoice in heaven. The fire will consume those who are enemies of the truth. The Paradise of God blooms for the martyrs; Gehenna will envelope those who deny—and eternal fire will burn them up. *Treatise on the Glory of Martyrdom (c. 255, W), 5.581.*

He relates that he saw under the altar of God—that is, under the earth—the souls of those who were slain. For both heaven and earth are called God's altar. *Lactantius (c. 304–313, W), 7.351.*

III. Baptism of blood

But Jesus answered and said, "You do not know what you ask. Are you able to drink the cup that I am about to drink, and be baptized with the baptism that I am baptized with?" Matt. 20:22.

I have a baptism to be baptized with, and how distressed I am till it is accomplished! Luke 12:50.

Who, after inquiry, does not embrace our doctrines? And when he has embraced them, who does not desire to suffer so that he may become a partaker of the fullness of God's grace—so that he may obtain complete forgiveness, by giving his blood in exchange? For [martyrdom] secures the remission of all offenses. *Tertullian (c. 197, W), 3.55*

We have indeed, likewise, a second font . . . of blood. . . . These two baptisms He sent out from the wound in His pierced side, in order that those who believed in His blood could be bathed with the water. Likewise, those who had been bathed in the water could likewise drink the blood. This is the baptism that both stands in lieu of the fontal bath—when that has not been received—and restores it when it has been lost. *Tertullian (c. 198, W), 3.677.*

When, however, a person is led forth unto the final proof of happiness, unto the occasion of the second baptism, unto the act of ascending the divine seat, no patience is more needed there than bodily patience. *Tertullian (c. 200, W), 3.716.*

If this is so, then martyrdom will be another baptism. For he says, "I have also another baptism." It was for this that there flowed out of the wound in the Lord's side water and blood, the materials of both baptisms. Now, if I could set someone else free through the second baptism [which I cannot], then, I should have the same right through the first baptism. *Tertullian (c. 212, W), 4.100.*

God had foreseen . . . that faith—even after baptism—would be endangered. He saw that most persons—after attaining unto salvation—would be lost again, through soiling the wedding dress, through failing to provide oil for their torches. . . . He therefore appointed as a

second supply of comfort—and the last means of succor—the fight of martyrdom and the baptism of blood—thereafter free from danger. *Tertullian (c. 213, W), 3.639.*

In the baptism [of blood], life itself is laid down. Thus, "love covers the multitude of sins." *Tertullian (c. 213, W), 3.639.*

With one bite [from the leopard], he was bathed with such a quantity of blood that the people shouted out to him as he was returning the testimony of his second baptism: "Saved and washed! Saved and washed!" Manifestly, he was assuredly saved who had been glorified in such a spectacle. *Passion of Perpetua and Felicitas (c. 205, W), 3.705.*

Let no one say, "He who accepts martyrdom is baptized in his own blood and, therefore, peace is not necessary to him from the bishop." *Cyprian (c. 250, W), 5.337.*

Can the power of [water] baptism be greater or of more avail than confession, than suffering—when a person confesses Christ before men and is baptized in his own blood? Yet, even this baptism does not benefit a heretic . . . because there is no salvation out of the church. *Cyprian (c. 250, W), 5.384.*

Some ask, "If one of these [catechumens]—before he is baptized—is arrested and slain after confessing the Name, does he lose the hope of salvation and the reward of confession, since he had not previously been born again of water?" . . . They certainly are not lacking the sacrament of baptism who are baptized with the most glorious and greatest baptism of blood. Concerning this baptism, the Lord also said that He had "another baptism to be baptized with." The same Lord declared in the Gospel that those who are baptized in their own blood and sanctified by suffering are perfected. They obtain the grace of the divine promise. He showed this when He spoke to the thief who believed and confessed in His very passion. Jesus promised him that he would be with Him in Paradise. *Cyprian (c. 250, W), 5.385.*

Let those of us who . . . have given the first baptism to believers, also prepare everyone for the second baptism. We should urge and teach that this is a baptism greater in grace, more lofty in power, and more precious in honor. . . . This is a baptism after which no one sins any more. . . . This is a baptism that immediately associates us with God when we withdraw from the world. In the baptism of water, there is received the remission of sins. In the baptism of blood, there is received the crown of life. *Cyprian (c. 250, W), 5.497.*

John made a distinction and said that he indeed baptized in water, but that one would come who would baptize in the Holy Spirit, by the grace and power of God. . . . They are also so [baptized] in the baptism of everyone in his own proper blood. *Treatise on Re-Baptism (c. 257, W), 5.668.*

"Are you able to drink of the cup that I drink of, or to be baptized with the baptism with which I am baptized?" For He knew that those men had to be baptized not only with water, but also in their own blood. . . . What was said by the Lord, "I have another baptism to be baptized with," signifies in this place not a second baptism, as if there were two baptisms, but demonstrates that there is a baptism of another kind given to us, conferring the same salvation. . . . Therefore, either one of the two, or both kinds, might afford to us this one twofold saving and glorifying baptism. . . . Also, to those who are made lawful believers, the baptism of their own blood is lacking without injury. For, being baptized in the name of Christ, they have been redeemed with the most precious blood of the Lord. . . . These are different kinds of the one and the same baptism that flows from one wound [of Christ] into water and blood. *Treatise on Re-Baptism (c. 257, W), 5.675.*

IV. Honor of Martyrs

You have seen before your eyes—not only in the case of the blessed Ignatius, Zosimus, and Rufus—but also in others among yourselves, and in Paul himself, and the rest of the apostles. . . . They are in their due place in the presence of the Lord, with whom they also suffered. *Polycarp (c. 135, E), 1.35.*

Polycarp was now crowned with the wreath of immortality, having beyond dispute received his reward. He [the wicked one] did his utmost that not the least memorial of Polycarp should be taken away by us. For many Christians desired to do this, and to become possessors of his holy flesh. . . . However, [Satan] is ignorant that it is neither possible for us ever to forsake Christ . . . nor to worship any other. For we worship Him indeed, as being the Son of God. However, as for the martyrs, as disciples and followers of the Lord, we worthily love them

on account of their extraordinary affections towards their own King. *Martyrdom of Polycarp (c. 135, E), 1.42, 43.*

Accordingly, we afterwards took up Polycarp's bones, as being more precious than the most exquisite jewels, and more purified than gold. We deposited them in a fitting place, where, being gathered together, as opportunity is allowed us, with joy and rejoicing, the Lord will permit us to celebrate the anniversary of his martyrdom. *Martyrdom of Polycarp (c. 135, E), 1.43.*

The blessed Polycarp suffered martyrdom on the second day of the month Xanthicus, the seventh day before the first of May, on the great Sabbath, at the eighth hour. *Martyrdom of Polycarp (c. 135, E), 1.43.*

The holy martyrs . . . were beheaded, and so they perfected their testimony in the confession of the Savior. Some of the faithful secretly removed their bodies and laid them in a suitable place. *The Martyrdom of the Holy Martyrs (c. 160, W), 1.306.*

The church does in every place, because of that love which she cherishes towards God, send forward at all times a multitude of martyrs to the Father. In contrast, all others not only have nothing of this kind to point to among themselves, but even maintain that such witness-bearing is not at all necessary. *Irenaeus (c. 180, E/W), 1.508.*

Some, not able to find this peace [i.e., ecclesiastical forgiveness] in the church, have been accustomed to seek it from the imprisoned martyrs. And so you should have it dwelling with you, cherish it, and guard it—that you may be able perhaps to bestow it upon others. *Tertullian (c. 197, W), 3.693.*

[What unbelieving husband] will permit her to creep into prison to kiss a martyr's chains? *Tertullian (c. 205, W), 4.46.*

At once, he put away the heavy cloak, and his disburdening began. He loosed from his foot the military shoe, beginning to stand upon holy ground. *Tertullian (c. 211, W), 3.93.*

You go so far as to lavish this power [of forgiveness of sins] on martyrs as well! No sooner has anyone . . . put on the chains . . . than adulterers beset him and fornicators gain access to him. Instantly prayers echo around him. Instantly, pools of tears. . . . Let it suffice to the martyr to have purged his *own* sins. . . . Who can redeem another's death by his own, except the Son of God alone? *Tertullian (c. 212, W), 4.100.*

The death of martyrs is also praised in song. . . . The death of His own saints is precious in His sight, as David sings. *Tertullian (c. 213, W), 3.639, 640.*

You who were concerned in these matters may be reminded of them again to the glory of the Lord, so that you who know them by report may have communion with the blessed martyrs, and through them with the Lord Jesus Christ. *Passion of Perpetua and Felicitas (c. 205, W), 3.699.*

Laurentius and Egnatius had also been once warring in the camps of the world. However, they were true and spiritual soldiers of God, casting down the devil by the confession of Christ. Therefore, they merited palms and crowns from the Lord by their illustrious passion. We always offer sacrifices for them (as you remember) as often as we celebrate the passions and days of the martyrs in the annual commemoration. *Cyprian (c. 250, W), 5.313.*

Indeed, we believe that the merits of martyrs and the works of the righteous are of great avail with the Judge. However, this will be when the Day of Judgment comes. It will be after the conclusion of this life and the end of this world—when His people will stand before the judgment seat of Christ. *Cyprian (c. 250, W), 5.442.*

Those who have received certificates from the martyrs . . . if they should be seized with any misfortune and peril of sickness, . . . and if a presbyter cannot be found and death begins to be imminent, they can make confession of their sin before even a deacon. *Cyprian (c. 250, W), 5.293.*

Cyprian, to the presbyters and deacons abiding at Rome, his brethren. . . . Our brother Lucian, who himself also is one of the confessors, is earnest indeed in faith and robust in virtue. However, he is but little established in the reading of the Lord's Word. He has attempted certain things, constituting himself for a time as an authority for unskilled people. Certificates written by his hand were given indiscriminately to many persons in the name of Paulus. Whereas Mappalicus the martyr, cautious and modest, mindful of the law and discipline,

wrote no letters contrary to the Gospel. Rather, only moved with filial affection for his mother, who had lapsed, he commanded peace to be given to her. *Cyprian (c. 250, W), 5.300.*

Take note of their days on which they depart, so that we may celebrate their commemoration among the memorials of the martyrs. . . . There are celebrated here by us oblations and sacrifices for their commemorations. *Cyprian (c. 250, W), 5.315.*

Let no one decry the dignity of martyrs! Let no one degrade their glories and their crowns! The strength of their uncorrupted faith abides sound. *Cyprian (c. 250, W), 5.443.*

When the blessed martyr Paulus was still in the body, he called me and said to me: "Lucian, in the presence of Christ I say to you, if anyone after my being called away will ask for peace from you, grant it in my name." *Lucian (c. 250, W), 5.299.*

Those holy martyrs, who were once with us, are now seated with Christ. They are sharers in His kingdom and partakers with Him in His judgment. They act as His judicial assessors. *Dionysius of Alexandria (c. 262, E), 6.100.*

The most joyful festival of all, however, has been celebrated by those perfect martyrs who have sat down at the feast in heaven. *Dionysius of Alexandria, as quoted by Eusebius (c. 262, E), 6.108.*

Now, concerning the martyrs, we say to you that they are to be held in all honor with you. *Apostolic Constitutions (compiled c. 390, E), 7.442.*

Sing for the martyrs that have fallen asleep, and for all the saints from the beginning of the world—as well as for your brothers who are asleep in the Lord. And offer the acceptable Eucharist, the representation of the royal body of Christ, both in your churches and in the dormitories. *Apostolic Constitutions (compiled c. 390, E), 7.464.*

Let [the slaves] rest on the day of the first martyr Stephen and of the other holy martyrs who preferred Christ to their own life. *Apostolic Constitutions (compiled c. 390, E), 7.495; see also 2.417, 2.427; extended discussion: 5.347–5.350, 5.579–5.587.*

SEE ALSO CONFESSORS; IGNATIUS; JUSTIN MARTYR; LAPSED; PERSECUTION; POLYCARP; RELICS OF MARTYRS AND SAINTS.

MARY

While He was still talking to the multitudes, behold, His mother and brothers stood outside, seeking to speak with Him. Then one said to Him, "Look, Your mother and Your brothers are standing outside, seeking to speak with You." But He answered and said to the one who told Him, "Who is My mother and who are My brothers?" And he stretched out His hand toward His disciples and said, "Here are My mother and My brothers! For whoever does the will of My Father in heaven is My brother and sister and mother." Matt. 12:46–50.

Now in the sixth month the angel Gabriel was sent by God to a city of Galilee named Nazareth, to a virgin betrothed to a man whose name was Joseph, of the house of David. The virgin's name was Mary. Having come in, the angel said to her, "Rejoice, highly favored one, the Lord is with you; blessed are you among women!" But when she saw him, she was troubled at his saying, and considered what manner of greeting this was. Then the angel said to her, "Do not be afraid, Mary, for you have found favor with God. And behold, you will conceive in your womb and bring forth a Son, and shall call His name Jesus." Luke 1:26–31.

Then Mary said, "Behold the maidservant of the Lord! Let it be to me according to your word." Luke 1:38.

And it came about while He said these things, one of the women in the crowd raised her voice, and said to Him, "Blessed is the womb that bore You, and the breasts at which You nursed." But He said, "On the contrary, blessed are those who hear the word of God, and observe it." Luke 11:27, 28 (nas).

And when they ran out of wine, the mother of Jesus said to Him, "They have no wine." Jesus said to her, "Woman, what does your concern have to do with Me? My hour has not yet come." John 2:3, 4.

In his works, Papias gives a description of the various persons named Mary who are mentioned in the writings of the apostles. Among them he lists:

Mary, the mother of the Lord. *Papias (c. 120, E), 1.155.*

There is One Physician who is possessed of both flesh and spirit, . . . both of Mary and of God. *Ignatius (c. 105, E), 1.52.*

Jesus Christ . . . was descended from David, and He was also of Mary. *Ignatius (c. 105, E), 1.70.*

He became man by the virgin, in order that the disobedience which began with the serpent might receive its destruction in the same manner in which it derived its origin. For Eve, who was a virgin and undefiled, having conceived the word of the serpent, brought forth disobedience and death. But the virgin Mary received faith and joy when the angel Gabriel announced the good tidings to her that the Spirit of the Lord would come upon her. *Justin Martyr (c. 160, E), 1.249.*

When Mary urged Him on to the wonderful miracle of the wine and was desirous to partake of the cup of emblematic significance before the proper time, the Lord restrained her untimely haste, saying, "Woman, what have I to do with you? My hour has not yet come." He was waiting for that hour that was foreknown by the Father. *Irenaeus (c. 180, E/W), 1.443.*

Mary the virgin is found obedient, saying, "Behold the handmaiden of the Lord; be it unto me according to your word." In contrast, Eve was disobedient. For she did not obey when she was still a virgin. . . . Having become disobedient, she was made the cause of death, both to herself and to the entire human race. Correspondingly, Mary, who was also a virgin (although betrothed to a man), by yielding obedience, became the cause of salvation, both to herself and the whole human race. . . . This demonstrates the corresponding reference from Mary back to Eve. . . . So it was that the knot of Eve's disobedience was loosed by the obedience of Mary. For what the virgin Eve had bound fast through unbelief, this did the virgin Mary set free through faith. *Irenaeus (c. 180, E/W), 1.455.*

The Lord then was manifestly coming to His own things, and was sustaining them by means of that creation that is supported by Himself. He was making a recapitulation of that disobedience that had occurred in connection with a tree, through the obedience that was upon a tree [i.e., the cross]. Furthermore, the original deception was to be done away with—the deception by which that virgin Eve (who was already espoused to a man) was unhappily misled. That this was to be overturned was happily announced through means of the truth by the angel to the virgin Mary (who was also [espoused] to a man). . . . So if Eve disobeyed God, yet Mary was persuaded to be obedient to God. In this way, the virgin Mary might become the advocate of the virgin Eve. And thus, as the human race fell into bondage to death by means of a virgin, so is it rescued by a virgin. Virginal disobedience has been balanced in the opposite scale by virginal obedience. For in the same way, the sin of the first created man received amendment by the correction of the First-Begotten, and the cunning of the serpent was conquered by the harmlessness of the dove. *Irenaeus (c. 180, E/W), 1.547.*

Enabling Him to gather up Adam from Mary, who was as yet a virgin. *Irenaeus (c. 180, E/W), 1.455.*

For this reason, the Law considers a woman who is betrothed to a man to be the wife of him who had betrothed her. This is so even though she was as yet a virgin. This indicates the reference from Mary back to Eve. *Irenaeus (c. 180, E/W), 1.455.*

Those [Gnostics], therefore, who allege that He took nothing from the virgin do greatly err. . . . For why did He come down into Mary if He were to take nothing of her? *Irenaeus (c. 180, E/W), 1.454.*

I have proved already that it is the same thing to say that He merely *seemed* to appear and to assert that He received nothing from Mary. *Irenaeus (c. 180, E/W), 1.527.*

The Lord Christ, the fruit of the virgin, did not pronounce the breasts of women blessed. *Clement of Alexandria (c. 195, E), 2.220.*

As it appears, many even down to our own time regard Mary, on account of the birth of her child, as having been in the puerperal state, although she was not. For some say that, after she brought forth, she was found, when examined, to still be a virgin. *Clement of Alexandria (c. 195, E), 2.551.*

In subsequent passages, the prophet evidently asserts that the virgin of whom it behooved Christ to be born must derive her lineage of the seed of David. He says, "And there will be born a rod from the root of Jesse"—which rod is Mary. *Tertullian (c. 197, W), 3.164.*

He was from the native soil of Bethlehem, and from the house of David. For, among the Romans, Mary is described in the census of whom Christ is born. *Tertullian (c. 197, W), 3.164.*

Was anything, again, concealed from John, the Lord's most beloved disciple, . . . whom He

commended to Mary as a son in His own place? *Tertullian (c. 197, W), 3.253.*

The following six passages were written against Marcion and others who claimed that Mary was not the natural mother of Christ.

A certain mother of the company exclaims, "Blessed is the womb that bore You, and the breasts which you have sucked." But the Lord said, "On the contrary, blessed are they who hear the Word of God and keep it." Now, He had in precisely similar terms rejected His mother and His brothers, while preferring those who heard and obeyed God. His mother, however, was not there present with Him. On that former occasion, therefore, He had not denied that He was her natural son. On hearing these words the second time, He once again transferred the blessedness (as He had done before) away from the womb and the breasts of His mother to His disciples. *Tertullian (c. 207, W), 3.393.*

There is some basis for thinking that Christ's answer denies His mother and brothers for the present, as even Apelles might learn. "The Lord's brothers had not yet believed in Him." This is contained in the Gospel that was published before Marcion's time. At the same time, there is also a lack of evidence of His mother's adherence to Jesus—although the Marthas and the other Marys were in constant attendance on Him. Indeed, in this very passage, their unbelief is evident. Jesus was teaching the way of life, preaching the kingdom of God . . . but, meanwhile, while strangers were intent on hearing Jesus, His very nearest relatives were absent. . . . They preferred to interrupt Him; they desired to call Him away from His great work. *Tertullian (c. 210, W), 3.528.*

In whatever sense He adopted as His own those who adhered to Him, in that same sense He denied as His own those who kept aloof from Him. . . . How strange, then, would it certainly have been, if, while he was teaching others not to esteem mother, father, or brothers, as highly as the word of God, He were Himself to leave the word of God as soon as His mother and brothers were announced to Him. He denied his parents, then, in the sense in which He has taught us to deny ours—for God's work. But there is also another view of the case: In the mother whom He denied, there is a symbol of the synagogue. In the unbelieving brothers, there is a symbol of the Jews. For, as a group, Israel remained outside. On the other hand, the new disciples who kept close to Christ within—hearing and believing Him—represented the church. Jesus called these disciples His "mother" in a preferable sense, and He called them a worthier "brotherhood." In doing so, He repudiated the fleshly relationship. It was in just the same sense, indeed, that He also replied to that other exclamation—not denying His mother's womb and breasts, but designating those persons as more "blessed who hear the word of God." *Tertullian (c. 210, W), 3.529.*

It was while Eve was yet a virgin that the ensnaring word had crept into her ear. And this word was to build the edifice of death. In like manner, the Word of God must be introduced into a virgin's soul—that Word who was to raise the fabric of life, so that what had been reduced to ruin by this sex, might by the self-same sex be recovered to salvation. As Eve had believed the serpent, so Mary believed the angel. *Tertullian (c. 210, W), 3.536.*

[If Mary was not truly Christ's mother], will not the angel's announcement also be subverted—that the virgin should "conceive in her womb and bring forth a son?" And will not in fact every Scripture be subverted that declares that Christ had a mother? For how could she have been His mother, unless He had been in her womb? . . . No flesh can speak of a mother's womb but that which is itself the offspring of that womb. *Tertullian (c. 210, W), 3.539.*

Now, as a wife, she was under the very law of "opening the womb." Under this law, it was quite immaterial whether the birth of the male was by virtue of a husband's co-operation or not. . . . Who could properly be said to "open" the womb, other than he who opened a *closed* one. But it is marriage that opens the womb in all cases. The virgin's womb, therefore, was specially opened, because it was specially closed. . . . And what must be said more on this point? Since it was in this sense that the apostle declared that the Son of God was born not of a *virgin,* but of a *woman.* In that statement, he recognized the condition of the "opened womb" that ensues in marriage. *Tertullian (c. 210, W), 3.541.*

No one can understand the meaning of [the Gospel of John] unless he has lain on Jesus' breast and from Jesus has received Mary to be his mother, too. Such a person must he become who is to be another John. . . . For if Mary—as those say who extol her with sound mind—had no other son but Jesus, then He virtually said to Her, "Look! This is Jesus, whom you did bear." (For He did not say to His mother, "Behold, you have this son *also,*" but "Woman, behold your son.") Is it not the case that everyone who is perfect, lives for himself no longer? Does not Christ live in him? And if Christ lives in him, then it is said of him to Mary, "Behold, your son, Christ." What a mind, then, we must have to enable us to interpret this work [the Gospel of John] in a worthy manner. *Origen (c. 228, E), 9.300.*

Some say, basing it on a tradition in the *Gospel According to Peter,* as it is entitled, or the *Book of James* [i.e., the spurious *Protevangelium of James*], that the brothers of Jesus were sons of Joseph by a former wife, whom he married before Mary. Now, those who say so wish to preserve the honor of Mary in virginity to the end, so that her body . . . might not know intercourse with a man after the Holy Spirit came into her and power from on high overshadowed her. And I think it is in harmony with reason that just as Jesus was the first-fruit among men of the purity that consists in chastity, so was Mary among women. For it was not pious to ascribe to any other than to her the first-fruit of virginity. *Origen (c. 245, E), 9.424.*

The parent of Your life—that unspotted grace and undefiled virgin—conceived in her womb without the aid of man, through a pure conception. She thus became suspected of having betrayed the marriage bed. *Methodius (c. 290, E), 6.353.*

The Spirit could not abide upon all men, but only on Him who was born of Mary, the God-bearer. *Disputation of Archelaus and Manes (c. 320, E), 6.208.*

[MANICHEAN SPEAKER:] Now, tell me whether these brethren were begotten by Joseph or by the same Holy Spirit. . . . If you say that these were not begotten by the same Holy Spirit, and yet acknowledge that He had brothers, then without a doubt we will have to understand that after the Spirit and after Gabriel, the most pure and spotless virgin formed an actual marriage connection with Joseph. However, if this is also a thing altogether absurd—I mean the supposition that she had any type of sexual relations with Joseph—tell me whether then He had brothers. Are you, therefore, going to attach the crime of adultery also on her, most wise Marcellus? However, if none of those suppositions suits the position of the virgin undefiled, how will you make it out that he had brothers?.... [REPLY OF ARCHELAUS, A BISHOP:] It does not seem to you, then, to be a pious thing to say that Jesus had a mother in Mary. And you hold a similar view on certain other positions that you have now been discussing in terms that I, for my part, altogether shrink from repeating. *Disputation of Archelaus and Manes (c. 320, E), 6.223.*

Our Lord Jesus Christ in very deed (and not merely in appearance) carried a body, which was of Mary, the God-bearer. *Alexander of Alexandria (c. 324, E), 6.296.*

SEE ALSO JESUS CHRIST (IV. MEDIATOR BETWEEN GOD AND MAN; VI. BROTHERS OF JESUS); MOTHER, SPIRITUAL; SINLESSNESS; THEOTOKOS; VIRGIN BIRTH; WOMAN CLOTHED WITH THE SUN.

MASS

SEE EUCHARIST.

MATERIALISM

No one can serve two masters.... You cannot serve God and mammon. Matt. 6:24.

Having food and clothing, with these we shall be content. But those who desire to be rich fall into temptation and a snare.... For the love of money is a root of all kinds of evil, for which some have strayed from the faith in their greediness. 1 Tim. 6:8–10.

Let your conduct be without covetousness, and be content with such things as you have. Heb. 13:5.

My child, do not be a money-lover, nor vainglorious. For out of these, thefts are born. *Didache (c. 80–140, E), 7.378.*

Foremost of all evil desires is the desire after another's wife or husband. There is also the desire after extravagance, many useless dainties and drinks, and many other foolish luxuries. For all luxury is foolish and empty to the servants of God. These, then, are the evil desires that slay the servants of God. *Hermas (c. 150, W), 2.28.*

Wealth, when not properly governed, is a stronghold of evil. Many, because of casting their eyes on it, will never reach the kingdom of heaven. For they are sick for the things of the world, and are living proudly through luxury.... Love of money is found to be the

stronghold of evil, which the apostle says "is the root of all evils." ... But the best riches is poverty of desires. And the true magnanimity is not to be proud of wealth, but to despise it. *Clement of Alexandria (c. 195, E), 2.248.*

It is not scanty means that ever constitute poverty, but greed. The good man, being free from this, will also be rich. *Clement of Alexandria (c. 195, E), 2.352.*

"Sell your possessions." And what is this? Jesus does not ask him to throw away the substance he possessed and to abandon his property (as some carelessly think). Rather, He asks him to banish from his soul his notions about wealth, his excitement and morbid feeling about it, and his anxieties. *Clement of Alexandria (c. 195, E), 2.594.*

Let us not interpret "covetousness" as consisting merely in the lust of what is another's. For even what seems *ours* is another's. For nothing is ours, since all things are God's, to whom we ourselves belong. *Tertullian (c. 200, W), 3.711.*

How will we make friends with mammon, if we love it so much as not to put up with its loss? We will perish together with the lost mammon. *Tertullian (c. 200, W), 3.712.*

It becomes us not to lay down our souls for money, but money for our souls—whether spontaneously in giving, or patiently in losing. *Tertullian (c. 200, W), 3.712.*

The more wealthy a woman is—inflated with the name of "matron"—the more spacious of a house she requires for her burdens. It is as if it were a field where ambition may run its course. To such a person, the churches look paltry. A rich husband is a difficult thing [to find] in the house of God.... To such a Christian woman, it is irksome to marry a believer inferior to herself in estate.... However, she will be dowered with an ampler dowry from the goods of him who is rich in God. *Tertullian (c. 205, W), 3.48.*

That many of us are called poor, this is not our disgrace, but our glory. For, as our mind is relaxed by luxury, so is it strengthened by frugality. Yet, who can be poor if he does not want—if he does not crave for—the possessions of others? Who can be poor if he is rich towards God? He, rather, is poor, who, although he has much, desires more. *Mark Minucius Felix (c. 200, W), 4.195.*

The words of the Gospel, although probably containing a deeper meaning, may yet be taken in their more simple and obvious sense, as teaching us not to be disturbed with anxieties about our food and clothing. Rather, while living in plainness and desiring only what is needful, we should put our trust in the providence of God. *Origen (c. 248, E), 4.620.*

Those whom you consider rich add forests to forests. They exclude the poor from their neighborhoods and stretch out their fields far and wide into space without any limits. They possess immense heaps of silver and gold, as well as mighty sums of money. . . . Such a person enjoys no security either in his food or in his sleep. In the middle of the banquet he sighs, although he drinks from a jeweled goblet. . . . He does not realize, poor wretch, that these things are merely gilded torments. He is held in bondage by his gold. He is the slave, not the master, of his luxury and wealth. . . . From him, there is no liberality to dependents, no giving to the poor. . . . His possession amounts to this only: that he can keep others from possessing it. *Cyprian (c. 250, W), 5.279.*

Whom He has made rich, none will make poor. For, in fact, there can be no poverty to him whose breast has once been supplied with heavenly food. Ceilings enriched with gold, and houses adorned with mosaics of costly marble, will seem crude to you now that you know that it is you yourself who are to be perfected, instead. . . . Let us embellish this "house" with the colors of innocence; let us enlighten it with the light of justice. *Cyprian (c. 250, W), 5.280.*

A blind love of one's own property has deceived many. How could they be prepared for fleeing [in persecution] . . . when their wealth fettered them like a chain? . . . For that reason, the Lord, . . . forewarning for the future time, said, "If you will be perfect, go, sell all that you have and give to the poor." If rich men did this, they would not perish because of their riches. . . . Heart, mind, and feeling would be in heaven, if the treasure were in heaven. *Cyprian (c. 250, W), 5.440.*

"Having therefore food and covering, let us be content with these." "But those who will be rich fall into temptation and a snare." . . . He teaches us that riches are not only to be scorned, but that they are also full of peril. The root of seducing evils is in them. . . . On the other hand, the Lord tells us that a person

becomes perfect and complete when he sells all his goods and distributes them for the use of the poor. Thereby, he lays up for himself treasure in heaven. *Cyprian (c. 250, W), 5.453.*

You are the captive and slave of your money! You are bound with the chains and bonds of covetousness. You, whom Christ had once loosed, are once more in chains! *Cyprian (c. 250, W), 5.479.*

The lust of possessing and of money are not to be sought for. . . . "We brought nothing into this world, and neither can we take anything away. Therefore, having maintenance and clothing, let us be content with these. But those who want to become rich fall into temptation and a snare." *Cyprian (c. 250, W), 5.550.*

Whoever has extended his hope beyond the present and has chosen better things will be without these earthly goods so that, being lightly equipped and without impediment, he may overcome the difficulty of the way. For it is impossible for a person who has surrounded himself with royal pomp, or loaded himself with riches, either to enter upon or to persevere in these difficulties. *Lactantius (c. 304–313, W), 7.165.*

To seek riches is not a virtue. *Lactantius (c. 304–313, W), 7.168.*

It is not a virtue to be frugal. This word beguiles and deceives under the appearance of virtue. . . . Frugality is a vice in this respect: that it arises from the love of possessing. In contrast, we should both abstain from pleasures and yet by no means withhold money. To use money sparingly, that is, moderately, is a type of weakness of the mind. It reveals someone fearing lest he will be in need. Or it reveals someone despairing of being able to recover it, or someone incapable of the contempt of earthly things. *Lactantius (c. 304–313, W), 7.182.*

SEE ALSO PROSPERITY.

MATINS

SEE MORNING AND EVENING PRAYER.

MATTHEW

They say in the traditions that Matthew the apostle constantly said that if the neighbor of an elect man sins, the elect man has sinned. For had he conducted himself as the Word prescribes, his neighbor also would have been filled with such reverence for the life he led as not to sin. *Clement of Alexandria (c. 195, E), 2.547.*

Marcion produces as proof the tax–collector [i.e., Matthew] who was chosen by the Lord. Marcion says that he was chosen as a stranger to the Law and that he was uninitiated in Judaism. Marcion also claims he was chosen by One who was an adversary to the Law. Apparently, the case of Peter escaped Marcion's memory—who, although he was a man of the Law—was not only chosen by the Lord, but also obtained the testimony of possessing knowledge that was given to him by the Father. *Tertullian (c. 207, W), 3.360.*

There is, first of all, Matthew, that most faithful chronicler of the Gospel, since he was the companion of the Lord. For no other reason . . . except to show us clearly the fleshly lineage of Christ, Matthew begins his Gospel in this manner: "The book of the generation of Jesus Christ, the son of David, the son of Abraham." *Tertullian (c. 210, W), 3.540.*

SEE ALSO APOSTLES, TWELVE; MATTHEW, GOSPEL OF.

MATTHEW, GOSPEL OF

Matthew put together the oracles [of the Lord] in the Hebrew language, and each one interpreted them as best he could. *Papias (c. 120, E), 1.155, as quoted by Eusebius.*

Matthew also issued a written Gospel among the Hebrews in their own dialect, while Peter and Paul were preaching at Rome. *Irenaeus (c. 180, E/W), 1.414.*

The Gospel according to Matthew was written to the Jews. For they laid particular stress upon the fact that Christ is of the seed of David. Matthew also, who had a still greater desire [to prove this], took particular pains to afford them convincing proof that Christ is of the seed of David. Therefore, Matthew begins with His genealogy. *Irenaeus (c. 180, E/W), 1.573.*

Matthew wrote for the Hebrews, who looked for the [Messiah] to come from the line of Abraham and of David. Therefore, he says, "the book of the generation of Jesus Christ, the son of David, the son of Abraham." *Origen (c. 228, E), 9.299.*

We will begin with Matthew, who is reported by tradition to have published his Gospel

before the others. [He wrote it] to the Hebrews, namely, those of the circumcision who believed. *Origen (c. 228, E), 9.366.*

SEE ALSO GOSPELS; MATTHEW.

MATTHIAS

Let his days be few, and let another take his office. Ps. 109:8.

And they cast their lots, and the lot fell on Matthias. And he was numbered with the eleven apostles. Acts 1:20.

Judas was deprived [of his office] and cast out. Matthias was ordained in his place. This was according to what had been written, "And let another take his bishopric." *Irenaeus (c. 180, E/W), 1.388.*

Matthias, accordingly, who was not chosen along with them, on showing himself worthy of becoming an apostle, was substituted for Judas. *Clement of Alexandria (c. 195, E), 2.504.*

Having . . . chosen Matthias by lot as the twelfth [apostle], in the place of Judas, they obtained the promised power of the Holy Spirit. *Tertullian (c. 197, W), 3.252.*

Matthias was chosen to be an apostle in the place of the betrayer. He took the position of Judas. For it was written, "Let another take his bishopric." *Apostolic Constitutions (compiled c. 390, E), 7.454.*

SEE ALSO APOSTLES, TWELVE.

MEAT SACRIFICED TO IDOLS

For it seemed good to the Holy Spirit, and to us, to lay upon you no greater burden than these necessary things: that you abstain from things offered to idols. Acts 15:28, 29.

I say that the things which the Gentiles sacrifice they sacrifice to demons and not to God, and I do not want you to have fellowship with demons. You cannot drink the cup of the Lord and the cup of demons. 1 Cor. 10:20, 21.

Eat whatever is sold in the meat market, asking no questions for conscience' sake. 1 Cor. 10:25.

If any of those who do not believe invites you to dinner, and you desire to go, eat whatever is set before you, asking no questions for conscience' sake. But if anyone says to you, "This was offered to idols," do not eat it for the sake of the one who told you. 1 Cor. 10:27, 28.

But I have a few things against you, because you have there those who hold the doctrine of Balaam, who taught Balak to put a stumbling block before the children of Israel, to eat things sacrificed to idols. Rev. 2:14.

I have a few things against you, because you allow that woman Jezebel, who calls herself a prophetess, to teach and beguile My servants to commit sexual immorality and to eat things sacrificed to idols. Rev. 2:20.

Against that which is sacrificed to idols, be exceedingly on your guard; for it is the service of dead gods. *Didache (c. 80–140, E), 1.379.*

Christians do not eat the food that is consecrated to idols, for they are pure. *Aristides (c. 125, E), 9.276.*

[JUSTIN SPEAKING:] "Those of the Gentiles who know God . . . through Jesus the crucified . . . abide every torture and vengeance even to the extremity of death, rather than to worship idols, or eat meat offered to idols." And Trypho [a Jew] said, "I believe, however, that many of those who say that they confess Jesus, and are called Christians, eat meats offered to idols, and declare that they are by no means injured in consequence." And I replied, "The fact that there are such men confessing themselves to be Christians . . . yet not teaching His doctrines . . . causes us who are disciples of the true and pure doctrine of Jesus Christ to be more faithful." *Justin Martyr (c. 160, E), 1.212.*

The "most perfect" among them [i.e., the Gnostics] addict themselves without fear to all those kinds of forbidden deeds of which the Scriptures assure us that "those who do such things will not inherit the kingdom of God." For instance, they make no scruple about eating meats offered in sacrifice to idols, imagining that they can in this way contract no defilement. *Irenaeus (c. 180, E/W), 1.324.*

The character of these men [the Nicolaitans] is very plainly pointed out in the Apocalypse of John. It shows they taught that it is a matter of indifference to practice adultery and to eat things sacrificed to idols. *Irenaeus (c. 180, E/W), 1.352.*

Others, again, following upon Basilides and Carpocrates, have introduced promiscuous intercourse and a plurality of wives, and are indifferent about eating meats sacrificed to idols, maintaining that God is not greatly concerned about such matters. *Irenaeus (c. 180, E/W), 1.353.*

The apostle says, "All other things buy out of the meat market, asking no questions"—with the exception of the things mentioned in the catholic epistle of all the apostles "with the consent of the Holy Spirit." That epistle was written in the Acts of the Apostles and was conveyed to the faithful by the hands of Paul himself. For they indicated "that they must of necessity abstain from things offered to idols, from blood, from things strangled, and from fornication." *Clement of Alexandria (c. 195, E), 2.427.*

That we despise the remains of sacrifices and the cups out of which drink offerings have been poured, is not a confession of fear, but an assertion of our true liberty. *Mark Minucius Felix (c. 200, W), 4.197.*

It must be very greatly guarded against in the use of food. And we must be warned lest anyone should think that liberty is permitted to the degree that he can even approach what has been offered to idols. For, as far as pertains to God's creation, every creature is clean. But when it has been offered to demons, it is polluted so long as it is offered to the idols. As soon as this is done, it belongs no longer to God, but to the idol. And when this creature is taken for food, . . . it makes the partaker a fellow guest with the idol, not with Christ. *Novatian (c. 235, W), 5.650.*

If we know that some things are used by demons (or if we do not know, but suspect and are in doubt about it), and if we use such things, we have not used them to the glory of God, nor in the name of Christ. . . . According to the apostle, "He who doubts is condemned if he eats, because he does not eat of faith." . . . He, then, eats in faith who believes that the food to be eaten has not been sacrificed in the temples of idols and that it is not strangled, nor is blood. But he does not eat of faith who is in doubt about any of these things. And the man who knows that they have been sacrificed to demons and still uses them becomes a communicant with demons. *Origen (c. 245, E), 9.441.*

The apostle concludes from the fact that "an idol is nothing in the world" that it is injurious to use things offered to idols. And he shows to those who have ears to hear on such subjects that he who partakes of things offered to idols is worse than a murderer. For such a person destroys his own brethren, for whom Christ died. . . . It has been clearly shown that we are forbidden to take part in these festivals, when we know the difference between the table of the Lord and the table of demons. *Origen (c. 248, E), 4.648.*

That which is offered to idols is sacrificed to demons, and a man of God must not join the table of demons. . . . In our opinion, a man can only be said to eat and drink with demons when he eats the flesh of what are called "sacred victims," and when he drinks the wine poured out to the honor of the demons. But [the pagan critic] Celsus thinks that we cannot eat bread or drink wine in any way whatever, or taste fruits, or even take a drink of water, without eating and drinking with demons. He also adds that the air that we breathe is received from demons. *Origen (c. 248, E), 4.650.*

[CONCERNING CHRISTIANS TAKEN CAPTIVE BY MARAUDING BARBARIANS:] The meats are no burden to us, most holy father, if the captives ate things that their conquerors set before them. This is particularly so since there is a united report from everyone that the barbarians who have made inroads into our parts have not sacrificed to idols. *Gregory Thaumaturgus (c. 255, E), 6.19.*

The mother of Galerius, a woman exceedingly superstitious, was a votary of the gods of the mountains. Being of such a character, she made sacrifices almost every day. And she feasted her servants on the meat offered to idols. However, the Christians of her family would not partake of those entertainments. So while she feasted with the Gentiles, they continued to fast and pray. On this account, she harbored ill-will against the Christians. *Lactantius (c. 320, W), 7.305.*

Abstain from things offered to idols, for they offer them in honor of demons. *Apostolic Constitutions (compiled c. 390, E), 7.469.*

SEE ALSO IDOLATRY; JERUSALEM COUNCIL.

MEDIATOR

SEE JESUS CHRIST (IV. MEDIATOR BETWEEN GOD AND MEN).

MEDICINE, MEDICAL SCIENCE

Luke the beloved physician and Demas greet you. Col. 4:14.

No longer drink only water, but use a little wine for your stomach's sake and your frequent infirmities. 1 Tim. 5:23.

But medicine and everything included in it is an invention of the same kind. If anyone is healed by matter, by trusting in it, much more will he be healed by having recourse to the power of God. *Tatian (c. 160, E), 2.73.*

Even if you are healed by drugs (I grant you that point by courtesy), yet it behooves you to give testimony for the cure to God. *Tatian (c. 160, E), 2.73.*

A physician is required for those of us who are diseased in body. Likewise, those who are diseased in soul require a mentor to cure their maladies. *Clement of Alexandria (c. 195, E), 2.209.*

People in health do not require a physician. They do not require him as long as they are strong. However, those who are ill need his skill. *Clement of Alexandria (c. 195, E), 2.213.*

The physician is not evil to the sick person simply because he tells him of his fever. For the physician is not the *cause* of the fever; he only points out the fever. *Clement of Alexandria (c. 195, E), 2.231.*

God has permitted the production of oil to mitigate human pains. *Clement of Alexandria (c. 195, E), 2.254.*

In the area of medicine, I have shown that, for healing, . . . the delight derived from flowers and the benefit derived from ointments and perfumes should not be overlooked. *Clement of Alexandria (c. 195, E), 2.257.*

For the sake of bodily health, we submit to incisions, cauterizations, and medicines. He who administers them is called a savior and a healer, even though he may have to amputate limbs. *Clement of Alexandria (c. 195, E), 2.339.*

What would be said if, when you thought a doctor was necessary, you began to find fault with his instruments because they cut, cauterize, amputate, or tighten? There could be no doctor of any value without his professional tools. *Tertullian (c. 207, W), 3.309.*

I have looked into medical science also, the sister of philosophy, which claims as her function the cure of the body, and thereby to have a special acquaintance with the soul. *Tertullian (c. 210, W), 3.183.*

Suppose Aesculapius was the first who sought and discovered cures. Isaiah mentions that he ordered Hezekiah medicine when he was sick.

Paul, too, knows that a little wine does the stomach good. *Tertullian (c. 211, W), 3.97.*

This stubbornness also applies to persons . . . who seem to be eager to die rather than to be healed. For there are many who flee from the aid of a physician, also. Many do this in folly; others, from fear and false modesty. And the healing art obviously has a seeming cruelty—such as the lancet, the burning iron, and the great heat of the mustard. Yet, to be cut and burned, to be pulled and bitten, is not on that account an evil thing. For it furnishes helpful pains. . . . In short, the man who is howling, groaning, and bellowing in the hands of a physician will soon afterwards load the same hands with a fee. *Tertullian (c. 213, W), 3.637.*

On account of those bad effects that we bring upon ourselves by eating and drinking, we deem it necessary for the health of the body to make use of some unpleasant and painful drug. If the nature of the disease demands it, it sometimes even requires the severe process of the amputating knife. And if the virulence of the disease transcends even these remedies, the evil at last has to be burned out by fire. *Origen (c. 225, E), 4.295.*

I indeed . . . would say that even those who are engaged in the healing of a number of sick persons do not attain their results without divine help. *Origen (c. 248, E), 4.407.*

These are analogous to the wine, oil, plasters, and other healing applications that belong to the art of medicine. *Origen (c. 248, E), 4.488.*

In seeking recovery from disease, a man may follow the more ordinary and simple methods, having recourse to the medical arts. On the other hand, if he would go beyond the common methods adopted by men, he must rise to the higher and better way of seeking the blessing of Him who is Governor over all, through piety and prayers. *Origen (c. 248, E), 4.662; see also 4.212.*

SEE ALSO HEALING, DIVINE.

MEN

A woman will not wear anything that pertains to a man, nor will a man put on a woman's garment, for all who do so are an abomination to the Lord your God. Deut. 22:5.

A true man must have no mark of effeminacy visible on his face, or any other part of his body. Let no blot on his manliness, then, ever be found either in his movements or habits. *Clement of Alexandria (c. 195, E), 2.289.*

And let not men, therefore, spend their time in barbers' shops and taverns, babbling nonsense. And let them give up hunting for the women who sit nearby, and ceaselessly talking slander against many to raise a laugh. *Clement of Alexandria (c. 195, E), 2.289.*

What is the purpose in the Law's prohibition against a man wearing woman's clothing? Is it not that the Law would have us to be masculine and not to be effeminate in either person or actions—or in thought and word? Rather, it would have the man who devotes himself to the truth to be masculine both in acts of endurance and patience—in life, conduct, word, and discipline. *Clement of Alexandria (c. 195, E), 2.365.*

In His Law, it declares that the man is cursed who wears female garments. *Tertullian (c. 197, W), 3.89.*

The Lord does not promise the grace of celibacy to men and pass over women. Rather, since the woman is a portion of the man, and is taken and formed from him, God in Scripture almost always speaks to the protoplast, the first formed, because they are two in one flesh. And in the male is at the same time signified the woman also. *Cyprian (c. 250, W), 5.431.*

SEE ALSO FATHERS; HUSBANDS; MAN, DOCTRINE OF; MARRIAGE; WOMEN.

MENANDER THE HERETIC

Menander (1st or 2nd century) was a heretical teacher from Samaria and a disciple of Simon Magus.

A man named Menander was also a Samaritan, of the town of Capparetaea. He was a disciple of Simon [Magus] and was possessed by devils. We know that he deceived many persons through his magical arts while he was in Antioch. He convinced those who followed him that they would never die. Even now, there are some still living who hold to this belief of his. *Justin Martyr (c. 160, E), 1.171.*

The Samaritans—Simon and Menander—did many mighty works by magic and deceived many. *Justin Martyr (c. 160, E), 1.182.*

The successor of [Simon Magus] was Menander, who was also a Samaritan by birth.

He, likewise, was a master in the practice of magic. He maintained that the primary Power remains unknown to everyone. But he said that he himself was the person who was sent forth from the presence of the invisible beings as a savior, for the deliverance of men. *Irenaeus (c. 180, E/W), 1.348.*

Some suppose that [souls] came down from heaven.... Saturninus, the disciple of Menander, who belonged to Simon's sect, introduced this opinion. He asserted that man was made by angels. *Tertullian (c. 210, W), 3.203.*

The insane opinion of the Samaritan heretic, Menander, is also rejected. He will have it that death has not only nothing to do with his disciples, but, in fact, that it never reaches them. He pretends to have received the following commission from the secret power of One above: that all who partake of his baptism become immortal, incorruptible, and instantaneously invested with the resurrection life. *Tertullian (c. 210, W), 3.227.*

SEE ALSO HERESIES, HERETICS; SIMON MAGUS.

MENANDER THE POET

Menander (342–291 B.C.) was the Greek poet whom Paul quotes in 1 Corinthians 15:33.

When we assert that men should not worship the works of their hands, we say the very things that have been said by the comic poet Menander. *Justin Martyr (c. 160, E), 1.170.*

The same Menander, in the *Sacerdos,* says: "There is no God, O woman, who can save one man by another." *Justin Martyr (c. 160, E), 1.292.*

Menander says, "There are none who provide for us, except God alone." *Theophilus (c. 180, E), 2.97.*

To me it seems that Menander erred when he said, "O sun! You, first of gods, should be worshipped." *Clement of Alexandria (c. 195, E), 2.191.*

Of such a one, Menander gives a comic description in *The Superstitious Man. Clement of Alexandria (c. 195, E), 2.529.*

SEE ALSO POETS, PAGAN.

MENTAL ILLNESS

The truth is that whenever a man is out of his mind, it is his soul that is demented. It is not because the mind is absent, but because it is a fellow-sufferer at the time. *Tertullian (c. 210, W), 3.198.*

·And in those who are insane, it is the mind that is not functioning; the soul continues to function. For that reason, they are said to be out of their *minds. Lactantius (c. 304–313, W), 7.209.*

MERIT

Do not marvel at this; for the hour is coming in which all who are in the graves will hear His voice and come forth—those who have done good, to the resurrection of life, and those who have done evil, to the resurrection of condemnation. John 5:28, 29.

I am coming quickly, and My reward is with Me, to give to every one according to his work. Rev. 22:12.

The award according to merit finds no place in the present existence. For many atheists ... live on to the end. *Athenagoras (c. 175, E), 2.159.*

The reward or punishment for lives that are either ill or well spent is proportionate to the merit of each. *Athenagoras (c. 175, E), 2.162.*

We affirm that a judgment has been ordained by God according to the merits of every man. *Tertullian (c. 197, W), 3.127.*

God would be unjust if anyone were not punished or else rewarded in that very condition by which the merit was itself achieved. *Tertullian (c. 207, W), 3.456.*

The order will be arranged individually, on account of individual merits. Furthermore, since merits must be ascribed to the body, it necessarily follows that the order must also be arranged in respect to bodies. This is so that it may correspond to their merits. *Tertullian (c. 210, W), 3.581.*

The blessed rest that is to be found in the kingdom of God is reserved for those who are worthy of becoming His subjects. *Origen (c. 248, E), 4.501.*

We indeed believe that the merits of martyrs and the works of the righteous are of great avail with the Judge. However, that will be when the Day of Judgment comes. *Cyprian (c. 250, W), 5.442.*

SEE ALSO FREE WILL AND PREDESTINATION; JUDGMENT, LAST; MAN, DOCTRINE OF; SALVATION.

MESSIAH, TWO ADVENTS OF THE

See Jesus Christ (II. Two Advents of Christ).

MESSIANIC PROPHECIES

Therefore the Lord himself will give you a sign: Behold, the virgin shall conceive and bear a Son, and shall call His name Immanuel. Isa. 7:14.

Before the child shall have knowledge to cry "My father" and "My mother," the riches of Damascus and the spoil of Samaria will be taken away. Isa. 8:4.

For unto us a Child is born, unto us a Son is given; and the government will be upon His shoulder. And His name will be called Wonderful, Counselor, Mighty God, Everlasting Father, Prince of Peace. Isa. 9:6, 7.

I gave My back to those who struck Me. Isa. 50:6.

I have stretched out My hands all day long to a rebellious people. Isa. 65:2.

But you, Bethlehem Ephrathah, though you are little among the thousands of Judah, yet out of you shall come forth to Me the One to be ruler in Israel, whose goings forth have been from of old, from everlasting. Mic. 5:2; see also Ps. 22:16–22, Ps. 69:21, Ps. 88:9, Isa. 53:2, Jer. 11:19, Zech. 9:9, and Zech. 12:10.

The prophet also says, "The stone that the builders rejected, the same has become the head of the corner." . . . What does the prophet say again? "The assembly of the wicked surrounded me; they encompassed me as bees do a honeycomb," and "upon my garments they cast lots." Therefore, since He was about to be manifested and to suffer in the flesh, His suffering was predicted. For the prophet speaks against Israel, "Woe to their soul, because they have counseled an evil counsel against themselves, saying, "Let us bind the just one, because he is displeasing to us." *Barnabas (c. 70–130), 1.140.*

And when the Spirit of prophecy speaks from the person of Christ, the utterances are of this sort: "I have spread out My hands to a disobedient and gainsaying people." . . . And again: "I gave My back to the scourges." *Justin Martyr (c. 160, E), 1.175.*

I have proved that all things that have already happened had been predicted by the prophets before they came to pass. . . . Although I could produce many other prophecies, I will forbear. For I think the ones [I have produced] are suf-ficient to persuade those who have ears to hear and understand. . . . Why else would we believe that a crucified man is the First-Born of the unbegotten God? Why else would we believe that He will pass judgment on the whole human race? We would not do so unless we had found testimonies about Him that were proclaimed before He came and before He was born as man. And we have seen that things have happened accordingly. I am referring to things such as the devastation of the land of the Jews and that men of every race are persuaded by His teaching through the apostles. *Justin Martyr (c. 160, E), 1.180.*

"The Lord said unto My Lord, 'Sit at My right hand, until I make your enemies your footstool.'" . . . I am not ignorant that you [Jews] venture to expound this Psalm as if it referred to king Hezekiah. However, that you are mistaken, I will prove to you. *Justin Martyr (c. 160, E), 1.210, 211.*

I will remind you of another Psalm, dictated to David by the Holy Spirit, which you [Jews] say refers to Solomon, who was also your king. But it refers also to our Christ. *Justin Martyr (c. 160, E), 1.211.*

In the ninety-eighth Psalm, the Holy Spirit reproaches you [Jews] and foretells Him whom you do not wish to be king, to be King and Lord—of Samuel, Aaron, and Moses. *Justin Martyr (c. 160, E), 1.213.*

In the forty-fourth Psalm, these words are in like manner referred to Christ: "My heart has brought forth a good matter; I tell my works to the King. . . . Thy throne, O God, is forever and ever." *Justin Martyr (c. 160, E), 1.213.*

[Speaking to Jews:] Show me yourselves first of all how it is said of Hezekiah that before he knew how to call father or mother, he received "the power of Damascus" and "the spoils of Samaria in the presence of the king of Assyria." . . . However, we are able to prove that it happened in the case of our Christ. For at the time of His birth, Magi who came from Arabia worshipped Him. *Justin Martyr (c. 160, E), 1.237.*

Now I will demonstrate to you that the whole Psalm refers in this manner to Christ. *Justin Martyr (c. 160, E), 1.248.*

That he also experienced that pre-eminent birth which is from the virgin, the divine Scriptures do in both respects testify of Him. They also testify that He was a man without comeliness and liable to suffering, that He sat upon the foal of a donkey, that He received vinegar and gall to drink, that He was despised among the people, and that He humbled Himself even to death. *Irenaeus (c. 180, E/W), 1.449.*

So also did all the prophets prefigure the one [Christ]. *Irenaeus (c. 180, E/W), 1.509.*

Daniel said that "visions and prophecy were sealed" inasmuch as He is the seal of all prophets, fulfilling all things which had been announced of Him in days gone by. For after the advent of Christ and His passion, there is no longer vision or prophet to announce Him as yet to come. *Tertullian (c. 197, W), 3.160.*

The Jews say: "Let us challenge that prediction of Isaiah and let us institute a comparison whether—in the case of the Christ who is already come—there is application to Him. First, let us inquire about the name that Isaiah foretold and, second, the signs of it that he announced. *Tertullian (c. 197, W), 3.161.*

Let those Eastern Magi be believed, endowing with gold and incense the infancy of Christ as a king. For thereby the infant has received "the power of Damascus" without battle and arms. *Tertullian (c. 197, W), 3.162.*

[ADDRESSED TO THE MARCIONITES:] Challenge us first, as is your custom, to consider Isaiah's description of Christ. For you contend that in no point does it fit. For, to begin with, you say that Isaiah's Christ will have to be called Emmanuel. *Tertullian (c. 207, W), 3.330, 331.*

What are we to say concerning the prophecies of Christ in the Psalms? For there is a certain ode there with the heading, "For the Beloved." . . . Also, the place of His birth has been foretold in Micah. *Origen (c. 225, E), 4.352, 353.*

While we thus briefly demonstrate the deity of Christ and make use of the prophetic declarations regarding Him, we demonstrate at the same time that the writings that prophesied of him were divinely inspired. *Origen (c. 225, E), 4.353.*

They are astounded at the voices of so many prophets before Him, who establish the place of his birth, the country of His upbringing, the power of his teaching, His working of wonder-

ful works, and His human passion, followed by His resurrection. . . . The prophetic testimonies do not merely declare the coming of the Messiah, . . . they teach a great deal of theology. The relationship of the Father to the Son and of the Son to the Father may be learned not less from what the prophets announce about Christ than from the apostles. *Origen (c. 228, E), 9.342.*

One of the strongest evidences in confirmation of the claims of Jesus is that His coming was predicted by the Jewish prophets. *Origen (c. 248, E), 4.417.*

It is the same person that Isaiah refers to when he exclaims concerning His passion, saying: "As a sheep He is led to the slaughter; and as a lamb before his shearer is dumb, so He did not open His mouth in His humility." Isaiah was speaking of Him when he described the blows and stripes of His scourgings: "By His bruises we were healed." Or His humiliation: "And we saw Him, and He had neither form nor comeliness, a man in suffering, and who knows how to bear infirmity." Or that the people would not believe on Him: "All day long I have spread out my hands to an unbelieving people." *Novatian (c. 235, W), 5.619.*

Although the cross had not yet even existed, He said, "All day long I have stretched out my hands to an unbelieving people." And although He had not yet been scornfully given [vinegar] to drink, the Scripture says, "In my thirst they gave me vinegar to drink." And although He had not yet been stripped, He said, "Upon my vesture they cast lots and they numbered my bones; they pierced my hands and my feet." For the divine Scripture speaks of things as already being done when it knows they shall be done, foreseeing the future. *Novatian (c. 235, W), 5.639.*

In Isaiah, "I have spread out my hands all day to a people disobedient and contradicting me, who walk in ways that are not good, but after their own sins." Also in Jeremiah: "Come, let us cast the tree into His bread, and let us blot out His life from the earth." . . . Also in the twenty-first Psalm: "They tore my hands and my feet; they numbered all my bones. They gazed upon me, and saw me, and divided my garments among them, and for my garments they cast lots." . . . Also, in Zechariah: "And they shall look upon me, whom they have pierced." Also in the eighty-seventh Psalm: "I have called unto you, O Lord, the whole day; I have stretched out my hands unto you." *Cyprian (c. 250, W), 5.524.*

In the twenty-first Psalm, David said: "They pierced my hands and my feet. They numbered all my bones. They themselves looked and stared upon me. They divided my garments among them. And upon my clothing they cast lots." *Lactantius (c. 304–313, W), 7.121.*

Christ was not believed by us to be God because He did wonderful things, but because we saw that all the things that had been announced to us by the prediction of the prophets were fulfilled in His life. *Lactantius (c. 304–313, W), 7.139.*

They will also discover that the birth of Him whom we preach, and His cross, and all of the things that have happened in the history of our Lord, are those very matters that had been predicted by that prophet. *Disputation of Archelaus and Manes (c. 320, E), 6.219.*

That He was to be born of a virgin, they read this prophecy: "Behold, a virgin shall be with child, and shall bring forth a Son, and they shall call His name Emmanuel." . . . Now, that because of their exceeding great wickedness they would not believe in Him, the Lord shows in these words: "Who has believed our report? And to whom has the arm of the Lord been revealed?" *Apostolic Constitutions (compiled c. 390, E), 7.446; extended discussion: 1.173–1.181, 1.221–1.225, 1.240–1.269, 1.473–1.475, 1.509–510, 3.165–3.171, 3.330–3.339, 3.417–3.421, 3.351–3.360, 3.364–3.367, 3.417–3.423, 7.446.*

SEE ALSO CHRIST, DIVINITY OF; JESUS CHRIST; JEW, JEWS (I. DESCRIPTION AND BELIEFS).

MICHAEL

Yet Michael the archangel, in contending with the devil, when he disputed about the body of Moses, dared not bring against him a reviling accusation, but said, "The Lord rebuke you!" Jude 9.

War broke out in heaven: Michael and his angels fought against the dragon. Rev. 12:7.

The great and glorious angel Michael is he who has authority over this people, and governs them. For this is he who gave them the law into the hearts of believers. He accordingly oversees them. *Hermas (c. 150, W), 2.40.*

"When Michael, the archangel, disputing with the devil, debated about the body of Moses." . . . He is here called Michael, who through an angel near to us debated with the devil. *Clement of Alexandria (c. 195, E), 2.573.*

Who is Michael but the angel assigned to the people? . . . "My angel will go with you." *Hippolytus (c. 205, W), 5.190.*

Christ is not on this account to be regarded as an angel—as a Gabriel or a Michael. *Tertullian (c. 210, W), 3.534.*

SEE ALSO ANGELS.

MILITARY LIFE

Do we believe it is lawful for a human oath to be added on top of one that is divine? Is it lawful for a man to come under promise to another master after Christ? Is it lawful to renounce father, mother, and all nearest kinsfolk—whom even the Law has commanded us to honor and to love next to God Himself? . . . Shall a Christian apply the chain, the prison, the torture, and the punishment, when he is not the avenger even of his own wrongs? Shall he stand guard for others, more than for Christ? Shall he do it on the Lord's Day, when he does not even do it for Christ Himself? Shall he stand guard before those temples that he has renounced? Shall he take a meal where the apostle has forbidden him? . . . You will see by a slight survey how many other offenses there are involved in the performances of camp offices. And we must hold them to involve a transgression of God's law. *Tertullian (c. 211, W), 3.99, 100.*

Does Venus Militaris also preside over the wickedness of [military] camps and the debaucheries of young men? *Arnobius (c. 305, E), 6.478.*

SEE ALSO NONRESISTANCE; WAR.

MILLENNIUM

The wolf also will dwell with the lamb, the leopard will lie down with the young goat, the calf and the young lion and the fatling together; and a little child will lead them. The cow and the bear will graze; their young ones will lie down together; and the lion will eat straw like the ox. Isa. 11:6–9.

Blessed are the meek, for they will inherit the earth. Matt. 5:5.

But I say to you, I will not drink of this fruit of the vine from now on until that day when I drink it new with you in My father's kingdom. Matt. 26:29.

And he cast him into the bottomless pit, and shut him up, and set a seal on him, so that he should deceive the nations no more till the thousand years were finished. . . . Then I saw the souls of those who had been beheaded for their witness to Jesus and for the word of God, who had not worshipped the beast or his image, and had not received his mark on their foreheads or on their hands. And they lived and reigned with Christ for a thousand years. But the rest of the dead did not live again until the thousand years were finished. Rev. 20:3–5.

The days will come in which vines having ten thousand branches will grow. In each branch, there will be ten thousand twigs, and in each shoot there will be ten thousand clusters. Each cluster will have ten thousand grapes, and every grape will give twenty-five metretes of wine, when pressed. . . . In like manner, a grain of wheat will produce ten thousand ears. *Irenaeus, citing Papias (c. 120, E), 1.153, 154.*

Among these things, Papias says that there will be a millennium after the resurrection from the dead, when the personal reign of Christ will be established on this earth. *Eusebius, citing Papias (c. 120, E), 1.154.*

I and others who are right-minded Christians on all points are assured that there will be a resurrection of the dead, and a thousand years in Jerusalem, which will then be built. . . . For Isaiah spoke in that manner concerning this period of a thousand years. *Justin Martyr (c. 160, E), 1.239.*

There was a certain man with us, whose name was John, one of the apostles of Christ, who prophesied by a revelation that was made to him, that those who believed in our Christ would dwell a thousand years in Jerusalem. *Justin Martyr (c. 160, E), 1.240.*

Therefore, when man will have again made his way back to his natural condition and no longer does evil, the [animals] will also be restored to their original gentleness. *Theophilus (c. 180, E), 2.101.*

It is fitting for the righteous to be the first to receive the promise of the inheritance that God promised to the fathers. It is fitting for them to reign in it, when they rise again to behold God in this creation that will have been renovated. It is fitting that the judgment should take place afterwards. For it is just that in that very same creation in which they toiled or were afflicted (being tested in every way by suffering) they should receive the reward of their suffering. . . . It is fitting, therefore, that the creation itself, being restored to its pristine condition, should be under the dominion of the righteous without restraint. *Irenaeus (c. 180, E/W), 1.561.*

The promise of God that He gave to Abraham remains steadfast. . . . God promised him the inheritance of the land. Yet, Abraham did not receive it during all the time of his journey there. Accordingly, it must be that Abraham, together with his seed (that is, those who fear God and believe in Him), will receive it at the resurrection of the just. *Irenaeus (c. 180, E/W), 1.561.*

Now God made promise of the *earth* to Abraham and his seed. Yet neither Abraham nor his seed (that is, those who are justified by faith) presently receive any inheritance in it. Therefore, they will receive it at the resurrection of the just. For God is true and faithful. For this reason, He said, "Blessed are the meek, for they will inherit the earth." *Irenaeus (c. 180, E/W), 1.562.*

"I will not drink henceforth of the fruit of this vine, until that day when I will drink it new with you in my Father's kingdom." Therefore, Christ will Himself renew the inheritance of the earth. . . . For He cannot by any means be understood as drinking of the fruit of the vine when settled down with his [disciples] above in a heavenly place. *Irenaeus (c. 180, E/W), 1.562.*

What are the hundredfold [rewards] in this world? . . . These are in the times of the kingdom. That is, they are upon the seventh day, which has been sanctified, in which God rested from the works which He created, which is the true Sabbath of the righteous. *Irenaeus (c. 180, E/W), 1.562.*

The predicted blessing, therefore, belongs unquestionably to the times of the kingdom, when the righteous will bear rule, after their rising from the dead. It is also the time when the creation will bear fruit with an abundance of all kinds of food, having been renovated and set free. . . . And all of the animals will feed on the vegetation of the earth. They will become peaceful and harmonious among each other, and they will be in perfect subjection to man. And these things are borne witness to in the fourth book of the writings of Papias, the hearer of John, and a companion of Polycarp. *Irenaeus (c. 180, E/W), 1.562, 563.*

Isaiah says, "The wolf also will feed with the lamb, and the leopard will take his rest with the kid." . . . I am quite aware that some persons attempt to apply these words to the situation of savage men, both of different nations and various habits, who come to believe. For, when they have believed, they act in harmony with the righteous. And this is presently [true] with regard to some men coming from various nations to the harmony of the faith. Nevertheless, in the resurrection of the just, [it applies] to those animals mentioned. And it is right that when the creation is restored, all the animals should obey and be subject to man, and revert to the food originally given by God. *Irenaeus (c. 180, E/W), 1.563.*

In the times of the kingdom, the earth will be called again by Christ. And Jerusalem will be rebuilt after the pattern of the Jerusalem above. *Irenaeus (c. 180, E/W), 1.565*

On the other hand, there is to be an end of evil when the chief of evil, the devil, will "go away into the fire that God has prepared for him and his angels," having first been cast into the bottomless pit. Likewise, at that time, the manifestation of the children of God will have delivered the animals from evil. For they had been "made subject to vanity." At that time, the cattle will be restored in the innocence and integrity of their nature and will be at peace with beasts of the field. At that time, also, little children will play with serpents. *Tertullian (c. 200, W), 3.483.*

The Sabbath is the type and symbol of the future kingdom of the saints, when they shall reign with Christ after He comes from heaven, as John says in his Revelation. For "a day with the Lord is as a thousand years." *Hippolytus (c. 205, W), 5.179.*

We do confess that a kingdom is promised to us upon the earth, although before heaven. Only, it will be in another state of existence. For it will be after the resurrection for a thousand years in the divinely-built city of Jerusalem "let down from heaven." *Tertullian (c. 207, W), 3.342.*

Cerinthus [a heretic], through written revelations by a "great apostle" (as he would have us

believe), brings before us marvelous things—which he pretends were shown to him by angels. He alleges that after the resurrection, the kingdom of Christ is to be on earth and that the flesh dwelling in Jerusalem will again be subject to desires and pleasures. *Eusebius, quoting Caius (c. 215, W), 5.601.*

Certain persons, . . . adopting a superficial view of the letter of the law, . . . are of the opinion that the fulfillment of the promises of the future are to be looked for in bodily pleasure and luxury. Therefore, they especially desire after the resurrection to have again bodies that will always have the power of eating, drinking, and performing all the functions of flesh and blood. . . . Consequently, they say that after the resurrection, there will be marriages and the begetting of children. They imagine to themselves that the earthly city of Jerusalem is to be rebuilt, its foundations being laid in precious stones. . . . Moreover, they think that the natives of other countries are to be given them as the servants of their pleasures. . . . They think that they are to receive the wealth of the nations to live on. These views they think to establish on the authority of the prophets, by those promises that are written regarding Jerusalem. . . . And from the New Testament, too, they quote the saying of the Savior . . . "Henceforth, I will not drink of this cup, until I drink it with you new in My Father's kingdom." . . .

[The millennialists] desire the fulfillment of all things looked for in the promises, all according to the manner of things in this life and in all similar matters. . . . However, those who receive the interpretations of Scripture according to the understanding of the apostles, entertain the hope that the saints will indeed eat—but that it will be the bread of life that can nourish the soul with the food of truth and wisdom. *Origen (c. 225, E), 4.297.*

The Amen sends flames on the nations. And the Medes and Persians burn for a thousand years, as the apocalyptic words of John declare. After a thousand years, they will be delivered over to Gehenna. And he whose work they were is burned up with them. *Commodianus (c. 240, W), 4.211.*

The city will descend from heaven in the first resurrection. . . . We who have been devoted to Him will arise again to Him. And they will be incorruptible, even already living without death. Neither will there be any grief nor any groaning in that city. They will also come who overcame cruel martyrdom under the Antichrist. And they themselves will live for the whole time and receive blessings because they have suffered evil things. And they themselves will marry, begetting for a thousand years. All the bounty of the earth will be prepared, because the earth will pour forth abundantly without end, being renewed. No rain and no cold will come into the golden camp. *Commodianus (c. 240, W), 4.212.*

They produce a certain composition written by Nepos. On this basis, as if it were incontestably proven, they insist very strongly that there will be a reign of Christ upon the earth. . . . They attempt to lead [our simpler brethren] to hope for things that are trivial and corruptible—that is, only those things that we might presently find in the kingdom of God. *Dionysius of Alexandria (c. 262, E), 6.81.*

The true Sabbath will be in the seventh millennium of years, when Christ will reign with His elect. *Victorinus (c. 280, W), 7.342.*

Those years during which Satan is bound are during the first coming of Christ—even to the end of the age. They are called a thousand years, in accord with that manner of speaking whereby a part is signified by the whole. . . . "And he cast him into the abyss." This is said because the devil began to take possession of the wicked, having been excluded from the hearts of believers. *Victorinus (c. 280, W), 7.358.*

I will put forth what my capacity enables me to judge [concerning the thousand year reign]. The tenfold number signifies the Decalogue. And the hundredfold means the crown of virginity. For the person who will have kept the undertaking of virginity completely and will have faithfully fulfilled the commandments of the Decalogue . . . he is the true priest of Christ, and he accomplishes the thousand year number completely. Therefore, he is said to reign with Christ. And truly, in his case, the devil is bound. . . . But in that it says that when the thousand years are finished, [Satan] is loosed, so the number of the perfect saints being completed . . . many will be overthrown, seduced by the love of earthly things. *Victorinus (c. 280, W), 7.359.*

They are not to be heard who assure themselves that there is to be an earthly reign of a thousand years. They think like the heretic Cerinthus. For the kingdom of Christ is already eternal in the saints—even though the glory of the saints will be manifested after the resurrection. *Victorinus (c. 280, W), 7.360.*

Taking my journey and going forth from the Egypt of this life, I came first to the resurrection, which is the true Feast of the Tabernacles. There, I set up my tabernacle, adorned with the fruits of virtue, on the first day of the resurrection, which is the Day of Judgment. And I celebrate with Christ the millennium of rest, which is called the seventh day, even the true Sabbath. *Methodius (c. 290, E), 6.347.*

Back then a mortal and imperfect man was formed from the earth, so that he might live a thousand years in this world. So, now, from this earthly age is formed a perfect man. And, being quickened by God, he will bear rule in this same world through a thousand years. *Lactantius (c. 304–313, W), 7.212.*

The dead will rise again . . . to reign with God for a thousand years. *Lactantius (c. 304–313, W), 7.218.*

When He will have destroyed unrighteousness and executed His great judgment, . . . He will be occupied among men for a thousand years. And He will rule them with a most just command. . . . Then, those who are alive in their bodies will not die. Rather, during these thousand years, they will produce an infinite multitude. Their offspring will be holy and beloved by God. However, those who are raised from the dead will preside over the living as judges. The nations will not be entirely extinguished. For some will be left as a victory for God. . . . They will be subjected to perpetual slavery. During that time, the ruler of the devils, who is the contriver of all evils, will be bound with chains. He will be imprisoned during the thousand years of this heavenly rule, in which righteousness will reign in the world. . . . After [Christ's] coming, the righteous will be collected from all the earth. When the judgment has been completed, the sacred city will be planted in the middle of the earth, in which God Himself, the Builder, may dwell together with the righteous. . . . The sun will become seven times brighter than it is now. And the earth will open its fruitfulness and bring forth most abundant fruits of its own accord. . . . The world itself will rejoice, and all nature will exult. For they will be rescued and set free from the dominion of evil, impiety, guilt, and error. Throughout this time, beasts will not be nourished by blood, nor will birds prey. Rather, all things will be peaceful and tranquil. Lions and calves will stand together at the hay trough. *Lactantius (c. 304–313, W), 7.219; see also 1.564–1.566.*

SEE ALSO ESCHATOLOGY; JERUSALEM; RESURRECTION OF THE DEAD.

MINISTRY

SEE CHURCH GOVERNMENT; EVANGELISM; ORDINATION.

MINOR ORDERS

The term "minor orders" refers to ministerial positions below those of bishop, presbyter, and deacon. Among such positions in the early church were subdeacon, reader, and acolyte.

Know, then, that I have made Saturus a reader, and Optatus, the confessor, a subdeacon. For already, by the general advice, we had made him next to the clergy. For we had entrusted the reading to Saturus on Easter, time and again. And when with the presbyter-teachers we were carefully testing readers, we appointed Optatus from among the readers to be a teacher of the hearers. First of all, though, we examined whether all things were found fitting in these men, which should be found on those who are in preparation for the clerical office. *Cyprian (c. 250, W), 5.301.*

. . . also your readers, your singers, your porters, your deaconesses, your widows, your virgins, and your orphans. *Apostolic Constitutions (compiled c. 390, E), 7.410.*

We do not permit the rest of the clergy to baptize: neither readers, singers, porters, nor ministers—but the bishops and presbyters alone. *Apostolic Constitutions (compiled c. 390, E), 7.429.*

SEE ALSO CHURCH GOVERNMENT; READER; SUBDEACON.

MINUCIUS FELIX

Mark Minucius Felix (c. 170–215) was a Roman lawyer who converted to Christianity. He composed one of the finest early Christian apologies, entitled Octavius, written in the form of a dialogue between a Christian and a pagan.

Of those who are known to me, Minucius Felix was of no low rank among apologists. His book, which bears the title of *Octavius,* declares how suitable a defender of the truth he might have been if he had given himself altogether to that pursuit [i.e., of being an apologist]. *Lactantius (c. 304–313, W), 7.136.*

MIRACLES

Papias relates that he had received a wonderful narrative from the daughters of Philip. For he reports that a dead man was raised to life in his day. He also mentions another miracle relating to Justus, surnamed Barsabas, how he swallowed a deadly poison, and received no harm, because of the grace of the Lord. *Eusebius, citing Papias (c. 120, E), 1.154.*

Our Savior's works, moreover, were always present. For they were real. They consisted of those who had been healed of their diseases and those who had been raised from the dead. These persons were not only seen while they were being healed and raised up, but they were afterwards constantly present. Nor did they remain only during the sojourn of the Savior on earth, but also a considerable time after His departure. Indeed, some of them have survived even down to our own times. *Quadratus (c. 125), 8.749.*

The heretics will, besides, add a great deal concerning the high authority of each teacher of heresy. They will relate how that these men strengthened belief in their own doctrine through mighty works, how that they raised the dead, restored the sick, foretold the future—so that they might deservedly be regarded as apostles. As if this warning were not also in the written record: that many would come who were to work even the greatest miracles, in defense of the deception of their corrupt preaching. *Tertullian (c. 197, W), 3.264, 265.*

I am acquainted with the case of a woman, the daughter of Christian parents, who in the very flower of her age and beauty slept peacefully [in death]. This was after a singularly happy, though brief, married life. Before they laid her in her grave, and when the presbyter began the prayers, at the very first breath of his prayer she withdrew her hands from her side, placed them in a posture of devotion, and after the holy service was concluded, she returned them to their lateral position. Then, again, there is that well-known story among our own people that a corpse voluntarily shifted in a certain cemetery to afford room for another body to be placed near to it. If, as is the case, similar stories are told among the pagans, God everywhere manifests signs of his power—to His own people for their comfort; to strangers, for a testimony unto them. *Tertullian (c. 210, W), 3.228.*

When, indeed, have not droughts been put away by our kneelings and our fastings? *Tertullian (c. 212, W), 3.107.*

Natalius was persuaded by them to let himself be chosen bishop of this heresy.... Connecting himself with the [heretics], he was admonished by the Lord in visions on many occasions.... But since he gave little heed to the visions, ... he was at last scourged by holy angels and severely beaten through a whole night. As a result, he rose early in the morning and threw himself, clothed with sackcloth and covered with ashes, before Zephyrinus the bishop. *Eusebius, quoting Caius (c. 215, W), 5.602.*

Things that are done by God may be (or may *appear* to some to be) unbelievable. However, they are not contrary to nature. *Origen (c. 248, E), 4.553.*

Those very persons whom we have shown to be no gods have often displayed their majesty both by prophecies, dreams, auguries, and oracles. Indeed, many miraculous things can be enumerated.... The immediate [supernatural] punishment of sacrilegious persons can also be mentioned, by which the gods are believed to have avenged the injury done to them.... Ceres of Miletus also gained for herself great veneration among men. For when the city had been taken by Alexander, and the soldiers had rushed in to plunder her temple, they were all blinded by a flame of fire suddenly thrown upon them. There are also dreams that seem to show the power of the gods. *Lactantius (c. 304– 313, W), 7.52.*

Christ's virtues have been made manifest to you, along with that unheard-of power ... that was used over the whole world by those who proclaimed Him. It has subdued the fires of passion and caused races, peoples, and nations that are most diverse in character to hasten with one accord to accept the same faith. For the deeds can be listed and numbered that have been done in India, as well as among the Seres, Persians, and Medes. *Arnobius (c. 305, E), 6.438.*

SEE ALSO GIFTS OF THE SPIRIT; UNCORRUPTED BODIES.

MIRIAM

Why was it, that when these two [Aaron and Miriam] had both acted with spite towards Moses, the latter alone was punished? The answer is, first, because the woman was the more culpable, since both nature and the Law place the woman in a subordinate position to the man. Or perhaps it was that Aaron was to a certain degree excusable, in consideration of his being the elder and his being adorned with the dignity of high priest. *Irenaeus (c. 180, E/W), 1.573.*

MISSIONS

SEE EVANGELISM.

MITHRAS

One of the more popular mystery religions in the Roman Empire, particularly among the military, was the worship of the Persian god Mithras.

Those who record the mysteries of Mithras say that he was begotten of a rock. And they call the place a "cave" where those who believe in him are initiated. *Justin Martyr (c. 160, E), 1.233.*

If my memory still serves me, Mithras there sets his marks on the foreheads of his soldiers, celebrates also the oblation of bread, and introduces a semblance of a resurrection. *Tertullian (c. 197, W), 3.262, 263.*

The soldier of Mithras is initiated in the gloomy cavern, in the camp ... of darkness. At the sword's point, a crown is presented to him, as though in mimicry of martyrdom. It is then put on his head. But he has been admonished to resist and cast it off or move it to his shoulder, saying that Mithras is his crown. Thereafter, he never allows himself to be crowned. And this is his mark to show who he is [i.e., a worshipper of Mithras].... So a person is immediately believed to be a soldier of Mithras if he throws a crown away, or if he says that he has his crown in his god. *Tertullian (c. 211, W), 3.103.*

SEE ALSO GODS, PAGAN; MYSTERY RELIGIONS.

MIXED MARRIAGES

SEE MARRIAGE (II. MARRIAGE TO UNBELIEVERS); UNBELIEVING SPOUSE.

MODESTY

In like manner also, [I desire] that the women adorn themselves in modest apparel, with propriety and mod-

eration, not with braided hair or gold or pearls or costly clothing. 1 Tim. 2:9.

Do not let your beauty be that outward adorning of arranging the hair, of wearing gold, or of putting on fine apparel; but let it be the hidden person of the heart, with the incorruptible ornament of a gentle and quiet spirit. 1 Pet. 3:3.

By no manner of means are women to be allowed to uncover and exhibit any part of their person. Otherwise, both may fall—the men by being excited to look; the women, by drawing to themselves the eyes of the men. *Clement of Alexandria (c. 195, E), 2.246.*

Much more must we keep pure from shameful deeds. On the one hand, we must keep from exhibiting and exposing parts of the body that we should not. And on the other hand, we must keep from looking at what is forbidden.... Now, the knee and leg, and such other members, are not obscene; nor are the names applied to them. In fact, the activity put forth by them is not obscene. And even the genitals are to be regarded as objects suggestive of *modesty,* not shame. It is their *unlawful* activity that is shameful. *Clement of Alexandria (c. 195, E), 2.251.*

Let [married women] be fully clothed: by garments on the outside and by modesty on the inside. *Clement of Alexandria (c. 195, E), 2.252.*

They must not do as some do. For some women imitate the acting of comedy. They practice the mincing motions of dancers, and they conduct themselves in society as if on the stage. That is, they go around with voluptuous movements and gliding steps, pretentious voices, and casting languishing glances round. *Clement of Alexandria (c. 195, E), 2.287.*

I would counsel the married men never to kiss their wives in the presence of their domestic servants. *Clement of Alexandria (c. 195, E), 2.291.*

Handmaids of the living God, my fellow-servants and sisters, the right that I enjoy with you emboldens me to address to you a discourse. However, I am the lowest in that right of fellow-servantship and brotherhood.... Salvation consists in the exhibition principally of modesty. I say this not only of women, but likewise of men. For ... we are all the "temple of God." *Tertullian (c. 198, W), 4.18.*

Most women ... have the boldness to walk as if modesty consisted only in the bare integrity of the flesh and in turning away from actual fornication.... They wear in their gait the same appearance as do the women of the nations, from whom the sense of true modesty is absent.... In short, how many women are there who do not earnestly desire to look pleasing even to strangers? Who does not on that very account take care to have herself painted out, yet denying that she has ever been an object of carnal appetite? *Tertullian (c. 198, W), 4.18, 19.*

Why, therefore, excite toward yourself that evil passion? Why invite that to which you profess yourself a stranger? *Tertullian (c. 198, W), 4.19.*

I know not whether He allows impunity to him who has been the cause of perdition to some other person. For that other person perishes—as soon as he has felt lust after your beauty and has mentally already committed the deed that his lust points to. And you have been made the sword that destroys him. So that, although you are free from the actual crime, you are not free from the infamy attaching to it. *Tertullian (c. 198, W), 4.19.*

Are we to paint ourselves out so that our neighbors may perish? What happened to, "You will love your neighbor as yourself"? *Tertullian (c. 198, W), 4.19.*

Let a holy woman, if naturally beautiful, give no one such a great occasion for carnal lust. Certainly, if even she is beautiful, she should not show off [her beauty], but should rather obscure it. *Tertullian (c. 198, W), 4.20.*

To blush if he sees a virgin is as much a mark of a holy man, as of a holy virgin if seen by a man. *Tertullian (c. 207, W), 4.28.*

So far, in fact, are Christians from indulging in incestuous desire, that with some Christians even the modest mingling of the sexes causes a blush. *Mark Minucius Felix (c. 200, W), 4.192.*

The dress of a modest woman should be modest. A believer should not be conscious of adultery even in the mixture of colors. *Novatian (c. 235, W), 5.591, formerly attributed to Cyprian.*

However, these things [i.e., adornments] are not necessary for modest women. Pierce your breast with chaste and modest feelings.... Wear the necessary clothes that the cold or the heat (or too much sun) demand, and so you may be approved as modest.... You married women, flee from the adornment of vanity. Such attire is fitting for women who haunt the brothels. O modest women of Christ, overcome the evil one. *Commodianus (c. 240, W), 4.214.*

But self-control and modesty do not consist only in purity of the flesh, but also in seemliness and in modesty of dress and adornment. *Cyprian (c. 250, W), 5.431.*

SEE ALSO CLOTHING; GROOMING; JEWELRY; VEIL.

MONARCHIANISM

The term "monarchianism" (or, more technically, "modalistic monarchianism") refers to the belief that the Father, Son, and Holy Spirit are all different modes or revelations of one and the same person. This belief is also known in theological circles as Modalism, Patripassianism, and Sabellianism. In popular use, this belief is generally referred to as "Jesus only" or "oneness" theology. This erroneous concept of the Trinity has perhaps come about partially because of the inadequacies of human language in speaking about God.

Undoubtedly the verse that causes the most confusion is John 1:1: "In the beginning was the Word, and the Word was with God, and the Word was God." The unwary reader does not realize that in this verse John uses the word "God" in two different senses. When John says that the Word was "with God," he is using "God" in the sense of "the Father." (In fact, the New Testament writers nearly always use the term "God" in the sense of "the Father.") When John says that the Word "was God," however, he is using the word "God" in a different sense. He is talking about the nature of the Word. The Word is divine; he has all the attributes of true divinity. He and the Father are two different persons, but they share the same nature.

To illustrate this somewhat confusing limitation of language, we can look at the Hebrew word *adam*. In Hebrew, *adam* means "mankind" or "human." Yet, it is also the proper name of the first human, Adam. Now, analogously to John 1:1, we could say, "Eve was with adam, and Eve was adam." That statement is true only if we understand that we are using the word adam in two different senses. When we say Eve was "with adam," we are using adam as a proper name, referring to Adam, Eve's husband. But when we say that Eve "was adam," we are using the term in the sense of "human." Eve was a different person from Adam, but both Adam and Eve were *adam*—human.

Similarly, not realizing that John was using the Greek word theos in two different senses in John 1:1, the unwary reader may think that John is saying, in essence, "the Word was with the Father and the Word was the Father." Such an interpretation is quite erroneous. Two of the early teachers of monarchianism were Noetus and Praxeas.

Go therefore and make disciples of all the nations, baptizing them in the name of the Father and of the Son and of the Holy Spirit. Matt. 28:19.

When you lift up the Son of Man, then you will know that I am He, and that I do nothing of Myself; but as My Father taught Me, I speak these things. John 8:28.

If I honor Myself, My honor is nothing. It is My Father who honors Me, of whom you say that He is your God. John 8:54.

My Father, who has given them to Me, is greater than all; and no one is able to snatch them out of My Father's hand. I and My Father are one. John 10:29, 30.

If you loved Me, you would rejoice because I said, "I am going to the Father," for My Father is greater than I. John 14:28.

I am ascending to My Father and your Father, and to My God and your God. John 20:17.

Those persons who declare that the Son is the Father are proved neither to have become acquainted with the Father, nor to know that the Father of the universe has a Son. *Justin Martyr (c. 160, E), 1.184.*

Some others are secretly introducing another doctrine and have become disciples of one Noetus who was a native of Smyrna and lived not very long ago. . . . He alleged that Christ was the Father Himself and that the Father Himself was born, suffered, and died. Yet, see what pride of heart and what a strange inflated spirit had insinuated themselves into him. From his other actions, then, the proof is already given us that he did not speak with a pure spirit. For he who blasphemes against the Holy Spirit is cast out from the holy inheritance. This same Noetus also alleged that he was himself Moses and that Aaron was his brother. When the blessed presbyters heard this, they summoned him before the church and examined him. . . . But he stood out against them, saying, "What evil, then, am I doing in glorifying Christ?" And the presbyters replied to him, "We too know in truth one God; we know Christ." . . . Then, after examining him, they expelled him from the church. And he was carried to such a pitch of pride, that he established a sect. *Hippolytus (c. 205, W), 5.223.*

They seek to exhibit the foundation for their dogma by citing the word in the Law, "I am the God of your fathers; you will have no other gods beside me." And, again, in another passage, He says: "I am the first and the last. And beside me there is no other." Thus they say they prove that God is one. Then, they answer in this manner: "If, therefore, I acknowledge Christ to be God, He must be the Father Himself—if indeed He is God. Now, Christ—being Himself God—suffered. Therefore, the Father suffered, for He was the Father Himself." However, the case does not stand through that logic. For the Scriptures do not set forth the matter in this manner. *Hippolytus (c. 205, W), 5.223, 224.*

If, again, Noetus alleges Christ's own words when He said, "I and the Father are one," let him attend to the fact and understand that He did not say, "I and the Father *am* one, but *are* one." For the word "are" is not said of one person. Rather, it refers to two persons, but one *power*. Christ has Himself made this clear, when He spoke to His Father concerning the disciples: "The glory which you gave me I have given them, that they may be one." . . . What have the Noetians to say to these things? Are we all one body in respect of person—or is it that we become one in the power and disposition of unity of mind? *Hippolytus (c. 205, W), 5.226.*

"He who has seen me has seen the Father." By which he means, "If you have seen me, you may know the Father through me. For the Father is made readily known through the image, which is like [the original]." *Hippolytus (c. 205, W), 5.226.*

There has appeared one Noetus by name; by birth, a native of Smyrna. This person introduced a heresy from the tenets of Heraclitus. . . . The school of these heretics during the succession of [these bishops] continued to acquire strength and augmentation from the fact that Zephrinus and Callistus [bishops of Rome] helped them to prevail. *Hippolytus (c. 225, W), 5.125.*

Now, that Noetus affirms that the Son and the Father are the same [Person], no one is ignorant. But he makes his statement in this manner: "When indeed, then, the Father had not been born, he was justly called 'Father.' And when it pleased him to undergo generation, He Himself became His own Son, not another's, having been begotten." For in this way, Noetus thinks he establishes the sovereignty of God, alleging that the Father and the Son are one and the same Person—not one individual produced from a different individual. Rather, He is from Himself. And He is called by the name "Father" or "Son," depending on the circumstances of the time. . . . So He commended His spirit to Himself, having died, yet not being dead. And he raised Himself up on the third day. *Hippolytus (c. 225, W), 5.127, 128.*

Now Callistus [bishop of Rome] brought forward Zephrinus himself [successor bishop of Rome] and induced him to publicly avow: "I know that there is one God, Jesus Christ." . . . And we, becoming aware of his sentiments, did not give place to him, but reproved and withstood him for the truth's sake. And he hurried headlong into folly . . . and called us worshippers of two Gods. *Hippolytus (c. 225, W), 5.128.*

Callistus [bishop of Rome] alleges that the Logos Himself is both the Son and also the Father Himself. Callistus says that although called by a different title, in reality He is one indivisible spirit. He says that the Father is not one Person and the Son another, but that they are one and the same Person. *Hippolytus (c. 225, W), 5.130.*

The devil has rivalled and resisted the truth in various ways. . . . Praxeas maintains that there is only one Lord, the Almighty Creator of the world. He says this in order that out of this unity he may fabricate a heresy. He says that the Father Himself came down into the virgin, was Himself born of her, Himself suffered, and indeed was Himself Jesus Christ. *Tertullian (c. 213, W), 3.597.*

The devil is himself a liar from the beginning, and so is whomever he instigates in his own way, such as Praxeas. For Praxeas was the first to import into Rome from Asia this kind of heretical depravity. *Tertullian (c. 213, W), 3.597.*

This heresy supposes itself to possess the pure truth, in thinking that one cannot believe in only one God in any other way than by saying that the Father, the Son, and the Holy Spirit are the very selfsame Person. *Tertullian (c. 213, W), 3.598.*

The Monarchians are constantly throwing out against us that we are preachers of two Gods and three Gods—while they take preeminent credit to themselves as being worshippers of the one God. . . . We say that they maintain the "Monarchy." . . . As for myself, however, if I have gleaned any knowledge of either language, I am sure that *monarchia* has no other meaning than single and individual rule. However, for all that, the term monarchy merely means the government of one. It does not preclude him whose government it is from having a son. . . . If, moreover, there is a son belonging to him whose monarchy it is, it does not thereby become divided and cease to be a monarchy, even if the son is taken as a sharer in it. *Tertullian (c. 213, W), 3.599.*

We have been already able to show that the Father and the Son are two—not only by the mention of their individual names as Father and Son, but also by the fact that He who delivered up the kingdom, and He to whom it is delivered up . . . must necessarily be two different Beings. But since the Monarchians will have the two to be but one (so that the Father is deemed to be the same as the Son), it is only right that the whole question respecting the Son should be examined. *Tertullian (c. 213, W), 3.600.*

The Father is distinct from the Son, being greater than the Son, inasmuch as He who begets is one, and He who is begotten is another. Likewise, He who sends is one, and He who is sent is another. He, again, who makes is one, and He through whom the thing is made is another. *Tertullian (c. 213, W), 3.604.*

Monarchians say that He Himself made Himself a Son to Himself. . . . A father must necessarily have a son in order to be a father. So, likewise, a son must have a father to be a son. However, it is one thing to *have,* and another thing to *be.* For example, in order to be a husband, I must have a wife. However, I can never myself be my own wife. In like manner, in order to be a father, I must have a son, for I never can be a son to myself. *Tertullian (c. 213, W), 3.604.*

If the number of the Trinity also offends you, as if it were not connected in the simple Unity, I ask you how it is possible for a Being who is merely and absolutely one and singular to speak in plural phrase, saying, "Let us make man in our own image, and after our own likeness"? . . . And "Behold, the man is become as one of us." *Tertullian (c. 213, W), 3.606.*

Jesus says, "My Father who gave them to me, is greater than all," adding immediately, "I and my Father are one." . . . This is an indication of two Beings—I *and* my Father. Furthermore, there is the plural verb, "are," which is inapplicable to only one person. . . . Two beings are still the subject in the masculine gender. He accordingly says "are *unum,*" a neuter term, which does not imply singularity of *number.* Rather, it implies unity of essence, likeness, conjunction, and affection on the Father's part. For the Father loves the Son. It also indicates submission on the Son's part, who obeys the Father's will. *Tertullian (c. 213, W), 3.618.*

In what sense was it said, "He that has seen me has seen the Father"? Even in the same sense in which it was said in a previous passage, "I and my Father are one." . . . For in all these passages, He had shown Himself to be the Father's agent, through whose agency even the Father could be seen in His works, heard in His words, and recognized in the Son's administration of the Father's words and deeds. *Tertullian (c. 213, W), 3.620.*

"Say unto them, I ascend unto my Father and your Father, and to my God and your God." [Does this mean I ascend] *as* the Father to the Father, and *as* God to God? Or, rather, does it mean as the Son to the Father, and as the Word to God? *Tertullian (c. 213, W), 3.621.*

Jesus commands them to baptize into the Father, the Son, and the Holy Spirit—not into a unipersonal God. *Tertullian (c. 213, W), 3.623.*

You blaspheme, for you allege not only that the Father died, but that He died the death of the cross. . . . Since you convert Christ into the Father, you are guilty of blasphemy against the Father. *Tertullian (c. 213, W), 3.626.*

There are some who fall into confusion on this matter of the Father and the Son, and I must devote a few words to them. They quote the text . . . "Destroy this temple and in three days I will raise it up," as if it proved that the Son does not differ in number from the Father.

Rather, they say that both are one—not only in the matter of substance but also of person. They say that the Father and the Son are said to be different in some of their aspects, but not in their persons. Against such views, we must in the first place produce the leading texts that prove the Son to be another person than the Father. We must show that the Son must of necessity be the son of a father, and the Father, the father of a son. Then we may very properly refer to Christ's declaration that He cannot do anything except what He sees the Father doing and saying. *Origen (c. 228, E), 9.402.*

Why do they shrink from being associated with the boldness of Sabellius, who says that Christ is the Father? *Novatian (c. 235, W), 5.622.*

Because it is so very clear that Christ is declared in the Scriptures to be God, many heretics—moved by the magnitude and truth of this divinity—exaggerate His honors above measure. And they have dared to declare or to think that He is not the Son, but God the Father Himself. *Novatian (c. 235, W), 5.634.*

The [heretics] say that if it is accepted that God is one and that Christ is God, then . . . the Father and Christ are one God, and Christ can be called the Father. But in this they are proved to be in error. They do not know Christ, but merely follow the sound of a name. For they are not willing that He should be the second Person after the Father, but the Father Himself. Since these things are easily answered, only a few words will be said. For who does not acknowledge that the Person of the Son is second after the Father? *Novatian (c. 235, W), 5.636.*

The [heretics] frequently urge upon us the passage where it is said, "I and the Father are one." But in this we all also overcome them just as easily. . . . Let the heretics understand that he did not say "one *person*." For the word "one," used in the neuter gender refers to social unity, not personal unity. Note that "one" is neuter, not masculine. . . . So this "one" has reference to agreement, to identity of judgment, and to the loving association itself. . . . For He would not have said *"are"* if He had meant that He, the one and only Father, had become the Son. . . . [Scripture has many examples of] this unity of agreement. . . . For in writing to the Corinthians, Paul said, "I have planted, Apollos watered, but God gave the increase. . . . Now he that plants and he that waters are one." Now,

who does not realize that Apollos is one person and Paul another? . . . Furthermore, the offices mentioned of each one of them are different. For he who plants is one, and he who waters is another. . . . Yet, as far as respects their agreement, both are one. *Novatian (c. 235, W), 5.637, 638.*

Be certain to contend about the fact that Christ is God also in such a way that it does not contradict the truth of Scripture. . . . For those who say that Jesus Christ Himself is God the Father have gathered from there the sources and reasons of their error and perversity—just the same as those who would have Him be only a man. *Novatian (c. 235, W), 5.642.*

There cannot be a hope of salvation except by knowing the two together. How, when God the Father is not known—nay, is even blasphemed—can they who among the heretics are said to be baptized in the name of Christ only, be judged to have obtained the remission of sins? . . . Christ Himself commands the pagans to be baptized in the full and united Trinity. Are we to believe that someone who denies Christ is denied by Christ, but that he who denies His Father . . . is not denied? Are we to believe that he who blasphemes against Him whom Christ called His Lord and His God is rewarded by Christ? Are we to believe that such a person obtains remission of sins and the sanctification of baptism? . . . Do you think that Christ grants impunity to the ungodly and profane, and the blasphemers of His Father? *Cyprian (c. 250, W), 5.383, 384.*

In summary, those who do not hold the true Lord, the Father, cannot hold the truth either of the Son or of the Holy Spirit. *Firmilian (c. 256, E), 5.392.*

Sabellius . . . blasphemes in saying that the Son Himself is the Father and vice versa. *Dionysius of Rome (c. 265, W), 6.365, as quoted by Athanasius.*

They have gone astray with regard to one of the three Persons of the Trinity. For example, some say, like Sabellius, that the Almighty Person of the Father Himself suffered. *Methodius (c. 290, E), 6.338.*

If any bishop or presbyter does not baptize according to the Lord's commandment—that is, into the Father, the Son, and the Holy Spirit—but baptizes into three Beings without beginning [i.e., into three Fathers], or into three Sons, or three Comforters, let him be removed. *Apostolic Constitutions (compiled c. 390, E), 7.503; extended discussion: 3.597–3.627, 5.223–5.231.*

SEE ALSO CHRIST, DIVINITY OF; TRINITY.

MONASTICISM

SEE VIRGINS.

MONEY

SEE ALMS, ALMSGIVING; MATERIALISM; PROSPERITY; TITHES, TITHING.

MONKS

SEE VIRGINS.

MONTANISTS

Montanism was a spiritual movement that began in the latter part of the second century. It was begun by a man named Montanus, who lived in Phrygia. After him, the movement was led by two alleged prophetesses, Priscilla and Maximilla. The Montantists referred to their movement as the New Prophecy. The church usually called them Phrygians, Cataphrygians, or Montanists.

I. Nature of Montanism and its teachings

II. Examples of Montanistic teachings from Tertullian
   A. New revelations from the Paraclete
   B. Christians should not flee from persecution
   C. No second marriages
   D. No forgiveness for postbaptismal sins

I. Nature of Montanism and its teachings

[WRITTEN CONCERNING THE MONTANISTS:] They do not admit that aspect presented by John's Gospel, in which the Lord promised that He would send the Paraclete. Rather, they set aside both the Gospel and the prophetic Spirit. Wretched men, indeed! They wish to be pseudo-prophets, for they set aside the gift of prophecy from the church. . . . They hold themselves aloof from the communion of the brethren. We must conclude, moreover, that these men cannot admit the apostle Paul, either. For, in his letter to the Corinthians, he speaks expressly of prophetical gifts. And he recognizes men and women prophesying *in the church. Irenaeus (c. 180, E/W), 1.429.*

Let not the above-mentioned people, then, call us "natural men" by way of reproach. Do not let the Phrygians, either. For these persons now use the term "natural men" to refer to those who do not apply themselves to the New Prophecy. We will discuss them in our remarks on prophecy. *Clement of Alexandria (c. 195, E), 2.426.*

There are others who are themselves even more heretical in nature [than the Quartodecimans] and are Phrygians by birth. These have been rendered victims of error because of being previously captivated by those wretched women called Priscilla and Maximilla, whom they supposed to be prophetesses. They claim that the Paraclete Spirit had come into these women. And prior to them, the Phrygians in like manner consider Montanus as a prophet. . . . They allege that they have learned more through [their books] than from the Law and Prophets, and from the Gospels. In fact, they magnify these wretched women above the apostles and every gift of grace. Moreover, some of them presume to assert that there is in them something superior to Christ. *Hippolytus (c. 225, W), 5.123.*

These persons acknowledge God to be the Father of the universe and Creator of all things—similarly with the church—and believe all the things that the Gospel testifies concerning Christ. However, they introduce the novelties of [certain] fasts, feasts, meals of parched food, and meals of radishes—alleging that they have been so instructed by these women. Some of them assent to the heresy of the Noetians, affirming that the Father Himself is the Son. *Hippolytus (c. 225, W), 5.123, 124.*

Those who are called Cataphrygians endeavor to claim to themselves new prophecies. They can have neither the Father nor the Son. For if we ask them what Christ they preach, they will reply that they preach Him who sent the Spirit that speaks by Montanus and Priscilla. However, when we observe that there has not been the spirit of truth in these persons, but a spirit of error, we know that they who maintain their false prophesying against the faith of Christ cannot have Christ. *Firmilian (c. 256, E), 5.392.*

Some had doubts about the baptism of those who appeared to recognize the same Father and Son with us, yet who received the New Prophets. Very many of us meeting together in Iconium very carefully examined the matter and we decided that every baptism was altogether to be rejected that was arranged for outside the church. *Firmilian (c. 256, E), 5.395.*

Even among them, too, he reveals that there are men of a lax disposition . . . who listen to new forms of prophesying. *Victorinus (c. 280, W), 7.347.*

II. Examples of Montanistic teachings from Tertullian

Most of Tertullian's writings after 206 exhibit strong Montanistic leanings, although Tertullian was still part of the church. Around 213, Tertullian may have left the church and joined a Montanist group. The following passages from Tertullian give us insight into how the Montanists viewed themselves, as well as some examples of their teachings. Among the Montanistic teachings reflected below are that (1) the Holy Spirit (the Paraclete) continues to give his people new commandments and teachings, (2) it is wrong to flee from persecution, (3) it is wrong to remarry for any reason, including the death of a spouse, and (4) there is no forgiveness for serious postbaptismal sins, such as adultery or denial of Christ in persecution.

A. New revelations from the Paraclete

The word of the New Prophecy, which is a part of our belief, attests how it foretold that there would be for a sign a picture of this very city [i.e., the new Jerusalem] exhibited to be seen previous to its manifestation. This prophecy, indeed, has been very lately fulfilled in an expedition to the East. For it is evident from the testimony of even pagan witnesses, that in Judea there was suspended in the sky a city early every morning for forty days. As the day advanced, the entire figure of its walls would wane gradually, and sometimes it would vanish instantly. *Tertullian (c. 207, W), 3.342, 343.*

Was his ignorance the result of simple error? Or was it on the principle which we maintain in the cause of the New Prophecy—that ecstasy or rapture is incidental to grace. For when a man is rapt in the Spirit (especially when he beholds the glory of God, or when God speaks through him), he necessarily loses his sensation. For he is overshadowed with the power of God. This is a point on which there is an issue between us and the "natural men." *Tertullian (c. 207, W), 3.383.*

Whatever savors of opposition to truth, this will be heresy, even [if it is] an ancient custom. *Tertullian (c. 207, W), 4.27.*

The law of faith being constant, the other succeeding points of discipline and manner of living allow the novelty of correction. For the grace of God operates and advances even to the end. For what kind of [belief] is it, that, while the devil is always operating and adding daily to the ingenuities of iniquity, the work of God should either have ceased, or else have desisted from advancing? . . . What, then, is the Paraclete's administrative office but this: the direction of discipline, the revelation of the Scriptures, the re-formation of the intellect, and the advancement toward the better things? *Tertullian (c. 207, W), 4.27.*

Now, through the Paraclete, it is settling into maturity. He will be, after Christ, the only one to be called and revered as Master. For He speaks not from Himself, but what is commanded by Christ. He is the only prelate, because He alone succeeds Christ. Those who have received Him set truth before custom. Those who have heard him prophesying even to the present time—not of old—bid virgins to be wholly covered. *Tertullian (c. 207, W), 4.28.*

To *us*, the Lord has—even by revelations—measured the space for the veil to extend over. For a certain sister of ours was thus addressed by an angel. *Tertullian (c. 207, W), 4.37.*

As for ourselves [i.e., the Montanists], indeed, we inscribe on the soul the lineaments of corporeity . . . also from the firm conviction that divine grace impresses us by revelation. For, seeing that we acknowledge spiritual *charismata*, or gifts, we too have merited the attainment of the prophetic gift, even though coming after John. We have now among us a sister whose lot it has been to be favored with sundry gifts of revelation, which she experiences in the Spirit by ecstatic vision amid the sacred rites of the Lord's Day in the church. She converses with angels and sometimes even with the Lord. . . . Whether it is in the reading of Scriptures, in the chanting of psalms, in the preaching of sermons, or in the offering up of prayers—in all these religious services, matter and opportunity are afforded to her for seeing visions. . . . After the people are dismissed at the conclusion of the sacred services, she is in the regular habit of reporting to us whatever things she may have seen in vision (for all her communications are examined with the most scrupulous care). . . . This was her vision; and for her witness, there was God. And the apostle most assuredly foretold that there were to be spiritual gifts in the church. *Tertullian (c. 207, W), 3.188.*

No one will hesitate to believe that the soul undergoes in Hades some compensatory discipline, without prejudice to the full process of the resurrection—when the recompense will be administered through the flesh as well. This point the Paraclete has also pressed home on our attention in most frequent admonitions, whenever any of us has admitted the force of His words from a knowledge of His promised spiritual disclosures. *Tertullian (c. 210, W), 3.235.*

It is a shrewd saying that the Paraclete utters concerning these persons [the Gnostics] by the mouth of the prophetess Priscilla: "They are carnal, and yet they hate the flesh." *Tertullian (c. 210, W), 3.552.*

It is plain enough that the ancient Holy Writ has furnished [the heretics] with sundry materials for their evil doctrine, which very materials indeed are refutable from the same Scriptures. It was fit and proper, therefore, that the Holy Spirit should no longer withhold the pouring forth of His gracious light upon these inspired writings, in order that He might be able to disseminate the seeds of truth with no adulteration of heretical subtleties, and pluck out from it their tares. He has accordingly now dispersed all the perplexities of the past, and their self-chosen allegories and parables, by the open and clear explanation of the entire mystery through the New Prophecy that descends in copious streams from the Paraclete. *Tertullian (c. 210, W), 3.594.*

In regard to every decision in matters we are called on to consider, the apostle also says, "If you are ignorant of anything, God will reveal it to you." [Paul] himself, too, was accustomed to afford counsel even though he did not have the command of the Lord and to dictate of himself as possessing the Spirit of God, who guides into all truth. Therefore, his advice has—by the warrant of divine reason—become equivalent to nothing less than a divine command. Earnestly now inquire of this teacher. *Tertullian (c. 211, W), 3.95.*

I would be surprised at the "natural men" if it was to voluptuousness alone that they were enthralled (which leads them to repeated marriages) and if they were not also bursting with gluttony, causing them to hate fasts. *Tertullian (c. 213, W), 4.102.*

It is these "natural men" who raise controversy with the Paraclete. It is on this account that the New Prophecies are rejected. It is not that Montanus, Priscilla, and Maximilla preach another God. Nor that they disjoin Jesus Christ, nor that they overturn any particular rule of faith or hope. It is because they plainly teach more frequent fasting than marrying. . . . They charge us with keeping fasts of our own, with prolonging our stations generally into the evening . . . with not eating or drinking anything with a wine flavor, and they teach abstinence from the bath, consistent with our dry diet. The Unspiritual are therefore constantly reproaching us with novelty. . . . [They say] it must either be judged as heresy, if it is attributed to human presumption, or else pronounced to be false prophecy, if it is a spiritual declaration. *Tertullian (c. 213, W), 4.102.*

[Paul is] the detester of those who—in like manner as they prohibit marrying—so bid us to abstain from meats created by God. And accordingly they think us [Montanists] to have been even then predicted as "in the last days departing from the faith, giving heed to spirits that seduce the world, having a conscience burned in with doctrines of liars." . . . Thus, too, they assert that we share with the Galatians the piercing rebuke as "observers of days, months, and years." *Tertullian (c. 213, W), 4.103.*

Of those things that are observed on the ground of tradition, we are bound to produce so much the more worthy reason that they lack the authority of Scripture—until by some manifest heavenly gift they are either confirmed or else corrected. *Tertullian (c. 213, W), 4.109.*

Grant that from the time of John, the Paraclete had grown mute. We ourselves would have arisen as prophets to ourselves, for this cause chiefly: . . . to secure by foreknowledge the moral position of the last days, exhorting every type of asceticism, since the prison must be familiarized to us, and hunger and thirst practiced. . . . In this way, the Christian may *enter* into prison in a similar condition as though he had just *left* it. *Tertullian (c. 213, W), 4.110.*

Why then do you hesitate to believe that the Paraclete, whom you deny in a Montanus, exists in an Apicius? *Tertullian (c. 213, W), 4.111.*

The Holy Spirit, when He was preaching in whatever lands He chose, and through whomever He chose, was—in His role as Paraclete—used to issuing mandates for observances of this nature. For example, at the present time, He issued mandates for the purpose of practicing the discipline of sobriety and abstinence. We who receive Him must necessarily observe also the appointments that He then made. *Tertullian (c. 213, W), 4.111.*

After the Bishop of Rome had acknowledged the prophetic gifts of Montanus, Priscilla, and Maximilla and after he had bestowed his peace on the churches of Asia and Phrygia (because of this acknowledgment), Praxeas by importunately urging false accusations against the prophets themselves and their churches ... compelled him to recall the letter of peace he had issued and to desist from ... acknowledging the said gifts. *Tertullian (c. 213, W), 3.597.*

"I still have many things to say unto you, but you are not yet able to bear them. When the Holy Spirit will come, he will lead you into all truth." ... You [in the church] say, "By this line of argument, it follows that anything you [Montanists] please that is novel and burdensome may be ascribed to the Paraclete—even if it has come from the adversary spirit!" *Tertullian (c. 217, W), 4.59.*

The New Law [i.e., Christianity] abrogated divorce—it had to abrogate. The New Prophecy abrogates second marriage—which is no less a divorce of the former spouse. *Tertullian (c. 217, W), 4.71.*

B. Christians should not flee from persecution

Just as [those in the church] have rejected the prophecies of the Holy Spirit, they are also purposing the refusal of martyrdom.... Nor do I doubt that some are already turning their back on the Scriptures, are making ready their luggage, and are equipped for flight from city to city. For this is all of the gospel they care to remember. *Tertullian (c. 211, W), 3.93.*

We must first come to a decision as to how the matter stands in regard to persecution itself—whether it comes on us from God or from the devil.... With respect to this, let me in the meantime say that nothing happens without God's will.... For what is the offspring of persecution, what other result comes from it, but the approving and rejecting of faith—in regard to which the Lord will certainly sift his people? Persecution is the judgment of the Lord. By means of it, one is declared either approved or

rejected. The judging properly belongs to God alone. This is that fan that even now cleanses the Lord's threshing floor (the church, I mean), winnowing the mixed heap of believers and separating the grain of the martyrs from the chaff of the deniers.... So persecution may be viewed as a contest. By whom is the conflict proclaimed, but by Him by whom the crown and the rewards are offered? *Tertullian (c. 212, W), 4.116.*

Do you not know that God is Lord of all? And if it is God's will, then you will suffer persecution. But if it is not, the pagan will be still. Believe it more surely, if indeed you believe in that God without whose will not even a sparrow, which a small coin can buy, falls to the ground.... Well, then, if it is evident from whom persecution proceeds, we are able at once to satisfy your doubts ... that men should not flee from it. For if persecution proceeds from God, in no way will it be our duty to flee from what has God as its author. *Tertullian (c. 212, W), 4.118.*

He says, "When they begin to persecute you, flee from city to city." We maintain that this applies only to the apostles personally, and to their times and circumstances. *Tertullian (c. 212, W), 4.119.*

Seek not to die on bridal beds, nor in miscarriages, nor in soft fevers, but to die the martyr's death—that He who has suffered for you may be glorified. *Tertullian (c. 212, W), 4.121.*

C. No second marriages

Moderation is to not regret something that has been taken away, and taken away by the Lord God, without whose will neither does a leaf glide down from a tree, nor does a sparrow of one coin's worth fall to the earth.... Accordingly, if we renew a marriage that has been taken away [by the death of a spouse], doubtlessly we strive against the will of God—willing to have once again a thing that He has not willed us to have. For had He willed it, he would not have taken it away. *Tertullian (c. 212, W), 3.50.*

Neither in the Gospels nor in Paul's own Epistles will you find a commandment of God as the source from which repetition of marriage is permitted.... That which is not found to be *permitted* by the Lord is acknowledged to be *forbidden. Tertullian (c. 212, W), 3.52.*

If we look deeply into his meanings, and interpret them, second marriages will have to be termed nothing other than a type of fornication. *Tertullian (c. 212, W), 4.55.*

Through the holy prophetess, Priscilla, the Gospel is thus preached that "the holy minister knows how to minister sanctity." She says, "For purity is harmonious, and they see visions. And turning their faces downwards, they even hear manifest voices, as salutary as they are secret." Now, this dulling [of the spiritual faculties] averts the Holy Spirit even when the carnal nature is allowed room for exercise in the first marriage. How much more so does it do this when it is brought into play in a second marriage! *Tertullian (c. 212, W), 4.56.*

By *us* [Montanists], precaution is thus also taken against the greatest or highest [sins] in that it is not permitted for us, after believing, to experience even a second marriage—differentiated though it is, to be sure, from the work of adultery and fornication by the marriage and dowry rules. Accordingly, with the utmost strictness, we excommunicate those who are twice-married. For they bring infamy upon the Paraclete by the irregularity of their discipline. *Tertullian (c. 212, W), 4.75.*

D. No forgiveness for postbaptismal sins

Those who have received another Paraclete in and through the apostles, and do not recognize Him even in His special prophets [i.e., the Montanists], no longer possess Him in the apostles either. Come, now, let them . . . teach us the possibility that the stains of a flesh that after baptism has been polluted again can be washed away by repentance. *Tertullian (c. 212, W), 4.85.*

Inasmuch as He puts such sins [i.e., adultery and fornication] on the paid side of the account *before* baptism, he thereby determines them to be irremissible *after* baptism. *Tertullian (c. 212, W), 4.91.*

Therefore, exhibit prophetic evidence even now to me, apostolic sir, that I may recognize your divine virtue and vindicate to yourself the power of remitting such sins! If, however, you have had the functions of *discipline* alone allotted to you . . . who are you, how great are you, to grant indulgence! For, by exhibiting neither the prophetic nor the apostolic character, you lack that virtue whose property it is to indulge. *Tertullian (c. 212, W), 4.99.*

You say, "But the church has the power of forgiving sins." This I acknowledge and adjudge more, I who have the Paraclete Himself in the persons of the New Prophets saying, "The church has the power to forgive sins. But I will not do it, lest they commit others besides." . . . Accordingly, it is true that the church will forgive sins. But this is the church *of the Spirit,* by means of a spiritual man. It is not the church that consists of a number of bishops. For the right and decision is the Lord's, not the servant's. It is God's Himself; not the priest's [Latin, *sacerdos*]. *Tertullian (c. 212, W), 4.99, 100.*

SEE ALSO HERESIES, HERETICS.

MORNING AND EVENING PRAYER

Morning Prayer and Evening Prayer were liturgical services held each day at the local church, during which psalms were sung and prayers offered to God.

Do not forget Christ's church. So go there in the morning before all your work. And meet there again in the evening to return thanks to God. *Apostolic Constitutions (compiled c. 390, E), 7.413.*

But assemble yourselves together every day, morning and evening, singing psalms and praying in the Lord's house. In the morning, say the sixty-second Psalm. And in the evening, say the hundred and fortieth Psalm, but particularly on the Sabbath day. *Apostolic Constitutions (compiled c. 390, E), 7.423.*

When they rise from sleep and have washed themselves, and before they go to work, let all of the faithful pray, whether they are men or women. And if any catechetical instruction is being held, let the faithful person prefer the word of piety before his work. *Apostolic Constitutions (compiled c. 390, E), 7.495; see also 7.478.*

SEE ALSO ASSEMBLIES, CHRISTIAN; EUCHARIST; LITURGY.

MOSES

Moses, who was the first of the prophets, spoke in these very words: "The scepter will not depart from Judah" [Gen. 49:10]. *Justin Martyr (c. 160, E), 1.173.*

Of all your teachers—whether sages, poets, historians, philosophers, or lawgivers—by far the oldest was Moses, our first religious teacher. The Greek histories show us this. For in the days of Ogyges and Inachus, whom some of your poets suppose to have been the original inhabitants of earth, Moses is mentioned as being the leader and ruler of the Jewish nation. *Justin Martyr (c. 160, E), 1.277.*

By this, you can easily recognize the antiquity of Moses. . . . From all manner of proofs, it is easy to see that the history of Moses is by far more ancient than all secular histories. . . . There is no ancient work that makes known any action of the Greeks or barbarians [before the era of the Olympiads]. So before that period, there only existed the history of the prophet Moses, which he wrote in the Hebrew characters by divine inspiration. For the Greek characters were not yet in use. *Justin Martyr (c. 160, E), 1.278.*

From these very old records, it is proved that the writings of the rest [i.e., the Greeks and other pagans] are more recent than the writings given to us through Moses. They are even more recent than the later prophets. *Theophilus (c. 180, E), 2.118.*

That which had been done typically through the actions of the prophet, the apostle demonstrates to have been done in reality by Christ in the church. For that reason, too, did Moses take an Ethiopian woman as his wife. For he thereby made her an Israelite woman. This prefigured the wild olive tree that is grafted into the cultivated olive tree, enabling the wild olive to partake of its richness. *Irenaeus (c. 180, E/W), 1.492.*

Josephus says that when Moses had been brought up in the royal palaces, he was chosen to be the general against the Ethiopians. And having proved victorious, he obtained in marriage the daughter of that king. *Irenaeus (c. 180, E/W), 1.573.*

Philo says in his "Life of Moses" that Greeks taught the rest of the usual course of instruction to Moses in Egypt, as a royal child. *Clement of Alexandria (c. 195, E), 2.335.*

Our Moses, then, was a prophet, a legislator, a man skilled in military tactics and strategy, a governor, and a philosopher. *Clement of Alexandria (c. 195, E), 2.336.*

The Greeks had the advantage of receiving from Moses all these things, coupled with the knowledge of how to use each of them. *Clement of Alexandria (c. 195, E), 2.337.*

Plato the philosopher was aided in legislation by the books of Moses. . . . Indeed, the philosophers would proclaim any man as being wise who was a king, a legislator, and a military general—and who was also just, holy, and loved by God. So if we discover these qualities in Moses (as shown from the Scriptures themselves) we may, with the greatest certainty, pronounce Moses to be truly wise. *Clement of Alexandria (c. 195, E), 2.338.*

It is then clear, too, that all the other virtues set forth in Moses supplied the Greeks with the basics of the whole department of morals. *Clement of Alexandria (c. 195, E), 2.365.*

If you happen to have heard of a certain Moses, I speak first of him. . . . By nearly four hundred years—only seven less—he precedes Danasus, your most ancient [Greek] name. . . . I might affirm, too, that he is five hundred years earlier than Homer. *Tertullian (c. 197, W), 3.33.*

Moses is certainly much more divine. For he recounts and traces the course of the human race from the very beginning of the world. And he indicates the many generations according to their names and their epochs. He thus gives plain proof of the divine character of his work, from its divine authority and word. *Tertullian (c. 210, W), 3.208, 209.*

Celsus [a pagan critic] says, . . . "Moses, having learned the doctrine that is to be found existing among wise nations and eloquent men, obtained the reputation of divinity." Now, in answer to this, we have to say that it may be allowed that Moses did indeed hear a somewhat ancient doctrine and transmitted the same to the Hebrews. *Origen (c. 248, E), 4.404, 405; see also 2.117; extended discussion: 2.335–2.338.*

SEE ALSO JOSEPHUS; LAW, MOSAIC; MOSES, ASSUMPTION OF; PENTATEUCH.

MOSES, ASSUMPTION OF

The *Assumption of Moses* was a Jewish spiritual work that is today usually included in the Old Testament Pseudepigrapha. The following verse from Jude is apparently referring to a passage in this work:

Yet Michael the archangel, in contending with the devil, when he disputed about the body of Moses, dared not bring against him a reviling accusation, but said, "The Lord rebuke you!" Jude 9.

As the mystics say, after his assumption, He had a third name in heaven, Melchi. *Clement of Alexandria (c. 195, E), 2.335.*

Joshua, the son of Nave, saw Moses in double when he was taken up. There was one Moses with the angels, and another one on the mountains, honored with burial in its ravines. *Clement of Alexandria (c. 195, E), 2.511.*

"When Michael, the archangel, disputing with the devil, debated about the body of Moses." Here he confirms the assumption of Moses. *Clement of Alexandria (c. 195, E), 2.573.*

In the work entitled the *Assumption of Moses,* the archangel Michael, when disputing with the devil regarding the body of Moses, says that the serpent, being inspired by the devil, was the cause of Adam and Eve's transgression. *Origen (c. 225, E), 4.328.*

SEE ALSO ENOCH, BOOK OF; PSEUDEPIGRAPHA, OLD TESTAMENT.

MOTHER, GREAT

Among the many gods and goddesses worshipped throughout the Roman Empire, one of the more popular was the Great Mother.

All honor to that king of the Scythians . . . who shot with an arrow one of his subjects who imitated among the Scythians the mystery of the Mother of the gods. *Clement of Alexandria (c. 195, E), 2.177.*

[SAID SARCASTICALLY:] Why, too, even in these days the Great Mother has given a notable proof of her greatness which she has conferred as a boon upon the city. *Tertullian (c. 197, W), 3.39.*

You have festivals bearing the name of the Great Mother. *Tertullian (c. 197, W), 3.82.*

These pagans constantly attend the mysteries called those of the Great Mother, supposing especially that they behold the entire mystery by means of the ceremonies performed there. *Hippolytus (c. 225, W), 5.57.*

When Hannibal, the Carthaginian, was plundering Italy and seeking the rulership of the whole world, is that not when you began to know . . . and to worship with remarkable honors the Phrygian Mother? Are not the sacred rites of the mother Ceres, which were adopted but a little while ago, called Graeca? *Arnobius (c. 305, E), 6.462.*

Some of you have said that the earth is the Great Mother, for it provides good for all living things. *Arnobius (c. 305, E), 6.472.*

The Great Mother, adorned with her sacred fillets, is represented by dancing. *Arnobius (c. 305, E), 6.488.*

The birth of the Great Mother of the gods and the origin of her rites are detailed . . . in Timotheus. *Arnobius (c. 305, E), 6.491.*

But the Great Mother . . . was a cause of safety and great joy to the people. *Arnobius (c. 305, E), 6.538; see also 6.493, 6.496, 6.538; extended discussion: 6.491–6.493.*

MOTHER, SPIRITUAL

The Jerusalem above is free, which is the mother of us all. Gal. 4:26.

The mother draws the children to herself; and we seek our mother, the church. *Clement of Alexandria (c. 195, E), 2.214.*

The virgin mother is one; I love to call her the church. . . . She is both virgin and mother. That is, she is as pure as a virgin, but as loving as a mother. Calling her children to her, she nurses them with holy milk. *Clement of Alexandria (c. 195, E), 2.220.*

He generated us from our mother—the water [of baptism]. *Clement of Alexandria (c. 195, E), 2.439.*

The mother is not, as some say, the essence from which we sprang, nor, as others teach, the church. Rather, it is the divine knowledge and Wisdom, as Solomon says, when he calls Wisdom "the mother of the just." *Clement of Alexandria (c. 195, E), 2.514.*

. . . along with the provision that our lady mother, the church, from her bountiful breasts, and each brother out of his private means, provides for your physical needs in the prison. *Tertullian (c. 197, W), 3.693.*

Therefore, blessed ones, whom the grace of God awaits, you ascend from that most sacred bath of your new birth and spread your hands for the first time in the house of your mother, together with your brethren. *Tertullian (c. 198, W), 3.679.*

Nor is even our mother, the church, passed by. *Tertullian (c. 198, W), 3.682.*

Do not depart far from your mother [i.e., the church], and the highest will be able to be merciful to you. . . . I exhort the adults that they should be born again and run in arms, as it were, to their mother from the womb. *Commodianus (c. 240, W), 4.212, 213.*

Cyprian, to the martyrs and confessors in Christ our Lord and in God the Father, everlasting salvation. I gladly rejoice and am thankful, most brave and blessed brethren, at hearing of your faith and virtue, by which the church, our mother, glories. *Cyprian (c. 250, W), 5.287.*

. . . we begin to be gathered together once more into the bosom of the church, our mother. *Cyprian (c. 250, W), 5.290.*

They have chosen to consent with you, so that they may remain with the church, their mother. *Cyprian (c. 250, W), 5.316.*

I wish I could persuade them, for the sake of our mutual affection, to return to their mother—that is, to the catholic church. *Cyprian (c. 250, W), 5.321.*

Can he have God as his Father, before he has had the church for his mother? *Cyprian (c. 250, W), 5.388.*

Munnulus of Girba said: "Brethren, the truth of our mother, the catholic church, has always remained and still remains with us—especially in the Trinity of baptism." *Seventh Council of Carthage (c. 256, W), 5.567.*

This is the desire and purpose of all heretics, to frame as many attacks of this kind as possible against our most holy mother, the church. *Treatise on Re-Baptism (c. 257, W), 5.667.*

SEE ALSO CHURCH, THE; WOMAN CLOTHED WITH THE SUN.

MURATORIAN FRAGMENT

SEE CANON, NEW TESTAMENT.

MUSIC, MUSICAL INSTRUMENTS

Praise Him with the sound of the trumpet; praise Him with the lute and harp! Ps. 150:3.

Be filled with the Spirit, speaking to one another in psalms and hymns and spiritual songs, singing and making melody in your heart to the Lord. Eph. 5:18, 19.

Your [pagan] public assembles I have come to hate. For there are excessive banquets and sub-

tle flutes that provoke people to lustful movements. *Justin Martyr (c. 160, E), 1.272.*

Of such persons, too, the Spirit has spoken through Isaiah: "They drink wine with harps, tablets, psalteries, and flutes. However, they do not regard the works of God." *Irenaeus (c. 180, E/W), 1.464.*

If people occupy their time with pipes, psalteries, choirs, dances, Egyptian clapping of hands, and such disorderly frivolities, they become quite immodest. . . . Let the pipe be resigned to the shepherds, and the flute to the superstitious ones who are engrossed in idolatry. For, in truth, such instruments are to be banished from the temperate banquet. . . . Man is truly a peaceful instrument. However, if you investigate, you will find other instruments to be warlike, inflaming to lusts, kindling up passion, or rousing wrath. . . . The Spirit, distinguishing the divine service from such revelry, says, "Praise Him with the sound of trumpet." For with the sound of the trumpet, He will raise the dead. "Praise him on the psaltery." For the tongue is the psaltery of the Lord. "And praise him on the lyre." By the lyre is meant the mouth struck by the Spirit. *Clement of Alexandria (c. 195, E), 2.248.*

The one instrument of peace, the Word alone by whom we honor God, is what we employ. We no longer employ the ancient psaltery, trumpet, timbrel, and flute. For those expert in war and scorners of the fear of God were inclined to make use of these instruments in the choruses at their festive assemblies. . . . Yet, even if you wish to sing and play to the harp or lyre, there is no blame. You will imitate the righteous Hebrew king in his thanksgiving to God. . . . Nevertheless, let love songs be banished far away. But let our songs be hymns to God. . . . Temperate harmonies are to be allowed. But we are to banish as far as possible from our robust mind those liquid harmonies. For, through pernicious arts in the modulations of tones, they lead persons to effeminacy and indecency. But serious and modest strains say farewell to the turbulence of drunkenness. Chromatic harmonies are therefore to be abandoned to immodest revels, and to ornate and tawdry music. *Clement of Alexandria (c. 195, E), 2.249.*

Outside [the assembly], they foolishly amuse themselves with impious amusements, . . . occupied with flute playing, dancing, intoxication, and all kinds of frivolity. Yet, those who sing in that manner . . . are the same ones who hymned immortality [a short time] before. *Clement of Alexandria (c. 195, E), 2.290.*

By music, we harmoniously relax the excessive tension of seriousness. *Clement of Alexandria (c. 195, E), 2.303.*

As an example of music, let us produce David, both playing and prophesying, melodiously praising God. Now the Enarmonic suits best the Dorian harmony; and the Diatonic, the Phrygian. . . . Music, then, is to be studied for the sake of the embellishment and composure of manners. For instance, at a banquet, we pledge each other while the music is playing. By song, we soothe the eagerness of our desires, and we glorify God for the copious gift of human enjoyments. . . . However, we must reject frivolous music, which weakens men's souls. *Clement of Alexandria (c. 195, E), 2.500, 501.*

The [theater and the arena] resemble each other also in their ceremony, having the same procession to the scene of their display from temples and altars, and that mournful profusion of incense and blood, with music of pipes and trumpets. *Tertullian (c. 197, W), 3.84.*

What trumpet of God is now heard—unless it is in the entertainments of the heretics? *Tertullian (c. 210, W), 3.562.*

If [Mercury] also first strung the chord to give forth melody, I will not deny—when listening to David—that this invention has been in use with the saints and has ministered to God. *Tertullian (c. 211, W), 3.97.*

One imitates the hoarse, warlike clanging of the trumpet. Another with his breath blowing into a pipe regulates its mournful sounds. . . . Why should I speak of . . . those great tragic vocal ravings? Why should I speak of strings set vibrating with noise? Even if these things were not dedicated to idols, they should not be approached and gazed upon by faithful Christians. *Novatian (c. 235, W), 5.578, formerly attributed to Cyprian.*

God also gave man a voice. Yet, love songs and indecent things are not to be sung merely on that account. *Cyprian (c. 250, W), 5.433.*

[Satan] presents to the eyes seductive forms and easy pleasures, by the sight of which he might destroy chastity. He tempts the ears with harmonious music, so that by the hearing of sweet sounds, he may relax and weaken Christian vigor. *Cyprian (c. 250, W), 5.491.*

Did He send souls so that beings of a sacred and majestic race should practice singing and piping here? Did he send them so that they would swell up their cheeks in blowing the flute? Or, that they would take the lead in singing impure songs and raising the loud clamor of the castanets? *Arnobius (c. 305, E), 6.450.*

SEE ALSO DANCING; ENTERTAINMENT; HYMNS; ORGAN.

MYSTERIES, CHRISTIAN

SEE SACRAMENTS.

MYSTERY RELIGIONS

The mystery religions were ancient cults that featured secret rites by which persons were initiated into the cult. They began in Greece but spread throughout the entire ancient world, adapting themselves to various foreign deities. Among the better-known mysteries were those of Dionysus, Isis, Serapis, Attis, and Mithras, along with the Eleusinian mysteries.

The initiatory rites of the Thracians—mysteries of deceit, are hallowed and celebrated in their hymns. *Clement of Alexandria (c. 195, E), 2.171.*

And what if I go over the mysteries? I will not divulge them in mockery, as they say Alcibiades did. Rather, I will accurately expose by the word of truth the sorcery hidden in them. . . . The bacchanals hold their origin in honor of the frenzied Dionysus, celebrating their sacred frenzy by the eating of raw flesh. They go through the distribution of the parts of butchered victims, crowned with snakes, shrieking out the name of that Eve by whom error came into the world. The symbol of the Bacchic orgies is a consecrated serpent. . . . Demeter and Proserpina have become the heroines of a mystic drama. Their wanderings, seizure, and grief, the Eleusis celebrates by torchlight processions. . . . [Some] say that Melampus the son of Amythaon imported the festivals of Ceres from Egypt into Greece, celebrating her grief in song. I would point to them as the prime authors of evil. They are the parents of ungodly fables and of deadly superstition. The mysteries sowed that seed of evil and ruin in human life. *Clement of Alexandria (c. 195, E), 2.175.*

For the initiated, the "holy night" is the telltale of the rites of licentiousness. The glare of torches reveals vicious indulgences. . . . The fire does not dissemble. Rather, it exposes and punishes what it is requested. Such are the mysteries of the atheists. I call them atheists for good reason. For they do not know the true God, and they pay shameless worship to a boy torn in pieces by the Titans. *Clement of Alexandria (c. 195, E), 2.177.*

In the honor of Pluto and Dionysus, they give themselves up to frenzy. In my opinion, they do not participate in the bacchanal for the sake of intoxication as much as for the sake of the shameless ceremonial practiced. *Clement of Alexandria (c. 195, E), 2.181.*

The Samothracian and Eleusinian mysteries make no disclosures. . . . It is a universal custom in religious initiations to keep out the profane and to beware of witnesses. *Tertullian (c. 197, W), 3.23.*

In the case of those Eleusinian mysteries—which are the very heresy of Athenian superstition—it is their secrecy that is their disgrace. Accordingly, they previously beset all access to their body with tormenting conditions. And they require a long initiation before they enroll. For their perfect disciples, they require instruction for five years. *Tertullian (c. 200, W), 3.503.*

This, he says, is what they affirm who have been initiated in the mysteries of the Eleusinians. It is, however, a regulation of law, that those who have been admitted into the lesser mysteries should again be initiated into the Great Mysteries. *Hippolytus (c. 225, W), 5.55*

The sacred rites of the Eleusinian Ceres are not unlike those [of Isis]. For just as in those (where the boy Osiris is sought with the wailing of his mother), so likewise in these, Proserpine is carried away to contract an incestuous marriage with her uncle. . . . Her sacred rites are celebrated with the throwing of torches. *Lactantius (c. 304–313, W), 7.35.*

We will pass by the wild Bacchanalia also. . . . Those secret mysteries of the Cyprian Venus we will also pass by. . . . It was our purpose to

also leave unnoticed those mysteries into which Phrygia is initiated and all that race. *Arnobius (c. 305, E), 6.496, 497; extended discussion: 6.496–6.498.*

SEE ALSO GODS, PAGAN; MITHRAS; WORSHIP, PAGAN.

MYSTICISM, CHRISTIAN

As used here, mysticism refers to experiencing God in depth through contemplation and through a deep love relationship that transcends human reason. In the pre-Nicene church, this type of mysticism is seen primarily in the writings of Origen. The following passages illustrate some of the mystical expressions found in the pre-Nicene Christian writings:

It becomes us now to seek for what we once had, but have lost. It becomes us to unite the soul with the Holy Spirit, and to strive after union with God. *Tatian (c. 160, E), 2.71.*

When the sun is shining, the moon and the stars lose their power of giving light. Likewise, those who are radiant in Christ Himself and receive His beams have no need of the ministering apostles and prophets, nor of the angels. We must have courage to declare this truth. . . . To those who do not receive the solar beams of Christ, the ministering saints afford an illumination much less than the former. *Origen (c. 228, E), 9.311.*

Among those who are under a king, there are differences. Some experience his rule in a more mystic, hidden, and divine way. However, others experience it in a less perfect fashion. Some are led by reason, apart from all agencies of sense. They have beheld incorporeal things (the things that Paul speaks of as "invisible" and "not seen"). Such ones are ruled by the leading nature of the Only-Begotten. *Origen (c. 228, E), 9.314.*

He came not to bring peace on the earth . . . but a sword to cut through . . . the disastrous friendship of soul and body, so that the soul—committing herself to the spirit that was against the flesh—may enter into friendship with God. *Origen (c. 228, E), 9.316.*

MYTHOLOGY, GREEK
SEE GODS, PAGAN; POETS, PAGAN.

NATIVITY OF JESUS

SEE BIRTH OF JESUS.

NATURAL LAW

SEE LAW, NATURAL.

NAZARENE

And he came and dwelt in a city called Nazareth, that it might be fulfilled which was spoken by the prophets, "He shall be called a Nazarene." Matt. 2:23.

The Christ of the Creator had to be called a Nazarene according to prophecy. On that very account, the Jews also designate us as "Nazarenes," after Him. For we are they of whom it is written, "Her Nazarites were whiter than snow." *Tertullian (c. 207, W), 3.354.*

NERO

Nero (A.D. 37–68) was the first Roman emperor to persecute Christians. Peter and Paul were evidently martyred during his reign.

The teaching of the apostles, encompassing the ministry of Paul, ended with Nero. *Clement of Alexandria (c. 195, E), 2.555.*

Nero was the first who attacked the Christian sect with the imperial sword. *Tertullian (c. 195, W), 3.22.*

Under Nero, Christianity was ruthlessly condemned. You may weigh its worth and nature even from the character of its persecutor. If that ruler was a godly man, then the Christians are ungodly. . . . If he was not a public enemy, we are enemies of our country. . . . Now, although every other practice that existed under Nero has been destroyed, yet this of ours [i.e., persecution of Christians] has firmly remained. *Tertullian (c. 197, W), 3.114.*

At Rome, Nero was the first [Emperor] who stained the rising faith with blood. *Tertullian (c. 213, W), 3.648.*

"And the beast that you saw is of the seven." Nero reigned before those kings. . . . Now [in saying] that one of the heads was, as it were, slain to death, . . . he speaks of Nero. *Victorinus (c. 280, W), 7.358.*

When Nero reigned, the apostle Peter came to Rome . . . and, by turning many to the true religion, he built up a faithful and steadfast temple unto the Lord. When Nero heard of those things, and observed that, not only in Rome, but in every other place, a great multitude turned daily from the worship of idols, . . . he sprang forward to decimate the heavenly temple and to destroy the true faith. For he was an abominable and evil tyrant. It was he who first persecuted the servants of God. He crucified Peter and slew Paul. Yet, he did not escape with impunity. For God looked on the affliction of His people. Therefore, this tyrant, bereaved of authority and thrown headlong from the height of empire, suddenly disappeared. Even the burial place of that noxious wild beast was nowhere to be seen. This has led some persons of extravagant imagination to suppose that—having been transported to a distant region—he is still reserved alive. To him, they apply the Sibylline verses concerning "the fugitive, who slew his own mother, who is to come from the uttermost boundaries of the earth." They believe that he who was the first persecutor should also be the last persecutor. They also believe that he will prove to be the forerunner of the Antichrist. But we should not believe those persons . . . who imagine that Nero is to appear hereafter as the forerunner of the devil, when he will come to lay waste the earth and overthrow mankind. *Lactantius (c. 320, W), 7.302.*

NEW BIRTH

Jesus answered and said to him, "Most assuredly, I say to you, unless one is born again, he cannot see the kingdom of God. . . . Most assuredly, I say to you, unless one is born of water and the Spirit, he cannot enter the kingdom of God." John 3:3, 5.

Do not lie to one another, since you have put off the old man with his deeds, and have put on the new man who is renewed in knowledge according to the image of Him who created him. Col. 3:9.

Everyone who loves is born of God and knows God. 1 John 4:7.

Having renewed us by the remission of our sins, He has made us after another pattern, that we should possess the souls of children, inasmuch as He has created us anew by His Spirit. *Barnabas (c. 70–130, E), 1.140.*

Having received the forgiveness of sins, and having placed our trust in the name of the Lord, we have become new creatures, formed again from the beginning. . . . He, then, who wishes to be saved, looks not to man, but to Him who dwells in him. *Barnabas (c. 70–130, E), 1.147.*

At our birth, we were born without our own knowledge or choice, but by our parents coming together. . . . In order that we may not remain the children of necessity and of ignorance, but may become the children of choice and knowledge, and may obtain in the water the remission of sins formerly committed, there is pronounced over him who chooses to be born again, and has repented of his sins, the name of God the Father and Lord of the universe . . . and the name of Jesus Christ . . . and the name of the Holy Spirit. *Justin Martyr (c. 160, E), 1.183.*

He himself formed man of the dust, regenerated him by water, made him grow by his Spirit, and trained him by His word to adoption and salvation, directing him by sacred commandments. This is in order that, transforming earth-born man into a holy and heavenly being by His advent, He might fulfill to the utmost that divine utterance, "Let Us make man in Our own image and likeness." *Clement of Alexandria (c. 195, E), 2.234.*

He says, "Everyone who does righteousness is born of God"—being regenerated, that is, according to faith. *Clement of Alexandria (c. 195, E), 2.576.*

"Unless a man is born of water and of the Spirit, he cannot enter into the kingdom of God." In other words, he cannot be holy. Every soul, then, by reason of its birth, has its nature in Adam until it is born again in Christ. Moreover, it is unclean all the while that it remains without this regeneration. And because it is unclean, it is actively sinful. *Tertullian (c. 210, W), 3.220.*

When the soul embraces the faith, being renewed in its second birth by water and the power from above, then the veil of its former corruption is taken away. And it sees the light in all its brightness. It is also taken up by the Holy Spirit. This is in contrast to its first birth, when it is embraced by the unholy spirit. The flesh follows the soul, which is now wedded to the Spirit, as a part of the bridal portion. The flesh is no longer the servant of the soul, but of the Spirit. *Tertullian (c. 210, W), 3.221.*

Hoodwinking multitudes, [Marcus, the heretic] misled many of this description who had become his disciples. He taught them that they were prone, no doubt, to sin, but that they were beyond the reach of danger because they belonged to the perfect power. . . . After baptism, these heretics promise another [rebirth], which they call Redemption. And by this, they wickedly subvert those who remain with them in expectation of redemption. As if persons, after they had once been baptized, could again obtain remission! *Hippolytus (c. 225, W), 5.92.*

Christ is the God above all, and He has arranged to wash away sin from human beings, regenerating the old man. *Hippolytus (c. 225, W), 5.153.*

Christ is called the Resurrection. For He causes those who sincerely attach themselves to Him to put away their deadness and rise again and put on newness of life. *Origen (c. 228, E), 9.319.*

The Logos, who cleanses the soul, must first have been in the soul. It is after Him and the cleansing that proceeds from Him that the pure life comes to everyone who has made himself a fit dwelling for the Logos, considered as God. Now, all that is dead or weak in the soul has been taken away. *Origen (c. 228, E), 9.334.*

The world is crucified to them. When they see the consummation of this world to be at hand (as far as their effort is concerned), then Jesus will no longer be *with* them. Rather, He will be *in* them, and they will say, "It is no longer I who live, but Christ who lives in me." *Origen (c. 228, E), 9.386.*

I used to regard it as a difficult matter (and especially difficult because of my character at that time) that a man could be capable of being born again. Yet, this was a truth that the divine mercy had announced for my salvation. I thought it difficult that a man quickened to a new life in the bath of saving water would be able to put off what he had previously been. That is, although retaining all his bodily structure, he himself could be changed in heart and soul. I said, "How is such a conversion possible, that there could be a sudden and rapid divestment of all [our corrupt habits]?" ... I used to indulge my sins as if they were actually parts of me and native to me. But after that, by the help of the water of new birth, the stain of former years had been washed away, and a light from above—serene and pure—had been infused into my reconciled heart. Then, by the agency of the Spirit breathed from heaven, a second birth had restored me to a new man. ... I was enabled to acknowledge that what had been previously living in the practice of sins (being born of the flesh) was of the earth and was earthly. But now it had begun to be of God and was enlivened by the Spirit of holiness. *Cyprian (c. 250, W), 5.275, 276.*

The new man is born again and restored to his God by His grace. *Cyprian (c. 250, W), 5.449.*

That which he makes us by a second birth, He wishes us to continue when we are newly born. So that we, who have begun to be sons of God, may abide in God's peace. *Cyprian (c. 250, W), 5.454.*

SEE ALSO BAPTISM; CONVERSION (II. TESTIMONIES OF CONVERSION); MAN, DOCTRINE OF; SALVATION.

NEW COVENANT

Behold, the days are coming, says the Lord, when I will make a new covenant with the house of Israel and with the house of Judah. Jer. 31:31.

... Jesus the Mediator of the new covenant. Heb. 12:24.

God promised that there would be another covenant, not like that old one. *Justin Martyr (c. 160, E), 1.232.*

"Now, as concerning virgins, I have no commandment from the Lord. Yet, I give my judgment as one who has obtained mercy of the Lord to be faithful." But further, in another place, he says: "That Satan tempt you not for your incontinence." Therefore, even in the New Testament, the apostles are found granting certain precepts in consideration of human infirmity. They did this because of the incontinence of some, lest such persons, having grown hardhearted, and despairing altogether of their salvation, might become apostates from God. Therefore, it should not be wondered at that also in the Old Covenant the same God permitted similar indulgences for the benefit of His people. *Irenaeus (c. 180, E/W), 1.480.*

These things, therefore, which were given for bondage, and for a sign to them, He cancelled by the new covenant of liberty. But He has increased and widened those laws which are natural, noble, and common to all. He has granted to men largely and without grudging, by means of adoption, to know God the Father, and to love Him with the whole heart. They are to follow His word unswervingly, while they abstain not only from evil deeds, but even from the desire for such deeds. But He has also increased the feeling of reverence. For sons should have more veneration than slaves, and greater love for their father. *Irenaeus (c. 180, E/W), 1.482.*

SEE ALSO ISRAEL OF GOD; LAW, MOSAIC; SALVATION.

NEW JERUSALEM

SEE JERUSALEM (II. JERUSALEM IN PROPHECY).

NEW TESTAMENT

Originally, Christians used the term "new testament" to refer to the new covenant. They referred to the Christian Scriptures as the "memoirs of the apostles," "the Gospels and Epistles," or some other designation. It was not until the third century that the term "New Testament" became common as a designation for the Christian Scriptures.

The words are recorded in the memoirs of His apostles. *Justin Martyr (c. 160, E), 1.249.*

This is recorded in the memoirs of the apostles. ... For in the memoirs which I say were drawn up by His apostles and those who followed them, [it is recorded] that His sweat fell down like drops of blood. *Justin Martyr (c. 160, E), 1.251.*

About to be offered up and giving himself a ransom, he left for us a new testament: My love I give unto you. And what and how great is it? For each of us, He gave His life—the equivalent for all. *Clement of Alexandria (c. 195, E), 2.601.*

One of these men was the initiator of the Old Testament [i.e., old covenant]; the other will be the consummator of the New. *Tertullian (c. 207, W), 3.383.*

We have it on the true tradition of the church that this epistle was sent to the Ephesians, not to the Laodiceans. *Tertullian (c. 207, W), 3.464, 465.*

In addition, for the proof of our statements, we take testimonies from that which is called the Old Testament and that which is called the New—which we believe to be divine writings. *Origen (c. 225, E), 4.349.*

One . . . should take his stand against historical fictions and oppose them with the true and lofty evangelical message in which the agreement of the doctrines found in both the so-called Old Testament and in the so-called New appears so clearly and completely. *Origen (c. 228, E), 9.348.*

"Unless the testator has died, a testament cannot be confirmed." . . . In other words, unless Christ had undergone death, the testament could not have been opened. That is, the mystery of God could not have been unveiled and understood. But all Scripture is divided into two Testaments. That which preceded the coming and passion of Christ (that is, the Law and the Prophets) is called the Old. But those things that were written after His resurrection are called the New Testament. The Jews make use of the Old, we of the New. However, they are not conflicting. For the New is the fulfilling of the Old. And in both there is the same testator, Christ. *Lactantius (c. 304–313, W), 7.122.*

SEE ALSO CANON, NEW TESTAMENT; GOSPELS; OLD TESTAMENT; PSEUDEPIGRAPHA, NEW TESTAMENT; SCRIPTURES; TESTAMENT.

NEW WINE

Nor do people put new wine into old wineskins, or else the wineskins break. Matt. 9:17.

The new wine that is put into new bottles is the faith that is in Christ, by which He has proclaimed the way of righteousness. *Irenaeus (c. 180, E/W), 1.511.*

NICOLAITANS

And they chose Stephen, a man full of faith and the Holy Spirit, and Philip, Prochorus, Nicanor, Timon, Parmenas, and Nicolas, a proselyte from Antioch. Acts 6:5.

But this you have, that you hate the deeds of the Nicolaitans, which I also hate. Rev. 2:6.

You also have those who hold the doctrine of the Nicolaitans, which thing I hate. Rev. 2:15.

Nevertheless I have a few things against you, because you allow that woman Jezebel, who calls herself a prophetess, to teach and seduce My servants to commit sexual immorality and eat things sacrificed to idols. Rev. 2:20.

The Nicolaitans are the followers of that Nicholas who was one of the seven first ordained to the diaconate by the apostles. The Nicolaitans lead lives of unrestrained indulgence. The character of these persons is very plainly pointed out in the Apocalypse of John. It shows that they teach that it is a matter of indifference to practice adultery and to eat things sacrificed to idols. *Irenaeus (c. 180, E/W), 1.352.*

John, the disciple of the Lord, preached this faith. And he sought, through the proclamation of the Gospel, to remove that error that had been disseminated among men by Cerinthus, and a long time previously by those called Nicolaitans. They are an offshoot of that "falsely called knowledge." *Irenaeus (c. 180, E/W), 1.426.*

Those who say that they follow Nicholas quote an adage of that man—"the flesh must be abused"—which they pervert. But that worthy man [Nicholas] actually meant that it was necessary to curtail pleasures and lusts. *Clement of Alexandria (c. 195, E), 2.373.*

John, however, in the Apocalypse is instructed to chastise those persons "who eat things sacrificed to idols" and "who commit fornication." There are even now another sort of Nicolaitans. *Tertullian (c. 197, W), 3.259.*

I do not aim at destroying the happiness of sanctity, as do certain Nicolaitans in their maintenance of lust and luxury. *Tertullian (c. 207, W), 3.294.*

Nicolas has been a cause of the widespread combination of these wicked men. He was appointed by the apostles as one of the seven for the diaconate. However, he departed from correct doctrine and was in the habit of inculcating indifference as to both life and food. And when his disciples continued to insult the Holy Spirit, John reproved them in the Apocalypse as being fornicators and partakers of food offered to idols. *Hippolytus (c. 225, W), 5.115.*

SEE ALSO HERESIES, HERETICS; MEAT SACRIFICED TO IDOLS; REVELATION, BOOK OF.

NOAH

What relates to Noah, who is called by some Deucalion, has been explained by us. *Theophilus (c. 180, E), 2.107.*

Noah not only preceded Bacchus, but also Saturn and Uranus, by many generations. . . . The descendants of Noah were called Hebrews, among whom the religion of the true God was established. . . . Those persons err, therefore, who maintain that the worship of the gods existed from the beginning of the world and that paganism was prior to the religion of God. *Lactantius (c. 304–313, W), 7.63.*

SEE ALSO ARK, NOAH'S; FLOOD, THE.

NONRESISTANCE

You have heard that it was said, "An eye for an eye and a tooth for a tooth." But I tell you not to resist an evil person. But whoever slaps you on your right cheek, turn the other to him also. If anyone wants to sue you and take away your tunic, let him have your cloak also. And whoever compels you to go one mile, go with him two. Matt. 5:38–41.

Beloved, do not avenge yourselves, but rather give place to wrath; for it is written, "Vengeance is Mine, I will repay," says the Lord. . . . Do not be overcome by evil, but overcome evil with good. Rom. 12:19, 21.

They comfort their oppressors and make them their friends. They do good to their enemies. *Aristides (c. 125, E), 9.276.*

We will not ask you to punish our accusers. Their present wickedness is sufficient punishment. *Justin Martyr (c. 160, E), 1.165.*

We have learned not to return blow for blow, nor to go to law with those who plunder and rob us. Not only that, but to those who strike us on one side of the face, we have learned to offer the other side also. *Athenagoras (c. 175, E), 2.129.*

He commanded [His followers] . . . not only not to strike others, but even, when they themselves are struck, to present the other cheek. . . . [He commanded them] not only not to injure their neighbors, nor to do them any evil, but also, when they are dealt with wickedly, to be long-suffering. *Irenaeus (c. 180, E/W), 1.408.*

The philosophers will then with propriety be taken up in a friendly exposure, . . . but not in the manner of avenging ourselves on our detractors. Rather, it will be for the purpose of their conversion. For vengeance is far from being the case with those persons who have learned to bless those who curse. *Clement of Alexandria (c. 195, E), 2.347.*

The spiritual man never cherishes resentment or harbors a grudge against anyone—even though deserving of hatred for his conduct. *Clement of Alexandria (c. 195, E), 2.540.*

Paul does not merely describe the spiritual man as being characterized by suffering wrong, rather than doing wrong. Rather, Paul teaches that a Christian does not keep count of injuries. For Paul does not allow him even to pray against the man who has done wrong to him. For he knows that the Lord expressly commanded us to pray for our enemies. *Clement of Alexandria (c. 195, E), 2.548.*

Christians are not allowed to use violence to correct the delinquencies of sins. *Clement of Alexandria (c. 195, E), 2.581.*

Hippias [a pagan] is put to death for laying plots against the state. No Christian ever attempted such a thing on behalf of his brethren, even when persecution was scattering them abroad with every atrocity. *Tertullian (c. 195, W), 3.51.*

If dragged to trial, he does not resist. *Tertullian (c. 197, W), 3.110.*

The practice of the old law was to avenge itself by the vengeance of the sword. It was to pluck out "eye for eye," and to inflict retaliatory revenge for injury. However, the practice of the new law points to clemency. *Tertullian (c. 197, W), 3.154.*

Men of old were used to requiring "eye for eye, and tooth for tooth" and to repay evil for evil, with usury! . . . But after Christ has supervened and has united the grace of faith with patience, now it is no longer lawful to attack others even with words, nor to merely say "fool," without danger of the judgment. . . . Christ says, "Love your enemies and bless your cursers, and pray for your persecutors." *Tertullian (c. 200, W), 3.711.*

If someone attempts to provoke you by physical violence, the admonition of the Lord is at hand. He says, "To him who strikes you on the face, turn the other cheek also." Let outrageousness be worn out by your patience. Whatever that blow may be, joined with pain and scorn, it will receive a heavier one from the Lord. *Tertullian (c. 200, W), 3.712.*

For what difference is there between provoker and provoked? The only difference is that the former was the first to do evil, but the latter did evil afterwards. Each one stands condemned in the eyes of the Lord for hurting a man. For God both prohibits and condemns every wickedness. In evil doing, there is no account taken of the order. . . . The commandment is absolute: evil is not to be repaid with evil. *Tertullian (c. 200, W), 3.713.*

Christ plainly teaches a new kind of long-suffering, when He actually prohibits the reprisals that the Creator permitted in requiring "an eye for an eye, and a tooth for a tooth." *Tertullian (c. 207, W), 3.370.*

The Lord will save them in that day—even His people—like sheep. . . . No one gives the name of "sheep" to those who fall in battle with arms in hand, or those who are killed when repelling force with force. Rather, it is given only to those who are slain, yielding themselves up in their own place of duty and with patience—rather than fighting in self-defense. *Tertullian (c. 207, W), 3.415.*

Moreover, the command about the right cheek being struck is most [literally] impossible, since everyone who strikes (unless he happens to have some bodily irregularity) strikes the *left* cheek with his *right* hand. *Origen (c. 225, E), 4.367.*

[Celsus, a pagan critic,] says, "They also have a teaching to this effect: that we should not avenge ourselves on one who injures us." Or, as Christ expresses it: "Whoever will strike you on the one cheek, turn the other to him also." *Origen (c. 248, E), 4.634.*

We revile no one, for we believe that "revilers will not inherit the kingdom of God." And we read, "Bless them that curse you; bless, and curse not." Also, "Being reviled, we bless." *Origen (c. 248, E), 4.654.*

Do not willingly use force and do not return force when it is used against you. *Commodianus (c. 240, W), 4.212.*

When a Christian is arrested, he does not resist. Nor does he avenge himself against your unrighteous violence—even though our people are numerous and plentiful. *Cyprian (c. 250, W), 5.462.*

We may not hate. And we please God more by rendering no return for wrong. Therefore, we exhort you to make satisfaction to God. Do this while you have the power, while there yet remains in you something of life. . . . We do not envy your comforts, nor do we conceal the divine benefits. We repay kindness for your hatred. In return for the torments and penalties that are inflicted on us, we point out to you the ways of salvation. *Cyprian (c. 250, W), 5.465.*

The Christian has departed from rage and carnal contention as if from the hurricanes of the sea. He has already begun to be tranquil and meek in the harbor of Christ. Therefore, he should allow neither anger nor discord within his breath. For he must neither return evil for evil, nor bear hatred. *Cyprian (c. 250, W), 5.488.*

Even our enemies are to be loved. *Cyprian (c. 250, W), 5.546.*

Do no one any injury at any time; provoke no one to anger. If an injury is done to you, look to Jesus Christ. And even as you desire Him to forgive your transgressions, also forgive others theirs. *Theonas of Alexandria (c. 300, E), 6.161.*

Religion is to be defended—not by putting to death—but by dying. Not by cruelty, but by patient endurance. Not by guilt, but by good faith. For the former belongs to evil, but the latter to the good. . . . For if you wish to defend religion by bloodshed, tortures, and guilt, it will no longer be defended. Rather, it will be polluted and profaned. . . . And, therefore, when we suffer such impious things, we do not resist even in word. Rather, we leave vengeance to God. We do not act as those persons who would have it appear that they are defenders of their gods, who rage without restraint against those who do not worship them. *Lactantius (c. 304-313, W), 7.157,158.*

If we all derive our origin from one man whom God created, we are clearly of one blood. Therefore, it must be considered the greatest wickedness to hate a man—even if he is guilty. On this account, God has forbidden us to ever contract enmities. Rather, they are to be eliminated, so that we sooth those who are our enemies by reminding them of their relationship. For, if we are all inspired and quickened by one God, what else are we except brothers? . . . Therefore, they are to be considered as savage beasts who injure man, who—in opposition to every law and right of human nature—plunder, torture, slay, and banish. On account of this relationship of brotherhood, God teaches us never to do evil, but always good. *Lactantius (c. 304–313, W), 7.172, 173.*

When we suffer such ungodly things, we do not resist even in word. Rather, we leave vengeance to God. *Lactantius (c. 304–313, W), 7.158.*

The Christian does injury to no one. He does not desire the property of others. If fact, he does not even defend his own property if it is taken from him by violence. For he knows how to patiently bear an injury inflicted upon him. *Lactantius (c. 304–313, W), 7.160.*

We do not resist those who injure us, for we must yield to them. *Lactantius (c. 304–313, W), 7.182.*

If anyone should be so shameless as to inflict injury on a good and just man, such a man must bear it with calmness and moderation. He will not take upon himself his revenge. Rather, he will reserve it for the judgment of God. He must maintain innocence at all times and in all places. And this commandment is not limited to merely his not [being the first to] inflict injury on another. Rather, he should not even avenge it when injury is inflicted on him. For there sits on the judgment-seat a very great and impartial Judge. *Lactantius (c. 304–313, W), 7.183.*

Why do contests, fights, and contentions arise among men? Is it because impatience against injustice often excites great tempests? However, if you meet injustice with patience, then no virtue can be found more true. . . . In contrast, if injustice . . . has met with impatience on the same level as itself, . . . it will ignite a great fire that no stream can extinguish, but only the shedding of blood. *Lactantius (c. 304–313, W), 7.184.*

In what respect, then, does the wise and good man differ from the evil and foolish one? Is it not that he has unconquerable patience, of which the foolish are destitute? Is it not that he knows how to govern himself and to mitigate his anger—which those are unable to curb because they are without virtue? . . . What if a man gives way to grief and anger and indulges these emotions (which he should struggle against)? What if he rushes wherever injustice will call him? Such a man does not fulfill the duty of virtue. For he who tries to return an injury desires to imitate that very person by whom he has been injured. In short, he who imitates a bad man cannot be good. *Lactantius (c. 304–313, W), 7.184.*

When provoked by injury, if he returns violence to his assailant, he is defeated. *Lactantius (c. 304–313, W), 7.185.*

"An eye for an eye, and a tooth for a tooth." That is the expression of *justice.* However, His injunction that a man who is struck on the one cheek should offer the other also—that is the expression of *goodness.* Now, are justice and goodness opposed to each other? Far from it! Rather, there has only been advancement from simple justice to positive goodness. *Disputation of Archelaus and Manes (c. 320, E), 6.216; see also 3.370–3.372.*

SEE ALSO LAWSUITS; PERSECUTION; SERMON ON THE MOUNT; WAR.

NOVATIAN, NOVATIANISTS

Novatian was a distinguished presbyter in the church at Rome, who eventually started a separate church, marked by its rigorous discipline. The Novatianists believed that the church should not pronounce ecclesiastical forgiveness to repentant Christians who denied Christ during persecution; rather, such forgiveness should only be given by Christ Himself. Unfortunately, all of the quotations in the Ante-Nicene Fathers about the Novatianists are from their opponents, who understandably present a one-sided view.

We discovered . . . that Novatian had been made bishop. Disturbed by the wickedness of an unlawful ordination made in opposition to the catholic church, we considered at once that such persons must be restrained from communion with us. . . . They burst into our solemn assembly with invidious abuse and turbulent clamor, demanding that the accusations (which they said they brought and would prove) should be publicly investigated by us and by the people. However, we said that it was not consistent with our gravity to allow the honor of our colleague [Cornelius] to be called into question any further by the abusive voice of rivals. For he had already been chosen, ordained, and approved by the laudable sentence of many. *Cyprian (c. 250, W), 5.319.*

The Novatianists are striving also to distract the members of Christ into schismatic parties and to cut and tear the one body of the catholic church. . . . They need to acknowledge and understand that when a bishop is once made and approved by the testimony and judgment of his colleagues and the people, another one can by no means be appointed. *Cyprian (c. 250, W), 5.319.*

Maximus, Urbanus, Sidonius, and several brethren who had joined themselves to them, came to the presbyters, desiring with earnest prayers that what had been done before [i.e., joining with Novatian] might fall into oblivion. . . . To quote their very own words, "We know that Cornelius is bishop of the most holy catholic church, elected by Almighty God and by Christ our Lord. We confess our error. . . . Although we seemed, as it were, to have held a kind of communion with a man who was a schismatic and a heretic, yet our mind was always sincere in the church. For we are not ignorant that there is one God, one Christ the Lord (whom we have confessed), and one Holy Spirit. So in the catholic church, there should be only one bishop." *Cyprian (c. 250, W), 5.323.*

You indicated that you did not hold communion with Novatian, but followed my advice and held one common agreement with Cornelius, our co-bishop. *Cyprian (c. 250, W), 5.327.*

[WRITTEN CONCERNING NOVATIAN:] Does he seem to you to be a bishop, who strives by bribery to be made an adulterous and extraneous bishop by the hands of deserters? Particularly, when a bishop has already been made in the church by sixteen co-bishops? *Cyprian (c. 250, W), 5.329.*

Novatian is sending his new apostles through very many cities, so that he can establish some new foundations of his own appointment. Throughout each city and all the provinces, there have already been ordained bishops old in years, sound in faith, proven in trial, and banished in persecution. Yet, Novatian dares to create against these other false bishops. As if he could either wander over the whole world with the persistence of his new endeavor, or else break asunder the structure of the ecclesiastical body by the spread of his own discord. *Cyprian (c. 250, W), 5.333.*

Novatian, you say to our brethren: "Mourn and shed tears, groan day and night, and labor largely and frequently for the washing away and cleansing of your sin. Nevertheless, after all these things, you will die outside the enclosure of the church." . . . This is to shut up and to cut off the way of grief and of repentance! *Cyprian (c. 250, W), 5.335.*

When Novatian sent ambassadors to us into Africa, asking to be received into our communion, he received back word from a council of several priests who were here present that he had excluded himself and could not be received into communion by any of us. *Cyprian (c. 250, W), 5.368.*

The Novatians re-baptize those whom they entice from us. *Cyprian (c. 250, W), 5.380.*

Beloved brethren, do not let the abrupt madness of that treacherous heretic move or disturb us. For he is placed in very great guilt of dissension and schism, and he is separated from the church. . . . Among them, shamelessly, and without any law of ordination, the episcopate is sought after. *Treatise against Novatian (c. 255, W), 5.657, 658.*

Whom will the Lord Christ chiefly deny—if not all of you heretics, schismatics, and strangers to His name? For you were at one time Christians, but you are now Novatianists. *Treatise against Novatian (c. 255, W), 5.659.*

Christ had previously forewarned Peter that he was about to deny Christ. Nevertheless, when he had denied Him, Christ did not deny Peter. Rather, He strengthened him. . . . What sort of folly is yours, Novatian, only to read what tends to the destruction of salvation and to pass by what tends to mercy. . . . You, O Novatian, judge and declare that the lapsed have no hope of peace and mercy. You do not incline your ear to the rebuke of the apostle, when he said, "Who are you, who judges another man's servant? To his own master he stands or falls." *Treatise against Novatian (c. 255, W), 5.659, 661.*

To Novatus [a companion of Novatian], his brother, greeting. It would have been but dutiful to have suffered any kind of ill, so as to avoid rending the church of God. . . . And now, if you can persuade or constrain the brethren to come to be of one mind again, your uprightness will be superior to your error. *Dionysius of Alexandria (c. 262, E), 6.97.*

We rightly reject Novatian, who has divided the church. And he has drawn away some of the brethren to impiety and blasphemies. He has brought into the world a most ungodly doctrine concerning God. And he slanders our most merciful Lord Jesus Christ as though he were unmerciful. And besides all these things, he holds the sacred bath as of no effect and rejects it. He overturns faith and confession, which precede baptism. And he utterly drives away the Holy Spirit from them. *Letter to Dionysius of Alexandria (c. 260, W), 6.103; extended discussion: 5.327–5.335, 5.657–5.663.*

SEE ALSO LAPSED; SCHISM.

NUMEROLOGY

Justin the martyr and philosopher comments with exceeding wisdom on the number six of the sixth day. He declares that the intelligent soul of man and his five susceptible senses were the six works of the sixth day. Having discussed at length the number six, Justin declares that all things that have been framed by God are divided into six classes. *Anastasius, post-Nicene writer, citing Justin Martyr (c. 160, E), 1.302.*

Fittingly, therefore, will his name possess the number six hundred and sixty-six, since the Antichrist sums up in his own person all the mixture of wickedness that took place previous to the deluge, due to the apostasy of the angels. For Noah was six hundred years old when the deluge came upon the earth. . . . Furthermore, that image which was set up by Nebuchadnezzar had indeed a height of sixty cubits, while the breadth was six cubits. . . . Thus, then, the six hundred years of Noah . . . indicate the number of the name of that man in whom is concentrated the whole apostasy of six thousand years. *Irenaeus (c. 180, E/W), 1.558.*

Ten is recognized as being the perfect number. *Clement of Alexandria (c. 195, E), 2.499.*

That ten is a sacred number, it is unnecessary to say now. *Clement of Alexandria (c. 195, E), 2.511.*

The whole world of creatures born alive, as well as things that grow, revolves in sevens. Likewise, the first-born princes of the angels, who have the greatest power, are seven. *Clement of Alexandria (c. 195, E), 2.513.*

A full-term and regular birth takes place, as a general rule, at the beginning of the tenth month. . . . For my own part, I prefer viewing this measure of time in reference to God, as if implying that the ten months rather initiated man into the ten commandments. For the numerical estimate of the time needed to consummate our natural birth corresponds to the numerical classification of the rules of our regenerate life. But inasmuch as birth can also take place at the seventh month, I more readily recognize in this number . . . the honor of a numerical agreement with the sabbatical period. *Tertullian (c. 210, W), 3.218.*

The first seven days in the divine arrangement contain seven thousand years. Likewise, there are seven spirits and seven angels that stand and go in and out before the face of God. And there is the seven-branched lamp in the tabernacle of witness, and there are the seven golden candlesticks in the Apocalypse. . . . And the apostle Paul, who refers to this lawful and certain number, wrote to the seven churches. Likewise, in the Apocalypse, the Lord directed his divine and heavenly commandments to the seven churches and their angels. *Cyprian (c. 250, W), 5.503.*

Now is manifested the reason of the truth why the fourth day is called Tetras. . . . Look, there are four living creatures before God's throne, four Gospels, four rivers flowing in Paradise. *Victorinus (c. 280, W), 7.341.*

Behold the seven horns of the Lamb, the seven eyes of God, . . . seven golden candlesticks, seven young sheep, the seven women in Isaiah, the seven churches in Paul, seven deacons, seven angels, seven trumpets, and seven seals to the book. *Victorinus (c. 280, W), 7.342.*

The day . . . is divided into two parts by the number twelve—by the twelve hours of day and night. . . . No doubt, there have been appointed twelve angels of the day and twelve angels of the night, in accordance with the number of hours. For these are the twenty-four elders of the days and nights that sit before the throne of God, having golden crowns on their heads. *Victorinus (c. 280, W), 7.343.*

Indeed, that he himself [i.e., Paul] also might maintain the type of seven churches, he did not exceed that number. Rather, he wrote to the Romans, the Corinthians, the Galatians, the Ephesians, the Thessalonians, the Philippians, and the Colossians. Afterwards, he wrote to individual persons, so as not to exceed the number of seven churches. *Victorinus (c. 280, W), 7.345.*

One thousand is a full and perfect number, and it is a symbol of the Father Himself—who made the universe by Himself and rules all things for Himself. The number, two hundred, represents two perfect numbers united together, and it is the symbol of the Holy Spirit. For He is the Author of our knowledge of the Son and the Father. But sixty is composed of the number six multiplied by ten, and it is a symbol of Christ. *Methodius (c. 290, E), 6.339; see also 2.499–2.502, 2.513; extended discussion: 7.341–7.343.*

SEE ALSO CHRONOLOGY; MARK OF THE BEAST; REVELATION, BOOK OF.

NUNS
SEE VIRGINS; WIDOWS, ORDER OF.

144, 000

SEE REVELATION, BOOK OF.

OATHS

You have heard that it was said to those of old, "You shall not swear falsely, but shall perform your oaths to the Lord." But I say to you, do not swear at all.... But let your "Yes" be "Yes," and your "No," "No." For whatever is more than these is from the evil one. Matt. 5:33, 34, 37.

But above all, my brethren, do not swear, either by heaven or by earth or with any other oath. But let your "Yes" be "Yes," and your "No," "No," lest you fall into judgment. Jas. 5:12.

And with regard to our not swearing at all, and always speaking the truth, He commanded as follows: "Swear not at all." *Justin Martyr (c. 160, E), 1.168.*

He commanded them not only not to swear falsely, but not even to swear at all. *Irenaeus (c. 180, E/W), 1.408.*

Above all, let an oath on account of what is sold be far from you. And let swearing on account of other things be banished. *Clement of Alexandria (c. 195, E), 2.290.*

[The saying] "Let your yes mean yes, and your no, no" may be compared to the following saying: "To admit a falsehood and to deny a truth, is in no way lawful." Also, the saying in the tenth book of the *Laws* [of Plato] agrees with the prohibition against swearing. *Clement of Alexandria (c. 195, E), 2.468.*

The man of proven character in such piety is far from being apt to lie and to swear. For an oath is a decisive affirmation, with the taking of the divine name. For how can he, who is once faithful, show himself unfaithful so as to require an oath.... But he does not even swear, preferring to make averment in affirmation by

"yes" and in denial by "no." For it is an oath to swear, or to produce anything from the mind in the way of confirmation in the form of an oath. It suffices, then, with him, to add to an affirmation or denial the expression, "I speak truthfully." ... The man of God swears truly, but he is not apt to swear. He rarely has recourse to an oath, just as we have said. And his speaking truth on oath arises from his accord with the truth. This speaking truth on oath, then, is found to be the result of correctness in duties. To him who lives in accordance with the extreme of truth, where, then, is the necessity for an oath? He, then, who does not even swear will be far from perjuring himself.... So he does not lie, nor does he do anything contrary to his agreements. And so he does not swear even when asked for his oath. *Clement of Alexandria (c. 195, E), 2.537.*

John pledged and assured him on oath that he would find forgiveness for himself from the Savior. *Clement of Alexandria (c. 195, E), 2.603.*

More than this, although we decline to swear by the genii of the Caesars, we swear by their safety.... To what God has willed, we desire all safety, and we count an oath by it a great oath. *Tertullian (c. 195, W), 3.43.*

Of perjury I am silent, since even swearing is not lawful. *Tertullian (c. 200, W), 3.67.*

Let us suppose that it is possible for anyone to succeed in functioning under the mere *name* of a public office, in whatever office. Let us suppose that he neither sacrifices nor lends his authority to sacrifices.... Suppose he makes no proclamations or edicts for any [pagan] festivals. Suppose he does not even take oaths. *Tertullian (c. 211, W), 3.72.*

In borrowing money from pagans under pledged securities, some Christians give a guarantee under oath. However, they deny to themselves to have done so.... However, Christ prescribes that there is to be no swearing. *Tertullian (c. 200, W), 3.75.*

There are commandments contained in the Gospel that allow no doubt whether they are to be observed according to the letter or not.... [For example,] "But I say unto you, Swear not at all." *Origen (c. 225, E), 4.368.*

They would swear not only rashly, but even worse, would swear *falsely!* *Cyprian (c. 250, W), 5.438.*

You are compelled to swear, which is not lawful. *Cyprian (c. 250, W), 5.470.*

We must not swear.... Of this same matter, according to Matthew: ... "I say unto you, 'Swear not at all.'" *Cyprian (c. 250, W), 5.536.*

Avoid swearing falsely, swearing often, and swearing in vain. *Apostolic Constitutions (compiled c. 390, E), 7.413.*

SEE ALSO SERMON ON THE MOUNT.

OBEDIENCE, ROLE IN SALVATION

SEE SALVATION (III. ROLE OF OBEDIENCE IN SALVATION).

OCCULT

SEE SPIRITISM.

OFFICE, PUBLIC

SEE PUBLIC OFFICE.

OFFICERS, CHURCH

SEE CHURCH GOVERNMENT.

OIL, ANOINTING WITH

Is anyone among you sick? Let him call for the elders of the church, and let them pray over him, anointing him with oil in the name of the Lord. Jas. 5:14.

We are called Christians for this reason: because we are anointed with the oil of God. *Theophilus (c. 180, E), 2.92.*

When we have come out of the [baptismal] font, we are thoroughly anointed with a blessed oil. ... The oils runs over the *body*, but it profits us *spiritually*. *Tertullian (c. 198, W), 3.672.*

"She said to her maids, 'Bring me oil.'" ... And what was the oil, but the power of the

Holy Spirit—with which believers are anointed as with ointment after the laver of washing. *Hippolytus (c. 205, W), 5.192.*

It is also necessary that he who is baptized should be anointed. This is so that, having received the chrism, that is, the anointing, he may be anointed of God and have the grace of Christ in him. Furthermore, the Eucharist is the place where the baptized are anointed with the oil sanctified on the altar. For he who has neither an altar nor a church cannot sanctify the oil. Therefore, there can be no spiritual anointing among heretics. *Cyprian (c. 250, W), 5.376.*

How dare any man speak against his bishop, by whom the Lord gave the Holy Spirit among you, upon the laying on of his hands.... By the bishop, you were sealed with the oil of gladness and the ointment of understanding. *Apostolic Constitutions (compiled c. 390, E), 7.412.*

You, O bishop, ... will anoint the head of those who are to be baptized—whether they are men or women—with the holy oil, as a representation of the spiritual baptism. *Apostolic Constitutions (compiled c. 390, E), 7.431.*

You should anoint the person beforehand with the holy oil and then baptize him with the water. Finally, you should seal him with the ointment. This is so that the anointing with oil may be the participation of the Holy Spirit, the water may be the symbol of death, and the ointment may be the seal of the covenants. *Apostolic Constitutions (compiled c. 390, E), 7.469.*

SEE ALSO BAPTISM (II. MODE AND DESCRIPTION OF BAPTISM); HANDS, LAYING ON OF.

OLD TESTAMENT

Originally, Christians used the term "old testament" to refer to the old covenant. They usually referred to the Jewish Scriptures as "the Law and the Prophets" or simply "the Scriptures." It was not until the third century that the term "Old Testament" became a common designation for the Scriptures written before Christ.

The Scriptures had perished in the captivity of Nebuchadnezzar. Therefore, Ezra, the Levite and priest, in the time of Artaxerxes (king of the Persians), became inspired in the exercise of prophecy. Therefore, he restored again the whole of the ancient Scriptures. *Clement of Alexandria (c. 195, E), 2.334.*

[The church] unites the Law and the Prophets in one volume with the writings of evangelists and apostles, from which she drinks in her faith. *Tertullian (c. 197, W), 3.260.*

You have the third book of the Kings. If you also turn to the fourth book, you will discover all this conduct of Christ pursued by that man of God who ordered ten barley loaves. *Tertullian (c. 207, W), 3.381.*

One of these men was the initiator of the Old Testament [i.e., old covenant]; the other will be the consummator of the New. *Tertullian (c. 207, W), 3.383.*

In addition, for the proof of our statements, we take testimonies from that which is called the Old Testament and that which is called the New—which we believe to be divine writings. *Origen (c. 225, E), 4.349.*

One . . . should take his stand against historical fictions and oppose them with the true and lofty evangelical message in which the agreement of the doctrines found in both the so-called Old Testament and in the so-called New appears so clearly and completely. *Origen (c. 228, E), 9.348.*

The announcement of the New Testament gains no faith unless it has the prophetical testimonies of the Old Testament, by which it is lifted from the earth and flies. *Victorinus (c. 280, W), 7.349.*

The Book of Job is by Moses. *Methodius (c. 290, E), 6.381, as quoted by Photius.*

All Scripture is divided into two Testaments. That which preceded the coming and passion of Christ (that is, the Law and the Prophets) is called the Old. *Lactantius (c. 304–313, W), 7.122.*

SEE ALSO CANON, OLD TESTAMENT; DEUTEROCANONICAL BOOKS; LAW, MOSAIC; NEW TESTAMENT; PENTATEUCH; PSALMS; SCRIPTURES; SEPTUAGINT; TESTAMENT.

OLYMPICS

The Olympian games are nothing more than the funeral sacrifices of Pelops. . . . So apparently the mysteries were games held in honor of the dead. *Clement of Alexandria (c. 195, E), 2.180.*

The games are called Olympian in honor of Jupiter. *Tertullian (c. 197, W), 3.84.*

It has now become clear in Africa, too, as to what enthusiasm the world celebrates those games: the combative festivals and superstitious contests of the Greeks. They involve both forms of worship and of pleasure. . . . By the world, it has been believed to be a most proper mode of testing proficiency in studies. *Tertullian (c. 213, W), 3.638.*

If the following persons come [to be baptized], whether they are men or women, let them leave off their employments, or else be rejected: someone belonging to the theater, a charioteer, . . . Olympic gamester, or one who plays at those games on the pipe, lute, or harp. *Apostolic Constitutions (compiled c. 390, E), 7.495.*

OMNIPRESENCE OF GOD

SEE GOD, ATTRIBUTES OF.

OMNISCIENCE OF GOD

SEE GOD, ATTRIBUTES OF.

ONE HUNDRED AND FORTY-FOUR THOUSAND

SEE REVELATION, BOOK OF.

ONESIPHORUS

The Lord grant mercy to the household of Onesiphorus, for he often refreshed me, and was not ashamed of my chains. The Lord grant to him that he may find mercy from the Lord in that Day. 2 Tim. 1:16, 18.

Concerning Onesiphorus, he also writes to Timothy: "The Lord grant unto him that he may find mercy on that Day." *Tertullian (c. 210, W), 3.562.*

And how can [Paul] bless those whom he praises as having done well? For he blesses the house of Onesiphorus in these words: "The Lord give mercy to the house of Onesiphorus. For he often refreshed me and was not ashamed of my chains. But, when he was in Rome, he sought me out very diligently, and found me. The Lord grant to him that he may find mercy of the Lord in that Day." *Origen (c. 225, E), 4.324, 325.*

SEE ALSO PRAYER (VI. SHOULD CHRISTIANS PRAY FOR THE DEAD?).

ONLY BEGOTTEN

SEE CHRIST, DIVINITY OF (II. BEGETTING OF THE SON).

OPHITES

The Ophites were a Gnostic sect that regarded the serpent in the garden of Eden as a friend of man, trying to help mankind escape from the domination of the oppressive Creator.

The Ophites declare that, on [Adam and Eve] thus eating [of the fruit], they obtained the knowledge of that Power who is above all, and that they departed from those who had created them.... Ialdabaoth, however, ... not paying any regard to these things, cast Adam and Eve out of Paradise, for they had transgressed his commandment. For he had a desire to beget sons by Eve. *Irenaeus (c. 180, E/W), 1.356.*

Although certain other heresies have been identified—such as the Cainites, Ophites, Noachites, and others of these types—I have not considered it necessary to explain the things taught or done by these heresies. Otherwise, on account of this work, they might consider themselves somebody. *Hippolytus (c. 225, W), 5.124.*

[Celsus, a pagan] next returns to the subject of the seven ruling demons. However, their names are not found among Christians. Rather, I think they are accepted by the Ophites. *Origen (c. 248, E), 4.586.*

To these are also added those heretics who are called Ophites. They magnify the serpent to such a degree, that they prefer him even to Christ Himself. For they say that it was he who gave us the beginning of the knowledge of good and evil. They say that Moses understood his power and majesty and therefore set up the bronze serpent. Whoever gazed upon him obtained health. They also say that in his gospel, Christ Himself imitates the sacred power of Moses' serpent. For He says, "And just as Moses lifted up the serpent in the desert, so it behooves the Son of man to be lifted up." They invoke the serpent to bless their eucharistic elements. *Anonymous work incorrectly attributed to Tertullian, 3.650; extended discussion: 1.354–1.358; extended discussion of the Naassenes, a similar sect: 5.47–5.58.*

SEE ALSO GNOSTICS, GNOSTICISM; HERESIES, HERETICS.

ORACLES, PAGAN

The oracles were the prophets and prophetesses of the Hellenic world. The most famous oracle was that of Apollo at Delphi. In time, the term "oracle" also came to mean the religious shrine where the prophet or prophetess prophesied.

[ADDRESSING PAGAN GREEKS:] This is your own story. When someone inquired at your oracle what religious men had ever lived, you say that the oracle answered in this manner: "Only the Chaldeans have obtained wisdom, along with the Hebrews, who worship God Himself, the self-begotten King." *Justin Martyr (c. 160, E), 1.278.*

[CONCERNING A PAGAN PROPHETESS:] A certain woman by drinking water gets into a frenzy, and loses her sense by the fumes of frankincense, and you [pagans] say that she has the gift of prophecy.... He who makes you fond of money also foretells your getting rich. He who incites to seditions and wars also predicts victory in war. *Tatian (c. 160, E), 2.73.*

[The oracles] who rave at Delphi do not marry. *Tertullian (c. 205, W), 4.42.*

As for all other oracles, ... what else must we declare about them than that they are the diabolical contrivance of those spirits who even at that time dwelled in eminent persons themselves.... They went so far as to counterfeit a divine power under their shape and form, and, with equal persistence in evil, to deceive men. *Tertullian (c. 210, W), 3.225.*

I could quote passages to show that even among the Greeks themselves there were some who utterly discredited the oracles that were recognized and admired throughout the whole of Greece.... There is no necessity to attribute these oracular responses to any divinities. On the other hand, they can be traced to wicked demons.... It is said of the Pythian priestess [i.e., the oracle of Delphi], whose oracle seems to have been the most celebrated, that when she sat down at the mouth of the Castalian cave, the prophetic spirit of Apollo entered her private parts. And when she was filled with that spirit, she gave utterance to responses, which are regarded with awe as divine truths.... If, then, the Pythian priestess is beside herself when she prophesies, what spirit must it be that fills her mind and clouds her judgment with darkness? Must it not be of the same order with those demons that many Christians cast out of persons possessed with them? *Origen (c. 248, E), 4.611, 612.*

Are we not compelled by reason to label as evil such spirits who use the power of prophesying for the purpose of deceiving men, and thus turning them away from God? (Now, prophecy itself is a power that is neither good nor bad). . . . If the Delphian Apollo were really a god, as the Greeks suppose, would he not rather have chosen as his prophet some wise man? . . . How is it that he came not to prefer a man to a woman for the utterance of his prophesies? And if he preferred the latter sex . . . why did he not choose from among women a virgin to interpret his will? But no! The Pythian . . . judged no wise man—in fact, no man at all—worthy of the divine possession. *Origen (c. 248, E), 4.612, 613.*

For this reason, we consider as nothing the oracles of the Pythian priestess, or those delivered at Dodona, Clarus, Branchidae, at the temple of Jupiter Ammon, or by a multitude of other so-called prophets. *Origen (c. 248, E), 4.613.*

It is related of the priestess of Apollo that she at times allowed herself to be influenced in her answers by bribes. However, our prophets were admired for their plain truthfulness. In fact, they were admired, not only by their contemporaries, but also by those who lived in later times. *Origen (c. 248, E), 4.656.*

They think Apollo to be divine above all others, and especially prophetic. . . . When someone asked him who he was, or what God existed at all, he replied in twenty-one verses. Of those verses, this is the beginning: "God is self-produced, untaught, without a mother, unshaken, having a name not even to be comprised in word, and dwelling in fire. This is God. And we His messengers are a slight portion of God." *Lactantius (c. 304–313, W), 7.17.*

[The demons] especially deceive in the case of oracles. However, the pagans cannot distinguish their deceptions from the truth. Therefore, the pagans imagine that rulership, victories, wealth, and prosperous issues of affairs are bestowed by the demons. . . . However, all these things are deceptions. For since demons have some foreknowledge of the arrangements of God (having been His ministers), they interpose themselves in these matters . . . so it will appear that they themselves are doing it. *Lactantius (c. 304–313, W), 7.66.*

SEE ALSO DEMONS, DEMON POSSESSION; SIBYL; SPIRITISM.

ORDERS, HOLY

SEE CHURCH GOVERNMENT; ORDINATION.

ORDINATION

And the saying pleased the whole multitude. And they chose Stephen, a man full of faith and the Holy Spirit, and Philip, . . . whom they set before the apostles; and when they had prayed, they laid hands on them. Acts 6:5, 6.

As they ministered to the Lord and fasted, the Holy Spirit said, "Now separate to Me Barnabas and Saul for the work to which I have called them." Then, having fasted and prayed, and laid hands on them, they sent them away. Acts 13:2, 3.

When they had appointed elders in every church, and prayed with fasting, they commended them to the Lord in whom they had believed. Acts 14:23.

For this reason I left you in Crete, that you should set in order the things that are lacking and appoint elders in every city. Tit. 1:5.

In ordinations of the clergy, beloved brethren, we usually consult you [the congregation] beforehand and weigh the character and deserts of individuals, with the general counsel [of all]. However, human testimonies must not be waited for when the divine approval comes first. Aurelius, our brother, an illustrious youth . . . has contended here in a double conflict, having twice confessed and twice been glorious in the victory of his confession. . . . Such a man is to be estimated not by his years, but by his deserts. He has merited higher degrees of clerical ordination and a greater advancement. But, in the meantime, I judged it appropriate that he should begin with the office of reading. . . . Know, then, most beloved brethren, that this man has been ordained by me and by my colleagues who were then present. *Cyprian (c. 250, W), 5.312.*

A man cannot have the ordination of the church if he does not hold the unity of the church. *Cyprian (c. 250, W), 5.329.*

Cornelius was made bishop by the judgment of God and of His Christ, by the testimony of almost all the clergy, by the election of the people who were then present, and by the assembly of ancient priests and good men. *Cyprian (c. 250, W), 5.329.*

[WRITTEN CONCERNING NOVATIAN:] Does he seem to you to be a bishop, who strives by bribery to be made an adulterous and extraneous bishop by the hands of deserters? Particularly, when a bishop has already been made in the church by sixteen co-bishops? *Cyprian (c. 250, W), 5.329.*

We observe it to have come from divine authority that the priest should be chosen in the presence of the people, under the eyes of all. And he should be approved worthy and suitable by public judgment and testimony. . . . God commands a priest to be appointed in the presence of all the assembly. That is, He instructs and shows that the ordination of priests should not be solemnized except with the knowledge of the people standing near. Thereby, in the presence of the people, either the sins of the wicked will be disclosed, or the merits of the good will be declared. That way, the ordination will be just and legitimate, for the man has been examined by the election and judgment of all. *Cyprian (c. 250, W), 5.370.*

For the proper celebration of ordinations, all the neighboring bishops of the same province should assemble with the people for whom a prelate is being ordained. And the bishop should be chosen in the presence of the people. For the local people have most fully known the life of each man, and they have looked into the doings of each one as respects his habitual conduct. *Cyprian (c. 250, W), 5.371.*

How can he be esteemed a pastor, who succeeds to no one, but begins from himself? For the true shepherd remains and presides over the church of God by successive ordination. Therefore, the other one becomes a stranger and a profane person, an enemy of the Lord's peace. *Cyprian (c. 250, W), 5.398.*

The following passage was written to several bishops who had performed ordinations outside their own local areas.

What agitation and sadness have been caused to all of us collectively and individually by the ordination carried through by you in parishes [Gr. *paroikia*] having no manner of connection with you! . . . However, we have not delayed to prove your practice wrong by this short statement. There is the law of our fathers and forefathers—of which you are not ignorant. That law has been established according to divine and ecclesiastical order. . . . By our forefathers, it has been established and settled that it is not lawful for any bishop to celebrate ordinations in other parishes than his own. This is a law that is

extremely important and wisely drawn up. In the first place, it is only right that the manner of life of those who are ordained should be examined with great care. In the second place, all confusion and turbulence should be done away with. For everyone will have enough to do in managing his own parish. . . .

But you . . . have not considered the law of our sainted fathers and those who have been taken to Christ time after time. Nor have you considered the honor of our great bishop and father, Peter [bishop of Alexandria], on whom we all depend. . . . Instead, you have ventured on subverting all things at once. . . . You should have waited for the judgment of the superior father [i.e., bishop Peter] and for his allowance of this practice. However, without giving any heed to these matters, but indulging a different expectation—and, indeed, denying all respect to us—you have provided certain rulers for the people. . . . Furthermore, you were not persuaded to delay this procedure or to restrain your purpose even by the word of the apostle Paul. Now, Paul is the most blessed seer, the man who put on Christ. And he is the man who is the Christ of all of us no less. For he, in writing to his dearly beloved son Timothy, says: "Lay hands suddenly on no man; neither be a partaker of other men's sins." So he immediately shows his own anxious consideration for Timothy and gives him his example. He reveals the law according to which persons are to be chosen for the honor of ordination, with all carefulness and caution. *Phileas (c. 307, E), 6.163, 164.*

A bishop is to be ordained by three bishops, or at least by two. For it is not lawful that he be set over you by one. For the testimony of two or three witnesses is more firm and secure. But a presbyter and a deacon are to be ordained by one bishop and the rest of the clergy. Nor should either a presbyter or a deacon ordain anyone from the laity into the clergy. *Apostolic Constitutions (compiled c. 390, E), 7.432.*

Not everyone who wants to is ordained—as was the case with that counterfeit priesthood of the calves under Jeroboam. Rather, only he who is called of God is ordained. . . . A presbyter may not perform ordinations. For it is not agreeable to holiness to have this order perverted. For "God is not the God of confusion." So subordinate persons should not tyrannically assume functions that belong to their superiors.

. . . However, someone may accuse Philip, the deacon, or Ananias, the faithful brother. For the first one [i.e., Philip] baptized the eunuch; the other baptized Paul. However, such a person does not understand what we are saying. We are only saying that no one snatches the priestly dignity to himself. He either receives it from God—as did Melchizedek and Job—or from a high priest—as did Aaron from Moses. Now, Philip and Ananias did not ordain themselves, but were appointed by Christ, the High Priest. *Apostolic Constitutions (compiled c. 390, E), 7.499, 500.*

Let a bishop be ordained by two or three bishops. Let a presbyter, as also a deacon and the rest of the clergy, be ordained by one bishop. *Apostolic Constitutions (compiled c. 390, E), 7.500.*

A bishop must not venture to ordain out of his own bounds in cities or countries that are not subject to him. *Apostolic Constitutions (compiled c. 390, E), 7.502.*

If any bishop, presbyter, or deacon receives a second ordination from anyone, let him be deprived, along with the person who ordained him—unless he can show that his former ordination was from the heretics. *Apostolic Constitutions (compiled c. 390, E), 7.504; see also 7.493.*

Post-Nicene forms of prayers for ordination: 7.482; 7.491–7.492.

SEE ALSO BISHOP; CHURCH, THE; CHURCH GOVERNMENT; PRESBYTER.

ORGAN

Look at that very marvelous piece of organic mechanism invented by Archimedes. I am referring to his hydraulic organ, with its many components, parts, bands, passages for the notes, outlets for their sounds, combinations for their harmony, and the array of its pipes. *Tertullian (c. 210, W), 3.193.*

SEE ALSO MUSIC, MUSICAL INSTRUMENTS.

ORIGEN

Origen (c. 185–251) was one of the most learned—and most original—Christian teachers of his day. For many years, he served as the teacher of catechumens in the church in Alexandria. He was also the most prolific writer of the pre-Nicene church, dictating around 2,000 works. He produced not only doctrinal and apologetic works but also commentaries on most of the books of the Bible. He also travelled widely, becoming acquainted with Christian leaders throughout the Roman world. Origen's writings often reflect brilliant spiritual insights; at other times, however, they exhibit strained or unsound theological speculations.

A common misconception today is that, during his lifetime, Origen was excommunicated from the church as a heretic. The available evidence does not, however, support this claim. What did happen is that Origen was expelled from Alexandria by his bishop, Demetrius. But this was not because Origen taught heresy. Rather, according to Eusebius, this was a result of the bishop's jealousy. Origen was only a layman, yet he was the most celebrated Christian teacher of his time. He was far better known than his bishop. Demetrius's resentment came to a head when, during Origen's travels through Palestine on church interests (c. 233), Origen was ordained as a presbyter by the bishop of Caesarea. This was a highly unusual proceeding, since Origen was a member of the church in Alexandria. When Demetrius heard of this, he was furious. He called a local church council, which decided that Origen could no longer serve in the church in Alexandria. The council, however, did not declare him to be a heretic.

Origen spent the remainder of his life as a presbyter at Caesarea in Palestine, where he publicly preached and taught. He also defended the church against heretics and pagan accusers. He died in the communion of the church as a confessor, having endured excruciating tortures for Christ during the Decian persecution.

I. Life and Character

II. Viewpoints unique to Origen
   A. Three-tier system of Scripture interpretation
   B. Preexistence of souls
   C. Universal reconciliation
   D. Heavenly bodies and powers

I. Life and Character

These are the thoughts that have occurred to me in addressing subjects of such difficulty as the incarnation and deity of Christ. If, indeed, there is anyone who can discover something better—and who can establish his assertions by clearer proofs from Holy Scriptures—let his opinion be received in preference to mine. *Origen (c. 225, E), 4.284.*

Solomon says in Ecclesiastes, "My son, beware of making many books. There is no end to it, and much study is a weariness of the flesh." However, unless that verse has some hidden meaning that I do not yet understand, I have directly transgressed that injunction. For I have not guarded myself against making many books. *Origen (c. 228, E), 9.346.*

As to the type of men who are slower intellectually, my answer is that I try to improve such ones, to the best of my ability. However, I do not seek to build up the Christian community out of such materials. Rather, I prefer those who are brighter and quicker. For they are able to understand the meaning of the hard sayings and of the passages in the Law, Prophets, and Gospels that are obscure in meaning. *Origen (c. 248, E), 4.493.*

The next three quotations are from Gregory Thaumaturgus, who, as a young man and as a pagan, came to Origen for his further education. Not only did Origen educate Gregory; he also led him to Christ.

It is my purpose to speak of one who has indeed the semblance and reputation of being a man, but who seems, to those who are able to grasp the greatness of his intellectual ability, to be endowed with powers more noble and nearly divine. *Gregory Thaumaturgus (c. 255, E), 6.22.*

He was also the first and only man who urged me to study the philosophy of the Greeks. And he persuaded me by his own moral example both to hear and to practice the teaching of morals. . . . This admirable man, this friend and advocate of the virtues, has long ago done for us perhaps all that it lay in his power to do for us, in making us lovers of virtue. *Gregory Thaumaturgus (c. 255, E), 6.33.*

With respect to these human teachers, indeed, he counseled us to attach ourselves to none of them—not even if they were attested as most wise by all men. Rather, he counselled us to devote ourselves to God alone and to the prophets. *Gregory Thaumaturgus (c. 255, E), 6.36.*

Origen also, the most learned of all, and the most discerning in making calculations, . . . has published in a very elegant manner a little book on Easter. *Anatolius (c. 270, E), 6.146; extended discussion on the man: 6.21–6.39.*

II. Viewpoints unique to Origen

Most of Origen's teachings were quite harmonious with the orthodoxy of the pre-Nicene church. Nevertheless, because of his brilliant mind, Origen came up with a number of theological speculations that most Christians have judged to be unsound. It must be remembered that the amount of defined dogma in the pre-Nicene church was quite small, and Origen was very careful not to teach contrary to any dogma defined by the church. Origen's modern critics often quote his speculative viewpoints out of their historical context, making it appear as though Origen were teaching such things as dogma. However, Origen made it clear that his speculations were not being presented as dogma, but as points of dialogue and reflection.

A. Three-tier system of Scripture interpretation
Origen taught that most Scripture passages can be interpreted on three levels: the literal, the moral, and the spiritual. He correlated these three levels to the threefold composition of man: body, soul, and spirit. Some of the passages of Scripture that influenced his thinking on this matter begin this section.

We know that the law is spiritual. Rom. 7:14.

For it is written in the law of Moses, "You shall not muzzle an ox while it treads out the grain." Is it oxen God is concerned about? Or does He say it altogether for our sakes? For our sakes, no doubt, this is written, that he who plows should plow in hope, and he who threshes in hope should be partaker of his hope. 1 Cor. 9:9, 10.

Moreover, brethren, I do not want you to be unaware that all our fathers were under the cloud, all passed through the sea, all were baptized into Moses in the cloud and in the sea, all ate the same spiritual food, and all drank the same spiritual drink. For they drank of that spiritual Rock that followed them, and that Rock was Christ. 1 Cor. 10:1–4.

The individual should, then, portray the ideas of Holy Scripture in a threefold manner upon his own soul. . . . For as man consists of body, soul, and spirit, so Scripture consists in the same way. *Origen (c. 225, E), 4.359.*

There are certain passages of Scripture that do not at all contain the "bodily" sense. . . . Therefore, there are passages where we must seek for only the "soul," as it were, and the "spirit" of Scripture. *Origen (c. 225, E), 4.360.*

The first level, then, is profitable in this respect: that it is capable of imparting edification. This is testified by the multitudes of genuine and simple believers. Second, of that interpretation that is likened to the "soul," there is an illustration in Paul's first Epistle to the Corinthians. The expression is, "You will not muzzle the mouth of the ox that treads out the corn." To which, he adds: "Does God care about oxen? Or does He say it altogether for our sakes? For our sakes, no doubt, this was written." *Origen (c. 225, E), 4.360, 361.*

The interpretation is "spiritual" when one is able to show the heavenly things of which the Jews served as an example "according to the flesh." . . . And Paul gives an opportunity for ascertaining of what things these were patterns, when he says: "For they drank of the spiritual Rock that followed them, and that Rock was Christ." *Origen (c. 225, E), 4.361.*

The Word of God has arranged for certain stumbling blocks (so to speak), offenses, and impossibilities to be introduced into the midst of the Law and the history. . . . For where the Word found that things done according to the history could be adapted to these mystical senses, He made use of them, concealing the deeper meaning from the multitude. However, [sometimes] . . . the Scripture interwove into the history some event that did not take place. Or sometimes it contains what could not have happened. Or sometimes it contains what could have happened, but did not. Furthermore, sometimes a few words are interpolated that are not true in their literal meaning. Sometimes, a larger number [of words are interpolated]. *Origen (c. 225, E), 4.364.*

What need is there to say more, since those who are not altogether blind can collect numerous instances of a similar kind that are recorded as having occurred. Yet, they did not literally take place. In fact, the Gospels themselves are filled with the same kind of narratives. One example is when the devil leads Jesus up into a high mountain in order to show him from there the kingdoms of the whole world. *Origen (c. 225, E), 4.365.*

However, let no one suppose that I am saying with respect to the whole [of Scripture] that no history is real, just because a certain one is not. Or that no commandment is to be literally observed, just because a certain one, as to the literal letter, is absurd or impossible. . . . With regard to certain things, it is perfectly clear to me that the historical account is true. . . . In fact, the passages that are true in their historical meaning are much more numerous than those

that are interspersed with a purely spiritual signification. *Origen (c. 225, E), 4.368.*

With respect to Holy Scripture, my opinion is that the whole of it has a "spiritual" meaning. However, all of it does not have a "bodily" [i.e., literal] meaning. For the "bodily" meaning is proved to be impossible in many places. *Origen (c. 225, E), 4.369.*

For how can anyone be said to believe the Scripture in the full sense when he does not see in it the mind of the Holy Spirit, which God would have us to believe, rather than the literal meaning? *Origen (c. 228, E), 9.407.*

While you devote yourself to this divine reading, seek aright and with unwavering faith in God the hidden sense that is present in most passages of the divine Scriptures. *Origen (c. 245, E), 9.296.*

The subjects of Adam and his son will be philosophically dealt with by those who are aware that in the Hebrew language Adam means "man." So in those parts of the narrative that appear to refer to Adam as an individual, Moses is talking about the nature of man in general. For, as the Scripture says, "in Adam all die," and all were condemned in the likeness of Adam's transgression. Now, the Word of God says this not so much of one particular individual as of the whole human race. . . . And the expulsion of the man and woman from Paradise . . . contains a certain secret and mystical doctrine of the soul's losing its wings and being borne downwards to earth. *Origen (c. 248, E), 4.516.*

Scripture frequently makes use of the histories of real events in order to present to view more important truths, which are but obscurely intimated. *Origen (c. 248, E), 4.517.*

From the prophetic Scriptures, in which historical events are recorded, it is possible to be convinced that the historical portions also were written with an allegorical purpose. . . . Since the very fathers and authors of the doctrines themselves give them an allegorical meaning, what other inference can be drawn but that they were composed so as to be allegorically understood in their chief meaning? *Origen (c. 248, E), 4.520.*

I hold, then, that the Law has a twofold sense: one literal, the other spiritual. . . . Of the first or literal sense, it is said (not by me, but by God, speaking through one of the prophets) that "the statutes are not good, and the judgments are not good" [Ezek. 20:25]. In like manner, Paul says that "the letter kills, but the spirit gives life." He means by "the letter," the literal sense, and by "the spirit," the spiritual sense of Scripture. *Origen (c. 248, E), 4.619.*

... "a land flowing with milk and honey." This promise is not to be understood to refer, as some suppose, to that part of the earth that we call Judea. For, however good it may be, it still forms part of the earth that was originally cursed for the transgression of Adam.... Both Judea and Jerusalem were the shadow and figure of that pure land ... in the pure region of heaven, in which is the heavenly Jerusalem. *Origen (c. 248, E), 4.622; extended discussion: 4.359–4.374.*

B. Preexistence of souls
Neither Scripture nor the pre-Nicene church had defined where human souls come from. Origen speculated that souls existed in another world prior to their birth in humans—a viewpoint that no other pre-Nicene writer shared. Nevertheless, as the quotations below demonstrate, Origen did not believe in reincarnation (as his modern detractors sometimes claim).

This world is itself called an "age," and it is said to be the conclusion of many ages. Now, the holy apostle teaches that in the age that preceded this one, Christ did not suffer. *Origen (c. 225, E), 4.273.*

When the Scriptures are carefully examined regarding Jacob and Esau, it is not found to be unrighteous of God to have said—before they were born, or had done anything in this life— that "the older will serve the younger." However, it is not unrighteous ... if we feel that Jacob was worthily beloved by God according to the deserts of his previous life.... Owing to causes that have previously existed, a different office is prepared by the Creator for each one in proportion to the degree of his merit. *Origen (c. 225, E), 4.292.*

It appears to me that this will be seen more clearly at last if each being—whether heavenly, earthly, or infernal—is said to have the causes of his diversity in himself, prior to his bodily birth.... There is no doubt that at the Day of Judgment, the good will be separated from the bad (and the just from the unjust) and all will be distributed according to their deserts, by the sentence of God.... Similarly, I am of the

opinion that such a state of things was the case in the past. *Origen (c. 225, E), 4.293.*

It is possible that someone who is now a vessel of dishonor is one because of reasons more ancient than the present life. After reformation, he may become a vessel of honor in the new creation. *Origen (c. 225, E), 4.327.*

I think it should be inquired into as to the reasons why a human soul is acted on sometimes by good and at other times by bad. I suspect the reason for this is older than the bodily birth of the individual.... To all these instances, those who maintain that everything in the world is under the administration of Divine providence can give no other answer (as it appears to me) to show that no shadow of injustice rests upon the divine government than to hold that there were certain causes of prior existence. And in consequence of this prior existence, our souls contracted a certain amount of guilt in their sensitive nature, before their birth in the body. *Origen (c. 225, E), 4.337.*

This is the objection which they generally raise: They say, "If the world had its beginning in time, what was God doing before the world began?" ... I say that God did not begin to work for the first time when he made this visible world. Just as there will be another world after its destruction, so also I believe that other worlds existed before the present one came into being. And both of these positions will be confirmed by the authority of Holy Scripture.... That before this world others also existed is shown by Ecclesiastes, in the words ... "Who will speak and say, 'Look! This is new'? It has already been in the worlds that have been before us" [Eccles. 1:9, 10, LXX]. *Origen (c. 225, E), 4.341, 342.*

There has been a descent from a higher to a lower condition on the part of certain souls. This is true not only of those souls who have deserved the change by the variety of their movements but also of those who (in order to serve the whole world) were brought down from those higher and invisible spheres to these lower and visible ones, although against their will. *Origen (c. 225, E), 4.342.*

"There was a man sent from God, whose name was John." ... John was sent from either heaven or Paradise—or from some other region to this place on the earth.... But there is a more convincing argument for the view that

John was sent from another region when he entered into the body. . . . John was "filled with the Holy Spirit even from his mother's womb." . . . This must necessarily assume that John's soul was older than his body, and subsisted by itself before it was sent on the ministry of the witness of the light. *Origen (c. 228, E), 9.339, 340.*

[REFERRING TO JOHN THE BAPTIST:] In this place, it does not seem to me that by the word "Elijah" the soul is being spoken of. Otherwise, I would fall into the doctrine of transmigration, which is foreign to the church of God. It is not handed down by the apostles, nor is it set forth in the Scriptures anywhere. *Origen (c. 245, E), 9.474.*

C. Universal reconciliation
More than most of the early Christian writers, Origen focused on God's love. He went so far as to speculate that through God's unfailing love and His just and wise discipline, all creatures—including perhaps Satan—might eventually be reconciled to God somewhere in eternity. Again, no other writer shared his view on this matter (except perhaps Clement of Alexandria). Origen's speculations on universal reconciliation should not be confused, however, with modern doctrines of universal salvation, which teach that everyone will be saved regardless of what they believe or how they live. Origen taught a very strict Christianity, in accord with the rest of the pre-Nicene church. Yet he also posited that God's disciplinary punishments after death would perhaps eventually reconcile all sinning humans and angels to God. Origen apparently based these speculations on Scriptures such as the passages beginning this section.

For as in Adam all die, even so in Christ all shall be made alive. 1 Cor. 15:22.

For it pleased the Father that in Him all the fullness should dwell, and by Him to reconcile all things to Himself, whether things on earth or things in heaven, having made peace through the blood of His cross. Col. 1:19, 20.

We trust in the living God, who is the Savior of all men, especially of those who believe. 1 Tim. 4:10.

The Lord is not slack concerning His promise, as some count slackness, but is longsuffering toward us, not willing that any should perish but that all should come to repentance. 2 Pet. 3:9; see also Rom. 5:18; Tit. 2:11; 1 John 2:2.

I think, indeed, that the goodness of God, through His Christ, may recall all His creatures to one end. For all of His enemies will be conquered and subdued. *Origen (c. 225, E), 4.260.*

Those [angelic creatures] who have been removed from their original state of blessedness have not been removed irrecoverably. Rather, they have been placed under the rule of those holy and blessed angelic orders that I have described. By availing themselves of this angelic help, and being remolded by salutary principles and discipline, they may recover themselves and be restored to their condition of happiness. . . . However, as to any of these powers who act under the direction of the devil and obey his wicked commands, whether or not they will be converted to righteousness in a future world (because of their possessing the faculty of freedom of the will) . . . is a result which you the reader may approve of. *Origen (c. 225, E), 4.261.*

D. Heavenly bodies and powers
Scripture sometimes speaks of the stars and other heavenly bodies as though they were living creatures. For example, it says, "the stars are not pure in His sight" (Job 25:5), and speaks of the time when "the morning stars sang together" (Job 38:7). The Psalms say, "Praise Him, all His angels; Praise Him, all His hosts! Praise Him, sun and moon; Praise Him, all you stars of light! Praise Him, you heavens of heavens, and you waters above the heavens!" (Ps. 148:24). Virtually all Christians understand these expressions to be figurative. Origen, however, speculated that these expressions may be literal and that perhaps the heavenly bodies are living creatures. (Many educated persons in Origen's day believed that the heavenly bodies were living beings.) Origen's speculation on this is rather ironic, for he so often interpreted Scriptures figuratively when the rest of the church interpreted them literally. In this one instance, he interpreted literally what the rest of the church interpreted figuratively.

Regarding the sun, moon, and stars—whether they are living beings or without life—there is no distinct teaching [of the church]. *Origen (c. 225, E), 4.241.*

Job appears to assert that not only may the stars be subject to sin, but even that they are actually unclean from the contagion of it. The following are his words: "The stars also are not clean in your sight." . . . We think, then, that they may be designated as living beings, for this reason: that they are said to receive commandments from God, which is ordinarily the case only with rational beings. "I have given a commandment to all the stars," says the Lord. What, now, are those commandments? Namely, that each star, in its order and course, should bestow upon the world the amount of splendor that has been entrusted to it. *Origen (c. 225, E), 4.263.*

It would surely be absurd to say that He tasted death for human sins and not for any other beings who had fallen into sin (besides man)— such as the stars. For not even the stars are clean in the eyes of God, as we read in Job. *Origen (c. 228, E), 9.319.*

We must also speak about powers, not about power. We frequently read, "Thus says the Lord of powers." So there are certain creatures, rational and divine, that are called powers. Christ is the highest and best of these. He is called not only the Wisdom of God, but also His Power. So, then, there are several powers of God—each of them in its own form. But the Savior is different from these. *Origen (c. 228, E), 9.321, 322.*

A third class of persons worship the sun, moon, and all the host of heaven, wandering (it is true) from God. However, their wandering is far different and is better than the wandering of those who invoke as gods the works of men's hands, such as silver and gold. *Origen (c. 228, E), 9.324.*

I am persuaded that the sun himself, the moon, and the stars all pray to the Supreme God through His Only-Begotten Son.... However, Celsus assumes that the sun, moon, and stars are regarded by us as of no account. ... However, Celsus had obviously not read the innumerable other passages that speak of the sun, moon, and stars. I am referring to passages such as, "Praise Him, all you stars" ... and "Praise Him, you heaven of heavens." If he had, he would not have said of us that we regard as of no account such mighty beings who "greatly praise" the Lord God. *Origen (c. 248, E), 4.548.*

ORIGINAL SIN

SEE ADAM; FALL OF MAN; MAN, DOCTRINE OF.

ORPHANS AND WIDOWS

Now in those days, when the number of the disciples was multiplying, there arose a murmuring against the *Hebrews by the Hellenists, because their widows were neglected in the daily distribution. Acts 6:1.*

Pure and undefiled religion before God and the Father is this: to visit orphans and widows in their trouble. Jas. 1:27.

Let the presbyters be compassionate and merciful to everyone—bringing back those who wander, visiting all the sick, and not neglecting the widow, the orphan, or the poor. *Clement of Rome (c. 96, W), 1.34.*

Do not let widows be neglected. After the Lord, be their protector and friend. *Ignatius (c. 105, E), 1.94.*

Christians love one another. They do not turn away their care from widows, and they deliver the orphan from anyone who treats him harshly. He who has, gives to him who has not. And this is done without boasting. *Aristides (c. 125, E), 9.277.*

Therefore, instead of lands, buy afflicted souls, according as each one is able. And visit widows and orphans. *Hermas (c. 150, W), 2.31.*

What is collected is deposited with the president, who gives aid to the orphans and widows. *Justin Martyr (c. 160, E), 1.186.*

Although keeping parrots and curlews, the [pagans] do not receive the orphan child. Rather, they expose children who are born at home and yet take up the young of birds. *Clement of Alexandria (c. 195, E), 2.279.*

I request that you be diligent to take care of the widows, the sick, and all of the poor. Moreover, you may supply from my own portion the expenses for strangers—if any should be indigent. *Cyprian (c. 250, W), 5.314.*

Everything that is given is conferred upon widows and orphans. *Cyprian (c. 250, W), 5.480.*

The widow and orphans should be protected. In Solomon, it says: "Be merciful to the orphans as a father, and as a husband to their mother" [Sir. 4:10]. *Cyprian (c. 250, W), 5.556.*

It is an equally great work of justice to protect and defend orphans and widows who are destitute and stand in need of assistance. Therefore, the divine law commands this to everyone. *Lactantius (c. 304–313, W), 7.177.*

When any Christian becomes an orphan, ... it is good that one of the brethren who is without a child should take the young man and value him in the place of a son. *Apostolic Constitutions (compiled c. 390, E), 7.433.*

OVERPOPULATION

The human race has progressed with a gradual growth of population. Some occupy different portions of the earth as natives. . . . Others occupy certain regions through emigration, which they call "colonies." These are established for the purpose of throwing off excess population, disgorging into other places their overcrowded masses. . . . What most frequently meets our eyes is our teeming population. Our numbers are burdensome to the world, which can hardly supply us from its natural elements. Our wants grow more and more acute, and our complaints more bitter in all mouths, while Nature fails in affording us her usual sustenance. In fact, pestilence, famine, wars, and earthquakes have to be regarded as a remedy for nations, as the means of pruning the abundance of the human race. *Tertullian (c. 210, W), 3.210.*

SEE ALSO PROCREATION.

OVERSEER

SEE BISHOP.

PACIFISM

SEE NONRESISTANCE; WAR.

PANTAENUS

Between c. 180 and 190, Pantaenus headed up the catechetical school in Alexandria. Eusebius reports that Pantaenus left Alexandria to go to India as a missionary. Clement of Alexandria, Pantaenus's best-known pupil, replaced him as head of the catechetical school.

[This work is] truly an image and outline of those vigorous and lively discourses that I was privileged to hear, from blessed and truly remarkable men. Of these, the first was in Greece, an Ionic man. . . . When I came upon the last teacher [i.e., apparently Pantaenus], I found him to be the first in power. Once I tracked him down, finding him concealed in Egypt, I found rest. He, the true teacher, was like a Sicilian bee. For he gathered the nectar of the flowers of the prophetic and apostolic meadow. And he engendered a timeless element of knowledge in the souls of his hearers. *Clement of Alexandria (c. 195, E), 2.301.*

We are well acquainted with those blessed fathers who have trodden the course before, and to whom we too will soon go: namely, Pantaenus, the truly blessed man, my master. *Alexander of Cappadocia (c. 250, E), 6.154.*

PAPACY

SEE BISHOP (II. ROME, BISHOP OF).

PAPIAS

Papias (c. 60–130) was a bishop of Hierapolis in Asia Minor, a disciple of John, and a friend of Polycarp. His testimony concerning the Gospels of Matthew and Mark has been invaluable to the church.

And these things are borne witness to in writing by Papias, the hearer of John, and a companion of Polycarp, in his fourth book. *Irenaeus (c. 180, E/W), 1.562, 563.*

Papias . . . affirms that he received the sayings of the apostles from those who accompanied them. Moreover, Papias asserts that he heard Aristion and the presbyter John in person. *Eusebius (c. 320, E), 1.154.*

Papias, an ancient man, was a hearer of John and a friend of Polycarp. He composed five books. *Eusebius (c. 320, E), 1.154.*

Papias of Hierapolis, the illustrious, was a disciple of the apostle who leaned on the bosom of Christ. *Anastasius Sinaita, post-Nicene writer, 1.155.*

PARABLES OF JESUS

I. Principles for interpreting parables

II. Interpretations of specific parables
    A. Dragnet
    B. Lost coin
    C. Marriage feast
    D. Mustard seed
    E. Pearl of great price
    F. Prodigal son
    G. Talents
    H. Wheat and tares
    I. Wise and foolish virgins
    J. Workers in the vineyard

I. Principles for interpreting parables

The parables should not be adapted to ambiguous expressions. If such a thing is avoided, he who explains them will do so without danger. Furthermore, the parables will receive a similar interpretation from everyone. *Irenaeus (c. 180, E/W), 1.398.*

In the case of the parables in the Gospel, when the kingdom of heaven is likened to anything, the comparison does not extend to all the features of that thing to which the kingdom is compared. Rather, it applies only to those features that are required by the argument at hand. *Origen (c. 245, E), 9.419.*

II. Interpretations of specific parables

A. Dragnet
Matt. 13:47–50.

Some persons desire that before the end of the age, and before the angels come to remove the wicked from among the righteous, there should not be evil persons of every kind in the dragnet. However, such a person seems not to have understood the Scripture. For he desires the impossible. Therefore, let us not be surprised if, before the removing of the wicked from among the righteous by the angels, . . . we see our gatherings filled with wicked persons. Let us hope that the number of those who will be cast into the furnace of fire will not be greater than the righteous! *Origen (c. 245, E), 9.421; see also 9.419–9.420.*

B. Lost coin
Luke 15:8–10.

You sinner, be of good cheer! See where it is written that there is joy at your return. What meaning for us do those themes of the Lord's parables have? A woman has lost a drachma, and she seeks and finds it. Then she invites her female friends to share her joy. Is this not an example of a restored sinner? *Tertullian (c. 203, W), 3.663.*

Fourteen years later, writing as a Montanist, Tertullian no longer applied this parable to a repentant Christian:

I interpret the parable of the drachma . . . as applying to the pagans. . . . For this whole world is the one house of everyone. And in this world, it is more the pagan who is found in darkness and whom the grace of God enlightens than it is the Christian, who is already in God's light. *Tertullian (c. 217, W), 4.80.*

C. Marriage feast
Matt. 22:2–14.

You should pay attention to this all the more, my brothers, when you reflect on and see that even after such great signs and wonders had been performed in Israel, they were still abandoned. Let us beware lest we be found to be, as it is written, the "many who are called," but not the "few who are chosen." *Barnabas (c. 70–130, E), 1.139.*

These are the holy spirits. Men cannot otherwise be found in the kingdom of God unless they have put their clothing upon them. For if you receive the name only, and do not receive from them the clothing, they are of no advantage to you. For these virgins are the powers of the Son of God. *Hermas (c. 150, W), 2.48.*

If, because of the disobedient and ruined Israelites, certain persons assert that the teacher of the Law was limited in power, they will find in our dispensation that "many are called, but few chosen." *Irenaeus (c. 180, E/W), 1.480.*

He called together from all the highways, that is, from all nations, guests to the marriage feast of His Son. *Irenaeus (c. 180, E/W), 1.516.*

He also made it clear that, after our calling, we should also be adorned with works of righteousness, so that the Spirit of God may rest upon us. For this is the wedding garment. *Irenaeus (c. 180, E/W), 1.517.*

If, however, you will not believe in Him and you flee from His hands, the cause of imperfection will be in you. For you did not obey. The cause is not in Him who called you. For He commissioned ones to call people to the marriage. However, those who did not obey Him deprived themselves of the royal supper. *Irenaeus (c. 180, E/W), 1.523.*

It is here that the preparation for entrance to the marriage to which we are invited must be accomplished. The person who has been made ready to enter will say, "My joy is now fulfilled." However, the unadorned and unsightly person will hear, "Friend, how did you come in here without having a wedding garment?" *Clement of Alexandria (c. 195, E), 2.582.*

Even in the gospel, the wedding garment may be regarded as the sanctity of the flesh. *Tertullian (c. 210, W), 3.565.*

The person who is not clothed at the marriage feast in the garment of good works will have to be bound hand and foot. *Tertullian (c. 210, W), 3.571.*

Christ saw that most—after attaining unto salvation—would be lost again, through soiling the wedding dress. *Tertullian (c. 213, W), 3.639.*

Such a person will recline on that couch from which those who are unworthily clad will be lifted by the jailers and cast out into darkness. *Tertullian (c. 217, W), 4.83.*

The soul that . . . is neither holy nor blameless because of wickedness . . . is not part of the church that Christ builds upon the rock. But if anyone wishes to embarrass us in regard to these things because of the great majority of those of the church who are thought to believe, it must be said to him that "many are called, but few chosen." . . . "Many, I say unto you, will seek to enter in and will not be able." You will understand that this refers to those who boast that they are of the church, but who live weakly and contrary to the Word. *Origen (c. 245, E), 9.457; see also 2.232.*

D. Mustard seed
Matt. 13:31, 32.

He Himself, speaking of Himself very beautifully, likened Himself to a grain of mustard seed. He pointed out the spirituality of the word that is sown, the productiveness of its nature, and the magnificence and conspicuousness of the power of the word. He also intimated that the pungency of the word and the purifying virtue of punishment are profitable because of its pungency. Through the little seed, as it is figuratively called, He abundantly bestows salvation on all humanity. *Clement of Alexandria (c. 195, E), 2.234.*

The growth of the Word increased to such a great size that the tree which sprang from it filled the world. This is the church of Christ, established over the whole earth. The birds of the air dwelled in the tree's branches. These birds are the divine angels and lofty souls. *Clement of Alexandria (c. 195, E), 2.578.*

The Lord has taught us that the word is like "a grain of mustard seed," which is of a fiery nature. If anyone uses it unskillfully, he will find it bitter. For in the mystical points, we should not be rash, but cautious. *Apostolic Constitutions (compiled c. 390, E), 7.427.*

E. Pearl of great price
Matt. 13:45, 46.

Jesus is a pearl of translucent and purest radiance. *Clement of Alexandria (c. 195, E), 2.578.*

There are many merchants engaged in many forms of merchandise. However, the kingdom of heaven is not likened to any of these except the one who is seeking beautiful pearls. And he has found one pearl equal in value to many—a very costly pearl that he has bought in place of many pearls. I consider it reasonable, then, to make some inquiry into the nature of the pearl. Please note that Christ did not say, "He sold all the *pearls* he had." For he had not only sold those pearls he had bought (as one who was seeking beautiful pearls), but he also sold everything that he had, in order to buy that beautiful pearl. *Origen (c. 245, E), 9.416, 417.*

In another place, He says that a merchant of the heavenly grace (one who would gain eternal salvation) should purchase the precious pearl—that is, eternal life—at the price of the blood of Christ, from the amount of his estate, parting with all his wealth for it. He says: "The kingdom of heaven is like a merchant seeking beautiful pearls. And when he found a precious pearl, he went away and sold all that he had and bought it." *Cyprian (c. 250, W), 5.478; see also 5.531; extended discussion (by Origen): 9.416–9.419.*

F. Prodigal son
Luke 15:11–32.

The kind father does not wait until the son comes to Him. For perhaps he would never be able to approach (or would never try) if he did not find the father so forgiving. Therefore, when the son is merely wishing, as soon as he made a beginning, when he took the first step, while he was yet a great way off, his father was moved with compassion, ran to him, fell upon his neck, and kissed him. And then the son, taking courage, confessed what he had done. *Clement of Alexandria (c. 195, E), 2.582.*

He, then, will receive you—His own son—back, even if you have squandered what you had received from Him. . . . But this is only if you heartily repent. He receives you only if you compare your own hunger with the plenty of your Father's hired servants. And you must leave behind you the swine—that unclean herd. *Tertullian (c. 203, W), 3.663.*

It will be no speech of a Jew to the Father, "Behold, how many years I have served you, and your teachings I have never transgressed." For when has the Jew *not* been a transgressor of the Law. . . . Likewise, it will be no speech of the Father to the Jew: "You are always with me and everything I have is yours." For the Jews are declared to be an apostate son. . . .

The Jew has had every tasty morsel torn from his throat, not to mention the very land of paternal promise. As a result, at the present day, the Jew (no less than the younger son) is a beggar in alien territory, having squandered God's substance. Even until now the Jew serves . . . the princes of this world. . . . Much more aptly would the Christian have fit the description of the elder son, and the Jew the younger son. . . . However, the conclusion would preclude this interpretation. For it would be fitting for the Christian to rejoice at the restoration of Israel, and not to grieve—if it is true that our whole hope is intimately entwined with the remaining expectation of Israel. *Tertullian (c. 212, W), 4.82.*

With deep perception, the Word has called the souls of the prophets concubines, for He did not marry them openly, as He did the church. For he killed the fatted calf for the church. *Methodius (c. 290, E), 6.333.*

If anyone returns and displays the fruits of repentance, you should receive him to prayer, as the lost son, the prodigal who had consumed his father's estate with harlots. *Apostolic Constitutions (compiled c. 390, E), 7.415; see also 1.479, 3.715; extended discussion: 2.581–2.584.*

G. Talents
Matt. 25:14–30.

The Savior reveals Himself, out of His abundance, to dispense goods to His servants according to the ability of each recipient. Thereby, His servants can increase them by useful activity and then return to account for them. . . . [Paul says,] "The things that you have heard from me among many witnesses, the same you should commit to faithful men, who will also be able to teach others." *Clement of Alexandria (c. 195, E), 2.299.*

That fate also that is mentioned in the Gospels as overtaking unfaithful stewards . . . undoubtedly indicates some type of punishment on those whose spirit (as it seems to me) is shown to be separated from the soul. For if this . . . is understood to be the Holy Spirit, we will understand this to be said of the gift of the Holy Spirit. For a gift may have been bestowed upon a man either by baptism or by the grace of the Spirit. I am referring to gifts such as the word of wisdom, word of knowledge, or any other gift that has been bestowed, but not rightly used. . . . In such an event, the gift of the Spirit will certainly be withdrawn from his

soul. And the other portion that remains—that is, the substance of the soul—will be assigned its place with the unbelievers. . . .

There is also a third sense in which that separation may be understood. This is that each believer (although he may be the humblest in the church) is said to be attended by an angel. The Savior declares that this angel always beholds the face of God the Father. Now, this angel has the purpose of being the guardian of the believer. So if that person is rendered unworthy by his lack of obedience, the angel of God is said to be taken from him. And then that part of him—the part belonging to his human nature—is torn away from the divine part. And it is assigned a place along with the unbelievers, for it has not faithfully observed the admonitions of the angel allotted it by God. . . . But the outer darkness, in my opinion, is to be understood—not so much of some dark atmosphere without any light—as of those persons who, being plunged in the darkness of profound ignorance, have been placed beyond the reach of any light of understanding. *Origen (c. 225, E), 4.296.*

Those who have received the ten talents are those who have been entrusted with the dispensing of the Word, which has been committed to them. *Origen (c. 245, E), 9.503; see also 1.445, 9.502.*

H. Wheat and tares
Matt. 13:24–30.

The Lord, indeed, sowed good seed in His own field. And He says, "The field is the world." However, while men slept, the enemy came and "sowed tares in the midst of the wheat, and went his way." From this we learn that this was the apostate angel who is the enemy. For he was envious of God's workmanship and took in hand to render this workmanship into something at enmity with God. For this reason, too, God has banished from His presence the one [Satan] who of his own accord stealthily sowed the tares. I am referring to the one who brought about the transgression. However, God took compassion upon man, who through lack of caution (no doubt), yet still wickedly, became involved in disobedience. *Irenaeus (c. 180, E/W), 1.524.*

The good olive, if neglected for a period of time and left to grow wild and to run to wood, will itself become a wild olive. . . . For when men sleep, the enemy sows the material of tares. For this reason, the Lord commanded His disciples to be on guard. *Irenaeus (c. 180, E/W), 1.536.*

That heresies would be sown among the truth, as "tares among the wheat," was foretold by the Lord. *Clement of Alexandria (c. 195, E), 2.549.*

Persecution is the judgment of the Lord. By means of it, one is declared either approved or rejected. The judging properly belongs to God alone. This is that fan that even now cleanses the Lord's threshing floor (the church, I mean), winnowing the mixed heap of believers and separating the grain of the martyrs from the chaff of the deniers. *Tertullian (c. 212, W), 4.116.*

However, by then the tares of Praxeas [a heretic] had dispersed their seeds everywhere. And having lain hidden for awhile, with its poison concealed under a mask, it has now broken out into fresh life. Nevertheless, it shall be rooted up even now, if the Lord so wills. However, if not now, then it will be rooted up in the day when all bundles of tares are gathered together, along with every other stumbling block. And they shall be burned up with unquenchable fire. *Tertullian (c. 213, W), 3.598.*

[SAID IN DISAPPROVAL:] Callistus alleged that the parable of the tares was uttered in reference to such a [sinning] person, saying, "Let the tares grow along with the wheat"! Or, in other words, let those in the church who are guilty of sin, remain in it! *Hippolytus (c. 225, W), 5.131.*

On the question of what is meant in Scripture by the word "world" [Gr. *kosmos*], I think it is proper to repeat this: I am aware that a certain scholar understands by "world" the church alone. For the church is the adornment of the world and is said to be the light of the world. . . . If those who hold the view in question cannot show this, then let them consider if my interpretation is not a sound one: that the light is the church and the "world" refers to those others who call on the Name. *Origen (c. 228, E), 9.380.*

The seed of the tares stand mingled in the church. . . . The Husbandman separates all those collected tares. *Commodianus (c. 240, W), 4.213.*

Although there seem to be tares in the church, yet neither our faith nor our charity should be hindered. Just because we see that there are tares in the church, we ourselves should not withdraw from the church. Rather, we only should labor that we may be wheat. In that manner, when the wheat begins to be gathered into the Lord's barns, we may receive fruit for our labor. *Cyprian (c. 250, W), 5.327.*

Those who departed from Christ perished by their own fault. Yet, the church that believes on Christ, and holds that which it has once learned, never departs from Him at all. They are the church who remain in the house of God. On the other hand, those whom we see blown about like chaff are not the plantation planted by God the Father. For they are not established with the stability of wheat. *Cyprian (c. 250, W), 5.341.*

"In the time of the harvest, I will say to the reapers to gather the tares and make bundles of them, and to burn them with everlasting fire. However, I will tell them to gather the wheat into my barns." The Apocalypse shows that these reapers, shepherds, and laborers are the angels. *Victorinus (c. 280, W), 7.352; see also 1.556; 6.187; 9.414–9.415.*

I. Wise and foolish virgins
Matt. 25:1–13.

The simple language of the Holy Scriptures has led the honest readers of them to be filled with a divine spirit. And this light is nourished within them by the oil that in a certain parable is said to have preserved the light of the torches of the five wise virgins. *Origen (c. 248, E), 4.575.*

Now five of them were prudent and wise. But five were foolish and unwise, for they did not have enough foresight to fill their vessels with oil—remaining destitute of righteousness. *Methodius (c. 290, E), 6.329.*

The virgins standing outside the chamber wail and mournfully lament with bitter tears and deep moans that their lamps have gone out. For they have failed to enter into the chamber of joy in time. . . . Turning from the sacred way of life, these unhappy ones have neglected to prepare enough oil for the path of life. Carrying lamps whose bright light is dead, they groan from the inward recesses of their mind. *Methodius (c. 290, E), 6.352.*

"Prepare your works for your exit, and provide all things beforehand in the field." Otherwise, some of the things necessary for your journey will be lacking, just as the oil of holiness was deficient in the five foolish virgins mentioned in the gospel. For because of their having extinguished their lamps of divine knowledge, they were shut out of the bridal chamber. Accordingly, he who values the security of his soul, will take care to be out of danger, by keeping free from sin. In that manner, he can preserve the advantage to himself of his former good works. *Apostolic Constitutions (compiled c. 390, E), 7.400; see also 1.395, 1.398, 1.518, 3.663, 6.329–6.330.*

J. Workers in the vineyard
Matt. 20:1–16.

Now for the parable of the workmen who were sent into the vineyard at different periods of the day. . . . He began by giving the hire to those who were hired last, for in the last times, when the Lord was revealed, He presented Himself to all. *Irenaeus (c. 180, E/W), 1.518.*

By the equal reward given to each of the laborers—that is, salvation (which is meant by the denarius)—He indicated the equality of justice. The difference of those called He indicated by those who worked for unequal portions of time. They will work, therefore, in accordance with the appropriate mansions of which they have been deemed worthy as rewards. *Clement of Alexandria (c. 195, E), 2.415.*

Although there are many mansions in the house of the same Father, all have labored for the one "denarius" of the same hire—that is, of eternal life. *Tertullian (c. 217, W), 4.67; see also 1.455, 1.500, 3.244.*

Parable of the king and his unforgiving servant: 9.497–9.504.

Parable of the treasure hidden in the field: 9.415–9.416.

PARACLETE

SEE HOLY SPIRIT; MONTANISTS.

PARADISE

The Lord God planted a garden eastward in Eden, and there He put the man whom He had formed. . . . Now a river went out of Eden to water the garden, and from there it parted and became four river heads. Gen. 2:8, 10.

Jesus said to him, "Assuredly, I say to you, today you will be with me in Paradise." Luke 23:43.

He was caught up into Paradise and heard inexpressible words, which it is not lawful for a man to utter. 2 Cor. 12:4.

God transferred man from the earth, out of which he had been produced, into Paradise, giving him means of advancement. . . . In respect of beauty, this place, Paradise, was made intermediate between earth and heaven. *Theophilus (c. 180, E), 2.104.*

"And God planted a garden eastward in Eden, and there He placed the man whom He had formed." And then afterwards, when man proved disobedient, he was cast out from there into this world. For that reason, the elders who were disciples of the apostles tell us that those who were translated [i.e., Enoch and Elijah] were transferred to that place. For Paradise has been prepared for righteous men, those who have the Spirit. Likewise, Paul the apostle, when he was translated, heard words in this place that are unspeakable. . . . So it is there that those who have been translated will remain until the consummation [of all things], as a prelude to immortality. *Irenaeus (c. 180, E/W), 1.531.*

Paradise is the place of heavenly bliss that has been appointed to receive the spirits of the saints, who are severed from the knowledge of this world by that fiery zone as by a sort of enclosure. *Tertullian (c. 195, W), 3.52.*

Some may venture strongly to contend that Paradise is the holy land—which it may be possible to designate as the land of our first parents, Adam and Eve. Nevertheless, it will even then follow that the restoration of Paradise will seem to be promised to the flesh. *Tertullian (c. 210, W), 3.564.*

Some choose to maintain that Paradise is in heaven, and that it forms no part of the system of creation. However, we see with our eyes the rivers that go forth from it. For they are open to inspection by anyone who chooses to see them even in our day. Accordingly, let everyone conclude from this that Paradise did not belong to heaven. . . . In truth, it is a locality in the east, and a select place. *Hippolytus (c. 205, W), 5.163.*

[Methodius] says that Paul had two revelations. He says that the apostle does not suppose Paradise to be in the third heaven. This is the opinion of those who knew how to observe the particularities of language. For Paul says, "I know such a man caught up to the third heaven; and I know such a man . . . who was caught up into Paradise." Here he indicates that he has seen two revelations, having been evidently taken up twice: once to the third heaven and once into Paradise. *Methodius (c. 290, E), 6.370, as quoted by Photius.*

SEE ALSO ASSUMPTIONS; DEAD, INTERMEDIATE STATE OF THE.

PARENTS, PARENTING

If anyone comes to Me and does not hate his father and mother, wife and children, brothers and sisters, yes, and his own life also, he cannot be My disciple. Luke 14:26.

Children, obey your parents in the Lord, for this is right. "Honor your father and mother," which is the first commandment with promise: "that it may be well with you and you may live long on the earth." And you, fathers, do not provoke your children to wrath, but bring them up in the training and admonition of the Lord. Eph. 6:1–4.

Children, obey your parents in all things, for this is well pleasing to the Lord. Fathers, do not provoke your children, lest they become discouraged. Col. 3:20, 21.

You shall not remove your hand from your son or from your daughter. Rather, from their youth, you shall teach them the fear of God. *Didache (c. 80-140, E), 7.378.*

Let your children be partakers of true Christian training. Let them learn that humility is of great avail with God. *Clement of Rome (c. 96, W), 1.11.*

Your household has committed iniquity against the Lord and against you, their parents. Although you love your children, yet you did not warn your household. Instead, you permitted them to be terribly corrupted. For this reason, the Lord is angry with you. Nevertheless, He will heal all the evils that have been committed in your house. . . . Only, do not be lax, but be of good courage and comfort your house. Just as a smith hammers out his work and accomplishes whatever he desires, so shall righteous daily speech overcome all wickedness. Therefore, do not cease to admonish your children. *Hermas (c. 150, W), 2.10.*

Therefore, the spiritual man will prefer neither children, nor marriage, nor parents over his love for God and righteousness in life. *Clement of Alexandria (c. 195, E), 2.503.*

"Whoever does not hate father, mother, and children, and his own life besides, cannot be My disciple." Now, the God of peace, who also exhorts us to love our enemies, does not introduce hatred and dissolution from those who are dearest to us. But if we are to love our enemies, it is in accordance with right reason that, ascending from them, we should love also those nearest in kinship. Or, if we are to hate our blood-relations, reason teaches us that we are to hate our enemies even more. *Clement of Alexandria (c. 195, E), 2.597.*

Who is there that does not feel a greater concern for his children than for himself? *Tertullian (c. 207, W), 3.309.*

I am also of the opinion that there were many persons of the same name with John the apostle, who by their love, admiration, and emulation of him . . . were induced to embrace the same name also. Similarly, we find many of the children of the faithful called by the names of Paul and Peter. *Dionysius of Alexandria (c. 262, E), 6.83.*

A son . . . who deserts his father in order not to pay him obedience is considered deserving of being disinherited and of having his name removed forever from his family. *Lactantius (c. 304-313, W), 7.155.*

We restrain the faults of those who are in our power. We do this so that the tender age may be formed by a severer discipline to integrity and justice. For if this period of life is not restrained by fear, the lack of discipline will produce presumption and will erupt into every disgraceful and daring action. *Lactantius (c. 304–313, W), 7.185.*

It is a failing not to restrain the faults of slaves and children. If they escape without punishment, they will go on to greater evils. In this instance, anger is not to be restrained. *Lactantius (c. 304–313, W), 7.275.*

Honor your parents as the authors of your life. *Apostolic Constitutions (compiled c. 390, E), 7.413.*

Therefore, let us renounce our parents, relatives, friends, wife, children, possessions, and all the enjoyments of life—when any of those things become an impediment to godliness. *Apostolic Constitutions (compiled c. 390, E), 7.439.*

SEE ALSO FATHERS; HUSBANDS; MARRIAGE; PROCREATION; WIFE, WIVES.

PAROUSIA

SEE SECOND COMING OF CHRIST.

PASCHA

SEE EASTER; PASCHAL CONTROVERSY.

PASCHAL CONTROVERSY

The Paschal controversy concerned the day on which the Christian Passover (Gr. *pascha*), known today as Easter, was to be celebrated. In the pre-Nicene church, the main issue about Easter was whether it was to be celebrated on a fixed date each year, Nisan 14, or whether it was to be celebrated on the Sunday following Nisan 14—regardless of the date on which that Sunday falls. In Asia Minor, Christians celebrated Easter on Nisan 14, and they testified that they received this custom from the apostle John. In most other places, the Christian Passover was celebrated on the Sunday following Nisan 14. Another minor paschal controversy concerned the calculation of the spring equinox under the Julian calendar—which ultimately affected the date that Easter would be observed.

Endeavor also to send abroad copies of our epistle among all the churches, so that those who easily deceive their own souls may not be able to lay the blame on us. We would have you know, too, that in Alexandria also they observe the festival on the same day as ourselves. For the Paschal letters are sent from us to them, and from them to us—so that we observe the holy day in unison and together. *Theophilus of Caesarea (c. 180), 8.774.*

When the blessed Polycarp was visiting in Rome in the time of Anicetus, . . . they were at once well inclined towards each other, not willing that any quarrel should arise between them upon this matter [the observance of Easter]. For Anicetus could not persuade Polycarp to forego the observance [of his Easter customs] inasmuch as these things had been always observed by John the disciple of our Lord, and by other apostles with whom he had been conversant. Nor, on the other hand, could Polycarp succeed in persuading Anicetus to keep [Easter in his way], for Anicetus maintained that he was bound to adhere to the usage of the presbyters who preceded him. And in this state of affairs they held fellowship with each other. *Irenaeus (c. 180, E/W), 1.569.*

As for us, then, we scrupulously observe the exact day, neither adding nor taking away. For in Asia great luminaries have gone to their rest, who will rise again on the day of the coming of the Lord. . . . These all kept Easter on the fourteenth day, in accordance with the Gospel. . . . Seven of my relatives were bishops, and I am the eighth, and my relatives always observed the day when the people put away the leaven. *Polycrates (c. 190, E), 8.773, 774.*

There are some diversities among the churches. Anyone may know this from the facts concerning the celebration of Easter. . . . He may see that here are some diversities among them. All things are not observed alike among the churches, such as are observed at Jerusalem. Similarly, in very many other provinces, many things are varied because of the difference of the places and names. Nevertheless, there is no departure at all from the peace and unity of the catholic church on this account. *Firmilian (c. 256, E), 5.391.*

Our predecessors, men most learned in the books of the Hebrews and Greeks (I refer to Isidore, Jerome, and Clement) . . . come harmoniously to one and the same most exact determining of Easter—the day, month, and season meeting in accord with the highest honor for the Lord's resurrection. But Origen also, the most learned of all, and the most discerning in making calculations, . . . has published in a very elegant manner a little book on Easter. . . . For this reason, also, we maintain that those who . . . determine the fourteenth day of the Paschal season by it make no trivial or common blunder. . . . Therefore, in this concurrence of the sun and moon, the Paschal festival is not to be celebrated. For as long as the [sun and moon] are found in this course, the power of darkness is not overcome. And as long as equality between light and darkness endures, and is not diminished by the light, it is shown that the Paschal festival is not to be celebrated. Accordingly, it is directed that the festival be kept after the equinox. *Anatolius (c. 270, E), 6.147.*

To us, however, with whom it is impossible for all these things to come aptly at one and the same time—namely, the moon's fourteenth day, the Lord's Day, and the passing of the equinox—it is granted that we may extend the beginning of our celebration even to the moon's twentieth day. For the obligation of the Lord's resurrection binds us to keep the Paschal festival on the Lord's Day. *Anatolius (c. 270, E), 6.148.*

But those who determine that the festival may be kept at this age of the moon, are unable to make that good by the authority of Scripture. Furthermore, they also turn into the crime of sacrilege and rebellion, and they incur the peril of their souls. For they say that the true light may be celebrated along with something of that power of darkness that dominates all. *Anatolius (c. 270, E), 6.148.*

But nothing was difficult to them with whom it was lawful to celebrate the Passover on any day when the fourteenth of the moon happened after the equinox. Following their example up to the present time, all the bishops of Asia were in the custom of celebrating the paschal feast every year whenever the fourteenth day of the moon had come and the lamb was sacrificed by the Jews, after the equinox was past. For they themselves also received the rule from an unimpeachable authority—the evangelist John, who leaned on the Lord's breast and drank in spiritual instructions without doubt. They did not acquiesce on this matter with the authority of some—namely, the successors of Peter and Paul, who had taught all the churches in which they sowed the spiritual seeds of the Gospel that the solemn festival of the resurrection of the Lord can only be celebrated on the Lord's Day.

From this, a certain contention broke out between the successors of these [apostles]. The contention was between Victor, at that time bishop of the city of Rome, and Polycrates, who then appeared to hold the primacy among the bishops of Asia. And this contention was adjusted most rightfully by Irenaeus, at that time president of a part of Gaul. The result was that both parties kept to their own order and did not decline from the original custom of antiquity. The one party, indeed, kept the Paschal day on the fourteenth day of the first month—in accordance with the Gospel, as they understood it. They added nothing of an extraneous kind, but kept the rule of faith through all things. And the other party—keeping the day of the Lord's passion as one replete with sadness and grief—hold that it should not be lawful to celebrate the Lord's mystery of Easter at any other time but on the Lord's Day, on which the resurrection of the Lord from death took place. *Anatolius (c. 270, E), 6.148, 149; extended discussion: 6.146–6.151.*

SEE ALSO EASTER; LENT; LORD'S DAY; QUARTODECIMANS.

PASSOVER, CHRISTIAN

SEE EASTER; PASCHAL CONTROVERSY.

PASSOVER, JEWISH

The Passover of the Jews consists of a sheep that is sacrificed, each taking a sheep according to his father's house. And the Passover is accompanied by the slaughter of thousands of rams and goats, in proportion to the number of the households of the people. But our Passover is sacrificed for us, namely, Christ. Another feature of the Jewish festival is unleavened bread. *Origen (c. 228, E), 9.389.*

These writers, in solving some questions that are raised concerning Exodus, say that everyone should sacrifice the Passover after the vernal equinox in the middle of the first month. *Anatolius (c. 270, E), 6.147; extended discussion: 9.387–9.391.*

PATEN

SEE VESSELS, EUCHARISTIC.

PATRIARCHS

It might seem to the men of the present day, who are ignorant of God's appointment, to be a thing incredible and impossible that any man could live for such a number of years, yet those who were before us did. *Irenaeus (c. 180, E/W), 1.531.*

Before the Law, Adam spoke prophetically concerning the woman and the naming of the creatures. Noah preached repentance. Abraham, Isaac, and Jacob gave many clear utterances about both present and future things. *Clement of Alexandria (c. 195, E), 2.331.*

The shepherd's tent that belonged to Jacob was preserved at Edessa up to the time of Emperor Antoninus of the Romans. But it was destroyed by a thunderbolt. *Julius Africanus (c. 245, E), 6.132.*

SEE ALSO ABRAHAM; MOSES; NOAH.

PATRIPASSIANISM

SEE MONARCHIANISM.

PATRIOTISM

My kingdom is not of this world. If My kingdom were of this world, My servants would fight, so that I should not be delivered to the Jews; but now My kingdom is not from here. John 18:36.

Our citizenship is in heaven, from which we also eagerly wait for the Savior. Phil. 3:20.

Beloved, I beg you as sojourners and pilgrims, abstain from fleshly lusts. 1 Pet. 2:11.

We have no country on earth. Therefore, we can despise earthly possessions. *Clement of Alexandria (c. 195, E), 2.281.*

All zeal in the pursuit of glory and honor is dead in us. So we have no pressing inducement to take part in your public meetings. Nor is there anything more entirely foreign to us than the affairs of state. We acknowledge one all-embracing commonwealth—the world. *Tertullian (c. 195, W), 3.46.*

As for you, you are a foreigner in this world, a citizen of Jerusalem, the city above. Our citizenship, the apostle says, is in heaven. *Tertullian (c. 212, W), 3.101.*

[LUCILIUS, A PAGAN:] "It is virtue to give that which is really due to honor.... That is, we should consider the interests of our country first, those of our parents should come next, and our own interests should be in the third and last place." ... [LACTANTIUS'S REPLY:] However, we will presently see how false these things are.... It is a virtue to restrain anger, to control desire, and to curb lust. For this is to flee from vice. For almost all things that are done unjustly and dishonestly arise from these affections.... Also, if desire is restrained, no one will use violence by land or by sea. Nor will anyone lead an army to carry off and lay waste the property of others.... It is not virtue, either, to be the "enemy of the bad" or "the defender of the good." ... When the agreement of men is taken away, virtue has no existence at all. For what are the interests of our country, but the hardships of another state or nation? To extend the boundaries that are violently taken from others, to increase the power of the state, to improve the revenues—all of these things are not virtues, but the overthrowing of virtues. *Lactantius (c. 304–313, W), 7.168, 169.*

How can a man be just who hates, who despoils, who puts to death? And those who strive to be serviceable to their country do all these things. *Lactantius (c. 304–313, W), 7.169.*

He is extolled with praises to heaven who gains these "goods" for his country! I speak of one who has filled the treasury with money by the overthrow of cities and the destruction of nations. In him there is said to be the greatest and most perfect virtue! And this is the error—not only of the people and the ignorant—but also of the philosophers. *Lactantius (c. 304–313, W), 7.169.*

When they speak of the "duties" relating to warfare, their speech pertains neither to justice nor to true virtue. Rather, it pertains only to this life and to civil institutions. And this is not justice. *Lactantius (c. 304–313, W), 7.169.*

SEE ALSO CHURCH AND STATE; NONRESISTANCE; PUBLIC OFFICE; WAR.

PAUL, APOSTLE

"Benjamin is a devouring wolf. In the morning, he will devour the prey, and at night he will divide the spoil." Gen. 49:27.

Through envy and jealousy, the greatest and most righteous pillars have been persecuted and put to death.... Owing to envy, Paul also obtained the reward of patient endurance, after being seven times thrown into captivity.... After preaching both in the east and the west, he gained the illustrious reputation due to his faith. For he had taught righteousness to the whole world, and he came to the extreme limit of the west. He finally suffered martyrdom under the prefects. *Clement of Rome (c. 96, W), 1.6.*

I do not, as Peter and Paul, issue commandments unto you. They were apostles. *Ignatius (c. 105, E), 1.75.*

For neither I, nor any other such one, can come up to the wisdom of the blessed and glorified Paul. *Polycarp (c. 135, E), 1.33.*

You have seen before your eyes—not only in the case of the blessed Ignatius, Zosimus, and Rufus—but also in others among yourselves, and in Paul himself, and the rest of the apostles. ... They are in their due place in the presence of the Lord, with whom they also suffered. *Polycarp (c. 135, E), 1.35.*

Matthew also issued a written Gospel among the Hebrews in their own dialect, while Peter and Paul were preaching at Rome, and laying the foundations of the church.... Luke also, the companion of Paul, recorded in a book the Gospel preached by Paul. *Irenaeus (c. 180, E/W), 1.414.*

The universally known church was founded and organized at Rome by the two most glorious apostles, Peter and Paul. *Irenaeus (c. 180, E/W), 1.415.*

As I have shown elsewhere through many examples, it was Paul's custom to transpose words. . . . From many other instances also, we can see that the apostle frequently used a transposed order in his sentences. This was due to the speed of his discourses and the impetus of the Spirit who was in him. *Irenaeus (c. 180, E/W), 1.420.*

Paradise has been prepared for righteous men, such as have the Spirit. In this place, also, Paul the apostle, when he was caught up, heard words which are unspeakable. *Irenaeus (c. 180, E/W), 1.531.*

Paul knew Epimenides the Cretan as a Greek prophet. Paul mentions him in the Epistle to Titus, where he says, "One of themselves, a prophet of their own, said, 'Cretans are always liars, evil beasts, slow bellies.'" . . . You see how even to the prophets of the Greeks he attributes something of the truth. Furthermore, he is not ashamed . . . to make use of Greek poems. Accordingly, while discoursing on the resurrection of the dead to the Corinthians (for that was not the only instance), he makes use of a tragic Iambic line, when he said, "What advantage is it to me if the dead are not raised? Let us eat and drink, for tomorrow we die." *Clement of Alexandria (c. 195, E), 2.314.*

Paul, in the Acts of the Apostles, is recorded to have said to the Areopagites . . . "As I passed by and beheld your devotions, I found an altar with the inscription, To The Unknown God. Whom therefore you ignorantly worship, Him I declare unto you." . . . Paul indicates that, by the unknown God, the Greeks in a roundabout way worshipped God the Creator. *Clement of Alexandria (c. 195, E), 2.321.*

Paul may be only recent in time—having flourished immediately after the Lord's ascension. Nevertheless, his writings depend on the Old Testament, breathing and speaking of them. *Clement of Alexandria (c. 195, E), 2.434.*

The teaching of the apostles, encompassing the ministry of Paul, ends with Nero. *Clement of Alexandria (c. 195, E), 2.555.*

"I die daily"—that is, no doubt, in the perils of the body, in which Paul even fought with beasts at Ephesus. He even fought with those beasts that caused him such peril and trouble in Asia, to which he alludes in his second epistle to the same church of Corinth: "For we would not, brothers, have you ignorant of our trouble which came to us in Asia, that we were pressed above measure, above strength, so much that we despaired even of life." *Tertullian (c. 195, W), 3.582.*

Now, with the view of branding the apostles with some mark of ignorance, the Gnostics put forth the case of when Peter and those who were with him were rebuked by Paul. . . . Still they should show, from the circumstance which they allege (of Peter's being rebuked by Paul), that Paul added yet another form of the gospel in addition to that which Peter and the rest had previously set forth. *Tertullian (c. 197, W), 3.253, 254.*

As Paul himself narrates, he "went up to Jerusalem for the purpose of seeing Peter." This was no doubt because of his office, and by right of a common belief and preaching. . . . They accordingly even gave him "the right hand of fellowship" as a sign of their agreement with him, and they arranged among themselves a distribution of office—not a diversity of gospel. *Tertullian (c. 197, W), 3.254.*

It is a happy fact that Peter is on the same level with Paul in the very glory of martyrdom. Now, although Paul was carried away even to the third heaven and was caught up to Paradise, and heard certain revelations there, yet these cannot possibly seem to have qualified him for [teaching] another doctrine. *Tertullian (c. 197, W), 3.254.*

The next three passages were written against Marcion, who exalted Paul above the twelve apostles. In fact, Marcion accepted in his New Testament only the writings of Paul, along with the Gospel of Luke (since Luke was Paul's companion).

Paul yielded his belief to that gospel which he found in existence. He so earnestly wished his own gospel to agree with that gospel, that he actually on that account went up to Jerusalem to know and consult the apostles, "lest he should run, or had been running in vain." In other words, he desired that the faith which he had learned and the gospel which he was preaching to be in accordance with theirs. Then, at last, having conferred with the authors, and having agreed with them concerning the rule of faith, they joined their hands in fellowship. *Tertullian (c. 207, W), 3.347, 348.*

The enlightener of Luke [i.e., Paul] himself desired the authority of his predecessors for both his own faith and preaching. *Tertullian (c. 207, W), 3.348.*

I need to know from Marcion the origin of his apostle [i.e., Paul]. . . . A man is asserted to me to be an apostle whom I do not find mentioned in the Gospel in the list of the apostles. Indeed, when I hear that this man was chosen by the Lord after he had obtained His rest in heaven, I feel that some kind of improvidence is being imputed to Christ, for not knowing beforehand that this man was necessary to Him. *Tertullian (c. 207, W), 3.429.*

Even the Book of Genesis so long ago promised me the apostle Paul. Among the types and prophetic blessings which Jacob pronounced over his sons, when he turned his attention to Benjamin, he exclaimed, "Benjamin will ravish as a wolf. In the morning He will devour the prey. And at night he will impart nourishment." He foresaw that Paul would arise out of the tribe of Benjamin—a voracious wolf, devouring his prey in the morning. In other words, in the early period of his life, he would devastate the Lord's sheep, as a persecutor of the churches. But in the evening, he would give them nourishment. This means that in his declining years, he would educate the flock of Christ, as the teacher of the Gentiles. *Tertullian (c. 207, W), 3.430.*

Paul is beheaded. . . . Then does Paul obtain a birth suited to Roman citizenship, when in Rome he springs to life again ennobled by martyrdom! *Tertullian (c. 213, W), 3.648.*

And [Luke] shows this clearly—i.e., that the principle on which he wrote was to write only of what fell under his own observation. This can be seen by his omission of the martyrdom of Peter and the journey of Paul, when he went from the city of Rome to Spain. *Muratorian Fragment (c. 200, W), 5.603.*

"Benjamin is a devouring wolf. In the morning, he will devour the prey, and at night he will apportion the food." This thoroughly fits Paul, who was of the tribe of Benjamin. For when he was young, he was a ravaging wolf. However, when he believed, he "apportioned the food." *Hippolytus (c. 205, W), 5.168.*

Paul was made fit to be a minister of the new covenant—not of the letter, but of the spirit. Although he fulfilled the gospel from Jerusalem round about to Illyricum, he did not write epistles to all the churches he taught. And to those to whom he did write, he sent no more than a few pages. *Origen (c. 228, E), 9.346.*

Paul became a Jew to the Jews so that he might gain Jews. . . . Paul, too, used a spirit of accommodation when he circumcised Timothy and offered sacrifice in accordance with a certain legal vow, as is written in the Acts of the Apostles. *Origen (c. 245, E), 9.437.*

Paul was, after Jesus, the founder of the churches that are in Christ. *Origen (c. 248, E), 4.425.*

Let them also follow the example of the apostle Paul, who, after often-repeated imprisonment, after scourging, after exposures to wild beasts, continued to be meek and humble in everything. Even after his rapture to the third heaven and Paradise, he did not proudly arrogate anything to himself. *Cyprian (c. 250, W), 5.283.*

Peter and Paul preached at Rome. *Lactantius (c. 304–313, W), 7.123.*

It was Nero who first persecuted the servants of God. He crucified Peter and slew Paul. *Lactantius (c. 320, W), 7.302.*

You were not persuaded to delay this procedure . . . even by the word of the apostle Paul—the most blessed seer, the man who put on Christ. He is the man who is the Christ of all of us, no less. *Phileas (c. 307, E), 6.164.*

The renowned Paul, having been oftentimes delivered up and brought in peril of death . . . was also himself beheaded in the same city [Rome]. *Peter of Alexandria (c. 310, E), 6.273.*

[The Spirit] did most abundantly impart Himself to Paul, whose testimony we also believe when he says, "Unto me only is this grace given" [Eph. 3:8]. . . . For who of us could have dreamed that Paul, the persecutor and enemy of the church, would prove to be its defender and guardian? Yes, and not only that, but that he would become also its ruler—the founder and architect of the churches? Therefore, after him, and after those who were with him (the disciples), we are not to look for the coming of any other, according to the Scriptures. For our Lord Jesus Christ says of this Paraclete, "He will receive of mine." Therefore, he selected him as an acceptable vessel. He sent this Paul to us in the Spirit. Into him, the Spirit was poured.... That Spirit, the Comforter, could not come into any other persons, but could only come upon the apostles and the holy Paul. *Disputation of Archelaus and Manes (c. 320, E), 6.208.*

That best master-builder of Christ, Paul himself, has laid our foundation, that is, the foundation of the church. And he has put us in trust of the law, ordaining deacons, presbyters, and bishops. *Disputation of Archelaus and Manes (c. 320, E), 6.229; see also 3.646.*

SEE ALSO APOSTLES, TWELVE; BARNABAS; JOHN, APOSTLE; NEW TESTAMENT; PETER.

PAUL OF SAMOSATA

Paul of Samosata, a bishop of Antioch (c. 260–268), surrounded himself with pomp and wealth. He also began teaching various heretical tenets. He apparently denied Christ's preexistence, teaching that Jesus was an ordinary man who obtained deification. Eventually Paul of Samosata was excommunicated by a council of bishops.

Firmilian came twice in person and condemned [Paul of Samosata's] innovations in doctrine. We who were present know and bear witness to this.... But when [Paul of Samosata] promised to give up these opinions, Firmilian believed him.... Although this Paul was formerly poor and beggarly, ... he has now come to have excessive wealth through his deeds of iniquity and sacrilege.... Neither do I need to say anything about the pride and haughtiness with which he assumed worldly dignities. He wishes to be called a "procurator," rather than a "bishop." He struts through the marketplaces, reading letters and reciting them as he walks in public. He is escorted by multitudes of people going before him and following him. *Malchion (c. 270, E), 6.169.*

[Paul of Samosata] set up for himself a lofty tribunal and throne—so unlike a disciple of Christ.... He discontinued the psalms sung in honor of our Lord Jesus Christ, as being the recent compositions of contemporary men. Instead, he trained women to sing psalms in honor of himself in the midst of the church, during the great day of the Paschal festival—which choristers one might shudder to hear! ... On account of these things, all are groaning and lamenting with themselves. Yet, they have such a

fear of his tyranny and power, that they do not dare to accuse him.... Therefore, we have been compelled to excommunicate this man ... and to appoint another bishop in his place. For he refuses submission. *Malchion (c. 270, E), 6.170.*

Nor is [Arianism] anything else but an imitation of Paul of Samosata, bishop of Antioch. And he [Paul] was put out of the church by the judgment and counsel of all the bishops. *Alexander of Alexandria (c. 324, E), 6.294; extended discussion: 6.169–6.171.*

PAX ROMANA

The Pax Romana (Roman Peace) was a period of about 200 years (27 B.C.–A.D. 180) during which time there were no major wars in the Mediterranean region or any serious threats to the Roman frontier. The early Christians believed that this unparalleled period of peace came through divine intervention.

Through the Romans' instrumentality, the world is at peace, and we walk on the highways without fear and sail where we will. *Irenaeus (c. 180, E/W), 1.503.*

The existence of many kingdoms would have been a hindrance to the spread of the doctrine of Jesus throughout the entire world.... This was because of the need of men everywhere to engage in war and to fight on behalf of their native country—which was the case before the times of Augustus.... How, then, was it possible for the Gospel doctrine of peace to prevail throughout the world? For it does not permit men to take vengeance even upon their enemies. It was only possible because, at the coming of Jesus, a milder spirit had been everywhere introduced into the conduct of things. *Origen (c. 248, E), 4.444.*

You allege that those wars of which you speak were sparked because of hatred of our religion. However, it would not be difficult to prove that (after the name of Christ was heard in the world) wars were not increased. In fact, they actually *diminished* in great measure by the restraining of furious passions.... As a result, an ungrateful world is now enjoying—and for a long period has enjoyed—a benefit from Christ. For by His means, the rage of savage ferocity has been softened and has begun to withhold hostile hands from the blood of a fellow creature. In fact, if all men without exception ... would lend an ear for a while to His salutary and peaceful rules, ... the whole world would be living in the most peaceful tranquility. The world would have turned the use of steel into more peaceful uses and would unite together in blessed harmony, maintaining inviolate the sanctity of treaties. *Arnobius (c. 305, E), 6.415.*

SEE ALSO ROMAN EMPIRE, ROMANS; WAR.

PEARL OF GREAT PRICE

SEE PARABLES OF JESUS (II. E. PEARL OF GREAT PRICE).

PEARLS, CASTING BEFORE SWINE

Do not give what is holy to the dogs; nor cast your pearls before swine, lest they trample them under their feet, and turn and tear you in pieces. Matt. 7:6.

Even now I fear "to cast the pearls before swine." . . . For it is difficult to display the truly pure and transparent words about the true light to swinish and untrained hearers. For, to the multitude, hardly anything that they hear could seem more ludicrous. *Clement of Alexandria (c. 195, E), 2.312.*

PEDAGOGUE

In ancient times, a pedagogue was a servant who accompanied the children of his master to and from school.

I understand, then, that the primary effort [of Manes, a heretic] was directed at proving that the Law of Moses is not harmonious with the law of Christ. . . . However, we proved that the whole Old Testament agrees with the New Testament and is in perfect harmony with it. . . . Do you think that a boy who is brought to the teachers of knowledge by his pedagogue should later view that pedagogue in dishonor, after he has grown up to adulthood? Should he dishonor him simply because he no longer needs his services, but can make his way to the schools without any assistance from that custodian? *Disputation of Archelaus and Manes (c. 320, E), 6.215.*

SEE ALSO LAW, MOSAIC.

PENANCE

SEE DISCIPLINE, CHURCH (II. PENITENTIAL DISCIPLINE).

PENTATEUCH

The Pentateuch consists of the first five books of the Old Testament. The early church maintained that Moses was the author of the Pentateuch.

As it is written in the Law of Moses, all this disaster has come upon us. Dan. 9:13.

Have you not read in the book of Moses, in the burning bush passage, how God spoke to him? Mark 12:26.

And beginning at Moses and all the Prophets, He expounded to them in all the Scriptures the things concerning Himself. Luke 24:27.

Moses, the servant of God, recorded, through the Holy Spirit, the very beginning of the creation of the world. First he spoke of the things concerning the creation and genesis of the world, including the first man and everything that happened afterwards in the order of events. He also indicated the number of years that elapsed before the Deluge. *Theophilus (c. 180, E), 2.118.*

The origin of that knowledge should not, on that account, be considered as originating with the Pentateuch. For knowledge of the Creator did not begin with the volume of Moses. Rather, from the very first, it is traced from Adam and Paradise. *Tertullian (c. 207, W), 3.278.*

What portion of Scripture can give us more information concerning the creation of the world than the account that Moses has transmitted? *Origen (c. 225, E), 4.341.*

The destruction of Sodom and Gomorrah by fire on account of their sins is related by Moses in Genesis. *Origen (c. 248, E), 4.505.*

Moses said, "And the Lord God saw that the wickedness of men was overflowing upon the earth" [Gen. 6:5–7]. *Novatian (c. 235, W), 5.658.*

It is contained in the book of Moses, which he wrote about creation, and which is called Genesis. *Victorinus (c. 280, W), 7.341.*

If you will look at the books of Moses, David, Solomon, Isaiah, or the prophets who follow, . . . you will see what offspring they have left. *Methodius (c. 290, E), 6.333.*

Let the following books be considered venerable and holy by you, both of the clergy and the laity. Of the Old Testament: the five books of Moses—Genesis, Exodus, Leviticus, Numbers, and Deuteronomy . . . *Apostolic Constitutions (compiled c. 390, E), 7.505.*

SEE ALSO CANON, OLD TESTAMENT; MOSES; PSALMS; SCRIPTURES.

PENTECOST

The Christian feast of Pentecost falls on the fiftieth day after Easter. It commemorates the outpouring of the Holy Spirit on the apostles and disciples.

Now this custom took its rise from apostolic times. The blessed Irenaeus, the martyr and bishop of Lyons, declares this in his treatise *On Easter*. In it, he makes mention of Pentecost also, upon which day we do not bend the knee, because it is of equal significance with the Lord's Day. *Eusebius, citing Irenaeus (c. 180, E/W), 1.569.*

We, however (just as we have received it), only on the day of the Lord's Resurrection, should guard not only against kneeling, but against every posture and office of solicitude. Similarly, too, the period of Pentecost we distinguish by the same solemnity of exultation. *Tertullian (c. 198, W), 3.689*

We consider fasting or kneeling in worship on the Lord's Day to be unlawful. We rejoice in the same privilege also from Easter to Pentecost. *Tertullian (c. 211, W), 3.94.*

If the apostle has erased all devotion absolutely of "seasons, days, months, and years," why do we . . . celebrate Easter by an annual rotation in the first month? Why in the fifty ensuing days do we spend our time in all exultation? *Tertullian (c. 213, W), 4.112.*

We ourselves are accustomed to observe certain days. For example, there is . . . Pentecost. . . . He who can truly say, "We are risen with Christ," and "He has exalted us and made us to sit with him in heavenly places in Christ," is always living in the season of Pentecost. *Origen (c. 248, E), 4.647.*

See also Calendar, Christian; Easter; Prayer (II. Prayer Postures and Customs).

PERFECTION, CHRISTIAN

Therefore you shall be perfect, just as your Father in heaven is perfect. Matt. 5:48.

Leaving the discussion of the elementary principles of Christ, let us go on to perfection. Heb. 6:1.

Let patience have its perfect work, that you may be perfect and complete, lacking nothing. Jas. 1:4.

According to the same apostle, those who strive after perfection, must "give no offense in anything, but in everything approve themselves not to men, but to God." *Clement of Alexandria (c. 195, E), 2.433.*

As I conceive it, sanctity is perfect pureness of mind, deeds, thoughts, and words. In its last degree, it is sinlessness in dreams. *Clement of Alexandria (c. 195, E), 2.435.*

What necessity is there for self-restraint to the one who has no need of it? For to have such desires that one must exercise self-restraint in order to control them is characteristic of someone who is not yet pure. Rather, he is still subject to lusts. Now, fortitude is taken on because of fear and cowardice. It is no longer fitting that the friend of God (whom "God has foreordained before the foundation of the world" to be enrolled in the highest adoption) should fall into pleasures or fears and be occupied with the repression of lusts. *Clement of Alexandria (c. 195, E), 2.497.*

Abstinence from sins is not sufficient for perfection, unless a person also assumes the work of righteousness—activity in doing good. *Clement of Alexandria (c. 195, E), 2.504.*

The spiritual man will pray that he may never fall from virtue, giving his most strenuous cooperation in order that he may become unfailing. . . . Now that he has made it his choice to live perfectly, he subjects himself to training, for the attainment of the stability of knowledge on each side. . . . Just as weight in a stone cannot be lost, so the knowledge of such a spiritual man is incapable of being lost. However, this is not apart from the exercise of will, or the force of reason, knowledge, and providence. Rather, it is through them that this knowledge reaches the point of being incapable of being lost. *Clement of Alexandria (c. 195, E), 2.536.*

He who holds conversation with God must have his soul immaculate and pure, without stain. It is essential to have made himself perfectly good. *Clement of Alexandria (c. 195, E), 2.537.*

In all circumstances, then, is the soul of the man of God strong. It is in a condition of extreme health and strength, like the body of an athlete. . . . This beauty of the soul becomes a temple of the Holy Spirit when it acquires a disposition in the whole of life corresponding to the gospel. Such a one consequently withstands all fear of everything terrible—not only of death, but also of poverty, disease, dishonor, and similar things. He is unconquered by pleasure and is lord over irrational desires. *Clement of Alexandria (c. 195, E), 2.541.*

If, through the necessity of life, he spends a small portion of time for his sustenance, the spiritual man thinks himself defrauded, being diverted by business. So, not even in dreams does he look on anything that is unsuitable to an elect man. For every such one is thoroughly a stranger and sojourner in the whole of life. Although inhabiting the city [of the world], he despises the things in the city that are admired by others. *Clement of Alexandria (c. 195, E), 2.545.*

He impoverishes himself in order that he may never overlook a brother who has been brought into affliction. . . . Accordingly, he considers the other's pain as his own grief. *Clement of Alexandria (c. 195, E), 2.545.*

"Be perfect as your father, perfectly." One does this by forgiving sins, forgetting injuries, and living in the habit of passionlessness. *Clement of Alexandria (c. 195, E), 2.549.*

For it is in this manner that one truly follows the Savior: by aiming at sinlessness and at His perfection. *Clement of Alexandria (c. 195, E), 2.597.*

Christ led them up along with Himself to the divine citizenship that is above the Law. For the imperfect and those who are still sinners, it contains sacrifices for the remission of sins. He, then, who is without sin and no longer stands in need of legal sacrifices, has perhaps passed even beyond the spiritual law when he has become perfect. He then comes to the Word beyond it. *Origen (c. 245, E), 9.452.*

I am persuaded that every action of the perfect man is a testimony to Christ Jesus and that abstinence from every sin is a denial of self, leading him after Christ. *Origen (c. 245, E), 9.464.*

So long as we are imperfect, and need someone to assist us so that we may be delivered from evils—we stand in need of an angel of whom Jacob said, "The angel who delivered me from all the evils." However, when we have become perfected, and have passed through the stage of being subject to nursing fathers, nursing mothers, guardians, and stewards, we are fit to be governed by the Lord himself. *Origen (c. 245, E), 9.490.*

Apart from the help of the Word, . . . it is impossible for a man to become free from sin. *Origen (c. 248, E), 4.492.*

When a man becomes "perfect, as our Father in heaven is perfect," . . . he receives into his virtuous soul the traits of God's image. *Origen (c. 248, E), 4.602.*

God allows Himself at all times to be comprehended in our thoughts. . . . This is so that we may receive a desire for purity and may free ourselves from every stain by the removal of all our shortcomings. *Arnobius (c. 305, E), 6.419; see also 2.434, 2.538–2.549.*

SEE ALSO CHRISTIAN LIFE; SALVATION; SINLESSNESS.

PERFUME

The use of crowns and ointments is not necessary for us. For it leads to pleasures and indulgences, especially on the approach of night. I know that the woman brought to the sacred supper "an alabaster box of ointment" and anointed the feet of the Lord, and refreshed Him. . . . But that woman had not yet received the Word, for she was still a sinner. So she honored the Lord with what she thought was the most precious thing in her possession—the ointment. *Clement of Alexandria (c. 195, E), 2.253.*

Let a woman breathe the odor of the true royal ointment—that of Christ, not of lotions and scented powders. *Clement of Alexandria (c. 195, E), 2.254.*

[PAGAN ANTAGONIST, SPEAKING OF CHRISTIANS:] You do not grace your bodies with perfume! You reserve ointments only for funeral rites! You even refuse garlands for your sepulchers! *Mark Minucius Felix (c. 200, W), 4.179.*

SEE ALSO COSMETICS; GROOMING; JEWELRY.

PERPETUA

Perpetua was a female catechumen who heroically died as a martyr c. 203, along with several other catechumens. The account of her death is recorded in the *Passion of Perpetua and Felicitas,* which seems to have Montanistic leanings.

Among them also was Vivia Perpetua, respectably born, liberally educated, a married woman, having a father, mother, and two brothers. One of her brothers, like herself, was a catechumen. She also had an infant son at the breast. She herself was about twenty-two years of age. From this point onward, she will herself narrate the whole course of her martyrdom. *Passion of Perpetua and Felicitas (c. 205, W), 3.699.*

PERSECUTION

I. Persecution of Christians

II. Christians do not persecute others

I. Persecution of Christians

Then they will deliver you up to tribulation and kill you, and you will be hated by all nations for My name's sake. Matt. 24:9.

All who desire to live godly in Christ Jesus will suffer persecution. 2 Tim. 3:12.

[The proconsul] tried to persuade him to deny [Christ], saying, . . . "Swear by the fortune of Caesar. Repent, and say, 'Away with the atheists.'" *Martyrdom of Polycarp (c. 135, E), 1.41.*

You have not treated us who are called Christians in like manner. We commit no wrong. In fact, as will appear in the rest of this discourse, we are of all men most piously and righteously disposed towards the Deity and towards your government. Nevertheless, you allow us to be harassed, plundered, and persecuted. The crowds make war upon us for our name alone. *Athenagoras (c. 175, E), 2.129.*

Gold which is hidden, as well as jewels, are dug up by those among us who are condemned to death. *Clement of Alexandria (c. 195, E), 2.268.*

They persecute us, not from the supposition that we are wrong-doers, but imagining that by the very fact of our being Christians we sin against life. This is because of the way we conduct ourselves, and because we exhort others to adopt a similar life. *Clement of Alexandria (c. 195, E), 2.423.*

If any one ruler whatever prohibits the Greek philosophy, that philosophy vanishes immediately. But our doctrine on its very first proclamation was prohibited by both kings and tyrants, as well as by local rulers and governors. . . . In fact, they tried as far as they could to exterminate it. However, it flourishes the more. For it does not die as does human doctrine. . . . Rather, it remains unchecked, although prophesied as destined to be persecuted to the end. *Clement of Alexandria (c. 195, E), 2.520.*

There is a persecution that arises externally—from men attacking the faithful. . . . However, the most painful is internal persecution, which proceeds from each man's own soul being vexed by ungodly lusts. *Clement of Alexandria (c. 195, E), 2.598.*

Christians alone are forbidden to say anything in exoneration of themselves. . . . All that is cared about is having what the public hatred demands! *Tertullian (c. 195, W), 3.18.*

Trajan wrote back that Christians were by no means to be sought after. But if they were brought before him, they should be punished. *Tertullian (c. 195, W), 3.18.*

You do not in that case deal with us in the ordinary way of judicial proceedings against offenders. For, in the case of [ordinary criminals] who deny, you use torture to make them *confess.* Christians alone do you torture to make them *deny!* Whereas, if we were guilty of any [real] crime, we would be sure to deny it, and you with your tortures would force us to confession. *Tertullian (c. 195, W), 3.19.*

You think that the Christian is a man of every crime, an enemy of the gods, of the emperor, of the laws, of good morals, and of all nature. Yet, you compel him to deny, that you may acquit him, which without his denial you could not do. In short, you play fast and loose with the laws. *Tertullian (c. 195, W), 3.19.*

What are we to think of the fact that most people so blindly knock their heads against the hatred of the Christian name? So that when they bear favorable testimony to anyone, they mingle with it abuse of the name he bears. For example, someone will say, "Gaius Seius is a good man, only he is a Christian." *Tertullian (c. 195, W), 3.20.*

It was in the days of Tiberius that the Christian name made its entry into the world. Having himself received intelligence from Palestine of events that had clearly shown the truth of Christ's divinity, Tiberius brought the matter before the Senate, with his own decision in favor of Christ. However, the senate rejected his proposal because it had not given the approval itself. Tiberius Caesar held to his opinion, threatening wrath against all accusers of the Christians. Consult your histories. You will there find that Nero was the first who attacked the Christian sect with the imperial sword. *Tertullian (c. 195, W), 3.22.*

We are daily beset by foes; we are daily betrayed! We are oftentimes surprised in our meetings and congregations. *Tertullian (c. 195, W), 3.23.*

You put Christians on crosses and stakes. . . . We are cast to the wild beasts. . . . We are burned in the flames. . . . We are condemned to the mines. . . . We are banished to islands. *Tertullian (c. 195, W), 3.28.*

Although torn and bleeding under your tortures, we cry out, "We worship God through Christ." *Tertullian (c. 195, W), 3.36.*

We alone are prevented from having a religion of our own. We give offense to the Romans and are excluded from the rights and privileges of Romans, because we do not worship the gods of Rome. *Tertullian (c. 195, W), 3.39.*

Some, indeed, think it is a mark of insanity that, when it is in our power to offer sacrifice at once and to go away unharmed (holding as ever our convictions), we prefer an obstinate persistence in our confession over our safety. *Tertullian (c. 195, W), 3.41.*

With our hands thus stretched out and up to God, rend us with your iron claws, hang us up on crosses, wrap us in flames, take our heads from us with the sword, let loose the wild beasts on us—the very attitude of a Christian praying is one of preparation for all punishment. *Tertullian (c. 195, W), 3.42.*

How often you inflict gross cruelties on Christians, partly because it is your own inclination, and partly in obedience to the laws. How often, too, the hostile mob, paying no regard to you, takes the law into its own hand, and attacks us with stones and flames. With the very frenzy of the Bacchanals, they do not even spare the Christian dead, but tear them from the rest of the tomb, now sadly changed, no longer entire. *Tertullian (c. 195, W), 3.45.*

Instead of taking into account what is due to us for the important protection we afford you, and though we are not merely no trouble to you, but in fact are necessary to your well-being, you prefer to view us as enemies. *Tertullian (c. 195, W), 3.45.*

Recently, in condemning a Christian woman to the pimp instead of to the lion, you acknowledged that a stain on our purity is considered among us something more terrible than any punishment or death. *Tertullian (c. 195, W), 3.55.*

If a Christian is pointed at, he glories in it. If dragged to trial, he does not resist. If accused, he makes no defense. When questioned, he confesses. When condemned, he rejoices. *Tertullian (c. 197, W), 3.109, 110.*

I know of various husbands, formerly anxious about their wives' conduct, . . . upon discovering the cause of their new diligence and their unwonted attention to the duties of home, offered the entire loan of their wives to others. . . . A father disinherited his son, with whom he had ceased to find fault. A master sent his slave to the workhouse, although he had even found the slave to be indispensable to him. As soon as they discovered that they were Christians, they preferred them to be criminals again! *Tertullian (c. 197, W), 3.112.*

Even in persecutions, it is better to take advantage of the permission granted and flee from town to town than—when apprehended and racked—to deny Christ. *Tertullian (c. 205, W), 4.40.*

Come, tell me what is your opinion of the flesh, when it has to contend for the name of Christ? When it is dragged out to public view and exposed to the hatred of all men? When it languishes in prisons under the cruellest deprivation of light, in banishment from the world, amidst squalor, filth, and foul-smelling food? When it has no freedom even in sleep, for it is bound on its very pallet and mangled in its bed of straw? When, at length before the public view, it is racked by every kind of torture that can be devised? *Tertullian (c. 210, W), 3.551.*

Every crowd in the popular assemblies is still shouting to "throw the Christians to the lions." *Tertullian (c. 210, W), 3.561.*

We can point you also to the deaths of some provincial rulers, who in their last hours had painful memories of their sin in persecuting the followers of Christ. . . . Claudius Lucius Herminianus in Cappadocia, enraged that his wife had become a Christian, had treated the Christians with great cruelty. Well, left alone in his palace, suffering under a contagious malady, he boiled out in living worms, and was heard exclaiming, "Let nobody know of it, lest the Christians rejoice, and Christian wives take encouragement." *Tertullian (c. 212, W), 3.106.*

We, who are without fear ourselves, are not seeking to frighten you. Rather, we would save all men, if possible, by warning them not to fight with God. You may perform the duties of your charge, and yet remember the claims of humanity. *Tertullian (c. 212, W), 3.106.*

But you say, "How will we assemble together [if we do not pay tribute to avoid persecution]?" To be sure, just as the apostles also did—who were protected by faith, not by money. . . . If you cannot assemble by day, you have the night—the light of Christ luminous against its darkness. . . . Be content with a church of threes. It is better that you sometimes should not see your crowds [of other Christians], than to subject yourselves [to paying tribute]. *Tertullian (c. 212, W), 4.125.*

Pagan assemblies have their own circus, where they readily join in the cry, "Death to the third race!" *Tertullian (c. 213, W), 3.643.*

We are regarded as persons to be hated by all men for the sake of the Name—just as it was written. And we are delivered up by our nearest of kin also—as it was written. We are brought before magistrates, examined, tortured, make confession [of Christ], and are ruthlessly killed—as it was written. *Tertullian (c. 213, W), 3.645.*

For the church is afflicted and pressed, not only by the Jews, but also by the Gentiles. It is also afflicted by those who are called Christians, but are not such in reality. *Hippolytus (c. 205, W), 5.193.*

In the case of the Christians, the Roman senate, the rulers of the time, the soldiers, the people, and the relatives of those who had become converts to the faith—they all made war upon their doctrine and would have defeated it. They would have overcome it by a confederacy of so powerful a nature, had it not escaped the danger by the help of God. It has risen above these forces, in order to defeat the whole world in conspiracy against it. *Origen (c. 248, E), 4.398.*

When God gives to the Tempter permission to persecute us, then we suffer persecution. And when God wishes us to be free from suffering—even in the middle of a world that hates us—we enjoy a wonderful peace. We trust in the protection of Him who said, "Be of good cheer, for I have overcome the world." *Origen (c. 248, E), 4.666.*

Part of you have already gone before us by the consummation of their martyrdom to receive from their Lord the crown of their deserts. Part still abide in the dungeons of the prison, or in the mines and in chains—exhibiting by the very delays of their punishments, greater examples for the strengthening and arming of the brethren. . . . The body is not cherished in the mines with couch and cushions. Rather, it is cherished with the refreshment and solace of Christ. The frame that is wearied with labors lies prostrate on the ground. Yet, it is no shame to lie down with Christ. Your unwashed limbs are foul and disfigured with filth and dirt. Yet, within, they are spiritually cleansed. . . . There the bread is scarce, but man does not live by bread alone, but by the Word of God. Shivering, you need clothing. But he who puts on Christ is both abundantly clothed and adorned. The hair of your half-shorn head seems repulsive. However, Christ is the head of the man, so anything is attractive to that head if it is illustrious on account of Christ's name. *Cyprian (c. 250, W), 5.403.*

[Emperor] Valerian had sent a rescript to the Senate, to the effect that bishops, presbyters, and deacons should immediately be punished. In addition, Christians who were senators, men of importance, or Roman knights were to lose their dignity and be deprived of their property. And if, when their means were taken away, they still persisted in being Christians, then they were to lose their heads. Matrons were to be deprived of their property and sent into banishment. People of Caesar's household, whoever of them had either confessed before or should now confess, were to have their property confiscated and be sent in chains by assignment to Caesar's estates. *Cyprian (c. 250, W), 5.408.*

The Lord has desired his family to be tested. Because a long peace had corrupted the discipline that had been divinely delivered to us, the heavenly rebuke has aroused our faith. For our faith was slipping and (I might say) slumbering. Although we deserved more for our sins, yet the most merciful Lord has so moderated all things that all that has happened has seemed more like a trial than a persecution. *Cyprian (c. 250, W), 5.438.*

Nor, indeed, are you Romans content with a brief endurance of our sufferings and with a simple and swift exhaustion of pains. You set in motion slow tortures, by tearing our bodies. You multiply numerous punishments by lacerating our vital organs. In fact, your brutality and fierceness cannot be content with ordinary tortures. Rather, ingenious cruelty devises new sufferings. *Cyprian (c. 250, W), 5.461.*

The Holy Spirit teaches and shows us that the army of the devil is not to be feared. And if the foe should declare war against us, our hope consists in that very war itself. . . . In Exodus, the Holy Scripture declares that we are actually multiplied and increased by afflictions. *Cyprian (c. 250, W), 5.501.*

There were many and frequent earthquakes, so that many places were destroyed throughout Cappadocia and Pontus. . . . From this, there also arose a severe persecution against those of us of the Christian name. And this persecution arose suddenly after the long peace of the previous age. . . . The faithful . . . fled here and there out of fear of the persecution. They left their country and passed over into other regions. . . . For the persecution was not over the whole world, but was local. *Firmilian (c. 256, E), 5.392, 393.*

Even up to the present day, the governor does not cease to put to death, in a cruel manner . . . some of those who are brought before him. Others, he wears out by torture. Others, he wastes away with imprisonment and chains. *Dionysius of Alexandria (c. 262, E), 6.97.*

The persecution with us did not begin with the imperial edict, but preceded it by a whole year. A certain prophet and poet, an enemy to this city, . . . had previously roused and exasperated the masses of the pagans against us, inflaming them anew with the fires of their native superstition. *Dionysius of Alexandria (c. 262, E), 6.97.*

They torture, put to death, and banish the worshippers of the Most High God—that is, the righteous. Yet, those who hate us so vehemently are unable to give a reason for their hatred. *Lactantius (c. 304–313, W), 7.135.*

If any persons, through fear of pain or death, or by their own treachery, have deserted the heavenly oath and have consented to deadly sacrifices, the pagans praise them and load them with honors. This is so that they may lure others by their example. But as for those persons who have highly esteemed their faith and have not denied that they are worshippers of God, the pagans attack with all the strength of their butchery, as though they thirsted for blood. . . . Could anything be more desperate than to tor-

ture and tear in pieces him whom you know to be innocent? *Lactantius (c. 304–313, W), 7.144.*

Some were swift to slaughter [the Christians]. For example, there was a certain individual in Phrygia who burned a whole assembly of Christians, together with their place of meeting. *Lactantius (c. 304–313, W), 7.147.*

Our number . . . is never lessened, not even in persecution itself. For men may commit sin and may be defiled by sacrifice. But they cannot be turned away from God. For the truth prevails by its own power. *Lactantius (c. 304–313, W), 7.148.*

Our persecutors act with a blind and unreasonable fury, which we see but they do not. For it is not the men themselves who persecute us. For they have no cause of anger against the innocent. Rather, it is those defiled and abandoned spirits by whom the truth is both known and hated. Those spirits infiltrate their minds and goad them to fury in their ignorance. For, as long as there is peace among the people of God, these spirits flee from the righteous and fear them. *Lactantius (c. 304–313, W), 7.159.*

Lest they should be as much corrupted by ease as their forefathers had been by indulgence, it was His will that they should be oppressed by those in whose power He placed them. . . . There is another reason why He permits persecutions to be carried on against us: so that the people of God may be increased. And it is not difficult to show how or why this happens. First of all, great numbers are driven from the worship of the false gods by their hatred of cruelty. . . . [Second,] someone will invariably desire to know what that good thing is that is defended even to death. What is it that is preferred to all things that are pleasant and beloved in this life? For neither the loss of goods or the deprivation of light, nor bodily pain, nor tortures of their vital organs can deter Christians from it. These things have a great effect! And these causes have always especially increased the number of our followers. *Lactantius (c. 304–313, W), 7.161.*

Therefore, whatever things wicked rulers plan against us, God Himself permits to be done. And yet these most unjust persecutors—to whom the name of God is a subject of reproach and mockery—must not think that they will escape with impunity. *Lactantius (c. 304–313, W), 7.161.*

[Emperor Daia] forbade the slaying of God's servants, but he did command that they should be mutilated. So the confessors of the faith had their ears and nostrils slit, their hands and feet cut off, and their eyes dug out of their sockets. *Lactantius (c. 304–313, W), 7.316.*

Behold, all the adversaries are destroyed and tranquility has been re-established throughout the Roman empire. The late oppressed church arises again. The temple of God, overthrown by the hands of the wicked, is built with more glory than before. For God has raised up rulers to rescind the ungodly and bloody edicts of the tyrants and provide for the welfare of mankind. So now the cloud of past times is dispelled and peace and serenity gladden all hearts. *Lactantius (c. 320, W), 7.301.*

While [Emperor Diocletian] sacrificed, some attendants of his, who were Christians, stood by and they put the immortal sign on their foreheads. At this, the demons were chased away, and the holy rites were interrupted. . . . Then Diocletian, in furious passion, ordered not only all who were assisting at the holy ceremonies, but also all who resided within the palace to sacrifice. And, if they refused, they were to be whipped. And further, by letters to the commanding officers, he ordered that all soldiers should be forced to the same impiety, under pain of being dismissed from the service. *Lactantius (c. 320, W), 7.304.*

Presbyters and other officers of the church were seized (without evidence by witnesses or confession), condemned, and together with their families led to execution. In burning alive, no distinction of sex or age was regarded. And because of their great multitude, they were not burned one after another, but a herd of them were encircled with the same fire. Servants, having millstones tied around their necks, were cast into the sea. *Lactantius (c. 320, W), 7.306.*

They thirst for our blood, and for a long time they have been eager to remove us from the generations of men. *Arnobius (c. 305, E), 6.419.*

No innocent person who is foully slain is ever disgraced thereby. Nor is he stained by the mark of any shame when he suffers severe punishment because of the savage nature of his persecutor, rather than because of his own deserts. *Arnobius (c. 305, E), 6.424.*

Rather than to be unfaithful to Christ and to cast off the oaths of the warfare of salvation,

slaves choose to be tortured by their masters as they please, wives to be divorced, and children to be disinherited by their parents. *Arnobius (c. 305, E), 6.435.*

The bitterness of persecution of which you speak is our deliverance and not our oppression. Your ill treatment will not bring evil upon us. Rather, it will lead us to the light of liberty. *Arnobius (c. 305, E), 6.463.*

Your flames, banishments, tortures, and monsters with which you tear in pieces and rend asunder our bodies do not rob us of life. They only free us from our flesh. *Arnobius (c. 305, E), 6.463.*

Why, indeed, have our writings deserved to be given to the flames? Why have our meetings deserved to be cruelly broken up? *Arnobius (c. 305, E), 6.488.*

Notice, he says that *they* will deliver you up, not *you* will deliver *yourselves* up. . . . For he would have us flee from place to place so long as there are those who persecute us for his name's sake. Even again we hear Him say, "But when they persecute you in this city, flee to another." For he would not have us deliberately approach the ministers and attendants of the devil—so that we might not be the cause to them of a multiple death. *Peter of Alexandria (c. 310, E), 6.273.*

It is not lawful [for Christians] to criticize those who have left everything and have retired for the safety of their life. *Peter of Alexandria (c. 310, E), 6.277.*

Do not overlook any Christian who, because of the name of Christ and his love and faith towards God, is condemned by the ungodly to the games, the beasts, or the mines. But provide for his sustenance through your labor and your very sweat, and for a reward to the soldiers. Do this so that he may be relieved and taken care of. It should be your goal that so far as it lies in your power, your blessed brother may not be afflicted. *Apostolic Constitutions (compiled c. 390, E), 7.437.*

Let us not think it strange when we are persecuted. *Apostolic Constitutions (compiled c. 390, E), 7.439.*

Receive those who are persecuted on account of the faith and who flee from city to city—being mindful of the words of the Lord. For, knowing that "the spirit is willing, but the flesh is weak," they flee, preferring the spoiling of their goods, so that they may preserve the name of Christ in themselves without denying it. *Apostolic Constitutions (compiled c. 390, E), 7.498.*

II. Christians do not persecute others

Repay no one evil for evil. . . . Do not be overcome by evil, but overcome evil with good. Rom. 12:17, 21.

Christians are not allowed to use violence to correct the delinquencies of sins. For God crowns those who abstain from wickedness by *choice,* not those who abstain by *compulsion. Clement of Alexandria (c. 195, E), 2.581.*

[Celsus has claimed that we] "utter against one another dreadful blasphemies, saying all manner of things shameful to be spoken." . . . Now, in answer to this, I have already said that in philosophy and medicine, sects are to be found warring against other sects. We, however, who are followers of the Word of Jesus, have exercised ourselves in thinking, saying, and doing what is in harmony with His words. "When reviled, we bless; being persecuted, we suffer it; being defamed, we entreat." So we would *not* utter "all manner of things shameful to be spoken" against those who have adopted different opinions from ours. Rather, if possible, we use every effort to raise them to a better condition. . . . Yet, if those who hold different opinions will not be convinced, we observe the injunction laid down for the treatment of such a person: "A man who is a heretic, after the first and second admonition, reject." . . . Moreover, we know the following teachings: "Blessed are the peacemakers" and "Blessed are the meek." Therefore, we would not regard with hatred the corrupters of Christianity. . . . We could also employ innumerable other quotations from the Scriptures, such as, "For though we walk in the flesh, we do not war after the flesh." *Origen (c. 248, E), 4.570, 571.*

Christians could not slay their enemies or condemn those who had broken the law to be burned or stoned, as Moses commands. *Origen (c. 248, E), 4.621.*

Torture and piety are widely different. Nor is it possible for truth to be united with violence, or justice with cruelty. *Lactantius (c. 304–313, W), 7.156.*

Religion is to be defended—not by putting to death—but by dying. Not by cruelty, but by patient endurance. *Lactantius (c. 304–313, W), 7.157.*

We, on the contrary, do not require that anyone should be compelled to worship our God, whether he is willing or unwilling. . . . Nor are we angry if anyone does not worship Him. For we trust in the majesty of Him who has power to avenge contempt shown towards Himself. . . . And, therefore, when we suffer such impious things, we do not resist even in word. Rather, we leave vengeance to God. We do not act as those persons who would have it appear that they are defenders of their gods, who rage without restraint against those who do not worship them. *Lactantius (c. 304–313, W), 7.158.*

The children who had gathered about the place set the example and began to pelt Manes [a heretic] and drive him off. And the rest of the crowd [of Christians] followed them and moved excitedly about, with the intention of compelling Manes to flee. However, when Archelaus [a Christian bishop] observed this, he raised his voice like a trumpet above the din, in his anxiety to restrain the crowd. He addressed them in this manner: "Stop, my beloved brethren, lest perhaps we are found to have bloodguilt on us at the Day of Judgment. For it is written of men like this, that "there must also be heresies among you, that those who are approved may be made manifest."" *Disputation of Archelaus and Manes (c. 320, E), 6.213; extended discussion: 5.457–5.465, 6.96–6.100.*

History of the major persecutions: 7.301–7.322.

See also Lapsed; Martyrs, Martyrdom; Nero; Nonresistance.

PERSEVERANCE OF THE SAINTS

See Salvation (VI. Can Those Who Are Saved Ever Be Lost?)

PERSIA, PERSIANS

O Greeks, do not be hostile towards the barbarians. Do not look on their opinions with ill will. For which of your institutions has not been derived from the barbarians? . . . To the Babylonians you owe astronomy; to the Persians, magic. *Tatian (c. 160, E), 2.65.*

Ctesias tells us that the Persians have illicit intercourse with their mothers. *Tertullian (c. 195, W), 3.26.*

The Persians have made themselves laws permitting them to take as wives their sisters, daughters, and granddaughters. There are some who go even further and take even their mothers. . . . There are many places, too, in the kingdom of Persia where men kill their wives, brothers, and children—yet incur no penalty. In contrast, among the Romans and the Greeks, he who kills one of these incurs capital punishment, the severest of penalties. *Bardesanes (c. 222, E), 8.730.*

In regard to the Persians, we have already said that though they do not build temples, yet they worship the sun and the other works of God. *Origen (c. 248, E), 4.637.*

If the gods willed that the Germans and the Persians would be defeated because Christians dwelled among their tribes, how did they grant victory to the Romans? For Christians dwelled among their peoples also. *Arnobius (c. 305, E), 6.417.*

You laugh because in ancient times the Persians worshiped rivers, as is told in the writings that hand these things down. *Arnobius (c. 305, E), 6.510.*

It is the manner and practice of the Persians for the people to yield themselves as slaves to their kings—and for the kings to treat their people as slaves. *Lactantius (c. 320, W), 7.309.*

The honorable report of Marcellus' name was carried into the territory of Persia. In this country dwelled a man named Manes. *Disputation of Archelaus and Manes (c. 320, E), 6.181.*

SEE ALSO MAGI.

PETER

Simon Peter answered and said, "You are the Christ, the Son of the living God." Jesus answered and said to him, "Blessed are you, Simon Bar-Jonah, for flesh and blood has not revealed this to you, but My Father who is in heaven. And I also say to you that you are Peter, and on this rock I will build My church, and the gates of Hades shall not prevail against it. And I will give you the keys of the kingdom of heaven, and whatever you bind on earth will be bound in heaven, and whatever you loose on earth will be loosed in heaven." Matt. 16:16–19.

"Most assuredly, I say to you when you were younger, you girded yourself and walked where you wished; but when you are old, you will stretch out your hands, and another will gird you and carry you where

you do not wish." This He spoke, signifying by what death [Peter] would glorify God. John 21:18, 19.

Do we have no right to take along a believing wife, as do also the other apostles, the brothers of the Lord, and Cephas? 1 Cor. 9:5.

But when Peter had come to Antioch, I withstood him to his face, because he was to be blamed. Gal. 2:11.

Through envy and jealousy, the greatest and most righteous pillars have been persecuted and put to death. Let us set before our eyes the illustrious apostles. Peter, through unrighteous envy, endured not one or two, but numerous labors; and when he had at length suffered martyrdom, he departed to the place of glory due to him. *Clement of Rome (c. 96, W), 1.6.*

I do not, as Peter and Paul, issue commandments to you. They were apostles. *Ignatius (c. 105, E), 1.75.*

Matthew also issued a written Gospel among the Hebrews in their own dialect, while Peter and Paul were preaching at Rome, and laying the foundations of the church. After their departure, Mark, the disciple and interpreter of Peter, also handed down to us in writing what had been preached by Peter. *Irenaeus (c. 180, E/W), 1.414.*

The universally known church was founded and organized at Rome by the two most glorious apostles, Peter and Paul. *Irenaeus (c. 180, E/W), 1.415.*

They say, accordingly, that the blessed Peter, on seeing his wife led to death, rejoiced on account of her call and conveyance home. He called to her very encouragingly and comfortingly, addressing her by name and saying, "Remember the Lord!" Such was the marriage of the blessed and their perfect disposition towards those dearest to them. *Clement of Alexandria (c. 195, E), 2.541.*

Mark was the follower of Peter, when Peter publicly preached the gospel at Rome before some of Caesar's equestrian knights. *Clement of Alexandria (c. 195, E), 2.573.*

[Clement of Alexandria] says that Peter, James, and John (after the Savior's ascension), although preeminently honored by the Lord, did not contend for glory. Rather, they appointed James the Just as bishop of Jerusalem. *Eusebius, citing Clement of Alexandria (c. 195, E), 2.579.*

To James the Just, John, and Peter, the Lord imparted knowledge after His resurrection. These imparted it to the rest of the apostles. And the rest of the apostles imparted it to the Seventy, of whom Barnabas was one. *Eusebius, citing Clement of Alexandria (c. 195, E), 2.579.*

The blessed Peter was the chosen, the pre-eminent, the first of the disciples for whom alone and himself the Savior paid tribute. So, on hearing those words, he quickly seized and comprehended the saying. *Clement of Alexandria (c. 195, E), 2.597.*

What man of sound mind can possibly suppose that these men were ignorant of anything, whom the Lord ordained to be teachers? . . . Was anything withheld from the knowledge of Peter, who is called the rock on which the church should be built, who also obtained "the keys of the kingdom of heaven" with the power of loosing and binding in heaven and on earth? Was anything, again, concealed from John, the Lord's most beloved disciple, who used to lean on His breast? *Tertullian (c. 197, W), 3.253.*

Now, with the view of branding the apostles with some mark of ignorance, the Marcionites put forth the case of when Peter and those who were with him were rebuked by Paul. . . . Still, they need to prove from the circumstance which they allege (of Peter's being rebuked by Paul), that Paul added yet another form of the gospel in addition to that which Peter and the rest had previously set forth. *Tertullian (c. 197, W), 3.253, 254.*

As Paul himself narrates, he "went up to Jerusalem for the purpose of seeing Peter." This was no doubt because of his office, and by right of a common belief and preaching. . . . They accordingly even gave Paul "the right hand of fellowship" as a sign of their agreement with him. They arranged among themselves a distribution of office—not a diversity of gospel. *Tertullian (c. 197, W), 3.254.*

Peter was rebuked because, after he had lived with the Gentiles, he proceeded to separate himself from their company out of respect for persons. The fault surely was one of his manner of living, not his preaching. *Tertullian (c. 197, W), 3.254.*

It is a happy fact that Peter is on the same level with Paul in the very glory of martyrdom. *Tertullian (c. 197, W), 3.254.*

Jesus changes the name of Simon to Peter. . . . But why to *Peter*? If it was because of the vigor of his faith, there were many solid materials that might lend a name from their strength. Was it because Christ was both a rock and a stone? For we read of His being placed "as a stone of stumbling and as a rock of offense." *Tertullian (c. 207, W), 3.365.*

From what source do *you* usurp this right to "the church"? Is it because the Lord has said to Peter, "Upon this rock I will build My church" and "to you have I given the keys of the heavenly kingdom"? Or "Whatever you will have bound or loosed in earth will be bound or loosed in the heavens"? You presume that the power of binding and loosing has come down to you—that is, to every church of Peter. What sort of man are you! You subvert and completely change the clear intention of the Lord. For He conferred this power personally upon Peter. . . . This would mean that in Peter himself the church was reared. *Tertullian (c. 212, W), 4.99.*

Peter is girded by another when he is fastened to the cross. *Tertullian (c. 213, W), 3.648.*

Peter alone do I find to have been married. And that is through [mention of] his "mother-in-law." I am led to presume that he was once-married, on consideration of the church, which, built upon him, was destined to appoint every grade of her order from those who are once-married. *Tertullian (c. 217, W), 4.65.*

And Luke shows clearly that the principle on which he wrote was to write only of what fell under his own notice. This is seen by his omission of the martyrdom of Peter. *Muratorian Fragment (c. 200, W), 5.603.*

Peter, on whom the church of Christ is built—against which the gates of Hades will not prevail—left one epistle of acknowledged authenticity. Suppose we allow that he left a second; yet, this is doubtful. *Origen (c. 228, E), 9.346.*

If we, too, have said like Peter, "You are the Christ, the Son of the living God"—not as if flesh and blood had revealed it to us, but by light from the Father in heaven having shone in our heart—we become a Peter. So to us there might be said by the Word, "You are Peter, etc." For every disciple of Christ is a rock. . . . And upon every such rock is built every word of the church and the polity in accordance with it. For in each of the perfect—who have the combination of words, deeds, and thoughts that fill up the blessedness—the church is built by God. *Origen (c. 245, E), 9.456.*

But if you suppose that upon only that one Peter the whole church is built by God, what would you say about John, the son of thunder, or about each one of the apostles? Shall we dare to say that the gates of Hades will not prevail against Peter in particular, but that they will prevail against the other apostles and the perfect? Does not the saying previously made, "The gates of Hades will not prevail against it," apply in regard to all? . . . Are the keys of the kingdom of heaven given by the Lord to Peter only and will none other of the blessed receive them? *Origen (c. 245, E), 9.456.*

In this place [Matt. 16:18, 19], these words seem to be addressed to only Peter—"Whatever you will bind on earth will be bound in heaven." However, in the Gospel of John, the Savior gave the Holy Spirit to the disciples by breathing upon them and said, "Receive the Holy Spirit, etc." Many then will say to the Savior, "You are the Christ, the Son of the living God." . . . And if anyone says this to Him . . . through the Father in heaven, he will obtain the things that were spoken according to the language of the gospel to Peter. . . . For all who are the imitators of Christ bear the surname of "rock." . . . Furthermore, as members of Christ, they derive their surname from Him, being called "Christians." And from the rock, they are called "Peters." *Origen (c. 245, E), 9.456.*

Peter himself seems to have observed for a considerable time the Jewish observances commanded by the Law of Moses. For he had not yet learned from Jesus to ascend from the Law that is regulated according to the letter to that which is interpreted according to the spirit. . . . Moreover, in the Epistle to the Galatians, Paul states that Peter, from fear of the Jews, ceased to eat with the Gentiles upon the arrival of James. *Origen (c. 248, E), 4.429.*

Peter, upon whom by the same Lord the church had been built, speaking one for all, and answering with the voice of the church, says, "Lord, to whom will we go?" *Cyprian (c. 250, W), 5.341.*

Peter, on whom the church was to be built, taught . . . that the church will not depart from Christ. *Cyprian (c. 250, W), 5.374.*

The Lord spoke to Peter, saying, "I say unto you, 'You are Peter; and upon this rock I will build my church.'" . . . And, again, to the same apostle He says after His resurrection, "Feed my sheep." And, after His resurrection, He gave an equal power to all the apostles, saying, "As the Father has sent me, even so I send you. Receive the Holy Spirit. Anyone's sins you forgive, they will be forgiven unto him. And anyone's sins you retain, they will be retained." Yet, that He might set forth unity, He arranged by His authority the origin of that unity, as beginning from one apostle. Assuredly, the rest of the apostles were also the same as was Peter—endowed with a like partnership, both of honor and power. Still, the beginning proceeds from unity. In the Song of Songs, in the person of our Lord, the Holy Spirit designated this as being one church, saying, "My dove, my spotless one, is but one." *Cyprian (c. 250, W), 5.422.*

Peter himself was the leader and chief of the apostles. *Treatise on Re-Baptism (c. 257, W), 5.672.*

They did not acquiesce on this matter with the authority of some—namely, the successors of Peter and Paul. For [those apostles] had taught all the churches in which they sowed the spiritual seeds of the Gospel that the solemn festival of the resurrection of the Lord can only be celebrated on the Lord's Day. *Anatolius (c. 270, E), 6.148, 149.*

Peter and Paul preached at Rome. *Lactantius (c. 304–313, W), 7.123.*

[The people of Rome] had seen the chariot of Simon Magus, his fiery car, blown into pieces by the mouth of Peter and vanish when Christ was named. *Arnobius (c. 305, E), 6.438.*

Peter, the first of the apostles, was often arrested, thrown into prison, and treated with dishonor. He was finally crucified at Rome. *Peter of Alexandria (c. 310, E), 6.273.*

While Nero reigned, the apostle Peter came to Rome. Through the power of God committed to him, he worked certain miracles. And by turning many to the true religion, he built up a faithful and steadfast temple unto the Lord. . . . It was Nero who first persecuted the servants of God. He crucified Peter and slew Paul. *Lactantius (c. 320, W), 7.301, 302.*

SEE ALSO APOSTLES, TWELVE; BINDING AND LOOSING; KEYS OF THE KINGDOM; PAUL, APOSTLE; SIMON MAGUS.

PHARISEES

Woe to you, scribes and Pharisees, hypocrites! For you are like whitewashed tombs which indeed appear beautiful outwardly, but inside are full of dead men's bones and all uncleanness. Even so you also outwardly appear righteous to men, but inside you are full of hypocrisy and lawlessness. Matt. 23:27, 28.

[The Pharisees] hold firmly to the ancient tradition and continue to pursue in an argumentative spirit a close investigation into the things that are clean and unclean according to the Law. And they interpret the Law and put forward teachers for such things. They assert the existence of fate and that some things are in our power, whereas others are under the control of destiny. In this way, they maintain that some things depend upon ourselves, whereas others depend upon fate. But they say that God is the cause of all things and that nothing is managed or happens without His will. These likewise acknowledge that there is a resurrection of the flesh, that the soul is immortal, and that there will be a judgment and conflagration. They say that the righteous will be imperishable, but that the wicked will endure everlasting punishment in unquenchable fire. *Hippolytus (c. 225, W), 5.137.*

Knowing their ruin, the Lord Jesus told them that they attended to only those things that are external and that they disdained as something foreign those things that are inside. *Disputation of Archelaus and Manes (c. 320, E), 6.194.*

Even the Jewish nation had wicked heresies. . . . There are the Pharisees, who ascribe the practice of sinners to fortune and fate. *Apostolic Constitutions (compiled c. 390, E), 7.452.*

SEE ALSO ESSENES; JEW, JEWS; SADDUCEES.

PHILIP

The Philip discussed below is the deacon Philip, spoken of in the book of Acts. Some of the quotations below appear to confuse him with the apostle Philip.

And the saying pleased the whole multitude. And they chose Stephen, a man full of faith and the Holy Spirit, and Philip, . . . whom they set before the apostles; and when they had prayed, they laid hands on them. Acts 6:5, 6.

On the next day we who were Paul's companions departed and came to Caesarea, and entered the house

of Philip the evangelist, who was one of the seven, and stayed with him. Now this man had four virgin daughters who prophesied. Acts. 21:8, 9.

The residence of the apostle Philip with his daughters in Hierapolis has been mentioned above. We must now point out how Papias, who lived at the same time, relates that he had received a wonderful narrative from the daughters of Philip. For he says that a dead man was raised to life in his day. *Eusebius, citing Papias (c. 120, E), 1.154.*

[I speak of] Philip, one of the twelve apostles, who is laid to rest at Hierapolis. Also his two daughters, who arrived at old age unmarried. His other daughter also, who passed her life under the influence of the Holy Spirit, reposes at Ephesus. *Polycrates (c. 190), 8.773.*

After this, there were four prophetesses—daughters of Philip, at Hierapolis in Asia. Their tomb is there, and so is that of their father. *Eusebius, quoting Caius (c. 215, W), 5.601.*

Those who had believed in Samaria . . . had been baptized by Philip the deacon, whom the same apostles had sent. *Cyprian (c. 250, W), 5.381.*

Philip, our fellow apostle, performed miracles of healing in Samaria by the gift of the Lord and the energy of His Spirit. As a result, the Samaritans were affected and embraced the faith of the God of the universe and of the Lord Jesus. *Apostolic Constitutions (compiled c. 390, E), 7.452.*

SEE ALSO ETHIOPIAN EUNUCH.

PHILO

Philo (c. 20 B.C.–A.D. 50) was an Alexandrian Jew who wrote numerous spiritual works, including commentaries on the Old Testament. He used Greek Platonic thought to give allegorical interpretations to many Old Testament passages. Centuries after his death, his methods greatly influenced Origen, who was also a native of Alexandria.

You men of Greece, these things about the antiquity of Moses have been recorded in writing by men who were not of our religion. . . . I am speaking of Philo and Josephus. For, in their account of the history of the Jews, these men say that Moses was descended from the race of the Chaldeans and was born in Egypt. *Justin Martyr (c. 160, E), 1.277.*

I have told you things so that you can also learn from others—and especially from those wise and esteemed men who have written of these things, Philo and Josephus. *Justin Martyr (c. 160, E), 1.278, 279.*

Philo says in his life of Moses that certain Greeks taught the rest of the usual course of instruction to Moses in Egypt as a royal child. *Clement of Alexandria (c. 195, E), 2.335.*

[CELSUS, A PAGAN CRITIC:] "However, the allegorical explanations that have been devised are much more shameful and absurd than the fables themselves." . . . [ORIGEN'S REPLY:] He seems to refer in these words to the works of Philo, or to those of still older writers, such as Aristobulus. But I conjecture that Celsus has not read their books. For it seems to me that in many passages, they have so successfully hit the meaning that even Grecian philosophers would have been captivated by their explanations. *Origen (c. 248, E), 4.521.*

This may be learned from what Philo, Josephus, and Musaeus have written. *Anatolius (c. 270, E), 6.147.*

SEE ALSO JOSEPHUS.

PHILOSOPHERS, PHILOSOPHY

I. Condemnation of Greek philosophy

II. Christians who viewed philosophy as having some value

III. Did the philosophers borrow from Moses and the Prophets?

IV. The teachings of the philosophers

I. Condemnation of Greek philosophy

Where is the wise? Where is the scribe? Where is the disputer of this age? Has not God made foolish the wisdom of this world? 1 Cor. 1:20.

Let no one deceive himself. If anyone among you seems to be wise in this age, let him become a fool that he may become wise. For the wisdom of this world is foolishness with God. 1 Cor. 3:18, 19.

Beware lest anyone cheat you through philosophy and empty deceit, according to the tradition of men, according to the basic principles of the world, and not according to Christ. Col. 2:8.

Great is the error that the philosophers among them have brought upon their followers. *Aristides (c. 125, E), 9.266.*

You [Romans] profess to despise death and to be sufficient of yourselves for everything. However, this is a discipline in which your philosophers are greatly deficient. In fact, some of them receive from the king of the Romans 600 aurei yearly. Yet, they perform no useful service. So they will not even wear a long beard without being paid for it! *Tatian (c. 160, E), 2.73.*

What great and wonderful things have your philosophers effected? They leave uncovered one of their shoulders. They let their hair grow long. They cultivate their beards. Their nails are like the claws of wild beasts. They say that they want nothing. However, like Proteus, they need a tanner for their wallet, a weaver for their mantle, a wood-cutter for their staff, rich patrons, and a cook for their gluttony. *Tatian (c. 160, E), 2.75.*

One of the philosophers asserts that God is body, but I assert that He is without body. One of the philosophers asserts that the world is indestructible, but I say that it is to be destroyed. *Tatian (c. 160, E), 2.76.*

And regarding lawless conduct, those who have blindly wandered into the choir of philosophy have, almost to a man, spoken with one voice. Certainly Plato did, to mention him first. He seems to have been the most respectable philosopher among them. Yet, he expressly legislates (so to speak) in his first book, entitled *The Republic,* that the wives of all should be held in common. *Theophilus (c. 180, E), 2.112.*

Who compels a philosopher to sacrifice or take an oath, or put out useless lamps at midday? Nay, they openly overthrow your gods. And in their writings, they attack your superstitions. Yet, you applaud them for it. *Tertullian (c. 195, W), 3.50.*

But it will be said that some of us, too, depart from the rules of our discipline. In that case, however, we count them no longer Christians. But the philosophers who do such things still retain the name and the honor of wisdom. So, then, where is there any likeness between the Christian and the philosopher? Between the disciple of Greece and the disciple of heaven? *Tertullian (c. 195, W), 3.51.*

The God whom they had so imperfectly admitted, they could neither know nor fear. Therefore, they could not be wise, since they wandered away indeed from "the beginning of wisdom"—that is, "the fear of God." *Tertullian (c. 197, W), 3.130.*

Heresies are themselves instigated by philosophy. *Tertullian (c. 197, W), 3.246.*

What indeed has Athens to do with Jerusalem? What agreement is there between the Academy and the church? . . . Away with all attempts to produce a mottled Christianity of Stoic, Platonic, and dialectic composition! *Tertullian (c. 197, W), 3.246.*

The philosophers are the patriarchs of all heresy. *Tertullian (c. 200, W), 3.482.*

[The philosophers] knocked at the door of truth. But they did not enter. *Tertullian (c. 210, W), 3.545.*

I would prefer to God that no "heresies had been ever necessary, in order that they who are approved may be made manifest!" For then we would never be required to test our strength in contests about the soul with philosophers—those patriarchs of heretics, as they may be fairly called. The apostle, so far back as his own time, foresaw, indeed, that philosophy would do violent injury to the truth. *Tertullian (c. 210, W), 3.183.*

Some of the philosophers deny the immortality of the soul. Others affirm that it is immortal, and something more. . . . The fault, I suppose, of the divine doctrine lies in its springing from Judea rather than from Greece! Christ made a mistake, too, in sending forth fishermen to preach, rather than the sophist! *Tertullian (c. 210, W), 3.184.*

I may tell you from my experience that not many "take from Egypt" only what is useful—that is, going away and using it for the service of God. . . . Rather, there are those who, from their Greek studies, produce heretical notions and set them up like the golden calf in Bethel. *Origen (c. 240, E), 4.393.*

We testify of certain Greek philosophers that they knew God, seeing "He manifested Himself to them," although "they did not glorify Him as God, neither were they thankful, but became vain in their imaginations; and professing themselves to be wise, they became foolish." *Origen (c. 248, E), 4.510.*

However, those who have written in this [praiseworthy] manner about the "chief good"

will still go down . . . and offer prayer to Artemis, as if she were God. . . . They pass from those great topics that God has revealed to them and adopt low and trifling thoughts. They even offer a rooster to Aesculapius! *Origen (c. 248, E), 4.574.*

We see that philosophers are neither lowly nor meek. Rather, they greatly please themselves. *Cyprian (c. 250, W), 5.484.*

This latter class [of philosophers], in proportion to their superior wisdom (in that they understood the error of false religion) rendered themselves so much the more foolish, for they did not realize that some religion was true. . . . Thus, philosophers have reached the height of human wisdom, in understanding that which does *not* exist. But they have failed in attaining the power of saying what truly *does* exist. It is a well-known saying of Cicero: "I wish that I could as easily find out the truth as I can refute false things." *Lactantius (c. 304–313, W), 7.44.*

It has been handed down to us in the sacred writings that the thoughts of philosophers are foolish. . . . Therefore, there is no reason why we should give so much honor to philosophers. *Lactantius (c. 304–313, W), 7.70.*

This is the way that philosophers *seek.* However, they do not *find.* That is because they prefer to seek it on the earth, where it cannot be found. *Lactantius (c. 304–313, W), 7.170.*

This is the reason why the philosophers—although they may be naturally good—have no knowledge and no intelligence. All of their learning and virtue is without a head. For they are ignorant of God, who is the head of virtue and knowledge. *Lactantius (c. 304–313, W), 7.172.*

II. Christians who viewed philosophy as having some value

Although most of the early Christian writers viewed philosophy primarily in a negative light, a few believed that God had planted seeds of truth in Greek philosophy as a tool to eventually bring the Greeks to Christ.

Do not the philosophers turn every discourse on God? Is not this truly the duty of philosophy, to investigate the Deity? *Justin Martyr (c. 160, E), 1.194.*

My book will not shrink from making use of what is best in philosophy and other preparatory instruction. According to the apostle, "For not only for the Hebrews and those who are under the Law is it right to become a Jew, but also a Greek for the sake of the Greeks, that we may gain all." *Clement of Alexandria (c. 195, E), 2.302, 303.*

The *Miscellanies* will contain the truth mixed up in the dogmas of philosophy—or rather covered over and hidden in them, as the edible part of the nut in the shell. . . . I am not oblivious of what is babbled by some, who in their ignorance are frightened at every noise, and say that we should occupy ourselves with what is most necessary and which contains the faith—and that we should pass over what is beyond and superfluous. *Clement of Alexandria (c. 195, E), 2.303.*

Others think that philosophy was introduced into life by an evil influence, for the ruin of men, by an evil inventor. But I will show, throughout the whole of these *Miscellanies,* that evil has an evil nature. It can never turn out to be the producer of what is good. This indicates that philosophy is, in a sense, a work of divine providence. *Clement of Alexandria (c. 195, E), 2.303.*

Before the advent of the Lord, philosophy was necessary to the Greeks for righteousness. And now it becomes conducive to piety. It is a kind of preparatory training to those who attain to faith through demonstration. . . . Perhaps, too, philosophy was given to the Greeks directly and primarily, until the Lord would call the Greeks. For this was a pedagogue to bring "the Hellenic mind" to Christ, as the Law did the Hebrews. *Clement of Alexandria (c. 195, E), 2.305.*

I do not mean the Stoic, or the Platonic, or the Epicurean, or the Aristotelian, but whatever has been well said by each of those sects that teaches righteousness along with a knowledge pervaded by piety. This eclectic whole I call philosophy. But the conclusions of human reasonings, that men have cut away and falsified, I would never call divine. *Clement of Alexandria (c. 195, E), 2.308.*

Some, who think themselves naturally gifted, do not wish to touch either philosophy or logic. In fact, they do not wish to learn natural science. They demand bare faith alone! *Clement of Alexandria (c. 195, E), 2.309.*

Hellenic philosophy does not comprehend the whole extent of the truth. Besides, it is destitute of strength to perform the command-ments of the Lord. Yet, it prepares the way for the truly royal teaching. *Clement of Alexandria (c. 195, E), 2.318.*

Philosophy, it is said, was not sent by the Lord, but came stolen, or given by a thief. It was then some power or angel who had learned something of the truth, but did not abide in it. He inspired and taught these things—not without the Lord's knowledge. . . . Now, the devil . . . was the author of the theft. *Clement of Alexandria (c. 195, E), 2.319.*

"He that does not enter in by the door into the sheepfold, but climbs up some other way, the same is a thief and a robber.". . . Men must be saved, then, by learning the truth through Christ, even if they attain philosophy. *Clement of Alexandria (c. 195, E), 2.465.*

We will not err in alleging that all things necessary and profitable for life came to us from God, and that philosophy more especially was given to the Greeks, as a covenant peculiar to them. *Clement of Alexandria (c. 195, E), 2.495.*

But the majority [of Christians] are frightened at the Hellenic philosophy, as children are at masks, being afraid lest it lead them astray. *Clement of Alexandria (c. 195, E), 2.498.*

This is the heresy of the barbarian philosophy: Although they speak of one God, although they sing the praises of Christ, they speak without accuracy, not in accordance with truth. For they follow another god, and they do not receive Christ as the prophecies deliver. *Clement of Alexandria (c. 195, E), 2.509.*

Philosophy is not, then, the product of vice, since it makes men virtuous. It follows, then, that it is the work of God. *Clement of Alexandria (c. 195, E), 2.517.*

Greek philosophy, as it were, purges the soul and prepares it beforehand for the reception of faith, on which the Truth builds up the edifice of knowledge. *Clement of Alexandria (c. 195, E), 2.528.*

I have set forth the opinions of almost all the philosophers whose more illustrious glory is that they have pointed out that there is one God, although with many names. So someone might think either that Christians are now philosophers, or that philosophers were then already Christians. *Mark Minucius Felix (c. 200, W), 4.184.*

Another branch of learning occupies my mind completely. . . . I refer to those admirable laws of our sages, by which the affairs of all the subjects of the Roman Empire are now directed. . . . These are wise and exact in themselves, as well as manifold and admirable. In a word, they are most thoroughly Grecian. *Gregory Thaumaturgus (c. 255, E), 6.21.*

III. Did the philosophers borrow from Moses and the Prophets?

Whatever both philosophers and poets have said concerning the immortality of the soul, or punishments after death, or contemplation of things heavenly, or doctrines of the like kind, they have received such suggestions from the prophets. And these have enabled them to interpret these things. And hence there seem to be seeds of truth among all men. *Justin Martyr (c. 160, E), 1.177.*

But now it seems proper for me to demonstrate that our philosophy is older than the systems of the Greeks. *Tatian (c. 160, E), 2.77.*

But let Homer be not later than the Trojan war. Let it be granted that he was contemporary with it. . . . Now, this Moses I have previously mentioned will be shown to have been many years older than the taking of Troy. . . . Therefore, from what has been said, it is evident that Moses was older than the ancient heroes, wars, and demons. And we should believe him, who stands before them in point of age—rather than the Greeks, who, without being aware of it, drew his doctrines as from a fountain. *Tatian (c. 160, E), 2.80, 81.*

We may show that the Hebrew philosophy was older by many generations. *Clement of Alexandria (c. 195, E), 2.315.*

Well, be it so that "the thieves and robbers" are the philosophies among the Greeks, who before the coming of the Lord received fragments of the truth from the Hebrew prophets. They claimed these as their own teachings, without complete understanding of them. *Clement of Alexandria (c. 195, E), 2.320.*

On the plagiarizing of the dogmas of the philosophers from the Hebrews, we will address a little afterwards. . . . Through that discussion, the philosophy of the Hebrews will be demonstrated beyond all contradiction to be the most ancient of all wisdom. *Clement of Alexandria (c. 195, E), 2.324.*

Numenius, the Pythagorean philosopher, expressly writes, "For what is Plato, but Moses speaking in Attic Greek?" *Clement of Alexandria (c. 195, E), 2.334, 335.*

It is then clear also that all the other virtues set forth in Moses supplied the Greeks with the rudiments of the whole department of morals. *Clement of Alexandria (c. 195, E), 2.365.*

The philosophers of the Greeks are called thieves, inasmuch as they have taken their principal dogmas from Moses and the Prophets, without acknowledgement. *Clement of Alexandria (c. 195, E), 2.446.*

Let me now display with greater clarity the plagiarism by the Greeks of barbarian philosophy. *Clement of Alexandria (c. 195, E), 2.465.*

The philosophers, having heard it from Moses, taught that the world was created. *Clement of Alexandria (c. 195, E), 2.466.*

There would not be enough years in my life to try to enumerate in detail and expose the selfish plagiarism of the Greeks. They claim to have discovered for themselves the best of their doctrines. However, they have actually received them from us. *Clement of Alexandria (c. 195, E), 2.486.*

Nor do we need to wonder if the speculations of philosophers have perverted the older Scriptures. Some of their brood, with their opinions, have even adulterated our new-given Christian revelation, and corrupted it into a system of philosophic doctrines. *Tertullian (c. 195, W), 3.52.*

In their inquisitive disposition to search into all kinds of learning, the philosophers seem to have investigated the sacred Scriptures themselves because of the antiquity of the Scriptures. And they seem to have derived from them some other opinions. Yet, because they have interpolated these deductions, they prove that they have either despised them wholly or have not fully believed them. *Tertullian (c. 197, W), 3.130.*

IV. The teachings of the philosophers

Some of the philosophers of the Porch say that there is no God at all; or, if there is, they say that He cares for no one but Himself. And the folly of Epicurus and Chrysippus has set forth these views at large. And others say that all things are produced without external agency, that the world is uncreated, and that nature is eternal. *Theophilus (c. 180, E), 2.95.*

The Sibyl, then, and the other prophets, yes, and the poets and philosophers have clearly taught concerning righteousness, judgment, and punishment. *Theophilus (c. 180, E), 2.110.*

I am not unaware of what a vast mass of literature the philosophers have accumulated concerning the subject before us [i.e., the soul]. Nor am I unaware of what various schools of principles there are, what conflicts of opinion, what prolific sources of questions, and what perplexing methods of solution. *Tertullian (c. 210, W), 3.183.*

There is nothing after death, according to the school of Epicurus. To like effect, Seneca says that after death, all things come to an end, even death itself. However, it is sufficient that the no less important philosophy of Pythagoras, Empedocles, and the Platonists, take the contrary view—and declare the soul to be immortal. Moreover, they affirm in a way that most nearly approaches [our own] that the soul actually returns into bodies—although [according to the philosophers] not the same bodies, and not invariably those of human beings. *Tertullian (c. 210, W), 3.545.*

Among the moral philosophers are Socrates . . . and Plato, the pupil of Socrates. He combined three systems of philosophy. Among the logicians is Aristotle, a pupil of Plato. He systematized the art of dialectics. Among the Stoics were Chrysippus and Zeno. Epicurus, however, advanced an opinion contrary to almost all philosophers. *Hippolytus (c. 225, W), 5.9.*

Is the universe one coherent whole? It seems to be in our own judgment, as well as in that of the wisest of the Greek philosophers—such as Plato, Pythagoras, the Stoics, and Heraclitus. Or is it a duality, as some may possibly have conjectured? *Dionysius of Alexandria (c. 262, E), 6.84.*

So much for the poets. Let us come to the philosophers, whose authority is of greater weight and their judgment more to be relied on. . . . For they paid attention, not to matters of fiction, but to the investigation of the truth. . . . Pythagoras defined the being of God in this manner: "as a soul passing to and fro, and diffused through all parts of the universe." . . .

Anaxagoras said that God was an infinite mind, which moves by its own power. *Lactantius (c. 304–313, W), 7.14.*

Other philosophers say things contrary to the [Epicureans and others]. They say that the soul survives after death. The chief among these are the Pythagoreans and Stoics. *Lactantius (c. 304–313, W), 7.88; extended discussion: 2.321–2.324, 2.465–2.476, 2.486–2.488, 2.518, 2.559–2.567, 3.52–3.54, 3.130–3.132, 4.183–4.184, 5.9–5.23, 7.70–7.100.*

Discussion of history of philosophy: 2.313–2.315.

SEE ALSO EPICUREANS; PLATO; POETS, PAGAN; PYTHAGORAS; SOCRATES; SOUL; STOICS, STOICISM.

PHOENIX

The works of Herodotus, Pliny the Elder, and other educated men of the ancient world described a bird, called the phoenix, that supposedly lived in the east. According to them, the bird lived for centuries, and upon dying, it was reborn from its own remains. The early Christians, like most Romans, believed these accounts to be true. So the Christians saw in the phoenix a natural depiction of the resurrection of the dead. Some modern Christians unfairly criticize the early Christians for believing in the phoenix, as if somehow those Christians were supposed to know more about natural science than the scientists of their day!

Let us consider that wonderful sign that takes place in eastern lands—that is, in Arabia and the countries around it. There is a certain bird that is called a phoenix. This is the only one of its kind, and it lives for five hundred years. When the time of its dissolution draws near for it to die, it builds itself a nest of frankincense, myrrh, and other spices. When the time has come, it enters into the nest and dies. But as the flesh decays, a certain kind of worm is produced, which, being nourished by the essence of the dead bird, produces feathers. *Clement of Rome (c. 96, W), 1.12.*

Take a most complete and unassailable symbol of our hope. . . . I refer to the bird that is peculiar to the East. It is famous for its singularity, and it is marvelous from its posthumous life. For it renews its life in a voluntary death. Its dying day is its birthday. For on that day, it departs and returns—once more a phoenix where just now there was none. . . . Must *men* die once for all time, while *birds* in Arabia are sure of a resurrection? *Tertullian (c. 210, W), 3.554.*

The phoenix builds for herself either a nest or a tomb. For she perishes so that she may live. Yet, she re-produces herself. . . . In the meantime, her body is destroyed by death. But this proves to be the source of life. . . . After this, it is formed again, such as its figure was before. And the phoenix, having burst her shell, springs forth—even as caterpillars in the fields . . . are changed into butterflies. *Probably Lactantius (c. 310, W), 7.325.*

They say that there is a unique bird that provides a copious demonstration of the resurrection. They say that it has no mate and that there is only one in the creation. They call it a phoenix and say that every five hundred years it comes to Egypt. It comes to the place that is called the altar of the sun. It brings with it a great quantity of cinnamon, cassia, and balsamwood. Standing towards the east and praying to the sun, it burns out of its own power and becomes ashes. However, a worm arises again out of those ashes. And when the worm is warmed, it becomes a newly born phoenix. When it is able to fly, it goes back to Arabia. *Apostolic Constitutions (compiled c. 390, E), 7.441; extended discussion: 7.324–7.326.*

PHYSICIANS

SEE MEDICINE, MEDICAL SCIENCE.

PILATE, PONTIUS

When they had bound Him, they led Him away and delivered Him to Pontius Pilate the governor. Matt. 27:2.

That these things did happen, you can verify from the Acts of Pontius Pilate. *Justin Martyr (c. 160, E), 1.175.*

All these things Pilate did to Christ. And now in fact a Christian in his own convictions, Pilate sent word of Him to the reigning Caesar, who was at the time Tiberius. *Tertullian (c. 195, W), 3.35.*

[Celsus] does not realize that it was not so much Pilate who condemned Christ, . . . as it was the Jewish nation, which has been condemned by God. *Origen (c. 248, E), 4.445.*

SEE ALSO ROMAN EMPIRE, ROMANS.

PLAN OF GOD

SEE SOVEREIGNTY AND PROVIDENCE OF GOD.

PLATO

Plato (429–347 B.C.) was the most famous of Socrates' pupils, and he has had a major influence on western thought. He established a school of philosophical teaching in Athens called the Academy.

I. Miscellaneous teachings

II. Teaching on the soul

III. Did Plato borrow from Moses and the Prophets?

I. Miscellaneous teachings

At any rate, Plato said at one time that there are three first principles of the universe: God, matter, and form. *Justin Martyr (c. 160, E), 1.276.*

[ADDRESSED TO PAGANS:] If then the Savior said this and proclaimed salvation to the soul alone, what new thing did He bring us, beyond what we heard from Pythagoras and Plato and all their band? *Justin Martyr (c. 160, E), 1.299.*

If, therefore, Plato is not an atheist for conceiving of one uncreated God—the Framer of the universe—neither are we. *Athenagoras (c. 175, E), 2.132.*

But Plato and those of his school acknowledge indeed that God is uncreated, and is the Father and Maker of all things. However, they also maintain that matter is uncreated, as well as God. They say that it is co-eternal with God. *Theophilus (c. 180, E), 2.95.*

Plato . . . legislates in his first book, entitled the *Republic*, that the wives of all should be held in common, using the precedent of the son of Jupiter. *Theophilus (c. 180, E), 2.112.*

Plato is proved to be more religious than those men [the Gnostics], for he allowed that the same God was both just *and* good, having power over all things. *Irenaeus (c. 180, E/W), 1.459.*

For my part, I approve of Plato, who plainly lays it down as a law that a man is not to labor for wealth of gold or silver, nor to possess a useless vessel that is not required for some necessary purpose. *Clement of Alexandria (c. 195, E), 2.247.*

In his *Timaeus*, Plato's God is by His very name the parent of the world, the artificer of the soul, the fabricator of heavenly and earthly things. *Mark Minucius Felix (c. 200, W), 4.184.*

Plato, in the *Timaeus*, declares the operations of the senses to be irrational. He says they are influenced by our opinions or beliefs. *Tertullian (c. 210, W), 3.195.*

Plato says that there are three originating principles of the universe: God, matter, and form. . . . He says that matter is an originating principle and co-eternal with the Deity, and that in this respect the world is uncreated. . . . He admits natures of demons and says that some of them are good, but that others are worthless. And some assert that Plato states that the soul is uncreated and immortal. . . . Others, however, [say that Plato believed the soul was] created, but that it is rendered imperishable through the will of God. *Hippolytus (c. 225, W), 5.18.*

Plato is judged the wisest of all [the philosophers]. He plainly and openly maintains the rule of one God. And he does not name Him Ether, Reason, or Nature—but, as He truly is, God. And he says that this universe, so perfect and wonderful, was created by Him. *Lactantius (c. 304–313, W), 7.14.*

II. Teaching on the soul

I may use, therefore, the opinion of a Plato, when he declares, "Every soul is immortal." *Tertullian (c. 210, W), 3.547.*

What remains now but for us to give the soul a figure? Plato refuses to do this, as if it would endanger the soul's immortality. *Tertullian (c. 210, W), 3.188.*

I am sorry from my heart that Plato has been the caterer to all these heretics. For in the *Phaedo*, he imagines that souls wander from this world to that, and then back again from there. . . . He says that the soul had formerly lived with God in the heavens above—sharing His ideas with Him. But he says that afterwards it came down to live with us on earth. While here, it recollects the eternal patterns of things which it had learned before. Now, to procure belief in all of that, he elaborated his new formula, saying that learning is actually reminiscence. He implies that the souls which come to us from there forget the things among which they formerly lived. However, the souls

afterwards recall them, instructed by the objects they see around them. *Tertullian (c. 210, W), 3.203.*

III. Did Plato borrow from Moses and the Prophets?

Plato says, "The blame is on the one who chooses, and God is blameless." However, he took this from the prophet Moses and uttered it. *Justin Martyr (c. 160, E), 1.177.*

Plato the philosopher was aided in his legislation by the books of Moses. *Clement of Alexandria (c. 195, E), 2.338.*

It is not very clear, indeed, if Plato fell in with these stories by chance—or if . . . he met during his visit to Egypt with certain individuals who philosophized on the Jewish mysteries. Learning some things from them, he may have preserved a few of their ideas and thrown others aside. For he was careful not to offend the Greeks by a complete adoption of all the points of the Jews' philosophy, for they were in bad repute with most persons. *Origen (c. 248, E), 4.515; see also: 1.283–1.287, 2.141, 2.375, 2.412; extended discussion: 1.281–1.287, 7.92–7.93.*

SEE ALSO ARISTOTLE; PHILOSOPHERS, PHILOSOPHY; REINCARNATION; SOCRATES; SOUL.

POETS, PAGAN

The myths are shallow tales that contain no depth whatever. *Aristides (c. 125, E), 9.275.*

Those who hand down the myths that the poets have made, produce no evidence to the youths who learn them. *Justin Martyr (c. 160, E), 1.181.*

You men of Greece, who do you say are your teachers of religion? The poets? It will certainly not help your case to say this to persons who are familiar with the poets. *Justin Martyr (c. 160, E), 1.273.*

[SAID SARCASTICALLY:] Admirable, too, are your lying poets, who beguile their listeners from the truth through their fictions! . . . Away with the mythical tales of Acusilaus and Menander! . . . We leave you to these worthless things. *Tatian (c. 160, E), 2.75.*

And these spirits of error themselves confess that they are demons who used to inspire these writers [i.e., the pagan poets]. *Theophilus (c. 180, E), 2.97.*

We are far from exhorting men to listen to tales such as these. In fact, we avoid the practice of soothing our crying children . . . by telling them myths. For we are afraid of fostering in their minds the impiety professed by those who have no more knowledge of the truth than do infants—even though they are wise in their own eyes. *Clement of Alexandria (c. 195, E), 2.191.*

We Christians get ourselves laughed at for proclaiming that God will one day judge the world. Yet, like us, the poets and philosophers set up a judgment seat in the realms below. *Tertullian (c. 195, W), 3.52.*

Homer (so dreamed Ennius) remembered that he was once a peacock. However, I cannot for my part believe poets, even when they are wide awake! *Tertullian (c. 210, W), 3.214.*

It should be observed, further, that all the legendary accounts that are considered especially remarkable by the Greeks because of their antiquity, are actually found to belong to a period *after* Moses. For example, I speak of their floods and conflagrations. *Julius Africanus (c. 245, E), 6.134.*

Maro was the first of our poets to approach the truth. He speaks in this manner respecting the highest God, whom he calls Mind and Spirit, saying: "Know first that the heaven and the earth . . . are nourished by a Soul, a Spirit, whose celestial flame glows in each member." *Lactantius (c. 304–313, W), 7.14.*

Ovid also, in the beginning of his remarkable work, without any disguising of the name, admits that the universe was arranged by God, whom he calls the Framer of the world, the Artificer of all things. *Lactantius (c. 304–313, W), 7.14.*

SEE ALSO GODS, PAGAN; MENANDER THE POET; PHILOSOPHERS, PHILOSOPHY.

POLITICS

SEE PUBLIC OFFICE

POLYCARP

Polycarp was a personal disciple of the apostle John, and he served as the bishop of Smyrna for many years. In his old age, he was arrested by the Romans and died heroically as a martyr.

I write to you, giving thanks unto the Lord and loving Polycarp, just as I love you. *Ignatius (c. 105, E), 1.58.*

The Ephesians from Smyrna . . . salute you, along with Polycarp, the bishop of Smyrna. *Ignatius (c. 105, E), 1.65.*

We have written to you, brethren, as to what relates to the martyrs, and especially to the blessed Polycarp, who put an end to the persecution, having—so the speak—set a seal upon it by his martyrdom. *Martyrdom of Polycarp (c. 135, E), 1.39.*

The blessed Polycarp was the twelfth person who was martyred in Smyrna (including those persons of Philadelphia). However, he occupies a place of his own in the memory of everyone. In fact, he is everywhere spoken of by the pagans themselves. He was not only a renowned teacher, but he was also a pre-eminent martyr. *Martyrdom of Polycarp (c. 135, E), 1.43.*

Polycarp also was instructed by apostles, and he spoke with many who had seen Christ. Not only that, but by apostles, in Asia he was appointed bishop of the church in Smyrna. I also saw him in my early youth, for he lived a very long time. When he was a very old man, he gloriously and most nobly suffered martyrdom and departed this life. He had always taught the things which he had learned from apostles, and which the church has handed down, and which alone are true. . . . It was he who, coming to Rome in the time of Anicetus, caused many persons to turn away from the aforesaid heretics to the church of God. . . . And Polycarp himself replied to Marcion, who met him on one occasion, and said, "Do you know me?" [Polycarp replied,] "I do know you, the first-born of Satan!" . . . There is also a very powerful epistle of Polycarp written to the Philippians, from which those who choose to do so, and are anxious about their salvation, can learn the character of his faith, and the preaching of the truth. *Irenaeus (c. 180, E/W), 1.416.*

And these things are borne witness to in writing by Papias, the hearer of John, and a companion of Polycarp, in his fourth book. *Irenaeus (c. 180, E/W), 1.562, 563.*

While I was yet a boy, I saw you in Lower Asia with Polycarp. . . . I can even describe the place where the blessed Polycarp used to sit and teach, . . . together with the discourses that he delivered to the people. I can remember also, how he would speak of his familiar relations with John, and with the rest of those who had seen the Lord. I remember how he would call their words to remembrance. Whatever things he had heard from them respecting the Lord, both with regard to His miracles and His teaching, Polycarp would recount them all in harmony with the Scriptures—having in that manner received it from the eye-witnesses of the Word of life. *Irenaeus (c. 180, E/W), 1.569.*

When the blessed Polycarp was visiting in Rome in the time of Anicetus, . . . he and Anicetus were at once well inclined towards each other, not willing that any quarrel should arise between them upon this matter. For Anicetus could not persuade Polycarp to forego the observance [of his Easter customs], inasmuch as these things had been always observed by John the disciple of our Lord, and by other apostles with whom he had been conversant. Nor, on the other hand, could Polycarp succeed in persuading Anicetus to keep [Easter in his way], for Anicetus maintained that he was bound to adhere to the usage of the presbyters who preceded him. And in this state of affairs, they held fellowship with each other. *Irenaeus (c. 180, E/W), 1.569.*

Then there is Polycarp, both bishop and martyr at Smyrna. *Polycrates (c. 190, E), 8.773.*

POLYGAMY

Let your fountain be blessed, and rejoice with the wife of your youth. Prov. 5:18.

Your imprudent and blind masters [i.e., Jewish teachers] even until this time permit each man to have four or five wives. And if anyone sees a beautiful woman and desires to have her, they quote the doings of Jacob. *Justin Martyr (c. 160, E), 1.266.*

If it were allowable to take any wife, or as many wives as one chooses—and how he chooses—David would have permitted this. Nevertheless, the men of your nation [i.e., the Jews] practice this over all the earth, wherever they sojourn. *Justin Martyr (c. 160, E), 1.270.*

Others, again, following upon Basilides and Carpocrates, have introduced promiscuous intercourse and a plurality of wives, and are indifferent about eating meats sacrificed to idols, maintaining that God is not greatly concerned about such matters. *Irenaeus (c. 180, E/W), 1.353.*

The contracting of marriage with several wives had been done away with from the times of the prophets. For we read, "Do not go after your lusts, but refrain yourself from your appetites" [Sir. 18:30]. . . . And in another place, "Let your fountain be blessed and rejoice with the wife of your youth." This plainly forbids a plurality of wives. *Methodius (c. 290, E), 6.312.*

SEE ALSO MARRIAGE; TWICE-MARRIED.

PONTIFEX MAXIMUS

The pontifex maximus was the pagan high priest of Rome. Tertullian applied the title satirically, as a term of reproach, to either the bishop of Carthage or the bishop of Rome. The bishop of Rome did not begin to regularly use this title until the fifteenth century.

I hear that there has even been an edict set forth—and a dogmatic one too. The pontifex maximus—that is, the bishop of bishops—issues an edict: "I remit the sins of both adultery and fornication to those who have fulfilled repentance!" O edict, on which cannot be inscribed, "Good deed!" And where will this liberality be posted up? On the very spot, I suppose, on the very gates of the sensual appetites! *Tertullian (c. 212, W), 4.74.*

[ADDRESSED TO PAGANS:] Did that great Jupiter Capitolinus of yours . . . endow any priest of a curia or the pontifex maximus with this right? *Arnobius (c. 305, E), 6.427.*

Also, at the public games, the colleges of all the [pagan] priests and magistrates take their places, along with the chief pontiffs and the chief priests of the curia. *Arnobius (c. 305, E), 6.488.*

POOR IN SPIRIT

Blessed are the poor in spirit, for theirs is the kingdom of heaven. Matt. 5:3.

Some persons hold possessions, gold, silver, and houses only as gifts of God, and they minister from them. . . . They are superior to the possession of them. They are not the slaves of the things they possess. . . . Furthermore, they are able to endure the loss of these things with a cheerful mind—the same as they can accept their abundance. These are the ones who are blessed by the Lord and are called "poor in spirit." *Clement of Alexandria (c. 195, E), 2.595.*

What about when Jesus calls the poor blessed? Well, in that saying, Jesus did not refer to those who are simply poor in worldly possessions. Rather, He referred to those who are poor in spirit—that is to say, those who are not puffed up with pride. Such ones have the gentle and lowly dispositions of humility, not thinking of themselves more than they should think. *Disputation of Archelaus and Manes (c. 320, E), 6.217.*

SEE ALSO MATERIALISM; PROSPERITY; SERMON ON THE MOUNT.

POPE

SEE BISHOP (II. BISHOP OF ROME).

PORNOGRAPHY

[ADDRESSED TO PAGANS:] On the other hand, what kind are your pictures? Diminutive Pans, naked girls, drunken Satyrs, and phallic tokens—painted naked in pictures disgraceful for filthiness! More than this, you are not ashamed before the eyes of all to look at representations of all types of licentiousness that are portrayed in public places. Rather, you set them up and guard them with scrupulous care. You consecrate these pillars of shamelessness at home as though they were the images of your gods. We denounce not only the *use* of them, but the very *sight* and *mention* of them. *Clement of Alexandria (c. 195, E), 2.189.*

PRAYER

I. Admonitions on and descriptions of prayer

II. Prayer postures and customs

III. Lifting hands in prayer

IV. Praying with the spirit

V. Should Christians pray to angels and saints?

VI. Should Christians pray *for* the dead?

VII. Should Christians pray *to* the dead?

I. Admonitions on and descriptions of prayer

When you pray, you shall not be like the hypocrites. For they love to pray standing in the synagogues. . . . But you, when you pray, go into your room, and when you have shut your door, pray to your Father who is in the secret place; and your Father who sees in secret will reward you openly. Matt. 6:5, 6.

Ask, and it will be given to you; seek, and you will find; knock, and it will be opened to you. For everyone who asks receives. Matt. 7:7, 8.

Pray without ceasing. 1 Thess. 5:17.

You ask and do not receive, because you ask amiss, that you may spend it on your pleasures. Jas. 4:3.

You should not go to prayer with an evil conscience. *Barnabas (c. 70–130, E), 1.149.*

To me, there is no doubt but that the earth abides because of the prayers of the Christians. *Aristides (c. 125, E), 9.278.*

On the soldiers giving him permission, Polycarp stood and prayed, being full of the grace of God. In fact, he could not cease for two full hours, to the astonishment of those who heard him. *Martyrdom of Polycarp (c. 135, E), 1.40.*

How can a person who does not serve the Lord ask and obtain anything from Him? Those who serve Him will obtain their requests. However, those who do not serve Him will receive nothing. *Hermas (c. 150, W), 2.33.*

For who of you does not know that the prayer of one who accompanies it with lamentation and tears, with the body prostrate, or with bended knees, propitiates God most of all? *Justin Martyr (c. 160, E), 1.244.*

As it is befitting, before partaking of food, we should bless the Creator of all. . . . Finally, before partaking of sleep, it is a sacred duty to give thanks to God, having enjoyed his grace and love. As a result, we can go straight to sleep. *Clement of Alexandria (c. 195, E), 2.249.*

The spiritual man prays in thought during every hour, being allied to God by love. First, he will ask forgiveness of sins; and afterwards, he asks that he may sin no more. *Clement of Alexandria (c. 195, E), 2.503.*

The spiritual man gives thanks always for all things to God—by righteous hearing and divine reading, by true investigation, by holy oblation, and by blessed prayer. Always lauding, hymning, blessing, and praising—such a soul is never separated from God at any time. *Clement of Alexandria (c. 195, E), 2.506.*

Someone may say that the voice does not reach God, but is rolled downward in the air. However, the thoughts of the saints pierce not only the air, but the whole world. And the divine power, with the speed of light, sees through the whole soul. . . . If we may be permitted to use the expression, God is "all ears and all eyes." In general, an unworthy opinion of God maintains no piety in hymns, discourses, writings, or doctrines. Rather, it digresses to grovelling and unseemly ideas and notions. *Clement of Alexandria (c. 195, E), 2.533.*

Prayer, then, to speak more boldly, is conversation with God. Though whispering (and consequently, not opening the lips), we speak in silence, yet we cry inwardly. For God hears continually all the inward conversation. So also we raise the head and lift the hands to heaven, and set the feet in motion at the closing utterance of the prayer, following the eagerness of the spirit directed towards the intellectual essence. Endeavoring to elevate the body from the earth along with our prayer—raising the soul aloft, winged with longing for better things—we compel it to advance to the region of holiness, magnanimously despising the chain of the flesh. *Clement of Alexandria (c. 195, E), 2.534.*

Thanksgiving and request for the conversion of our neighbors is the function of the spiritual man. . . . If any occasion of conversation with God becomes prayer, no opportunity of access to God should be omitted. *Clement of Alexandria (c. 195, E), 2.534.*

God does not wait for talkative tongues . . . but knows absolutely the thoughts of all. What the voice communicates to *us*, our thoughts speak to *God*. For, even before the creation, He knew what would come into our minds. So prayer may be uttered without the voice. *Clement of Alexandria (c. 195, E), 2.535.*

The whole life of the spiritual man is a holy festival. His sacrifices are prayers, praises, and readings in the Scriptures before meals. They are psalms and hymns during meals and before bed—and prayers also again during night. By these, the spiritual man unites himself to the divine choir. *Clement of Alexandria (c. 195, E), 2.537.*

The spiritual man does not use wordy prayer by his mouth. For he has learned to ask of the Lord what is necessary. In every place, therefore, but not ostensibly and visibly to the multitude, he will pray. While engaged in walking, in conversation, while in silence, while engaged in reading and in works according to reason, he prays in every situation. *Clement of Alexandria (c. 195, E), 2.537.*

His whole life is prayer and conversation with God. And if he is pure from sins, he will by all means obtain what he wishes. For God says to the righteous man, "Ask, and I will give you." . . . But if someone says to us that some sinners even obtain according to their requests, [we reply] that this takes place only rarely. *Clement of Alexandria (c. 195, E), 2.544.*

But they are not yet obedient if they do not pray even for their enemies, having become entirely free of resentment. *Clement of Alexandria (c. 195, E), 2.548.*

Let us consider His heavenly wisdom: first, addressing the teaching of praying secretly, whereby He exacted man's faith. . . . Further, we should not think that the Lord must be approached with a train of words. *Tertullian (c. 198, W), 3.681.*

The exercise of prayer should not only be free from anger, but from all mental disturbances whatever. Prayer should be uttered from a spirit like the Spirit to whom it is sent. For a defiled spirit cannot be acknowledged by a holy Spirit, nor a sad one by a joyful one, nor a fettered one by a free one. . . . But what reason is there to go to prayer with hands indeed washed, but the spirit foul? *Tertullian (c. 198, W), 3.685.*

The sounds of our voice, likewise, should be subdued. For, if we are to be heard for our noise, what large windpipes we would need! But God is the hearer—not of the *voice*—but of the *heart.* . . . What superior advantage will those who pray too loudly gain—except that they annoy their neighbors? Nay, by making their petitions audible, what less error do they commit than if they were to pray in public? *Tertullian (c. 198, W), 3.686.*

How [can we pray] "in every place," since we are prohibited from praying in public? He means in every place that opportunity or even necessity may have rendered suitable. For that which was done by the apostles (who, in jail, in the hearing of the prisoners "began praying and singing to God") is not considered to have been done contrary to this teaching. *Tertullian (c. 198, W), 3.689.*

529

You will not dismiss a brother who has entered your house without prayer.... But again, when received yourself by brethren, you will not make earthly refreshments more important than heavenly. *Tertullian (c. 198, W), 3.690.*

Those who are more diligent in prayer are used to adding to the end of their prayers the "Hallelujah" and similar psalms. *Tertullian (c. 198, W), 3.690.*

In days gone by, prayer used to call down plagues, scatter the armies of foes, and withhold the wholesome influences of showers. Now, however, the prayer of righteousness averts all of God's anger, keeps patrol on behalf of personal enemies, and makes supplication on behalf of persecutors. *Tertullian (c. 198, W), 3.691.*

Prayer is the wall of faith. It is her arms and missiles against the foe, who keeps watch over us on all sides. And so we never walk unarmed. *Tertullian (c. 198, W), 3.691.*

When He recommends perseverance and earnestness in prayer, He sets before us the parable of the judge who was compelled to listen to the widow. *Tertullian (c. 207, W), 3.409.*

"If two of you will agree on earth as regarding anything that they will ask, it will be done for them." ... This is the cause why we are not heard when we pray—because we do not agree with one another on earth, neither in opinions nor in life. *Origen (c. 245, E), 9.495.*

Let each one pray to the Word of God and still more to His Father. *Origen (c. 248, E), 4.548.*

Be constant in both prayer and reading. First, speak with God; then let God speak with you. Let Him instruct you in His teachings, let Him direct you. *Cyprian (c. 250, W), 5.279, 280.*

Let us ask and we will receive. And if there is delay and tardiness in our receiving—since we have grievously offended—let us knock, for "to him that knocks it will also be opened." But our prayers, our groanings, and our tears must knock at the door. And with these, we must be urgent and persevering, even though prayer is offered with one mind.... Let us urgently pray and groan with continual petitions. Know this, beloved brethren, that I was not long ago reproached in a vision about this—that we were lethargic in our prayers and did not pray with watchfulness.... Therefore, let us strike off and break away from the bonds of sleep and pray with urgency and watchfulness. *Cyprian (c. 250, W), 5.286.*

Let each one of us pray to God, not only for himself, but for all the brethren. For this is as the Lord has taught us to pray. For He ... directed us when we pray to pray for everyone in a common prayer and joint supplication.... Let us beseech the Lord in simplicity and unanimity. Let us ask without ceasing, with full faith that we will receive. We should entreat not only with groanings, but with tears. *Cyprian (c. 250, W), 5.287.*

I ask that you will grant my desire and that you will grieve with me at the [spiritual] death of my sister. For in this time of devastation, she has fallen from Christ. She has sacrificed [to idols] and provoked the Lord, as it seems clear to us. Although this is the day of Paschal rejoicing, I have spent the days in tears for her deeds, weeping day and night—in sackcloth and ashes. *Cyprian (c. 250, W), 5.298.*

With mutual prayers, let us by turns cherish, guard, and arm one another. Let us pray for the lapsed, that they may be raised up. Let us pray for those who stand, that they may not be tempted to such a degree as to be destroyed. Let us pray that those who are said to have fallen may acknowledge the greatness of their sin. *Cyprian (c. 250, W), 5.310.*

When we pray, we should let our speech and petition be under discipline, observing quietness and modesty.... For it is characteristic of a shameless man to be noisy with his cries. On the other hand, it is fitting to the modest man to pray with moderated petitions. In fact, in His teaching, the Lord has told us to pray in secret, ... which is best suited to faith. *Cyprian (c. 250, W), 5.448.*

When we meet together with the brethren in one place, and celebrate divine sacrifices with God's priest, we should be mindful of modesty and discipline. We should not throw out our prayers indiscriminately, with unsubdued voices. ... He does not need to be clamorously reminded, for he sees men's thoughts.... Hannah prayed to God, not with clamorous petition, but silently and modestly—within the very recesses of her heart. She spoke with hidden prayer, but with open faith. She spoke with her heart, not her voice. *Cyprian (c. 250, W), 5.448.*

Beloved brethren, let the worshipper not be ignorant of the manner the tax collector prayed with the Pharisee in the temple. The tax collector did not pray with eyes lifted up boldly to heaven, nor with hands proudly raised. *Cyprian (c. 250, W), 5.449.*

If He who was without sin prayed, how much more should sinners pray. He prayed *continually*, watching through the whole night in uninterrupted petitions. Therefore, how much more should we watch nightly in constantly repeated prayer. *Cyprian (c. 250, W), 5.455.*

That he may obtain the favor of God and be free from every stain, let him always implore the mercy of God and pray for nothing else but pardon for his sins, even though he has none. If he desires anything else, there is no need of expressing it in word to One who knows what we wish. If anything good has happened to him, let him give thanks. If any evil has come, let him make amends and let him confess that the evil has happened to him because of his faults. . . . And let him not think that this is to be done by him only in the temple—but at home and even in his very bed. In short, let him always have God with himself, consecrated in his heart. *Lactantius (c. 304–313, W), 7.193.*

Before God, we all prostrate ourselves, according to our custom. We adore Him in joint prayers. We beg from Him things that are just and honorable—and worthy of His ear. Not that He needs our supplications, or that He loves to see the homage of so many thousands laid at His feet. Rather, it is all to our benefit, and it is to our advantage. For we are prone to err, and to yield to various lusts and appetites through the fault of our innate weakness. Therefore, He allows Himself at all times to be comprehended in our thoughts . . . so that we may receive a desire for purity and may free ourselves from every stain by the removal of all our shortcomings. *Arnobius (c. 305, E), 6.419; extended discussion: 2.532–2.537, 3.681–3.691.*

II. Prayer postures and customs

In his upper room, with his windows open toward Jerusalem, [Daniel] knelt down on his knees three times that day. Dan. 6:10.

The tax collector, standing afar off, would not so much as raise his eyes to heaven, but beat his breast, saying, "God be merciful to me a sinner!" I tell you, this man went down to his house justified. Luke 18:13, 14.

Now Peter and John went up together to the temple at the hour of prayer, the ninth hour. Acts 3:1.

[Cornelius] gave alms generously to the people, and prayed to God always. About the ninth hour of the day he saw clearly in a vision an angel of God. Acts 10:2, 3.

The next day, as they went on their journey and drew near the city, Peter went up on the housetop to pray, about the sixth hour. Acts 10:9.

On coming to that place, I bowed my knees and began to pray to the Lord. *Hermas (c. 150, W), 2.11.*

Who of you do not know that the prayer of someone who accompanies it with lamentation and tears—with the body prostrate or with bended knees—propitiates God the most? *Justin Martyr (c. 160, E), 1.244.*

If some persons assign definite hours for prayer—as, for example, the third, sixth, and ninth—yet the spiritual man prays throughout his whole life, endeavoring by prayer to have fellowship with God. . . . Those who know the blessed triad of the holy abodes, are acquainted with the distribution of the hours into a three-fold division. *Clement of Alexandria (c. 195, E), 2.534.*

Corresponding with the manner of the sun's rising, prayers are made looking towards the sunrise in the east. *Clement of Alexandria (c. 195, E), 2.535.*

We more commend our prayers to God when we pray with modesty and humility—with not even our hands too loftily elevated—but elevated temperately and becomingly. And not even our countenance should be uplifted too boldly. For that publican who prayed with humility and dejection—not merely in his supplication, but in his countenance too—went his way more justified than the shameless Pharisee. *Tertullian (c. 198, W), 3.686.*

Prayer is also subject to diversity of observance in the matter of kneeling, through the act of some few who abstain from kneeling on the Sabbath [i.e., Saturday]. Since this diversity is particularly on its trial before the churches, the Lord will give His grace that the dissidents may either yield or else follow their opinion without offense to others. We, however, have received this practice: that we refrain from kneeling only on the day of the Lord's resurrection. In fact, we not only refrain from kneeling, but also from every posture and office of solicitude. *Tertullian (c. 198, W), 3.689*

But who would hesitate every day to prostrate himself before God, at least in the first prayer with which we enter on the daylight? At both fasts and stations, no prayer should be made without kneeling and the other customary marks of humility. For we are not only *praying*, but also pleading and making satisfaction to God our Lord. *Tertullian (c. 198, W), 3.689.*

As for *times* of prayer, nothing at all has been prescribed except clearly "to pray at every time and every place." . . . However, the outward observance of certain hours will not be unprofitable. I mean those common hours that mark the intervals of the day—the third, the sixth, and the ninth—which we may find in the Scriptures to have been more solemn than the rest. *Tertullian (c. 198, W), 3.689.*

Just as we read this to have been observed by Daniel, . . . we also pray at a minimum of not less than three times during the day. For we are debtors to Three: Father, Son, and Holy Spirit. Of course, in addition to our regular prayers that are due without any admonition, [we should pray] at the entrance of light and of night. Furthermore, it is becoming for believers not to take food nor go to the bath before interposing a prayer. For the refreshments and nourishments of the spirit are to be held prior to those of the flesh. *Tertullian (c. 198, W), 3.690.*

We consider fasting or kneeling in worship on the Lord's Day to be unlawful. We rejoice in the same privilege also from Easter to Pentecost. *Tertullian (c. 211, W), 3.94.*

In Luke's writings, the third hour is demonstrated as an hour of prayer. It was about this hour that those who had received the inaugural gift of the Holy Spirit were thought to be drunkards. And then there is the sixth hour, at which hour Peter went up on the roof. Finally, there is the ninth, at which hour they entered the temple. Why should we not understand that, with absolutely perfect indifference, we must pray always, everywhere, and at every time. Still, these three hours are distinguished in human affairs. For they divide the day, distinguish businesses, and reverberate in the public ear. They have likewise always been of special solemnity in divine prayers. This is a practice that is sanctioned also by the corroborating fact of Daniel praying three times in the day. *Tertullian (c. 213, W), 4.108.*

The three children, with Daniel, . . . observed the third, sixth, and ninth hours—as a type of sacrament of the Trinity. . . . The worshippers of God in times past . . . made use of these intervals of hours for determined and lawful times for prayer. . . . But for us, beloved brethren, besides the hours of prayer observed of old, both the times and the sacraments have now increased in number. For we must also pray in the morning—that the Lord's resurrection may be celebrated by morning prayer. . . . Also, at the setting of the sun and at the decline of the day, we must necessarily pray again. . . . Still, if in the Holy Scriptures the true Sun and the true Day are Christ, there is no hour excepted in which Christians should not frequently and always worship God. . . . Let us who are in Christ (and therefore always in the Light), not cease from praying even during night. *Cyprian (c. 250, W), 5.456, 457.*

Offer up your prayers in the morning, at the third hour, the sixth, the evening, and at cockcrowing. *Apostolic Constitutions (compiled c. 390, E), 7.496.*

III. Lifting hands in prayer

Lift your hands toward Him. Lam. 2:19.

I desire therefore that the men pray everywhere, lifting up holy hands. 1 Tim. 2:8.

Full of holy designs, you . . . stretched forth your hands to God Almighty. *Clement of Rome (c. 96, W), 1.5*

Let us then draw near to Him with holiness of spirit, lifting up pure and undefiled hands unto Him. *Clement of Rome (c. 96, W), 1.12.*

We also raise the head and lift the hands to heaven. *Clement of Alexandria (c. 195, E), 2.534.*

We lift our eyes to [heaven], with hands outstretched. *Tertullian (c. 195, W), 3.42.*

With our hands thus stretched out and up to God, you tear us apart with your iron claws and hang us up on crosses. . . . The very posture of a Christian praying is one of preparation for all punishment. *Tertullian (c. 195, W), 3.42.*

[The Jews] do not even dare to raise their hands to the Lord. . . . We, however, not only raise them, but even expand them. Taking our model from the Lord's passion, even in prayer we confess to Christ. *Tertullian (c. 198, W), 3.685.*

We commend our prayers to God better when we pray with modesty and humility—with not even our hands too loftily elevated—but elevated temperately and becomingly. *Tertullian (c. 198, W), 3.686.*

[CONCERNING CHRISTIANS WHO MAKE IDOLS FOR A LIVING:] The zeal of faith will direct its pleadings to this quarter, lamenting the fact that a Christian would come from idols into the church. . . . It laments that he would raise to God the Father hands that are the mothers of idols. *Tertullian (c. 200, W), 3.64.*

I should think that no one is more shameless than he who is baptized unto his God in water that belongs to another [God], who stretches out his hands to his God towards a heaven that is another's. *Tertullian (c. 207, W), 3.289.*

We assuredly see the sign of a cross . . . when a man adores God with a pure mind, with hands outstretched. *Mark Minucius Felix (c. 200, W), 4.191.*

[The tax collector] did not pray with eyes lifted up boldly to heaven, nor with hands proudly raised. *Cyprian (c. 250, W), 5.449.*

IV. Praying with the spirit

If I pray in a tongue, my spirit prays, but my understanding is unfruitful. What is the result then? I will pray with the spirit, and I will also pray with the understanding. 1 Cor. 14:14, 15.

We are the true worshippers and the true priests who, praying in spirit, offer a sacrifice in spirit: prayer, a victim that is proper and acceptable to God. *Tertullian (c. 198, W), 3.690.*

It is not lawful to declare that the saying, "Everyone who asks receives," is a lie. Who then is he that asks? It is he who has obeyed Jesus when he said, "If you stand praying, believe that you receive, and you will receive." But he that asks must do everything in his power so that he may pray "with the spirit," and pray also "with the understanding," and also pray "without ceasing." *Origen (c. 245, E), 9.512.*

V. Should Christians pray to angels and saints?

In this manner, therefore, pray: Our Father in heaven. Matt. 6:9.

Let no one defraud you of your reward, taking delight in false humility and worship of angels. Col. 2:18.

Having thus learned to call these beings "angels" [i.e., messengers] from their employments, we find that because they are divine, they are sometimes called "gods" in the sacred Scriptures. But this is not said in the sense that we are commanded to honor and worship them in place of God—even though they minster to us and bear His blessings to us. For every prayer, supplication, intercession, and thanksgiving is to be sent up to the Supreme God through the High Priest—the living Word and God, who is above all the angels. . . . To invoke angels, without having obtained a greater knowledge of their nature than is possessed by men, would be contrary to reason. But . . . even if we had this knowledge, . . . it would not permit us to pray with confidence to anyone other than to the Supreme God, who is sufficient for all things, through our Savior, the Son of God. *Origen (c. 225, E), 4.544.*

We judge it improper to pray to those beings who themselves offer up prayers. For even they themselves would prefer that we should send up our requests to the God to whom they pray, rather than to send them downwards to themselves, or to apportion our power of prayer between God and them. *Origen (c. 248, E), 4.548*

Celsus forgets that he is addressing Christians, who pray to God alone through Jesus. *Origen (c. 248, E), 4.653.*

In the Apocalypse, the angel resists John, who wishes to worship him, and says, "See that you do not do this. For I am your fellow-servant and your brother. Worship Jesus the Lord." *Cyprian (c. 250, W), 5.491.*

VI. Should Christians pray *for* the dead?

Under the tunic of each of the dead they found amulets sacred to the idols of Jamnia, which the law forbids the Jews to wear. So it was clear to all that this was why the men had been slain. . . . Turning to supplication, they prayed that the sinful deed might be fully blotted out. 2 Macc. 12:40–42.

The Lord grant to [Onesiphorus] that he may find mercy from the Lord in that Day—and you know very well how many ways he ministered to me at Ephesus. 2 Tim. 1:18.

On that very night, this was shown to me in a vision: I saw Dinocrates going out from a gloomy place, where also there were several others. . . . And I was aroused and knew that my brother was in suffering. But I trusted that my prayer would bring help to his suffering. And I prayed for him every day. . . . Then, on the day on which we remained in chains, this was shown to me: I saw that the place which I had formerly observed to be in gloom was now bright. And Dinocrates—with a clean body well clad—was finding refreshment. . . . Then I understood that he was transported from the place of punishment. *Passion of Perpetua and Felicitas (c. 205, W, probably Montanistic), 3.701.*

There is not a soul that can at all procure salvation, unless it believes while it is still in the flesh. For it is an established truth that the flesh is the very condition on which salvation hinges. *Tertullian (c. 210, W), 3.551.*

As often as the anniversary comes around, we make oblations for the dead as birthday honors. *Tertullian (c. 211, W), 3.94.*

For you cannot hate the first wife [who has died]. In fact, you retain an even more religious affection for her, since she is already received into the Lord's presence. You make request for her spirit. You render annual oblations for her. Will you, then, stand before the Lord with as many wives as you commemorate in prayer? Will you offer for two? *Tertullian (c. 212, W), 4.56.*

Indeed, she prays for the soul [of her deceased husband] and requests refreshment for him in the meanwhile—and fellowship with him in the first resurrection. She also offers on the anniversaries of his falling asleep. For, unless she does these deeds, she has in the true sense divorced him, so far as in her lies. *Tertullian (c. 217, W), 4.67.*

Since he has dared to appoint Geminius Faustinus, a presbyter, as his executor, you are not permitted to make any offering for his repose. Nor should any prayers be made in the church in his name. *Cyprian (c. 250, W), 5.367.*

You cruelly break up our meetings, in which prayer is made to the Supreme God and in which peace and pardon are asked for all those in authority—for soldiers, kings, friends, and enemies, for those still in life and for those who are freed from the bondage of the flesh. *Arnobius (c. 305, E), 6.488.*

Let us pray for our brethren who are at rest in Christ. Let us pray that God, . . . who has received his soul, may forgive him every sin—both voluntary and involuntary. Let us pray that He may be merciful and gracious to him and give him his lot in the land of the righteous, who are sent into the bosom of Abraham, Isaac, and Jacob. *Apostolic Constitutions (compiled c. 390, E), 7.497.*

Let the third day of the departed be celebrated with psalms, lessons, and prayers—on account of Him who arose within the space of three days. And let the ninth day be celebrated in remembrance of the living and of the departed. Do this also on the fortieth day, according to the ancient pattern. For the people lamented Moses in this manner. Also the anniversary day should be kept in memory of him. And let alms be given to the poor out of his goods, for a memorial to him. Now, we say these things concerning the godly. As for the ungodly person—if you gave the whole world to the poor, you would not benefit him at all. For to whom the Deity was an enemy while he was alive, it is certain it will be the same way when he is departed. *Apostolic Constitutions (compiled c. 390, E), 7.498.*

VII. Should Christians pray *to* the dead?

We speak of Paradise, the place of divine bliss appointed to receive the spirits of the saints. There, the saints are cut off from the knowledge of this world by that fiery zone, as by a sort of enclosure. *Tertullian (c. 197, W), 3.52.*

It is clear that those who make prayers to the dead . . . do not act as becomes men. They will suffer punishment for their impiety and guilt. Rebelling against God, the Father of the human race, they have undertaken unforgivable rites. They have violated every sacred law. *Lactantius (c. 304–313, W), 7.67.*

SEE ALSO EAST; HEARING FROM GOD; ONESIPHORUS; WORSHIP, CHRISTIAN (II. WORSHIP CUSTOMS).

PRAYER VEIL

SEE VEIL.

PREACHING

Whether it is in the reading of Scriptures . . . or the preaching of sermons, . . . opportunity is afforded to her of seeing visions. *Tertullian (c. 210, W), 3.188, Montanistic writing.*

PREDESTINATION

SEE FREE WILL AND PREDESTINATION.

PRESBYTER

Do not neglect the gift that is in you, which was given to you by prophecy with the laying on of the hands of the presbytery. 1 Tim. 4:14.

Let the elders [Gr. presbyteroi] who rule well be counted worthy of double honor, especially those who labor in the word and doctrine. 1 Tim. 5:17.

For this reason I left you in Crete, that you should set in order the things that are lacking, and appoint elders [Gr. presbyteroi] in every city. Tit. 1:5.

Be obedient to those who had the rule over you, and give all fitting honor to the presbyters among you. *Clement of Rome (c. 96, W), 1.5.*

It is disgraceful, beloved, yes, highly disgraceful, and unworthy of your Christian profession, that such a thing should be heard of as that the most steadfast and ancient church of the Corinthians should . . . engage in sedition against its presbyters. *Clement of Rome (c. 96, W), 1.18.*

Let the flock of Christ live on terms of peace with the presbyters set over it. *Clement of Rome (c. 96, W), 1.19.*

Being subject to the bishop and the presbyters, you may in all respects be sanctified. *Ignatius (c. 105, E), 1.50.*

Obey the bishop and the presbyters with an undivided mind. *Ignatius (c. 105, E), 1.58.*

I exhort you to study to do all things with a divine harmony, while your bishop presides in the place of God, and your presbyters in the place of the assembly of the apostles, along with your deacons. *Ignatius (c. 105, E), 1.61.*

As therefore the Lord did nothing without the Father, being united to Him, . . . so neither should you do anything without the bishop and presbyters. *Ignatius (c. 105, E), 1.62.*

It is therefore necessary that you should do nothing without the bishop (just as you already practice). And you should also be subject to the presbyters. *Ignatius (c. 105, E), 1.66.*

He who does anything apart from the bishop, presbyters, and deacons, such a man is not pure in his conscience. *Ignatius (c. 105, E), 1.69.*

Polycarp, and the presbyters with him, to the church of God sojourning at Philippi. *Polycarp (c. 135, E), 1.33.*

Let the presbyters be compassionate and merciful to all, bringing back those who wander, visiting all the sick—and not neglecting the widow, the orphan, or the poor. *Polycarp (c. 135, E), 1.34.*

The old woman came and asked me if I had yet given the book to the presbyters. . . . You will read the words in this city, along with the presbyters who preside over the church. *Hermas (c. 150, W), 1.12.*

It is necessary to obey the presbyters who are in the church—those who, as I have shown, possess the succession from the apostles. For they are those who, together with the succession of the bishops, have received the certain gift of truth, according to the good pleasure of the Father. *Irenaeus (c. 180, E/W), 1.497.*

However, there are those who are believed to be presbyters by man, but serve their own lusts. They do not place the fear of God supreme in their hearts. Rather, they conduct themselves with contempt towards others. . . . Such men will be convicted by the Word. *Irenaeus (c. 180, E/W), 1.497.*

The church nourishes the type of presbyter of whom the prophet says: "I will give your rulers in peace and your bishops in righteousness." *Irenaeus (c. 180, E/W), 1.498.*

I have heard from a certain presbyter who had heard it from those who had seen the apostles (and from those who had been their disciples) that the punishment in Scripture was sufficient for the ancients in regard to what they did without the Spirit's guidance. *Irenaeus (c. 180, E/W), 1.498.*

Those, therefore, who desert the preaching of the church, call into question the knowledge of the holy presbyters. *Irenaeus (c. 180, E/W), 1.548.*

[SPEAKING TO HERETICS:] Those presbyters who preceded us, and who were conversant with the apostles, did not hand down those opinions to you! *Irenaeus (c. 180, E/W), 1.568.*

Those presbyters who preceded you, and who did not observe [this custom], sent the Eucharist to those of other presbyters' churches who did observe it. *Irenaeus (c. 180, E/W), 1.569.*

Nor, on the other hand, could Polycarp succeed in persuading Anicetus to keep [Easter in his way]. For Anicetus maintained that he was bound to adhere to the usage of the presbyters who preceded him. And in this state of affairs, they held fellowship with each other. *Irenaeus (c. 180, E/W), 1.569.*

Those, then, also now, who have exercised themselves in the Lord's commandments, and lived perfectly and knowledgeably according to the Gospel, may be enrolled in the chosen body of the apostles. Such a man is in reality a presbyter of the church, and a true deacon of the will of God—if he does and teaches what is the Lord's. This is not as being ordained by men, nor regarded righteous because a presbyter, but enrolled in the presbyterate because he is righteous. And although here upon earth he is not honored with the chief seat, he will sit down on the twenty-four thrones, judging the people, as John says in the Apocalypse. *Clement of Alexandria (c. 195, E), 2.504.*

The improvement of the body is the object of the medical art; the improvement of the soul is the object of philosophy. Ministerial service is rendered to parents by children, to rulers by subjects. Similarly, in the church, the elders attend to the ministry that has improvement [of the flock] for its object; the deacons attend to the physical things. *Clement of Alexandria (c. 195, E), 2.523.*

The tried men of our elders preside over us, obtaining that honor not by purchase, but by established character. There is no buying and selling of any sort in the things of God. *Tertullian (c. 195, W), 3.46.*

Do you lead him into the midst and prostrate him—all in haircloth and ashes, a compound of disgrace and horror, before the widows, before the presbyters, begging for the tears of all? *Tertullian (c. 212, W), 4.86.*

A command was given to Hermas to write two books. After so doing, he was to announce to the presbyters of the church what he had learned from the Spirit. *Origen (c. 225, E), 4.359.*

To the presbyters of the whole church of God, who have become gray through wisdom. *Origen (c. 225, E), 4.360.*

The purpose for his remaining behind, as we see, was this: that the Lord might add him to our clergy and might adorn with glorious priests the number of our presbyters that had been desolated by the lapse of some. *Cyprian (c. 250, W), 5.314.*

Since he has dared to appoint Geminius Faustinus, a presbyter, as his executor, you are not permitted to make any offering for his repose. Nor should any prayers be made in the church in his name. *Cyprian (c. 250, W), 5.367.*

He called to him his grandchild and said, . . . "Hurry, I entreat you, and absolve me quickly. Summon one of the presbyters to me." . . . The boy ran for the presbyter. *Dionysius of Alexandria (c. 262, E), 6.101.*

Neither a presbyter nor a deacon should ordain anyone from the laity into the clergy. *Apostolic Constitutions (compiled c. 390, E), 7.432.*

A presbyter blesses. . . . He lays on hands, but he does not ordain. *Apostolic Constitutions (compiled c. 390, E), 7.494.*

If any presbyter despises his own bishop and assembles separately and prepares another altar—when he has nothing to condemn in his bishop either as to piety or righteousness—let him be deprived as an ambitious person. *Apostolic Constitutions (compiled c. 390, E), 7.502.*

SEE ALSO BISHOP; CHURCH GOVERNMENT; DEACON.

PRIESTHOOD OF ALL BELIEVERS

SEE CHURCH GOVERNMENT (XI. PRIESTHOOD OF ALL BELIEVERS).

PROCREATION

Be fruitful and multiply; fill the earth and subdue it. Gen. 1:28.

If we marry, it is only so that we may bring up children. *Justin Martyr (c. 160, E), 1.172.*

We despise the things of this life, even to the pleasures of the soul. Each of us considers her his wife whom he has married according to the laws laid down by us—and he marries only for the purpose of having children. After throwing the seed into the ground, the farmer awaits the harvest. He does not sow more seed on top of it. Likewise, to us the procreation of children is the limit of our indulgence in [sexual] appetite. *Athenagoras (c. 175, E), 2.146.*

God made the male and female for the propagation of the human race. *Irenaeus (c. 180, E/W), 1.353.*

Scripture does not regard it as right for sexual relations to take place either in wantonness or for hire like prostitutes. Rather, it is only for the birth of children. *Clement of Alexandria (c. 195, E), 2.367.*

What cause is there for the exposure of a child? The man who did not desire to beget children had no right to marry at all. He certainly did not have the right to become the murderer of his children, because of licentious indulgence. *Clement of Alexandria (c. 195, E), 2.368.*

Since pleasure and lust seem to fall under marriage, it must also be addressed. Marriage is the first union of man and woman for the procreation of legitimate children. *Clement of Alexandria (c. 195, E), 2.377.*

To such a spiritual man, after conception, his wife is as a sister and is treated as if of the same father. *Clement of Alexandria (c. 195, E), 2.503.*

Further reasons for marriage that men allege for themselves arise from anxiety for posterity, and the bitter, bitter pleasure of children. To *us,* this is idle. For why should we be eager to bear children, whom, when we have them, we desire to send before us [to glory]. For we are desirous, too, to be taken out of this most wicked world and to be received into the Lord's presence, which was the desire even of an apostle. . . . Are we secure enough of our own salvation that we have leisure for children? Should we seek burdens for ourselves that are avoided even by the majority of the Gentiles? *Tertullian (c. 205, W), 4.41.*

He bestowed His blessing on matrimony also, as on an honorable estate, for the increase of the human race—just as He did likewise as to the entirety of His creation, for wholesome and good uses. *Tertullian (c. 207, W), 3.294.*

Although the previous two quotations from Tertullian show some indication of his Montanistic leanings, the ensuing two quotations, written later, definitely represent more of a Montanistic view than the view of the church.

By enjoining continence and restraining sexual desire, . . . God has abolished the command, "Grow and multiply." . . . For the extremity of the times has restrained [that command] which He had sent out. It has taken back the indulgence that He had granted. *Tertullian (c. 212, W), 4.53.*

The extremity of the times has canceled the command, "Grow and multiply." For the apostle gives another command, "It remains that those who have wives so be as if they did not," because the time is short. *Tertullian (c. 212, W), 4.64.*

Women who were reputed believers began to resort to drugs for producing sterility. They also began to gird themselves around, so as to expel what was being conceived. For they did not wish to have a child by either a slave or by any paltry fellow—for the sake of their family and excessive wealth. Behold, into how great an impiety the lawless one has proceeded: inculcating adultery and murder at the same time! *Hippolytus (c. 225, W), 5.131.*

It is a source of joy and glory to humans to have children like themselves. *Cyprian (c. 250, W), 5.495.*

When the predestined number of humans is fulfilled, humans will afterwards abstain from the generation of children. However, at the present, man must cooperate in the forming of the image of God. . . . And we must not be offended at the ordinance of the Creator. For from that ordinance, we ourselves have our being. *Methodius (c. 290, E), 6.313.*

If God still forms man, we will be guilty of audacity if we think of the procreation of children as something offensive. For the Almighty Himself is not ashamed to make use of it, in working with His undefiled hands. *Methodius (c. 290, E), 6.314.*

When one thoroughly examines and understands these things that happen to man according to his nature, he will know not to disdain the procreation of children—although he applauds celibacy and prefers it in honor. *Methodius (c. 290, E), 6.316.*

The Divine Word considers chastity to be the crown of those virtues and duties that have been mentioned. . . . They, too, possess it who live chastely with their wives. . . . However, those who are goaded on by their lusts, . . . through the heat of unsubdued lust, are excessive in embracesóeven though they do not commit fornication and even though they remain within the things that are permitted with a lawful wife. . . . How will they rejoice . . . who have not listened to that which has been said: "they who have wives should be as though they had none"? [1 Cor. 7:29]. *Methodius (c. 290, E), 6.347.*

There would be no adulteries, debaucheries, and prostitution of women if everyone knew that whatever is sought beyond the desire of procreation is condemned by God. *Lactantius (c. 304–313, W), 7.143.*

Sexual desire is given to us for the procreation of offspring. *Lactantius (c. 304–313, W), 7.185.*

We believe that lawful marriage and the begetting of children is honorable and undefiled. The difference of the sexes was established in Adam and Eve for the increase of mankind. *Apostolic Constitutions (compiled c. 390, E), 7.454.*

When the menstrual purgations appear in the wives, their husbands should not approach them, out of regard to the children to be begotten. For the Law has forbidden it when it says: "You will not come near your wife when she is in her separation" [Lev. 18:19]. Nor, indeed, let them have relations when their wives are with child. For [in that case] they are not doing it for the begetting of children, but only for the sake of pleasure. Now a lover of God should not be a lover of pleasure. *Apostolic Constitutions (compiled c. 390, E), 7.463.*

SEE ALSO ABORTION, INFANTICIDE; CONCEPTION; MARRIAGE; OVERPOPULATION.

PROPHECY, PROPHETS

I. Prophecy in the early church

II. How to identify a true prophet

III. Old Testament prophets

I. Prophecy in the early church

In these days prophets came from Jerusalem to Antioch. Then one of them, named Agabus, stood up and showed by the Spirit that there was going to be a great famine throughout all the world, which also happened in the days of Claudius Caesar. Acts 11:27, 28.

Tongues are for a sign, not to those who believe but to unbelievers; but prophesying is not for unbelievers but for those who believe. 1 Cor. 14:22.

Let two or three prophets speak, and let the others judge. 1 Cor. 14:29.

Do not despise prophecies. 1 Thess. 5:20.

He Himself is prophesying in us. *Barnabas (c. 70–130, E), 1.147.*

Every true prophet who wishes to abide among you is worthy of his support. So also a true teacher is himself worthy, as the workman of his support. Every first-fruit, therefore, of the products of the wine-press and threshing-floor, of oxen and of sheep, you will take and give to the prophets, for they are your high priests. *Didache (c. 80–140, E), 7.381.*

The ensuing quotation was written in reference to the Montanists, who said that the gift of prophecy had left the church.

Others, again, try to set at nought the gift of the Spirit, which in the latter times has been poured out upon the human race, by the good pleasure of the Father. For they do not admit that aspect presented by John's Gospel, in which the Lord promised that He would send the Paraclete. Rather, they set aside at once both the Gospel and the prophetic Spirit. Wretched men indeed! They wish to be pseudo-prophets, but they set aside the gift of prophecy from the church. . . . We must conclude, moreover, that these men cannot admit the apostle Paul either. For, in his Epistle to the Corinthians, he speaks expressly of prophetical gifts, and recognizes men and women prophesying in the church. *Irenaeus (c. 180, E/W), 1.429.*

Prophecy is a prediction of future things. That is, it is a declaration beforehand of things that will happen later. *Irenaeus (c. 180, E/W), 1.489.*

[I speak of] Philip, one of the twelve apostles, who is laid to rest at Hierapolis. Also his two daughters, who arrived at old age unmarried. His other daughter also, who passed her life under the influence of the Holy Spirit, reposes at Ephesus. *Polycrates (c. 190, E), 8.773.*

Prophecy has been fulfilled through His advent. . . . That is the reason why Daniel said, "Vision and prophet were sealed." For Christ is the seal of all prophets, fulfilling all that had in former days been announced concerning Him. For, since His advent and personal passion, there is no longer vision or prophet. *Tertullian (c. 197, W), 3.168.*

After this, there were four prophetesses—daughters of Philip, at Hierapolis in Asia. Their tomb is there, and that, too, of their father. *Eusebius, quoting Caius (c. 215, W), 5.601.*

Never have any of those who have not embraced our faith done anything similar to what was done by the ancient prophets. And in more recent times, since the coming of Christ, no prophets have arisen among the Jews, who have confessedly been abandoned by the Holy Spirit. *Origen (c. 248, E), 4.614.*

Celsus is not to be believed when he says that he has heard such men prophesy. For no prophets bearing any resemblance to the ancient prophets have appeared in the time of Celsus [i.e., the second century]. *Origen (c. 248, E), 4.615.*

Besides the vision of the night, by day also, the innocent age of boys is among us filled with the Holy Spirit—seeing in an ecstasy with their eyes, and hearing and speaking those things by which the Lord warns and instructs us. And you will hear all things when the Lord, who bade me to withdraw, will bring me back again to you. *Cyprian (c. 250, W), 5.290.*

The apostles have overcome unbelief though powers, signs, portents, and mighty works. After them, there is now given to the same completed churches the comfort of having the prophetic Scriptures subsequently interpreted. As I said, after [the apostles] there would be *interpreting* prophets. For the apostle says: "And he placed in the church first, apostles; secondly, prophets; thirdly, teachers." . . . And when he says, "Let two or three prophets speak, and let the others judge," he is not speaking about the universal prophecy of things unheard and unknown. Rather, he is speaking of things that have been both known and announced. But let them judge whether or not the interpretation is consistent with the testimonies of the prophetic utterance. It is plain, therefore, that to John—armed as he was with superior virtue [as an apostle]—this was not necessary. *Victorinus (c. 280, W), 7.353.*

II. How to identify a true prophet

Many will say to Me in that day, "Lord, Lord, have we not prophesied in Your name." . . . And then I will declare to them, "I never knew you; depart from Me, you who practice lawlessness." Matt. 7:22, 23.

Many false prophets will rise up and deceive many. Matt. 24:11.

Let every apostle that comes to you be received as the Lord. But he will not remain except one day; but if there be need, also the next. But if he remains three days, he is a false prophet. And when the apostle goes away, let him take nothing but bread until he lodges. However, if he asks for money, he is a false prophet. *Didache (c. 80–140, E), 7.380.*

But not everyone who speaks in the Spirit is a prophet. Rather, only if he holds the ways of the Lord. Therefore, from their ways will the false prophet and the [true] prophet be known. . . . Every prophet who teaches the truth, if he does not do what he teaches, he is a false prophet. . . . But whoever says in the Spirit, "Give me money," or something else, you should not listen to him. But if he says to you to give for the sake of others who are in need, let no one judge him. *Didache (c. 80–140, E), 7.380, 381.*

The false prophet does not have the power of a divine Spirit in him. Therefore, he answers his hearers according to their inquiries, and according to their wicked desires. He fills their souls with expectations, according to their own wishes. For being himself empty, he gives empty answers to empty inquirers. *Hermas (c. 150, W), 2.27.*

He says, "I will tell you about both kinds of prophets, and then you can test the true and the false prophet according to my directions. Test the man who has the divine Spirit by his life. First of all, he who has the divine Spirit proceeding from above is meek, peaceable, humble, and refrains from all iniquity and the vain desires of this world. He contents himself with fewer needs than those of other men, and when asked he makes no reply. Nor does he prophesy privately. The Holy Spirit does not speak when man wishes the Spirit to speak. Instead, it speaks only when God wishes Him to speak. When, then, a man having the divine Spirit comes into an assembly of righteous men who have faith in the divine Spirit, and this assembly of men offers up prayer to God, then the angel of the prophetic Spirit, who is destined for him, fills the man. When the man is filled with the Holy Spirit, he speaks to the multitude as the Lord wishes." . . . He says, "Hear then, in regard to the spirit which is earthly, empty, powerless, and foolish. First, the man who *seems* to have the Spirit exalts himself, and wishes to have the first seat. He is bold, impudent, and talkative. He lives in the midst of many luxuries and many other delusions, and he takes rewards for his prophecy. If he does not receive rewards, he will not prophesy." *Hermas (c. 150, W), 2.27, 28.*

Test the man who says that he is inspired—by his deeds and his life. *Hermas (c. 150, W), 2.28.*

It appears probable enough that this man [Marcus, a heretic] possesses a demon as his familiar spirit. By means of this spirit, he seems to be able to prophesy. He also enables others to prophesy—as many as he counts worthy to be partakers of his *charis.* . . . However, the gift of prophecy is not conferred on men by Marcus, the magician. Rather, only those to whom God sends His grace from above possess the divinely-bestowed power of prophesying. And they speak where and when God wishes, not when Marcus orders them to do so. *Irenaeus (c. 180, E/W), 1.334, 335.*

He will also judge false prophets, who have not received the gift of prophecy from God. They are not possessed of the fear of God, either. Instead, either for the sake of vainglory, or with a view to some personal advantage (or acting in some other way under the influence of a wicked spirit), they pretend to utter prophecies, while all the time they lie against God. *Irenaeus (c. 180, E/W), 1.508.*

The prophets of old did not speak of their own power—let there be no mistake as to that. Nor did they declare what pleased themselves. But, first of all, they were endowed with wisdom by the Word. And then again, they were rightly instructed in the future by means of visions. And then, when they themselves were fully convinced, they spoke those things that were revealed by God to them alone, and concealed from all others. For with what reason should the prophet be called a prophet, unless he in spirit foresaw the future? For, if the prophet spoke of any chance event, he would not then be a prophet. For he would be speaking of things that were under the eye of all. But one who set forth in detail things yet to be, he was rightly judged a prophet. *Hippolytus (c. 200, W), 5.204, 205.*

Let [Marcion] know that, whatever it may be, we will challenge it to the rule of the grace and power of the Spirit and the prophets. That is, we will challenge it to foretell the future, to reveal the secrets of the heart, and to explain mysteries. *Tertullian (c. 207, W), 3.462.*

Show me your authority. If you are a prophet, foretell something for us. *Tertullian (c. 210, W), 3.522.*

Even among them, too, he reveals that there are men of a lax disposition . . . who listen to new forms of prophesying [i.e., the Montanists]. *Victorinus (c. 280, W), 7.347.*

III. Old Testament prophets

No prophecy of Scripture is of any private interpretation, for prophecy never came by the will of man, but holy men of God spoke as they were moved by the Holy Spirit. 2 Pet. 1:20, 21.

Men of God sustained in them a Holy Spirit, and they became prophets. They were inspired and made wise by God, and so they became divinely instructed, holy, and righteous. Moreover, they were also deemed worthy of receiving this reward, so that they could become instruments of God. . . . And there was not one or two prophets, but many, at various times and seasons among the Hebrews. Also, among the Greeks there was the Sibyl. And they all have spoken things consistent and harmonious with each other. *Theophilus (c. 180, E), 2.97.*

The prophets used to prophesy, not by word alone, but in visions also, and in their manner of life, and in the actions which they performed, according to the suggestions of the Spirit. *Irenaeus (c. 180, E/W), 1.490.*

Among the Hebrews, the prophets were moved by the power and inspiration of God. *Clement of Alexandria (c. 195, E), 2.331.*

The [Old Testament] preachers of whom we have spoken are called prophets, from the office that belongs to them of predicting the future. *Tertullian (c. 195, W), 3.32.*

In regard to the prophets among the Jews, some of them were wise men before they became divinely inspired prophets. Others became wise by the illumination that their minds received when divinely inspired. They were selected by divine providence to receive the Divine Spirit and to be the depositaries of His holy oracles. For they led a life of almost unapproachable excellence. *Origen (c. 248, E), 4.613.*

As God has commanded them, the prophets had therefore declared with all plainness those things that it was desirable for their hearers to understand at present for the governing of their conduct. In regard to deeper and more mysterious subjects (which lay beyond the reach of the common understanding), the prophets set them forth in the form of enigmas and allegories.... They have followed this plan so that those who are ready to spare no labor and no pains in their quest after truth and virtue might search into their meaning. *Origen (c. 248, E), 4.614, 615.*

The inclination to feign and to speak falsely belongs to those who covet riches and eagerly desire gains. But such a disposition was far removed from those holy men.... They were so far from laying up store for the future, that they did not even labor for the day.... They not only had no gains, but they even endured torments and death.... Those who had no desire for gain, had neither the inclination nor the motive for deceit. *Lactantius (c. 304–313, W), 7.13.*

The prophets are found to be of much greater antiquity than the Greek writers. *Lactantius (c. 304–313, W), 7.105.*

SEE ALSO GIFTS OF THE SPIRIT; HEARING FROM GOD; MONTANISTS; ORACLES, PAGAN; SCRIPTURE; SIBYL; VISIONS.

PROSPERITY

You still lack one thing. Sell all that you have and distribute to the poor, and you will have treasure in heaven; and come, follow Me. Luke 18:22.

Do not lay up for yourselves treasures on earth, where moth and rust destroy and where thieves break in and steal; but lay up for yourselves treasures in heaven.... For where your treasure is, there your heart will be also. Matt. 6:19–21.

Now he who received seed among the thorns is he who hears the word, and the cares of this world and the deceitfulness of riches choke the word. Matt. 13:22.

He said to them, "Take heed and beware of covetousness, for one's life does not consist in the abundance of the things he possesses." Luke 12:15.

Command those who are rich in this present age not to be haughty nor to trust in uncertain riches but in the living God. 1 Tim. 6:17.

But do not let it trouble your understanding, that we see the unrighteous having riches and the servants of God in need.... For if God immediately gave the reward to the righteous, immediately we would be engrossing ourselves in business, not in godliness. *Second Clement (c. 150), 7.523.*

But who are those persons who are white and round, and yet do not fit into the building of the tower?... These are the ones who have

faith indeed, but they also have the riches of this world. As a result, when tribulation comes, they deny the Lord on account of their riches and business.... So also those who are rich in this world cannot be useful to the Lord unless their riches are cut down. *Hermas (c. 150, W), 2.15.*

Give heed, therefore, you who glory in your wealth, lest those who are needy should groan, and their groans should ascend to the Lord, and you should be shut out with all your goods beyond the gate of the tower. *Hermas (c. 150, W), 2.16.*

So the use of cups made of silver and gold, and other ones inlaid with precious stones, is out of place.... The elaborate vanity, too, of vessels in etched glass—more apt to break on account of the art, teaching us to fear while we drink—is to be banished from our well-ordered constitution.... Bed-clothes of purple and other colors difficult to produce should be banished.... Tell me, does the table knife not cut unless it is studded with silver and unless its handle is made of ivory?... Will the lamp not dispense light because it is the work of the potter, not of the goldsmith? I attest that a trundle bed provides just as much rest as does the ivory couch.... The Lord ate from a common bowl, and He made the disciples recline on the grass, on the ground. Furthermore, He washed their feet girded with a linen towel—He the lowly-minded God and Lord of the universe. He did not bring down a silver footbath from heaven! *Clement of Alexandria (c. 195, E), 2.246, 247.*

Riches are then to be partaken of rationally and given lovingly. *Clement of Alexandria (c. 195, E), 2.279.*

The good man, being temperate and just, treasures up his wealth in heaven. He who has sold his worldly goods and given them to the poor, finds the imperishable treasure "where there is neither moth nor robber."... It is not jewels, gold, clothing, or beauty of person that are of high value, but virtue. *Clement of Alexandria (c. 195, E), 2.280.*

Delicacies spent on pleasures become a dangerous shipwreck to men. *Clement of Alexandria (c. 195, E), 2.280.*

The Scripture vouches "that the true riches of the soul are a man's ransom." In other words, if he is rich, he will be saved by distributing his wealth. *Clement of Alexandria (c. 195, E), 2.281.*

For example, it is a sin to live luxuriously and licentiously. *Clement of Alexandria (c. 195, E), 2.361.*

Wealth is of itself sufficient to puff up and corrupt the souls of its possessors and to turn them from the path by which salvation is to be attained. *Clement of Alexandria (c. 195, E), 2.591.*

Let not the man who has been invested with worldly wealth think that he is excluded at the outset from the Savior's contest—provided he is a believer and one who contemplates the greatness of God's philanthropy. On the other hand, he should not expect to grasp the crowns of immortality without struggle and effort. *Clement of Alexandria (c. 195, E), 2.592.*

If no one had anything, what room would be left among men for giving? . . . Riches, then, which benefit also our neighbors, are not to be thrown away. *Clement of Alexandria (c. 195, E), 2.594, 595.*

Let no man destroy wealth. Rather, let him destroy the passions of the soul. For these are incompatible with the better use of wealth. For, becoming virtuous and good, he may be able to make good use of those riches. The renunciation, then, and selling of all possessions, is to be understood as spoken of the passions of the soul. *Clement of Alexandria (c. 195, E), 2.595.*

It was difficult for the soul not to be seduced and ruined by the luxuries and flowery enchantments that beset remarkable wealth. *Clement of Alexandria (c. 195, E), 2.596.*

I doubt that the leg that has rejoiced in the anklet will allow itself to be squeezed into the shackle. I fear that the neck beset with pearl and emerald nooses will give no room to the broadsword. For that reason, blessed ones, let us meditate on hardships, so we will not feel them. Let us abandon luxuries, and we will not regret them. Let us stand ready to endure every violence, having nothing which we may fear to leave behind. It is these things that are the bonds which retard our hope. *Tertullian (c. 198, W), 4.25.*

The endowing of a man with riches is not an incongruity to God. For by the help of riches, even rich men are comforted and assisted. Moreover, by them, many a work of justice and charity are carried out. Yet, there are serious faults that accompany riches. And it is because

of these that woes are denounced on the rich, even in the Gospel. *Tertullian (c. 207, W), 3.368.*

Rich men—attached to their means—have been accustomed to gaze more upon their gold than upon heaven. In contrast, our sort of people [i.e., Christians]—though poor—have both discovered wisdom and have delivered their teaching to others. *Mark Minucius Felix (c. 200, W), 4.181.*

As he who treads a road is happier the lighter he walks, so happier is he in this journey of life who lifts himself along in poverty and does not breathe heavily under the burden of riches. Yet, even if we thought wealth to be useful to us, we would ask it of God. Assuredly, He is able to indulge us in some measure, since His is the whole. But we would rather scorn riches than possess them. *Mark Minucius Felix (c. 200, W), 4.195.*

Are you rich? But fortune is ill trusted. And with a large travelling baggage the brief journey of life is not *furnished*, but *burdened*. *Mark Minucius Felix (c. 200, W), 4.196.*

Luxury does not entertain the fear of God. *Novatian (c. 235, W), 5.648.*

Luxury and the short-lived joys of the world are ruining you. *Commodianus (c. 240, W), 4.207.*

When the letter of the law promises riches to the just, Celsus [a pagan] may follow the letter that kills and understand it of worldly riches, which blind men. However, we say that it refers to those riches that enlighten the eyes and which enrich a man "in all utterance and in all knowledge." In this sense, we "charge those who are rich in this world, that they be not high-minded, nor trust in uncertain riches." *Origen (c. 248, E), 4.619.*

You say that you are wealthy and rich. You say you think that you should use those things that God has willed you to possess. Use them, certainly, but for the things of salvation! . . . Let the poor feel that you are wealthy. Let the needy feel that you are rich. Lend your estate to God. Give food to Christ. . . . In this very matter you are sinning against God if you think that riches were given you by Him for the purpose of thoroughly enjoying them, without a view to salvation. For God also gave man a voice. Yet love songs and indecent things are not on that account to be sung. God willed iron to be for the culture of the earth. However, on that account, must murders be committed? ... A large estate is a temptation, unless one's wealth ministers to good use. *Cyprian (c. 250, W), 5.433.*

How can they follow Christ, who are held back by the chain of their wealth? ... They think that they possess, but they are *possessed* instead. They are the bond-slaves of their money, not the lords of their money. They are slaves of their profit. *Cyprian (c. 250, W), 5.440.*

Riches do not make men illustrious—except that they are able to make them more conspicuous by good works. No one is truly rich simply because he possesses riches—but only if he employs them on works of justice. *Lactantius (c. 304–313, W), 7.151.*

If you esteem justice so highly, lay aside the burdens that oppress you. Follow justice instead. Free yourself from fetters and chains, so that you can run to God without any hindrance. *Lactantius (c. 304–313, W), 7.177, 178.*

He who desires to obtain justice, God, perpetual life, everlasting light, and all those things that God promises to man—he will scorn those riches, honors, commands, and kingdoms themselves. *Lactantius (c. 304–313, W), 7.182.*

Someone may now reason with us, saying that it is *not* a good thing to give up riches. Well, I reply that it is a good thing for those who are capable of it. However, at the same time, to use riches for the work of righteousness and mercy is a thing as acceptable as giving up the whole of our riches at once. *Disputation of Archelaus and Manes (c. 320, E), 6.217; see also 2.36–2.37, 2.591–2.604, 3.368–3.370.*

SEE ALSO JEWELRY; MATERIALISM.

PROVIDENCE OF GOD

SEE SOVEREIGNTY AND PROVIDENCE OF GOD.

PSALMS

The Book of Psalms contains new doctrine after the Law of Moses. And after the writing of Moses, it is the second book of doctrine.... After the judges, David arose, ... and he first gave to the Hebrews a new style of psalmody. Through it, he abrogates the ordinances established by Moses with respect to sacrifices, and he introduces the new hymn and new style of jubilant praise in the worship of God. And

throughout his whole ministry, he teaches very many other things that went beyond the Law of Moses. *Hippolytus (c. 205, W), 5.170.*

PSEUDEPIGRAPHA, NEW TESTAMENT

The New Testament Pseudepigrapha are writings that are falsely ascribed to the apostles or other New Testament figures. Most of these writings are Gnostic in origin. Included among the New Testament Pseudepigrapha are the Preaching of Peter, the Preaching of Paul, the Gospel of Thomas, and the Protevangelium of James.

They bring forward an endless number of apocryphal and spurious writings, which they themselves have forged. They use them to bewilder the minds of foolish men and those who are ignorant of the Scriptures of truth. *Irenaeus (c. 180, E/W), 1.344.*

In the *Preaching of Peter*, you will find the Lord called Law and Word. *Clement of Alexandria (c. 195, E), 2.341.*

Peter says in the *Preaching:* "Know then that there is one God." *Clement of Alexandria (c. 195, E), 2.489.*

In addition to Peter's *Preaching*, the apostle Paul will show, saying: "Take also the Hellenic books, read the Sibyl, how it is shown that God is one." *Clement of Alexandria (c. 195, E), 2.490.*

There are also in circulation an epistle to the Laodiceans and another one to the Alexandrians. However, these were forged under the name of Paul, addressed against the heresy of Marcion. *Muratorian Fragment (c. 200, W), 5.603.*

Someone may quote to us out of the little work entitled the *Preaching of Peter*, in which the Savior seems to say to His disciples, "I am not an incorporeal spirit." If so, I have to reply that in the first place, that work is not included among the ecclesiastical books. For we can show that it was not composed either by Peter or by any other person inspired by the Spirit of God. *Origen (c. 225, E), 4.241.*

Basing it on a tradition in the *Gospel according to Peter*, as it is entitled, or the *Book of James* [i.e., the *Protevangelium of James*], some say that the brothers of Jesus were sons of Joseph by a former wife, whom he married before Mary. *Origen (c. 245, E), 9.424.*

If there is any author of this adulterous, yes, murderous baptism [i.e., some type of heretical baptism in fire], it is certainly a book devised by these same heretics concerning this error, which is entitled the *Preaching of Paul. Treatise on Re-Baptism (c. 257), 5.677; see also 2.362, 2.363, 2.491, 2.510.*

SEE ALSO CANON, NEW TESTAMENT; PSEUD-EPIGRAPHA, OLD TESTAMENT.

PSEUDEPIGRAPHA, OLD TESTAMENT

The Old Testament Pseudepigrapha (usually referred to simply as the Pseudepigrapha) is the name usually given to spiritual writings that are ascribed to various Old Testament figures, such as Enoch and Moses, but that were not included in the Old Testament canon. In general, the Jewish scribes thought that these writings were falsely ascribed to their purported authors—which, no doubt, most of them were. Some of these works, however, are quoted or alluded to in the New Testament. For example, Jude refers to events described in both Enoch and the Assumption of Moses (two works usually included in the Pseudepigrapha). Jude specifically quotes a prophecy from Enoch and states that it was made by "Enoch, the seventh from Adam" (Jude 14). The Epistle to the Hebrews mentions someone being "sawn in two" (Heb. 11:37). This refers to the death of Isaiah, which is described in the Martyrdom of Isaiah, another work usually included in the Pseudepigrapha. Paul mentions Jannes and Jambres (2. Tim. 3:8), who are discussed in the Book of Jannes and Jambres.

The Lord is near to them who return unto Him, as it is written in Eldad and Modat, who prophesied to the people in the wilderness. *Hermas (c. 150, W), 2.12.*

I have not attempted to establish proof about Christ from the passages of Scripture that are not admitted by you [Jews]—which I quoted from the words of Jeremiah the prophet, Esdras, and David. But [I have proved this] from those which are even now admitted by you. However, had your teachers comprehended these things, be well assured they would have deleted them, too, just as they did those writings about the death of Isaiah, whom you sawed asunder with a wooden saw. *Justin Martyr (c. 160, E), 1.259.*

With this strength of patience, Isaiah is cut asunder, but ceases not to speak concerning the Lord. Stephen is stoned and prays for pardon for his foes. *Tertullian (c. 200, W), 3.716.*

[The Jewish scribes] hid from the knowledge of the people as many of the passages as they could that contained any scandal against the elders, rulers, and judges. Some of these have been preserved in hidden writings. Take, for example, the story told about Isaiah. This is corroborated by the Epistle to the Hebrews. Yet, it is found in none of their public books. For the author of the Epistle to the Hebrews, in speaking of the prophets, and what they suffered, says, "They were stoned; they were sawn asunder." To whom, I ask, does the "sawn asunder" refer? Now, we know very well that tradition says that Isaiah the prophet was sawn asunder. And this is found in one of the hidden works. The Jews have probably purposely tampered with this work, introducing some phrases that are manifestly incorrect, so that discredit might be thrown on the whole. *Origen (c. 240, E), 4.388.*

Isaiah is reported to have been sawn asunder by the people. And if anyone does not accept the statement because of its being found in the hidden Isaiah, let him believe what is written thus in the Epistle to the Hebrews: "they were stoned; they were sawn asunder." . . . For the phrase, "they were sawn asunder," refers to Isaiah, just as the words, "They were slain with the sword," refer to Zechariah. For he was slain "between the sanctuary and the altar," as the Savior taught. This bears testimony, I think, to a Scripture that is not extant in the common and widely circulated books, but is perhaps in hidden books. *Origen (c. 245, E), 9.425.*

The Jews most cruelly slew Isaiah, cutting him in half with a saw. *Lactantius (c. 304–313, W), 7.110.*

And among the ancients, also, some have written spurious books of Moses, Enoch, Adam, Isaiah, David, Elijah, and the three patriarchs. These are evil and repugnant to the truth. *Apostolic Constitutions (compiled c. 390, E), 7.457.*

SEE ALSO CANON, OLD TESTAMENT; DEU-TEROCANONICAL BOOKS; ENOCH, BOOK OF; MOSES, ASSUMPTION OF.

PUBLIC OFFICE

When Jesus perceived that they were about to come and take him by force to make Him king, He departed again to a mountain by Himself alone. John 6:15.

The Caesars too would have believed on Christ, if either the Caesars had not been necessary for the world, or if Christians could have been Caesars. *Tertullian (c. 195, W), 3.35.*

In us, all ardor in the pursuit of glory and honor is dead. So we have no pressing inducement to take part in your public meetings. Nor is there anything more entirely foreign to us than affairs of state. *Tertullian (c. 195, W), 3.45.*

If we remember this rule [to avoid idolatry], we can render service even to magistrates and rulers, according to the example of the patriarchs and the other forefathers. They obeyed idolatrous kings up to the point of idolatry. Therefore, very recently, there arose a dispute as to whether a servant of God should take upon himself the administration of any dignity or power—if he can keep himself (through adroitness or some special grace) from every type of idolatry. For there is the example of both Joseph and Daniel, who kept clean from idolatry and yet administered both dignity and power in . . . Egypt and Babylonia. Let us suppose that it is possible for anyone to succeed in operating under the mere *name* of the office, in whatever office. Let us also suppose the following: He neither sacrifices nor lends his authority to sacrifices. He does not farm out sacrificial victims. He does not assign to others the care of the temples. He does not look after their tributes. He does not give spectacles at his own or the public expense, nor preside over them. He makes no proclamation or edict for any [pagan] festivals. He does not even take oaths. Furthermore, he does not sit in judgment on anyone's life or character (for you might allow his judging about *money*). He neither condemns nor indicts. He chains no one. He neither imprisons nor tortures anyone. Now, is it believable that all this is possible? *Tertullian (c. 200, W), 3.72.*

Shall he apply the chain, the prison, the torture, and the punishment—he who is not the avenger even of his own wrongs? *Tertullian (c. 211, W), 3.99.*

Celsus [a pagan] also urges us to "take office in the government of the country, if that is necessary for the maintenance of the laws and the support of religion." However, we recognize in each state the existence of another national organization that was founded by the Word of God. And we exhort those who are mighty in word and of blameless life to rule over churches. . . . It is not for the purpose of escaping public duties that Christians decline public offices. Rather, it is so they may reserve themselves for a more divine and necessary service in the church of God—for the salvation of men. *Origen (c. 248, E), 4.668.*

[Emperor] Valerian had sent a rescript to the senate, to the effect that bishops, presbyters, and deacons should immediately be punished. In addition, Christians who were senators, men of importance, or Roman knights were to lose their dignity and be deprived of their property. *Cyprian (c. 250, W), 5.408.*

It is impossible for him who has surrounded himself with royal pomp . . . to enter upon or to persevere in these difficulties. *Lactantius (c. 304–313, W), 7.165.*

Satan causes others to swell with ambitious desires. These are those who direct the whole occupation and care of their life to the holding of magistracies—so they can set a mark upon the annals and give a name to the years. The desire of other persons mounts even higher. They do not wish to merely rule provinces with the temporal sword, but to have boundless and perpetual power and to be called lords of the whole human race! *Lactantius (c. 304–313, W), 7.166.*

SEE ALSO CAPITAL PUNISHMENT; CRIME AND PUNISHMENT; NONRESISTANCE; WAR.

PUNISHMENT, ETERNAL

SEE ETERNAL PUNISHMENTS AND REWARDS.

PURGATORY

SEE DEAD, INTERMEDIATE STATE OF THE; PRAYER (VI. SHOULD CHRISTIANS PRAY FOR THE DEAD?).

PYTHAGORAS

Pythagoras was a Greek philosopher who lived in the sixth century B.C. He is best known today for his discovery that the universe obeys mathematical laws. He taught the transmigration of souls, and he formed a group of disciples who lived by an ascetic rule of life.

Alexander, in his book *On the Pythagorean Symbols,* relates that Pythagoras was a pupil of Nazaratus the Assyrian. *Clement of Alexandria (c. 195, E), 2.316.*

This is then the significance of the silence of five years prescribed by Pythagoras, which he commanded to his disciples: It was so that, removing themselves from the objects of sense, they might contemplate the Deity with the mind alone. *Clement of Alexandria (c. 195, E), 2.460.*

How can I help but believe that Pythagoras is a deceiver, for he practices deceit to win my belief? How will he convince me that (before he was Pythagoras) he had been Aethalides, Euphorbus, the fisherman Pyrrhus, and Hermotimus? He says this to make us believe that men live again after they have died. *Tertullian (c. 210, W), 3.209.*

However, as for Pythagoras, he was such a recluse and so unwarlike, that he shrank from the military exploits of which Greece was then so full. He preferred to devote himself in the quiet retreat of Italy, to the study of geometry, astrology, and music. *Tertullian (c. 210, W), 3.211.*

There was also ... another philosophy that Pythagoras originated—which they call "Italian"—because Pythagoras, fleeing from the king of Samos, took up residence in a city of Italy and passed the entirety of his remaining years there. ... And this man, instituting an investigation concerning natural phenomena, combined together astronomy, geometry, and music. *Hippolytus (c. 225, W), 5.11.*

Pythagoras and his disciples do not eat beans, nor anything that contains life. *Origen (c. 248, E), 4.561.*

Pythagoras was not the only one who duly honored arithmetic. His best known disciples did so too. *Anatolius (c. 270, E), 6.153.*

The Pythagoreans and Stoics claim that the soul is not born with the body. Rather, they say it is introduced into it and that it migrates from one body to another. ... That foolish old man [i.e., Pythagoras] falsely said that he had lived before and that in his former life he had been named Euphorbus. *Lactantius (c. 304–313, W), 7.88, 89.*

Pythagoras of Samos was burned to death in a temple, under an unjust suspicion of grasping at sovereign power. *Arnobius (c. 305, E), 6.424; extended discussion: 5.82–5.85.*

SEE ALSO PHILOSOPHERS, PHILOSOPHY; REINCARNATION.

QUARTODECIMANS

The Quartodecimans were Christians who celebrated the Christian Passover (later called Easter) on Nisan 14 every year—regardless on which day of the week that Nisan 14 fell. This practice was primarily followed in Asia Minor, and the Christians there testified that the apostle John had handed down this practice to them. For the first few centuries, this practice was tolerated within the church. Later, however, when the rest of the church attempted to force the Quartodecimans to follow the practice of celebrating Easter on the Sunday following Nisan 14, some Quartodecimans formed their own separate church, which lasted until the fifth century.

Certain other ones, contentious by nature, . . . say that Easter should be kept on the fourteenth day of the first month, according to the commandment of the Law, regardless of what day [of the week] it may occur. . . . In other respects, however, these persons consent to all the traditions delivered to the church by the apostles. *Hippolytus (c. 225, W), 5.123.*

The allegation that [the Quartodecimans] sometimes make against us is that, if we pass the moon's fourteenth day, we cannot celebrate the beginning of the Paschal feast in light. However, this allegation neither moves nor disturbs us. For, although they lay it down as a thing unlawful that the beginning of the Paschal festival should be extended so far as to the moon's twentieth day, they cannot deny that it should be extended to the sixteenth and seventeenth, which coincide with the day on which the Lord rose from the dead. *Anatolius (c. 270, E), 6.149; extended discussion: 6.146–6.151.*

See also Easter; Paschal Controversy.

QUOTABLE QUOTES FROM THE EARLY CHRISTIANS

Some of the following quotations have been condensed.

Only request on my behalf that I may not merely be *called* a Christian, but may really be found to be one. *Ignatius (c. 105, E), 1.74.*

Sound doctrine does not enter into a hard and disobedient heart. *Justin Martyr (c. 160, E), 1.302.*

I am in the habit of *walking* on the earth, not of *worshipping* it. *Clement of Alexandria (c. 195, E), 2.188.*

Their preconceived ideas incline them to disbelieve. *Clement of Alexandria (c. 195, E), 2.320.*

We should select and possess what is useful out of all cultures. *Clement of Alexandria (c. 195, E), 2.348.*

To be subjected to our lusts, and to yield to them, is the most extreme form of slavery. To keep those lusts in subjection is the only liberty. *Clement of Alexandria (c. 195, E), 2.378.*

Does not he who denies the Lord deny himself? For he does not rob his Master of His authority, but deprives himself of his relationship to Him. *Clement of Alexandria (c. 195, E), 2.417.*

Loving one's enemies does not mean loving wickedness, ungodliness, adultery, or theft. Rather, it means loving the thief, the ungodly, and the adulterer. *Clement of Alexandria (c. 195, E), 2.426.*

The soul that has chosen the best life—the life that is from God and righteousness—exchanges earth for heaven. *Clement of Alexandria (c. 195, E), 2.440.*

If one expects to comprehend all things by the senses, he has fallen far from the truth. *Clement of Alexandria (c. 195, E), 2.445.*

We are commanded to be lords over not only the wild beasts outside of us, but also over the wild lusts within ourselves. *Clement of Alexandria (c. 195, E), 2.507.*

Every place and every time in which we entertain the idea of God is in reality sacred. *Clement of Alexandria (c. 195, E), 2.535.*

Not a single thing we possess is properly our own. We are truly owners of one possession alone—godliness. When death overtakes us, death will not rob us of this. But from all else, it will eject us. *Clement of Alexandria (c. 195, E), 2.577.*

A man *becomes* a Christian; he is not *born* one. *Tertullian (c. 197, W), 3.32.*

The more often we are mown down by you, the more in number we grow. The blood of Christians is seed. *Tertullian (c. 197, W), 3.55*

You cannot know either the will or the adversary of a God you do not know. *Tertullian (c. 197, W), 3.80.*

We were not given eyes to lust with, nor the tongue for speaking evil. *Tertullian (c. 197, W), 3.80.*

You have your joys where you have your longings. *Tertullian (c. 197, W), 3.90.*

The more inclined you are to maliciousness, the more ready you are to believe evil. *Tertullian (c. 197, W), 3.114.*

Condemn the truth if you have the heart, but only after you have examined it. *Tertullian (c. 197, W), 3.128.*

In the presence of God, there will be no idleness. *Tertullian (c. 197, W), 3.592.*

The leg does not feel the chain when the mind is in heaven. *Tertullian (c. 197, W), 3.694.*

If the bit of glass is so precious, what must the true pearl be worth? *Tertullian (c. 197, W), 3.695.*

He who does not fear to lose, does not find it difficult to give. *Tertullian (c. 200, W), 3.712.*

If we draw up wills for [material] matters, should we not take even more forethought for our posterity in things divine and heavenly? *Tertullian (c. 205, W), 4.39.*

We read that "the flesh is weak" and, hence, we soothe ourselves in some cases. Yet, we read, too, that "the spirit is strong." . . . Why, then, do we (being overly prone to excuse ourselves) put forward the *weak* part of us? Why do we not look at the *strong?* Why should not the earthly yield to the heavenly? *Tertullian (c. 205, W), 4.41.*

Superlative is their folly, for they prejudge divine things from human. *Tertullian (c. 207, W), 3.309.*

Wide are men's inquiries into uncertainties. Wider still are their disputes about conjectures. *Tertullian (c. 210, W), 3.183.*

It is, of course, foolish if we are to judge God by our own conceptions. *Tertullian (c. 210, W), 3.524.*

Christ was buried and rose again. This fact is certain—because it is impossible! *Tertullian (c. 210, W), 3.525.*

Those persons have but a poor knowledge of God, who suppose Him to be capable of doing only what comes within the boundaries of their own thoughts. *Tertullian (c. 210, W), 3.573.*

What is needed is not the authority of the *one who argues,* but the truth of the argument itself. *Mark Minucius Felix (c. 200, W), 4.181.*

The more unskilled the discourse, the more evident the reasoning is. For it is not colored by the pomp of eloquence and grace. *Mark Minucius Felix (c. 200, W), 4.181.*

But how unjust it is to form a judgment on things unknown and unexamined, as you do! *Mark Minucius Felix (c. 200, W), 4.190.*

Among Christians, he who is most just is he who is most religious. *Mark Minucius Felix (c. 200, W), 4.193.*

Calamity is very often the discipline of virtue. *Mark Minucius Felix (c. 200, W), 4.195.*

It is a vain mistake of man to glitter in purple and yet be sordid in mind. *Mark Minucius Felix (c. 200, W), 4.196.*

We bear wisdom in our mind, not in our dress. *Mark Minucius Felix (c. 200, W), 4.197.*

We do not *speak* great things—we *live* them. *Mark Minucius Felix (c. 200, W), 4.197.*

Evil thoughts are the wellspring of all sins. They can pollute even those actions that would have justified the man who did them—if they had been done without any evil thoughts. *Origen (c. 245, E), 9.444.*

Peter is called a stumbling block by Jesus for not minding the things of God in what he said. For he minded the things of men. Accordingly, what is to be said about all those who profess to be disciples of Jesus, but do not mind the things of God? They do not look to things unseen and eternal. Rather, they mind the things of man. *Origen (c. 245, E), 9.463.*

You will observe the difference between the crowds, who simply "followed" Christ, and Peter and the others who "gave up everything and followed." *Origen (c. 245, E), 9.505.*

We are to "put off the old man with his deeds and put on the new man, which is renewed in knowledge after the image of Him who has created him." In taking upon them the image of Him who has created them, they raise within themselves an image in accord with what the Most High God Himself desires. Now, among sculptors, there are some who are marvelously perfect in their art, while others make inferior statues. In the same way, there are some who form images of the Most High in a better manner and with a more perfect skill. *Origen (c. 248, E), 4.646.*

When the soul, in its gaze into heaven, has recognized its Author, it rises higher than the sun and far transcends all this earthly power. It then begins to be that which it believes itself to be. *Cyprian (c. 250, W), 5.279.*

There cannot be a victory unless first there comes a battle. *Cyprian (c. 250, W), 5.472.*

The tree that is deeply founded in its root is not moved by the onset of winds. *Cyprian (c. 250, W), 5.472.*

When the threshing floor brings out the grain, the strong and robust grains ignore the winds, while the empty chaff is carried away by the blast that falls upon it. *Cyprian (c. 250, W), 5.472.*

Suppose the walls of your house were shaking with age, the roofs above you were trembling, and the house (now worn out and wearied) was threatening to immediately collapse? Would you not leave with all haste? Look, the world is changing and passing away! It testifies to its

ruin now—not by its age—but by the end of things. *Cyprian (c. 250, W), 5.475.*

Why is a person who does not completely trust in Christ called a Christian? The name of Pharisee is more fitting! *Cyprian (c. 250, W), 5.479.*

The state does not take away the property entrusted to God, nor does the tax collector intrude on it. *Cyprian (c. 250, W), 5.481.*

You care more about your children's earthly estate than you do about their heavenly estate! *Cyprian (c. 250, W), 5.481.*

We are philosophers—not in words—but in deeds! . . . We do not speak great things; we live them! *Cyprian (c. 250, W), 5.484.*

Jealousy has no limit. It is an evil that continually endures. It is a sin without end. *Cyprian (c. 250, W), 5.493.*

It is then that we are truly fashioned in the likeness of God—when we represent his features in our human life. *Methodius (c. 290, E), 6.312.*

There is more weight in a smaller number of learned men than in a greater number of ignorant persons. *Lactantius (c. 304–313, W), 7.68.*

The power of truth is so great that it defends itself by its own clarity. *Lactantius (c. 304–313, W), 7.69.*

Simple and undisguised truth is the most clear, for it has sufficient ornament of itself. For this reason, it is corrupted when it is embellished with external ornamentation. *Lactantius (c. 304–313, W), 7.69.*

Virtue united with knowledge is wisdom. *Lactantius (c. 304–313, W), 7.76.*

Piety is nothing else than the recognition of God as a parent. *Lactantius (c. 304–313, W), 7.77.*

Men either undertake religion and pay no attention to wisdom, or else they devote themselves to wisdom alone and pay no attention to religion. However, the one cannot be true without the other. *Lactantius (c. 304–313, W), 7.78.*

The fountain of wisdom and religion is God. And if those two streams turn aside from Him, they will dry up. For those who are ignorant of Him cannot be wise or religious. *Lactantius (c. 304–313, W), 7.104.*

The things that you teach cannot have any weight unless you will be the first to practice them. *Lactantius (c. 304–313, W), 7.125.*

You may call those truly deaf who do not hear the things that are heavenly and true. *Lactantius (c. 304–313, W), 7.127.*

Those persons are most foolish who think it is a crime that we are willing to die for *God.* Yet, they themselves extol to the heavens with the highest praises the person who was willing to die for a *man. Lactantius (c. 304–313, W), 7.154.*

Religion is to be defended—not by putting to death—but by dying. Not by cruelty, but by patient endurance. *Lactantius (c. 304–313, W), 7.157.*

This is true worship: when the mind of the worshipper presents itself as an undefiled offering to God. *Lactantius (c. 304–313, W), 7.163.*

Pleasures of short duration are followed by eternal evils. And evils of short duration are followed by eternal pleasures. *Lactantius (c. 304–313, W), 7.166.*

The course of virtue consists in acquiring those things that neither man nor death can take away. *Lactantius (c. 304–313, W), 7.168.*

Whoever strives to hold the right course of life should not look to the earth, but to the heavens. *Lactantius (c. 304–313, W), 7.170.*

He who is ignorant of God must also be ignorant of justice. *Lactantius (c. 304–313, W), 7.171.*

He who is rich towards God can never be poor. *Lactantius (c. 304–313, W), 7.178.*

The rewards of vices are temporal; those of virtues are eternal. *Lactantius (c. 304–313, W), 7.194.*

There is nothing built by human strength that cannot equally be destroyed by human strength. The works of mortals are mortal. *Lactantius (c. 304–313, W), 7.212.*

We should consider *what* is said—not with what *eloquence* it is said. Nor should we look at how it tickles the ears. Instead, we should look at the benefits that it confers on its hearers. *Arnobius (c. 305, E), 6.430.*

The credibility of a religion must not be determined by its age, but by its divinity. *Arnobius (c. 305, E), 6.461.*

You say that my *religion* did not exist four hundred years ago. I reply that your *gods* did not exist two thousand years ago! *Arnobius (c. 305, E), 6.461.*

RACES OF MAN

In truth I perceive that God shows no partiality. But in every nation whoever fears Him and works righteousness is accepted by Him. Acts 10:34, 35.

He has made from one blood every nation of men to dwell on all the face of the earth, and has determined their preappointed times and the boundaries of their habitation. Acts 17:26.

There are four classes of men in this world: Barbarians, Greeks, Jews, and Christians. *Aristides (c. 125, E), 9.264.*

At the same time, it teaches us not to wrong anyone belonging to another race and to bring him under the yoke. For there is no other reason to justify such a thing than difference of race. But that is no reason at all. *Clement of Alexandria (c. 195, E), 2.368.*

We admit that the same nature exists in every race, and the same virtue. *Clement of Alexandria (c. 195, E), 2.419.*

SEE ALSO EQUALITY OF HUMANKIND; TOWER OF BABEL.

RANSOM

SEE ATONEMENT.

RAPTURE

We who are alive and remain until the coming of the Lord will by no means precede those who are asleep. For the Lord Himself will descend from heaven with a shout, with the voice of an archangel, and with the trumpet of God. And the dead in Christ will rise first. Then we who are alive and remain will be caught up together with them in the clouds to meet the Lord in the air. 1 Thess. 4:15–17.

When in the end the church will suddenly be caught up from this, it is said, "There will be tribulation such as has not been since the beginning, nor will be." For this is the last con-

test of the righteous. When they overcome in this contest, they are crowned with incorruption. *Irenaeus (c. 180, E/W), 1.558.*

I will then see whether it will be women thus decked out [in cosmetics] whom the angels carry up to meet Christ in the air! If these things are now good, and of God, they will then also present themselves to the rising bodies. *Tertullian (c. 198, W), 4.22.*

In the crisis of the last moment, and from their instantaneous death while encountering the oppression of the Antichrist, these persons will also undergo a change. They obtain thereby, not so much a divestiture of the body, as a clothing superimposed upon it with the garment that is from heaven. These persons will put on this heavenly garment over their bodies. Meanwhile, the dead, for their part, will also recover their bodies. Over their bodies, they too have a garment to put on—the incorruption of heaven. . . . The one group puts on this apparel when they recover their bodies. The others put it on as overcoats, for indeed they hardly lose their bodies. *Tertullian (c. 207, W), 3.455.*

He says that those who remain unto the coming of Christ, along with the dead in Christ, shall rise first, being "caught up in the clouds to meet the Lord in the air." . . . By the mouth of Isaiah, it was said long ago: "Who are these that fly as clouds unto me, as doves with their young ones?" *Tertullian (c. 207, W), 3.462.*

How, indeed, will the soul mount up to heaven, . . . when as yet those whom the coming of the Lord is to find on the earth have not yet been caught up into the air to meet Him at His coming? For they will be in company with the dead in Christ, who will be the first to rise. *Tertullian (c. 210, W), 3.231.*

When we read, "Go, my people, enter into your closets for a little season, until my anger passes away," we understand the closets to be graves, in which will rest for a little while those who—at the end of the world—have departed this life in the last furious onset of the power of the Antichrist. *Tertullian (c. 210, W), 3.565.*

Before we put off the garment of the flesh, we wish to be clothed with the celestial glory of immortality. Now, the privilege of this favor awaits those who are found in the flesh at the coming of the Lord. These—owing to the oppression of the times of the Antichrist—deserve by an instantaneous death (which is accomplished by a sudden change) to become qualified to join the rising saints. Paul writes of this to the Thessalonians. *Tertullian (c. 210, W), 3.575.*

For who is there that will not desire, while he is in the flesh, to put on immortality and to continue his life by a happy escape from death through the transformation that must be experienced instead of [death]—without encountering too that Hades that will exact the very last farthing? *Tertullian (c. 210, W), 3.575; see also 3.473, 3.562, 3.584.*

SEE ALSO ANTICHRIST; ESCHATOLOGY; LAST DAYS; RESURRECTION OF THE DEAD.

READER

In the early church, readers were men who were appointed to publicly read from the Scriptures during the assembly of the church.

After the reading of the Law and the Prophets, the rulers of the synagogue sent to them, saying, "Men and brethren, if you have any word of exhortation for the people, say on." Acts 13:15.

Till I come, give attention to reading, to exhortation, to doctrine. 1 Tim. 4:13.

Blessed is he who reads and those who hear the words of this prophecy. Rev. 1:3.

And so it came to pass that [among the heretics] today one man is their bishop, tomorrow another. Today he is a deacon who tomorrow is a reader. *Tertullian (c. 197, W), 3.263.*

I warn certain readers . . . to set an example of life for others. Avoid strife and shun many quarrels. . . . Be among the lilies of the field by your benefits. You have become blessed when you bear the edicts. *Commodianus (c. 240, W), 4.216.*

The trumpet of the heralds sounds forth, while the reader is reading, so that the ears may be open. *Commodianus (c. 240, W), 4.218.*

Such a man is to be estimated not by his years, but by his deserts. He has merited higher degrees of clerical ordination and a greater advancement. But, in the meantime, I judged it appropriate that he should begin with the office of reading. . . . Know, then, most beloved brethren, that this man has been ordained by me and by my colleagues who were then present. *Cyprian (c. 250, W), 5.312.*

Of those who come into the clergy unmarried, we permit only the readers and singers to marry afterwards, if they so desire. *Apostolic Constitutions (compiled c. 390, E), 7.501.*

SEE ALSO CHURCH GOVERNMENT; MINOR ORDERS.

REAL PRESENCE

SEE EUCHARIST.

REBAPTISM

SEE BAPTISM (V. BAPTISM BY HERETICS).

RECAPITULATION

SEE ATONEMENT (II. RECAPITULATION IN CHRIST).

REDEMPTION

SEE ATONEMENT; BLOOD OF CHRIST; SALVATION.

REGENERATION

SEE BAPTISM; NEW BIRTH.

REINCARNATION

Souls neither see God nor transmigrate into other bodies. For, if they did, they would know why they were punished, and they would be afraid to commit even the most trivial sin afterwards. *Justin Martyr (c. 160, E), 1.197.*

[The Gnostics] deem it necessary, therefore, that by means of transmigration from body to body, souls should experience every kind of life. *Irenaeus (c. 180, E/W), 1.351.*

We may subvert [the Gnostics'] doctrine as to transmigration from body to body by this fact: that souls remember nothing whatever of the events which took place in their [supposed] previous states of existence. *Irenaeus (c. 180, E/W), 1.409.*

Plato, that ancient Athenian, . . . was the first to introduce this opinion [i.e., reincarnation]. *Irenaeus (c. 180, E/W), 1.410.*

The hypothesis of Basilides [a Gnostic teacher] says that the soul, having sinned before in another life, endures punishment in this life. *Clement of Alexandria (c. 195, E), 2.424.*

How much more worthy of acceptance is our belief that maintains that souls will return to the same bodies. And how much more ridiculous is your inherited [pagan] teaching that the human spirit is to reappear in a dog, mule, or a peacock! *Tertullian (c. 197, W), 3.127.*

It is sufficient that the no less important philosophy of Pythagoras, Empedocles, and the Platonists, take the contrary view—and declare that the soul is immortal. Moreover they say this in a way that most nearly approaches [our own teaching,] that the soul actually returns into bodies. However, [according to the philosophers] it is not the same bodies, and it is not necessarily those of human beings. *Tertullian (c. 210, W), 3.545.*

What does it mean, that ancient saying (mentioned by Plato) concerning the reciprocal migration of souls? He says they leave here and go yonder, and then return here and pass through life. Yet, they again depart from this life, and afterwards become alive from the dead. Some will have it that this is a saying of Pythagoras. *Tertullian (c. 210, W), 3.208.*

Now our position is this: that the human soul cannot by any means at all be transferred to beasts. *Tertullian (c. 210, W), 3.212.*

Homer (so dreamed Ennius) remembered that he was once a peacock. However, I cannot for my part believe poets, even when they are wide awake! *Tertullian (c. 210, W), 3.214.*

Souls do not transmigrate into animals. Rather, they return to their own proper bodies. . . . No belief, indeed, under cover of any heresy, has as yet burst upon us that embodies any such extravagant fiction as that the souls of human beings pass into the bodies of wild beasts. *Tertullian (c. 210, W), 3.215.*

However, it is not for you alone [Simon Magus], that the transmigration philosophy has invented this story. Carpocrates also makes equally good use of it. *Tertullian (c. 210, W), 3.216.*

Pythagoras first, and Plato chiefly, have delivered the doctrine of resurrection with a corrupt and divided faith. . . . They add also this, by way of misrepresenting the truth: that the souls of men return into cattle, birds, and beasts. *Mark Minucius Felix (c. 200, W), 4.194.*

He will accomplish a resurrection of all—not by transferring souls into other bodies—but by raising the bodies themselves. *Hippolytus (c. 205, W), 5.222.*

[REFERRING TO JOHN THE BAPTIST:] In this place, it does not seem to me that by the name "Elijah," the soul is being spoken of. Otherwise, I would fall into the doctrine of transmigration, which is foreign to the church of God. It is not handed down by the apostles, nor is it set forth in the Scriptures anywhere. *Origen (c. 245, E), 9.474.*

The Pythagoreans and Stoics claimed that the soul is not born with the body. Rather, they say it was introduced into it and that it migrates from one body to another. *Lactantius (c. 304–313, W), 7.88, 89.*

What crimes could we have committed when we did not even exist? Unless we will happen to believe that foolish old man [i.e., Pythagoras], who falsely said that he had lived before and that in his former life he had been named Euphorbus. . . . O wonderful and remarkable memory of Pythagoras! What miserable forgetfulness on the part of the rest of us! For we do not remember who we were in our former lives! *Lactantius (c. 304–313, W), 7.89.*

Pythagoras contends that souls migrate from bodies that are worn out with old age and death. He says they gain admission into bodies that are new and recently born. He also says the same souls are reproduced at one time in a man, another time in a sheep, another in a wild beast, and another in a bird. He says that they are accordingly immortal, for they often change their habitations—which consist of various and dissimilar bodies. This opinion of a senseless man is ridiculous. It is more worthy of a stage-player than of a school of philosophy. *Lactantius (c. 304–313, W), 7.210; see also 6.440.*

SEE ALSO ORIGEN; PLATO; PYTHAGORAS; RESURRECTION OF THE DEAD; SOUL.

RELICS OF MARTYRS AND SAINTS

So it was, as they were burying a man, that suddenly they spied a band of raiders; and they put the man in the tomb of Elisha; and when the man was let down and touched the bones of Elisha, he revived and stood on his feet. 2 Ki. 13:21.

Now God worked unusual miracles by the hands of Paul, so that even handkerchiefs or aprons were brought from his body to the sick, and the diseases left them and the evil spirits went out of them. Acts 19:11, 12.

We afterwards took up Polycarp's bones—as being more precious than the most exquisite jewels and more purified than gold. We deposited them in a fitting place. *Martyrdom of Polycarp (c. 135, E), 1.43.*

I can show the trophies [i.e., relics] of the apostles. For if you choose to go to the Vatican or to the Ostian Road, you will find the trophies of those who founded this church. *Eusebius, quoting Caius (c. 215, W), 5.601.*

Do not seek after Jewish separations . . . or purifications upon touching a dead body. . . . For as to those who live with God, even their very relics are not without honor. For even Elisha the prophet, after he had fallen asleep, raised up a dead man who had been slain by the raiders of Syria. For his body touched the bones of Elisha, and he arose and returned to life. Now, this would not have happened unless the body of Elisha were holy. And chaste Joseph embraced Jacob after he was dead upon his bed. And Moses and Joshua, the son of Nun, carried away the relics of Joseph and did not consider it a defilement. *Apostolic Constitutions (compiled c. 390, E), 7.464.*

SEE ALSO MARTYRS, MARTYRDOM; PRAYER (V. SHOULD CHRISTIANS PRAY TO ANGELS AND SAINTS?).

RELIGION

It is clear that no other hope is set before man, except that he lay aside all vanities and wretched error, and come to know God and to serve Him. He must renounce this transitory life and train himself by the principles of righteousness, for the cultivation of true religion. For we were created on this condition: that we pay just and due obedience to God, who created us. We should know and follow Him alone. We are bound and tied *[religare]* to God by this chain of piety. And the word "religion" *[religio]* is derived from this. . . . Religion is the cultivation of truth. In contrast, superstition is the cultivation of what is false. . . . The worshippers of the gods imagine themselves to be religious. However, they are actually superstitious. They are unable to distinguish religion from superstition. Nor are they able to correctly define the meaning of the names [of religion and superstition]. As I have said, the name of religion is derived from the bond of piety. *Lactantius (c. 304–313, W), 7.131.*

REMARRIAGE

Moses, because of the hardness of your hearts, permitted you to divorce your wives, but from the beginning it was not so. And I say to you, whoever divorces his wife, except for sexual immorality, and marries another, commits adultery; and whoever marries her who is divorced commits adultery. Matt. 19:8, 9.

Now to the married I command, yet not I but the Lord: A wife is not to depart from her husband. But even if she does depart, let her remain unmarried or be reconciled to her husband. And a husband is not to divorce his wife. 1 Cor. 7:11.

A wife is bound by law as long as her husband lives; but if her husband dies, she is at liberty to be married to whom she wishes, only in the Lord. 1 Cor. 7:39.

And I said, "If a wife or husband dies, and the widower or widow marries, does he or she commit sin?" "There is no sin in marrying again," he said. "However, if they remain unmarried, they gain greater honor and glory with the Lord. Still, if they marry, they do not sin." *Hermas (c. 150, W), 2.22.*

A person should either remain as he was born, or be content with one marriage. For a second marriage is only a specious adultery. Jesus says, "For whoever puts away his wife and marries another, commits adultery." He does not permit a man to send her away whose virginity he has brought to an end, nor to marry again. A man who deprives himself of his first wife, even though she is dead, is a cloaked adulterer, resisting the hand of God. For in the beginning, God made one man and one woman. *Athenagoras (c. 175, E), 2.146, 147.*

That erring Samaritan woman did not remain with one husband. Rather, she committed fornication by many marriages. *Irenaeus (c. 180, E/W), 1.445.*

Being a heretic by his very nature, . . . he maintains repeated marriages. *Tertullian (c. 200, W), 3.477.*

The Lord ... hurled His denunciation against Herod in the form of unlawful marriages and of adultery. For he pronounced as an adulterer even the man who married a woman who had been put away by her husband. He said this in order the more severely to load Herod with guilt. For Herod had taken his brother's wife after she had been loosed from her husband—by death rather than by divorce. For he had been impelled thereto by his lust—not by the commandment of the Law. For his brother had left a daughter. Therefore, the marriage with his widow could not be lawful. *Tertullian (c. 207, W), 3.405, 406.*

The next two quotations reflect the Montanistic teaching that all remarriages are forbidden.

Now, if any limitation is set to marrying, it is the spiritual rule, which prescribes but one marriage under the Christian obedience, maintained by the authority of the Paraclete. *Tertullian (c. 207, W), 3.294.*

The modest restraint in secret on the marriage bed—and the once only adoption of it—are fragrant offerings to God. *Tertullian (c. 210, W), 3.551.*

"If you are bound to a wife, do not seek to be loosed. If you have been loosed from a wife, do not seek a wife. But even if you have taken a wife, you have not sinned." [1 Cor. 7:27, 28]. He says that because to a man who had been loosed from a wife prior to his believing [in Christ], his wife will not be counted as a "second wife." Because she is his first wife after his believing. *Tertullian (c. 217, W), 4.68.*

[SAID IN DISAPPROVAL:] About the time of this man [i.e., Callistus], bishops, presbyters, and deacons who had been twice married—even *thrice* married—began to retain their place among the clergy. *Hippolytus (c. 225, W), 5.131.*

But now, contrary to what was written, even some of the rulers of the church have permitted a woman to marry—even when her husband was living, doing contrary to what was written. For it is said, "A wife is bound so long as her husband lives." *Origen (c. 245, E), 9.510.*

A woman is an adulteress—even though she seems to be married to a man—if the former husband is still living. Likewise, also, the man who seems to marry the woman who has been put away, does not so much marry her as commit adultery with her—according to the declaration of our Savior. *Origen (c. 245, E), 9.511.*

"To the unmarried and widows, it is good for them if they can remain even as I am. But if they cannot contain themselves, let them marry. For it is better to marry than to burn." Here Paul also persisted in giving the preference to continence. ... He challenged his hearers to this state of life, teaching that it was better that a man who had been bound to one wife should from then on remain single, just as he did. On the other hand, ... on account of the strength of animal passion, Paul allows "by permission" one who is in such a condition to contract a second marriage. ... He allows a second marriage to those who are burdened with the disease of the passions, lest they should be wholly defiled by fornication. *Methodius (c. 290, E), 6.321.*

Let not the younger widows be placed in the order of widows, lest ... they come to a second marriage and become subject to sin. ... For you should know this, that marrying once according to the law is righteous, as being according to the will of God. But second marriages, made after the promise, are wicked—not because of the marriage itself, but because of the falsehood. Third marriages are indications of incontinency. But any marriages beyond the third are manifest fornication. ... But to the younger women, let a second marriage be allowed after the death of their first husband. *Apostolic Constitutions (compiled c. 390, E), 7.426.*

SEE ALSO HEROD; MONTANISTS; TWICE-MARRIED; WIDOWS, ORDER OF.

REPENTANCE

Repent therefore and be converted, that your sins may be blotted out. Acts 3:19.

They should repent, turn to God, and do works befitting repentance. Acts 26:20.

If anyone sins, we have an Advocate with the Father, Jesus Christ the righteous. 1 John 2:1.

If we sin willfully after we have received the knowledge of the truth, there no longer remains a sacrifice for sins. Heb. 10:26.

Remember therefore from where you have fallen; repent and do the first works, or else I will come to you quickly and remove your lampstand. Rev. 2:5.

Repentance is great wisdom. For he who has sinned understands that he acted wickedly in the sight of the Lord. He remembers the actions he has done, and he repents. He no longer acts wickedly, but he does good generously. He humbles and torments his soul because he has sinned. *Hermas (c. 150, W), 2.22.*

"I heard, sir, that some teachers maintain that there is no other repentance than that which takes place when we descended into the water and received remission of our former sins." He said to me, "That was sound doctrine which you heard; for that is really the case. For he who has received remission of his sins should not sin any more, but should live in purity. . . . And therefore I say to you, that if anyone is tempted by the devil, and he sins after that great and holy calling in which the Lord has called His people to everlasting life, he has opportunity to repent but once. But if he should sin frequently after this, and then repent, to such a man his repentance will be of no avail." *Hermas (c. 150, W), 2.22.*

Trust God, then, you who on account of your sins have despaired of life, and who add to your sins and weigh down your life. For if you return to the Lord with all your heart, and practice righteousness the rest of your days, and serve him according to his will, He will heal your former sins, and you will have power to hold sway over the works of the devil. *Hermas (c. 150, W), 2.30.*

It is impossible for him to be saved who now intends to deny his Lord. But to those who denied Him long ago, repentance seems to be possible. *Hermas (c. 150, W), 2.52.*

These are the ones who have now heard my commandments, and repented with their whole hearts. When the Lord saw that their repentance was good and pure, and that they were able to remain in it, He ordered their former sins to be blotted out. *Hermas (c. 150, W), 2.54.*

God welcomes the repentance of the sinner, for He loves the repentance that follows sins. For this Word of whom we speak alone is sinless. For to sin is natural and common to all. But to return [to God] after sinning is characteristic not of any man, but only of a man of worth. *Clement of Alexandria (c. 195, E), 2.293.*

Repentance, then, is a result of faith. For unless a man believes that to which he was addicted to be sin, he will not abandon it. And he must believe that punishment looms over the transgressor. He must believe that salvation belongs to the one who lives according to the commandments. Otherwise, he will not reform. *Clement of Alexandria (c. 195, E), 2.353.*

He that repents of what he did, no longer does or says the things he did. . . . He, then, who has received the forgiveness of sins should sin no more. *Clement of Alexandria (c. 195, E), 2.360.*

Being very merciful, God has promised a second repentance for those who fall into some transgression yet remain in the faith. In that manner, if anyone is tempted after his calling, and is overcome by force and fraud, he may still receive repentance. But he must not turn away from that repentance. "For if we sin wilfully after we have received the knowledge of the truth, there remains no more sacrifice for sins." . . . But continual and successive repentings of sins does not differ at all from the case of those who have not believed at all. *Clement of Alexandria (c. 195, E), 2.360.*

He, then, who from among the Gentiles and from that old life has come to faith, has obtained forgiveness of sins once. But he who has sinned after this should fear, even though he may obtain pardon because of his repentance, for he is as one no longer washed to the forgiveness of sins. . . . The frequent asking of forgiveness, then, for those things in which we often transgress is only the imitation of repentance. It is not repentance itself. *Clement of Alexandria (c. 195, E), 2.361.*

There are two kinds of repentance. The more common is one of fear [of punishment] because of what has been done. The other kind, which is more special, is the shame that the spirit feels in itself, arising from the conscience. *Clement of Alexandria (c. 195, E), 2.416.*

Those who fall into sin after baptism are those who are subjected to discipline. For the deeds done before baptism are remitted [in baptism]. However, those committed after baptism are purged [through discipline]. *Clement of Alexandria (c. 195, E), 2.438.*

If one introduces [love] into his soul, although he is born in sins and has done many forbidden things, he is able to retrieve his mistakes. He does this by increasing his love and by adopting a pure repentance. *Clement of Alexandria (c. 195, E), 2.602.*

True repentance means to be no longer bound in the same sins for which He denounced death against Himself. Rather, it is to eradicate them completely from the soul. For on their extirpation, God takes up His abode again in you. *Clement of Alexandria (c. 195, E), 2.602.*

God gives forgiveness of past sins. However, as to future sins, each one procures this for himself. He does this by repenting, by condemning the past deeds, and by begging the Father to blot them out. For only the Father is the one who is able to undo what is done. *Clement of Alexandria (c. 195, E), 2.602.*

John pledged and assured the young man on oath that he would find forgiveness for himself from the Savior. He beseeched him and fell on his knees. John kissed his right hand itself, as now purified by repentance, and led him back to the church. John then supplicated the Lord with godly prayers, strove along with him in continual fastings, and subdued his mind by various utterances of words. And he did not let up, as they say, until he restored the man to the church. *Clement of Alexandria (c. 195, E), 2.603, 604.*

At the end of the world, the angels, radiant with joy, hymning and opening the heavens, will receive into the celestial abodes those who truly repent. *Clement of Alexandria (c. 195, E), 2.604.*

Where there is no fear, in like manner there is no conversion. Where there is no conversion, repentance is of necessity vain. For it lacks the fruit for which God sowed it—that is, man's salvation. *Tertullian (c. 203, W), 3.657.*

Seize the opportunity of unexpected joy—that you, who at one time were in God's sight nothing but "a drop of a bucket," and "dust of the threshing floor," and "a potter's vessel," may from now on become that "tree that is sown beside the waters, is perennial in leaves, bears fruit at its own time," and will not see fire or axe. Having found the truth, repent of errors. *Tertullian (c. 203, W), 3.659.*

A man commits no small sin against the Lord when, after he has by repentance renounced the Lord's rival, the devil, . . . he again raises him by his own return [to the devil]. For such a person becomes a basis of exultation to [the devil]. . . . For he who has known both [God and Satan] seems to have made a comparison. Therefore, he who . . . had begun to make satisfaction to

the Lord, will, by repenting of his repentance, make satisfaction to the devil. He will therefore be the more hateful to God in proportion as he is the more acceptable to His rival. *Tertullian (c. 203, W), 3.660.*

Repentance is the price for which the Lord has determined to award pardon. . . . Sellers first examine the coin with which they make their bargains to see if it is cut, scraped, or counterfeit. Likewise, we believe that the Lord, when about to grant us such costly merchandise—eternal life—first tests our repentance. *Tertullian (c. 203, W), 3.661.*

He, then, will receive you—His own son—back, even if you have squandered what you had received from Him. . . . But He does this only if you heartily repent. He does this only if you contrast your own hunger with the plenty of your Father's hired servants. And you must leave behind you the swine—that unclean herd. *Tertullian (c. 203, W), 3.663.*

In Greek, the root meaning of "repentance" is not the "confession of a sin"—but a "change of mind." *Tertullian (c. 207, W), 3.316.*

Sometimes a sinner who has become conscious of his own sin and therefore repents . . . is preferred over one who is considered a lesser sinner, but who . . . prides himself on the ground of certain good qualities that he thinks he possesses. *Origen (c. 248, E), 4.489.*

Those who have passed severe condemnation upon themselves because of their sins, and who—on that account—lament and bewail themselves as lost . . . are received by God because of their repentance. *Origen (c. 248, E), 4.492.*

"Behold! I will cast her into a bed. And those who commit adultery with her, into great tribulation—unless they repent of their deeds." Certainly, the Lord would not have exhorted them to repent, if He did not promise mercy to those who repent. *Cyprian (c. 250, W), 5.333.*

After all these things, Christ still receives His own murderers—if they will be converted and come to Him. . . . He closes His church to no one. . . . Even he who has shed Christ's blood can be made alive by Christ's blood! How great is the patience of Christ. Had it not been so great, the church would never have possessed Paul as an apostle. *Cyprian (c. 250, W), 5.486.*

All sins may be forgiven the one who has turned to God with his whole heart. . . . Zechariah says, "Be converted unto me, and I will be turned unto you." . . . Also, in Ecclesiasticus: "Turn to the Lord and forsake your sins." . . . Also, in the second Epistle of the blessed Paul to the Corinthians: "For the sorrow that is according to God works a steadfast repentance unto salvation. However, the sorrow of the world works death." . . . Also, in the Apocalypse: "Remember from where you have fallen and repent. But if not, I will come to you quickly and remove your candlestick out of its place." *Exhortation to Repentance (c. 255, W), 5.592–5.595.*

Repentance erases every sin when there is no delay after the fall of the soul. It erases every sin when the disease is not allowed to go on for an extended time. For then evil will not have power to leave its mark on us. *Methodius (c. 290, E), 6.382.*

In that circumcision [of the heart], He has set before us repentance. If we lay open our hearts—that is, if we confess our sins and make satisfaction to God—we will obtain pardon. Such pardon is denied to those who are obstinate and conceal their faults. *Lactantius (c. 304–313, W), 7.119.*

God especially desires for men to be cleansed from their sins. Therefore, he commands them to repent. Yet, to repent is nothing else than to profess and to affirm that one will sin no more. Therefore, the ones who are pardoned are those who slip into sin unintentionally and incautiously. He who sins wilfully has no pardon. *Lactantius (c. 304–313, W), 7.178.*

Let no one be disheartened. Let no one despair concerning himself if he has turned aside to the way of unrighteousness because he was overcome by passion, impelled by desire, deceived by error, or compelled by force. For it is possible for such a one to be brought back and to be set free. It is possible if he repents of his actions and makes satisfaction to God, turning to better things. *Lactantius (c. 304–313, W), 7.190.*

God is not appeased by incense, victims, or costly offerings. For these things are all corruptible. Rather, he is appeased by a reform of the morals. He who ceases to sin renders the anger of God extinguishable. *Lactantius (c. 304–313, W), 7.277.*

A sinner avoids destruction by repentance. *Apostolic Constitutions (compiled c. 390, E), 7.399.*

Judge with authority as does God. Yet receive the repentant person, for God is a God of mercy. *Apostolic Constitutions (compiled c. 390, E), 7.400.*

If any bishop or presbyter does not receive a person who returns from his sins, but rejects him, let him be deprived. For he grieves Christ, who says, "There is joy in heaven over one sinner who repents." *Apostolic Constitutions (compiled c. 390, E), 7.503; see also 2.41–2.43, 2.48, 2.114; extended discussion: 3.657–3.666, 5.592–5.595.*

SEE ALSO ABSOLUTION; DISCIPLINE, CHURCH; SALVATION.

RESURRECTION OF CHRIST

They were terrified and frightened, and supposed they had seen a spirit. And He said to them, "Why are you troubled? And why do doubts arise in your hearts? Behold My hands and My feet, that it is I Myself. Handle Me and see, for a spirit does not have flesh and bones as you see I have." Luke 24:37–39.

He, foreseeing this, spoke concerning the resurrection of the Christ, that His soul was not left in Hades, nor did His flesh see corruption. This Jesus God has raised up, of which we are all witnesses. Acts 2:31, 32.

Jesus Christ, the faithful witness, the firstborn from the dead. Rev. 1:5.

God has made the Lord Jesus Christ the firstfruits by raising Him from the dead. *Clement of Rome (c. 96, W), 1.11.*

For I know that after His resurrection also, He was still possessed of flesh. And I believe that He is so now. *Ignatius (c. 105, E), 1.87.*

The remainder of the Psalm makes it clear that Christ knew His Father would grant to Him all things that He asked and that His Father would raise Him from the dead. *Justin Martyr (c. 160, E), 1.252.*

You will also allow that it was in the flesh that Christ was raised from the dead. For the very same body that fell in death, and which lay in the sepulcher, did rise again. *Tertullian (c. 197, W), 3.581.*

We profess our belief that [the flesh of Christ] is sitting at the right hand of the Father in heaven. And we further declare that it will come again from there in all the grandeur of the Father's glory. It is, therefore, just as impossible for us to say that [his flesh] was abolished, as it is for us to maintain that it was sinful. *Tertullian (c. 210, W), 3.535.*

Jesus is still sitting there at the right hand of the Father—man, yet God. He is the last Adam; yet, He is also the original Word. He is flesh and blood, yet His body is purer than ours. *Tertullian (c. 210, W), 3.584.*

His resurrection is more miraculous than that of the others in this one respect: The others had been raised by the prophets Elijah and Elisha. However, He was raised by none of the prophets, but by His Father in heaven. *Origen (c. 248, E), 4.455.*

After His resurrection, Christ existed in an intermediate body, as it were. For it was somewhere between the physicalness of the body He had before his sufferings and the appearance of a soul uncovered by such a body. It was for this reason that when His disciples were together and Thomas was with them, Jesus came and stood in their midst, even though the doors were shut. . . . And in the Gospel of Luke also, while Simon and Cleopas were conversing with each other concerning all that had happened to them, Jesus "drew near and went with them." . . . And when their eyes were opened and they knew Him, then the Scripture says, in express words, "And He vanished out of their sight." *Origen (c. 248, E), 4.456.*

On the third day, He freely rose again from the dead. He appeared to His disciples as He had been. . . . However, He tarried for forty days, so that they might be instructed by Him in the precepts of life and so that they might learn what they were to teach. Then, in a cloud spread around Him, He was lifted up into heaven—so that as a conqueror, He might bring man to the Father. For Christ loved man, He became man, and He shielded man from death. *Cyprian (c. 250, W), 5.468.*

The allegation that they sometimes make against us is that, if we pass the moon's fourteenth, we cannot celebrate the beginning of the Paschal feast in light. However, . . . they cannot deny that it should be extended to the sixteenth and seventeenth, which coincide with the day on which the Lord rose from the dead. *Anatolius (c. 270, E), 6.149.*

When He was risen from the dead, He appeared first to Mary Magdalene and Mary the mother of James. He then appeared to Cleopas on the way. After that, He appeared to His disciples. *Apostolic Constitutions (compiled c. 390, E), 7.445.*

RESURRECTION OF THE DEAD

Do not marvel at this; for the hour is coming in which all who are in the graves will hear His voice and come forth—those who have done good, to the resurrection of life, and those who have done evil, to the resurrection of condemnation. John 5:28, 29.

There will be a resurrection of the dead, both of the just and the unjust. Acts 24:15.

We shall not all sleep, but we shall all be changed—in a moment, in the twinkling of an eye, at the last trumpet. For the trumpet will sound, and the dead will be raised incorruptible, and we shall be changed. For this corruptible must put on incorruption, and this mortal must put on immortality. 1 Cor. 15:51–53.

The Lord Himself will descend from heaven with a shout, with the voice of an archangel, and with the trumpet of God. And the dead in Christ will rise first. 1 Thess. 4:16.

They lived and reigned with Christ for a thousand years. But the rest of the dead did not live again until the thousand years were finished. This is the first resurrection. Rev. 20:4, 5.

I saw the dead, small and great, standing before God, and books were opened. And another book was opened, which is the Book of Life. And the dead were judged according to their works, by the things which were written in the books. Rev. 20:12.

There will be a future resurrection. *Clement of Rome (c. 96, W), 1.11.*

If we please Him in this present world, we will also inherit the future world. For He promised to us that He will raise us again from the dead. *Polycarp (c. 135, E), 1.34.*

I give you thanks . . . that I can have a part . . . in the resurrection of eternal life, both of soul and body. *Martyrdom of Polycarp (c. 135, E), 1.42.*

Let none of you say that this very flesh will not be judged, nor rise again. . . . For just as you were called in the flesh, you will also come to be judged in the flesh. *Second Clement (c. 150), 7.519.*

We expect to receive again our own bodies. *Justin Martyr (c. 160, E), 1.169.*

Even if anyone is laboring under a defect of body, yet if he is an observer of the doctrines delivered by Christ, He will raise him up at His second advent perfectly sound. He will make him immortal, incorruptible, and free from grief. *Justin Martyr (c. 160, E), 1.233.*

Those who believed in our Christ will dwell a thousand years in Jerusalem. After that, the general (and in short, the eternal) resurrection and judgment of all men will likewise take place. *Justin Martyr (c. 160, E), 1.240.*

He will raise all men from the dead. He will appoint some to be incorruptible, immortal, and free from sorrow in the everlasting and imperishable kingdom. However, He will send others away to the everlasting punishment of fire. *Justin Martyr (c. 160, E), 1.257.*

Those who maintain the wrong opinion say that there is no resurrection of the flesh. *Justin Martyr (c. 160, E), 1.294.*

In truth, Christ has even called the flesh to the resurrection. He promises everlasting life to it. . . . Why did He rise in the flesh in which He suffered, unless it was to demonstrate the resurrection of the flesh? *Justin Martyr (c. 160, E), 1.297.*

We believe that there will be a resurrection of bodies after the consummation of all things. *Tatian (c. 160, E), 2.67.*

Having been born, I will exist again. Death will exist no longer, and it will be seen no longer. Similarly, there was a time that I did not exist; yet, afterwards I was born. So even though fire may destroy all traces of my flesh, the earth still receives the vaporized matter. And though [my body] may be dispersed through rivers and seas, or torn in pieces by wild beasts, I am laid up in the storehouses of a wealthy Lord. *Tatian (c. 160, E), 2.67.*

That same power can reunite what is dissolved. It can raise up what is prostrate, and restore the dead to life again. It can put the corruptible into a state of incorruption. And the same Being, and the same power and skill, can separate that which has been broken up and distributed among a multitude of animals. . . . He can separate this, I say, and unite it again with the proper members and parts of members. And this is whether it has passed into one animal, or into many, or even if it has passed again from one animal into others. *Athenagoras (c. 175, E), 2.150.*

The whole nature of men in general is composed of an immortal soul and a body. . . . One living being is formed from the two. . . . This proves that a resurrection will follow of those dead and dissolved bodies. For without this, neither could the same parts be united according to nature with one another, nor could the nature of the same men be reconstituted. . . . But that which has received both understanding and reason is *man,* not the soul by itself. Man, therefore, who consists of the two parts, must continue forever. . . . The conclusion is unavoidable, that, along with the eternal duration of the soul, there will be a perpetual continuance of the body according to its proper nature. *Athenagoras (c. 175, E), 2.157.*

It is impossible for the same men to be reconstituted unless the same bodies are restored to the same souls. *Athenagoras (c. 175, E), 2.162.*

God will raise your flesh immortal with your soul; and then, having become immortal, you will see the Immortal, if you now believe on Him. *Theophilus (c. 180, E), 2.91.*

When the number is completed that He had predetermined in His own counsel, all those who have been enrolled for life will rise again. They will have their own bodies, their own souls, and their own spirits, in which they had pleased God. On the other hand, those who deserve punishment will go away into it, they too having their own souls and their own bodies. . . . Both classes will then cease from any longer begetting and being begotten, from marrying and being given in marriage. *Irenaeus (c. 180, E/W), 1.411.*

The Father did not exercise His providence only for the men who are now alive. Rather, he exercised it for all men who from the beginning (according to their capacity), in their generation, have both feared and loved God, have practiced justice and piety towards their neighbors, and have earnestly desired to see Christ and to hear His voice. For that reason, at His second coming, He will first rouse from their sleep all persons of this description. And He will raise them up (as well as the rest who will be judged) and give them a place in His kingdom. *Irenaeus (c. 180, E/W), 1.494.*

But vain in every respect are they [i.e., the Gnostics] who despise the entire dispensation of God, and disallow the salvation of the flesh, and treat with contempt the regeneration of the flesh, maintaining that it is not capable of incorruption. *Irenaeus (c. 180, E/W), 1.528.*

Our bodies, being nourished by it [the Eucharist], and deposited in the earth, and although suffering decomposition there, will rise at their appointed time. For the Word of God will grant them resurrection to the glory of God, even the Father, who freely gives immortality to this which is mortal. *Irenaeus (c. 180, E/W), 1.528.*

Surely it was much more difficult and incredible [to have originally created man out of nothing] ... than to re-integrate again that which had been created and then afterwards decomposed into earth, ... having thus passed into those [elements] from which man ... was formed. *Irenaeus (c. 180, E/W), 1.529.*

"Flesh and blood cannot inherit the kingdom of God." This is put forward by all the heretics in support of their folly [i.e., their denial of the resurrection of the body]. They do this to try to annoy us and to point out that the handiwork of God [i.e., the flesh] is not saved. ... However, by "flesh and blood," Paul refers to all of those (as many as there are) who do not have that [Spirit] which saves and forms us into life. These are the ones who do not have the Spirit of God in themselves. For that reason, men of this mold are spoken of by the Lord as "dead." For He says, "Let the dead bury their dead." *Irenaeus (c. 180, E/W), 1.534, 535.*

Although the body is dissolved at the appointed time because of that original disobedience, it is placed, as it were, in the crucible of the earth, to be re-cast again. When it is re-cast, it will not be as this corruptible body. Rather, it will be pure, and no longer subject to decay. To each body, its own soul will be restored. *Irenaeus (c. 180, E/W), 1.570.*

In Asia, great luminaries have gone to their rest, who will rise again in the day of the coming of the Lord. This is when He comes with glory from heaven and when He will raise again all the saints. *Polycrates (c. 190, E), 8.773.*

In the resurrection, the soul returns to the body. *Clement of Alexandria (c. 195, E), 2.571.*

Every man must come forth [in the resurrection] as the very same person who had once existed. This is so that he may receive at God's hands a judgment, whether of good desert or the opposite. And, therefore, the body too will appear. For the soul is not capable of suffering without the solid substance (that is, the flesh). So it is not right that souls [by themselves] should bear the wrath of God. They did not sin without the body. *Tertullian (c. 197, W), 3.53.*

We maintain that after life has passed away, you still remain in existence and anticipate a Day of Judgment. [In the Judgment], according to your deserts, you are assigned to misery or to bliss. Either way, it will be forever. To be capable of this, your former substance must return to you—the matter and memory of the very same human being. For if you were not endowed again with that sensitive bodily organization, you could feel neither good nor evil. And there would be no grounds for judgment without the presentation of the very person to whom the sufferings of judgment were due. *Tertullian (c. 197, W), 3.177.*

If the flesh is to be repaired after its dissolution, much more will it be restored after some violent injury. ... Is not the amputation or the crushing of a limb the death of that limb? Now, if the death of the whole person is rescinded by its resurrection, what must we say of the death of a part of him? ... Accordingly, for a dead man to be raised again, amounts to nothing short of his being restored to his entire condition. Otherwise, he would still be dead in that part in which he has not risen again. God is quite capable of remaking what He once made. *Tertullian (c. 197, W), 3.589, 590.*

Isaiah says, "Everlasting joy will be upon their heads." Well, there is nothing eternal until after the resurrection. ... If sorrow, mourning, sighing, and death itself attack us from the afflictions both of soul and body, how will they be removed? Must it not be by the cessation of their causes? ... Where will you find adversities in the presence of God? ... What plague awaits the redeemed from death, after their eternal pardon? What wrath is there for the reconciled, after grace? *Tertullian (c. 197, W), 3.590.*

As respects their body and soul, there will be no difference of condition between the people who believe and those who do not believe. *Tertullian (c. 197, W), 3.591.*

They ask, "[In the resurrection,] what will be the use of the cavity of our mouth, and its rows of teeth? ... For there will no longer be any need for eating and drinking. ... What purpose will be served by loins?" ... In short, they ask what will be the purpose of [resurrecting] the entire body, when the entire body will become useless. In reply to all this, we have then already settled the principle that the dispensation of the future state should not be compared with that of the present world. ... The sole question, therefore, ... is whether the Lord—when He ordains salvation for man—intends it for his flesh. In other words, is it His will that the self-same flesh will be renewed? ... If, indeed, the body has existence, it is quite possible for it also to be useful. For in the presence of God, there will be no idleness. *Tertullian (c. 197, W), 3.592.*

There will be no more meat, because there will be no more hunger. There will be no more drink, for there will be no more thirst. There will be no more marriage, because there will be no more child-bearing. There will be no more eating and drinking, because there will be no more labor and toil. Death, too, will cease. So there will be no more need of the nutriment of food. *Tertullian (c. 197, W), 3.593.*

No restoration of marriage is promised in the day of the resurrection. For they will be transformed into the condition and sanctity of angels. *Tertullian (c. 205, W), 4.39.*

Addressing the resurrection of the dead, let us first inquire how some persons denied it back then [i.e., in the days of Paul]. No doubt, they denied it in the same way in which it is even now denied—since the resurrection of the flesh has always had men who denied it. ... The word "dead" expresses simply what has lost the vital principle, by means of which it used to live. Now, the body is that which loses life. As the result of losing it, the body becomes dead. Only to the *body*, then, is the term "dead" suitable. *Tertullian (c. 207, W), 3.447.*

The resurrection is first, and afterwards the kingdom. We say, therefore, that the flesh rises again. We say that when it has changed, it obtains the kingdom. "For the dead will be raised incorruptible" ... and "we will be changed, in a moment, in the twinkling of an eye." *Tertullian (c. 207, W), 3.451.*

Having then become something else by its change, the body will obtain the kingdom of God—no longer the [same] flesh and blood, but the body that God will have given it. Rightly then does the apostle declare, "flesh and blood cannot inherit the kingdom of God." For he ascribes this to the changed condition that follows the resurrection. *Tertullian (c. 207, W), 3.452.*

[THE GNOSTICS ASK:] Since Christ's flesh has both risen and returned to heaven, why is not ours also taken up at once? For it is like His, is it not? Or, on the other hand, they ask, why did His flesh (if it is like ours) not return in like manner to the ground and suffer dissolution? *Tertullian (c. 210, W), 3.535.*

If the resurrection of the flesh is denied, a prime article of the faith is shaken. ... He, therefore, will not be a Christian who will deny this doctrine. For it is confessed by Christians. *Tertullian (c. 210, W), 3.547.*

Day dies into night and is buried everywhere in darkness. ... Yet, it again revives, with its own beauty, its own dowry, its own sun—the same as ever. ... In a word, I would say that all creation is instinct with renewal. ... The whole, therefore, of this revolving order of things bears witness to the resurrection of the dead. *Tertullian (c. 210, W), 3.553.*

God would be unjust if He were to exclude from reward the flesh that is associated in good works. God would be idle if He were to exempt it from punishment—when it has been an accomplice in evil deeds. *Tertullian (c. 210, W), 3.555.*

After all this, we must turn our attention also to those Scriptures that prevent our believing in such a resurrection as is held by your [heretics]. ... For [the heretical resurrection] is either assumed to be taking place now (as soon as men come to the knowledge of the truth) or else to be accomplished immediately after their departure from this life. *Tertullian (c. 210, W), 3.560.*

I understand that in the case of Jonah we have a satisfactory proof of this divine power, when Jonah comes forth from the fish's belly uninjured in both his natures—his flesh and his soul. *Tertullian (c. 210, W), 3.568.*

The flesh that has been committed to the ground is able, in like manner, to rise again by the will of the same God. For although this is not allowed to the sparrows, yet "we are of more value than many sparrows." This is said because, when fallen, we rise again. *Tertullian (c. 210, W), 3.571.*

After that, they marry no more, but in their risen life are equal to the angels. They are not to marry because they are not to die. Rather, they are destined to pass into the angelic state by putting on the garment of incorruption, with a change in the substance that is restored to life. *Tertullian (c. 210, W), 3.571.*

Before we put off the garment of the flesh, we wish to be clothed with the celestial glory of immortality. Now, the privilege of this favor awaits those who at the coming of the Lord are found in the flesh. Because of the oppression of the time of the Antichrist, these deserve by an instantaneous death (which is accomplished by a sudden change) to become qualified to join the rising saints. It is as he writes to the Thessalonians. *Tertullian (c. 210, W), 3.575.*

He who has already traveled through Hades is destined also to obtain the change after the resurrection. It is from this circumstance that we definitively declare that the flesh will by all means rise again. Because of the change that is to come over it, it will assume the condition of angels. *Tertullian (c. 210, W), 3.575.*

The very same flesh that was once sown in death will bear fruit in the resurrection life. It will be the same in essence, only it will be more full and perfect. It will not be another body, although reappearing in another form. For it will receive in itself the grace and adornment that God desires to spread over it, according to its merits. *Tertullian (c. 210, W), 3.585.*

Do you think that when anything is withdrawn from our feeble eyes, it perishes to God? Every body is withdrawn from us, but it is reserved for God in the custody of the elements. This is so regardless of whether it is dried up into dust, dissolved into water, compressed into ashes, or is vaporized into smoke. *Mark Minucius Felix (c. 200, W), 4.194.*

For our consolation, all nature suggests a future resurrection. The sun sinks down and arises, the stars pass away and return, the flowers die and revive again. *Mark Minucius Felix (c. 200, W), 4.194*

We therefore believe that the body also is raised. For even if it decays, it is not in the least bit destroyed. That is because the earth that receives its remains, will preserve them. They become like seed and are wrapped up in the richer part of the earth. Thereafter, they spring up and bloom. . . . However, the body is not raised the same thing as it is now. Rather, it becomes pure and no longer corruptible. And to every body, its own proper soul will be given again. . . . But the unrighteous will receive their bodies unchanged. They will not be freed from suffering and disease. They will be unglorified, with all the ills in which they died. *Hippolytus (c. 205, W), 5.222.*

The apostolic teaching is . . . that there is to be a time of the resurrection from the dead, when this body—which now is sown in corruption—will rise in incorruption; and when that which "is sown in dishonor will rise in glory." *Origen (c. 225, E), 4.240.*

It will appear to be a necessary consequence that if bodily nature is annihilated, it must also be restored and created again. *Origen (c. 225, E), 4.272.*

If [the heretics] also admit that there is a resurrection of the dead, let them answer us this: What is it that died? Was it not the *body*? It is of the *body*, then, that there will be a resurrection. *Origen (c. 225, E), 4.293.*

We now turn our attention to some of our own [believers] who . . . adopt a very low and abject view of the resurrection of the body. . . . Now, the apostle says that a body which arises in glory, power, and incorruptibility has already become spiritual. Therefore, if they believe the apostle, it appears absurd and contrary to his meaning to say that the body can again be entangled with the lusts of flesh and blood. . . . But how do they understand the declaration of the apostle, "We will all be changed?" This transformation certainly is to be looked for. *Origen (c. 225, E), 4.294.*

Certain persons . . . adopt a superficial view of the letter of the law. . . . They are of the opinion that the fulfillment of the promises of the future are to be looked for in bodily pleasure and luxury. Therefore, they especially desire after the resurrection to have again such bodies as will always have the power of eating and drinking, and performing all of the functions of flesh and blood. *Origen (c. 225, E), 4.297.*

Ignorant men and unbelievers suppose that our flesh is destroyed after death to such a degree that it retains no relic at all of its former substance. However, we who believe in its res-urrection understand that only a change has been produced by death. . . . It will again be raised from the earth. And after this, it will advance to the glory of a spiritual body—according to the merits of the indwelling soul. We are to believe, then, that all this bodily sub-stance will be brought into this condition. This will be when all things will be re-established into a state of unity and when God will be "all in all." And this result must be understood as being brought about, not suddenly, but slowly and gradually. *Origen (c. 225, E), 4.346, 347.*

When it has cast away the infirmities in which it is now entangled, this same body will be changed into a condition of glory, being ren-dered spiritual, so that what was a vessel of dis-honor may (when cleansed) become a vessel of honor and an abode of blessedness. We are to believe also that it will abide forever in this con-dition, without any change. *Origen (c. 225, E), 4.347.*

Neither we, nor the Holy Scriptures, assert that those who were long dead will arise from the earth and will live again with the same bod-ies—without any change to a higher condition. *Origen (c. 248, E), 4.551.*

Therefore, we do not maintain that the body that has undergone corruption will resume its original nature. For the grain of wheat that has decayed does not return to its former condition. Rather, we maintain that—just as a stalk arises above the grain of wheat—so a certain power is implanted in the body, which is not destroyed, and from which the body is raised up in incor-ruption. *Origen (c. 248, E), 4.553.*

We do not assert, however, that God will raise men from the dead with the same flesh and blood. . . . For we do not maintain that the nat-ural body, which is sown in corruption, dis-honor, and weakness, will rise again just as it was sown. *Origen (c. 248, E), 4.586.*

A law of resurrection is established in that Christ was raised up in the substance of the body as an example for the rest. *Novatian (c. 235, W), 5.620.*

Believe in the one God, so that when you are dead, you may live and may rise in His king-dom, when there will be the resurrection of the just. *Commodianus (c. 240, W), 4.209.*

Christ descends to His elect, who have been darkened from our view for so long a time. *Commodianus (c. 240, W), 4.211.*

There are two resurrections. The first resur-rection takes place now. It is of the souls that are in the faith. For this faith does not permit men to pass over to the second death. Of this resurrection, the apostle says, "If you have risen with Christ, seek those things that are above." *Victorinus (c. 280, W), 7.359.*

It is patently absurd to think that the body will not co-exist with the soul in the eternal state. *Methodius (c. 290, E), 6.364.*

It is the body that dies; the soul is immortal. So, then, if the soul is immortal, and the body is the corpse, then those who say that there is not a resurrection of the flesh deny any resurrection at all. *Methodius (c. 290, E), 6.367.*

He is not of sound mind who—without having any greater hope set before him—prefers labors, torments, and miseries to those good things that others enjoy in life. *Lactantius (c. 304–313, W), 7.172.*

The [faithful dead] will rise again and be clothed by God with bodies. They will remem-ber their former life and all of its actions. Being placed in the possession of heavenly goods and enjoying the pleasure of innumerable resources, they will give thanks to God in His immediate presence. *Lactantius (c. 304–313, W), 7.218.*

The Almighty God Himself will . . . grant us a resurrection with all those who have slept from the beginning of the world. And we will then be such as we are now in this present form, but without any defect or corruption. For we will rise incorruptible. *Apostolic Consti-tutions (compiled c. 390, E), 7.439; see also 1.542–1.543, 2.158–2.162, 3.590; extended discussion: 3.545–3.594, 7.439–7.441.*

SEE ALSO DEAD, INTERMEDIATE STATE OF THE; ESCHATOLOGY; ETERNAL PUNISHMENTS AND REWARDS; JUDGMENT, LAST; MILLEN-NIUM; RAPTURE; RESURRECTION OF CHRIST; SECOND COMING OF CHRIST.

REVELATION, BOOK OF

I. Authorship and general references

II. Interpretation of specific passages

I. Authorship and general references

The Revelation of Jesus Christ, which God gave him to show His servants—things which must shortly take place. And He sent and signified it by His angel to His servant John. Rev. 1:1.

I, John, both your brother and companion in tribulation, and in the kingdom of patience of Jesus Christ, was on the island that is called Patmos for the word of God and for the testimony of Jesus Christ. Rev. 1:9.

There was a certain man with us, whose name was John, one of the apostles of Christ, who prophesied by a revelation that was made to him. He prophesied that those who believed in our Christ would dwell a thousand years in Jerusalem. *Justin Martyr (c. 160, E), 1.240.*

When John could not endure the sight (for he says, "I fell at his feet as dead"), . . . the Word revived him. Christ reminded him that it was He upon whose bosom he had leaned at supper. *Irenaeus (c. 180, E/W), 1.491.*

. . . those which John, the disciple of the Lord, saw in the Apocalypse. *Irenaeus (c. 180, E/W), 1.504.*

In a still clearer light has John, in the Apocalypse, indicated to the Lord's disciples what will happen in the last times, and concerning the ten kings who will then arise. *Irenaeus (c. 180, E/W), 1.554.*

This number is found in all the most approved and ancient copies [of Revelation]. And those men who saw John face to face bear their testimony. *Irenaeus (c. 180, E/W), 1.558.*

And although here upon earth a spiritual man is not honored with the chief seat, he will sit down on the twenty-four thrones, judging the people, as John says in the Apocalypse. *Clement of Alexandria (c. 195, E), 2.504.*

If you doubt, unravel the meaning of what the Spirit says to the churches. He charges the Ephesians with having forsaken their love. He reproaches the Thyatirenes for fornication and for eating things sacrificed to idols. *Tertullian (c. 203, W), 3.663.*

We have also John's foster churches. For although Marcion rejects his Apocalypse, the order of the bishops (when traced up to their origin) will yet rest on John as their author. *Tertullian (c. 207, W), 3.350.*

In the Revelation of John, again, the order of these times is spread out to view. *Tertullian (c. 210, W), 3.563.*

John sees, when on the Isle of Patmos, a revelation of awe-inspiring mysteries, which he freely recounts and makes known to others. Tell me, blessed John—apostle and disciple of the Lord—what did you see and hear concerning Babylon? *Hippolytus (c. 200, W), 5.211.*

Some persons before our time have set this book aside and entirely rejected it. They have criticized it chapter by chapter, trying to demonstrate that it is without either sense or reason. They have also alleged that its title is false. For they deny that John is the author. . . . They claim that none of the apostles, nor indeed any of the saints, nor any person belonging to the church, could be its author. Rather, they say that Cerinthus and the heretical sect founded by him . . . attached that title to the book. . . . However, I, for my part, could not venture to set this book aside. For there are many brethren who value it highly. *Dionysius of Alexandria (c. 262, E), 6.82.*

I regard it as containing a kind of hidden and wonderful intelligence on the various subjects that come under it. Although I cannot comprehend it, I still believe that there is some deeper sense underlying the words. . . . I do not abruptly reject what I do not understand. Rather, I am that much more filled with wonder at it. *Dionysius of Alexandria (c. 262, E), 6.82.*

I do not deny that this person was called John, therefore, and that this was the writing of someone named John. I also acknowledge that it was the work of some holy and inspired man. However, I could not so easily acknowledge that the author was one of the apostles. I cannot so easily acknowledge that it is the same person who wrote the Gospel that bears the title, "According to John," and the author of the general epistle. Rather, from the character of both those works and the forms of expression in them, . . . I draw the conclusion that the authorship is not his. For the evangelist nowhere else affixes his name [to his works]. He never proclaims himself either in the Gospel or in the epistle. *Dionysius of Alexandria (c. 262, E), 6.83.*

The Gospel and the Epistle agree with each other. They both begin in the same way. . . . However, the Revelation is totally different and altogether distinct. . . . Neither does it contain a syllable in common with these other books. . . . Furthermore, on the ground of difference in diction, it is possible to prove a distinction between the Gospel and the Epistle on the one hand, and the Revelation on the other. For the former are written without actual errors as regards the Greek language. In fact, they were written with the greatest elegance. . . . However, as to the author of the latter, . . . his dialect and language are not of the precise Greek type. He even uses barbarous idioms. *Dionysius of Alexandria (c. 262, E), 6.85.*

The Apocalypse of John the apostle and evangelist calls these persons "elders." *Victorinus (c. 280, W), 7.343.*

Those seven stars are the seven churches. . . . This does not mean that they themselves are the only churches—or even the main churches. Rather, what he says to one, he says to all. For they are in no respect different. *Victorinus (c. 280, W), 7.345.*

When John said these things, he was on the island of Patmos. . . . It was there, therefore, that he saw the Revelation. . . . When John was dismissed from the mines, he later delivered [to the churches] this same Revelation that he had received from God. *Victorinus (c. 280, W), 7.353.*

With regard to the inspiration of the book [i.e., Revelation], we deem it unnecessary to add another word. For the blessed Gregory Theologus and Cyril, and even men of still older date—Papias, Irenaeus, Methodius, and Hippolytus—bore entirely satisfactory testimony to it. *Eusebius (c. 324, E), 1.155.*

II. Interpretation of specific passages

[REV. 1:12:] The church preaches the truth everywhere, and she is the seven-branched candlestick that bears the light of Christ. *Irenaeus (c. 180, E/W), 1.548.*

[REV. 2:5:] Unless this were done, he threatened to remove their candlestick out of its place—that is, to disperse the congregation. *Victorinus (c. 280, W), 7.346.*

[REV. 2:17–4:6:] The hidden manna is immortality. The white gem is adoption as a son of God. The new name written on the stone is "Christian." . . . The morning star is the first resurrection. . . . By saying, "They are neither cold nor hot," He means they are neither unbelieving nor believing. Rather, they try to be all

things to all men. . . . "A door was opened in heaven." The new covenant is announced as an open door in heaven. . . . "A sea of glass like crystal." This represents the gift of baptism that He sheds forth through his Son at the time of repentance. *Victorinus (c. 280, W), 7.346–348.*

[REV. 4:7:] The cherubim, too, had four faces, and their faces were representations of the dispensation of the Son of God. For it says, "The first living creature was like a lion." This symbolizes Christ's effectual working, His leadership, and His royal power. The second one was like a calf, signifying His sacrificial and priestly order. "The third had, as it were, the face of a man." This is a clear depiction of His coming as a human being. "The fourth was like a flying eagle." This points out the gift of the Spirit, who hovers with His wings over the church. Therefore, the Gospels are in accord with these things, among which Christ Jesus is seated. For [the Gospel] according to John describes His original, effectual, and glorious generation from the Father, declaring, "In the beginning was the Word, and the Word was with God, and the Word was God." . . . However, [the Gospel] according to Luke takes up His priestly character, beginning with Zachariah the priest offering sacrifice to God. . . . Now, Matthew describes His birth as a man, saying, "The book of the generation of Jesus Christ, the son of David, the son of Abraham." . . . This, then, is the Gospel of his humanity. . . . On the other hand, Mark begins with the prophetical Spirit coming down from on high to men, saying, "The beginning of the Gospel of Jesus Christ, as it is written in Isaiah the prophet." This points to the winged aspect of the Gospel. *Irenaeus (c. 180, E/W), 1.428, 429.*

[REV. 4:7:] The four living creatures are the four Gospels. . . . The lion designates Mark, in whom is heard the voice of the lion roaring in the desert. And in the figure of a man, Matthew strives to declare to us the genealogy of Mary, from whom Christ took flesh. . . . Therefore, his announcement sets forth the image of a man. Luke, in narrating the priesthood of Zachariah as he offers a sacrifice for the people, . . . bore the likeness of a calf. John the evangelist is like an eagle speeding on uplifted wings to greater heights. For he writes about the Word of God. As an evangelist, Mark thus begins: "The beginning of the Gospel of Jesus Christ, as it is written in Isaiah the prophet." "The voice of one crying in the wilderness." This has the figure of a lion. And Matthew, "The book of the generation of Jesus Christ, the son of David, the son of Abraham." This is the form of a man. But Luke begins, "There was a priest by the name of Zechariah. . . . This is the likeness of a calf. But John begins, "In the beginning was the Word, and the Word was with God, and the Word was God." Here he resembles the likeness of a flying eagle. *Victorinus (c. 280, W), 7.348.*

[REV. 4:10:] The twenty-four elders are the twenty-four books of the Law and the Prophets, which give testimonies of the Judgment. *Victorinus (c. 280, W), 7.348.*

[REV. 5:1:] "And I saw . . . a book written inside and out, sealed with seven seals." This book signifies the Old Testament, which has been given into the hands of our Lord Jesus Christ, who received judgment from the Father. *Victorinus (c. 280, W), 7.350.*

[REV. 5:9:] The proclamation of the Old Testament associated with the new, points out the Christian people singing a "new song," that is, bearing their confession publicly. It is a new thing that the Son of God should become man. It is a new thing to ascend into the heavens with a body. It is a new thing to give remission of sins to men. It is a new thing for men to be sealed with the Holy Spirit. It is a new thing to receive the priesthood of sacred observance and to look for a kingdom of limitless promise. *Victorinus (c. 280, W), 7.350.*

[REV. 6:9:] He relates that he saw under the altar of God—that is, under the earth—the souls of those who were slain. For both heaven and earth are called God's altar. *Lactantius (c. 304–313, W), 7.351.*

[REV. 6:11:] He says they received "white robes," that is, the gift of the Holy Spirit. *Victorinus (c. 280, W), 7.351.*

[REV. 6:12:] The moon of blood represents the church of the saints, who pours out her blood for Christ. *Victorinus (c. 280, W), 7.351.*

[REV. 7:4–8:] The number of believers who belong to Israel according to the flesh is small. One might venture to assert that they would not nearly make up the number of a hundred and forty-four thousand. It is evident, therefore, that the hundred and forty-four thousand who have not defiled themselves with women must be made up of those who have

come to the divine Word out of the Gentile world. *Origen (c. 228, E), 9.298.*

[REV. 7:9:] The great multitude out of every tribe . . . represent the number of the elect out of all believers. Having been cleansed by baptism in the blood of the Lamb, they have made their robes white, keeping the grace that they have received. *Victorinus (c. 280, W), 7.352.*

[REV. 8:13:] The angel flying through the middle of heaven signifies the Holy Spirit bearing witness. *Victorinus (c. 280, W), 7.352.*

[REV. 12:1, 2:] The woman clothed with the sun and having the moon under her feet . . . is the ancient church of fathers, prophets, saints, and apostles. It had the groans and torments of its longing until it saw that Christ had taken flesh out of the selfsame people—the fruit of its people according to the flesh that had long ago been promised to it. *Victorinus (c. 280, W), 7.355.*

[REV. 12:3, 14:] The seven heads [of the red dragon] were the seven kings of the Romans, of whom also is the Antichrist. . . . The aid of the great eagle's wings is the gift of the prophets that was given to the catholic church. *Victorinus (c. 280, W), 7.355, 356.*

[REV. 12:4:] The stars that are dark, obscure, and falling are the assemblies of the heretics. For they, too, desire to be acquainted with the heavenly ones . . . and to come near to the stars as children of light. However, they are dragged down, being shaken out by the folds of the dragon. For they did not remain within the triangular [i.e., Trinitarian] forms of godliness. . . . They are called the third part of the stars, for they have gone astray with regard to one of the three Persons of the Trinity. *Methodius (c. 290, E), 6.338.*

[REV. 13:11:] By the beast coming up out of the earth, he means the kingdom of the Antichrist. And by the two horns, he means Antichrist and the false prophet after him. *Hippolytus (c. 200, W), 5.214.*

[REV. 14:1–5:] John shows us, saying in the Book of the Revelation, "And I looked, and lo, . . . with Him a hundred and forty-four thousand. . . . These are those who were not defiled with women. For they are virgins. These are those who follow the Lamb wherever he goes." This shows that the Lord is the Leader of the choir of virgins. In addition to this, notice how very great in the sight of God is the dignity of virginity: "These were redeemed from among men, being the first-fruits unto God and to the Lamb." . . . And he clearly intends by this to teach us that the number of virgins was, from the beginning, restricted to a certain number—a hundred and forty-four thousand. In contrast, the multitude of the other saints is innumerable. *Methodius (c. 290, E), 6.313.*

[REV. 17:5:] So, again, Babylon, in our own John, is a figure of the city Rome, as being equally great and proud of her sway. *Tertullian (c. 197, W), 3.162.*

[REV. 17:5:] Babylon is the Roman state. *Victorinus (c. 280, W), 7.351.*

[REV. 17:10, 11:] [The harlot] is the city of Rome. "And there are seven kings. Five have fallen, and one is, and the other is not yet come." . . . The date that the Apocalypse was written must be remembered. For at that time, Caesar Domitian reigned. But before him, there had been Titus (his brother), Vespasian, Otho, Vitellius, and Galba. These are the five who have fallen. One remains—Domitian, under whom the Apocalypse was written. "The other has not yet come." This refers to Nerva. "And when he is come, he will be for a short time." Nerva did not even reign two full years. "And the beast that you saw is of the seven." Nero reigned before those kings. . . . Now [in saying] that one of the heads was, as it were, slain to death . . . he speaks of Nero. *Victorinus (c. 280, W), 7.358.*

[REV. 22:1:] The river of life means the grace of spiritual doctrine that has flowed through the minds of the faithful. *Victorinus (c. 280, W), 7.359; extended discussion (interpretation): 7.344–7.360.*

SEE ALSO ANTICHRIST; BABYLON THE GREAT; BOOK OF LIFE; CANON, NEW TESTAMENT; ESCHATOLOGY; DANIEL, BOOK OF; JOHN, APOSTLE; MARK OF THE BEAST; NICOLAITANS; NUMEROLOGY; TREE OF LIFE; WOMAN CLOTHED WITH THE SUN.

REVENGE

SEE NONRESISTANCE.

RICHES

SEE MATERIALISM; PROSPERITY.

RIGHTEOUSNESS OF GOD

SEE SALVATION.

RING

The Word, then, allows wives to have a finger ring of gold. However, this is not for adornment. Rather, it is for sealing things that are worth keeping safe in the house, in the exercise of their charge of housekeeping. For if all were well trained, there would be no need of seals—that is, if servants and masters were equally honest. But since lack of training produces an inclination to dishonesty [in servants], we require seals. *Clement of Alexandria (c. 195, E), 2.285.*

While engaged in public business or discharging other avocations in the country, and if we are often away from our wives, it may be necessary for us to seal something for the sake of safety. He therefore allows us a signet for this purpose only. Other finger rings are to be cast off. *Clement of Alexandria (c. 195, E), 2.285.*

Men are not to wear the ring on the joint, for this is feminine. Rather, they are to place it on the little finger at its root. *Clement of Alexandria (c. 195, E), 2.285.*

The things I have named above [the toga, marriage engagements, and marriage ceremonies] I take to be clean in themselves. For neither manly garb, nor the marital ring, nor marital union comes from honors done to any idol. *Tertullian (c. 200, W), 3.71.*

SEE ALSO CLOTHING; GROOMING; JEWELRY.

ROMAN EMPIRE, ROMANS

Through the instrumentality of the Romans, the world is at peace. As a result, we walk on the highways without fear, and we sail wherever we want. *Irenaeus (c. 180, E/W), 1.503.*

I will not avoid the controversy that is invited by the following groundless assertion: There are those [unbelievers] who maintain that, as a reward for their singular devotion to religion, the Romans have been raised to such heights of power as to have become masters of the world. . . . This, supposedly, is the wages the gods have paid the Romans for their devotion. *Tertullian (c. 197, W), 3.39.*

How utterly foolish it is to attribute the greatness of the Roman name to religious merits. For it was after Rome had become an empire (or call it still a kingdom) that the religion she professes made its chief progress.... The Romans, therefore, were not distinguished for their devotion to the gods before they attained to greatness. Therefore, their greatness was not the result of their religion.... Indeed, how could religion make a people great who have owed their greatness to their irreligion? ... You cannot have wars and victories without the capturing (and often the destruction) of cities. In such things, the gods receive their share of calamity. Houses and temples suffer alike. There is indiscriminate slaughter of priests and citizens. The hand of plunder reaches both sacred and common treasure. Thus the sacrileges of the Romans are as numerous as their trophies. *Tertullian (c. 197, W), 3.40.*

There is also another and a greater necessity for our offering prayer on behalf of the emperors. In fact, we should pray for the complete stability of the empire, and for Roman interests in general. That is because we know that a mighty cataclysm hangs over the whole earth. In fact, the very end of all things threatens dreadful woes. And this is only held back by the continued existence of the Roman empire. We have no desire, then, to be overtaken by these dire events. In praying that their coming may be delayed, we are lending our aid to Rome's duration. *Tertullian (c. 197, W), 3.42, 43.*

So, again, Babylon, in our own John, is a figure of the city of Rome. For she is equally great and proud of her sway. *Tertullian (c. 197, W), 3.162.*

But when the urn of worldly lots varied, God favored the Romans. *Tertullian (c. 200, W), 4.5.*

[A DESCRIPTION OF THE ROMAN EMPIRE:] If one looks at the whole world, it is surely obvious enough that it is daily becoming better cultivated and more fully populated than it was in ancient times. All places are now accessible. All are well known. All are open to commerce. Most pleasant farms have obliterated all traces of what were once dreary and dangerous wastelands. Cultivated fields have subdued forests. Flocks and herds have expelled wild beasts. Sandy deserts are sown. Rocks are planted; marshes are drained. Where there were once barely even solitary cottages, there are now large cities. No longer are islands dreaded, nor their rocky shores feared. Everywhere, there are houses, inhabitants, stable government, and civilized life. *Tertullian (c. 210, W), 3.210.*

And the Christian must necessarily desire [the emperor's well-being], along with that of the empire over which the emperor reigns. He desires this so long as the world will stand. For Rome will continue so long as that. *Tertullian (c. 212, W), 3.105.*

[PAGAN SPEAKER:] While in the city of an enemy that the Romans have captured, while still in the fury of victory, the Romans venerate the conquered deities. In all directions, they seek for the gods of strangers in order to make them their own. They build altars even to unknown divinities, and to the Manes. For that reason, they have deserved their dominion. For they acknowledge the sacred institutions of all nations.... Look at the temples and sanctuaries of the gods by which the Roman city is both protected and armed. They are made more venerable by the deities who are their inhabitants. For those deities are present and are constantly dwelling in them. *Mark Minucius Felix (c. 200, W), 4.176.*

[PAGAN SPEAKER:] Do not the Romans—without any help from your God—govern, reign, and have the enjoyment of the whole world? In fact, do they not even have dominion over you [Christians]? *Mark Minucius Felix (c. 200, W), 4.179.*

[CHRISTIAN SPEAKER:] You will say that this very superstition itself gave, increased, and established their empire for the Romans. You say they prevailed not so much by their valor as by their religion and piety.... However, whatever the Romans hold, cultivate, and possess is the spoil of their audacity. All their temples are built from the spoils of violence. ... Therefore, the Romans have become so great, not because they were religious, but because they were *sacrilegious* with impunity. *Mark Minucius Felix (c. 200, W), 4.188.*

Our countrymen have always claimed for themselves the glory of gentleness and civilization. However, are they not found to be more inhuman by these sacrilegious rites? *Lactantius (c. 304–313, W), 7.34.*

The difference between utility and justice is demonstrated by the Roman people themselves.... For, by always desiring and carrying off the property of others, they have gained for themselves the possession of the whole world! *Lactantius (c. 304–313, W), 7.171.*

It should not appear incredible to anyone that a kingdom founded with such vastness, and increased by so many and such men . . . will, nevertheless, fall at some time. There is nothing built by human strength that cannot equally be destroyed by human strength. *Lactantius (c. 304–313, W), 7.212.*

The Sibyls openly say that Rome is doomed to perish—and that, indeed, it will perish by the judgment of God. For it held His name in hatred. Being the enemy of righteousness, it destroyed the people who kept the truth. *Lactantius (c. 304–313, W), 7.213.*

However, while the city of Rome remains, it appears that nothing of this kind [the end of the world] is to be feared. But when the capital of the world falls, . . . who can doubt that the end will have now arrived to the affairs of men and the whole world? It is that city, and only that city, that still sustains all things. *Lactantius (c. 304–313, W), 7.220.*

Like some swollen torrent, the Romans, of late, have overthrown all nations, sweeping them beneath the flood. *Arnobius (c. 305, E), 6.415.*

SEE ALSO AUGUSTUS CAESAR; CHURCH AND STATE; GOVERNMENT; LAW, ROMAN; MARCUS AURELIUS; PILATE, PONTIUS; TIBERIUS CAESAR.

ROME

SEE ROMAN EMPIRE, ROMANS.

ROME, BISHOP OF

SEE BISHOP (II. BISHOP OF ROME).

ROME, CHURCH AT

SEE CHURCHES, APOSTOLIC (VI. CHURCH AT ROME).

RULE OF FAITH

SEE APOSTOLIC FAITH; CREEDS, EARLY.

SABBATH

Bring no more futile sacrifices; incense is an abomination to Me. The New Moons, the Sabbaths, and the calling of assemblies—I cannot endure iniquity and the sacred meeting. Your New Moons and your appointed feasts My soul hates. Isa. 1:13, 14.

How is it that you turn again to the weak and beggarly elements, to which you desire again to be in bondage? You observe days and months and seasons and years. Gal. 4:9–11.

. . . having abolished in His flesh the enmity, that is, the law of commandments contained in ordinances. Eph. 2:15.

. . . having wiped out the handwriting of requirements that was against us. . . . Therefore let no one judge you in food or in drink, or regarding a festival or a new moon or sabbaths. Col. 2:14, 16.

. . . no longer observing the Sabbath, but living in the observance of the Lord's Day. *Ignatius (c. 105, E), 1.62.*

However, [the Jews,] too, have erred from true knowledge. In their imagination, they think that it is God whom they serve. Actually, by their type of worship, they render their service to the angels and not to God. For example, they do this when they celebrate Sabbaths. *Aristides (c. 125, E), 9.276.*

Their scrupulosity concerning meats, and their superstition as respects the Sabbaths, and their boasting about circumcision, and their fancies about fasting and the new moons . . . are utterly ridiculous and unworthy of notice. . . . And to speak falsely of God, as if He forbade us to do what is good on the Sabbath-days—how is this not ungodly? *Letter to Diognetus (c. 125–200), 1.26.*

Is there any other matter, my [Jewish] friends, in which we Christians are blamed, than this:

that we do not live after the Law . . . and do not observe Sabbaths, as you do? *Justin Martyr (c. 160, E), 1.199.*

You [a Jew] now have need of a second circumcision, although you glory greatly in the flesh. The new law requires you to keep a perpetual Sabbath. However, you, because you are idle for one day, suppose you are godly. . . . The Lord our God does not take pleasure in such observances. If there is any perjured person or a thief among you, let him cease to be so. . . . Then he has kept the sweet and true Sabbaths of God. *Justin Martyr (c. 160, E), 1.200.*

All those righteous men already mentioned, though they kept no Sabbaths, were pleasing to God. *Justin Martyr (c. 160, E), 1.204.*

There was no need of circumcision before Abraham. Nor was there need of the observance of Sabbaths, or of feasts and sacrifices, before Moses. Accordingly, there is no more need of them now. *Justin Martyr (c. 160, E), 1.206.*

If some, through weak-mindedness, wish to observe the laws given by Moses, . . . yet choose to live with the Christians and the faithful, as I said before, not inducing the Gentiles either to be circumcised like themselves, or to keep the Sabbath, or to observe any other such ceremonies, then I hold that we should join ourselves with such persons. *Justin Martyr (c. 160, E), 1.218.*

"You will observe My Sabbaths; for it will be a sign between Me and you for your generations." These things, then, were given for a sign. . . . The Sabbaths taught that we should continue day by day in God's service, . . . abstaining from all avarice and not acquiring or possessing treasures upon earth. . . . However, man was not justified by these things. Rather, they were given as a sign to the people. This fact is evident, for Abraham himself—without circumcision and without observance of Sabbaths—"believed God, and it was imputed to him for righteousness." *Irenaeus (c. 180, E/W), 1.481.*

The seventh day is recognized as sacred, not only by the Hebrews, but also by the Greeks. *Clement of Alexandria (c. 195, E), 2.469.*

We do not follow the Jews in their peculiarities in regard to food nor in their sacred days. *Tertullian (c. 197, W), 3.34.*

Let the one who contends that the Sabbath is still to be observed as a balm of salvation, . . . prove to us that in times past righteous men kept the Sabbath, or practiced circumcision, and were thereby made "friends of God." God created Adam uncircumcised and non-observant of the Sabbath. . . . Also, God freed from the deluge Noah, who was uncircumcised and did not observe the Sabbath. Enoch, too, He transported from this world, even though that most righteous man was uncircumcised and did not observe the Sabbath. . . . Melchizedek also, "the priest of the most high God," although uncircumcised and not observing the Sabbath, was chosen to the priesthood of God. *Tertullian (c. 197, W), 3.153.*

Just as the abolition of fleshly circumcision and of the old Law is demonstrated as having been consummated at its specific times, so also the observance of the Sabbath is demonstrated to have been temporary. *Tertullian (c. 197, W), 3.155.*

We [Christians] understand that we still more should observe a sabbath from all "servile work" always. This is not only every seventh day, but at all times. *Tertullian (c. 197, W), 3.155.*

It was not with a view to its observance in perpetuity that God formerly gave them such a law. *Tertullian (c. 197, W), 3.156.*

Prayer is also subject to diversity of observance in the matter of kneeling, through the act of some few who abstain from kneeling on the Sabbath [i.e., Saturday]. . . . We, however, have received this practice: that we refrain from kneeling only on the day of the Lord's resurrection. In fact, we not only refrain from kneeling, but also from every posture and office of solicitude. *Tertullian (c. 198, W), 3.689.*

The Holy Spirit rebukes the Jews for their holy days. He says, "Your Sabbaths, new moons, and ceremonies my soul hates." Yet some of us—to whom Sabbaths are strange (as are the new moons and festivals formerly loved by God)— are frequenting the Saturnalia! *Tertullian (c. 200, W), 3.70.*

And let this become a rigorous fast, lest we should appear to observe any Sabbath with the Jews. For concerning [their Sabbath], Christ himself, the Lord of the Sabbath, says by His prophets that "His soul hates." In His body, He abolished this Sabbath. *Victorinus (c. 280, W), 7.341.*

The Lawgiver also desires that every individual among us should be devoted unceasingly to this kind of work, even as God Himself is. Consequently, He directs us to continuously rest from secular things and to engage in no worldly sort of work whatever. This is called *our* Sabbath. *Disputation of Archelaus and Manes (c. 320, E), 6.203.*

You will observe the Sabbath on account of Him who ceased from His work of creation. However, He did not cease from His work of providence. So the Sabbath is a rest in order to meditate on the law; it is not a day for idleness of the hands. *Apostolic Constitutions (compiled c. 390, E), 7.413.*

He had given the commandment to keep the Sabbath, by resting on it for the sake of meditating on the laws. However, He has now commanded us to meditate on the law of creation and of providence *every* day. *Apostolic Constitutions (compiled c. 390, E), 7.461.*

Keep the Sabbath and the Lord's Day festival. The first is the memorial of the creation; the latter, of the Resurrection. However, there is only one Sabbath to be observed by you during the whole year—that of our Lord's burial. On that day, men should keep a fast, but not a festival. *Apostolic Constitutions (compiled c. 390, E), 7.469.*

Let the slaves work five days. But on the Sabbath day and the Lord's Day, let them have rest in order to go to church for instruction in piety. We say the Sabbath, on account of creation, and the Lord's Day, on account of the resurrection. *Apostolic Constitutions (compiled c. 390, E), 7.495; see also 3.362–3.364.*

SEE ALSO EIGHTH DAY; LAW, MOSAIC; LORD'S DAY.

SABELLIANISM

See Monarchianism.

SACRAMENTS

The Latin-speaking church referred to baptism and communion as "sacraments." The Greek-speaking church referred to these same rites as "mysteries."

It is fitting also that the deacons, as being [the ministers] of the mysteries of Jesus Christ, should in every respect be pleasing to all. *Ignatius (c. 105, E), 1.67.*

The mysteries are not exhibited indiscriminately to everyone. *Clement of Alexandria (c. 195, E), 2.449.*

It is a universal custom in religious initiations to keep out the profane and to beware of witnesses. *Tertullian (c. 197, W), 3.23.*

It is not to be doubted that God has caused the material elements to obey Him also in His own peculiar sacraments. . . . The material substance that governs earthly life acts as an agent likewise in the heavenly. *Tertullian (c. 198, W), 3.670.*

The flesh, indeed, is washed in order that the soul may be cleansed. The flesh is anointed so that the soul may be consecrated. The flesh is signed [with the cross] so that the soul too may be fortified. The flesh is shadowed with the imposition of hands so that the soul also may be illuminated by the Spirit. The flesh feeds on the body and blood of Christ so that the soul likewise may feed on God. *Tertullian (c. 210, W), 3.551.*

When those who have been turned towards virtue have made progress, and have shown that they have been purified by the Word, and have led as far as they can a better life—then (and not before) do we invite them to participate in our sacraments. "For we speak wisdom among those who are perfect." *Origen (c. 248, E), 4.488.*

Whoever is pure not only from all defilement, but from what are regarded as lesser transgressions, let him be boldly initiated into the mysteries of Jesus. For they are properly made known only to the holy and the pure. *Origen (c. 248, E), 4.488.*

[Celsus, a pagan] does not know the difference between inviting the wicked to be healed and initiating into the sacred mysteries those

who are already purified. We do not invite the wicked man to participate in our mysteries. . . . Nor do we invite those others whom Celsus might list in his exaggerated style. Rather, we invite such persons only to be *healed. Origen (c. 248, E), 4.488.*

Being led away from the darkness of error, and enlightened by His pure and shining light, we may keep the way of life through the saving sacraments. *Cyprian (c. 250, W), 5.507.*

In the Gospel according to John, it says: "Unless a man is born again of water and the Spirit, he cannot enter into the kingdom of God." . . . Also in the same place: "Unless you eat the flesh of the Son of man and drink His blood, you will not have life in you." Yet, it is of little use to be baptized and to receive the Eucharist, unless one profits by them both in deeds and works. *Cyprian (c. 250, W), 5.542.*

See also Baptism; Eucharist; Hands, Laying on of; Oil, Anointing with.

SACRIFICES, SPIRITUAL

See Eucharist.

SADDUCEES

Some Sadducees, who say there is no resurrection, came to Him. Mark 12:18.

The Sadducees say that there is no resurrection—and no angel or spirit; but the Pharisees confess both. Acts 23:8.

The Sadducees, however, are for abolishing fate. And they teach that God does nothing that is wicked, nor exercises providence. Rather, they say that the choice between good and evil lies within the power of men. They not only deny that there is a resurrection of the flesh, but they also suppose that the soul does not continue on [after death]. . . . While the Pharisees are full of mutual affection, the Sadducees, on the other hand, are motivated by self-love. This sect had its stronghold especially around Samaria. And they, too, adhere to the customs of the Law, saying that one should live by it, so that he may conduct himself virtuously and leave children behind him on earth. They do not, however, devote attention to the Prophets, nor to any other sages, but only to the Law of Moses. *Hippolytus (c. 225, W), 5.137.*

Let no one charge us with Jewish fables and those of the sect of the Sadducees—as though we, too, attribute forms to the Deity. For this is supposedly taught in their writings. *Arnobius (c. 305, E), 6.467.*

Even the Jewish nation had wicked heresies. Of them were the Sadducees, who do not confess the resurrection of the dead. *Apostolic Constitutions (compiled c. 390, E), 7.452.*

SEE ALSO ESSENES; JEW, JEWS; PHARISEES.

SAINTS, VENERATION OF

SEE MARTYRS, MARTYRDOM (IV. MARTYRS, VENERATION OF).

SALT AND LIGHT

SEE CHRISTIANITY (VII. CHRISTIANS AS SALT AND LIGHT).

SALVATION

I. Salvation through Christ alone

II. Role of grace and faith in salvation

III. Role of obedience in salvation

IV. The violent who storm the kingdom of heaven

V. Righteousness of God vs. righteousness of the Law

VI. Can those who are saved ever be lost?

VII. Universal salvation?

I. Salvation through Christ alone

Jesus said to him, "I am the way, the truth, and the life. No one comes to the Father except through Me. John 14:6.

Nor is there salvation in any other, for there is no other name under heaven given among men by which we must be saved. Acts 4:12.

A man cannot otherwise enter into the kingdom of God than by the name of His beloved Son. *Hermas (c. 150, W), 2.48.*

Open your heart to the Lord, believing that you can be saved by no other name than by His great and glorious name. *Hermas (c. 150, W), 2.18.*

But there is no other [way] than this: to become acquainted with this Christ, to be washed in the fountain spoken of by Isaiah for the remission of sins, and for the rest, to live sinless lives. *Justin Martyr (c. 160, E), 1.217.*

Those who did that which is universally, naturally, and eternally good are pleasing to God. Therefore, in the resurrection, they will be saved through this Christ. They will be saved equally with those righteous men who were before them—namely, Noah, Enoch, Jacob, and whoever else there may be—along with those who have known this Christ. *Justin Martyr (c. 160, E), 1.217.*

If you repent of your sins, and recognize Him to be Christ, and observe His commandments, then you may assert [that you have done no wrong]. For, as I have said before, remission of sins will be yours. *Justin Martyr (c. 160, E), 1.247.*

No man can know God without both the goodwill of the Father and the agency of the Son. *Irenaeus (c. 180, E/W), 1.470.*

Christ is present with all those who were approved by God from the beginning. He granted them His Word to be present with them. *Irenaeus (c. 180, E/W), 1.496.*

At what time, then, did Christ pour out upon the human race the life-giving seed—that is, the Spirit of the remission of sins, by whom we are given life? Was it not then, when He was eating with men, and drinking wine upon the earth? *Irenaeus (c. 180, E/W), 1.505.*

If one loves himself, he loves the Lord, and he confesses unto salvation, so that he may save his soul. *Clement of Alexandria (c. 195, E), 2.417.*

Christians have learned that their eternal life consists in knowing the only true God, who is over all, and Jesus Christ, whom He has sent. *Origen (c. 248, E), 4.479.*

By this alone can the Jews obtain pardon of their sins: if they wash away the blood of the slain Christ in His baptism, come into the church, and obey His commandments. *Cyprian (c. 250, W), 5.508.*

It is impossible to reach the Father except by His Son Jesus Christ. *Cyprian (c. 250, W), 5.542.*

All those who deny the true Christ or introduce or follow another, . . . leave themselves no hope of salvation. They are no different than those who have denied Christ before men, who will necessarily be denied by Christ. *Treatise on Re-Baptism (c. 257, W), 5.674.*

"The law of the Spirit of life," which is the Gospel, is different from earlier laws. For, by its preaching, it leads to obedience and the remission of sins. It has delivered us from the law of sin and death, having entirely conquered sin that reigned over our flesh. *Methodius (c. 290, E), 6.373, as quoted by Photius.*

No hope of gaining immortality is given to man, unless he will believe on Him and will take up that cross that is to be carried and endured. *Lactantius (c. 304–313, W), 7.122.*

Let us suppose that it is possible for someone—by natural and innate goodness—to gain true virtues. We have heard that Cimon who lived in Athens was such a man. He gave alms to the needy, entertained the poor, and clothed the naked. However, when that one thing is lacking that is of the greatest importance—the acknowledgement of God—then all those good things are superfluous and empty. In pursuing them, he has labored in vain. For all of his justice will resemble a human body that has no head. *Lactantius (c. 304–313, W), 7.171.*

[YOU SAY:] "Unless, then, I become a Christian, I cannot hope for salvation." It is just as you say. . . . The Almighty Master of the world has determined that this should be the way of salvation. This is the door of life. There is access to the light through Him alone. Men cannot either sneak in or enter somewhere else. For all other ways are barred and are secured by an impenetrable barrier. *Arnobius (c. 305, E), 6.459.*

By believing in Him you will live. But by disbelieving, you will be punished. For "he that is disobedient to the Son will not see life." *Apostolic Constitutions (compiled c. 390, E), 7.449; see also 2.29, 2.36, 2.55.*

II. Role of grace and faith in salvation

No one can come to Me unless the Father who sent Me draws him; and I will raise him up at the last day. John 6:44.

Having been justified by faith, we have peace with God through our Lord Jesus Christ. Rom. 5:1.

What shall we say then? Shall we continue in sin that grace may abound? Certainly not! How shall we who died to sin live any longer in it? Rom. 6:1, 2.

As workers together with Him also plead with you not to receive the grace of God in vain. 2 Cor. 6:1.

Even when we were dead in trespasses, [God] made us alive together with Christ (by grace you have been saved). Eph. 2:5.

By grace you have been saved through faith, and that not of yourselves; it is the gift of God. Eph. 2:8.

Who has saved us and called us with a holy calling, not according to our works, but according to His own purpose and grace which was given to us in Christ Jesus. 2 Tim. 1:9.

. . . not by works of righteousness which we have done, but according to His mercy He saved us, through the washing of regeneration and renewing of the Holy Spirit. Tit. 3:5.

What does it profit, my brethren, if someone says he has faith but does not have works? Can faith save him? Jas. 2:14; see also Rom. 4:1–4; 5:15, 16; Gal. 3:1–3.

All of these persons, therefore, were highly honored, and were made great. This was not for their own sake, or for their own works, or for the righteousness which they wrought, but through the operation of His will. And we, too, being called by His will in Christ Jesus, are not justified by ourselves. Nor are we justified by our own wisdom, understanding, godliness, or works that we have done in holiness of heart. Rather, we are justified by that faith through which, from the beginning, Almighty God has justified all men. *Clement of Rome (c. 96, W), 1.13.*

For what reason was our father Abraham blessed? Was it not because he worked righteousness and truth through faith? *Clement of Rome (c. 96, W), 1.13*

Therefore, let us not be ungrateful for His kindness. For if He were to reward us according to our works, we would cease to be. *Ignatius (c. 105, E), 1.63.*

Being convinced at that time of our unworthiness of attaining life through our own works, it is now, through the kindness of God, graciously given to us. Accordingly, it is clear that in ourselves we were unable to enter into the kingdom of God. However, through the power of God, we can be made able. *Letter to Diognetus (c. 125–200), 1.28.*

Into this joy, many persons desire to enter. They know that "by grace you are saved, not of works," but by the will of God through Jesus Christ. . . . But He who raised Him up from the dead will raise up us also—if we do His will, and walk in His commandments, and love what He loved, keeping ourselves from all unrighteousness. *Polycarp (c. 135, E), 1.33.*

For Abraham was declared by God to be righteous, not on account of circumcision, but on account of faith. *Justin Martyr (c. 160, E), 1.245.*

"Blessed is the man to whom the Lord does not impute sin" [Ps. 32:2]. That is, having repented of his sins, he can receive remission of them from God. But this is not as you [Jews] deceive yourselves, and some others who resemble you in this. For they say, that even though they remain sinners, the Lord will not impute sin to them, because they know God. *Justin Martyr (c. 160, E), 1.270.*

The Lord himself, who is Emmanuel from the virgin, is the sign of our salvation. It was the Lord Himself who saved them. For they could not be saved by their own instrumentality. Therefore, when Paul explains human infirmity, he says, "For I know that there dwells in my flesh no good thing" [Rom. 7:18]. He thus shows that the "good thing" of our salvation is not from us, but from God. And again: "Wretched man that I am, who will deliver me from the body of this death?" [Rom. 7:24]. . . . Here we see that we must be saved by the help of God, not by ourselves. *Irenaeus (c. 180, E/W), 1.450.*

No one, indeed, while placed out of reach of the Lord's benefits, has power to procure for himself the means of salvation. So the more we receive His grace, the more we should love Him. *Irenaeus (c. 180, E/W), 1.478.*

These men [the prophets] did not impute unto us [the Gentiles] our transgressions, which we did before Christ was manifested among us. Therefore, it is not right for us to lay blame upon those who sinned before Christ's coming. For "all men fall short of the glory of God," and are not justified of themselves. Rather, they are justified by the coming of the Lord—those who earnestly direct their eyes towards His light. *Irenaeus (c. 180, E/W), 1.499.*

Those men who are devoid of sense [i.e., the Gnostics] . . . endeavor to bring in another Father. They point to [the punishments of the Old Testament]. They then contrast this with the great things the Lord did at His coming to save those who received Him, taking compassion upon them. However, they keep silent

with regard to His judgments and all those things which will come upon those who have heard His words, but have not done them. For it would be better for them if they had not been born. *Irenaeus (c. 180, E/W), 1.501.*

He confers His free gifts upon those who should [receive them]. *Irenaeus (c. 180, E/W), 1.517.*

Christ redeems us righteously from [the apostasy] by His own blood. But as regards those of us who have been redeemed, [He does this] by grace. For we have given nothing to Him previously. Nor does He desire anything from us, as if He stood in need of it. *Irenaeus (c. 180, E/W), 1.528.*

When man is grafted in by faith and receives the Spirit of God, he certainly does not lose the substance of flesh, but changes the quality of the fruit of his works. *Irenaeus (c. 180, E/W), 1.536.*

Now he says that the things that save us are the name of our Lord Jesus Christ and the Spirit of our God. *Irenaeus (c. 180, E/W), 1.537.*

The apostolic Scripture speaks in this manner: "After that, the kindness and love of God our Savior to man appeared, not by works of righteousness that we have done, but according to His mercy, He saved us." Behold the might of the new song! It has made men out of stones and out of beasts! Furthermore, those who were as dead (since they were not partakers of the true life) have come to life again! *Clement of Alexandria (c. 195, E), 2.172.*

Rightly, then, to those who have believed and obey, grace will abound beyond measure. *Clement of Alexandria (c. 195, E), 2.196.*

Now the Lord Himself has most clearly revealed the equality of salvation, when He said: "For this is the will of my Father, that everyone who sees the Son, and believes on Him, should have everlasting life." *Clement of Alexandria (c. 195, E), 2.216.*

"Abraham was not justified by works, but by faith." It is therefore of no advantage to persons after the end of life, even if they do good works now, if they do not have faith. *Clement of Alexandria (c. 195, E), 2.308.*

We have discovered faith to be the first movement towards salvation. After faith, fear, hope, and repentance (accompanied by temperance and patience) lead us to love and knowledge. *Clement of Alexandria (c. 195, E), 2.354.*

Faith is power for salvation and strength to eternal life. *Clement of Alexandria (c. 195, E), 2.360.*

This is what it means to "be drawn by the Father": It means to become worthy to receive the power of grace from God, so as to run without hindrance. *Clement of Alexandria (c. 195, E), 2.435.*

"For by grace we are saved"—but not, indeed, without good works. Rather, we must be saved by being molded for what is good, acquiring an inclination for it. And we must possess the healthy mind that is fixed on the pursuit of the good. For this, we have the greatest need of divine grace, of right teaching, of holy susceptibility, and of the drawing of the Father to Himself. *Clement of Alexandria (c. 195, E), 2.445.*

Perhaps it is, then, that the Father Himself draws to Himself everyone who has led a pure life and has reached the conception of the blessed and incorruptible nature. Or perhaps the free will that is in us, by reaching the knowledge of the good, leaps and bounds over the barriers—as the gymnasts say. Either way, it is not without eminent grace that the soul is winged, soars, and is raised above the higher spheres. *Clement of Alexandria (c. 195, E), 2.464.*

The apostle exhorts, "your faith should not be in the wisdom of men," who profess to persuade, "but in the power of God," who alone is able to save without proofs, but by mere faith. *Clement of Alexandria (c. 195, E), 2.446.*

The same from the foundation of the world is each one who at different periods is saved, and will be saved by faith. *Clement of Alexandria (c. 195, E), 2.491.*

The covenant of salvation, reaching down to us from the foundation of the world, through different generations and times, is one—although it is conceived as different in respect of the gift. For it follows that there is one unchangeable gift of salvation given by one God, through one Lord, benefiting in many ways. *Clement of Alexandria (c. 195, E), 2.504.*

Choice depended on the man as being free. But the gift depended on God as the Lord. And He gives to those who are willing, are exceed-ingly earnest, and who ask. In this manner, their salvation can become their own. For God does not compel. *Clement of Alexandria (c. 195, E), 2.593.*

Christ admonished [the rich man] to leave his busy life and to cleave to One, adhering to the grace of Him who offered everlasting life. *Clement of Alexandria (c. 195, E), 2.594.*

Into the impure soul, the grace of God finds no entrance. *Clement of Alexandria (c. 195, E), 2.595.*

To him who directs his eye to salvation and desires it, asking with boldness and vehemence for its bestowal, the good Father who is in heaven will give the true purification and the changeless life. *Clement of Alexandria (c. 195, E), 2.604.*

We make petition, then, that He supply us with the substance of His will and the capacity to do it—so that we may be saved both in the heavens and on earth. For the sum of His will is the salvation of those whom He has adopted. *Tertullian (c. 198, W), 3.682.*

Grace with the Lord, when once learned and undertaken by us, should never afterward be cancelled by repetition of sin. *Tertullian (c. 203, W), 3.660.*

Her repentance as a sinner deserved forgiveness according to the mind of the Creator, who is accustomed to prefer mercy to sacrifice. But even if the stimulus of her repentance proceeded from her faith, she heard her justification by faith pronounced through her repentance, in the words, "Your faith has saved you." This was by Him who had declared by Habakkuk, "The just man will live by his faith." *Tertullian (c. 207, W), 3.376.*

It is the office of Christ's Gospel to call men from the Law to grace. *Tertullian (c. 207, W), 3.432.*

He exhorts those who are justified by faith in Christ, and not by the Law, to have peace with God. *Tertullian (c. 207, W), 3.458.*

There is not a soul that can at all procure salvation, unless it believes while it is still in the flesh. For it is an established truth that the flesh is the very condition on which salvation hinges. *Tertullian (c. 210, W), 3.551.*

He seeks all and desires to save all. He wishes to make everyone the children of God. He calls all the saints unto one perfect man. *Hippolytus (c. 200, W), 5.205.*

Some of the [heretics] . . . simply deny the Law and the Prophets for the sake of their lawless and impious doctrine. And under the pretense of grace, they have sunk down to the lowest abyss of perdition. *Eusebius, quoting Caius (c. 215, W), 5.602.*

It seems a possible thing that rational natures, from whom the faculty of free will is never taken away, may be again subjected to movements of some kind, through the special act of the Lord Himself. Otherwise, if they were always to occupy a condition that was unchangeable, they might not know that it is by the grace of God—and not by their own merit—that they have been placed in that final state of happiness. *Origen (c. 225, E), 4.272.*

It is advantageous to each one for him to perceive his own particular nature and the grace of God. For he who does not perceive his own weakness and the divine favor, . . . not having tested himself nor having condemned himself, will imagine that the benefit conferred upon him by the grace of heaven is his own doing. And this imagination also produces vanity, which will be the cause of his downfall. . . . They have been revealed to babes—to those who after childhood have come to better things. These are those who remember that it is not so much from their own effort as by the unspeakable goodness [of God] that they have reached the greatest possible extent of blessedness. *Origen (c. 225, E), 4.313.*

How could Christ ever be the Advocate, the Atonement, and the Propitiation without the power of God? For it makes an end of our weakness and flows over the souls of believers. It is administered by Jesus, who indeed is prior to it and is Himself the Power of God. He enables a man to say: "I can do all things through Jesus Christ, who strengthens me." *Origen (c. 228, E), 9.317.*

The passage declares that before God, no living being will be justified. This shows that in comparison with God—and the righteousness that is in Him—no one (even of the most perfect saints) will be justified. We might take an illustration from another scenario, saying that no candle can give light before the sun. By that,

we do not mean that the candle will not give out light, but only that it will not be seen when the sun outshines it. *Origen (c. 228, E), 9.333.*

The strength of our will is not sufficient to procure the perfectly pure heart. For we need God to create it. He, therefore, who prays as he should, offers this petition to God: "Create in me a clean heart, O God." *Origen (c. 248, E), 4.624.*

When the Word of God says, "No man knows the Father but the Son, and he to whom the Son will reveal Him," he declares that no one can know God except by the help of divine grace coming from above, with a certain divine inspiration. Indeed, it is reasonable to suppose that the knowledge of God is beyond the reach of human nature. This is the reason for the many errors into which men have fallen in their views of God. [Our knowledge of God], then, is through the goodness and love of God to mankind and by a marvelous exercise of divine grace. *Origen (c. 248, E), 4.629.*

The first law of God is the foundation of the subsequent law. To you [Gentiles], indeed, it has been assigned to believe in the second law. . . . Now astounded, swear that you will believe in Christ. For the Old Testament proclaims Him. It is necessary only to believe in Him who was dead to be able to rise again to live for all time. . . . You reject, unhappy one, the advantage of heavenly discipline. You rush into death, wishing to stray without a bridle. Luxury and the short-lived joys of the world are ruining you. *Commodianus (c. 240, W), 4.207.*

It is not necessary to pay a price either in the way of bribery or of labor—such that man's elevation or dignity or power would be begotten in him with elaborate effort. Rather, it is a gratuitous gift from God and is accessible to all. *Cyprian (c. 250, W), 5.279.*

. . . that the sanctification and quickening that is received from the grace of God may be preserved by His protection. *Cyprian (c. 250, W), 5.450.*

Implore God, who is the one and true God, in confession and faith of acknowledgment of Him. Pardon is granted to the man who confesses. And saving mercy is given from the divine goodness to the believer. . . . Christ bestows this grace. This gift of His mercy He confers upon us—by overcoming death in the trophy of the cross, by redeeming the believer with the price of His blood, by reconciling man to God the Father, and by giving life to our mortal nature with a heavenly regeneration. *Cyprian (c. 250, W), 5.465.*

We must boast in nothing, since nothing is our own. In the Gospel according to John: "No one can receive anything unless it were given him from heaven." *Cyprian (c. 250, W), 5.533.*

He who does not believe is judged already. *Cyprian (c. 250, W), 5.543.*

Our Lord says to the paralytic man, "Be of good cheer, my son, your sins are forgiven you." He said this so that He could show that hearts were purified by faith for the forgiveness of sins, which would follow. Similarly, the woman who was a sinner in the city obtained this same remission of sins. For the Lord said to her, "Your sins are forgiven you." . . . From all of these things, it is shown that hearts are purified by faith, souls are washed by the Spirit, and bodies are washed by water. Finally, by blood we may more readily attain at once to the rewards of salvation. *Treatise on Re-Baptism (c. 257, W), 5.677.*

There is need of humility, fear, and devotion in the greatest degree—lest anyone should put his confidence in his integrity and innocence. For, in doing this, he may incur the charge of pride and arrogance. *Lactantius (c. 304–313, W), 7.193.*

Must we beg you to "lower yourselves" to accept the gift of salvation from God? And must God's gracious mercy be poured into your bosom, while you reject it with disdain and flee very far from it? . . . You will only have robbed yourself of the benefit of the gift. God compels no one; He terrifies no one with overpowering fear. *Arnobius (c. 305, E), 6.458.*

. . . I, who have been made [spiritually] rich by the grace of God. *Disputation of Archelaus and Manes (c. 320, E), 6.218; see also 1.537.*

III. Role of obedience in salvation

Not everyone who says to Me, "Lord, Lord," shall enter the kingdom of heaven, but he who does the will of My Father in heaven. Matt. 7:21.

Strive to enter through the narrow gate, for many, I say to you, will seek to enter and will not be able. Luke 13:24.

Most assuredly, I say to you, if anyone keeps My word he shall never see death. John 8:51.

Moreover, brethren, I declare to you the gospel . . . by which also you are saved, if you hold fast that word which I preached to you—unless you believed in vain. 1 Cor. 15:1, 2.

For this you know, that no fornicator, unclean person, nor covetous man, who is an idolater, has any inheritance in the kingdom of Christ and God. Let no one deceive you with empty words. Eph. 5:5, 6.

Take heed to yourself and to the doctrine. Continue in them, for in doing this you will save both yourself and those who hear you. 1 Tim. 4:16.

Let us therefore be diligent to enter that rest, lest anyone fall after the same example of disobedience. Heb. 4:11.

You see then that a man is justified by works, and not by faith only. JAS. *2:24; see also Matt. 25:33–35; John 8:31; 15:10; Acts 24:15–16; Rom. 2:6, 7.*

The way of light, then, is as follows. If anyone desires to travel to the appointed place, he must be zealous in his works. *Barnabas (c. 70–130, E), 1.148.*

He who keeps them will be glorified in the kingdom of God. However, he who chooses other things will be destroyed with his works. *Barnabas (c. 70–130, E), 1.149.*

We are justified by our works, and not our words. *Clement of Rome (c. 96, W), 1.13*

Take heed, beloved, lest His many kindnesses lead to the condemnation of us all. [For thus it must be] unless we walk worthy of Him, and with one mind do those things which are good and well-pleasing in His sight. *Clement of Rome (c. 96, W), 1.11.*

Let us therefore earnestly strive to be found in the number of those that wait for Him, in order that we may share in His promised gifts. But how, beloved, will this be done? It will be done only by the following things: If our understanding is fixed by faith towards God. If we earnestly seek the things that are pleasing and acceptable to Him. If we do the things that are in harmony with His blameless will. And if we follow the way of truth, casting away from us all unrighteousness and iniquity. *Clement of Rome (c. 96, W), 1.14.*

. . . that He may both hear you, and perceive by your works that you are indeed the members of His Son. *Ignatius (c. 105, E), 1.51.*

Faith cannot do the works of unbelief, nor unbelief the works of faith. *Ignatius (c. 105, E), 1.53.*

The tree is made manifest by its fruit. So those who profess themselves to be Christians will be recognized by their conduct. . . . It is better for a man to be silent and be [a Christian], than to talk and not be one. *Ignatius (c. 105, E), 1.55.*

This, then, is our reward if we will confess Him by whom we have been saved. But in what way will we confess Him? We confess Him by doing what He says, not transgressing His commandments, and by honoring Him not only with our lips, but with all our heart and all our mind. . . . Let us, then, not only call Him Lord, for that will not save us. For He says, "Not everyone who says to Me, Lord, Lord, will be saved, but he that works righteousness." For that reason, brethren, let us confess Him by our works, by loving one another. *Second Clement (c. 150), 7.518.*

Therefore, brethren, by doing the will of the Father, and keeping the flesh holy, and observing the commandments of the Lord, we will obtain eternal life. *Second Clement (c. 150), 7.519.*

He will bestow on them the blessing which He has promised them, with much glory and joy, if only they will keep the commandments of God, which they have received in great faith. *Hermas (c. 150, W), 2.10.*

The first of them, who is clasping her hands, is called Faith. Through her, the elect of God are saved. . . . Self-restraint is the daughter of Faith. Whoever then follows Self-restraint will become happy in his life, because he will restrain himself from all evil works, believing that, if he restrains himself from all evil desire, he will inherit eternal life. *Hermas (c. 150, W), 2.15.*

And he said to me, "You will live if you keep my commandments, and walk in them; and whoever will hear and keep these commandments, will live to God." *Hermas (c. 150, W), 2.22.*

Only those who fear the Lord and keep His commandments have life with God; but as for those who do not keep His commandments, there is no life in them. *Hermas (c. 150, W), 2.25.*

Life is the possession of all who keep the commandments of the Lord. *Hermas (c. 150, W), 2.42.*

We . . . hasten to confess our faith, persuaded and convinced as we are that those who have proved to God by their works that they followed Him, and loved to abide with Him where there is no sin to cause disturbance, can obtain these things. *Justin Martyr (c. 160, E), 1.165.*

If men by their works show themselves worthy of His design, they are deemed worthy of reigning in company with Him, being delivered from corruption and suffering. This is what we have received. . . . Those who choose what is pleasing to Him are, on account of their choice, deemed worthy of incorruption and of fellowship with Him. *Justin Martyr (c. 160, E), 1.165.*

Each man goes to everlasting punishment or salvation according to the value of his actions. *Justin Martyr (c. 160, E), 1.166.*

Let those who are not found living as He taught, be understood not to be Christians, even though they profess with the lips the teachings of Christ. For it is not those who make profession, but those who do the works, who will be saved. *Justin Martyr (c. 160, E), 1.168.*

The Son of God has promised again to deliver us and invest us with prepared garments—if we do His commandments. And He has undertaken to provide an eternal kingdom [for us]. *Justin Martyr (c. 160, E), 1.257.*

The matters of our religion lie in works, not in words. *Justin Martyr (c. 160, E), 1.288.*

He has set before you all these things, and shows you that, if you follow after evil, you will be condemned for your evil deeds. But, if you follow goodness, you will receive from Him abundant good, together with immortal life forever. *Melito (c. 170, E), 8.754.*

To those who by patient continuance in well-doing seek immortality, He will give life everlasting. *Theophilus (c. 180, E), 2.93.*

That, then, which man brought upon himself through carelessness and disobedience, God now vouchsafes to him as a gift through His own philanthropy and pity, when men obey Him. For man drew death upon himself by disobeying. So, by obeying the will of God, he who wants to can procure for himself life everlasting. For God has given us a law and holy commandments. And everyone who keeps them can be saved. And, obtaining the resurrection, he can inherit incorruption. *Theophilus (c. 180, E), 2.105.*

To believe in Him is to do His will. *Irenaeus (c. 180, E/W), 1.468.*

The Lord did not abrogate the natural teachings of the Law, by which man is justified. For those who were justified by faith, and who pleased God, observed those teachings previous to the giving of the Law. *Irenaeus (c. 180, E/W), 1.477.*

We will give account to God not only of deeds (as slaves), but even of words and thoughts (as being those who have truly received the power of liberty). For under liberty, a man is more severely tested as to whether he will reverence, fear, and love the Lord. . . . God desires obedience, which renders [His worshippers] secure—rather than sacrifices and burnt-offerings, which avail men nothing towards righteousness. *Irenaeus (c. 180, E/W), 1.482.*

Those who believe God and follow His word receive that salvation that flows from Him. On the other hand, those who depart from Him, and despise His teachings, and by their deeds bring dishonor on Him who made them . . . heap up against themselves most righteous judgment. *Irenaeus (c. 180, E/W), 1.511.*

With respect to obedience and doctrine, we are not all the sons of God. Rather, it is only those who truly believe in Him and do His will. Now, those who do not believe, and do not obey His will, are sons and angels of the devil. . . . Those who do not obey Him, being disinherited by Him, have ceased to be His sons. *Irenaeus (c. 180, E/W), 1.525.*

All of humanity stands in need of Jesus, so that we may not continue intractable and remain sinners to the end—and thus fall into condemnation. *Clement of Alexandria (c. 195, E), 2.230.*

To obey the Word, whom we call the Instructor, is to believe Him, going against him in nothing. *Clement of Alexandria (c. 195, E), 2.350.*

"Now the just will live by faith," which is according to the covenant and the commandments. *Clement of Alexandria (c. 195, E), 2.354.*

It is the will of God that he who repents of his sins and is obedient to the commandments should be saved. *Clement of Alexandria (c. 195, E), 2.363.*

Salvation is from a change due to obedience; it is not from nature. *Clement of Alexandria (c. 195, E), 2.372.*

To keep from wrong is the beginning of salvation. *Clement of Alexandria (c. 195, E), 2.410.*

He who does not believe God is cheated of his own hope. And he does not believe God, who does not do what God has commanded. *Clement of Alexandria (c. 195, E), 2.416.*

He says, "Why do you call me Lord, Lord, and do not do the things that I say?" For "the people who love with their lips, but have their heart far away from the Lord" are another people. They trust in another god and have willingly sold themselves to another. But those who perform the commandments of the Lord, in every action "testify" by doing what He wishes, and consistently naming the Lord's name. They testify by deed to Him in whom they trust. *Clement of Alexandria (c. 195, E), 2.417.*

Sinners are called enemies of God—enemies, that is, of the commandments that they do not obey. In contrast, those who obey become friends. The one group [of friends] are named so from their fellowship; the others from their estrangement, which is the result of free choice. *Clement of Alexandria (c. 195, E), 2.426.*

When we hear, "Your faith has saved you," we do not understand Him to say absolutely that those who have believed in any way whatever will be saved. For works must also follow. But it was to the Jews alone that He spoke this utterance. Those persons were Jews who kept the Law and lived blamelessly. All they lacked was faith in the Lord. No one, then, can be a believer and at the same time be licentious. *Clement of Alexandria (c. 195, E), 2.505.*

It is well-pleasing to Him that we should be saved. And salvation is effected through both well-doing and knowledge. *Clement of Alexandria (c. 195, E), 2.508.*

He who obtains the mastery in these struggles [against fleshly desires], and overthrows the tempter, . . . wins immortality. . . . The one who has obeyed the directions of the trainer wins the day. . . . We are born to obey the commandments, if we choose to be willing to be saved. Such is the nemesis, through which there is no escaping from God. Man's duty, then, is obedience to God. For He has proclaimed salvation manifold by the commandments. *Clement of Alexandria (c. 195, E), 2.528.*

God ministers eternal salvation to those who cooperate for the attainment of knowledge and good conduct. Since what the commandments command are in our own power, along with the performance of them, the promise is accomplished. *Clement of Alexandria (c. 195, E), 2.536.*

Such is the reward of knowledge . . . abstinence from what is evil, activity in doing good, by which salvation is acquired. *Clement of Alexandria (c. 195, E), 2.543.*

Whoever obtains this and distinguishes himself in good works will gain the prize of everlasting life. . . . Others, attaching slight importance to the works that tend to salvation, do not make the necessary preparation for attaining to the objects of their hope. *Clement of Alexandria (c. 195, E), 2.591.*

Salvation does not depend on external things—whether they are many or few, small or great, illustrious or obscure, esteemed or not esteemed. Rather, it depends on the virtue of the soul—on faith, hope, love, brotherliness, knowledge, meekness, humility, and truth, the reward for which is salvation. *Clement of Alexandria (c. 195, E), 2.596.*

That surrounding circle of angels do not cease to say, "Holy, holy, holy." In like manner, therefore, we, too, are candidates for angelhood—if we succeed in deserving it. So we must begin even here on earth to learn by heart that melody. *Tertullian (c. 198, W), 3.682.*

It is for this reason that [the Gnostics] neither regard works as necessary for themselves, nor do they observe any of the calls of duty, eluding even the necessity of martyrdom on any pretense that may suit their pleasure. *Tertullian (c. 200, W), 3.517.*

This shows that transgressions are blotted out and that reconciliation is made for sins. But who are the ones who have reconciliation made for their sins—except those who believe on His name and propitiate His countenance by good works? *Hippolytus (c. 205, W), 5.181.*

It is to His saints who fear Him—and to them alone—that He reveals himself. For if anyone seems to be living now in the church and yet does not have the fear of God, his companionship with the saints will avail him noth-

ing. "Your words were heard." See how much the piety of a righteous man avails! For to him alone (as to one worthy) things are revealed that are not yet to be manifested in the world. *Hippolytus (c. 205, W), 5.190.*

Who are they who are chosen, but those who believe the word of truth? For they are to be made white thereby, to cast off the filth of sin, and to put on the heavenly, pure, and glorious Holy Spirit. In this manner, when the Bridegroom comes, they may go in straightaway with Him. *Hippolytus (c. 205, W), 5.191.*

You will resemble Him—provided you obey His solemn injunctions and become a faithful follower of Him who is good. *Hippolytus (c. 225, W), 5.153.*

The apostolic teaching is that the soul, . . . after its departure from the world, will be recompensed according to its deserts. It is destined to obtain either an inheritance of eternal life and blessedness (if its actions will have procured this for it) or to be delivered up to eternal fire and punishments—if the guilt of its crimes will have brought it down to this. *Origen (c. 225, E,), 4.240.*

The Son of God, . . . taking the form of a servant, was made obedient unto death so that He might teach obedience to those who could not obtain salvation other than by obedience. *Origen (c. 225, E), 4.343.*

We might interpret the saying [of Jesus] as follows: "If anyone who has grasped what salvation really is, and wishes to procure the salvation of his own life, let him do this: Bid farewell to this life, deny himself, take up his own cross, follow me, and lose his own life to the world." . . . If, then, we wish our life to be saved, let us lose it to the world. Let us be as one of those who have been crucified with Christ . . . so that we may gain our end—even the salvation of our lives. For such salvation begins from the time when we lose our life for the sake of the Word. . . . Therefore, let each one lose his own sinning life, that having lost that which is sinful, he may receive that which is saved by right actions. *Origen (c. 245, E), 9.465.*

The conclusion of the parable, however, is adapted also to the simpler. For all of us who have obtained the forgiveness of our own sins, but have not forgiven our brethren, are taught at once that we will suffer the lot of the servant who was forgiven, but did not forgive his fellow servant. *Origen (c. 245, E), 9.504.*

It is those who not only believe, but also enter upon the life that Jesus taught. This life elevates everyone who lives according to the commandments of Jesus. It elevates them to friendship with God and communion with Him. *Origen (c. 248, E), 4.475.*

We do not teach concerning the unrighteous man that it is sufficient for him to humble himself on account of his wickedness. Rather, God will accept him only if—after passing condemnation upon himself for his past conduct—he walks humbly on account of it and in a righteous manner for his remaining days. *Origen (c. 248, E), 4.489.*

We entertain the hope that by a virtuous life, and by acting agreeably to reason in all things, we may rise to a likeness with all these persons. *Origen (c. 248, E), 4.509.*

It is the Son alone who leads to God those who are striving to come near to God—by the purity of their thoughts, words, and deeds. *Origen (c. 248, E), 4.641.*

Our bodies are the temples of God. If anyone by lust or sin defiles the temple of God, he will himself be destroyed for acting impiously towards the true temple. *Origen (c. 248, E), 4.646.*

Whoever was willing to follow Him and to be His disciple would obtain the reward of being able to see the Father. *Novatian (c. 235, W), 5.639.*

Place, occasion, and person are now given to you; but only if you believe. . . . Bring yourself into obedience; go to Christ and place your neck under Him. *Commodianus (c. 240, W), 4.209.*

If you wish to live, surrender yourselves to the second law. . . . Turn yourselves to Christ, and you will be co-workers with God. *Commodianus (c. 240, W), 4.210.*

I designate you as barren Christians. In the Word of the Lord, the fig tree without fruit was cursed. And immediately it withered away. You do no works! You prepare no gift for the treasury! And yet you vainly think you will deserve well of the Lord! *Commodianus (c. 240, W), 4.213.*

Why, then, has the law itself gone forth with so much pains? You abuse the commandments of the Lord and yet you call yourself His sons. . . . The Almighty seeks the meek to be his sons, those who are upright with a good heart—those who are devoted to the divine law. *Commodianus (c. 240, W), 4.214.*

Abraham believed in God and it was accounted to him as righteousness. Assuredly, then, whoever believes in God and lives in faith is found righteous and is already blessed in faithful Abraham. *Cyprian (c. 250, W), 5.359.*

How can a man say that he believes in Christ, if he does not do what Christ commanded him to do? From where will he attain the reward of faith, if he will not keep the faith of the commandment? . . . He will make no advancement in his walk toward salvation, for he does not keep the truth of the way of salvation. *Cyprian (c. 250, W), 5.422.*

To prophesy, to cast out devils, and to do great acts upon the earth—these are all certainly a sublime and an admirable thing. However, one does not attain the kingdom of heaven even though he is found in all these things, unless he walks in the observance of the right and just way. *Cyprian (c. 250, W), 5.426.*

"Depart from me, you workers of iniquity." There is need of righteousness, that one may deserve well of God the Judge. We must obey His teachings and warnings, so that our merits may receive their reward. *Cyprian (c. 250, W), 5.426.*

He that is freed owes obedience to his deliverer. *Cyprian (c. 250, W), 5.432*

By enduring suffering and by going forward to Christ by the narrow way that Christ trod, we may receive the reward of His life. *Cyprian (c. 250, W), 5.472.*

He who has not been merciful will not be able to deserve the mercy of the Lord. *Cyprian (c. 250, W), 5.477.*

When the servant does not do what is commanded, the Lord will do what he threatens. . . . "I was hungry and you gave me nothing to eat. I was thirsty, and you gave me nothing to drink. . . . And these will go away into everlasting burning." *Cyprian (c. 250, W), 5.483.*

He follows Christ who stands in His commandments, who walks in the way of His teaching, who follows His footsteps and His ways, who imitates that which Christ both did and taught. . . . To put on the name of Christ, and yet not to go in the way of Christ—what else is this but a mockery of the divine name! It is a desertion of the way of salvation. For He Himself teaches and says that the persons who keep His commandments will come into life. *Cyprian (c. 250, W), 5.494.*

"But if the wicked man will turn from all his sins that he has committed, and will do righteousness, he will live in eternal life and will not die in his wickedness." For the sins that he has committed will be abolished from memory by the good deeds that follow. *Treatise against Novatian (c. 255, W), 5.661.*

"Unless you repent, you will all likewise perish." Let us then arouse ourselves as much as we can, beloved brethren. Breaking away from the slumber of laziness and security, let us be watchful for the observance of the Lord's commandments. *Treatise against Novatian (c. 255, W), 5.662.*

To serve God is nothing else than to maintain and preserve justice by good works. *Lactantius (c. 304–313, W), 7.77.*

Labors that are endured and overcome all the way up until death, cannot fail to obtain a reward. . . . And this reward can be nothing else but immortality. *Lactantius (c. 304–313, W), 7.79.*

The spirit must earn immortality by works of righteousness. *Lactantius (c. 304–313, W), 7.127.*

By walking in the way of righteousness and following his Teacher, man can attain to eternal life. *Lactantius (c. 304–313, W), 7.128.*

He who follows truth and righteousness will enjoy perpetual light, having received the reward of immortality. But he who prefers vices to virtues and falsehood to truth (being enticed by that evil guide) must be carried to the setting of the sun and to darkness. . . . The heavenly way is described as being difficult and hilly. It is also rough with dreadful thorns, entangled with stones jutting out. As a result, everyone must walk with the greatest labor and wearing of the feet, and with great precautions against falling. *Lactantius (c. 304–313, W), 7.165.*

We must be on the watch, must post guards, must undertake military expeditions, must shed our blood to the uttermost. In short, we must patiently submit to all things that are unpleasant and grievous. We should do this all the more readily because God our Commander has appointed for us eternal rewards for our labors. . . . Assuredly, no labor should be refused by us. For by it, that is gained which cannot be lost. *Lactantius (c. 304–313, W), 7.166.*

God calls man to life only through virtue and labor. But the other one calls us to death by delights and pleasures. *Lactantius (c. 304–313, W), 7.189.*

Man cannot attain to immortality by a delicate and easy course of life. Rather, he can arrive at that unspeakable reward of eternal life with only the utmost difficulty and great labors. *Lactantius (c. 304–313, W), 7.200.*

Why, then, did God make man frail and mortal? . . . He did so in order that He might set before man virtue—that is, the endurance of evils and labors by which man might be able to gain the reward of immortality. For man consists of two parts, body and soul. . . . And two lives have been assigned to man. The one is temporal, which is appointed for the body. The other is everlasting, and it belongs to the soul. We receive the first life at our birth. We attain to the latter by striving, so that immortality might not exist to man without any difficulty. . . . For this reason, He has given us this present life: that we may either lose that true and eternal life by our vices, or win it by virtue. *Lactantius (c. 304–313, W), 7.200.*

We worship Him for this end: that we may receive immortality as the reward of our labors. For the worship of God consists of the greatest labors. *Lactantius (c. 304–313, W), 7.203.*

Those who have known God will be judged. Their deeds—that is, their evil works—will be compared and weighed against their good ones. So that if those that are good and just are more numerous and more weighty, they will be given to a life of blessedness. But if the evil ones exceed the good ones, they will be condemned to punishment. *Lactantius (c. 304–313, W), 7.216.*

Persons cannot be partakers of this heavenly and eternal reward if they have polluted their consciences by acts of violence, fraud, robbery, and dishonesty. By their ungodly actions and by the injuries they have inflicted upon others, they have branded themselves with indelible stains. *Lactantius (c. 304–313, W), 7.279.*

Many are still perishing—those who have not chosen to devote themselves to works of righteousness. For only those who have received Him . . . "have obtained power to become the sons of God." *Disputation of Archelaus and Manes (c. 320, E), 6.201.*

If we consider that man is justified without the works of the Law, and if Abraham was counted righteous, how much more will those persons obtain righteousness who have fulfilled the law that contains the things that are expedient for men. *Disputation of Archelaus and Manes (c. 320, E), 6.201.*

If there is to be no judgment, then the keeping of God's commandments will be to no purpose. If that is the case, there is no reason for abstinence. Rather, we can say, "Let us eat and drink, for tomorrow we will die." *Disputation of Archelaus and Manes (c. 320, E), 6.225.*

If anyone follows unrighteousness and does those things that are contrary to the will of God—such a person will be considered by God the same as the disobedient unbeliever. *Apostolic Constitutions (compiled c. 390, E), 7.391.*

IV. The violent who storm the kingdom of heaven

From the days of John the Baptist until now the kingdom of heaven suffers violence, and the violent take it by force. Matt. 11:12.

Strive to enter through the narrow gate, for many, I say to you, will seek to enter and will not be able. Luke 13:24.

The Lord declared that the kingdom of heaven was the portion of "the violent." He says, "The violent take it by force." By "the violent," He means those who by strength and earnest striving are on the watch to snatch it away on the moment. . . . This able Wrestler, therefore, exhorts us to enter the struggle for immortality. He does this so that we may be crowned, and so we may deem the crown precious—for it is that which is acquired by our struggle. . . . Since, then, this power has been conferred upon us, the Lord has taught us and the apostle has commanded us even more to love God, so that we may reach this for ourselves by striving after it. *Irenaeus (c. 180, E/W), 1.520.*

The "violent who storm the kingdom" are not persons who are argumentative in speeches. Rather, they are said "to take it by force" because they continue in a right life and in unceasing prayers. They thereby wipe away the blots left by their previous sins. *Clement of Alexandria (c. 195, E), 2.448.*

The kingdom belongs pre-eminently to the violent. They reap this fruit from investigation, study, and discipline, so that they may become kings. *Clement of Alexandria (c. 195, E), 2.515.*

The kingdom of heaven does not belong to sleepers and sluggards. Rather, "the violent take it by force." For this alone is commendable violence—to struggle with God and to take life from God by force. And He knows those who persevere firmly, or rather violently, and He yields and grants. For God delights in being conquered in such things. *Clement of Alexandria (c. 195, E), 2.597.*

Offering up prayer to God as with united force, we wrestle with Him in our supplications. God delights in this "violence." *Tertullian (c. 197, W), 3.46.*

V. Righteousness of God vs. righteousness of the Law

For they being ignorant of God's righteousness, and seeking to establish their own righteousness, have not submitted to the righteousness of God. . . . For Moses writes about the righteousness which is of the law, "The man who does those things shall live by them." Rom. 10:3, 5.

Christ did not label the Law given by Moses as "commandments of men." Rather, the [commandments of men] were the traditions of the elders that they themselves had invented. In upholding those traditions, they made the Law of God of no effect. And they were on this account also not subject to His Word. For this is also what Paul says concerning these men: "For they, being ignorant of God's righteousness, and going about to establish their own righteousness, have not submitted themselves to the righteousness of God." *Irenaeus (c. 180, E/W), 1.476.*

To those who were righteous according to the Law, faith was lacking. For that reason, the Lord, in healing them, said, "Your faith has saved you." *Clement of Alexandria (c. 195, E), 2.490.*

By the "righteousness of God," he means that judgment that we will have to undergo as the recompense of our deeds. *Tertullian (c. 210, W), 3.562.*

VI. Can those who are saved ever be lost?

The Lord is with you while you are with Him. If you seek Him, He will be found by you; but if you forsake Him, He will forsake you. 2 Chron. 15:2.

The righteousness of the righteous man shall not deliver him in the day of his transgression. Ezek. 33:12.

You will be hated by all for My name's sake. But he who endures to the end will be saved. Matt. 10:22.

Jesus said to him, "No one, having put his hand to the plow, and looking back, is fit for the kingdom of God." Luke 9:62.

If we endure, we shall also reign with Him. If we deny Him, He also will deny us. 2 Tim. 2:12.

If we sin willfully after we have received the knowledge of the truth, there no longer remains a sacrifice for sins, but a certain fearful expectation of judgment. Heb. 10:26.

For if, after they have escaped the pollutions of the world through the knowledge of the Lord and Savior Jesus Christ, they are again entangled in them and overcome, the latter end is worse for them than the beginning. For it would have been better for them not to have known the way of righteousness, than having known it, to turn from the holy commandment delivered to them. 2 Pet. 2:20, 21; see also Matt. 24:13; Luke 17:31, 32; John 8:31, 32; 15:1, 6; Gal. 6:9; Jas. 1:12; Heb. 6:4–6; 10:36.

We ought therefore, brethren, carefully to inquire concerning our salvation. Otherwise, the wicked one, having made his entrance by deceit, may hurl us forth from our life. *Barnabas (c. 70–130, E), 1.138.*

The whole past time of your faith will profit you nothing, unless now in this wicked time we also withstand coming sources of danger. . . . Take heed, lest resting at our ease, as those who are the called, we fall asleep in our sins. For then, the wicked prince, acquiring power over us, will thrust us away from the kingdom of the Lord. . . . And you should pay attention to this all the more, my brothers, when you reflect on and see that even after such great signs and wonders had been performed in Israel, they were still abandoned. Let us beware lest we be found to be, as it is written, the "many who are called," but not the "few who are chosen." *Barnabas (c. 70–130, E), 1.139.*

[WRITTEN TO CHRISTIANS:] Since all things are seen and heard [by God], let us fear Him

and forsake those wicked works that proceed from evil desires. By doing that, through His mercy, we may be protected from the judgments to come. For where can any of us flee from His mighty hand? *Clement of Rome (c. 96, W), 1.12.*

Let us therefore repent with the whole heart, so that none of us perish by the way. *Second Clement (c. 150), 7.522.*

Let us then practice righteousness so that we may be saved unto the end. *Second Clement (c. 150), 7.523.*

For the Lord has sworn by His glory, in regard to His elect, that if any one of them sin after a certain day which has been fixed, he will not be saved. For the repentance of the righteous has limits. Filled up are the days of repentance to all the saints. But to the unbeliever, repentance will be possible even to the last day. . . . For the Lord has sworn by His Son, that those who denied their Lord have abandoned their life in despair. *Hermas (c. 150, W), 2.11.*

There is but one repentance to the servants of God. *Hermas (c. 150, W), 2.21.*

If you do not guard yourself against [anger], you and your house will lose all hope of salvation. *Hermas (c. 150, W), 2.23.*

Put away doubting from you, and do not hesitate to ask of the Lord, saying to yourself, "How can I ask of the Lord and receive from Him, seeing I have sinned so much against Him?" Do not reason with yourself in this manner. Instead, with all your heart turn to the Lord, and ask of Him without doubting. For then you will know the multitude of His tender mercies and that He will never leave you, but will fulfil the request of your soul. For He is not like men, who remember evils done against them. *Hermas (c. 150, W), 2.26.*

The apostates and traitors of the church have blasphemed the Lord in their sins. Moreover, they have been ashamed of the name of the Lord by which they were called. These persons, therefore, at the end were lost unto God. *Hermas (c. 150, W), 2.41.*

I hold further, that those of you who have confessed and known this man to be Christ, yet who have gone back for some reason to the legal dispensation [i.e., the Mosaic Law], and have denied that this man is Christ, and have not repented before death—you will by no means be saved. *Justin Martyr (c. 160, E), 1.218.*

These men of old time, . . . for whom the Son of God had not yet suffered, when they committed any sin and served fleshly lusts, were rendered objects of great disgrace. Accordingly, what will the men of the present day suffer, who have despised the Lord's coming, and have become the slaves of their own lusts? Truly, the death of the Lord brought healing and remission of sins to the former. However, Christ will not die again on behalf of those who now commit sin. For death will no more have dominion over Him. . . . We should not, therefore, as that presbyter remarks, be puffed up, nor be severe upon those of olden times. Rather, we should fear ourselves, least perchance, after [we have come to] the knowledge of Christ, if we do things displeasing to God, we obtain no further forgiveness of sins, but are shut out from His kingdom. And for that reason, Paul said, "For if [God] spared not the natural branches, [take heed] lest He also not spare you." *Irenaeus (c. 180, E/W), 1.499.*

It was not to those who are on the outside that he said these things, but to us—lest we should be cast forth from the kingdom of God, by doing any such thing. *Irenaeus (c. 180, E/W), 1.500.*

Knowing that what preserves his life, namely, obedience to God, is good, he may diligently keep it with all earnestness. *Irenaeus (c. 180, E), 1.522.*

Those who do not obey Him, being disinherited by Him, have ceased to be His sons. *Irenaeus (c. 180, E/W), 1.525.*

God's greatest gift is self-restraint. For He Himself has said, "I will never leave you, nor forsake you," as having judged you worthy according to the true election. Thus, then, while we attempt piously to advance, we will have put on us the mild yoke of the Lord from faith to faith, one charioteer driving each of us onward to salvation. *Clement of Alexandria (c. 195, E), 2.374.*

He who hopes for everlasting rest knows also that the entrance to it is toilsome and narrow. So let him who has once received the Gospel not turn back, like Lot's wife, as is said—even in the very hour in which he has come to the knowledge of salvation. And let him not go back either to his former life (which adheres to the things of sense) or to heresies. *Clement of Alexandria (c. 195, E), 2.550.*

It is neither the faith, nor the love, nor the hope, nor the endurance of one day; rather, "he that endures to the end will be saved." *Clement of Alexandria (c. 195, E), 2.600.*

God gives forgiveness of past sins. However, as to future sins, each one procures this for himself. He does this by repenting, by condemning the past deeds, and by begging the Father to blot them out. For only the Father is the one who is able to undo what is done. . . . So even in the case of one who has done the greatest good deeds in his life, but at the end has run headlong into wickedness, all his former pains are profitless to him. For at the climax of the drama, he has given up his part. *Clement of Alexandria (c. 195, E), 2.602.*

No one is a Christian but he who perseveres even to the end. *Tertullian (c. 197, W), 3.244.*

The world returned to sin . . . and so it is destined to fire. So is the man who after baptism renews his sins. *Tertullian (c. 198, W), 3.673.*

We ought indeed to walk so holily, and with so entire substantiality of faith, as to be confident and secure in regard of our own conscience, desiring that it may abide in us to the end. Yet, we should not presume [that it will]. For he who presumes, feels less apprehension. He who feels less apprehension, takes less precaution. He who takes less precaution, runs more risk. Fear is the foundation of salvation. Presumption is an impediment to fear. . . . More useful, then, is it to apprehend that we may possibly fail, than to presume that we cannot. For apprehending will lead us to fear, fear to caution, and caution to salvation. On the other hand, if we presume, there will be neither fear nor caution to save us. *Tertullian (c. 198, W), 4.19.*

[The Valentinians claim] that since they are already naturalized in the brotherly bond of the spiritual state, they will obtain a certain salvation—one which is on all accounts their due. *Tertullian (c. 200, W), 3.517.*

Some think that God is under a necessity of bestowing even on the unworthy what He has promised [to give]. So they turn His liberality into His slavery. . . . For do not many afterwards fall out of [grace]? Is not this gift taken away from many? These, no doubt, are they who, . . . after approaching to the faith of repentance, build on the sands a house doomed to ruin. *Tertullian (c. 203, W), 3.661.*

God had foreseen . . . that faith—even after baptism—would be endangered. He saw that most persons—after obtaining salvation—would be lost again, by soiling the wedding dress, by failing to provide oil for their torches. *Tertullian (c. 213, W), 3.639.*

Hoodwinking multitudes, [Marcus, the heretic] deceived many persons of this description who had become his disciples. He taught them that they were prone, no doubt, to sin. However, he said that they were beyond the reach of danger because they belonged to the perfect Power. . . . Subsequent to baptism, these [heretics] promise another, which they call Redemption. And by this, they wickedly subvert those who remain with them in expectation of redemption. As if persons, after they had once been baptized, could again obtain remission. *Hippolytus (c. 225, W), 5.92.*

A man may possess an acquired righteousness, from which it is possible for him to fall away. *Origen (c. 225, E), 4.266.*

Certain ones of those [heretics] who hold different opinions misuse these passages. They essentially destroy free will by introducing ruined natures incapable of salvation and by introducing others as being saved in such a way that they cannot be lost. *Origen (c. 225, E), 4.308.*

The same reply must be given to them with respect to the statement of the apostle. . . . On whom does He have mercy? . . . He has it on those who are capable of incurring destruction if they did not receive mercy. They will obtain mercy in order that they may not incur that destruction of which they are capable. That way, they will remain in the condition of those who are saved. *Origen (c. 225, E), 4.309.*

He who has not denied himself, but denied Christ, will experience the saying, "I also will deny him." *Origen (c. 245, E), 9.464.*

Being a believing man, if you seek to live as the Gentiles do, the joys of the world remove you from the grace of Christ. *Commodianus (c. 240, W), 4.214.*

Let fear be the keeper of innocence, so that the Lord, who of His mercy has flowed into our hearts in the access of celestial grace, may be kept by righteous submissiveness in the home of a grateful mind. Otherwise, the assurance we have gained may beget carelessness, and so the old enemy will creep upon us again. *Cyprian (c. 250, W), 5.276.*

There remains more than what is yet seen to be accomplished. For it is written, "Praise not any man before his death." And again, "Be faithful unto death, and I will give you a crown of life." And the Lord also says, "He that endures to the end, the same will be saved." *Cyprian (c. 250, W), 5.283.*

You are still in the world. You are still in the battlefield. You daily fight for your lives. So you must be careful, that . . . what you have begun to be with such a blessed commencement will be consummated in you. It is a small thing to have first received something. It is a greater thing to be able to *keep* what you have attained. Faith itself and the saving birth do not make alive by merely being received. Rather, they must be *preserved*. It is not the actual attainment, but the perfecting, that keeps a man for God. The Lord taught this in His instruction when He said, "Look! You have been made whole. Sin no more, lest a worse thing come upon you." . . . Solomon, Saul, and many others were able to keep the grace given to them so long as they walked in the Lord's ways. However, when the discipline of the Lord was forsaken by them, grace also forsook them. *Cyprian (c. 250, W), 5.284.*

I ask . . . that you will grieve with me at the [spiritual] death of my sister. For in this time of devastation, she has fallen from Christ. *Cyprian (c. 250, W), 5.298.*

He who wills that no one should perish, desires that sinners should repent, and by repentance, should return again to life. *Cyprian (c. 250, W), 5.333.*

They should not think that the way of life or of salvation is still open to them if they have refused to obey the bishops and priests. For in Deuteronomy, the Lord God says, "And the man that will do presumptuously and will not listen to the priest or judge, . . . that man will die." *Cyprian (c. 250, W), 5.358.*

[ADDRESSED TO CHRISTIAN LEADERS:] Endeavor that the undisciplined ones should not be consumed and perish. As much as you can, by your salutary counsels, you should rule the brotherhood and take counsel of each one with a view to this salvation. Strait and narrow is the way through which we enter into life. *Cyprian (c. 250, W), 5.358.*

It is clear that the devil is driven out in baptism by the faith of the believer. But he returns if the faith should afterwards fail. *Cyprian (c. 250, W), 5.402.*

Although they forsake the fountain of life, the [heretics] promise the grace of living and saving water. . . . Begotten of treachery, they lose the grace of faith. *Cyprian (c. 250, W), 5.425.*

Whoever that confessor is, he is not greater, better, or dearer to God than Solomon. Solomon retained the grace that he had received from the Lord, as long as he walked in God's ways. However, after he forsook the Lord's way, he also lost the Lord's grace. For that reason it is written, "Hold fast that which you have, lest another take your crown." Assuredly, the Lord would not threaten that the crown of righteousness might be taken away if it were not that the crown must depart when righteousness departs. . . . "He that endures to the end, the same will be saved." So whatever comes before the end is a step by which we ascend to the summit of salvation. It is not the *finish*, where the full result of the ascent is already gained. *Cyprian (c. 250, W), 5.428.*

To anyone who is born and dies, is there not a necessity at some time . . . to suffer the loss of his estate? Only let not Christ be forsaken, so that the loss of salvation and of an eternal home would be feared. *Cyprian (c. 250, W), 5.439.*

We pray that this sanctification may abide in us. For our Lord and Judge warns the man who was healed and quickened by Him to sin no more—lest a worse thing happen to him. So we make this supplication in our constant prayers, . . . that the sanctification and quickening that is received from the grace of God may be preserved by His protection. *Cyprian (c. 250, W), 5.450.*

There is need of continual prayer and supplication so that we do not fall away from the heavenly kingdom, as the Jews fell away, to whom this promise had first been given. *Cyprian (c. 250, W), 5.451.*

The quarrelsome and disunited . . . will not be able to escape the crime of brotherly dissension. For it is written, "He who hates his brother is a murderer." And no murderer

attains to the kingdom of heaven. Nor does he live with God. A person cannot be with Christ if he had rather be an imitator of Judas than of Christ. How great is the sin that cannot even be washed away by a baptism of blood! *Cyprian (c. 250, W), 5.454.*

What a wonderful providence, how great the mercy, that by a plan of salvation it is provided for that more abundant care should be taken for preserving a man after he is already redeemed. . . . Nor would the infirmity and weakness of human frailty have any resource, unless the divine mercy, coming once more in aid, should open some way of securing salvation, by pointing out works of justice and mercy. So, by almsgiving, we may wash away whatever foulness we subsequently contract. *Cyprian (c. 250, W), 5.476.*

You are afraid that perhaps your estate might fail if you begin to act generously from it. Do you not know, miserable man, that while you are worrying that your family property may fail, life itself and salvation are failing! *Cyprian (c. 250, W), 5.478.479.*

He says, "He that endures to the end, the same will be saved." And again He says, "If you continue in my word, you will truly be my disciples" [John 8:31, 32]. . . . So there needs to be patience in order that hope and faith may attain their result. *Cyprian (c. 250, W), 5.487.*

Let us press onward and labor, watching with our whole heart. Let us be steadfast with all endurance; let us keep the Lord's commandments. Thereby, when that day of anger and vengeance comes, we may not be punished with the ungodly and the sinners. Rather, we may be honored with the righteous and with those who fear God. *Cyprian (c. 250, W), 5.491.*

Those who are snatched from the jaws of the devil and delivered from the snares of this world, should not return to the world again, lest they should lose the advantage of their leaving it in the first place. . . . The Lord admonishes us of this in His Gospel. He taught that we should not return again to the devil and to the world. For we have renounced them and have escaped from them. He says, "No man looking back after putting his hand to the plough is fit for the kingdom of God." And again, "Let him that is in the field not return back. Remember Lot's wife." . . . So we must press on and persevere in faith and virtue. We must complete the heavenly and spiritual grace so that we may attain to the palm and the crown. In the book of Chronicles it says, "The Lord is with you so long as you also are with him; but if you forsake him, he will forsake you." Also in Ezekiel: "The righteousness of the righteous man will not deliver him in whatever day that he may transgress." Furthermore, in the Gospel, the Lord speaks and says: "He that endures to the end, the same will be saved." And again: "*If* you will abide in my word, you will be my disciples indeed." *Cyprian (c. 250, W), 5.500.*

In the Gospel according to Matthew: "Every tree that does not bring forth good fruit will be cut down and cast into the fire" [Matt. 3:10]. . . . Even a baptized person loses the grace that he has attained, unless he remains innocent. In the Gospel according to John: "Look, you are made whole. Sin no more, lest a worse thing happens to you" [John 5:14]. Also, in the first Epistle of Paul to the Corinthians: "Do you not know that you are the temple of God, and the Spirit of God abides in you? If anyone violates the temple of God, God will destroy him" [1 Cor. 3:16, 17]. Of this same thing in the Chronicles: "God is with you, while you are with Him. If you forsake Him, he will forsake you" [2 Chron. 15:2]. *Cyprian (c. 250, W), 5.542.*

As to one who again denies Christ, no special previous standing can be effective to him for salvation. For anyone of us will hold it necessary that whatever is the last thing to be found in a man in this respect, that is where he will be judged. All of those things that he has previously done are wiped away and obliterated. *Treatise on Re-Baptism (c. 257, W), 5.674.*

He put a seal upon him, for it is concealed as to who belong to the side of the devil and who to the side of Christ. For we do not know out of those who seem to stand whether they will fall or not. And of those who are down, it is uncertain whether they might rise. *Victorinus (c. 280, W), 7.358.*

A son . . . who deserts his father in order not to pay him obedience is considered deserving of being disinherited and of having his name removed forever from his family. How much more so does a person [deserve to be disinherited] who forsakes God—in whom the two names meet that are entitled to equal reverence: Lord and Father? . . . Of what punish-

ments, therefore, is he deserving who forsakes Him who is both the true Master and Father? *Lactantius (c. 304–313, W), 7.155.*

The righteous man, since he has entered upon a hard and rugged way, must be an object of contempt, derision, and hatred. . . . Therefore, he will be poor, humble, low, subject to injury, and yet enduring all things that are grievous. And if he will continue his patience unceasingly to that last step and end, the crown of virtue will be given to him and he will be rewarded by God with immortality for the labors that he has endured in life for the sake of righteousness. *Lactantius (c. 304–313, W), 7.165.*

We believe that our children have been corrected when we see that they repent of their errors. And though we may have disinherited them and cast them off, we again receive, cherish, and embrace them. Why, then, should we despair as if the mercy of God our Father might not be appeased by repentance? He who is both the Lord and a most indulgent Parent promises that He will remit the sins of the penitent. He promises that He will blot out all the iniquities of the one who begins afresh to practice righteousness. The uprightness of one's past life is to no avail to him who lives badly, for the subsequent wickedness has destroyed his works of righteousness. Likewise, former sins do not stand in the way of him who has amended his life. For the subsequent righteousness has wiped away the stain of his former life. *Lactantius (c. 304–313, W), 7.191.*

[True] repentance makes a man cautious and diligent to avoid the faults into which he has once fallen through treachery. No one can be so prudent and so cautious as not at some time to slip. Therefore, God, knowing our weakness, out of His compassion has opened a harbor of refuge for man—that the medicine of repentance might aid this necessity to which our frailty is liable. *Lactantius (c. 304–313, W), 7.191.*

If they tear themselves away from this pernicious slavery, all their error will be forgiven them—if they have corrected their error by a better life. *Lactantius (c. 304–313, W), 7.191.*

He who sins after his baptism, unless he repents and forsakes his sins, will be condemned to Gehenna. *Apostolic Constitutions (compiled c. 390, E), 7.398.*

How do you know, O man, when you sin, whether you will live a sufficient number of days in this present state in order that you will have time to repent? For the time of your departure out of this world is uncertain. And if you die in sin, there will remain no repentance for you. *Apostolic Constitutions (compiled c. 390, E), 7.400.*

The Holy Spirit always abides with those who are possessed of Him, so long as they are worthy. . . . The Holy Spirit remains with a person so long as he is doing good, and He fills him with wisdom and understanding. *Apostolic Constitutions (compiled c. 390, E), 7.462; see also 2.42, 2.422.*

VII. Universal salvation?

As is quite clear from the preceding quotations, the early church, as a whole, did not believe in universal salvation. But two early Christian writers—Clement of Alexandria and Origen—speculated that, after the disciplinary punishments of Gehenna, perhaps all persons would eventually be reconciled to God. Neither of these men, however, taught this dogmatically. They apparently based their viewpoint on the following Scriptures:

For as in Adam all die, even so in Christ all shall be made alive. 1 Cor. 15:22.

We trust in the living God, who is the Savior of all men, especially of those who believe. 1 Tim. 4:10.

He Himself is the propitiation for our sins, and not for ours only but also for the whole world. 1 John 2:2.

The Lord is not slack concerning His promise, as some count slackness, but is longsuffering toward us, not willing that any should perish but that all should come to repentance. 2 PET. 3:9; see also Rom. 5:18; Col. 1:20; Tit. 2:11.

"And in Him is no darkness at all,"—that is, no passion, no keeping up of evil respecting anyone. He destroys no one, but grants salvation to all. *Clement of Alexandria (c. 195, E), 2.575.*

He says that the Lord is the Propitiator, "not only for our sins"—that is, for those of the faithful—"but also for the whole world." He, indeed, saves all. But [He saves] some by converting them through punishments. However, those who follow voluntarily, [He saves] with dignity of honor. *Clement of Alexandria (c. 195, E), 2.575.*

I think, indeed, that the goodness of God, through His Christ, may recall all His creatures to one end. For all of His enemies will be conquered and subdued. *Origen (c. 225, E), 4.260.*

Those [angelic creatures] who have been removed from their original state of blessedness have not been removed irrecoverably. Rather, they have been placed under the rule of those holy and blessed orders that I have described. By availing themselves of this angelic help, and being remolded by salutary principles and discipline, they may recover themselves and be restored to their condition of happiness. . . . However, as to any of these powers who act under the direction of the devil and obey his wicked commands, whether or not they will be converted to righteousness in a future world, because of their possessing the faculty of freedom of the will, . . . is a result which you the reader may approve of. *Origen (c. 225, E), 4.261.*

"Behold the Lamb of God who takes away the sin of the world." Is the "world" here to be taken spiritually to mean the church? Is the taking away of sin limited to the church? If so, what are we to make of the saying of the same disciple? . . . Paul's words appear to me to be to the same effect, when he says, "Who is the Savior of all men, especially of the faithful." *Origen (c. 228, E), 9.380.*

SEE ALSO ATONEMENT; BLOOD OF CHRIST; DESCENT INTO HADES; ETERNAL PUNISHMENTS AND REWARDS; FAITH; FALL OF MAN; FOREKNOWLEDGE OF GOD; FREE WILL AND PREDESTINATION; MAN, DOCTRINE OF; ORIGEN (II. C. UNIVERSAL RECONCILIATION); SINLESSNESS; TWO WAYS.

SAMUEL

Then Saul said to his servants, "Find me a woman who is a medium, that I may go to her and inquire of her." . . . Then the woman said, "Whom shall I bring up for you?" And he said, "Bring up Samuel for me." When the woman saw Samuel, she cried out with a loud voice. 1 Sam. 28:7, 11, 12.

That souls survive, I have shown to you from the fact that the soul of Samuel was called up by the witch, as Saul demanded. And it appears also, that all the souls of similar righteous men and prophets fell under the dominion of such powers. This, indeed, can be inferred from the very facts in the case of that witch. *Justin Martyr (c. 160, E), 1.252.*

The question is raised whether Samuel rose by the hand of the sorceress or not. Now, if, indeed, we were to say that he did rise, we would be propounding what is false. For how could a demon call back the soul—I say not only of a righteous man, but of anyone whomever—when it had gone and was tarrying, one knew not where? . . . It would have been no difficult matter for the demon to conjure up the form of Samuel, for Samuel's form was known to him. How then, he says, did he foretell the calamities that were to befall Saul and Jonathan at the same time? He actually did foretell the end of the war and how Saul would be overcome, drawing that as an inference from the wrath of God against [Saul]. *Hippolytus (c. 205, W), 5.169.*

It was no less than this that was anciently permitted to the Pythonic spirit: it was allowed even to represent the soul of Samuel, when Saul consulted the dead, after God. God forbid, however, that we should suppose that the soul of any saint—much less of a prophet—can be dragged out of [Hades] by a demon. We know that Satan himself is "transformed into an angel of light." . . . You must not imagine that he who produced the apparition was one person, and he who consulted it was another. Rather, it was one and the same spirit that was in both the sorceress and the apostate [i.e., Saul]—which easily pretended to be an apparition. *Tertullian (c. 210, W), 3.234.*

SEE ALSO SAUL; SPIRITISM.

SATAN

Now there was a day when the sons of God came to present themselves before the Lord, and Satan also came among them. Job 1:6.

You were the seal of perfection, full of wisdom and perfect in beauty. You were in Eden, the garden of God; every precious stone was your covering. . . . You were the anointed cherub who covers; I established you; you were on the holy mountain of God; you walked back and forth in the midst of fiery stones. You were perfect in your ways from the day you were created, till iniquity was found in you. Ezek. 28:12–15.

And the Lord said, "Simon, Simon! Indeed, Satan has asked for you, that he may sift you as wheat. But I have prayed for you, that your faith should not fail. Luke 22:31, 32.

Resist the devil and he will flee from you. Jas. 4:7.

So the great dragon was cast out, that serpent of old, called the Devil and Satan, who deceives the whole world; he was cast to the earth, and his angels were cast out with him. Rev. 12:9.

Fear not the devil. By fearing the Lord, you will have dominion over the devil. For there is no power in him. . . . Nevertheless, fear the *deeds* of the devil, since they are wicked. *Hermas (c. 150, W), 2.24, 25.*

He says, "[The devil] cannot hold dominion over the servants of God, who with all their heart place their hopes in Him. The devil can wrestle against them. But he cannot overthrow them." *Hermas (c. 150, W), 2.29*

The devil goes to all the servants of God to test them. The ones who are full in the faith resist him strongly. So he withdraws from them, having no way to enter them. He goes, then, to the empty. Finding a way of entrance into them, he produces in them whatever he wishes, and they become his servants. *Hermas (c. 150, W), 2.29, 30.*

Because she was in the beginning deceived by the serpent, this Eve become the author of sin. Actually, it was the wicked demon, who also is called Satan, who then spoke to her through the serpent. And he works even to this day in those men who are possessed by him. They even call him "Eve" in their invocations. And he is also called "demon" and "dragon" on account of his revolting from God. For at first he was an angel. *Theophilus (c. 180, E), 2.105.*

Eternal fire was not originally prepared for man, but for him who beguiled man, and caused him to offend. I say, it was prepared for him, who is chief of the apostasy, and for those angels who became apostates along with him. *Irenaeus (c. 180, E/W), 1.456.*

The apostate angel, having caused the disobedience of mankind by means of the serpent, imagined that he escaped the notice of the Lord. As a result, God assigned him the form and name [of a serpent]. *Irenaeus (c. 180, E/W), 1.462.*

From this we learn that this was the apostate angel and the enemy. For he was envious of God's workmanship and took in hand to render this workmanship into something at enmity with God. For this reason, too, God has banished from His presence the one who of his own accord stealthily sowed the tares. I am referring to the one who brought about the transgression. *Irenaeus (c. 180, E/W), 1.524.*

We do not find that the devil created anything whatsoever. For, indeed, he is himself a creature of God, like the other angels. *Irenaeus (c. 180, E/W), 1.524.*

The Hebrew word *Satan* means an apostate. *Irenaeus (c. 180, E/W), 1.549.*

The creation is not subjected to his power, since indeed he is himself but one among created things. *Irenaeus (c. 180, E/W), 1.551.*

The devil was one of those angels who are placed over the spirit of the air. . . . However, becoming envious of man, he was rendered an apostate from the divine law. . . . The Word of God, however, the Maker of all things, conquered him by means of human nature. So, showing him to be an apostate, Christ has, on the contrary, put him under the power of man. *Irenaeus (c. 180, E/W), 1.553.*

You have Satan constantly upon your lips— the very one we hold to be the angel of evil. He is the source of error and the corrupter of the whole world. By him, in the beginning, man was entrapped into breaking the commandment of God. *Tertullian (c. 197, W), 3.177.*

He deceived [man] because he had envied him. *Tertullian (c. 200, W), 3.709.*

That most stubborn Foe never gives his malice a rest. Indeed, he is then the most savage when he fully feels that a man is freed from his clutches. He then flames fiercest while he is fast becoming extinguished. He must of necessity grieve and groan over the fact that, by the grant of pardon, so many works of death in man have been overthrown. He grieves that so many marks of condemnation (which formerly was his own) have now been erased. He grieves that this [former] sinner, [who is now] Christ's servant, is destined to judge him and his angels. And so the Foe observes, assaults, and attacks him. *Tertullian (c. 203, W), 3.662, 663.*

No doubt it was an angel who was the seducer. *Tertullian (c. 207, W), 3.303.*

From where did this malice of lying and deceit towards man—and slandering of God— originate? Most certainly not from God! For He made the angel good after the fashion of His good works. Indeed, before he became the devil, he stood forth as the wisest of creatures.

And wisdom is no evil. If you turn to the prophecy of Ezekiel, you will at once realize that this angel was good by creation. It was by choice that he became corrupt. For in the person of the prince of Tyre, it says things in reference to the devil. *Tertullian (c. 207, W), 3.305.*

From the devil comes the incentive to sin. *Tertullian (c. 210, W), 3.194.*

The devil, it must be acknowledged, seems indeed to have power—in this case, really his own—over those who do not belong to God. . . . But against those who belong to the household of God, he may not do anything through any right of his own. *Tertullian (c. 212, W), 4.117.*

Regarding the devil, his angels, and the opposing forces, the teaching of the church is that these beings do indeed exist. However, the church has not explained with sufficient clarity what they are, or how they exist. Most Christians, however, hold this opinion: that the devil was an angel and that, having become an apostate, he induced as many of the angels as possible to fall away with him. *Origen (c. 225, E), 4.240.*

The names, then, of Devil, Satan, Wicked One, and Enemy of God are mentioned in many passages of Scripture. Moreover, certain angels of the devil are mentioned. There is also mentioned a prince of this world. Whether this prince is the devil himself or someone else, is not yet clearly manifest. *Origen (c. 225, E), 4.257.*

We find in the prophet Ezekiel two prophecies written to the king of Tyre. . . . The second is clearly of such a kind that it cannot be at all understood about a man. It must refer to some superior power who had fallen away from a higher position and had been reduced to a lower and worse condition. I will take from it an illustration by which it may be demonstrated with the utmost clearness that those opposing and malignant spiritual powers were not formed or created so by nature. Rather, they fell from a better to a worse position and were converted into wicked beings. . . .

"From the day when you were created with the cherubim, I placed you in the holy mountain of God." Who could so water down the meaning of this passage so as to suppose that this language was referring to some man or saint—not to mention the prince of Tyre? Who could imagine that any man could live in the midst of fiery stones? Who could be supposed to be stainless from the very day of his creation, wickedness only being discovered in him at a later time? No, this must be said of someone who was cast down to the earth? . . .

I have shown, then, that what I have quoted concerning the prince of Tyre from the prophet Ezekiel refers to an adverse power. And it clearly shows that this power was once holy and happy. Yet, he fell from this state of happiness from the time that evil was found in him. So he was hurled to the earth. Yet, [this evil] was not in him by nature or by creation. I am of the opinion that these words are spoken of a certain angel who had received the office of governing the nation of Tyre. *Origen (c. 225, E), 4.258, 259.*

He compares [Satan] to lightning and says that he fell from heaven. He shows by this that Satan had at one time been in heaven and had enjoyed a place among the saints. He had enjoyed a portion of that light in which all the saints participate, by which they are made angels of light. *Origen (c. 225, E), 4.259.*

In our view, not even the devil himself was incapable of good. *Origen (c. 225, E), 4.265.*

In the prophecies of Ezekiel, the prince of Tyre is shown unmistakenly to be a type of spiritual power. *Origen (c. 225, E), 4.335.*

What is said about the ruler of Tyre cannot be understood of a certain man who ruled over Tyre. *Origen (c. 225, E), 4.372.*

In respect that he is the devil, he is not the work of God. Yet, he who is the devil is a created being. Since there is no other Creator except our God, he is a work of God. *Origen (c. 228, E), 9.330.*

In the Book of Job, which is older even than Moses himself, the devil is distinctly described as presenting himself before God and asking for power against Job—so that he might involve him in trials of the most painful kind. *Origen (c. 248, E), 4.593.*

The Apostle Peter, in his epistle, forewarns and teaches, saying, "Be sober and watch. For your adversary the devil goes about as a roaring lion, seeking anyone to devour." He goes about each one of us. He is like an enemy besieging those who are shut up [in a city]. He examines the walls and tests to see if any part of the walls

are less firm and less trustworthy. For perhaps, he can make a breach and penetrate to the inside. He presents to the eyes seductive forms and easy pleasures, by the sight of which he might destroy chastity. He tempts the ears with harmonious music, so that by the hearing of sweet sounds, he may relax and weaken Christian vigor. . . . He promises earthly honors, so he can deprive us of heavenly ones. . . . And when he cannot deceive us secretly, he threatens plainly and openly—brandishing the fear of fierce persecution to conquer God's servants. He is always restless and always hostile. He is crafty in peace and fierce in persecution. *Cyprian (c. 250, W), 5.491.*

At the very beginning of the world, the devil was the first one to perish and to destroy. . . . When he saw man made in the image of God, he broke forth into jealous and malevolent envy. . . . How great an evil it was, beloved brethren, that caused an angel to fall! *Cyprian (c. 250, W), 5.492.*

God had foretold that this seed would proceed from the woman, and that he would trample on the head of the devil. *Cyprian (c. 250, W), 5.519.*

The devil has no power against man unless God has allowed it. In the Gospel according to John, it is written: "Jesus said, 'You could have no power against me unless it were given you from above.'" *Cyprian (c. 250, W), 5.553.*

There is a strong conflict to be waged against the devil. Therefore, we should stand bravely, so that we may be able to conquer. *Cyprian (c. 250, W), 5.556.*

"Behold a red dragon, having seven heads." Now, that he says that this dragon was of a red color, . . . it was the result of his works that give him such a color. For, from the beginning, he was a murderer. And he has oppressed the entire human race. . . . He seduced the third part of the angels who were subject to him, for he was still a ruler when he descended from his estate. . . . He approached Jesus to tempt Him as man. But when he found that Jesus was not what he thought Him to be, he departed from Him. *Victorinus (c. 280, W), 7.355.*

God made another being, in whom the disposition of the divine origin did not remain. Therefore, he was infected with his own envy, as with poison. So he passed from good to evil. Through his own will, which had been given to him by God unfettered, he acquired for himself a contrary name. From this, it appears that the source of all evils is envy. For he envied his predecessor [i.e., the Son], who through His steadfastness is acceptable and dear to God the Father. This person, who from good became evil by his own act, is called by the Greeks *diabolos* [i.e., slanderer]. We call him the Accuser, for he reports to God the faults to which he himself entices us. *Lactantius (c. 304–313, W), 7.52, 53.*

From the beginning, He had given the devil power over the earth. *Lactantius (c. 304–313, W), 7.64.*

Satan lays plots against everyone. . . . Those who know God, he attacks with wiles and craftiness, so he can ensnare them with desire and lust. . . . Or if that strategy does not work, he attempts to overthrow them by force and violence. *Lactantius (c. 304–313, W), 7.99.*

Certain of the angels, refusing to submit themselves to the commandment of God, resisted his will. And one of them indeed fell like a flash of lightning upon the earth. . . . And that angel who was cast down to earth, finding no further admittance into any of the regions of heaven, now flaunts about among men, deceiving them and luring them to become transgressors like himself. Even to this day, he is an adversary to the commandments of God. . . . For this reason, he has also obtained the name of "devil," because he has passed over from the heavenly places and appeared on earth as the disparager of God's commandment. *Disputation of Archelaus and Manes (c. 320, E), 6.205.*

The Serpent, envying the glory of the first man, made his way into Paradise . . . and began to . . . generate death for the men who had been fashioned by God and who had received the gift of life. The devil, however, was not able to manifest himself completely through the serpent. . . . On the one hand, through the serpent, he displayed his hypocrisies and lies to Eve. On the other hand, through Cain, he brought about the beginning of murder. *Disputation of Archelaus and Manes (c. 320, E), 6.206; extended discussion: 4.258–4.260.*

SEE ALSO ANGEL, ANGELS (III. WICKED ANGELS); DEMONS, DEMON POSSESSION; EVIL, PROBLEM OF; FALL OF MAN; LUCIFER.

SAUL

Saul is chosen, for he is not yet the despiser of the prophet Samuel. . . . In the case of Saul, the Creator had made no mistake in selecting him for the kingdom. He made no mistake in endowing him with His Holy Spirit. Rather, God made a statement concerning the [initial] goodness of Saul's character. God had most appropriately chosen Saul as being the most suitable man at that moment. For, as He says, there was not his equal among the children of Israel. Yet, God was not ignorant of how he would afterwards turn out. *Tertullian (c. 207, W), 3.315.*

SEE ALSO SAMUEL; SPIRITISM.

SCHISM

Where there are envy, strife, and divisions among you, are you not carnal and behaving like mere men? 1 Cor. 3:3.

Now the works of the flesh are evident, which are . . . contentions, jealousies, outbursts of wrath, selfish ambitions, dissensions, heresies. Gal. 5:19, 20.

Reject a divisive man after the first and second admonition, knowing that such a person is warped and sinning, being self-condemned. Tit. 3:10, 11.

You will not make a schism. Rather, you should make peace between those who contend, by bringing them together. *Barnabas (c. 70–130, E), 1.148.*

Under the inspiration of the Spirit, Paul wrote to you [Corinthians] concerning himself, Cephas, and Apollos. For even then parties had been formed among you. However, that inclination for one above another entailed less guilt upon you back then, inasmuch as your partialities were then shown towards apostles (already of high reputation) and towards a man whom they had approved. In contrast, now reflect on who those are that have perverted you and lessened the renown of your celebrated brotherly love. It is disgraceful, beloved, that such a thing should be heard of as that the most steadfast and ancient church of the Corinthians would engage in sedition against its presbyters on account of one or two persons. *Clement of Rome (c. 95, W), 1.18.*

If any man follows him who makes a schism in the church, he will not inherit the kingdom of God. *Ignatius (c. 105, E), 1.80.*

Heal and take way from you those wicked schisms, so that if the Lord of the flocks comes, He may rejoice concerning you. *Hermas (c. 150, W), 2.53.*

. . . acting like those who, on account of such as come in hypocrisy, hold themselves aloof from the communion of the brethren. *Irenaeus (c. 180, E/W), 1.429.*

It is incumbent to obey the presbyters who are in the church—those who, as I have shown, possess the succession from the apostles. These are those who, together with the succession of the episcopate, have received the certain gift of truth, according to the good pleasure of the Father. But it is incumbent to hold in suspicion others who depart from the primitive succession, and assemble themselves together in any place whatsoever, either as heretics of perverse minds, or as schismatics puffed up and self-pleasing, or again as hypocrites, acting in such a manner for the sake of money and vainglory. . . . But those who cut asunder and separate the unity of the church will receive from God the same punishment as Jeroboam did. *Irenaeus (c. 180, E/W), 1.497.*

He will also judge those who give rise to schisms, who are destitute of the love of God, and who look to their own special advantage rather than to the unity of the church. They, for trifling reasons, or any kind of reason which occurs to them, cut in pieces and divide the great and glorious body of Christ. . . . They are men who . . . do in truth strain out a gnat, but swallow a camel. For no reformation of so great importance can be effected by them, as will compensate for the mischief arising from their schism. *Irenaeus (c. 180, E/W), 1.508.*

The whole passage points to the maintenance of unity and the curtailing of division, inasmuch as heresies sever men from unity no less than schisms and dissensions. *Tertullian (c. 197, W), 3.245.*

The following quotation was written by Tertullian as a Montanist:

Repudiation of fellowship is never a certain indication of sin. After all, it would be easier to err with the majority. But it is in the company of the few that truth is loved! . . . I am not embarrassed about an error that I have ceased to hold, because I am delighted at having ceased to hold it. *Tertullian (c. 212, W), 4.75.*

[The pagan critic, Celsus, says that] "Christians were few in numbers at first, and they held the same opinions. But when they grew to be a great multitude, they were divided and separated, each wishing to have his own individual party." [ORIGEN'S REPLY:] . . . However, from the beginning, there were differences of opinion among believers regarding the meaning of the books held to be divine. At all events, while the apostles were still preaching, . . . there was no small discussion among the converts from Judaism regarding Gentile believers. The issue was whether they should observe Jewish customs. . . . In fact, even in the Epistles of Paul, . . . certain matters are mentioned as having been the subject of dispute, such as respecting the resurrection (whether it was already past) and the day of the Lord (whether it was at hand or not). . . . This is enough to show that from the very beginning . . . there were certain doctrines interpreted in different ways. *Origen (c. 248, E), 4.468, 469.*

Factions have never originated from any matter in which the principle involved was not important and beneficial to human life. For example, the science of medicine is useful and necessary to the human race, . . . and there are admittedly found, for this reason, numerous schools of thought prevailing in the science of medicine. . . . Therefore, seeing that Christianity appeared to be an object of veneration to men, . . . there necessarily originated differing factions. However, these did not all come about as the result of dissension and strife. Rather, some came about because of the earnest desire of many educated men to become acquainted with the doctrines of Christianity. The consequence of this was that . . . there arose sects. These sects received their names from those individuals who admired, indeed, the origin of Christianity, but who were led . . . by certain plausible reasons to discordant views. Still, no one would rationally avoid medicine because of its factions. *Origen (c. 248, E), 4.469.*

Whoever will ally himself with this man's conspiracy and faction, let him know that he will not communicate in the church with us, since he has preferred to be separated from the church of his own accord. *Cyprian (c. 250, W), 5.316.*

I find that you there had consented to the making of another bishop. This was contrary to ecclesiastical order, evangelical law, and the unity of the catholic institution. It was neither right nor allowable to be done. It means that another church has now been set up and that Christ's members are to be torn asunder. The one mind and body of the Lord's flock will be lacerated by a divided rivalry! *Cyprian (c. 250, W), 5.321.*

Because we see that there are tares in the church, we ourselves should not withdraw from the church. Rather, we should only labor that we may be wheat. *Cyprian (c. 250, W), 5.327.*

He may pass over to the heretics and schismatics. If so, although he might afterwards be put to death on account of the Name, still, he could not in his death be crowned. For he is placed outside the church; he is divided from unity and from charity. *Cyprian (c. 250, W), 5.331.*

Whoever he may be, and whatever he may be, he who is not in the church of Christ is not a Christian. . . . He who has not maintained brotherly love or ecclesiastical unity has lost even what he previously had been. *Cyprian (c. 250, W), 5.333.*

What kind of people do you think they are who are the enemies of the priests and are rebels against the catholic church? They are frightened neither by the threatening of a forewarning Lord, nor by the vengeance of a coming judgment. Heresies have arisen and schisms have originated from no other source than this: that God's priest is not obeyed. *Cyprian (c. 250, W), 5.340.*

Those who departed from Christ perished by their own fault. Yet, the church that believes on Christ, and holds that which it has once learned, never departs from Him at all. They are the church who remain in the house of God. On the other hand, they are not the plantation planted by God the Father whom we see blown about like chaff, rather than being established with the stability of wheat. *Cyprian (c. 250, W), 5.341.*

A people who are obedient to the Lord's commandments and who fear God should separate themselves from a sinful prelate. They should not associate themselves with the sacrifices of a sacrilegious priest. This is especially so since they themselves have the power of either choosing worthy priests or of rejecting unworthy ones. *Cyprian (c. 250, W), 5.370.*

How inseparable is the sacrament of unity. And how hopeless are they—and what exces-sive ruin they earn for themselves from the indignation of God—who make a schism and, forsaking their bishop, appoint another false bishop for themselves from outside. *Cyprian (c. 250, W), 5.399.*

The episcopate is one, each part of which is held by each one for the whole. The church also is one, which is spread abroad far and wide. . . . There are many rays of the sun, but only one light. There are many branches of a tree, but one strength based in its tenacious root. . . . If you separate a ray of the sun from its body of light, its unity will not allow a division of light. Break a branch from a tree, and when broken it will not be able to bud. Cut off the stream from its fountain and the portion that is cut off dries up. *Cyprian (c. 250, W), 5.423.*

A person can no longer have God for his Father, who does not have the church for his mother. If anyone could escape who was outside the ark of Noah, then he also may escape who will be outside of the church. *Cyprian (c. 250, W), 5.423.*

A person cannot possess the garment of Christ if he parts and divides the church of Christ. *Cyprian (c. 250, W), 5.423.*

These are those who of their own accord, without any divine arrangement, set themselves to preside among the presumptuous strangers assembled. They appoint themselves prelates without any law of ordination. They assume to themselves the name of bishop, although no one gives them the episcopate. *Cyprian (c. 250, W), 5.424.*

Even if such men were slain in confession of the Name, that stain is not even washed away by blood. The inexpiable and grave sin of dissension is not even purged by suffering. A person cannot be a martyr if he is not in the church. *Cyprian (c. 250, W), 5.425.*

What unity does he keep? What love does he maintain or consider—who, savage with the madness of dissension, divides the church? *Cyprian (c. 250, W), 5.426.*

The quarrelsome and disunited man, and he who does not have peace with his brethren, . . . even if he has been slain for the name of Christ, will not be able to escape the crime of brotherly dissension. For it is written, "He who hates his brother is a murderer." And no murderer attains to the kingdom of heaven. *Cyprian (c. 250, W), 5.454.*

How greatly he sins who divides unity and peace. . . . Christ knew that dissension cannot come into the kingdom of God. *Cyprian (c. 250, W), 5.455.*

A schism must not be made—even though he who withdraws [from the church] remains in one faith and in the same tradition. . . . In the 132nd Psalm, it says: "Behold how good and how pleasant a thing it is that brethren should dwell in unity." Also in the Gospel according to Matthew: "He that is not with me is against me. And he that does not gather with me, scatters." *Cyprian (c. 250, W), 5.553.*

The apostle condemns, along with all the wicked, those also who cause division—that is, schismatics and heretics. *Seventh Council of Carthage (c. 256, W), 5.566.*

It would have been but dutiful to have suffered any kind of ill, so as to avoid rending the church of God. A martyrdom endured for the sake of preventing a division of the church would have been just as glorious as one endured for refusing to worship idols. *Dionysius of Alexandria (c. 262, E), 6.97.*

Those whose faith was unsettled, when they pretended that they knew and worshipped God, . . . aspired to the highest priestly power. And when overcome by others more powerful, they preferred to secede with their supporters than to endure those who were set up over them. *Lactantius (c. 304–313, W), 7.133.*

God inflicted punishment immediately on those who made a schism. *Apostolic Constitutions (compiled c. 390, E), 7.451.*

If any presbyter despises his own bishop and assembles separately and prepares another altar, when he has nothing to condemn in his bishop either as to piety or righteousness, let him be deprived as an ambitious person. *Apostolic Constitutions (compiled c. 390, E), 7.502; see also 5.321; extended discussion: 5.421–5.429, 7.450–7.453.*

SEE ALSO CHURCH, THE; HERESIES, HERETICS; NOVATIAN, NOVATIANISTS; ORDINATION.

SCHOOLS

SEE EDUCATION.

SCRIPTURES

I. The need to study the Scriptures

II. Antiquity and authority of the Scriptures

III. Inspiration of the Scriptures

IV. Humble diction and candor of the Scriptures

V. Scripture difficulties

VI. Defending the Scriptures

VII. Miscellaneous thoughts on Scripture

I. The need to study the Scriptures

These words which I command you today shall be in your heart; you shall teach them diligently to your children, and shall talk of them when you sit in your house, when you walk by the way, when you lie down, and when you rise up. Deut. 6:6, 7.

From childhood you have known the Holy Scriptures, which are able to make you wise for salvation. 2 Tim. 3:15.

Beloved, you understand the sacred Scriptures. In fact, you understand them well. You have looked very earnestly into the prophecies of God. *Clement of Rome (c. 96, W), 1.19.*

I trust that you are well versed in the sacred Scriptures. *Polycarp (c. 135, E), 1.35.*

We are . . . very earnest in desiring to converse according to the Scriptures. *Justin Martyr (c. 160, E), 1.240.*

Renouncing the error of your fathers, you should read the prophecies of the sacred writers. . . . Learn from them what will give you everlasting life. *Justin Martyr (c. 160, E), 1.288.*

Give reverential attention to the prophetic Scriptures, and they will make your way plainer for escaping the eternal punishments and for obtaining the eternal prizes of God. *Theophilus (c. 180, E), 2.93.*

A sound mind . . . that is devoted to piety and love of truth will eagerly meditate upon those things that God has placed within the power of mankind and has subjected to our knowledge. . . . Such a mind will advance in the knowledge of those things . . . by means of daily study. I am referring to those things that fall under our observation and are clearly and unambiguously set forth in the sacred Scriptures in clear terms. *Irenaeus (c. 180, E/W), 1.398.*

The sacrifices of the spiritual man are prayers, praises, and readings in the Scriptures before meals. *Clement of Alexandria (c. 195, E), 2.537.*

Let the faithful Christian . . . devote himself to the sacred Scriptures. There he will find worthy exhibitions for his faith. *Novatian (c. 235, W), 5.578, formerly attributed to Cyprian.*

More strength will be given you, and the knowledge of the heart will be increased more and more, as you examine more fully the Scriptures, old and new, and read through the complete volumes of the spiritual books. *Cyprian (c. 250, W), 5.507.*

Let no day pass by without reading some portion of the sacred Scriptures—at such convenient hour as offers. And give some time to meditation. Never cast off the habit of reading in the Holy Scriptures. For nothing feeds the soul and enriches the mind as much as those sacred studies do. *Theonas of Alexandria (c. 300, E), 6.161.*

When you stay at home, read the books of the Law, the Kings, and the Prophets. Sing the hymns of David and diligently study the Gospel, which is the completion of the other works. *Apostolic Constitutions (compiled c. 390, E), 7.393.*

II. Antiquity and authority of the Scriptures

It is written, "Man shall not live by bread alone, but by every word that proceeds from the mouth of God." Matt. 4:4.

For this reason we also thank God without ceasing, because when you received the word of God which you heard from us, you welcomed it not as the word of men, but as it is in truth, the word of God. 1 Thess. 2:13.

All Scripture is given by inspiration of God, and is profitable for doctrine, for reproof, for correction, for instruction in righteousness. 2 Tim. 3:16.

I heard some persons saying, "If I do not find it in the ancient Scriptures [i.e., Old Testament], I will not believe the gospel." So I replied, "It is written." They answered me, "That remains to be proved." However, to me, Jesus Christ is in the place of all that is ancient. *Ignatius (c. 105, E), 1.84.*

From these very old records, it is proved that the writings of the rest [i.e., the Greeks and other pagans] are more recent than the writings given to us through Moses. They are even more recent than the later prophets. *Theophilus (c. 180, E), 2.118.*

We have learned the plan of our salvation from no one else other than from those through whom the gospel has come down to us. For they did at one time proclaim the gospel in public. And, at a later period, by the will of God, they handed the gospel down to us in the Scriptures—to be "the ground and pillar of our faith." *Irenaeus (c. 180, E/W), 1.414.*

When, however, the Gnostics are confuted from the Scriptures, they turn round and accuse these same Scriptures as if they were not correct, nor of authority. They say that they are ambiguous, and that the truth cannot be extracted from them by those who are ignorant of tradition. . . . But, again, when we refer them to that tradition which originates from the apostles, . . . they object to tradition. *Irenaeus (c. 180, E/W), 1.415.*

Since, therefore, the tradition from the apostles does thus exist in the church, and is permanent among us, let us revert to the Scriptural proof furnished by those apostles who did also write the gospel. *Irenaeus (c. 180, E/W), 1.417.*

In this manner, I have shown it to be, if anyone reads the Scriptures. For it was in that manner that the Lord discoursed with the disciples after His resurrection from the dead, proving to them from the Scriptures themselves. *Irenaeus (c. 180, E/W), 1.497.*

There will be no light punishment upon him who either adds or subtracts anything from Scripture. *Irenaeus (c. 180, E/W), 1.559.*

Faith will lead you. Experience will teach you. Scripture will train you. *Clement of Alexandria (c. 195, E), 2.196.*

I have demonstrated that the Scriptures which we believe are valid from their omnipotent authority. *Clement of Alexandria (c. 195, E), 2.409.*

Those who are ready to toil in the most excellent pursuits will not desist from the search after truth until they get the demonstration from the Scriptures themselves. *Clement of Alexandria (c. 195, E), 2.550.*

We have the Lord as the source of teaching—both by the Prophets, the Gospel, and the blessed apostles. . . . He, then, who of himself believes the Scripture and the voice of the Lord (which by the Lord acts to the benefit of men) is rightly [regarded] as being faithful. Certainly we use it as a criterion in the discovery of things. *Clement of Alexandria (c. 195, E), 2.551.*

The heretics go the length of impiety by disbelieving the Scriptures! *Clement of Alexandria (c. 195, E), 2.552.*

In fact, the heretics stitch together a multitude of lies and figments so that they might appear to be acting in accordance with reason in their not accepting the Scriptures. *Clement of Alexandria (c. 195, E), 2.552.*

Having grown old in the Scriptures and maintaining apostolic and ecclesiastic orthodoxy in doctrines, the spiritual man lives most correctly in accordance with the Gospel. *Clement of Alexandria (c. 195, E), 2.554.*

To those who thus ask questions, in the Scriptures there is given from God . . . the gift of the God-given knowledge. *Clement of Alexandria (c. 195, E), 2.558.*

In order that we might acquire an ampler and more authoritative knowledge of Himself, His counsels, and His will, God has added a written revelation for the benefit of everyone whose heart is set on seeking Him. *Tertullian (c. 197, W), 3.32.*

We bring under your notice something of even greater importance: we point to the majesty of our Scriptures, if not to their antiquity. If you doubt that they are as ancient as we say, we offer proof that they are divine. . . . For all that is taking place around you was foretold. All that you now see with your eye was previously heard by the ear: The swallowing up of cities by the earth; the theft of islands by the sea; wars, bringing external and internal convulsions; the collision of kingdoms with kingdoms; famines and pestilences. . . . It was all foreseen and predicted before it came to pass. While we suffer the calamities, we read of them in the Scriptures. They are written in the same books, for the same Spirit inspires them. *Tertullian (c. 197, W), 3.33.*

Examine our sacred books, which we do not keep in hiding, and which many accidents put into the hands of those who are not of us. Learn from them that a large benevolence is enjoined upon us. *Tertullian (c. 197, W), 3.42.*

The Scriptures of God, whether belonging to Christians or to Jews (into whose olive tree we have been grafted) are much more ancient than any secular literature. *Tertullian (c. 197, W), 3.178.*

Now, what is there in our Scriptures that is contrary to us? What of our own have we introduced? Is there anything that we need to take away again, or else add to it, or alter it—in order to restore to its natural soundness anything that is contrary to it and contained in the Scriptures? What we are ourselves, that also is what the Scriptures are, and have been from the beginning. *Tertullian (c. 197, W), 2.261.*

If it is nowhere written, then let him fear the woe that comes on all who add to or take away anything [from the written Word]. *Tertullian (c. 200, W), 3.490.*

However, the statements of Holy Scripture will never be discordant with truth. *Tertullian (c. 210, W), 3.202.*

It will be your duty, however, to present your proofs out of the Scriptures, as plainly as we do. *Tertullian (c. 213, W), 3.605.*

Brethren, there is one God, the knowledge of whom we gain from the Holy Scriptures and from no other source. . . . Even as He has chosen to teach them by the Holy Scriptures, so let us discern them. *Hippolytus (c. 205, W), 5.227.*

Perhaps what [the heretics] allege might be credible, if—in the first place—the Holy Scriptures did not contradict them. *Eusebius, quoting Caius (c. 215, W), 5.601.*

The heretics have boldly falsified the sacred Scriptures, rejected the canons of the ancient faith, and ignored Christ. *Eusebius, quoting Caius (c. 215, W), 5.602.*

We . . . believe that it is possible in no other way to explain and bring within the reach of human knowledge this higher and diviner Logos as the Son of God, than by means of those Scriptures, which alone were inspired by the Holy Spirit: the Gospels and Epistles, and the Law and the Prophets, according to the declaration of Christ Himself. *Origen (c. 225, E), 4.252.*

I do not want to appear to build my assertions on the basis of inference alone, particularly concerning subjects of such importance and difficulty. Nor do I wish for my listeners to agree to what is only conjectural. So let us see if we can obtain any declarations from Holy Scripture. For by its authority, these positions can be more credibly maintained. *Origen (c. 225, E), 4.258.*

If, indeed, there is anyone who can discover something better—and who can establish his assertions by clearer proofs from Holy Scriptures—let his opinion be received in preference to mine. *Origen (c. 225, E), 4.284.*

Every divine Scripture is gospel. *Origen (c. 228, E), 9.305.*

One . . . should take his stand against historical fictions and oppose them with the true and lofty evangelical message in which the agreement of the doctrines found in both the so-called Old Testament and in the so-called New appears so clearly and completely. *Origen (c. 228, E), 9.348.*

Let him listen to our sacred writings themselves, and, as far as possible, form an opinion as to the purpose of the writers from their contents, and from their consciences and disposition of mind. For he will discover that they were men who strenuously contend for what they upheld. Some of them show that the history that they narrate is one that they have both seen and experienced—and which was miraculous and worthy of being recorded for the advantage of their future hearers. *Origen (c. 248, E), 4.521, 522.*

With respect to certain matters, the same teachings can be found among the Greeks as in our own Scriptures. However, they do not possess the same power of attracting and disposing the souls of men to follow them. *Origen (c. 248, E), 4.574.*

Moses . . . is much older than the Greek literature. *Origen (c. 248, E), 4.622.*

It is no objection to the principles of Jews or Christians that the same things were also said by the Greeks. Especially, if it is proved that the writings of the Jews are older than those of the Greeks. *Origen (c. 248, E), 4.634.*

I will, as is needed, collect into one collection whatever passages of the Holy Scriptures are pertinent to this subject. And I will manifestly harmonize, as far as possible, those which seem to be differing or of various meanings. *Treatise on Re-Baptism (c. 257, W), 5.668.*

In all sincerity and with open hearts before God, we accepted all that could be established by the demonstrations and teachings of the Holy Scriptures. *Dionysius of Alexandria (c. 262, E), 6.82.*

There is no contradiction nor absurdity in Holy Scripture. *Methodius (c. 290, E), 6.366.*

We, whom the Holy Scriptures instruct to the knowledge of the truth, know the beginning and the end of the world. *Lactantius (c. 304–313, W), 7.211.*

III. Inspiration of the Scriptures

Men and brethren, this Scripture had to be fulfilled, which the Holy Spirit spoke before by the mouth of David. Acts 1:16.

God has spoken by the mouth of all His holy prophets since the world began. Acts 3:21.

All Scripture is given by inspiration of God. 2 Tim. 3:16.

No prophecy of Scripture is of any private interpretation, for prophecy never came by the will of man, but holy men of God spoke as they were moved by the Holy Spirit. 2 Pet. 1:20

Look carefully into the Scriptures, which are the true utterances of the Holy Spirit. *Clement of Rome (c. 96, W), 1.17.*

Take up the epistle of the blessed apostle Paul. What did he write to you at the time when the Gospel first began to be preached? Truly, he wrote to you under the inspiration of the Spirit. *Clement of Rome (c. 96, W), 1.18.*

These were spoken from the person of the Father, through Isaiah the prophet. *Justin Martyr (c. 160, E), 1.175.*

It is impossible to learn anything true about religion from your [pagan] teachers. For, by their mutual disagreement, they have furnished you with sufficient proof of their own ignorance. Therefore, I think it is reasonable to return to our forefathers. For they have precedence over your teachers in a great way. First, they precede them in time. Second, they have taught us nothing from their own private opinions. They have not differed with one another, nor have they attempted to overturn each other's position. Rather, without any wrangling or contention, they received from God the knowledge that they also taught to us. For neither by nature nor by human conception is it possible for men to know things that are so great and divine. It is possible only by the gift that descended from above upon the holy men. These men had no need of the rhetorical arts, nor of uttering anything in a contentious or quarrelsome manner. Rather, they presented themselves in a pure manner to the energy of the Divine Spirit, so that the divine plectrum itself could descend from heaven and use these righteous men as an instrument like a harp or lyre. Thereby, the Divine Spirit could reveal to us the knowledge of things divine and heavenly. Accordingly, they have taught us in succession as though with one mouth and one tongue. They have taught us in harmony with each other concerning God, the creation of the world, the formation of man, the immortality of the human soul, and the judgment that is to be after this life. *Justin Martyr (c. 160, E), 1.276.*

We have the prophets as witnesses of the things we comprehend and believe. These were men who declared things about God and the things of God. They were guided by the Spirit of God. . . . It would be irrational for us to disbelieve the Spirit from God and to give heed to mere human opinions. For He moved the mouths of the prophets like musical instruments. *Athenagoras (c. 175, E), 2.132.*

Prophets were lifted in ecstasy above the natural operations of their minds by the impulses of the Divine Spirit, and they spoke the things with which they were inspired. The Spirit operated through them just as a flute player breathes into a flute. *Athenagoras (c. 175, E), 2.133.*

Through the Holy Spirit, Moses, the servant of God, recorded the very beginning of the creation of the world. *Theophilus (c. 180, E), 2.118.*

I could produce ten thousand Scriptures of which not "one tittle will pass away" without being fulfilled. For the mouth of the Lord, the Holy Spirit, has spoken these things. *Clement of Alexandria (c. 195, E), 2.195.*

Truly holy are those letters that sanctify and deify. For that reason, the same apostle calls the writings or volumes that consist of those holy letters and syllables as being "inspired of God, and profitable for doctrine, for reproof, for correction." . . . No one will be as impressed by the exhortations of any of the saints as he is by the words of the Lord himself, the lover of man. *Clement of Alexandria (c. 195, E), 2.196.*

He, then, who believes the divine Scriptures with sure judgment, receives in them the voice of God, who bestowed the Scriptures. *Clement of Alexandria (c. 195, E), 2.349.*

Let him know that it was God Himself who promulgated the Scriptures by His Son. *Clement of Alexandria (c. 195, E), 2.464.*

The apostle has used the same word in writing. For he was guided, of course, by the same Spirit by whom the book of Genesis was drawn up—as were all the divine Scriptures. *Tertullian (c. 198, W), 3.687.*

Moses thus gives plain proof of the divine character of his work, from its divine authority and word. *Tertullian (c. 210, W), 3.209.*

Although Paul did not have a specific commandment of the Lord [to cite], he was accustomed to give counsel and to dictate matters from his own authority, for he possessed the Spirit of God, who guides into all truth. For that reason, his advice has, by the authority of the Divine Word, become equivalent to nothing less than a divine command. *Tertullian (c. 211, W), 3.95.*

Although different matters are taught us in the various books of the Gospels, there is no difference as regards the faith of believers. For in all of them, all things are related under one imperial Spirit. *Muratorian Fragment (c. 200, W), 5.603.*

These fathers were furnished with the Spirit, and they were largely honored by the Word Himself. They were similar to instruments of music. For they had the Word always in union with them, like a plectrum [the small implement by which a lyre was plucked]. When moved by Him, the prophets spoke what God willed. For they did not speak of their own power. Let there be no mistake about that. Nor did they speak the things that pleased themselves. *Hippolytus (c. 200, W), 5.204.*

For this reason, [the heretics] have boldly laid their hands upon the divine Scriptures, alleging that they have corrected them. . . . And as to the great audacity implied in this offense, it is not likely that even they themselves can be ignorant. For either they do not believe that the divine Scriptures were dictated by the Holy Spirit (and are thus infidels), or else they think that they themselves are wiser than the Holy Spirit (which makes them demoniacs). *Eusebius, quoting Caius (c. 215, W), 5.602.*

This work [the *Teaching of Peter*] is not included among ecclesiastical books. For we can show that it was composed neither by Peter nor by any other person inspired by the Spirit of God. *Origen (c. 225, E), 4.241.*

A man receives the energy—i.e., the work—of a good spirit when he is stirred and incited to good and is inspired to heavenly or divine things. For example, the holy angels and God Himself worked in the prophets, arousing them to a better way of life and exhorting them by their holy suggestions. Yet, [this was done in a way] that it remained within the will and judgment of the individual to be either willing or unwilling to follow the call to divine and heavenly things. *Origen (c. 225, E), 4.336.*

In addition, for the proof of our statements, we take testimonies from that which is called the Old Testament and that which is called the New—which we believe to be divine writings. *Origen (c. 225, E), 4.349.*

While we thus briefly demonstrate the deity of Christ and make use of the prophetic declarations regarding Him, we demonstrate at the same time that the writings that prophesied of Him were divinely inspired. *Origen (c. 225, E), 4.353.*

Before the advent of Christ, it was not entirely possible to present clear proofs of the divine inspiration of the ancient Scripture. However, His coming led those who might think the Law and the Prophets were not divine to the clear conviction that they were composed by heavenly grace. And he who reads the words of the prophets with care and attention . . . will be led by his own emotions to believe that those words that have been deemed to be the words of God are not the compositions of men. *Origen (c. 225, E), 4.353, 354.*

The men who are wise in Christ have profited by those epistles that are current. They recognize them to be vouched for by the testimonies deposited in the Law and the Prophets. So it is the conviction of these men that the apostolic writings are to be pronounced wise and worthy of belief and that they have great authority. However, they are not on the same level with that "thus says the Lord Almighty." For example, consider the language of Paul. When he declares that "All Scripture is inspired of God and profitable," does he include his own writings? Or does he not include his remark, "*I say, and not the Lord.*" . . . And he writes similar things by virtue of his own authority—which do not quite possess the character of words flowing from divine inspiration. . . . The Savior says, "Call no man Teacher upon the earth." However, the apostle says that teachers have been appointed in the church. Accordingly, these latter persons will not be "teachers" in the strict sense of the language of the Gospel. In the same way, the gospel in the Epistles will not extend to every word of them—not when they are compared with the narrative of Jesus' actions and sufferings and discourses. *Origen (c. 228, E), 9.299.*

The object of Christianity is that we should become wise. This can be proved—not only from the ancient Jewish writings, which *we* also use—but particularly from those writings that were composed after the time of Jesus. The churches believe these writings to be divine. *Origen (c. 248, E), 4.482.*

The Holy Spirit also is not silent in the Psalms on the sacrament of this thing, when He makes mention of the Lord's cup. Cyprian (c. 250, W), 5.361.

IV. Humble diction and candor of the Scriptures

Now when they saw the boldness of Peter and John, and perceived that they were uneducated and untrained men, they marveled. Acts 4:13.

Not with wisdom of words, lest the cross of Christ should be made of no effect. 1 Cor. 1:17.

God has chosen the foolish things of the world to put to shame the wise. 1 Cor. 1:27.

We have this treasure in earthen vessels, that the excellence of the power may be of God and not of us. 2 Cor. 4:7.

Renouncing the error of your fathers, you should read the prophecies of the sacred writers, not expecting to find in them polished diction. *Justin Martyr (c. 160, E), 1.288.*

I was led to put faith in the Scriptures by the unpretentious nature of the language, the candid character of the writers, and the foreknowledge displayed of future events. *Tatian (c. 160, E), 2.77.*

The divinity of Scripture—which extends to all of it—is not [lost] because of the inability of our weakness to discover in every expression the hidden splendor of the doctrines veiled in common and unattractive phraseology. For we have the "treasure in earthen vessels" so that the excellency of the power of God may shine forth. For if the usual methods of demonstration used by men . . . had been successful in convincing us, then our faith would rightly have been thought to rest on the wisdom of men—not on the power of God. However, now it is evident to everyone who lifts up his eyes that the word and preaching have not prevailed among the multitude "by persuasive words of wisdom, but by demonstration of the Spirit and of power." *Origen (c. 225, E), 4.354, 355.*

[The Gospel of John] has been committed to the earthly treasure house of common speech—a writing that anybody can read. And, when it is read aloud, it can be understood by anyone. *Origen (c. 228, E), 9.300.*

By "earthen vessels," we understand the humble diction of the Scriptures, which the Greeks are so ready to despise, but in which the excellency of God's power appears so clearly. *Origen (c. 228, E), 9.345.*

Now, if the apostles had not been lovers of truth, but had been fabricators of fables (as Celsus supposes), they would not have represented Peter as denying [Christ]. Nor would they have portrayed His disciples as stumbling over Him. For although those events actually happened, who would have been able to prove it later? *Origen (c. 248, E), 4.437.*

If anyone gives himself to the attentive study of [Paul's words], I am well assured that he will be amazed at the understanding of the man who can clothe great ideas in common language. *Origen (c. 248, E), 4.471.*

Celsus should have recognized the love of truth displayed by the writers of sacred Scripture, who have not concealed even what is to their discredit. He should have thereby been led to accept the other and more marvelous accounts as true. *Origen (c. 248, E), 4.518.*

It should be the object of the ambassadors of the truth to confer benefits upon the greatest possible number . . . everyone, without exception—intelligent as well as simple—not only Greeks, but also barbarians. . . . Therefore, it is apparent that they must adopt a style of address fitted to do good to all—that is, one to gain over to them men of every kind. On the other hand, they [pagan philosophers and writers] turn away from ignorant persons as being mere slaves who are unable to understand the flowing intervals of a polished and logical discourse. Therefore, the philosophers devote their attention solely to those who have been brought up among literary pursuits. So they confine their views of "the public good" within very strait and narrow limits. *Origen (c. 248, E), 4.573.*

Our prophets, the apostles, and Jesus Himself, were careful to adopt a style of speech that would not only convey the truth, but that would be suitable to gain over the multitude. . . . For, if I may venture to say so, few have benefited from the beautiful and polished style of Plato and others who have written like him. . . . It is easy, indeed, to observe that Plato is found only in the hands of those who profess to be literary men. *Origen (c. 248, E), 4.573.*

Notice the difference between the polished diction of Plato concerning the "chief good," and the declarations of our prophets concerning the "light" of the blessed. Notice also that what truth is contained in Plato on this subject did not help his readers in any way to attain to a pure worship of God. It did not even help Plato himself, who could philosophize so majestically about the "chief good." In contrast, the simple language of the Holy Scriptures has led the honest readers of these Scriptures to be filled with a divine spirit. *Origen (c. 248, E), 4.575.*

We are not to imagine that a truth adorned with the graces of Grecian speech is necessarily better than the same when expressed in the more humble and unpretentious language used by Jews and Christians. *Origen (c. 248, E), 4.634.*

See, then, if Plato and the wise men among the Greeks, in the beautiful things they say, are not like those physicians who confine their attentions to what are called the "better classes of society," and despise the multitudes. In contrast, the prophets among the Jews and the disciples of Jesus scorn mere elegances of style and what is called in Scripture "the wisdom according to the flesh." . . . They resemble those who investigate to provide the most wholesome food for the largest number of persons. For this purpose, they adapt their language and style to the capacities of the common people. *Origen (c. 248, E), 4.635.*

When learned men have studied the religion of God, they do not believe—unless they have been instructed by some skillful teacher. For, being accustomed to sweet and polished speeches or poems, they disdain the simple and common language of the sacred writings as being menial. . . . With the greatest foresight, He wished those things that are divine to be without adornment, that everyone might understand the things that He Himself spoke to all. *Lactantius (c. 304–313, W), 7.188.*

[You say] they were written by unlearned and ignorant men and that, therefore, they should not be readily believed. But is this not rather a stronger reason to believe? For they have not been adulterated by any false statements. Rather, they were produced by men of simple mind, who did not know how to make their accounts deceitful with flashy language. For truth never seeks deceitful polish. *Arnobius (c. 305, E), 6.429.*

You accuse our writings of having disgraceful blemishes. However, do not your most perfect and wonderful books contain these grammatical errors as well? *Arnobius (c. 305, E), 6.430.*

V. Scripture Difficulties

The first quotation below addresses the seeming contradiction between John and the writers of the Synoptic Gospels concerning the day of Jesus' death. John's account of the trial and crucifixion of Jesus seems to indicate that Jesus died on the afternoon before the Passover meal (John 18:28; 19:14). The Synoptic writers, however, seem to say that Jesus was crucified on the afternoon after the Passover meal had been eaten (Matt. 26:17–20; Mark 14:12; Luke 22:7, 8).

In the previous years, Jesus had eaten the Passover sacrificed by the Jews, keeping the feast. However, He was the true Passover, the Lamb of God, who was led as a sheep to the slaughter. Therefore, when He had accomplished His preaching mission, He then taught His disciples the mystery of [what the Passover prefigured], on the thirteenth day. It was on that day that the apostles asked, "Where do you wish us to prepare for you to eat the Passover?" So it was on that day [i.e., Nisan 13] that both the consecration of the unleavened bread and the preparation for the feast took place. . . . And on the following day, our Savior suffered. . . . On the fourteenth day, on which He also suffered, in the morning, the chief priests and the

scribes, who brought Him to Pilate, did not enter the Praetorium. This was so that they would not be defiled and could freely eat the Passover that evening. *Clement of Alexandria (c. 195, E), 2.581.*

Never mind if there does occur some variation in the order of their [Gospel] narratives. What matters is that there is agreement in the essential doctrine of the faith. *Tertullian (c. 207, W), 3.347.*

A person becomes a third type of peacemaker when he demonstrates that the things that appear to others to be a conflict in the Scriptures are actually no conflict at all. He demonstrates their harmony and peace—whether of the Old Scriptures with the New, or of the Law with the Prophets, or of the Gospels with the apostolic Scriptures, or of the apostolic Scriptures with each other. . . . For he knows that all Scripture is the one perfect and harmonized instrument of God, from which different sounds give forth one saving voice to those who are willing to learn. *Origen (c. 245, E), 9.413.*

Celsus finds fault with our Lord's genealogy. In truth, there are certain points that cause some difficulty even to Christians. Some persons present arguments against their correctness, because of the discrepancy between the genealogies. *Origen (c. 248, E), 4.444; extended discussion: 9.382–9.391.*

VI. Defending the Scriptures

It would be tedious to enumerate now the most ancient prophecies concerning every future event so that the skeptic—being impressed by their divinity—may lay aside all hesitation and distraction and devote himself with his whole soul to the words of God. *Origen (c. 225, E), 4.354.*

[Celsus, a pagan critic] gives credence to the histories of barbarians and Greeks concerning the antiquity of those nations of whom he speaks. Yet, he stamps the histories of this nation alone [Israel] as false. . . . Notice, then, the arbitrary procedure of this individual. He believes the histories of certain nations on the grounds that those nations are "learned." And he condemns others as being wholly "ignorant." . . . It seems, then, that Celsus makes these statements, not from a love of truth, but from a spirit of hatred. His object is to disparage the origin of Christianity, which is connected with Judaism. . . . The Egyptians, then, when they boastfully give their own account of the divinity of animals, are to be considered "wise." However, if any Jew ... credits everything to the Creator of the universe and the only God, he is deemed "inferior" in the opinion of Celsus and those like him. *Origen (c. 248, E), 4.402, 404.*

Observe in what a spirit of hatred and falsehood Celsus collects together the statements of the sacred history. Wherever it appeared to him to contain a ground of accusation, he produces the passage. However, wherever there is any exhibition of virtue worthy of mention, he does not even mention the circumstance! For example, there is the account of Joseph not gratifying the lust of his mistress, refusing alike her allurements and her threats. *Origen (c. 248, E), 4.518.519.*

VII. Miscellaneous thoughts on Scripture

He says, "Your *faith* has saved you"—not your skill in the Scriptures. *Tertullian (c. 197, W), 3.250.*

[The church] unites the Law and the Prophets in one volume with the writings of evangelists and apostles, from which she drinks in her faith. *Tertullian (c. 197, W), 3.260.*

Solomon says in Ecclesiastes, "My son, beware of making many books. There is no end to it, and much study is a weariness of the flesh." ... Sacred history seems to agree with the text in question, inasmuch as none of the saints composed numerous works, or set forth his views in a number of books. *Origen (c. 228, E), 9.346; see also 2.119, 2.511.*

SEE ALSO CANON, NEW TESTAMENT; CANON, OLD TESTAMENT; GOSPELS; HERESIES, HERETICS; HERMENEUTICS; NEW TESTAMENT; OLD TESTAMENT; PENTATEUCH; TEXTUAL CRITICISM.

SCRIPTURES, INTERPRETATION OF

SEE HERMENEUTICS.

SECOND COMING OF CHRIST

When the Son of Man comes in His glory, and all the holy angels with Him, then he will sit on the throne of His glory. Matt. 25:31.

For the Lord himself will descend from heaven with a shout, with the voice of an archangel, and with the trumpet of God. And the dead in Christ will rise first. 1 Thess. 4:16.

Behold, He is coming with clouds, and every eye will see him, and they also who pierced Him. And all the tribes of the earth will mourn because of Him. Rev. 1:7.

But be ready, for you do not know the hour in which our Lord comes. *Didache (c. 80–140, E), 7.382.*

He speaks of the day of His appearing, when He will come and redeem us, each one according to his works. *Second Clement (c. 150), 7.522.*

Believing on Him, we may be saved in His second glorious advent. *Justin Martyr (c. 160, E), 1.212.*

Two advents of Christ have been announced. In the first one, He is set forth as suffering, inglorious, dishonored, and crucified. However, in the other advent, He will come from heaven with glory, when the man of apostasy ... speaks strange things. *Justin Martyr (c. 160, E), 1.253.*

All the prophets announced His two advents. ... In the second one, He will come on the clouds, bringing on the day which burns as a furnace. *Irenaeus (c. 180, E/W), 1.506.*

When He comes from heaven with His mighty angels, the whole earth will be shaken, as He Himself declares. *Irenaeus (c. 180, E/W), 1.510.*

Already His second coming draws near to us. *Cyprian (c. 250, W), 5.363.*

He will soon come from heaven for the punishment of the devil and for the judgment of the human race, with the force of an avenger and with the power of a judge. *Cyprian (c. 250, W), 5.468.*

At His coming, only the righteous will rejoice. For they look for the things that have been promised them. And the subsistence of the affairs of this world will no longer be maintained. Rather, all things will be destroyed. *Disputation of Archelaus and Manes (c. 320, E), 6.211; extended discussion: 3.414–3.417.*

SEE ALSO ESCHATOLOGY; JESUS CHRIST (II. TWO ADVENTS OF CHRIST); JUDGMENT DAY; RAPTURE; RESURRECTION OF THE DEAD.

SENECA

Seneca (c. A.D. 1–65) was the tutor of young Nero, and he was able to provide good guidance to Nero's government during its early years. Seneca was eventually forced to commit suicide for allegedly plotting against Nero's life. Seneca's writings contain some good moral counsel and insights, but he himself did not live by his own strict teachings.

As Seneca says (whom we so often find on our side): "There are implanted within us the seeds of all the arts and periods of life. And God, our Master, secretly produces our mental dispositions." *Tertullian (c. 210, W), 3.200.*

Seneca says: "After death, all comes to an end, even [death] itself." *Tertullian (c. 210, W), 3.221.*

How often, also, does Annaeus Seneca, who was the keenest Stoic of the Romans, give deserved praise to the supreme Deity. . . . He said, "You do not understand the authority and majesty of your Judge, the Ruler of the world, and the God of heaven and of all gods, on whom those deities that we separately worship and honor are dependent." *Lactantius (c. 304–313, W), 7.15.*

SEPTUAGINT

The Septuagint was the first Greek translation made of the Old Testament. According to tradition, it was made in Alexandria, Egypt, during the third century B.C. by seventy (or seventy-two) translators. (The word "Septuagint" comes from the Latin word for "seventy.") When the New Testament writers quoted from the Old Testament, they nearly always quoted from the Septuagint, not from the Hebrew text. Indeed, the Septuagint soon became the Old Testament of the church. After its enthusiastic acceptance by Christians, however, the Jews eventually discontinued using it—preferring the second-century translation made by a Jewish convert, Aquila.

I. History and use of the Septuagint

II. Differences between the Septuagint and other Old Testament texts

III. Examples of quotations from the Septuagint

I. History and use of the Septuagint

When Ptolemy, king of Egypt, formed a library and sought to collect the writings of all men, he also heard of these prophets. So he sent to Herod, who was the king of the Jews at that time, requesting that the books of the prophets be sent to him. And Herod the king did indeed send them, written, as they were, in the Hebrew language. Now, when their contents were found to be unintelligible to the Egyptians, he again sent and requested that men be commissioned to translate them into the Greek language. And when this was done, the books remained with the Egyptians, where they are until now. They are also in the possession of all Jews throughout the world. *Justin Martyr (c. 160, E), 1.173.*

Ptolemy, king of Egypt, had built the library in Alexandria and had filled it by gathering books from every place. He then learned that the very ancient histories written in Hebrew happened to be carefully preserved. Wishing to know their contents, he sent for seventy wise men from Jerusalem, who were acquainted with both the Greek and Hebrew languages. He directed them to translate the books. So that they could more speedily complete the translation by being free from all disturbances, he ordered the construction of as many cottages as there were translators—not in the city itself, but seven stadia away. . . . He ordered the officers overseeing this . . . to prevent any communication [of the translators] with one another. This was so the accuracy of the translation could be verified by their agreement [of one translation with another]. When Ptolemy discovered that the seventy men not only had all given the same meanings, but had even used the same words, . . . he believed that the translation had been written by divine power. . . . You men of Greece, this is no fable. Nor have I narrated something fictitious. Rather, I myself have been in Alexandria and have seen the remains of the little cottages at the Pharos, which are still preserved. And I have heard these things from the inhabitants [of Alexandria], who had received them as part of their country's tradition. I have told you things that you can also learn from others—and especially from those wise and esteemed men who have written of these things: Philo and Josephus. *Justin Martyr (c. 160, E), 1.278, 279.*

Before the Romans possessed their kingdom (while as yet the Macedonians held Asia), Ptolemy, the son of Lagus, was anxious to adorn the library which he had founded in Alexandria with a collection of the writings of all men that were of merit. So he requested the people of Jerusalem to have their Scriptures translated into the Greek language. And they

... sent to Ptolemy seventy of their elders, who were thoroughly skilled in the Scriptures and in both languages [i.e., Hebrew and Greek], to carry out what Ptolemy had desired. . . . However, Ptolemy wished to test them individually. For he feared that they might perhaps, by taking counsel together, conceal the truth in the Scriptures by their translation. So he separated them from each other, and commanded them all to write the same translation. He did this with respect to all the books. But when they came together in the same place before Ptolemy, and each of them compared his own translation with that of every other, God was indeed glorified, and the Scriptures were acknowledged as truly divine. For all of them read out the same translation in the very same words. *Irenaeus (c. 180, E/W), 1.451, 452.*

The apostles are of more ancient date than all these [heretics]. And they agree with this aforesaid translation [i.e., the LXX]. And the translation harmonizes with the tradition of the apostles. For Peter, John, Matthew, and Paul, and the rest in turn, as well as their followers, quoted all prophecies just as the interpretation of the elders contains them. *Irenaeus (c. 180, E/W), 1.452.*

The Scriptures were translated into the language of the Greeks, in order that the Greeks might never be able to allege the excuse of ignorance. *Clement of Alexandria (c. 195, E), 2.308.*

It is said that the Scriptures, both of the Law and of the Prophets, were translated from the language of the Hebrews into the Greek language during the reign of Ptolemy, the son of Lagos. Or, according to others, it was a Ptolemy surnamed Philadelphus. . . . For the Macedonians were still in possession of Asia, and the king was ambitious to adorn his library at Alexandria with all writings. So he desired the people of Jerusalem to translate the prophecies they possessed into the Greek language. And, they, being the subjects of the Macedonians, selected seventy elders from those of highest character among them. And each one individually translated each prophetic book. However, when all the translations were compared together, they agreed both in meaning and expression. For it was the counsel of God carried out for the benefit of Grecian ears. It was not alien to the inspiration of God (who originally gave the prophecy) also to produce

the translation and make it, as it were, Greek prophecy. *Clement of Alexandria (c. 195, E), 2.334.*

That the understanding of their books might not be lacking, this also the Jews supplied to Ptolemy. For they gave him seventy-two interpreters. . . . The same account is given by Aristeas. So the king left these works unlocked to all, in the Greek language. To this day, at the temple of Serapis, the libraries of Ptolemy are to be seen, with the identical Hebrew originals in them. The Jews, too, read them publicly. *Tertullian (c. 197, W), 3.32.*

He will endeavor to praise the divine Scriptures, which, with marvelous care and the most generous expenditure, Ptolemy Philadelphus caused to be translated into our language. *Theonas of Alexandria (c. 300, E), 6.160.*

II. Differences between the Septuagint and other Old Testament texts

The first quotation concerns Isaiah 7:14, where the Septuagint reads, "virgin," while the Masoretic Text reads, "young woman."

But you [Jews] and your teachers venture to declare that in the prophecy of Isaiah it does not say, "Behold, the *virgin* will conceive," but, "Behold, the *young woman* will conceive, and bear a son." Furthermore, you explain the prophecy as if [it referred] to Hezekiah, who was your king. Therefore, I will endeavor to discuss shortly this point in opposition to you. *Justin Martyr (c. 160, E), 1.216.*

Shall I not in this matter, too, compel you not to believe your [Jewish] teachers—who venture to assert that the explanation given by your seventy elders, who were with Ptolemy, the king of the Egyptians, is untrue in certain respects. *Justin Martyr (c. 160, E), 1.233.*

But I am far from putting reliance in your [Jewish] teachers, who refuse to admit that the interpretation made by the seventy elders who were with Ptolemy of the Egyptians is a correct one. . . . I wish you to observe, that the Jewish teachers have altogether taken away many Scriptures from the translations made by those seventy elders who were with Ptolemy, and by which this very man who was crucified is proved to have been set forth expressly as God and man. *Justin Martyr (c. 160, E), 1.234.*

The Lord Himself saved us, giving us the sign of the virgin. But it is not as some allege, who are now presuming to expound the Scripture as "Behold, a *young woman* will conceive, and bring forth a son," as Theodotion the Ephesian has interpreted, and Aquila of Pontus, both Jewish proselytes. *Irenaeus (c. 180, E/W), 1.451.*

At this point, we have an asterisk. The words are found in the Hebrew, but do not occur in the Septuagint. *Hippolytus (c. 205, W), 5.163.*

"For the Lord is righteous, and He loved righteousnesses" [Ps. 11:7]. This is the reading in the exact copies and in the other versions besides the Septuagint, and in the Hebrew. *Origen (c. 228, E), 9.353.*

In many other of the sacred books, I sometimes found more in our copies [i.e., the LXX] than in the Hebrew, sometimes less. I will give a few examples, since it is impossible to give them all. Of the Book of Esther, neither the prayer of Mordecai nor that of Esther—both intended to edify the reader—is found in the Hebrew. *Origen (c. 240, E), 4.387.*

I make it my endeavor not to be ignorant of their various readings. Otherwise, in my controversies with the Jews, I might quote to them what is not found in their copies. Also, I want to be able to make use of what is found there—even though it is not in *our* Scriptures [i.e., the LXX]. *Origen (c. 240, E), 4.387.*

III. Examples of quotations from the Septuagint

Where the New Testament writers quote from the Old Testament, their quotations often read differently than do the Old Testament passages found in most English Bibles. That is because the New Testament writers generally quote from the Septuagint. In contrast, most English Old Testaments have been translated from the Hebrew Masoretic Text. Take, for example, Hebrews 10:5, 6: "Therefore, when He came into the world, he said: 'Sacrifice and offering You did not desire, but a body You have prepared for Me.'" Here, the writer of Hebrews is quoting from Psalm 40:6 of the Septuagint. But in most English translations of the Old Testament, Psalm 40:6 reads: "Sacrifice and offering You did not desire; My ears You have opened." Similarly, when the early Christian writers quote from the Old Testament, they nearly always quote from the Septuagint.

"He set the bounds of the nations according to the numbers of the children of Israel" [Deut. 32:7, *quoting from the Hebrew text of his day*]. . . .

Having said this, I added: "The Seventy have translated it, 'He set the bounds of the nations according to the number of the angels of God.'" *Justin Martyr (c. 160, E), 1.265.*

"No one is pure from defilement, not even if his life were but for one day" [Job 14:4, 5, LXX]. *Clement of Alexandria (c. 195, E), 2.428.*

"Come, let us put wood into his bread, and let us wear him away from out of the land of the living. And his name will be remembered no more" [Jer. 11:19, LXX]. *Tertullian (c. 197, W), 3.166.*

Jeremiah declares: "Then I saw their devices. I was led as an innocent lamb to the sacrifice. They meditated a plan against me, saying, 'Come, let us send wood into his bread and let us sweep away his life from the earth, and his name will no more be remembered'" [Jer. 11:18, 19, LXX]. *Lactantius (c. 304–313, W), 7.121.*

Let us learn, therefore, how the divine word triumphs over such women, saying, . . . "As a worm in wood, so does a wicked woman destroy her husband" [Prov. 12:4, LXX]. *Apostolic Constitutions (compiled c. 390, E), 7.395.*

"Divination is iniquity" [1 Sam. 15:23, LXX]. *Apostolic Constitutions (compiled c. 390, E), 7.424.*

SEE ALSO AQUILA, TRANSLATION OF; ARISTEAS; ARISTOBULUS; CANON, OLD TESTAMENT; DEUTEROCANONICAL BOOKS; HEXAPLA; TOWER OF BABEL (II. ANGELIC DIVISION OF THE NATIONS).

SERMON, SERMONS
SEE PREACHING.

SERMON ON THE MOUNT
SEE MATT. 5:1–7:29.

The teaching [of the way of life] is this: Bless those who curse you and pray for your enemies. Fast for those who persecute you. For what reward is there, if you love only those who love you? Do not the Gentiles also do the same? Rather, love those who hate you, and you will not have an enemy. Abstain from fleshly and worldly lusts. If someone gives you a blow upon your right cheek, turn the other to him also. *Didache (c. 80–140, E), 7.377.*

We have learned not to return blow for blow, nor to go to law with those who plunder and rob us. Not only that, but to those who strike us on one side of the face, we have learned to offer the other side also. *Athenagoras (c. 175, E), 2.129.*

What, then, are the teachings in which we Christians are brought up? "I say unto you, 'Love your enemies; bless those who curse you. Pray for those who persecute you.'" *Athenagoras (c. 175, E), 2.134.*

We are so far from practicing promiscuous intercourse, that it is not lawful among us to indulge even a lustful look. Jesus says, "He that looks on a woman to lust after her has committed adultery already in his heart." *Athenagoras (c. 175, E), 2.146.*

With the Lord, not only is the adulterer rejected, but also the person who *desires* to commit adultery. Not only is the actual murderer considered guilty of having killed another person (to his own damnation), but also the man who is angry with his brother without a reason. Jesus commanded [His followers] not only not to hate men, but also to love their enemies. He commanded them not only not to swear falsely, but not even to swear at all. . . . He commanded . . . not only not to strike others, but even, when they themselves are struck, to present the other cheek. . . . He commanded not only not to injure their neighbors, nor to do them any evil, but also, when they are dealt with wickedly, to be long-suffering. *Irenaeus (c. 180, E/W), 1.408.*

Instead of the prohibition that says, "You shall not kill," Jesus prohibits even anger. Instead of the law commanding the giving of tithes, He taught us to share *all* our possessions with the poor. He taught us to love not only our neighbors, but even our enemies. We should not only be generous givers and bestowers, but should even give a free gift to those who take away our goods. For He says, "To him that takes away your coat, give to him your cloak also. And from him that takes away your goods, do not ask for them back. As you would have men do unto you, do unto them also. . . . If anyone will compel you to go a mile, go with him two." In that way, you will not follow that person as a slave, but as a free man. *Irenaeus (c. 180, E/W), 1.477.*

[Celsus, a pagan critic,] says, "They also have a teaching to this effect: that we should not avenge ourselves on one who injures us. Or, as

Christ expresses it: 'Whoever will strike you on the one cheek, turn the other to him also.'" *Origen (c. 248, E), 4.634.*

SEE ALSO BEATITUDES; DIVORCE; LORD'S PRAYER; LUST; NONRESISTANCE; OATHS; WAR.

SERPENT, BRONZE

Then the Lord said to Moses, "Make a fiery serpent, and set it on a pole; and it shall be that everyone who is bitten, when he looks at it, shall live." So Moses made a bronze serpent, and put it on a pole; and so it was, if a serpent had bitten anyone, when he looked at the bronze serpent, he lived. Num. 21:8, 9.

Why, again, did the same Moses—after the prohibition of any likeness of anything—exhibit a bronze serpent, placed on a tree? . . . Is it not that in this case he was exhibiting the Lord's cross on which the serpent, the devil, was defeated? *Tertullian (c. 197, W), 3.166.*

But someone says, . . . "Why, then, did Moses in the desert make a likeness of a serpent out of bronze?" The types [of future things] stand in a class by themselves. For they were laid as the groundwork for some unrevealed, future dispensation, not with a view to the repeal of the Law. . . . Does anyone pretend ignorance of the fact that the figure of the bronze serpent, after the manner of one hung up, pictured the shape of the Lord's cross? *Tertullian (c. 200, W), 3.63.*

When forbidding the likeness to be made of all things that are in heaven, in earth, and in the waters, He also gave the reason: as prohibiting all material display of an unseen idolatry. For He adds: "You will not bow down to them, nor serve them." The form, however, of the bronze serpent that the Lord afterwards commanded Moses to make, afforded no excuse for idolatry. Rather, it was meant for the cure of those who were plagued with the fiery serpents. I say nothing of what was pre-figured by this cure. *Tertullian (c. 207, W), 3.314.*

SEE ALSO IDOLATRY; IMAGES; TYPE; TYPOLOGY.

SERVANTS

SEE EQUALITY OF HUMANKIND; SLAVES.

SEVENTH DAY OF CREATION

And on the seventh day God ended His work which He had done, and He rested on the seventh day from all His work which he had done. Gen. 2:2.

For we who have believed do enter that rest, as He has said: "So I swore in My wrath, 'They shall not enter My rest,'" although the works were finished from the foundation of the world. For He has spoken in a certain place of the seventh day in this way: "And God rested on the seventh day from all His works"; and again in this place: "they shall not enter My rest." Heb. 4:3–5.

It was not said of the seventh day the same as the other days, "And there was evening, and there was morning." This fact is a distinct indication of the consummation which is to take place in it before [the seventh day] is finished. *Justin Martyr (c. 160, E), 1.301.*

God's resting is not, then, as some conceive, that God ceased from doing. For, being good, if He should ever cease from doing good, then He would cease to be God, which is a sacrilege even to say. *Clement of Alexandria (c. 195, E), 2.513.*

He knows nothing of the day of the Sabbath and God's rest, which follows the completion of the world's creation. This day lasts during the duration of the world. In it, all those who have done all their works in their six days will keep festival with God. Because they have omitted none of their duties, they will ascend to the contemplation and to the assembly of righteous and blessed beings. *Origen (c. 248, E), 4.601.*

Who that is filled with the Holy Spirit does not see in his heart that on the same day that the dragon seduced Eve, the angel Gabriel brought the glad tidings to the virgin Mary. . . . On the same day that the Son made the land and water, He was incarnate in the flesh. *Victorinus (c. 280, W), 7.343.*

This world will be terminated at the seventh thousand years. At that time, God will have completed the world and will rejoice in us. *Methodius (c. 290, E), 6.344.*

SEE ALSO CHRONOLOGY; CREATION.

SEVENTY, THE (DISCIPLES)

At Elim were twelve springs of water and seventy palm trees; so they camped there. Num. 33:9.

After these things the Lord appointed seventy others also, and sent them two by two before His face into every city and place where He Himself was about to go. Luke 10:1.

He chose also seventy other apostles besides the twelve. Now, the twelve followed the number of the twelve fountains of Elim. Therefore, why should not the seventy correspond to the like number of the palms of that place? *Tertullian (c. 207, W), 3.387.*

After He was risen from the abode of the dead and was received into heaven, Thomas the apostle, . . . by an impulse from God, sent Thaddaeus to Edessa to be a preacher and proclaimer of the teaching of Christ. Now, this Thaddaeus was himself also numbered among the seventy disciples of Christ. And the promise of Christ was fulfilled through him. *Eusebius (c. 315, E), 8.651.*

SEE ALSO APOSTLES, TWELVE; BARNABAS.

SEVENTY (SEPTUAGINT)
SEE SEPTUAGINT.

SEVENTY WEEKS OF DANIEL
SEE DANIEL, BOOK OF.

SEXUAL RELATIONS
SEE PROCREATION.

SHEPHERD OF HERMAS
SEE HERMAS, SHEPHERD OF.

SHUNNING
SEE DISCIPLINE, CHURCH.

SIBYL

In the Greek and Roman world, the sibyls were elderly prophetesses who usually prophesied in a state of ecstasy. The writings attributed to them often contain various prophecies that support Christian beliefs. Modern scholars usually explain this fact by saying that either the Jews or the Christians tampered with the Sibylline Oracles. The early Christians, however, believed that God had planted seeds of truth in the Greek and Roman cultures through the sibyls.

The Sibyl and Hystaspes said that there would be a dissolution of all corruptible things by God. *Justin Martyr (c. 160, E), 1.169.*

[ADDRESSED TO PAGANS:] You may in part easily learn the right religion from the ancient Sibyl. For, by some kind of powerful inspiration, she teaches you. Through her oracular predictions, she teaches truths that seem to be similar to the teaching of the prophets. They say that she was of Babylonian lineage, being the daughter of Berosus, who wrote the *History of the Chaldeans.* Justin Martyr (c. 160, E), 1.288.

But I have to remark further, that the Sibyl also has said concerning them that they worship the images of deceased kings. *Melito (c. 170, E), 8.752.*

Also, among the Greeks there was the Sibyl. They all have spoken things consistent and harmonious with each other. *Theophilus (c. 180, E), 2.97.*

From that time [i.e., of the tower of Babel], God confused the languages of men, giving to each a different dialect. And the Sibyl speaks similarly of this: . . . "In the Assyrian land they built a tower, and all were of one speech, and wished to rise even until they climbed unto the starry heavens." *Theophilus (c. 180, E), 2.106.*

The Sibyl was a prophetess among the Greeks and the other nations. In the beginning of her prophecy, she reproaches the race of men, saying, . . . "Do you not tremble, nor fear God Most High? . . . There is only one uncreated God, who reigns alone, all-powerful, very great, from whom nothing is hid." *Theophilus (c. 180, E), 2.108, 109.*

It is manifestly from the prophetess of the Hebrews [i.e., the Sibyl] who prophesies in the following manner: "What flesh can see with the eye the celestial, the true, the immortal God, who inhabits the vault of heaven?" *Clement of Alexandria (c. 195, E), 2.192.*

[Celsus claims] that certain Christians believe in the Sibyl. He probably misunderstood someone who *censured* those who believed in the existence of a prophetic Sibyl. *Origen (c. 248, E), 4.570.*

Marcus Varro [an ancient Roman writer] . . . says that the Sibylline Books were not the production of one Sibyl only. Rather, they were called by one name, Sibylline, because all prophetesses were called Sibyls by the ancients. . . . So all these Sibyls proclaim one God. . . . Now, in these verses that the ambassadors brought to Rome, there are these testimonies respecting the one God: "One God, who is alone, most mighty, uncreated." This is the only supreme God, who made the heaven, and decked it with lights. "But there is only one God of pre-eminent power, who made the heaven, the sun, the stars, the moon, the fruit-

ful earth, and the waves of the water of the sea." . . . "Worship Him who is alone the ruler of the world, who alone was and is from age to age." Also, another Sibyl, whoever she was, said that she conveyed the voice of God to men. On His behalf, she said: "I am the one only God, and there is no other God." *Lactantius (c. 304–313, W), 7.15, 16.*

There is a Son of the Most High God, who is possessed of the greatest power. This is shown not only by the unanimous utterances of the prophets, but also by . . . the predictions of the Sibyls. . . . The Erythraean Sibyl, in the beginning of her poem (which she began with the Supreme God), proclaims the Son of God as the leader and commander of all, in the following verses: "The Nourisher and Creator of all things, who placed the sweet breath in all, and made God the Leader of all." And again, at the end of the same poem: "But whom God gave for faithful men to honor." And another Sibyl declares that He should be known: "Know Him as your God, who is the Son of God." *Lactantius (c. 304–313, W), 7.105.*

The Sibyl had foretold in advance that the miracle would take place, whose verses are related to this effect: "With five loaves at the same time, and with two fishes, He will satisfy five thousand men in the wilderness." . . . And again, another says, "He will walk on the waves. He will release men from disease. He will raise the dead and drive away many pains. And from the bread of one pouch, there will be a satisfying of men." Being refuted by these testimonies, some are accustomed to fall back on the claim that these poems were not written by the Sibyls, but were invented and composed by our own writers, instead. However, he who has read Cicero, Varro, and other ancient writers will assuredly not think this. For they make mention of the Erythraean and the other Sibyls, from whose books we bring forth these examples. And those authors died before the birth of Christ according to the flesh. However, I do not doubt that in former times these poems were regarded as ravings. For, at that time, no one understood them. . . . Therefore, they were neglected for many ages. But they received attention after the birth and passion of Christ. *Lactantius (c. 304–313, W), 7.116.*

The Sibyl also showed that the same things would happen: "He will afterwards come into the hands of the unjust and the faithless. And they will inflict blows with impure hands on God." *Lactantius (c. 304–313, W), 7.120.*

SEE ALSO ORACLES, PAGAN.

SIGNING

As used here, signing refers to making the sign of the cross on a person's forehead.

Go through the midst of Jerusalem, and set a mark [Gr. tau] on the foreheads of the men that groan and that grieve for all the iniquities that are done in the midst of them. Ezek 9:4 (LXX). [NOTE: THE GREEK LETTER *TAU*, EQUIVALENT TO THE ENGLISH CAPITAL "T," IS IN THE SHAPE OF A CROSS.]

From which ruin no one will be freed except he who has been sealed in front with the passion of Christ. *Tertullian (c. 197, W), 3.167.*

Shall you escape notice when you sign your bed or your body [with the cross]? . . . Will you not be thought to be engaged in some work of magic? *Tertullian (c. 205, W), 4.46.*

The Greek letter *Tau* and our own letter T is the very form of the cross. He predicted this would be the sign on our foreheads in the true catholic Jerusalem. *Tertullian (c. 207, W), 3.340, 341.*

The flesh is signed so that the soul too may be fortified. *Tertullian (c. 210, W), 3.551.*

At every forward step and movement, at every going in and out, when we put on our clothes and shoes, when we bathe, when we sit at the table, when we light the lamps, when on the couch, on a seat, and in all the ordinary actions of daily life, we trace the sign upon our foreheads. *Tertullian (c. 211, W), 3.94, 95*

We have faith for a defense . . . in immediately making the sign and adjuring. . . . We often aid in this manner even the pagan, seeing that we have been endowed by God with that power that the apostle first used when he despised the viper's bite. *Tertullian (c. 213, W), 3.633.*

[Uzziah] was marked upon his forehead with the spot of leprosy. He was thus marked by an offended Lord on that part of his body where those who deserve well of the Lord are signed. *Cyprian (c. 250, W), 5.427.*

Only those can escape who have been born anew and signed with the sign of Christ. "Have no pity upon old or young. And slay the virgins, the little ones, and the women, that they may be utterly destroyed. But do not touch any man upon whom is written the mark." What this mark is and in what part of the body it is placed, God sets forth in another place, saying, "Go through the midst of Jerusalem and set a mark [*tau*] upon the foreheads of the men who sigh and cry for all the abominations that are done in the midst thereof." This sign pertains to the passion and blood of Christ. Whoever is found in this sign is kept safe and unharmed. *Cyprian (c. 250, W), 5.464.*

Women did not benefit from that sign [of circumcision]. However, all are sealed by the sign of the Lord. *Cyprian (c. 250, W), 5.510.*

In His suffering, He stretched forth His hands and measured out the world—so that even then He might show that a great multitude . . . was about to come under His wings and to receive on their foreheads that great and lofty sign. And the Jews even now display a symbol of this transaction when they mark their thresholds with the blood of a lamb. *Lactantius (c. 304–313, W), 7.129.*

He is the salvation of all who have written on their foreheads the sign of blood. I am referring to the sign of the cross, on which He shed His blood. . . . But I will show in the last book in what manner or in what region all will be safe who have marked on the highest part of their body this sign of the true and divine blood. *Lactantius (c. 304–313, W), 7.129.*

When the pagans sacrifice to their gods, if anyone bearing a marked forehead stands by, the sacrifices are by no means favorable. . . . And this has often been the cause of punishment to wicked kings. For some of their attendants who were of our religion were standing by their masters as the masters sacrificed. Because the attendants had the sign placed on their foreheads, this caused the gods of their masters to flee. As a result, they could not observe future events in the entrails of the victims. *Lactantius (c. 304–313, W), 7.129.*

Today, His followers, in the name of their Master, and by the sign of His passion, banish the same polluted spirits from men. *Lactantius (c. 304–313, W), 7.129.*

Since the demons can neither approach those in whom they will see the heavenly mark, nor injure those whom the immortal sign protects like an impregnable wall, they harass them by men and persecute them by the hands of others. *Lactantius (c. 304–313, W), 7.130.*

While [Emperor Diocletian] sacrificed, some attendants of his, who were Christians, stood by and they put the immortal sign on their foreheads. At this, the demons were chased away, and the holy rites were interrupted. *Lactantius (c. 320, W), 7.304.*

SEE ALSO CROSS.

SIGN OF THE CROSS
SEE SIGNING.

SIMON AND CLEOPAS
Now behold, two of them were traveling that same day to a village called Emmaus, which was about seven miles from Jerusalem.... Then the one whose name was Cleopas answered and said to Him, "Are You the only stranger in Jerusalem?" Luke 24:13, 18.

Simon and Cleopas bear witness to this power when they say, "Were not our hearts burning within us by the way, as he opened to us the Scriptures?" *Origen (c. 228, E), 9.302.*

And in the Gospel of Luke also, while Simon and Cleopas were talking to each other concerning all that had happened to them, Jesus "drew near and went with them." ... And when their eyes were opened and they knew Him, then the Scripture says, in express words, "And He vanished out of their sight." *Origen (c. 248, E), 4.456.*

When He was risen from the dead, He appeared first to Mary Magdalene and Mary the mother of James. He then appeared to Cleopas on the way. *Apostolic Constitutions (compiled c. 390, E), 7.445.*

SIMON MAGUS
But there was a certain man called Simon, who previously practiced sorcery in the city and astonished the people of Samaria, claiming that he was someone great, to whom they all gave heed, from the least to the greatest, saying, "This man is the great power of God." ... Then Simon himself also believed; and when he was baptized he continued with Philip, and was amazed, seeing the miracles and signs which were done.... Now when Simon saw that through the laying on of the apostles' hands the Holy Spirit was given, he offered them money, saying, "Give me this power also, that anyone on whom I lay hands may receive the Holy Spirit." But Peter said to him, "Your money perish with you, because you though that the gift of God could be purchased with money! You have neither part nor portion in this matter, for your heart is not right in the sight of God." Acts 8:9–21.

There was a Samaritan, Simon, a native of the village called Gitto, who in the reign of Claudius Caesar, and in your royal city of Rome, did mighty acts of magic.... He was considered a god, and as a god was honored by you with a statue. This statue was erected on the Tiber River, between the two bridges. It bore the following inscription in the language of Rome: "To Simon, the holy God." ... And almost all the Samaritans, and a few even of other nations, worship him. They acknowledge him as the first god. *Justin Martyr (c. 160, E), 1.171.*

The Samaritans, Simon and Menander, did many mighty works by magic and deceived many. They remain deceived. Even among yourselves [i.e., the pagan Romans], as I said before, Simon was in the royal city of Rome in the reign of Claudius Caesar. He so greatly astonished the sacred Senate and the Roman people that he was considered a god. He was honored with a statue, just like the others whom you honor as gods.... I advise you to destroy that statue. *Justin Martyr (c. 160, E), 1.182.*

When I communicated in writing with Caesar, I gave no thought to any of my people, that is, the Samaritans. Rather, I stated that they were in error to trust in the magician Simon of their own nation. They say that he is God above all power, authority, and might. *Justin Martyr (c. 160, E), 1.260.*

Simon the Samaritan was the magician of whom Luke, the disciple and follower of the apostles, [writes].... He set himself eagerly to contend against the apostles, in order that he himself might seem to have been a supernatural being. So he applied himself with still greater zeal to the study of the entirety of magic arts, so he could bewilder and overpower multitudes of men. This was his method during the reign of Claudius Caesar, who honored Simon with a statue because of his magical power, according to what is said. This man, then, was glorified by many persons as if he were a god. And he taught that it was himself who appeared among the Jews as the Son.... All sorts of heresies derive their origin from this Simon of Samaria. He formed his sect in the following manner: At Tyre, a city of Phoenicia, he redeemed from slavery a certain woman named Helena. He used to take her along with him. He declared that this woman was the first conception of his mind. *Irenaeus (c. 180, E/W), 1.347, 348.*

God will also judge the vain speeches of the perverse Gnostics, by showing that they are the disciples of Simon Magus. *Irenaeus (c. 180, E/W), 1.507.*

You install Simon Magus in your Pantheon, giving him a statue and the title of holy God. *Tertullian (c. 197, W), 3.29.*

The doctrine of Simon's sorcery taught the worship of angels. It was itself actually reckoned among idolatries and condemned by the apostle Peter in Simon's own person. *Tertullian (c. 197, W), 3.259.*

From that point forward, Simon Magus, who had just become a believer, was cursed by the apostles and ejected from the faith. For he was still thinking somewhat of his juggling sect. That is, he wanted to buy even the gift of the Holy Spirit through imposition of hands, so that he could include it among the miracles of his profession. *Tertullian (c. 200, W), 3.66.*

There is the Simon of Samaria in the Acts of the Apostles, who bargained for the Holy Spirit. He had only a vain remorse that he and his money must perish together. After his condemnation, he applied his energies to the destruction of the truth, as if to console himself by revenge. In addition to the support with which his own magic arts furnished him, he had recourse to deception. He purchased a Tyrian woman of the name of Helen out of a brothel, with the same money that he had offered for the Holy Spirit—a transaction worthy of the wretched man. He actually pretended that he was the Supreme Father, and he further pretended that the woman was his own Primary Conception. *Tertullian (c. 210, W), 3.215.*

At this very time, even the heretical dupes of this same Simon are so much elated by the extravagant pretension of their art, that they try to bring up from Hades the souls of the prophets themselves. *Tertullian (c. 210, W), 3.234.*

The disciples, then, of this [Simon Magus] celebrate magical rites, and they resort to incantations. They transmit both love spells and charms.... This Simon, deceiving many in Samaria by his sorceries, was reproved by the apostles, and he was put under a curse. All of this has been written in the Acts. But Simon

afterwards renounced the faith.... And journeying as far as Rome, he came in conflict with the apostles. Peter offered repeated opposition to him, for Simon was deceiving many by his sorceries. *Hippolytus (c. 225, W), 5.80, 81.*

We know that Simon Magus gave himself the title of the "Power of God." *Origen (c. 228, E), 9.317.*

[Simon Magus] was successful on that one occasion. But today I think it would be impossible to find thirty of his followers in the entire world. In fact, I am probably overstating the number. There are exceedingly few in Palestine. And in the rest of the world (throughout which he desired to spread the glory of his name), you find him nowhere mentioned. Where his name is found, it is found quoted from the Acts of the Apostles. So he owes the preservation of his name to Christians. This clearly proves that Simon was in no respect divine. *Origen (c. 248, E), 4.422.*

[Celsus] next pours down upon us a heap of names, saying that he knows of the existence of certain Simonians, who worship Helen ... as their teacher. They are called Helenians. However, it has escaped the notice of Celsus that the Simonians do not at all acknowledge Jesus to be the Son of God. Rather, they consider Simon to be the Power of God. *Origen (c. 248, E), 4.570.*

Simonians are now found [practically] nowhere throughout the world. Yet, in order to gain many followers to himself, Simon protected his disciples from the danger of death [through martyrdom] ... by teaching them to regard idolatry as a matter of indifference. So even at the beginning of their existence, the followers of Simon were not exposed to persecution. After all, the wicked demon who was conspiring against the teachings of Jesus was well aware that none of his own teachings would be weakened by the teachings of Simon. *Origen (c. 248, E), 4.578.*

[The people of Rome] had seen the chariot of Simon Magus, his fiery car, blown into pieces by the mouth of Peter and vanish when Christ was named. They had seen Simon, I say, trusting in false gods. Yet, being abandoned by them in their terror, borne down headlong by his own weight, Simon lay prostrate with his legs broken. *Arnobius (c. 305, E), 6.438.*

Simon Magus believed and was baptized with many others. *Pamphilus (c. 309, E), 6.167.*

Simon the magician, . . . as he flew in the air in an unnatural manner, was dashed against the earth. *Apostolic Constitutions (compiled c. 390, E), 7.401.*

The first of the new [i.e., Christian] heresies began in this manner: The devil entered into one Simon, a Samaritan of a village called Gitthae. He was a magician by profession. . . . Simon himself, when he saw the signs and wonders that were done without any magic ceremonies, fell into admiration, believed, was baptized, and continued in fasting and prayer. . . . But when Simon saw that the Spirit was given to believers by the laying on of hands, he took money and offered it. *Apostolic Constitutions (compiled c. 390, E), 7.452.*

When he was in Rome, he disturbed the church severely and subverted many, bringing them over to himself. He astonished the Gentiles with his skill in magic. *Apostolic Constitutions (compiled c. 390, E), 7.453; see also 5.143; extended discussion: 5.74–5.81, 7.452–7.453.*

SEE ALSO HERESIES, HERETICS; MENANDER THE HERETIC.

SIMONY

Simony is the practice of buying or selling sacred things.

Now when Simon saw that through the laying on of the apostles' hands the Holy Spirit was given, he offered them money, saying, "Give me this power also, that anyone on whom I lay hands may receive the Holy Spirit." But Peter said to him, "Your money perish with you, because you thought that the gift of God could be purchased with money!" Acts 8:18–20.

The grace of God should be without price. In the Acts of the Apostles, it says: "Let your money perish with you, for you have thought that the grace of God could be bought with money." Also, in the Gospel: "Freely you have received, freely give." Also in the same place: "You have made my Father's house a house of merchandise." *Cyprian (c. 250, W), 5.554, 555.*

The participation of the Holy Spirit was not given for money, nor to hypocrites—but to saints by faith. *Pamphilus (c. 309, E), 6.167.*

If any bishop, or even a presbyter or deacon, obtains his office through money, let him and the person who ordained him be deprived. And let him be entirely cut off from communion, as Simon Magus was by Peter. *Apostolic Constitutions (compiled c. 390, E), 7.501.*

SIN

I. Classes of sins

II. Unforgivable sin

I. Classes of sin

Anyone who sees his brother sinning, if the sin is not deadly, should petition God, and thus life will be given to the sinner. This is only for those whose sin is not deadly. There is such a thing as a deadly sin; I do not say that one should pray about that. True, all wrongdoing is sin, but not all sin is deadly. 1 John 5:16, 17 (NA).

John, too, clearly teaches the differences of sins, in his larger Epistle. He does so in these words: "If any man sees his brother sin a sin that is not unto death, he will ask and he will give him life." *Clement of Alexandria (c. 195, E), 2.362.*

Of sins, some are carnal, that is, physical. Others are spiritual. . . . The source by which sins are named "spiritual" and "physical" is the fact that every sin is a matter either of *action* or else of *thought*. *Tertullian (c. 203, W), 3.658, 659.*

The next three quotations from Tertullian reflect the Montanistic view that the church cannot extend pardon for mortal sins (i.e., sins "unto death"):

We divide sins into two classes. Some sins are remissible; some are irremissible. Accordingly, no one will doubt that some sinners deserve chastisement; others, condemnation. Every sin is dischargeable, either by pardon or by penalty. By pardon, as the result of chastisement; by penalty, as the result of condemnation. Addressing this difference, we have already premised certain opposing passages of the Scriptures. On the one hand, sins are retained; on the other hand, sins are remitted. *Tertullian (c. 212, W), 4.76.*

It is tantamount to saying that John has forgotten himself: asserting in the first part of his Epistle that we are not without sin, but later saying that we do not sin at all. In the one case, flattering us somewhat with hope of pardon; but in the other, asserting with all strictness that those who have sinned are not sons of God. But away with this! We must not forget the distinction between sins that was the starting point of our digression. And John has sanctioned this [distinction]. For there are some sins we commit daily, to which we are all liable. For who will be free from sins such as being angry unjustly, retaining one's anger after sunset, using manual violence, carelessly speaking evil, or rashly swearing? . . . In business, in official duties, in trade, in food, in sight, in hearing—what a great number of temptations beset us. Accordingly, if there were no pardon for these types of sins, no one could obtain salvation. Of these [types of sins], then, there will be pardon through Christ—the successful Intercessor of the Father. *Tertullian (c. 212, W), 4.97.*

"Every unrighteousness is sin. And there is a sin unto death. But we know that every one who has been born of God does not sin"—that is, the sin which is unto death. Therefore, there is no course left for you but to either deny that adultery and fornication are mortal sins, or else acknowledge that they are irremissible. *Tertullian (c. 212, W), 4.97.*

Writing to the Corinthians, who had diverse sicknesses, the apostle says, "For this reason, many among you are weak and sickly, and not a few sleep." In these words, hear him knitting a band and pleating it with different types of sin. In his analogy, the first group are "weak." However, others are "sickly," which is more serious than the "weak." Finally, others are "asleep," in comparison to the first two. . . . Those who are "asleep" are the ones who are not taking notice and watching with their souls, as they should be doing. Rather, they . . . are drowsy in their reflections. *Origen (c. 245, E), 9.430.*

I think that, just as a man can commit adultery in his heart—not actually proceeding with the physical act—so likewise he can commit in his heart the rest of the things that are forbidden. . . . He who has done in his heart any of the things forbidden will not be punished the same as will the person who has actually sinned in deed. Take, for example, the case of someone who has stolen only in his heart. . . . Adultery that takes place in the heart is a lesser sin than if one were to add to it the act itself. *Origen (c. 245, E), 9.454.*

In the case of the least of the sins of men, he who has not repented after the public announcement of the sin is to be reckoned as a Gentile and a tax collector. This applies to sins that are "not unto death." Or as the Law has described them in the Book of Numbers, not "death bringing." *Origen (c. 245, E), 9.492.*

The principle of the philosophers and Stoics is different, dearest brother. For they say that all sins are equal. . . . However, there is a wide difference between Christians and philosophers. *Cyprian (c. 250, W), 5.331.*

Adultery, fraud, and manslaughter are mortal sins. *Cyprian (c. 250, W), 5.488.*

II. Unforgivable sin

Every sin and blasphemy will be forgiven men, but the blasphemy against the Spirit will not be forgiven men. Anyone who speaks a word against the Son of Man, it will be forgiven him; but whoever speaks against the Holy Spirit, it will not be forgiven him, either in this age or in the age to come. Matt. 12:31, 32.

If we sin willfully after we have received the knowledge of the truth, there no longer remains a sacrifice for sins, but a certain fearful expectation of judgment. Heb. 10:26, 27.

Who, then, is not amazed at the exceeding majesty of the Holy Spirit, when he hears that he who speaks a word against the Son of man may hope for forgiveness, but that he who is guilty of blasphemy against the Holy Spirit has no forgiveness—either in the present world or in that which is to come? *Origen (c. 225, E), 4.252.*

I think it follows that he who has committed a sin against the Son of man is deserving of forgiveness for the following reason: If he who participates in the Word or Reason [i.e., Logos] of God ceases to live agreeably to reason, he seems to have fallen into a state of ignorance or folly. Therefore, he deserves forgiveness. On the other hand, he who has been deemed worthy to have a portion of the Holy Spirit but has lapsed into sin again, he is—by this very act and work—said to be guilty of blasphemy against the Holy Spirit. *Origen (c. 225, E), 4.254.*

In the Gospel, Christ declares that there is forgiveness for the sin committed against Himself. However, for blasphemy against the Holy Spirit there is no forgiveness—either in this age or in the age to come. What is the reason for this? Is it because the Holy Spirit is of more worth than Christ? Is that why the sin against Him cannot be forgiven? Rather, is it not that . . . the only persons who have part in the Holy Spirit are those who have been found worthy of it. As a result, there appropriately cannot be any forgiveness for such persons who later fall away into evil—despite such a great and powerful co-operation. For they defeat the counsels of the Spirit who is in them. *Origen (c. 228, E), 9.329.*

After inspiration and revelation have come to a person, there is no pardon on account of ignorance for him—that is, if he has wilfully and knowingly continued in that course in which he has erred. For he resists [God] with a certain presumption and obstinacy. *Cyprian (c. 250, W), 5.382.*

It is not on account of the superiority of the Spirit over the Son that the blasphemy against the Spirit is a sin beyond discipline and pardon. Rather, it is because there is pardon for the imperfect. But for those who have tasted the heavenly gift and have been made perfect, there remains no plea or prayer for pardon. *Theognostus of Alexandria (c. 260, E), 6.156; see also 2.361.*

SEE ALSO ABSOLUTION; DISCIPLINE, CHURCH; REPENTANCE; SINLESSNESS.

SINGING

SEE MUSIC, MUSICAL INSTRUMENTS.

SINLESSNESS

All have sinned and fall short of the glory of God. Rom. 3:23.

[Jesus] was in all points tempted as we are, yet without sin. Heb. 4:15.

[Jesus] committed no sin, nor was guile found in His mouth. 1 Pet. 2:22.

If we say that we have no sin, we deceive ourselves, and the truth is not in us. 1 John 1:8.

In Him there is no sin. 1 John 3:5.

Christ alone is sinless. However, as far as we are able, let us try to sin as little as possible. *Clement of Alexandria (c. 195, E), 2.210.*

Christ welcomes the repentance of the sinner, for He loves the repentance that follows sins. For this Word of whom we speak alone is sinless. For to sin is natural and common to all. But to return [to God] after sinning is characteristic not of any man, but only of a man of worth. *Clement of Alexandria (c. 195, E), 2.293.*

I know of no one among men who is perfect in all things at once, as long as he is still human.

. . . The only exception is He alone who clothed Himself with humanity for us. *Clement of Alexandria (c. 195, E), 2.433.*

To the Son of God alone was it reserved to persevere to the end without sin. *Tertullian (c. 197, W), 3.244.*

The Lord knew Himself to be the only guiltless One, and so He teaches us to beg "to have our debts remitted us." *Tertullian (c. 198, W), 3.684.*

Now, who is so faultless among men, that God could always have him in His choice? *Tertullian (c. 207, W), 3.315.*

In Christ, that same flesh was maintained without sin—which in man was *not* maintained without sin. *Tertullian (c. 210, W), 3.535.*

God alone is without sin. And the only human without sin is Christ, since Christ is also God. *Tertullian (c. 210, W), 3.221.*

I do not inquire as to His own redemption. For, though He was tempted in all things just as we are, He was without sin. His enemies never reduced Him to [spiritual] captivity. *Origen (c. 228, E), 9.318.*

If by the phrase, "those who were without sin," [the pagan critic Celsus] means those who have never at any time sinned, . . . we reply that it is impossible for a human to be without sin in that manner. In saying this, we except, of course, the man understood to be in Christ Jesus, who did not sin. *Origen (c. 248, E), 4.489.*

[Celsus] alleges . . . that "they who are without sin are partakers of a better life." . . . [ORIGEN'S REPLY:] Of those who were without sin from the beginning of their lives, there cannot possibly be any. Even those who are so after their conversion are found to be few in number—being those who have become such after giving their allegiance to the saving Word. *Origen (c. 248, E), 4.492.*

Lest anyone should flatter himself that he is innocent—and should more deeply perish by exalting himself—he is instructed and taught that he sins daily. For he is told to pray daily for his sins. *Cyprian (c. 250, W), 5.453.*

Let no one flatter himself with the notion of a pure and immaculate heart. Let no one depend on his own innocence. Let no one think that the medicine does not need to be applied to his wounds.... In his epistle, John lays it down and says, "If we say that we have no sin, we deceive ourselves and the truth is not in us." If no one can be without sin, whoever should say that he is without fault is either proud or foolish. *Cyprian (c. 250, W), 5.476.*

No one is without stain and without sin.... In the Epistle of John, it says: "If we say that we have no sin, we deceive ourselves and the truth is not in us." *Cyprian (c. 250, W), 5.547.*

No one can boast of being so free from sin as not even to have an evil thought. *Methodius (c. 290, E), 6.365.*

No one can be without defect as long as he is burdened with a covering of flesh. For the infirmity of the flesh is subject to the dominion of sin in a threefold manner: in deeds, words, and thoughts. *Lactantius (c. 304–313, W), 7.178.*

No one can be so prudent and so cautious as not at sometime to slip. *Lactantius (c. 304–313, W), 7.191.*

SEE ALSO FALL OF MAN; MAN, DOCTRINE OF; PERFECTION, CHRISTIAN; SALVATION.

SIX HUNDRED SIXTY-SIX
SEE MARK OF THE BEAST.

SLAVES

Were you a slave when your call came? Give it no thought. Even supposing you could go free, you would be better off making the most of your slavery. The slave called in the Lord is a freedman of the Lord. 1 Cor. 7:21, 22 (NA).

There is neither Jew nor Greek, there is neither slave nor free, there is neither male nor female; for you are all one in Christ Jesus. Gal. 3:28.

Servants, be obedient to those who are your masters according to the flesh, with fear and trembling, in sincerity of heart, as to Christ.... And you, masters, do the same things to them, giving up threatening, knowing that your own Master also is in heaven, and there is no partiality with Him. Eph. 6:5, 9.

You will not issue orders with bitterness to your maidservant or your man-servant, who trust in the same God. *Barnabas (c. 70–130, E), 1.148.*

You shall not command anything in bitterness to your bondsman or maidservant, who hope in the same God. Otherwise, they perhaps will not fear God, who is over both. For He does not call

according to the outward appearance, but He calls those whom the Spirit has prepared. You servants, be subject to your masters as to a type of God, in modesty and fear. *Didache (c. 80–140, E), 7.378.*

We know many among ourselves who have given themselves up to slavery, in order that they could ransom others. Many others have surrendered themselves to slavery, so that with the price that they received for themselves, they might provide food for others. *Clement of Rome (c. 96, W), 1.20.*

Do not disdain either male or female slaves. Yet, neither let those slaves be puffed up with pride.... Let them not long to be set free at the communal expense. Otherwise, they may be found to be slaves to their own desires. *Ignatius (c. 105, E), 1.94, 95.*

If any Christians have male or female slaves or children, out of love towards them, they persuade them to become Christians. When they have done so, they call them brothers, without any distinction. *Aristides (c. 125, E), 9.276.*

If I am a slave, I endure servitude. If I am free, I do not make a boast of my good birth. *Tatian (c. 160, E), 2.69.*

We have slaves, some more and some fewer. *Athenagoras (c. 175, E), 2.147.*

The Greeks arrested the slaves of Christian catechumens.... These slaves had nothing to say that would meet the wishes of their tormentors, except that they had heard from their masters that the divine communion was the body and blood of Christ. *Irenaeus (c. 180, E/W), 1.570.*

Immediately take away, then, the adornments from women, and domestic servants from masters, and you will find masters in no respect different from bought slaves. *Clement of Alexandria (c. 195, E), 2.280.*

A man in health is not to use his servants as horses to carry him. *Clement of Alexandria (c. 195, E), 2.289.*

Domestic servants, too, are to be treated like ourselves. For they are human beings, as we are. God is the same to free and slave. *Clement of Alexandria (c. 195, E), 2.293.*

[The Law] prohibits those who are in servitude for their subsistence to be branded with disgrace. To those who have been reduced to slavery through money borrowed, the Law gives a complete release in the seventh year. *Clement of Alexandria (c. 195, E), 2.367.*

It is a crime needing atonement [under Roman law] for a slave even to be present at some [pagan] ceremonies. *Mark Minucius Felix (c. 200, W), 4.187.*

But what will believing servants or children do? Likewise, what will officials do when they attend their lords, patrons, or superiors who are sacrificing? Well, if anyone will have handed the wine to a sacrificer, nay, if he will have aided him by any single word necessary or belonging to a sacrifice—he will be held to be a minister of idolatry. Mindful of this rule, we can render service even to magistrates and powers—after the example of the patriarchs and the other forefathers, who obeyed idolatrous kings up to the point of idolatry. *Tertullian (c. 200, W), 3.71, 72.*

Servants, when they have believed, should serve their fleshly masters the better. In the Epistle of Paul to the Ephesians, it says: "Servants, obey your fleshly masters with fear and trembling." . . . Moreover, masters should be the more gentle. Also in the same place, it says: "And you masters, do the same things to them, forbearing anger." *Cyprian (c. 250, W), 5.552.*

Someone will say, "Are there not among you some who are poor and others who are rich? Are not some servants and others masters? Is there not some difference between individuals?" There is none. Nor is there any other cause why we mutually bestow upon each other the name of brethren, except that we believe ourselves to be equal. We measure all human things by the spirit, not by the body. Although the condition of bodies is different, yet we have no servants. For we both regard and speak of them as brothers in spirit and as fellow-servants in religion. *Lactantius (c. 304–313, W), 7.151.*

I praise [the master] if, when he is enraged, he allows his anger some time to cool, so that the agitation of his mind might calm down over the passage of time. In that manner, his chastisement will be confined within moderate limits. . . . But it is an error not to restrain the faults of slaves and children. *Lactantius (c. 304–313, W), 7.275.*

[CONCERNING CHRISTIANS WHO COMPROMISED DURING PERSECUTION:] Other Chris-

tians have sent Christian slaves to offer sacrifice for them. The slaves . . . being threatened by their masters . . . and having lapsed, will during the year display the works of penitence, learning for the future to do the will of Christ, as the slaves of Christ. . . . However, their masters will be tried by penance for three years—both for their deception and for having forced their fellow-servants to offer sacrifice. For these masters have not obeyed the apostle, who would have the masters do the same things unto the servant, forbearing threatening. He says they should know that our Master and theirs is in heaven, and there is no partiality of persons with Him. *Peter of Alexandria (c. 310, E), 6.271.*

A believer should not go to any of those public meetings, unless to purchase a slave and to save a soul. *Apostolic Constitutions (compiled c. 390, E), 7.424.*

As for such sums of money as are collected from them in the aforesaid manner, designate them to be used for the redemption of the saints and the deliverance of slaves and captives. *Apostolic Constitutions (compiled c. 390, E), 7.435.*

The slave should bring good will to his master, with the fear of God—even if his master is unholy and wicked. However, the slave should not yield in any way as to his worship. And let the master love his servant, although he is his superior. Let him consider how they are equal, for he too is a man. And let him who has a believing master love him both as his master and . . . as a father—although still preserving his authority as his master. . . . In like manner, let a master who has a believing servant love him as a son or as a brother—on account of their communion in the faith. *Apostolic Constitutions (compiled c. 390, E), 7.436.*

You will not give commands with bitterness of soul to your male or female servants who trust in the same God. Otherwise, they may groan against you, and the wrath of God will be upon you. And you servants, be subject to your masters, as to the representatives of God, with diligence and fear. *Apostolic Constitutions (compiled c. 390, E), 7.468.*

Let the faithful person, whether man or woman, treat servants kindly. . . . Let the slaves work five days. But on the Sabbath day and the Lord's Day, let them have rest, in order to go to church for instruction in piety. We say the

Sabbath, on account of creation, and the Lord's Day, on account of the resurrection. *Apostolic Constitutions (compiled c. 390, E), 7.495.*

We do not permit slaves to be ordained into the clergy without their masters' consent. For this would grieve those who owned them. . . . However, if at any time a slave appears worthy to be ordained into a high office (such as Onesimus appeared to be), and if his master allows it, gives him his freedom, and dismisses him from his house—let him be ordained. *Apostolic Constitutions (compiled c. 390, E), 7.505.*

SEE ALSO EQUALITY OF HUMANKIND.

SLEEP

Those who have the sleepless Word dwelling in them should not sleep the livelong night. Rather, they should rise while it is still dark, especially when the days are coming to an end. *Clement of Alexandria (c. 195, E), 2.259.*

Sleep is a temporary suspension of the activity of the senses, procuring rest for only the body, not for the soul also. For the soul is always in motion and always active. It never succumbs to rest. *Tertullian (c. 210, W), 3.222; see also 2.257–2.259.*

SEE ALSO DREAMS.

SOCRATES

Practically all of the philosophical schools of the Hellenistic age can be traced to the Greek philosopher Socrates (469–399 B.C.). He challenged the mythical stories about the gods, and he attempted to motivate people to have as much concern for their souls as they did for their bodies. Because of his innovative views and challenges to the existing religious and sociological beliefs, the council of Athens put Socrates to death by forcing him to drink poison. His ideas lived on, however, particularly through his greatest pupil, Plato.

Socrates endeavored by true reason and examination to bring these things to light and to deliver men from the demons. So the demons themselves (by means of men who rejoiced in iniquity) plotted his death, accusing him of being an atheist and a profane person. *Justin Martyr (c. 160, E), 1.164.*

Socrates, who was more zealous in this direction than all of them, was accused of the very same crimes as ourselves. For his accusers said that he was introducing new divinities. They said he did not consider those to be gods whom the state recognized. . . . He exhorted his fellowmen to become acquainted with the God who was unknown to them. *Justin Martyr (c. 160, E), 1.191.*

Socrates was the teacher of Plato, and Plato of Aristotle. Now, these men flourished in the time of Philip and Alexander of Macedonia. *Justin Martyr (c. 160, E), 1.278.*

Socrates was the wisest of your wise men. As you yourselves admit, your oracle bears witness to him, saying, "Of all men, Socrates is the wisest." Yet, he confessed that he knew nothing. So how did those who came after him profess to know even heavenly things? *Justin Martyr (c. 160, E), 1.288.*

Socrates, . . . in contempt of the gods, was in the habit of swearing by an oak, a goat, or a dog. In fact, for this very thing Socrates was condemned to death, because he overthrew the worship of the gods. *Tertullian (c. 197, W), 3.30.*

The philosophers acknowledge there are demons; Socrates himself waited on a demon's will. Why not? For it is said that an evil spirit attached itself especially to him even from his childhood—no doubt, turning his mind from what was good. *Tertullian (c. 197, W), 3.36.*

If we challenge you to a comparison in the virtue of chastity, I turn to a part of the sentence passed by the Athenians against Socrates, who was pronounced a corrupter of youth. In contrast, the Christian confines himself to the female sex. *Tertullian (c. 197, W), 3.51.*

Socrates was condemned on the point in which he came nearest in his search to the truth, by destroying your gods. *Tertullian (c. 197, W), 3.112.*

Socrates, as no one can doubt, was actuated by a different spirit. For they say that a demon clung to him from his boyhood. *Tertullian (c. 210, W), 3.182.*

Socrates was a hearer of Archelaus, the natural philosopher. Socrates reverenced the rule, "Know thyself." He also assembled a large school. Plato was far superior to all his pupils. Socrates himself left no writings after him. Plato, however, taking notes of all Socrates' wisdom, established a school, combining together natural, ethical, and logical philosophy. *Hippolytus (c. 225, W), 5.17.*

Socrates, condemned by the decision of his fellow citizens, suffered capital punishment. *Arnobius (c. 305, E), 6.424; extended discussion: 7.91–7.92.*

SEE ALSO PHILOSOPHERS, PHILOSOPHY; PLATO.

SODOM

Its neighbors, Sodom and Gomorrah, were consumed by fire from heaven. The country still smells of that conflagration. And if there are apples there upon the trees, it is only a mirage. For when you touch them, they turn to ashes. *Tertullian (c. 205, W), 4.48.*

SOLDIERS

SEE MILITARY LIFE; WAR.

SON OF GOD

SEE CHRIST, DIVINITY OF; TRINITY.

SONG OF SOLOMON

SEE SONG OF SONGS.

SONG OF SONGS

The sacrament of this unity we also see expressed in the Canticles, in the person of Christ, who says, "A garden enclosed is my sister, my spouse, a fountain sealed, a well of living water, a garden with the fruit of apples." If His church is a garden enclosed, and a fountain sealed, how can he who is not in the church enter into the same garden or drink from its fountain? *Cyprian (c. 250, W), 5.389.*

This one church, also, the Holy Spirit in the Song of Songs designated in the person of our Lord and says, "My dove, my spotless one, is but one." *Cyprian (c. 250, W), 5.422.*

This is quite clear in the Song of Songs, . . . where Christ Himself praises those who are firmly established in virginity. He says, "As the lily among thorns, so is my love among the daughters." *Methodius (c. 290, E), 6.331; extended discussion: 6.331–6.334.*

SOPHIA

SEE GNOSTICS, GNOSTICISM (II. FEMALE DEITIES OF THE GNOSTICS); WISDOM.

SORCERY

SEE SPIRITISM.

SOUL

I. Nature of the soul

II. Origin of souls

III. Tripartite distinction of body, soul, and spirit

IV. Tertullian's teaching on the corporeality of the soul

I. Nature of the soul

Do not fear those who kill the body but cannot kill the soul. But rather fear him who is able to destroy both soul and body in hell. Matt. 10:28.

His soul was not left in Hades, nor did His flesh see corruption. Acts 2:31.

May your whole spirit, soul, and body be preserved blameless at the coming of our Lord Jesus Christ. 1 Thess. 5:23.

The word of God is living and powerful, and sharper than any two-edged sword, piercing even to the division of soul and spirit. Heb. 4:12.

When He opened the fifth seal, I saw under the altar the souls of those who had been slain for the word of God and for the testimony which they held. Rev. 6:9.

The soul is dispersed throughout all the members of the body, and Christians are scattered throughout all the cities of the world. The soul dwells in the body, yet is not *of* the body. . . . The invisible soul is guarded by the visible body. . . . The flesh hates the soul, and wars against it. . . . The soul loves the flesh that hates it. . . . The soul is imprisoned in the body, yet preserves that very body. . . . The immortal soul dwells in a mortal tabernacle. *Letter to Diognetus (c. 125–200), 1.27.*

The souls of the wicked, being endowed with sensation even after death, are punished. . . . Those of the good are delivered from punishment and spend a blessed existence. *Justin Martyr (c. 160, E), 1.170.*

There are some others [the Platonists], who, having supposed the soul to be immortal and immaterial, believe that though they have committed evil they will not suffer punishment (for that which is immaterial is insensible). They also say that the soul, in consequence of its immortality, needs nothing from God. *Justin Martyr (c. 160, E), 1.194.*

Souls neither see God nor transmigrate into other bodies. For, if they did, they would know why they are punished, and they would be afraid to commit even the most trivial sin afterwards. But they can perceive that God exists and that righteousness and piety are honorable. *Justin Martyr (c. 160, E), 1.197.*

If the world is begotten, souls also are necessarily begotten. Perhaps at one time they were not in existence. For they were made on account of men and other living creatures—that is, if you will say that souls have been begotten wholly apart, and not along with their respective bodies. . . . "They are not, then, immortal?" No, since the world has appeared to us to be begotten. But I do not say, indeed, that all souls die. For that would truly be a piece of good fortune to evil persons. *Justin Martyr (c. 160, E), 1.197.*

The soul partakes of life, since God wills it to live. Thus, then, it will not even partake [of life] when God does not will it to live. For to live is not the soul's innate attribute, as it is God's. But a man does not live always, and the soul is not forever joined with the body. Whenever this union must be broken up, the soul leaves the body, and the man exists no longer. Even so, whenever the soul must cease to exist, the spirit of life is removed from it, and there is no more soul. Rather, it goes back to the place from where it was taken. *Justin Martyr (c. 160, E), 1.198.*

He prayed that His soul should be saved from the sword, the lion's mouth, and the hands of the dog. This was a prayer that no one should take possession of His soul. So when we arrive at the end of life, we may ask the same petition from God, who is able to turn away every shameless evil angel from taking our souls. And that the souls survive, I have shown to you from the fact that the soul of Samuel was called up by the witch, as Saul demanded. And it appears also, that all the souls of similar righteous men and prophets fell under the dominion of such powers. This can indeed be inferred from the very facts in the case of that witch. Hence also God, by His Son, teaches us (for whose sake these things seem to have been done) always to strive earnestly and at death to pray that our souls will not fall into the hands of any such power. For when Christ was giving up His spirit on the cross, He said, "Father, into your hands I commend my spirit." *Justin Martyr (c. 160, E), 1.252.*

It becomes us now to seek for what we once had, but have lost. It becomes us to unite the soul with the Holy Spirit, and to strive after union with God. The human soul consists of many parts, and is not simple. It is composite, so as to manifest itself through the body. For neither could it ever appear by itself without the body, nor does the flesh rise again without the soul. *Tatian (c. 160, E), 2.71.*

The demons who rule over men are not the souls of men. For how could these souls be capable of action after death? Otherwise, we would have to believe that man, who while living is void of such understanding and power, is endowed with more active power when he is dead. . . . And it is difficult to believe that the immortal soul, which is impeded by the members of the body, becomes more intelligent when it has migrated from it. *Tatian (c. 160, E), 2.72.*

Understand how that there is within you that entity that is called the soul. By it, the eye sees; by it, the ear hears; by it, the mouth speaks. Understand how it makes use of the whole body. Understand how, whenever He pleases to remove the soul from the body, the body falls to decay and perishes. *Melito (c. 170, E), 8.754.*

Our belief rests on a most infallible guarantee—the purpose of Him who fashioned us, according to which He made man of an immortal soul and a body. *Athenagoras (c. 175, E), 2.156.*

God made man of the dust of the earth, and breathed into his face the breath of life. And man became a living soul. Therefore, the soul is called immortal by most persons. *Theophilus (c. 180, E), 2.102.*

The body is not possessed of greater power than the soul. For indeed the body is inspired, vivified, increased, and held together by the soul. The soul possesses and rules over the body. . . . For the body may be compared to an instrument; but the soul is like . . . an artist [who uses the instrument]. *Irenaeus (c. 180, E/W), 1.410.*

Death is the fellowship of the soul in a state of sin with the body. Life is the separation from sin. . . . "For the world is crucified to me, and I to the world," the apostle says. "And now I live, though in the flesh, as having my conversation in heaven." *Clement of Alexandria (c. 195, E), 2.411.*

Souls, by themselves, are equal. When they no longer marry nor are given in marriage, souls are neither male nor female. And woman is transformed into man, when she has become equally unfeminine, manly, and perfect. *Clement of Alexandria (c. 195, E), 2.503.*

It appears that the soul is not naturally immortal. Rather, it is made immortal by the grace of God, through faith, righteousness, and knowledge. *Clement of Alexandria (c. 195, E), 2.571.*

Man is the very image and likeness of himself, and, by the origin of his soul, his own substance, too. *Tertullian (c. 207, W), 3.300.*

We must explain the nature of the soul. At the outset, we must hold fast the meaning of the Greek Scripture, which has "breath," not "Spirit" [in Gen. 2:7]. Some interpreters of the Greek, without reflecting on the difference of the words, and careless about their exact meaning, substitute "Spirit" for "breath." . . . Observe then that "breath" is less than the Spirit, although it comes from the Spirit. It is the Spirit's gentle breeze. But it is not the Spirit. . . . One may call a breeze the image of wind. In the same manner, man is the image of God, that is, of spirit. For God is spirit. "Breath" is therefore the image of the spirit. Now the image is not in any case equal to the very thing. . . . The "breath" possesses beyond doubt the true marks of divinity. I am referring to things such as an immortal soul, freedom and its own mastery over itself, foreknowledge in a great degree, reasonableness, and capacity of understanding and knowledge. Nevertheless, it is even in these respects still an image. It never amounts to the actual power of deity, nor to absolute exemption from fault. For that is a property that is conceded to God alone. *Tertullian (c. 207, W), 3.304.*

Without the soul, we are nothing. There is not even the name of a human being—only that of a carcass. *Tertullian (c. 210, W), 3.532.*

Some things are known even by nature. The immortality of the soul, for instance, is held by man. . . . I may use, therefore, the opinion of Plato, when he declares, "Every soul is immortal." *Tertullian (c. 210, W), 3.547.*

The soul is supported by the entire apparatus of the senses: sight, hearing, taste, smell, and touch. . . . Also, all work, business, and duties of life are accomplished by the flesh. So utterly are the living acts of the soul the work of the flesh, that for the soul to cease to do living acts, would be nothing else than to remove itself from the flesh. Similarly, the very act of dying is a function of the flesh—even as is the process of life. *Tertullian (c. 210, W), 3.551.*

I will go further and say that the soul does not even fall into sleep along with the body, nor does it with its companion even lie down in repose. For it is agitated in dreams. *Tertullian (c. 210, W), 3.558.*

Some of [the philosophers] deny the immortality of the soul. Others affirm that it is immortal, and something more. . . . It will be for Christians to clear away whatever noxious vapors (exhaled from philosophy) obscure the clear and wholesome atmosphere of truth. *Tertullian (c. 210, W), 3.184.*

If it had been possible to construct the soul and to destroy it, it would no longer be immortal. Since, however, it is not mortal, it is also incapable of dissolution and division. *Tertullian (c. 210, W), 3.193.*

And here, therefore, we draw our conclusion: that all the natural properties of the soul are inherent in it as parts of its substance. They grow and develop along with it, from the very moment of its own origin at birth. *Tertullian (c. 210, W), 3.200.*

The attributes that belong to the soul's own proper condition are these: immortality, rationality, sensibility, intelligence, and freedom of the will. All of these endowments of the soul are bestowed on it at birth. However, they are still obscured and corrupted by the malignant being who, in the beginning, regarded them with envious eye. Therefore, these attributes are never seen in their spontaneous action, nor are they administered as they should be. *Tertullian (c. 210, W), 3.219.*

As for "the man within," indeed, the apostle prefers its being regarded as the mind and heart rather than the soul. *Tertullian (c. 210, W), 3.574.*

All souls and all rational natures—whether holy or wicked—were formed or created. And all of them are incorporeal, according to their proper nature. *Origen (c. 225, E), 4.262.*

Only the flesh suffers the effects of wasting and death. But the soul is uncorrupted and beyond the laws of destruction and death. *Novatian (c. 235, W), 5.636.*

Abraham, Isaac, and Jacob were admittedly only men. Yet, they are demonstrated to be alive. For he says that all such ones "live unto God." So death in them does not destroy the soul.... The [soul] in them was immortal. Therefore, it is understood not to have been extinguished. For that reason, they are ... said to live unto God. *Novatian (c. 235, W), 5.636.*

The souls of the dead exist in a separate state. And he who adopts such an opinion does not believe without good reason in the immortality, or at least the continued existence, of the soul. *Origen (c. 248, E), 4.455.*

If, then, on the one hand, you suppose that souls do *not* exist, we will have to prove the doctrine of the soul's immortality. This is to us a doctrine of pre-eminent importance. If, on the other hand, they *do* exist, we still have to prove the doctrine of immortality, not only by what the Greeks have said so well regarding it but also in a manner agreeable to the teaching of Holy Scripture. *Origen (c. 248, E), 4.472.*

That the human soul lives and subsists after its separation from the body is believed not only among Christians and Jews, but also by many others among the Greeks and barbarians. *Origen (c. 248, E), 4.612.*

Celsus makes an unfounded charge against us when he ascribes to us the opinion that "there is nothing in our complex nature better or more precious than the body." For we hold that the soul is far beyond all bodies. *Origen (c. 248, E), 4.658.*

It is the body that dies; the soul is immortal. *Methodius (c. 290, E), 6.367.*

If we ask concerning the tongue, the finger, Abraham's bosom, and the reclining in Abraham's bosom, it may perhaps be that the soul receives in the change a form similar in appearance to its gross and earthly body. *Methodius (c. 290, E), 6.377, as quoted by Photius.*

Every animate creature consists of soul and body. *Lactantius (c. 304–313, W), 7.58.*

Being Himself immortal, God wills that the soul should also be everlasting. *Lactantius (c. 304–313, W), 7.77.*

When overcome by its enemies, the body suffers death. Likewise, the soul, when overpowered by vices, must die. *Lactantius (c. 304–313, W), 7.79.*

Immortality of the soul may be discerned from the fact that there is no other animal that has any knowledge of God. *Lactantius (c. 304–313, W), 7.206.*

The body can do nothing without the soul. But the soul can do many and great things without the body.... The soul is not the same thing as the mind. For it is one thing to *live* and another thing to *think*. And it is the mind of the sleeping person that is at rest—not the soul. And in those who are insane, it is the mind that is not functioning; the soul continues to function. For that reason, they are said to be out of their *minds*. *Lactantius (c. 304–313, W), 7.208, 209.*

The soul cannot entirely perish, for it received its origin from the Spirit of God, which is eternal.... So long as the soul is united with the body, it is destitute of virtue, and it grows sick by the contagion of the body and from sharing its frailty.... However, once the soul is disunited from the body, it will flourish by itself. ... It is not the soul that becomes senseless when the body fails. Rather, it is the body that becomes senseless when the soul takes its departure. *Lactantius (c. 304–313, W), 7.209.*

We acknowledge with us a soul that is incorporeal and immortal. *Apostolic Constitutions (compiled c. 390, E), 7.454; extended discussion: 3.181–3.220; 4.286–4.289.*

II. Origin of souls

And the Lord God formed man of the dust of the ground, and breathed into his nostrils the breath of life; and man became a living being. Gen. 2:7.

Some persons at this point may maintain that souls, if they only began a little while ago to exist, cannot endure for any length of time. They may say that souls must, on the one hand, either be unborn in order to be immortal, or if they have had a beginning in the way of generation, then they must die with the body itself. However, let them learn that God alone, who is Lord of all, is without beginning and without end. *Irenaeus (c. 180, E/W), 1.411.*

Anyone who thinks in this manner concerning souls and spirits, and, in fact, concerning all created things, will not by any means go far astray. For, indeed, all things that have been made had a beginning when they were formed. And they endure as long as God wills that they should have an existence and continuance.... But he who rejects this, proves himself ungrateful to his Maker. For, although he has been created, he has not recognized Him who bestowed [life]. Therefore, he deprives himself of continuance forever and ever. *Irenaeus (c. 180, E/W), 1.411, 412.*

Both [body and soul] are revealed to the world as but one. For the soul was not prior to the body in its essence. Nor, in regard to its formation, did the body precede the soul. But both of these were produced at one time. *Irenaeus (c. 180, E/W), 1.576.*

The soul, then, which is produced along with the body, is corruptible, as some think. *Clement of Alexandria (c. 195, E), 2.571.*

Stand forth, O soul, whether you are a divine and eternal substance (as most philosophers believe) . . . or whether you are the very opposite of divine—a mortal thing, as Epicurus alone thinks. . . . Are you received from heaven, or sprung from earth? . . . Does your existence begin with that of the body, or are you put into it at a later stage? *Tertullian (c. 197, W), 3.175.*

From that time, ever since the blessing was pronounced upon man's generation, the flesh and the soul have had a simultaneous birth—without any calculable difference in time. Therefore, the two have been even generated together in the womb. . . . Contemporaneous in the womb, they are also temporally identical in their birth. The two are no doubt produced by human parents of two substances—but not at two different periods. Rather, they are so entirely one that neither is before the other. *Tertullian (c. 197, W), 3.578.*

The soul is formed by the breathing of God. It is not formed out of matter. . . . For when we acknowledge that the soul originates in the breath of God, it follows that we attribute a beginning to it. However, Plato refuses to assign this to it. For he would have the soul be both unborn and unmade. *Tertullian (c. 210, W), 3.184.*

But Scripture—which has a better knowledge of the soul's Maker, or rather God—has told us nothing more than that God breathed on man's face the breath of life, and that man became a living soul. *Tertullian (c. 210, W), 3.191.*

It does not matter whether the question is begun by the philosopher, the heretic, or the crowd. . . . This is especially true of those of them who begin by maintaining that the soul

is not conceived in the womb, nor formed and produced when the flesh is molded. Rather, they say that it is impressed externally upon the infant before his complete vitality, but after the process of childbirth. *Tertullian (c. 210, W), 3.205.*

He here shows us that the soul proceeds from human seed, not from the first breath of the new-born child. If we are not produced from this seed of the soul, pray tell me how it happens that, from similarity of soul, we resemble our parents in disposition? *Tertullian (c. 210, W), 3.206.*

I indeed maintain that both [body and soul] are conceived and formed perfectly simultaneously. They are also born together. Not a moment's interval occurs in their conception. Therefore, neither one can be assigned a prior place. *Tertullian (c. 210, W), 3.207.*

The flesh and the soul have had a simultaneous birth, without any calculable difference in time, so that the two have even been generated together in the womb. . . . The two are no doubt produced by human parents. *Tertullian (c. 210, W), 3.578.*

If someone should teach that the immortal being of the soul is also sown along with the mortal body, he will not be believed. For the Almighty alone breathes into man the undying and undecaying part. . . . For He says that He "breathed into his nostrils the breath of life, and man became a living soul." *Methodius (c. 290, E), 6.316.*

Man consists of soul and body—that is, from heaven and earth. For the soul (by which we live) has its origin, as it were, out of heaven from God. But the body has its origin out of the earth, from the dust of which we have said that it was formed. *Lactantius (c. 304–313, W), 7.61.*

A question may also arise respecting this: whether the soul is produced from the father, or from the mother, or from both. Now, I think the following answer should be given, although not dogmatically: None of those three possibilities are correct. Rather, souls are produced neither from both parents or from either one alone. Of course, a body may be produced from a body, for something is contributed from both. But a soul cannot be produced from souls. . . . Therefore, the manner of the production of souls belongs entirely to God alone. . . . Nothing but what is mortal can be produced from mortals. . . . From this, it is evident that souls are not given by parents, but by one and the same God and Father of all. He alone knows the law and method of their birth, for He alone produces them. *Lactantius (c. 314, W), 7.298, 299.*

When Christians deny that souls are the off-spring of God Supreme, it does not necessarily follow that we have to declare from what parent they have sprung or by what causes they have been produced. . . . But what crime is it either to be ignorant of something, or to openly confess that you do not know that of which you are ignorant? *Arnobius (c. 305, E), 6.452, 453.*

III. Tripartite distinction of body, soul, and spirit

May your whole spirit, soul, and body be preserved blameless at the coming of our Lord Jesus Christ. 1 Thess. 5:23.

The word of God is living and powerful, and sharper than any two-edged sword, piercing even to the division of soul and spirit. Heb. 4:12.

We recognize two kinds of spirits. One kind is called the soul, but the other is greater than the soul. It is an image and likeness of God. Both existed in the first men. So in one sense, those men were material. But, in another sense, they were superior to matter. *Tatian (c. 160, E), 2.70.*

The soul is not in itself immortal, O Greeks, but mortal. Yet it is possible for it not to die. To be sure, if it does not know the truth, it dies. It is dissolved with the body, but rises again at last at the end of the world with the body, receiving death by punishment in immortality. But, again, if it acquires the knowledge of God, it does not die, although for a time it is dissolved. . . . The soul does not preserve the spirit, but is preserved by it. . . . The dwelling place of the spirit is above, but the origin of the soul is from beneath. *Tatian (c. 160, E), 2.70, 71.*

When the number is completed that He had predetermined in His own counsel, all those who have been enrolled for life will rise again. They will have their own bodies, their own souls, and their own spirits, in which they had pleased God. *Irenaeus (c. 180, E/W), 1.411.*

What was his object in praying that these three—that is, the soul, body, and spirit—might be preserved to the coming of the Lord, unless he was aware of the reintegration and union of the three? *Irenaeus (c. 180, E/W), 1.532.*

To die is to lose vital power and to become thereafter breathless, inanimate, and devoid of motion. . . . But this event happens neither to the soul (for it is the breath of life) nor to the spirit, for the spirit . . . cannot be decomposed, and is itself the life of those who receive it. *Irenaeus (c. 180, E/W), 1.533.*

The complete man is composed of flesh, soul, and spirit. One of these does indeed preserve and fashion [the man]—the spirit. It is united and formed to another—the flesh. Then there is that which is between these two—the soul. The soul is sometimes indeed raised up by it, when it follows the spirit. But sometimes the soul sympathizes with the flesh and falls into carnal lusts. *Irenaeus (c. 180, E/W), 1.534.*

Some maintain that there is within the soul a natural substance—the spirit—which is different from it. If this were so, to have life (the function of the soul) would be one thing, and to breathe (the alleged function of the spirit) would be another thing. . . . Man, indeed, although organically furnished with lungs and windpipes, will not on that account be proved to *breathe* by one process, and to *live* by another. . . . How much firmer ground have you for believing that the soul and the spirit are actually one and the same—since you assign to them no difference. *Tertullian (c. 210, W), 3.189, 190.*

The mind is nothing else than an apparatus or instrument of the soul. And the spirit is not another faculty separate from the soul, but it is the soul itself when exercised in respiration. . . . The truth is that whenever a man is out of his mind, it is his soul that is demented—not because the mind is absent, but because it is a fellow-sufferer at the time. *Tertullian (c. 210, W), 3.198.*

The apostolic teaching is that the soul, after its departure from the world, will be recompensed according to its deserts. For it has a substance and life of its own. . . . However, with respect to the soul, there is not distinguished with sufficient clearness in the teaching of the church whether it is derived from the seed by a process of traducianism (whereby the reason or substance of it may be considered as contained in the seminal particles of the body themselves) or whether it has some other beginning (and if so, whether this beginning is by birth or not, or whether it is bestowed upon the body from outside). *Origen (c. 225, E), 4.240.*

It appears that the soul is something intermediate between the weak flesh and the willing spirit. *Origen (c. 225, E), 4.289.*

IV. Tertullian's teaching on the corporeality of the soul

Tertullian believed that the soul has some type of nonfleshly body that corresponds to the fleshly body, although the soul's body is not visible to human eyes. Since the early church had no specific dogma about the nature and origin of the soul, Tertullian's theory was not considered heretical. Nevertheless, it was a minority view. Some of Irenaeus's understandings of the soul are similar to Tertullian's, although Irenaeus does not go as far with the theory of the soul's corporeality as does Tertullian.

Every simple-minded person who agrees with our opinion will be apt to suppose that the flesh will have to be present at the final judgment. . . . Otherwise, the soul would be incapable of suffering pain or pleasure—for it is incorporeal. Now, this is the common opinion. I, on my part, however, maintain here, and in a special treatise on the subject, . . . that the soul is corporeal. *Tertullian (c. 210, W), 3.557.*

The soul certainly sympathizes with the body and shares in its pain. . . . The body, too, suffers with the soul and is united with it. . . . When the body is deserted by the soul, it is overcome by death. The soul, therefore, is endowed with a body. For if it were not corporeal, it could not desert the body. *Tertullian (c. 210, W), 3.185*

Soranus, who is a most accomplished authority in medical science, provides us with an answer when he asserts that the soul is even nourished by corporeal food. In fact, when the soul is ailing and weak, it is oftentimes refreshed by food. Indeed, when deprived of all food, does not the soul entirely leave the body? *Tertullian (c. 210, W), 3.186.*

In the Gospel itself, there is found the clearest evidence for the corporeal nature of the soul. In Hades, the soul of a certain man is in torment, punished in flames, suffering excruciating thirst, and imploring from the finger of a happier soul the solace of a drop of water for his tongue. . . . Unless the soul possessed corporeality, the shadow of a soul could not possibly contain a finger of a bodily substance. . . . It must be a body to be able to experience punishment and refreshment. *Tertullian (c. 210, W), 3.187.*

Concerning the soul's corporeality, it is invisible to the flesh, but perfectly visible to the spirit. Thus John, being "in the Spirit of God," plainly beheld the souls of the martyrs. *Tertullian (c. 210, W), 3.187, 188.*

This is the inner man—different from the outer, yet one in the twofold condition. It, too, has eyes and ears of its own. . . . Thus it happens that the rich man in Hades has a tongue, and the poor man has a finger. Abraham has a bosom. By these features, also, the souls of the martyrs under the altar are distinguished and known. *Tertullian (c. 210, W), 3.189; see also 3.175–3.179.*

SEE ALSO DEAD, INTERMEDIATE STATE OF THE; FLESH; FREE WILL AND PREDESTINATION; MAN, DOCTRINE OF; ORIGIN (II. Viewpoints Unique to Origen); RESURRECTION OF THE DEAD.

SOUL SLEEP
SEE DEAD, INTERMEDIATE STATE OF.

SOVEREIGNTY AND PROVIDENCE OF GOD

The providence of God refers to His direction and care over all creation. God's sovereignty refers to the fact that God is the supreme Ruler and Lawgiver of the universe.

Unless the Lord builds the house, they labor in vain who build it; unless the Lord guards the city, the watchman stays awake in vain. Ps. 127:1.

Are not two sparrows sold for a copper coin? And not one of them falls to the ground apart from your Father's will. But the very hairs of your head are all numbered. Do not fear therefore; you are of more value than many sparrows. Matt. 10:29–31.

My Father, who has given them to Me, is greater than all; and no one is able to snatch them out of My Father's hand. John 10:29.

Jesus answered, "You could have no power at all against Me, unless it had been given you from above. John 19:11.

We know that all things work together for good to those who love God, to those who are the called according to His purpose. Rom. 8:28.

So then it is not of him who wills, nor of him who runs, but of God who shows mercy. . . . You will say to me then, "Why does He still find fault? For who has resisted His will?" But indeed, O man, who are you to reply against God? Will the thing formed say to him who formed it, "Why have you made me like this?" Rom. 9:19.

Instead you ought to say, "If the Lord wills, we shall live and do this or that." Jas. 4:15.

Accept as a blessing all of the things that befall you. For nothing comes to pass apart from God. *Didache (c. 80–140, E), 7.378.*

I hope as a prisoner in Christ Jesus to salute you—if indeed it is the will of God that I am thought worthy of attaining to the end. *Ignatius (c. 105, E), 1.73.*

All the martyrdoms were blessed and noble, and they took place according to the will of God. For it befits those of us who profess greater piety than others to ascribe to God the authority over all things. *Martyrdom of Polycarp (c. 135, E), 1.39.*

Not a single thing that has been made, or that will be made, escapes the knowledge of God. Rather, through His providence, every single thing has obtained its nature, rank, number, and special quantity. Nothing whatever has been produced (or is produced) in vain or by accident. Instead, everything has been made with precise suitability and through the exercise of transcendent knowledge. *Irenaeus (c. 180, E/W), 1.398.*

They were convinced that they should call the Maker of this universe the Father, for He exercises a providence over all things and arranges the affairs of our world. *Irenaeus (c. 180, E/W), 1.459.*

God rules over men and Satan too. In fact, without the will of our Father in heaven not even a sparrow falls to the ground. *Irenaeus (c. 180, E/W), 1.551.*

The will and the energy of God is the effective and foreseeing cause of every time, place, and age—and of every nature. *Irenaeus (c. 180, E/W), 1.569.*

Nothing happens without the will of the Lord of the universe. It remains to say that such things happen without the prevention of God. For this alone saves both the providence and the goodness of God. We must not, therefore, think that He actively produces afflictions. . . . Rather, we must be persuaded that He does not

prevent those beings who cause them. Yet, He overrules for good the crimes of His enemies. *Clement of Alexandria (c. 195, E), 2.424.*

Now, then, many things in life take their rise in some exercise of human reason, having received the kindling spark from God. Some examples are health by medicine, soundness of body through gymnastics, and wealth by trade. Now, all these things truly have their origin and existence because of divine providence—yet, not without human cooperation as well. *Clement of Alexandria (c. 195, E), 2.517.*

Although disease, accident, and . . . death come upon the spiritual man, . . . by the power of God they become the medicine of salvation. Through discipline, such things benefit those who are difficult to reform. They are allotted according to what is deserved by providence, which is truly good. *Clement of Alexandria (c. 195, E), 2.540.*

Rightly, then, the spiritual man is not disturbed by anything that happens. Nor does he suspect those things that, through divine arrangement, take place for good. *Clement of Alexandria (c. 195, E), 2.547.*

I wish then, that these heretics would learn and be set right by these notes and turn to the sovereign God. *Clement of Alexandria (c. 195, E), 2.553.*

We wound Christ when we do not accept with equanimity the summoning out of this world of any by Him, as if they were to be pitied. *Tertullian (c. 200, W), 3.713.*

God hardened the heart of Pharaoh. However, he deserved to be influenced to his destruction, for he had already denied God. *Tertullian (c. 207, W), 3.308.*

The next quotation reflects the Montanist view that it is wrong to remarry after the death of one's spouse.

Moderation is to not regret something that has been taken away, and taken away by the Lord God. For, without His will, neither does a leaf glide down from a tree, nor does a sparrow of one small coin's worth fall to the earth. . . . Accordingly, if we renew a marriage that has been taken away [by the death of a spouse], we are no doubt striving against the will of God. For we wish to have once again a thing that He has not willed us to have. For had He willed it, he would not have taken it away. Unless we interpret this, too, to be the will of God—as if

He again willed us to have what He just now did not will. It is not the part of good and solid faith to refer all things to the will of God in such a manner as that. Nor should any person so flatter himself by saying that "nothing is done without His permission," so as to make us fail to understand that there is something in our own power. Otherwise, every sin will be excused if we persist in contending that nothing is done by us without the will of God. . . . Accordingly, we should not lay to the account of the Lord's will anything that lies subject to our own choice. *Tertullian (c. 212, W), 4.50, 51.*

Some things seem to indicate the will of God, seeing that they are *allowed* by Him. However, it does not necessarily follow that everything that is *permitted* proceeds out of the unqualified and absolute will of Him who permits it. *Tertullian (c. 212, W), 4.51.*

[PAGAN SPEAKER:] All things flow back again into their source. They are turned again into themselves—without any Designer, Judge, or Creator. . . . If the world were governed by divine providence and by the authority of any deity, Phalaris and Dionysius would never have deserved to reign, . . . and Socrates would never have deserved the poison. *Mark Minucius Felix (c. 200, W), 4.175.*

I comforted him, saying, "On that scaffold, whatever God wills will happen. For know that we are not placed in our own power, but in that of God." *Passion of Perpetua and Felicitas (c. 205, W), 3.701.*

Although the whole world is arranged into offices of different kinds, nevertheless, its condition is not to be supposed as one of internal discrepancies and discordance. Rather, just as our one body is provided with many members—and is held together by one soul—so I am of the opinion that the whole world also should be regarded as some huge and immense creature that is kept together by the Power and Reason of God as by one soul. . . . For how do we live, move, and have our being in God—except by His comprehending and holding together the whole world by His power? *Origen (c. 225, E), 4.269.*

[After the resurrection] a person will also learn the judgment of Divine providence on each individual thing. He will learn that among those events that happen to men, none occur by accident or chance, but in accordance with a plan so carefully considered and so stupendous that it does not overlook even the number of the hairs of the heads. I speak not only of the saints, but perhaps of all human beings. A person will learn that the plan of this Providential government extends even to caring for the sale of two sparrows for a denarius. *Origen (c. 225, E), 4.299.*

Some say that we are moved externally, and they put the blame away from ourselves by declaring that we are like stones and pieces of wood. They say we are dragged about by those forces that act upon us externally. However, this is neither true nor in conformity with reason. Rather, it is the statement of someone who desires to destroy the conception of free will. *Origen (c. 225, E), 4.304.*

By [the things written regarding Job], we are taught that it is not by any accidental attacks that we are persecuted when we are visited with any such loss of property. When one of us is taken prisoner, it is not because of chance. . . . For in respect of all of these occurrences, every believer should say, "You would have no power at all against me, unless it were given you from above." For notice that the house of Job did not fall upon his sons until the devil had first received power against them. *Origen (c. 225, E), 4.333, 334.*

The result of all the preceding remarks is to show that all the occurrences in the world that are considered to be of an intermediate kind—whether they are mournful or otherwise—are not indeed brought about *by* God. Yet, neither do they happen *without* Him. For He not only does not prevent those wicked and opposing powers who are desirous to bring these things about, but He even permits them to do so. . . . Therefore, Holy Scripture teaches us to receive all that happens as though sent by God, knowing that without Him no event occurs. *Origen (c. 225, E), 4.334.*

Now this seems to me to be like the argument of those who oppose the doctrine of providence and who arrange things differently from what they are. Then they allege that the world would be better if it were as *they* would arrange it. *Origen (c. 248, E), 4.459.*

We have to say that God preserves the free will of each individual. However, He may make use of the evil of a wicked person for the administration of the world. . . . Even so, such a wicked individual deserves condemnation. *Origen (c. 248, E), 4.528.*

We should . . . express our admiration of man, who is capable of considering and admiring all things. For he executes not only the works that are determined by the providence of God, but also those that are the consequences of his own foresight. *Origen (c. 248, E), 4.534.*

Now is the time for you . . . either to overturn the belief in a God who visits the human race and exercises a providence over each individual man—or else to believe this and prove the falsity of Celsus' assertions. *Origen (c. 248, E), 4.544.*

Kings are not appointed by the son of Saturn . . . but by God, who governs all things and who wisely arranges whatever belongs to the appointment of kings. *Origen (c. 248, E), 4.665.*

We are far from setting aside the notion of a providence and that things happen directly or indirectly through the agency of providence. . . . As the Scripture says, "Two sparrows are sold for an assarion [1/16th of a denarius], yet not one of them falls to the ground without our Father in heaven." So completely does the divine providence embrace all things, that not even the hairs of our head fail to be numbered by Him. *Origen (c. 248, E), 4.666.*

We should not think that such an inexhaustible providence of God does not reach to even the very least of things. For the Lord says, "One of two sparrows will not fall without the will of the Father. For even the very hairs of your head are all numbered." His care and providence did not permit even the clothes of the Israelites to be worn out. . . . Since He embraces all things and contains all things, . . . His care consequently extends to every single thing. For His providence encompasses the whole, whatever it is. *Novatian (c. 235, W), 5.617.*

He allows these things to happen for this reason: that our faith may be tested. *Cyprian (c. 250, W), 5.355.*

"And allow us not to be led into temptation." In these words, it is shown that the adversary can do nothing against us unless God has first permitted it. So all of our fear, devotion, and obedience should be turned towards God. For in our temptations, nothing is permitted to do evil unless power is given from Him. . . . But power is given to evil ones against us according to our sins. *Cyprian (c. 250, W), 5.454.*

This pestilence and plague, which seems horrible and deadly, searches out the righteousness of each one. . . . It reveals whether those who are in health will tend the sick. It reveals whether relatives affectionately love their kindred. It reveals whether masters pity their languishing servants. *Cyprian (c. 250, W), 5.473.*

Apart from divine providence and power, nature is absolutely nothing. However, if they are going to call God "nature," what perverseness it is to use the name of "nature," rather than of God! *Lactantius (c. 304–313, W), 7.97.*

The Most High Father arranged from the beginning, and ordained all things that were accomplished . . . in Christ. *Lactantius (c. 304–313, W), 7.127.*

SEE ALSO DISASTERS; EVIL, PROBLEM OF; FOREKNOWLEDGE OF GOD; FREE WILL AND PREDESTINATION.

SPAIN

Whenever I journey to Spain, I shall come to you. Rom. 15:24.

After preaching both in the east and west, [Paul] gained the illustrious reputation due to his faith, having taught righteousness to the whole world, and having come to the extreme limit of the west. [The "extreme limit of the west" probably refers to either Spain or Britain.] *Clement of Rome (c. 96, W), 1.6.*

The churches which have been planted in Germany do not believe or hand down anything different, nor do those in Spain, nor those in Gaul. *Irenaeus (c. 180, E/W), 1.330, 331.*

[The name of Christ has reached] the various confines of the Moors, all the limits of Spain, and the diverse nations of the Gauls. *Tertullian (c. 197, W), 3.158.*

The principle on which Luke wrote was to write only of what fell under his own notice. And he shows this clearly by the omission of the martyrdom of Peter, and also of the journey of Paul, when he went from the city of Rome to Spain. *Muratorian Fragment (c. 200, W), 5.603.*

If the gods willed that mice and locusts should swarm forth in prodigious numbers in Asia and in Syria because Christians dwelled among their tribes, why then was there likewise no such phenomenon in Spain and in Gaul? For innumerable Christians lived in those provinces also. *Arnobius (c. 305, E), 6.417.*

SEE ALSO BRITAIN; CHRISTIANITY (II. GROWTH OF CHRISTIANITY); EVANGELISM; GERMANS.

SPIRIT, HOLY

SEE HOLY SPIRIT.

SPIRIT, HUMAN

SEE SOUL (III. TRIPARTITE DISTINCTION OF BODY, SOUL, AND SPIRIT).

SPIRITISM

There shall not be found among you anyone who makes his son or his daughter pass through the fire, or one who practices witchcraft, or a soothsayer, or one who interprets omens, or a sorcerer, or one who conjures spells, or a medium, or a spiritist, or one who calls up the dead. For all who do these things are an abomination to the Lord. Deut. 18:10–12.

Now the works of the flesh are evident, which are: adultery, . . . idolatry, sorcery; . . . of which I tell you beforehand, just as I also told you in time past, that those who practice such things will not inherit the kingdom of God. Gal. 5:19–21.

But the cowardly, unbelieving, abominable, murderers, sexually immoral, sorcerers, idolaters, and all liars shall have their part in the lake which burns with fire. Rev. 21:8.

My child, do not be an observer of omens, for it leads the way to idolatry. Likewise, do not be an enchanter nor an astrologer. *Didache (c. 80– 140, E), 7.378.*

Sorcerers call forth spirits and even bring up what seem to be the souls of the dead. They put boys to death in order to get a response from an oracle. With their juggling illusions, they pretend to do various miracles. They put dreams into people's minds by the power of the angels and demons, whose assistance they have invoked. *Tertullian (c. 197, W), 3.37.*

Sometimes the demons animate the fibers of the entrails, control the flights of birds, direct the lots, and are the cause of oracles involved in many falsehoods. *Mark Minucius Felix (c. 200, W), 4.190.*

As we have already suggested, there is hardly a human being who is unattended by a demon. And it is well known to many that premature and violent deaths (which men ascribe to accidents) are in fact brought about by demons. This deception of the evil spirits lying concealed in the persons of the dead, we are able to prove by actual facts (if I am not mistaken). For in cases of exorcism, [the evil spirit] sometimes claims to be one of the relatives of the persons possessed by him. . . . And, yet, for all that, the demon—after trying to circumvent the bystanders—is vanquished by the pressure of divine grace. And painfully against his will, he confesses the whole truth. The situation is similar in the other kind of sorcery that is supposed to bring up from Hades the souls now resting there. *Tertullian (c. 210, W), 3.233.*

Neither will I be silent respecting that piece of knavery of these sorcerers, which consists in divination by means of a cauldron. *Hippolytus (c. 225, W), 5.38.*

The wisdom of the princes of this world . . . we understand to be things like the secret and occult philosophy (as they call it) of the Egyptians and the astrology of the Chaldeans and Indians. *Origen (c. 225, E), 4.335.*

And what are we to say also of those whom they call diviners? By the working of those demons who have the mastery over them, these persons give answers in carefully constructed verses. Likewise, by invoking demons, those persons whom they term Magi or Malevolent have often caused boys of tender years to repeat poetical compositions that were the admiration and amazement of all. *Origen (c. 225, E), 4.335, 336.*

Since [the demons] are without bodies of earthly material, they possess some power of foretelling future events. So they engage in works of this kind, desiring to lead the human race away from the true God. They also secretly enter the bodies of the more predatory, savage, and wicked of animals and stir them up to do *whatever* they choose, *whenever* they choose. They can turn the fancies of these animals to make flights and movements of various kinds, in order to entrap men by such power of divination. *Origen (c. 248, E), 4.538.*

Magic and sorcery derive their power from evil demons, who are spell-bound by elaborate incantations and become subject to sorcerers. *Origen (c. 248, E), 4.451.*

The names of Abraham, Isaac, and Jacob possess such efficacy when united with the name of God, that those belonging to the nation [of Israel] employ in their prayers to God, and in the exorcising of demons, the words, "God of Abraham, God of Isaac, and God of Jacob." Not only do they use those words, but so also do almost all those who occupy themselves with incantations and magical rites. For there is found in treatises on magic in many countries such an invocation of God ... as implies a familiar use of it by these men in their dealings with demons. *Origen (c. 248, E), 4.512.*

[The Israelites] abhorred all kinds of divination, as something that bewitches men to no purpose and that actually comes from wicked demons. *Origen (c. 248, E), 4.562.*

Divination must not be used. *Cyprian (c. 250, W), 5.553.*

The demons were the inventors of astrology, soothsaying, divination, ... oracles, necromancy, the arts of magic, and whatever evil practices men exercise in addition to those things. *Lactantius (c. 304–313, W), 7.64.*

By itself, fortune is nothing. And we must not regard it as though it had any perception. For fortune is merely the sudden and unexpected occurrence of accidents. ... We also know that there is a wicked and crafty spirit who is unfriendly to the good. *Lactantius (c. 304–313, W), 7.98, 99.*

Avoid ... their enchantments, observations of omens, soothsayings, purgations, divinations, observations of birds, their necromancies, and their invocations. *Apostolic Constitutions (compiled c. 390, E), 7.424; see also 5.553; extended discussion: 5.35–5.40.*

SEE ALSO ASTROLOGY; DEMONS, DEMON POSSESSION; EXORCISM; ORACLES, PAGAN; SAMUEL.

SPIRITUAL GIFTS

SEE GIFTS OF THE SPIRIT.

SPIRITS IN PRISON

SEE DESCENT INTO HADES.

SPORTS

Bodily exercise profits a little, but godliness is profitable for all things. 1 Tim. 4:8.

For men to prefer gymnastic exercises to the baths is perhaps not bad. For such exercises are in some respects conducive to the health of young men. ... Nor are women to be deprived of bodily exercise. ... Reading aloud is often an exercise to many. However, do not let the athletic contests that I have allowed be undertaken for the sake of vainglory. Rather, they should be undertaken only for manly sweat. ... We must always aim at moderation. *Clement of Alexandria (c. 195, E), 2.283.*

Playing at ball not only depends on someone throwing the ball skillfully, but it also requires one to catch it dexterously, so that the game may be gone through according to the rules for ball. *Clement of Alexandria (c. 195, E), 2.353.*

[CONCERNING THE PUBLIC GAMES:] To the testimony of antiquity is added that of later games instituted in their place. ... Now, it is imprinted, as if on their very faces, for what idol and for what religious object these games of one kind or another were designed. ... The others have their religious origin in the birthdays and solemnities of kings, in public successes in municipal holidays. *Tertullian (c. 197, W), 3.82.*

Now let me address the kind of performances peculiar to the circus exhibitions [i.e., chariot races]. In former days, equestrianism was practiced in a simple way on horseback. Certainly, its ordinary use had nothing sinful in it. But when it was dragged into the games, it passed from the service of God into the employment of demons. *Tertullian (c. 197, W), 3.83.*

You will never give your approval to those foolish racing and throwing feats, and yet more foolish leapings. You will never find pleasure in injurious or useless exhibitions of strength. Certainly you will not regard with approval the strivings after an artificial body that aim at surpassing the Creator's work. ... And the wrestler's art is a devil's thing. *Tertullian (c. 197, W), 3.87.*

How idle are the contests themselves: strifes in colors, contentions in races, acclamations in mere questions of honor, rejoicing because a horse has been faster, grieving because it was more sluggish, reckoning up the years of animals, knowing the consuls, learning their ages, tracing their breeds, recording their very grandsires and great-grandsires! *Novatian (c. 235, W), 5.577, formerly attributed to Cyprian.*

Those who come for the sake of beholding the spectacle actually display more of a spectacle themselves. I am referring to when they begin to shout ... and to leap from their seats. . . . The celebrations of the games are festivals in honor of the gods, for they were instituted on account of their birthdays, or the dedication of new temples. . . . Therefore, if anyone is present at the spectacles to which men assemble for the sake of religion, he has departed from the worship of God. *Lactantius (c. 304–313, W), 7.188.*

We may not join in their feasts, which are celebrated in honor of demons, being partakers of them in their impiety. You are also to avoid their public meetings and those sports that are celebrated in them. *Apostolic Constitutions (compiled c. 390, E), 7.424.*

SEE ALSO ENTERTAINMENT; GLADIATORS; GYMNASIUM; OLYMPICS.

STAR OF BETHLEHEM

SEE BIRTH OF JESUS; MAGI.

STATIONS

SEE FASTING.

STATUES

SEE IMAGES.

STEPHEN

Stephen was the first man elected into the diaconate by the apostles, and he was the first slain for the testimony of Christ. *Irenaeus (c. 180, E/W), 1.480.*

STOICS, STOICISM

Stoicism was a philosophical school founded by Zeno (335–263 B.C.) in Athens. The Stoics believed that everything in the universe, including God, is material. They also believed that all things are predestined. Most Stoic teachers taught the importance of virtuous living. In the first and second centuries, Stoicism became the dominant philosophy of the Romans.

The philosophers called Stoics teach that even God Himself will be resolved into fire. They also say that the world is to be formed anew by this revolution. *Justin Martyr (c. 160, E), 1.169.*

Not taking note of this, the Stoics maintained that all things take place according to the necessity of fate. *Justin Martyr (c. 160, E), 1.190.*

Why, then, do Epicurus and the Stoics teach incest and sodomy, with which doctrines they have filled libraries? *Theophilus (c. 180, E), 2.112.*

The Stoics say that God, like the soul, is essentially body and spirit. You will find all this explicitly in their writings. *Clement of Alexandria (c. 195, E), 2.465.*

Turning away from Christians to the philosophers, from the church to the Academy and the Porch, he learned there from the Stoics how to place Matter on the same level with the Lord—just as if Matter too had eternally existed, neither being born nor made, having no beginning at all nor end. *Tertullian (c. 200, W), 3.477.*

I call on the Stoics also to help me, who, while declaring almost in our own terms that the soul is a spiritual essence, will yet have no difficulty in persuading us that the soul is a corporeal substance. Indeed, Zeno defines the soul as a spirit generated with the body. *Tertullian (c. 210, W), 3.185.*

The Stoics are very fond of saying that God—in His most watchful providence over every institution—gave us dreams among other preservatives of the arts and sciences of divination. *Tertullian (c. 210, W), 3.225.*

The Stoics themselves also imparted growth to philosophy, in respect of a greater development of the art of syllogism. . . . They likewise supposed God to be the one originating Principle of all things. They said He was a body of the utmost refinement and that His providential care pervaded everything. These speculators were positive about the existence of fate everywhere. . . . The same, of course, holds true in the case of men. For though not willing to follow, men will altogether be compelled to enter upon what has been decreed for them [according to the Stoics]. The Stoics, however, do assert that the soul abides after death, but that it is a body. *Hippolytus (c. 225, W), 5.20.*

The Stoics assign all things to destruction by fire. *Origen (c. 248, E), 4.606.*

The Stoics say that the world and all things that are in it, were made for the sake of men. The sacred writings teach us the same thing. . . . Zeno the Stoic taught that there were infernal regions and that the abodes of the good were separated from the wicked. He said the good enjoy peaceful and delightful regions, but that the wicked suffer punishment in dark places. *Lactantius (c. 304–313, W), 7.204; see also 2.375.*

SEE ALSO MARCUS AURELIUS; PHILOSOPHERS, PHILOSOPHY.

SUBDEACON

In the early church, a subdeacon was an assistant to a deacon, and in some churches he performed similar functions to that of a deacon.

We have been informed by Crementius the subdeacon, who came to us from you, that the blessed father Cyprian has withdrawn for a certain reason. *Letter from the clergy of Rome to Cyprian (c. 250, W), 5.280.*

The presbyters and deacons abiding at Rome, to father Cyprian, greetings. Beloved brother, we carefully read your letter that you had sent by Fortunatus, the subdeacon. *Letter from the clergy of Rome to Cyprian (c. 250, W), 5.307.*

. . . the letter that you sent to us by Herennianus, the sub-deacon, and Lucian, Maximus, and Amantius, the acolytes. *Letter of Lucius to Cyprian (c. 250, W), 5.405.*

SEE ALSO DEACON; MINOR ORDERS.

SUBSTANCE

SEE CHRIST, DIVINITY OF (III. Relationship of the Son to the Father).

SUICIDE

If a murderer is guilty because he is a destroyer of man, he who kills himself is under the same guilt. For he also kills a man. In fact, this crime can be considered to be greater, for the punishment of it belongs to God alone. We did not come into this life of our own accord. Therefore, we can withdraw from this habitation of the body . . . only by the command of Him who placed us in this body. We are to inhabit it until He orders us to depart from it. *Lactantius (c. 304–313, W), 7.89.*

It is a virtue to despise death. Not that we seek death, or of our own accord inflict it upon ourselves. . . . For this would be a wicked and ungodly thing. *Lactantius (c. 304–313, W), 7.183.*

SUN WORSHIP

When you look up to the heavens and behold the sun or the moon or any star among the heavenly hosts, do not be led astray into adoring them and serving them. These the Lord, your God, has left fall to the lot of all other nations under the heavens. Deut. 4:19.

It is written that God has given the sun and moon to the nations to worship as gods. *Justin Martyr (c. 160, E), 1.222.*

Not only the believer, but even the pagan, is judged most righteously. For God knew by virtue of His foreknowledge that the Gentile would not believe. Nevertheless, in order that the Gentile might receive his own perfection, God gave him philosophy. However, He gave it him previous to faith. And He gave the sun, the moon, and the stars to be worshipped. For the Law says God made them for the nations, so that they might not become altogether atheistic and so utterly perish. Nevertheless, the Gentiles, even in the instance of this commandment, became devoid of sense and addicted themselves to graven images. Therefore, they are judged unless they repent. . . . This was the way given to the nations to rise up to God, by means of the worship of the heavenly bodies. But there were those who would not abide by those heavenly bodies that had been assigned to them. Rather, they fell away from them to wooden blocks and stones. So they were considered . . . beyond salvation. *Clement of Alexandria (c. 195, E), 2.505.*

SEE ALSO GODS, PAGAN; HEAVENLY BODIES.

SUPERSTITION

It is natural, then, that having a superstitious dread of those quick-tempered gods, the pagans imagine that all events are signs and causes of evils. . . . If a cock that is being fattened crows in the evening, they think this is a sign of something. . . . The same people who worship every stick and greasy stone (as the saying goes) dread tufts of tawny wool, lumps of salt, and torches. *Clement of Alexandria (c. 195, E), 2.529.*

SEE ALSO SPIRITISM.

SUPPORT OF CLERGY

SEE CHURCH GOVERNMENT.

SURSUM CORDA

The expression sursum corda is Latin for "lift up your hearts." It is an expression that appears in most early liturgies.

The Lord's priest commanded with "sursum corda" when prayer was to be made, so that you would be silent. *Commodianus (c. 240, W), 4.218.*

The priest, by way of preface before his prayer, prepares the minds of the brethren by saying, "Lift up your hearts." The people respond, "We lift them up unto the Lord." He does this so he may be reminded that he himself should think of nothing but the Lord. *Cyprian (c. 250, W), 5.455.*

SEE ALSO LITURGY.

SUSANNA

Susanna was a virtuous Jewish woman who was a contemporary of Daniel. She was wrongfully charged with adultery by two elders. In the Septuagint, the account of her life is included either as an additional chapter in Daniel or as a separate book following the book of Daniel.

We find that the blessed Daniel prophesied in Babylon and appeared as the vindicator of Susannah. *Hippolytus (c. 205, W), 5.178.*

Susanna prefigured the church. Her husband, Joachim, prefigured Christ. *Hippolytus (c. 205, W), 5.192.*

When she heard these words, the blessed Susanna was troubled in her heart and watched her tongue. For she did not wish to be defiled by the wicked elders. *Hippolytus (c. 205, W), 5.193.*

Susanna was subjected to unveiling on her trial. *Tertullian (c. 211, W), 3.95.*

As we read of her, Susanna . . . was exceedingly beautiful [in appearance]. However, she was still more beautiful in character. Her outward appearance added no charm to her. For she was simple. Chastity had cultivated her. *Novatian (c. 235, W), 5.590, formerly attributed to Cyprian.*

The History of Susanna is found in every church of Christ in that Greek copy which the Greeks use [i.e., the Septuagint], but it is not in the Hebrew copies. *Origen (c. 240, E), 4.386.*

There was a learned Hebrew, who was said to be the son of a wise man and to have been specially trained to succeed his father. I had conversations with him on many subjects. I remember hearing from him the names of those elders. This indicated that he did not reject the history of Susanna. *Origen (c. 240, E), 4.388; extended discussion: 5.191–5.194.*

Discussion of canonicity of Susanna: 4.385–4.390.

SEE ALSO DEUTEROCANONICAL BOOKS.

SWEARING

SEE OATHS.

SYNAGOGUE

Even if Jesus had the general right of entering the synagogue (like other Jews), yet the function of giving instruction was allowed only to a man who was extremely well known. It had to be a man who had been examined and tested. Such a man was for some time invested with the privilege after duly attested by experience elsewhere. *Tertullian (c. 207, W), 3.352.*

SEE ALSO JEW, JEWS; TEMPLE, JEWISH.

SYNERGISM

SEE FREE WILL AND PREDESTINATION (IV. SYNERGISM).

SYNODS

SEE COUNCILS, CHURCH.

TABERNACLE

The Holy Spirit indicating this, that the way into the Holiest of All was not yet made manifest while the first tabernacle was still standing. It was symbolic for the present time in which both gifts and sacrifices are offered. Heb. 11:10.

The Hebrews were commanded to furnish the tabernacle as a type of the church. In this manner, by means of visible things, they could announce in advance the image of divine things. A pattern was shown to Moses on the mountain. He was to follow this in making the tabernacle. For the pattern was a type of accurate representation of the heavenly dwelling. We now understand this more clearly than we did through the types. Yet, we still perceive it more darkly than if we saw the reality. *Methodius (c. 290, E), 6.328.*

The Jews flutter about the bare letter of Scripture. . . . They believe that these words and ordinances were spoken concerning a tabernacle such as they erected. As if God delighted in those trivial adornments which they prepared. . . . In reality, those things . . . foretell the resurrection and the putting up of our tabernacle that had fallen upon the earth. *Methodius (c. 290, E), 6.344; extended discussion of what the tabernacle typified: 2.452–2.454.*

SEE ALSO ARK OF THE COVENANT; SYNAGOGUE; TEMPLE, JEWISH; TYPE, TYPOLOGY.

TACITUS

Cornelius Tacitus was a notable Roman historian who provided an accurate historical account of the Roman Empire in the first century. Tacitus, however, was not favorably disposed towards Christians, calling them "enemies of the human race."

Like some others, you are under the delusion that our god is an ass's head. Cornelius Tacitus first put this notion into people's minds. *Tertullian (c. 197, W), 3.31.*

Some among you have dreamed that our god is an ass's head—an absurdity that Cornelius Tacitus first suggested. In the fourth book of his *Histories*, . . . he begins his description with the origin of the [Jewish] nation. *Tertullian (c. 197, W), 3.121.*

TALENTS, PARABLE OF

SEE PARABLES OF JESUS.

TARTARUS

God did not spare the angels who sinned, but cast them down to hell [Tartarus] and delivered them into chains of darkness, to be reserved for judgment. 2 Pet. 2:4.

I would have you, then, consider whether the merits of your deities are of a kind to have raised them to the heavens, and not rather to have sunk them down into the lowest depths of Tartarus. It is the place that you regard, with many, as the prison of infernal punishments. *Tertullian (c. 197, W), 3.28.*

In order to teach us this, He uses the examples of Hades, the love of women, Tartarus, and the earth that is not filled with water. . . . Tartarus, which is situated in a doleful and dark locality, is not touched by a ray of light. *Hippolytus (c. 205, W), 5.174.*

By means of this knowledge, you will escape the approaching threat of the fire of judgment and the black scenery of gloomy Tartarus, where a beam from the radiant voice of the Word never shines. *Hippolytus (c. 225, W), 5.153; see also 6.445.*

SEE ALSO ANGEL, ANGELS (III.WICKED ANGELS); ETERNAL PUNISHMENTS AND REWARDS.

TATIAN

Tatian (2nd century) was a disciple of Justin Martyr, and he produced several Christian works, including the Diatessaron, a harmony of the four Gospels. After the death of Justin Martyr, however, Tatian embraced heretical Encratite teachings. All of the quotations from Tatian in the Ante-Nicene Fathers are from Tatian's orthodox writings.

A certain man named Tatian first introduced the blasphemy [i.e., denial of Adam's salvation]. He was a hearer of Justin [Martyr]. Now, as long as he continued with Justin, he expressed no such views. But after Justin's martyrdom, Tatian separated from the church. Excited and puffed up by the thought of being a teacher (as if he were superior to others), he composed his own peculiar type of doctrine. He invented a system of certain invisible Aeons, like the followers of Valentinus. Furthermore, like Marcion and Saturninus, he declared that marriage was nothing else than corruption and fornication. But his denial of Adam's salvation was an opinion that was entirely due to himself. *Irenaeus (c. 180, E/W), 1.353.*

Besides, there are writings of certain brethren older than the times of Victor, which they wrote against the pagans in defense of the truth and against the heresies of their day. I mean Justin, Miltiades, Tatian, Clement, and many others. In all their writings, divinity is ascribed to Christ. *Eusebius, quoting Caius (c. 215, W), 5.601.*

Although he himself was a disciple of Justin the Martyr, Tatian did not hold similar opinions with his master. Rather, he attempted to introduce certain novelties and stated that there existed certain invisible Aeons.... Similarly with Marcion, he stated that marriage is destruction. He also alleged that Adam is not saved, because he was the author of disobedience. *Hippolytus (c. 225, W), 5.122.*

There exists the *Discourse to the Greeks,* written by Tatian the younger. With very great learning, he lists in this work those historians who have

written about the antiquity of the Jewish nation and of Moses. *Origen (c. 248, E), 4.403.*

On this basis, perhaps, Tatian, the chief of the Encratites, endeavors to build his heresy, asserting that wine is not to be drunk. His rationale is that it was commanded in the Law that the Nazarites were not to drink wine. *Jerome (c. 400, W), 2.83; see also 5.146.*

SEE ALSO ENCRATITES; HERESIES, HERETICS; JUSTIN MARTYR.

TAXES

"Is it lawful to pay taxes to Caesar, or not?" ... And He said to them, "Whose image and inscription is this?" They said to Him, "Caesar's." And He said to them, "Render therefore to Caesar the things that are Caesar's, and to God the things that are God's." Matt. 22:17–21.

Because of this you also pay taxes, for they are God's ministers attending continually to this very thing. Render therefore to all their due: taxes to whom taxes are due, customs to whom customs, fear to whom fear, honor to whom honor. Rom. 13:6, 7.

And of civil government, it says: "Render to Caesar the things that are Caesar's; and unto God, the things that are God's." *Clement of Alexandria (c. 195, E), 2.293.*

Your other taxes will acknowledge a debt of gratitude to Christians. For in the faithfulness that keeps us from fraud upon a brother, it is a matter of conscience that we pay all our taxes. *Tertullian (c. 197, W), 3.49.*

No doubt the apostle admonishes the Romans to be subject to all powers, for there is no power but of God.... Then he goes on to show also how he wishes you to be subject to the powers, exhorting you to pay "tribute to whom tribute is due, custom to whom custom [is due]." In other words, give the things that are Caesar's back to Caesar, and the things that are God's to God. *Tertullian (c. 213, W), 3.647.*

Do not be owing the pagans anything in the nature of tribute or fear. Instead, "render to Caesar the things that are Caesar's, and to God the things that are God's." I am speaking of tribute, taxes, or head-money. For our Lord was freed from disturbance by giving a piece of money. *Apostolic Constitutions (compiled c. 390, E), 7.417.*

Be subject to all royal power and dominion in things that are pleasing to God. . . . Render to everyone the fear that is due to them, all offerings, all customs, all honor, gifts, and taxes. *Apostolic Constitutions (compiled c. 390, E), 7.436.*

SEE ALSO CHURCH AND STATE; GOVERNMENT.

TEMPERANCE

SEE WINE.

TEMPLE, JEWISH

Then the Jews said, "It has taken forty-six years to build this temple, and will You raise it up in three days?" John 2:20.

Concerning the building of the temple in Judea, Solomon the king built this 566 years after the exodus of the Jews from Egypt. Among the people of Tyre, there is a record of how the temple was built. In their archives, writings have been preserved that prove the temple existed 143 years and 8 months before the Tyrians founded Carthage. This record was made by Hiram, the king of the Tyrians, the son of Abimalus. There was a hereditary friendship that existed between Hiram and Solomon . . . because of the surpassing wisdom that Solomon had. For they continually engaged with each other in discussing difficult problems. Proof of this exists in their correspondence, which has been preserved to this day among the Tyrians. *Theophilus (c. 180, E), 2.117, 118.*

The Jews therefore said, "Forty-six years was this temple in building, and will you raise it up in three days?" If we adhere to the history, we are unable to discern why the Jews said that the temple had taken forty-six years to build. For it is written in the third Book of Kings . . . that the building of it took less than eleven years. So why did the Jews say that the temple took forty-six years to build? A person could stretch the words to literally fit a period of forty-six years at all costs. He could do this by counting the time from when David planned the building of the temple. . . . However, someone else might say that the temple spoken of was not the one built by Solomon (since it was destroyed at the beginning of the captivity), but rather the temple built during the time of Ezra. And, perhaps, that temple took forty-six years to build. Still, things were very unsettled during the Maccabean period with regards to the people

and the temple. So I do not know if the [second] temple was really built in that number of years. *Origen (c. 228, E), 9.403.*

TEMPLES

SEE CHURCH BUILDINGS.

TEN COMMANDMENTS

SEE DECALOGUE.

TERTULLIAN

Septimius Tertullian (c. 160–240) wrote numerous apologies, works against heretics, and exhortations to other Christians. Nearly all of his works were written in Latin. A convert to Christianity when he was middle-aged, Tertullian apparently served as a presbyter in the church at Carthage, North Africa. Around 200, he became interested in the Montanist movement, and Montanistic influences are apparent in his writings after that date. Although many scholars believe that Tertullian eventually left the church to join a Montanist group, this matter cannot be established with any degree of certainty.

Septimius Tertullian was also skilled in literature of every kind. Yet, he had little inclination to eloquence. He was not very polished and was very obscure [in his rhetoric]. So he did not find great renown. *Lactantius (c. 304–313, W), 7.136.*

Tertullian fully pleaded the same cause in that treatise that is entitled the *Apology. Lactantius (c. 304–313, W), 7.140.*

SEE ALSO MONTANISTS; SOUL (IV. TERTULLIAN'S TEACHING ON THE CORPOREALITY OF THE SOUL).

TESTAMENT

In English, the term "testament" originally meant a will, as in "last will and testament." The Greek word *diathēkē* is translated as both "covenant" and "testament." So when the Christians of the second century spoke of the New Testament, they usually meant either the new covenant or the legacy left to us by Christ. It was not until around the third century that the terms "Old Testament" and "New Testament" took on the meaning of the two divisions of Scripture.

All the apostles taught that there were indeed two testaments among the two peoples. However, it was one and the same God who appointed both for the advantage of those men . . . who were to believe in God. . . . The first testament was not given without reason, or to no purpose, or in an accidental sort of manner. Rather, it subdued those to whom it was given to the service of God. *Irenaeus (c. 180, E/W), 1.506.*

No law is called a testament. Nor is anything else called a testament except what persons make who are about to die. And whatever is contained in the testament is sealed up through the day of the testator's death. *Victorinus (c. 280, W), 7.350.*

SEE ALSO NEW COVENANT; NEW TESTAMENT; OLD TESTAMENT.

TESTIMONIES

SEE CONVERSION.

TETRAGRAMMATON

The term "Tetragrammaton" refers to the four Hebrew letters (corresponding to YHWH) that represent the name of God in the Old Testament. In Latin, the Tetragrammaton is written as JHVH.

That mystic name is called the Tetragrammaton, by which those alone who had access to the Holy of Holies were protected. It is pronounced Jehovah, which means, "Who is and who will be." *Clement of Alexandria (c. 195, E), 2.585, from a Latin translation.*

TEXTUAL CRITICISM

In reference to Scripture, textual criticism is the discipline of comparing various ancient Bible texts for the purpose of determining which text is more likely to represent the original version. Quotations from the pre-Nicene writers play an important role in textual criticism, as they provide evidence of how various texts read in the centuries immediately following the apostles.

I. Evidence of divergent readings in early centuries

II. Isaiah 7:14

III. John 1:18

IV. Longer ending of Mark

I. Evidence of divergent readings in early centuries

"But I am far from putting reliance in your [Jewish] teachers, who refuse to admit that the interpretation made by the seventy elders who were with Ptolemy of the Egyptians is a correct one. . . . I wish you to observe, that they have altogether taken away many Scriptures from the translations effected by those seventy elders who were with Ptolemy." . . . Trypho, the Jew, said, "We ask you first of all to show us some of the Scriptures which you allege have been completely cancelled." And I said, "I will do as you ask. From the statements that Ezra made in reference to the law of the Passover, they have taken away the following: 'And Ezra said to the people, "This Passover is our Savior and our refuge."' . . . From the sayings of the same Jeremiah, the following words have been cut out: 'The Lord God remembered His dead people of Israel, who lay in the graves; and He descended to preach to them His own salvation.' . . . And from the ninety-fifth [ninety-sixth] Psalm, they have taken away this short saying of the words of David, . . . 'the Lord has reigned *from the wood*.'" *Justin Martyr (c. 160, E), 1.234, 235.*

This number [666] is found in all the most approved and ancient copies [of Revelation]. Furthermore, those men who saw John face to face bear their testimony. Reason also leads us to conclude that the number of the name of the beast, according to the Greek mode of calculation by the letters contained in it, will amount to six hundred and sixty-six. . . . I do not know how it is that some have erred following the ordinary mode of speech and have corrupted the middle number in the name. . . . Afterwards, others received this reading without examination. *Irenaeus (c. 180, E/W), 1.558.*

It is as incredible to every man of sense that we [i.e., orthodox Christians] would have introduced any corrupt text into the Scriptures. For we have existed from the very first. *Tertullian (c. 197, W), 3.262.*

For this reason, the heretics have boldly laid their hands upon the divine Scriptures, alleging that they have corrected them. . . . And many such copies can be obtained, for their disciples were very zealous in inserting these "corrections," as they call them. . . . Nor can they deny that the crime is theirs, when the copies have been written with their own hands.

Nor did they receive such copies of the Scriptures from those by whom they were first instructed in the faith. For they cannot produce the originals from which they were transcribed. *Eusebius, quoting Caius (c. 215, W), 5.602.*

"These things were done in Bethabara, beyond the Jordan, where John was baptizing." I am aware that the reading found in almost all the copies is: "These things were done in Bethany." Moreover, this appears to have been the reading at an earlier time.... However, I am convinced that we should not read "Bethany," but "Bethabara." For I have visited the places, in order to investigate.... Now, Bethany ... is fifteen stadia [1.8 miles] from Jerusalem. And the river Jordan is about a hundred and eighty stadia [21.5 miles] distant from it. *Origen (c. 228, E), 9.370.*

Thus we see that he who aims at a complete understanding of the Holy Scriptures must not neglect the careful examination of the proper names in it. In the matter of proper names, the Greek copies are often incorrect. In the Gospels, one might be misled by their authority. The event about the swine ... is said to have taken place in the country of the Gerasenes. Now, Gerasa is a town of Arabia, and it has neither a sea nor a lake. The evangelists would not have made a statement so obviously and demonstrably false. For they were men who informed themselves carefully of all matters connected with Judea. But in a few copies, we have found: "into the country of the Gadarenes." ... The same inaccuracy with regard to proper names is also to be observed in many passages of the Law and the Prophets, as I have been at pains to learn from the Hebrews. I have compared our own copies with theirs that have the confirmation of the versions never subjected to the corruption of Aquila, Theodotion, and Symmachus. *Origen (c. 228, E), 9.371.*

According to some of the manuscripts, Matthew has written, "Then He *commanded* His disciples that they should tell no man that He was the Christ." ... You must know, however, that some manuscripts of the Gospel according to Matthew have, "He *charged.*" *Origen (c. 245, E), 9.459.*

The ensuing quotation, in which Cyprian quotes from a Latin translation, may be a reference to 1 John 5:7.

It is written of the Father, of the Son, and of the Holy Spirit, "And these three are one." *Cyprian (c. 250, W), 5.423.*

In Ezra it is written in this manner: "And Ezra said to the people, 'This Passover is our Savior and our refuge.... And after these things, we will hope in Him, lest this place be deserted forever.'" *Lactantius (c. 304–313, W), 7.121, quoting a verse not found in our present texts.*

II. Isaiah 7:14

A key verse that differs between the Septuagint and the Masoretic text is Isaiah 7:14, where the Septuagint reads "virgin," while the Masoretic Text reads "young woman."

Behold, the virgin shall conceive and bear a Son, and shall call His name Immanuel. ISA. 7:14 [LXX].

But you [Jews] and your teachers venture to claim that in the prophecy of Isaiah it is not said, "Behold, the *virgin* will conceive," but, "Behold, the *young woman* will conceive, and bear a son." Furthermore, you explain the prophecy as if [it referred] to Hezekiah, who was your king. Therefore, I will endeavor to discuss shortly this point in opposition to you. *Justin Martyr (c. 160, E), 1.216.*

The Lord did Himself save us, giving us the token of the virgin. But this was not as some allege—who presume to expound the Scripture as: "Behold, a *young woman* will conceive, and bring forth a son." For this is the way that Theodotion the Ephesian has translated it, and Aquila of Pontus—both of whom are Jewish proselytes. The Ebionites, following these men, assert that Jesus was begotten by Joseph. *Irenaeus (c. 180, E/W), 1.451.*

He says, "Therefore, the Lord himself will give you a *sign.* Behold, a virgin will conceive, and bear a son." Now a sign from God would not have been a sign unless it had been some new and wonderful thing. However, Jewish cavillers, in order to annoy us, boldly pretend that Scripture does not hold that a *virgin* is to conceive and bring forth—but only a young woman. *Tertullian (c. 207, W), 3.331, 332.*

III. John 1:18

In the Textus Receptus (as translated in the King James Version), John 1:18 reads: "No man hath seen God at any time; the only begotten Son, which is in the bosom of the Father, he hath declared him." In the Alexandrine text, however, John 1:18 reads: "No man has seen

God at any time; the only begotten God, who is in the bosom of the Father, He has explained Him." Somewhat puzzling is the fact that in Irenaeus both versions of John 1:18 appear. It is generally believed that in Irenaeus the reading of "the only begotten Son" is a later alteration attempting to make it fit the Latin Vulgate:

There is one God the Father, who contains all things and who grants existence to all, as is written in the Gospel: "No man has seen God at any time, except the only-begotten Son, who is in the bosom of the Father; He has declared Him." *Irenaeus (c. 180, E/W), 1.489.*

"No man has seen God at any time." However, as He Himself desired it (and for the benefit of those who beheld the Word), His Word has shown the Father's brightness and explained His purposes (as also the Lord said): "The only-begotten God, who is in the bosom of the Father, He has declared Him." *Irenaeus (c. 180, E/W), 1.491.*

John also says, "No man has seen God at any time. The Only-Begotten Son, who is in the bosom of the Father, He has declared Him." *Hippolytus (c. 205, W), 5.225.*

"No one has seen God at any time. The Only-Begotten God, who is in the bosom of the Father, He has declared Him." *Origen (c. 228, E), 9.343.*

"The Only-Begotten Son of God, who is in the bosom of the Father, He has declared Him." *Origen (c. 228, E), 9.350.*

It is also supported by this Scripture: "No man has seen God at any time, except the only begotten Son, who is in the bosom of the Father." *Disputation of Archelaus and Manes (c. 320, E), 6.205.*

IV. Longer ending of Mark

The last twelve verses of Mark, as contained in the King James Version, do not appear in the two oldest Greek manuscripts in existence. Many of the pre-Nicene writers seem to be unfamiliar with these verses. On the other hand, Irenaeus quotes from some of them, and Tatian includes some of these verses in his Diatessaron.

"For whoever believes and is baptized shall be saved; but whoever does not believe shall be rejected. And the signs which will attend those who believe in me are these: they will cast out devils in my name; and they will speak with new tongues; and they will take up serpents; and if they drink deadly poison, it will not injure them; and they will lay their hands on the diseased, and they will be healed." [QUOTING MARK 16:15–18]. *Tatian (c. 160, E), 9.128, 129.*

Also, towards the conclusion of his Gospel, Mark says: "So then, after the Lord Jesus had spoken to them, He was received up into heaven, and sits on the right hand of God." [QUOTING MARK 16:19]. *Irenaeus (c. 180, E/W), 1.426.*

For the Lord says, . . . "He who believes and is baptized will be saved. But he who does not believe will be condemned." [QUOTING MARK 16:16.] *Apostolic Constitutions (compiled c. 390, E), 7.457.*

With good reason did He say . . . "They will cast out demons; they will speak with new tongues; they will take up serpents; and if they drink any deadly thing, it will by no means hurt them. They will lay their hands on the sick and they will recover." [QUOTING MARK 16:17, 18]. *Apostolic Constitutions (compiled c. 390, E), 7.479.*

SEE ALSO SCRIPTURES; SEPTUAGINT; VIRGIN BIRTH.

THADDAEUS

SEE SEVENTY, THE (DISCIPLES).

THECLA

Thecla, a Christian virgin, is the primary character in the apocryphal work, the Acts of Paul and Thecla. According to these Acts, Thecla cut her hair and dressed like a man. After this, Paul commissioned Thecla to teach.

I do not permit a woman to teach or to have authority over a man, but to be in silence. 1 Tim. 2:12.

The writings that wrongly go under Paul's name may claim Thecla's example as a license for women's teaching and baptizing. However, let them know that in Asia, the presbyter who composed that writing (as if he were augmenting Paul's fame from his own storehouse) confessed that he had done it from love of Paul. He was convicted and removed from his office. *Tertullian (c. 198, W), 3.677.*

SEE ALSO WOMEN (V. ROLE IN THE CHURCH).

THEOPHANY

A theophany is a temporary appearance of God in visible form. The early church taught that in all of the Old Testament theophanies, it was the pre-incarnate Son of God who appeared, not the Father.

They heard the sound of the Lord God walking in the garden in the cool of the day. Gen. 3:8.

The Lord came down to see the city and the tower which the sons of men had built. Gen. 11:5.

"Look!" he answered, "I see four men loose, walking in the midst of the fire; and they are not hurt, and the form of the fourth is like the Son of God." Dan. 3:25.

"How do you now say that He walked in Paradise?" Hear what I say: The God and Father of all, indeed, cannot be contained. He is not found in a place, for there is no place of His rest. Instead, His Word, through whom He made all things, being His Power and His Wisdom, assumed the character of the Father and Lord of all. He went to the garden in the person of God, and conversed with Adam.... The Word, then, being God, and being naturally produced from God, whenever the Father of the universe wills, He sends Him to any place. And when the Word appears, He is both heard and seen, being sent by Him. And He is found in a specific place. *Theophilus (c. 180, E), 2.103.*

The Son of God is implanted everywhere throughout Moses' writings. At one time, indeed, He spoke with Abraham, when about to eat with him. At another time, He was with Noah, giving to him the dimensions [of the ark]. At another time, He inquired after Adam. At another time, He brought down judgment upon the Sodomites. And again, He became visible and directed Jacob on his journey and spoke with Moses from the bush. *Irenaeus (c. 180, E/W), 1.473.*

He confesses himself to be the Instructor: "I am the Lord your God, who brought you out of the land of Egypt." ... This was He who appeared to Abraham and said to him, "I am your God, be accepted before Me." ... Furthermore, Jacob is said to have wrestled with Him. ... Jacob called the name of the place, "Face of God." He says, "For I have seen God face to face; and my life is preserved." The "face of God" is the Word by whom God is manifested and made known. Then also was Jacob given

the name Israel, because he saw God the Lord. It was God, the Word. *Clement of Alexandria (c. 195, E), 2.223, 224.*

This Word is called His Son. Under the name of "God," He was seen in various ways by the patriarchs, and He was heard at all times in the prophets. *Tertullian (c. 197, W), 3.249.*

It was Christ who was seen by the king of Babylon in the furnace with His martyrs—"the fourth, who was like the Son of man." He also was revealed to Daniel himself expressly as "the Son of man, coming in the clouds of heaven" as a Judge. *Tertullian (c. 207, W), 3.359.*

It was the Son, therefore, who was always seen, and the Son who always conversed with men. This is the Son who has always worked by the authority and will of the Father. For "the Son can do nothing of Himself, but what He sees the Father do." ... Therefore, it is the Son who has been from the beginning administering judgment, throwing down the pompous tower, confusing the languages, punishing the whole world by the violence of the deluge, raining fire and sulphur upon Sodom and Gomorrah, as the Lord from the Lord. *Tertullian (c. 213, W), 3.611.*

Moses everywhere introduces God the Father as infinite and without end. He is not enclosed in any place.... So, with reason, He can neither descend nor ascend, because He Himself both contains and fills all things. However, Moses speaks of God descending to consider the tower that the sons of men were building.... Whom do they pretend here to have been the God who descended to that tower? ... God the Father? But then He is enclosed in a place. So how does He embrace all things? ... Accordingly, neither did the Father descend ... nor did an angel command these things.... Then it remains that He must have descended, of whom the apostle Paul says, "He who descended is the same who ascended above all the heavens, that He might fill all things,"—that is, the Son of God, the Word of God. Yet, the Word of God was made flesh and dwelt among us. This must be Christ. Therefore, Christ must be declared to be God. *Novatian (c. 235, W), 5.627.*

SEE ALSO ANGEL OF THE LORD; ANTHROPOMORPHISMS; CHRIST, DIVINITY OF.

THEOPHILUS

In his book written to Autolycus concerning the *Times,* Theophilus says that Thalus relates in his history that Belus . . . lived 322 years before the Trojan war. *Lactantius (c. 304–313, W), 7.39.*

THEOTOKOS

The Greek term *Theotokos* means "God-bearer." As a title of Mary, it is used in the *Ante-Nicene Fathers* only by fourth-century writers. In the post-Nicene Latin-speaking church, *Theotokos* was generally rendered *Dei Genitrix,* which means "Mother of God"—a term that has been frequently misunderstood in popular usage.

The Spirit could not abide upon all men, but only on Him who was born of Mary, the God-bearer. *Disputation of Archelaus and Manes (c. 320, E), 6.208.*

Our Lord Jesus Christ in very deed (and not merely in appearance) carried a body, which was of Mary, mother of God. *Alexander of Alexandria (c. 324, E), 6.296.*

SEE ALSO MARY.

THOMAS

If, then, anyone who had attended on the elders came, I asked them in detail what was said [by the apostles]. What did Andrew or Peter say? Or what was said by Philip, Thomas, or James? *Papias (c. 120, E), 1.153.*

After He was risen from the abode of the dead and was received into heaven, Thomas the apostle, . . . by an impulse from God, sent Thaddaeus to Edessa to be a preacher and proclaimer of the teaching of Christ. Now, this Thaddaeus was himself also numbered among the seventy disciples of Christ. And the promise of Christ was fulfilled through him. *Eusebius (c. 315, E), 8.651.*

SEE ALSO APOSTLES, TWELVE; SEVENTY, THE (DISCIPLES).

TIBERIUS CAESAR

Tiberius (42 B.C.–A.D. 37), the stepson of Caesar Augustus, was the reigning Roman emperor when John the Baptist began his ministry, and he continued as emperor through the period of Jesus' ministry and the conversion of Paul.

It was in the days of Tiberius that the Christian name made its entry into the world. Having himself received intelligence from Palestine of events that had clearly shown the truth of Christ's divinity, Tiberius brought the matter before the senate, with his own decision in favor of Christ. However, the senate rejected his proposal because it had not given the approval itself. Tiberius Caesar held to his opinion, threatening wrath against all accusers of the Christians. Consult your histories! *Tertullian (c. 197, W), 3.22.*

We date the origin of our religion . . . from the reign of Tiberius. *Tertullian (c. 197, W), 3.23.*

All these things Pilate did to Christ. And now in fact a Christian in his own convictions, he sent word of Him to the reigning Caesar, who was at the time Tiberius. *Tertullian (c. 197, W), 3.35.*

SEE ALSO AUGUSTUS CAESAR; ROMAN EMPIRE, ROMANS.

TIME

SEE ETERNITY.

TITHES, TITHING

Bring all the tithes into the storehouse, that there may be food in My house. Mal. 3:10.

Nor was there anyone among them who lacked; for all who were possessors of lands or houses sold them, and brought the proceeds of the things that were sold and laid them at the apostles' feet. Acts 4:34, 35.

On the first day of the week let each one of you lay something aside, storing up as he may prosper. 1 Cor. 16:2.

Let each one give as he purposes in his heart, not grudgingly or of necessity; for God loves a cheerful giver. 2 Cor. 9:7.

Every true prophet that wishes to abide among you is worthy of his support. Likewise, a true teacher is himself worthy, as the workman of his support. Every first-fruit, therefore, of the products of the wine-press and the threshing-floor, of oxen and of sheep, you will take and give to the prophets, for they are your high priests. But if you have no prophet, give it to the poor. If you make a batch of dough, take the first-fruit and give according to the commandment. So also when you open a jar of wine or of oil, take the first-fruit and give it to the prophets. *Didache (c. 80–140, E), 7.381.*

The wealthy among us help the needy. . . . As for the persons who are prosperous and are willing, they give what each thinks fit. *Justin Martyr (c. 160, E), 1.185, 186.*

Instead of the Law commanding the giving of tithes, He taught us to share all *our* possessions with the poor. *Irenaeus (c. 180, E/W), 1.477.*

The class of oblations in general has not been set aside. For there were both oblations there [among the Jews] and there are oblations here [among the Christians]. Sacrifices there were among the [Israelite] people; sacrifices there are, too, in the church. Only the outward form has been changed. For the offering is now made, not by slaves, but by free men. . . . [The Jews] had indeed the tithes of their goods consecrated to Him. In contrast, those who have received liberty set aside *all* their possessions for the Lord's purposes, bestowing joyfully and freely not the less valuable portions of their property, since they have the hope of better things. *Irenaeus (c. 180, E/W), 1.484, 485.*

At the beginning, God accepted the gifts of Abel, because he offered with single-mindedness and righteousness. However, He had no respect for the offering of Cain, because his heart was divided with envy and malice. . . . For if anyone will endeavor to offer a sacrifice merely for outward appearances, . . . such an oblation will not profit him anything. . . . Sacrifices, therefore, do not sanctify a man. For God stands in no need of sacrifice. But it is the conscience of the person offering that sanctifies the sacrifice when it is pure. *Irenaeus (c. 180, E/W), 1.485.*

On the monthly day, if he likes, each puts in a small donation—but only if it is his pleasure and only if he is able. For there is no compulsion; all is voluntary. *Tertullian (c. 197, W), 3.46.*

They used to sell houses and estates so that they might lay up for themselves treasures in heaven. They presented the proceeds from them to the apostles, to be distributed for the use of the poor. However, now, we do not even give the tenths from our patrimony! *Cyprian (c. 250, W), 5.429.*

Let the bishop use as a man of God those tithes and first-fruits that are given according to the command of God. Let him also dispense in a right manner the free-will offerings that are brought in for the poor. *Apostolic Constitutions (compiled c. 390, E), 7.408.*

Give to the priest those things that are due to him—the first-fruits of your [threshing] floor and of your wine-press. *Apostolic Constitutions (compiled c. 390, E), 7.413.*

SEE ALSO ALMS, ALMSGIVING.

TONGUES, SPEAKING IN

SEE GIFTS OF THE SPIRIT.

TOTAL DEPRAVITY

SEE FALL OF MAN; FREE WILL AND PREDESTINATION; MAN, DOCTRINE OF.

TOWER OF BABEL

I. Confusion of languages

II. Angelic division of the nations

I. Confusion of languages

Therefore its name is called Babel, because there the Lord confused the language of all the earth; and from there the Lord scattered them abroad over the face of all the earth. Gen. 11:9.

Not at the instigation of God, [their plan was] to build a city, with a tower whose top might reach into heaven. They desired this so that they could make a glorious name to themselves. . . . From that time, He confused the languages of men, giving to each a different dialect. And the Sibyl speaks similarly of this. *Theophilus (c. 180, E), 2.106.*

At first, there were only a few men, situated in the land of Arabia and Chaldea. However, after their languages were divided, they gradually began to multiply and spread over all the earth. And some of them moved towards the east, to dwell there. Others went to parts of the great continent. Still others went northwards, so as to go as far as Britain. *Theophilus (c. 180, E), 2.107.*

II. Angelic division of the nations

According to most English translations, God set the boundaries of the nations according to the "number of the children of Israel" (Deut. 32:8). The Septuagint, however, states that he set the boundaries according to the "number of the angels of God." Based on that Scripture, together with passages from Ezekiel, Daniel, and other Scriptures, the early Christians believed that each nation is subject to the oversight of one of the angels.

When the Most High divided the nations, when he separated the sons of Adam, he set the bounds of the nations according to the number of the angels of God. Deut. 32:8 (lxx).

"He set the boundaries of the nations according to the numbers of the children of Israel." . . . Having said this, I added: "The Seventy have translated it, 'He set the boundaries of the nations according to the number of the angels of God.'" *Justin Martyr (c. 160, E), 1.265.*

"He set the boundaries of the nations after the number of the angels of God." However, the people who believe in God are not now under the power of angels, but under the Lord's [rule]. "For His people Jacob were made the portion of the Lord." *Irenaeus (c. 180, E/W), 1.434.*

Regiments of angels are distributed over the nations and cities. *Clement of Alexandria (c. 195, E), 2.517.*

By an ancient and divine order, the angels are distributed among the nations. *Clement of Alexandria (c. 195, E), 2.524.*

Moreover, other nations are called a part of the angels. This is because "when the Most High divided the nations and dispersed the sons of Adam, He fixed the boundaries of the nations according to the number of the angels of God." *Origen (c. 225, E), 4.241.*

Our prophet of God and His genuine servant Moses, in his song in the Book of Deuteronomy, makes a statement regarding the portioning out of the earth in the following terms: "When the Most High divided the nations, when He dispersed the sons of Adam, he set the boundaries of the people according to the number of the angels of God. And the Lord's portion was His people, Jacob." *Origen (c. 248, E), 4.555.*

All the people upon the earth are to be regarded as having originally used one divine language. As long as they lived harmoniously together, they were preserved in the use of this divine language. They remained without moving from the east, as long as they were imbued with the sentiments of the light. . . . [After the confusion of languages,] each one was handed over . . . to angels of character more or less severe . . . until the peoples had paid the penalty for their brash deeds. The angels imprinted on each his native language. And they were con-

ducted by those angels to the different parts of the earth according to their deserts. For example, some were taken to a region of burning heat. Others, to a country that chastises its inhabitants by its cold. Again, others, to a land exceedingly difficult to cultivate. . . . Those who preserved their original language continued . . . in possession of the east and of their eastern language. Take note that these people alone became the portion of the Lord. And His people were called Jacob and Israel. . . . These alone were governed by an [angelic] ruler who did not receive those who were placed under him for the purpose of punishment—as was the case with the others. *Origen (c. 248, E), 4.556.*

To every nation is sent an angel, as the Law says: "He determined them by the number of the angels of God," until the number of the saints should be filled up. They do not overstep their boundaries, because in the end they shall come with the Antichrist. *Victorinus (c. 280, W), 7.352; see also 5.500, 5.627.*

SEE ALSO FLOOD, THE.

TRADITION

Scripture speaks of two types of tradition: human tradition and apostolic tradition. On the one hand, Christians are warned not to be deceived by the "tradition of men" (Col. 2:9). On the other hand, Christians are commanded to "keep the traditions as I delivered them to you" (1 Cor. 11:2).

I. Traditions of men

II. Apostolic tradition

I. Traditions of men

"Why do Your disciples transgress the tradition of the elders? For they do not wash their hands when they eat bread." But He answered and said to them, "Why do you also transgress the commandment of God because of your tradition?" Matt. 15:2, 3.

And he said to them, "All too well you reject the commandment of God, that you may keep your tradition." Mark 7:9.

Beware lest anyone cheat you through philosophy and empty deceit, according to the tradition of men, according to the basic principles of the world, and not according to Christ. Col. 2:8.

The tradition of the elders, which they pretend to observe from the Law, was contrary to the Law given by Moses. For that reason, Isaiah also declares: "Your dealers mix the wine with water," showing that the elders were in the habit of mingling a watered tradition with the simple command of God. That is, they set up a spurious Law, one contrary to the true Law. The Lord also made this plain when He said to them, "Why do you transgress the commandments of God for the sake of your tradition?" *Irenaeus (c. 180, E/W), 1.475.*

The Pharisees rebelled from the Law by introducing human teachings. *Clement of Alexandria (c. 195, E), 2.494.*

The Lord warns us in His Gospel, saying, "You reject the commandment of God, that you may establish your own tradition." Those who reject the commandment of God and who attempt to keep their own tradition—let them be firmly and courageously rejected by you. *Cyprian (c. 250, W), 5.318.*

What presumption there is to prefer human tradition to divine ordinance! How can we not see that God is indignant and angry every time a human tradition relaxes the divine commandments and passes them by. *Cyprian (c. 250, W), 5.387.*

Custom without truth is simply the antiquity of error. *Cyprian (c. 250, W), 5.389.*

II. Apostolic tradition

Now I praise you, brethren, that you remember me in all things and keep the traditions as I delivered them to you. 1 Cor. 11:2.

The things which you learned and received and heard and saw in me, these do, and the God of peace will be with you. Phil. 4:9.

Therefore, brethren, stand fast and hold the traditions which you were taught, whether by word or our epistle. 2 Thess. 2:15.

But we command you, brethren, in the name of our Lord Jesus Christ, that you withdraw from every brother who walks disorderly and not according to the tradition which he received from us. 2 Thess. 3:6.

The things that you have heard from me among many witnesses, commit these to faithful men who will be able to teach others also. 2 Tim. 2:2.

If, then, anyone who had attended on the elders came, I asked minutely after their sayings. I asked what Andrew or Peter said, or what was said by Philip, Thomas, James, John, Matthew, or any other of the Lord's disciples—

things which Aristion and presbyter John, the disciples of the Lord, say. I concluded that what was to be got from books was not so profitable to me as what came from the living and abiding voice. *Papias (c. 120, E), 1.153, as quoted by Eusebius.*

For although the languages of the world are different, yet the import of the tradition is one and the same. For the churches which have been planted in Germany do not believe or hand down anything different, nor do those in Spain, nor those in Gaul. *Irenaeus (c. 180, E/W), 1.330, 331.*

Nor, on the other hand, will he who is deficient in power of expression inflict injury on the tradition. For the faith is ever one and the same. Accordingly, neither does he who is able at great length to discourse regarding it, make any addition to it. Nor does one who can say but little, diminish it. *Irenaeus (c. 180, E/W), 1.331.*

When, however, they [the Gnostics] are confuted from the Scriptures, they turn around and accuse these same Scriptures as if they were not correct. . . . But, again, when we refer them to that tradition which originates from the apostles, which is preserved by means of the successions of presbyters in the churches, they object to tradition, saying that they themselves are wiser not merely than the presbyters, but even than the apostles. *Irenaeus (c. 180, E/W), 1.415.*

It is within the power of all, therefore, in every church, who may wish to see the truth, to contemplate clearly the tradition of the apostles manifested throughout the whole world. And we are in a position to reckon up those who were by the apostles instituted bishops in the churches, and the succession of these men to our own times. . . . For if the apostles had known hidden mysteries, . . . they would have delivered them especially to those to whom they themselves were also committing the churches. *Irenaeus (c. 180, E/W), 1.415.*

In the third place from the apostles, Clement was allotted the bishopric. This man had seen the blessed apostles and had been conversant with them. Therefore, he might be said to have the preaching of the apostles still echoing [in his ears] and their traditions before his eyes. Nor was he alone in this. For there were many persons still remaining who had received instructions from the apostles. *Irenaeus (c. 180, E/W), 1.416.*

In this order, and by this succession, the ecclesiastical tradition from the apostles and the preaching of the truth have come down to us. And this is most abundant proof that there is one and the same life-giving faith, which has been preserved in the church from the apostles until now, and handed down in truth. *Irenaeus (c. 180, E/W), 1.416.*

Polycarp also was instructed by apostles, and he spoke with many who had seen Christ. Not only that, but by apostles, in Asia he was appointed bishop of the church in Smyrna. I also saw him in my early youth, for he lived a very long time. When he was a very old man, he gloriously and most nobly suffered martyrdom and departed this life. He had always taught the things which he had learned from the apostles, and which the church has handed down, and which alone are true. *Irenaeus (c. 180, E/W), 1.416.*

The church in Ephesus was founded by Paul. Furthermore, John remained among them permanently until the times of Trajan. That church is a true witness of the tradition of the apostles. *Irenaeus (c. 180, E/W), 1.416.*

It is not necessary to seek the truth among others, for it is easy to obtain it from the church. That is because the apostles, like a rich man [depositing his money] in a bank, lodged in her hands most lavishly all things pertaining to the truth. Therefore, every man, whosoever will, can draw from her the water of life. *Irenaeus (c. 180, E/W), 1.416, 417.*

For how does the case stand? Suppose there arises a dispute relative to some important question among us? Should we not have recourse to the most ancient churches with which the apostles had constant communication? Should we not learn from them what is certain and clear in regard to the question at hand? For how would it be if the apostles themselves had not left us writings? Would it not be necessary to follow the course of the tradition that they handed down to those to whom they committed the churches? To which course, many nations of those barbarians who believe in Christ do agree. For they have salvation written in their hearts by the Spirit, without paper or ink. And they care-

fully preserve the ancient tradition. . . . Therefore, the tradition from the apostles exists in the church in this manner. And it is permanent among us. Accordingly, let us revert to the Scriptural proof furnished by those apostles who also wrote the gospel. *Irenaeus (c. 180, E/W), 1.417.*

I have pointed out the truth, and I have shown the preaching of the church, which the prophets proclaimed. . . . Now, Christ brought this preaching to perfection, and the apostles have handed it down. The church has received it from the apostles, and she alone preserves it in its integrity throughout all the world. She has transmitted it to her sons. *Irenaeus (c. 180, E/W), 1.526.*

These opinions [i.e., that God created evil] . . . are not of sound doctrine. These opinions do not harmonize with the [teaching of] the church. . . . In fact, even the heretics beyond the church's pale have never ventured to broach these opinions. It is certain that those presbyters who preceded us, and who were conversant with the apostles, did not hand these opinions down to you. *Irenaeus (c. 180, E/W), 1.568.*

Polycarp would speak of his familiar relations with John, and with the rest of those who had seen the Lord. He would call their words to remembrance. So Polycarp received it in this manner from the eye-witnesses of the Word of life. Whatever things he had heard from them respecting the Lord (concerning both His miracles and His teaching), he would recount—all in harmony with the Scriptures. *Irenaeus (c. 180, E/W), 1.569.*

They preserved the tradition of the blessed doctrine derived directly from the holy apostles—Peter, James, John, and Paul. So the sons received it from the father, but few were like the fathers. And it came by God's will to us also to deposit those ancestral and apostolic seeds. *Clement of Alexandria (c. 195, E), 2.301.*

I think such a sketch as this will be agreeable to a soul desirous of preserving from loss the blessed tradition. *Clement of Alexandria (c. 195, E), 2.301.*

The dogmas taught by strange sects will be brought forward. And against these dogmas will be opposed all those things that should be premised in accordance with the profoundest contemplation of the knowledge that will advance to our view, as we proceed to the renowned and venerable canon of tradition. *Clement of Alexandria (c. 195, E), 2.302.*

It is necessary for men to abandon impious opinion and turn from there to the true tradition. *Clement of Alexandria (c. 195, E), 2.530.*

He, who has spurned the ecclesiastical tradition and darted off to the opinions of heretical men—he has ceased to be a man of God and to remain faithful to the Lord. *Clement of Alexandria (c. 195, E), 2.551.*

We call those heretics "empty," for they are destitute of the counsels of God and the traditions of Christ. In truth, they are bitter like the wild almond, for their dogmas originate with themselves. *Clement of Alexandria (c. 195, E), 2.552.*

Those who have a craving for glory voluntarily evade (by arguments of a diverse sort) the things delivered by the blessed apostles and teachers, which things are wedded to inspired words. They use human teaching to oppose the divine tradition, in order to establish the heresy. . . . They do not have the key of entrance, but rather a false or counterfeit key. With this, they do not enter in, as we do. For we enter through the tradition of the Lord. *Clement of Alexandria (c. 195, E), 2.553, 554.*

The tradition of the apostles was one. *Clement of Alexandria (c. 195, E), 2.555.*

In the Lord's apostles, we possess our authority. For even they did not of themselves choose to introduce anything new, but faithfully delivered to the nations the teaching that they had received from Christ. *Tertullian (c. 197, W), 3.246.*

Wherever it will be evident that the true Christian faith and rule exist, there will also be the true Scriptures and explanations thereof, and all the Christian traditions. *Tertullian (c. 197, W), 3.251, 252.*

Error of doctrine in the churches must necessarily have produced various issues. When, however, that which is deposited among many is found to be one and the same—it is not the result of error, but of tradition. Can anyone, then, be reckless enough to say that they were in error who handed on the tradition? *Tertullian (c. 197, W), 3.256.*

The truth may be adjudged to belong to us, for we are the "many" who "walk according to the rule." The church has handed this down from the apostles, the apostles from Christ, and Christ from God. . . . Since the heretics are not Christians, they have no right to the Christian Scriptures. . . . [The church says,] "Indeed, Marcion, by what right do you carve my wood? Valentinus, by whose permission are you diverting the streams of my fountain? . . . This is my property. I have long possessed it. I possessed it before you. I hold reliable title-deeds from the original owners themselves, to whom the estate belonged. I am the heir of the apostles. For they carefully prepared their will and testament, committed it to a trust, and solemnly charged the trustee. Therefore, I hold it in trust." *Tertullian (c. 197, W), 3.261.*

Such are the conclusive arguments that we use . . . maintaining both the rule of time (which decrees that a late date is the mark of forgers) and the authority of churches (which lends support to the tradition of the apostles). For truth must necessarily precede the forgery, since it proceeds directly from those from whom it has been handed down. *Tertullian (c. 207, W), 3.351.*

Show me your authority. . . . If you are an ordinary Christian [not an apostle], believe what has been handed down to us. . . . That which had been handed down was true. For it has been transmitted by those whose duty it was to hand it down. Therefore, when you rejected that which had been handed down, you rejected that which was true. You had no authority for what you did. *Tertullian (c. 210, W), 3.522.*

If, for these and other such rules, you insist upon having positive Scripture injunction, you will find none. Tradition will be held forth to you as the originator of them. Custom is their strengthener, and faith is their observer. . . . These instances, therefore, will make it sufficiently plain that you can vindicate the keeping of even unwritten tradition established by custom. The proper witness for tradition is its demonstration by long-continued observance. *Tertullian (c. 211, W), 3.95.*

You [the church] lay down a rule that this faith has its solemnities appointed by either the Scriptures or the tradition of the forefathers. No further addition in the way of observance must be added, because innovation is unlawful. *Tertullian (c. 213, W), 4.111.*

Dear brethren, let us believe according to the tradition of the apostles. *Hippolytus (c. 205, W), 5.230.*

They have boldly falsified the sacred Scriptures, rejected the canons of the ancient faith, and ignored Christ. *Eusebius, quoting Caius (c. 215, W), 5.602.*

There are many who *think* they hold the opinions of Christ. However, some of these men think differently than their predecessors. Therefore, that alone is to be accepted as the truth which differs in no respect from ecclesiastical and apostolic tradition. For the teaching of the church—transmitted in orderly succession from the apostles—remains in the churches to the present day and is still preserved. *Origen (c. 225, E), 4.239.*

It should be known that the holy apostles—in preaching the faith of Christ—delivered themselves with the utmost clearness on certain points. For they believed those points to be necessary to everyone—even to those who seemed somewhat dull in the investigation of divine knowledge. *Origen (c. 225, E), 4.239.*

Know that we do not depart from the traditions of the Gospel and of the apostles. Rather, with constancy and firmness, we ... maintain the discipline of the church. *Cyprian (c. 250, W), 5.357.*

The bishops who are set over the churches of the Lord by divine grace, throughout the whole world, maintain the plan of evangelical truth and of the tradition of the Lord. They do not depart, by human and novel institution, from that which Christ our Master both commanded and did. *Cyprian (c. 250, W), 5.359.*

You must diligently observe and keep the practice delivered from divine tradition and apostolic observance, which is also maintained among us and almost throughout all the provinces. *Cyprian (c. 250, W), 5.371.*

SEE ALSO CHURCHES, APOSTOLIC; CREEDS, EARLY; APOSTOLIC FAITH.

TRANSFIGURATION

So when Aaron and all the children of Israel saw Moses, behold, the skin of his face shone, and they were afraid to come near him. Ex. 34:30.

Assuredly, I say to you, there are some standing here who shall not taste death till they see the son of Man coming in His kingdom. Now after six days Jesus took Peter, James, and John his brother, brought them up on a high mountain by themselves, and was transfigured before them. Matt. 16:28; 17:1, 2.

Even the Holy Scriptures give us instances of this form of change. . . . For example, the face of Moses was changed, with a brightness that the eyes could not bear. But he was still Moses, even when he was not visible. So also Stephen had already put on the appearance of an angel—even though it was still his human knees that bent beneath the stoning. The Lord, again, in the retirement of the mountain, had changed His clothing for a robe of light. Yet, He still retained features that Peter could recognize. In that same scene, Moses also and Elijah gave proof that the same condition of bodily existence may continue even in glory. *Tertullian (c. 197, W), 3.588, 589.*

"Truly I say unto you that some of you that stand here will not taste of death [until they see the Son of man coming in His kingdom]." Some interpret these words to the going up . . . of the three disciples into the high mountain with Jesus alone. Those who adopt this interpretation say that Peter and the other two apostles did not taste of death before they saw the Son of man coming in His own kingdom and in His own glory. For when they saw Jesus transfigured before them, so that His face shone, "they saw the kingdom of God coming with power." . . . However, this interpretation about the three apostles . . . is adapted to those who are designated by Peter as "new-born babes." *Origen (c. 245, E), 9.466.*

Jesus did not invite all His apostles [to the transfiguration], but only Peter, James, and John. For they alone were capable of beholding His glory on that occasion and seeing the glorified appearance of Moses and Elijah. . . . I am of the opinion that . . . He ascended the same mountain where His disciples had previously come to Him alone, which was where He taught them the beatitudes. *Origen (c. 248, E), 4.457; extended discussion: 3.382–3.385, 9.466–9.473.*

SEE ALSO ELIJAH; MOSES.

TRANSLATION OF ENOCH AND ELIJAH

SEE ASSUMPTIONS.

TRANSMIGRATION OF SOULS

See Reincarnation.

TRANSUBSTANTIATION

See Eucharist.

TREE OF KNOWLEDGE

And the Lord God commanded the man, saying, "Of every tree of the garden you may freely eat; but of the tree of the knowledge of good and evil you shall not eat, for in the day that you eat of it you shall surely die." Gen. 2:16, 17.

The tree of knowledge itself was good, and its fruit was good. For it was not the tree that had death in it, as some think. Rather, it was the disobedience. For there was nothing else in the fruit except knowledge. But knowledge is good when one uses it discreetly. But Adam, being yet an infant in age, was on this account as yet unable to receive knowledge worthily.... However, there was not any evil in the tree of knowledge. *Theophilus (c. 180, E), 2.104.*

Who is so foolish as to think that God, in the manner of a gardener, planted a paradise in Eden, towards the east, and . . . that a person could be a partaker of good and evil by eating what was taken from the tree? . . . I do not suppose that anyone doubts that these things figuratively indicate certain mysteries. *Origen (c. 225, E), 4.365.*

Man was taught that there was no evil in the fruit of the tree. Rather, he was forewarned that evil would arise if man were to exercise his free will in contempt of the law that had been given him. *Novatian (c. 235, W), 5.612.*

See also Adam; Eve; Fall of Man; Tree of Life.

TREE OF LIFE

Then the Lord God said, "Behold, the man has become like one of us, to know good and evil. And now, lest he put out his hand and take also of the tree of life, and eat, and live forever." Gen. 3:22.

To him who overcomes I will give to eat from the tree of life, which is in the midst of the Paradise of God. Rev. 2:7.

That He will come again in glory after His crucifixion was symbolized . . . by the tree of life, which was said to have been planted in Paradise. *Justin Martyr (c. 160, E), 1.242.*

Moses, allegorically describing the divine prudence, called it the tree of life planted in Paradise. *Clement of Alexandria (c. 195, E), 2.461.*

The act of reclining at the feast in the kingdom of God, sitting on Christ's thrones, finally standing on His right hand and His left, and eating of the tree of life: what are all of these things but most certain proofs of a bodily placement and destination? *Tertullian (c. 210, W), 3.571.*

Who is so foolish as to think that God, in the manner of a gardener, planted a paradise in Eden, towards the east, and placed in it a tree of life: visible and tangible, so that one who tasted of the fruit with physical teeth obtained life? . . . I do not suppose that anyone doubts that these things figuratively indicate certain mysteries. *Origen (c. 225, E), 4.365.*

See also Paradise; Tree of Knowledge.

TRIBULATION, GREAT

See Great Tribulation.

TRINITY

Go therefore and make disciples of all the nations, baptizing them in the name of the Father and of the Son and of the Holy Spirit. Matt. 28:19.

In the beginning was the Word, and the Word was with God, and the Word was God. John 1:1.

Most assuredly, I say to you, the Son can do nothing of Himself, but what He sees the Father do; for whatever He does, the Son also does in like manner. For the Father loves the Son, and shows Him all things that He Himself does. John 5:19, 20.

For us there is only one God, the Father, of whom are all things, and we for Him; and one Lord Jesus Christ, through whom are all things, and through whom we live. 1 Cor. 8:6.

I want you to know that the head of every man is Christ, the head of woman is man, and the head of Christ is God. 1 Cor. 11:3.

The grace of the Lord Jesus Christ, and the love of God, and the communion of the Holy Spirit be with you all. 2 Cor. 13:14.

According to the foreknowledge of God the Father, in sanctification of the Spirit, for obedience and sprinkling of the blood of Jesus Christ. 1 Pet. 1:2.

Do we not have one God and one Christ? Is there not one Spirit of grace poured out upon us? *Clement of Rome (c. 96, W), 1.17.*

The most true God, is the Father of righteousness. . . . We worship and adore Him, the Son (who came forth from Him and taught us these things, along with the host of the other good angels who follow and are made like Him), and the prophetic Spirit. *Justin Martyr (c. 160, E), 1.164.*

Who, then, would not be astonished to hear men called atheists who speak of God the Father, and of God the Son, and of the Holy Spirit, and who declare both their power in union and their distinction in order? *Athenagoras (c. 175, E), 2.133.*

Christians know God and His Logos. They also know what type of oneness the Son has with the Father and what type of communion the Father has with the Son. Furthermore, they know what the Spirit is and what the unity is of these three: the Spirit, the Son, and the Father. They also know what their distinction is in unity. *Athenagoras (c. 175, E), 2.134.*

We acknowledge a God, and a Son (His Logos), and a Holy Spirit. These are united in essence—the Father, the Son, and the Spirit. Now, the Son is the Intelligence, Reason, and Wisdom of the Father. And the Spirit is an emanation, as light from fire. *Athenagoras (c. 175, E), 2.141.*

The three days which were before the luminaries are types of the Triad of God, His Word, and His Wisdom. *Theophilus (c. 180, E), 2.101.*

It is the Father who anoints, and it is the Son who is anointed by the Spirit. The Spirit is the unction. *Irenaeus (c. 180, E/W), 1.446.*

I have also largely demonstrated that the Word, namely the Son, was always with the Father. Now, that Wisdom also, who is the Spirit, was present with Him before all creation, He declares by Solomon: "God by Wisdom founded the earth, and by understanding He has established the heaven. By His knowledge, the depths burst forth, and the clouds dropped down the dew." And again: "The Lord created me the beginning of His ways in His work. He set me up from everlasting, in the beginning, before He made the earth." . . .

There is therefore one God, who by His Word and Wisdom created and arranged all things. *Irenaeus (c. 180, E/W), 1.488.*

God is powerful in all things. At that time, He was seen *prophetically* through the Spirit and *adoptively* through the Son. However, he will be seen *paternally* in the kingdom of heaven. The Spirit truly prepares a man in the Son of God, and the Son leads him to the Father. Finally, the Father confers upon him incorruption for eternal life. *Irenaeus (c. 180, E/W), 1.489.*

It is after the image and likeness of the uncreated God: the Father planning everything well and giving His commands, the Son carrying these into execution and performing the work of creating, and the Spirit nourishing and increasing. *Irenaeus (c. 180, E/W), 1.521, 522.*

One God the Father is declared, who is above all, through all, and in all. The Father is indeed above all, and He is the Head of Christ. But the Word is through all things and is Himself the Head of the church. While the Spirit is in us all, and He is the living water. *Irenaeus (c. 180, E/W), 1.546.*

They ascend through the Spirit to the Son, and through the Son to the Father. And in due time, the Son will yield up His work to the Father, even as it is said by the apostle. *Irenaeus (c. 180, E/W), 1.567.*

The universal Father is one. The universal Word is one. And the Holy Spirit is one. *Clement of Alexandria (c. 195, E), 2.220.*

Thank the one only Father and Son, Son and Father. The Son is the Instructor and Teacher, along with the Holy Spirit. They are all in One, in whom is all, for whom all is One, for whom is eternity. *Clement of Alexandria (c. 195, E), 2.295.*

It is protected by the power of God the Father, and the blood of God the Son, and the dew of the Holy Spirit. *Clement of Alexandria (c. 195, E), 2.601.*

We pray at a minimum not less than three times in the day. For we are debtors to Three: Father, Son, and Holy Spirit. *Tertullian (c. 198, W), 3.690.*

For the very church itself is—properly and principally—the Spirit Himself, in whom is the Trinity of the One Divinity: Father, Son, and Holy Spirit. *Tertullian (c. 212, W), 4.99.*

We . . . believe that there is only one God, but under the following dispensation or "economy" [Gr. *oikonomia*], as it is called. We believe that this one only God has also a Son, His Word, who proceeded from Himself, by whom all things were made, and without whom nothing was made. Him we believe to have been sent by the Father into the virgin, and to have been born of her—being both man and God, the Son of man and the Son of God. . . . And the Son also sent from heaven from the Father, according to His own promise, the Holy Spirit, the Paraclete, the sanctifier of the faith of those who believe in the Father, the Son, and the Holy Spirit. *Tertullian (c. 213, W), 3.598.*

This heresy [Monarchianism] supposes itself to possess the pure truth, in thinking that one cannot believe in only one God in any other way than by saying that the Father, the Son, and the Holy Spirit are the very selfsame Person. As if in this way also One were not All, in that All are of One, by unity of substance. In this manner, the mystery of the "economy" is still guarded, which distributes the Unity into a Trinity, placing in their order the three: Father, Son, and Holy Spirit. However, this is not in condition, but in degree. It is not in substance; but in form. It is not in power, but in aspect. Yet, they are of one substance, one condition, and one power—for as He is one God from whom these degrees, forms, and aspects are reckoned under the name of the Father, the Son, and the Holy Spirit. How they are susceptible of number without division will be shown. . . . The simple, . . . who always constitute the majority of believers, are startled at the "economy," on the ground that their very rule of faith withdraws them from the world's plurality of gods to the only true God. They do not understand that, although He is the one only God, He must yet be believed in with His own "economy." . . . How does it come to pass that God is thought to suffer division and severance in the Son and in the Holy Spirit, who have the second and the third places assigned to them, and who are so closely joined with the Father in His substance? . . . Do you really suppose that those, who are naturally members of the Father's own substance, pledges of His love, instruments of His might, . . . are the overthrow and destruction thereof? You are not right in thinking so. *Tertullian (c. 213, W), 3.598, 3.599.*

As for me, I derive the Son from no other source than from the substance of the Father. And I believe He does nothing without the Father's will and that He received all power from the Father. So how can I possibly be destroying the Monarchy from the faith, when I preserve it in the Son just as it was committed to Him by the Father? . . . Likewise with the Third Degree, for I believe the Spirit is from no other source than from the Father through the Son. *Tertullian (c. 213, W), 3.599.*

For God sent forth the Word, as the Paraclete also declares. This is just as the root puts forth the tree, the fountain the river, and the sun the ray. For these are emanations of the substances from which they proceed. I should not hesitate, indeed, to call the tree the son or offspring of the root; or the river, that of the fountain; or the ray, that of the sun. . . . Now, the Spirit indeed is third from God and the Son. Just as the fruit of the tree is third from the root, or as the stream out of the river is third from the fountain, or as the apex of the ray is third from the sun. Nothing, however, is alien from that original source from which it derives its own properties. In like manner, the Trinity, flowing down from the Father through intertwined and connected steps, does not at all disturb the "Monarchy," while it at the same time guards the state of the "Economy." *Tertullian (c. 213, W), 3.603.*

I testify that the Father, the Son, and the Spirit are inseparable from each other. . . . My assertion is that the Father is one, the Son is one, and the Spirit is one—and that they are all distinct from each other. . . . The Father is not the same as the Son, for they differ one from the other in the mode of their being. For the Father is the entire substance, but the Son is a derivation and portion of the whole, as He Himself acknowledges: "My Father is greater than I." *Tertullian (c. 213, W), 3.603, 604.*

However, that there are two Gods or two Lords, is a statement that at no time proceeds out of our mouths. Not as if it were untrue that the Father is God, the Son is God, and the Holy Spirit is God, and each is God. . . . Now, if there were found in the Scriptures but one Personality of Him who is God and Lord, Christ would justly enough be inadmissible to the title of God and Lord. For there was declared to be none other than one God and one Lord. *Tertullian (c. 213, W), 3.608.*

In the "Economy" itself, the Father willed that the Son should be regarded as being on earth, and the Father Himself as being in heaven. Actually, however, He is everywhere present. *Tertullian (c. 213, W), 3.619.*

Thus the connection of the Father in the Son, and of the Son in the Paraclete, produces three coherent Persons, distinct one from another. These Three are one in essence—not one in Person. For it is said, "I and my Father are One," in respect of unity of substance, not singularity of number. *Tertullian (c. 213, W), 3.621.*

He commands them to baptize into the Father, the Son, and the Holy Spirit—not into a unipersonal God. *Tertullian (c. 213, W), 3.623.*

The earth is moved by three things: the Father, the Son, and the Holy Spirit. *Hippolytus (c. 205, W), 5.174.*

Who will not say that there is one God? Yet, he will not on that account deny the Economy. *Hippolytus (c. 205, W), 5.224.*

Therefore, a man ... is compelled to acknowledge God the Father Almighty, and Christ Jesus the Son of God—who, being God, became man, to whom also the Father made all things subject (Himself excepted)—and the Holy Spirit; and that these are three [Persons]. However, if he desires to know how it is shown that there is still one God, let him know that His power is one. As far as regards the power, therefore, God is one. But as far as regards the Economy, there is a threefold manifestation. *Hippolytus (c. 205, W), 5.226.*

We accordingly see the incarnate Word. And we know the Father through Him. We also believe in the Son, and we worship the Holy Spirit. *Hippolytus (c. 205, W), 5.228.*

If, then, the Word was with God and was also God, what follows? Would one say that I speak of two Gods? I will not indeed speak of two Gods, but of one. I speak of two Persons, however, and of a third Economy—the grace of the Holy Spirit. For the Father indeed is one, but there are two Persons, because there is also the Son. And then there is the third, the Holy Spirit. The Father decrees, the Word executes, and the Son is manifested, through whom the Father is believed on. The Economy of harmony is led back to one God. For God is one. It is the Father who commands, and the Son who obeys, and the Holy Spirit who gives understanding. The

Father is *above* all, the Son is *through* all, and the Holy Spirit is *in* all. *Hippolytus (c. 205, W), 5.228.*

"Go and teach all nations, baptizing them in the name of the Father, and of the Son, and of the Holy Spirit." By this, He showed that whoever omits any one of these three, fails in glorifying God perfectly. For it is through this Trinity that the Father is glorified. For the Father willed, the Son did, and the Spirit manifested. *Hippolytus (c. 205, W), 5.228.*

However, many of those who profess to believe in Christ differ from each other not only on small and trifling matters but also on subjects of the highest importance. I mean, for example, the things concerning God, or the Lord Jesus Christ, or the Holy Spirit. . . . For that reason, therefore, it seems necessary first of all to fix a definite limit and to lay down an unmistakable rule regarding each one of these [Persons]. . . . The particular points that are clearly delivered in the teaching of the apostles are as follows: First, that there is one God, who created and arranged all things, and who, when nothing existed, called all things into being. . . . Secondly, that Jesus Christ Himself, who came, was born of the Father before all creatures and that—after He had been the minister of the Father in the creation of all things ("for by Him all things were made"), He in the last times divested Himself and became a man. He was incarnate although still God. . . . And thirdly, the apostles related that the Holy Spirit was associated in honor and dignity with the Father and the Son. But in His case it is not clearly distinguished whether He is to be regarded as born or unborn—or also as a Son of God nor not. *Origen (c. 225, E), 4.240.*

The Savior Himself rightly says in the Gospel: "There is no one good but only one, God the Father." By such an expression, it should be understood that the Son is not of a different goodness, but of that one goodness that exists in the Father, of whom He is rightly called the Image. For He proceeds from no other source than from that primal goodness. Otherwise, there might appear to be in the Son a different goodness than that which is in the Father. . . . Therefore it is not to be imagined that there is a kind of blasphemy, as it were, in the words, "There is no one good except one only, God the Father." For it is not as if thereby it might be supposed to be denying that either Christ or the Holy Spirit are good. Rather, as we have already said, the primal goodness is to be understood as residing in God the Father, from whom both the Son is born and the Holy Spirit proceeds. *Origen (c. 225, E), 4.251.*

Saving baptism was not complete except by the authority of the most excellent Trinity of them all. That is, it is made complete by naming the Father, Son, and Holy Spirit. In this, we join the name of the Holy Spirit to the Unbegotten God (the Father) and to His Only-Begotten Son. *Origen (c. 225, E), 4.252.*

Having made these declarations regarding the Unity of the Father, the Son, and the Holy Spirit, let us return to the order in which we began the discussion. God the Father bestows existence upon all. Participation in Christ, in respect of His being the Word of reason, renders them rational beings. . . . To begin with, they derive their existence from God the Father. Secondly, they derive their rational nature from the Word. Thirdly, they derive their holiness from the Holy Spirit. *Origen (c. 225, E), 4.255.*

There is no nature, then, that may not admit of good or evil—except the nature of God, the Fountain of all good things, and of Christ. . . . In like manner also, the nature of the Holy Spirit—being holy—does not allow pollution. For it is holy by nature, or essential being. *Origen (c. 225, E), 4.266.*

The Father generates an uncreated Son and brings forth a Holy Spirit—not as if He had no previous existence, but because the Father is the origin and source of the Son or Holy Spirit. *Origen (c. 225, E), 4.270.*

As to what movements of their will leads God so to arrange all these things, this is known to God alone, and to His Only-Begotten Son (through whom all things were created and restored), and to the Holy Spirit (through whom all things are sanctified). He proceeds from the Father, to whom be glory forever and ever. *Origen (c. 225, E), 4.344.*

Isaiah, too, knowing that the beginnings of things could not be discovered by a mortal nature—not even by those natures which are more divine than human, yet were nevertheless created or formed themselves. . . . For my Hebrew teacher also used to teach in this same manner. [He said] that the beginning or end of all things could be comprehended by no one,

except only our Lord Jesus Christ and the Holy Spirit. *Origen (c. 225, E), 4.375, 376.*

Let everyone, then, who cares for truth not be concerned about words and language. For in every nation there prevails a different usage of speech. Rather, let him direct his attention to the *meaning* conveyed by the words (rather than to the nature of the words that convey the meaning), especially in matters of such importance and difficulty. . . . The "substance" of the Trinity that is the beginning and cause of all things . . . is altogether incorporeal. *Origen (c. 225, E), 4.376.*

All things that exist were made by God and there was nothing that was not made—except for the nature of the Father, the Son, and the Holy Spirit. . . . For the Father alone knows the Son. And the Son alone knows the Father. And the Holy Spirit alone searches even the deep things of God. *Origen (c. 225, E), 4.380.*

The Savior and the Holy Spirit were sent by the Father for the salvation of men. *Origen (c. 245, E), 9.486.*

We are not ignorant that there is one God; and one Christ, the Lord (whom we have confessed); and one Holy Spirit. *Cyprian (c. 250, W), 5.323.*

"Go therefore and teach all nations, baptizing them in the name of the Father, the Son, and the Holy Spirit." He suggests the Trinity, in whose sacrament the nations were to be baptized. *Cyprian (c. 250, W), 5.380.*

If a person baptized by heretics were sanctified, he would also be made the temple of God. I ask, "of what God?" If of the Creator, he could not be. For he has not believed in Him. If of Christ, he could not become His temple, since he denies that Christ is God. If of the Holy Spirit, how can the Holy Spirit be at peace with him who is the enemy either of the Son or of the Father? For the three are one. *Cyprian (c. 250, W), 5.382.*

The Lord says, "I and the Father are one." And, again, it is written of the Father, the Son, and the Holy Spirit: "And these three are one." *Cyprian (c. 250, W), 5.423.*

The three children, along with Daniel, . . . observed the third, sixth, and ninth hours (as it were) for a sacrament of the Trinity, which was to be manifested in the last times. For the first hour in its progress to the third declares the completed number of the Trinity. *Cyprian (c. 250, W), 5.456.*

... baptizing them in the name of the Father, the Son, and the Holy Spirit. The very same Trinity who operated figuratively through the dove in Noah's days, now operates spiritually in the church through the disciples. *Treatise against Novatian (c. 255, W), 5.658.*

The false and wicked baptism of heretics ... is a blasphemy of the Trinity. *Seventh Council of Carthage (c. 256, W), 5.568.*

... the invocation of the Trinity—of the names of the Father, the Son, and the Holy Spirit. *Firmilian (c. 256, E), 5.392.*

The individual names uttered by me can neither be separated from one another, nor parted. ... They are ignorant that the Father, in that He is a father, cannot be separated from the Son. For that name is the obvious grounds of bonding.... Nor can the Son be separated from the Father, for the word "father" indicates an association between them. Furthermore, there is obviously a Spirit who can not be disjoined from the One who sends.... Thus, indeed, we expand the indivisible Unity into a Trinity. *Dionysius of Alexandria (c. 262, E), 6.93, as quoted by Athanasius.*

As the next two quotations illustrate, eastern pre-Nicene writers often used the Greek word hypostasis to mean "person," while western writers often used it to mean "substance." This caused much confusion between east and west.

If there are three Persons [Gr. *hypostases*], this does not mean that they are divided. There are three whether they like it or not. Otherwise, let them get rid of the divine Trinity altogether. *Dionysius of Alexandria (c. 262, E), 6.94, as quoted by Athanasius.*

It would be just to dispute against those who destroy the Monarchy by dividing and rending it ... into three powers and distinct substances [Gr. *hypostases*] and deities. ... In a certain manner, these men declare three Gods, in that they divide the Holy Unity into three different substances, absolutely separated from one another. For it is essential that the Divine Word should be united to the God of all, and that the Holy Spirit should abide and dwell in God. Therefore, the Divine Trinity should be reduced and gathered into one, into a certain Head—that is,

into the Omnipotent God of all. For the doctrine of the foolish Marcion, which cuts and divides the Monarchy into three elements, is certainly of the devil. It is not of Christ's true disciples, ... for these indeed correctly know that the Trinity is declared in the divine Scripture. However, the doctrine that there are three Gods I find neither taught in the Old nor in the New Testament. *Dionysius of Rome (c. 265, W), 7.365, as quoted by Athanasius.*

That admirable and divine unity, therefore, must not be separated into three divinities. Nor must the dignity and eminent greatness of the Lord be diminished by the name of creation. Rather, we must believe on God the Father omnipotent, and on Christ Jesus His Son, and on the Holy Spirit. *Dionysius of Rome (c. 265, W), 7.365, 366, as quoted by Athanasius.*

The thousand two hundred and sixty days [Rev. 12:6] ... is the accurate and complete understanding concerning the Father, the Son, and the Spirit.... A thousand embraces a full and perfect number and is a symbol of the Father Himself. He made the universe by Himself and rules all things for Himself. Two hundred embraces two perfect numbers united together, and it is the symbol of the Holy Spirit. For He is the Author of our knowledge of the Son and the Father. Sixty is composed of the number six multiplied by ten, and it is a symbol of Christ.... He came from the fullness of Godhood into a human life. For having emptied Himself and taken upon Him the form of a slave, He was restored again to his former perfection and dignity. *Methodius (c. 290, E), 6.339.*

Methodius thinks that the following are types of the holy and consubstantial Trinity: the innocent and unbegotten Adam is a type and resemblance of God the Father Almighty, who is uncaused and is the cause of all. Adam's begotten son [Abel or Seth] pictures the image of the begotten Son and Word of God. And Eve, who proceeded forth from Adam, signifies the person and procession of the Holy Spirit. *Reference to Methodius (c. 290, E), 6.402, from a post-Nicene writer.*

The Father is the God over all. Christ is the Only-Begotten God—the beloved Son, the Lord of glory. The Holy Spirit is the Comforter, who is sent by Christ, taught by Him, and proclaimed by Him. *Apostolic Constitutions (compiled c. 390, E), 7.431.*

656

Now, God, who alone is Unbegotten, and the Maker of the whole world . . . grants to you eternal life with us, through the mediation of His beloved Son, Jesus Christ, our God and Savior. With whom glory be to You, the God over all and the Father, in the Holy Spirit, the Comforter. *Apostolic Constitutions (compiled c. 390, E), 7.505; extended discussion: 3.597–3.627.*

See also Christ, Divinity of; Father, God the; Filioque; God; Holy Spirit; Jesus Christ; Monarchianism; Theophanies; Wisdom; Word of God (Christ).

TWICE-MARRIED

A bishop then must be blameless, the husband of one wife. 1 Tim. 3:2.

Let deacons be the husband of one wife. 1 Tim. 3:12.

Do not let a widow under sixty years old be taken into the number, and not unless she has been the wife of one man. 1 Tim. 5:9.

From the beginning, the church understood the verses above to apply to any second marriage—including a remarriage after one's spouse had died. If a person had been remarried for any reason, that person was disqualified from being ordained into the clergy or being enrolled as a widow. The Montanists, however, went a step further, prohibiting even laypersons from re-marrying after the death of their spouses. The following six quotations were written by Ter-tullian as a Montanist. They reveal both the po-sition of the church and the position of the Montanists on this topic.

In the old Law, I find the pruning knife applied to the permission of repeated marriages. There is a caution in Leviticus: "My priests will not pluralize marriages." . . . Therefore, among *us* the prescript is more fully and more carefully laid down: that they who are chosen into the priestly order must be men of one marriage. This rule is so rigidly observed that I remember some removed from their office for a second marriage. *Tertullian (c. 212, W), 4.54.*

If you have the *right* of a priest in your own persons in cases of necessity, it behooves you to have likewise the *discipline* of a priest when-ever it may be necessary to have the right of a priest. If you are twice-married, do you bap-tize? If you are twice-married, do you offer? How much more serious is it for a twice-mar-ried layman to act as a priest, when the priest himself, if he becomes twice-married, is

deprived of the power of acting as a priest? But you say, "to necessity, indulgence is granted." *Tertullian (c. 212, W), 4.54.*

We are bound to contend that the command to abstain from second marriages relates first to the layman. For no other man can be a presby-ter than a layman, provided he has been a hus-band once for all. *Tertullian (c. 212, W), 4.54.*

I am led to presume that Peter was once-mar-ried—on consideration of the church, which, built upon him, was destined to appoint every grade of her order from those who are once-married. *Tertullian (c. 217, W), 4.65.*

You [i.e., the church] say, "It is true that the apostle has permitted remarriage [after the death of a spouse]." You also say that it is only those who are of the clerical order that he has strin-gently bound to the yoke of one marriage. For that which he prescribes to certain persons, he does not prescribe to all. *Tertullian (c. 217, W), 4.69*

Why, how many twice-married men, too, pre-side in your churches! They insult the apostle, of course! At all events, apparently they do not blush when these passages are read under their presidency! *Tertullian (c. 217, W), 4.69.*

Paul wishes no one in the church who has attained to any eminence beyond the many (as is attained in the administration of the sacra-ments) to make trial of a second marriage. For laying down the law in regard to bishops in the first Epistle to Timothy, he says, . . . "The bishop, therefore, must be without reproach, the husband of one wife." . . . He also says, "Let the deacons be the husbands of one wife." . . . Yes, and also when appointing widows, he says, "Let there be no one as a widow under sixty years old, having been the wife of one man." *Origen (c. 245, E), 9.509.*

Now, when I saw that some who have been married twice may be much better than those who have been married once, I was perplexed why Paul does not at all permit those who have been twice married to be appointed to ecclesias-tical dignities. It seemed to me that such a thing was worthy of examination. For it was possible that a man, who had been unfortunate in two marriages, and had lost his second wife while he was yet young, might have lived for the rest of his years up to old age in great self-control and chastity. Who, then, would not naturally be perplexed why at all, when a ruler of the church is being sought for, we do not appoint such a man, even though he has been twice married? [ORIGEN THEN GIVES HIS THEORY OF WHY THIS RULE MUST BE FOLLOWED.] *Origen (c. 245, E), 9.510.*

He selects for the episcopate a man who has been once married—rather than he who has twice entered into the married state. *Origen (c. 248, E), 4.483.*

A bishop should be a man who has been the husband of one wife, who herself has had no other husband. He should "rule well in his own house." In this manner, let examination be made. *Apostolic Constitutions (compiled c. 390, E), 7.396.*

We have already said that a bishop, a presbyter, and a deacon, when they are constituted, must be married but once—whether their wives are alive or whether they are dead. *Apostolic Constitutions (compiled c. 390, E), 7.457.*

Let the deaconess be a pure virgin. Or, at the least, let her be a widow who has been married but once and who is faithful and well-esteemed. *Apostolic Constitutions (compiled c. 390, E), 7.457.*

He who has been twice married after his baptism, or has had a concubine, cannot be made a bishop, presbyter, or deacon—or indeed any of the priestly category. *Apostolic Constitutions (compiled c. 390, E), 7.501.*

SEE ALSO CHURCH GOVERNMENT; REMARRIAGE.

TWO ADVENTS OF CHRIST

SEE JESUS CHRIST (II. TWO ADVENTS OF CHRIST).

TWO KINGDOMS

SEE CHURCH AND STATE; GOVERNMENT; NONRESISTANCE; PUBLIC OFFICE; WORLD, SEPARATION FROM THE.

TWO WAYS

I have set before you today life and good, death and evil. Deut. 30:15.

No one can serve two masters; for either he will hate the one and love the other, or else he will be loyal to the one and despise the other. Matt. 6:24.

Whoever hears these sayings of Mine, and does them, I will liken him to a wise man who built his house on

the rock. . . . Everyone who hears these sayings of Mine, and does not do them, will be like a foolish man who built his house on the sand. Matt. 7:24, 26.

There are two ways of doctrine and authority: one of light and the other of darkness. And there is a great difference between these two ways. *Barnabas (c. 70–130, E), 1.148.*

There are two ways: one of life and one of death. And there is a great difference between the two ways. The way of life is this: First, love God who created you. Second, love your neighbor as yourself. And all things that you should not want done to you, do not do to someone else. *Didache (c. 80–140, E), 7.377.*

The same is declared by Barnabas in his Epistle, where he says there are two ways—one of light and one of darkness. *Origen (c. 225, E), 4.332.*

There are two ways, O Emperor Constantine, by which human life must proceed: the one that leads to heaven and the other that leads to Hades. *Lactantius (c. 304–313, W), 7.164.*

This is the way things are: those who are happy in this life (as pertaining to the body and the earth) are about to be miserable forever. For they have already enjoyed the good things that they preferred. *Lactantius (c. 304–313, W), 7.207.*

The lawgiver Moses said to the Israelites, "Look! I have set before your face the way of life and the way of death." And he added, "Choose life that you may live." . . . The Lord Jesus also rightly said: "No one can serve two masters." . . . There are two ways: the one of life, the other of death. They have nothing in common with one another, for they are very different. In fact, they are entirely separate. The way of life is the original one. The way of death was introduced later. For it is not in accordance with the mind of God. Rather it comes from the snares of the enemy. *Apostolic Constitutions (compiled c. 390, E), 7.465.*

SEE ALSO CHRISTIAN LIFE; SALVATION; WORLD, SEPARATION FROM THE.

TYPE, TYPOLOGY

A type is a person, object, or event that symbolizes or represents something that is to come at a later date. For example, the Passover lamb was a type of Jesus; the tabernacle was a type of heaven.

Moreover, brethren, I do not want you to be unaware that all our fathers were under the cloud, all passed through the sea, all were baptized into Moses in the cloud and in the sea, all ate the same spiritual food, and all drank the same spiritual drink. For they drank of that spiritual Rock that followed them, and that Rock was Christ. 1 Cor. 10:1–4.

It is written that Abraham had two sons: the one by a bondwoman, the other by a freewoman. But he who was of the bondwoman was born according to the flesh, and he of the freewoman through promise, which things are symbolic. For these are the two covenants. Gal. 4:22–24.

Therefore let no one judge you in food or in drink, or regarding a festival or a new moon or sabbaths, which are a shadow of things to come, but the substance is of Christ. Col. 2:17.

There are priests who offer the gifts according to the law; who serve the copy and shadow of the heavenly things. Heb. 8:4, 5.

The law, having a shadow of the good things to come, and not the very image of the things. Heb. 10:1.

This was so that the type established in Isaac when he was offered on the altar might be fully accomplished. . . . But why is it that they place the wool in the midst of thorns? It is a type of Jesus set before the view of the church. *Barnabas (c. 70–130, E), 1.141, 142.*

Now what do you suppose this is a type of: that a command was given to Israel that men of the greatest wickedness should offer a heifer, slay, it and burn it? . . . The calf is Jesus. The sinful men who offered it are those who led Him to the slaughter. *Barnabas (c. 70–130, E), 1.142.*

This was so that he might reveal a type of Jesus. Moses then made a bronze serpent, and placed it upon a beam. *Barnabas (c. 70–130, E), 1.145.*

You should understand who Isaac was and who Rebecca was. And you should understand concerning what persons He declared that this people should be greater than that. *Barnabas (c. 70–130, E), 1.145.*

The Passover was a type of Christ. . . . The lamb, which is roasted, is roasted and dressed up in the form of the cross. . . . And the offer-ing of fine flours . . . was a type of the bread of the Eucharist. *Justin Martyr (c. 160, E), 1.214, 215.*

The commandment that twelve bells were to be attached to the [robe] of the high priest . . . was a symbol of the twelve apostles, who depend on the power of Christ, the eternal Priest. *Justin Martyr (c. 160, E), 1.215.*

By enumerating all the other appointments of Moses, I can demonstrate that they were types, and symbols, and declarations of those things that would happen to Christ. *Justin Martyr (c. 160, E), 1.216.*

That He will come again in glory after His crucifixion was symbolized . . . by the tree of life, which was said to have been planted in Paradise. *Justin Martyr (c. 160, E), 1.242.*

It was declared by symbol, even in the time of Moses, that there would be two advents of this Christ. . . . [This is evident] from the symbol of the goats presented for sacrifice during the fast. *Justin Martyr (c. 160, E), 1.254.*

The Holy Spirit sometimes brought about some-thing that was a type of the future. *Justin Martyr (c. 160, E), 1.256.*

Now Leah is your people [Jews] and your synagogue; but Rachel is our church. *Justin Martyr (c. 160, E), 1.267.*

God called them to the things of primary importance by means of those which were secondary. That is, He called them to things that are real, by means of those that are typical. . . . For by means of types, they learned to fear God. *Irenaeus (c. 180, E/W), 1.479.*

It is reasonable that those earthly things, indeed, which are spread all around us, should be types of the celestial. *Irenaeus (c. 180, E/W), 1.486.*

The three spies, who were spying out all the land, . . . doubtless [were a type of] the Father and the Son, together with the Holy Spirit. *Irenaeus (c. 180, E/W), 1.492.*

Although Abraham was one, he did in himself prefigure the two covenants. *Irenaeus (c. 180, E/W), 1.496.*

The whole exodus of the people out of Egypt, which took place under divine guid-ance, was a type and image of the exodus of the church that would take place among the Gentiles. *Irenaeus (c. 180, E/W), 1.504.*

By these things, Christ was typified and acknowledged and brought into the world. For He was prefigured in Joseph, then by Levi and Judah. *Irenaeus (c. 180, E/W), 1.571.*

So the ark is declared a type of the body of Christ, which is both pure and immaculate. *Irenaeus (c. 180, E/W), 1.576.*

He is Isaac . . . who is a type of the Lord. *Clement of Alexandria (c. 195, E), 2.215.*

In the Septuagint, Joshua the son of Nun is known as Jesus the son of Nave. "Jesus" is the Greek equivalent of the Hebrew name "Joshua."

. . . Jesus the son of Nave. For the name of Jesus predicted in the Law was a shadow of Christ. *Clement of Alexandria (c. 195, E), 2.224.*

God, in a figure, selected Isaac for himself as a consecrated sacrifice, to be a type to us of the plan of salvation. *Clement of Alexandria (c. 195, E), 2.351.*

The younger, having won his father's favor and receiving his prayers, became the heir. And the elder served him. . . . Now, this arrangement was prophetical and typical. *Clement of Alexandria (c. 195, E), 2.369.*

It would be tedious to go over all the Prophets and the Law, specifying what is spoken in enigmas. For almost the whole Scripture gives its utterances in this way. *Clement of Alexandria (c. 195, E), 2.452.*

Perhaps the two tablets themselves may signify the two covenants. *Clement of Alexandria (c. 195, E), 2.511.*

That blended incense that is mentioned in the Law is that which consists of many tongues and voices in prayer. *Clement of Alexandria (c. 195, E), 2.532.*

From the beginning, the earthly things were foreshadowed in the person of Cain to be those of the "elder son"—that is, Israel. And the opposite sacrifices were demonstrated to be those of the "younger son," Abel—that is, our people. *Tertullian (c. 197, W), 3.156.*

Isaac, when led by his father as a victim, carried his own wood himself. He was even at that early period pointing to Christ's death.

. . . Joseph, again, was also made a figure of Christ. . . . For he suffered persecution at the hands of his brothers and was sold into Egypt. *Tertullian (c. 197, W), 3.165.*

What had formerly perished through the tree in Adam, should be restored through the tree in Christ. *Tertullian (c. 197, W), 3.170.*

The people were set unconditionally free. They escaped the violence of the Egyptian king by crossing over through water. And it was water that extinguished the king himself, with his entire forces. What figure is more manifestly fulfilled in the sacrament of baptism? *Tertullian (c. 198, W), 3.673.*

The cleansing of the Syrian signified the cleansing of the nations of the world in Christ their Light. For they were steeped in the stains of the seven deadly sins: idolatry, blasphemy, murder, adultery, fornication, false witness, and fraud. Seven times, therefore, as if once for each sin, Naaman washed in the Jordan. . . . So the virtue and fullness of the one baptism was thus solemnly imputed to Christ. For He alone was someday to establish on earth—not only revelation—but also a baptism that would be endowed with bounteous power. *Tertullian (c. 207, W), 3.356.*

Christ still would have observed the figurative signs of the Law in its types, because of their prophetic significance. *Tertullian (c. 207, W), 3.357.*

The two goats that were presented on the great day of atonement prefigure the two advents of Christ. *Tertullian (c. 210, W), 3.327.*

Isaac portrays a figure of God the Father. Rebecca prefigures the Holy Spirit. Esau prefigures the first people [the Jews] and the devil. Jacob prefigures the church, or Christ. *Hippolytus (c. 205, W), 5.168.*

Someone may be ready to say, "How will you prove to me that the Savior was born in the year 5500 [i.e., as counted from the beginning of Creation]? Learn that easily, O man, from the things that took place of old in the wilderness under Moses—in the case of the tabernacle. For they were made types and emblems of spiritual mysteries. . . . [The Ark of the Covenant's] measurements, when summed up together, make five cubits and a half, so that the 5500 years might be signified thereby. *Hippolytus (c. 205, W), 5.179.*

Hannah, in the first Book of Kings, was a type of the church. *Cyprian (c. 250, W), 5.448.*

The Hebrews were commanded to furnish the tabernacle as a type of the church. In this manner, by means of visible things, they could announce in advance the image of divine things. A pattern was shown to Moses on the mountain. He was to follow this in making the tabernacle. For the pattern was a type of accurate representation of the heavenly dwelling. We now understand this more clearly than we did through the types. Yet, we still perceive it more darkly than if we saw the reality. *Methodius (c. 290, E), 6.328.*

SEE ALSO CROSS; HERMENEUTICS; TABERNACLE.

UNBELIEVING SPOUSE

A woman who has a husband who does not believe, if he is willing to live with her, let her not divorce him. For the unbelieving husband is sanctified by the wife, and the unbelieving wife is sanctified by the husband. 1 Cor. 7:13, 14.

Likewise you wives, be submissive to your own husbands, that even if some do not obey the word, they, without a word, may be won by the conduct of their wives. 1 Pet. 3:1.

A certain woman lived with an intemperate husband. She, too, had once been intemperate. But when she came to the knowledge of the teachings of Christ, she became sober-minded. She tried to persuade her husband, too, to be temperate.... But he continued in the same excesses, and he alienated his wife from him through his actions. So she desired to be divorced from him. But she changed her mind because of her [Christian] friends, who advised her to remain with him, with the thought that some time or other her husband might give some hope of change. *Justin Martyr (c. 160, E), 1.188.*

The wise woman, then, will first choose to persuade her husband to be her associate in what is conducive to happiness. And should that be found impracticable, let her by herself earnestly aim at virtue, gaining her husband's consent in everything. She should never do anything against his will—with the exception of what is reckoned as necessary to virtue and salvation. *Clement of Alexandria (c. 195, E), 2.432.*

The following passage of Tertullian was written to discourage Christian women from marrying outside the faith.

Each and every believing woman must of necessity obey God. How can she serve two lords—the Lord, and her husband (a Gentile, to boot)? For in obeying a Gentile, she will carry out Gentile practices: personal attractiveness, dressing of the head, worldly elegancies, and blandishments that are even more corrupt. The very secrets of matrimony will be tainted.... If a station is to be kept, the [unbelieving] husband makes an appointment with his wife at daybreak to meet him at the baths. If there are fasts to be observed, the husband holds a lively banquet that same day. If a charitable expedition has to be made, never is family business more urgent. For who would permit his wife to go around from street to street to other men's ... cottages, for the sake of visiting the brethren? Who will willingly tolerate her being taken from his side for meetings at night, if the need is there? Finally, who will without anxiety endure her absence all the night long at the Paschal solemnities? Who will, without some suspicion of his own, dismiss her to attend that Lord's supper that they defame? Who will permit her to creep into prison to kiss a martyr's chains? Nay, truly, to meet any one of the brothers to exchange the kiss? Will he permit her to offer water for the saints' feet? ... If a pilgrim brother arrives, what hospitality for him will there be in an alien home? If goods are to be distributed to any, the granaries and the storehouses are closed in advance.... Now, these things may happen to those women likewise who continue in that state—having come to the faith while in a Gentile marriage. In that situation, they are excused, as having been chosen by God in these very circumstances. And they are directed to persevere in their married state. They are sanctified, and they have held out to them the hope of making a "gain" [by winning over their spouse]. *Tertullian (c. 205, W), 4.47.*

When a man and his wife are both unbelievers, sometimes it is the man who first believes and in time saves his wife. And sometimes it is the wife who begins to believe and afterwards in time persuades her husband. *Origen (c. 245, E), 9.491.*

Be sure to curb any spirit of contention as to all men—but particularly as to your husband. Otherwise, if he is an unbeliever or a pagan, he may have a cause of scandal or of blaspheming God. *Apostolic Constitutions (compiled c. 390, E), 7.395.*

SEE ALSO HUSBANDS; MARRIAGE; WIFE, WIVES.

UNCORRUPTED BODIES
An uncorrupted body is a corpse that, because of miraculous or natural reasons, does not decay.

In his *Republic,* [Plato] presents to us the corpse of an unburied person, which was preserved a long time without corruption. Plato says it was preserved because the soul remained unseparated from the body. . . . Now, it is quite possible that the nature of the atmosphere tended to the preservation of the above-mentioned corpse. What if the air were particularly dry, and the ground were of a saline nature? *Tertullian (c. 210, W), 3.228.*

UNFORGIVABLE SIN
SEE SIN (II. UNFORGIVABLE SIN).

UNION WITH GOD
SEE DEIFICATION OF MAN; MYSTICISM, CHRISTIAN.

USURY
Although the word "usury" has come to mean an exorbitant rate of interest on a loan, it originally meant any interest on a loan.

You shall not lend him your money for usury, nor lend him your food at a profit. Lev. 25:37.

Lord, who may abide in Your tabernacle? . . . He who does not put out his money at usury, nor does he take a bribe against the innocent. Ps. 15:1, 5.

"His money he will not give on usury and will not take interest." . . . These words contain a description of the conduct of Christians. *Clement of Alexandria (c. 195, E), 2.233.*

Let it suffice to remark that the Law prohibits a brother from taking usury. *Clement of Alexandria (c. 195, E), 2.366.*

Now, on the subject of a loan, He asks, "And if you lend to those from whom you hope to receive, what reward have you?" Compare this with the following words of Ezekiel, in which He says of the aforementioned just man: "He has not given his money upon usury, nor will he take any increase." That is, he will not take the excessiveness of interest, which is usury. The first step was to eradicate the fruit of the money lent. [This made it] more easy to accustom a man to the loss (should it happen) of the money itself. *Tertullian (c. 207, W), 3.372.*

The next two quotations were written to rebuke certain Christians:

In borrowing money from pagans under pledged securities, Christians give a guarantee under oath! Yet, they deny to themselves that they have done so! *Tertullian (c. 200, W), 3.75*

You have lent on usury, taking twenty-four percent! Yet, now you wish to bestow charity that you may purge yourself . . . with that which is evil. The Almighty absolutely rejects such works as these. *Commodianus (c.240, W), 4.216.*

We must not take usury. . . . "You will not lend to your brother with usury of money" [Deut. 23:19]. *Cyprian (c. 250, W), 5.546.*

If a Christian has lent any money, he will not receive interest—so that the benefit that relieved necessity may be unimpaired. . . . For it is his duty in other respects not to be sparing of his property, in order that he may do good. But to receive more than he has given is unjust! *Lactantius (c. 304–313, W), 7.183.*

Let a bishop, presbyter, or deacon who charges usury to those to whom he lends either cease doing so, or else let him be deprived. *Apostolic Constitutions (compiled c. 390, E), 7.502.*

SEE ALSO CHRISTIAN LIFE.

VALENTINUS, VALENTINIANS

Valentinus, who was a native of Egypt, was one of the foremost Gnostic teachers of the early second century. He constructed an elaborate cosmology of male-female aeons who supposedly govern the universe.

The Valentinians maintain, then, that in the invisible and ineffable heights above there exists a certain perfect, pre-existent Aeon. They call it Proarche, Propator, and Bythus. They describe it as being invisible and incomprehensible.... Each of these Aeons is masculo-feminine, as follows: Propator was united by a conjunction with his Ennoea. Then Monogenes (that is Nous) was united with Aletheia. Logos was united with Zoe, and Anthropos was united with Ecclesia. *Irenaeus (c. 180, E/W), 1.316.*

The Father afterwards produces, in his own image, by means of Monogenes, the above-mentioned Horos, without conjunction, masculo-feminine.... They tell us that Monogenes, acting in accordance with the prudent forethought of the Father, gave origin to another conjugal pair, namely Christ and the Holy Spirit. *Irenaeus (c. 180, E/W), 1.318.*

They go on to say that the Demiurge imagined that he created all these things of himself. However, he actually made them in conjunction with the productive power of Achamoth. He formed the heavens, yet was ignorant of the heavens. He fashioned man, yet did not know man. *Irenaeus (c. 180, E/W), 1.322.*

At the same time, the Valentinians deny that Christ assumed anything material [into His nature], since indeed matter is incapable of salvation. They further hold that the consummation of all things will take place when all that is spiritual has been formed and perfected by gnosis [i.e., knowledge]. And by this, they mean spiritual men who have attained to the perfect

knowledge of God, and been initiated into these mysteries by Achamoth. And they consider themselves to be these persons.... On the other hand, they say that carnal men are instructed in carnal things. Such "carnal men" can be recognized by their works and their simple faith. For they do not have perfect knowledge [gnosis]. The Valentinians say that we who belong to the church are such carnal persons. Therefore, they maintain that good works are necessary for us. Otherwise, it would be impossible for us to be saved. But as to themselves, they hold that they will be entirely saved for a certainty—not by means of their conduct, but because they are spiritual by nature. *Irenaeus (c. 180, E/W), 1.324.*

The "most perfect" among the Valentinians addict themselves without fear to all kinds of forbidden deeds. I mean, the deeds of which the Scriptures assure us that "those who do such things will not inherit the kingdom of God." ... Then, again, at every pagan festival celebrated in honor of the idols, the Valentinians are the first to assemble. And to such a degree do they go, that some of them do not even keep away from that bloody spectacle hateful both to God and men, in which gladiators either fight with wild beasts, or singly encounter one another. Others of them yield themselves up to the lusts of the flesh with the utmost greediness. For they maintain that carnal things apply only to the carnal nature, while spiritual things apply to the spiritual. *Irenaeus (c. 180, E/W), 1.324.*

The Valentinians conceive, then, of three kinds of men: spiritual, material, and carnal. These three kinds are represented by Cain, Abel, and Seth.... This, then, is their system, which neither the prophets announced, nor the Lord taught, nor the apostles delivered. However, they boast that they have a perfect knowledge, beyond all others. They gather their views from other sources than the Scriptures. *Irenaeus (c. 180, E/W), 1.326.*

Valentinus adapted the principles of the heresy called "Gnostic" to the distinctive character of his own school. *Irenaeus (c. 180, E/W), 1.332.*

On the other hand, those who are from Valentinus are altogether reckless. They create their own Scriptures, boasting that they possess more Gospels than there really are. Indeed, they have gone to such a degree of audacity, as to entitle their comparatively recent writing the *Gospel of Truth. Irenaeus (c. 180, E/W), 1.429.*

All the followers of Valentinus, therefore, lost their case, when they said that man was not created out of this earth, but from a fluid and diffused substance. *Irenaeus (c. 180, E/W), 1.543.*

The followers of Valentinus assign *faith* to us—the "simple." However, they claim that *knowledge* [gnosis] sprang up in themselves. *Clement of Alexandria (c. 195, E), 2.349.*

Valentinus, in a sermon, writes in these words: "You are originally immortal and children of eternal life. And you would have death distributed to you that you may spend and lavish it, and so that death may die in you and by you." . . . For Valentinus, like Basilides, also supposes there is a class who are saved by nature and that this different race has come here to us from above, for the abolition of death. *Clement of Alexandria (c. 195, E), 2.425.*

Where was Valentinus then, the disciple of Platonism? For it is evident that those men lived not so long ago . . . and that they at first were believers in the doctrine of the catholic church. For they were in the church of Rome under the episcopate of the blessed Eleutherus, until on account of their ever restless curiosity . . . they were more than once expelled. *Tertullian (c. 197, W), 3.257.*

The apostle directs a similar blow against those who said that "the resurrection was already past." Such an opinion do the Valentinians assert. *Tertullian (c. 197, W), 3.259.*

One man perverts the Scriptures with his hand; another perverts their meaning by his exegesis. For although Valentinus seems to use the entire volume [of Scripture], he has none the less laid violent hands on the truth. Only, he does it with more cunning mind and skill than Marcion. *Tertullian (c. 197, W), 3.262.*

The Valentinians . . . are no doubt a very large body of heretics. *Tertullian (c. 200, W), 3.503.*

If you ask sincere and honest questions to the Valentinians, they answer you with a stern look and wrinkled brow, and say, "The subject is profound." . . . For this reason, we are branded by them as the "simple." *Tertullian (c. 200, W), 3.503, 504.*

However, let any man approach the subject from a knowledge of the faith that he has learned from other sources. Now, as soon as the [honest inquirer] finds so many names of Aeons, so many marriages, so many offsprings, so many exits . . . of a dispersed and mutilated Deity, that man will not hesitate to immediately proclaim that these are "the fables and endless genealogies" that the inspired apostle condemned by foreknowledge—back when these seeds of heresy were even then sprouting. *Tertullian (c. 200, W), 3.505.*

I say, we know most fully their actual origin. And we are quite aware of why we call them Valentinians, although they pretend to disavow their name. It is true that they have departed from their founder. Nevertheless, their origin is still there. *Tertullian (c. 200, W), 3.505.*

Valentinus had expected to become a bishop, because he was an able man both in genius and eloquence. Being indignant, however, that another obtained the dignity by reason of a claim of being a confessor, he separated from the church of the true faith. Just like those spirits who (when roused by ambition) are usually inflamed with the desire for revenge, he devoted himself with all his might to exterminate the truth. *Tertullian (c. 200, W), 3.505.*

Axionicus at Antioch is the only man who at the present time honors the memory of Valentinus, by keeping his rules to the full. However, this heresy is permitted to change itself into as many various shapes as does a prostitute who changes and adjusts her dress every day. *Tertullian (c. 200, W), 3.505.*

Whenever the Valentinians have hit upon any novelty, they immediately call their presumption a "revelation"! They call their own perverse ingenuity a "spiritual gift"! *Tertullian (c. 200, W), 3.505.*

I now bring forward what they say concerning Christ. . . . They say He was produced *by means of* a virgin, rather than *of* a virgin. By this, they mean that He descended into the virgin and passed through her, instead of receiving a birth by her. In short, Jesus came into existence *through* her, not *of* her. In other words, He did not experience a mother in her, but only a conduit. *Tertullian (c. 200, W), 3.516.*

It is for this reason that they do not regard works as necessary for themselves. Nor do they observe any of the calls of duty. They even elude the necessity of martyrdom on any pretense that may suit their fancy. *Tertullian (c. 200, W), 3.517.*

Valentinus was more consistent and more liberal [than Marcion]. For, having once imagined two deities, Bythos and Sige, he then poured forth a swarm of divine essences—a brood of no less than thirty Aeons. *Tertullian (c. 207, W), 3.274.*

. . . or else holding, after the heretical tenets of Valentinus, . . . that [the body of Christ] had qualities unique to itself. *Tertullian (c. 210, W), 3.546.*

Of the writings of Arsinous, also called Valentinus, . . . we receive nothing at all [as canonical]. *Muratorian Fragment (c. 200, W), 5.604.*

The heresy of Valentinus is certainly, then, connected with the Pythagorean and Platonic theory. *Hippolytus (c. 225, W), 5.81.*

Valentinus says that all the prophets, therefore, and the Law, spoke by means of the Demiurge—a silly god. They were fools, who knew nothing. He says it was for this reason that the Savior states, "All who came before me are thieves and robbers." *Hippolytus (c. 225, W), 5.89; see also 1.507, 1.513, 2.355, 2.372; extended discussion: 1.316–1.328, 1.439–1.442, 3.502–3.520, 5.85–5.91.*

See also Gnostics, Gnosticism; Heresies, Heretics; Marcion.

VALERIAN, EMPEROR

The Roman emperor Valerian (c. 200–c. 260), issued edicts in 257 and 258 against Christians. These edicts resulted in a short but intense wave of persecution against the church. Valerian was captured by the Persians in 260, however, and his fierce persecution came to an abrupt end.

One finds both things to wonder at in Valerian's case. Particularly, one has to consider how different it was with him before those events happened. Consider how mild and well-disposed he was towards the men of God. For among the emperors who preceded him, there was not one who displayed such a kindly and favorable disposition toward the Christians as he did. . . . At that time, his whole house was filled with godly persons. It was practically itself a church of God. But the master and president of the Magi of Egypt prevailed on him to abandon that course and urged him to slay and persecute those pure and holy men. . . . [Soon after doing that,] Valerian speedily perished, with his whole family, root and branch. *Eusebius, quoting Dionysius of Alexandria (c. 262, E), 6.106, 107.*

Soon [after Decius], Valerian also, in a mood just as frantic, lifted up his unholy hands to attack God. And although his time was short, he shed much righteous blood. But God punished him in a new and extraordinary manner. . . . Having been made prisoner by the Persians, he lost not only that power that he had exercised without moderation, but he also lost the liberty of which he had deprived others. So he spent the remainder of his days in the vilest condition of slavery. *Lactantius (c. 320, W), 7.302.*

VEIL

Every woman who prays or prophesies with her head uncovered dishonors her head, for that is one and the same as if her head were shaved. . . . For this reason the woman ought to have a symbol of authority on her head, because of the angels. 1 Cor. 11:5, 10.

A virgin meets me, adorned as if she were proceeding from the bridal chamber. She was clothed entirely in white and wore white sandals. She was veiled up to her forehead, and her head was covered by a hood. *Hermas (c. 150, W), 2.18.*

Such a covering should be worn as is necessary for covering the eyes of women. *Clement of Alexandria (c. 195, E), 2.264, 265.*

It has also been commanded that the head should be veiled and the face covered. For it is a wicked thing for beauty to be a snare to men. Nor is it appropriate for a woman to desire to make herself conspicuous by using a purple veil. *Clement of Alexandria (c. 195, E), 2.266.*

And a Christian woman will never fall, if she puts before her eyes modesty and her veil. Nor will she invite another to fall into sin by uncovering her face. For this is the wish of the Word, since it is becoming for her to pray veiled. *Clement of Alexandria (c. 195, E), 2.290.*

"Because of the angels." By the "angels," he means righteous and virtuous men. Let her be veiled then, so that she may not lead them to stumble into fornication. For the real angels in heaven see her, even though she is veiled. *Clement of Alexandria (c. 195, E), 2.578.*

The quotations below from Tertullian address the issue whether the apostolic commandment concerning veiling applies only to married women or whether it applies to virgins as well:

That matter must now be dealt with that is inconsistently observed throughout the churches. I am referring to the issue of whether virgins should be veiled or not. For those persons who give virgins immunity from a head covering appear to rest their position on this: that the apostle has not specified "virgins" to be veiled—but "women." . . . Indeed, he says women must be veiled "because of the angels." This refers to the event, when, on account of "the daughters of men," angels revolted from God. Now, who would argue that it was only "women" (that is, those who were already married and had lost their virginity) who were the objects of angelic lust. Are virgins incapable of excelling in beauty and finding lovers? . . . Why do you uncover before God what you cover before men? Will you be more modest in public than in the church? . . . Be veiled, virgin, if you really are a virgin. For you should blush. If you are a virgin, shrink from the gaze of many eyes. Let no one admire your face. Let no one perceive your falsehood. *Tertullian (c. 198, W), 3.687–3.689.*

Some persons disputed about eating idol sacrifices; others about the veiled dress of women. *Tertullian (c. 207, W), 3.286.*

But why "should the woman have power over her head, because of the angels"? If it is because she was created for the man, and taken out of the man, according to the Creator's purpose, then in this way too has the apostle maintained the discipline of that God. . . . He adds: "Because of the angels." What angels? In other words, whose angels? If he means the fallen angels of the Creator, there is great propriety in his meaning. It is right that the face which was a snare to them should

wear some mark of a humble guise and veiled beauty. *Tertullian (c. 207, W), 3.445.*

It behooves our virgins to be veiled from the time that they have passed the turning point of their age. This observance is required by truth. Therefore, no one can impose any condition on it: no space of time, no influence of persons, and no privilege of regions. . . . Throughout Greece, and certain of its barbaric provinces, the majority of churches keep their virgins covered. There are places, too, beneath this [North African] sky, where this practice is also followed (lest anyone ascribe the custom to Greek or barbarian Gentilehood). But I have proposed as models those churches which were founded by apostles or apostolic men. . . . Still, until very recently, among us, females following either custom were admitted to communion with comparative indifference. The matter had been left up to choice—for each virgin either to veil herself or expose herself. *Tertullian (c. 207, W), 4.27, 4.28.*

But insofar as it is the custom to argue even from the Scriptures in opposition to truth, there is immediately urged against us the fact that no mention of "virgins" is made by the apostle when he is prescribing about the veil. Rather, only "women" are named. *Tertullian (c. 207, W), 4.29.*

Likewise, the Corinthians themselves understood him in this manner. In fact, at this very day, the Corinthians do veil their virgins. What the apostles taught, their disciples approve. *Tertullian (c. 207, W), 4.33.*

Even if it is on account of the angels that she is to be veiled, the age from which the law of the veil will come into operation will no doubt be that from which the "daughters of men" were able to invite lust of their persons and to experience marriage. *Tertullian (c. 207, W), 4.34.*

Since they veil their heads in the presence of pagans, let them at all events conceal their virginity *in the church.* After all, they veil themselves outside the church. If they fear strangers, let them stand in awe of their brothers too. *Tertullian (c. 207, W), 4.35.*

For some, with their turbans and woollen bands, do not *veil* their heads, but *bind* them up. They are protected, indeed, in front. However, they are bare where the head properly lies. Others are to a certain extent covered over the region of the brain with linen doilies of small dimensions ... which do not quite reach the ears.... Let them know that the whole head constitutes the woman. Its limits and boundaries reach as far as the place where the robe begins. The region of the veil is co-extensive with the space covered by the hair when unbound.... Arabia's pagan females will be your judges. For they cover not only the head, but the face also. *Tertullian (c. 207, W), 4.37.*

How severe a chastisement will they likewise deserve, who during the Psalms—and at any mention of God—remain uncovered. Even when about to spend time in prayer itself, with the utmost readiness they place a fringe, tuft, or any thread whatever on the crown of their heads and suppose themselves to be covered! *Tertullian (c. 207, W), 4.37.*

Among the Jews, so usual is it for their women to have the head veiled, that they may thereby be recognized. *Tertullian (c. 211, W), 3.95.*

In respect of the woman's veil, he says, "Does not even nature teach you?" *Tertullian (c. 211, W), 3.96.*

A woman should not appear with her head uncovered—on account of the angels. *Tertullian (c. 211, W), 3.102.*

When you are in the streets, cover your head. For by such a covering, you will avoid being viewed by idle persons.... Look downward when you walk in public, veiling yourself, as becomes women. *Apostolic Constitutions (compiled c. 390, E), 7.395; see also 3.687–3.689.*

SEE ALSO CLOTHING; MODESTY.

VENERATION OF RELICS

SEE RELICS OF MARTYRS AND SAINTS.

VENERATION OF SAINTS

SEE MARTYRS, MARTYRDOM (IV. VENERATION OF MARTYRS).

VESSELS, EUCHARISTIC

Let the very paintings upon your cups come forward to show whether even in them the figurative meaning of that sheep will shine through. *Tertullian (c. 212, W), 4.80.*

The utensils and furniture of the church were abandoned to pillage. *Lactantius (c. 320, W), 7.305.*

Let no one appropriate to his own use a vessel of silver, gold, or linen that is sanctified. And if anyone is caught, let him be punished with suspension. *Apostolic Constitutions (compiled c. 390, E), 7.504.*

SEE ALSO LITURGY; VESTMENTS, RELIGIOUS.

The pagans approach [their altars] so that they may gaze upon the gold and look at the brilliancy of polished marble and ivory. They approach so that they can study with unwearied contemplation the garments adorned with precious stones and colors, or cups studded with glittering jewels. *Lactantius (c. 304–313, W), 7.50.*

VESTMENTS, RELIGIOUS

In the first quotation below, Polycrates refers to John as being a "priest wearing the petalon." There is no consensus among scholars as to what Polycrates means. The Septuagint uses the word petalon to refer to the breastplate worn by the Jewish high priest. Is Polycrates claiming that John served as a Jewish priest? Does he mean that John wore some type of special garment? Or does Polycrates mean it only in a symbolic sense?

John, who reclined on the Lord's breast, became a priest wearing the *petalon*, a martyr, and a teacher. He rests at Ephesus. *Polycrates (c. 190, E), 8.773.*

[John the Baptist] was preparing the lowly and chaste ways of the Lord. For how could he possibly have worn a purple robe? After all, he turned away from the pomp of cities. Instead, he retired to the solitude of the desert to live in serenity with God. *Clement of Alexandria (c. 195, E), 2.266.*

I will mention that often in the houses of the temple-keepers and [pagan] priests (under the sacrificial head-bands, sacred hats, and the purple robes), deeds of licentiousness are done amid the fumes of incense. *Tertullian (c. 197, W), 3.30.*

How is it that, even with the garland of Ceres on the brow, wrapped in the purple cloak of Saturn, wearing the white robe of the goddess Isis, you invoke God as judge? *Tertullian (c. 197, W), 3.176.*

That famous purple and the gold used as an ornament of the neck—these were marks of dignity among the Egyptians and Babylonians. ... The purple and other marks of dignities and powers were originally dedicated to idolatry. They were later engrafted as marks of dignity and power. So they carry the stain of their own profanation. . . . What is the point, then, to use the garment, if you do not administer the functions of it? *Tertullian (c. 200, W), 3.72.*

The Lord walked in humility and obscurity, . . . unadorned in dress. Otherwise, He would not have said, "Behold! Those who are clad in soft raiment are in kings' houses." In short, He was lowly in countenance and appearance, just as Isaiah had also prophesied. . . . He shrank back from being made a king, for He was conscious of His own kingdom. Therefore, He in the fullest manner gave us the example of turning completely from all the pride, dignity, and garments of power. *Tertullian (c. 200, W), 3.73.*

Christ shrank back from being made a king. He, in the fullest manner, gave Himself as an example for turning coldly from all the pride and garb, as well of dignity as of power. For who would rather have used them than the Son of God? . . . What kind of purple would bloom from his shoulders? What kind of gold would radiate from His head? However, Christ judged the glory of the world to be alien both to Himself and to His followers. Therefore, what He was unwilling to accept, He has rejected. *Tertullian (c. 200, W), 3.73.*

What apostle, preacher of the gospel, or bishop do you ever find wearing a crown? I do not think that even the temple of God itself was crowned. Neither was the ark of the covenant, nor the tabernacle of witness. *Tertullian (c. 211, W), 3.98.*

If the smell of some place or other offends me, I burn the Arabian product myself. However, I do not do this with the same ceremony nor in the same dress, nor with the same ceremony, with which it is done to idols. *Tertullian (c. 211, W), 3.99.*

The blood of the Lord serves as your purple robe. *Tertullian (c. 211, W), 3.101.*

[PAGAN ANTAGONIST:] They despise the temples as dead houses. They reject the gods. They laugh at sacred things. Wretched, they pity the priests—if they are allowed. Half naked themselves, they despise honors and purple robes. *Mark Minucius Felix (c. 200, W), 4.177.*

We do not, at once, stand on the level of the lowest of the people, just because we refuse your honors and purple robes. *Mark Minucius Felix (c. 200, W), 4.193.*

The martyrs were brought to the gate, and were forced to put on the clothing. The men were forced to wear the clothing of the priests of Saturn. The women were forced to wear those which were consecrated to Ceres. However, that noble-minded woman resisted even to the end. *Passion of Perpetua and Felicitas (c. 205, W), 3.704.*

The pagans approach [the pagan altars] so that they may gaze upon the gold and look at the brilliancy of polished marble and ivory. They approach so that they can study with unwearied contemplation the garments adorned with precious stones and colors, or cups studded with glittering jewels. *Lactantius (c. 304–313, W), 7.50.*

Among the Romans, the robe of purple is a sign of the assumption of royal dignity. *Lactantius (c. 304–313, W), 7.106.*

If anyone thinks that vestments, jewels, and other things that are considered precious [by men] are valued by God, he is altogether ignorant of what God is. *Lactantius (c. 304–313, W), 7.192.*

Emperor Daia commanded that all of those newly instituted [pagan] priests should appear in white garments, for that was the most honorable distinction of dress. *Lactantius (c. 304–313, W), 7.316.*

POST-NICENE REFERENCE TO EUCHARISTIC VESTMENTS: 7.486.

SEE ALSO VESSELS, SACRED (PAGAN); WORSHIP, CHRISTIAN (II. WORSHIP CUSTOMS); WORSHIP, PAGAN.

VICAR OF CHRIST

A vicar is a person who acts in the place of someone else.

[SAID SARCASTICALLY:] Grant . . . that the Holy Spirit had no such respect for any one [church] so as to lead it into truth—even though He was sent by Christ for this purpose! . . . Grant, also, that He, the Steward of God, the Vicar of Christ, neglected His office! . . . [If so,] is it likely that so many churches—and they so great—would have gone astray into one and the same faith? *Tertullian (c. 197, W), 3.256.*

Discipline is to be . . . carried on to perfection by the Vicar of the Lord, the Holy Spirit. *Tertullian (c. 207, W), 4.27.*

VIOLENT WHO STORM HEAVEN

See Salvation (IV. The Violent Who Storm the Kingdom of Heaven).

VIRGIN BIRTH

Therefore the Lord Himself will give you a sign: Behold, the virgin shall conceive and bear a Son, and shall call His name Immanuel. Isa. 7:14.

Now the birth of Jesus Christ was as follows: After His mother Mary was betrothed to Joseph, before they came together, she was found with child of the Holy Spirit. Matt. 1:18.

Then Mary said to the angel, "How can this be, since I do not know a man?" And the angel answered and said to her, "The Holy Spirit will come upon you, and the power of the highest will overshadow you: therefore, also, that Holy One who is to be born will be called the Son of God. Luke 1:34, 35.

He was truly born of a virgin. *Ignatius (c. 105, E), 1.86.*

We even affirm that He was born of a virgin. *Justin Martyr (c. 160, E), 1.170.*

Hear again how Isaiah in express words foretold that He would be born of a virgin. *Justin Martyr (c. 160, E), 1.174.*

But you [Jews] and your teachers venture to claim that in the prophecy of Isaiah it is not said, "Behold, the *virgin* will conceive," but, "Behold, the *young woman* will conceive, and bear a son." Furthermore, you explain the prophecy as if [it referred] to Hezekiah, who was your king. Therefore, I will endeavor to soon discuss this point in opposition to you. *Justin Martyr (c. 160, E), 1.216.*

Christ Jesus, the Son of God, because of His surpassing love towards His creation, humbled Himself to be born of the virgin. Thereby, He united man through Himself to God. *Irenaeus (c. 180, E/W), 1.417.*

The Lord Himself did save us, giving us the token of the virgin. But this was not as some allege—who presume to expound the Scripture as: "Behold, a *young woman* will conceive, and bring forth a son." For this is as Theodotion the Ephesian has translated it, and Aquila of Pontus—both of whom are Jewish proselytes. The Ebionites, following these men, assert that He was begotten by Joseph. *Irenaeus (c. 180, E/W), 1.451.*

He was born Emmanuel of the virgin. To this effect, they testify that before Joseph had come together with Mary, while she remained in virginity, "she was found with child by the Holy Spirit." ... By what has been said, the Holy Spirit has carefully pointed out His birth from a virgin. *Irenaeus (c. 180, E/W), 1.452.*

Isaiah said, "The Lord Himself will give you a sign." Accordingly, he declared something unexpected with regard to His conception—something which could not have been accomplished in any other way than by God, the Lord of all. God Himself gave us a sign in the house of David. For what great thing or what sign would it have been if merely a *young woman* conceived by a man and gave birth? After all, this is a thing that happens to all women who produce offspring. However, since an unexpected salvation was to be provided for men through the help of God, so also was the unexpected birth from a virgin accomplished. *Irenaeus (c. 180, E/W), 1.453.*

He will also judge the Ebionites [who denied the virgin birth]. ... How will man escape from the birth that is subject to death, if it is not by means of a new birth, given in a wonderful and unexpected manner by God—that regeneration that flows from the virgin through faith? *Irenaeus (c. 180, E/W), 1.507.*

He declared that the Word would become flesh. He declared that the Son of God would become the Son of man. For the pure One opened purely that pure womb that regenerates men unto God. For He Himself made it pure. *Irenaeus (c. 180, E/W), 1.509.*

Vain also are the Ebionites, who do not receive by faith into their soul the union of God and man. Rather, they remain in the old leaven of [the natural] birth. For they do not choose to understand that the Holy Spirit came upon Mary and the power of the Most High overshadowed her. *Irenaeus (c. 180, E/W), 1.527.*

The heretics ... do not acknowledge His incarnation. Others ignore the arrangement of a virgin and maintain that He was begotten by Joseph. *Irenaeus (c. 180, E/W), 1.547.*

The Son of God—He who made the universe—assumed flesh and was conceived in the virgin's womb. *Clement of Alexandria (c. 195, E), 2.509.*

Some say that, after Mary brought forth, she was found, when examined, to be a virgin. "And she brought forth, and yet brought not forth," says the Scripture—as having conceived of herself, rather than from union [with a man]. *Clement of Alexandria (c. 195, E), 2.551.*

. . . Jesus, whom of the lightning flash of Divinity the virgin bore. *Clement of Alexandria (c. 195, E), 2.578.*

This ray of God, then, as it was always foretold in ancient times, descended into a certain virgin. And He was made flesh in her womb. So, in His birth, God and man were united. *Tertullian (c. 197, W), 3.34, 35.*

You [Jews] have the audacity to lie, as if the Scriptures actually said "a young female" was to conceive and bring forth, rather than "a virgin." You are refuted even by the fact that something that is a daily occurrence—the pregnancy and giving birth of a young female—cannot possibly be anything of a *sign*. *Tertullian (c. 197, W), 3.161.*

He says, "Therefore, the Lord himself will give you a *sign*. Behold, a virgin will conceive, and bear a son." Now a sign from God would not have been a sign unless it had been some new and wonderful thing. However, Jewish cavillers, in order to annoy us, boldly pretend that Scripture does not hold that a *virgin* is to conceive and bring forth—but only a young woman. They are, however, refuted by this consideration: that nothing of the nature of a sign can possibly come out of what is a daily occurrence—the pregnancy and child-bearing of a young woman. Instead, a virgin mother is justly deemed to be proposed by God as a sign. *Tertullian (c. 207, W), 3.331, 332.*

Whoever wishes to see Jesus, the Son of David, must believe in Him through the virgin's birth. He who will not believe this will not hear from Him the commendation, "Your faith has saved you." *Tertullian (c. 207, W), 3.411.*

However, a word of caution must be addressed to all who refuse to believe that our flesh was in Christ, on the grounds that it did not come from the seed of a human father. Let them remember that Adam himself received this flesh of ours without the seed of a human father. *Tertullian (c. 210, W), 3.536.*

A sign has been given to the house of David. For the virgin conceived, was pregnant, and brought forth a Son. *Origen (c. 225, E), 4.352.*

A Jew might split words and say that the words are not, "Look, a virgin [will give birth]," but, "Look, a young woman . . . " I reply that the word *olmah*—which the Septuagint has rendered by "virgin," but others by "young woman," occurs . . . in Deuteronomy, being applied [clearly] to a virgin, in the following passage: "If a woman who is a virgin [Heb. *olmah*] is betrothed unto a husband . . ." *Origen (c. 248, E), 4.411.*

The Lord is recounted to have spoken to Ahaz as follows: "Ask a sign for yourself from the Lord, your God, either in the depth or height above." And afterwards the sign is given: "Behold, a virgin will conceive and bear a son." What kind of sign would that have been, if it were merely a young woman—not a virgin—giving birth to a child? *Origen (c. 248, E), 4.411.*

Surely it is appropriate only to a virgin to produce a being at whose birth it is said, "God [is] with us." . . . I will ask, "Who in the times of Ahaz bore a son at whose birth the expression Immanuel was made use of"? *Origen (c. 248, E), 4.411.*

He had made these remarks because he did not know the pure and virgin birth of that body that was to minister to the salvation of men, unaccompanied by any corruption. *Origen (c. 248, E), 4.606.*

The parent of your life—that unspotted grace and undefiled virgin—conceived in her womb without the aid of man, through a pure conception. She thus became suspected of having betrayed the marriage bed. *Methodius (c. 290, E), 6.353.*

He chose the holy virgin, so that He might enter into her womb. And she, being filled by the possession of the Divine Spirit, conceived. Without any intercourse with a man, her virgin womb was suddenly impregnated. . . . The words of the prophet Isaiah are these: "Therefore, God himself will give you a sign. Behold, a virgin will conceive and bear a son." *Lactantius (c. 304–313, W), 7.110; see also 3.537–3.542.*

SEE ALSO CHRIST, DIVINITY OF; INCARNATION; JESUS CHRIST; MARY.

VIRGINS, ORDER OF

In most of the early churches, there was a recognized order of virgins—celibate men and women who pledged themselves to remain single and to be betrothed to Christ. The order of virgin women were closely associated with the order of widows. These orders were the precursors of the orders of monks and nuns that developed later.

There are eunuchs who have made themselves eunuchs for the kingdom of heaven's sake. He who is able to accept it, let him accept it." Matt. 19:12.

Now this man [Philip] had four virgin daughters who prophesied. Acts 21:9.

There is a difference between a wife and a virgin. The unmarried woman cares about the things of the Lord, that she may be holy both in body and in spirit. But she who is married cares about the things of the world—how she may please her husband. . . . So then he who gives [his virgin] in marriage does well, but he who does not give her in marriage does better. 1 Cor. 7:38.

Now she who is really a widow, and left alone, trusts in God and continues in supplications and prayers night and day. But she who lives in pleasure is dead while she lives. 1 Tim. 5:5, 6.

Refuse to put younger widows on the list, for when they feel sensual desires in disregard of Christ, they want to get married, thus incurring condemnation, because they have set aside their previous pledge. 1 Tim. 5:11, 12 [NAS].

Then I looked, and behold, a Lamb standing on Mount Zion, and with Him one hundred and forty-four thousand. . . . These are the ones who were not defiled with women, for they are virgins. These are the ones who follow the Lamb wherever he goes. Rev. 14:1, 4.

I salute . . . the virgins who are called widows. *Ignatius (c. 105, E), 1.92.*

The virgins also must walk in a blameless and pure conscience. *Polycarp (c. 135, E), 1.34.*

[I speak of] Philip, one of the twelve apostles, who is laid to rest at Hierapolis. I speak also of his two daughters, who arrived at old age unmarried. His other daughter also, who passed her life under the influence of the Holy Spirit, lies at Ephesus. *Polycrates (c. 190, E), 8.773.*

The second Epistle of John, which is written to virgins, is very simple. *Clement of Alexandria (c. 195, E), 2.576.*

How many voluntary eunuchs are there! How many virgins espoused to Christ! *Tertullian (c. 197, W), 3.593.*

So many male virgins—so many voluntary eunuchs—carry their glory in secret, carrying no token to make them, too, illustrious. *Tertullian (c. 207, W), 4.33.*

Sometimes [virgins are motivated] by that god, their stomachs. For the brotherhood readily undertakes the maintenance of virgins. . . . They are brought forth into the midst [of the church] and elated by the public approval of their status. They are laden by the brothers with every honor and charitable gift, so long as they do not fall. *Tertullian (c. 207, W), 4.35, 36.*

Do not belie yourself in appearing as a bride. For you are wedded to Christ. To Him you have surrendered your flesh. To Him you have espoused your maturity. Walk in accordance with the will of your Espoused. *Tertullian (c. 207, W), 4.37.*

Virginity, likewise, and widowhood . . . are fragrant offerings to God. *Tertullian (c. 210, W), 3.551.*

In the Revelation of John, it is said: "These are the ones who have not defiled their clothes with women"—indicating, of course, virgins and those who have become "eunuchs for the kingdom of heaven's sake." Therefore, they will be "clothed in white garments," that is, in the bright beauty of the unmarried flesh. *Tertullian (c. 210, W), 3.563, 564.*

How many men, therefore, and how many women in ecclesiastical orders owe their position to chastity, who have preferred to be wedded to God. *Tertullian (c. 212, W), 4.58.*

What else is virginity than the freedom of liberty? It has no husband for a master. Virginity is freed from all affections. It is not given up to marriage, nor to the world, nor to children. *Novatian (c. 235, W), 5.589, formerly attributed to Cyprian.*

For even a time of repentance is granted by us to adulterers, and peace is given. Yet, virginity is not deficient in the church because of that. . . . The church, crowned with so many virgins, flourishes. *Cyprian (c. 250, W), 5.332.*

We should faithfully care for the life of each one and not allow virgins to dwell with men. I am not speaking of just *sleeping* together, but of *living* together. For both their weak sex and their age . . . should be bridled in all things and ruled by us [i.e., the bishops]. Otherwise, an occasion may be given to the devil, who ensnares us. . . . If they have faithfully dedicated themselves to Christ, let them persevere in modesty and chastity, without incurring any evil report. Thereby, in courage and steadiness, they can await the reward of virginity. However, if they are unwilling or unable to persevere, it is better for them to marry, than that by their crimes they should fall into the fire. *Cyprian (c. 250, W), 5.357.*

You have acted advisedly and with vigor, dearest brother, in excommunicating the deacon who has often lived with a virgin—together with the others who had been regularly sleeping with virgins. But if they repented of their unlawful lying together, and have mutually withdrawn from one another, let the virgins meanwhile be carefully inspected by midwives. And if they should be found to still be virgins, let them be received to communion and admitted to the church. *Cyprian (c. 250, W), 5.358.*

My address is now to virgins, whose glory, as it is more eminent, excites the greater interest. This is the flower of the ecclesiastical seed, the grace and ornament of spiritual endowment. . . . This is the more illustrious portion of Christ's flock. . . . These have dedicated themselves to Christ. They have departed from carnal immorality and have vowed themselves to God, in both the flesh and the spirit. In order to complete their work, which is destined to a great reward, they should no longer explore how to be adorned or how to please anybody [by their appearance], except their Lord. For it is from Him that they expect to receive the reward for virginity. As He himself says, "All men cannot receive this word, but those to whom it is given. . . . There are eunuchs that have made themselves eunuchs for the kingdom of heaven's sake." Again, also, by this word of the angel, the gift of chastity is set forth and virginity is preached: "These are those who have not defiled themselves with women, for they have remained virgins. These are those who follow the Lamb wherever he goes." *Cyprian (c. 250, W), 5.431.*

A virgin should not only be so in fact, but she should also be recognized so [by others] and believed to be so. No one on seeing a virgin should have any doubt as to whether she is one. . . . Why should she walk out adorned? Why should she have hair that has been styled—as if she either had a husband or was seeking one? . . . For it is not right for a virgin to have her hair braided for the appearance of her beauty or to boast of her flesh and of its beauty. *Cyprian (c. 250, W), 5.431.*

It is not becoming for *any* Christian—and especially it is not becoming for a virgin—to seek any glory and honor of the flesh. . . . Or, if she must glory in the flesh, then certainly let her glory when she is tortured in confession of the Name—when a woman is found to be stronger than the tortures. *Cyprian (c. 250, W), 5.432.*

[The Scriptures] also warn us that the women who are accustomed to make an excuse for their dress by reference to their husbands should be restrained and limited by religious observance to the church's discipline. Accordingly, how much more is it right that the virgin should keep that observance. For she has no excuse for adorning herself. . . . Your shameful dress and immodest adornment accuse you. Nor can you be counted now among Christ's maidens and virgins, since you live in such a manner as to make yourselves objects of desire. *Cyprian (c. 250, W), 5.432.*

I think that virgins . . . who have adorned themselves with arts of this kind should not be counted among the virgins. Rather, like infected sheep and diseased cattle, they should be driven from the holy and pure flock of virginity. Otherwise, because of living together, they might pollute the rest with their disease. *Cyprian (c. 250, W), 5.435.*

Some virgins are not ashamed to be present at marriage parties, and in that freedom of wanton discourse to mingle in unchaste conversation. They are not ashamed to hear what is not becoming, or to say what is not lawful. They are not ashamed to expose themselves and be present in the midst of disgraceful words and drunken banquets. . . . When virgins wish to be more carefully adorned and to wander with more liberty, they cease to be virgins. . . . In the same proportion as they had been destined to great rewards as virgins, so will they experience greater punishments for the loss of their virginity. *Cyprian (c. 250, W), 5.435.*

[ADDRESSED TO VIRGINS:] The first fruit for the martyrs is a hundred-fold. The second is yours, sixty-fold. . . . With you, whose reward is second in grace [next to the martyrs], let there be the strength in endurance next to theirs. . . . Do you wish to know what ill the virtue of celibacy avoids and what good it possesses? God said to the woman, "I will multiply your sorrows and your groanings. And in sorrow you will bring forth children. And your desire will be for your husband, and he will rule over you." You are free from this sentence. You do not fear the sorrows and the groans of women. You have no fear of childbearing. Nor is your husband lord over you. Rather, your Lord and Head is Christ, after the likeness and in the place of the man. For your lot and your condition is the same [as the man]. . . . You pass through the world without the pollution of the world. In that you continue chaste and as virgins, you are like the angels of God [who do not marry or bear children]. . . . When He says that in His Father's house there are many mansions, He indicates there are dwellings of better habitation. You are seeking those better habitations. *Cyprian (c. 250, W), 5.436.*

The hundredfold reward means the crown of virginity. For he who undertakes virginity completely and has faithfully fulfilled the precepts of the Decalogue, . . . he is the true priest of Christ. He accomplishes the thousand-year number completely. Therefore, he is said to reign with Christ. And truly, in his case, the devil is bound. *Victorinus (c. 280, W), 7.359.*

They will enter upon an eternal kingdom with an immortal King. For they are virgins in more than body. They have equally protected themselves from wickedness in tongue and in thought. *Victorinus (c. 280, W), 7.359.*

I will now endeavor to explain to you, O virgins, the rest of the things that are prescribed. For this is attached to your duties. . . . "When either a man or woman will separate themselves to vow a vow of a Nazarite, to separate themselves unto the Lord, he will separate himself from wine and strong drink" [Num. 6:1–4]. . . . This means that he who has devoted and offered himself to the Lord will not partake of the fruits of the plant of evil, for its natural tendency is to produce intoxication and distraction of mind. . . . Moreover, it is forbidden to virgins not only to in any way

touch those things that are *made* from that vine, but even to avoid such things as *resemble* them. *Methodius (c. 290, E), 6.327.*

A virgin who has no charity, mercy, or humanity is much inferior to those who honorably exercise chastity [within marriage]. . . . All the bodily members are to be preserved intact and free from corruption. This means not only those members that are sexual, but those other members, too, that minister to the service of lusts. For it would be ridiculous to keep pure the reproductive organs, but not the tongue. It would be ridiculous to preserve the tongue, but not the eyes, ears, or hands. Lastly, it would be ridiculous to keep all of these members pure, but not the mind, defiling it with pride and anger. *Methodius (c. 290, E), 6.351.*

She that vows [celibacy] should do works that are suitable to her vow. This shows that her vow is real and made for the purpose of having time for piety. It was not made to cast a reproach on marriage. *Apostolic Constitutions (compiled c. 390, E), 7.436.*

A virgin is not *ordained,* for we have no such commandment from the Lord. Rather, virginity is a state of voluntary discipline—not for the reproach of marriage, but to have more time for godly service. *Apostolic Constitutions (compiled c. 390, E), 7.493; extended discussion: 5.430–5.436, 6.309–6.355.*

SEE ALSO CELIBACY; MARRIAGE; WIDOWS, ORDER OF.

VISIONS

Three days before Polycarp was arrested, while he was praying, a vision came to him. Behold, the pillow under his head seemed to him to be on fire. Upon seeing this, he turned to those who were with him and said to them prophetically, "I must be burned alive." *Martyrdom of Polycarp (c. 135, E), 1.40.*

God also declares through Hosea the prophet: "I have multiplied visions and have used parables by the ministry of the prophets" [Hos. 12:10]. Now, the apostle expounded this very passage when he said, "Now, there are diversities of gifts." *Irenaeus (c. 180, E/W), 1.489.*

Because of visions, many have come to make their abode with Jesus. *Hippolytus (c. 205, W), 5.203.*

Then my brother said to me, "My dear sister, you are already in a position of great dignity, and are such that you may ask for a vision." . . . And I, who knew that I was privileged to converse with the Lord, whose kindnesses I had found to be so great, boldly promised him. *Passion of Perpetua and Felicitas (c. 205, W), 3.700.*

Without delay, on that very night, this was shown to me in a vision. . . . The day before that day on which we were to fight, I saw in a vision that Pomponius the deacon came here to the gate of the prison. . . . Moreover, the blessed Saturus also related this his vision. *Passion of Perpetua and Felicitas (c. 205, W), 3.701, 702.*

Then Perpetua was received by a certain one who was still a catechumen, Rusticus by name. And he kept close to her. And she, as if aroused from sleep, so deeply had she been in the Spirit and in an ecstasy, began to look around her. *Passion of Perpetua and Felicitas (c. 205, W), 3.705.*

Whether it is in the reading of Scriptures . . . or in the preaching of sermons, . . . in all these religious services matter and opportunity are given to her for seeing visions. *Tertullian (c. 210, W, Montanistic), 3.188.*

Natalius was persuaded by them to let himself be chosen bishop of this heresy. . . . Connecting himself with the heretics, he was admonished by the Lord in visions on many occasions. . . . But he gave little heed to the visions. *Eusebius, quoting Caius (c. 215, W), 5.602.*

Here, during the day in waking vision, I have access to the mysteries of God. *Gregory Thaumaturgus (c. 238, E), 6.38.*

Know this, beloved brethren, that not long ago I was reproached in a vision because we were sleepy in our prayers. *Cyprian (c. 250, W), 5.286.*

Besides the visions of the night, by day also, the innocent age of boys is among us filled with the Holy Spirit—seeing in an ecstasy with their eyes and hearing and speaking those things by which the Lord warns and instructs us through His grace. *Cyprian (c. 250, W), 5.290.*

By the suggestion of the Holy Spirit and the admonition of the Lord, conveyed by many and manifest visions, we have determined . . . to gather the soldiers of Christ within the camp and to examine the case of each one. *Cyprian (c. 250, W), 5.338.*

Among other things that He has kindly shown and revealed, He also added this: "Whoever, therefore, does not believe Christ, who ordains the priest, will hereafter begin to believe Him when He avenges the priest." I know that to some men, dreams seem ridiculous, and visions seem foolish. Nevertheless, assuredly it so seems to those who would rather believe in *opposition* to the priest, than to believe the priest. *Cyprian (c. 250, W), 5.375.*

As the dying man prayed, and when he was near the point of death, a youth stood by him— venerable in honor and majesty, lofty in stature and shining in aspect. As he stood by, the human sight could hardly look upon him with fleshly eyes. However, he who was about to depart from the world could already behold such a one. And the youth . . . rebuked him, saying, "You fear to suffer; you do not want to depart. What will I do to you?" . . . Now, what the dying man heard, he heard for the very purpose that he might relate it to others. He did not hear it for himself, but for us. *Cyprian (c. 250, W), 5.474.*

I was strengthened by a vision that was sent me from God. And a word spoken to me, expressly commanded me, saying, "Read everything that will come into your hands. For you are fit to do so." *Dionysius of Alexandria (c. 262, E), 6.102, 103.*

SEE ALSO DREAMS; GIFTS OF THE SPIRIT; HEARING FROM GOD; MIRACLES; MONTANISTS; PROPHECY, PROPHETS.

VISITORS (ECCLESIASTICAL)

In the early church, a visitor was a bishop or presbyter who ministered to a congregation that was temporarily without a bishop or presbyters.

They revealed to Meletius certain presbyters, who were then in hiding [because of persecution], to whom the blessed Peter [bishop of Alexandria] had given power to act as parish visitors. *Phileas (c. 307, E), 6.164.*

VOICE OF GOD

SEE HEARING FROM GOD.

WAR

I. Opposition to war

II. References to Christians in the army

I. Opposition to war

For out of Zion shall go forth the law, and the word of the Lord from Jerusalem. He shall judge between the nations, and shall rebuke many people; they shall beat their swords into plowshares, and their spears into pruning hooks; nation shall not lift up sword against nation, neither shall they learn war anymore. Isa. 2:3, 4.

You have heard that it was said, "An eye for an eye and a tooth for a tooth." But I tell you not to resist an evil person. But whoever slaps you on your right cheek, turn the other to him also. If anyone wants to sue you and take away your tunic, let him have your cloak also. And whoever compels you to go one mile, go with him two. Matt. 5:38–41.

Then Jesus said to him, "Put your sword in its place, for all who take the sword will perish by the sword. Matt. 26:52.

Jesus answered, "My kingdom is not of this world. If My kingdom were of this world, My servants would fight, so that I should not be delivered to the Jews; but now My kingdom is not from here." John 18:36.

For though we walk in the flesh, we do not war according to the flesh. For the weapons of our warfare are not carnal but mighty in God for pulling down strongholds. 2 Cor. 10:3, 4.

We who formerly murdered one another now refrain from making war even upon our enemies. *Justin Martyr (c. 160, E), 1.176.*

We used to be filled with war, mutual slaughter, and every kind of wickedness. However, now all of us have, throughout the whole earth, changed our warlike weapons. We have changed our swords into plowshares, and our spears into farming implements. *Justin Martyr (c. 160, E), 1.254.*

I do not wish to be a king. I am not anxious to be rich. I decline military command. *Tatian (c. 160, E), 2.69.*

We have learned not to return blow for blow, nor to go to law with those who plunder and rob us. Instead, even to those who strike us on one side of the face, we offer the other side also. *Athenagoras (c. 175, E), 2.129.*

The new covenant that brings back peace and the law that gives life have gone forth over the whole earth, as the prophets said: "For out of Zion will go forth the law, and the word of the Lord from Jerusalem; and he will rebuke many people; and they will break down their swords into plowshares, and their spears into pruning-hooks, and they will no longer learn to fight." . . . These people [i.e., Christians] formed their swords and war-lances into plowshares, . . . that is, into instruments used for peaceful purposes. So now, they are unaccustomed to fighting. When they are struck, they offer also the other cheek. *Irenaeus (c. 180, E/W), 1.512.*

It is not in war, but in peace, that we are trained. *Clement of Alexandria (c. 195, E), 2.234.*

The Scythians, the Celts, the Iberians, and the Thracians are all warlike races. They are also greatly addicted to intoxication and think that drunkenness is an honorable, happy pursuit to engage in. But we, the people of peace, feast for lawful enjoyment, not to wantonness. We drink sober cups of friendship. *Clement of Alexandria (c. 195, E), 2.246*

The one instrument of peace is what we employ: the Word alone, by whom we honor God. We no longer use the ancient psaltery, trumpet, timbrel, and flute. For those who are expert in war and are scorners of the fear of God were accustomed to make use of them. *Clement of Alexandria (c. 195, E), 2.249.*

Let our seals be either a dove, a fish, or a ship scudding before the wind. . . . If there is anyone fishing, he will remember the apostle, and the children drawn out of the water. We are not to draw an outline of . . . a sword or a bow, since we follow peace. Nor should we draw an outline of . . . drinking cups, since we are temperate. *Clement of Alexandria (c. 195, E), 2.286.*

He bids us to "love our enemies, bless them who curse us, and pray for those who despitefully use us." And He says: "If anyone strikes you on the one cheek, turn to him the other also; and if anyone takes away your coat, do not hinder him from taking your cloak also." *Clement of Alexandria (c. 195, E), 2.293.*

An enemy must be aided, so that he may not continue as an enemy. For by help, good feeling is compacted and enmity dissolved. *Clement of Alexandria (c. 195, E), 2.370.*

We do not train our women like Amazons to manliness in war, for we wish even the men to be peaceable. *Clement of Alexandria (c. 195, E), 2.420.*

If, then, we are commanded to love our enemies (as I have remarked above), whom have we to hate? If injured, we are forbidden to retaliate, lest we become just as bad ourselves. Who can suffer injury at our hands? *Tertullian (c. 197, W), 3.45.*

How often you inflict gross cruelties on Christians. You do this, partly because it is your own inclination, and partly in obedience to the laws. . . . Yet, banded together as we are, ever so ready to sacrifice our lives, what single case of revenge for injury are you able to point to? However, if it were held to be right for us to repay evil by evil, a single night with a torch or two could achieve an ample vengeance. But away with the idea of a divine sect avenging itself by human fires! *Tertullian (c. 197, W), 3.45.*

We willingly yield ourselves to the sword. So what wars would we not be both fit and eager to participate in (even against unequal forces), if in our religion it were not counted better to be slain than to slay? *Tertullian (c. 197, W), 3.45.*

The Christian does no harm even to his enemy. *Tertullian (c. 197, W), 3.51.*

God puts His prohibition on every sort of man-killing by that one inclusive commandment: "You shall not kill." *Tertullian (c. 197, W), 3.80.*

"Nation will not take up sword against nation, and they will no more learn to fight." Who else, therefore, does this prophecy apply to, other than *us?* For we are fully taught by the new law, and therefore observe these practices. . . . The teaching of the new law points to clemency. It changes the primitive ferocity of swords and lances to tranquility. It remodels the primitive execution of war upon the rivals and enemies of the Law into the peaceful actions of plowing and cultivating the land. *Tertullian (c. 197, W), 3.154.*

Now inquiry is made about the point of whether a believer may enter into military service. The question is also asked whether those in the military may be admitted into the faith—even the rank and file (or any inferior grade), who are not required to take part in sacrifices or capital punishments. . . . A man cannot give his allegiance to two masters—God and Caesar. . . . How will a Christian man participate in war? In fact, how will he serve even in *peace* without a sword? For the Lord has taken the sword away. It is also true that soldiers came to John [the Baptist] and received the instructions for their conduct. It is true also that a centurion believed. Nevertheless, the Lord afterward, in disarming Peter, disarmed every soldier. *Tertullian (c. 200, W), 3.73.*

"And they will beat their swords into plowshares, and their spears into pruning hooks." In other words, they will change the dispositions of injurious minds, hostile tongues, blasphemy, and all kinds of evil into pursuits of moderation and peace. "Nation will not lift up sword against nation." That is, they will not stir up conflict. "Neither will they learn war any more"—that is, the provocation of hostilities. So you should learn from this that Christ was not promised to be powerful in war. Rather, He was promised to pursue peace. Now, you must deny either that these things were foretold (although they are plainly seen) or that they have been fulfilled (although you read of them). *Tertullian (c. 207, W), 3.339, 340.*

I think we must first inquire whether warfare is proper at all for Christians. What point is there in discussing the merely incidental, when that on which it rests is to be condemned? Do we believe it is lawful for a human oath to be added to one that is divine? Is it lawful for a man to come to be pledged to another master after Christ has become his Master? Is it lawful to renounce father, mother, and all nearest kinsfolk, whom even the Law has commanded us to honor and love next to God himself? . . . Is it lawful to make an occupation of the sword, when the Lord proclaims that he who uses the sword will perish by the sword? Will the son of peace take part in the battle when it does not become him even to sue at law? Will he who is not the avenger even of his own wrongs, apply the chain, the prison, the torture, and the punishment? *Tertullian (c. 211, W), 3.100.*

Is the [military] laurel of triumph made of leaves, or of corpses? Is it adorned with ribbons, or with tombs? Is it wet with ointments, or with the tears of wives and mothers? It may be made of some [dead] Christians too. For Christ is also believed among the barbarians. *Tertullian (c. 211, W), 3.101.*

Our religion commands us to love even our enemies, and to pray for those who persecute us. *Tertullian (c. 212, W), 3.105.*

The existence of many kingdoms would have been a hindrance to the spread of the doctrine of Jesus throughout the entire world. . . . This was because of the need for men everywhere to engage in war and fight on behalf of their native country—which was the case before the times of Augustus. . . . How, then, was it possible for the Gospel doctrine of peace to prevail throughout the world? For it does not permit men to take vengeance even upon their enemies. It was only possible because, at the coming of Jesus, a milder spirit had been everywhere introduced into the conduct of things. *Origen (c. 248, E), 4.444.*

The statement [of Celsus, a pagan critic] is false "that in the days of Jesus, others who were Jews rebelled against the Jewish state and became His followers." For neither Celsus, nor those who think like him, are able to point out any act on the part of Christians that hints of rebellion. In fact, if a revolt had led to the formation of the Christian commonwealth, the Christian Lawgiver would not have altogether forbidden the putting of men to death. So it could not have derived its existence in such a way from the Jews. For they were permitted to take up arms in defense of the members of their families and to slay their enemies. Yet, Christ nowhere teaches that it is right for His own disciples to offer violence to anyone, no matter how wicked. For He did not consider it to be in accord with His laws to allow the killing of any individual whomever. For His laws were derived from a divine source. Indeed, if the Christians truly owed their origin to a rebellion, they would not have adopted laws of so exceedingly mild a character. For their laws do not allow them on any occasion to resist their persecutors, even when it was their fate to be slain as sheep. *Origen (c. 248, E), 4.467.*

Christians were taught not to avenge themselves upon their enemies. . . . They would not have made war (although capable) even if they had received authority to do so. For they have obtained this reward from God: that He has always warred on their behalf. On certain occasions, he has restrained those who rose up against them and desired to destroy them. . . . On special occasions, some have endured death for the sake of Christianity, and those individuals can be easily numbered. However, God has not permitted the whole nation [of Christians] to be exterminated. *Origen (c. 248, E), 4.467, 468.*

Perhaps the so-called wars among the bees convey instructions as to the manner in which wars should be waged in a just and orderly way among men—if ever there arise a necessity for them. *Origen (c. 248, E), 4.533.*

To those who inquire of us from where we come, or who is our founder, we reply that we have come agreeably to the counsels of Jesus. We have cut down our hostile, insolent, and wearisome swords into plowshares. We have converted into pruning hooks the spears that were formerly used in war. For we no longer take up "sword against nation," nor do we "learn war any more." That is because we have become children of peace for the sake of Jesus, who is our Leader. *Origen (c. 248, E), 4.558.*

Celsus [a pagan critic] adds . . . "How could God command the Israelites through Moses to gather wealth, to extend their dominion, to fill the earth, to put their enemies of every age to the sword, and to destroy them utterly? . . . For, on the other hand, His Son, the man of Nazareth, promulgated laws quite opposed to these. He declared that no one can come to the Father who loves power, riches, or glory. Jesus said that to anyone who has given them one blow, they should offer to receive another. So is it Moses or Jesus who taught falsely? When the Father sent Jesus, did He forget the commands that He had given to Moses? Or did He change his mind, condemn His own laws, and send forth a Messenger with opposite instructions?" . . .

[ORIGEN'S REPLY:] We would observe that it must be impossible for the legislation of Moses, taken literally, to harmonize with the calling of the Gentiles and with their subjection to the Roman government. On the other hand, it would be impossible for the Jews to preserve their civil economy unchanged if they were to embrace the gospel. For Christians could not slay their enemies. Nor could they condemn those who had broken the law to be burned or stoned, as Moses commands. . . . In the case of the ancient Jews, who had a land and a form of government of their own, to take from them the right of making war upon their enemies, of fighting for their country, of putting to death or otherwise punishing adulterers, murderers, or others who were guilty of similar crimes, would have been to subject them to sudden and utter destruction whenever the enemy fell upon them. For, in that case, their very laws would restrain them and prevent them from resisting the enemy. Yet, that same providence that of old gave the Law, and has now given the gospel of Jesus Christ, has destroyed their city and their temple, not wishing the Jewish state to continue any longer. . . . However, this providence has extended the Christian religion day by day, so that it is now preached everywhere with boldness. And this is in spite of the numerous obstacles that oppose the spread of Christ's teaching in the world. However, since it was the purpose of God that the nations should receive the benefits of Christ's teaching, all the devices of men against Christians have been brought to nothing. For the more that kings, rulers, and peoples have persecuted them everywhere, the more Christians have increased in number and grown in strength. *Origen (c. 248, E), 4.617, 618, 621.*

[CELSUS:] "You surely do not say that if (in compliance with your wish) the Romans were to neglect their customary duties to gods and men, and were to worship the Most High, . . . that He would come down and fight for them, so that they would not need any other help than His. For this same God . . . promised of old this and much more to those who served Him. Yet, see in what way He has helped the Jews and

you! Instead of being masters of the whole word, the Jews are left with not so much as a patch of ground or a home."

[ORIGEN'S REPLY:] What would happen if, instead of only a relatively few persons believing (as at the present), the entire empire of Rome believed? They would pray to the Word, who of old said to the Hebrews, when they were pursued by the Egyptians: "The Lord will fight for you, and you will hold your peace." And if all the Romans united in prayer with one accord, they would be able to put to flight far more enemies than those who were defeated by the prayer of Moses. . . . However, He had made the fulfillment of His promises dependent on certain conditions—namely, that they would observe and live according to His Law. . . . But if all the Romans embraced the Christian faith (according to the supposition of Celsus), they would overcome their enemies when they prayed. Or rather, they would not war at all. For they would be guarded by that divine power that promised to save five entire cities for the sake of fifty righteous persons. Men of God are assuredly the salt of the earth. They preserve the order of the world. And society is held together as long as the salt is uncorrupted. . . . When God gives to the Tempter permission to persecute us, then we suffer persecution. And when God wishes us to be free from suffering—even in the middle of a world that hates us—we enjoy a wonderful peace, trusting in the protection of Him who said, "Be of good cheer, for I have overcome the world." *Origen (c. 248, E), 4.666.*

In the next place, Celsus urges us "to help the king with all our might, to labor with him in the maintenance of justice, and to fight for him. Or if he demands it, to fight under him or lead an army along with him." To this, our answer is that we do give help to kings when needed. But this is, so to speak, a divine help, "putting on the whole armor of God." And we do this in obedience to the commandment of the apostle: "I exhort, therefore, that first of all, supplications, prayers, intercessions, and thanksgiving be made for all men; for kings, and for all who are in authority." So the more anyone excels in godliness, the more effective the help is that he renders to kings. This is a greater help than what is given by soldiers who go forth to fight and kill as many of the enemy as they can. And to those enemies of our faith who demand us to bear arms for the commonwealth and to slay men, we reply: "Do not those who are the priests at certain shrines . . . keep their hands free from blood, so that they may offer the appointed sacrifices to your gods with unstained hands that are free from human blood? Even when war is upon you, you never enlist the priests in the army. If, then, that is a praiseworthy custom, how much more so that—when others are engaged in battle—Christians engage as the priests and ministers of God, keeping their hands pure. For they wrestle in prayers to God on behalf of those who are fighting in a righteous cause, and for the king who reigns righteously. They pray that whatever is opposed to those who act righteously may be destroyed.

Our prayers defeat all demons who stir up war. Those demons also lead persons to violate their oaths and to disturb the peace. Accordingly, in this way, we are much more helpful to the kings than those who go into the field to fight for them. And we do take our part in public affairs when we join self-denying exercises to our righteous prayers and meditations, which teach us to despise pleasures and not to be led away by them. So none fight better for the king than we do. Indeed, we do not fight *under* him even if he demands it. Yet, we fight on his behalf, forming a special army—an army of godliness—by offering our prayers to God. And if Celsus would have us "lead armies in defense of our country," let him know that we do this too. And we do not do it for the purpose of being seen by men or for vainglory. For in secret, and in our own hearts, our prayers ascend on behalf of our fellow-citizens, as from priests. And Christians are benefactors of their country more than others. For they train up citizens and inculcate piety to the Supreme Being. And they promote to a divine and heavenly city those whose lives in the smallest cities have been good and worthy. *Origen (c. 248, E), 4.667, 668.*

Wars are scattered all over the earth with the bloody horror of camps. The whole world is wet with mutual blood. And murder—which is admitted to be a crime in the case of an individual—is called a virtue when it is committed wholesale. Impunity is claimed for the wicked deeds, not because they are guiltless—but because the cruelty is perpetrated on a grand scale! *Cyprian (c. 250, W), 5.277.*

Christians do not attack their assailants in return, for it is not lawful for the innocent to kill even the guilty. *Cyprian (c. 250, W), 5.351.*

The hand must not be spotted with the sword and blood—not after the Eucharist is carried in it. *Cyprian (c. 250, W), 5.488.*

When the worship of God was taken away, men lost the knowledge of good and evil. . . . They then began to fight with one another, to plot, and to achieve glory for themselves from the shedding of human blood. *Lactantius (c. 304–313, W), 7.141.*

If only God were worshipped, there would not be dissensions and wars. For men would know that they are the sons of one God. *Lactantius (c. 304–313, W), 7.143.*

Why would [the just man] carry on war and mix himself with the passions of others when his mind is engaged in perpetual peace with men? Would he be delighted with foreign merchandise or with human blood—he who does not know how to seek gain? For the Christian is satisfied with his standard of living. He considers it unlawful not only to commit slaughter himself, but also to be present with those who do it. *Lactantius (c. 304–313, W), 7.153.*

If desire is restrained, no one will use violence by land or by sea. No one will lead an army to carry off and lay waste the property of others. . . . For what are the interests of our country, but the detriments of another state or nation? To extend the boundaries that are violently taken from others, to increase the power of the state, to improve the revenues—all of these things are not virtues. Rather, they are the overthrowing of virtues. *Lactantius (c. 304–313, W), 7.169.*

How can a man be just who hates, who despoils, who puts to death? Yet, those who strive to be serviceable to their country do all these things. . . . When they speak of the "duties" relating to warfare, their speech pertains neither to justice nor to true virtue. *Lactantius (c. 304–313, W), 7.169.*

The Stoics say that the emotion of anger is the whetstone of virtue. As though no one could fight bravely against enemies unless he were excited by anger. By this, they plainly show that they neither know what virtue is, nor why God gave anger to man. If it were given to us for the purpose of using it to slay men, then what creature can be considered more savage than man? Who resembles the wild beasts more than that creature whom God formed for communion and innocence? *Lactantius (c. 304–313, W), 7.185.*

Therefore, it is not befitting that those who strive to keep to the path of justice should be companions and sharers in this public homicide. For when God forbids us to kill, He prohibits more than the open violence that is not even allowed by the public laws. He also warns us against doing those things that are considered lawful among men. For that reason, it will not be lawful for a just man to engage in warfare, since his warfare is justice itself. Nor is it lawful for him to accuse anyone of a capital charge. For it makes no difference whether you put a man to death by word, or by the sword instead. That is because it is the act of putting to death itself that is prohibited. Therefore, with regard to this commandment of God, there should be no exception at all. Rather, it is always unlawful to put a man to death, whom God willed to be a sacred creature. *Lactantius (c. 304–313, W), 7.187.*

It is not right that a worshipper of God should be injured by a another worshipper of God. *Lactantius (c. 304–313, W), 7.271.*

You allege that those wars of which you speak were sparked because of hatred of our religion. However, it would not be difficult to prove that (after the name of Christ was heard in the world), wars were not increased. In fact, they actually *diminished* in great measure by the restraining of furious passions. A numerous band of men as we are, we have learned from His teaching and His laws that evil should not be repaid with evil. Rather, it is better to suffer wrong than to inflict it. We would rather shed our own blood than stain our hands and our conscience with that of another. As a result, an ungrateful world is now enjoying—and for a long period has enjoyed—a benefit from Christ. For by His means, the rage of savage ferocity has been softened and has begun to withhold hostile hands from the blood of a fellow creature. In fact, if all men without exception ... would lend an ear for a while to His salutary and peaceful rules, ... the whole world would be living in the most peaceful tranquillity. The world would have turned the use of steel into more peaceful uses and would unite together in blessed harmony, maintaining inviolate the sanctity of treaties. *Arnobius (c. 305, E), 6.415.*

Those soldiers were filled with wonder and admiration at the grandeur of the man's piety and generosity and were struck with amazement. They felt the force of this example of pity. As a result, very many of them were added to the faith of our Lord Jesus Christ and threw off the belt of military service. *Disputation of Archelaus and Manes (c. 320, E), 6.179.*

II. References to Christians in the army

The quotations above clearly demonstrate the early church's opposition to war. Yet, the early Christian writings also mention the existence of Christian soldiers. The quotation from Tertullian below [3.100] explains this seeming contradiction. Although disallowing Christians to join the military, the church (at least by the close of the second century) permitted converted soldiers to remain in the army after baptism—so long as they did not use the sword, take oaths, or engage in idolatrous practices.

Hippolytus bears witness to this practice in his Apostolic Tradition (c. 200, W). *The Ante-Nicene Fathers* does not contain this passage, for Hippolytus's work was not uncovered until after *The Ante-Nicene Fathers* had originally been published. Concerning persons coming to baptism, Hippolytus writes: "A soldier of the civil authority must be taught not to kill men and to refuse to do so if he is commanded, and to refuse to take an oath. If he is unwilling to comply, he must be rejected for baptism. A military commander or civic magistrate who wears the purple must resign or be rejected. If an applicant or a believer seeks to become a soldier, he must be rejected, for he has despised God." (Apostolic Tradition 16).

I summoned those who among us go by the name of Christians. And having made inquiry, I discovered a great number and vast host of Christians. So I raged against them. However, this was by no means becoming. For afterwards, I learned of their power. Because of that power, they did not begin the battle by preparing weapons, nor arms, nor bugles. In fact, such preparation is hateful to them—because of the God they bear about in their conscience.... For having prostrated themselves on the ground, they prayed not only for me, but also for the whole army as it stood. They prayed that they might be delivered from the present thirst and famine. *Marcus Aurelius (c. 172), 1.187. Most scholars regard this letter as spurious.*

But for a man, bare feet are quite in keeping—except when he is on military service. *Clement of Alexandria (c. 195, E), 2.267.*

We, on the contrary, bring before you an emperor who was their protector. You will see this by examining the letters of Marcus Aurelius, that most serious of emperors. For, in his letters, he bears witness that the Germanic drought was removed by the rains obtained through the prayers of the Christians, who happened to be fighting under him. *Tertullian (c. 197, W), 3.22.*

We sail with you, serve in the military with you, and cultivate the ground with you. *Tertullian (c. 197, W), 3.49.*

The soldiers, crowned with laurels, were approaching. However, one of them was more a soldier of God. In fact, he was more steadfast than the rest of his brethren, who had imagined that they could serve two masters. His head alone was uncovered, for he held the useless wreath in his hand. By that peculiarity alone, he was recognized by everyone as being a Christian. *Tertullian (c. 211, W), 3.93.*

Of course, if faith comes later and finds someone already occupied with military service, their case is different. For example, there is the instance of those whom John [the Baptist] received for baptism, and of those most faithful centurions. I mean the centurion whom Christ approved, and the centurion whom Peter instructed [i.e., Cornelius]. Yet, at the same time, when a man has become a believer and faith has been sealed, there must be either an immediate abandonment of the military office, which has been the course of many—or else all sorts of quibbling will have to be resorted to in order to avoid offending God. And such quibbling is not allowed even outside of military service. *Tertullian (c. 211, W), 3.100.*

Marcus Aurelius, also, in his expedition to Germany, got rain in that well-known thirst by the prayers that his Christian soldiers offered to God. *Tertullian (c. 212, W), 3.107.*

Only understand that [the martyrs] include men and women, both young men and old, both maidens and elderly matrons, both soldiers and private citizens. *Dionysius of Alexandria (c. 262, E), 6.96.*

There was also a body of soldiers. . . . Along with them, there was an old man, Theophilus. These men had taken up their position in a

group in front of the tribunal. A certain person was on trial as a Christian, and he was about to deny [Christ]. As a result, these men stood round about and ground their teeth and made signs with their faces and stretched out their hands. . . . Eventually, they quickly ran up to the bench of judgment and declared themselves to be Christians, too. *Dionysius of Alexandria (c. 262, E), 6.100.*

Then Diocletian, in furious passion, ordered not only all who were assisting at the holy ceremonies, but also all who resided within the palace, to sacrifice. And, if they refused, they were to be whipped. And further, by letters to the commanding officers, he ordered that all soldiers should be forced to the same impiety, under pain of being dismissed from the service. *Lactantius (c. 320, W), 7.304, 305.*

Diocletian said that it would be enough for him to exclude persons of that religion [i.e., Christians] from the court and the army. *Lactantius (c. 320, W), 7.305.*

Let a bishop, presbyter, or deacon who goes to the army and desires to retain both the Roman government and the priestly administration be deprived. For "the things of Caesar belong to Caesar and the things of God to God." *Apostolic Constitutions (compiled c. 390, E), 7.505.*

SEE ALSO CAPITAL PUNISHMENT; MILITARY LIFE; NONRESISTANCE; PATRIOTISM; PAX ROMANA; PUBLIC OFFICE.

WEALTH
SEE MATERIALISM; PROSPERITY.

WEDDING GARMENT (SPIRITUAL)
SEE PARABLES OF JESUS (II. C. MARRIAGE FEAST).

WHEAT AND TARES, PARABLE OF
SEE PARABLES OF JESUS (II. H. WHEAT AND TARES).

WIDOWS, ORDER OF
Now she who is really a widow, and left alone, trusts in God and continues in supplications and prayers night and day. . . . Do not let a widow under sixty years old be taken into the number, and not unless she has been the wife of one man, well reported for good works; if she has brought up children, if she has lodged strangers, if she has washed the saints' feet, if she has

relieved the afflicted, if she has diligently followed every good work. But refuse the younger widows; for when they have begun to grow wanton against Christ, they desire to marry, having condemnation because they have cast off their first faith. And besides they learn to be idle, wandering about from house to house, and not only idle but also gossips and busybodies, saying things which they ought not. 1 Tim. 5:5, 9–13.

I salute . . . the virgins who are called widows. *Ignatius (c. 105, E), 1.92.*

Teach the widows to be discreet as respects the faith of the Lord, praying continually for all, . . . knowing that they are the altar of God. *Polycarp (c. 135, E), 1.34.*

Innumerable commands such as these are written in the Holy Scriptures pertaining to chosen persons—some to presbyters, some to bishops, some to deacons, other to widows (of whom we will have another opportunity of speaking). *Clement of Alexandria (c. 195, E), 2.294.*

He who has exercised sexual desire and then restrained himself is like a widow who becomes a virgin again by continence. *Clement of Alexandria (c. 195, E), 2.543.*

Follow the examples of those sisters of ours whose names are with the Lord, who—when their husbands have died before them—have given neither beauty nor age precedence over holiness. They prefer to be wedded to God. To God, they give their beauty; to God, they give their youth. With Him, they live. With Him, they converse. They handle Him by day and by night. To the Lord, they assign their prayers as dowries. From Him, as often as they desire it, they receive His approval as dowry gifts. Thus, they have laid hold for themselves of an eternal gift of the Lord. And while on earth—by abstaining from marriage—they are already counted as belonging to the angelic family. *Tertullian (c. 205, W), 4.41.*

I know plainly that in a certain place a virgin of less than twenty years of age has been placed in the order of *widows!* Whereas, if the bishop had been bound to accord her any relief, he could, of course, have done it in some other way without detriment to the respect due to discipline. . . . But the [nonexistent] authority that allows her to sit in that seat [of a widow] *uncovered* is the same authority that allows her to sit there as a *virgin.* For it is a seat that is limited not only to those with one husband (that is, *married* women), but also to *mothers* as well. In

fact, [they must be] "educators of children," in order that their training by experience in all the affections may . . . have rendered them capable of readily aiding all others with counsel and comfort. *Tertullian (c. 207, W), 4.33.*

Therefore, how many men and how many women in ecclesiastical orders owe their position to continence? [A REFERENCE TO VIRGINS AND WIDOWS.] *Tertullian (c. 212, W), 4.58.*

Do you yourself lead him into the midst and prostrate him—all in haircloth and ashes, a compound of disgrace and horror, before the widows, before the presbyters, begging for the tears of all? *Tertullian (c. 212, W), 4.86.*

All widows who are approved are to be held in honor. *Cyprian (c. 250, W), 5.552.*

The bronze altar [in the tabernacle] can be compared to the company and circuit of widows. For they are a living altar of God. *Methodius (c. 290, E), 6.328.*

Choose your "widows not under sixty years of age," that in some measure the suspicion of a second marriage may be prevented by their age. For if you admit a younger woman into the order of widows . . . and she marries, she will bring indecent reflections on the glory of the order of the widows. And she will give an account to God—not because she married a second time, but because she has "waxed wanton against Christ," and has not kept her promise. . . . Therefore, such a promise should not be rashly made, but with great caution. *Apostolic Constitutions (compiled c. 390, E), 7.426.*

Let every widow be meek, quiet, gentle, sincere, free from anger, and not talkative. . . . And let the widow attend to nothing but to pray for those who give and for the whole church. And when she is asked anything by anyone, let her not easily answer, . . . referring to the leaders those who desire to be instructed in the doctrines of godliness. *Apostolic Constitutions (compiled c. 390, E), 7.427.*

Let the widow, therefore, acknowledge herself to be the "altar of God," and let her sit in her house and not enter into the houses of the faithful to receive anything, for any reason. For the altar of God never runs about. Rather, it is fixed in one place. Therefore, let the virgin and the widow be ones who do not run about, or gad about the houses of those who are alien from the faiths. . . . They should be content with their subsistence from the church, having moderate desires. However, some widows run from one of their neighbors' houses to another and disturb them. They heap up to themselves plenty of money, and they even lend at bitter usury. *Apostolic Constitutions (compiled c. 390, E), 7.428; extended discussion: 7.426–7.430.*

SEE ALSO CELIBACY; ORPHANS AND WIDOWS; REMARRIAGE; TWICE-MARRIED; VIRGINS, ORDER OF.

WIFE, WIVES

Who can find a virtuous wife? For her worth is far above rubies. The heart of her husband safely trusts her; so he will have no lack of gain. She does him good and not evil all the days of her life. She seeks wool and flax, and willingly works with her hands. Prov. 31:10–13.

A wife is bound by law as long as her husband lives; but if her husband dies, she is at liberty to be married to whom she wishes, only in the Lord. 1 Cor. 7:39.

Wives, submit to your own husbands, as to the Lord. For the husband is head of the wife, as also Christ is head of the church; and he is the Savior of the body. Therefore, just as the church is subject to Christ, so let the wives be to their own husbands in everything. Eph. 5:22–24.

Wives, submit to your own husbands, as is fitting in the Lord. Col. 3:18.

Likewise their wives must be reverent, not slanderers, temperate, faithful in all things. 1 Tim. 3:11.

Admonish the young women to love their husbands, to love their children. Tit. 2:4.

You wives, be submissive to your own husbands, that even if some do not obey the word, they, without a word, may be won by the conduct of their wives, when they observe your chaste conduct accompanied by fear. . . . For in this manner, in former times, the holy women who trusted in God also adorned themselves, being submissive to their own husbands, as Sarah obeyed Abraham, calling him lord. 1 Pet. 3:1, 5, 6.

You instructed your wives to do all things with a blameless, worthy, and pure conscience. You instructed them to love their husbands, to which they are duty bound. You taught them that they should manage their household affairs appropriately, living in the rule of obedience. *Clement of Rome (c. 96, W), 1.5.*

Let us direct our wives to that which is good. Let them exhibit the lovely habit of purity. Let them display the sincere disposition of meekness. *Clement of Rome (c. 96, W), 1.11.*

The wife who loves her husband must be furnished for the pilgrimage similarly to her husband. A fair provision for the journey to heaven belongs to those who bear simplicity with chaste seriousness. *Clement of Alexandria (c. 195, E), 2.281.*

It is no disgrace for wives to apply themselves to the mill. Nor is it a reproach for a wife—who is a housekeeper and helpmate—to occupy herself in cooking, so that it may be palatable to her husband. *Clement of Alexandria (c. 195, E), 2.283.*

The labor of their own hands, above all, adds genuine beauty to women. . . . They should not bring non-ornamental adornment made by others, which is vulgar and flashy. Rather, she should bring the adornment of every good woman—clothing supplied and woven by her own hands, whenever she has need. It is never suitable for women whose lives are framed according to God, to appear arrayed in things bought from the market. Rather, they should appear in their own homemade work. For a thrifty wife, who clothes both herself and her husband, is a most beautiful thing. *Clement of Alexandria (c. 195, E), 2.287.*

In brief, "A store of excellence is a woman of worth, who eats not the bread of idleness." . . . And again, "A virtuous woman is a crown to her husband." *Clement of Alexandria (c. 195, E), 2.287.*

A wife's care and the diligence of her constancy appear to exceed the endurance of all other relations and friends. She also excels them in sympathy. Most of all, she takes kindly to patient watching. And in truth, according to Scripture, she is a needed helper. *Clement of Alexandria (c. 195, E), 2.378.*

She should not deck and adorn herself beyond what is becoming. By avoiding this, a wife is free from slanderous suspicion, while she devotes herself constantly to prayers and supplications. She should avoid frequent departures from the house, closing herself as far as possible from the view of all persons who are not related to her. For she considers housekeeping of more importance than impertinent trifling. *Clement of Alexandria (c. 195, E), 2.379.*

The wise woman, then, will first choose to persuade her husband to be her associate in what is conducive to happiness. And should that be found impracticable, let her by herself earnestly aim at virtue, gaining her husband's consent in everything. She should never to do anything against his will—with the exception of what is reckoned as necessary to virtue and salvation. *Clement of Alexandria (c. 195, E), 2.432.*

For with perfect propriety, Scripture has said that woman is given by God as a helper to man. It is evident, then, in my opinion, that she will charge herself with remedying, by good sense and persuasion, each of the annoyances that originate with her husband in domestic economy. And if he does not yield, then she will endeavor, as far as possible for human nature, to lead a sinless life. *Clement of Alexandria (c. 195, E), 2.432.*

Let the wife be obedient to her own proper husband, for "the husband is the head of the wife." But Christ is the head of that husband who walks in the way of righteousness. And "the head of Christ is God," even His Father. Therefore, O wife, next to the Almighty . . . and His beloved Son . . . fear your husband and reverence him. Please him alone, rendering yourself acceptable to him in the various affairs of life. *Apostolic Constitutions (compiled c. 390, E), 7.394.*

Be sure to curb any spirit of contention as to all men—but particularly as to your husband. Otherwise, if he is an unbeliever or a pagan, he may have a cause for scandal or for blaspheming God. . . . Or, if your husband is a Christian, he will be forced (from his knowledge of the Scriptures) to say that which is written in the book of Wisdom: "It is better to dwell in the wilderness than with a contentious and an angry woman." You wives, then, demonstrate your piety by your modesty and meekness to all persons outside the church, whether they are women or men. *Apostolic Constitutions (compiled c. 390, E), 7.395.*

Wives, be subject to your own husbands and hold them in esteem. Serve them with fear and love, just as holy Sarah honored Abraham. For she was not comfortable in calling him by his name. Rather, she called him lord. *Apostolic Constitutions (compiled c. 390, E), 7.463; extended discussion: 7.394, 395.*

SEE ALSO HUSBANDS; MARRIAGE; WOMEN.

WIGS

SEE GROOMING.

WINE

And when they ran out of wine, the mother of Jesus said to Him, "They have no wine." . . . Jesus said to them, "Fill the water pots with water." And they filled them up to the brim. And`He said to them, "Draw some out now, and take it to the master of the feast." And they took it. When the master of the feast had tasted the water that was made wine, and did not know where it came from (but the servants who had drawn the water knew), the master of the feast called the bridegroom. And he said to him, "Every man at the beginning sets out the good wine, and when the guests have well drunk, then the inferior. You have kept the good wine until now!" John 2:3, 7–10.

But now I have written to you not to keep company with anyone named a brother, who is sexually immoral, or covetous, or an idolater, or a reviler, or a drunkard. 1 Cor. 5:11.

For in eating, each one takes his own supper ahead of others; and one is hungry and another is drunk. 1 Cor. 11:21.

Do not be drunk with wine. Eph. 5:18.

Likewise deacons must be reverent, not double-tongued, not given to much wine. 1 Tim. 3:8.

No longer drink only water, but use a little wine for your stomach's sake and your frequent infirmities. 1 Tim. 5:23.

The wine, which was produced by God in a vineyard and which was consumed first [at the wedding feast], was good. None of those who drank of it found fault with it. And the Lord partook of it also. But that wine was even better that the Word made from water, on the spur of the moment, and simply for the use of those who had been called to the marriage. *Irenaeus (c. 180, E/W), 1.427.*

It was when Christ was eating with men and drinking wine. *Irenaeus (c. 180, E/W), 1.505.*

The vine produces wine, as the Word produces blood. And both drink health to men: wine for the body; blood for the spirit. *Clement of Alexandria (c. 195, E), 2.213.*

It is good, then, neither to eat flesh nor to drink wine. . . . Yet, if one partakes of them, he does not sin. Only let him partake temperately, not being dependent on them. *Clement of Alexandria (c. 195, E), 2.240.*

Therefore, I admire those who have adopted an austere life, and who are fond of water, the medicine of temperance. I admire those who flee as far as possible from wine, shunning it as they would the danger of fire. It is proper, therefore, that boys and girls should keep away from this medicine as much as possible.... And, besides, it suits divine studies not to be heavy with wine.... But towards evening, about supper time, wine may be used, when we are no longer engaged in more serious reading. ... But even then it must only be a little wine that is to be used. *Clement of Alexandria (c. 195, E), 2.243.*

Although Jesus made water into wine at the marriage, He did not give permission to get drunk.... The Scripture has named wine as the symbol for the sacred blood. However, reproving the sordid excessive drinking with the dregs of wine, it says: "Intemperate is wine and insolent is drunkenness" [Prov. 20:1]. Therefore, it is agreeable to right reason to drink on account of the cold of winter, until the numbness is dispelled from those who are subject to feel it. And, on other occasions, it serves as a medicine for the intestines. Just as we are to use food to satisfy hunger, so also are we to use liquid to satisfy thirst, taking the most careful precautions against a slip. For the introduction of wine is perilous.... We must not trouble ourselves to procure Chian wine if it is absent, or Ariousian wine when it is not at hand.... Importations of wines from beyond the seas are for an appetite enfeebled by excess.... For why should not the wine of their own country satisfy men's desires? Are they going to import water also? *Clement of Alexandria (c. 195, E), 2.245.*

He says, "Be not mighty at wine; for wine has overcome many." The Scythians, the Celts, the Iberians, and the Thracians are all warlike races, and they are greatly addicted to intoxication. They think that it is an honorable, happy pursuit to engage in. But we, the people of peace, feast for lawful enjoyment, not to wantonness. We drink sober cups of friendship. *Clement of Alexandria (c. 195, E), 2.246*

In what manner do you think the Lord drank when He became man for our sakes? ... Rest assured, He Himself also partook of wine. For He, too, was man. And He blessed the wine, saying, "Take, drink; this is my blood." ... And that a person who drinks should observe moderation, He clearly showed by what He taught at feasts. For He did not teach while influenced by wine. And that it was wine that was the thing

blessed, He showed again, when He said to his disciples, "I will not drink of the fruit of this vine, until I drink it with you in the kingdom of my Father." And that it was wine that was drunk by the Lord, He tells us again, ... "For the Son of man came and they say, 'Behold a glutton and a wine-bibber.'" *Clement of Alexandria (c. 195, E), 2.246.*

We not only are forbidden to drink with others to the point of intoxication, but we are not even to indulge in *much* wine. *Clement of Alexandria (c. 195, E), 2.256.*

We are not to draw an outline of ... drinking cups, since we are temperate. *Clement of Alexandria (c. 195, E), 2.286.*

In order for you to discover how wine was anciently used as a figure for blood, turn to Isaiah. *Tertullian (c. 207, W), 3.418.*

Expend upon them what is sufficient—wine and food. *Commodianus (c. 240, W), 4.218.*

Bread nourishes and makes a person strong. It is said to strengthen the heart of man. In contrast, wine pleases, rejoices, and softens man. *Origen (c. 228, E), 9.314.*

It is not from demons that men receive any of the things that meet the necessities of life.... So those who partake of corn, wine, the fruits of trees, water, and air do not eat with demons. Rather, they feast with divine angels.... We are not to refuse to enjoy those things that have been created for our use. Rather, we should receive them with thanksgiving to the Creator. *Origen (c. 248, E), 4.651.*

Be sparing of an abundance of wine, lest by means of it you should go wrong. *Commodianus (c. 240, W), 4.215.*

I very much wonder where this practice has originated. That is, contrary to evangelical and apostolic discipline, in some places water is offered in the Lord's cup. But water by itself cannot represent the blood of Christ. The Holy Spirit also is not silent in the Psalms on the sacrament of this thing, when He makes mention of the Lord's cup and says, "Your inebriating cup, how excellent it is." Now the cup that inebriates is certainly mingled with wine. For water cannot inebriate anybody. And the cup of the Lord inebriates in the same way as Noah also was intoxicated by drinking wine, in Genesis. However, the intoxication of the Lord's cup and blood is not the same as is the intoxication of the world's wine. . . . The Lord's cup inebriates those who drink it in such a manner as to make them sober. It restores their minds to spiritual wisdom. *Cyprian (c. 250, W), 5.361.*

[ADDRESSED TO VIRGINS WHO HAD TAKEN A VOW OF CELIBACY:] I will now endeavor to explain to you, O virgins, the rest of the things that are prescribed. For this is attached to your duties. . . . "When either a man or woman will separate themselves to vow a vow of a Nazarite, to separate themselves unto the Lord, he will separate himself from wine and strong drink" [Num. 6:1–4]. . . . This means that he who has devoted and offered himself to the Lord will not take of the fruits of the plant of evil, for its natural tendency is to produce intoxication and distraction of mind. . . . Moreover, it is forbidden to virgins not only to in any way touch those things that are *made* from that vine, but even to avoid such things as *resemble* them. *Methodius (c. 290, E), 6.327.*

Give to the priest those things that are due to him—the first-fruits of your [threshing] floor and of your wine-press. *Apostolic Constitutions (compiled c. 390, E), 7.413.*

When you are invited to their memorials, feast with good order, with the fear of God. . . . Since you are the presbyters and deacons of Christ, you should always be sober. . . . We say this, not that they are not to drink at all. Otherwise, it would be to reproach what God has made for cheerfulness. Rather, we say that they should not be *disordered* with wine. For the Scripture does not say, "Do not drink wine." What does it say? It says, "Do not be *drunk* with wine." *Apostolic Constitutions (compiled c. 390, E), 7.498.*

If a bishop, presbyter, or deacon indulges himself in dice or drinking, he must either leave off those practices or else let him be deprived. If a subdeacon, a reader, or a singer does the same, he must either cease to do so or else let him be suspended. And the same is true for one of the laity. *Apostolic Constitutions (compiled c. 390, E), 7.502.*

If any bishop, presbyter, or deacon (or indeed any of the priestly category) abstains from marriage, meat, and wine—not for his own discipline—but because he abominates these things, he forgets that "all things were very good" and that "God made man male and female." So he blasphemously abuses the creation. Therefore,

either let him reform, or else let him be deprived and be cast out of the church. The same is true for any of the laity. *Apostolic Constitutions (compiled c. 390, E), 7.503.*

On this, perhaps, Tatian, the chief of the Encratites, endeavors to build his heresy, asserting that wine is not to be drunk—since it was commanded in the Law that the Nazarites were not to drink wine. *Jerome (c. 400, W), 2.83; see also 2.242–2.246.*

WISDOM

In quotations below where Wisdom refers to the Son of God, masculine pronouns have been appropriately used although the Greek word for "wisdom," sophia, is actually feminine in gender and the English word "wisdom" is neuter.

I. The Son as Wisdom

II. The Holy Spirit as Wisdom

I. The Son as Wisdom

I, wisdom, dwell with prudence, and find out knowledge and discretion. . . . The Lord possessed me at the beginning of His way, before His works of old. I have been established from everlasting. Prov. 8:12, 22, 23.

Wisdom has built her house, she has hewn out her seven pillars. Prov. 9:1.

Christ the power of God and the wisdom of God. 1 Cor. 1:24.

The Word of Wisdom is Himself this God begotten of the Father of all things. He is Word, Wisdom, Power, and the Glory of the Begetter. *Justin Martyr (c. 160, E), 1.227.*

The Wisdom of the Lord is His Son. The apostle says: "Christ, the Power of God, and the Wisdom of God." Solomon says: "The wisdom of the Lord reaches from one end to the other mightily." *Melito (c. 170, E), 8.761.*

Pointing to the First-Begotten Son, Peter writes, accurately comprehending the statement, "In the beginning God made the heaven and the earth." And He is called Wisdom by all the prophets. This is He who is the Teacher of all created beings. *Clement of Alexandria (c. 195, E), 2.493.*

For if that, which from its being inherent in the Lord was of Him and in Him, was yet not without an origin—I mean His Wisdom, which was then born and made, when in the thought of God He began to assume motion for the arrangement of His creative works—how much more impossible is it that anything should have been without an origin that was extrinsic to the Lord. *Tertullian (c. 200, W), 3.487.*

This power and disposition of the Divine Intelligence is set forth also in the Scriptures under the name of Sophia—Wisdom. For what can be better entitled to the name of Wisdom than the Reason or the Word of God? Listen therefore to Wisdom, expressed in the character of the Second Person: "At the first, the Lord created me as the beginning of His ways, with a view to His own works, before He made the earth, before the mountains were settled. Moreover, before all the hills did He beget me." That is to say, "He created and generated me in His own intelligence." *Tertullian (c. 213, W), 3.601.*

We need not dwell any longer on this point, as if it were not the very Word Himself, who is spoken of under the name of both Wisdom and Reason, and of the entire Divine Soul and Spirit. He became also the Son of God and was begotten, when He proceeded forth from Him. *Tertullian (c. 213, W), 3.602.*

"Wisdom has built her house." By this, he means Christ, the Wisdom and Power of God the Father. Christ has built His "house," which is His nature in the flesh derived from the virgin. *Hippolytus (c. 205, W), 5.175.*

Seeing that He is called by many different names, we, therefore, must first ascertain who the Only-Begotten Son of God is. . . . For He is called Wisdom, according to the expression of Solomon: "The Lord created me—the beginning of His ways, and among His works before He made any other thing." . . . He is also called Firstborn, for the apostle has declared, "who is the Firstborn of every creature." The Firstborn, however, is not a different person by nature than Wisdom. They are one and the same. Finally, the apostle Paul says that Christ is "the Power of God and the Wisdom of God." However, let no one imagine that we mean anything impersonal when we call him the Wisdom of God. For instance, let no one suppose that we understand Him to be something that makes men wise, rather than a living Being. *Origen (c. 225, E), 4.246.*

Who that is capable of entertaining reverential thoughts or feelings regarding God can suppose or believe that God the Father ever existed—even for a moment of time—without having generated this Wisdom? For in that case we would have to say one of two things: Either God was *unable* to generate Wisdom before He produced Him—so that He afterwards called into being Him who formerly did not exist. Or He indeed possessed the power, . . . but was unwilling to use it. *Origen (c. 225, E), 4.246.*

What need is there to speak of Wisdom, which "the Lord created the beginning of His ways, for His works"? This is the One in whom His Father rejoiced. The Father delighted in His manifold intellectual beauty, seen by the eyes of the mind alone. Whoever discerns His divine and heavenly charm is incited to love. *Origen (c. 228, E), 9.303.*

The Wisdom of God, who is above every creature, speaks of Himself, when He says: "God created me the beginning of His ways for His works." By this creating act, the whole creation was enabled to exist, being receptive of that divine Wisdom. *Origen (c. 228, E), 9.317.*

The Son of God is the Word by whom all things were made. He exists in substance throughout the underlying nature of things, being the same as Wisdom. For He permeated all creation from the beginning. *Origen (c. 228, E), 9.369.*

It is because Christ was the Power of God and the Wisdom of the Father that He accomplished and still accomplishes such results. *Origen (c. 248, E), 4.464.*

His Son is God the Word, and Wisdom, and Truth, and Righteousness, and everything else that the sacred Scriptures call Him when speaking of God. *Origen (c. 248, E), 4.541.*

We must not regard Wisdom and Righteousness as females, simply because of their feminine name and grammatical gender. For these things are in our view the Son of God. *Origen (c. 248, E), 4.561.*

We have put on Christ, the Wisdom of God the Father. *Cyprian (c. 250, W), 5.421.*

He is that Wisdom who says, "I was the thing in which He delighted, and I was daily his delight before his face at all times." *Dionysius of Alexandria (c. 262, E), 6.92, as quoted by Athanasius.*

This Word, therefore, when He made light, is called Wisdom. *Victorinus (c. 280, W), 7.342.*

The Beginning is Wisdom. For Wisdom is said by one of the Divine company to speak in this manner concerning itself: "The Lord created me the beginning of His ways for His works." *Methodius (c. 290, E), 6.381, as quoted by Photius.*

II. The Holy Spirit as Wisdom

The three days which were before the luminaries are types of the Triad—being God, His Word, and His Wisdom. *Theophilus (c. 180, E), 2.101.*

The Father always had present with Him the Word and Wisdom, the Son and the Spirit, by whom and in whom He made all things, freely and spontaneously. *Irenaeus (c. 180, E/W), 1.487, 488.*

I have also largely demonstrated that the Word, namely the Son, was always with the Father. And that Wisdom also, who is the Spirit, was present with Him before all creation. *Irenaeus (c. 180, E/W), 1.488.*

SEE ALSO CHRIST, DIVINITY OF; HOLY SPIRIT; JESUS CHRIST (III. TITLES OF JESUS); LOGOS; WORD OF GOD (CHRIST).

WOMAN CLOTHED WITH THE SUN

But the Jerusalem above is free, which is the mother of us all. Gal. 4:26.

Now a great signed appeared in heaven: a woman clothed with the sun, with the moon under her feet, and on her head a garland of twelve stars. Then being with child, she cried out in labor and in pain to give birth. . . . And the dragon stood before the woman who was ready to give birth, to devour her Child as soon as it was born. She bore a male Child who was to rule all nations with a rod of iron. And her Child was caught up to God and his throne. Then the woman fled into the wilderness, where she has a place prepared by God, that they should feed her there one thousand two hundred and sixty days. Rev. 12:1, 2, 4–6.

Now, concerning the tribulation of the persecution that is to fall upon the church from the adversary, John also speaks in this manner: "And I saw a great and wondrous sign in heaven: a woman clothed with the sun, and the moon under her feet, and upon her head a crown of twelve stars." . . . By the "woman clothed with the sun," he most obviously meant the church,

endued with the Father's Word, whose brightness is above the sun. And by "the moon under her feet," he referred to her being adorned like the moon, with heavenly glory. The phrase, "upon her head a crown of twelve stars," refers to the twelve apostles by whom the church was founded. And the passage, "she, being with child, cries, travailing in birth, and pained to be delivered," means that the church will not cease to bear from her heart the Word that is persecuted by the unbelievers in the world. He says, "And she brought forth a male child, who is to rule all the nations." By this is meant that the church—always bringing forth Christ, the perfect male child of God (who is declared to be God and man)—becomes the instructor of all the nations. *Hippolytus (c. 200, W), 5.217.*

"The woman was given two wings of the great eagle, that she might fly into the wilderness, where she is nourished for a time, and times, and half a time, from the face of the serpent." That refers to the one thousand two hundred and sixty days during which the tyrant is to reign and to persecute the church, which flees from city to city, and seeks concealment in the wilderness among the mountains. It possesses no other defense than the two wings of the great eagle, that is to say, the faith of Jesus Christ. *Hippolytus (c. 200, W), 5.217.*

The woman clothed with the sun and having the moon under her feet . . . is the ancient church of fathers, prophets, saints, and apostles. It had the groans and torments of its longing until it saw that Christ had taken flesh out of the selfsame people—the fruit of its people according to the flesh that had long ago been promised to it. *Victorinus (c. 280, W), 7.355.*

John, in the course of the Apocalypse, says: "And there appeared a great wonder in heaven, a woman clothed with the sun, and the moon under her feet." . . . The woman who appeared in heaven clothed with the sun . . . is certainly, according to the accurate interpretation, our mother, . . . whom the prophets . . . have sometimes called Jerusalem, sometimes a Bride, sometimes Mount Zion, and sometimes the Temple and Tabernacle of God. . . . It is the church, whose children will come to her with all haste after the resurrection. . . . The statement that she stands upon the moon, as I consider it, represents the faith of those who are cleansed from corruption in the bath [i.e., baptism]. For the light of the moon resembles moderately warm water. And all watery substances are dependent upon the moon [i.e., the tides]. So the church stands upon our faith and adoption . . . until the fullness of the nations come in. She labors and brings forth natural men as spiritual men. For this reason, she is also a mother. . . . The church conceives those who flee to the Word and forms them according to the likeness and image of Christ. *Methodius (c. 290, E), 6.336, 337; extended discussion: 6.336–6.340.*

SEE ALSO GREAT TRIBULATION; MOTHER, SPIRITUAL; REVELATION, BOOK OF.

WOMEN

I. Counsel to women

II. Examples of godly women

III. Equality with men in nature and salvation

IV. Differences between men and women

V. Role in the church

VI. Role among heretics and pagan religions

I. Counsel to women

Charm is deceitful and beauty is vain, but a woman who fears the Lord, she shall be praised. Prov. 31:30.

You wives, be submissive to your own husbands, that even if some do not obey the word, they, without a word, may be won by the conduct of their wives, when they observe your chaste conduct accompanied by fear. . . . For in this manner, in former times, the holy women who trusted in God also adorned themselves, being submissive to their own husbands, as Sarah obeyed Abraham, calling him lord. 1 Pet. 3:1, 5, 6.

But if any necessity arises, commanding the presence of married women, let them be well clothed—by garments on the outside, but by modesty within. But as for those women who are unmarried, it is the most extreme scandal for them to be present at a banquet of men, especially men under the influence of wine. *Clement of Alexandria (c. 195, E), 2.252.*

Love of display is not for a lady, but a prostitute. Such women care little for keeping at home with their husbands. Instead, loosing their husbands' purse-strings, they spend its supplies on their lusts, so that they may have many witnesses of their seemingly fair appearance. And, devoting the whole day to their dressing table, they spend their time with their bought slaves. . . . So they dishonor the Creator of men, as if the beauty given by Him was

nothing worthwhile. As you might expect, they become lazy in housekeeping, sitting like painted things to be looked at, not as if made for domestic work. *Clement of Alexandria (c. 195, E), 2.272.*

These [pagan] women are carried about around the temples, sacrificing and practicing divination every day. They spend their time with fortune-tellers, mendicant priests, and disreputable old women. They keep up old wives' tales over their cups. They learn charms and incantations from soothsayers, to the ruin of the nuptial bonds. They keep some men, and they are kept by others. Others are promised to them by the diviners. *Clement of Alexandria (c. 195, E), 2.278.*

Women are not to be deprived of bodily exercise. Nevertheless, they are not to be encouraged to engage in wrestling or running. Instead, they are to exercise themselves in spinning, weaving, and overseeing the cooking, if necessary. They should fetch with their own hands what is necessary from the store. Furthermore, it is no disgrace for them to apply themselves to the handmill. Nor is it a reproach for a wife to occupy herself in cooking, so that the food will be palatable to her husband. For she is a housekeeper and a helper. . . . She who imitates Sarah will not be ashamed of that highest of ministries—helping travelers. *Clement of Alexandria (c. 195, E), 2.283.*

If there dwelt upon earth a faith as great as is the reward of faith that is expected in the heavens, all of you, best beloved sisters [would rather] walk about as Eve, mourning and repentant. This would be in order that by every garb of satisfaction she might the more fully expiate that which she derives from Eve—the shame, I mean, of the first sin, and the odium attaching to her as the cause of human ruin. *Tertullian (c. 198, W), 4.14.*

Submit your head to your husbands and you will be sufficiently adorned! Busy your hands with spinning. Keep your feet at home, and you will please better than by dressing yourselves in gold. Clothe yourselves with the silk of uprightness, the fine linen of holiness, and the purple of modesty. If you are adorned in this manner, you will have God as your Lover! *Tertullian (c. 198, W), 4.25.*

The devil has taught his disciples also a patience of his own. I am referring to the practice that makes husbands mercenary for dowry. It teaches them to trade in pandering, and it makes them subject to the power of their wives—which, with feigned affection, undergoes every toil of forced obedience. *Tertullian (c. 200, W), 3.717.*

The more wealthy anyone is—inflated with the name of "matron"—the more spacious house she requires for her burdens. It is as if her house were a field where ambition may run its course. To such, the churches look paltry. A rich man is a difficult thing [to find] in the house of God. . . . To such a Christian woman, it is irksome to wed a believer inferior to herself in estate. . . . Yet, she will be dowered with an ampler dowry from the goods of a husband who is rich in God. *Tertullian (c. 205, W), 4.48.*

Woman was immediately condemned to bring forth in sorrow, and to serve her husband. In contrast, previously she had heard without pain the increase of her race proclaimed with the blessing, "Increase and multiply." Previously, she had been destined to a be a helper and not a slave to her male partner. Immediately, the earth was also cursed, which before was blessed. *Tertullian (c. 207, W), 3.306.*

Moreover, the women assemble as if they were about to enter the bath. They press closely together and treat God's house as if it were a fair. . . . They speak in an undisciplined manner, as if God were absent. *Commodianus (c. 240, W), 4.218.*

The question concerns women in the time of their menstrual period. When they are in that condition, is it proper for them to enter the house of God? I consider this is an unnecessary question. For, if they are believing and godly women, I do not think they will themselves be rash enough in such a condition to either approach the holy table or to touch the body and blood of the Lord. *Dionysius of Alexandria (c. 262, E), 6.96.*

The Holy Spirit always abides with those who are possessed of Him, so long as they are worthy. And when He departs, he leaves them desolate and exposed to the wicked spirit. . . . Therefore, O woman, if you say that in the days of your menstruation that you are void of the Holy Spirit, then you must be filled with the unclean spirit. For by neglecting to pray and to read [at that time], you will invite the unclean spirit to you. *Apostolic Constitutions (compiled c. 390, E), 7.462.*

II. Examples of godly women

And many women who followed Jesus from Galilee, ministering to Him, were there looking on from afar. Matt. 27:55.

Now this man [Philip] had four virgin daughters who prophesied. Acts 21:8.

By faith Sarah herself also received strength to conceive seed, and she bore a child when she was past the age, because she judged Him faithful who had promised. Heb. 11:11.

Many women, also, being strengthened by the grace of God, have performed numerous manly exploits. The blessed Judith, when her city was besieged, asked the elders for permission to go forth into the camp of the strangers, . . . and the Lord delivered Holofernes into the hands of a woman. Esther also, being perfect in faith, exposed herself to no less danger, in order to deliver the twelve tribes of Israel from impending destruction. *Clement of Rome (c. 96, W), 1.20.*

Contemporaneous with the Law, Moses and Aaron [prophesied]. And after these, the following men prophesied: Joshua the son of Nun, Samuel, Gad, Nathan. . . . And of women (for these also prophesied), there were Sarah, Rebecca, Miriam, Deborah, and Huldah. *Clement of Alexandria (c. 195, E), 2.331.*

[I speak of] Philip, one of the twelve apostles, who is laid to rest at Hierapolis. I speak also of his two daughters, who arrived at old age unmarried. His other daughter also, who passed her life under the influence of the Holy Spirit, lies at Ephesus. *Polycrates (c. 190, E), 8.773.*

It is related in the Gospels that there were certain women who had been healed of their diseases. Among these was Susanna. From their own possessions, these women provided the disciples the means of support. *Origen (c. 248, E), 4.426.*

For such was the charm of Jesus' words, that not only were *men* willing to follow him to the wilderness, but *women* also, forgetting the weakness of their sex and a regard for outward propriety in so following their Teacher into desert places. *Origen (c. 248, E), 4.468.*

There are blessed women, too, who are established with you in the same glory of confession. For they have maintained the Lord's faith and are braver than their sex. Not only are they near to the crown of glory themselves, but they have provided an example to other women by their constancy. *Cyprian (c. 250, W), 5.407.*

Women prophesied also. Of old, there was Miriam, the sister of Moses and Aaron; and after her, Deborah. Then there were later Huldah and Judith—the first under Josiah, the second under Darius. The mother of the Lord prophesied as well, as did Anna and Mary's kinswoman, Elizabeth. Furthermore, in the days of the apostles, there were the daughters of Philip. Yet, these women were not puffed up against their husbands. Rather, they preserved their own bounds. Therefore, if there is among you a man or a woman who has obtained any gift, let that person be humble, that God may be pleased with him. *Apostolic Constitutions (compiled c. 390, E), 7.481.*

III. Equality with men in nature and salvation

There is neither Jew nor Greek, there is neither slave nor free, there is neither male nor female; for you are all one in Christ Jesus. Gal. 3:28.

Who would not laugh when you tell us that the Amazons, and Semiramis, and certain other warlike women existed? Yet, you cast reproaches on our maidens! . . . You say that we talk nonsense among women and boys, and among maidens and old women. You scoff at us for not being with you. However, let us look at what silliness prevails among the Greeks: Their works of art are devoted to worthless objects. Nevertheless, they are held in higher esteem by you than even your gods. And you behave unbecomingly in what relates to woman. For Lysippus cast a statue of Praxilla, whose poems contain nothing useful. . . . My object in referring to these women is so that you will not regard what you find among us as something strange. Rather, in comparing the statues that are before your eyes, perhaps you will not treat with scorn the women who among us pursue philosophy. *Tatian (c. 160, E), 2.78, 79.*

This Sappho is a lewd, love-sick female, and sings her own wantonness. In contrast, all our women are chaste, and the maidens at their weaving sing of divine things more nobly than that damsel of yours. For that reason, be ashamed, for you are professed disciples of women! Yet, you scoff at those of the sex who hold our doctrine. You also scoff at the solemn assembles they frequent. . . . A certain Melanippe was a wise woman, and for that reason Lysistratus made a statue of her. However, you will not believe that among us there are wise women! . . . How is it that you are not ashamed to slander the reputation of our women? After all, you have so many poetesses whose productions are mere trash. You have innumerable prostitutes and worthless men. *Tatian (c. 160, E), 2.79.*

The virtue of man and woman is the same. For if the God of both is one, the Master of both is also one. There is one church, one temperance, and one modesty. Their food is common; marriage is an equal yoke. . . . All those whose life is common, have common graces and a common salvation. Common to them are love and training. "For in this world," He says, "they marry, and are given in marriage," in which alone the female is distinguished from the male. "But in that world, it is so no more." There the rewards of this social and holy life, which is based on conjugal union, are laid up. . . . Common therefore, too, to men and women is the name of human. *Clement of Alexandria (c. 195, E), 2.211.*

Woman does not possess one nature, and man, another. Rather, they have the same. So also it is with virtue. Therefore, if self-restraint and righteousness (and whatever qualities are regarded as following them) are virtues of the male, then it would belong to the male alone to be virtuous. It would accordingly belong to the woman to be licentious and unjust. But it is offensive even to say this! Accordingly, a woman is to practice self-restraint and righteousness, and every other virtue, the same as a man. This applies to both slave and free. For it is a fitting consequence that the same nature should possess one and the same virtue. *Clement of Alexandria (c. 195, E), 2.419, 420.*

But as it is noble for a man to die for virtue, for liberty, and for himself, so also is it for a woman. For this is not unique to the nature of males, but to the nature of the good. *Clement of Alexandria (c. 195, E), 2.421.*

In this perfection, it is possible for man and woman to share equally. *Clement of Alexandria (c. 195, E), 2.431.*

For you [women], too, have the same angelic nature promised as your reward, and the same sex, as do men. The Lord promises you the same advancement to the dignity of judging. *Tertullian (c. 198, W), 4.15.*

For no man will love the picture of his wife without taking care of it, honoring it, and crowning it. The likeness partakes with the reality in the privileged honor. *Tertullian (c. 207, W), 3.469.*

Let him know that all persons are begotten alike, with a capacity and ability of reasoning and feeling—without any preference of age, sex, or rank. *Mark Minucius Felix (c. 200, W), 4.181.*

[THE PAGAN CRITIC CELSUS SAYS:] "Christians carefully incite young boys to wickedness and women to forsake their fathers and teachers, and to follow them." . . . [ORIGEN REPLIES:] Celsus will not be able to make good any such accusation against us. For, on the contrary, we turn women away from an immoral life. We turn them away from being at enmity with those with whom they live. We turn them away from all mad desires after theaters and dancing, and from superstition. *Origen (c. 248, E), 4.486.*

It appeared that the mercy of Christ, and the heavenly grace that would subsequently follow, was equally divided among everyone—without difference of sex, without distinction of years, and without distinction of persons. *Cyprian (c. 250, W), 5.401.*

IV. Differences between men and women

I want you to know that the head of every man is Christ, the head of woman is man, and the head of Christ is God. 1 Cor. 11:3.

Wives, submit to your own husbands, as to the Lord. For the husband is head of the wife, as also Christ is head of the church; and he is the Savior of the body. Therefore, just as the church is subject to Christ, so let the wives be to their own husbands in everything. Eph. 5:22–24.

Why was it, that when those two [Aaron and Miriam] had both acted with spite towards Moses, the latter alone was punished? The answer is, first, because the woman was the more culpable, since both nature and the Law place the woman in a subordinate condition to the man. *Irenaeus (c. 180, E/W), 1.573.*

Since woman's soul is the same as man's, she will attain to the same virtue. However, as there is difference as respects the distinctive construction of the body, she is destined for child-bearing and housekeeping. The apostle says, "For I would have you know that the head of every man is Christ, and the head of the woman is the man, for the man is not of the woman, but the woman of the man." . . . We say that the man should be continent and superior to pleasures. Therefore, we also reckon that the woman should be continent and practiced in fighting against pleasures, too. . . . Women are therefore to philosophize equally with men, though the males are preferable at everything, unless they have become effeminate. To the whole human race, then, discipline and virtue are a necessity, if they would pursue after happiness. . . . The ruling power is therefore the head. And if "the Lord is head of the man and the man is head of the woman," the man, "being the image and glory of God, is lord of the woman." Therefore also in the Epistle to the Ephesians it is written: "Subject yourselves one to another in the fear of God. Wives, submit yourselves to your own husbands, as to the Lord. For the husband is head of the wife, as also Christ is the head of the church. And He is the Savior of the body. Husbands, love your wives, as also Christ loved the church." *Clement of Alexandria (c. 195, E), 2.419, 420.*

Contrary to the custom of humans and contrary to nature, [Plato] . . . thought that women should also engage in warfare, take a share in public counsels, undertake magistracies, and assume commands. Therefore, he assigned horses and weapons to them. It follows that he should have assigned to men wool, the loom, and the carrying of infants. He did not foresee the impossibility of what he said, even though no nation has existed in the world that is so foolish or so vain as to live in this manner. *Lactantius (c. 304–313, W), 7.93.*

V. Role in the church

Every woman who prays or prophesies with her head uncovered dishonors her head. 1 Cor. 11:5.

Let your women keep silent in the churches, for they are not permitted to speak; but they are to be submissive, as the law also says. And if they want to learn something, let them ask their own husbands at home; for it is shameful for women to speak in church. 1 Cor. 14:34, 35.

Let a woman learn in silence with all submission. And I do not permit a woman to teach or to have authority over a man, but to be in silence. For Adam was formed first, then Eve. And Adam was not deceived, but the woman being deceived, fell into transgression. 1 Tim. 2:11, 12.

Paul did not hesitate to mention his "companion" in one of his epistles. . . . He says in his epistle, "Do I not have the right to take along a sister-wife, as do the other apostles?" However, the other apostles, in harmony with their particular ministry, devoted themselves to preaching without any distraction. Their spouses went with them, not as wives, but as sisters, in order to minister to housewives. *Clement of Alexandria (c. 195, E), 2.390, 391.*

But the woman of pertness, who has usurped the power to teach, will of course not give birth for herself likewise to a right of baptizing! . . . For how credible would it seem, that he who has not permitted a woman even to learn with over-boldness, should give a female the power of teaching and of baptizing! He says, "Let them be silent and consult their husbands at home." *Tertullian (c. 198, W), 3.677.*

Paul instructs women to be silent in the church, not speaking for the mere sake of learning. In doing so, he goes to the Law for his authority that women should be under obedience. However, when he veils the woman who prophesies, he demonstrates that even they have the right of prophesying. *Tertullian (c. 207, W), 3.446.*

It is not permitted to a woman to speak in the church, nor to teach, baptize, offer, or to claim to herself a lot in any manly function, not to mention the priestly office. *Tertullian (c. 207, W), 4.33.*

A woman should be silent in the church. In the first Epistle of Paul to the Corinthians: "Let women be silent in the church. But if any wish to learn anything, let them ask their husbands at home." Also to Timothy: "Let a woman learn with silence, in all subjection. But I do not permit a woman to teach, nor to be set over the man, but to be in silence." *Cyprian (c. 250, W), 5.546.*

We do not permit our women "to teach in the church." Rather, they are only permitted to pray and hear those who teach. For Jesus Himself, our Master and Lord, when He sent out the twelve to make disciples of the people and of the nations, nowhere sent out women to preach—even though there was no lack of women available. For there were with Him the mother of our Lord and His sisters; Mary Magdalene; Mary, the mother of James; Martha and Mary, the sisters of Lazarus; Salome; and certain others. . . . For "the head of the wife is the man," and it is not reasonable that the rest of the body should govern the head. *Apostolic Constitutions (compiled c. 390, E), 7.427, 428.*

As to women baptizing, we let you know that there is no small peril to those who undertake it. Therefore, we do not advise you to do it. For it is dangerous, or rather wicked and impious. . . . For if in the foregoing constitutions, women have not been permitted to teach, how will anyone allow them . . . to perform the office of a priest? For such is not one of the institutions of Christ, but is one of the ignorant practices of the Gentile atheism. For they ordain women priests for the female deities. After all, if baptism were to be administered by women, certainly our Lord would have been baptized by His own mother and not by John. Or when He sent [the apostles] to baptize, he would have also sent along women for this purpose. *Apostolic Constitutions (compiled c. 390, E), 7.429.*

VI. Role among heretics and pagan religions

Nevertheless I have a few things against you, because you allow that woman Jezebel, who calls herself a prophetess, to teach and beguile My servants to commit sexual immorality and to eat things sacrificed to idols. Rev. 2:20.

Handing mixed cups to the women, [Marcus, a heretic,] instructs them to consecrate these cups in his presence. . . . He devotes himself especially to women, and particularly to those women who are well-bred, elegantly attired, and of great wealth. *Irenaeus (c. 180, E/ W), 1.334.*

The very women of these heretics, how wanton they are! For they are bold enough to teach, to dispute, to enact exorcisms, to undertake cures—it may be even to baptize. *Tertullian (c. 197, W), 3.263.*

That most monstrous creature [a female heretical teacher], who had no right to teach even sound doctrine, knew full well how to kill the little fishes [i.e., new believers]. *Tertullian (c. 198, W), 3.669.*

Gentiles, in honor of their own Satan, endure priestly offices that involve both virginity and widowhood. . . . [The oracles] who rave at Delphi abstain from marriage. Moreover, we know that "widows" minister to the African Ceres—enticed away, indeed, from matrimony by a most stern oblivion. For not only do they withdraw from their still living husbands, but they even introduce other wives to them in their own room. *Tertullian (c. 205, W), 4.42.*

There is one place [i.e., a pagan temple] where a man may not go, and there are some that are sacred from women. . . . Some sacred places are crowned by a woman having one husband; some by a woman with many. And she who can reckon up the most adulteries is sought after with most religious zeal. *Mark Minucius Felix (c. 200, W), 4.187.*

Jupiter . . . has rejected the male sex, and, as Celsus observes, employs the women of Dodona for the prophetic office. *Origen (c. 248, E), 4.613.*

There suddenly arose among us a certain woman, who in a state of ecstasy declared herself as a prophetess and acted as though she were filled with the Holy Spirit. She was so empowered by the impetus of the principal demons that for a long time she . . . deceived the brotherhood. And she accomplished certain wonderful and marvelous things. She even promised that she would cause the earth to be shaken. . . . She deceived one of the presbyters, who was a man of the country. She also deceived another man, a deacon. These men had sexual relations with that same woman, which was detected shortly afterwards. For suddenly she was confronted by one of the exorcists. He was an approved man and was always of a good manner of living as to religious discipline. . . .

That exorcist, inspired by God's grace, bravely resisted and showed that what was previously thought to be holy was indeed a most wicked spirit. However, among others things by which she had deceived many, that woman also had frequently dared these things: to pretend that with an invocation not to be scorned she sanctified bread and celebrated the Eucharist. And she offered sacrifice to the Lord, not without the sacrament of the accustomed utterance. She also baptized many, making use of the usual and lawful words of interrogation, so that nothing might seem to be different from the ecclesiastical rule. What, then, will we say about the baptisms performed by this woman, by which a most wicked demon baptized through means of a woman? . . . Can it be believed that either remission of sins was given, or the regeneration of the saving bath was duly completed—when all things were done by a demon, even though they were done in a manner resembling the image of truth? *Firmilian (c. 256, E), 5.393.*

[Paul of Samosata] put a stop to the psalms sung in honor of our Lord Jesus Christ. For he said they were the recent compositions of contemporary men. Instead, he trained women to sing psalms in honor of himself in the midst of the church, during the great day of the Paschal festival. One would shudder to hear such choristers! *Malchion (c. 270, E), 6.170; see also 2.287–2.288, 2.431; extended discussion: 7.393–7.395, 7.429–7.431.*

SEE ALSO CLOTHING; COSMETICS; EVE; GROOMING; JEWELRY; MARRIAGE; MEN; MODESTY; THECLA; VEIL; WIFE, WIVES.

WORD OF GOD (CHRIST)

My heart has uttered a good word. Ps. 45:1 [LXX].

In the beginning was the Word, and the word was with God, and the Word was God. John 1:1.

The word of God is living and powerful, and sharper than any two-edged sword. Heb. 4:12.

He was clothed with a robe dipped in blood, and His name is called The Word of God. Rev. 19:13.

Jesus Christ, His Son, is His eternal Word. The Son did not proceed forth from silence. He in all things pleased Him who sent Him. *Ignatius (c. 105, E), 1.62.*

The Word Himself, who took shape and became man, was called Jesus Christ. *Justin Martyr (c. 160, E), 1.164.*

The first power after God the Father and Lord of all is the Word, who is also the Son. *Justin Martyr (c. 160, E), 1.173.*

Not one of the created and subject things shall ever be compared to the Word of God, by whom all things were made, who is our Lord Jesus Christ. *Irenaeus (c. 180, E/W), 1.421.*

Those persons hold a far more appropriate [view of Christ] than do those others who equate the begetting of the eternal Word of God to the begetting of words to which men give utterance. For they assign to Him a beginning and course of production similar to their own words. If that were true, in what respect would the Word of God—yes, God Himself, since He is the Word—differ from the words of men? For He would follow the same order and process of generation. *Irenaeus (c. 180, E/W), 1.488.*

For with Him were always present the Word and Wisdom, the Son and the Spirit, by whom and in whom, freely and spontaneously, He made all things. He speaks to this one, saying, "Let Us make man after Our image and likeness." *Irenaeus (c. 180, E/W), 1.488.*

By this work of His, he confounded the unbelievers, and showed that He is Himself the Voice of God, by whom man received commandments. *Irenaeus (c. 180, E/W), 1.545.*

Ignorance does not apply to the God who, before the foundation of the world, was the counselor of the Father. For He was the Wisdom in which the Sovereign God delighted. For the Son is the Power of God, as being the Father's most ancient Word before the production of all things, and His Wisdom. *Clement of Alexandria (c. 195, E), 2.525.*

That the Son was always the Word is signified by saying, "In the beginning was the Word." *Clement of Alexandria (c. 195, E), 2.574.*

In the Gospel, moreover, I discover a minister and witness of the Creator, even His Word. *Tertullian (c. 200, W), 3.490.*

In this good work, God employs a most excellent minister, even His own Word. He says, "My heart has emitted my most excellent Word." *Tertullian (c. 207, W), 3.299.*

But someone will say to me, "You introduce a strange thing to me when you call the Son the Word. For John, indeed, speaks of the Word, but it is by a figure of speech." No, it is not by a figure of speech! *Hippolytus (c. 205, W), 5.229.*

I wonder at the stupidity of the general run of Christians in this matter. I do not mince words. It is nothing but stupidity. . . . The passage they employ most is that in the Psalms, "My heart has produced a good Word." So they imagine that the Son of God is the utterance of the Father that has been deposited (as it were) in syllables. As a result, if we examine them further, we find they do not allow Him to be an independent Person [Gr. *hypostasis*], nor are they clear about His essence. I do not mean that

they confuse its qualities, but the fact of His having an essence of His own. For such persons cannot understand how that which is said to be "Word" can be a Son. For such an animated "Word" is not a Son, for it is not a separate entity from the Father and does not have its own subsistence. Therefore, if He is a Son, let them say that God the Word is a separate Being and has an essence of His own. *Origen (c. 228, E), 9.308–310.*

The mouth of the Son of God is a sharp sword, for "The Word of God is living and active, and sharper than any two-edged sword." *Origen (c. 228, E), 9.316.*

"The Word of the Lord that came to Hosea, the son of Beeri." "The Word that came to Isaiah, the son of Amos." . . . The crowd simply looks at what the prophets said, as if what they said was the "Word of the Lord," or "the Word" that came to the prophets. However, could it not be, that as we say that this person comes to that person, so the Son (the Word) . . . came to Hosea, being sent to him by the Father? *Origen (c. 228, E), 9.322.*

This same Christ is the Word of God. In the forty-fourth Psalm: "My heart has breathed out a good Word." *Cyprian (c. 250, W), 5.516.*

The author of the whole creation is Jesus. His name is the Word. For thus His Father says: "My heart has emitted a good word." Therefore, John the evangelist says: "In the beginning was the Word, and the Word was with God, and the Word was God." *Victorinus (c. 280, W), 7.342.*

He who hears the Son of God mentioned should not conceive in his mind so great an impiety as to think that God begat Him by marriage and union with a woman. . . . In what manner, then, did God beget Him? First of all, divine operations cannot be known or declared by anyone. Nevertheless, the sacred writings teach us . . . that this Son of God is the Speech, or even the Reason of God. . . . With good reason, therefore, He is called the Speech and the Word of God. For, by a certain incomprehensible energy and power of His majesty, God enclosed the vocal spirit proceeding from His mouth into a form that has life through its own perception and wisdom. So God did not conceive the Word in His womb, but in His mind. . . . Now, our human words are mingled with the air and they fade away. However, they can still be preserved in writing. How much more must we believe that the voice of God both remains forever and is accompanied with perception and power. It has derived this from God the Father like a stream from a fountain. Someone may be puzzled that God could be produced from God [the Father] by a putting forth of the voice and breath. However, if such a person is acquainted with the sacred utterances of the prophets, he will cease to wonder. ... The Greeks speak of Him as the Logos, more appropriately than we [Romans] do as the "Word" or "Speech." For *logos* means both speech and reason. And He is both the Voice and the Wisdom of God. *Lactantius (c. 304–313, W), 7.106, 107.*

SEE ALSO CHRIST, DIVINITY OF; JESUS CHRIST; LOGOS; TRINITY; WISDOM.

WORK

SEE EMPLOYMENT.

WORKS

SEE SALVATION (III. ROLE OF OBEDIENCE IN SALVATION).

WORLD, SEPARATION FROM THE

They are not of the world, just as I am not of the world. John 17:16.

Do not be conformed to this world, but be transformed by the renewing of your mind. Rom. 12:2.

Come out from among them and be separate, says the Lord. Do not touch what is unclean, and I will receive you. 2 Cor. 6:17.

Pure and undefiled religion before God and the Father is this: to visit orphans and widows in their trouble, and to keep oneself unspotted from the world. Jas. 1:27.

Adulterers and adulteresses! Do you not know that friendship with the world is enmity with God? Whoever therefore wants to be a friend of the world makes himself an enemy of God. Jas. 4:4.

Do not love the world or the things in the world. If anyone loves the world, the love of the Father is not in him. For all that is in the world—the lust of the flesh, the lust of the eyes, and the pride of life—is not of the Father but is of the world. 1 John 2:15, 16; see also John 17:14; 1 Cor. 7:31; 2 Tim. 4:10; 2 Pet. 2:20.

This world and the next are two enemies. . . . We cannot therefore be the friends of both. *Second Clement (c. 150), 7.518.*

He continues, "You know that you who are the servants of God dwell in a strange land. For your city is far away from this one. If, then, you know your city in which you are to dwell, why do you here provide lands, and make expensive preparations, and accumulate dwellings and useless buildings? He who makes such preparations for this city cannot return again to his own. . . . Do you not understand that all these things belong to another, and are under the power of another? . . . Take note, therefore. As one living in a foreign land, make no further preparations for yourself than what is merely sufficient. And be ready to leave this city, when the master of this city will come to cast you out for disobeying his law. *Hermas (c. 150, W), 2.31.*

Refrain from much business, and you will never sin, for those who are occupied with much business commit also many sins. For they are distracted about their affairs, and they are not serving their Lord at all. *Hermas (c. 150, W), 2.33.*

Your [pagan] public assemblies I have come to hate. For there are excessive banqueting, subtle flutes that provoke people to lustful movements, useless and luxurious anointings, and crownings with garlands. *Justin Martyr (c. 160, E), 1.272.*

I do not wish to be a king. I am not anxious to be rich. I decline military command. I detest fornication. I am not impelled by an insatiable love of gain to go to sea. I do not contend for chaplets. I am free from a mad thirst for fame. I despise death. I am superior to every kind of disease. Grief does not consume my soul. If I am a slave, I endure servitude. If I am free, I do not boast about my good birth. . . . Die to the world, repudiating the madness that is in it! Live to God! *Tatian (c. 160, E), 2.69.*

If you are superior to the passions, you will scorn all worldly things. *Tatian (c. 160, E), 2.73.*

Christ has not merely related to us a story about a poor man and a rich one. Rather, He has taught us some things: In the first place, He has taught that no one should lead a luxurious life. No one should live in worldly pleasures and perpetual feasting. No one should be the slave of his lusts and forget God. *Irenaeus (c. 180, E/W), 1.464.*

We have no country on earth. Therefore, we can disdain earthly possessions. *Clement of Alexandria (c. 195, E), 2.281.*

If you would loose, withdraw, and separate your soul from the delight and pleasure that is in this life (for this is what the cross means), you will possess it. It will be found resting in the looked-for hope. *Clement of Alexandria (c. 195, E), 2.371.*

"God stood in the congregation of the gods; he judges in the midst of the gods." Who are these "gods"? They are those who are superior to pleasure, who rise above the passions.... It is those who are greater than the world. *Clement of Alexandria (c. 195, E), 2.374.*

On the day of gladness [i.e., a pagan festival], why do we neither cover our door-posts with laurels, nor intrude upon the day with lamps? Is it a proper thing, at the call of public festivity, to dress your house up like some new brothel? ... We do not celebrate along with you the holidays of the Caesars in a manner forbidden alike by modesty, decency, and purity. *Tertullian (c. 197, W), 3.44.*

[ADDRESSED TO PAGANS:] All zeal in the pursuit of glory and honor is dead in us. So we have no pressing inducement to take part in your public meetings. Nor is there anything more entirely foreign to us than the affairs of state. We acknowledge one all-embracing commonwealth—the world. We renounce all your spectacles. ... Among us, nothing is ever said, seen, or heard that has anything in common with the madness of the circus, the immodesty of the theater, the atrocities of the arena, or the useless exercise of the wrestling ground. Why do you take offense at us because we differ from you in regard to your pleasures? *Tertullian (c. 197, W), 3.46.*

The following quotation was written to encourage Christians who had been imprisoned because of their faith.

Let us compare the life of the world and of the prison—and see if the spirit does not gain more in the prison than the flesh loses. ... In prison, you have no occasion to look on strange gods; you do not bump into their images. You have no part in pagan holidays, even by mere bodily mingling in them. You are not annoyed by the foul fumes of idolatrous solemnities. You are not pained by the noise of the public shows, nor by the atrocity, madness, or immodesty of

their celebrants. ... The prison does the same service for the Christian that the desert did for the prophet. *Tertullian (c. 197, W), 3.694.*

Moreover, what causes have you for appearing in public in excessive grandeur? After all, you are removed from the occasions that call for such exhibitions. For you neither make the circuit of the temples, nor demand to be present at public shows. Furthermore, you have no acquaintance with the festivals of the Gentiles. Now, it is for the sake of all these public gatherings—and of much seeing and being seen—that all ceremonies are exhibited before the public eye.... You, however, have no cause for appearing in public, except such as is serious. Either some brother who is sick is visited, or else the sacrifice is offered, or else the Word of God is dispensed. *Tertullian (c. 198, W), 4.24.*

So long as you deem yourself a Christian, you are a different man from a pagan. Give him back his own views of things! After all, he does not himself learn from your views. Why lean upon a blind guide, if you have eyes of your own? Why be clothed by one who is naked, if you have put on Christ? *Tertullian (c. 210, W), 3.547.*

As for you, you are a foreigner in this world, a citizen of Jerusalem, the city above. Our citizenship, the apostle says, is in heaven. You have your own registers, your own calendar. You have nothing to do with the joys of this world. In fact, you are called to the very opposite—for "the world will rejoice, but you will mourn." *Tertullian (c. 212, W), 3.101.*

It is not possible for anyone to enter into the kingdom of heaven who has not been turned away from the affairs of this world and made like the little children who possess the Holy Spirit. *Origen (c. 245, E), 9.485.*

The one peaceful and trustworthy tranquility, the one solid, firm, and constant security is this: for a man to withdraw from this whirlpool of a distracting world and to lift his eyes from earth to heaven, anchored on the ground of the harbor of salvation. ... He who is actually greater than the world can crave nothing or desire nothing from the world. How stable, how free from all shocks is that safeguard. How heavenly ... to be loosed from the snares of this entangling world and to be purged from earthly dregs and be fitted for the light of eternal immortality. *Cyprian (c. 250, W), 5.279.*

Whatever things are earthly and have been received in this world (and will remain here with the world) should be scorned, even as the world itself is scorned. For we have already renounced its ceremonies and delights when we came to God through a blessed passage [i.e., baptism]. John stimulates and exhorts us.... He says, "Love not the world, neither the things that are in the world." *Cyprian (c. 250, W), 5.432.*

We should ever and a day reflect that we have renounced the world and are in the meantime living here as guests and strangers. *Cyprian (c. 250, W), 5.475.*

He who has attained to trust, having put off the former man, should reflect on only heavenly and spiritual things. He should give no heed to the world that he has already renounced. *Cyprian (c. 250, W), 5.535.*

Of this same thing, it is written in Matthew: ... "He who does not forsake all that he has cannot be my disciple." ... "The time is limited. It remains, therefore, that those who have wives be as though they do not have them." ... Of this very matter, he wrote to the Galatians: "But be it far from me to boast, except in the cross of our Lord Jesus Christ, by whom the world is crucified to me." ... Of the same thing in the Epistle of Peter: "As strangers and pilgrims, abstain from carnal lusts, which war against the soul." ... Of the same thing in the Epistle of John: ... "Love not the world, neither the things that are in the world." *Cyprian (c. 250, W), 5.536.*

A person who has gloried in the life of the world could not enjoy eternal salvation. That is the very voice of Christ, who says: "He that loves his life in this world will lose it in the world to come. But he that hates his life in this world, will find it in the world to come." *Treatise on the Glory of Martyrdom (c. 255, W), 5.586.*

We must not join in their feasts, which are celebrated in honor of demons, being partakers of them in their impiety. You are also to avoid their public meetings and those sports that are celebrated in them. *Apostolic Constitutions (compiled c. 390, E), 7.424.*

SEE ALSO CHRISTIAN LIFE; CHRISTIANITY; EDUCATION; EMPLOYMENT; ENTERTAINMENT; HOLIDAYS, PAGAN; PUBLIC OFFICE; WAR.

WORSHIP, CHRISTIAN

I. Principles of worship

II. Worship customs

I. Principles of worship

God is Spirit, and those who worship Him must worship in spirit and truth. John 4:24.

Present your bodies a living sacrifice, holy, acceptable to God, which is your reasonable service. Rom. 12:2.

Let all things be done decently and in order. 1 Cor. 14:40.

It behooves us to do all things in order, which the Lord has commanded us to perform at stated times. He has commanded offerings [to be presented] and service to be performed [to Him]. And these things are not to be performed thoughtlessly or irregularly, but at the appointed times and hours. *Clement of Rome (c. 96, W), 1.16.*

We are commanded to reverence and to honor the same One, being persuaded that He is Word.... We do not do this just on special days, as some other persons do. Rather, we do this continually in our whole life, and in every way.... For that reason, not in a specified place, or selected temple, or at certain festivals and on appointed days, but during his whole life, the spiritual man honors God. He does this in every place—even if he is alone by himself. He does this wherever he has with him any of those brethren who have exercised the same faith. *Clement of Alexandria (c. 195, E), 2.532.*

The honor that we pay to the Son of God, as well as that which we render to God the Father, consists of an upright course of life. This is plainly taught us by the passage, "You that boast of the Law, through breaking the Law dishonor God." ... For if he who transgresses the law dishonors God by his transgression, ... it is evident that he who keeps the law honors God. So the worshipper of God is he whose life is regulated by the principles and teachings of the Divine Word. *Origen (c. 248, E), 4.643.*

Plato says, "Ivory is not a pure offering to God." What then? Are embroidered and costly textures? Nay, rather nothing is a pure offering to God that can be corrupted or taken away secretly. *Lactantius (c. 304–313, W), 7.192.*

If anyone thinks that vestments, jewels, and other things that are considered precious [by men] are valued by God, he is altogether ignorant of what God is.... That which is spiritual must be offered to God, for he accepts this. His offering is innocency of soul. His sacrifice is praise and hymns. Since God is not seen, He should be worshipped with things that are not seen. . . . Therefore, the chief ceremonial in the worship of God is the praise from the mouth of a just man directed towards God. *Lactantius (c. 304–313, W), 7.192, 193.*

II. Worship Customs

Now I praise you, brethren, that you remember me in all things and keep the traditions as I delivered them to you. 1 Cor. 11:1.

This custom of not bending the knee on Sunday is a symbol of the resurrection, through which we have been set free by the grace of Christ. . . . Now this custom took its rise from apostolic times, as the blessed Irenaeus, the martyr and bishop of Lyons, declares in his treatise *On Easter*. *Eusebius, citing Irenaeus (c. 180, E/W), 1.569.*

Others . . . believe that the sun is our god. The idea no doubt has originated from our being known to turn to the east in prayer. *Tertullian (c. 197, W), 3.31.*

But what reason is there in going to prayer with hands indeed washed, but the spirit foul? These are the things that are truly pure. They are not those which most persons are superstitiously careful about—such as washing with water at every prayer, even when they are coming from a bath of the whole body. *Tertullian (c. 198, W), 3.685.*

But since we have addressed one special point of empty observance, it will not be irksome to set our mark likewise on the other points against which the reproach of vanity may deservedly be laid. If, that is, they are observed without the authority of any commandment either of the Lord, or else of the apostles. For matters of this kind belong not to religion, but to superstition. . . . [For example,] there is the custom of some persons to make prayer with cloaks off, for the nations approach their idols in this manner. . . . However, if the observance of this practice were becoming, the apostles would have included it in their instructions. For they teach us concerning the garment of prayer [1 Cor. 11:4, 5]. . . . Again, I can see no reason for the custom that some persons have of sitting when prayer is ended, other than the reason that children give. *Tertullian (c. 198, W), 3.685, 686.*

In congregations before daybreak, we take from the hand of no one but the presidents the sacrament of the Eucharist. For the Lord com-

manded this to be eaten at mealtimes, and He commanded it to be taken by all alike. As often as the anniversary comes around, we make oblations for the dead as birthday honors. We consider fasting or kneeling in worship on the Lord's Day to be unlawful. We rejoice in the same privilege also from Easter to Pentecost. We feel pained should any wine or bread—even though it is our own—falls upon the ground. At every forward step and movement, at every going in and out, when we put on our clothes and shoes, when we bathe, when we sit at the table, when we light the lamps, when on the couch, on a seat, and in all the ordinary actions of daily life, we trace the sign upon our foreheads. If, for these and other such rules, you insist upon having positive Scripture injunction, you will find none. Tradition will be held forth to you as the originator of them. Custom is their strengthener, and faith is their observer. *Tertullian (c. 211, W), 3.94, 95.*

SEE ALSO ASSEMBLIES, CHRISTIAN; CANDLES; EAST; EUCHARIST; IMAGES; INCENSE; LITURGY; MUSIC, MUSICAL INSTRUMENTS; PRAYER; TRADITION; VEIL; WORSHIP, PAGAN.

WORSHIP, PAGAN

I. Descriptions of pagan worship

II. Imitation of Christian practices

I. Descriptions of pagan worship

It is the aforementioned demons who draw men to idols. For they are eager for the blood of the sacrifices, and they lick them up. But the gods who please the multitude, and whose names are given to the images, were only men. This can be learned from their history. Yet, that it is the demons who act under their names is proved by the nature of their operations. For some castrate, as does Rhea. Others wound and slaughter, as does Artemis. The Tauric goddess puts all strangers to death. I will skip those who lacerate with knives and scourges of bones. *Athenagoras (c. 175, E), 2.143.*

Let anyone look at those persons who minister before the idols! Their hair is matted and their bodies are disgraced with filthy and tattered clothes. They never come near a bath, and they let their nails grow to an extraordinary length—like wild beasts. Many of them are castrated. They demonstrate that the idol's temples are actually graves or prisons. It appears to me that they *bewail* the gods, instead of *worshiping* them. Their sufferings are a matter of *pity* rather than *piety*. *Clement of Alexandria (c. 195, E), 2.197.*

I wish now to review your sacred rites. . . . You offer the worn-out, the scabbed, the corrupting. *Tertullian (c. 197, W), 3.29.*

I will add . . . that in the temples, adulteries are arranged, and that at the altars pimping is practiced. I will mention that often in the houses of the temple-keepers and priests (under the sacrificial head-bands, sacred hats, and the purple robes), deeds of licentiousness are done amid the fumes of incense. I am not sure but that your gods have more reason to complain of *you* than of Christians. *Tertullian (c. 197, W), 3.30.*

On the day of gladness [a pagan festival], why do we neither cover our door-posts with laurels, nor intrude upon the day with lamps? Is it a proper thing, at the call of public festivity, to dress your house up like some new brothel? . . . We do not celebrate along with you the holidays of the Caesars in a manner forbidden alike by modesty, decency, and purity. *Tertullian (c. 197, W), 3.44.*

You say that the temple revenues are every day falling off! How few persons now throw in a contribution!. . . . Let Jupiter then hold out his hand and receive. For our compassion spends more in the streets than yours does in the temples! *Tertullian (c. 197, W), 3.49.*

Gentiles, in honor of their own Satan, endure priestly offices that involve both virginity and widowhood. . . . [The oracles] who rave at Delphi abstain from marriage. Moreover, we know that "widows" minister to the African Ceres—enticed away, indeed, from matrimony by a most stern oblivion. For not only do they withdraw from their still living husbands, but they even introduce other wives to them in their own room. *Tertullian (c. 205, W), 4.42.*

The handmaid of God dwells amid alien labors [if married to an unbelieving husband]. And among these, she will be agitated by the odor of incense on all the memorial days of demons, at all solemnities of kings, at the beginning of the year, and at the beginning of the month. She will have to exit by a gate wreathed with laurel and hung with lanterns, as from some new meeting place of public lusts. *Tertullian (c. 205, W), 4.47.*

And if you reconsider the rites of these gods—see how many things are laughable, and how many are also pitiable! Naked people run about in the raw winter. Some walk bonneted and carry around old shields, beat drums, or lead their gods begging through the streets. It is permitted to approach some sanctuaries once a year. Some it is forbidden to visit at all. There is one place where a man may not go, and there are some that are sacred from women. It is a crime needing atonement for a slave even to be present at some ceremonies. *Mark Minucius Felix (c. 200, W), 4.187.*

A man makes offerings of his own blood and invokes his god by his own wounds. Would it not be better if he were completely irreverent than to be religious in such a way as this? And he whose private parts are cut off—how greatly does he wrong God in seeking to propitiate Him in this manner! *Mark Minucius Felix (c. 200, W), 4.187.*

We have spoken of the gods themselves who are worshipped. We must now speak a few words concerning their sacrifices and mysteries. Among the people of Cyprus, Teucer sacrificed a human victim to Jupiter. He handed that practice to posterity, until it was recently abolished by Hadrian when he was emperor. There was a law among the people of Tauris . . . that strangers should be sacrificed to Diana. And this sacrifice was practiced for many ages. The Gauls used to appease Hesus and Teutas with human blood. *Lactantius (c. 304–313, W), 7.34.*

The priests of Bellona . . . cut their shoulders. Thrusting forth drawn swords in each hand, they run, and are beside themselves, and are frantic. . . . Is it not better to live like cattle than to worship deities so impious, profane, and blood-thirsty? *Lactantius (c. 304–313, W), 7.35.*

In Egypt, there are sacred rites in honor of Isis, since she either lost or found her little son. At first, her priests (having made their bodies smooth) beat their breasts and lament—as the goddess herself had done when her child was lost. Afterwards, the boy is brought forward, as if found, and their mourning is changed into joy. *Lactantius (c. 304–313, W), 7.35.*

They do not approach the gods so much on account of *religion*. For religion can have no place in things corruptible and acquired through evil. Rather, they approach so that they may gaze upon the gold, look at the brilliancy of polished marble and ivory, and so that they can study with unwearied contemplation garments adorned with precious stones and colors, or cups studded with glittering jewels. The more ornate the temples are, and the more beautiful the images are, the greater majesty they have, according to their beliefs. So their religion is entirely confined to those things that the desires of men admire. *Lactantius (c. 304–313, W), 7.50.*

They sacrifice fine and fat victims to God, as though He were hungry. They pour forth wine to Him, as though he were thirsty. They kindle lights to Him, as though He were in darkness. *Lactantius (c. 304–313, W), 7.163; see also 3.119–3.121, 7.34–7.38.*

II. Imitation of Christian practices

Satan himself transforms himself into an angel of light. 2 Cor. 11:14.

The devil . . . vies even with the essential portions of the sacraments of God. He, too, baptizes some—that is, his own believers and faithful followers. He promises the putting away of sins by a bath. And if my memory still serves me, Mithras there sets his mark on the foreheads of his soldiers. He also celebrates the oblation of bread, and he introduces an image of a resurrection. And before a sword, he wreathes a crown. What also must we say to Satan's limiting his chief priest to a single marriage? He, too, has his virgins. He, too, has his masters of celibacy. *Tertullian (c. 197, W), 3.262, 263.*

The nations, who are strangers to all understanding of spiritual powers, ascribe to their idols the imbuing of waters with the self-same efficacy. . . . For washing is the channel through which they are initiated into some sacred rites—of some notorious Isis or Mithras. . . . We recognize here also the zeal of the devil in rivalling the things of God. For we find him, too, practicing baptism on his subjects. *Tertullian (c. 198, W), 3.671.*

Let us take note of the devices of the devil. For he is inclined to mimic some of God's things. He does this for no other purpose than to put us to shame and to condemn us through the faithfulness of his servants. *Tertullian (c. 211, W), 3.103.*

By his power, the enemy always imitates the forms of virtue and righteousness. He does not do this for the purpose of truly promoting the

exercise of these things, but for deception and hypocrisy. . . . He is "transformed into an angel of light," ensnaring many persons by the appearance of piety. *Methodius (c. 290, E), 6.349.*

SEE ALSO GODS, PAGAN; HOLIDAYS, PAGAN; IDOLATRY; IMAGES; MYSTERY RELIGIONS; WREATHS.

WRATH OF GOD

SEE ANGER OF GOD.

WREATHS

On the day of gladness, why do we neither cover our door-posts with wreaths, nor intrude upon the day with lights? Is it a proper thing, because of a public festival, to dress your house up like some new brothel? *Tertullian (c. 197, W), 3.44.*

The Minervalia are as much Minerva's as the Saturnalia are Saturn's. . . . The schools must be wreathed with flowers. *Tertullian (c. 200, W), 3.66.*

He says, "Let your works shine." But now all our shops and gates shine! Nowadays, you will find more doors of pagans without lights and laurel wreaths than those of Christians! . . . Do you say, "But the lights in front of my doors, and the wreaths on my gate-posts, are an honor to God"? However, they are not there as an honor to *God*, but to him who is honored in God's place through ceremonial observances of this kind. *Tertullian (c. 200, W), 3.70.*

I know that a brother was severely chastised through a vision on the very same night that his servants had wreathed his gates because of the sudden announcement of public rejoicing. Yet, he himself had neither wreathed them, nor commanded them to be wreathed. . . . So we are strictly judged by God in matters of this kind, even with regard to the discipline of our family. *Tertullian (c. 200, W), 3.71.*

Indeed, A Christian will not even dishonor his own gate with laurel wreaths! *Tertullian (c. 211, W), 3.102.*

SEE ALSO CROWNS; HOLIDAYS, PAGAN.

WRITING, ORIGIN OF

O Greeks, do not be hostilely disposed towards the barbarians. Do not look on their opinions with ill will. For which of your institutions has not been derived from the barbarians? . . . To the Babylonians, you owe astronomy. . . . To the Phoenicians, you owe instruction by alphabetic writing. *Tatian (c. 160, E), 2.65.*

Let us, then, do a comparison between them. We will find that our doctrines are older—not only than those of the Greeks—but than the invention of letters. *Tatian (c. 160, E), 2.77.*

The Greeks make no mention of the histories which give the truth. The reason is that, first, they themselves only recently became partakers of the knowledge of letters. And they themselves admit it. For some of them allege that let-ters were invented by the Chaldeans. Others say it was by the Egyptians. And still others say that they were derived from the Phoenicians. *Theophilus (c. 180, E), 2.121.*

Cadmus, the inventor of letters among the Greeks, was a Phoenician, as Euphorus says. For that reason, Herodotus writes that they were called Phoenician letters. And they say that the Phoenicians and the Syrians first invented letters. *Clement of Alexandria (c. 195, E), 2.317.*

SEE ALSO INVENTIONS.

ZODIAC

SEE ASTROLOGY.

ZOROASTER, ZOROASTRIANISM

Zoroaster (c. 628–551 B.C.) was the reputed founder of Zoroastrianism, which became the dominant religion of Persia. Zoroastrianism was marked by a strong dualism between the Wise Lord and the Evil Spirit.

Pythagoras showed that Zoroaster the Magus was a Persian. Those who follow the heresy of Prodicus boast that they are in possession of the secret books of this man. *Clement of Alexandria (c. 195, E), 2.316.*

Plato says that this Zoroaster was placed on a funeral pyre, but that he rose to life again in twelve days. *Clement of Alexandria (c. 195, E), 2.469.*

Between the Assyrians and Bactrians, under the leadership of Ninus and Zoroaster of old, a struggle was maintained not only by the sword and by physical power, but also by magicians, and by the mysterious learning of the Chaldeans. *Arnobius (c. 305, E), 6.415.*